EXPLORING

Cases, Readings,

ORGANIZATIONAL

and Experiences

BEHAVIOR

BARRY ALLEN GOLD

Pace University

THE DRYDEN PRESS

Harcourt Brace College Publishers

*Fort Worth Philadelphia San Diego New York Orlando Austin San Antonio
Toronto Montreal London Sydney Tokyo*

Acquisitions Editor	Ruth Rominger
Developmental Editor	Van Strength
Project Editor	Jon Gregory
Art Director	Melinda Huff
Production Manger	Marilyn Williams
Publisher	Elizabeth Widdicombe
Director of Editing, Design, and Production	Diane Southworth

Text Designer	Gina Sample
Copy Editor	Dee Salisbury
Indexer	Paula Pratt
Compositor	Octavo Design
Text Type	10.5/12 Adobe Garamond

Cover Image	Piet Mondrian, *Composition.* 1921, Courtesy of The Emanuel Hoffman Foundation, Basel, Kunstmuseum Basel.

Requests for permission to make copies of any part of the work should be mailed to: Permissions Department, Harcourt Brace & Company, 6277 Sea Harbor Drive, Orlando, FL 32887–6777.

Permission acknowledgements appear on pages 583–585, which constitute a continuation of the copyright page.

Address for Editorial Correspondence
The Dryden Press, 301 Commerce Street, Suite 3700, Fort Worth, TX 76102

Address for Orders
The Dryden Press, 6277 Sea Harbor Drive, Orlando, FL 32887–6777
1-800-782-4479, or 1-800-433-0001 (in Florida)

ISBN: 0-03-075472-0

Library of Congress Catalog Card Number: 93-72064

Printed in the United States of America

3 4 5 6 7 8 9 0 1 2 069 9 8 7 6 5 4 3 2 1

The Dryden Press
Harcourt Brace College Publishers

For my parents

The Dryden Press Series in Management

Holley and Jennings
THE LABOR RELATIONS PROCESS
Fifth Edition

Huseman, Lahiff, and Penrose
BUSINESS COMMUNICATION:
STRATEGIES AND SKILLS
Fourth Edition

Jauch and Coltrin
THE MANAGERIAL EXPERIENCE:
CASES AND EXERCISES
Sixth Edition

Kemper
EXPERIENCING STRATEGIC
MANAGEMENT

Kuehl and Lambing
SMALL BUSINESS: PLANNING AND
MANAGEMENT
Third Edition

Kuratko and Hodgetts
ENTREPRENEURSHIP: A
CONTEMPORARY APPROACH
Second Edition

Kuratko and Welsch
ENTREPRENEURIAL STRATEGIES:
TEXT AND CASES

Lewis
IO ENTERPRISES SIMULATION

Luthans and Hodgetts
BUSINESS
Second Edition

McMullen and Long
DEVELOPING NEW VENTURES: THE
ENTREPRENEURIAL OPTION

Matsuura
INTERNATIONAL BUSINESS:
A NEW ERA

Mauser
AMERICAN BUSINESS: AN
INTRODUCTION
Sixth Edition

Montanari, Morgan, and Bracker
STRATEGIC MANAGEMENT: A
CHOICE APPROACH

Northcraft and Neale
ORGANIZATIONAL BEHAVIOR: A
MANAGEMENT CHALLENGE
Second Edition

Penderghast
ENTREPRENEURIAL SIMULATION
PROGRAM

Sandburg
CAREER DESIGN SOFTWARE

Sawyer
BUSINESS POLICY AND
STRATEGIC MANAGEMENT:
PLANNING, STRATEGY,
AND ACTION

Schoderbek
MANAGEMENT
Second Edition

Schwartz
INTRODUCTION TO MANAGEMENT:
PRINCIPLES, PRACTICES, AND
PROCESSES
Second Edition

Varner
CONTEMPORARY BUSINESS REPORT
WRITING
Second Edition

Vecchio
ORGANIZATIONAL BEHAVIOR
Second Edition

Walton
CORPORATE ENCOUNTERS: LAW,
ETHICS, AND THE BUSINESS
ENVIRONMENT

Wolford and Vanneman
BUSINESS COMMUNICATION

Wolters and Holley
LABOR RELATIONS: AN
EXPERIENTIAL AND CASE APPROACH

Zikmund
BUSINESS RESEARCH METHODS
Fourth Edition

**The Harcourt Brace College
Outline Series**

Pentico
MANAGEMENT SCIENCE

Pierson
INTRODUCTION TO BUSINESS
INFORMATION SYSTEMS

Sigband
BUSINESS COMMUNICATION

About the Author

Barry Allen Gold is a professor of management at the Lubin School of Business, Pace University at New York City. He received his Ph.D. from Columbia University in 1978. His research interests include organization change, organizational conflict, and qualitative data collection and analysis techniques. Dr. Gold is the coauthor of *Whose School Is It, Anyway?*, and numerous articles in professional journals. Dr. Gold is a member of several professional organizations including the Academy of Management, the American Sociological Association, and the North American Case Research Association.

Preface

Exploring Organizational Behavior is an introduction to the major topics in the theory and practice of contemporary organizational behavior and management. It is aimed at upper-level undergraduate and M.B.A. courses. Reflecting the multidisciplinary tradition of organizational behavior, this textbook draws on perspectives from psychology, social psychology, psychoanalytic theory, political science, sociology, and management theory. The Readings balance theory, research, and practice as well as micro and macro approaches to organizational behavior. The Cases develop analytical skills by expanding concepts and ideas presented in the readings. And the Experiences offer students an opportunity to explore their own and others' behavior.

Four themes emerge from the readings in this book and are reflected in the cases and experiences:

Organization Behavior and Management Can Be Viewed from Multiple—Often Conflicting—Perspectives. No intellectual discipline or theory has a monopoly on the description and explanation of organizational behavior. For example, conflicting views are found in Merton's "The Ambivalence of Organizational Leaders" and Conger's "Leadership: The Art of Empowering Others." Merton, using a sociological framework, identifies structurally generated incompatible norms that produce uncertainty in leaders, regardless of their personal traits and skills. From the perspective of management theory, Conger describes the leader as self-confident and capable of transferring power to subordinates, thereby empowering them.

U.S. Organizations Are in a Process of Fundamental Change. Among the pressures creating change are globalization, multiculturalism, feminism, a renewal of concern with ethics, the total quality movement, and innovations in technology and communications. It is not clear, however, what type of managerial and organizational behavior are required to create change, react to changes, or, more importantly, what new forms organizations will or should take. An illustration of this can be seen by comparing Elliott Jaques' "In Praise of Hierarchy" with Robert Reich's "The New Web of Enterprise." Both authors recognize that U.S. organizations require redesign to become more competitive. However, their observations and prescriptions are diametrically opposed. Jaques claims that hierarchy is poorly understood in modern organizations and suggests that it is essential for coordination. Reich views the pyramidal form of organization—hierarchy—as an anachronism that is rapidly being replaced by "webs" of temporary alliances that are appropriate for new economic conditions.

Various Processes Are Creating Convergence—Homogenization—of Organizational Behaviors and Structures across National Boundaries. For example, Florida and Kenney in "Transplanted Organizations" provide evidence that Japanese companies in the United States change the U. S. environment to conform to Japanese business practices. Adler and Bartholomew's "Managing Globally Competent People" suggests that U.S. firms are in the process of adapting to the culture, organizational behavior, and management techniques of other countries.

Ways in Which Organizational Behavior and Management Are Understood Are Changing. Intellectual change is the product of the changes in organizations. At the same time, of course, new ideas influence social activity. Among recent developments are the study of organizational culture, the population ecology approach to organizations, evolutionary theories, ethnographic research methods, deconstruction, and postmodernism. In this textbook, Barley's article "Technology as an Occasion for Structuring" and Gersick's "Time and Transition in Work Teams" are examples of the fruitfulness of qualitative methodology. Alvesson and Willmott reformulate the Frankfort School's Critical Theory for understanding and prescribing emerging trends in organizational research, theory, and practice.

These are only some possible ways to gather the common threads of the readings collected here. Students undoubtedly will discover yet other integrating themes.

Audience

This textbook can be used by itself or with a text for upper level undergraduate and M.B.A. courses in organization behavior and principles of management. It contains 36 Readings, 12 Cases, and 12 Experiences, organized into the following five parts:

Part I. Introduction
Part II. Individual Behavior
Part III. Behavior in Groups
Part IV. Managing for Performance
Part V. The Larger Context of Organizational Behavior

The part and chapter sequence is the same as Gregory B. Northcraft and Margaret A. Neale's *Organization Behavior: A Management Challenge* (second edition) Fort Worth: The Dryden Press, 1994. Because Northcraft and Neale cover the major topics found in organization behavior textbooks by various authors, this book can be used to accompany any text by rearranging the part and chapter sequences.

Pedagogic Features

The philosophy of teaching that guides this textbook is that students learn from a variety of approaches. The readings, cases, and experiences provide diverse teaching and learning strategies. Of course, they also complement each other. For example, to analyze a case or interpret behavior observed in a classroom simulation, it is essential to understand organizational behavior and management theory. This approach helps to create the wide range of skills neccessary to manage people effectively in complex organizations.

Readings

Each reading is preceded by Learning Objectives and followed by Discussion Questions. The Learning Objectives are designed to alert students to the major issues in each reading. The Discussion Questions offer students an opportunity to test their mastery of each reading. At the end of each chapter, in the For Further Reading section, there is a selective list of additional studies.

Cases

By placing organizational behavior in context, the cases extend key issues found in each section. The cases are field researched, contain multiple issues, and can be interpreted from a variety of perspectives. Cases such as these provide a graphic account of actual managerial and organizational behavior and promote meaningful classroom discussion. In addition, following long-established practice, the cases are not followed by questions; one challenge of a case is for students to pose penetrating questions themselves. However, the *Instructor's Manual* that accompanies this text has suggested discussion questions and teaching notes for each case.

Experiences

Each experience is designed to either illustrate or extend a concept or theory found in a reading. In several cases, the experience develops concepts not included in the readings. The new concepts are introduced at the beginning or discovered in the process of the experience. The experiences are self-explanatory. When necessary, however, additional instructions are contained in the *Instructor's Manual.*

Acknowledgments

Many people played a role in shaping this book. I would like to thank Lenny Bambina for his gracious assistance with library work, and Monica Zeigler, who always made the administrative tasks of life easy and even enjoyable. Lou Seagull, Ann Marie Franchesco, Joe Russo, and Nahrendra Bhandari, colleagues at Pace University, New York, supplied intellectual and social support at various times. Butch Gemin, Barbara Rosenberg, Ruth Rominger, Jon Gregory, Van Strength, and Dee Salisbury of The Dryden Press were friendly and supportive of this project. Finally, but of course, not least, Bonnie, Lauren, and Ian deserve grateful thanks for everything.

Barry Allen Gold

Brief Contents

Contents

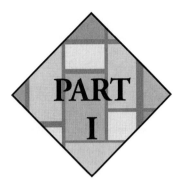

PART
I

INTRODUCTION

1

CONTEMPORARY PERSPECTIVES ON ORGANIZATIONAL BEHAVIOR

Perspectives on Action in Organizations

KARL E. WEICK

LEARNING OBJECTIVES

After reading "Perspectives on Action in Organizations" by Karl Weick, the student will be able to:

1. Develop preliminary definitions of organizations and organizational behavior

2. Understand how action links organizational behavior theory and managerial practice

3. Appreciate the intellectual demands involved in the analysis of organizational behavior

4. Begin to construct a critical, empirically grounded model of organizational behavior

This chapter describes how action provides a link between the worlds of theory and practice. Four properties of action are salient in organized settings and determine much of what happens there.

1. Actions evoke justifications.
2. Actions displace thinking.
3. Actions create environments.
4. Actions require interaction.

When people act in organized settings they search for reasons that transform their actions into responses to some stimulus yet to be identified; they guide their actions by routines, direct perception, and situational demands rather than by prospective thought; they respond to environ-ments of their own construction; and they act interdependently with others.

The Setting for Action

To ground organizational theory in the particulars of managerial action is also to say more about the settings within which those actions take place. Organizational settings only intermittently and locally cohere as if they were systems (Simon 1962; Katz 1974; Weick 1976). These settings are often tied together hypocritically by the rhetoric of rationality and goal attainment, a rhetoric that is usually mocked by the practices that actually work. Stated more compactly, organizations are misnamed. To understand this inaccuracy is to understand the essence of managerial action and how managers might cope better.

The term *organization* implies more orderliness, coordination, and systematization than is commonly discovered when people look closely at joint action (Morgan 1981). The commonly used data collection procedures smooth over the irregularities, imperfections, and discontinuities that occur in daily organizational life (Kimberly 1980;

Source: Karl E. Weick, "Perspectives on Action in Organizations," Jay W. Lorsch, ed., *Handbook of Organizational Behavior,* ©1987, pp. 10-28. Reprinted by permission of Prentice-Hall, Inc., Englewood Cliffs, New Jersey.

Leach 1967), and so we researchers persist in using a term that exaggerates order. Researchers who study large organizations try to capture their size and apparent complexity by using surveys, averages, and synoptic measures in an attempt to say something about everything they observe. The costs of these strategic decisions are becoming clearer in the deepening irrelevance of organizational researchers for organizational participants (Perrow 1981; Thoenig 1982).

Managers work amidst a great deal of chaos. Order imposed upon conditions of divergent self-interest, career competition, turnover, shifting definitions of self, and uncertain resources is unstable and must continually be reestablished.

> *The real world of management is not orderly, well-defined, or clear as to its practices. It is a jungle of ideas, methods, techniques, and divergent philosophies that one might be tempted to call a mess. Textbook principles of organization, authority, command, and strategies for getting results comprise a logical and persuasive set of assumptions. The real world of management, however, is loaded with confusion, stress, uncertainty, politics, trial and error, frustration, disappointment, and emotional disturbances, and in many cases is a maze of "the rat race of survivability." The real world of management contains upheavals, redirections, and realignments because of new threats, new vibrations, new conflicts, new concerns. (Mali 1981, 49)*

Unpredictability is high in organizations, as in life. Managers who themselves are unpredictable must work continuously to make sense of unpredictable environments. Neither the managerial group, the organization, nor the environment is unitary. Failure is inevitable if we try to understand organizations by aggregating into higher units elements that themselves are not unitary (Mayhew 1980).

The managerial group is not unitary because concerns with career advancement keep people apart (Watson 1982, 271; Wilson 1982). The organization is not unitary because it is a field of interests (Borum 1980), a set of procedures for arguing, shifting alliances presided over by a dominant coalition, which spends its time maintaining dominance rather than seeking profit. The environment itself is not unitary (Zey-Ferrell 1981, 193) because it is defined relative to differing organizational interests and contains shifting amounts of resources managed by shifting interorganizational alliances (Robbins 1983, 154-56).

The combination of incentives, turnover, role ambiguity, and role overload threatens whatever order and equi-

librium people are able to build on a short-run basis. Thus they need continual interaction, phoning, and meeting to reassure themselves and others that yesterday's routines are still in place and that the organization is unfolding today pretty much the way it unfolded yesterday.

Arrangements continually need to be renegotiated because of our inevitable uncertainty as to who will show up tomorrow, in what frame of mind, capable of doing what, and remembering which episodes from the past to use as precedents for and warnings about the future. Managers need to reassure themselves and their colleagues that things today are basically the way they were yesterday, that past agreements and understandings are still in force, and that it is okay to act as if it were "business as usual." In the flow of ongoing organizations, business as usual is a major accomplishment, not an automatic outcome. Business as usual reflects an overdetermined state, most of whose determinants are neither known nor understood.

The disorder found in most organizations is held together by a combination of cognition and action. Action is energized, directed, and intensified by the labels that are attached to it, labels that originate in cognitive activity. But action leads and constrains cognition, and provides the raw material around which cognition is organized (Weick 1979). Because order in organizations is transient, managers need to make a strong and continuing effort to stabilize shifting events. Order is produced, contested, repaired, organized, and displayed in concrete situations by active people who are continually defining what that situation is about (Knorr-Cetina 1981, 6).

Action is a crucial source of order, not just because managers act, but because organizations themselves are action generators.

> *Automatic, nonreflective action is built into organizations. They advertise not because they have identified a specified problem and have decided that advertising is the best solution, but because they have set up advertising departments and there are people whose sole responsibility is to advertise. Organizations create budgets because they possess forms and procedures and specialists for making budgets, not because they have explicitly decided that budgets will solve clearly identified problems that exist here and now. The action-generating mechanisms are copied from other organizations or learned in schools of management or carried forward by tradition, and claims that they solve problems are afterthoughts arising from the desires to appear rational and legitimate. (Starbuck 1982. 20–21)*

The observation that organizations are successful generators of action often is lost on those who feel that a key issue in organizational theory is to explain what motivates people and why most people are not motivated (White and Locke 1981). The problem within organizations may be misdirected activity, fruitless activity, incorrect activity, or noncumulative activity, but the problem is not *in*activity.

Elapsed action becomes the stimulus for people in organizations to develop theories of what they have done and what will happen if they do it again (Dutton and Starbuck 1963; Meyer 1982). The assertion that organizations generate action thus becomes the start, not the end of an explanation of what is required to manage organizations. Left with unexplained action, managers need to explain its origins. Constructing consistent justifications that accommodate visible implications of the prior action is a prominent way managers explain what they have done.

Actions Evoke Justification

Societal ideologies insist that actions ought to be responses—actions taken unreflectively without specific reasons are irrational and irrationality is bad . . . so organizations justify their actions with problems, threats, successes, or opportunities. Bureaucrats, for instance, attribute red tape to legal mandates or to sound practice. (Starbuck 1983, 94)

Organizations are action generators, but they also give and require reasons for doing things. Typically these reasons become salient after the action has occurred (retrospective rationality) rather than before (prospective rationality). Once action has been justified, subsequent explanations and options are restricted.

The most powerful set of ideas concerning the justification process originated in cognitive-dissonance theory (Festinger 1957; Wicklund and Brehm 1976). There is evidence that, during the period of time preceding a decision, people focus attention on the alternatives they eventually do not choose, whereas in the postdecisional state they concentrate on the chosen alternative (Jones and Gerard 1967). They are usually aware that in some respects the chosen alternative may be less attractive than the rejected one. To neutralize these jarring facts, once people make a decision they realign their cognitions and do such things as enhance the value of the chosen alternative,

devalue the rejected alternative, deny that the decision was volitional ("I really had no choice"), minimize the importance of the outcome, enlarge the degree of overlap between the chosen and rejected alternatives, or persuade other people that the choice was a good one. Each of these resolutions has different implications for what the person will do next. More important, because these resolutions reduce tension, the person has some investment in preserving these altered views, especially in organizations where norms of rationality are pervasive.

People are disturbed by postdecision dissonance when they feel personally responsible for bringing about an aversive event—one that produces an undesirable outcome (Cooper, Zanna, and Taves 1978). To be responsible means that the person acted freely, cannot plead force, and could have foreseen what might happen (Goethals, Cooper, and Naficy 1979).

In addition to the combination of arousal, responsibility, and aversiveness, three other conditions can also create pressures to justify action. The first is inconsistencies between actions and one's self-concept (Aronson 1980; Bramel 1968). If people believe they are incompetent (e.g., qualitative overload), then discovering that they have been undercompensated or have made errors should not be disturbing. However, if people believe they are competent, then working for insufficient rewards, using simple skills, and investing in failing enterprises all should be disturbing because they do not follow from the belief that one is a competent person who makes good decisions.

Dissonance effects can also be created by the frustration of motives such as (in an organizational context) the desire for power or achievement.

When a person has the cognition that he has voluntarily chosen to commit himself to a behavior which has negative consequences for the satisfaction of some relevant, salient motive, a state of cognitive dissonance is created. The knowledge that the tension associated with a given motive is uncomfortable is inconsistent with the knowledge that one has agreed to accept it, continue to enter into more of it, and postpone behavior directed to available goals which could reduce their drive. (Zimbardo 1969, 15)

If I agree to postpone being reviewed for a promotion, this voluntary commitment to deprivation of achievement motives is dissonant *unless* I decrease the intensity of that motive. If I am able to do that, then even if someone suddenly presents an opportunity to achieve, I will reject it and act like someone for whom achievement is no longer an incentive (Weick and Prestholdt 1968; Zimbardo 1969).

Most managers confront inconsistent cognitions most of the time. Organizations are infused with the ideology that rational action is good and necessary and possible, but that ideology is very much at odds with what actually happens (Pfeffer 1981b, 194). The standards to which managers are held and the behavior that is held up to them as an example are impossible to attain and are seldom exhibited even by the people who enforce these standards. Hypocrisy is ubiquitous in organizations, and this necessitates continuous dissonance reduction. Because dissonance is so prevalent, one might hypothesize that managers would become accustomed to it, so that it would have little continuing effect on action. Dissonance probably retains its power to affect action, however, partly because self-concepts are involved, partly because Western ideologies treat inconsistency as error, and partly because self-concepts of managers are invested so heavily with themes of rationality and competence.

The third and most useful way to understand justification is by means of Salancik's (1977) extension of Kiesler's (1971) analysis of commitment. The starting point for Salancik's analysis is the assertion that beliefs align themselves with actions taken. It will be recalled that action *starts* the sequences we are interested in, it does not end them. The chronic error that economists make is to suggest that most relevant determinants occur before action takes place and that action flows automatically from correct analyses. However, action typically generates its own dynamics, constraints, and pressures for redefinition, most of which are missed by so-called rational models of decision making.

Salancik's assertion that beliefs align themselves with completed actions rests on three assumptions.

1. People like what they do.
2. People believe in the value of what they do.
3. People become what they do.

These three assumptions are usually invoked to explain choices: people choose things they like over things they dislike, things they value over things they reject, and things that flatter their self-concept over things that do not. Thus, a knowledge of preferences should enable us to predict choices. That is the way a rational analysis sets up the problem and that is precisely why we have such a poor understanding of managerial action.

When managers complete the actions encouraged by organizational conditions, they work backward (retrospectively) and use the *actions* to search for patterns of likes, values, and definitions of self that explain the outcome.

Cognitions become defined *after* the action, not before it. The action becomes an excuse to reexamine the situation. But the action also serves as a constraint, because only certain likes, preferences, and self-definitions will justify the action (O'Reilly and Caldwell 1981).

Salancik argues that three conditions—visibility, irrevocability, volition—determine the degree to which a manager feels pressure to justify an action. When an action is visible, the person cannot deny that the behavior occurred. When an action is irrevocable, the behavior cannot be changed. The joint realities of visibility and irrevocability both signify that the action *has* taken place. When an action is also volitional, it becomes the responsibility of a specific person or group, who must then explain it.

Beliefs constructed in the service of justification tend to ride roughshod over evidence. Hence organizations are often described as collections of myths, stories, avoided tests, anecdotes, and beliefs that have only a modest fit with realities described by more detached observers (Boland 1982).

The implications of commitment are substantial. For example, commitment affects control systems. Accountability, a hallmark of rational organizations, can erode flexibility through the mechanism of commitment. Control systems make action visible, which increases commitment, which then decreases flexibility, experimentation, and early detection of failing courses of action. Control systems that emphasize visibility and accountable discretion may encourage concealment of failure through increased investment in faltering enterprises—something control systems supposedly prevent (Staw and Ross 1978; Staw 1976).

If accountability is less visible because it is diffused rather than concentrated, if experimentation and incrementalism are institutionalized so that resources are invested in small quantities, and if individual choice is left slightly ambiguous, then organizations should remain flexible because commitments are softer.

So far we have argued that people's explanations of actions tend to be inaccurate and self-serving. That implication understates the complexity of cognition in organizations. When people search for justification, they often find real attractions as well as fictitious ones. People may trap themselves into unsatisfying jobs and failing projects when they justify earlier decisions, but they also may discover unexpected rewards.

At a time when promotion opportunities within firms have dwindled, people need to view career advancement as something other than simply ascending a hierarchy. Driver (1979), for example, urges people to cultivate spiral careers, in which they perform several different activities at a single organizational level, and forgo the idea of an upward linear career. As hierarchies become flatter and promotion less frequent, extra attractions discovered while justifying effort expenditure become more an important source of personal job enrichment tailored to the person's own unique interests.

Saying that an assignment "isn't so bad after all" can represent an effort to gloss over negative qualities, but it can also reflect discovery of subtle attractions that no one else noticed. The line between self-deception and genuine discovery is exceedingly thin, and there are no clear guidelines by which one can judge when one trails off into the other.

While some features of organizations seem highly committing (e.g., visibility and accountability of individual action), others suggest that commitment should be rare. For example, it is not clear how much choice managers actually have in their jobs (Marshall and Stewart 1981). Informal role prescriptions, formal job descriptions, and orders from the boss all imply that actions were forced rather than volitional, and therefore need no explanation. In many organizations managers speak the truth when they say, "I had no choice but to . . . ." To stress researchers, such statements signify occasions of low personal control and high stress (Miller 1980; Wortman and Brehm 1975); they are also significant to effectiveness researchers because they signify that organizations are not tied up by a set of commitments that will be defended at all costs. Ironically, some flexibility is preserved when people do things under duress because then they do not have to defend their actions personally.

Organizations may be more adaptable when commitments are harder to develop, because ambiguous events can be reversed with relative ease and because their consequences can be redefined in ways that favor revocation or adaptation. The very organizational chaos that people treat as evidence of poor management and lack of foresight can also favor adaptation, because people are less pressured to justify what they do. The fact that managers are tentative and seldom make irreversible decisions can be viewed as evidence of timidity, risk aversion, or confusion. At the same time, they may feel less pressure to develop myths that distort evidence. People who avoid irreversible action preserve adaptability.

In summary, organizations generate action in settings teeming with norms of rationality; organization members feel they must explain those actions as rational responses. Pressures to justify action intensify when there is evidence that attractive opportunities have been forgone, that outcomes are of questionable value, that incompetence may

be perceived, or that what was chosen has no overlap with what was rejected (negative features of the chosen alternative can make this discomfort quite pronounced). Under these conditions, people search for exonerating explanations, reevaluate outcomes, and attempt to recoup losses by escalating commitment (Staw 1980).

Each of these resolutions squeezes some flexibility out of the organization's response repertoire (Bell 1967) and some accuracy out of the organization's perceptions of its environments and itself (Weick 1978). While justifications may uncover unsuspected skills, resources, and missions, they can also cause people to lose touch with themselves, what they are capable of doing, and what they want to do. As managers lose touch with their skills and their preferences and defend increasingly tenuous visions, they invite crises and collapse. The same explanations that prospectively may assist in planning, strategy making, and analysis often operate retrospectively to conceal assets and troubles. Managers who practice unselective justification can become estranged from themselves and the settings within which they operate (Lewicki 1981).

In disorderly organizational worlds, actions unfold in ways that are not predictable. Justification is an attempt to rationalize action and add predictability. When people attempt to live solely by norms of rationality, however, they too often try to recoup losses by escalating commitments and end up losing flexibility and judgment.

Actions Displace Thinking

Action can make thinking less necessary for several reasons, two of which are explored here. First, action can provide direct perceptual data that obviate the need for further thinking. Second, action can incorporate over-learned routines that do not require thoughtful monitoring.

Ecological Action

Most managers are active, manage by walking about, thrive on face-to-face interaction, and are suspicious of any media that are less direct and less immediate (Mintzberg 1973, 1975). In contrast, our knowledge of perception, social knowing, and analysis is based primarily on studies of people who are *not* mobile (e.g., they rest their head on a chin rest while observing a static display).

To make sense of these drastically restricted stimuli, the experimental subject must use complicated cognitive operations (e.g., inference) that require considerable time and effort. Observing people under these conditions, researchers have concluded that human beings in general have to think about their world a great deal to cope with it (Huber 1980). This conclusion, however, is an artifact of the ecologically invalid displays with which they have been presented. Social knowing may require less cognitive inference than anyone has realized.

The possibility that action can substitute for cognitive inference has been discussed recently by Baron (1981), Neisser (1977), and Knowles and Smith (1982). In the following discussion, "perception" refers to the pickup of environmental information and "cognition" refers to the encoding, storage, and recall of this environmental information. Perception is usually viewed as a process that follows cognitive activities such as analysis, synthesis, inference, extrapolation, active construction, and the like ("Oh, now I see what's out there"). Direct perception, however, occurs before cognition and often renders cognition unnecessary. Orderly information is available to guide perception, especially when the person is allowed to move about. When movement is permitted, perception becomes more accurate, occurs more quickly, and involves less cognitive work.

If this line of analysis is plausible, it explains why detailed analyses of cognition and thinking explain so little of how managers act and what they know (Nugent 1981). Barnard, in his famous essay "Mind in Everyday Affairs" (1938, 308–309), observed that most managerial thought was so rapid that it was simply not possible to explain it by conventional processes of reflection and contemplation—processes perhaps used by most academics, and erroneously attributed to everyone else as well.

The importance of mobility for perception cannot be overemphasized.

There is little danger of overload when information is obtained through exploration. Indeed, the more information that is available, the less confused the Gibsonian perceiver [person using direct perception] becomes. For example, the more perspectives one has on an object, the easier it is to know its essential identity; the more complete the rotation or the more contexts in which one sees an entity, the easier it is to establish what is invariant from what is changing. . . . Thus, the existence of overload may be more of a commentary on the lack of opportunity for adequate observation than any limitations of the perceiver. (Baron 1981, 66)

Multiple perspectives should facilitate the discovery of invariants, which reduces overload and increases accuracy. From an information-processing view, however, multiple perspectives should strain channel capacity more than a redundant viewing done from the same perspective (Axelrod 1973). Of particular importance for the exploration argument is the finding that when perceivers are not constrained and the context surrounding objects is not eliminated, visual illusions do *not* occur (Knowles and Smith 1982, 58). It is only when people have to use inferential processes in a fabricated environment that their senses play tricks on them and generate conclusions they would never make in the world outside the laboratory.

Managers seldom report being overloaded, perhaps because they observe events from several perspectives, see what is common, and base their actions on that core. None of this requires detailed analysis. The person who may be forced to analyze is the one who is confined to an office, a work station, a terminal, a printout, summarized data, or written words, all of which are incomplete fragments that require effort to synthesize. Conclusions drawn from these less-direct modes of knowing are more subject to error because they require more processing, with more fallible cognitive operations.

This line of reasoning predicts that the people who report the most stress from qualitative or quantitative overload should be those whose situation most closely resembles that of a subject in a classical perception experiment—those who are in a stationary position, given incomplete cues, and forced to make complex judgments in a contextless setting.

Managers are less active in the head, more active in the world. This difference used to be a source of ridicule because it was presumed that being highly active in the head was the only way to cope with the world. That view is slowly being replaced by perspectives that are more sensitive to the ecology that surrounds perception and more awareness of the considerable amount of information that is out there and available with a minimum of inference. The important question for managers is how far they can get with unelaborated information before they have to resort to higher-order cognitive processes.

Daft and Lengel (1984) postulate that rich informational media are needed to register rich, complex environments. They argue that face-to-face contact has the most richness, followed by phone conversations, letters, and memos, with computer printout having the least richness because there is no feedback, it is dated, and it appeals to only one sensory modality. As we move back up the hierarchy, there is an increase in immediacy and accuracy of feedback, the number of sensory modalities being used, and the extent to which the data are acquired in real time. The rank ordering proposed by Daft and Lengel also corresponds with variations in observer mobility, which should mean that richness correlates negatively with the necessity to resort to higher-order cognitive processes and positively with the accuracy of judgments.

Mindless Action

A second major explanation for the mindless quality of managerial action is that it consists of overlearned routines triggered by simple categories and coarse attributions of causality. All of these tactics insure that relatively little thought occurs unless situations are novel, difficult to typify, or have little precedent (e.g., an employee brings on infant to work to care for it).

The relative importance of nonthinking in interaction has been discussed from time to time, but it is only recently that investigators such as Langer (1978) and Thorngate (1976) have begun to pull these ideas together and extend them.

Langer quotes Alfred N. Whitehead to illustrate the major themes associated with investigation of mindless action.

> By relieving the brain of all necessary work, a good rotation sets it free to concentrate on more advanced problems, and in effect increases the mental powers of the race. . . . It is a profoundly erroneous truism, repeated by all copy-books and by eminent people making speeches, that we should cultivate the habit of thinking what we are doing. The precise opposite is the case. Civilization advances by extending the number of operations which we can perform without thinking about them. Operations of thought are like cavalry charges in battle—they are strictly limited in number, they require fresh horses, and must only be made at decisive moments. (Langer 1978, 40)

Action changes as it shifts from being consciously organized to more automatic. Over time, as an action is repeated, the number of cues that guide it is steadily reduced. In the early consciously monitored stages, numerous cues are noticed and influence the form of the action. As the same situation recurs, the person overlearns only that information that is seen to be available repeatedly. Thus, each time the event is repeated, less information is processed and actions gradually become guided by less information. The person eventually needs only enough information to trigger the complete action. Everything beyond this minimum is ignored, including cues suggest-

ing that the old responses are no longer appropriate. When responses become overlearned, people become more confident, earlier in the unfolding of a situation, that they know what is occurring (Dailey 1971). As a result, they activate a full response more quickly and with less revision to fit particulars of the situation.

This is one reason why managers' judgments and decisions often do not improve as time passes. When they act on the basis of fewer cues with more confidence, they ignore more data, much of which implies the necessity to change the action. In most organizations, the combination of impression management, ambiguity, and multiple meanings reduces temporarily the trouble that can occur when nonroutine situations are treated as if they were routine.

Langer (1978) raises the interesting question of why we have come to feel that so much action is mediated by thought. It is relevant to consider her explanation, because so much description in organizational behavior assumes that managers think, analyze, and plan most of the time.

> When we think about people, since we ourselves are thinking, we are not likely to assume their behavior to be automatic. If that behavior is not correspondent with the information the situation presents to us, we may be led to erroneous conclusions about why they behaved the way they behaved. It is probably because of this—that people think they, or others were thinking; that we when behaving as people, think we are thinking; and when, we behaving as psychologists studying people, may actually be thinking—that we have overlooked all the non-thinking that takes place. (p. 39)

It is clear that people do think and do become aware of the fine grain of their ongoing action when situations are unfamiliar. Because most observers study relatively unfamiliar situations in order to learn more about them, they are flooded with unexpected events that require conscious effort to understand, and they are likely to assume that participants have to make the same effort.

This is why sustained direct observation is one of the few research techniques that can be relied upon to approximate the understanding that practitioners eventually have of their own situation (Bogdan 1972; Schwartz and Jacobs 1979). This is also why participant observers are so crucial to improve our understanding of managerial behavior. Managers take more for granted than researchers do, and thereby free their attention for more novel issues. We need to understand the routines of management so we can discover what kinds of cognitive and attentional resources are left for managers to direct at issues that no one has encountered before.

The final importance of understanding mindless action derives from the supposition that when people think about their behavior as they enact it, they destroy the spontaneous continuity of the action, produce a less-skilled performance, and become more dissatisfied with the outcomes. People who become self-conscious while delivering a speech find that this consciousness disrupts the flow of speech. Langer (1978, 41) hypothesized that "the positivity of postactivity evaluation varies inversely with the degree of conscious awareness of the activity. That is, the more one is involved in the event, the more one enjoys the event; and increased levels of involvement are achieved by not paying attention to the particulars of the situation [by not thinking]."

In summary, much interaction in organizations is rehearsed rather than spontaneous. People know in advance that the district manager is going to visit; they rehearse what they will say, tours are planned, people are coached on the answers to questions most likely to be asked—all of which restricts spontaneity and information exchange. People take turns saying their lines, suggesting the relevance of a dramaturgical model (Overington and Mangham 1982; and Overington 1982) concerned with rehearsing, backstage, frontstage, scripts, cues, muffed lines, and so on.

If organizations are heavily dramaturgical and if people play parts carefully worked out in advance, interest then focuses on the extent to which managers become what they have acted. When people believe they had some choice in performing their script, they may come to believe it.

Mindless routines are more likely to occur in mechanistic organizations operating in stable environments than in organic organizations operating in dynamic environments (Carroll and Tosi 1977). In organic organizations, processes are negotiated and assembled in different ways, depending on the problem (Argote 1982). If organizations are loosely coupled, it is more difficult to use routines unless they concern fundamentals of interaction. The only routines that work are simple rules: when in doubt, do something; if you're confused, ask someone; search in the vicinity of the problem.

Actions Create Environments

Environments, like organizations, may be either loosely or tightly coupled. Some organizational theorists assume that environments are coupled more tightly than organizations are, so that to survive, organizations must accommodate to

the rate of change in those tight environments (e.g., Brittain and Freeman 1980; Hannan and Freeman 1977). Loosely coupled organizations survive in tightly coupled environments to the extent that their managers are skilled at sensing and diagnosing themselves and their environment (Hambrick 1981), that they can establish organizational structures that exploit attractive environmental niches, and that they can produce large-scale change swiftly when the attractive niches change. The valued manager is perceptive, with strong skills in organizational design and organizational development. In a tightly coupled environment, the organization most likely to survive is one with skilled people in boundary role positions who can distinguish between transient and permanent environmental changes (Aldrich and Herker 1977; Miles 1980) and flexible people in the technical core who are willing to do things differently with little forewarning in response to intelligence picked up at the boundary.

Other organizational theorists assume that organizations, or parts of them, are coupled more tightly than environments are (e.g., Schreyogg 1980; Colignon and Cray 1980). Specific coalitions or even forceful individuals can create environments when they modify regulations, build interorganizational alliances (Stern 1979, 1981), create demand (Ewen 1976), alter perceptions of the organization (Dunkerly, Spybey, and Thrasher 1981), and deter competitors.

A significant portion of the organization's environment consists of nothing more than talk, symbols, promises, lies, interest, attention, threats, agreements, expectations, memories, rumors, economic indicators, supporters, detractors, good faith, suspicion, trust, appearances, loyalties, and commitments—all of which are more intangible and more influenceable than material goods (Peters 1980; Gronn 1968; Weick 1980). Focused action within these less tangible environments attracts attention, induces avoidance, pulls concessions, forestalls competition, induces monitoring, and alters resource flows (Pfeffer 1981a). Whenever action is focused within largely symbolic environments, unrelated events become more closely associated with one another and their covariation increases. As managerial action varies, events cohere in different ways, which means that the environments that confront the organization also change. In this sense, the organization creates its environment.

When organizations exist in more pliant environments, the crucial managerial skill becomes the ability to focus action (Hirsch 1975) so as to rearrange loosely coupled environmental elements. Characteristics such as persistence, confidence, assertiveness, and visibility now become more crucial. In tightly coupled environments, forcefulness is wasted and may even be detrimental because it can preclude accurate sensing (Suedfeld, Tetlock, and Ramirez 1977). But in loosely coupled environments, assertion should be more predictive of organizational success. Important managerial characteristics are persistence, visibility, durability, consistency (Moscovici 1976, 1980), and interpersonal skills associated with gaining and holding attention (e.g., ingratiation, inducing obligations, physical attractiveness).

Finally, some organizational theorists argue that organizations and environments are both either tightly coupled or loosely coupled (e.g., Cherns 1980; Leifer and Delbecq 1978). Many people argue for reciprocal effects, but they fail to state whether they assume that tight or loose entities are affecting one another. That is not a trivial assumption, because when loose entities affect one another, environment-organization fit should be higher than when tight entities interact.

If reciprocal relationships are postulated, the theorist has to begin the sequence somewhere. The identity of that starting point makes a great deal of difference (Harrison 1981).

If, in the beginning, the environment determined structure, then the structure from which the next response is generated does not contain all the resources, capabilities, and options that it did before the environment imposed the initial constraint. Instead, a partially biased structure exerts an effect back on the environment—an effect that is always slightly weaker, slightly less forceful, slightly less deterministic, because the organization operates with a slightly less complete response repertoire. Since environments consist of other organizations and other people, it is not stretching the point to say that when the environment is the first mover, it exerts some influence over what the organization will demand and forgo in the next period by virtue of its initial effect on structure.

If the first mover is the organization, then the environment feeds back to it a more coherent and predictable set of demands than was likely before the organization took the first action. Again, there is reciprocity, but the reciprocity favors the organization in the sense that it shapes the environmental demands toward its own strengths.

The mechanism associated with a first mover resembles a self-fulfilling prophecy. The initial response, whether by the environment or the organization, pulls a second response that *preserves* the original definition of the situation implied by the original action. The second response is constructed to be a sensible act within that original framework. That serves to unbalance the control over reciprocal relationships. Each entity partially determines the response of the other entity, but the second response is generated on a field controlled by the initial responder and therefore accommodates to that initial response.

If the reciprocal relationship between organization and environment begins with an environmental influence on structure, then the reciprocity has a stronger thread of environmental determinism than of organizational determination, and the effective managerial actions will be those associated with sensing and internal design. If, however, the reciprocal influence starts in the organization, then the reciprocity favors organizational determination, and forcefulness and visibility become more crucial managerial qualities.

External Environments

Both organizations and environments are loosely coupled. Managerial actions are a crucial input that organizes these fragmented settings. Thus, it is important to look more closely at what happens when managers confront external situations of modest orderliness. In many loosely coupled settings, the gaps that exist among events must be filled in at least by thought, if not by action. One way to do so is by presuming that there is a logic by which events cohere. These presumptions of logic are evident in the inferences about cause and effect that are assembled into cause maps (e.g., Ashton 1976; Bougon, Weick, and Binkhorst 1977; Goodman 1968; Axelrod 1977; Roos and Hall 1980; Porac 1981).

When managers act as if loosely coupled events were tied together as they are in a cause map, events often *become* more tightly coupled, more orderly, or less variable.

Thus the administrator of an extended-care unit in a hospital (Roos and Hall 1980) may presume that increased public relations activities directed at influential outsiders will stave off mounting internal pressures to follow the rules. Having presumed that the world hangs together like this, the pressured administrator spends more time away from the hospital, which makes him more visible to outsiders. The outsiders think about the hospital more than they did before they saw the administrator, which makes the outsiders' actions more predictable and focused. Their actions previously had been under the control of multiple agendas, which have now been edited down to a smaller set of items, with the hospital being more salient on all those lists. Through the simple act of becoming visible, the administrator makes more homogeneous the "environment" with which the hospital must deal. The administrator also makes the diverse outsiders more mutually relevant to one another, because each now needs some of the information that the others have. Furthermore, the administrator is in an advantageous position to resolve whatever uncertainties his contacts create, which means that he has acquired more power (Hinings et al. 1974).

This entire sequence draws together diverse forces into a more focused scenario that now has more effect on significant actors. The hospital becomes constrained by an environment that did not exist until the administrator changed the salience of events for outsiders. Demands on the hospital became more orderly under the influence of administrative action that itself was launched on the basis of presumptions that just such orderliness would and did exist. At the time the administrator first acted, none of the orderliness was in place nor was there any guarantee that this particular order, or any order for that matter, would be "there" to validate the initial presumption.

In the beginning, presumptions cognitively bridged the gaps among events outside the hospital. Confident action addressed to this presumptively logical world then gave it a tangible form that resembled the presumptive forms stored in the *a priori* maps in the administrator's head.

It is crucial to see that the issue here is *not* one of accuracy. Cause maps could be wrong and still be an important part of managerial action. The important feature of a cause map is that it leads people to anticipate some order "out there." It matters less what particular order is portrayed than that an order of some kind is portrayed. The crucial dynamic is that the prospect of order lures the manager into ill-formed situations that then accommodate to forceful actions and come to resemble relations contained in the cause map. The map animates managers, and the fact of animation, not the map itself, imposes order on situations.

Thus, trappings of rationality, such as strategic plans, are important largely as binding mechanisms. They hold events together long enough and tight enough in people's heads so that they do something in the belief that their action will be influential. To a significant extent, the order they find is an order created by the very actions thought to be *reactions* to demands that were there before action was even contemplated.

This enactment mechanism works precisely because environments are loosely coupled. Looseness by itself is often difficult to understand because causes produce effects only suddenly (rather than continuously), occasionally (rather than constantly), negligibly (rather than significantly), indirectly (rather than directly), and eventually (rather than immediately) (Weick 1982, 380). Such an

unpredictable world cannot be relied upon or controlled. Presumptions, expectations, justifications, and commitments span the breaks in a loosely coupled system and encourage confident actions that tighten settings. The conditions of order and tightness in organizations exist as much in the mind as they do in the field of action. The field of action becomes transformed into something that resembles the mind's image whenever action takes place. But the order that is "discovered" is usually misattributed to external conditions rather than to the *a priori* mental images that triggered the actions of consolidation in the first place.

Such mundane properties of managerial action as confidence, assertion, and optimism now can be recognized as crucial resources by which organizational events are made orderly (March 1975; Zaleznik 1977). Confidence becomes more important the more pliant the setting, the greater the amount of uncertainty, the younger the organization, the higher the turnover, the more intensive the technology. All of these variables weaken the ties among events, which then increases the extent to which presumptions of order and consistent actions impose whatever structure exists among those events.

Consider the activity of divestment (Nees 1981). The presumption that it is possible to sell a firm, when put into action ("Do you want to buy my firm?"), may coalesce the fragments of the environment into homogeneous suspicion, which generates a uniform and forceful no. No then becomes the environment to which the divestor must accommodate. Top management's obsession with secrecy attests to the ease with which the act of inquiring shapes the environment with which they then must deal.

Problems often turn out to be environmental residues of managers' inquiring styles (Mitroff and Kilmann 1978). Changes in those styles of inquiring change the ways in which environments cohere, which in turn changes the problems that are "discovered."

Work on cognitive styles (e.g., McKenney and Keen 1974), for example, may be important because different styles of action flow from these inquiring styles and have differential effects on the environments being examined. For example, consider the Myers-Briggs Type Indicator (Myers 1980). An extroverted sensing type who takes in data by direct inspection, processes these data by thinking, and orients to the world through the dominant perceptual process of sensing (ESTP), will be more active and more conspicuous than will an introverted intuitive type who processes data by feeling and reserves the dominant process of intuition for his or her own thoughts while orienting to the world through personal feelings (INFJ). If the ESTP is more successful in top management than the INFJ, the critical factor may not be analytical style but rather the greater ease with which the ESTP dominates and creates the environments through which he or she moves.

The environment is less crucial to the functioning of an intuitive type than it is to the functioning of a sensing type who relies on direct sensory data. Intuitives, in contrast, often imagine environments that have only a modest fit with what the sensing type would observe. Intuitives are interested in possibilities, not in sensed objects, because the sensed objects are interesting only in terms of what they might become. If sensing types are more attuned to environment, then theories that postulate environmental determinism might be supported when they are tested with CEOs (chief executive officers) who are sensing types but not when they are tested with CEOs who are intuitive types.

Internal Environments

Top management in complex organizations does not design operating structures; it designs decision structures. It essentially divides the organization into subunits that then design the operating structures (Boschken 1982). Instead of managing the organization, management manages the process that then manages the organization; Kuhn and Beam (1982, 325–26) refer to this as "metamanagement."

To design a decision structure is not a simple matter. Top management selects the people who will be in the decision-making group. Thus personnel selection is a key means by which top management creates the environments that will constrain it in the future. This is a tricky issue, however. Just as top management does not know enough to make certain decisions, and hence forms the decision structure, it does not necessarily know enough to dictate who the members of the decision-making group might need for advice. Accordingly, top management must give up some of its control over the list of people who will be its agents. There is a big difference between the statements "I am in control" and "Things are under control" (Antonovsky 1979). To manage complex systems is to know the difference and to relinquish individual control to gain system stability.

While top management is accustomed to saying, "Do what I tell you and I will reward you in proportion as you do it to my satisfaction," it adopts a different philosophy to manage dynamic complexity. The manager who sacrifices personal control by pushing decision making downward to subgroups says essentially,

Do what you collectively think best in light of the objectives I have stated. I will try to reward you collectively as I will have no real way of knowing which persons had what effect in your decisions. In fact, you are probably better judges than I of whether your methods were the most effective available and which of your members are most effective. All I can do is to tell you whether your accomplishment as a group strikes me as reasonably satisfactory relative to my purposes.[1]

Abandoning unity of command (VanFleet and Bedeian 1977), the manager essentially says, "See what you can do and do your best." The manager does retain some control over the purse strings and over decisions to hire, fire, and promote people. However, since individual contributions are concealed within the group product, even personnel decisions will be difficult to make under this arrangement.

The manager still exerts some influence by seeing that wider organizational considerations are kept in mind when decisions are made between units, keeping decision makers informed of relevant constraints, replacing agents, and handling situations that exceed the range for which the group was designed.

This model of delegated control under conditions of dynamic complexity very much resembles the control structure found in universities (Bess 1982; Wilson1981). The president of a university is unable to evaluate the intellectual products of the faculty. The best research goes the way the researcher wants it to go, not the way the administrator wants it to go. It is not possible for administrators to manage hunches or the pursuit of hunches, so they say essentially, "Keep busy and do research." Subsystems within the university decide most of the key issues, such as teaching and admissions requirements, and the only control presidents have over these subgroups is money and final approval of personnel decisions.

Questions of authority, legitimacy, and insubordination are greatly attenuated in universities, but the same attenuation occurs in other organizations where the ties among subsystems are loose and responsibility is delegated to groups rather than to individuals (Blau and Alba 1982). It is sometimes objected that much organizational theory has limited generality because it is based on universities. But in fact the loosely coupled university structure is a prototype for complex organi-

---

[1] From A. Kuhn and R. D. Beam. *The Logic of Organization.* (San Francisco: Jossey-Bass, 1982), 327, by permission.

zations in general, where lower levels make top-management decisions.

Top management creates its own environment when it designs the internal structure that will generate recommendations and monitor the external environment. The degrees of freedom in this creation are limited, but they are not zero. To cope with complexity, top management does not have to give up completely nor does it have to settle for mere tactics. It does have to attend closely to structural and personnel matters and then walk away from them (Padget 1980, 602).

Actions Require Interaction

People generate actions. And people are needed by one another when they generate these actions (Leavitt and Lipman-Blumen 1980). Whether imagined or actually present, people surround all managerial action.

To manage action amidst other people is to (1) identify the basic form in which this interaction operates, the "double interact"; (2) use others more intentionally in the process of self-definition; (3) provide conditions for constructing a sufficiently stable social reality, so that people can do what they are expected to do; and (4) offset the tendency for social cohesion to distort perceptions of external environments.

The Double Interact

The basic form of action when two or more people are involved is the double interact (Allport 1962). Person A does something in the presence of person B (B can be either physically present or imagined, as when one tries to anticipate top-management reaction to a presentation); B then responds to this action; and finally, on the basis of what B did, A either modifies or retains the initial act. What A's act meant initially is *not* known fully by A until he or she sees what B does. The act by itself means nothing apart from B's response. When B does respond, A knows what he or she has done and then can either reaffirm or modify that action to bring it closer to the initial intentions, which themselves are now clearer. Because the first action serves as an anchor and the second action is designed relative to the first, the double interact concludes with the second act by A. Additional acts merely trigger different processes that are less

basic (e.g., when the sequence is extended to a fourth, fifth, or sixth act, the situation now becomes a debate).

The double-interact concept allows analysts to distinguish four basic ways in which action is coordinated. Consider Table 1.1, which has been adapted from Willis and Hollander.

When a manager gives an order, the subordinate's reaction indicates what the original action meant, what is likely to happen, and what revisions are needed. Thus, if the manager says, "I think we need to cut costs," and the associate says, "I think we need to increase market share," the manager can then say either, "You're right" (conforming to the colleague's view) or "You're wrong; cost is the issue" (demonstrating independence). If the associate had said, "I agree with you; the problem is cost," then the manager might have kept this diagnosis, believing that the colleague was credible (uniformity), or might have changed his or her view, saying, "He's never agreed with me before so there must be something wrong"—an example of anticonformity.

The value of the double interact to explain managerial action is that managers often assume that their influence is unilateral and fail to realize the power of subordinates to withhold compliance and jeopardize joint outcomes (Knights and Roberts 1982; Dubois 1981; Butler and Snizek 1976).

TABLE 1.1

Act	Interact	Double Interact	Type of Influence
Affirm A	Affirm A	Affirm A	Uniformity
		Affirm B	Anticonformity
Affirm A	Affirm B	Affirm A	Independence
		Affirm B	Conformity

From R.H. Willis and E. P. Hollander, "An Experimental Study of Three Response Modes in Social Influence Situation," *Journal of Abnormal and Social Psychology* 69 (1964): 150–56. Copyright 1964 by the American Psychological Association. Adapted by permission of the authors.

Self-definition through
Self-fulfilling Prophecies

Double interacts often unfold in face-to-face interaction, making action more complex.

> [A] great deal of the work of organization—decision making, the transmission of information, the close coordination of physical tasks—is done face to face, requires being done in this way, and is vulnerable to face-to-face effects. Differently put, insofar as agents of social organizations of any scale from states to households, can be persuaded, cajoled, flattered, intimidated, or otherwise influenced by effects only achievable in face-to-face dealings, then here, too, the interaction order bluntly impinges on macroscopic entities. (Goffman 1983, 8)

Goffman (p. 8) suggests that many interactions in organizations can be viewed as people-processing encounters during which the impressions that are conveyed affect life chances. As a metaphor for interaction in organizations, he suggests the placement interview, a situation in which there is a quiet sorting that reproduces the social structures associated with statuses such as gender, race, physical attractiveness, class, and age. He argues that people processing such as is done institutionally by school counselors, personnel departments, psychiatric diagnosticians, or courtroom officials is ubiquitous. "Everyone is a gatekeeper in regard to something. Thus, friendship relationships and marital bonds (at least in our society) can be traced back to an occasion in which something more was made of an incidental contact than need have been" (p. 8).

Face-to face interaction has a promissory, evidential quality in which people read indicators to guide subsequent interactions. Organizations are heavily evaluative contexts in which accountability, responsibility, blame, and credit are accorded freely and consequentially (Perry and Barney 1981). In that sense, it is relevant to assume that every day at work is like a placement interview during which a mixture of fact and fantasy influences how people read one another for indications of status and character.

A significant portion of what people know about themselves originates in how they are treated and labeled by others (Maines 1977). This process is especially complicated because the definitions other people send back to the original actor, who incorporates them as parts of the self, often are implanted in those others by the original actions of the original actor. People do create environments, and that means they often create the other people who then create them. Thus we begin to see the profound sense in which social behavior has a solitary core (Bateson 1975).

Self-fulfilling prophecies control much interaction with others (e.g., King 1974; Jones 1977; Snyder, Tanke, and Berscheid 1977). We interact with expectations of how events will unfold based on rumors, reputations, and nonverbal signals that are immediately visible. These expectations often control what we get back. For example, anticipating hostility, we walk guardedly into a situation and give off signals that *stimulate* the hostility we predicted would be there (Schwartz and Lever 1976).

Thus people create themselves by biasing the interactions in which they participate. Personal character does not exist until other people begin to define it for us by their actions and labels. But those actions and labels (e.g., "*He* is hostile, we are not") are often implanted by the person in search of character. Thus, I become the prophecies I project on others, which they redirect back to me. Since expectations are so prominent in organizations, conditions there seem ripe to encourage self-validating definitions of character that are essentially closed to the discovery of new data.

Social Comparison and Social Reality

Because loosely coupled organizations generate uncertainty (Downey and Slocum 1975; Duncan 1972), people must rely more heavily on one another to define a workable reality (Pfeffer, Salancik, and Leblebici 1976). Social-comparison processes should be especially salient in loosely coupled systems where people find it difficult to assess their abilities and beliefs (Festinger 1954). If social comparison is crucial, then we would expect to find that people are especially sensitive to issues of similarity and dissimilarity, because these are the fundamental judgments that determine the appropriateness of comparison with others (Salancik and Pfeffer 1978).

When people are uncertain about an opinion or an ability, they select for comparison someone judged to be in rough agreement with what they believe or roughly at their level of competence. To fine-tune the comparison and validate the belief, they then communicate with the comparison person to move his or her position even closer or they change their own position so that it agrees even more with that of the comparison person. If neither of these mechanisms works, they reject the comparison and try again.

Out of these interactions people build a social reality with which they can cope. If comparable others are not available, or if similarities occur on marginal issues, then beliefs become unstable, actions become erratic, prediction and control decrease, and stress increases. Under conditions of high uncertainty managers should be sensitive to the necessity to build a social reality and the fact that people can do this more readily when there are salient bases for similarity. Highlighting existing similarities, providing conditions where people can disclose more information safely, making it more likely that they will discover similarities, or manufacturing similarities by putting people through intense socializations (Van Maanen and Schein 1979), all can facilitate comparison, which facilitates reality construction, which increases predictability, control, and satisfaction.

Uncertainty directly creates one form of role stress—role ambiguity—and is indirectly involved in at least two other forms—quantitative and qualitative role overload (VanSell, Brief, and Schuler 1981). Often when people complain that they do not have sufficient skills to do their job (qualitative overload) or that they are asked to do too much (quantitative overload), it is not clear to them what is to be done, what skills are relevant, or what is important.

When social realities are built through the process of social comparison, ambiguities get resolved long enough for forceful action to be taken, which then consolidates a more certain environment. The extent of similarity determines the speed with which social reality is built, its stability, and its resistance to competing realities advanced by dissimilar people.

All of these social-comparison processes become less important when there is a physical reality to which questions of belief and ability can be referred. To the extent that organizations rely on tangible indicators that require a minimum of judgment, and to the extent that environments are stable and structures are predictable, then social comparison is less crucial and the organization should be able to tolerate a more diverse set of actors over longer periods of time with fewer negative effects on productivity. Diversity should be less troublesome in mechanistic systems than in organic systems because there is less need to construct reality. Similar others in a mechanistic system are redundant. Diverse others in an organic system amplify uncertainty and may encourage cliques among those people who are similar on at least some dimensions (e.g., all graduates of Seattle University), even if those dimensions are not central to task accomplishment.

A recent concept that highlights the necessity for social comparison is the suggestion that organizations are like paradigms (Pfeffer 1982, Chapter 7; Brown 1978; Lodahl and Gordon 1972). "A paradigm is a technology, including the beliefs about cause-effect relations and standards of practice and behavior, as well as specific examples of these, that constitute how an organization goes about doing things" (Pfeffer 1982, 227-28). The importance of a paradigm is that it infuses day-to-day activity with meaning and purpose. Paradigms control the interpretations people impose on new information and often determine whether they will even gather any new information. When paradigms are well developed, there is consensus on preferences and on definitions of the situation, which means that people within a subunit can speak with one voice and pursue a consistent course of action. This consolidated position can have substantial advantages in political struggles. When paradigms are less well developed and when uncertainty is higher, social comparison becomes more crucial, conflict is more likely, and forcefulness is compromised.

Thus social comparison and the social influence processes that accompany it are crucial means to develop the paradigms that solidify organizations.

Cohesion and Accuracy

The complexities of interaction can be summarized in the form of a dilemma that confronts most managers, a dilemma we will call the "cohesion-accuracy trade-off." Emphasizing social cohesion risks establishing a biased, unreliable, misleading perception of the world. But to maintain perceptual accuracy is to run the risk of alienation and turnover when social cohesion is kept at a minimum.

The social systems in most groups in organizations are vulnerable to fragmentation and dissolution (Campbell 1972). To prevent this fragmentation members strive for at least four things.

1. Some degree of uniformity of belief
2. Some degree of acceptance of leadership and traditional authority
3. Willingness to learn vicariously from the reports of others (trust)
4. Willingness to participate in collective action

Honesty, dissent, innovation, and variation can threaten these four requirements. People who see things differently from other group members pose a threat to uniformity in belief, reject leadership and authority, imply a distrust for the reports of others, and resist collective action. Under these conditions, honesty has the potential to splinter the group or to invite rejection.

If a cohesive system tries to test reality it may fail, because the preference and beliefs that hold the system together bias how people test reality and interpret what they find. People see what validates the group's view, not what others outside the group might verify independently (Janis 1972; Tetlock 1979).

This bias can be reduced by designing a social system so that outcomes in the external world—those things people want to learn more about—occur *independently* of the preferences of individuals. The way to do this is to use norms and procedures in which no one—whether boss or colleague—can affect the answers. Obviously this is an ideal.

Organizations rely heavily on authority of position, precedent, prestige, and the majority view to influence decisions. It makes little difference who produces the evidence: it is the evidence itself that counts. If the value of evidence is defined by who found it, then accuracy is sacrificed to cohesion. The only way to break free of ideas that preserve cohesion, continuity, and consensus is to make them vulnerable to experimental probes (e.g., Staw 1977). Then empirical evidence will be taken seriously whether presented by a very young person, a disliked person, or a minority group member.

The chronic danger in organizations is that the constructed social reality may be nothing but a wishful construction. It all depends on the degree to which the manager either imposes norms that neutralize the more severe effects of cohesion on accuracy or reduces cohesion to the minimum level necessary to sustain a group.

Accuracy can be promoted by following a series of norms in management (adapted from Campbell 1979, 192-96).

1. Tradition is a source of error rather than truth; be suspicious of received wisdom.
2. Stubborn, insubordinate, young geniuses are to be listened to even if their ideas go against the prevailing views of older, more established people.
3. Competence rather than likableness should be rewarded.
4. Contribution to effectiveness is the only legitimate basis on which to bestow status.
5. Dishonesty should be punished with ruthlessness and finality.

Many of these norms run contrary to the political nature of organizations in which information is "bent" to individual advantage. The very fact that these norms seem so unrealistic makes the point that accuracy will be in short supply unless interpersonal ties are overlaid with a set of restrictions that favor accuracy, are monitored continuously, and are firmly enforced.

A different approach is to weaken social ties. Compromises that favor accuracy over cohesion occur when there is less group to preserve. There are several ways to weaken social ties: recruit loners, tolerate high turn-over, design tasks so that people can perform them with relatively little instruction and relatively short apprenticeships, recruit people who have been similarly socialized and who therefore can coordinate and mesh their activities without much face-to-face supervision, assign individual projects that are basically self-contained, reward disagreement and conflict, develop a culture favoring individualism, use diverse reference groups as comparisons, and review performance at infrequent intervals (allow long spans of time within which people can exercise discretion).

These tactics minimize the necessity for close attention to the social system by reducing its scope and what is required to maintain it. Norms are not needed to offset social threats to validity, because the social threats themselves are minimal. In a thinned system, a combination of culture, group composition, division of labor, delegation of authority, and a broad definition of mission create a sensing mechanism with multiple sensors but fewer internal constraints that distort what is registered. The danger is that the manager will go too far and create disoriented, alienated employees who adopt every suggestion they hear.

Conclusions

The purpose of this chapter has been to lay the groundwork for more general understanding of managerial action in organizations. We now know a good deal about what managers actually do (Metcalfe 1982; Kotter 1982; Davis and Luthans 1980), but we know less about the adequacy with which they do it, what they might be doing instead, how these actions address the dimly sensed problems associated with coordination and control in joint action, why these particular forms and not other ones persist, and what the lingering and larger effects are of repeated activation of these limited forms.

Answers to some of these puzzles may lie in illuminating the mechanisms by which theories such as population ecology, institutionalization, interorganizational relations, resource dependence, systems theory, loose coupling, or organized anarchies flow through, give form to, and constrain daily managerial actions. The relationship between theory and reality is seldom clear-cut. Consider the "mushy ice problem" described by Kuhn and Beam:

The law of levers states that weight times distance on one side of a fulcrum will equal weight times distance on the other side. If a restless polar bear walks toward one end of a slab of mushy ice that rests roughly centered on top of a mound of snow while a seal rests on the other end, any one or a combination of a number of things may happen. The bear's end of the slab may go down and the seal's end go up, like a true lever, or the slab of ice may break in one or more places so that the bear goes down but the seal does not go up. The snow may compress so that both go down, or the snow fulcrum may be so broad and the ice so strong that the slab does not move at all. . . . If the slab of ice does not always behave as the law of levers prescribes, that fact does not invalidate the law. It merely means that the situation does not closely resemble the theoretical model of a lever. . . . [2]

When the facts are mushy, no theoretical model provides precise analysis and no seasoned investigator would try to find one that does. But one should not throw out perfectly good principles when the problems of application lie in the setting rather than the theory.

Principles of action bear on actual organizations just as principles of mechanics bear on mushy ice. Organization theory often discards useful ideas like dissonance in the face of unclear facts and then replaces the ideas with other flawed ideas. When the substitutes do not work either, the field is then left with nothing. It simply shuffles among formulations, all of which fare poorly because they are applied to disorderly events.

To ground an understanding of organizations in justified, interdependent action between two or more persons is to start with basics that do not evaporate whenever facts become less clear. To start with action is not to make reductionistic assertions that psychology is sufficient to understand organizational behavior. Action is no more psychological than it is sociological or economic. Action cuts across all disciplines and is fully understood by none of them.

Ultimately, organizational theories must be tested against what managers do and the consequences of their actions. The theories most likely to prove valid will be those that focus explicitly on what managers do when they construct, maintain, and use constantly shifting arrangements to acquire constantly shifting scarce resources.

---

[2] From A. Kuhn and R. D. Beam. *The Logic of Organization.* 287–88, by permission.

REFERENCES AND ADDITIONAL READINGS

Aldrich, H., and D. Herker. 1977. "Boundary Spanning Roles and Organizational Structure." *The Academy of Management Review* 2:217–30.

Allport, F. H. 1962. "A Structuronomic Conception of Behavior: Individual and Collective." *Journal of Abnormal and Social Psychology* 64:3–30.

Antonovsky, A. 1979. *Health, Stress and Coping.* San Francisco: Jossey-Bass.

Argote, L. 1982. "Input Uncertainty and Organizational Coordination in Hospital Emergency Units." *Administrative Science Quarterly* 27:420–34.

Aronson, E. 1980. "Persuasion via Self-Justification: Large Commitments for Small Rewards." In *Retrospections on Social Psychology,* ed. L. Festinger, 3–21. New York: Oxford University Press.

Ashton, R. H. 1976. "Deviation-Amplifying Feedback and Unintended Consequences of Management Accounting Systems." *Accounting, Organizations and Society* 1:289–300.

Axelrod, R. 1973. "Schema Theory: An Informative Processing Model of Perception and Cognition." *American Political Science Review* 67:1248–66.

———. 1977. "Argumentation in Foreign Policy Settings." *Journal of Conflict Resolution* 21:727–56.

Barnard, C. I. 1938. "Mind in Everyday Affairs." In *The Functions of the Executive,* 301–22. Cambridge, Mass.: Harvard University Press.

Baron, R. M. 1981. "Social Knowing from an Ecological-Event Perspective: A Consideration of the Relative Domains of Power for Cognitive and Perceptual Modes of Knowing." In *Cognition, Social Behavior, and the Environment,* ed. J. H. Harvey, 61–89. Hillsdale, N. J.: Erlbaum.

Bateson, G. 1975. "Counsel for a Suicide's Friend." *CoEvolution Quarterly* (Spring): 135.

Bell, G. D. 1967. "Formality versus Flexibility in Complex Organizations." In *Organizations and Human Behavior,* ed. G. D. Bell, 97–106. Englewood Cliffs, N.J.: Prentice-Hall.

Benson, J. K. 1977. "Innovation and Crisis in Organizational Analysis," In *Organization Analysis: Critique and Innovation,* ed. J. K. Benson, 5–18. Beverly Hills, Calif.: Sage.

Berg, P.O. 1979. *Emotional Structures in Organizations.*

Farnborough, England: Teakfield.

Bess, J. L. 1982. *University Organization.* New York: Human Sciences Press.

Blau, J. R., and R. D. Alba. 1982. "Empowering Nets of Participation." *Administrative Science Quarterly* 27:363–79.

Bogdan R. 1972. *Participant Observation in Organizational Settings.* Syracuse, N.Y.: Syracuse University Press.

Boland, R. J., Jr. 1982. "Myth and Technology in the American Accounting Profession." *Journal of Management Studies* 19:109–27.

Borum, F. 1980. "A Power-Strategy Alternative to Organization Development." *Organization Studies* 1:123–46.

Boschken, H. L. 1982. "Organization Theory and Federalism: Interorganizational Networks and the Political Economy of the Federalist." *Organization Studies* 3:335–73.

Bougon, M., K. E. Weick, and D. Binkhorst. 1977. "Cognition in Organizations: An Analysis of the Utrecht Jazz Orchestra." *Administrative Science Quarterly* 22:606–39.

Bramel, D. 1968. "Dissonance, Expectation, and the Self." In *Theories of Cognitive Consistency: A Sourcebook,* ed. R. P. Abelson, E. Aronson, W. J. McGuire, T. M. Newcomb, M. J. Rosenberg, and P. H. Tannenbaum, 355–65. Chicago: Rand McNally.

Brittain, J. W., and J. H. Freeman. 1980. "Organizational Proliferation and Density Dependent Selection: Organizational Evolution in the Semiconductor Industry." In *The Organizational Life Cycle,* ed. J. R. Kimberly and R. H. Miles, 291–338. San Francisco: Jossey-Bass.

Brown, R. H. 1978. "Bureaucracy as Praxis: Toward a Political Phenomenology of Formal Organizations." *Administrative Science Quarterly* 23:365–82.

Brunesson, N. 1982. "The Irrationality of Action and Action Rationality: Decisions, Ideologies, and Organizational Actions." *Journal of Management Studies* 19:29–44.

Butler, S. R., and W. E. Snizek. 1976. "The Waitress-Diner Relationship: A Multimethod Approach to the Study of Subordinate Influence." *Sociology of Work and Occupations* 3:209–22.

Campbell, D. T. 1972. "Objectivity and the Social Locus of Scientific Knowledge." In *Studies in the Philosophy of Science,* vol. 10, ed. R.S. Cohen and M. N. W. Wartofsky. Dordrecht, Netherlands: Redi Reidel.

———. 1979. "A Tribal Model of the Social System Vehicle Carrying Scientific Knowledge." *Knowledge: Creation, Diffusion, Utilization* 1:181–201.

Carroll, S. J., and H. L. Tosi. 1977. *Organizational Behavior.* Chicago: St. Clair.

Cherns, A. 1980. "Organizations as Instruments of Social Change in Postindustrial Societies." *Organization Studies* 1:109–22.

Cohen, M. D., and J. G. March. 1974. *Leadership and Ambiguity.* New York: McGraw-Hill.

Cohen, M. D., J. G. March, and J. P. Olsen. 1972. "A Garbage Can Model of Organizational Choice." *Administrative Science Quarterly* 17:1–25.

Colignon, R., and D. Cray. 1980. "Critical Organizations." *Organization Studies* 1:349–65.

Cooper, J., M. P. Zanna, and P. A. Taves. 1978. "Arousal as a Necessary Condition for Attitude Change Following Induced Compliance." *Journal of Personality and Social Psychology* 36:1101–6.

Daft, R. L., and R. H. Lengel. 1984. "Information Richness: A New Approach to Manager Behavior and Organization Design." In *Research in Organizational Behavior,* ed. B. Staw and L. L. Cummings, vol. 6. Greenwich, Conn.: Jai Press.

Dailey, C. A. 1971. *Assessment of Lives.* San Francisco: Jossey-Bass.

Davis, T. R. B., and F. Luthans. 1980. "Managers in Action: A New Look at Their Behavior and Operating Modes." *Organizational Dynamics* 9, no. 1:64–80.

Downey, H. K., and J. W. Slocum. 1975. "Uncertainty: Measures, Research, and Sources of Variation." *Academy of Management Journal* 18:562–78.

Driver, M. J. 1979. "Career Concepts and Career Management in Organizations." In *Behavioral Problems in Organizations,* ed. C. L. Cooper, 79–139. Englewood Cliffs, N.J.: Prentice-Hall.

Dubois, P. 1981. "Workers' Control Over the Organization of Work: French and English Maintenance Workers in Mass Production Industry." *Organization Studies* 2:347–60.

Duncan, R. 1972. "Characteristics of Organizational Environments and Perceived Environmental Uncertainty." *Administrative Science Quarterly* 17:313–27.

Dunkerly, D., T. Spybey, and M. Thrasher. 1981. "Interorganizational Networks: A Case Study of Industrial Location." *Organization Studies* 2:229–47.

Dutton, J. M., and W. H. Starbuck. 1963. "On Managers and Theories." *Management International* 6:1–11.

Ewen S. 1976. *Captains of Consciousness.* New York: McGraw-Hill.

Feldman, M. S., and J. G. March. 1981. "Information in Organizations as Signal and Symbol." *Administrative Science Quarterly* 26:171– 86.

Festinger, L. 1954. "A Theory of Social Comparison Processes." *Human Relations* 7:117–40.

———. 1957. *A Theory of Cognitive Dissonance.* Evanston, Ill.: Row, Peterson.

Fisch, R., J. H. Weakland, and L. Segal. 1982. *The Tactics of Change.* San Francisco: Jossey-Bass.

Glassman, R. B. 1973. "Persistence and Loose Coupling in Living Systems." *Behavioral Science* 18:83–98.

Goethals, G. R., J. Cooper, and A. Naficy. 1979. "Role of Foreseen, Foreseeable, and Unforeseeable Behavior Consequences in the Arousal of Cognitive Dissonance." *Journal of Personality and Social Psychology* 37:1179–85.

Goffman, E. 1983. "The Interaction Order." *American Sociological Review* 48:1–17.

Goodman, P. S. 1968. "The Measurement of an Individual's Organization Map." *Administrative Science Quarterly* 13:246–65.

Gronn, P. S. 1968. "Talk as the Work: The Accomplishment of School Administration." *Administrative Science Quarterly* 13:246–65.

Hage, J. 1980. *Theories of Organizations.* New York: Wiley.

Hall, P. M. 1972. "A Symbolic Interactionist Analysis of Politics." *Sociological Inquiry* 42, nos. 3–4:35–75.

Hambrick, D. C. 1981. "Specialization of Environmental Scanning Activities Among Upper Level Executives." *Journal of Management Studies* 18:299– 320.

Hannan, M. T., and J. Freeman. 1977. "The Population Ecology of Organizations." *American Journal of Sociology* 82:929–64.

Harrison, R. 1981. "Startup: The Care and Feeding of Infant Systems." *Organizational Dynamics* 10, no. 1:5–29.

Herr, J. J., and J. H. Weakland. 1977. *Counseling Elders and Their Families.* New York: Springer.

Hinings, C. R., D. J. Hickson, J. M. Pennings, and R. E. Schneck. 1974. "Structural Conditions of Intraorganizational Power." *Administrative Science Quarterly* 19:22–44.

Hirsch, P. M. 1975. "Organizational Effectiveness and the Institutional Environment." *Administrative Science Quarterly* 20:327–44.

Huber, G. P. 1980. *Managerial Decision Making.* Glenview, Ill.: Scott, Foresman.

Janis, I. R. 1972. *Victims of Groupthink.* Boston: Houghton Mifflin.

Jones, E. E., and H. B. Gerard. 1967. *Foundations of Social Psychology.* New York: Wiley.

Jones, R. A. 1977. *Self-Fulfilling Prophecies.* Hillsdale, N.J.: Erlbaum.

Katz, F. E. 1974. "Interdeterminancy in the Structure of Systems." *Behavorial Science* 19:394–403.

Kiesler, C. A. 1971. *The Psychology of Commitment.* New York: Academic.

Kimberly, J. R. 1980. "Data Aggregation in Organizational Research: The Temporal Dimension." *Organization Studies* 1:367–77.

King, A. S. 1974. "Expectation Effects in Organizational Change." *Administrative Science Quarterly* 19:221–30.

Knights, D., and J. Roberts. 1982. "The Power of Organization or the Organization of Power?" *Organization Studies* 3:47–63.

Knorr-Cetina, K. D. 1981. "Introduction: The Micro-Sociological Challenge of Macro-Sociology: Toward a Reconstruction of Social Theory and Methodology." In *Advances in Social Theory and Methodology,* ed. K. Knorr-Cetina and A. V. Cicourel, 1–47. Boston: Routledge & Kegan Paul.

Knowles, P. L., and D. L. Smith. 1982. "The Ecological Perspective Applied to Social Perception: Revision of a Working Paper." *Journal for the Theory of Social Behavior* 12:53–78.

Kotter, J. 1982. *The General Managers.* New York: Free Press.

Kuhn, A., and R. D. Beam. 1982. *The Logic of Organization.* San Francisco: Jossey-Bass.

Langer, E. J. 1978. "Rethinking the Role of Thought in Social Interaction." In *New Directions in Attribution Research,* ed. J. H. Harvey, W. J. Ickes, and R. F. Kidd, vol. 2: 35–58. Potomac, Md.: Erlbaum.

Leach, E. R. 1967. "An Anthropologist's Reflections in a Social Survey." In *Anthropologists in the Field,* ed. D. G. Jongmans and P. C. Gutking, 75–88. Atlantic Highlands, N. J.: Humanities Press.

Leavitt, H. J., and J. Lipman-Blumen. 1980. "A Case for the Relational Manager," *Organizational Dynamics* 9, no. 1:27–41.

Leifer, R., and A. Delbecq. 1978. "Organizational/Environmental Interchange: A Model of Boundary Spanning Activity." *Academy of Management Review* 3:40–50.

Lewicki, R. J. 1981. "Organizational Seduction: Building Commitment to Organizations." *Organizational Dynamics* 10, no. 2:5–21.

Lodahl, J. B., and G. Gordon. 1972. "The Structure of Scientific Fields and the Functioning of University Graduate Departments." *American Sociological Review* 37:57–73.

Maines, D. R. 1977. "Social Organization and Social Structure in Symbolic Interactionist Thought." *Annual Review of Sociology* 3:235–59.

Mali, P., ed. 1981. *Management Handbook.* New York: Wiley.

Mangham, I. L., and M. A. Overington. 1982. "Performance and Rehearsal: Social Order and Organizational Life." *Symbolic Interaction* 5:205–23.

March, J. G. 1975. "Education and the Pursuit of Optimism." *Texas Tech Journal of Education* 2:5–17.

Marshall, J., and R. Stewart. 1981. "Managers' Job Perceptions. Part I: Their Overall Frameworks and Working Strategies." *Journal of Management Studies* 18:177–90.

Mayhew, B. H. 1981. "Structuralism versus Individualism: Part I, Shadowboxing in the Dark." *Social Forces* 59:335–75.

McKenney, J. L., and P. G. W. Keen. 1974. "How Managers' Minds Work." *Harvard Business Review* (May-June) pp. 79–90.

Metcalfe, B. M. A. 1982. "Leadership: Extrapolating from Theory and Research to Practical Skills Training." *Journal of Management Studies* 19:295–305.

Meyer, A. D. 1982. "Adapting to Environmental Jolts." *Administrative Science Quarterly* 27:515–37.

Meyer, J. W., and B. Rowan. 1977. "Institutionalized Organizations: Formal Structure as Myth and Ceremony." *American Journal of Sociology* 83:340–63.

Meyer, M. W. 1979. "Organizational Structure as Signaling." *Pacific Sociological Review* 22:481–500.

Miles, R. H. 1980. "Organization Boundary Roles." In *Current Concerns in Occupational Stress,* ed. C. L. Cooper and R. Payne, 61–96. New York: Wiley.

Miller, S. M. 1980. "Why Having Control Reduces Stress: If I Can't Stop the Roller Coaster I Don't Want to Get Off." In *Human Helplessness,* ed. J. Garber and M. E. P. Seligman, 71–95. New York: Academic.

Mintzberg, H. 1973. *The Nature of Managerial Work.* New York: Harper & Row.

———. 1985. "The Manager's Job: Folklore and Fact." *Harvard Business Review* 53, no. 4:49–61.

Mitroff, I. I., and R. H. Kilmann. 1978. *Methodological Approaches to Social Science.* San Francisco: Jossey–Bass.

Morgan, G. 1981. "The Schismatic Metaphor and Its Implications for Organizational Analysis." *Organization Studies* 2:23–44.

Moscovici, S. 1976. *Social Influence and Social Change.* New York: Academic.

———. 1980. "Toward a Theory of Conversion Behavior." In *Advances in Experimental Social Psychology,* ed. L. Berkowitz, vol. 13: 209–39. New York: Academic.

Myers, I. B. 1980. *Introduction to Type.* Palo Alto, Calif.: Consulting Psychologists Press.

Nees, D. 1981. "Increase Your Divestment Effectiveness." *Strategic Management Journal* 2:119–30.

Neisser, U. 1972. "Gibson's Ecological Optics: Consequences of a Different Stimulus Description." *Journal for the Theory of Social Behavior* 7:17–28.

Neruda, P. 1968. *We Are Many.* Trans. Alistair Reid. London: Grossman.

Nugent, P. S. 1981. "Management and Modes of Thought." *Organizational Dynamics* 9, no. 4:45–59

O'Reilly, C. A., and D. F. Caldwell. 1981. "The Commitment and Job Tenure of New Employees: Some Evidence of Postdecisional Justification." *Administrative Science Quarterly* 26: 597–616.

Overington, M. A., and I. L. Mangham. 1982. "The Theatrical Perspective in Organizational Analysis." *Symbolic Interaction* 5:173–85.

Padget, J. F. 1980. "Managing Garbage Can Hierarchies." *Administrative Science Quarterly* 25:583–604.

Perrow, C. 1981. "Disintegrating Social Sciences." *New York University Educational Quarterly* 12 no. 2:2–9.

Perry, L. T., and J. B. Barney. 1981. "Performance Lies Are Hazardous to Organizational Health." *Organizational Dynamics* 9, no. 3:68–80.

Peters, T. J. 1980. "Management Systems: The Language of Organizational Character and Competence." *Organizational Dynamics* 9, no. 1:3–26.

Pfeffer, J. 1981a. "Management as Symbolic Action: The Creation and Maintenance of Organizational Paradigms." In *Research in Organizational Behavior,* vol. 3, ed. L. L. Cummings and B. Staw, 1–52. Greenwich, Conn.: Jai Press.

———. 1981b. *Power in Organizations.* Marshfield, Mass.: Pitman.

———. 1982. *Organizations and Organization Theory.* Marshfield, Mass.: Pitman.

Pfeffer, J., G. R. Salancik, and H. Leblebici. 1976. "The Effect of Uncertainty on the Use of Social Influence in Organizational Decision Making." *Administrative Science Quarterly* 21:227–45.

Porac, J. F. 1981. "Causal Loops and Other Intercausal Perceptions in Attributions for Exam Performance." *Journal of Educational Psychology* 73:587–601.

Rados, D. L. 1972. "Selection and Evaluation of Alternatives in Repetitive Decision Making." *Administrative Science Quarterly* 17:196–206.

Reynolds, D. K. 1976. *Morita Psychotherapy.* Berkeley, Calif.: University of California Press.

———. 1981. "Morita Psychotherapy." In *Handbook of Innovative Psychotherapies,* ed. R. J. Corsini, 489–501. New York: Wiley.

Robbins, S. P. 1983. *Organization Theory: The Structure and Design of Organizations.* Englewood Cliffs, N. J.: Prentice-Hall.

Roos, L. L., and R. I. Hall. 1980. "Influence Diagrams and Organizational Power." *Administrative Science Quarterly* 25:57–71.

Ross, J., and K. R. Ferris. 1981. "Interpersonal Attraction and Organizational Outcomes: A Field Examination." *Administrative Science Quarterly* 26:617–32.

Salancik, G. R. 1977. "Commitment and the Control of Organizational Behavior and Belief." In *New Directions in Organizational Behavior,* ed. B. M. Staw and G. R. Salancik, 1–54. Chicago: St. Clair.

Salancik, G. R., and J. Pfeffer. 1978. "Uncertainty, Secrecy, and the Choice of Similar Others." *Social Psychology* 41, no. 3:246–55.

Schreyogg, G. 1980. "Contigency and Choice in Organization Theory." *Organization Studies:* 305–26.

Schwartz, H., and J. Jacobs. 1979. *Qualitative Sociology: A Method to the Madness.* New York: Free Press.

Schwartz, P., and J. Lever. 1976. "Fear and Loathing at a College Mixer." *Urban Life* 4:413–31.

Scott, W. R. 1981. *Organizations: Rational, Natural, and Open Systems.* Englewood Cliffs, N. J.: Prentice-Hall.

Simmel, G. 1971. "How Is Society Possible?" In *George Simmel on Individuality and Social Forms,* ed. D. N. Levine, 6–22. Chicago: University of Chicago Press.

Simon, H. A. 1962. "The Architecture of Complexity." *Proceedings of the American Philosophical Society* 106, no. 6: 467–82.

Snyder, M., E. D. Tanke, and E. Berscheid. 1977. "Social Perception and Interpersonal Behavior: On the Self-Fulfilling Nature of Social Stereotypes." *Journal of Personality and Social Psychology* 35:656–66.

Starbuck, W. H. 1982. "Congealing Oil: Inventing Ideologies to Justify Acting Ideologies Out." *Journal of Management Studies* 19:3–27.

———. 1983. "Organizations as Active Generators." *American Sociological Review* 48:91–102.

Staw, B. M. 1976. "Knee Deep in the Big Muddy: A Study of Escalating Commitment to a Chosen Course of Action." *Organizational Behavior and Human Performance* 16:27–44.

———. 1977. "The Experimenting Organization." *Organizational Dynamics* 6, no. 1:3–18.

———. 1980. "Rationality and Justification in Organizational Life." In *Research in Organizational Behavior,* vol. 2, ed. B. M. Staw and L. L. Cummings, 45–80. Greenwich, Conn.: Jai Press.

Staw, B. M., and J. Ross. 1978. "Commitment to a Policy Decision: A Multitheoretical Decision." *Administrative Science Quarterly* 23:40–64.

Stern, R. N. 1979. "The Development of an Interorganizational Control Network: The Case of Intercollegiate Athletics." *Administrative Science Quarterly* 24:242–66.

———. 1981. "Competitive Influences on the Interorganizational Regulation of College Athletics." *Administrative Science Quarterly,* 26:15–32.

Suedfeld, P., P. E. Tetlock, and C. Ramirez. 1977. "War, Peace, and Integrative Complexity." *Journal of Conflict Resolution* 21:427–42.

Tetlock, P. E. 1979. "Identifying Victims of Groupthink from Public Statements of Decision Makers." *Journal of Personality and Social Psychology* 37:1314–24.

Thoenig, J. C. 1982. "Discussion Note: Research Management and Management Research." *Organization Studies* 3:269–75.

Thoits, P. A. 1982. "Conceptual, Methodological, and Theoretical Problems in Studying Social Support as a Buffer Against Life Stress," *Journal of Health and Social Behavior* 23:145–59

Thorngate, W. 1976. "Must We Always Think Before We Act?" *Personality and Psychology Bulletin* 2:31–35.

Van Fleet, D. D., and A. G. Bedeian. 1977. "A History of the Span of Management." *Academy of Management Review* 2:356–72.

Van Maanen, J., and E. H. Schein. 1979. "Toward a Theory of Organizational Socialization." In *Research in Organizational Behavior,* ed. B. M. Staw, vol. 1: 209–64. Greenwich, Conn.: Jai Press.

Van Sell, M., A. P. Brief, and R. S. Schuler. 1981. "Role Conflict and Role Ambiguity: Integration of the Literature and Direc-

tions for Future Research." *Human Relations* 34:43–71.

Watson, T. J. 1982. "Group Ideologies and Organizational Change." *Journal of Management Studies* 19:259–75.

Weick, K. E. 1976. "Educational Organizations as Loosely Coupled Systems." *Administrative Science Quarterly* 21:1–19.

———. 1978. "The Spines of Leaders." In *Leadership: Where Else Can We Go?* ed. M. W. McCall, Jr., and M. M. Lombardo, 37–61. Durham: Duke University Press.

———. 1979. *The Social Psychology of Organizing.* 2d ed. Reading, Mass.: Addison–Wesley.

———. 1980. "The Management of Eloquence." *Executive* 6, no. 3:18–21.

———. 1982. "Management of Organizational Change Among Loosely Coupled Elements." In *Change in Organizations,* ed. P. Goodman, 375–408. San Francisco: Jossey–Bass.

Weick, K. E., and P. Prestholdt. 1968. "Realignment of Discrepant Reinforcement Value." *Journal of Personality and Social Psychology* 8:180–87.

Weiss, C. H. 1980. "Knowledge Creep and Decision Accretion." *Knowledge: Creation, Diffusion, Utilization* 1:381–404.

White, F. M., and E. A. Locke. 1981. "Perceived Determinants of High and Low Productivity in Three Occupational Groups: A Critical Incident Study." *Journal of Management Studies* 18:375–87.

Wicklund, R. A., and J. W. Brehm, 1976. *Perspectives on Cognitive Dissonance.* Hillsdale, N. J.: Erlbaum.

Willis, R. H., and E. P. Hollander. 1964. "An Experimental Study of Three Response Modes in Social Influence Situations." *Journal of Abnormal and Social Psychology* 69:150–156.

Wilson, D. C. 1982. "Electricity and Resistance: A Case Study of Innovation and Politics." Organization Studies 3:119–40.

Wilson, J. A., ed., 1981. *Management Science Applications to Academic Administration.* San Francisco: Jossey–Bass.

Wortman, C. B., and J. W. Brehm. 1975. "Responses to Uncontrollable Outcomes: An Integration of Reactance Theory and the Learned Helplessness Model." In *Advances in Experimental Social Psychology,* ed. L. Berkowitz, vol. 8:277–336. 1977. New York: Academic.

Zaleznik, A. 1977. "Managers and Leaders: Are They Different?" *Harvard Business Review* (May–June).

Zey–Ferrel, M. 1981. "Criticisms of the Dominant Perspective on Organizations." *Sociological Quarterly* 22:18–205.

Zimbardo, P. G. 1969. *The Cognitive Control of Motivation.* Glenview, Ill.: Scott, Foresman.

Discussion Questions

1. What are the distinctions between rationality and retrospective rationality?

2. Discuss Weick's observation that "Hypocrisy is ubiquitous in organizations, and this necessitates continuous dissonance reduction."

3. How does action displace thinking?

4. What is "loose coupling" and what are its implications, positive and negative, for organizations?

5. What are the processes managers use to enact environments?

6. Describe the elements of the double interact.

7. Evaluate Weick's depiction of managerial action, behavior in organizations, and the nature of organizations. Is it an accurate model or a distortion that misrepresents human collective effort as non-rational and underorganized?

A Model for Diagnosing Organizational Behavior

DAVID A. NADLER AND MICHAEL T. TUSHMAN

LEARNING OBJECTIVES

After reading Nadler and Tushman's "A Model for Diagnosing Organizational Behavior," the student will:

1. Understand the concept of organizational effectiveness

2. Understand the open systems perspective of organizational behavior

3. Be able to diagnose organizational behavior

4. Develop action steps to constructively change organizational behavior

Management's primary job is to make organizations operate effectively. Society's work gets done through organizations and management's function is to get organizations to perform that work. Getting organizations to operate effectively is difficult, however. Understanding one individual's behavior is challenging in and of itself; understanding a group that's made up of different individuals and comprehending the many relationships among those individuals is even more complex. Imagine, then, the mind-boggling complexity of a large organization made up of thousands of individuals and hundreds of groups with myriad relationships among these individuals and groups.

But organizational behavior must be managed in spite of this overwhelming complexity; ultimately the organization's work gets done through people, individually or collectively, on their own or in collaboration with technology. Therefore, the management of organizational behavior is central to the management task—a task that involves the capacity to *understand* the behavior patterns of individuals, groups, and organizations, to *predict* what behavioral responses will be elicited by various managerial actions, and finally to use this understanding and these predictions to achieve *control*.

How can one achieve understanding and learn how to predict and control organizational behavior? Given its inherent complexity and enigmatic nature, one needs tools to unravel the mysteries, paradoxes, and apparent contradictions that present themselves in the everyday life of organizations. One tool is the conceptual framework or model. A model is a theory that indicates which factors (in an organization, for example) are most critical or important. It also shows how these factors are related—that is, which factors or combination of factors cause other factors to change. In a sense then, a model is a roadmap that can be used to make sense of the terrain of organizational behavior.

The models we use are critical because they guide our analysis and action. In any organizational situation, problem solving involves the collection of information about the problem, the interpretation of that information to determine specific problem types and causes, and the development of action plans accordingly. The models that individuals use influence the kind of data they collect and the kind they ignore; models guide people's approach to analyzing or interpreting the data they have; finally, models help people choose their course of action.

Indeed, anyone who has been exposed to an organization already has some sort of implicit model. People develop these roadmaps over time, building on their own experiences. These implicit models (they usually are not explicitly written down or stated) guide behavior; they vary in quality, validity, and sophistication depending on the nature and extent of the experiences of the model builder, his or her perceptiveness, his or her ability to conceptualize and generalize from experiences, and so on.

We are not solely dependent, however, on the implicit and experience-based models that individuals develop. Since there has been extensive research and theory development on the subject of organizational behavior over the last four decades, it is possible to use scientifically developed explicit models for analyzing organizational behavior and solving organizational problems.

We plan to discuss one particular model, a general model of organizations. Instead of describing a specific phenomenon or aspect of organizational life (such as a model of motivation or a model of organizational design), the general model of organization attempts to provide a framework for thinking about the organization as a total system. The model's major premise is that for organizations to be effective, their subparts or components must be consistently structured and managed: they must approach a state of congruence.

In the first section of this article, we will discuss the basic view of organizations that underlies the model—that is, systems theory. In the second section, we will present and discuss the model itself. In the third section, we will present an approach to using the model for organizational problem analysis. Finally, we will discuss some of the model's implications for thinking about organizations.

A Basic View of Organizations

There are many different ways of thinking about organizations. When a manager is asked to "draw a picture of an organization," he or she typically draws some version of a pyramidal organizational chart. This is a model that views the stable, formal relationships among the jobs and formal work units as the most critical factors of the organization. Although this clearly is one way to think about organizations, it is a very limited view. It excludes such factors as leadership behavior, the impact of the environment, informal relations, power distribution, and so on. Such a model can capture only a small part of what goes on in organizations. Its perspective is narrow and static.

The past two decades have seen a growing consensus that a viable alternative to the static classic models of organizations is to envision the organization as a social system. This approach stems from the observation that social phenomena display many of the characteristics of natural or mechanical systems. In particular, as Daniel Katz and Robert L. Kahn have argued, organizations can be better understood if they are considered as dynamic and open social systems.

What is a system? Most simply, a system is a set of interrelated elements—that is, a change in one element affects other elements. An *open system* is one that interacts with its environment; it is more than just a set of interrelated elements. Rather, these elements make up a mecha-nism that takes input from the environment, subjects it to some form of transformation process, and produces output. At the most general level, it should be easy to visualize organizations as systems. Let us consider a manufacturing plant, for example. It is made up of different related components (a number of departments, job technologies, and so on). It receives inputs from the environment—that is, labor, raw material, production orders, and so on—and transforms these inputs into products.

As systems, organizations display a number of basic systems characteristics. Some of the most critical are these:

1. *Internal interdependence.* Changes in one component or subpart of an organization frequently have repercussions for other parts; the pieces are interconnected. Again, as in the manufacturing plant example, changes made in one element (for example, the skill levels of those hired to do jobs) will affect other elements (the productiveness of equipment used, the speed or quality of production activities, the nature of supervision needed, and so on).

2. *Capacity for feedback*—that is, information about the output that can be used to control the system. Organizations can correct errors and even change themselves because of this characteristic. If in our plant example plant management receives information that the quality of its product is declining, it can use this information to identify factors in the system itself that contribute to this problem. However, it is important to note that, unlike mechanized systems, feedback information does not always lead to correction. Organizations have the potential to use feedback to become self-correcting systems, but they do not always realize this potential.

3. *Equilibrium*—that is, a state of balance. When an event puts the system out of balance the system reacts and moves to bring itself back into balance. If one work group in our plant example were suddenly to increase its performance dramatically, it would throw the system out of balance. This group would be making increasing demands on the groups that supply it with the information or materials it needs; groups that work with the high-performing group's output would feel the pressure of work-in-process inventory piling up in front of them. If some type of incentive is in effect, other groups might perceive inequity as this one group begins to earn more. We would predict that some actions would be taken to put the system back into balance. Either the rest of the plant would be changed to increase production and thus be back in balance with the single group, or (more likely) there would be pressure to get this group to modify its behavior in line with the performance levels of the rest of the system (by removing

workers, limiting supplies, and so on). The point is that somehow the system would develop energy to move back toward a state of equilibrium or balance.

4. *Equifinality.* This characteristic of open systems means that different system configurations can lead to the same end or to the same type of input-output conversion. Thus there's no universal or "one best way" to organize.

5. *Adaptation.* For a system to survive, it must maintain a favorable balance of input or output transactions with the environment or it will run down. If our plant produces a product for which there are fewer applications, it must adapt to new demands and develop new products; otherwise, the plant will ultimately have to close its doors. Any system, therefore, must adapt by changing as environmental conditions change. The consequences of not adapting are evident when once-prosperous organizations decay (for example, the eastern railroads) because they fail to respond to environmental changes.

Thus systems theory provides a way of thinking about the organization in more complex and dynamic terms. But although the theory provides a valuable basic perspective on organizations, it is limited as a problem-solving tool. This is because a model systems theory is too abstract for use in day-to-day analysis of organizational behavior problems. Because of the level of abstraction of systems theory, we need to develop a more specific and pragmatic model based on the concepts of the open systems paradigm.

A Congruence Model of Organizational Behavior

Given the level of abstraction of open theory, our job is to develop a model that reflects the basic systems concepts and characteristics, but that is more specific and thus more usable as an analytic tool. We will describe a model that specifies the critical inputs, the major outputs, and the transformation processes that characterize organizational functioning.

The model puts its greatest emphasis on the transformation process and specifically reflects the critical system property of interdependence. It views organizations as made up of components or parts that interact with each other. These components exist in states of relative balance, consistency, or "fit" with each other. The different parts of an organization can fit well together and function effec-

tively, or fit poorly and lead to problems, dysfunctions, or performance below potential. Our *congruence model of organizational behavior* is based on how well components fit together—that is, the congruence among the components; the effectiveness of this model is based on the quality of these "fits" or congruence.

The concept of congruence is not a new one. George Homans, in his pioneering work on social processes in organizations, emphasized the interaction and consistency among key elements of organizational behavior. Harold Leavitt, for example, identified four major components of organization as being people, tasks, technology, and structure. The model we will present here builds on these views and also draws from fit models developed and used by James Seiler, Paul Lawrence and Jay Lorsch, and Alan Sheldon.

It is important to remember that we are concerned about creating a model for *behavioral* systems of the organization—the system of elements that ultimately produce behavior patterns and, in turn, organizational performance. Put simply, we need to deal with questions of the inputs the system has to work with, the outputs it must produce, the major components of the transformation process, and the ways in which these components interact.

Inputs

Inputs are factors that, at any one point in time, make up the "givens" facing the organization. They're the material that the organization has to work with. There are several different types of inputs, each of which presents a different set of "givens" to the organization (see Figure 1.1 for an overview of inputs).

The first input is the *environment*, or all factors outside the organization being examined. Every organization exists within the context of a larger environment that includes individuals, groups, other organizations, and even larger social forces, all of which have a potentially powerful impact on how the organization performs. Specifically, the environment includes markets (clients or customers), suppliers, governmental and regulatory bodies, labor unions, competitors, financial institutions, special interest groups, and so on. As research by Jeffrey Pfeffer and Gerald Salancik has suggested, the environment is critical to organizational functioning.

The environment has three critical features that affect organizational analysis. First the environment makes demands on the organization. For example, it may require certain products or services at certain levels of quality or

FIGURE 1.1

KEY ORGANIZATIONAL INPUTS

INPUT	ENVIRONMENT	RESOURCES	HISTORY	STRATEGY
Definition	All factors, including institutions, groups, individuals, events, and so on, that are outside the organization being analyzed, but that have a potential impact on that organization	Various assets to which the organization has access, including human resources, technology, capital, information, and so on, as well as less tangible resources (recognition in the market, and so forth)	The patterns of past behavior, activity, and effectiveness of the organization that may affect current organizational functioning	The stream of decisions about how organizational resources will be configured to meet the demands, constraints, and opportunities within the context of the organization's history
Critical Features for Analysis	1. What demands does the environment make on the organization? 2. How does the environment put constraints on organizational action?	1. What is the relative quality of the different resources to which the organization has access? 2. To what extent are resources fixed rather than flexible in their configuration(s)?	1. What have been the major stages or phases of the organization's development? 2. What is the current impact of such historical factors as strategic decisions, acts of key leaders, crises, and core values and norms?	1. How has the organization defined its core mission, including the markets it serves and the products/services it provides to these markets? 2. On what basis does it compete? 3. What supporting strategies has the organization employed to achieve the core mission? 4. What specific objectives have been

quantity. Market pressures are particularly important here. Second, the environment may place constraints on organizational action. It may limit the activities in which an organization may engage. These constraints range from limitations imposed by scarce capital to prohibitions set by government regulations. Third, the environment provides opportunities that the organization can explore. When we analyze an organization, we need to consider the factors in the organization's environment and determine how those factors, singly or collectively, create demands, constraints, or opportunities.

The second input is the organization's *resources*. Any organization has a range of different assets to which it has access. These include employees, technology, capital, information, and so on. Resources can also include less

tangible assets, such as the perception of the organization in the marketplace or a positive organizational climate. A set of resources can be shaped, deployed, or configured in different ways by an organization. For analysis purposes, two features are of primary interest. One concerns the relative quality of those resources or their value in light of the environment. The second concerns the extent to which resources can be reshaped or how fixed or flexible different resources are.

The third input is the organization's *history*. There is growing evidence that the way organizations function today is greatly influenced by past events. It is particularly important to understand the major stages or phases of an organization's development over a period of time, as well as the current impact of past events—for example, key strategic decisions, the acts or behavior of key leaders, the nature of past crises and the organization's responses to them, and the evolution of core values and norms of the organization.

The final input is somewhat different from the others because in some ways it reflects some of the factors in the organization's environment, resources, and history. The fourth input is *strategy*. We use this term in its broadest context to describe the whole set of decisions that are made about how the organization will configure its resources against the demands, constraints, and opportunities of the environment within the context of its history. Strategy refers to the issue of matching the organization's resources to its environment, or making the fundamental decision of "What business are we in?" For analysis purposes, several aspects of strategy are important to identify. First, what is the core mission of the organization, or how has the organization defined its basic purpose or function within the larger system or environment? The core mission includes decisions about what markets the organization will serve, what products or services it will provide to those markets, and how it will compete in those markets. Second, strategy includes the specific supporting strategies (or tactics) the organization will employ or is employing to achieve its core mission. Third, it includes the specific performance or output objectives that have been established.

Strategy may be the most important single input for the organization. On one hand, strategic decisions implicitly determine the nature of the work the organization should be doing or the tasks it should perform. On the other hand, strategic decisions, and particularly decisions about objectives, determine the system's outputs.

In summary, there are three basic inputs—environment, resources, and history—and a fourth derivative input, strategy, which determines how the organization responds to or deals with the basic inputs. Strategy is critical because it determines the work to be performed by the organization and it defines desired organizational outputs.

Outputs

Outputs are what the organization produces, how it performs, and how effective it is. There has been a lot of discussion about the components of an effective organization. For our purposes, however, it is possible to identify several key indicators of organizational output. First, we need to think about system output at different levels. In addition

to the system's basic output—that is, the product—we need to think about other outputs that contribute to organizational performance, such as the functioning of groups or units within the organization or the functioning of individual organization members.

At the organizational level, three factors must be kept in mind when evaluating organizational performance: (1) goal attainment, or how well the organization meets its objectives (usually determined by strategy), (2) resource utilization, or how well the organization makes use of available resources (not just whether the organization meets its goals, but whether it realizes all of its potential performance and whether it achieves its goals by building resources or by "burning them up"), and (3) adaptability, or whether the organization continues to position itself in a favorable position vis-à-vis its environment—that is, whether it is capable of changing and adapting to environmental changes.

Obviously, the functioning of groups or units (departments, divisions, or other subunits within the organization) contribute to these organizational-level outputs. Organizational output is also influenced by individual behavior, and certain individual-level outputs (affective reactions such as satisfaction, stress, or experienced quality of working life) may be desired outputs in and of themselves.

The Organization as a Transformation Process

So far, we've defined the nature of inputs and outputs of the organizational system. This leads us to the transformation process. Given an environment, a set of resources, and history, "How do I take a strategy and implement it to produce effective performance in the organization, in the group/unit, and among individual employees?"

In our framework, the organization and its major component parts are the fundamental means for transforming energy and information from inputs and outputs. On this basis, we must determine the key components of the organization and the critical dynamic that shows how those components interact to perform the transformation function.

Organizational Components

There are many different ways of thinking about what makes up an organization. At this point in the development of a science of organizations, we probably do not know the one right or best way to describe the different components of an organization. The task is to find useful approaches for describing organizations, for simplifying complex phenomena, and for identifying patterns in what may at first blush seem to be random sets of activity. Our particular approach views organizations as composed of four major components: (1) the task, (2) the individuals, (3) the formal organizational arrangements, and (4) the informal organization. We will discuss each of these individually (see Figure 1.2 for overviews of these components).

The first component is the organization's *task*—that is, the basic or inherent work to be done by the organization and its subunits or the acivity the organization is engaged in, particularly in light of its strategy. The emphasis is on the specific work activities or functions that need to be done and their inherent characteristics (as opposed to characteristics of the work created by how the work is organized or structured in this particular organization at this particular time). Analysis of the task would include a description of the basic work flows and functions with

attention to the characteristics of those work flows—for example, the knowledge or skills demanded by the work, the kinds of rewards provided by the work, the degree of uncertainty associated with the work, and the specific constraints inherent in the work (such as critical time demands, cost constraints, and so on). Since it is assumed that a primary (although not the only) reason for the organization's existence is to perform the task consistent with strategy, the task is the starting point for the analysis. As we will see, the assessment of the adequacy of other components depends to a large degree on an understanding of the nature of the tasks to be performed.

A second component of organizations involved the *individuals* who perform organizational tasks. The issue here is identifying the nature and characteristics of the organization's employees (or members). The most critical aspects to consider include the nature of individual knowledge and skills, the different needs or preferences that individuals have, the perceptions or expectancies that

---

FIGURE 1.2

KEY ORGANIZATIONAL COMPONENTS

COMPONENT	TASK	INDIVIDUAL	FORMAL ORGANIZATIONAL ARRANGEMENTS	INFORMAL ORGANIZATION
Definition	The basic and inherent work to be done by the organization and its parts	The characteristics of individuals in the organization	The various structures, processes, methods, and so on that are formally created to get individuals to perform tasks	The emerging arrangements, including structures, processes, relationships, and so forth
Critical Features for Analysis	1. The types of skill and knowledge demands the work poses 2. The types of rewards the work can provide 3. The degree of uncertainty associated with the work, including such factors as interdependence, routineness, and so on 4. The constraints on performance demands inherent in the work (given a strategy)	1. Knowledge and skills individuals have 2. Individual needs and preferences 3. Perceptions and expectancies 4. Background factors	1. Organization design, including grouping of functions, structure of subunits and coordination and control mechanisms 2. Job design 3. Work environment 4. Human resource management systems	1. Leader behavior 2. Intragroup relations 3. Intergroup relations 4. Informal working arrangements 5. Communication and influence patterns

they develop, and other background factors (such as demographics) that may potentially influence individual behavior.

The third component is the formal *organizational arrangements*. These include the range of structures, processes, methods, procedures, and so forth that are explicitly and formally developed to get individuals to perform tasks consistent with organizational strategy. The broad term, organizational arrangements, encompasses a number of different factors. One factor is organizational design—that is, the way jobs are grouped together into units, the internal structure of those units, and the coordination and control mechanisms used to link those units together. A second factor is the way jobs are designed within the context of organizational designs. A third factor is the work environment, which includes a number of factors that characterize the immediate environment in which work is done, such as the physical working environment, the available work resources, and so on. A final factor includes the organization's formal systems for attracting, placing, developing, and evaluating human resources.

Together, these factors create the set of formal organizational arrangements—that is, they are explicitly designed and specified, usually in writing.

The final component is the *informal organization*. Despite the set of formal organizational arrangements that exists in any organization, another set of arrangements tends to develop or emerge over a period of time. These arrangements are usually implicit and unwritten, but they influence a good deal of behavior. For lack of a better term, such arrangements are frequently referred to as the informal organization and they include the different structures, processes, and arrangements that emerge while the organization is operating. These arrangements sometimes complement formal organizational arrangements by providing structures to aid work where none exist. In other situations they may arise in reaction to the formal structure, to protect individuals from it. They may therefore either aid or hinder the organization's performance.

Because a number of aspects of the informal organization have a particularly critical effect on behavior, they need to be considered. The behavior of leaders (as opposed to the formal creation of leader positions) is an important feature of the informal organization, as are the patterns of relationships that develop both within and between groups. In addition, different types of informal working arrangements (including rules, procedures, methods, and so on) develop. Finally, there are the various communication and influence patterns that combine to create the informal organization design.

Organizations can therefore be thought of as a set of components—the task, the individuals, the organizational arrangements, and the informal organization. In any system, however, the critical question is not what the components are, but what the nature of their interaction is. This model raises the question: What are the dynamics of the relationships among the components? To deal with this issue, we must return to the concept of congruence or fit.

The Concept of Congruence

A relative degree of congruence, consistency, or fit exists between each pair of organizational inputs. The congruence between two components is defined as "the degree to which the needs, demands, goals, objectives, and/or structures of one component are consistent with the needs, demands, goals, objectives and/or structures of another component."

Congruence, therefore, is a measure of how well pairs of componenets fit together. Consider, for example, two components—the task and the individual. At the simplest level, the task presents some demands on individuals who would perform it (that is, skill/knowledge demands). At the same time, the set of individuals available to do the tasks have certain characteristics (their levels of skill and knowledge). Obviously, if the individual's knowledge and skill match the knowledge and skill demanded by the task, performance will be more effective.

Obviously, too, the individual-task congruence relationship encompasses more factors than just knowledge and skill. Similarly, each congruence relationship in the model has its own specific characteristics. Research and theory can guide the assessment of fit in each relationship. For an overview of the critical elements of each congruence relationship, see Figure 1.3.

The Congruence Hypothesis

The aggregate model, or whole organization, displays a relatively high or low degree of system congruence in the same way that each pair of components has a high or low degree of congruence. The basic hypothesis of the model, which builds on this total state of congruence, is as follows: Other things being equal, the greater the total degree of congruence or fit between the various components, the more effective will be the organization—effectiveness being defined as the degree to which actual organization outputs at individual, group, and organizational levels are

FIGURE 1.3

DEFINITION OF FITS

FIT	ISSUES
Individual/Organization	How are individual needs met by the organizational arrangements? Do individuals hold clear or distorted perceptions of organizational structures? Is there a convergence of individual and organizational goals?
Individual/Task	How are individual needs met by the tasks? Do individuals have skills and abilities to meet task demands?
Individual/Informal organization	How are individual needs met by the informal organization? How does the informal organization make use of individual resources consistent with informal goals?
Task/Organization	Are organizational arrangements adequate to meet the demands of the task? Do organizational arrangements motivate behavior that is consistent with task demands?
Task/Informal organization	Does this informal organization structure facilitate task performance or not? Does this hinder or help meet the demands of the task?
Organization/Informal organization	Are the goals, rewards, and structures of the informal organization consistent with those of the formal organization?

similar to expected outputs, as specified by strategy.

The basic dynamic of congruence sees the organization as most effective when its pieces fit together. If we also consider strategy, this view expands to include the fit between the organization and its larger environment; that is, an organization is most effective when its strategy is consistent with its environment (in light of organizational resources and history) and when the organizational components are congruent with the tasks necessary to implement that strategy.

One important implication of the congruence hypothesis is that organizational problem analysis (or diagnosis) involves description of the system, identification of problems, and analysis of fits to determine the causes of problems. The model also implies that different configurations of the key components can be used to gain outputs (con-

sistent with the systems characteristic of equifinality). Therefore the question is not how to find the "one best way" of managing but how to find effective combinations of components that will lead to congruent fits among them.

The process of diagnosing fits and identifying combinations of components to produce congruence is not necessarily intuitive. A number of situations that lead to congruence have been defined in the research literature. Thus in many cases fit is something that can be defined, measured, and even quantified; there is, in other words, an empirical and theoretical basis for assessing fit. The theory provides considerable guidance about what leads to congruent relationships (although in some areas the research is more definitive and helpful than others). The implications is that the manager who wants to diagnose behavior must become familiar with critical aspects of relevent organizational behavior models or theories so that he or she can evaluate the nature of fits in a particuar system.

The congruence model provides a general organizing framework. The organizational analyst will need other, more specific "submodels" to define high and low congruence. Examples of such submodels that might be used in the context of this general diagnostic model include the following:

1. The job characteristics model to assess and explain the fit between individuals and organizational arrangements (job design)
2. Expectancy theory models of motivation to explain the fit between individuals and the other three components
3. The information processing model of organizational design to explain the task-formal organization and task-informal organization fits
4. An organizational climate model to explain the fit between the informal organization and the other components

These models and theories are listed as illustrations of how more specific models can be used in the context of the general model. Obviously, those mentioned above are just a sampling of possible tools that could be used.

In summary, then, we have described a general model for the analysis of organizations (see Figure 1.4). The organization is seen as a system or transformation process that takes inputs and transforms them into outputs, a process that is composed of four basic components. The critical dynamic is the fit or congruence among the components. We now turn our attention to the pragmatic question of how to use this model for analyzing organizational problems.

A Process for Organizational Problem Analysis

The conditions that face organizations frequently change; consequently, managers are required to continually engage in problem-identification and problem-solving activities. Therefore, managers must gather data on organizational performance, compare the data with desired performance levels, identify the causes of problems, develop and choose action plans, and, finally, implement and evaluate these action plans. These phases can be viewed as a generic problem-solving process. For long-term organizational viability, some type of problem-solving process must operate—and operate continuously.

Experience with using the congruence model for organizations for problem analysis in actual organizational settings has led to the development of an approach to using the model that's based on these generic problem-solving processes (see Figure 1.5). In this section, we will "walk through" this process, describing each step in the process and discussing how the model can be used at each stage. Here are the steps in the problem-analysis process.

1. *Identify symptoms.* In any situation, initial information (symptomatic data) may indicate that there are problems but not what the problems are or what the causes are. Symptomatic data are important because the symptoms of problems may indicate where to look for more complete data.

2. *Specify inputs.* Once the symptoms are identified, the starting point for analysis is to identify the system and the environment in which it functions. This means collecting data about the nature of environment, the type of resources the organization has, and the critical aspects of its history. Input analysis also involves identifying the overall strategy of the organization—that is, its core mission, supporting strategies, and objectives.

3. *Identify outputs.* The third step is an analysis of the organization's outputs at the individual, group, and organizational levels. Output analysis actually involves two elements: (1) defining the desired or planned output through an analysis of strategy that explicitly or implicitly defines what the organization

wants to achieve in terms of output or performance indicators, and (2) collecting data that indicate the type of output the organization is actually achieving.

4. *Identify problems.* Symptoms may indicate problems—in this case, significant difference between desired or planned output and actual output. Such problems might be discrepancies (actual vs. expected) in organizational performance, group functioning, individual behavior, or affective reactions. These data tell us what problems exist, but they still don't tell us the causes. (Note: Where data are available, it is frequently also useful to identify the costs associated with the problems or the *penalties* the organization incurs by not fixing the problem. Penalties might be actual costs—increased expenses, and so on—or opportunity costs, such as revenue lost because of the problem.)

5. *Describe organizational components.* At this step the analysis to determine the causes of problems begins. Data are collected about the nature of each of the four major organizational components, including information about the component and its critical features in this organization.

6. *Assess congruence (fits).* Using the data collected in step 5 as well as applicable submodels or theories, an assessment is made of the positive or negative fit between each pair of components.

7. *Generate hypotheses about problem causes.* Once the components are described and their congruence assessed, the next step is to link together the congruence analysis with the problem identification (step 4). After analyzing to determine which are the poor fits that seem to be associated with, or account for, the output problems that have been identified, the patterns of congruence and incongruence that appear to cause the patterns of problems are determined.

8. *Identify action steps.* The final step in problem analysis is to identify possible action steps. These steps might range from specific changes to deal with relatively obvious

FIGURE 1.4

A CONGRUENCE MODEL FOR ORGANIZATION ANALYSIS

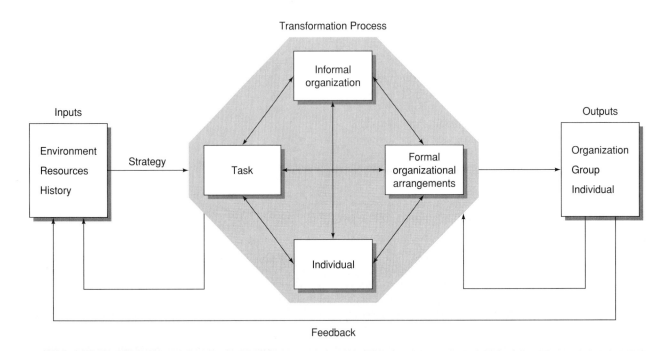

In addition to these eight steps, some further steps need to be kept in mind. After possible actions are identified, problem solving involves predicting the consequence of various actions, choosing the course of action, and implementing and evaluating the impact of the chosen course of action. It is, of course, important to have a general diagnostic framework to monitor the effects of various courses of action.

The congruence model and this problem-analysis process outline are tools for structuring and dealing with the complex reality of organizations. Given the indeterminate nature of social systems, there is no one best way of handling a particular situation. The model and the process could, however, help the manager in making a number of decisions and in evaluating the consequences of those decisions. If these tools have merit, it is up to the manager to use them along with his or her intuitive sense (based on experience) to make the appropriate set of diagnostic, evaluative, and action decisions.

Future Directions

The model we have presented here reflects a particular way of thinking about organizations. If that perspective is significant, the model might be used as a tool for handling more complex problems or for structuring more complex situations. Some directions for further thought, research, and theory development could include these:

1. *Organizational change.* The issue of organizational change has received a good deal of attention from both managers and academics. The question is how to effectively implement organizational change. The prob-

problem causes to a more extensive data collection designed to test hypotheses about relatively more complex problems and causes.

FIGURE 1.5

Basic Problem Analysis Steps Using the Congruence Model

Step	Explanation
1. Identify symptoms.	List data indicating possible existence of problems.
2. Specify inputs.	Identify the system.
	Determine the nature of environment, resources, and history.
	Identify critical aspects of strategy.
3. Identify outputs.	Identify data that define the nature of outputs at various levels (individual, group/unit, organizational). This should include desired outputs (from strategy) and actual outputs being obtained.
4. Identify problems.	Identify areas where there are significant and meaningful differences between desired and actual outputs.
	To the extent possible, identify penalties; that is, specific costs (actual and opportunity costs) associated with each problem.
5. Describe components of the organization.	Describe basic nature of each of the four components with emphasis on their critical features.
6. Assess congruence (fits).	Conduct analysis to determine relative congruence among components (draw on submodels as needed).
7. Generate and identify causes.	Analyze to associate fit with specific problems.
8. Identify action steps.	Indicate the possible actions to deal with problem causes.

lem seems to center on the lack of a general model of organizational change. It is hard to think about a general model of organizational change without a general model of organizations. The congruence perspective outlined here may provide some guidance and direction toward the development of a more integrated perspective on the processes of organizational change. Initial work in applying the congruence model to the change issue is encouraging.

2. *Organizational development over time.* There has been a growing realization that organizations grow and develop over time, and that they face different types of crises, evolve through different stages, and develop along some predictable lines. A model of organizations such as the one presented here might be a tool for developing typology of growth patterns by indicating the different configurations of tasks, individuals, organizational arrangements, and informal organizations that might be most appropriate for organizations in different environments and at different stages of development.

3. *Organizational pathology.* Organizational problem solving ultimately requires some sense of the types of problems that may be encountered and the kinds of patterns of causes one might expect. It is reasonable to assume that most problems encountered by organizations are not wholly unique but are predictable. The often expressed view that "our problems are unique" reflects in part the lack of a framework of organizational pathology. The question is: Are there basic "illnesses" that organizations suffer? Can a framework of organizational pathology, similar to the physician's framework of medical pathology, be developed? The lack of a pathology framework, in turn, reflects the lack of a basic functional model of organizations. Again, development of a congruence perspective might provide a common language to use for the

identification of general pathological patterns of organizational functioning.

4. *Organizational solution types.* Closely linked to the problem of pathology is the problem of treatment, intervention, or solutions to organizational problems. Again, there is a lack of a general framework in which to consider the nature of organizational interventions. In this case, too, the congruence model might be a means for conceptualizing and ultimately describing the different intervention options available in response to problems.

Summary

This article has presented a general approach for thinking about organizational functioning and a process for using a model to analyze organizational problems. This particular model is only one way of thinking about organizations; it clearly is not the only model, nor can we claim it is definitely the best model. It is one tool, however, that may be useful for structuring the complexity of organizational life and helping managers create, maintain, and develop effective organizations.

BIBLIOGRAPHY

For a comprehensive review and synthesis of research in organizational behavior, see Marvin Dunnette's *Handbook of Industrial and Organizational Psychology* (Rand-McNally, 1976). Daniel Katz and Robert Kahn's seminal work on organizations as systems, *The Social Psychology of Organizations* (Wiley, 1966), has been revised, updated, and extended in their 1978 edition. See their new book for an extensive discussion of organizations as open systems and for a unique synthesis of the literature in terms of systems ideas.

For a broad analysis of organizational behavior, see David Nadler, J. Richard Hackman, and Edward E. Lawler's *Managing Organizational Behavior* (Little, Brown, 1979), and see Charles Hofer and Daniel Schendel's *Strategy Formulation: Analytical Concepts* (West, 1978) for a discussion of strategy.

For an extensive discussion of output and effectiveness, see Paul Goodman and Johannes Pennings's *New Perspectives on Organizational Effectiveness* (Jossey-Bass, 1977), and Andrew Van de Ven and Diane Ferry's *Organizational Assessment* (Wiley Interscience, 1980).

For more detail on organizational arrangements, see Jay R. Galbraith's *Designing Complex Organizations* (Addison-Wesley, 1973); on job design and motivation, see J. Richard Hackman and Greg Oldham's *Work Redesign* (Addison-Wesley, 1979); and on informal organizations, see Michael Tushman's "A Political Approach to Organizations: A Review and Rationale" (*Academy of Management Review*, April 1977), and Jeffrey Pfeffer's new book, *Power and Politics in Organizations* (Pittman Press, 1980).

Submodels corresponding to the various components of our congruence model would include: J. Richard Hackman and Greg Oldham's job design model; Victor Vroom and Edward Lawler's work on expectancy theory of motivation and decision making—see Vroom's *Work and Motivation* (Wiley, 1964) and Lawler's *Motivation in Work Organizations* (Wadsworth Publishing Co., 1973); Jay R. Galbraith, Michael Tushman, and David Nadler's work on information processing models of organizational design; and George Litwin and Robert Stringer's work on organization climate—see Litwin and Stringer's *Motivation and Organizational Climate* (Harvard University Graduate School of Business Administration, 1968).

David Nadler's "Managing Organizational Change: An Integrated Perspective" (*Journal of Applied Behavioral Science* 17, no. 2 (1981): 191–211) uses the congruence model to think about the general problems of organizational change and dynamics. Several distinct levers for change are developed and discussed. Other pertinent books of interest include: Jay R. Galbraith's *Organization Design* (Addison-Wesley, 1979); Jay R. Galbraith and Daniel A. Nathanson's *Strategy Implementation: The Role of Structure and Process* (West, 1978); George C. Homan's *The Human Group* (Harcourt Brace Jovanovich, 1950); Paul R. Lawrence and Jay W. Lorsch's *Developing Organizations: Diagnosis and Action* (Addison-Wesley, 1969); Harold J. Leavitt's "Applied Organization Change in Industry" in J. G. March's (Ed.) *Handbook of Organizations* (Rand McNally, 1965); Harry Levinson's *Organizational Diagnosis* (Harvard University Press, 1972); Harry Levinson's *Psychological Man* (Levinson Institute, 1976); J. W. Lorsch and Alan Sheldon's "The Individual in the Organization: A Systems View" in J. W. Lorsch and P. R. Lawrence's (Eds.) *Managing Group and Intergroup Relations* (Irwin-Dorsey, 1972); David A. Nadler and Noel M. Tichy's "The Limitations of Traditional Intervention Technology in Health Care Organizations" in N. Margulies and J. A. Adams's (Eds.) *Organization Development in Health Care Organizations* (Addison-Wesley, 1980); Edgar H. Schein's *Organizational Psychology* (Prentice-Hall, 1970); and James A. Seiler's *Systems Analysis in Organizational Behavior* (Irwin-Dorsey, 1967).

DISCUSSION QUESTIONS

1. List the elements in Nadler and Tushman's definition of organizational behavior.

2. What is the role of a model for understanding organizational behavior and efforts to improve organizations?

3. What is an open system?

4. Distinguish inputs, outputs, and transformational processes. How do each of these affect organizational effectiveness?

5. What are the components of an organization?

6. Explain the concept of congruence, its relationship to open systems theory, and the concept of effectiveness.

7. What is the basic hypothesis of Nadler and Tushman's model?

8. What are the steps in the problem-analysis process for diagnosing organizations?

9. Compare and contrast Weick's understanding of organizations and organizational behavior with that of Nadler and Tushman.

10. In what ways would a diagnosis of organizational behavior by Weick differ from that of Nadler and Tushman?

11. Using the descriptions and theories in these readings, diagnose an organization with which you are familiar. Examples are the university or college that you attend, a voluntary organization you are a member of, or where you work.

FOR FURTHER READING

Blau, P., and Meyer, M. *Bureaucracy in Modern Society*, 3rd ed. New York: Random House, 1987.

Hannan, M., and Freeman, J. *Organizational Ecology*. Cambridge: Harvard University Press, 1989.

Kanter, R. "The New Managerial Work." *Harvard Business Review* (November-December 1989) 85–92.

Katz, D., and Kahn, R. *The Social Psychology of Organizations*, 2nd ed. New York: Wiley, 1978.

Levinson, H. *Organizational Diagnosis*. Cambridge: Harvard University Press, 1972.

Lorsch, J. (ed.). *Handbook of Organizational Behavior*. New Jersey: Prentice Hall, 1987.

Northcraft, G., and Neale, M. *Organizational Behavior: A Management Challenge*. Fort Worth: Dryden, 1994.

O'Reilly, C. "Organizational Behavior: Where We've Been, Where We're Going." *Annual Review of Psychology* 42, (1990) 427–58.

Ott, J. *Classic Readings in Organizational Behavior*. Pacific Grove, CA: Brooks/Cole, 1989.

Perrow, C. *Complex Organizations: A Critical Essay,* 3rd ed. New York: Random House, 1986.

Singh, J. (ed.). *Organizational Evolution*. California: Sage, 1990.

Sullivan, J. "Human Nature, Organizations, and Management Theory." *Academy of Management Review* 11, (1986) 534-49.

Weick, K. *The Social Psychology of Organizing*, 2nd ed. Reading, Mass: Addison-Wesley, 1979.

2

HISTORICAL PERSPECTIVES ON ORGANIZATIONAL BEHAVIOR

From Human Relations to Organizational Behavior: Reflections on the Changing Scene

WILLIAM FOOTE WHYTE

LEARNING OBJECTIVES

After reading "From Human Relations to Organizational Behavior: Reflections on the Changing Scene" by Whyte, a student will be able to:

1. Understand the history of the scientific study of organizational behavior

2. Identify the two streams of organizational behavior that have developed since the 1960s: A mainstream, characterized by a sharp separation between research and practice and rigorous specification and measurement of variables, and an alternate stream, with more applied research and sometimes active involvement in organizational change

3. Identify which of the two streams is dominant at the present time

4. Understand Whyte's preference for the alternate approach to studying organizational behavior

We are now in the midst of the most drastic and fundamental changes in industrial relations of any era since the great CIO organizing drives in the 1930s. I was in college (1932–36) at the height of the CIO campaigns, but I began my first study in industry not long after (in 1942) and I have continued active in this field since that time.

Thus, what I am presenting can be considered the report of a participant observer on what we behavioral scientists have been doing in studies of industrial relations and on how we have related our work to that in other disciplines and to labor and management.

When and How Did It Begin?

I trace the beginnings of behavioral science research in industrial relations to Elton Mayo and his colleagues at the Harvard Business School who worked on the Western Electric research program in the 1920s and early 1930s, culminating with the publication in 1939 of *Management and the Worker* (Roethlisberger and Dickson). Many sociologists prefer to trace the origins back to Max Weber, who indeed did make his important contribution decades before Mayo, but Weber's writings on bureaucracy did not lead directly to the development of a new field of study. It was the Harvard–Western Electric collaboration that launched research in the field first called human relations

Source: William Foote Whyte, "From Human Relations to Organizational Behavior: Reflections on the Changing Scene," *Industrial and Labor Relations Review,* Vol. 40, No. 4, (1987), pp. 487-500. © Cornell University, 1987. Reprinted by permission.

in industry or industrial sociology and now more generally known as organizational behavior.

I first became acquainted with the Western Electric program in a seminar with Elton Mayo in the fall of 1937. I read and discussed with him his books on the Hawthorne plant, which presented earlier interpretations than the more solid and systematic *Management and the Worker*. It was this experience with Mayo, reinforced by associations with social anthropologists Conrad M. Arensberg, Eliot D. Chapple, and F. L. W. Richardson, that led me away from community studies (Whyte 1943) and into industrial relations.

In 1940 I moved from Harvard to the University of Chicago to study under social anthropologist W. Lloyd Warner, then known particularly for his Yankee City studies. As I later learned, while at Harvard he had led the Mayo group from the famous experiment of the test room girls in the Hawthorne plant to a study of a work group in its natural factory setting: the bank wiring room (Roethlisberger and Dickson 1939). This still seems to me one of the finest work group studies ever carried out. The test room experiments excited public attention because of the surprising finding that the young women continued to increase their production when the conditions of work were made more favorable *or* less favorable. Since Roethlisberger (1977) himself later offered seventeen full or partial explanations of that result, the scientific significance of the test room studies seems to me to have been greatly overrated. On the other hand, the bank wiring room study suggested the importance of examining a group of workers in its natural hierarchical structural working conditions—a line of research more compatible with social anthropology than with the psychological orientation of Mayo.

In fact, Mayo himself derailed these promising beginnings in what I have called a monumental misinterpretation of the practical implications of the Hawthorne plant studies (Whyte 1978). I like to startle my students with the claim that, though there may be a phenomenon such as "the Hawthorne effect," it did not appear in the Western Electric research at the Hawthorne plant. The Hawthorne effect interpretation is based on the notion that the increasing productivity of the test room women was a response to the friendly interest in them and in their work by the research observer and therefore indirectly by management. As Arensberg (1951) pointed out, however, the men in the bank wiring room, like the women in the test room, were provided by management with a friendly and sympathetic observer, and yet their productivity ran in a straight line throughout the observation period.

How can we explain these productivity differences?

We can believe either that women are more gullible than men or (as I think more likely) that the explanation lies in the markedly different *structural conditions* within which the two cases were embedded. The bank wiring room was designed to operate just like a regular department—with the constant presence of the observer being the only deviation from that norm. The men worked under the close supervision of the foreman and had frequent and predominantly negatively tinged interactions with their inspector. In contrast, no inspector was ever present in the test room, and the foreman only appeared to deliver materials and pick up the output. In today's terminology, the test room functioned as an autonomous work group.

Unfortunately, Elton Mayo never sought to explain the striking output differences between the two cases. The hypothesis of the Hawthorne effect to explain the results of the test room study was attractive to him because it fitted in with his previously stated convictions that the human problems of industry arose out of boredom and obsessive reveries suffered by workers in repetitive jobs. The company and the workers, he believed, would benefit by the establishment of a personnel counseling program to enable individuals to achieve catharsis by unburdening themselves to a sympathetic nondirective interviewer.

In effect, the inauguration of the personnel counseling program blocked off social research at Western Electric. Whatever benefits workers or the company gained through the 20 years and many millions of dollars Western Electric invested in personnel counseling, that program bore little resemblance to research. Social research had also been on the shelf in the Harvard Business School for a decade or more, while the professors went about gathering case materials for teaching.

Revival came in 1943 under the leadership of two social anthropologists who formed the Committee on Human Relations in Industry at the University of Chicago. Picking up the neglected leads from the bank wiring room case, they committed themselves to studying industrial life in its natural settings. W. Lloyd Warner chaired the Committee and Burleigh B. Gardner served as its executive secretary until 1946, when he left the University to form his own research and consulting organization. Warner and Gardner were joined by Everett C. Hughes (Sociology Department), Allison Davis and Robert J. Havighurst (Department of Human Development), and George Brown (School of Business). In 1944 I joined the Committee to direct a study on human relations in the restaurant industry, and I stayed on to become executive secretary from 1946 to 1948.

I believe the Committee was the first instance of an interdisciplinary group of professors and students planning and carrying out a research program in what we then called human relations in industry. The program was initially supported by six industrial companies providing $3,600 a year each. Shortly after the beginning, Sears, Roebuck and Company joined in supporting the Committee, and small pieces of support were picked up elsewhere.

The Chicago initiative was followed up shortly by the Labor-Management Center of E. Wight Bakke and the Technology Project of Charles Walker at Yale and the work of Douglas McGregor and others at MIT.

Reactions among Sociologists and Economists

This sudden opening of a new field of study attracted wide attention and enthuiasm among students. It was greeted with some apprehension, however, among our colleagues in sociology and economics at Chicago and elsewhere. Some sociologists concluded that they too should move into teaching and research in this new field, which they preferred to call industrial sociology. Tracing the origins of the field to Max Weber, they focused attention on broad studies of management and labor, with emphasis on the macro- or societal-level aspects.

Meanwhile, those of us pursuing human relations were involved in intensive field work in factories and even with small work groups. Some sociologists and labor economists attacked us for being both unethical and unscientific. Since we were then entirely supported by management, they claimed we were not really engaged in scientific pursuits but were rather creating a managerial sociology, helping management to manipulate workers and to undermine unions or avoid unionization. And since workers and union leaders knew that our work was supported by management, they would not talk frankly to our interviewers. Therefore, we could only get a one-sided and unscientific view of the topics we were studying.

We were also accused of disregarding the role of unions. When we did study rare cases in which local unions and management had resolved their conflicts and developed cooperative relations, critics claimed that our conception of cooperation meant simply having union leaders and workers agree to do whatever management wanted done. Our critics also charged us with believing that all conflicts between labor and management could be resolved through "good communications"—that panacea being provided by the management people who learned from our research.

Academic Turf Problems

Before the human relations boom, the field of industrial relations had been monopolized by labor economists and industrial psychologists, who were concentrating on the measurement of individual skills and aptitudes. As the human relations people opened up the new approach, many industrial psychologists joined in the trend and began calling themselves industrial social psychologists.

Although some labor economists joined in the attack on the ethics of the human relations researchers, there were others who were more puzzled than hostile. In fact, some of them—particularly Frederick Harbison and Charles Meyers—went out of their way to try to fit us in, and leaders of the Industrial Relations Research Association have periodically tried to encourage behavioral scientists to get involved with IRRA, which still remains predominantly an association for labor economists.

The difficulty in fitting us in can be traced in part to a problem of the differing scale of studies on the two sides of the divide. In the 1940s and 1950s, when labor economists thought of doing a case study, they would have in mind something like labor relations in the steel industry. If they wanted to really narrow the field down, they might settle for a study of labor relations in United States Steel. In contrast, behavioral scientists approached the field with a much more micro focus. For us, a case study was likely to be limited to a particular factory or even to a single department in that factory or a single work group. Instead of studying an international union as a whole, we were more inclined to do intensive studies of local unions (Sayles and Strauss 1951).

The mixed reactions to what we were then doing were well expressed in a 1948 Cornell summer institute on industrial relations. When I had finished my report, a labor economist expressed his concern about the lack of a firm theoretical framework guiding our research: "You people in human relations are certainly doing interesting research, but do you know enough yet to teach courses?" I replied rather undiplomatically, "In your studies of labor relations you are constantly having to point out that the orthodox theories of economics don't apply. We are trying to build theory from the ground up in the field."

Common Misinterpretations of Management Interest in Human Relations Research

Many years later, perhaps it is possible to state with some detachment that such attacks were largely based on misinterpretations of management's interest in and utilization of our research, as well as on a misunderstanding of the way we went about our work. To be sure, the people who decided to contribute to the financing of our research must have thought their companies would get some benefits out of the relationship, but their initial expectations were both modest and vague. In a period of high profits during World War II, $3,600 a year was a trifling sum. Some executives who had intellectual and cultural interests beyond the bottom line may have been attracted by the part of the program that brought them together for dinner every six weeks with the professors to engage in high-level discussions of labor, management, and society.

If executives had an immediate practical interest in our research, it concerned the problem of absenteeism and labor turnover. In the very tight wartime labor market, they had difficulty filling their orders because workers were not showing the expected discipline in coming to work or were simply leaving in search of openings elsewhere. Even that interest, however, did not at first open any doors for research. It was a year from the beginning of the Committee before its members were able to gain permission for in-plant research from any of the six companies supporting the program.

There were two common answers to researchers' requests for permission to launch in-plant studies. One answer was that things were going so smoothly in the plant that management did not want any outsiders to come in and ask workers how they felt about their jobs because such probing might get workers to think about reasons to be unhappy. The other answer was that the situation was so tense on the shop floor that the introduction of an outsider could set off an explosion.

Lacking access to the plants, our researchers could learn about worker-management relations only through house-to-house interviews in working-class neighborhoods. The data collected in this way were miscellaneous, but at least the interviews did furnish stories that might

have some bearing on what led workers to consider a job good or bad, a supervisor good or bad, and so on.

The breakthrough to in-plant studies occurred suddenly in one of the evening meetings shortly before I joined the Committee. After expressing his concern and frustrations about his company's labor relations, Walter Paepke, chief executive officer of Container Corporation of America, said, "The situation in our 35th Street plant is so fouled up that no outsider could possibly make things worse. Why don't you come in and see if there is anything you can do?" Burleigh Gardner went through this open door and began the first of a series of field studies that was eventually extended to several of the other supporting companies.

Paradoxical as it may seem, in those years with the Committee, we found many workers and local union officers and even some international representatives more open and interested than most managers in what we were doing. Since we always told them at the outset about our source of support, they initially viewed us with suspicion. But once a skillful field worker had spent some time getting acquainted with workers on the factory floor and talking with local union leaders, and they had encountered no negative consequences from our presence in the plant, the barriers began to go down. Many workers came to express themselves freely and frankly. Why? Again and again we got the same explanation. Workers and local union leaders had tried to get management to take action on problems they were facing. Either they could not get anybody in management to listen or else people listened but then nothing happened. So they would say to us, "You talk to the management people. Maybe you can get them to understand our problems."

My entry into the program in 1944 was made possible by a $10,000 grant from the National Restaurant Association. But the giving of that grant did not mean that members of the association had any strong interest in understanding human relations in their industry. They had approached the University of Chicago to negotiate for the establishment of a master's program in restaurant administration. George Brown reported to the Committee on Human Relations in Industry that the School of Business was prepared to accept financial support from the National Restaurant Association to build such a program, but only if a small portion of the funds were set aside to support research. Brown reported that no one in the School of Business had any interest in research in the restaurant industry. Did the Committee members have anything to suggest? I believe it was Everett Hughes who suggested to the School of Business that I direct a study of human relations in the restaurant industry.

Toward the end of our field work, I was invited to give talks in several cities to groups of restaurant management people. For that purpose I focused on what I was calling "human elements in supervision" in the draft of a book, and that subject did evoke some interest. When the NRA members read the first draft of the manuscript, however, they were distressed by my discussion of the low prestige of the industry and the low social status of waiters, waitresses, countermen, dishwashers, and so on. Regarding the motivation of the NRA sponsors for supporting the grant to the University of Chicago, the most revealing comment on my manuscript was phrased in three blunt sentences: "I thought that the reason we wanted to work with the University of Chicago was to raise the status of our industry. If this book is published it will have the opposite effect. Therefore it should not be published." If the University's contract with the NRA had not included a clause protecting the author's right to publish, I doubt that it would have been possible to arrive at any agreement for revisions of the manuscript that would have satisfied the NRA people and would have satisfied me and our Committee.

The Management Resistance Problem

In the early postwar years, I saw no change in the general indifference or even hostility of most operating managers to our human relations research. To be sure, there were notable exceptions. For example, James C. Worthy (1950, 1984) of Sears, Roebuck and Company had a lively intellectual and practical interest in our research and worked with people from our Committee in developing the Sears attitudinal survey program and on further projects. But such exceptions were few.

At first I attributed our failure to stir up more interest and support from managers to our inability to talk their language, but now I think that was a misdiagnosis. Some of us were able to speak and write in rather clear and simple terms. I think the problem was rather that top management people saw no need to change their styles of management. These were the years following World War II in which the U.S. "great arsenal of democracy" had achieved an enormous international reputation. Productivity teams from all over the world were visiting the United States to learn the secrets of our know-how. As late as 1968, when Japan was already beginning to make serious inroads into our industrial dominance, the French journalist Jean-Jacques Servan-Schreiber published the best-selling *The American Challenge,* in which he claimed that U.S. management people were so much more efficient than those in Europe that the United States was taking over economic dominance of that part of the world.

Since top management people were being told by their admirers elsewhere that they had all the answers, why should they listen to people from the ivory tower who might point out problems they were not mastering? In that era, we barely got to talk to a plant manager, let alone to any line manager at higher levels. We had better access to personnel administrators, who were looking for some new gimmicks that might help them gain status in their companies. But when personnel administrators would say, "What we want you to tell us is how can we make the workers feel they are participating," we had to answer that we were not into impression management. And when we explained that the way to make workers feel that they were participating was to open up opportunities for them to exert influence on decisions of importance to them, the personnel administrators generally lost interest in further discussion.

The situation in Japan was dramatically different. Having suffered the disastrous loss of World War II, Japanese intellectuals and business and government leaders were looking around the world for new ideas that might help them to rebuild. They discovered the growing academic human relations literature and translated and read the writings of Douglas McGregor, Rensis Likert, Chris Argyris, and others. This led to what Robert Cole has described as "a creative misunderstanding" (personal communication). The Japanese assumed that the participative management styles espoused by these authors were actually being implemented by the leading U.S. companies. They concluded that if Japan wished to compete with the United States and other industrialized nations, it must develop its own system of participation. Thus, whereas the works of the university people were viewed in U.S. management circles as more ornamental than practical, the Japanese went to work seriously to reshape industrial management and labor relations.

For example, Hideo Kawabuchi in 1951 was one of the first contingent of Japanese students to come for graduate study in the United States following World War II. He remained only one year at the New York State School of Industrial and Labor Relations at Cornell, where I had moved in 1948, but in that year he became an enthusiastic convert to human relations and participative management. Returning to Japan, he persuaded an old friend to defect from a regional government program promoting scientific management to enlist with him in converting Japanese management to the human relations approach. They founded the Japan Human Relations Association—which still goes by that title, untranslated. Today, more than 4,000 industrial companies belong to JHRA. The association has a central office staff of about thirty people, publishes a monthly supervisor's journal, and conducts conferences and publishes other studies designed to promote what the Japanese still call human relations.

But I should not exaggerate the impact of my tangential relationship, through my student Kawabuchi, with these Japanese developments. Probably the Japan Federation of Employers' Associations and the Japan Union of Scientists and Engineers were more influential than JHRA in stimulating and guiding Japan's development of its program of employee involvement (Cole 1985).

In the 1940s and 1950s, the prevailing relationships between unions and management were sharply adversarial. Many managements were still trying to avoid unionization or to undermine their unions. Those managements accepting collective bargaining in principle nevertheless seemed to act as if the relationship were a necessary evil. They were trying to run the companies as much as possible as if unions were not there.

This meant that the New York State School of Industrial and Labor Relations, which had been created by the state government in 1945 to gain knowledge to help both labor and management, was necessarily suspect. In those early years, in some management quarters in New York State this new college was called "the cardboard Kremlin"—"cardboard" because of the temporary quarters we occupied until 1961, and "Kremlin" because of the school's general commitment to the institution of collective bargaining (which, of course, never had any place in the Soviet system).

In that era, professors of industrial relations were assumed to be either pro-labor or pro-management. It was hard to find practitioners who could accept the idea that a professor might be interested in helping the parties to develop mutually advantageous ways of working together.

The Withering Away of Human Relations

In the 1940s and 1950s, those identified with human relations had a dominant influence in laying out what was becoming our field of study. Why did "human relations in industry" give way to "organizational behavior" and other

labels? I trace the roots of that shift back to the academic debates of the 1950s, particularly reflected in an exchange of views I had with labor economist John Dunlop (Dunlop and Whyte 1950). Emphasizing the great influence of the institutional framework in shaping the human relations we studied, Dunlop conceded only that our microlevel studies could cast light "in the area of the relation of individuals to organizations" (p. 391). He wrote that "the 'human relations' approach is more or less identified here with the study of communications" (p. 383). He added, "The communication and human relations approach seems to proceed from the premise that conflict can be reduced in industrial relations if individuals have more accurate information" (p. 392).

At that time, I rejected the Dunlop critique as based on a well-meant but misguided interpretation of our work. I had never believed that communication of more accurate information was a major force in reducing conflict. My interest in communication was focused not only on interpersonal interactions but also on the *actions* that followed the interactions. We expected to observe frequent occasions when managers initiated actions for workers, but did workers and union leaders also initiate actions for managers? If so, how often, in what circumstances, and on what types of problems?

I now have a clearer view of the weaknesses of my 1950 position than I did then. I had argued that

> [w]e must have a means of dealing with influences from outside the plant. But at the same time, we are not dealing with influences in general. We must study them at the point of contact: where they actually enter the plant. (p. 400)

The weakness of that position is that it fostered a concentration on human relations as if the interactions were occurring in an economic, technological, and structural vacuum. That is, we had to deal with the external elements when they became so obvious that we could not ignore them; but we dealt with elements outside our social systems framework on an ad hoc basis, having no systematic means of integrating them into our thinking.

Perhaps that confession overstates the case against us. Through the pioneering work of Charles Walker, Robert Guest, and Arthur Turner (1952, 1956) we recognized that the automotive assembly line was one of the most oppressive systems of getting work done that had ever been devised, but we assumed that this mode of production was so economically efficient that it would be impossible to produce efficiently under any other system of work organization. We knew it would be impossible economically to go back to the earlier methods in which craftsmen had built cars, but we did not see ahead to the more flexible systems of organizing work that developed years later. In other words, we treated technology as a constant rather than as a set of variables. (Nor did we learn until many years later the importance of treating *ownership* as a set of variables rather than as a constant.)

We did give some attention to the impact of economic incentives on workers, in our studies of piece rates (Whyte et al. 1955), but we had no way of integrating the economics of the firm into our framework. We knew that the behavior of managers was influenced by the way they interpreted the numbers that purported to reflect the performance of the firm, but, with few exceptions (Argyris 1952), we did not focus on the point where economic analysis and behavioral analysis come together.

In discovering that the formal organization structure did not determine behavior, as the exponents of scientific management had argued, we concentrated particularly on what we then called "informal organization." We neglected the importance of the formal hierarchical and departmental and divisional structures in shaping behavior.

It was the growing awareness of the limitations of "the human relations approach" that led even some of us old-timers to accept other labels, such as "organizational behavior" or "complex organizations."

From the 1950s to the 1980s

During the past thirty years or so, we have seen a growing interest in organizational behavior research on the part of practitioners. We have also seen a great proliferation of research articles and books.

Do we now have more to offer to science and practice than we did in the days of human relations? Any attempt to answer such a general question within the scope of an article will necessarily be more provocative than comprehensive and balanced. Here I opt to sketch out what I see as major trends in the hope of focusing debates on the future of our field.

What has become the main stream of research in *organizational theory* contrasts with the human relations approach in several important respects:

1. A shift of emphasis from the micro to the macro: from interpersonal relations to formal organizational structures, technologies, and the impact of markets and other environmental factors on the organization.
2. A shift from the study of general patterns of relations toward the definition of variables, and the specification of hypotheses to be tested by rigorous quantitative methods.
3. A shift from intensive interviewing and observational studies toward questionnaire or survey research.
4. A sharp separation between theory and practice, with the researchers generally avoiding any linking of research to practice.

Main stream researchers do not all share the same interests and methodologies, of course, but they have enough in common to be identified as a group by most scholars studying the development of organization theory (see, for example, Hall 1982).

There is also an alternate stream of development that groups together those concentrating on *organizational change.* In a sense, this research stream arose out of the human relations approach instead of representing a sharp break away from it. Like those of us active in the 1940s and 1950s, the alternate stream researchers reject the separation of theory from practice, arguing that science can best be advanced when the two are linked together. The difference is that today's organizational change researchers have sharper action tools and better theoretical frameworks than we did in those earlier decades.

Although the main stream and the alternate stream are clearly different in some ways, they also have certain interests in common. Researchers of both kinds accept the influence on organizations of formal structure, markets, and other environmental conditions, but the alternate stream researchers go on to study how organizational performance can be improved within those limiting conditions. Both streams have strong interests in worker participation, but they pursue that interest in quite different ways (a point I discuss below).

Until Joan Woodward (1965) came on the scene, the only theory of organizational structures was that handed down by the scientific management school: that for any organization of a given size there was just one best way of designing its structure. The studies of the Woodward group demonstrated that plants with different technologies and work processes required distinctively different organizational structures.

For the main stream (organization theory), the Woodward studies set off a flood of research on organizational structures. Paul Lawrence and Jay Lorsch (1967) extended this analysis into the relations of the organization and its markets. Howard Aldrich (1979) went further to argue that the environment tended to select those organizational characteristics that best fit it.

Those developing the alternate stream (organizational change) picked up the Woodward lead on organizational structures to work on the theory and practice of changing structures, technologies, and social systems so as to fit them more fruitfully together. Having begun his research career in England long before Woodward, Eric Trist went on to formulate the concept of socio-technical systems (Trist 1981). The idea is basically simple: the most effective organizations will be those in which the technology and the organization structure and social processes are designed to fit together. If this idea now seems obvious, note that it departs radically from all of past practice and most current practice. In the past, designers of organizations laid out the technology and assumed that work and social processes must be designed (generally by other people) to fit the requirements of the technology.

From England to Scandinavia and America, Trist and his social systems framework have had an enormous influence on organizational change theory and practice. In Norway, Einar Thorsrud created and guided for many years the Industrial Democracy project, bringing together Norwegian and foreign social scientists with Norwegian workers, managers, and union leaders to learn how to design (or redesign) organizations so as to enhance both economic efficiency and the quality of working life (Thorsrud 1977; Elden 1979). In Oslo in June 1987, hundreds of social scientists and practitioners gathered to honor the memory of Thorsrud and to discuss how best to contribute to the flow of research and action on socio-technical systems.

That the main and the alternate streams have diverged sharply from each other is most readily demonstrated by picking up a textbook from a mainstream social scientist. Consider, for example, Richard H. Hall's *Organizations: Structure and Process* (1982), in which leading figures in the alternate stream are almost completely overlooked. Eric Trist is mentioned only briefly in reference to his earliest study, and Einar Thorsrud and other leading figures in the alternate stream do not even rate footnotes. Or consider the leading action researchers focusing on the problems of changing leader behavior in organizations: Donald Schön (1983) is not mentioned by Hall, and the only mentions of Chris Argyris (1986) are in connection with his critiques of main stream research.

Can these two streams be brought together? Since researchers in both streams continue to study worker participation in decision making, let us examine the prospects provided by that focus.

Solving the Participation-Productivity Puzzle

Those in both streams would like to believe that increases in worker participation are positively correlated with increases in productivity. Research does support the conclusion that job satisfaction is favorably affected by worker participation, but main stream studies on the participation-productivity relationship have yielded mixed results (Brett and Hammer 1982; Hammer 1983).

What accounts for the ambiguous findings? Apart from the technical difficulties of measuring productivity and generalizing across a wide range of technologies and organization structures, we face three major problems: how to define participation; how to determine to what extent participation has taken place; and how to link a particular form of participation with a specific target for productivity improvement (or cost savings).

Regarding the first problem, participation can and does occur in many different forms, determined both by the particular problems being addressed and by the means chosen to handle those problems. For example, instead of just giving orders, the boss may informally consult individual subordinates before acting. Or he may hold group discussions and allow his decisions to be influenced by those discussions. In practice, there are enormous differences in time devoted to employee involvement activities. In the typical quality circle in the United States, worker members may hold a one-hour meeting every week or every two weeks. At the other extreme, Xerox study action teams of workers and management people spend full time for up to six months working out concrete solutions to pressing cost and productivity problems (Lazes and Costanza 1984).

The scope of the problems addressed by worker participation may also vary widely. At one extreme, worker involvement may be limited to housekeeping issues (company parking lot, vending machines, cafeteria, etc.); at the other extreme, workers may be involved in decisions on key industrial relations issues (incentive rates, gains sharing, work redesign, work rule changes, and productivity/cost issues).

Regarding the second problem, most main stream researchers have finessed the task of determining whether participation has taken place by measuring participation subjectively: asking survey respondents to what extent they *feel* they have been participating. The measurements can be refined further by asking how they *feel* about their participation regarding specified issues. This approach gives us a rich yield of numbers, but those numbers do not tell us what *behavior* has given rise to the subjective responses.

With exceptions that are just beginning to occur, research has not focused on participation projects designed to produce specific and measurable productivity improvements. The research design has been based on the assumption that participation will have an *indirect* effect on productivity. Researchers cannot hope to accurately measure direct effects on productivity when the parties have not established any target for their efforts. In that case, if productivity increases occur following a particular form of participation, we may assume only at our peril that participation led to this result, since it may well be that other variables intervened to produce a spurious relationship.

Under these conditions, it should not be expected that the main stream research strategy will yield any meaningful results. Tracking the impact of participation through measures keyed to any single variable or any set of variables is bound to be fruitless.

What other research design is more promising? We can seek answers through *patterns* rather than through discrete variables. We begin with the recognition that, although participation could conceivably occur in an almost infinite variety of forms, by now the work of practitioners and researchers has sorted out a small number of forms that appear to have promise (Lawler 1986).

Consistent with those considerations is the following research design. We examine a case in which people in labor and management are implementing a *participatory action research strategy* designed to achieve certain concrete objectives in productivity improvements or cost reductions. We then describe systematically the actions and interpersonal interactions constituting that strategy and, finally, measure whether and to what extent the objectives have been achieved. If the strategy has been successful in those terms, we have established a direct relationship between participation and productivity. (To be sure, it is possible that the outcome could be produced by factors not observed by the researchers, but such an event is much less likely when we are studying the attainment of explicitly specified goals than when we are studying the indirect impact of participation on productivity.)

The example cited above is not simply hypothetical. Such a case occurred in the wire harness department of a Xerox factory (Lazes and Costanza 1984; Kochan et al. 1984:13-33). In the wire harness case, the challenge to a labor-management study action team (working full time for six months) was to save 180 jobs through reducing departmental costs by $3.2 million—more than 25 percent. People in higher management could not believe that such an outcome was possible, yet the team overshot the target, producing a plan to save $3.7 million. While implementing the wire harness plan, Xerox and the Amalgamated Clothing and Textile Workers Union proceeded to carry out (with similar ultimate success) the same participatory action strategy with other departments in which Xerox's costs substantially exceeded those available from vendors. Xerox's experience has led Cornell's Programs for Employment and Workplace Systems (PEWS), under the leadership of Peter Lazes, to make this general strategy the central thrust in PEWS projects currently being carried out with labor and management in other companies.

The significance of this participatory action research strategy is not limited to establishing a relationship between participation and productivity, important as that may be. These cases demonstrate the importance of linking up human relations with the economics of the firm. Not only are we incorporating cost measures into our research, we are also strengthening our understanding of the way management and union people react to economic measures. Of course, this breakthrough simply points to future theoretical and practical problems to be studied—but that is the nature of scientific progress. We can describe the social processes leading to the economic results, and we can report the economic figures, but to behavioral scientists the technical economic and engineering analysis that went into the determination of the cost savings figures remains a black box. A next step in the advancement of organizational science is to open that black box.

A colleague in managerial economics tells me that there have been no basic advances in teaching or research in accounting in business schools since 1929 (personal communication from Alan McAdams; see also Anthony 1986). Those conventional methods are clearly not well adapted to solving the cost accounting problems of modern industry in a highly competitive environment. The Xerox study action teams have apparently developed innovative methods of accounting and engineering analysis that have made it possible to save millions of dollars and preserve hundreds of jobs. Though we now know the results in terms of dollars and jobs saved, the technical and financial analyses generating those results are filed away in company reports. A university team could work with members of the study action teams to abstract from their reports the methods of technical and financial analysis they developed. The data thus recovered could serve as the basis for future teaching and research in accounting, engineering, managerial economics, and organizational behavior, opening up exciting new fields of interdisciplinary study.

For such new research, the alternate stream has clearcut advantages over the main stream in several respects. First, main stream research tends to be disciplinebound. The planning process begins with a review of the literature, which may go somewhat beyond the scholar's discipline but tends to be concentrated within that discipline. Variables are specified and hypotheses formulated so as to maximize the chance that the research will build on the body of knowledge within the discipline. Since very few problems in the complex field of modern industry lend themselves to solution with the tools of any single discipline, this disciplinary focus is bound to be counterproductive, theoretically and practically.

In contrast, alternate stream researchers approach the field with a general interest: for example, the problem of reconciling management's aim to cut costs with the union's aim to maintain employment. The researcher then looks over the scene to find cases in which the people in the organization are trying to find new and interesting ways of coping with their problems. He or she approaches the gatekeepers to see whether the researcher's involvement in the search and coping process promises to be mutually advantageous. If so, the researcher then seeks to work out a role that combines gathering of data with participation in the change process. The researcher must then stretch his or her mind to grasp at least some of the general lines of analysis in other disciplines—or else collaborate with specialists in those disciplines. As this type of research breaks through traditional disciplinary barriers, it is bound to have an unsettling but stimulating effect across a wide range of disciplines.

The alternate stream strategy also makes it possible to study some change processes that would not have occurred without the researcher's personal involvement. For example, it was Peter Lazes, serving as consultant to both union and management at Xerox, who first proposed the idea of study action teams as a means of balancing management's aim to cut costs and the union's aim to preserve jobs.

Industrial Relations Research in the 1980s

In the 1980s, we do our research and consulting in an industrial relations environment drastically different from that of earlier decades. To be sure, there are many managers who see

weakening of the union movement and pressures of international competition as enhancing opportunities to maintain a "union free environment" or to undermine existing unions. Those academics who choose to do research or consulting with such companies cannot escape the charge that they are anti-union. On the other hand, we find a number of companies—and even major companies—whose managements have decided not only to tolerate unions but actually to try to work jointly with union leaders and workers on cooperative activities designed to strengthen the firm's competitive position and thereby to save jobs.

Those who study jointly developed cooperative programs find that they are now no longer regarded by the parties as either pro-labor or pro-management. Accepting money from a company for research or technical assistance does not automatically brand a professor or student as anti-union. Even a project wholly financed by the company can be accepted by workers and the union–provided that the union leaders are fully involved with management in providing access and guidance to the researchers and know that, if they refuse to endorse it, that project will not go forward.

The turbulence of the industrial relations scene in the 1980s is also accompanied by unprecedented changes in the ownership of corporations, ranging from battles to take over corporations to the rapid growth of employee ownership in various forms. When industrial relations and managements and unions are in such a state of rapid change, there is an urgent need for social scientists to go into the field so as to document new lines of development and help practitioners to understand trends and possibilities.

In organizational behavior, we can no longer say that we could help management and labor to solve their problems if they would only listen to us. They are now ready to listen and to work with us. The question is: will we be up to the challenge of providing them with the help they so urgently need?

A distinguished sociologist, reviewing the current state of his discipline, has written,

> the dominant mood today is one of discouragement—a feeling that researchers go around in circles, that conceptual clarity is lacking, that theory is uninformed by empirical findings, that blind empiricism is rampant, that knowledge fails to accumulate, and that the former consensus about the core of the discipline has largely broken down. (Inkeles 1986)

I believe the same judgment applies to research in the main stream of organizational behavior, whether the research is done by sociologists or psychologists. The refined measurement of discrete variables at the micro level and the further exploration of macro level elements appear to be adding constantly to our knowledge—until we ask what use can be made of that knowledge. If asked how they can help union leaders or managers to solve the problems of their organizations, main stream researchers would have to fall back on broad, general statements regarding the institutional and environmental constraints within which the practitioners are working. Since the practitioners are likely to be more attuned to their organization's particular constraints than are researchers, they are unlikely to find such orientations useful.

I am not arguing that every research project should yield significant practical implications. But even those most dedicated to pure science goals would hardly deny that advancing science should *eventually* yield payoffs in practical applications. As I see it, the main stream has been running now for about 30 years. Rather than gener-ating useful knowledge, the main stream seems to me to be running dry.

I see the alternate stream in a disorderly but vigorous period of growth. When the alternate stream is ignored by those in the main stream, that is unhealthy for the future development of organizational behavior. Criticisms of aspects of theory and methodology used in the alternate stream can be healthy, but they should not be based on the implicit assumption that there is just one best way to advance a science of organizational behavior. Is it possible to do acceptable scientific research focused on participatory action strategies? If the answer from main streamers is negative, then clearly the two streams can never come fruitfully together. If the answer is affirmative, then the quantitative skills and theoretical sophistication of the main streamers can greatly strengthen the scientific base for the study of participatory action strategies, to our mutual advantage.

REFERENCES

Aldrich, Howard E. *Organizations and Environments.* Englewood Cliffs, N.J.: Prentice-Hall, 1979.

Anthony, Robert N. 1987 "We Don't Have the Accounting Concepts We Need." *Harvard Business Review,* Vol. 65 (Jan.-Feb., 1987), pp. 70–83.

Argyris, Chris. *The Impact of Budgets on People.* Ithaca, N.Y.: School of Business and Public Administration, Cornell University, 1952.

Argyris, Chris, Robert Putnam, and Diana McLain Smith. *Action Science.* San Francisco: Jossey-Bass, 1986.

Brett, Jeanne M., and Tove Helland Hammer. "Organizational Behavior and Industrial Relations." In Thomas Kochan, Daniel J. B. Mitchell, and Lee Dyer, eds., *Industrial Relations Research in the 1970s: Review and Appraisal.* Madison, Wis.: IRRA, 1982, pp. 221-81.

Cole, Robert. "The Macropolitics of Organizational Change: A Comparative Analysis of the Spread of Small-Group Activities." *Administrative Science Quarterly,* 1985, Vol. 30, pp. 560–85.

Dunlop, John T., and William F. Whyte. "Framework for the Analysis of Industrial Relations: Two Views." *Industrial and Labor Relations Review,* Vol. 3, No. 3 (April 1950), pp. 383–401.

Elden, Max. "Three Generations of Worker Democracy Research in Norway." In C. L. Cooper and E. Mumford, eds., *The Quality of Work Life in Europe.* London: Associated Business Press, 1979, pp. 226-57.

Hall, Richard H. *Organizations: Structure and Process.* 3d Edition. Englewood Cliffs, N.J.: Prentice-Hall, 1982.

Hammer, Tove Helland. "Worker Participation Programs: Do They Improve Productivity?" *ILR Report,* 1983, Vol. 21, No. 1, pp. 15–20.

Inkeles, Alex. "Advances in Sociology: A Critique." In Karl W. Deutsch, Andrei S. Markovits, and John Platt, eds., *Advances in the Social Sciences, 1900-1980.* Lanhan, Md.: University Press of America (Abt Books), pp. 13–31.

Kochan, Thomas A., Harry C. Katz, and Nancy R. Mower. *Worker Participation and American Unions.* Kalamazoo, Mich.: Upjohn Institute for Employment Research, 1984.

Lawler, Edward E. *High Involvement Management.* San Francisco: Jossey-Bass, 1986.

Lawrence, Paul R., and Jay W. Lorsch. *Organizations and Environment.* Cambridge, Mass.: Harvard University Press, 1967.

Lazes, Peter, and Tony Costanza. "Cutting Costs Without Layoffs Through Union-Management Collaboration." *National Productivity Review,* Vol. 2, No. 4 (Autumn 1983), pp. 362–70.

Roethlisberger, F. J. *The Elusive Phenomena.* Cambridge, Mass.: Harvard University Press, 1977.

Roethlisberger, F. J., and William J. Dickson. *Management and Worker.* Cambridge, Mass.: Harvard University Press, 1939.

Sayles, Leonard, and George Strauss. *The Local Union: Its Place in the Industrial Plant.* New York: Harper & Bros., 1953.

Schön, Donald A. *The Reflective Practitioner: How Professionals Think in Action.* New York: Basic Books, 1983.

Servan-Schreiber, J. J. *The American Challenge.* New York: Harper & Row, 1968.

Thorsrud, Einar. "Democracy at Work: Norwegian Experience with Non-Bureaucratic Forms of Organization." *Applied Behavior Science,* 1977, Vol. 13. No. 3, pp. 410–21.

Trist, Eric. *The Evolution of Socio-Technical Systems: A Conceptual Framework and Action Research Program.* Toronto: Ontario Ministry of Labour, 1981.

Walker, Charles, and Robert H. Guest. *The Man on the Assembly Line.* Cambridge, Mass.: Harvard University Press, 1952.

Walker, Charles, Robert H. Guest, and Arthur Turner. *The Fore-man on the Assembly Line.* Cambridge, Mass.: Harvard University Press, 1956.

Woodward, Joan. *Industrial Organization: Theory and Practice.* London: Oxford University Press, 1965.

Whyte, W. F. "Review of *The Elusive Phenomena.*" *Human Organization,* 1978, Vol. 37, No. 4, pp. 412–20.

———. *Money and Motivation.* New York: Harper Bros, 1955.

———. *Street Corner Society.* Chicago: University of Chicago Press, 1943.

Worthy, James C. *Shaping an American Institution: Robert E. Wood and Sears, Roebuck.* Urbana: University of Illinois Press, 1984.

———. "Organization Structure and Employee Morale." *American Sociological Review,* 1950, Vol. 15 (April).

DISCUSSION QUESTIONS

1. According to Whyte, what research marked the beginning of behavioral science interest in industrial relations? Why?

2. What were the contributions of Max Weber to the study of industrial sociology?

3. What were the different research interests among labor economists, industrial psychologists, sociologists, and human relations researchers? What controversies resulted from these different interests?

4. What is a case study? What is field work?

5. Why did managers resist studies of their organizations?

6. What important intellectual discovery does Whyte attribute to Japanese students who studied in the United States after World War II?

7. Why did "human relations in industry" change to "organizational behavior"?

8. What are the major differences between the main stream of research in organization theory and the human relations approach?

9. What are the current interests of what Whyte identifies as the "alternate" stream of organizational research?

10. Why does Whyte view the alternate approach to research as more promising than the main stream approach?

Business Ethics Past and Present

David Vogel

LEARNING OBJECTIVES

After reading "Business Ethics Past and Present" by Vogel, a student will be able to:

1. Recognize that concern with ethical behavior in organizations—particularly businesses—is historical and not only an issue raised by the highly publicized scandals of the 1980s

2. Appreciate that ethical issues in organizations are framed by the value system of society, which is to a large extent derived from religious principles

3. Understand the interactions of business, government, and society in shaping ethical behavior

4. Understand the importance of ethics for interpreting and responsibly managing the behavior of individuals and organizations

While both public and scholarly interest in business ethics have increased significantly over the last decade, the subject itself is not new; in fact business ethics is an integral part of the Western ethical tradition. The public has been concerned with the ethics of business ever since a market economy began in the West more than 750 years ago.

Unfortunately, most contemporary writing on business ethics is ahistorical. Aside from the obligatory references to Kant and Mill, one rarely finds any serious discussion of concepts or ideas that date back more than a few decades. The relevant writings of Aristotle and of the Catholic and Protestant theologians who thought long and hard about the ethics of business are rarely cited. One also finds remarkably few references in the contemporary business-ethics literature to the works of scholars such as Max Weber, Albert Hirschman, and Michael Walzer—all of whom have written extensively about the historical roots of capitalism as an ethical system.

While there is a rich secondary literature on business ethics, it is significant that it includes few historical works. Nor do any of the widely used business-ethics texts extensively discuss the history of the use of ethical concepts to evaluate business behavior during the last few centuries. The last decade was certainly not the first in which the ethics of American business was widely criticized: the moral shortcomings of financiers, bankers, and investors have been noted recurrently in American history. Yet to date, no one has understood the contemporary resurgence of ethical criticism of business historically, by examining the interactions of business with government and society in earlier times.

In many important respects, the ethical standards to which we hold business have remained remarkably constant over a long period of time—though obviously many of the specific aspects of business conduct that trouble us today are new. Moreover, many of our contemporary debates about the nature of business ethics are centuries old. By drawing upon this rich intellectual history, we will be better able to appreciate the nature and significance of many current concerns.

The Protestant Ethic

The emergence of capitalism in sixteenth-century Europe was closely associated with the Protestant Reformation. In an important sense, Protestantism made business ethics possible. To the extent that medieval Catholic theology held that moneymaking was morally suspect, it could not establish moral standards for its pursuit. As St. Augustine put it, "[T]he businessman . . . may conduct himself without sin, but cannot be pleasing to God." And St. Thomas Aquinas believed that most forms of trade conducted for profit were inherently immoral, holding that "he who in trading sells a thing for more than he paid for it must have paid less than it was worth or be selling it for more."

Source: David Vogel, "Business Ethics Past and Present," Reprinted with permission of the publisher and the author from: *The Public Interest*, No. 102 (Winter 1991), pp. 49-84. ©1991 by National Affairs, Inc.

Catholic theologians did distinguish among types of economic activity. They regarded producing a good for sale as less ethically suspect than either trading in goods or extending loans, for example. But for the most part, business activity was regarded as beyond the moral pale: the only ethical advice given by Christ to the merchants and tradesmen that he encountered was to abandon their work and follow him. A moral businessman was thus a contradiction in terms. In a way, a Catholic could no more have been an ethical moneylender six centuries ago than he could be a socially responsible drug dealer today.

If an activity is reagarded as inherently immoral, the only moral course of action is to disengage from it entirely. The contemporary moral case against such business activities as investing in South Africa, manufacturing and marketing cigarettes, or producing strategic weapons represents an echo of the more sweeping medieval case against finance in particular and the pursuit of profit in general. During the intervening centuries the specific sources of profit regarded as inherently unethical have changed, but the moral standard for evaluating the ethics of business activities has remained remarkably stable.

Not surprisingly, many medieval merchants did in fact act like contemporary drug dealers. After all, if their activity was thought to be immoral to begin with, why should they have tried to perform it ethically? As the sociologist Paul Blumberg notes, pre-Reformation capitalism was rooted in a "rampant individualism which knew few scruples. . . . The capitalist mentality of the medieval business classes rested on the dictum: 'A profit is a profit, however it is acquired.'" For example, merchants in Italian city-states thought nothing of putting the bodies of diseased animals into the shops of their competitors in order to make them, their employees, and their customers ill.

It was by morally sanctifying the pursuit of profit that Protestantism made business ethics possible. While traditional Catholic theology viewed work at worst as a curse and at best as a distraction, Protestantism held that a businessman's work could be pleasing to God. Not only could one serve God by working, but the correct use of wealth was precisely to increase it for the glory of God. Consequently, the pursuits of profit and of heaven became not only compatible but mutually reinforcing. A diligent worker, for instance, was less likely to be tempted by the devil. And being rewarded with financial success was now understood as a sign of God's favor. In short, the Reformation made it possible for a successful businessman to be an ethical individual as well.

John Calvin's radical doctrine of predestination was never widely shared, even among Protestants. But a more secular version of Protestant business ethics did become important in Western popular culture. It is to this Protestant ethic that we owe our contemporary effort to understand the relationship between personal virtue and financial success, between corporate ethics and profitability.

Irving Kristol has described nineteenth-century America as "a society in which it was agreed that there was a strong correlation between certain personal virtues—frugality, industry, sobriety, reliability, piety—and the way in which power, privilege and property were distributed." Success was associated with the performance of duty—a point made repeatedly in the Benjamin Franklin homilies and Horatio Alger novels that were read by literally tens of thousands of schoolchildren then.

Kristol correctly notes that nineteenth-century Americans were extremely interested in the relationship between good moral character and success in business. But he appears to have exaggerated the extent to which they regarded the two as closely related. By the end of the century numerous successful industrialists were certainly repugnant to many Americans. In Gustavus Myers's 1909 work *History of the Great American Fortunes,* Jay Gould—an extremely successful financial operator—is described as a "freebooter, . . . a pitiless human carnivore, glutting on the blood of his numerous victims, . . . [and] a gambler destitute of the usual gambler's codes of fairness in abiding by the rules"—hardly the portrait of a man whose accumulation of wealth would have been pleasing to God.

A Secularized Ethic

Contemporary discussions of business ethics focus less on questions of individual character than was true a century ago. Indeed, we appear to have almost completely lost sight of the fact that the word "ethics" is derived from the Greek term *ethos,* meaning "character." Because much economic activity now takes place through organizations, today we are less interested in the character of individual businessmen than in the decision-making processes of business firms. Consequently we tend to use the terms corporate social responsibility and business ethics almost interchangeably.

In addition, contemporary discussions of business ethics are overwhelmingly cast in secular terms. The profound Judeo-Christian roots of the Western tradition of business ethics are rarely examined. Even those theologians who write about business ethics seldom refer to the concepts of sin, evil, or divine judgment. Nevertheless, we remain no less preoccupied with the relationship between morality and profits than Weber's Calvinist merchants or Kristol's nineteenth-century schoolchildren.

Indeed, one's assessment of the relationship between morality and profits is a virtual litmus test of one's overall appraisal of the ethics of American business. The harshest critics of American business ethics tend to assume that the relationship between ethics and profits is either random or negative; members of this camp include the large percentage of Americans who believe that companies often behave irresponsibly in order to increase their profits. Many certainly believe that financially successful firms are apt to be less ethical than those less favored by the invisible hand. Though their reasoning may differ, those who hold this view reach a conclusion akin to that of Augustine and Aquinas.

On the other hand, a secular variant of the Protestant ethic has now been revived by the mainstream business community. The reports on business ethics issued by such organizations as the Business Roundtable and Touche Ross argue that good ethics is good business. They claim that it is possible to be both virtuous and successful, and even that moral virtue is necessary for success. Thus former Securities and Exchange Commission chairman John Shad asserts that "ethics pays. It's smart to be ethical."

To hold this view is not to insist that socially responsible firms are always profitable. But then even the Protestant clergymen of seventeenth-century Europe and nineteenth-century America did not preach that good people invariably prospered or achieved salvation. The claim instead is that being "good" or "responsible" is a necessary though not sufficient condition for succeeding in the marketplace. In other words, not all virtuous firms and individuals will succeed, but all successful ones are likely to have been virtuous.

There is also an equally important implicit corollary, which is that those who behave badly will be punished. This punishment takes the form of customer and employee dissatisfaction, criticism in the media (all presumably resulting in reduced profits), and—in extreme cases—civil or criminal prosecution. For the Protestant clergy punishment was deferred to the afterlife, though its form was both more consequential and more enduring than that commonly meted out by secular authorities and the market.

Many scholars have attempted to measure the relationship between the social responsibility of a company and its financial performance. Important as this research is,

in a way it is also beside the point: the appeal of Calvinism and Horatio Alger did not rest on the demonstrated validity of their causal models. It may make more sense to regard the Business Roundtable's view as the contemporary, secular equivalent of a Protestant sermon. Like many of the statements on business ethics made by businessmen, its real purpose is to exhort the business community to improve its moral behavior. And just as the Protestant clergy promised salvation as a reward for virtue, so does the Roundtable promise improved profits as a reward for ethical business conduct.

In principle, the Roundtable's position may be more demonstrable than that of the Protestant clergy; but in the final analysis, both rest on faith. Equally important is that both predictions are meant to be self-fulfilling. Thus if large numbers of executives are persuaded that good ethics is good business, the two in fact are likely to turn out to be positively correlated. Alternatively, if many executives believe in a trade-off between them, the ethics of business is less likely to improve.

In sum, people have been interested in the relationship between ethics and profits for a long time. The debate over the nature of their relationship remains central to our appraisal of the moral legitimacy of business. Just as the Protestant ethic played an important role in legitimating capitalism, so are the efforts of today's business community to correlate ethics with profits important as an attempt to firm up the moral legitimacy of our contemporary business system. Alternatively, those who argue that a good person cannot succeed in business, or that a socially responsible company is handicapped in the marketplace, are challenging the ethical foundations of our market economy; in effect they are arguing, as did many medieval Catholic theologians, that business ethics is an oxymoron.

The emergence of ethical or socially responsible investment funds and programs can also be understood in this context. Like Calvin's sermons and Alger's novels, these funds appeal to the desire of the public to be both virtuous and prosperous. The funds are based on the assumption that not only is there no trade-off between virtue and prosperity, but that in many cases they are mutually reinforcing. For all the progressive political rhetoric that surrounds these funds, their core assumptions are actually quite similar to those of the Business Roundtable. And their depiction of the relationship between ethics and profits, like the Roundtable's, is also meant to be self-fulfilling: presumably if many investors act on the belief that a responsible firm will likely be more profitable, then the price of its shares will rise accordingly. The popularity of these funds suggests that the moral issues that troubled Aquinas and Calvin remain: evidently many people are still searching for a way to accumulate capital without sin.

The Capitalist Legitimation of Economic Success

The notion that successful businessmen could be good human beings constituted an important dimension of the original moral case for capitalism. A second dimension involved a new understanding of the relationship between economic success and the public good.

In pre-market economics, the acquisition of wealth was primary a zero-sum game. One became wealthy primarily by fighting or taxing others, so as to take their resources. What made capitalism unique was its claim to have developed a mechanism though which it was possible for an individual to acquire wealth that not only did not harm others, but actually benefited them. This mechanism was, of course, the market. In principle, the only way to acquire wealth in a market economy is to satisfy the material needs of others; profits reward businessmen for successfully fulfilling the legitimate expectations of their employees, customers, and investors.

Wealth accumulated through the market does not lessen the total volume of available goods and services: the consumer is no worse off for having exchanged his money for a commodity than is the merchant who now has fewer goods and more money. Thanks to the market, both are better off than they would otherwise have been, though not necessarily in the same proportion.

Prior to capitalism, virtually all profit tended to be regarded as profiteering; it appeared to be rooted in extortion rather than fair exchange. Accordingly, it was morally suspect. What capitalism did was to provide an ethical justification for moneymaking; capitalism's claim to be the world's first fair economic system was predicated on the understanding that the merchant, unlike the Roman warrior or the feudal lord, actually deserved his material wealth. In short, capitalism purported to be the first social system in which the wealthy could claim that they simply received a just reward for performing a socially useful function.

Centuries after the birth of capitalism, we continue to judge the acquisition of wealth by this standard. For many free-market economists, the moral case against govern-

ment intervention in the economy is that government divorces acquiring wealth from serving the needs of society as expressed through the market Protective tariffs, subsidies, tax breaks, legally sanctioned cartels, and monopolies—all can be viewed as relics of mercantilism, the system of business-government relations whose abuses and inequities were denounced by Adam Smith in *The Wealth of Nations.* Government intervention does create wealth, of course; that is precisely why there are so many lobbyists in Washington. But the moral claim of its critics is that much of the wealth created by government intervention is extorted rather than earned; it reflects political influence rather than social contribution.

Many contemporary economists and political economists tend to regard government as the primary if not the exclusive source of illegitimate wealth in capitalist societies. Even though this perspective tends to overlook the numerous regulations and public expenditures that clearly benefit society, it is not unreasonable. Newspapers are replete with examples of bankers or developers who have used their political influence to acquire huge sums of money—in each case clearly harming significant numbers of their fellow citizens. Adam Smith would surely not have been surprised by the savings-and-loan debacle or the recent scandals at HUD; he would likely have regarded them as the inevitable outgrowth of a system of political economy that rewards political privilege rather than economic performance.

The Continuing Critique of Market Profits

For much of the American public, however, government is not the only source of illegitimate wealth. Many citizens deny that wealth accumulated through the market is inherently moral. Instead they subject market profits to the same ethical standards that Smith employed in criticizing mercantilist profits.

Consider, for example, the response of the American public to the increased earnings of the major integrated oil companies following the oil-price rise of 1973. Were these profits deserved? The vast majority of gasoline consumers did not think so. Responding to pressures from the electorate, the federal government established controls on energy prices in an effort to limit oil company profits. And when energy prices were subsequently deregulated, the government imposed a "windfall" or "excess" profits tax on the integrated oil firms in order to prevent them from benefiting from the removal of price controls.

Now from the point of view of neoclassical economics, the notion of an "excess" or "windfall" profit is meaningless. (One is reminded of the *New Yorker* cartoon in which an elderly executive reading the paper at his club turns to his friend and exclaims: "In all my many years in business, I have yet to see an excess profit!") In fact, the terms reflect not an economic analysis but a moral critique.

Why did so many Americans regard the oil companies' earnings as an example of "profiteering"? In other words, why did they consider them to be "undeserved"? Two reasons seem particularly significant. First, the profits did not reflect any additional effort on the part of the oil companies, which had not discovered new oil reserves or improved their operating efficiency in 1974. Instead their increased earnings were largely inventory profits: substantial wealth was being transferred to them for no other reason than that a group of Arab oil ministers had suddenly discovered how to form a successful cartel. The companies' profits were due less to their economic contribution than to the fact that they happened to be in the right place at the right time; in short, they made a fortune only because they had been fortunate.

Secondly, the good fortune of the oil producers had important distributive consequences: it was accompanied by substantial suffering on the part of American consumers. Indeed, the fortune and the suffering appeared to be almost physically linked: it was as if the increased price of gasoline at the pump represented a direct transfer of wealth from consumers to shareholders and executives. The proposed deregulation of energy prices promised to raise gasoline prices still further: many regarded it as unfair for a small group of executives and stockholders to benefit from the sacrifices of millions of ordinary Americans.

Not surprisingly, the maintenance of price controls on energy in the recent past evokes the medieval concept of the "just price." This term, too, has no economic meaning. Rather it derives from the notion, widely shared in medieval Europe, that those who controlled access to certain critical commodities, particularly when their control was due to an "act of God" rather than their own initiative, were not entitled to all the profits that the "normal" workings of the market allowed.

Critics have also raised questions about social contribution and fairness in connection with the profits received by investment bankers in return for their efforts to restructure the American economy. Robert Reich has described some members of the American financial community as "paper entrepreneurs"—yet another term of moral opprobrium rather than economic analysis. Reich's criticism of financiers who have made large fortunes by buying and selling, or by putting together and breaking up existing companies, is remarkably similar to the medieval Church's strictures against usurers.

The Church, although it frowned upon all forms of money-making, was particularly critical of banking or money lending. It argued that it was wrong for people to be paid back more money than they had lent, since they had not improved their commodity in any way. Gold and silver were essentially "sterile": they represented a convenient way to measure wealth, but they themselves were incapable of adding to the resources available to sustain life. Accordingly, while farmers or craftsmen were entitled to charge for their labors, bankers were not.

This, of course, is precisely why Reich is so critical of the profits earned by Wall Street firms from restructuring the American economy. Reich regards producers of goods and services as the exclusive source of "real" wealth: their profits are legitimate because they derive from their efforts to deploy human material resources to meet various private and public needs. Those who make their living from buying and selling these companies, however, are in a different moral category: paper entrepreneurs are predators, not creators of value.

Fairness at Issue

As in the case of the oil-company profits of the 1970s, the extraordinary profits earned by many lawyers, investment bankers, managers, and stockholders during the 1980s also raise the issue of fairness. If restructuring is essentially a zero-sum game, as its critics allege, then the wealth accumulated by its beneficiaries must be counterbalanced by a reduction in wealth on the part of various other constituencies. The latter include not only the holders of various financial assets, but—more importantly from the point of view of the public—large numbers of employees. Paper entrepreneurship appears unfair to many Americans because it has allegedly benefited some by harming others—precisely the pre-capitalist definition of profiteering.

More generally, people's appraisal of the ethics of restructuring has to do with their perception of its contribution to economic efficiency and productivity. If, on balance, the dramatic changes in the governance of the

American economy that took place during the 1980s made business less productive and efficient, then the profits earned from this activity are clearly not deserved; after all, the moral case for profits rests on the claim that they reward only those activities that increase society's overall material abundance. Alternatively, if paper entrepreneurship has, on balance, strengthened the long-term performance of the American economy, then its critics are as short-sighted as the medieval Church was in prohibiting the payment of interest on the grounds that "time belongs to God."

It is in this context that the legitimacy of the substantial fortune accumulated by Michael Milken should be viewed. Milken's defenders have pointed out that he raised a huge amount of money for companies through the sale of junk bonds, so that his compensation—though larger in 1988 than the profits of all but a handful of corporations—was not excessive. On the other hand, the amount of Milken's personal wealth was specifically referred to in the opening pages of the U.S. Attorney's indictment of him for violating the securities laws. Both the defense and the indictment miss the point, however; at issue is not the amount of money that Milken raised for others (or received himself), but the results produced by his labors.

If junk-bond financing helped many American corporations in accumulating funds needed for growth and expansion, then Milken's compensation was not unreasonable. But if junk-bond financing instead is little more than asset reshuffling at best (and asset stripping at worst), then Milken's compensation was not deserved—regardless of its amount. In this context, it is striking that the unethical corporate raider played by Michael Douglas in the movie *Wall Street* explicitly justifies his financial machinations in zero-sum terms. As he puts it, "Somebody wins and somebody loses. Money isn't gained, it's transferred. I create nothing. I own." It would be hard for anyone to come up with a clearer ethical indictment of restructuring.

Milken's violations of the law obviously deserved punishment. But the size of his gain per se is irrelevant to his guilt or innocence; in a capitalist system, making a lot of money is not a crime. It is true that if the sums made by Milken or the oil industry were insignificant, hardly anyone would care whether they were deserved. But many athletes, entertainers, and "real" entrepreneurs make substantial sums of money without their ethics being questioned by the public. And certainly during the 1980s many high-tech firms reported increases in profits comparable to those enjoyed by the oil industry during the previous decade, yet no one ever suggested subjecting them to a "windfall" profits tax.

In this context, it is also worth noting that many home owners in New York, California, and Washington, D.C., recently experienced dramatic increases in wealth due to their good fortune in having bought a home in the right place at the right time. Their profits were clearly no more—or less—deserved than those of the oil industry. And yet no one wanted to impose a "windfall home-profits tax" on them, although Henry George—who wrote before home ownership became widespread—advocated a tax on land for precisely this reason. And while housing is as critical a commodity as energy, no one outside of Berkeley, California, has seriously proposed establishing price controls on the sale of private homes. In assessing the ethics of business, the public evidently is not immune to calculations of its own material interests.

The distinction between the wealth accumulated by Bill Cosby and Apple Computer on the one hand, and Michael Milken and Exxon on the other, has no basis whatsoever in economic theory. Rather it demonstrates the hold that medieval economic thought continues to exercise on our collective moral imagination. Many people continue to believe that not all profits are created equal; some profits, they think, are more deserved than others.

Intentions and Results

Adam Smith wrote in *The Wealth of Nations*:

> *It is not from the benevolence of the butcher, the brewer, or the baker, that we expect our dinner, but from their regard to their own self-interest. We address ourselves, not to their humanity but to their self-love, and never talk to them of our own necessities but of their advantages.*

These often-quoted lines capture the moral contradiction that lies at the heart of capitalism, in which morally dubious intentions combine to produce morally beneficial results. On the one hand, we do get the food that we need to survive—certainly no mean accomplishment in a world in which hunger was once commonplace. But on the other hand, the way we achieve this happy outcome is by paradoxically assuming that the providers of food are indifferent as to whether or not we are actually fed.

If one judges the ethics of capitalism by its results, then the system deserves our unequivocal moral approbation. By any conceivable criterion, appealing to the self-interest of humanity "works": market economies have produced more wealth and greater economic security for more individuals than even their most ardent eighteenth- and nineteenth-century defenders thought possible. Capitalism's improvement in the quality of life is equally impressive. And no other economic system has proven even remotely so compatible with liberty and democracy.

However, the issue of motives constitutes the moral Achilles heel of capitalism. This is because of the appeal to self-interest that is at the core of a market economy. Notwithstanding capitalism's impressive results, many remain uncomfortable with a system in which economic action is motivated by selfishness.

Numerous scholars have tried to address this moral issue, without much success. In *The Passions and the Interests,* Albert Hirschman presents the ideas of a number of eighteenth- and nineteenth-century thinkers who argued for the ethical superiority of capitalist motives. They favorably contrasted a society in which people sought to maximize their interests with one in which people were ruled by their passions. As Montesquieu wrote in praising market economies, "[I]t is fortunate for men to be in a situation in which, though their passions may prompt them to be wicked, they have nevertheless an interest in not being so."

Now it may well be the case, to cite Samuel Johnson's famous epigram, that "there are few ways in which a man can be more innocently employed than in getting money." Certainly, when one compares the profit motive to the homicidal and genocidal passions that have motivated so much human behavior, the moral case for the profit motive is clear. John Maynard Keynes's judgment is surely correct: "It is better that a man should tyrannize over his bank balance than over his fellow citizens."

The last few centuries, however, have also demonstrated that far from calming men's passions, the pursuit of money can just as easily inflame them. Writing in *The Predator's Ball,* Connie Bruck portrays Michael Milken as a man driven less by the rational pursuit of self-interest than by megalomania; he is hardly the kind of individual that Montesquieu had in mind, one presumes.

Moreover, while the pursuit of material self-interest may be preferable to some motives, it is hardly superior to all of them. Much of the ethical appeal of socialism in the West has derived precisely from the moral superiority of the motives that it would substitute for the pursuit of material self-interest. It remains far more uplifting to exhort people to "love one another" than to "maximize utility," even though the latter may in fact be more socially beneficial.

Perhaps the most audacious effort to reconcile the motives of capitalists with the results of capitalism can be found in George Gilder's *Wealth and Poverty.* Gilder argues that capitalism begins not with material self-interest, but with "giving." Because the investor has no guarantee of return on his investment, his investment effectively constitutes a gift to the community. And like the gifts of the South Sea Islanders, it is given in the hope that it will be reciprocated. This argument has persuaded no one: as one of his numerous critics put it, Gilder's attempt to equate giving with investing is as likely to give philanthropy a bad name as capitalism a good one.

Yet at the same time, his analysis—perhaps unwittingly—also helps make sense of both the pervasiveness and widespread public appeal of corporate philanthropy. In fact, corporate philanthropy fits Gilder's model far better than does business investment. Philanthropy clearly involves giving, with no guarantee of return. Yet at the same time, the gifts given by corporations are commonly understood to be motivated not simply by altruism, but by the firms' long-terms interests. They thus represent a kind of happy medium between a genuine gift, whose primary purpose is to improve the welfare of the recipient, and an investment, whose only purpose is to maximize the wealth of the investor.

Not surprisingly, corporate philanthropy has been criticized from both the left and the right. One set of critics has attacked it for failing to serve the objectives of the firm's stockholders: they argue that too much corporate philanthropy goes to organizations and institutions that are hostile to business. Another group of critics attacks it for precisely the opposite reason: they claim that its real purpose is to improve the image of the company, so that it is misleading to describe it as philanthropic. The paradox of corporate philanthropy is that the more the public perceives it as altruistic, the more effectively it serves the self-interest of the company that provides it.

Michael Novak's *The Spirit of Democratic Capitalism* represents another contemporary effort to improve the moral status of capitalism by redefining the motives that underlie it. Novak notes that "like prudence in Aristotelian thought, self-interest in democratic capitalist thought has an inferior reputation among moralists." He argues, however, that it is misleading to evaluate "self-interest" with greed or acquisitiveness. Rather, self-interest also encompasses "religious and moral interests, artistic and scientific interests, and interests in peace and justice," as well as concern for the well-being of one's family, friends, and country.

But while it is certainly true that much behavior in capitalist societies is self-interested in Novak's broader sense, this is decidedly not true of economic behavior proper. The predictive power of neoclassical economics rests precisely on the fact that consumers, investors, and employers do define their self-interest primarily—if not exclusively—in pecuniary terms. It is possible to deplore the extent to which our economic system rests on economic self-interest; it is not, however, appropriate to deny it.

Corporate Social Responsibility

The doctrine of corporate social responsibility can also be understood as part of the ongoing effort to reconcile the intentions and results of capitalism. It does this in part by fudging the issue: no small part of the nearly universal appeal of corporate social responsibility rests on the doctrine's ambiguity. Proponents of corporate social responsibility do not deny the legitimacy of the profit motive; instead they redefine the profit motive to encompass other, more public-spirited purposes. The notion of the "corporate conscience" represents an attempt to humanize the firm, to endow its managers with a range of motivations that transcend the selfish pursuit of wealth. Likewise, speaking of "enlightened" self-interest is clearly meant to soften self-interest, which itself is employed as a euphemism for selfishness.

But the term "enlightened self-interest" begs a critical issue. What happens when a manager's concern for the welfare of society conflicts with the material interests of his company's shareholders? Supporters of the free market believe that society is best served when executives try to maximize the interests of their shareholders. Thus an important conservative criticism of corporate social responsibility is precisely that it gives businessmen "credit" for serving society only when they are engaged in activities that are not primarily motivated by shareholder interests—thus undermining a central moral *raison d'être* of a market economy.

The response of the advocates of corporate responsibility is to deny that there is a tension between intentions and results: common to virtually every exposition of the doctrine of corporate responsibility is the belief that in the long run the interests of society and of business converge, so that those firms that intend to do good also wind up doing well, and vice versa.

This is also the position of the movement for socially responsible investment: much of the popularity of "socially responsible" investment vehicles rests on their claim to resolve the tension between "bad" intentions and "good" results that characterizes a market economy, by enabling investors to hold on to their good intentions without sacrificing their rate of return. Much of the claim for the need to instruct businessmen in ethics rests on a similar social vision.

Appealing as this position evidently is, unfortunately it is not terribly persuasive. If corporate social responsibility amounts to nothing more than enlightened self-interest, why would anyone need to devote special effort to understand it or to urge others to pursue it? For that matter, what would be the point of teaching ethics to present or future managers? Why not simply teach them how to become more intelligent or sophisticated profit maximizers? Likewise, if socially responsible funds offer their investors a market rate of returns, then why is it praiseworthy to invest in them?

The fact that so much effort is devoted to preaching to both executives and investors about their social and moral responsibilities suggests that we are still uncomfortable with an economic system that relies so heavily on the motive of selfishness to achieve its goals—however laudable they may be. The moral paradox that Adam Smith so insightfully described more than two centuries ago remains with us; we are no closer than he to resolving it.

DISCUSSION QUESTIONS

1. What is the Protestant ethic? How does it influence contemporary business and organizational practices?

2. What is the secular version of the Protestant ethic?

3. Evaluate the statements: "Good ethics is good business" and "Ethics pays. It's smart to be ethical."

4. What is the relationship between ethics and profit?

5. What is the moral legitimation for capitalism?

6. Are ethical criticisms of the "paper entrepreneurs"—investment bankers, lawyers, managers, stockholders—who restructured many companies in the 1980s morally defensible?

7. What are the moral contradictions of capitalism?

8. Discuss the idea of corporate social responsibility. What responsibility do individual managers have within corporations, particularly within the context of corporate social responsibility?

For Further Reading

Barley, S., and Kunda, G. "Design and Devotion: Surges of Rational and Normative Ideologies of Control in Managerial Discourse." *Administrative Science Quarterly* 37 (1992) 363-399.

Bell, D. *The Cultural Contradictions of Capitalism.* New York: Basic Books, 1976.

Bendix. R. *Work and Authority in Industry.* California: University of California, 1956.

Jackall, R. *Moral Mazes: The World of Corporate Managers.* New York: Oxford University Press, 1988.

Weber, M. *The Protestant Ethic and the Spirit of Capitalism.* New York: Scribner, 1958.

Wrege, D., and Perroni, A. "Taylor's Pig-Tale: A Historical Analysis of Frederick W. Taylor's Pig-Iron Experiments." *Academy of Management Journal* 17 (1974) 627.

Yin, R. *Case Study Research: Design and Methods.* California: Sage, 1989.

PART II

INDIVIDUAL BEHAVIOR

3

FOUNDATIONS: PERCEPTION, ATTITUDES, AND PERSONALITY

On Work and Alienation

KAI ERIKSON

LEARNING OBJECTIVES

After reading Erickson's "On Work and Alienation," a student will be able to:

1. Understand the historical development of the concept of alienation

2. Identify the causes of alienation in industrialized societies

3. Apply the concept of alienation to behavior in modern organizations

4. Consider ways that managers and workers can reduce alienation in the workplace

My intention in the paragraphs to follow is to consider once again the familiar concept of alienation. I do not plan to report on a completed piece of research here or to argue for any particular way of doing sociological work on the subject. I hope, rather, to engage in the kind of aerial reconnaissance sociologists often undertake before they move on foot into a new research terrain.[1] This will mean that I cannot help being more attentive to the broader contours of the subject than to its finer grains and textures; and it will mean, too, that in sweeping across so wide a surface I am bound to skim past scholarly contributions of crucial importance to the sociology of work. Scouting expeditions are like that.

My remarks are in three parts: first, a field-worker's reading of Karl Marx's views on the nature of human alienation; second, a few thoughts on alienation in the increasingly automated and computerized workplaces of today; and third, a note of vaguely methodological intent on how one can know when one is in the presence of alienation.

When done, I hope to have demonstrated that the idea of alienation, despite the heavy philosophical and ideological cargo it is often asked to carry, can serve as a sensitive conceptual device for helping us understand the way people relate to the work they do.[2]

The very term *alienation* is so closely identified with the work of Karl Marx that one is almost required to begin a reconnaissance with him. The genealogy of the concept, of

---

[1] The new research terrain in my case is a study of workers in the telecommunications industry. The working title of the project is "The Culture of the Workplace." Cynthia Fuchs Epstein and I serve as principal investigators, and support has been provided by a grant from the Russell Sage Foundation.

Source: Kai Erickson, "On Work and Alienation," from *The Nature of Work: Sociological Perspectives,* ed. Kai Erikson and Steven Peter Vallas pp.19–35 (Yale University Press, 1990). Reprinted by permission.

I owe a special debt to the generosity of Marvin Bressler, Cynthia Fuchs Epstein, William Form, Richard H. Hall, David Montgomery, and especially, Steven Peter Vallas. I have more than the usual reasons, though, for wanting to make clear that I alone am to blame for errors of fact, tone, and imagination.

[2] See Archibald, 1978, for a good review of some of the issues involved in even so gentle a claim as this.

course, can be traced past Marx to Feuerbach, Hegel, Fichte, and a number of others, so it had been toughening for years in the heavy brine of German metaphysics before Marx turned to it; and, moreover, he may have eyed the concept more warily in his later writings than in his earlier ones. I do not want to enter the ongoing discussions about these matters here, even supposing that I knew enough to do so. But it may be useful (to borrow a wonderful image from Jaroslav Pelikan) to pass a magnet lightly across Marx's writings on alienation in the hope of drawing out from them those scraps of metal, those filings, that may have special value to sociologists trying to find grounding in the world of work.

Human beings, says Marx, are, quite literally, made for work. This is not because we are doomed to toil as a result of the Fall ("Cursed is the ground for thy sake . . . in the sweat of thy face shalt thou eat bread"), but, on the contrary, because working is in our bones, in the very tissues of our being. The human animal emerged as a species from an environment in which laboring already played a prominent evolutionary part, and to that extent humankind is shaped by work, molded by it. The human hand, the human eye, the human brain have all evolved in response to the nature of work, and so, of course, have the human nervous system and the human imagination.[3] Hannah Arendt (1958:86) called this "the seemingly blasphemous notion of Marx that labor (and not God) created man or that labor (and not reason) distinguishes man from other animals."

Human beings reach out, gather the materials of nature, and fashion them into objects of one kind or another. We collect an armful of wood, pick up a piece of flint, extract a stone from a quarry—or, for that matter, capture a sight or a sound that happens to move us. The true character of humankind is reflected in the objects we produce as a result of that process: a campfire, an axe, a cathedral, a sonnet. Work of that kind is necessary for humans to fulfill their true nature. That is how, Marx said, they "develop" their "slumbering powers" ([1906] 1967: 177). Now the energy and skill invested in the object are the very stuff of the person who created it, a part of his life's blood. And in a very real sense, he sees himself, evaluates himself, measures himself—even knows himself—by the things he makes. He "sees his own reflection in a world which he has constructed," Marx put

it (1964:128). The producer, then, and the thing he produces are of the same flesh. Or at least that is the way nature intended it to be.

In the age of industrialization and capitalism, however, three developments have conspired to disturb that natural arrangement. The first is the institution of private property. Both the means by which objects are produced and the objects themselves are owned by somebody else in a functioning capitalist system, with the result that the worker is drawn apart from the work itself. They are of a flesh, the worker and the work, but that flesh is severed by the cruel wedge of private ownership.

The second is the development of a more and more complex division of labor. Workers play a reduced role when a task is broken up into minute segments; they apply but a fraction of their skill and knowledge to the task at hand and often lose their sense of the larger logic of the productive process in the bargain.

The third is the process by which human labor becomes a commodity like all other commodities. Workers in a capitalist economy do not ordinarily manufacture things for their own consumption, nor, presumably, do they do so for the joy of it. They manufacture things for money, for cold tender. Their experience and ability—their very selves, in fact—are sold at market prices in much the same way as a side of beef or a sack of onions, and in that sense they become commodities themselves. They are objects, things of a measured worth, without any greater value than the denomination of the coin used to purchase them.

Alienation, then, is disconnection, separation—the process by which human beings are cut adrift from their natural moorings in the world as the result of unnatural, alien work arrangements, and, Marx thought, it can take a number of forms.

For one thing, people can be said to be alienated when they lose contact with the product of their own labor. The things people fashion become an extension of their persons, a part of themselves, because they have breathed life into them. In the process of shaping a bowl or working a piece of leather or stitching a garment, they have poured some of themselves into it—a portion of their inventiveness, energy, humanity. And when the objects they have created are taken away to be stored in someone else's warehouse or sold on someone else's terms, the qualities they had invested in those objects are simply lost to them. They are reduced in stature, diminished in spirit. And as this raid on their personalities is repeated every day of their working lives, they become more and more incomplete human beings, facing life with dulled moral reflexes, blurred perceptions, and an impaired ability to think matters through.

---

[3] "Thus the hand is not only the organ of labour, it is also the product of labour," wrote Frederick Engels in a section of *Dialectics of Nature* entitled "The Part Played by Labour in the Transition from Ape to Man" (1987:453).

People can also be said to be alienated when they lose their involvement in the activity of working itself and no longer experience it as a meaningful act of creation. This can happen, for example, when a worker feels dominated by the machinery with which she works. It can happen when the work of the hand is separated from the work of the brain, when the rhythms of a particular set of tasks are choreographed by a planner in some distant office and carried out with wooden compliance by workers on the shop floor. It can happen when a person's working hours are sharply differentiated from the other hours of the daily round: most modern workers can draw the line between the hours that belong to work and the hours that belong to them with a fierce precision, punching in and punching out on the dot of the minute. And it can happen, finally, when a person comes to see work as a means to an end, as an instrumentality. It does not nourish the worker's spirit but depletes it, and he becomes like a machine senselessly grinding out something for the food it will bring to his table. "From being a man," said Marx somewhat starchily, "he becomes merely an abstract activity and a belly" (1964:72).

People can also be said to be alienated when they become estranged from their fellow creatures, as, says Marx, is inevitable in capitalism. Being commodities for sale, people are always in competition with one another. and that understandably helps reduce whatever feelings of comradeship and communality might otherwise emerge. Workers tend to be so brutalized and depleted by the experience of work, moreover, that they are largely incapable of authentic relations with others anyway.

And, finally, people can be said to be alienated when they find themselves separated from their own nature as members of the human species. Since they are not engaged in creating life but are merely earning the wherewithal to stay alive, they are no longer an active part of nature, no longer participants in its rhythms. They are, then, less than human, alienated even from themselves. (That thought has always had a good deal of appeal to critics like Erich Fromm, who want to talk about the existential crisis of modern times, but I will abandon it here, a bit prematurely, with the observation that, whatever its other virtues, it will not yield our magnet many scraps of the sort we need for a venture into the field.)

So all of the methods devised under capitalism to increase production, said Marx with a fine flourish,

mutilate the labourer into a fragment of a man, degrade him to the level of an appendage of a machine, destroy every remnant of charm in his work and turn it into a hated toil: they estrange

from him the intellectual potentialities of the labour-process to a despotism the more hateful for its meanness: they transform his lifetime into a working-time, and drag his wife and child beneath the wheels of the Juggernaut of capital. (1906:708)

Whew! Thus the views of Karl Marx on alienation—or a version of them anyway.

Now suppose for a moment that we were to take those views with us into the new research terrain and use them to inform our inquiry. From what regions of the modern workplace should we most expect alienation to emerge? Where should we look for those sensitive zones in the structure of work that seem most capable of inducing it?[4]

If he followed his own texts as closely as those who now think themselves his heirs, Marx's belief would presumably be that alienation is most likely to issue from those overlapping spheres in the workplace (a) where workers are separated both from the products of their labor and from the means of production, (b) where people contributing to the overall production process do not have a clear sense of the pattern of the whole and are not really sure what their own role is in it, (c) where the work process is controlled by an external force or condition to which the worker has to adapt her own movements, and (d) where the work task has been splintered into so many specialties that only a fraction of the worker's intelligence and skill is required for its completion.

The first of those considerations has a rather antique sound in this day and age. Workers in industrialized countries everywhere can be said to have lost whatever claim they might otherwise have had to the product of their own labor, even if we knew what product meant in an economy increasingly devoted to service; and few persons can be said to own the means of production, except in the somewhat remote sense that they are among "the people" in whose name the title has been drawn up.[5] The main issue in any event is not whether workers have legal claim to the equipment they use but whether they exercise some real measure of control over it, as Braverman (1975), among others, has

---

[4] I do not want to commit myself to an awkward new term here, so I will duck into the nearest footnote to point out that if "pathogenic" refers to conditions that appear to induce pathology, then "alienogenic" could serve as a way to refer to those zones of sensitivity that seem to induce alienation.

[5] The thinning but still sturdy ranks of the "self-employed" provide an exception, of course, and owning the means of production in their case really seems to matter. See Archibald 1981 for one view.

been at pains to point out. So the first and third considerations really collapse into one. And, in a like way, the second and fourth considerations overlap so greatly that they, too, can merge.

The key sources of alienation, then, from this point of view, reduce to two—first, those structures in the modern workplace that subdivide labor into narrower and narrower specialties, and, second, those structures in the modern workplace that limit the amount of control workers exercise over the conditions in which they work.

II

To the extent that Marx's observations were meant to serve as notes on the history of capitalism, he was asking us to envision a transformation from the gentler rhythms and more intimate scales of the artisanal past to the clatter and brutality of the industrial present. It is a story of the ways in which a system of production based on craft is replaced by a system of production based on a finely calibrated division of labor.

If we were to try to portray that transformation as drama, our first scene would almost have to take place in a craft workshop, where a cobbler or spinner or barrel maker fashions an object, invests something of himself in it, and either figuratively or literally leaves his signature on it; and our last scene would almost have to take place in a modern factory, especially one engaged in line assembly. Those are the images, after all, around which most of us organize our sense of that critical passage. The song of the craftsman would be drawn from such testimony as this (Sturt 1923:78):

> But no higher wage, no income, will buy for men
> that satisfaction which of old—until machinery
> made drudges of them—streamed into their
> muscles all day long from close contact with iron,
> timber, clay, wind and wave, horse-strength. It
> tingled up in the niceties of touch, sight, scent. The
> very ears unawares received it, as when the plane
> went singing over the wood. or the exact chisel
> went tapping in (under the mallet) to the hard ash
> with gentle sound. But these intimacies are now
> over. Although they have much for leisure men can
> now taste little solace in life, of the sort that skilled
> handwork used to yield to them. . . . In what was
> once the wheelwright's shop, where Englishmen
> grew friendly with the grain of timber and with
> sharp tool, nowadays youths wait upon machines.

And the song of the factory operative would be drawn from any of the hundreds of interviews that abound in contemporary social studies. "God, I hated that assembly line," a mechanic says to Lillian Breslow Rubin (1976: 155): "I hated it. I used to fall asleep on the job standing up and still keep doing my work. There's nothing more boring and more repetitious in the world. On top of it, you don't feel human. The machine's running you, you're not running it." And another operative says to Charles Walker and Robert Guest (1952:54): "The assembly line is no place to work, I can tell you. There is nothing more discouraging than having a barrel beside you with 10,000 bolts in it and using them all up. Then you get a barrel with another 10,000 bolts, and you know every one of those 10,000 bolts has to be picked up and put in exactly the same place as the last 10,000 bolts."

The problem with that way of portraying the transformation is that the craft workshop and the assembly line can hardly be understood as much more than symbols. To speak of handicrafts in the preindustrial age is to speak of the economy of the towns and the occupations of a select few, not of the vast stretches of farmland in which most of the population scratched out a living. To speak of the assembly line in our own time is to speak of a rather special form of manufacture. For all the celebrity of the automobile industry among social scientists, a decreasing number of workers are involved in manufacturing of any kind, and even at its moment of glory, no more than a fraction of manual workers in the United States were engaged in line assembly. Nor can we take for granted that even that minority has been as abused by the ways of the workplace as is often supposed (Form 1976, 1987). The world we have lost is a world of agriculture; the world we are in the process of becoming is a world in which manufacture is yielding to service and both are becoming automated.

It is hard to know how to speak of the toil of the peasant when our subject is alienation. It is a form of craft work, to be sure, conducted at one's own pace and involving an intimate association with tools and materials; and to the extent that one extracts a living from the land one works, one can be said to be retaining at least a portion of the product of one's labor. There is personality in a good thatch, presumably, craft in a well-fashioned harness, art in a clean furrow. Ferdinand Toennies (1963:164) thought, "The Gemeinschaft, to the extent that it is capable of doing so, transforms all repulsive labor into a kind of art, giving it style, dignity, and charm, and a rank in its order, denoted as a calling and an honor." Well, maybe; but how many peasants, gnarled and leathery and bent to the hoe after decades in the fields, knew of that charm and honor? Somehow we need a different conceptual vocabulary than the one from which the term *alienation* comes to deal with the preindustrial countryside.

It is also hard to know how to speak about alienation as workers leave the satanic mills and move into the automated workplaces of our own period. There have been many expressions of hope in the last two or three decades that the coming of automation would reduce the amount of alienation in the modern workplace by replacing labor of the most mechanical and mindless kind with activities that require skill, judgment, and a sense of craft. Workers in charge of automated equipment, so the argument goes, rely on quick intelligence and sure perceptions rather than on raw strength, are freed from the unrelenting rhythms of a machine, can wander around the larger workplace and develop some feeling for what the whole enterprise is about, and, in general, escape from the pinched and narrow niches into which a complicated division of labor would otherwise have confined them. These expressions of hope have been nourished by just enough empirical evidence to make it one of the more important hypotheses under consideration in the sociology of work (see, for example, Bell 1973: Blauner 1964; Shepard 1971).

There is a contrary position, however, also nourished by enough data to protect its standing in the field. For if it is reasonable to point out, as Blauner and others have, that the division of labor is likely to become less problematic in automated work settings because more aspects of the productive process are gathered into a single set of hands, then it is also reasonable to note that automation may have a pronounced potential for sharpening other aggravations in the workplace that appear to induce alienation (for example Braverman 1974; Burawoy 1979a; Edwards 1979; Glenn and Feldberg 1977; Feldberg and Glenn 1983; Noble 1984; Wallace and Kalleberg 1982; Zuboff 1988). Let me review some of those reasons, moving lightly across the surface.

To begin with, the work required in most automated settings, though largely free of muscular exertion, can replace the boredom that comes from endlessly repeating the same rote activity ("then you get a barrel with another 10,000 bolts") with the boredom that comes from doing nothing at all. That is sometimes a blessing, to be sure. "When the machine is working," said one operative happily, "I am not" (Shaiken 1984:134). His job is to attend the machine, to be at its service. He is, as David Halle (1984) puts it, "on guard duty." But monitoring the workings of some machine can be profoundly tedious when things go right, which is most of the time; and if the worker finds other things to engage her mind—reading, musing, telling tales—the activity itself is clearly alien from the substance of the work.

Even when the process is complex and demanding, however, the skills called for in many automated procedures are really a quickness of reflex, a sureness of eye, and, maybe most important, an ability to pay attention—not the mastery of materials and the command of pace that is usually implied by the word *craft*. In such settings, the finer tunings of the human body—its deftness, artistry, cunning, versatility—are simply not brought to bear at all.

Nor, for that matter, are most of the human senses. The day is clearly long past when more than a handful of workers actually sight down the grain of the wood, feel the texture of the weave, or otherwise remain in touch with the materials they use by listening, smelling, tasting; but it should be noted that those who work with certain kinds of automation become yet another step removed from things they are shaping. In continuous process plants, for example, it is not uncommon for workers to never see or touch the raw materials that come in one end of the cycle or the finished products that come out the other. And in computerized offices, similarly, it is not uncommon for workers to see nothing but the images on a screen or to touch nothing but the keys on a keyboard, rarely coming into physical contact with the letters they type, the files they prepare, and so on.

Moreover, information flows both back and forth along the circuits of a computer. They send programmed instructions out to the office or the shop floor, and, at the same time, they bring intelligence back. In the process, they have the capacity to drain workers of what may well have been their most important lever of control—the wisdom and lore that come from years of seasoning. "Any self-respecting machinist," says Harley Shaiken (1984:54), "has a legendary 'black book' that records the problems encountered and the short cuts discovered on the previous jobs." It is a special kind of knowledge, "enriched over time." The same is true, of course, though less formally so, of coal miners, short order cooks, filing clerks, salespeople, and anyone else who becomes more skilled with experience. Computers, though, can appropriate such experience and store it permanently, and they can do so for every worker who enters a computer network. So the computer's black book can easily contain the lore of thousands of minds, and as all that information is sorted out, experience becomes a matter of formula, intuition and judgment become matters of computation. It is almost as if the computer's black book does for human workers what genetic codes do for social insects: give creatures the accumulated experience of generations without asking from them so much as a trace of thought.

In a sense, then, computerized procedures can draw away most of the faculties that are the stuff of humanhood. People have been operating machines since the beginning of the industrial era, of course, and under the right circumstances the largest of them is like a hand tool, an extension of the person. It clearly makes a huge difference, though, in the almost organic relationship between person and machine whether you master it or it masters you. When the machine is yours to command, you turn it on and thereby give it life; you adjust it and thereby make it an annex of your hand; you instruct it and thereby make it an expansion of your brain. But when it does its own calculations, monitors its own performance, consults its own immense bank of experience, applies its own logics, reviews its own thinking, makes its own decisions, and even turns itself on and off, then it is like a willful creature with its own motives whom you must serve. It is an unrelenting, massively stubborn, inexhaustible intelligence.

So the operator of a really smart machine enters the process only in the sense that she occupies a work station. Her intelligence is not engaged, her motor skills are not engaged, her fund of past experience is not engaged, her sense organs are not engaged. She is hardly there at all. "Lobotomized" is Harry Braverman's word for her condition (1975:25), but that is not quite right: the properties of her humanhood have been absorbed by the machine, and in that sense she has been emptied of content. It is a kind of evisceration, a kind of decortication, and that, surely, comes close to what Marx meant by alienation (cf. Zuboff 1988).

For all of the reasons just cited, then, automated processes in general and computerized processes in particular can become an almost perfect instrument of control over *process*. If the goal of the old Scientific Management movement was to control the muscle activity of the worker from the distant removes of the front office, to eliminate flourish and personality and lazy rhythms from the doing of everyday tasks, then it should be noted that the computer can program not only the behavior of the machine, but, in a very real sense, the behavior of the operator.

And, for all the reasons just cited, automated procedures in general and computerized processes in particular can become an almost perfect instrument of control over persons. This is true not only in the sense that automation offers a means of programming almost everything that happens in the workplace, but also in the sense that it makes possible a remarkably efficient system of surveillance. A computer can count and measure and time virtually everything its operator does, down to the number of keys he strikes in any given quarter minute; and it can keep a record of his performance for as long a stretch of time as the most curious of managers could ask. "Once computers are linked," Barbara Garson (1988:205) notes, "anyone who touches the keyboard is automatically reporting on himself." It is a continuous, tireless time and motion study.

Now I need to pause for a moment before the momentum of these thoughts carries me beyond the sight of shore to repeat that I am not talking here about *inevitable properties* of the smart new machines but of *potentialities* that seem often to be taken advantage of. The computer *need* not behave in the manner I have been suggesting, but it *can;* and its capacity to monitor the activities of the persons who monitor it, to keep a running log of their performance, is likely to prove irresistible.

It may really matter, too. If the grinding pace of the assembly line, say, makes one into a kind of motor, a torpid technical instrument, so can supervision. At its rawest, in fact, supervision can feel like a kind of automation, if only in the sense that when it is too mechanical, too automatic, too relentless, it becomes machinelike. Harry Braverman complains that clerical workers are too often

> *subjected to routines, more or less mechanized according to current possibilities, that strip them of their former grasp of even a limited amount of office information, divest them of the need or ability to understand and decide, and make of them so many mechanical eyes, fingers, and voices whose functioning is, insofar as possible, predetermined by both rules and machinery. (1974:340)*

The dominion of the machinery to which Braverman refers has been remarked any number of times: the dominion of the rules less often. Yet workers who are pressed in on all sides by quotas, indices, routines, and all those forms of monitoring that managers can turn to when they are under pressure themselves are, for all practical purposes, being exposed to a major source of alienation. To be reproved for minor lapses, to have every working minute measured and evaluated, to be paced by routines wholly unresponsive to the realities of the moment, to be judged against quotas of someone else's making, to need to ask permission to leave a work station for even a moment—these can feel demeaning and infantilizing. The logic of supervision (at its worst, anyway) is the logic of childhood. So it scarcely ranks as good news to those who work at the nonmanagement level that the number of supervisors seems to be growing at a much faster rate throughout the labor force than other employees and that the tools of their trade are becoming ever more sensitive and precise.

My own fledgling study, for what it may be worth at this early stage, suggests that supervision may be a key element in this kind of routinization, and there are quite a few studies in the literature, the work of Melvin L. Kohn and his associates being prominent among them, that alert us to expect as much (Kohn 1976, 1985; Kohn and Schooler 1973, 1978, 1982, 1983; Monimer and Lorence 1979; Mottaz 1981; Walsh 1982).

There is no easy answer, then, to the question as to whether automation serves to restrict the range of a worker's skill and autonomy or serves to free him from the old tyrannies of work (for a balanced view see Form 1981, 1987; Spenner 1979, 1983). There is every reason to suppose, however, that the effects of automation are spread very unevenly throughout the workplace, not only from industry to industry or from occupation to occupation, but from one work station to another (see Vallas 1988).

III

I have been trying to review here some of the structural conditions of the modern workplace that may be especially productive of alienation. But in order for that to be a useful contribution to the sociology of work, we need to consider another matter. Where does alienation reside? How does one know when one is in its presence? That is a tougher question than might appear on the surface, because so many different currents of thought have converged on it from so many different ideological directions.

Joachim Israel (1971) distinguishes between "estranging processes"—those conditions in the structure of the workplace that induce alienation—and "states of estrangement"—those psychological dispositions that result. I have been speaking more or less of the former; I am turning now—more or less—to the latter.

There are those who argue that one ought to be able to determine when a person is alienated by taking a look at the objective conditions in which she works. The worker exposed to estranging conditions is alienated almost by definition no matter what she says she thinks or even what she thinks she thinks. Harry Braverman, for example, would accuse us of doing the work of the personnel administrator if we dealt with "the reaction of the worker" rather than with the nature of the work (1971:29), by which he means, apparently, that certain forms of work can be understood as

alienating no matter how that condition is registered in the person of the worker.[6] That view, whatever else one might want to say about it, has the effect of closing off sociological investigation rather than inviting it. Alienation, in order to make empirical sense, has to reside somewhere in or around the persons who are said to experience it.

Yet it sounds rather naive to assume, as many sociologists have, that a state like alienation can be discerned by so simple a procedure as asking people about their degree of job satisfaction—which is essentially what Blauner, for all the other riches of his analysis, actually did. People can think themselves satisfied by work that degrades them in countless ways, and, of course, they can grumble incessantly about work that would appear on the face of it to be enhancing. Michel Crozier (1971), for instance, discovered in his study of Parisian office workers that the employees who expressed the most interest in their work were often the ones who complained the most about it, an observation others have made as well; and in general, there are many reasons to suppose that the relationship between expressions of satisfaction and the facts of the workday is, to say the least, an inexact one (see, for example, Kahn 1972).

Robert Blauner and Harry Braverman, as a matter of fact, mark the two poles very well. Virtually all of Blauner's data come from surveys on job satisfaction conducted by Elmo Roper, while Braverman reports no data at all on the way workers *feel* about work, how they experience it, or what it does to them.

So we need something in between. The concept alienation, let's say, has a limited number of uses for sociology unless it refers to a condition that is registered somewhere in the person's mind or spirit or body and is reflected in actual behavior. On the face of it, at least, that would seem like easily defended ground, but in fact it cuts off friends on both ends of the conceptual continuum. On the one hand, we have to jettison the idea that situations rich in the kinds of detail that appear degrading by some external standard or another can be assumed to generate alienation. That must be shown, not taken as given. Otherwise we would be in much the same logical position as a physician prepared to diagnose malaria on hearing the news that someone passed through an especially virulent swamp. On the other hand, we have to jettison a lot of what we think

---

[6] In the "usage" of "official sociology and popular journalism," Braverman writes elsewhere with evident scorn (1975:20), "alienated labor is understood to mean the worker who suffers from a feeling of distress, a malaise, a bellyache about his or her work."

we have learned from surveys, for we dare not assume that the effects of alienation are readily apparent even to those who experience it. The kinds of questions we ask in the usual survey on job satisfaction would seem like rather frail instruments for probing into all those layers of emotional scar tissue which, if Marx is even half right, can be formed over the injuries of work.[7] I would argue, in fact, that qualitative field studies, for all their widely advertised imprecisions, offer by far our best opportunity to understand how the ways of work are impressed on the persons exposed to them.

If alienation is a state of being, it is not a creature of the workplace alone, and that raises other questions. How do the degradations of the workplace bleed into the larger fabric of a person's life? How do the activities people engage in outside the realm of work aggravate or compensate for whatever dissatisfactions are generated in the workplace? Karl Marx obviously thought of work as near the core of a person's moral life, the forge in which the self is tempered. And much depends, as I have been suggesting, on the way a worker's mind and spirit are affected by the logics, the cadences, the pressures of the workplace. But it should be noted, if only in passing, that while the structures of modern life make it easy to distinguish between the world of work and the world of leisure, the structures of the human mind do not operate in the same way. The moods of the workplace are carried across the threshold into the rest of life, and, of course, the moods of the rest of life are carried back, and the ways in which the two are played off in the organization of a person's life are a critical piece of the larger puzzle.

Within the narrower confines of the work station itself, moreover—cubicle, cab, desk, compartment, niche—one can decorate and improvise, become involved in acts of passive resistance or outright sabotage, and in a thousand other ways introduce a sense of self in settings that would otherwise seem to exclude it. The wider communalities of the workplace, too, from informal kinds of camaraderie to more formal associations like trade unions, have a major impact on the character of work. And, obviously, persons who enter the office or shop floor for scheduled hours of work bring with them imaginations that have been nourished and lives that have been given meaning by activities engaged in elsewhere. These are all ways in which personality, intelligence, playfulness, and whim are brought to bear on the workplace, and more important, they are all means of

coping with, drawing insulation around, or making an argument against the pains of work.[8]

Keeping in mind the larger wholes of human life, then, one notes there are many forms of behavior that might alert an observer to the possibility that alienation is lurking somewhere below the surface. One can begin, as sociologists traditionally have, with the standard indices of dissatisfaction: calling in sick, filing grievances, and quitting altogether have long been regarded as hidden protest votes on the quality of work life, and most of the available data seem to indicate that such votes are cast far more often in the kinds of work setting that can reasonably be described as alienating. One can try to assess the long-range effects of various working conditions on the personalities of those exposed to them, as Kohn and his associates have been doing for years. Then one can attend to the things people do—and the things that happen to them—outside the immediate precincts of work: we have every reason in the world to think, for example, that taking drugs and drinking too much and sinking into a kind of numbed depression are correlated with alienating work conditions.

All of which raises a darker point as I bring these remarks to a close. We have to assume, as I noted a moment ago, that alienated work leaves some sort of mark on the persons affected by it, and that those marks are at least in principle detectable by the right kind of geiger counter. We also have to assume—this too is repetition—that the persons so marked are not usually the ones best equipped to understand what has happened to them. Indeed, it is one of Marx's major contributions to our thinking that lack of insight into one's true condition can itself be a consequence of alienation. The condition furnishes its own camouflage.

We are, then, engaged in a haughty business, for we are declaring for all practical purposes that trained and thoughtful observers can see traces in the conduct of fellow human beings of something they are not aware of and, in fact, cannot be aware of. That prospect did not bother Marx for one moment. His language crackles with feeling when he describes what he thinks the capitalist mode of production does to a worker exposed to it. It "mortifies his body and ruins his mind," said he, leaving "idiocy" and "cretinism" in its wake. It makes of the

[7] For a helpful and wise discussion, see Archibald 1978.

[8] A good reading list on this general subject could begin (but ought not end) with Burawoy 1979a, Garson 1977, Halle 1984, Molstad 1986, Moorhouse 1987, Nash 1976, and the papers in this volume by Epstein, Freidson, and Wheeler. The opening pages of Moorhouse's article are particularly instructive.

worker "a crippled monstrosity"—"mutilated," "degraded," "stunted," "broken," "emasculated," "stupefied," "debased."

Now that is a sharp diagnosis by any standard, and I, for one, do not plan to walk onto a shop floor somewhere and ask hulking operatives whether the conditions under which they work have stupefied them or made idiots of them. But there may be an important world to be discovered there as soon as we learn to ask the right questions about it. The work of Melvin Seeman in particular gives us a secure place to stand when we consider the anatomy of alienation (see 1959, 1972, 1975, and especially 1983).

But being raised now is the question of what it does to the human spirit in other ways. Do the conditions that Marx encouraged us to think of as alienating add in any appreciable way to the sum of human indifference, brutality, exhaustion, cruelty, numbness? Is there any relationship between alienation and the passion with which capital punishment is promoted, guns and other weapons cherished, insults to national honor resented, people of other kinds demeaned? I have no idea. I only know that such questions are important, sympathetic, and, in principle, answerable.

References

Archibald, W. Peter. 1978. "Using Marx's Theory of Alienation Empirically." *Theory and Society* 6:119–32.

Archibald, W. Peter, Owen Adams, and John W. Gartrell. 1981. "Propertylessness and Alienation: Reopening a 'Shut' Case." In *Alienation: Problems of Meaning, Theory and Method,* edited by R. Felix Geyer and David Schweitzer. London: Routledge and Kegan Paul.

Arendt, Hannah. 1958. *The Human Condition.* Chicago: University of Chicago Press.

Bell, Daniel. 1973. *The Coming of Post-Industrial Society.* New York: Basic Books.

Blauner, Robert. 1964. *Alienation and Freedom.* Chicago: University of Chicago Press.

Braverman. Harry. 1974. *Labor and Monopoly Capital.* New York: Monthly Review Press.

———. (1975). "Work and Unemployment." *Monthly Review* July: 18–31.

Burawoy, Michael. 1979a. *Manufacturing Consent: Changes in the Labor Process under Monopoly Capitalism.* Chicago: University of Chicago Press.

———. 1979b. "The Anthropology of Industrial Work." *Annual Review of Sociology* 8:231–66.

Crozier, Michel. 1971. *The World of the Office Worker.* Chicago: University of Chicago Press.

Edwards, Richard. 1979. *Contested Terrain: The Transformation of the Workplace in the Twentieth Century.* New York: Basic Books.

Engels, Frederick. 1987 [1896]. "The Part Played by Labour in the Transition from Ape to Man." Karl Marx and Frederick Engels, *Selected Works,* vol. 24, pp. 452–63. New York: International Publishers.

Feldberg, Roslyn L., and Evelyn Nakano Glenn. 1983. "Technology and Work Degradation: Effects of Office Automation on Women Clerical Workers." In *Machina Ex Dea: Feminist Perspectives on Technology,* edited by Joan Rothschild. Oxford: Pergamon.

Form, William. 1973. "Auto Workers and Their Machines: A Study of Work, Factory, and Job Satisfaction in Four Countries." *Social Forces* 52:1–15.

———. 1976. *Blue-Collar Stratification: Auto Workers in Four Countries.* Princeton: Princeton University Press.

———. 1981. "Resolving Ideological Issues on the Division of Labor." In *Theory and Research in Sociology,* edited by Hubert M. Blalock, Jr. New York: Free Press.

———. 1987. "On the Degradation of Skills." *Annual Review of Sociology* 13.

Garson, Barbara. 1977. *All the Livelong Day.* London: Penguin.

———. 1988. *The Electronic Sweatshop,* New York: Simon and Schuster.

Glenn, Evelyn Nakano, and Roslyn L. Feldberg. 1977. "Degraded and Deskilled: The Proletarianization of Clerical Work." *Social Problems* 25:52–64.

Halle, David. 1984. *America's Working Man.* Chicago: University of Chicago Press.

Howard, Robert. 1985. *Brave New Workplace.* New York: Viking.

Israel, Joachim. 1971. *Alienation.* New York: Allyn and Bacon.

Kahn, Robert L. 1972. "The Meaning of Work: Interpretation and Proposals for Measurement." In *The Human Meaning of Social Change,* edited by Angus Campbell and Philip E. Converse. New York: Russell Sage Foundation.

Kohn, Melvin L. 1976. "Occupational Structure and Alienation." *American Journal of Sociology* 82:111–30.

———. 1985. "Unresolved Interpretive Issues in the Relationship between Work and Personality." Paper presented at the annual meeting of the American Sociological Association. Washington, D.C.

Kohn, Melvin L., and Carmi Schooler. 1973. "Occupational Experience and Psychological Functioning: An Assessment of Reciprocal Effects." *American Sociological Review* 38:97–118.

———. 1978. "The Reciprocal Effects of the Substantive Complexity of Work and Intellectual Flexibility: A Longitudinal Assessment." *American Journal of Sociology* 84:24-52.

———. 1982. "Job Conditions and Personality: A Longitudinal Assessment of Their Reciprocal Effects." *American Journal of Sociology* 87:1257-86.

———. 1983. *Work and Personality: An Inquiry into the Impact of Social Stratification.* Norwood, N.J.: Ablex Publishing.

Marx, Karl. 1906 [1867]. *Capital,* volume 1, edited by Frederick Engels, translated by Samuel Moore and Edward Aveling. London: Charles H. Kerr.

———. 1964 [1844]. ''Economic and Philosophical Manuscripts." In *Karl Marx: Early Writings,* edited and translated by T. B. Bottomore. New York: McGraw-Hill.

Molstad, Clark. 1986. "Choosing and Coping With Boring Work." *Urban Life* 15:215–36.

Moorhouse, H. F. 1987. "The 'Work Ethic' and 'Leisure' Activity: The Hot Rod in Post-War America." In *The Historical Meanings of Work,* edited by Patrick Joyce. Cambridge: Cambridge University Press.

Mortimer, Jeylan T., and Jon Lorence. 1979. "Work Experience and Occupational Value Socialization: A Longitudinal Study." *American Journal of Sociology* 84: 1361–85.

Mottaz, Clifford J. 1981. "Some Determinants of Work Alienation." *Sociological Quarterly* 22:515–29.

Nash, Al. 1976. "Job Satisfaction: A Critique." In *Auto Work and Its Discontents,* edited by B. J. Widick. Ann Arbor: University Microfilms International.

Noble, David F. 1984. *Forces of Production: A Social History of Industrial Automation.* New York: Knopf.

Roy, Donald F. 1960. "Banana Time: Job Satisfaction and Informal Interaction." *Human Organization* 18:158–68.

Rubin, Lillian Breslow. 1976. *Worlds of Pain: Life in the Working-Class Family.* New York: Basic Books.

Seeman, Melvin. 1959. "On the Meaning of Alienation." *American Sociological Review* 24:783–91.

———. 1972. "Alienation and Engagement." In *The Human Meaning of Social Change,* edited by Angus Campbell and Philip E. Converse. New York: Russell Sage Foundation.

———. 1975. "Alienation Studies." In *Annual Review of Sociology,* edited by Alex Inkeles, James Coleman, and Neil Smelser, 1:91–123.

———. 1983. "Alienation Motifs in Contemporary Theorizing: The Hidden Continuity of the Classic Themes." *Social Psychology Quarterly* 46:171–84.

Shaiken, Harley. 1984. *Work Transformed.* New York: Holt, Rinehart and Winston.

Shepard, Jon M. 1971. *Automation and Alienation: A Study of Office and Factory Workers.* Cambridge: MIT Press.

Spenner, Kenneth I. 1979. "Temporal Changes in Work Content." *American Sociological Review* 44:968–75.

———. 1983. "Deciphering Prometheus: Temporal Change in the Skill Level of Work." *American Sociological Review* 48:824–37.

Sturt, George. 1923. *The Wheelwright's Shop.* Excerpted in *Work and Community in the West,* edited by Edward Shorter. New York: Harper and Row, 1973.

Toennies, Ferdinand. 1963. *Community and Society.* Edited and translated by Charles P. Loomis. New York: Harper Torchbooks.

Vallas, Steven Peter. 1988. "New Technology, Job Content and Worker Alienation: A Test of Two Rival Perspectives." *Work and Occupations.*

———. 1989. "Computers, Managers and Control at Work." *Sociological Forum* 4:291–303.

Walker, Charles R., and Robert H. Guest. 1952. *The Man on the Assembly Line.* Cambridge: Harvard University Press.

Wallace, Michael, and Arne L. Kalleberg. 1982. "Industrial Transformation and Decline of Craft: The Decomposition of Skill in the Printing Industry." *American Sociological Review* 47: 307–24.

Walsh, Edward J. 1982. "Prestige, Work Satisfaction, and Alienation." *Work and Occupations* 9:475–96.

Zuboff, Shoshana. 1988. *In the Age of the Smart Machine.* New York: Basic.

DISCUSSION QUESTIONS

1. What did Marx view as human's relationship to work?

2. How does the division of labor contribute to the alienation of workers?

3. Is labor a commodity like other non-human commodities? If so, what is its significance for organizational behavior? Also, how does this affect interpersonal relations in a post-industrial society?

4. What are the forms that alienation can take according to Marx?

5. What historic changes in the nature of work have modified working conditions and thus the original meaning of alienation as Marx formulated it?

6. What conditions exist in modern work that create alienation? In particular, what is the role of computerization and automation? Do they create alienation or freedom from the dull routine of work?

7. How can alienation be identified in a workplace?

8. What actions, if any, can managers and workers take to reduce either objective or subjectively experienced alienation?

Untangling the Relationship between Displayed Emotions and Organizational Sales: The Case of Convenience Stores

Robert I. Sutton and Anat Rafaeli

LEARNING OBJECTIVES

"Untangling the Relationship between Displayed Emotions and Organizational Sales: The Case of Convenience Stores" by Sutton and Rafaeli should provide the student with:

1. An understanding of the role of displayed emotions in organizations

2. An understanding of the complexity of large scale quantitative and qualitative empirical research

3. Awareness that many important ideas in organizational behavior and management are counterintuitive; that is, common sense understandings of human activity are often incorrect or at least unsupported by research

4. The ability to reformulate a research study to improve its design and findings (see the Appendix)

People want to be happy! Be happy and they will be glad they came to your store.

Loyal, regular customers are a source of steady sales for your store. Smile!! Service with a smile and a friendly attitude will keep them loyal and keep them coming back!
—From "Effective Customer Service Increases Sales,"
a training program used by a chain of convenience stores

Much theory and research has focused on the role of emotion in organizational life. Emotions are typically viewed as intrapsychic states caused by factors such as job characteristics (Hackman & Oldham, 1980), stress (Kahn, 1981), relationships with supervisors (Bass, 1982), or compensation (Lawler, 1981). Such studies most frequently have examined the determinants of job satisfaction, which Locke defined as "a pleasurable or positive emotional state" (1976: 1300).

Recent theoretical work, however, has emphasized that employees' emotions are displayed as well as felt (Hochschild, 1979,1983; Rafaeli & Sutton, 1987, 1989). A variety of forces may explain variation in organizational members' displayed emotions. Internal feelings certainly influence such behavior: Satisfied employees may display genuine broad smiles and laughter during interactions with co-workers and customers; dissatisfied or tense employees may frown and groan during such transactions.

Yet there is an imperfect match between the emotions people feel and emotions they express on the job because employees are often expected to display emotions that are unrelated, or even in conflict, with their true feelings. Many organizations use practices, including recruitment and selection, socialization, and rewards and punishments, to assure that their members will conform to normative expectation, or "display rules" (Ekman, 1980: 87–88), that specify which emotions should be expressed and which should be hidden.

Organizations can support display rules by recruiting and selecting employees who are predisposed to express required emotions. Hochschild (1983) reported, for example, that Delta Airlines tries to select new flight attendants who will display good cheer to passengers and who have the emotional stamina to endure long, crowded flights

We wish to thank Mary Kay Benson, David Bowen, Larry Ford, Connie Gersick, James Jucker, Benjamin Schneider, Caren Siehl, Barry Staw, Lorna Weisinger, Tim Whitten, and John Van Maanen for their help with this article. We thank the Department of Industrial Engineering and Engineering Management at Stanford and the Mutual Fund of the Hebrew University of Jerusalem for supporting this research. Portions of this paper were prepared while Robert Sutton was a fellow at the Center for Advanced Study in the Behavioral Sciences. He is grateful for financial support provided by the Carnegie Corporation of New York and the William and Flora Hewlett Foundation.

Source: Robert Sutton and Anat Rafaeli, "Untangling the Relationship between Displayed Emotions and Organizational Sales: The Case of Convenience Stores," *Academy of Management Journal,* 1988; Vol. 31; No. 3. Copyright © 1988. Reprinted by permission.

without abandoning their smiles. Organizations may use socialization practices to teach display rules to newcomers. For example, a woman who supervises bill collectors reported that her subordinates learn—through both formal and informal means—to be pleasant to clients who are a month or two late on their Visa and MasterCard payments, to express firm disapproval to clients who are three or four months late, and to use nasty insults (e.g., "Why do you keep lying to me?") when speaking with clients who are five or six months late (Rafaeli & Sutton, 1989).

Organizations may also use reward and punishment systems to maintain display rules once socialization has been completed. Many service organizations like airlines, telephone companies, department stores, and grocery stores monitor their employees to assure that they are conveying correct emotions to customers (Hochschild, 1983; Rafaeli & Sutton, 1987). Employees who display the wrong emotions may be punished, and those who covey the right emotions may be rewarded. Management may even invite customers to help enforce display rules. For example, a store in Hayward, California, offers customers a five-dollar reward if a clerk does not offer them a "friendly greeting" and a "cheerful smile."

A primary reason that organizations develop and enforce display rules is that displayed emotions are thought to operate as "control moves." Goffman (1969:12) defined control moves as an individual's strategic manipulation of expressions, including emotional expressions, to influence the behavior of others. Along those lines, the emotions displayed by employees in organizational settings can function as control moves that influence the behavior of clients and fellow organizational members (Rafaeli & Sutton, 1987).

A modest body or evidence confirms that expressed negative, neutral, and positive emotions can serve as control moves for individuals. Police interrogators convey negative and esteem-degrading emotions to suspects in an effort to gain confessions (Arther & Caputo, 1959). In the same vein, the incomes of professional poker players depend heavily on their ability to display neutral emotion, regardless of their internal feelings (Hayano, 1982). Furthermore, field stimulations (Salancik, 1979) have suggested that smiling cocktail waitresses receive larger tips than unsmiling ones (Tidd & Lockhard, 1978) and that smiling nuns garner larger donations than glum nuns (Bradshaw, 1980).

Our contention is that displayed emotions are not only descriptors of individual employees; conveyed emotions can also be attributes of organizations. Specifically, we proposed that displayed pleasant emotions can act as control moves at the organizational level of analysis.

Displayed Emotions as Organizational Attributes

Customers of service organizations often interact with only one or two boundary-spanning employees during a given visit (Bowen & Schneider, 1985: Shamir, 1980). Furthermore, the emotions encountered by customers are displayed by individual employees. Yet customers typically develop an overall image of the emotions that members of a given organization will display. Such overall images arise because stimuli generalization occurs. Indeed, stimuli generalization enables authors of guidebooks to publish overall judgments about the level of courtesy that can be expected at hotels and restaurants (e.g., Birnbaum, 1987; Unterman & Sesser, 1984). After patronizing a service organization, customers may develop opinions about the emotional front they expect to encounter.

Those opinions—whether based on slight or extensive experience with an organization—reflect a characteristic of the organization because customers do not usually expect to be served by the same employee during each visit. Customers may also discern differences in emotional fronts because organizations differ in norms about displayed emotions (Hochschild, 1983; Rafaeli & Sutton, 1987). Norms are attributes of social systems rather than of individuals (Katz & Kahn, 1978).

Writings intended for managerial audiences also imply that the emotional front is a meaningful organizational attribute. Indeed, some recent managerial folklore suggests that employees who display good cheer to customers can enhance sales and customer loyalty (Ash, 1984; Hochschild, 1983: Peters & Austin, 1985; Peters & Waterman, 1982; Richman, 1984). The emerging literature on customer service (Czepiel, Solomon, & Surprenant, 1985; Parasuraman, Zeithamal, & Berry, 1985) also implies that belief. Those writings suggest that, when all other factors are held equal, the display of positive emotions by employees can, in the aggregate, act as control moves that bring about gains for an organization. The implication is that to the extent each potential customer associates a positive emotional front with a given organization, a larger proportion of the potential population will patronize that organization.

Theories of learning may explain why displaying warm feelings to customers can promote sales. Encountering employees who display warm, socially desirable feelings may be reinforcing for most people. Initial encounters with friendly employees may mark the start of an operant conditioning cycle

(Skinner, 1953) in which the emotions displayed by employees are the reinforcers and patronizing the organization is the reinforced behavior. The probability that a given customer will visit an organization a second time is increased by employees' display of positive emotions. The organization's emotional front may also reinforce customer behavior indirectly through vicarious learning (Bandura, 1977). A customer may watch other customers encounter positive emotions or may visit a service organization after reading that its employees are nice, friendly, or polite.

Empirical support for this conceptual perspective was sought through study of a sample of 576 convenience stores. Specifically, we hypothesized that store sales would be greater to the extent that clerks displayed positive emotions during transactions with customers.

Quantitative and Deductive Study: Methods

Research Context

These data were collected as part of an evaluation of employee courtesy in a large national chain of convenience stores. The corporation's human resources staff conducted this research as part of a chain-wide effort to enhance employee courtesy; top executives had decided that they could gain an advantage over their competitors by improving customer service in their stores. A primary reason that executives made this decision was that they had read *In Search of Excellence* and were swayed by Peters and Waterman's arguments that staying "close to the customer" (1982: 156) and having a "service obsession" (1982:157) are characteristics of excellent firms.

During the year before these data were collected, the human resources staff had changed employee handbooks and the classroom training provided to new employees so that—rather than vaguely encouraging clerks to be friendly to customers—the training clerks received instructed them to greet, smile at, establish eye contact with, and say "thank you" to every customer. In addition, a variety of local and corporation-wide training programs were developed to teach store managers about how they could improve courtesy among their clerks. For example, the introduction to this article quotes a program entitled "Effective Customer Service Increases Sales" that included lectures, readings, role-plays, and group discussions to help managers improve the level of courtesy in their stores.

A variety of local and corporate-wide practices were used, both before and after the collection of the data, to reward clerks who acted friendly during transactions with customers. Clerks in most regions were informed that "mystery shoppers" would be used to observe levels of employee courtesy. In some regions, clerks who were caught displaying the required good cheer to customers received a $25 bonus. In other regions, clerks who were observed greeting, smiling, establishing eye contact, and saying "thank you" could win a new automobile instantly.

The corporation held a contest, costing over $10 million, in which the owners of franchised stores and the managers of corporation-owned stores could qualify to enter a drawing for a million dollars if their clerks consistently offered good cheer to customers. The corporation also awarded large bonuses (over 25 percent of base salary) to regional managers when a high percentage of sales clerks in the stores they managed were observed greeting, smiling at, establishing eye contact with, and saying "thank you" to customers.

We had no influence over the design and implementation of this data gathering. The firm gave us the data because one of us had attended graduate school with the firm's director of field research. Other corporate executives were also interested in our findings because most of them believed that employee courtesy led to increased sales. They were curious to discover if quantitative evidence would support their beliefs. Small but significant relationships between displayed emotions and store sales could mean millions of dollars of sales for this national chain. For example, 2 percent increase in sales would increase corporate revenues by over $100 million.

Sample

The sample comprised 576 of the convenience stores in this national chain. There are over 7,000 stores in the United States and Canada, 36 percent of which are franchised. The corporation owns the remainder. The typical store has 8 to 10 employees, with a range of 6 to 20 employees. The stores sell a wide range of items, including food, drinks, cigarettes, and magazines. The corporation uses a variety of rules and inducements to assure that there will be similarity in the products sold in each of these stores, but there is variation because people who manage the corporation's stores and people who own franchised stores have some authority to decide what products will be sold. The stores with greater sales tend to carry larger inventories. Yet, compared to supermarkets, these stores all carry tiny inventories because they have little storage space. Thus, they must be replenished frequently by suppliers.

A random sample of 576 urban stores was selected for the study. The stores selected were from all 18 divisions in the United States and Canada. The corporation defines divisions, which include between 300 and 600 stores, by geographical boundaries. The firm chose the four most heavily populated urban districts (35–40 stores) from each division for the research, for a total of 72 districts. Rural districts were excluded to reduce travel costs. Eight stores were randomly selected from each district, for a total of 576 stores. Thus, the sample is representative of the urban stores in this national chain.

The extent to which employees display positive emotions to customers can be considered a store, or organization, attribute, as we suggested earlier. Yet this attribute can only be observed in the behaviors of individual employees. Thus, displayed emotions were measured by observers who coded clerks' behavior during transactions with customers. These observations were made during three months in 1984. Observers visited each of the 576 stores twice: once during the day shift and once during the swing shift. They visited 25 percent of the stores (144 stores) a third time during the night shift (11:00 p.m.–7:00 a.m.). A store visit could occur at any juncture in each eight-hour shift since observers also worked shifts that were approximately eight hours. The most efficient route of travel usually determined the order in which selected stores were visited.

Observers coded as many as 20 transactions between customers and clerks during each store visit, for a total of up to 60 transactions per store. The number of transactions coded during a visit ranged from 1 to 20 and was determined primarily by the number of customers in the store during the visit. The modal number of transactions coded at each visit was 8 and the mean was 9. The final sample included 11,805 clerk-customer transactions. A total of 1,319 clerks were observed; 44 percent were men, and about 75 percent of the customers were men.

Procedures

Observers acted as incognito participant observers (Webb, Campbell Schwartz, Sechrest, & Grove, 1981: 200). They were participant observers since they acted like typical customers. The firm notified store managers that mystery

shoppers might be visiting their stores during the spring or summer of 1984 to observe employee courtesy, but managers received no specific information about the timing of the visits.

The firm's marketing information indicated that typical customers were working class men and, less often, women, 18 to 34 years old. Observers were selected accordingly and instructed how to dress. The firm did not hire observers especially for this task. Rather, members of the corporate staff, particularly of the human resources staff, who fit the profile of a typical customer were asked to spend one to four weeks working as observers. The people who gathered the data held a wide range of jobs in the corporation, including those of organizational development specialist, executive development specialist, director of field research, secretary, and marketing manager.

The corporation's director of field research trained the other corporate employees who volunteered to help gather the data. Before visiting stores included in the study, each volunteer observer visited some pretest stores with the director of field research. They coded clerks' behaviors and compared observations after each visit. The volunteers and the director discussed and clarified differences in coding until they agreed consistently.

Observers visited each store in pairs. They acted independently and did not communicate with each other while inside the store. Observations were noted on preformatted three-by-five-inch cards. Only one clerk, the operator of the primary cash resister, was observed during each visit even if more than one register was operating. Observers walked around the store for a few minutes and noted how well the store was stocked with merchandise. They also noted whether the clerk was wearing a name tag and a smock and whether the smock was clean. Typically, the observers then walked to the magazine rack or coffee pots, which were usually close to the primary cash register. Observers usually coded clerks' behaviors toward customers from those vantage points. The observers then selected a small item like a candy bar and stood in line. They continued to note employees' behaviors toward customers while standing in line. Observers left the store after paying for their purchases.

The amount of time in each store varied from 4 to 12 minutes: the amount of time could not be predetermined because observers were instructed to stay in each store as long as possible. But they also had to avoid evoking suspicion. The visit was kept short if there were few customers in the store to prevent the clerk's becoming suspicious. Observers also noted if they felt that a clerk suspected that they were not ordinary customers. Clerks were thought suspicious in less than 3 percent of the observations; we excluded these observations from the analyses.

The firm's director of field research, an experienced organizational researcher who had responsibility for designing and implementing this study, established the interobserver reliability of this method. The director visited a sample of 274 stores and observed a clerk at each store. During each of those visits, one of seven other members of the data-gathering team accompanied the director. Interobserver reliability was assessed by comparing the research director's coding of clerks' emotional displays with the coding of the seven second observers. The correlations between the research director's coding and the second observers ranged from .94 to .67. The mean correlation was .82 and the median correlation was .85.

Predictor Variable: Display of Positive Emotion

The concept of displayed positive emotions is related to employee courtesy, an idea mentioned often in the literature on service organizations (Czepiel et al., 1985; Schneider, Parkington, & Buxton, 1980). The concept of courtesy, however, is broader than displayed positive emotion, since courtesy may also include working quickly, dressing neatly (Parasuraman et al., 1985), and doing favors for customers (Shamir, 1980). The display of positive emotion refers specifically to presenting a warm outward demeanor during transactions with customers.

The corporate researchers gathered evidence about two social amenities, greeting and thanking, and two forms of nonverbal behavior, smiling and establishing eye contact, that reflected the presentation of a warm outward demeanor. These four aspects of clerks' displayed positive emotion were observed at the transaction level of analysis and were operationally defined as follows. (1) Greeting: only "Hello," "how are you today," or another polite phrase at the outset of a transaction was considered to be a greeting. "Is that all for you?" and "Anything else?" were not coded as greetings. (2) Thanking: the word thank or a derivative had to be used. (3) Smiling: a smile was considered a noticeable uptwist of the lips (Tidd & Lockard, 1978). (4) Eye contact: a direct gaze by a clerk was coded as a sincere attempt at eye contact, regardless of whether a customer reciprocated.

The observers assigned a value of 1 if a behavior was displayed and a value of 0 if it was not displayed. Thus, each transaction was coded as to whether the clerk smiled at, greeted, thanked, and maintained eye contact with the customer. The data were aggregated to the store level of analysis to form an index of display of positive emotion as a store attribute.

For each store. a score was computed for each of the four emotional expressions by calculating the proportion of transactions in which the behaviors were displayed over the total number of transactions coded. For each store, the variable measuring the display of positive emotion was an index composed of the mean level of greeting, thanking, smiling, and eye contact observed in that store ($\alpha = .76$).

The aggregation of transaction-level data to an organizational level can be justified if the ratio of between-group variance to within-group variance is statistically significant. A significant ratio suggests that the aggregated variable is measuring an organizational-level construct (Rousseau, 1985). We performed an ANOVA with display of positive emotion as the dependent variable and store identifiers as the independent variable. The between-store variance was significantly greater than the within-store variance (ms = .82 and .06, respectively; $F_{576, 11,804} = 14,311$; $p < .01$).

Control Variables

This study sought to document the effects of a store's emotional front above and beyond the effects of other factors. Thus, it was important to control for the effects of other store attributes on store sales. Observers gathered data for five control variables: clerks' gender composition, customers' gender composition, clerks' image, store's stock level, and length of line. Data for three other control variables were obtained from company records: store ownership, supervision costs, and geographical region. We operationally defined those variables as follows. (1) Clerks' gender composition was defined as the proportion of a store's clerks who were women. Observers noted the gender of the clerk during each visit. In order to aggregate to the store level of analysis, we computed the proportion of women over the total number of clerks observed across all visits as an index of the store's gender composition. We used this measure to control for variation in displayed emotion due to gender (Deaux, 1985; Putnam & McCallister, 1980). (2) Customers' gender composition referred to the proportion of customers who were women. The observers noted the gender of the customer in each transaction. We aggregated those observations to the organizational level by computing the proportion of woman customers in each store over all the customers present during all observations in the store. This variable was introduced to help account for the different buying patterns of men and women (Engel, Blackwell, & Miniard, 1986). (3) Clerks' image was the degree to which clerks in a store maintained the dress code specified by corporate guidelines. This variable had three items: whether clerks wore a smock, whether their smock was clean, and whether they wore a name tag. Ratings were on a 2-point scale with 1 = no and 2 = yes (α = .74). This variable was used to help control for compliance with other corporate norms. (4) For store's stock level, three items were used to rate how well each store was stocked with merchandise. Observers used 5-point Likert scales to rate the extent to which the shelves, snack stands, and refrigerators were fully stocked (α = .81). We controlled for this variable because high stock levels may promote strong sales regardless of displayed emotions. (5) For average line length, observers recorded the largest number of customers in line at the primary cash register during each store visit. Average line length reflects the mean number of people standing in line across all visits to a store. We controlled for this variable because stores with longer lines may sell more than others, regardless of displayed emotions. (6) Store ownership captured whether a store was franchised (coded 1) or corporation owned (coded 0). The firm's executives have the authority to enforce policies about employee courtesy in corporate stores but can only encourage such practice in franchised stores. (7) Store supervision costs was the amount of money spent by the corporation on salaries, benefits, and training costs for the field supervisors who dealt directly with each store manager. This corporation provided us with standardized data about the number of dollars spent on each store for such supervision. A field supervisor typically oversees the operation of eight to ten stores, but such supervision costs varied considerably across stores in the sample. Variation occurred because regional, district, and division managers have some autonomy over how many stores each supervisor oversees, the amount such supervisors are paid, and how much training they receive. This variable was used to help control for the influence of quality of supervision on store sales. (8) Region reflected the corporation's grouping of stores into four geographical regions, each under the authority of a regional vice president; the northeastern region was coded 1; the western, 2; the midwestern, 3; and the southern, 4. We used this variable to control for variability in administrative practices and for differences in regional norms about displayed emotion. The variable was dummy-coded so that it could be used in multiple regression analysis.

Criterion Variable: Total Store Sales

The criterion variable used in this study was total store sales during the same year that the observational data were gathered. Total store sales was the dollar value of sales for each store from all products sold during the 1984 calendar year, including grocery items, cigarettes, dispensed drinks, hot food, video games, oil, and gasoline. This measure was obtained from company records and was standardized among the stores included in the sample. We received standardized rather than raw data because executives preferred not to release that sensitive financial information. Standardization was accomplished by transforming total store sales into a new variable by assigning a value of 0 to the mean of each variable and a value of 1 to the standard deviation. The value for each store was the number of standard deviations that the store's sales deviated from the mean.

Results of the Quantitative and Deductive Study

Table 3.1 presents the means, standard deviations, and intercorrelations of study variables. We performed multiple regression analyses to determine the relationship between the display of positive emotion and total store sales following a hierarchical procedure. The eight control variables were entered simultaneously into the first equation, which yielded a multiple R of .28 and an adjusted R-square of .06. The second regression equation included the eight control variables along with the index of displayed positive emotion. Total store sales was the criterion variable in both equations.

Table 3.2 reports results for the complete model. The control variables significantly related to total sales were store supervision costs, customers' gender composition, clerks' gender composition, and average line length. The second equation yielded a significant beta for the display of positive emotion, an R of .30, and an adjusted R-square of .07.

The statistically significant beta weight of the variable measuring display of positive emotion indicates a significant increment in R-square. That is, compared to the variance explained by the first equation, which included only control variables, the new variable included in the second equation contributed significantly to the variance explained (Cohen & Cohen, 1975). But the direction of the observed relationship contradicted our hypothesis: higher levels of displayed positive emotion were associated

TABLE 3.1

Means, Standard Deviations, and Intercorrelations of Quantitative Variables [a]

Variables [b]	Means	Standard Deviations	1	2	3	4	5	6	7	8
1. Display of positive emotion	0.51	0.23								
2. Store ownership	0.36	0.48	−.06							
3. Stock level	3.26	0.59	.26	.23						
4. Customers' gender composition	0.19	0.13	−.04	.07	.08					
5. Clerks' gender composition	0.56	0.37	.13	−.11	−.07	−.08				
6. Clerks' image	0.74	0.34	.13	−.67	−.04	−.05	.10			
7. Supervision costs	0.00	1.00	−.01	.16	.00	−.00	.08	−.13		
8. Average line length	2.88	1.16	−.18	.04	.10	.28	−.00	−.02	.06	
9. Total sales	0.00	1.00	−.06	.00	.09	.10	.09	−.02	.13	.18

[a] $n = 576$.

[b] Store ownership was coded 0 for corporation-owned stores and 1 for franchised stores. Customers' gender composition is the proportion of woman customers. Clerks' gender composition is the pro-portion of woman clerks. Supervision costs and total sales were standardized for all stores included in the sample; thus, the mean is 0.00, and the standard deviation is 1.00.

with lower levels of store sales. This finding was unexpected and confusing; it was also thought-provoking.

The modest positive relationship between line length and total store sales, along with the modest negative relationship between line length and the display of positive emotions (see Table 3.1), gave us a hint that by thinking about the difference between slow and busy settings we might be able untangle the relationship between displayed emotion and store sales. A a result, we gathered evidence about the differences between slow and busy settings as part of the qualitative research conducted to help understand why the quantitative evidence contradicted our central hypothesis.

The Qualitative and Inductive Study

Scholarly knowledge is developed through alternating phases of induction and deduction. When empirical obser-vations do not confirm a theory, investigators should embark on a new phase of theory building so that they can revise or reject the inadequate framework and replace it with a new framework (Merton, 1957; Wallace, 1971). As a result, our paper does not end with the usual discussion of quantitative findings. Instead, we conducted a qualitative and inductive study to help explain the unexpected negative relationship between the expression of positive emotion and store sales. The qualitative data provided rich information that helped us to view the convenience stores in a different light and to develop new predictions that could be tested in a reanalysis of the quantitative data.

Qualitative Methods

The qualitative phase included case studies, a day spent working as a clerk, conversations with managers, a customer service workshop, and about 40 visits to different stores.

Case studies of four stores in Northern California were conducted. We used data on employee courtesy and

TABLE 3.2

BETA WEIGHTS OF STORE EMOTIONAL DISPLAY AND CONTROL VARIABLES AS PREDICTORS OF TOTAL STORE SALES[a]

VARIABLES[b]	TOTAL SALES
Store ownership	−.10
Supervision costs	.13**
Stock level	.06
Customers' gender composition	.07†
Clerks' gender composition	.11**
Clerks' image	−.07
Average line length	.14**
Region 1	−.07
Region 2	.11
Region 3	.08
Display of positive emotion	−.10*
Multiple R	.30
Adjusted R-Square	.07**

[a] $n = 576$.

[b] Store ownership was coded 0 for corporation-owned stores and 1 for franchised stores. Customers' gender composition is the proportion of woman customers. Clerks' gender composition is the proportion of woman sales clerks. Region 1, region 2, and region 3 are dummy codes representing four regions.

†$p < .10$, two-tailed test.
*$p < .05$, two-tailed test.
**$p < .01$, two-tailed test.

store sales collected by the corporation to select cases that fit each of following four categories: (1) high sales and clerks who typically displayed positive emotions to customers, (2) high sales and clerks who typically did not display positive emotions, (3) low sales and clerks who typically displayed positive emotions, and (4) low sales and clerks who typically did not display positive emotions.

A pair of one-hour observations of transactions between clerks and customers were conducted in each of the four stores, one during a busy time and one during a slow time. Clerks working during each observation consented to participate in the study. An observer stood or sat near the cash register and took notes on predetermined topics, including customer demographics, line length, the number of customers in the store, customer behavior, and pressure from other tasks (e.g., stocking, cleaning, and dealing with vendors). The observers also had informal conversations with clerks about customer service.

A semistructured interview was conducted with the manager of each store. The interview contained 17 open-ended questions about the manager's prior experience; the selection, socialization, and reward systems used in the store; employee courtesy; and its influence on store sales. These questions appear in the Appendix. Interviews lasted between 30 and 60 minutes.

The qualitative study included a brief but instructive experience in which one of the authors spent a day working as a clerk in a store. About 30 minutes of training was provided, which included viewing a film on employee courtesy. This store had previously been rated as having low sales and frequent display of positive emotions.

We also had extensive in-person and telephone conversations with managers about the expression of emotion by store employees. At least 150 hours of conversations took place with corporate executives, customer service representatives, field supervisors, and store managers. These informal conversations focused on employee courtesy, especially the negative relationship we had observed between displayed positive emotion and sales. We also discussed interventions that could be used to enhance courtesy.

One of the authors attended a customer service workshop designed for franchisees and store managers. The two-hour program focused on methods for coaching and rewarding clerks in order to enhance their courtesy and satisfaction. It also provided an opportunity to hear managers discuss the role that expressed emotions play in the stores. Finally, the qualitative phase included approximately 40 visits to different stores located in three geographical regions. We made small purchases during those visits in order to observe clerks' displayed emotions.

The method of qualitative analysis used here draws on descriptions of how to generate theory by Glaser and Strauss (1967) and Miles and Huberman (1984). This juncture in the research was primarily inductive since facts were gathered to help us generate new theory. Nonetheless, as Miles and Huberman suggested, the data gathering and the interpretations attached to the data were guided by our explicit prior assumptions. Specifically, since the quantitative results suggested the importance of a store's average line length, we gathered qualitative data about store pace. We also made initial conceptual speculations about the differences between slow and busy stores.

We had frequent conversations during and after the collection of the qualitative data to discuss how we should modify the theory in light of the evidence. We traveled back and forth between the qualitative evidence and our conceptual explanations about why a negative relationship had emerged between displayed positive emotions and sales. Collecting and analyzing the five new sources of data led us to refine our understanding of differences between busy and slow settings and the implications of store pace for displayed emotions.

The Revised Perspective: Busy and Slow Times as Cues for Expressed Emotions

Customer:	Can I please have a plastic bag for my merchandise?
Sales Clerk:	Lady, we don't have time for your please and thank you. Can't you see how busy we are? just say what you want.

—*A transaction between one of the authors and a clerk in a very busy store.*

The qualitative evidence led us to conclude that the expression of positive emotion by clerks may not be a control move that influences the buying behavior of customers who visit these stores. The "service ideal"—the aspects of service that customers should expect to receive when they patronize an organization—portrayed in advertising and promotions for this national chain had historically emphasized speedy service and name-brand products rather than good cheer. Our conversations with executives also indicated that encounters with friendly clerks had only recently been included as part of the corporate marketing strategy.

Store managers throughout the corporation had received literature emphasizing the importance of offering smiles, greetings, eye contact, and thanks to customers only a few months before the quantitative data were gathered. Training programs for new employees had also recently been changed to include segments encouraging those behaviors. Further, some regional managers had implemented new customer service training programs like the one quoted at the outset of this article.

Yet the qualitative evidence that we encountered led us to question whether this new service ideal had been accepted. Managers and clerks typically believed that outright rudeness drove away customers. But they often contended that friendliness and warmth were unnecessary because "our customers just want to get in and out quickly" and "our customers don't care if the clerk is perky."

Nonetheless, the qualitative evidence did help us untangle the relationship between expressed emotion and store sales. The data led us to propose that store sales reflect store pace, or the amount of time pressure on clerks and customers. It also led us to propose that store pace is a cause, rather than an effect, of expressive behavior in the convenience stores studied.

Qualitative comparisons of stores during slow and busy times suggested that store pace is a cue for norms about expressed emotions. We followed Bettenhausen and Murnighan's (1985) view that norms are implicit agreements among members of a social system concerning which scripts they should and should not use to guide their behavior. Scripts are cognitive structures that specify "basic actions that can be executed in a range of possible manners and contexts" (Nisbett & Ross, 1980: 34). Scripts help people decide how to act in given situations.

Novel situations require participants to engage in considerable trial and error before they reach tacit agreement, or develop norms, about which scripts should guide actions (Bettenhausen & Murnighan, 1985). But the settings examined in this research were not novel. The membership of these stores is in constant flux as customers come and go, but both customers and clerks have well-developed scripts because of their extensive experience with such settings. Corporate records indicate that the average clerk serves hundreds of customers each day. Customers also have extensive experience with such stores; the average customer visits three times a week. Moreover, customers have much related experience with other businesses designed for convenience, such as fast-food restaurants. As a result, the scripts that guide behavior in these transactions are enacted quickly and frequently.

Indeed, there is usually instant, tacit agreement between clerks and customers about which norms of emotional expression should guide their behavior in such stores. Store pace is a primary cue that determines which norms apply at a given moment. During busy times, both clerks and customers tacitly agree that the expression of pleasant emotions is not essential. Conversely, both clerks and customers tacitly expect that pleasant emotions should be expressed during slow times.

Norms During Busy Times: Customers as Objects for Rapid Processing

Data from the five sources summarized in Table 3.3 led us to conclude that a set of tacitly agreed upon, but well-defined, norms exist during busy times that encourage

TABLE 3.3

QUALITATIVE EVIDENCE ABOUT THE INFLUENCE OF STORE PACE ON DISPLAYED EMOTIONS

SOURCES OF DATA	EVIDENCE ABOUT DISPLAYED EMOTIONS IN STORES DURING BUSY TIMES	EVIDENCE ABOUT DISPLAYED EMOTIONS IN STORES DURING SLOW TIMES
Four case studies	One store manager reported that clerks were less likely to be friendly during busy times. Customers are "more stressed and tense," as another store manager put it. Observers also noted that clerks tended to become less friendly during busy times. In both stores that were low on expressed positive emotion, there was a tendency to wait longer to open a second register than in the two stores that were high on the expression of positive emotion. Thus, during busy times, lines tended to be longer in the two "unfriendly" stores than in the two "friendly" stores.	The store managers reported that clerks were likely to be friendly during slow times; the observers noted that clerks tended to become more friendly during slow times. The observers also noted that extended conversations took place between clerks and regular customers during slow times, especially in the two "friendly" stores.
Day spent working as a clerk	The field notes reveal the following: [when the line of customers got long] "I never looked up at the customers. I never established eye contact. I never said thank you. I was breaking the rules, and I knew it. But I couldn't help it."	The field notes reveal the following: [during slow times] "There were regular customers. And my co-workers and I would often engage in brief, friendly banter, and sometimes even extended conversations, with these folks."
Conversations with managers	The negative relationship between positive emotion and performance was attributed to the "Manhattan effect," the notion that New Yorkers are less polite than people in other parts of the country because they are under greater time pressure.	There was widespread agreement that lack of courtesy should not be tolerated when it was slow because there are no excuses for such behavior.
Customer service workshop	A store manager remarked, "Customers who are in a long line don't care if we smile or not. They just want us to run like hell."	There was a general discussion about slow and busy stores. All agreed that it was easy to smile, greet, establish eye contact, and thank customers when it was slow, but being courteous was thought to be a challenge when it was busy.
Store visits	We noticed that clerks and customers tried to move as fast as possible when the store was busy. Everyone was less friendly. We also found that our own irritation from waiting in long lines was sometimes expressed to clerks.	We noticed that clerks tended to be more friendly when there were fewer customers in the store; customers and we ourselves also tended to be more friendly during slow times.

clerks in convenience stores to view customers as inputs for rapid processing. We also propose that those norms are reflected in differences at the store level of analysis because busy stores have a higher proportion of times during which clerks view customers—and customers view themselves—as inputs for rapid processing.

Isenberg (1981) reported a pilot study in which he found that people under time pressure expected themselves to be more task-oriented and less friendly. The pattern observed in the qualitative data was consistent with Isenberg's findings. When there were many customers in a store

and lines were long, both clerks and customers usually tried to move as quickly as possible to speed transactions. We heard clerks apologize for moving slowly during busy times. We also heard customers apologize for making large purchases when a long line of customers was waiting behind them. Such apologies by clerks and customers were heard even if only two or three people were standing in line because these stores are so strongly oriented towards convenience.

Consistent with Isenberg's findings, data from the case studies indicated that both clerks and customers in the busiest of the four stores were the least likely to display positive emotions; this store had the highest proportion of busy times. Moreover, visits to all four stores during busy times revealed that employees were less likely to offer greetings, eye contact, smiles, and thanks to customers than they were during slow times. Indeed, as Table 3.3 reveals, all five data sources suggested that positive emotions were less likely to be expressed during busy times.

Two reasons may explain why such norms are in place during busy times. First, such norms help maintain efficiency. Katz and Kahn (1978) and Feldman (1984) proposed that norms are enforced when they express core values of an organization or group and clarify what is distinctive about a social system. Efficiency is a core value for these convenience stores. Advertisements for the chain emphasize how quickly customers can get in and out of the stores. Indeed, speed of service is perhaps the primary reason that customers visit these stores.

Greeting, smiling at, thanking, and establishing eye contact with customers take only a small amount of extra time. But displaying those simple behaviors can encourage customers to prolong a transaction. One experienced clerk who worked in a store that was often busy told us that he learned not to smile or establish eye contact with customers because "being friendly" often caused customers to start prolonged conversations that he did not have time to finish. We also observed that people waiting in line are less likely to become irritated at "no nonsense" clerks who focus only on moving customers along quickly. Courteous clerks may be able to process customers just as quickly as clerks who do not interact with customers, but they appear to be slower. In short, customers and clerks are not likely to exchange good cheer during busy times because such acts hamper objective and perceived efficiency.

Second, a busy pace can create stress. Several of the clerks we spoke with reported feeling tense when lines were long. Table 3.3 also quotes a store manager who reported that customers feel tense when lines are long. Overloaded clerks who are displaying their inner feelings—rather than trying to follow corporate display rules—are not likely to be smiling. Even the display of anger or irritation may be acceptable during busy times; it is clearly more acceptable than it is during slow times. Expressing irritation toward people who hampered efficiency was found to be especially legitimate during busy times.

Indeed, we encountered some evidence that sanctions are applied to both clerks and customers who hamper efficiency during busy times. The following incident occurred during the day that one of us worked as a clerk: A customer initially requested only a hot dog and a soft drink. In the middle of his purchase, however, he decided to "grab a few things" including two Bic lighters, two toothbrushes, Ex-Lax, and aspirin; the three people waiting in line started glaring at this customer. To make things worse, the clerk did not have the skill to process this complicated order rapidly; he was also sanctioned. One impatient customer commented pointedly that "it is hard to get good help these days."

Along similar lines, a customer service manager told us about a time when—even though there was a line of seven customers at the primary cash register—the second clerk continued an animated conversation with his friend rather than open a second cash register. Both the clerk operating the cash register and a regular customer who was in line reacted by taunting the chatty clerk.

Norms during Slow Times: Customers as Entertainment

Norms during slow times contrast strongly with those during busy times. As with busy times, a set of tacitly agreed upon, but well-defined, behavioral expectations can be identified for slow times. Isenberg's (1981) previously cited laboratory research suggests that people under low time pressure expect themselves to be less task-oriented and more friendly than those under high time pressure. Findings from the five sources of qualitative evidence summarized in Table 3.3 are consistent with those findings. Clerks were more likely to greet, smile at, establish eye contact with, and say "thank you" to customers during slow times. Customers were also more likely to be friendly. Moreover, the norms for expressive behavior during slow times are also reflected at the store level because slow stores have a high proportion of slow times.

We identified three primary reasons why norms in slow stores support the expression of positive emotion. First, pressure on clerks for speed and efficiency is low during slow times. Clerks can take the time to greet customers, establish eye contact, smile, and say "thanks" without suffering the negative consequences that occur during busy times. Indeed, as Table 3.3 indicates, managers believe that lack of courtesy should not be tolerated during slow times because there is no excuse for such behavior.

Second, our observations suggested that customers who enter stores during slow times have different expectations about what constitutes correct behavior. In contrast to scripts for busy times, scripts for slow times have more "scenes" (Nisbett & Ross, 1980: 34) that emphasize interpersonal exchanges and the display of positive and esteem-enhancing emotions. Customers who entered stores that had few other customers were more likely to offer greetings and smiles to clerks. We also noticed this pattern in our own behavior when we visited stores.

Third, and perhaps more important, clerks in slow stores were often genuinely happy to see customers enter the store. They were most enthusiastic about seeing regular customers, but they acted happy even if it was someone they had never met. Recalling Roy's (1959) classic discussion of "banana time," our data indicated that informal social interaction with customers was an important means for introducing variety into a boring job. Clerks are especially friendly during slow times because they view customers as entertainment. Thus, the expression of positive emotions during slow times—and, in the aggregate, in stores that are usually slow—may be influenced more strongly by true feelings than by corporate display rules.

Field notes from the day one of us spent working as a clerk illustrate that point:

> There weren't a lot of customers. I was bored with the jobs they were giving me. When no customers were around, I'd spend my time putting prices on things, putting cans on shelves, and doing thrilling jobs such as cleaning the nacho machine. I'd get excited when a customer walked into the store because talking to customers was the only vaguely interesting thing to do.

In short, norms for slow times encourage the expression of positive and esteem-enhancing emotions. But such expectations do not appear to stem from efforts by the formal organization to increase sales.

Reanalysis of the Quantitative Data: Testing the Revised Theoretical Perspective

The revised theoretical perspective presented above provided considerable guidance for reanalysis of the quantitative data. A comparison of busy and slow times facilitated interpretation of the qualitative data. It appeared that stores with a high proportion of busy times were less likely to have a set of clerks who displayed positive emotions to customers and that stores with a low proportion of busy times were more likely to have a set of clerks who did display good cheer to customers. Stores could be placed on a

continuum from rapidly to slowly paced. Thus, we proposed that clerks working in a store that was usually busy would be guided less frequently by norms supporting the display of positive emotions. We came to view store pace—time pressure placed on clerks and customers—as cause of displayed emotion. Thus, although the display of positive emotion was a predictor variable in the initial analysis of the quantitative data, our revised perspective suggested that it be used as the criterion variable.

The revised perspective also suggested that we use two indicators of store pace—store sales and line length—as the predictor variables. Compared to stores with low sales, stores with high sales have more customers, more vendors coming and going, more telephone calls, and more people playing video games. Thus, stores with high sales have a high proportion of busy times. Furthermore, busy stores usually have longer lines than slow stores. Thus, average line length, one of the control variables used in the initial analysis, also indicates how much objective and subjective time pressure is usually placed on clerks and customers in a store.

Table 3.1 presents a modest positive relationship between sales and line length. But the small magnitude of that correlation, along with findings based on our observations of the stores, suggested that line length is a distinct indicator of store pace. High store sales may reflect large purchases rather than long lines. Moreover, stores with high sales place other demands on clerks that line length does not reflect, such as more frequent visits by vendors and more pressure to restock shelves.

In short, we proposed that stores with a high proportion of busy times would be less likely to have clerks who greeted, smiled at, established eye contact with, and said "thank you" to customers. Specifically, we expected that (1) store sales would be negatively related to the expression of positive emotion and (2) a store's average line length would be negatively related to the expression of positive emotion.

These expectations were tested in the same data set used for the first quantitative analyses; multiple regression analyses were again used in the sample of 576 stores. A hierarchical procedure similar to that used in the first quantitative analysis was employed. The first equation included seven control variables—ownership, supervision costs, stock level, customers' gender composition, clerks' gender composition, clerks' image, and region—as predictors of the display of positive emotion. This analysis yielded a multiple R of .40 and an adjusted R-square of .15 ($p < .001$). In the second equation, we added the predictor variables of line length and total store sales to the seven control variables used in the first equation. Table 3.4 presents the results of this equation; a multiple R of .44 and an adjusted R-square of .18 were obtained. Table 3.4 indicates that both store sales and average line length were significantly and negatively related to the display of positive emotion. The significant beta weights for both total store sales and average line length indicate that these variables make a significant contribution to the variance explained by the model. That is, the increment in R-square is statistically significant. These results support our revised perspective.[1]

Several control variables were also significantly related to the display of positive emotion: store ownership, stock level, clerks' gender composition, and region. Clerks in corporation-owned stores presented positive emotions more often than clerks in franchised stores. This finding may occur because executives can enforce policies about emotional expression in corporate stores but can only encourage such behavior in franchised stores. Stock level was positively related to pleasant displays: both maintaining well-stocked shelves and displaying good cheer may reflect general adherence to corporate guidelines. The positive relationship between clerks' gender composition and expressed positive emotions is consistent with prior findings that women are more likely to smile and display warmth than men (Deaux, 1985). Finally, as Table 3.4 shows, two of the three dummy-coded region variables had significant beta weights. A comparison of means (Pedhauzer, 1982: 289) for the regions indicated that clerks in the West were the most likely to express positive emotions and clerks in the Northeast were the least likely to do so. The negative relationship shown in Table 3.4 between the two indicators of store pace and the expression of positive emotion are consistent with our revised perspective. A key underlying assertion of this perspective is that clerks are

---

[1] We also conducted additional analyses to rule out nonlinear relationships between total store sales and displayed emotion and between line length and displayed emotion. An argument based on activation theory (Scott, 1966) suggested that, if store pace was a stressor and decrement in displayed positive emotion was a form of on-the-job performance, there would be an inverted-U-shaped relationship between store pace and the display of positive emotion. We used multiple regression analyses with quadratic (X^2) terms of store sales and line length to explore that hypothesis (Cohen & Cohen, 1975). The squared variable did not bear a significant relationship to displayed emotion ($p < .10$) in either of the analyses. Thus, we found no support for a U-shaped or an inverted-U-shaped relationship between sales and displayed emotion or between line length and displayed emotion.

TABLE 3.4

RESULTS OF REGRESSION ANALYSIS OF STORE PACE AS A PREDICTOR OF DISPLAY OF POSITIVE EMOTION [a]

VARIABLE [b]	BETAS
Control variables	
Store ownership	−.14†
Supervision costs	.01
Stock level	.23**
Customers' gender composition	.04
Clerks' gender composition	.15**
Clerks' image	.06
Region 1	−.03
Region 2	.25*
Region 3	.12**
Store pace	
Total store sales	−.09*
Average line length	−.20**
Multiple R = .44	
Adjusted R-square = .18**	

[a] $n = 576$.
[b] Store ownership was coded 0 for corporation-owned stores and 1 for franchised stores. Customers' gender composition is the proportion of woman customers. Clerks' gender composition is the proportion of woman sales clerks. Region 1, region 2, and region 3 are dummy codes representing the four regions.
† $p < .10$, two-tailed test.
* $p < .05$, two-tailed test.
** $p < .01$, two-tailed test.

less likely to display positive emotions during busy times than during slow times.

Further evidence for this assertion was obtained by comparing clerks' behavior during busy and slow times. The line-length variable, which was gathered at the clerk level of analysis, is an indicator of store pace at a given time. If norms about expressed emotions were linked to pace in the convenience stores studied, we expected that, across the 1,319 clerks who were observed for this study, there would be a negative relationship between the length of the line a clerk faced and his or her display of positive emotions.

A hierarchical multiple regression procedure at the individual level of analysis confirmed that expectation. We introduced the relevant control variables into the first equation: clerks' gender composition, proportion of woman customers, clerks' image, and store's stock level during the observation. This analysis yielded an R of .27 and an adjusted R-square of .07. In the second equation, we added average line length as an additional predictor. Line length was significantly and negatively related to the display of positive emotion by clerks (beta = −.14, $p < .001$, $n = 1,319$). The complete model yielded an R of .32 and an adjusted R-square of .10.

These analyses did not, however, address the question of whether constant exposure to busy or slow times influences all transactions in a store regardless of whether a particular time happens to be slow or busy. If recurring pace does influence store norms about expressive behavior, the relationship between line length and the display of positive emotion is likely to be different in typically busy stores than in typically slow stores.

The qualitative evidence led us to expect that clerks in stores that are usually busy will be less sensitive to the number of customers standing in line than clerks in stores that are usually slow. During slow times in typically busy stores, clerks may be indifferent or even unhappy about seeing customers because they must use slow times to cope with other demands such as stocking shelves, dealing with vendors, and answering phone calls. But such distracting demands are lower in stores that are typically slow. During slow times in stores that are usually slow, clerks are more likely to offer good cheer because they are bored and need the entertainment provided by customers.

In addition, we proposed that clerk in stores that are usually slow are less likely to offer pleasant emotions during busy times than clerks in stores that are usually busy. Clerks in stores that are usually slow have less experience in coping with the pressure of busy times. Thus, clerks in stores that are usually slow may be more likely to feel and thus express neutral, or even negative, feelings when lines do get long.

Thus, we expected a stronger negative relationship between the line lengths faced by individual clerks and their display of positive emotion in stores that are usually slow than in stores that are usually busy. Store sales is an indicator of whether a store is typically busy or slow. The expected relationship implies a significant interaction effect at the individual level of analysis between the length of a line that clerks face and the level of total sales of the store in which they work. We expected that interaction to have a significant effect on the display of positive emotion by clerks. Thus, an additional regression equation was examined. In this equation, the interaction term (line length × total sales) was included, in addition to the

individual-level control variable—clerks' gender composition, customers' gender composition, clerks' image, and store's stock level during the observation. As expected, the interaction term bore a significant relationship to displayed positive emotion (beta = −.07, $p < .001$), and the equation yielded a multiple R of .29 and an adjusted R-square of .08, compared to a multiple R of .27 and an adjusted R-square of .07 obtained with the model including only the control variables.

Subgroup analyses were conducted in order to understand the pattern of this interaction. Specifically, we split the sample of 576 stores at the mean of store sales, classifying 326 stores as slow and 250 stores as busy. We then conducted multiple regression analyses within each subsample on the relationship between line length and the expression of positive emotion by individual clerks.

As with the other multiple regressions at the clerk level of analysis, we first introduced clerks' gender, customers' gender, clerks' image, and store's stock level as control variables. Line length was then introduced as the predictor variable. The display of positive emotion by clerks was the criterion variable. In slow stores, the relationship between line length and the display of positive emotions was negative and significant (beta = −.19, $p < .001$, $n = 708$ clerks). In busy stores, that relationship was not nearly as strong and was only marginally significant (beta = −.06, $p < .10$, $n = 611$ clerks). Those results affirm that there is a stronger negative relationship between line length and the display of positive emotion by individual clerks in typically slow stores than in typically busy stores. We repeated this analysis with the sample split at the median of store sales and observed the same pattern of results.

Discussion

Our initial conceptual perspective focused on expressed positive emotions as control moves that influence the shopping behavior of customers. We hypothesized that stores in which employees were more likely to offer positive emotion to customers would have greater sales. But a quantitative study of 576 convenience stores revealed a negative relationship between displayed positive emotions and store sales.

Our revised perspective emphasized that store sales reflect store pace and that store pace is a cause, rather than an effect, of expressed emotions. We found some empirical support for the revised perspective. But our sample included only one variety of convenience stores; the service ideal associated with these stores has not traditionally included friendly service. Emotions expressed in organizations in which a different service ideal is present may act as control moves that influence sales. That is, a warm emotional front may promote sales when customers expect that it should and will be a central part of a firm's service. Examples of organizations where customers expect to receive good cheer from employees include Nordstrom's (Peters & Austin, 1985), Disneyworld (Tyler & Nathan, 1985), and Delta Airlines (Hochschild, 1983). Furthermore, expectations of fast service need not exclude warmth and friendliness; McDonald's is an example of a national chain in which the service ideal includes both rapid and friendly service.

The convenience stores studied are settings in which transactions between employees and customers are very brief. Expressed emotions may also be more powerful control moves during long transactions between employees and customers. When waiters serve customers in restaurants, for example, the interaction may last anywhere from 30 minutes to one and a half hours (Mars & Nicod, 1984), far longer than the 2 or 3 minutes that a typical customer spends in the stores we studied. There is more time during a long transaction for the customer to notice and react to the emotional behavior of an employee; thus, the operant conditioning cycle we discussed earlier is more likely to become established.

Our initial conceptual perspective had a far different focus than our revised perspective. The initial perspective emphasized control moves and corporate display rules. The revised perspective emphasized store pace, widely held norms for convenience settings, and employees' inner feelings. Nonetheless, some integration of those two perspectives on the expression of emotion in organizational life may have benefits for both organizational theory and managerial practice.

First, the qualitative evidence suggested that the concept of control moves might still be useful for understanding the convenience stores we studied but that future research might benefit from considering how expressed emotions influence variables other than sales volume. Evidence about busy times suggested that an emotionally neutral demeanor discouraged customers from initiating extended conversations. Presenting a neutral demeanor can act as a control move because it helps clerks influence the behavior of their customers and thus helps clerks provide fast service. Further, evidence about slow times suggested that pleasant displays can encourage customers to engage in conversations that are an important source of variety in a boring job. Thus, the display of good cheer

during slow times may be a control move that promotes individual rather than organizational goals.

Second, organizational theorists have not extensively studied the emotions displayed by organizational members (Hochschild, 1983; Rafaeli & Sutton, 1987). One central question for this emerging area is the extent to which leaders can prescribe employees' expressive behavior. Our initial perspective emphasized emotions expressed on the job as the outcome of corporate practices. But our revised perspective emphasizes that, although corporate display rules do constrain displayed emotions, store norms and inner feelings can sometimes be a more powerful influence over such behavior.

One combination of the initial and revised perspectives has direct implications for managers who want to design jobs so that subordinates who work in busy settings will be pleasant towards customers. Organizational norms specifying the display of good cheer to customers may be easier to enforce if managers take steps to reduce the objective and subjective stress placed on employees and customers. For example, the introduction of a single line for multiple clerks may reduce the perceived pressure on both employees and customers in busy environments. The physical distance between clerks and customers waiting in line may act as a buffer; clerks can offer polite and friendly service to the customer they are serving without risking sanctions from other customers. The single-line system with multiple clerks also reduces customer anxiety about having chosen the fastest clerk and discourages customers from focusing anger and irritation on any single clerk.

In closing, we would like to return to the methods used in this study. The observational methods used here are not widely employed in organizational research. Thus, questions may arise about whether it is ethical to secretly observe employees. Procedures used in the present research were, however, consistent with ethical guidelines on the conduct of nonreactive research and contrived observations (Salancik, 1979; Sechrest & Phillips, 1979; Webb et al., 1981). The American Psychological Association discourages "covert investigations in private places" (American Psychological Association, 1973:13). The convenience stores used in the present research are, however, public places. Moreover, the corporation's use of incognito observers and our own use of that method during the qualitative phase were only partly covert. Although specific, informed consent was not obtained from each clerk observed, all clerks had been informed that encounters with mystery shoppers were part of the job: the corporate training program explained the use of mystery shoppers and the expected expressive behaviors. Furthermore, the names of individual clerks were not recorded in either the quantitative research conducted by the corporation or in our own qualitative research. Thus, in terms of a harms-benefit analysis, such data were not, and could not, be used to harm any individual clerk.

Finally, we learned much about the role of expressed emotion in organizational life from this research because it entailed two complete cycles of induction and deduction. Unfortunately, however, it is not normative in the organizational studies literature, nor in other scholarly areas, to report unsuccessful efforts at induction or deduction.

Studies that find no significant relationships are usually not published. Moreover, we occasionally hear of studies in which the findings contradict initial hypotheses but that are written as if the unexpected results were predicted at the outset of the investigation. The tendency to report only successful predictions persists even though failed predictions offer important lessons about the research process and about organizational life (Mirvis & Berg, 1977). We hope that, in some small way, this research is a step toward changing those norms.

APPENDIX

Guide for Semistructured Interviews with Store Managers

1. How long have you been the manager of this store?

2. Why did you become a store manager?

3. Have you worked at the cash register in this store? (Prompts: How frequently? In another store?)

4. What qualities do you look for in selecting employees?

5. What sort of training do employees get? (Prompts: From the store? From the corporation?)

6. How are employees rewarded? (Prompts: How much pay? Anything other than pay? From the corporation? From the store?)

7. Do employees act differently when the store is busy? When the store is not busy?

8. Do customers act differently when the store is busy? When the store is not busy?

9. What do difficult customers do to make the clerk's work difficult? Tell me about a time when a really difficult customer entered the store. What are examples of good management of such customers? What are examples of bad management of such customers?

10. Is there anything special you tell employees about handling difficult customers?

11. Do you think there is a relationship between sales and courtesy?

12. What do you think of the corporation's push for courtesy?

13. What things do you do as a store manager to affect employee courtesy?

14. Is there any special employee training that emphasizes courtesy?

15. What do you think influences how courteous employees are?

16. Have you ever fired anyone for being rude to a customer?

17. In closing, are there any other important issues that we should have mentioned, but have not?

REFERENCES

American Psychological Association. 1973. *Code of ethics of the American Psychological Association.* Washington, D.C.: American Psychological Association.

Arther, R. O., & Caputo, R. R. 1959. *Interrogation for investigators,* New York: William C. Copp and Associates.

Ash, M. K. 1984. *Mary Kay on people management.* New York: Warner Books.

Bandura, A. 1977. *Social learning theory.* Englewood Cliffs, N.J.: Prentice-Hall.

Bass, B. M. 1982. *Stogdill's handbook of leadership.* New York: The Free Press.

Bettenhausen, K., & Murnighan, J. K. 1985. The emergence of norms in competitive decision-making groups. *Administrative Science Quarterly,* 30: 350–372.

Birnbaum, S. 1987. *Birnbaum's Italy.* Boston: Houghton-Mifflin.

Bowen, D. E., & Schneider, B. 1985. Boundary-spanning-role employees and the service encounter: Some guidelines for management and research. In J. A. Czepiel, M. R. Solomon, & C. F. Surprenant (Eds.), *The service encounter:* 3–15. Lexington, Mass.: Lexington Books.

Bradshaw, D. 1980. Sister can you spare a smile? *New York,* 13(8): 7.

Cohen, J., & Cohen, P. 1975. *Applied multiple regression/correlation analysis for the behavioral sciences.* New York: Wiley.

Czepiel, J. A., Solomon, M. R., & Surprenant, C. F. (Eds.). 1985. *The service encounter.* Lexington, Mass.: Lexington Books.

Deaux, K. 1985. Sex differences. *Annual Review of Psychology,* 36: 49–82.

Ekman, P. 1980. Biological and cultural contributions to body and facial movement in the expression of emotion. In A. O. Rorty (Ed.), *Explaining emotions:* 73–102. Berkeley, Calif.: California Press.

Engel, J. F., Blackwell, R. D., & Miniard, P. W. 1986. *Consumer behavior.* New York: The Dryden Press.

Feldman, D. C. 1984. The development and enforcement of group norms. *Academy of Management Review,* 9: 47–53.

Glaser, B., & Strauss, A. 1967. *The discovery of grounded theory: Strategies for qualitative research.* London: Wiedenfeld and Nicholson.

Goffman, E. 1969. *Strategic interaction.* Philadelphia: University of Pennsylvania Press.

Hackman, J. R., & Oldham, G. R. 1980. *Work redesign.* Reading, Mass.: Addison-Wesley.

Hayano, D. M. 1982. *Poker faces.* Berkeley, Calif.: University of California Press.

Hochschild, A. R. 1979. Emotion work, feeling rules and social structure. *American Journal of Sociology,* 85: 551–575.

Hochschild, A. R. 1983. *The managed heart.* Berkeley, Calif.: University of California Press.

Isenberg, D. J. 1981. Some effects of time pressure on vertical structure and decision making accuracy in small groups. *Organizational Behavior and Human Performance,* 27:119–134.

Kahn, R. L. 1981. *Work and health.* New York: Wiley.

Katz, D., & Kahn, R. L. 1978. *The social psychology of organizations* (2d ed.). New York: John Wiley & Sons.

Lawler, E. E. III. 1981. *Pay and organization development.* Reading, Mass.: Addison-Wesley.

Locke, E. A. 1976. The nature and causes of job satisfaction. In M. D. Dunnette (Ed.), *Handbook of industrial and organizational psychology:* 1297–1349. Chicago: Rand McNally & Co.

Mars, G., & Nicod, M. 1984. *The world of waiters.* London: George Allen & Unwin.

Merton, R. 1957. *Social theory and social stucture.* Glencoe, Ill.: Free Press.

Miles, M. B., & Huberman, A. M. 1984. *Qualitative data analysis.* Beverly Hills, Calif.: Sage Publications.

Mirvis, P., & Berg, P. 1977. *Failures in organizational development.* New York: Wiley.

Nisbett, R., & Ross, L. 1980. *Human inference: Strategies and shortcomings of social judgment.* Englewood Cliffs, N.J.: Prentice Hall.

Parasuraman, A., Zeithamal, V. A., & Berry, L. L. 1985. A conceptual model of service quality and its implications for future research. *Journal of Marketing,* 49 (4): 41–50.

Pedhauzer, E. J. 1982. *Multiple regression in behavioral research: Explanation and prediction.* New York: Holt, Rinehart & Winston.

Peters, T. J., & Austin, N. 1985. *A passion for excellence.* New York: Random House.

Peters, T. J., & Waterman, R. H., Jr. 1982. *In search of excellence.* New York: Harper & Row Publisher.

Putnam, L., & McCallister, L. l980. Situational effects of task and gender on nonverbal display. In D. Nimmo (Ed.), *Communications yearbook,* vol. 4: 679–697.

Rafaeli, A., & Sutton. R. I. 1987. The expression of emotion as part of the work role. *Academy of Management Review,* 12: 23–37.

Rafaeli, A., & Sutton, R. I. 1989. The expression of emotion in organizational life. In L. L. Cummings & B. M. Staw (Eds.), *Research in organizational behavior,* vol. 11: Forthcoming. Greenwich, Conn.: JAI Press.

Richman, T. 1984. *A tale of two companies. INC.,* 6(7): 38–43.

Rousseau, D. M. 1985. Issues of level in organizational research: Multi-level and cross-level perspectives. In L. L. Cummings & M. Staw (Eds.), *Research in organization behavior,* vol. 7: 1–37. Greenwich, Conn.: JAI Press.

Roy, D. F. 1959. "Banana time": Job satisfaction and informal interaction. *Human Organization,* 18 (4):158–168.

Salancik, G. R. 1979. Field stimulations for organizational behavior research. *Administrative Science Quarterly,* 24: 638–649.

Schneider, B., Parkington, J. J., & Buxton, V. M. 1980. Employee and customer perceptions of service in banks. *Administrative Science Quarterly,* 25: 252–260.

Scott, W. E. 1966. Activation theory and task design. *Organizational Behavior and Human Performance,* 1: 3–30.

Shamir, B. 1980. Between service and servility: Role conflict in subordinate service roles. *Human Relations,* 33: 741–756.

Skinner, B. F. 1953. *Science and human behavior.* New York: Macmillan Book Publishing Co.

Tidd, K. L., & Lockhard, J. S. 1978. Monetary significance of the affiliative smile. *Bulletin of the Psychonomic Society,* 11: 344–346.

Tyler, S., & Nathan, J. 1985. *In search of excellence* (film). New York: Public Broadcast System.

Unterman, P., & Sesser, S. 1984. *Restaurants of San Francisco.* San Francisco: Chronicle Books.

Wallace, W. 1971. *The logic of science in sociology.* New York: Aldine Publishing.

Webb, E. J., Campbell, D. T., Schwartz, D. S., Sechrest, L., & Grove, G. B. 1981. *Nonreactive measures in the social sciences.* Boston: Houghton-Mifflin.

DISCUSSION QUESTIONS

1. State the hypothesis that Sutton and Rafaeli wanted to test.

2. What are the central features of the quantitative deductive approach to organizational research?

3. What are the central features of the qualitative inductive approach to organizational research?

4. What are the central findings of this study?

5. What role, if any, does displayed emotion play in organizations?

6. What are the implications of this study for training employees who have direct contact with customers?

7. Using the concept of alienation as developed by Erikson, consider how it might affect the convenience store workers analyzed in Sutton and Rafaeli's article. For example, would motivational techniques and training in customer relations reduce worker alienation? Are the workers who are hostile to customers displaying symptoms of alienation? Do the structural conditions of work in a convenience store promote alienation?

FOR FURTHER READING

Gioia, D. and Poole, P. "Scripts in Organizational Behavior." *Academy of Management Review* 9 (1984) 449–459.

Goffman, E. *The Presentation of Self in Everyday Life.* Garden City, New York: Anchor Books, 1959.

Kanungo, R. "Work Alienation: A Pancultural Perspective." *International Studies of Management and Organization* 13 (1983) 129–138.

Marx, K. *The Economic and Philosophic Manuscripts of 1844.* New York: International, 1964.

Organ, D. "A Restatement of the Satisfaction-Performance Hypothesis." *Journal of Management* 14 (1988) 547–557.

Seeman, M. "On the Meaning of Alienation." *American Sociological Review* 24 (1959) 783-791.

4

LEARNING AND MOTIVATION

Organizational Learning

BARBARA LEVITT AND JAMES G. MARCH

LEARNING OBJECTIVES

After reading "Organizational Learning" by Barbara Levitt and James March, a student will be able to:

1. List and explain the various types of organizational learning

2. Understand how organizational learning differs from theories of analysis and choice, conflict and bargaining, and ecological perspectives on organizations

3. Understand how organizational learning works despite the turnover of personnel and the passage of time

4. Conceptualize the limitations of organizational learning as well as its possibilities as a form of intelligence

Introduction

Theories of organizational learning can be distinguished from theories of analysis and choice which emphasize anticipatory calculation and intention (Machina 1987), from theories of conflict and bargaining which emphasize strategic action, power, and exchange (Pfeffer 1981), and from theories of variation and selection which emphasize differential birth and survival rates of invariant forms (Hannan & Freeman 1977). Although the actual behavioral processes and mechanisms of learning are sufficiently intertwined with choice, bargaining, and selection to make such theoretical distinctions artificial at times, ideas about organizational learning are distinct from, and framed by, ideas about the other processes (Grandori 1987, Scott 1987).

Our interpretation of organizational learning builds on three classical observations drawn from behavioral studies of organizations. The first is that behavior in an organization is based on routines (Cyert & March 1963, Nelson & Winter 1982). Action stems from a logic of appropriateness or legitimacy more than from a logic of consequentiality or intention. It involves matching procedures to situations more than it does calculating choices. The second observation is that organizational actions are history-dependent (Lindblom 1959, Steinbruner 1974). Routines are based on interpretations of the past more than anticipations of the future. They adapt to experience incrementally in response to feedback about outcomes. The third observation is that organizations are oriented to targets (Simon 1955, Siegel 1957). Their behavior depends on the relation between the outcomes they observe and the aspirations they have for those outcomes. Sharper distinctions are made between success and failure than among gradations of either.

Within such a framework, organizations are seen as learning by encoding inferences from history into routines that guide behavior. The generic term "routines" includes the forms, rules, procedures, conventions, strategies, and

Source: Reproduced with permission, from the *Annual Review of Sociology*, Vol. 14, ©1988 by Annual Reviews Inc.

Author's note: All the case material in this article is disguised.

technologies around which organizations are constructed and through which they operate. It also includes the structure of beliefs, frameworks, paradigms, codes, cultures, and knowledge that buttress, elaborate, and contradict the formal routines. Routines are independent of the individual actors who execute them and are capable of surviving considerable turnover in individual actors.

The experiential lessons of history are captured by routines in a way that makes the lessons, but not the history, accessible to organizations and organizational members who have not themselves experienced the history. Routines are transmitted through socialization, education, imitation, professionalization, personnel movement, mergers, and acquisitions. They are recorded in a collective memory that is often coherent but is sometimes jumbled, that often endures but is sometimes lost. They change as a result of experience within a community of other learning organizations. These changes depend on interpretations of history, particularly on the evaluation of outcomes in terms of targets.

In the remainder of the present paper we examine such processes of organizational learning. The perspective is narrower than that used by some (Starbuck 1976, Hedberg 1981, Fiol & Lyles 1985) and differs conceptually from that used by others. In particular, both the emphasis on routines and the emphasis on ecologies of learning distinguish the present formulation from treatments that deal primarily with individual learning within single organizations (March & Olsen 1975, Argyris & Schön 1978) and place this paper closer to the traditions of behavioral theories of organizational decision making (Winter 1986, House & Singh 1987), and to population level theories of organizational change (Carroll 1984, Astley 1985).

Learning from Direct Experience

Routines and beliefs change in response to direct organizational experience through two major mechanisms. The first is trial-and-error experimentation. The likelihood that a routine will be used is increased when it is associated with success in meeting a target, decreased when it is associated with failure (Cyert & March 1963). The underlying process by which this occurs is left largely unspecified. The second mechanism is organizational search. An organization draws from a pool of alternative routines, adopting better ones when they are discovered. Since the rate of discovery is a function both of the richness of the pool and of the intensity and direction of search, it depends on the history of success and failure of the organization (Radner 1975).

Learning by Doing

The purest example of learning from direct experience is found in the effects of cumulated production and user experience on productivity in manufacturing (Dutton et al. 1984). Research on aircraft production, first in the 1930s (Wright 1936) and subsequently during World War II (Asher 1956), indicated that direct labor costs in producing airframes declined with the cumulated number of airframes produced. If C_i is the direct labor cost of the ith airframe produced, and a is a constant, then the empirical results are approximated by: $C_n = C_1 n^{-a}$. This equation, similar in spirit and form to learning curves in individuals and animals, has been shown to fit production costs (in constant dollars) reasonably well in a relatively large number of products, firms, and nations (Yelle 1979). Much of the early research involved only simple graphical techniques, but more elaborate analyses have largely confirmed the original results (Rapping 1965). Estimates of the learning rate, however, vary substantially across industries, products, and time (Dutton & Thomas 1984).

Empirical plots of experience curves have been buttressed by three kinds of analytical elaborations. First, there have been attempts to decompose experience curves into several intercorrelated causes and to assess their separate contributions to the observed improvements in manufacturing costs. Although it has been argued that important elements of the improvements come through feedback from customers who use the products, particularly where those products are complex (Rosenberg 1982), most of the research on experience curves has emphasized the direct effects of cumulative experience on production skills. Most studies indicate that the effects due to cumulative production are greater than those due to changes in the current scale of production, transformation of the technology, increases in the experience of individual production workers, or the passage of time (Preston & Keachie 1964, Hollander 1965, Argote et al. 1987); but there is evidence that the latter effects are also involved (Dutton & Thomas 1984, 1985). Second, there have been attempts to use experience curves as a basis for pricing strategies. These efforts have led to some well-publicized successes but also to some failures attributable to an inadequate specification of the basic model, particularly as it relates to the sharing of experience across organizations (Day & Montgomery

1983, Dutton & Freedman 1985). Third, there have been attempts to define models that not only predict the general log-linear result but also accommodate some of the small but theoretically interesting departures from that curve (Muth 1986). These efforts are, for the most part, variations on themes of trial-and-error learning or organizational search.

Competency Traps

In simple discussions of experiential learning based on trial-and-error learning or organizational search, organizations are described as gradually adopting those routines, procedures, or strategies that lead to favorable outcomes; but the routines themselves are treated as fixed. In fact, of course, routines are transformed at the same time as the organization learns which of them to pursue, and discrimination among alternative routines is affected by their transformations (March 1981, Burgelman 1988).

The dynamics are exemplified by cases in which each routine is itself a collection of routines, and learning takes place at several nested levels. In such multilevel learning, organizations learn simultaneously both to discriminate among routines and to refine the routines by learning within them. A familiar contemporary example is the way in which organizations learn to use some software systems rather than others and simultaneously learn to refine their skills on the systems that they use. As a result of such learning, efficiency with any particular procedure increases with use, and differences in success with different procedures reflect not only differences in the performance potentials of the procedures but also an organization's current competencies with them.

Multilevel learning typically leads to specialization. By improving competencies within frequently used procedures, it increases the frequency with which those procedures result in successful outcomes and thereby increases their use. Provided this process leads the organization both to improve the efficiency and to increase the use of the procedure with the highest potential, specialization is advantageous. However, a competency trap can occur when favorable performance with an inferior procedure leads an organization to accumulate more experience with it, thus keeping experience with a superior procedure inadequate to make it rewarding to use. Such traps are well-known both in their new technology version (Cooper & Schendel 1976) and in their new procedures version (Zucker 1977).

Competency traps are particularly likely to lead to maladaptive specialization if newer routines are better than older ones. One case is the sequential exposure to new procedures in a developing technology (Barley 1988). Later procedures are improvements, but learning organizations have problems in overcoming the competencies they have developed with earlier ones (Whetten 1987). The likelihood of such persistence in inferior procedures is sensitive to the magnitude of the difference between the potentials of the alternatives. The status quo is unlikely to be stable if the differences in potential between existing routines and new ones are substantial (Stinchcombe 1986). The likelihood of falling into a competency trap is also sensitive to learning rates. Fast learning among alternative routines tends to increase the risks of maladaptive specialization, while fast learning within a new routine tends to decrease the risks (Herriott et al. 1985).

The broader social and evolutionary implications of competency traps are considerable. In effect, learning produces increasing returns to experience (thus typically to scale) and leads an organization, industry, or society to persist in using a set of procedures or technologies that may be far from optimal (Arthur 1984). Familiar examples are the standard typewriter keyboard and the use of the internal combustion gasoline engine to power motor vehicles. Since they convert almost chance actions based on small differences into stable arrangements, competency traps result in organizational histories for which broad functional or efficiency explanations are often inadequate.

Interpretation of Experience

The lessons or experience are drawn from a relatively small number or observations in a complex, changing ecology of learning organizations. What has happened is not always obvious, and the causality or events is difficult to untangle. What an organization should expect to achieve, and thus the difference between success and failure, is not always clear. Nevertheless, people in organizations form interpretations of events and come to classify outcomes as good or bad (Thompson 1967).

Certain properties of this interpretation of experience stem from features of individual inference and judgment. As has frequently been observed, individual human beings are not perfect statisticians (Kahneman et al. 1982). They make systematic errors in recording the events of history and in making inferences from them. They overestimate the probability of events that actually occur and of events that are available to attention because of their recency or saliency. They are insensitive to sample size. They tend to overattribute events to the intentional actions of individuals. They use simple linear and functional rules, associate causality with spatial and temporal contiguity, and assume that big effects must have big causes. These attributes of individuals as historians are important to the present topic because they lead to systematic biases in interpretation, but they are reviewed in several previous publications (Slovic et al. 1977, Einhorn & Hogarth 1986, Starbuck & Milliken 1988) and are not discussed here.

Stories, Paradigms, and Frames

Organizations devote considerable energy to developing collective understandings of history. These interpretations of experience depend on the frames within which events are comprehended (Daft & Weick 1984). They are translated into, and developed through, story lines that come to be broadly, but not universally, shared (Clark 1972, Martin et al. 1985). This structure of meaning is normally suppressed as a conscious concern, but learning occurs within it. As a result, some of the more powerful phenomena in organizational change surround the transformation of givens, the redefinition of events, alternatives, and concepts through consciousness raising, culture building, double-loop learning, or paradigm shifts (Argyris & Schön 1978, Brown 1978, Beyer 1981).

It is imaginable that organizations will come to discard ineffective interpretive frames in the very long run, but the difficulties in using history to discriminate intelligently among alternative paradigms are profound. Where there are multiple, hierarchically arranged levels of simultaneous learning, the interactions among them are complex, and it is difficult to evaluate higher order alternatives on the basis of experience. Alternative frames are flexible enough to allow change in operational routines without affecting organizational mythology (Meyer & Rowan 1977, Krieger 1979), and organizational participants collude in support of interpretations that sustain the myths (Tirole 1986). As a result, stories, paradigms, and beliefs are conserved in the face of considerable potential disconfirmation (Sproull 1981); and what is learned appears to be influenced less by history than by the frames applied to that history (Fischoff 1975, Pettigrew 1985).

Although frameworks for interpreting experience within organizations are generally resistant to experi-ence—indeed, may enact that experience (Weick 1979)—they are vulnerable to paradigm peddling and paradigm politics. Ambiguity sustains the efforts of theorists and therapists to promote their favorite frameworks, and the process by which interpretations are developed makes it relatively easy for conflicts of interest within an organization to spawn conflicting interpretations. For example, leaders of organizations are inclined to accept paradigms that attribute organizational successes to their own actions and organizational failures to the actions of others or to external forces, but opposition groups in an organization are likely to have the converse principle for attributing causality (Miller & Ross 1975). Similarly, advocates of a particular policy, but not their opponents, are likely to interpret failures less as a symptom that the policy is incorrect than as an indication that it has not been pursued vigorously enough (Ross & Staw 1986). As a result, disagreements over the meaning of history are possible, and different groups develop alternative stories that interpret the same experience quite differently.

The Ambiguity of Success

Both trial-and-error learning and incremental search depend on the evaluation of outcomes as successes or failures. There is a structural bias toward post-decision disappointment in ordinary decision-making (Harrison & March 1984), but individual decisionmakers often seem to be able to reinterpret their objectives or the outcomes in such a way as to make themselves successful even when the shortfall seems quite large (Staw & Ross 1978).

The process is similar in organizational learning, particularly where the leadership is stable and the organization is tightly integrated (Ross & Staw 1986). But where such conditions do not hold, there are often differences stemming from the political nature of an organization. Goals are ambiguous, and commitment to them is confounded by their relation to personal and subgroup objectives (Moore & Gates 1986). Conflict and decision advocacy within putatively rational decision processes lead to inflated expectations and problems of implementation and thus to disappointments (Olsen 1976, Sproull et al. 1978). Different groups in an organization often have different targets and evaluate the same outcome differently. Simple euphoria is constrained by the presence of individuals and groups who opposed the direction being pursued, or who at least feel no need to accept responsibility for it (Brunsson 1985). New organizational leaders are inclined to define previous outcomes more negatively than are the leaders who preceded them (Hedberg 1981). As a result, evaluations of outcomes are likely to be more negative or more mixed in organizations than they are in individuals.

Organizational success is ordinarily defined in terms of the relation between performance outcomes and targets. Targets, however, change over time in two ways. First, the indicators of success are modified. Accounting definitions change (Burchell et al. 1985); social and policy indicators are redefined (MacRae 1985). Second, levels of aspiration with respect to any particular indicator change. The most common assumption is that a target is a function of some kind of moving average of past achievement, the gap between past achievement and past targets, or the rate of change of either (Cyert & March 1963, Lant 1987).

Superstitious Learning

Superstitious learning occurs when the subjective experience of learning is compelling, but the connections between actions and outcomes are misspecified. Numerous opportunities exist for such misunderstandings in learning from experience in organizations. For example, it is easy for technicians to develop superstitious perceptions of a new technology from their experience with it (Barley 1988). Cases of superstition that are of particular interest to students of organizations are those that stem from special features of life in hierarchical organizations. For example, the promotion of managers on the basis of performance produces self-confidence among top executives that is partly superstitious, leading them to overestimate the extent to which they can control the risks their organizations face (March & Shapira 1987).

Superstitious learning often involves situations in which subjective evaluations of success are insensitive to the actions taken. During very good times, or when post-outcome euphoria reinterprets outcomes positively, or when targets are low, only exceptionally inappropriate routines will lead an organization to experience failure. In like manner, during very bad times, or when post-outcome pessimism reinterprets outcomes negatively, or when targets are high, no routine will lead to success. Evaluations that are insensitive to actions can also result from adaptive aspirations. Targets that adapt very rapidly will be close to the current performance level. This makes being above or below the target an almost chance event. Very slow adaptation, on the other hand, is likely to keep an organization either successful for long periods of time or unsuccessful for long periods of time. A similar result is realized if targets adapt to the performance of other organizations. For example, if each firm

in an industry sets its target equal to the average performance of firms in that industry, some firms are likely to be persistently above the target and others persistently below (Levinthal & March 1981, Herriott et al. 1985).

Each of these situations produces superstitious learning. In an organization that is invariantly successful, routines that are followed are associated with success and are reinforced; other routines are inhibited. The organization becomes committed to a particular set of routines, but the routines to which it becomes committed are determined more by early (relatively arbitrary) actions than by information gained from the learning situation (Nystrom & Starbuck 1984). Alternatively, if failure is experienced regardless of the particular routine that is used, routines are changed frequently in a fruitless search for some that work. In both cases, the subjective feeling of learning is powerful, but it is misleading.

Organizational Memory

Organizational learning depends on features of individual memories (Hastie et al. 1984, Johnson & Hasher 1987), but our present concern is with organizational aspects of memory. Routine-based conceptions of learning presume that the lessons of experience are maintained and accumulated within routines despite the turnover of personnel and the passage of time. Rules, procedures, technologies, beliefs, and cultures are conserved through systems of socialization and control. They are retrieved through mechanisms of attention within a memory structure. Such organizational instruments not only record history but shape its future path, and the details of that path depend significantly on the processes by which the memory is maintained and consulted. An accounting system, whether viewed as the product of design or the residue of historical development, affects the recording and creation of history by an organization (Johnson & Kaplan 1987, Røvik 1987). The ways in which military routines are changed, maintained, and consulted contribute to the likelihood and orchestration of military engagement (Levy 1986).

Recording of Experience

Inferences drawn from experience are recorded in documents, accounts, files, standard operating procedures, and rule books; in the social and physical geography of organizational structures and relationships; in standards of good professional practice; in the culture of organizational stories; and in shared perceptions of "the way things are done around here." Relatively little is known about the details by which organizational experience is accumulated into a structure of routines, but it is clearly a process that yields different kinds of routines in different situations and is only partly successful in imposing internal consistency on organizational memories.

Not everything is recorded. The transformation of experience into routines and the recording of those routines involve costs. The costs are sensitive to information technology, and a common observation is that modern computer-based technology encourages the automation of routines by substantially reducing the costs of recording them. Even so, a good deal of experience is unrecorded simply because the costs are too great. Organizations also often make distinction between outcomes that will be considered relevant for future actions and outcomes that will not. The distinction may be implicit, as for example when comparisons between projected and realized returns from capital investment projects are ignored (Hägg 1979). It may be explicit, as for example when exceptions to the rules are declared not to be precedents for the future. By creating a set of actions that are not precedents, an organization gives routines both short-term flexibility and long-term stability (Powell 1986).

Organizations vary in the emphasis placed on formal routines. Craft-based organizations rely more heavily on tacit knowledge than do bureaucracies (Becker 1982). Organizations facing complex uncertainties rely on informally shared understandings more than do organizations dealing with simpler, more stable environments (Ouchi 1980). There is also variation within organizations. Higher level managers rely more on ambiguous information (relative to formal rules) than do lower level managers (Daft & Lengel 1984).

Experiential knowledge, whether in tacit form or in formal rules, is recorded in an organizational memory. That memory is orderly, but it exhibits inconsistencies and ambiguities. Some of the contradictions are a consequence of inherent complications in maintaining consistency in inferences drawn sequentially from a changing experience. Some, however, reflect differences in experience, the confusions of history, and conflicting interpretations of that history. These latter inconsistencies are likely to be organized into deviant memories, maintained by subcultures, subgroups, and subunits (Martin et al. 1985). With a change in the fortunes of the dominant coalition, the deviant memories become more salient to action (Martin & Sichl 1983).

Conservation of Experience

Unless the implications of experience can be transferred from those who experienced it to those who did not, the lessons of history are likely to be lost through turnover of personnel. Written rules, oral transitions, and systems of formal and informal apprenticeships implicitly instruct new individuals in the lessons of history. Under many circumstances, the transfer of tradition is relatively straightforward and organizational experience is substantially conserved. For example, most police officers are socialized successfully to actions and beliefs recognizable as acceptable police behavior, even in cases where those actions and beliefs are substantially different from those that were originally instrumental in leading an individual to seek the career (Van Maanen 1973).

Under other circumstances, however, organizational experience is not conserved. Knowledge disappears from an organization's active memory (Neustadt & May 1986). Routines are not conserved because of limits on the time or legitimacy of the socializing agents, as for example in deviant subgroups or when the number of new members is large (Sproull et al. 1978); because of conflict with other normative orders, as for example with new organization members who are also members of well-organized professions (Hall 1968); or because of the weaknesses of organizational control, as for example in implementation across geographic or cultural distances (Brytting 1986).

Retrieval of Experience

Even within a consistent and accepted set of routines, only part of an organization's memory is likely to be evoked at a particular time, or in a particular part of the organization. Some parts of organizational memory are more available for retrieval than others. Availability is associated with the frequency of use of a routine, the recency of its use, and its organizational proximity. Recently used and frequently used routines are more easily evoked than those that have been used infrequently. Thus, organizations have difficulty retrieving relatively old, unused knowledge or skills (Argote et al. 1987). In cases where routines are nested within more general routines, the repetitive use of lower level routines tends to make them more accessible than the more general routine to which they are related (Merton

1940). The effects of proximity stem from the ways the accumulation of history is linked to regularized responsibility. The routines that record lessons of experience are organized around organizational responsibilities and are retrieved more easily when actions are taken through regular channels than when they occur outside those channels (Olsen 1983). At the same time, organizational structures create advocates for routines. Policies are converted into responsibilities that encourage rule zealotry (Mazmanian & Nienaber 1979).

Availability is also partly a matter of the direct costs of finding and using what is stored in memory. Particularly where there are large numbers or routines bearing on relatively specific actions, modern information technology has reduced those costs and made the routinization of relatively complex organizational behavior economically feasible, for example in the preparation of reports or presentations, the scheduling of production or logistical support, the design of structures or engineering systems, or the analysis of financial statements (Smith & Green 1980). Such automation of the recovery of routines makes retrieval more reliable. Reliability is, however, a mixed blessing. It standardizes retrieval and thus typically underestimates the conflict of interest and ambiguity about preferences in an organization. Expert systems of the standard type have difficulty capturing the unpredictable richness, erratic redundancy, and casual validity checking of traditional retrieval procedures, and they reduce or eliminate the fortuitous experimentation of unreliable retrieval (Simon 1971, Wildavsky 1983). As a result, they are likely to make learning more difficult for the organization.

Learning from the Experience of Others

Organizations capture the experience of other organizations through the transfer of encoded experience in the form of technologies, codes, procedures, or similar routines (Dutton & Starbuck 1978). This diffusion of experience and routines from other organizations within a community of organizations complicates theories of routine-based learning. It suggests that understanding the relation between experiential learning and routines, strategies, or technologies in organizations will require attention to organizational networks (Håkansson 1987) as well as to the experience of the individual organization. At the

same time, it makes the derivation of competitive strategies (e.g., pricing strategies) more complex than it would otherwise be (Hilke & Nelson 1987).

Mechanisms for Diffusion

The standard literature on the epidemiology of disease or information distinguishes three broad processes of diffusion. The first is diffusion involving a single source broadcasting a disease to a population of potential, but not necessarily equally vulnerable, victims. Organizational examples include rules promulgated by governmental agencies, trade associations, professional associations, and unions (Scott 1985). The second process is diffusion involving the spread of a disease through contact between a member of the population who is infected and one who is not, sometimes mediated by a host carrier. Organizational examples include routines diffused by contacts among organizations, by consultants, and by the movement of personnel (Biggart 1977). The third process is two-stage diffusion involving the spread of a disease within a small group by contagion and then by broadcast from them to the remainder of a population. Organizational examples include routines communicated through formal and informal education institutions, through experts, and through trade and popular publications (Heimer 1985a). In the organizational literature, these three processes have been labeled *coercive, mimetic,* and *normative* (DiMaggio & Powell 1983). All three are involved in a comprehensive system of information diffusion (Imai et al. 1985).

Dynamics of Diffusion

The possibilities for learning from the experience of others, as well as some of the difficulties, can be illustrated by looking at the diffusion of innovations among organizations. We consider here only some issues that are particularly important for organizational learning. For more general reviews of the literature, see Rogers & Shoemaker (1971) and Kimberly (1981).

Although it is not easy to untangle the effects of imitation from other effects that lead to differences in the time of adoption, studies of the spread of new technologies among organizations seem to indicate that diffusion through imitation is less significant than is variation in the match between the technology and the organization (Mansfield 1968), especially as that match is discovered and molded through learning (Kay 1979). Imitation, on the other hand, has been credited with contributing substantially to diffusion of city manager plans among American cities (Knoke 1982) and multidivisional organizational structures among American firms (Fligstein 1985). Studies of the adoption of civil service reform by cities in the United States (Tolbert & Zucker 1983) and of high technology weaponry by air forces (Eyre et al. 1987) both show patterns in which features of the match between the procedures and the adopting organizations are more significant for explaining early adoptions than they are for explaining later ones, which seem better interpreted as due to imitation. The latter result is also supported by a study of the adoption of accounting conventions by firms (Mezias 1987).

The underlying ideas in the literature on the sociology of institutionalization are less epidemiological than they are functional, but the diffusion of practices and forms is one of the central mechanisms considered (Zucker 1987). Pressure on organizations to demonstrate that they are acting on collectively valued purposes in collectively valued ways leads them to copy ideas and practices from each other. The particular professions, policies, programs, laws, and public opinion that are created in the process of producing and marketing goods and services become powerful institutionalized myths that are adopted by organizations to legitimate themselves and ensure public support (Meyer & Rowan 1977, Zucker 1977). The process diffuses forms and procedures and thereby tends to diffuse organizational power structures as well (Fligstein 1987).

The dynamics of imitation depend not only on the advantages that come to an organization as it profits from the experience of others, but also on the gains or losses that accrue to those organizations from which the routines or beliefs are drawn (DiMaggio & Powell 1983). In many (but not all) situations involving considerations of technical efficiency, diffusion or experience has negative consequences for organizations that are copied. This situation is typified by the case of technical secrets, where sharing leads to loss of competitive position. In many (but not all) situations involving considerations of legitimacy, diffusion of experience has positive consequences for organizations that are copied. This situation is typified by the case of accounting practices, where sharing leads to greater legitimacy for all concerned.

The critical factor for the dynamics is less whether the functional impetus is a concern for efficiency or legitimacy than whether the feedback effects are positive or negative (Wiewel & Hunter 1985). Where concerns for technical efficiency are associated with positive effects of sharing, as for example in many symbiotic relations within an industry, the process will unfold in ways similar to the process of institutionalization. Where concerns for legitimacy are associated with negative effects of sharings as for example in cases of diffusion where mimicking by other organizations of lower status reduces the lead organization's status, the process will unfold in ways similar to the spread of secrets.

Ecologies of Learning

Organizations are collections of subunits learning in an environment that consists largely of other collections of learning subunits (Cangelosi & Dill 1965). The ecological structure is a complication in two senses. First, it complicates learning. Because of the simultaneously adapting behavior of other organizations, a routine may produce different outcomes at different times, or different routines may produce the same outcome at different times. Second, an ecology of learners complicates the systematic comprehension and modeling of learning processes. Environments change endogenously, and even relatively simple conceptions of learning become complex.

Learning in a World of Learners

Ecologies of learning include various types of interactions among learners, but the classical type is a collection of competitors. Competitors are linked partly through the diffusion of experience, and understanding learning within competitive communities of organizations involves seeing how experience, particularly secrets, are shared (Sitkin 1986), and how organizational actors come to trust one another, or not (Zucker 1986). Competitors are also linked through the effects of their actions on each other. One organization's action is another organization's outcome. As a result, even if learning by an individual organization were entirely internal and direct, it could be comprehended only by specifying the competitive structure.

Suppose competitors learn how to allocate resources to alternative technologies (strategies, procedures) in a world in which the return received by each competitor from the several technologies is a joint consequence of the potentials of the technologies, the changing competencies of the several competitors within the technologies, and the allocations of effort by the several competitors among the technologies (Khandwalla 1981). In a situation of this type, it has been shown that there are strong ecological effects (Herriott et al. 1985). The learning outcomes depend on the number of competitors, the rates at which they learn from their own experience, the rates at which they adjust their targets, the extent to which they learn from the experience of others, and the differences in the potentials of the technologies. There is a tendency for organizations to specialize and for faster learners to specialize in inferior technologies.

Learning to Learn

Learning itself can be viewed as one of the technologies within which organizations develop competence through use and among which they choose on the basis of experience. The general (nonecological) expectation is that learning procedures will become common when they lead to favorable outcomes and that organizations will become effective at learning when they use learning routines frequently. The ecological question is whether there are properties of the relations among interacting organizations that lead some of them to learn to learn and others not to do so.

In competitive situations, small differences in competence at learning will tend to accumulate through the competency multiplier, driving slower learners to other procedures. If some organizations are powerful enough to create their own environments, weaker organizations will learn to adapt to the dominant ones, that is they will learn to learn (Heimer 1985b). By the same token, powerful organizations, by virtue of their ability to ignore competition, will be less inclined to learn from experience and less competent at doing so (Engwall 1976). The circumstances under which these learning disabilities produce a disadvantage, rather than an advantage, are more complicated to specify than might appear, but there is some chance that a powerful organization will become incapable of coping with an environment that cannot be arbitrarily enacted (Hannan & Freeman 1984).

Learning as a Form of Intelligence

Organizational learning from experience is not only a useful perspective from which to describe organizational change; it is also an important instrument of organiza-

tional intelligence. The speculation that learning can improve the performance, and thus the intelligence, of organizations is confirmed by numerous studies of learning by doing, by case observations, and by theoretical analyses. Since we have defined learning as a process rather than as an outcome, the observation that learning is beneficial to organizations is not empty. It has become commonplace to emphasize learning in the design of organizations, to argue that some important improvements in organizational intelligence can be achieved by giving organizations capabilities to learn quickly and precisely (Starbuck & Dutton 1973, Duncan & Weiss 1979). As we have seen, however, the complications in using organizational learning as a form of intelligence are not trivial.

Nor are those problems due exclusively to avoidable individual and organizational inadequacies. There are structural difficulties in learning from experience. The past is not a perfect predictor of the future, and the experimental designs generated by ordinary life are far from ideal for causal inference (Brehmer 1980). Making organizational learning effective as a tool for comprehending history involves confronting several problems in the structure of organizational experience: (*a*) The paucity of experience problem: Learning from experience in organizations is compromised by the fact that nature provides inadequate experience relative to the complexities and instabilities of history, particularly when the environment is changing rapidly or involves many dangers or opportunities each of which is very unlikely. (*b*) The redundancy of experience problem: Ordinary learning tends to lead to stability in routines, to extinguish the experimentation that is required to make a learning process effective. (*c*) The complexity of experience problem: Organizational environments involve complicated causal systems, as well as interactions among learning organizations. The various parts of the ecology fit together to produce learning outcomes that are hard to interpret.

Improving the Structure of Experience

The problems of paucity, redundancy, and complexity in experience cannot be eliminated, but they can be ameliorated. One response to the paucity of experience is the augmentation of direct experience through the diffusion of routines. Diffusion increases the amount of experience from which an organization draws and reduces vulnerability to local optima. However, the sharing of experience through diffusion can lead to remarkably incomplete or flawed understandings. For example, if the experiences that are combined are not independent, the advantages of sharing are attenuated, and organizations are prone to exaggerate the experience base of the encoded information. Indeed, part of what each organization learns from others is likely to be an echo of its own previous knowledge (Anderson 1848).

Patience is a virtue. There is considerable evidence that organizations often change through a sequence of small, frequent changes and inferences formed from experience with them (Zald 1970). Since frequent changes accentuate the sample size problem by modifying a situation before it can be comprehended, such behavior is likely to lead to random drift rather than improvement (Lounamaa & March 1987). Reducing the frequency or magnitude of change, therefore, is often an aid to comprehension, though the benefits of added information about one situation are purchased at a cost of reduction in information about others (Levinthal & Yao 1988).

The sample size problem is particularly acute in learning from low probability, high consequence events. Not only is the number of occurrences small, but the organizational, political, and legal significance of the events, if they occur, often muddies the making of inferences about them with conflict over formal responsibility, accountability, and liability. One strategy for moderating the effects of these problems is to supplement history by creating hypothetical histories of events that might have occurred (Tamuz 1987). Such histories draw on a richer, less politically polarized set of interpretations, but they introduce error inherent in their hypothetical nature.

Difficulties in overcoming the redundancy of experience and assuring adequate variety of experience is a familiar theme for students of organizational change (Tushman & Romanelli 1985). Organizational slack facilitates unintentional innovation (March 1981), and success provides self-confidence in managers that leads to risk-taking (March & Shapira 1987); but in most other ways success is the enemy of experimentation (Maidique & Zirger 1985). Thus, concern for increasing experimentation in organizations focuses attention on mechanisms that produce variations in the failure rate, preferably independent of the performance level. One mechanism is noise in the measurement of performance. Random error or confusion in performance measurement produces arbitrary experiences of failure without a change in (real) performance (Hedberg & Jönsson 1978). A second mechanism is aspiration level adjustment. An aspiration level that tracks past performance (but not too closely) produces a failure rate—thus a level of search and risk taking—that is relatively

constant regardless of the absolute level of performance (March 1988).

A second source of experimentation in learning comes from imperfect routine-maintenance—failures of memory, socialization, or control. Incomplete socialization of new organizational members leads to experimentation, as do errors in execution of routines or failures of implementation (Pressman & Wildavsky 1973). Although it seems axiomatic that most new ideas are bad ones (Hall 1976), the ideology of management and managerial experience combine to make managers a source of experimentation. Leaders are exhorted to introduce change; they are supposed to make a difference (MacCrimmon & Wehrung 1986). At the same time, individuals who have been successful in the past are systematically more likely to reach top level positions in organizations than are individuals who have not. Their experience gives them an exaggerated confidence in the chances of success from experimentation and risk taking (March & Shapira 1987).

Overcoming the worst effects of complexity in experience involves improving the experimental design of natural experience. In particular, it involves making large changes rather than small ones and avoiding multiple simultaneous changes (Miller & Friesen 1982, Lounamaa & March 1987). From this point of view, the standard version of incrementalism with its emphasis on frequent, multiple, small changes cannot be, in general, a good learning strategy, particularly since it also violates the patience imperative discussed above (Starbuck 1983). Nor, as we have suggested earlier, is it obvious that fast, precise learning is guaranteed to produce superior performance. Learning that is somewhat slow and somewhat imprecise often provides an advantage (Levinthal & March 1981, Herriott et al. 1985).

The Intelligence of Learning

The concept of intelligence is ambiguous when action and learning occur simultaneously at several nested levels of a system (March 1987). For example, since experimentation often benefits those who copy successes more than it does the experimenting organization, managerial illusions of control, risk taking, and playful experimentation may be more intelligent from the point of view of a community of organizations than from the point of view of organizations that experiment. Although legal arrangements, such as patent laws, attempt to reserve certain benefits of experimentation to those organizations that incur the costs, these complications seem, in general, not to be resolved by explicit contracts but through sets of evolved practices that implicitly balance the concerns of the several levels (March 1981). The issues involved are closely related to similar issues that arise in variation and selection models (Holland 1975, (Gould 1982).

Even within a single organization, there are severe limitations to organizational learning as an instrument of intelligence. Learning does not always lead to intelligent behavior. The same processes that yield experiential wisdom produce superstitious learning, competency traps, and erroneous inferences. Problems in learning from experience stem partly from inadequacies of human cognitive habits, partly from features of organization, partly from characteristics of the structure of experience. There are strategies for ameliorating some of those problems, but ordinary organizational practices do not always generate behavior that conforms to such strategies.

The pessimism of such a description must, however, be qualified by two caveats. First, there is adequate evidence that the lessons of history as encoded in routines are an important basis for the intelligence of organizations. Despite the problems, organizations learn. Second, learn-ing needs to be compared with other serious alternatives, not with an ideal of perfection. Processes of choice, bargaining, and selection also make mistakes. If we calibrate the imperfections of learning by the imperfections of its competitors, it is possible to see a role for routine-based, history-dependent, target-oriented organizational learning. To be effective, however, the design of learning organizations must recognize the difficulties of the process and in particular the extent to which intelligence in learning is often frustrated, and the extent to which the comprehension of history may involve slow rather than fast adaptation, imprecise rather than precise responses to experience, and abrupt rather than incremental changes.

Acknowledgments

This research has been supported by grants from the Spencer Foundation, the Stanford Graduate School of Business, and the Hoover Institution. We are grateful for the comments of Robert A. Burgelman, Johan P. Olsen, W. Richard Scott, and William H. Starbuck.

REFERENCES

Anderson, H. C. 1848. Det er ganske vist. In *H. C. Andersens Eventyr*, ed. P. Høybe, pp. 72–75. Copenhagen: Forlaget Notabene.

Argote, L., Beckman, S., Epple, D. 1987. The persistence and transfer of learning in industrial settings. Paper presented at the St. Louis meetings of the Institute of Management Sciences (TIMS) and the Operations Research Society of America (ORSA).

Argyris, C., Schön, D. 1978. *Organizational Learning*. Reading, MA: Addison-Wesley.

Arthur, W. B. 1984. Competing technologies and economic prediction. *IIASA Options* 2:10–13.

Asher, H. 1956. *Cost-Quantity Relationships in the Airframe Industry*. Santa Monica, CA: Rand.

Astley, W. G. 1985. The two ecologies: population and community perspectives on organizational evolution. *Admin. Sci. Q.* 30: 224–41.

Barley, S. R. 1988. The social construction of a machine: ritual, superstition, magical thinking and other pragmatic responses to running a CT Scanner. In *Knowledge and Practice in Medicine: Social Cultural and Historical Approaches*, ed. M. Lock, D. Gordon. Hingham, MA: Reidel. In press.

Becker, H. S. 1982 *Art Worlds*. Berkeley, CA: Univ. Calif. Press.

Beyer, J. M. 1981. Ideologies, values, and decision making in organizations. See Nystrom & Starbuck 1981, 2:166–202.

Biggart, N. W. 1977. The creative-destructive process of organizational change: the case of the post office. *Admin. Sci.* Q., 22:410–26.

Brehmer, B. 1980. In one word: not from experience. *Acta Psychol.* 45:223–41.

Brown R. H. 1978. Bureaucracy as praxis: toward a political phenomenology of formal organizations. *Admin. Sci. Q.* 23:365–82.

Brunsson, N. 1985. *The Irrational Organization: Irrationality as a Basis for Organizational Action and Change*. Chichester, UK: Wiley.

Brytting, T. 1986. The management of distance in antiquity. *Scand. J. Mgmt. Stud.* 3:139–55.

Burchell S., Colin, C., Hopwood, A. G. 1985. Accounting in its social context: towards a history of value added in the United Kingdom. *Account. Organ. Soc.,* 10:381–413.

Burgelman, R. A. 1988. Strategy-making as a social learning process: the case of internal corporate venturing. *Interfaces* 18: In press.

Cangelosi, V. E., Dill, W. R. 1965. Organizational learning: observations toward a theory. *Admin. Sci. Q.* 10:175–203.

Carroll, G. R. 1984. Organizational ecology. *Ann. Rev. Sociol.* 10:71–93.

Clark, B. R. 1972. The organizational saga in higher education. *Admin. Sci. Q.* 17:178–84.

Cooper, A. C., Schendel, D. E. 1976. Strategic responses to technological threats. *Bus. Horizons* Feb: 19(1):61–63.

Cyert, R. M., March, J. G. 1963. *A Behavioral Theory of the Firm.* Englewood Cliffs, NJ: Prentice-Hall.

Daft, R. L., Lengel. R. H. 1984. Information richness: a new approach to managerial behavior and organization design. In *Research in Organizational Behavior,* ed. B. M. Staw, L. L. Cummings, 6:191–223. Greenwich, CT: JAI Press.

Daft, R. L., Weick, K. E. 1984. Toward a model of organizations as interpretation systems. *Acad. Mgmt. Rev.* 9:284–95.

Day, G. S., Montgomery, D. B. 1983. Diagnosing the experience curve, *J. Mark.* 47:44–58.

DiMaggio, P. J., Powell, W. W. 1983. The iron cage revisited: institutional isomorphism and collective rationality in organizational fields. *Am. Sociol. Rev.* 48:147–60.

Duncan, R., Weiss. A. 1979. Organizational learning: implications for organizational design. In *Research in Organizational Behavior,* ed. B. M. Staw, 1:75–123. Greenwich, CT: JAI Press.

Dutton, J. M., Freedman, R. D. 1985. External environment and internal strategies: calculating, experimenting, and imitating in organizations. In *Advances in Strategic Management,* ed. R. B. Lamb 3:39–67. Greenwich, Conn: JAI.

Dutton, J. M., Starbuck, W. H. 1978. Diffusion of an intellectual technology. In *Communication and Control in Society,* ed. K. Krippendorff, pp. 489–511. New York: Gordon & Breach.

Dutton, J. M., Thomas, A. 1984. Treating progress functions as a managerial opportunity. *Acad. Mgmt. Rev.* 9:235–47.

Dutton, J. M., Thomas, A. 1985. Relating technological change and learning by doing. In *Research on Technological Innovation, Management and Policy,* ed. R. S. Rosenbloom, 2:187–224 . Greenwich, Conn: JAI.

Dutton, J. M., Thomas, A., Butler, J. E. 1984. The history of progress functions as a managerial technology. *Bus. Hist. Rev.* 58:204–33.

Einhorn, E. J., Hogarth, R. M. 1986. Judging probable cause. *Psychol. Bull.* 99:3–19.

Engwall, L. 1976. Response time of organizations. *J. Mgmt. Stud.* 13:1–15.

Eyre, D. P., Suchman, M. C., Alexander, V. D. 1987. The social construction of weapons procurement: proliferation as rational myth. Pap. pres. Ann. Meet. Am. Sociol. Assoc. Chicago.

Fiol, C. M., Lyles, M. A. 1985. Organizational learning. *Acad. Mgmt. Rev.* 10:803–13.

Fischhoff, B. 1975. Hindsight or foresight: The effect of outcome knowledge on judgment under uncertainty. *J. Exper. Psychol.* 1:288-99.

Fligstein, N. 1985. The spread of the multidivisional form among large firms, 1919–1979. *Am. Sociol. Rev.* 50:377–91.

Fligstein, N. 1987. The intraorganizational power struggle: rise of finance personnel to top leadership in large corporations, 1919–1979. *Am. Sociol. Rev.* 52:44–58.

Gould, S. J. 1982. Darwinism and the expansion of evolutionary theory. *Science* 216:38–87.

Hägg, I. 1979. Reviews of capital investments: empirical studies. *Finn. J. Bus. Econ.* 28:211–25.

Häkansson, H. 1987. *Industrial Technological Development: A Network Approach.* London: Croom Helm.

Hall, R. H. 1968. Professionalization and bureaucratization. *Am. Sociol. Rev.* 33:92–104.

Hall, R. I. 1976. A system pathology of an organization: the rise and fall of the old Saturday Evening Post. *Admin. Sci. Q.* 21:185–211.

Hannan, M. T., Freeman, J. 1977. The population ecology of organizations. *Am. J. Sociol.* 82:929–64.

Hannan, M. T., Freeman, J. 1984. Structural inertia and organizational change. *Am. Sociol. Rev.* 49:149–64.

Harrison, J. R., March, J. G. 1984. Decision making and post-decision surprises. *Admin. Sci. Q.* 29:26–42.

Hastie, R., Park, B.,Weber, R. 1984. Social memory. In *Handbook of Social Cognition,* ed. R. S. Wyer, T. K. Srull, 2:151–212. Hillsdale, NJ: Erlbaum.

Hedberg, B. L. T. 1981. How organizations learn and unlearn. See Nystrom & Starbuck 1981, 1:3–27.

Hedberg, B. L. T., Jönsson, S. 1978. Designing semi-confusing information systems for organizations in changing environments. *Account. Organ. Soc.* 3:47–64.

Heimer C. A. 1985a. *Reactive Risk and Rational Action: Managing Moral Hazard in Insurance Contracts.* Berkeley, CA: Univ. Calif. Press.

Heimer, C. A. 1985b. Allocating information costs in a negotiated information order: in interorganizational constraints on decision making in Norwegian oil insurance. *Admin. Sci. Q.* 30:395–417.

Herriott, S. R., Levinthal, D., March, J. G. 1985. Learning from experience in organizations. *Am. Econ. Rev.* 75:298–302.

Hilke, J. C., Nelson, P. B. 1987. Caveat innovator: strategic and structural characteristics of new product innovations. *J. Econ. Behav. Organ.* 8:213-29.

Holland, J. H. 1975. *Adaptation in Natural and Artificial Systems: An Introductory Analysis with Applications to Biology, Control and Artificial Intelligence.* Ann Arbor, MI: Univ. Mich. Press.

Hollander, S. 1965. *The Sources of Increased Efficiency: A Study of DuPont Rayon Manufacturing Plants.* Cambridge, MA: MIT Press.

House, R. J., Singh, J. V. 1987. Organizational behavior: some new directions for i/o psychology. *Ann. Rev. Psychol.* 38:669–718.

Imai, K., Nonaka, I., Takeuchi, H. 1985. Managing the new product development process: how Japanese companies learn and unlearn. In *The Uneasy Alliance,* ed. K. Clark, R. Hayes, C. Lorentz, pp. 337–75. Boston: Harvard Grad. Sch. Bus.

Johnson, H. T., Kaplan, R. S. 1987. *Relevance Lost: The Rise and Fall of Management Accounting.* Boston, MA: Harvard Bus. Sch. Press.

Johnson, M . K., Hasher, L. 1987 . Human learning and memory. *Ann. Rev. Psychol.* 38:631–68.

Kahneman, D., Slovic, P., Tversky, A., eds. 1982. *Judgment under Uncertainty: Heuristics and Biases.* Cambridge: Cambridge Univ. Press.

Kay, N. M. 1979. *The Innovating Firm: A Behavioral Theory of Corporate R&D.* New York: St. Martin's Press.

Khandwalla, P. N. 1981. Properties of competing organizations. See Nystrom & Starbuck 1981, 1:409–32.

Kimberly, J. R. 1981. Managerial innovation. See Nystrom & Starbuck 1981, 1:84–104.

Knoke, D. 1982. The spread of municipal reform: temporal, spatial, and social dynamics. *Am. J. Sociol.* 87:1314–39.

Krieger, S. 1979 . *Hip Capitalism* . Beverly Hills, CA: Sage.

Lant, T. K. 1987. *Goals, search, and risk taking in strategic decision making.* Ph.D. thesis. Stanford Univ.

Levinthal, D. A., March, J. G. 1981. A model of adaptive organizational search. *J. Econ. Behav. Organ.* 2:307–33.

Levinthal, D. A., Yao, D. A. 1988. The search for excellence: organizational inertia and adaptation. *Unpubl. ms.* Carnegie Mellon Univ. In press.

Levy, J. S. 1986. Organizational routines and the causes of war. *Int. Stud. Q.* 30:193–222.

Lindblom, C. E. 1959. The "science" of muddling through. *Public Admin. Rev.,* 19:79–88.

Lounamaa, P. H.. March, J. G. 1987. Adaptive coordination of a learning team. *Mgmt. Sci.,* 33:107–23.

Machina, M. J. 1987. Choice under uncertainty: problems solved and unsolved. *J. Econ. Perspect.* 1:121–54.

MacCrimmon, K. R., Wehrung, D. A. 1986. *Taking Risks: The Management of Uncertainty.* New York: Free Press.

MacRae, D. 1985. *Policy Indicators.* Chapel Hill, NC: Univ. North Carolina Press.

Maidique, M. A., Zirger, B. J. 1985. The new product learning cycle. *Res. Policy* 14:299–313.

Mansfield, E. 1968. *The Economics of Technological Change.* New York: Norton.

March, J. G. 1981. Footnotes to organizational change. *Admin. Sci. Q.* 26:563–77

March, J. G. 1987. Ambiguity and accounting: the elusive link between information and decision making. *Account Organ. Soc.* 12:153–68.

March, J. G. 1988. Variable risk preferences and adaptive aspirations. *J. Econ. Behav. Organ.* 9:5–24.

March, J. G., Olsen. J. P. 1975. The uncertainty of the past: organizational learning under ambiguity. *Eur. J. Polit. Res.* 3: 147–71.

March, J. G., Shapira, Z. 1987. Managerial perspectives on risk and risk taking. *Mgmt. Sci.* 33:1404–18.

Martin, J., Siehl, C. 1983. Organizational culture and counterculture: an uneasy symbiosis. *Organ. Dynam.* Autumn:52–64.

Martin, J., Sitkin, S. B., Boehm, M. 1985. Founders and the elusiveness of a culture legacy. In *Organizational Culture,* ed. P. J. Frost, L. F. Moore, M. R. Louis, C. C. Lundberg, J. Martin. pp. 99-124. Beverly Hills, CA: Sage.

Mazmanian, D. A., Nienaber, J. 1979. *Can Organizations Change? Environmental Protection Citizen Participation and the Corps of Engineers.* Washington, DC: The Brookings Inst.

Merton, R. K. 1940. Bureaucratic structure and personality. *Soc. Forces* 18:560–68.

Meyer, J. W., Rowan, B. 1977. Institutionalized organizations: formal structure as myth and ceremony. *Am. J. Social.* 83:340–63.

Mezias, S. J. 1987. *Technical and Institutional Sources of Organizational Practices: The Case of a Financial Reporting Method.* Ph.D. thesis. Stanford Univ.

Miller, D. T., Ross, M. 1975. Self-serving biases in the attribution of causality. *Psychol. Bull* 82:213–25.

Miller, D., Friesen, P. 1982. Structural change and performance: quantum vs. piecemeal-incremental approaches. *Acad. Mgmt. J.* 25:867–92.

Moore, M. H., Gates, M. J. 1986. *Inspector-General: Junkyard Dogs or Man's Best Friend?* New York: Russell Sage Found.

Muth, J. F. 1986. Search theory and the manufacturing progress function. *Mgmt. Sci.* 32:948–62.

Nelson, R. R. Winter, S. G. 1982. *An Evolutionary Theory of Economic Change.* Cambridge, MA: Harvard Univ.

Neustadt, R. E., May, E. R. 1986. *Thinking in Time: The Uses of History for Decision Makers.* New York, NY: Free Press.

Nystrom, N. C., Starbuck, W. H., eds. 1981. *Handbook of Organizational Design.* Oxford Univ. Press.

Nystrom, N. C., Starbuck, W. H. 1984. To avoid organizational crisis, unlearn. *Organ. Dynam.* Spring:53–65.

Olsen, J. P. 1976. The process of interpreting organizational history. In *Ambiguity and Choice in Organizations,* ed. J. G. March, J. P. Olsen, pp. 338–50. Bergen, Norway: Universitetsforlaget.

Olsen, J. P. 1983. *Organized Democracy.* Bergen, Norway: Universitetsforlaget.

Ouchi, W. G. 1980. Markets, bureaucracies and clans. *Admin. Sci. Q.* 25:129–41.

Pettigrew, A. M. 1985. *The Awakening Giant: Continuity and Change in Imperial Chemical Industries.* Oxford: Blackwell.

Pfeffer, J. 1981. *Power in Organizations.* Marshfield, MA: Pitman.

Powell, W. W. 1986. How the past informs the present: the uses and liabilities of organizational memory. Paper read at the Conference on Communication and Collective Memory, Annenberg School, University of Southern California.

Pressman, J. L., Wildavsky, A. B. 1973. *Implementation.* Berkeley: Univ. Calif. Press.

Preston, L., Keachie, E. C. 1964. Cost functions and progress functions: an integration. *Am. Econ. Rev.* 54:100–7.

Radner, R. 1975. A behavioral model of cost reduction . *Bell J. Econ.* 6:196-215.

Rapping, L. 1965. Learning and World War II production functions. *Rev. Econ. Stat.* 47:81–86.

Rogers, E. M., Shoemaker, F. F. 1971. *Communication of Innovations.* New York: Free Press.

Rosenberg, N. 1982. *Inside the Black Box: Technology and Economics.* Cambridge: Cambridge Univ. Press.

Ross, J., Slaw, B. M. 1986. Expo 86: an escalation prototype. *Admin. Sci. Q.* 31:274–97.

Scott, W. R. 1985. Conflicting levels of rationality: regulators, managers, and professionals in the medical care sector. *J. Health Admin. Educ.* 3:113–31.

Scott, W. R. 1987. *Organizations: Rational, Natural, and Open Systems.* Englewood Cliffs: NJ: Prentice-Hall. 2nd ed.

Siegel, S. 1957. Level of aspiration and decision making. *Psychol. Rev.* 64:253–62.

Simon, H. A. 1955. A behavioral model of rational choice. *Q. J. Econ.* 69:99–118.

Simon, H. A. 1971. Designing organizations for an information rich world. In *Computers, Communications and the Public Interest,* ed. M. Greenberger, pp. 37–52. Baltimore, MD: Johns Hopkins Univ. Press.

Sitkin, S. B. 1986. *Secrecy in Organizations: Determinants of Secrecy Behavior among Engineers in Three Silicon Valley Semiconductor Firms.* Ph.D. thesis. Stanford Univ.

Slovic, P., Fischhoff, B., Lichtenstein, S. 1977. Behavioral decision theory. *Ann. Rev Psychol.* 28:1–39.

Smith, H. T., Green, T. R. G., eds. 1980. *Human Interaction with Computers.* New York: Academic.

Sproull, L. S. 1981. Beliefs in organizations. See Nystrom & Starbuck 1981. 2:203–24.

Sproull, L. S., Weiner, S., Wolf, D. 1978. *Organizing an Anarchy: Belief, Bureaucracy, and Politics in the National Institute of Education.* Chicago, IL: Univ. Chicago Press.

Starbuck W. H. 1983. Organizations as action generators. *Am. Sociol. Rev.* 48:91–102.

Starbuck, W. H. 1976. Organizations and their environments. In *Handbook of Industrial and Organizational Psychology,* ed. M. D. Dunnette, pp. 1067–1123. Chicago: Rand McNally.

Starbuck, W. H., Dutton, J. M. 1973. Designing adaptive organizations. *J. Bus. Policy* 3:21–28.

Starbuck, W. H., Milliken, F. J. 1988. Executives' perceptual filters; what they notice and how they make sense. In *Executive Effect: Concepts and Methods for Studying Top Managers,* ed. D. Hambrick. Greenwich, Conn: JAI. In press.

Staw, B. M. Ross, J. 1978. Commitment to a policy decision: a multi-theoretical perspective. *Admin. Sci. Q.* 23:40–64.

Steinbruner, J . D. 1974. *The Cybernetic Theory of Decision.* Princeton, NJ: Princeton Univ. Press.

Stinchcombe, A. L. 1986. *Stratification and Organization.* Cambridge: Cambridge Univ. Press.

Tamuz, M. 1987. The impact of computer surveillance on air safety reporting. *Columbia J. World Bus.* 22:69–77.

Thompson, J. D. 1967. *Organizations in Action.* New York: McGraw-Hill.

Tirole, J. 1986. Hierarchies and bureaucracies on the role of collusion in organizations. *J. Law Econ. Organ.* 2:181–214.

Tolbert, P. S., Zucker, L. G. 1983. Institutional sources of change in the formal structure of organizations: the diffusion of civil service reform, 1880-1935. *Admin. Sci. Q.* 28:22–39.

Tushman, M. L.; Romanelli, E. 1985. Organizational evolution: a metamorphosis model of convergence and reorientation. In *Research in Organizational Behavior,* ed. L. L. Cummings, B. M. Staw, 7:171–222. Greenwich, CT: JAI Press.

Van Maanen, J. 1973. Observations on the making of policemen. *Hum. Organ.* 32:407–18.

Weick, K. E. 1979. *The Social Psychology of Organizing.* Reading, MA: Addison-Wesley. 2nd ed.

Whetten, D. A. 1987. Organizational growth and decline processes. *Ann. Rev. Sociol.* 13:335–58.

Wiewel, W., Hunter, A. 1985. The interorganizational network as a resource: a comparative case study on organizational genesis. *Admin. Sci. Q.* 30:482–96.

Wildavsky, A. 1983. Information as an organizational problem. *J. Mgmt. Stud.* 20:29–40.

Winter, S. G. 1986. The research program of the behavioral theory of the firm: orthodox critique and evolutionary perspective. In *Handbook of Behavioral Economics,* ed. B. Gilad, S. Kaish, 1:151–87. Greenwich, CT: JAI Press.

Wright, T. P. 1936. Factors affecting the cost of airplanes. *J. Aeronautical Sci.* 3:122–28.

Yelle, L. E. 1979. The learning curve: historical review and comprehensive survey. *Decision Sci.* 10:302–28.

Zald, M. N. 1970. *Organizalional Change: The Political Economy of the YMCA.* Chicago, IL: Univ. Chicago Press.

Zucker, L. G. 1977. The role of institutionalization in cultural persistence. *Am. Sociol. Rev.* 42:726–43.

Zucker, L. G. 1986. Production of trust: institutional sources of economic structure, 1840 to 1920. In *Research in Organizational Behavior,* ed. L. L. Cummings, B. M. Staw, 8:55–111. Greenwich, CT: JAI Press.

Zucker, L. G. 1987. Institutional theories of organization. *Ann. Rev. Sociol.* 13:443–64.

Discussion Questions

1. What classical observations from behavioral studies of organizations do Levitt and March base their theory of organizational learning on?

2. What is the role of routines in organizational learning? How do routines change?

3. Explain what a competency trap is and provide an illustration from an organization of which you are a member.

4. How do interpretive frameworks form and change?

5. Define superstitious learning and locate examples of it in the college or university that you attend.

6. What are the mechanisms through which organizational memory develops, is retrieved, and changes?

7. What are the ways that organizations learn from other organizations? Specifically, how does the diffusion of innovation operate?

8. Discuss the statement, "powerful organizations, by virtue of their ability to ignore competition, will be less inclined to learn from experience and less competent at doing so."

9. According to Levitt and March, why doesn't organizational learning always result in organizational intelligence?

Power Is the Great Motivator

DAVID C. MCCLELLAND AND DAVID H. BURNHAM

LEARNING OBJECTIVES

David McClelland and David Burnham's "Power Is the Great Motivator" will help students:

1. Consider what factors motivate managers

2. Understand the differences between the need for achievement and the need for power

3. Learn how managerial styles can be changed

4. Appreciate and understand the constructive uses of power in organizations

What makes or motivates a good manager? The question is so enormous in scope that anyone trying to answer it has difficulty knowing where to begin. Some people might say that a good manager is one who is successful; and by now most business researchers and businesspeople themselves know what motivates people who successfully run their own small businesses. The key to their success has turned out to be what psychologists call "the need for achievement," the desire to do something better or more efficiently than it has been done before. Any number of books and articles summarize research studies explaining how-the achievement motive is necessary for people to attain success on their own.[1]

But what has achievement motivation got to do with good management? There is no reason on theoretical grounds why a person who has a strong need to be more efficient should make a good manager. While it sounds as if everyone ought to have the need to achieve, in fact, as psychologists define and measure achievement motivation, it leads people to behave in very special ways that do not necessarily lead to good management.

For one thing, because they focus on personal improvement, on doing things better by themselves, achievement-motivated people want to do things themselves. For another, they want concrete short-term feedback on their performance so that they can tell how well they are doing. Yet a manager, particularly one of or in a large complex organization, cannot perform all the tasks necessary for success by him or herself. Managers must manage others so that they will do things for the organization. Also, feedback on subordinates' performance may be a lot vaguer and more delayed than it would he if they were doing everything themselves.

The manager's job seems to call more for people who can influence others than for those who do things better on their own. In motivational terms, then, we might expect the successful manager to have a greater "need for power" than need to achieve. But there must be other qualities beside the need for power that go into the makeup of a good manager. Just what these qualities are and how they interrelate is the subject of this article.

To measure the motivations of managers, good and bad, we studied a number of individual managers from different large U.S. corporations who were participating in management workshops designed to improve their managerial effectiveness. (The workshop techniques and research methods and terms used are described in the shaded box on page 104.)

The general conclusion of these studies is that the top manager of a company must possess a high need for power, that is, a concern for influencing people. However, this need must be disciplined and controlled so that it is directed toward the benefit of the institution as a whole and not toward the manager's personal aggrandizement. Moreover, top managers' need for power ought to be greater than their need for being liked by people.

---

[1]For instance, see my books *The Achieving Society* (New York: Van Nostrand, 1961) and (with David Winter) *Motivating Economic Achievement* (New York: Free Press, 1969).

Now let us look at what these ideas mean in the con-
t_____viduals in real situations and see what com-
_____e of the good manager. Finally, we will look
_____ops themselves to determine how they go
about chang ng behavior.

Measuring Managerial Effectiveness

First off, what does it mean when we say that a good manager has a greater need for "power" than for "achievement"?
To get a more concrete idea, let us consider the case of Ken
Briggs, a sales manager in a large U.S. corporation who
joined one of our managerial workshops (see the shaded
box on page 104). Some six or seven years ago, Ken Briggs
was promoted to a managerial position at corporate headquarters, where he had responsibility for salespeople who
service his company's largest accounts.

In filling out his questionnaire at the workshop, Ken
showed that he correctly perceived what his job required of
him, namely, that he should influence others' success more
than achieve new goals himself or socialize with his subordinates. However, when asked with other members of the
workshop to write a story depicting a managerial situation,
Ken unwittingly revealed through his fiction that he did
not share those concerns. Indeed, he discovered that his
need for achievement was very high—in fact over the 90th
percentile—and his need for power was very low, in about
the 15th percentile. Ken's high need to achieve was no surprise—after all, he had been a very successful salesman—
but obviously his motivation to influence others was much
less than his job required. Ken was a little disturbed but
thought that perhaps the measuring instruments were not
too accurate and that the gap between the ideal and his
score was not as great as it seemed.

Then came the real shocker. Ken's subordinates confirmed what his stories revealed: he was a poor manager,
having little positive impact on those who worked for
him. Ken's subordinates felt that they had little responsibility delegated to them, that he never rewarded but only
criticized them, and that the office was not well organized
but confused and chaotic. On all three of these scales, his
office rated in the 10th to 15th percentile relative to
national norms.

As Ken talked the results over privately with a workshop leader, he became more and more upset. He finally

agreed, however, that the results of the survey confirmed
feelings he had been afraid to admit to himself or others.
For years, he had been miserable in his managerial role. He
now knew the reason: he simply did not want to nor had
he been able to influence or manage others. As he thought
back, he realized that he had failed every time he had tried
to influence his staff, and he felt worse than ever.

Ken had responded to failure by setting very high
standards—his office scored in the 98th percentile on
this scale—and by trying to do most things himself,
which was close to impossible; his own activity and lack
of delegation consequently left his staff demoralized.
Ken's experience is typical of those who have a strong
need to achieve but low power motivation. They may
become very successful salespeople and, as a consequence, may be promoted into managerial jobs for which
they, ironically, are unsuited.

If achievement motivation does not make a good
manager, what motive does? It is not enough to suspect
that power motivation may be important; one needs hard
evidence that people who are better managers than Ken
Briggs do in fact possess stronger power motivation and
perhaps score higher in other characteristics as well. But
how does one decide who is the better manager?

Real-world performance measures are hard to come by
if one is trying to rate managerial effectiveness in production marketing finance, or research and development. In
trying to determine who the better managers were in Ken
Briggs's company, we did not want to rely only on the
opinions of their superiors. For a variety of reasons, superiors' judgments of their subordinates' real-world performance may be inaccurate. In the absence of some standard
measure of performance, we decided that the next best
index of managers' effectiveness would be the climate they
create in the office reflected in the morale of subordinates.

Almost by definition, a good manager is one who,
among other things, helps subordinates feel strong and
responsible, who rewards them properly for good performance, and who sees that things are organized in such a way
that subordinates feel they know what they should be doing.
Above all, managers should foster among subordinates a
strong sense of team spirit, of pride in working as part of a
particular team. If a manager creates and encourages this
spirit, the subordinates certainly should perform better.

In the company Ken Briggs works for, we have direct
evidence of a connection between morale and performance in the one area where performance measures are
easy to come by—namely, sales. In April 1973, at least
three employees from this company's 16 sales districts

WORKSHOP TECHNIQUES

The case studies and data on companies used in this article were derived from a number of workshops we conducted where executives came to learn about their managerial styles and abilities as well as how to change them. The workshops had a dual purpose, however. They provided an opportunity for us to study which motivation pattern. whether it be a concern for achievement, power, people, or a combination thereof, makes the best managers.

When the managers first arrived at the workshops, they were asked to fill out a questionnaire about their job. Participants analyzed their jobs. explaining what they thought it required of them. The managers were asked to write a number of stories to pictures of various work situations. The stories were coded for the extent to which individuals were concerned about achievement, affiliation, or power, as well as for the amount of inhibition or self-control they revealed. The results were then matched against national norms. The differences between people's job requirements and their motivational patterns can often help assess whether they are in the right job, whether they are candidates for promotion to another job, or whether they are likely to be able to adjust to fit their present positions.

At the workshops and in this article, we use the technical terms "need for achievement," "need for power," and "need for affiliation" as defined in the books *The Achieving Society* and *Power: The Inner Experience.* The terms refer to measurable factors in groups and individuals. Briefly, these characteristics are measured by coding an individual's spontaneous thoughts for the frequency with which he thinks about doing something better or more efficiently than before (need for achievement), about establishing or maintaining friendly relations with others (need for affiliation), or about having impact on others (need for power). (When we talk about power, we are not talking about dictatorial power, but about the need to be strong and influential.) As used here, therefore. the motive labels are precise terms, referring to a particular method of defining and measuring, much as "gravity" is used in physics, or "gross national product" is used in economics.

To find out what kind of managerial style the participants had, we gave them a questionnaire in which they had to choose how they would handle various realistic work situations in office settings. Their answers were coded for six different management styles or ways of dealing with work situations. The styles depicted were democratic, affiliative, pacesetting, coaching, coercive, and authoritarian. The managers were asked to comment on the effectiveness of each style and to name the style that they prefer.

One way to determine how effective managers are is to ask the people who work for them. Thus, to isolate the characteristics that good managers have, we surveyed at least three subordinates of each manager at the workshop to see how they answered questions about their work situations that revealed characteristics of their supervisors along several dimensions, namely: (1) the amount of conformity to rules required, (2) the responsibility they feel they are given, (3) the emphasis the department places on standards of performance, (4) the degree to which they feel rewards are given for good work as opposed to punishment for something that goes wrong, (5) the degree of organizational clarity in the office. and (6) its team spirit.[1] The managers who received the highest morale scores (organizational clarity plus team spirit) from their subordinates were determined to be the best managers, possessing the most desirable motive patterns.

The subordinates were also surveyed six months after the managers returned to their offices to see if the morale scores rose after the workshop.

One other measure was obtained from the participants to find out which managers had another characteristic deemed important for good management: maturity. Scores were obtained for four stages in the progress toward maturity by coding the stories which the managers wrote for such matters as their attitudes toward authority and the kinds of emotions displayed over specific issues.

People in Stage I are dependent on others for guidance and strength. Those in Stage II are interested primarily in autonomy, in controlling themselves. In Stage III, people want to manipulate others; in Stage IV, they lose their egotistic desires and wish to selflessly serve others.[2]

The conclusions presented in this article are based on workshops attended by over 500 managers from over 25 different U.S. corporations. However, the data in the exhibits are drawn from just one of these companies for illustrative purposes.

---

[1]Based on G.H. Litwin and R.A. Stringer's *Motivation and Organizational Climate* (Boston: Division of Research, Harvard Business School, 1966).

[2]Based on work by Abigail Stewart reported in David C. McClelland's *Power: The Inner Experience* (New York: Irvington Publishers, 1975).

filled out questionnaires that rated their office for organizational clarity and team spirit (see the shaded box). Their scores were averaged and totaled to give an overall morale score for each office. The percentage gains or losses in sales for each district in 1973 were compared with those for 1972. The difference in sales figures by district ranged from a gain of nearly 30% to a loss of 8%, with a median gain of around 14%. Exhibit 4.1 shows the average gain in sales performance plotted against the increasing averages in morale scores.

In Exhibit 4.1 we can see that the relationship between sales and morale is surprisingly close. The six districts with the lowest morale early in the year showed an average sales gain of only around 7% by years' end (although there was wide variation within this group), whereas the two districts with the highest morale showed an average gain of 28%. When morale scores rise above the 50th percentile in terms of national norms, they seem to lead to better sales performance. In Ken Briggs's company, at least, high morale at the beginning is a good index of how well the sales division actually performed in the coming year.

And it seems very likely that the manager who can create high morale among salespeople can also do the same for employees in other areas (production, design, and so on), leading to better performance. Given that high morale in an office indicates that there is a good manager present, what general characteristics does he or she possess?

A Need for Power

In examining the motive scores of over 50 managers of both high and low morale units in all sections of the same large company, we found that most of the managers—over 70%—were high in power motivation compared with men in general. This finding confirms the fact that power motivation is important for management. (Remember that as we use the term "power motivation," it refers not to dictatorial behavior, but to a desire to have impact, to be strong and influential.) The better managers, as judged by the morale of those working for them, tended to score even higher in power motivation. But the most important determining factor of high morale turned out not to be how their power motivation compared to their need to achieve but whether it was higher than their need to be liked. This relationship existed for 80% of the better sales managers as compared with only 10% of the poorer managers. And the same held true for other managers in nearly all parts of the company.

In the research, product development, and operations divisions, 73% of the better managers had a stronger need for power than a need to be liked (or what we term "affiliation motive") as compared with only 22% of the poorer managers. Why should this be so? Sociologists have long argued that, for a bureaucracy to function effectively, those who manage it must be universalistic in applying rules. That is, if they make exceptions for the particular needs of individuals, the whole system will break down.

The manager with a high need for being liked is precisely the one who wants to stay on good terms with everybody, and, therefore, is the one most likely to make exceptions in terms of particular needs. If an employee asks for time off to stay home with a sick spouse to help look after the kids, the affiliative manager, feeling sorry for the person, agrees almost without thinking.

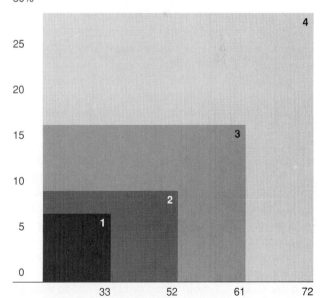

EXHIBIT 4.1

CORRELATION BETWEEN MORALE SCORE AND SALES PERFORMANCE FOR A LARGE U.S. CORPORATION

Average percent gain in sales by district from 1972 to 1973

Morale score (perceived organizational clarity plus team spirit)

1 = 6 districts   2 = 4 districts   3 = 4 districts   4 = 2 districts

When President Ford remarked in pardoning ex-President Nixon that he had "suffered enough," he was responding as an affiliative manager would, because he was empathizing primarily with Nixon's needs and feelings. Sociological theory and our data both argue, however, that the person whose need for affiliation is high does not make a good manager. This kind of person creates poor morale because he or she does not understand that other people in the office will tend to regard exceptions to the rules as unfair to themselves, just as many U.S. citizens felt it was unfair to let Richard Nixon off and punish others less involved than he was in the Watergate scandal.

Socialized Power

But so far our findings are a little alarming. Do they suggest that the good manager is one who cares for power and is not at all concerned about the needs of other people? Not quite, for the good manager has other characteristics which must still be taken into account.

Above all, the good manager's power motivation is not oriented toward personal aggrandizement but toward the institution which he or she serves. In another major research study, we found that the signs of controlled action or inhibition that appear when a person exercises his or her imagination in writing stories tell a great deal about the kind of power that person needs.[2] We discovered that, if a high power motive score is balanced by high inhibition, stories about power tend to be altruistic. That is, the heroes in the story exercise power on behalf of someone else. This is the "socialized" face of power as distinguished from the concern for personal power, which is characteristic of individuals whose stories are loaded with power imagery but which show no sign of inhibition or self-control. In our earlier study, we found ample evidence that these latter individuals exercise their power impulsively. They are more rude to other people, they drink too much, they try to exploit others sexually, and they collect symbols of personal prestige such as fancy cars or big offices.

Individuals high in power and in control, on the other hand, are more institution minded; they tend to get elected to more offices, to control their drinking, and to want to serve others. Not surprisingly, we found in the workshops that the better managers in the corporation also tend to score high on both power and inhibition.

[2]David C. McClelland, William N. Davis, Rudolf Kalin, and Erie Warner, *The Drinking Man* (New York: The Free Press, 1972).

Profile of a Good Manager

Let us recapitulate what we have discussed so far and have illustrated with data from one company. The better managers we studied are high in power motivation, low in affiliation motivation, and high in inhibition. They care about institutional power and use it to stimulate their employees to be more productive. Now let us compare them with affiliative managers—those in whom the need for affiliation is higher than the need for power—and with the personal power managers—those in whom the need for power is higher than for affiliation but whose inhibition score is low.

In the sales division of our illustrative company, there were managers who matched the three types fairly closely. Exhibit 4.2 shows how their subordinates rated the offices they worked in on responsibility, organizational clarity, and team spirit. There are scores from at least three subordinates for each manager, and several managers are represented for each type, so that the averages shown in the exhibit are quite stable. Note that the manager who is concerned about being liked by people tends to have subordinates who feel that they have very little personal responsibility, that organizational procedures are not clear, and that they have little pride in their work group.

In short, as we expected, affiliative managers make so many ad hominem and ad hoc decisions that they almost totally abandon orderly procedures. Their disregard for procedure leaves employees feeling weak, irresponsible, and without a sense of what might happen next, of where they stand in relation to their manager, or even of what they ought to be doing. In this company, the group of affiliative managers portrayed in Exhibit 4.2 were below the 30th percentile in morale scores.

The managers who are motivated by a need for personal power are somewhat more effective. They are able to create a greater sense of responsibility in their divisions and, above all, a greater team spirit. They can be thought of as managerial equivalents of successful tank commanders such as General Patton, whose own daring inspired admiration in his troops. But notice how in Exhibit 4.2 these men are still only in the 40th percentile in the amount of organizational clarity they create, as compared to the high power, low affiliation, high inhibition managers, whom we shall term "institutional."

Managers motivated by personal power are not disciplined enough to be good institution builders, and often their subordinates are loyal to them as individuals rather than to the institution they both serve. When a personal power manager leaves, disorganization often follows. His subordinates' strong group spirit, which the manager has personally inspired, deflates. The subordinates do not know what to do for themselves.

Of the managerial types, "institutional" managers are the most successful in creating an effective work climate. Exhibit 4.2 shows that their subordinates feel that they have more responsibility. Also, these managers create high morale because they produce the greatest sense of organizational clarity and team spirit. If such a manager leaves, he or she can be more readily replaced by another manager, because the employees have been encouraged to be loyal to the institution rather than to a particular person.

Managerial Styles

Since it seems undeniable from Exhibit 4.2 that either kind of power orientation creates better morale in subordinates than a "people" orientation, we must consider that a concern for power is essential to good management. Our findings seem to fly in the face of a long and influential tradition of organizational psychology which insists that authoritarian management is what is wrong with most businesses in this country. Let us say frankly that we think the bogeyman of authoritarianism has in fact been wrongly used to downplay the importance of power in management. After all management is an influence game. Some proponents of democratic management seem to have forgotten this fact, urging managers to be primarily concerned with people's human needs rather than with helping them to get things done.

But a good deal of the apparent conflict between our findings and those of other behavioral scientists in this area arises from the fact that we are talking about *motives,* and behaviorists are often talking about *actions.* What we are saying is that managers must be interested in playing the influence game in a controlled way. That does not necessarily mean that they are or should be authoritarian in action. On the contrary, it appears that power motivated managers make their subordinates feel strong rather than weak. The true authoritarian in action would have the reverse effect, making people feel weak and powerless.

Thus another important ingredient in the profile of a manager is his or her managerial style. In the illustrative company, 63% of the better managers (those whose subordinates had higher morale) scored higher on the democratic or coaching styles of management as compared with only 22% of the poorer managers, a statistically significant difference. By contrast, the latter scored higher on authoritarian or coercive management styles. Since the better

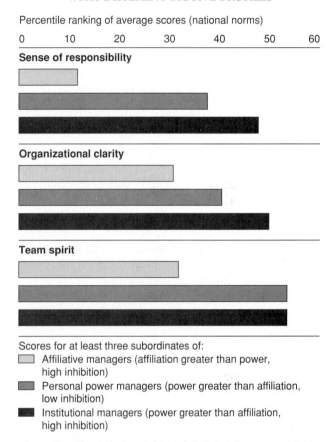

EXHIBIT 4.2

AVERAGE SCORES ON SELECTED CLIMATE DIMENSIONS BY SUBORDINATES OF MANAGERS WITH DIFFERENT MOTIVE PROFILES

Percentile ranking of average scores (national norms)

Scores for at least three subordinates of:
- Affiliative managers (affiliation greater than power, high inhibition)
- Personal power managers (power greater than affiliation, low inhibition)
- Institutional managers (power greater than affiliation, high inhibition)

managers were also higher in power motivation, it seems that, in action, they express their power motivation in a democratic way, which is more likely to be effective.

To see how motivation and style interact, let us consider the case of George Prentice, a manager in the sales division of another company. George had exactly the right motive combination to be an institutional manager. He was high in the need for power, low in the need for affiliation, and high in inhibition. He exercised his power in a controlled, organized way. His stories reflected this fact. In one, for instance, he wrote, "The men sitting around the table were feeling pretty good; they had just finished plans for reorganizing the company; the company has been beset with a number of organizational problems. This group, headed by a hard-driving, brilliant young executive, has completely reorganized the company structurally with new jobs and responsibilities. . . ."

This described how George himself was perceived by the company, and shortly after the workshop he was promoted to vice president in charge of all sales. But George was also known to his colleagues as a monster, a tough guy who would "walk over his grandmother" if she stood in the way of his advancement. He had the right motive combination and, in fact, was more interested in institutional growth than in personal power, but his managerial style was all wrong. Taking his cue from some of the top executives in the corporation, he told people what they had to do and threatened them with dire consequences if they didn't do it.

When George was confronted with his authoritarianism in a workshop, he recognized that this style was counterproductive—in fact, in another part of the study we found that it was associated with low morale—and he subsequently changed to acting more like a coach, which was the scale on which he scored the lowest initially. George saw more clearly that his job was not to force other people to do things but to help them to figure out ways of getting their job done better for the company.

The Institutional Manager

One reason it was easy for George Prentice to change his managerial style was that in his imaginative stories he was already having thoughts about helping others, characteristic of people with the institution-building motivational pattern. In further examining institution builders' thoughts and actions, we found they have four major characteristics:

1. They are more organization-minded; that is, they tend to join more organizations and to feel responsible for building up these organizations. Furthermore, they believe strongly in the importance of centralized authority.
2. They report that they like to work. This finding is particularly interesting, because our research on achievement motivation has led many commentators to argue that achievement motivation promotes the "Protestant work ethic." Almost the precise opposite is true. People who have a high need to achieve like to get out of work by becoming more

efficient. They would like to see the same result obtained in less time or with less effort. But managers who have a need for institutional power actually seem to like the discipline of work. It satisfies their need for getting things done in an orderly way.
3. They seem quite willing to sacrifice some of their own self-interest for the welfare of the organization they serve. For example, they are more willing to make contributions to charities.
4. They have a keen sense of justice. It is almost as if they feel that if people work hard and sacrifice for the good of the organization, they should and will get a just reward for their efforts.

It is easy to see how each of these four concerns helps a person become a good manager, concerned about what the institution can achieve.

Maturity

Before we go on to look at how the workshops can help managers to improve their managerial style and recognize their own motivations, let us consider one more fact we discovered in studying the better managers at George Prentice's company. They were more mature (see the box on page 104). Mature people can be most simply described as less egotistic. Somehow their positive self-image is not at stake in what they are doing. They are less defensive, more willing to seek advice from experts, and have a longer range view. They accumulate fewer personal possessions and seem older and wiser. It is as if they have awakened to the fact that they are not going to live forever and have lost some of the feeling that their own personal future is all that important.

Many U.S. businesspeople fear this kind of maturity. They suspect that it will make them less hard driving, less expansion-minded, and less committed to organizational effectiveness. Our data do not support their fears. These fears are exactly the ones George Prentice had before he went to the workshop. Afterward he was a more effective manager, not despite his loss of some of the sense of his own importance, but because of it. The reason is simple: His subordinates believed afterward that he genuinely was more concerned about the company than about himself. Where once they respected his confidence but feared him, they now trust him. Once he supported their image of him as a "big man" by talking about the new Porsche and the new Honda he had bought; when we saw him recently he said, almost as an aside, "I don't buy things anymore."

Changing Managerial Style

George Prentice was able to change his managerial style after learning more about himself in a workshop. But does self-knowledge generally improve managerial behavior?

Some people might ask, "What good does it do to know, if I am a manager, that I should have a strong power motive, not too great a concern about being liked, a sense of discipline, a high level of maturity, and a coaching managerial style? What can I do about it?" The answer is that workshops for managers that give information to them in a supportive setting enable them to change.

Consider the results shown in Exhibit 4.3 where "before" and "after" scores are compared. Once again we use the responses of subordinates to give some measure of the effectiveness of managers. To judge by their subordinates' responses, the managers were clearly more effective afterward. The subordinates felt that they were given more responsibility, that they received more rewards, that the organizational procedures were clearer, and that morale was higher. These differences are all statistically significant.

But what do these differences mean in human terms? How did the managers change? Sometimes they decided they should get into another line of work. This happened to Ken Briggs, for example, who found that the reason he was doing so poorly as a manager was because he had almost no interest in influencing others. He understood how he would have to change if he were to do well in his present job, but in the end decided, with the help of management, that he would prefer to work back into his first love, sales.

Ken Briggs moved into "remaindering," to help retail outlets for his company's products get rid of last year's stock so that they could take on each year's new styles. He is very successful in this new role; he has cut costs, increased dollar volume, and in time has worked himself into an independent role selling some of the old stock on his own in a way that is quite satisfactory to the business. And he does not have to manage anybody anymore.

In George Prentice's case, less change was needed. He was obviously a very competent person with the right motive profile for a top managerial position. When

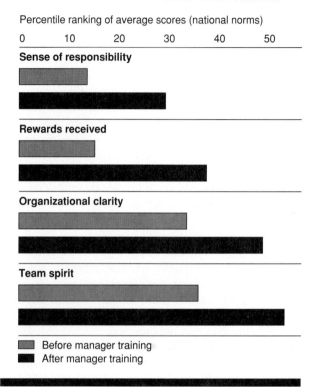

EXHIBIT 4.3

AVERAGE SCORES ON SELECTED CLIMATE DIMENSIONS BY OVER 50 SALESPEOPLE BEFORE AND AFTER THEIR MANAGERS WERE TRAINED

he was promoted, he performed even more successfully than before because he realized the need to become more positive in his approach and less coercive in his managerial style.

But what about people who do not want to change their jobs and discover that they do not have the right motive profile to be managers?

The case of Charlie Blake is instructive. Charlie was as low in power motivation as Ken Briggs, his need to achieve was about average, and his affiliation motivation was above average. Thus he had the affiliative manager profile, and, as expected, the morale among his subordinates was very low. When Charlie learned that his subordinates' sense of responsibility and perception of a reward system were in the 10th percentile and that team spirit was in the 30th, he was shocked. When shown a film depicting three managerial climates, Charlie said he preferred what turned out to be the authoritarian climate.

He became angry when the workshop trainer and other members in the group pointed out the limitations of this managerial style. He became obstructive in the group process and objected strenuously to what was being taught.

In an interview conducted much later, Charlie said, "I blew my cool. When I started yelling at you for being all wrong, I got even madder when you pointed out that according to my style questionnaire, you bet that that was just what I did to my salespeople. Down underneath I knew something must be wrong. The sales performance for my division wasn't so good. Most of it was due to me anyway and not to my salespeople. Obviously their reports that they felt very little responsibility was delegated to them and that I didn't reward them at all had to mean something. So I finally decided to sit down and try to figure what I could do about it. I knew I had to start being a manager instead of trying to do everything myself and blowing my cool at others because they didn't do what I thought they should. In the end, after I calmed down on the way back from the workshop, I realized that it is not so bad to make a mistake; it's bad not to learn from it."

After the course, Charlie put his plans into effect. Six months later, his subordinates were asked to rate him again. He attended a second workshop to study these results and reported, "On the way home I was very nervous. I knew I had been working with those people and not selling so much myself, but I was very much afraid of what they were going to say about how things were going in the office. When I found out that the team spirit and some of those other low scores had jumped from around 30th to the 55th percentile, I was so delighted and relieved that I couldn't say anything all day long."

When he was asked how he acted differently from before, he said, "In previous years when the corporate headquarters said we had to make 110% of our original goal, I had called the salespeople in and said, in effect, 'This is ridiculous; we are not going to make it, but you know perfectly well what will happen if we don't. So get out there and work your tail off.' The result was that I worked 20 hours a day and they did nothing.

"This time I approached it differently. I told them three things. First, they were going to have to do some sacrificing for the company. Second, working harder is not going to do much good because we are already working about as hard as we can. What will be required are special deals and promotions. You are going to have to figure out some new angles if we are to make it. Third, I'm going to back you up. I'm going to set a realistic goal with each of you. If you make that goal but don't make the company goal, I'll see to it that you are not punished. But if you do

make the company goal, I'll see to it that you will get some kind of special rewards."

When the sales people challenged Charlie saying he did not have enough influence to give them rewards, rather than becoming angry Charlie promised rewards that were in his power to give—such as longer vacations.

Note that Charlie has now begun to behave in a number of ways that we found to be characteristic of the good institutional manager. He is, above all, higher in power motivation, the desire to influence his salespeople, and lower in his tendency to try to do everything himself. He asks the salespeople to sacrifice for the company. He does not defensively chew them out when they challenge him but tries to figure out what their needs are so that he can influence them. He realizes that his job is more one of strengthening and supporting his subordinates than of criticizing them. And he is keenly interested in giving them just rewards for their efforts.

The changes in his approach to his job have certainly paid off. The sales figures for his office in 1973 were up more than 16% over 1972 and up still further in 1974 over 1973. In 1973 his gain over the previous year ranked seventh in the nation; in 1974 it ranked third. And he wasn't the only one in his company to change managerial styles. Overall sales at his company were up substantially in 1973 as compared with 1972, an increase which played a large part in turning the overall company performance around from a $15 million loss in 1972 to a $3 million profit in 1973. The company continued to improve its performance in 1974 with an 11% further gain in sales and a 38% increase in profits.

Of course not everyone can be reached by a workshop. Henry Carter managed a sales office for a company which had very low morale (around the 20th percentile) before he went for training. When morale was checked some six months later, it had not improved. Overall sales gain subsequently reflected this fact since it was only 2% above the previous year's figures.

Oddly enough, Henry's problem was that he was so well liked by everybody that he felt little pressure to change. Always the life of the party, he is particularly popular because he supplies other managers with special hard-to-get brands of cigars and wines at a discount. He uses his close ties with everyone to bolster his position in the company, even though it is known that his office does not perform well compared with others.

His great interpersonal skills became evident at the workshop when he did very poorly at one of the business games. When the discussion turned to why he had done so badly and whether he acted that way on the job, two prestigious participants immediately sprang to his defense, explaining away Henry's failure by arguing that the way he did things was often a real help to others and the company. As a result, Henry did not have to cope with such questions at all. He had so successfully developed his role as a likable, helpful friend to everyone in management that, even though his salespeople performed badly, he did not feel under any pressure to change.

Checks and Balances

What have we learned from Ken Briggs, George Prentice, Charlie Blake, and Henry Carter? Principally, we have discovered what motive combination makes an effective manager. We have also seen that change is possible if a person has the right combination of qualities.

Oddly enough, the good manager in a large company does not have a high need for achievement, as we define and measure that motive, although there must be plenty of that motive somewhere in the organization. The top managers shown here have a high need for power and an interest in influencing others, both greater than their interest in being liked by people. The manager's concern for power should be socialized—controlled so that the institution as a whole, not only the individual, benefits. People and nations with this motive profile are empire builders; they tend to create high morale and to expand the organizations they head.

But there is also danger in this motive profile; empire building can lead to imperialism and authoritarianism in companies and in countries.

The same motive pattern which produces good power management can also lead a company or a country to try to dominate others, ostensibly in the interests of organizational expansion. Thus it is not surprising that big business has had to be regulated from time to time by federal agencies. And it is most likely that international agencies will perform the same regulative function for empire-building countries.

For an individual, the regulative function is performed by two characteristics that are part of the profile of the very best managers—a greater emotional maturity, where there is little egotism, and a democratic, coaching managerial style. If an institutional power motivation is checked by maturity, it does not lead to an aggressive, egotistic expansiveness.

For countries, this checking means that they can control their destinies beyond their borders without being aggressive and hostile. For individuals, it means they can control their subordinates and influence others around them without resorting to coercion or to an authoritarian management style. Real disinterested statesmanship has a vital role to play at the top of both countries and companies.

Summarized in this way, what we have found out through empirical and statistical investigations may just sound like good common sense. But the improvement over common sense is that now the characteristics of the good manager are objectively known. Managers of corporations can select those who are likely to be good managers and train those already in managerial positions to be more effective with more confidence.

Whatever else organizations may be (problem-solving instruments, sociotechnical systems, reward systems, and so on), they are political structures. This means that organizations operate by distributing authority and setting a stage for the exercise of power. It is no wonder, therefore, that individuals who are highly motivated to secure and use power find a familiar and hospitable environment in business.
From "Power and Politics in Organizational Life," by Abraham Zaleznik, HBR May-June 1970, p. 47.

DISCUSSION QUESTIONS

1. What makes or motivates a good manager?
2. What is the achievement motive? What is the relationship of the achievement motive to good management?
3. What is the need for affiliation? How does it affect management?
4. What is the need for power? Why is it necessary for managers to have power?
5. What behavior is characteristic of managers who have a high need for achievement and a low need for power?
6. What do McClelland and Burnham mean by "socialized" power? What other type of power is there?
7. In what ways do effective managers differ from affiliative managers?

8. How does the use of power as McClelland and Burnham understand it differ from authoritarian management?

9. What are some techniques that can be used to change management styles?

10. Discuss implications of the statement: "The same motive pattern which produces good power management can also lead a company or a country to try to dominate others, ostensibly in the interests of organizational expansion."

For Further Reading

Alderfer, C. *Existence, Relatedness, and Growth: Human Needs in Organizational Settings.* New York: Free Press, 1972.

Bandura, A. *Social Foundations of Thought and Action: A Social Cognitive View.* New Jersey: Prentice Hall, 1986.

Herzberg, F. *Work and the Nature of Man.* New York: Crowell, 1966.

Katzell, R. "Work Motivation: Theory and Practice." *American Psychologist* 45 (1990)144-153.

Maslow, A. *Motivation and Personality,* 2nd ed. New York: Harper and Row, 1954.

McClelland, D. *The Achieving Society.* New Jersey: Van Nostrand Reinhold, 1961.

Skinner, B. *Science and Human Behavior.* New York: Free Press, 1953.

5

INDIVIDUAL DECISION MAKING

The Role of the Manager: What's Really Important in Different Management Jobs

ALLEN I. KRAUT, PATRICIA R. PEDIGO, D. DOUGLAS MCKENNA, AND MARVIN D. DUNNETTE

LEARNING OBJECTIVES

After reading "The Role of the Manager: What's Really Important in Different Management Jobs," by Kraut, Pedigo, McKenna, and Dunnette, a student will be able to:

1. Understand the roles and tasks of managers as they are practiced in organizations

2. Identify the different functions of management jobs at various levels in organizations

3. Recognize that the decision-making responsibilities in an organization differ with the level and function

4. Understand that decision making is an important aspect of managerial work but not the dominant task for most managers in an organization

Can we safely assume (to paraphrase Gertrude Stein) that "a manager is a manager is a manager"? Should we expect the jobs of all managers to be pretty much the same? And should managers expect their colleagues' jobs to be like their own? Well, "yes" and "no," according to the research described below. An analogy to team sports may help illustrate this answer, and suggest implications for organizational performance.

One of the signs of a successful athletic team is its almost uncanny ability to perform as a single unit, with the efforts of individual members blending seamlessly together. When this level of teamwork exists, unusual things happen. Quarterbacks complete blind passes, throwing the ball to spots on the field where they "know" their favorite receiver will be. The point guard playing basketball lobs a pass high above the basket, which enables a leaping teammate to catch it in midair and make a spectacular slam dunk. This level of teamwork requires a great deal of practice and natural ability, but members of the team must also have a clear understanding of their own roles, the roles of their teammates, and the way they must work together to be successful.

In addition to understanding specialized roles and assignments, players must also recognize the things that everyone, regardless of his or her position, must be ready and willing to do if the team is to win. When necessary, the quarterback must block like a lineman to allow the halfback to break free of the defense; diminutive kickers must tackle kick return specialists twice their size to stop a touchdown. The point is that the demands of a team sport call for each participant to be both a specialist and a generalist.

Management, we believe, is a team sport that makes similar demands of its players. Unfortunately, many executives (the "team captains") and managers do not recognize how managerial jobs are similar and yet different across organizational levels and functions. This lack of mutual understanding among management players can make it very difficult for

Source: Allen I. Kraut, Patricia R. Pedigo, D. Douglas McKenna, and Marvin D. Dunnette, "The Role of the Manager: What's Really Important in Different Management Jobs," *Academy of Management Executive* 1989; Vol. 3; No. 4. Copyright ©1989. Reprinted by permission.

them to appreciate one another's work and coordinate their work activities. It can make winning that much harder.

In addition to being able to coordinate work more effectively, executives who understand similarities and differences in managerial jobs gain other advantages. For example, they are better able to:

- Communicate performance expectations and feedback to subordinate managers.
- Prepare others and themselves for transitions to higher organizational levels or different functions.
- Forecast how different managers would perform if promoted or moved into a new function.
- Ensure that management training and development programs are targeted to fit the needs of managers as they change positions.
- Diagnose and resolve confusion regarding managerial roles, responsibilities, and priorities.

For the most part, research on managerial work has focused on the common denominators of management jobs. Indeed, a considerable amount of research has been published on this subject.[1] We, however, have recently completed a study designed to shed light on the *differences in management roles and activities across different levels and functions.* We started with a sample of 1,412 managers[2] and asked them to rate the relative importance of 57 managerial tasks to their jobs. Their choices included "Of utmost importance," "Of considerable importance," "Of moderate importance," "Of little importance," "Of no importance," and "I do not perform this task." Almost all tasks were rated "Of moderate importance" or higher.

Using these importance ratings, we statistically identified seven major factors or groups of management tasks[3]:

- Managing individual performance,
- Instructing subordinates
- Planning and allocating resources,
- Coordinating interdependent groups,
- Managing group performance,
- Monitoring the business environment, and
- Representing one's staff.

We then studied how important these seven factors and their component tasks were to managers at different levels and functions.

First-Level Managers: One-to-One with Subordinates

The first two factors involve supervising others. These activities are most important to first-level managers and decline in importance as one rises in management. (See Exhibit 5.1.)

"Managing individual performance" was rated the single most important set of activities by first-level management. Such tasks include motivating and disciplining subordinates, keeping track of performance and providing feedback, and improving communications and individual productivity. These tasks are traditionally associated with lower-level management. Although Exhibit 5.1 shows that many executives continue to see these tasks as very important, it is clear that their importance drops off as one moves up the management hierarchy.

The tasks in the "managing individual performance" set are listed in order of the percentage of the total sample who rated each as of "utmost" or "considerable" importance."

EXHIBIT 5.1

SUPERVISING INDIVIDUALS*

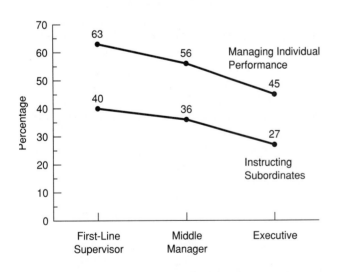

*Numbers refer to the percentage of managers who said the task was of "the utmost" or "considerable" importance.

76% Motivate subordinates to change or improve their performance.

76% Provide ongoing performance feedback to subordinates.

69% Take action to resolve performance problems in your work group.

69% Blend subordinates' goals (e.g., career goals, work performance) with company's work requirements.

63% Identify ways of improving communications among subordinates.

50% Keep track of subordinates' training and special skills as they relate to job assignments to aid their growth and development.

48% Resolve conflicts among subordinates.

40% Discipline and/or terminate personnel.

37% Review subordinates' work methods to identify ways to increase productivity.

The cluster "*instructing subordinates*" includes training, coaching, and instructing employees in how to do their job. Of moderate importance to most first-level managers, this cluster is considerably less important to executives.

For the "instructing subordinates" set, the items are listed below:

52% Inform subordinates about procedures and work assignments.

46% Explain work assignments to subordinates.

44% Provide technical expertise to help subordinates resolve work problems or questions.

43% Train subordinates in new technique or procedures.

6% Schedule daily activities of subordinates.

Middle Managers: Linking Groups

The concept of linking groups seems to drive the middle manager's work. Three task factors involve linking groups. The importance of these tasks jumps sharply (an average of 19 points) from first- to middle-level management. Thus, managers going from the lowest level of supervision to middle management need to develop skills in several new areas if they are to link groups successfully. The

importance of these drops slightly for executives (see Exhibit 5.2).

The most important tasks for middle management involve *"planning and allocating resources"* among different groups. Examples include estimating group resource requirements and making decisions about how resources should be distributed. One part of this cluster includes translating general directives into specific plans and communicating their benefits. Middle managers and executives see these tasks as crucial to their jobs.

The relative importance of the "planning and allocating resources" tasks is shown below:

72% Establis.h target dates for work products or services.

70% Estimate resource requirements for operational needs.

67% Develop evaluation criteria to measure progress and performance of operations.

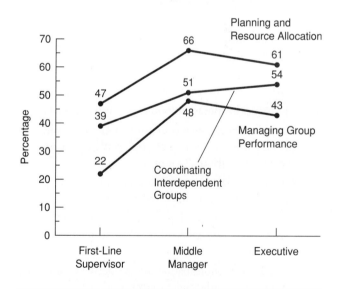

EXHIBIT 5.2

LINKING GROUPS*

*Numbers refer to the percentage of managers who said the task was of "the utmost" or "considerable" importance.

65% Decide which programs should be provided with resources (e.g., manpower, materials, funds, etc.).

63% Translate general directives (e.g., strategic plans) from superiors into specific operational plans/schedules/procedures, etc.

58% Communicate the benefits or opportunities posed by a new idea, proposal, project, or program.

40% Distribute budgeted resources.

Both middle managers and executives also rate *"coordinating interdependent groups"* as highly important to their jobs. This cluster includes reviewing the work and plans of various groups and helping them set priorities as well as negotiating and integrating various group plans and activities. This cluster—which involves bringing several efforts together to create a final product—jumps sharply in importance when a supervisor moves into higher management.

The tasks in "coordinating interdependent groups" were rated in this way:

70% Stay informed of the goals, actions, and agendas of top management.

60% Persuade other organizational groups to provide the information/products/resources needed by your work group.

58% Monitor events, circumstances, or conditions outside your work group that may affect its goals and/or performance.

53% Persuade other managers to provide support and/or resources for a new project or program.

51% Set priorities for responding to other groups.

50% Determine the possible effects of changes in the activities or outputs of your work group on other organizational groups.

45% Maintain awareness of the goals and plans of other groups within the organization.

44% Negotiate working agreements with other groups for the exchange of information, products, and/or services.

43% Ensure coordination of the activities and outputs of interdependent groups.

42% Provide advice or assistance to managers of other organizational groups.

39% Disseminate information about the activities of your work group to other groups.

27% Gather information on the needs/capabilities/resources (e.g., information, services) of other groups in the company.

Of the three factors most important to middle management, the biggest shift in importance occurs for the factor *"managing group performance."* This includes managing the performance of various work groups and working with subordinate managers on this performance.

Rated low in importance by first-level managers, "managing group performance" increases sharply (by 26 percentage points) in importance for those in middle management. It is the hallmark change for those going into middle management. While the middle manager must still monitor the performance of individual supervisors, measuring and managing group-level performance indicators becomes a significantly more important part of his or her responsibilities.

The items in "managing group performance," and their level of importance are as follows:

57% Define areas of responsibility for managerial personnel.

50% Inform managers when performance in their groups does not meet established goals or standards.

48% Meet with managers to discuss the likely effects of changes on their groups.

44% Monitor your work group's performance by reading reports, information system outputs, or other documents.

25% Prepare production and productivity reports.

23% Gather or review information on the activities and progress of several different work groups.

Executives: An Eye on the Outside

The activities encompassed in *"monitoring the business environment"* are a sharp shift in emphasis for managers reaching the executive ranks (see Exhibit 5.3). These activities require the executive to have an increased awareness of sales, business, economic, and social trends.

For managers below the executive ranks, these tasks rate the lowest in importance. At what point do managers need to become aware of and proficient in adopting new viewpoints for their high-level jobs? Clearly, executives find that this expanded perspective is a key requirement of their position.

The tasks involved in "monitoring the business environment" and their importance ratings are as follows:

47% Develop/maintain relationships with management-level customers or clients from the outside business community.

38% Participate in task forces to identify new business opportunities.

37% Monitor sales performance and promotional activities.

36% Gather information about trends outside your organization.

35% Identify developing market trends.

32% Develop/maintain relationships with management-level vendors or consultants in the business community.

31% Consult on companywide problems.

26% Attend outside meetings as a company representative.

20% Monitor multinational business and economic trends.

15% Release company information to the public (e.g., the news media).

Managers at All Levels: The Ambassador

Unlike the factors discussed earlier, which rise or drop in importance as the manager moves up the corporate ladder, *"representing your staff"* is ranked equally high by all levels of management (see Exhibit 5.4). This is the spokesperson role, noted in earlier studies by Henry Mintzberg. It involves representing one's work group to others and includes communicating the needs of one's work group to others, helping subordinates interact with other groups, and acting as the work group's representative.

The importance ratings of tasks involved in "representing your staff" are as follows:

68% Develop relationships with managers of other organizational groups that may be able to provide your work group with information/products/services/resources.

59% Communicate the needs or requirements of your work group to managers of other organizational groups.

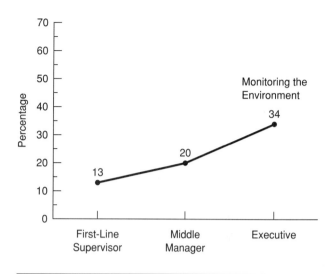

EXHIBIT 5.3

MONITORING THE BUSINESS ENVIRONMENT*

*Numbers refer to the percentage of managers who said the task was of "the utmost" or "considerable" importance.

58% Provide information on the status of work in your work group to managers of groups that depend on you for information/products/services/resources.

57% Determine the appropriate response(s) to managers demanding information/products/services/other resources from your work group.

48% Provide information or assistance to subordinates interacting with other organizational groups.

46% Communicate capabilities and resources of your work group to other managers in the organization.

39% Serve as an intermediary between your subordinates and managers of other organizational groups.

One might speculate that a big transition regarding such activities takes place when one is initially promoted into management. Until then individuals may have spoken only for themselves; thus, some ad adjustment is required before the manager will recognize and take on the role of group ambassador.

EXHIBIT 5.4

REPRESENTING PEOPLE*

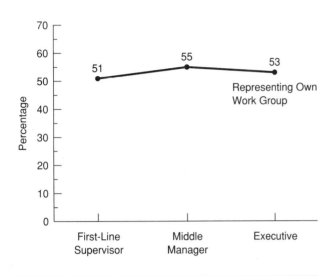

*Numbers refer to the percentage of managers who said the task was of "the utmost" or "considerable" importance.

Differences across Organizational Functions

Most managers would argue that different functions present significantly different management challenges. Our data permit some tests of this hypothesis.

We examined the importance of management tasks across three functions: (1) *marketing,* which includes managers in the sales and related support organization; (2) *manufacturing,* which includes managers in all phases of the manufacturing process; and (3) administration. which includes managers in finance, planning, and related staffs such as personnel.

As Exhibit 5.5 shows, the importance levels of managerial task factors are remarkably similar across functions, although some noteworthy differences exist. (The three levels of management are weighted equally in each function so that no one level has undue influence.) Marketing and administration appear to differ most in their rating of factors, with manufacturing falling in between.

"Instructing subordinates" is least important among marketing managers (27% said it was of "the utmost" or "considerable importance"), perhaps because so much of the training of marketing employees is done in corporate-sponsored programs. In administration, however, where many highly specific staff jobs and relatively little formal corporate training exists (at least in this company), "instructing subordinates" is a relatively more important management activity.

On the other hand, we suspect that a high level of professionalism among most administrative staff reduces the emphasis that their managers place on "managing individual performance" (50%). This factor, by contrast, is considerably more important in marketing (59%).

"Representation" is rated highest in importance by managers in marketing (59%). Obviously, these managers represent the company's products to others, mainly customers. By contrast. the demand for representing one's staff is 11 points lower among managers in administration. These relative differences apply also for "planning and allocating resources," which is rated highest by marketing (63%) and manufacturing (59%), and lowest by administration (52%). The activities involved in coordinating interdependent work groups is equally important for all three functions (47%).

"Managing group performance" is of somewhat higher importance to the managers in manufacturing (43%) and somewhat lower to managers in administration (32%). Presumably the administration function is made up of more specialists and professionals who work alone.

The activities involved in "monitoring the outside business environment" take on the highest importance for managers in marketing (32%). This external orientation, which results from their interaction with customers and need to remain current on competitors' products and marketing strategies, should not be too surprising.

Overall, our data suggest there are indeed differences in the importance of various managerial tasks across functions. Nevertheless, the similarities across the entire spectrum of functions are clearly more striking. (Such conclusions are also suggested in the findings of Cynthia M. Pavett and Alan W. Lau in their extension of Mintzberg's work.[4]) This suggests that a common approach to selecting, training, and developing managers may be both feasible and desirable for many functions in an organization.

Where significant differences do exist across functions, a common management development program or cross-functional work assignments may make managers more aware of different functions' perspectives, and help them avoid seeing all managers' jobs as either the same or

EXHIBIT 5.5

THE IMPORTANCE OF MANAGERIAL ACTIVITIES*

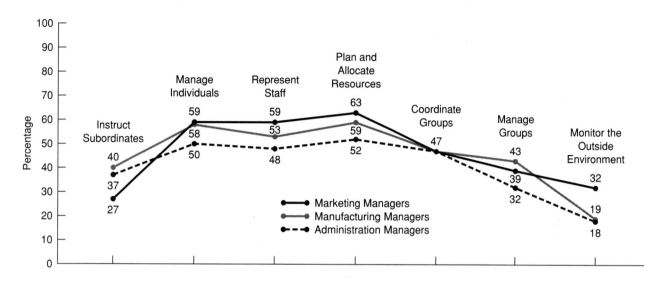

*Numbers refer to the percentage of managers who said the task was of "the utmost" or "considerable" importance.

unique. As John Kotter has noted in his work on executive behavior, people with narrow functional backgrounds who are promoted into general management positions may face a very difficult transition.[5]

Appropriate preparation may minimize such hardships.

Theoretical Implications

While we think this study has a number of practical implications that can help organizations make more effective use of their managerial resources, it is important to consider its limitations as well. First, the data are based on managers' own perceptions of the importance of various tasks. Certainly their bosses, peers, and subordinates may have a different view of things.[6] Second because we took a "snapshot" of managers at different levels, rather than following a group of managers over time, we cannot be certain that managers will experience the differences we describe as they move to higher-level management jobs; however, because the company whose managers we surveyed strictly follows a "promote from within" policy, it seems likely that the differences we note are indeed changes accompanying upward moves.

Despite these limitations, the study provides a carefully gathered record of the role and task perceptions of a large sample of real managers working in a diverse array of positions. As we noted at the beginning of this article, the results can be interpreted as supportive of Mintzberg's view that managerial jobs involve essentially the same managerial roles[7] as well as Katz and Kahn's argument that managers do different things at different levels.[8]

In support of Mintzberg, we found that managers at all levels rated most of the tasks on the questionnaire of some importance. The differences we observed were typically differences in the degree of importance of the tasks, not differences in whether the tasks were important at all. Yet, as Katz and Kahn would maintain, these differences are significant. Considering the costs of a manager's time, the difference between outstanding and average performance may well depend on the priority he or she assigns to each of the many tasks that are basically important.[9]

Practical Implications

How should we prepare our managers to meet the various demands that different managerial roles place on them? Who should we select to move up the management hierarchy? What training can we provide? How can we develop the skills essential for the manager's and team's success? The findings of this study provide some clues as to how a winning team can be fostered by training, development, and selection.

Training

Typically, management training has emphasized the basics of management: individually focused supervision, motivation, career planning, and performance feedback. All of these aspects should clearly be a central focus in the training of first-level managers. Given that managers continue to use these skills as they move up the hierarchy, periodic reinforcement also seems appropriate. Our study, however, indicates that training for managers above the first level must cover more than these one-to-one skills.

To help middle managers deal successfully with their responsibilities for managing and linking groups, training at this level should focus on skills needed for designing and implementing effective group and inter-group work and information systems; defining and monitoring group-level performance indicators; diagnosing and resolving problems within and among work groups; negotiating with peers and superiors; and designing and implementing reward systems that support cooperative behavior. As these topics suggest, the psychology of the individual, so important to the first-level manager, gives way to social psychology and sociology when one reaches middle management. Since the latter topics are generally less well known and more abstract than the former, it is not surprising that the transition to middle management can be very confusing and disorienting.

The executive's need to emphasize the external environment can also be partially addressed through training. The curriculum should focus on broadening the executive's understanding of the organization's competition, world economies, politics, and social trends. A number of executive training institutes and university-based programs are geared toward providing these broadening experiences; however, we think it is a serious mistake to wait until a person becomes an executive before teaching him or her to recognize the importance of attending to the relationship between the business and its environment. Consider the potential advantages of having middle and lower-level managers who understand the nature and strategic direction of their organization's business and are constantly on the lookout for opportunities and threats in the environment. We think this perspective should receive continuous attention in management training and development efforts at all levels.

Development

Planned development programs can also contribute to expanding the skill base of managers. At the first level, experiences such as filling in for the middle manager during vacation times, acting as a liaison between linked functions, or representing the entire function at important meetings can build group management and coordination skills.

For the middle manager, increased customer contact, visits to other organizations, and subscriptions to important business and trade publications can help impart the skills necessary for the executive ranks.

Selection

The results of this study also have implications for the selection of managers. Given our findings, it should not be surprising that executives are often chosen from the marketing function; these people have had their eyes on the outside environment for the majority of their careers. Yet through planned development, employees and managers from other functions can also acquire the skills required in executive management, and their contribution to overall decision making can be significant.

A Winning Team

The results of this study clearly identify the different roles that managers play and can provide organizations with the framework for building management training and development programs. By understanding the common and different roles played by managers as they move up the management hierarchy, we can develop programs that ensure that these managers have the skills needed to put together a winning team.

NOTES

[1] The questionnaire used in this study was based on an extensive review of research on managerial activities. A classic work in this area is *Management Behavior, Performance, and Effectiveness,* by J. P. Campbell, M. D. Dunnette, E. E. Lawler. and K. Weick, New York: McGraw-Hill, 1970. Another work that strongly influenced The questionnaire because of its depiction of The dynamic quality of managerial work, is L. Sayles's *Leadership,* New York: McGraw-Hill, 1979, aptly subtitled "What Effective Managers Really Do and How They Do It."

[2] This study was conducted by the authors in a large U.S. business enterprise. A random sample, designed to overrepresent higher-strata managers, resulted in 1,412 respondents: 658 first-line managers, 553 middle managers, and 201 executives. After extensive pretesting, a list of 65 activities was used on The final survey questionnaire. Through statistical analyses, these activities were "factored." or grouped, into seven sets, which comprised 57 activities. (Eight activities fit poorly into the seven sets and were dropped.)

Despite, or perhaps because, we used a literature search as the basis for our list of activities, some activities valued in this and other organizations may not have appeared in our survey. In passing we might mention that the importance placed on various activities is not necessarily related to "good" performance. The correlation between importance and effectiveness has simply not been examined in this study. By the same token, these activities are not necessarily the "correct" or "best" ones for any particular position. It remains to be determined which activities are desirable or appropriate, especially for the future.

[3] Other investigators have studied patterns of management tasks. For example, James MacDonald and his colleagues (Charles Youngblood and Kerry Glum report their comprehensive effort to determine training needs of first- and second-level supervisors working at AT&T in their book *Performance Based Supervisory Development,* Amherst, MA: Human Resource Development Press, 1982. Since they were concerned specifically with developing training guidelines, their categories of management (listed below) are much more focused on knowledge and skill development than are The seven behavioral factors developed in our investigation. Their categories of supervision include the following:

Planning the job
Controlling the job
Providing performance feedback
Managing time
Decision making
Problem solving
Maintaining upward communications
Maintaining downward communications
Maintaining peer communications
Creating a motivating atmosphere
Developing subordinates
Self-development

Providing written communications
Involvement with meetings
Community relations

Of more direct relevance to our work is the recent work reported by Fred Luthans, Stuart Rosenkrantz, and Harry Hennessey in "What Do Successful Managers Really Do? An Observation Study of Managerial Activities," *The Journal of Applied Behavioral Science,* 21(2), l9BS, 255-270. See also Fred Luthans, Successful vs. Effective Real Managers," *The Academy of Management Executive.* May 1988, 127-132. Luthans and his colleagues observed and recorded the actual activities of managers at all management levels and in many types of organizations. Observations were recorded according to four categories: *communication,* consisting of exchanging information and processing paperwork; *traditional management,* consisting of planning, decision making, and controlling; *human resource management,* consisting of motivating, disciplining, managing conflict, staffing, and training/developing: and *networking,* consisting of socializing, politicking, and interacting with outsiders.

It should be noted that the seven factors developed from our investigation encompass all the categories studied by MacDonald and Luthans in their earlier investigations.

[4] See C. M. Pavett and A. W. Lau, "Managerial Work: The Influence of Hierarchical Level and Functional Specialty." *Academy of Management Journal,* 26(1),1963, 170-177.

[5] See J. P. Kotter, *The General Managers,* New York: Free Press, 1982.

[6] An excellent review of The pro's and con's of various means to study managerial work is The report "Studies of Managerial Work: Results and Methods," by M. W. McCall, A. M. Morrison, and R. L. Kaplan, Greensboro, NC: Center for Creative Leadership, 1975.

[7] A well-known book on this subject, Henry Mintzberg's *The Nature of Managerial Work,* New York, Harper, 1973, is based on observations of a dozen chief executive officers. His work has been replicated by others, such as L. B. Kurke and H. E. Aldrich, "Mintzberg Was Right!: A Replication and Extension of the Nature of Managerial Work, *Management Science,* 29, 8, l983, 975-984.

[8] D. Katz and R. L. Kahn's *Social Psychology of Organizations* (2nd Ed.), New York: Wiley, 1978, presents a view of very different demands, cognitive and emotional, on managers at various levels in an organization.

[9] Finally, some further support for the argument that managers do some things differently al various levels was shown in one of Luthans' earlier investigations based on observations of some 53 managers (see Note 3). Comparisons between top executives and front-line supervisors revealed that executives engaged in much more networking, considerably more planning and decision making, and less staffing than front-line supervisors. These results are certainly compatible with ours.

DISCUSSION QUESTIONS

1. What is the reason for studying *differences* in management jobs?

2. What are the most important activities of first-level managers?

3. What is the central task of middle managers? How is this task accomplished?

4. What is the main concern of managers at the executive level?

5. Define the spokesperson role that managers play and discuss its importance to organization members.

6. Discuss implications of the finding that "the importance levels of managerial task factors are remarkably similar across functions."

7. In what way is decision making different at first-level supervisory jobs, middle-level management and the executive level?

8. What are the limitations of the findings in this study? How could the data be improved?

Making Management Decisions: The Role of Intuition and Emotion

Herbert A. Simon

LEARNING OBJECTIVES

After reading Herbert Simon's "Making Management Decisions: The Role of Intuition and Emotion," students will:

1. Understand the role of intuition and emotion in decision making

2. Differentiate highly structured decision-making opportunities from those that are loosely structured and those that occur during interpersonal interaction

3. Become familiar with the contributions of cognitive science and artificial intelligence in the study of decision making and management

4. Apply the insights of cognitive science and artificial intelligence research to the analysis of decision making in organizations

The work of a manager includes making decisions (or participating in their making), communicating them to others, and monitoring how they are carried out. Managers must know a great deal about the industry and social environment in which they work and the decision-making process itself to make decisions well. Over the past 40 years, the technique of decision making has been greatly advanced by the development of a wide range of tools—in particular, the tools of operations research and management science, and the technology of expert systems.

But these advances have not applied to the entire domain of decision making. They have had their greatest impact on decision making that is well-structured, deliberative, and quantitative; they have had less impact on decision making that is loosely structured, intuitive, and qualitative; and they have had the least impact on face-to-face interactions between a manager and his or her coworkers—the give and take of everyday work.

In this article, I will discuss these two relatively neglected types of decision making: "intuitive" decision making and decision making that involves interpersonal interaction. What, if anything, do we know about how judgmental and intuitive processes work and how they can be made to work better? And why do managers often fail to do what they know they should do—even what they have decided to do? What can be done to bring action into closer accord with intention?

My article will therefore have the form of a diptych, with one half devoted to each of these topics. First, I will discuss judgmental and intuitive decision making; then I will turn to the subject of the manager's behavior and the influence of emotions on that behavior.

Sometimes the term rational (or logical) is applied to decision making that is consciously analytic, the term nonrational to decision making that is intuitive and judgmental, and the term irrational to decision making and behavior that responds to the emotions or that deviates from action chosen "rationally." We will be concerned, then, with the nonrational and the irrational components of managerial decision making and behavior. Our task, you might say, is to discover the reason that underlies unreason.

Intuition and Judgment

As an appendix to *The Functions of the Executive* (Harvard University Press, 1938), Chester I. Barnard published an essay, based on a talk he had given in 1936 at Princeton, entitled "Mind in Everyday Affairs."[1] The central motif of that essay was a contrast between what Barnard called

Source: Herbert A. Simon, "Making Management Decisions: The Role of Intuition and Emotion," *Academy of Management Executive,* February, 1987, pp. 57–64. Copyright ©1987. Reprinted by permission.

"logical" and "nonlogical" processes for making decisions. He speaks of "the wide divergence of opinion . . . as to what constitutes a proper intellectual basis for opinion or deliberate action." And he continues:

> By "logical processes" I mean conscious thinking which could be expressed in words or by other symbols, that is, reasoning. By "non-logical processes" I mean those not capable of being expressed in words or as reasoning, which are only made known by a judgment, decision or action.

Barnard's thesis was that executives, as contrasted, say, with scientists, do not often enjoy the luxury of making their decisions on the basis of orderly rational analysis, but depend largely on intuitive or judgmental responses to decision-demanding situations.

Although Barnard did not provide a set of formal criteria for distinguishing between logical and judgmental decision making, he did provide a phenomenological characterization of the two styles that make them easily recognizable, at least in their more extreme forms. In logical decision making, goals and alternatives are made explicit, the consequences of pursuing different alternatives are calculated, and these consequences are evaluated in terms of how close they are to the goals.

In judgmental decision making, the response to the need for a decision is usually rapid, too rapid to allow for an orderly sequential analysis of the situation, and the decision maker cannot usually give a veridical account of either the process by which the decision was reached or the grounds for judging it correct. Nevertheless, decision makers may have great confidence in the correctness of their intuitive decisions and are likely to attribute their ability to make them rapidly to their experience.

Most executives probably find Barnard's account of their decision processes persuasive; it captures their own feelings of how processes work. On the other hand, some students of management, especially those whose goal is to improve management-decision processes, have felt less comfortable with it. It appears to vindicate snap judgments and to cast doubt on the relevance of management-science tools, which almost all involve deliberation and calculation in decision making.

Barnard did not regard the nonlogical processes of decision as magical in any sense. On the contrary, he felt they were grounded in knowledge and experience:

> The sources of these non-logical processes lie in physiological conditions or factors, or in the physical and social environment, mostly impressed upon us unconsciously or without conscious effort on our part. They also consist of he mass of facts, patterns, concepts, techniques, abstractions, and generally what we call formal knowledge or beliefs, which are impressed upon our minds more or less by conscious effort and study. This second source of nonlogical mental processes greatly increases with directed experience, study and education. (p. 302)

At the time I wrote *Administrative Behavior* (1941–42), I was troubled by Barnard's account of intuitive judgment (see the footnote on p. 51 of *AB*), largely, I think, because he left no clues as to what subconscious processes go on while judgments are being made.[2] I was wholly persuaded, however, that a theory of decision making had to give an account of both conscious and subconscious processes (see the end of p. 75 to the top of p. 76). I finessed the issue by assuming that both the conscious and the unconscious parts of the process were the same, that they involve drawing on factual premises and value premises, and operating on them to form conclusions that became the decisions.

Because I used logic (drawing conclusions from premises) as a central metaphor to describe the decision-making process, many readers of *Administrative Behavior* have concluded that the theory advanced there applies only to "logical" decision making, not to decisions that involve intuition and judgment. That was certainly not my intent. But now, after nearly 50 years, the ambiguity can be resolved because we have acquired a solid understanding of what the judgmental and intuitive processes are. I will take up the new evidence in a moment; but first, a word must be said about the "two brains" hypothesis, which argues that rational and intuitive processes are so different that they are carried out in different parts of the brain.

Split Brains and Forms of Thought

Physiological research on "split brains" brains in which the corpus callosum, which connects the two hemispheres of the cerebrum, has been severed—has provided encouragement to the idea of two qualitatively different kinds of decision making—the analytical, corresponding to Barnard's "logical," and the intuitive or creative, corresponding to his "non-logical." The primary evidence behind this dichotomy is that the two hemispheres exhibit a division of labor: in right-handed people, the right hemisphere plays a special role in the recognition of visual patterns, and the left hemisphere in analytical processes and the use of language.

Other evidence in addition to the split-brain research suggests some measure of hemispheric specialization. Electrical activity in the intact brain can be measured by EEG techniques. Activity in a brain hemisphere is generally associated with partial or total suppression in the hemisphere of the alpha system, a salient brain wave with a frequency of about ten vibrations per second. When a hemisphere is inactive, the alpha rhythm in that hemisphere becomes strong. For most right-handed subjects, when the brain is engaged in a task involving recognition of visual pattern, the alpha rhythm is relatively stronger in the left than in the right hemisphere; with more analytical tasks, the alpha rhythm is relatively stronger in the right hemisphere. (See Doktor and Hamilton, 1973, and Doktor, 1978, for some experiments and a review of the evidence.[3])

The more romantic versions of the split-brain doctrine extrapolate this evidence into the two polar forms of thought labeled above as analytical and creative. As an easy next step, evaluative nuances creep into the discussion. The opposite of "creative," after all, is "pedestrian." The analytical left hemisphere, so this story goes, carries on the humdrum, practical, everyday work of the brain, while the creative right hemisphere is responsible for those flights of imagination that produce great music, great literature, great art, great science, and great management. The evidence for this romantic extrapolation does not derive from the physiological research. As I indicated above, that research has provided evidence only for some measure of specialization between the hemispheres. It does not in any way imply that either hemisphere (especially the right hemisphere) is capable of problem solving, decision making, or discovery independent of the other. The real evidence for two different forms of thought is essentially that on which Barnard relied: the observation that, in everyday affairs, men and women often make competent judgments or reach reasonable decisions rapidly—without evidence indicating that they have engaged in systematic reasoning, and without their being able to report the thought processes that took them to their conclusion.

There is also some evidence for the very plausible hypothesis that some people, confronted with a particular problem, make more use of intuitive processes in solving it, while other people make relatively more use of analytical processes (Doktor, 1978).[3]

For our purposes, it is the differences in behavior, and not the differences in the hemispheres, that are important. Reference to the two hemispheres is a red herring that can only impede our understanding of intuitive, "non-logical" thought. The important questions for us are "What is

intuition?" and "How is it accomplished?" not "In which cubic centimeters of the brain tissue does it take place?"

New Evidence on the Processes of Intuition

In the 50 years since Barnard talked about the mind in everyday affairs, we have learned a great deal about the processes human beings use to solve problems, to make decisions, and even to create works of art and science. Some of this new knowledge has been gained in the psychological laboratory; some has been gained through observation of the behavior of people who are demonstrably creative in some realm of human endeavor; and a great deal has been gained through the use of the modern digital computer to model human thought processes and perform problem-solving and decision-making functions at expert levels.

I should like to examine this body of research, which falls under the labels of "cognitive science" and "artificial intelligence," to see what light it casts on intuitive, judgmental decision making in management. We will see that a rather detailed account can be given of the processes that underlie judgment, even though most of these process are not within the conscious awareness of the actor using them.

The Expert's Intuition

In recent years, the disciplines of cognitive science and artificial intelligence have devoted a great deal of attention to the nature of expert problem solving and decision making in professional-level tasks. The goal of the cognitive science research has been to gain an understanding of the differences between the behavior of experts and novices, and possibly to learn more about how novices can become experts. The goal of the artificial intelligence research has been to build computer systems that can perform professional tasks as competently as human experts can. Both lines of research have greatly deepened our understanding of expertise.[4]

Intuition in Chessplaying

One much studied class of experts is the grandmasters in the game of chess. Chess is usually believed to require a high level of intellect, and grandmasters are normally full-time professionals who have devoted many years to acquiring their mastery of the game. From a research standpoint, the advantage of the game is that the level of skill of players can be calibrated accurately from their official ratings, based on their tournament success.

From the standpoint of studying intuitive thinking, chess might seem (at least to outsiders) an unpromising research domain. Chess playing is thought to involve a highly analytical approach, with players working out systematically the consequences of moves and countermoves, so that a single move may take as much as a half hour's thought, or more. On the other hand, chess professionals can play simultaneous games, sometimes against as many as 50 opponents, and exhibit only a moderately lower level of skill than in games playing under tournament conditions. In simultaneous play, the professional takes much less than a minute, often only a few seconds, for each move. There is no time for careful analysis.

When we ask the grandmaster or master how he or she is able to find good moves under these circumstances, we get the same answer that we get from other professionals who are questioned about rapid decisions: It is done by "intuition," by applying one's professional "judgment" to the situation. A few seconds' glance at the position suggests a good move, although the player has no awareness of how the judgment was evoked.

Even under tournament conditions, good moves usually come to a player's mind after only a few seconds' consideration of the board. The remainder of the analysis time is generally spent verifying that a move appearing plausible does not have a hidden weakness. We encounter this same kind of behavior in other professional domains where intuitive judgments are usually subjected to tests of various kinds before they are actually implemented. The main exceptions are situations where the decision has to be made before a deadline or almost instantly. Of course we know that under these circumstances (as in professional chess when the allowed time is nearly exhausted), mistakes are sometimes made.

How do we account for the judgment or intuition that allows the chess grandmaster usually to find good moves in a few seconds? A good deal of the answer can be derived from an experiment that is easily repeated. First, present a grandmaster and a novice with a position from an actual, but unfamiliar, chess game (with about 2S pieces on the board). After five or ten seconds, remove the board and pieces and ask the subjects to reproduce it. The grandmaster will usually reconstruct the whole position correctly, and on average will place 23 or 24 pieces on their correct squares. The novice will only be able to replace, on average, about 6 pieces.

It might seem that we are witnessing remarkable skill in visual imagery and visual memory, but we can easily dismiss that possibility by carrying out a second experiment. The conditions are exactly the same as in the first experiment, except that now the 25 pieces are placed on the board at random. The novice can still replace about 6 pieces and the grandmaster—about 6! The difference between them in the first experiment does not lie in the grandmaster's eyes or imagery, but in his knowledge, acquired by long experience, of the kinds of patterns and clusters of pieces that occur on chessboards in the course of games. For the expert, such a chess board is not an arrangement of 25 pieces but an arrangement of a half dozen familiar patterns, recognizable old friends. On the random board there are no such patterns, only the 25 individual pieces in an unfamiliar arrangement.

The grandmaster's memory holds more than a set of patterns. Associated with each pattern in his or her memory is information about the significance of that pattern—what dangers it holds, and what offensive or defensive moves it suggests. Recognizing the pattern brings to the grandmaster's mind at once moves that may be appropriate to the situation. It is this recognition that enables the professional to play very strong chess at a rapid rate. Previous learning that has stored the patterns and the information associated with them in memory makes this performance possible. This, then, is the secret of the grandmaster's intuition or judgment.

Estimates have been made, in a variety of ways, of the number of familiar patterns (which psychologists now call chunks) that the master or grandmaster must be able to recognize. These estimates fall in the neighborhood of 50,000, give or take a factor of two. Is this a large number? Perhaps not. The natural language vocabularies of college graduates have been estimated to be in the range of 50,000 to 200,000 words, nearly the same range as the chess expert's vocabularies of patterns of pieces. Moreover, when we recognize a word, we also get access to information in our memories about the meaning of the word and to other information associated with it as well. So our ability to speak and understand language has the same intuitive or judgmental flavor as the grandmaster's ability to play chess rapidly.

Intuition in Computerized Expert Systems

A growing body of evidence from artificial intelligence research indicates that expert computer systems, capable of matching human performance in some limited domain, can be built by storing in computer memory tens of thousands of *productions.* Productions are computer instructions that take the form of "if-then" pairs. The "if" is a set of conditions or patterns to be recognized; the "then" is a body of information associated with the "if" and evoked from memory whenever the pattern is recognized in the current situation.

Some of our best data about this organization of expert knowledge come from the areas of medical diagnosis. Systems like CADUCEUS and MYCIN consist of a large number of such if-then pairs, together with an inference machine of modest powers. These systems are capable of medical diagnosis at a competent clinical level within their respective limited domains. Their recognition capabilities, the if-then pairs, represent their intuitive or judgmental ability; their inferencing powers represent their analytical ability.

Medical diagnosis is just one of a number of domains for which expert systems have been built. For many years, electric motors, generators, and transformers have been designed by expert systems developed by large electrical manufacturers. These computer programs have taken over from professional engineers many standard and relatively routine design tasks. They imitate fairly closely the rule-of-thumb procedures that human designers have used, the result of a large stock of theoretical and practical information about electrical machinery. Recognition also plays a large role in these systems. For example, examination of the customer's specifications "reminds" the program of a particular class of devices, which is then used as the basis for the design parameters for the design are then selected to meet the performance requirements of the device.

In chemistry, reaction paths for synthesizing organic molecules can be designed by expert systems. In these systems, the process appears relatively analytic, for it is guided by reasoning in the form of means-ends analyses, which work backward from the desired molecule, via a sequence of reactions, to available raw materials. But the reasoning scheme depends on a large store of knowledge of chemical reactions and the ability of the system to recognize rapidly that a particular substance can be obtained as the output of one or more familiar reactions. Thus, these chemical synthesis programs employ the same kind of mixture of intuition and analysis that is used in the other expert systems, and by human experts as well.

Other examples of expert systems can be cited, and all of them exhibit reasoning or analytic processes combined with processes for accessing knowledge banks with the help of recognition cues. This appears to be a universal scheme for the organization of expert systems—and of expert human problem solving as well.

Notice that there is nothing "irrational" about intuitive or judgmental reasoning based on productions. The conditions in a production constitute ; set of premises. Whenever these conditions are satisfied, the production draws the appropriate conclusion—it evokes from memory information implied by these conditions or even initiates motor responses. A person learning to drive a car may notice a red light, be aware that a red light calls for a stop, and be aware that stopping requires applying the brakes. For an experienced driver, the sight of the red light simply evokes the application of brakes. How conscious the actor is of the process inversely, how automatic the response is, may differ, but there is no difference in the logic being applied.

Intuition in Management

Some direct evidence also suggests that the intuitive skills of managers depend on the same kinds of mechanisms as the intuitive skills of chessmasters or physicians. It would be surprising if it were otherwise. The experienced manager, too, has in his or her memory a large amount of knowledge, gained from training and experience and organized in terms of recognizable chunks and associated information.

Marius J. Bouwman has constructed a computer program capable of detecting company problems from an examination of accounting statements.[5] The program was modeled on detailed thinking-aloud protocols of experienced financial analysts interpreting such statements, and it captures the knowledge that enables analysts to spot problems intuitively, usually at a very rapid rate. When a comparison is made between the responses of the program and the responses of an expert human financial analyst, a close match is usually found.

In another study, R. Bhaskar gathered thinking-aloud protocols from business school students and experienced businessmen, who were all asked to analyze a business policy case.[6] The final analyses produced by the students and the businessmen were quite similar. What most sharply discriminated between the novices and the experts was the time required to identify the key features of the case. This was done very rapidly, with the usual appearances of intuition, by the experts; it was done slowly, with much conscious and explicit analysis, by the novices.

These two pieces of research are just drops of water in a large bucket that needs filling. The description, in detail, of the use of judgmental and analytical processes in expert problem solving and decision making deserves a high priority in the agenda of management research.

Can Judgment Be Improved?

From this and other research on expert problem solving and decision making, we can draw two main conclusions. *First,* experts often arrive at problem diagnoses and solutions rapidly and intuitively without being able to report how they attained the result. *Second,* this ability is best explained by postulating a recognition and retrieval process that employs a large number—generally tens of thousands or even hundreds of thousands—of chunks or patterns stored in long-term memory.

When the problems to be solved are more than trivial, the recognition processes have to be organized in a coherent way and they must be supplied with reasoning capabilities that allow inferences to be drawn from the information retrieved, and numerous chunks of information to be combined. Hence intuition is not a process that operates independently of analysis; rather, the two processes are essential complementary components of effective decision-making systems. When the expert is solving a difficult problem or making a complex decision, much conscious deliberation may be involved. But each conscious step may itself constitute a considerable leap, with a whole sequence of automated productions building the bridge from the premises to the conclusions. Hence the expert appears to take giant intuitive steps in reasoning, as compared with the tiny steps of the novice.

It is doubtful that we will find two types of managers (at least, of good managers), one of whom relies almost exclusively on intuition, the other on analytic techniques. More likely, we will find a continuum of decision-making styles involving an intimate combination of the two kinds of skill. We will likely also find that the nature of the problem to be solved will be a principal determinant of the mix.

With our growing understanding of the organization of judgmental and intuitive processes, of the specific knowledge that is required to perform particular judgmental tasks, and of the cues that evoke such knowledge in situations in which it is relevant, we have a powerful new tool for improving expert judgment. We can specify the knowledge and the recognition capabilities that experts in a domain need to acquire as a basis for designing appropriate learning procedures.

We can also, in more and more situations. design expert systems capable of automating the expertise, or alternatively, of providing the human decision maker with an expert consultant. Increasingly, we will see decision aids for managers that will be highly interactive, with both knowledge and intelligence being shared between the human and the automated components of the system.

A vast research and development task of extracting and cataloging the knowledge and cues used by experts in different kinds of managerial tasks lies ahead. Much has been learned in the past few years about how to do this. More needs to be learned about how to update and improve the knowledge sources of expert systems as new knowledge becomes available.

Progress will be most rapid with expert systems that have a substantial technical component. It is no accident that the earliest expert systems were built for such tasks as designing motors, making medical diagnoses, playing chess, and finding chemical synthesis paths. In the area of management, the analysis of company financial statements is a domain where some progress has been made in constructing expert systems. The areas of corporate policy and strategy are excellent candidates for early development of such systems.

What about the aspects of executive work that involve the managing of people? What help can we expect in improving this crucial component of the management task?

Knowledge and Behavior

What managers know they should do—whether by analysis or intuitively is very often different from what they actually do. A common failure of managers, which all of us have observed, is the postponement of difficult decisions. What is it that makes decisions difficult and hence tends to cause postponement? Often, the problem is that all of the alternatives have undesired consequences. When people have to choose the lesser of two evils, they do not simply behave like Bayesian statisticians, weighing the bad against the worse in the light of their respective possibilities. Instead, they avoid the decision, searching for alternatives that do not have negative outcomes. If such alternatives are not available, they are likely to continue to postpone making a choice. A choice between undesirables is a dilemma, something to be avoided or evaded.

Often, uncertainty is the source of the difficulty. Each choice may have a good outcome under one set of environmental contingencies, but a bad outcome under another. When this occurs, we also do not usually observe Bayesian behavior; the situation is again treated as a dilemma.

The bad consequences of a manager's decision are often bad for other people. Managers sometimes have to dismiss employees or, even more frequently, have to speak; to them about unsatisfactory work. Dealing with such matters face to face is stressful to many, perhaps most, executives. The stress is magnified if the employee is a close associate or friend. If the unpleasant task cannot be delegated, it may be postponed.

The manager who has made a mistake (that is to say, all of us at one time or another) also finds himself or herself in a stressful situation. The matter must be dealt with sooner or later, but why not later instead of sooner? Moreover, when it is addressed, it can be approached in different ways. A manager may try to avoid blame—"It wasn't my fault!" A different way is to propose a remedy to the situation. I know of no systematic data on how often the one or the other course is taken, but most of us could probably agree that blame-avoiding behavior is far more common than problem-solving behavior after a serious error has been made.

The Consequences of Stress

What all of these decision-making situations have in common is stress, a powerful force that can divert behavior from the urgings of reason. They are examples of a much broader class of situations in which managers frequently behave in clearly nonproductive ways. Nonproductive responses are especially common when actions have to be made under time pressure. The need to allay feelings of guilt, anxiety, and embarrassment may lead to behavior that produces temporary personal comfort at the expense of bad long-run consequences for the organization.

Behavior of this kind is "intuitive" in the sense that it represents response without careful analysis and calculation. Lying, for example, is much more often the result of panic than of Machiavellian scheming. The intuition of the emotion-driven manager is very different from the intuition of the expert whom we discussed earlier. The latter's behavior is the product of learning and experience, and is largely adaptive; the former's behavior is a response to more primitive urges, and is more often than not inappropriate. We must not confuse the "nonrational" decisions of the experts—the decisions that derive from expert intuition and judgment—with the irrational decisions that stressful emotions may produce.

I have made no attempt here to produce a comprehensive taxonomy of the pathologies of organizational decision making, but simply have given some examples of the ways that stress interacts with cognition to elicit counterproductive behavior. Such responses can become so habitual for individuals or even for organizations that they represent a recognizable managerial "style."

Organizational psychologists have a great deal to say about ways of motivating workers and executives to direct their efforts toward organizational goals. They have said less about ways of molding habits so that executives can handle situations in a goal-directed manner. When it comes to handling situations, two dimensions of behavior deserve particular attention: the response to problems that arise, and the initiation of activity that looks to the future.

Responding to Problems

The response of an organization to a problem or difficulty, whether it results from a mistake or some other cause, is generally one that looks both backward and forward. It looks backward to establish responsibility for the difficulty and to diagnose it, and forward to find a course of action to deal with it.

The backward look is an essential part of the organization's reward system. The actions that have led to difficulties, and the people responsible for those actions, need to be identified. But the backward look can also be a source of serious pathologies. Anticipation of it—particularly anticipation that it will be acted on in a punitive way—is a major cause for the concealment of problems until they can no longer be hidden. It can also be highly divisive, as individuals point fingers to transfer blame to others. Such outcomes can hardly be eliminated, but an organization's internal reputation for fairness and objectivity can mitigate them. So can a practice of subordinating the blame finding to a diagnosis of causes as a first step toward remedial action.

Most important of all, however, is the forward look: the process of defining the problem and identifying courses of action that may solve it. Here also the reward system is critically important. Readiness to search for problem situations and effectiveness in finding them need to be recognized and rewarded.

Perhaps the greatest influence a manager can have on the problem-solving style of the organization as a role model is making the best responses to problems. The style the manager should aim for rests on the following principles:

1. Solving the problem takes priority over looking backward to its causes. Initially, backward looks should be limited to diagnosing causes; fixing responsibility for mistakes should be postponed until a solution is being implemented.
2. The manager accepts personal responsibility for finding and proposing solutions instead of seeking to shift that responsibility either to superiors or to subordinates, although the search for solutions may, of course, be a collaborative effort involving many people.
3. The manager accepts personal responsibility for implementing action solutions, including securing the necessary authority from above if required.
4. When it is time to look backward, fixing blame may be an essential part of the process, but the primary focus of attention should be on what can be learned to prevent similar problems from arising in the future.

These principles are as obvious as the Ten Commandments and perhaps not quite as difficult to obey. Earlier, I indicated that stress might cause departures from them, but failure to respond effectively to problems probably derives more from a lack of attention and an earlier failure to cultivate the appropriate habits. The military makes much use of a procedure called "Estimate of the Situation." Its value is not that it teaches anything esoteric, but that through continual training in its use, commanders become habituated to approaching situations in orderly ways, using the checklists provided by the formal procedure.

Habits of response to problems are taught and learned both in the manager's one-on-one conversations with subordinates and in staff meetings. Is attention brought back repeatedly to defining the problems until everyone is agreed on just what the problem is? Is attention then directed toward generating possible solutions and evaluating their consequences? The least often challenged and most reliable base of managerial influence is the power to set the agenda, to focus attention. It is one of the most effective tools the manager has for training organization members to approach problems constructively by shaping their own habits of attention.

The perceptive reader will have discerned that "shaping habits of attention" is identical to "acquiring intu-itions." The habit of responding to problems by looking for solutions can and must become intuitive—cued by the presence of the problem itself. A problem-solving style is a component of the set of intuitions that the manager acquires, one of the key components of effective managerial behavior.

Looking to the Future

With respect to the initiation of activity, the organizational habit we would like to instill is responsiveness to cues that signal future difficulties as well as to those that call attention to the problems of the moment. Failure to give sufficient attention to the future most often stems from two causes. The first is interruption by current problems that have more proximate deadlines and hence seem more urgent; the second is the absence of sufficient "scanning" activity that can pick up cues from the environment that long-run forces not impinging immediately on the organization have importance for it in the future.

In neither case is the need for sensitivity to the future likely to be met simply by strengthening intuitions. Rather, what is called for is deliberate and systematic allocation of organizational resources to deal with long-range problems, access for these resources to appropriate input from the environment that will attract their attention to new prospects, and protection of these planning resources from absorption in current problems, however urgent they may be. Attention to the future must be institutionalized; there is no simpler way to incorporate it into managerial "style" or habit.

It is a fallacy to contrast "analytic" and "intuitive" styles of management. Intuition and judgment—at least good judgment—are simply analyses frozen into habit and into the capacity for rapid response through recognition. Every manager needs to be able to analyze problems systematically (and with the aid of the modern arsenal of analytical tools provided by management science and operations research). Every manager needs also to be able to respond to situations rapidly, a skill that requires the cultivation of intuition and judgment over many years of experience and training. The effective manager does not have the luxury of choosing between "analytic" and "intuitive" approaches to problems. Behaving like a manager means having command of the whole range of management skills and applying them as they become appropriate.

NOTES

[1] Chester I. Barnard's (1938) *The Functions of the Executive* (Cambridge, Mass.: Harvard University Press), contains the essay on the contrast between logical and nonlogical processes as bases for decision making.

[2] H. A. Simon, (1978) *Administrative Behavior,* 2nd ed. New York: Free Press for a review of the artificial intelligence research on expert systems, see A. Barr and E. A. Figenbaum's (eds.) *The Handbook of Artificial Intelligence.* Vol. 2, Los Alamos, Cal.: William Kaufmann, 1982, pp. 77-294.

[3] Two works that examine the split brain theory and forms of thought are R. H. Doktor's "Problem Solving Styles of Executives and Management Scientists," in A. Charnes, W. W. Cooper, and R. J. Niehaus's (eds.) *Management Science Approaches to Manpower*

Planning and Organization Design (Amsterdam: North-Holland, 1978); and R. H. Doktor and W. F. Hamilton's Cognitive Style and the Acceptance of Management Science Recommendations" *(Management Science,* 19:884-894, 1973).

[4] For a survey of cognitive science research on problem solving and decision making, see H. A. Simon, (1979) *The Sciences of the Artificial,* 2nd ed., Cambridge, Mass.: The MIT Press, Chapters 3 and 4.

[5] Marius J. Bouwman's doctoral dissertation, *Financial Diagnosis* (Graduate School of Industrial Administration, Carnegie-Mellon University, 1978).

[6] R. Bhaskar's doctoral dissertation, *Problem Solving in Semantically Rich Domains* (Graduate School of Industrial Administration, Carnegie-Mellon University, 1978).

DISCUSSION QUESTIONS

1. According to Barnard, what are the major differences between logical and judgmental decision making?
2. What is the" split–brain" hypothesis? What are some misinterpretations of it?
3. What has been the goal of cognitive science research?
4. What implications for managerial decision making can be drawn from the experiments with chess players?
5. What does the term *production* mean as used in the creation of artificial intelligence?
6. In what ways can research findings improve judgment?
7. What effect does emotion—for example, stress—have on the ability of managers to make decisions?
8. List some of the things a manager can do to respond to problems.
9. Discuss the idea that managers at different levels use different decision-making pro-cesses. For example, do executives rely more on intuition than first-line supervisors?

FOR FURTHER READING

Beyer, J. "Ideologies, Values, and Decision Making in Organizations." In P. Nystrom and W. Starbuck (eds.). *Handbook of Organizational Design,* Vol. 2. New York: Oxford University Press, 1981.

Kotter, J. *The General Managers.* New York: Free Press, 1982.

March, J. "Bounded Rationality, Ambiguity, and the Engineering of Choice" *Bell Journal of Economics* Autumn (1978) 587-608.

Mintzberg, H. *The Nature of Managerial Work.* New York: Harper & Row, 1973.

Tversky, A., and Kahneman, D. "Rational Choice and the Framing of Decisions," *Journal of Business,* 59 (1986) 251–278.

6

CONFLICT AND STRESS IN ORGANIZATIONS

Managing Conflict

LEONARD GREENHALGH

LEARNING OBJECTIVES

After reading Greenhalgh's "Managing Conflict," a student will be able to:

1. Understand the dynamics of conflict in organizations

2. Identify sources of conflict in organizations, particularly under conditions of organizational change

3. Understand the basic principles of conflict management

4. Formulate interventions that can be used to resolve or control conflict

Managers or change agents spend a substantial proportion of their time and energy dealing with conflict situations. Such efforts are necessary because any type of change in an organization tends to generate conflict. More specifically, conflict arises because change disrupts the existing balance of resources and power, thereby straining relations between the people involved. Since adversarial relations may impede the process of making adaptive changes in the organization, higher level managers may have to intervene in order to implement important strategies. Their effectiveness in managing the conflict depends on how well they understand the underlying dynamics of the conflict—which may be very different from its expression—and whether they can identify the crucial tactical points for intervention.

Conflict Management

Conflict is managed when it does not substantially interfere with the ongoing functional (as opposed to personal) relationships between the parties involved. For instance, two executives may agree to disagree on a number of issues and yet be jointly committed to the course of action they have settled on. There may even be some residual hard feelings—perhaps it is too much to expect to manage feelings in addition to relationships—but as long as any resentment is at a fairly low level and does not substantially interfere with other aspects of their professional relationship, the conflict could be considered to have been managed successfully.

Conflict is not an objective, tangible phenomenon; rather, it exists in the minds of the people who are party to it. Only its manifestations, such as brooding, arguing, or fighting, are objectively real. To manage conflict, therefore, one needs to empathize, that is, to understand the situation as it is seen by the key actors involved. An important element of conflict management is persuasion, which may well involve getting

Source: Leonard Greenhalgh, "SMR Forum: Managing Conflict," *Sloan Management Review,* Summer 1986. Copyright ©1986. Reprinted by permission.

participants to rethink their current views so their perspective on the situation will facilitate reconciliation rather than divisiveness.

Influencing key actors' conceptions of the conflict situation can be a powerful lever in making conflicts manageable. This approach can be used by a third party intervening in the conflict or, even more usefully, by the participants themselves. But using this perceptual lever alone will not always be sufficient. The context in which the conflict occurs, the history of the relationship between the parties, and the time available will have to be taken into account if such an approach is to be tailored to the situation. Furthermore, the conflict may prove to be simply unmanageable: one or both parties may wish to prolong the conflict or they may have reached emotional states that make constructive interaction impossible; or, perhaps the conflict is "the tip of the iceberg" and resolving it would have no significant impact on a deeply rooted antagonistic relationship.

Table 6.1 presents seven perceptual dimensions that form a useful diagnostic model that shows what to look for in a conflict situation and pinpoints the dimensions needing high-priority attention. The model can thus be used to illuminate a way to make the conflict more manageable. The point here is that conflict becomes more negotiable between parties when a minimum number of dimensions are perceived to be at the "difficult-to-resolve" pole and a maximum number to be at the "easy-to-resolve" pole. The objective is to shift a viewpoint from the difficult-to-resolve pole to the easy-to-resolve one. At times, antago-

nists will deliberately resist "being more reasonable" because they see tactical advantages in taking a hard line. Nevertheless, there are strong benefits for trying to shift perspectives; these benefits should become apparent as we consider each of the dimensions in the model.

Issues in Question

People view issues on a continuum from being a matter of principle to a question of division. For example, one organization needed to change its channel of distribution. The company had sold door-to-door since its founding, but the labor market was drying up and the sales force was becoming increasingly understaffed. Two factions of executive sprung up: the supporters were open to the needed change; the resisters argued that management made a commitment to the remaining sales force and, as a matter of principle, could not violate the current sales representatives' right to be the exclusive channel of distribution.

Raising principles makes conflict difficult to resolve because by definition one cannot come to a reasonable compromise; one either upholds a principle or sacrifices one's integrity. For some issues, particularly those involving ethical imperatives, such a dichotomous view may be justified. Often, however, matters of principle are raised for the purpose of solidifying a bargaining stance. Yet, this tactic may work *against* the party using it since it tends to invite an impasse. Once matters of principle are raised, the parties try to argue convincingly that the other's point of

TABLE 6.1

CONFLICT DIAGNOSTIC MODEL

DIMENSION	VIEWPOINT CONTINUUM	
	DIFFICULT TO RESOLVE	EASY TO RESOLVE
Issue in Question	Matter of Principle	Divisible Issue
Size of Stakes	Large	Small
Interdependence of the Parties	Zero Sum	Positive Sum
Continuity of Interaction	Single Transaction	Long-term Relationship
Structure of the Parties	Amorphous or Fractionalized, with Weak Leadership	Cohesive, with Strong Leadership
Involvement of Third Parties	No Neutral Third Party Available	Trusted, Powerful, Prestigious, and Neutral
Perceived Progress of the Conflict	Unbalanced: One Part Feeling the More Harmed	Parties Having Done Equal Harm to Each Other

view is wrong. At best, this approach wastes time and saps the energy of the parties involved. A useful intervention at this point may be to have the parties acknowledge that they understand each other's view but still believe in their own, equally legitimate point of view. This acknowledgment alone often makes the parties more ready to move ahead from arguing to problem solving.

At the other extreme are divisible issues where neither side has to give in completely; the outcome may more or less favor both parties. In the door-to-door selling example, a more constructive discussion would have ensued had the parties been able to focus on the *economic* commitment the company had to its sales force, rather than on the *moral* commitment. As it was, the factions remained deadlocked until the company had suffered irrevocable losses in market share, which served no one's interests. Divisible issues in this case might have involved how much of the product line would be sold through alternative channels of distribution, the extent of exclusive territory, or how much income protection the company was willing to offer its sales force.

Size of Stakes

The greater the perceived value of what may be lost, the harder it is to manage a conflict. This point is illustrated when managers fight against acquisition attempts. If managers think their jobs are in jeopardy, they subjectively perceive the stakes as being high and are likely to fight tooth and nail against the acquisition. Contracts providing for continued economic security, so-called golden parachutes, reduce the size of the stakes for those potentially affected. Putting aside the question of whether such contracts are justifiable when viewed from other perspectives, they do tend to make acquisition conflicts more manageable.

In many cases the perceived size of the stakes can be reduced by persuasion rather than by taking concrete action. People tend to become emotionally involved in conflicts and as a result magnify the importance of what is really at stake. Their "egos" get caught up in the winning/losing aspect of the conflict, and subjective values become inflated.

A good antidote is to postpone the settlement until the parties become less emotional. During this cooling-off period they can reevaluate the issues at stake, thereby restoring some objectivity to their assessments. If time does not permit a cooling off, an attempt to reassess the demands and reduce the other party's expectations may be possible: "There's no way we can give you 100 percent of what you want, so let's be realistic about what you can live with." This approach is really an attempt to induce an atti-

tude change. In effect, the person is being persuaded to entertain the thought, "If I can get by with less than 100 percent of what I was asking for, then what is at stake must not be of paramount importance to me."

A special case of the high-stakes/low-stakes question is the issue of precedents. If a particular settlement sets a precedent, the stakes are seen as being higher because future conflicts will tend to be settled in terms of the current settlement. In other words, giving ground in the immediate situation is seen as giving ground for all time. This problem surfaces in settling grievances. Thus, an effective way to manage such a conflict is to emphasize the uniqueness of the situation to downplay possible precedents that could be set. Similarly, the perceived consequences of organizational changes for individuals can often be softened by explicitly downplaying the future consequences: employees are sometimes assured that the change is being made "on an experimental basis" and will later be reevaluated. The effect is to reduce the perceived risk in accepting the proposed change.

Interdependence of the Parties

The parties to a conflict can view themselves on a continuum from having "zero-sum" to "positive-sum" interdependence. Zero-sum interdependence is the perception that if one party gains in an interaction, it is at the expense of the other party. In the positive-sum case, both parties come out ahead by means of a settlement. A zero-sum relationship makes conflict difficult to resolve because it focuses attention narrowly on personal gain rather than on mutual gain through collaboration or problem solving.

Consider the example of conflict over the allocation of limited budget funds among sales and production when a new product line is introduced. The sales group fights for a large allocation to promote the product in order to build market share. The production group fights for a large allocation to provide the plant and equipment necessary to turn out high volume at high-quality levels. The funds available have a fixed ceiling, so that a gain for sales appears to be a loss for production and vice versa. From a zero-sum perspective, it makes sense to fight for the marginal dollar rather than agree on a compromise.

A positive-sum view of the same situation removes some of the urgency to win a larger share of the spoils at the outset. Attention is more usefully focused on how one party's allocation in fact helps the other. Early promotion allocations to achieve high sales volume, if successful, lead to high production volume. This, in turn, generates revenue that can be invested in the desired improvements to plant and equipment. Similarly, initial allocations to improve plant and equipment can make a high-quality product readily available to the sales group, and the demand for a high-quality product will foster sales.

The potential for mutual benefit is often overlooked in the scramble for scarce resources. However, if both parties can be persuaded to consider how they can both benefit from a situation, they are more likely to approach the conflict over scarce resources with more cooperative predispositions. The focus shifts from whether one party is getting a fair share of the available resources to what is the optimum initial allocation that will jointly serve the mutual long-run interests of both sales and production.

Continuity of Interaction

The continuity-of-interaction dimension concerns the time horizon over which the parties see themselves dealing with each other. If they visualize a long-term interaction—a continuous relationship—the present transaction takes on minor significance, and the conflict within that transaction tends to be easy to resolve. If, on the other hand, the transaction is viewed as a one-shot deal—an episodic relationship—the parties will have little incentive to accommodate each other, and the conflict will be difficult to resolve.

This difference in perspective is seen by contrasting how lawyers and managers approach a contract dispute. Lawyers are trained to perceive the situation as a single episode: the parties go to court, and the lawyers make the best possible case for their party in an attempt to achieve the best possible outcome. This is a "no-holds-barred" interaction in which the past and future interaction between the parties tends to be viewed as irrelevant. Thus the conflict between the parties is not really resolved; rather, an outcome is imposed by the judge.

In contrast, managers are likely to be more accommodating when the discussion of a contract is viewed as one interaction within a longer-term relationship that has both a history and a future. In such a situation, a manager is unlikely to resort to no-holds-barred tactics because he or she will have to face the other party again regarding future deals. Furthermore, a continuous relationship permits the bankrolling of favors: "We helped you out on that last problem; it's your turn to work with us on this one."

Here, it is easy, and even cordial, to remind the other party that a continuous relationship exists. This tactic works well because episodic situations are rare in real-world business transactions. For instance, people with substantial business experience know that a transaction is usually not completed when a contract is signed. No contract can be comprehensive enough to provide unambiguously for all possible contingencies. Thus trust and goodwill remain important long after the contract is signed. The street-fighting tactics that may seem advantageous in the context of an episodic orientation are likely to be very costly to the person who must later seek accommodation with the bruised and resentful other party.

Structure of the Parties

Conflict is easier to resolve when a party has a strong leader who can unify his or her constituency to accept and implement the agreement. If the leadership is weak, rebellious subgroups who may not feel obliged to go along with the overall agreement that has been reached are likely to rise up, thereby making conflict difficult to resolve.

For example, people who deal with unions know that a strong leadership tends to be better than a weak one, especially when organizational change needs to be accomplished. A strongly led union may drive a hard bargain, but once an agreement is reached the deal is honored by union members. If a weakly led union is involved, the agreement may be undermined by factions within the union who may not like some of the details. The result may well be chronic resistance to change or even wildcat strikes. To bring peace among such factions, management may have to make further concessions that may be costly. To avoid this, managers may find themselves in a paradoxical position of needing to boost the power of union leaders.

Similar actions may be warranted when there is no union. Groups of employees often band together as informal coalitions to protect their interests in times of change. Instead of fighting or alienating a group, managers who wish to bring about change may benefit from considering ways to formalize the coalition, such as by appointing its opinion leader to a task force or steering committee. This tactic may be equivalent to cooptation, yet there is likely to be a net benefit to both the coalition and management. The coalition benefits because it is given a formal channel in which the opinion leader's viewpoint is expressed; management benefits because the spokesperson presents the conflict in a manageable form, which is much better than passive resistance or subtle sabotage.

Involvement of Third Parties

People tend to become emotionally involved in conflicts. Such involvement can have several effects: perceptions may become distorted, nonrational thought processes and arguments may arise, and unreasonable stances, impaired communication, and personal attacks may result. These effects make the conflict difficult to resolve.

The presence of a third party, even if the third party is not actively involved in the dialogue, can constrain such effects. People usually feel obliged to appear reasonable and responsible because they care more about how the neutral party is evaluating them than about how the opponent is. The more prestigious, powerful, trusted, and neutral the third party, the greater is the desire to exercise emotional restraint.

While managers often have to mediate conflicts among lower-level employees, they are rarely seen as being neutral. Therefore, consultants and change agents often end up serving a mediator role, either by design or default. This role can take several forms, ranging from an umpire supervising communication to a messenger between parties for whom face-to-face communication has become too strained. Mediation essentially involves keeping the parties interacting in a reasonable and constructive manner. Typically, however, most managers are reluctant to enlist an outsider who is a professional mediator or arbitrator, for it is very hard for them to admit openly that they are entangled in a serious conflict, much less one they cannot handle themselves.

When managers remain involved in settling disputes, they usually take a stronger role than mediators: they become arbitrators rather than mediators. As arbitrators, they arrive at a conflict-resolving judgment after hearing each party's case. In most business conflicts, mediation is preferable because the parties are helped to come to an agreement in which they have some psychological investment. Arbitration tends to be more of a judicial process in which the parties make the best possible case to support their position: this tends to further polarize rather than reconcile differences.

Managers can benefit from a third-party presence, however, without involving dispute-resolution professionals per se. For example, they can introduce a consultant into the situation, with an *explicit* mission that is not conflict intervention. The mere presence of this neutral witness will likely constrain the disputants' use of destructive tactics.

Alternatively, if the managers find that they themselves are party to a conflict, they can make the conflict more public and produce the same constraining effect that a third party would. They also can arrange for the presence of relatively uninvolved individuals during interactions; even having a secretary keep minutes of such interactions encourages rational behavior. If the content of the discussion cannot be disclosed to lower-level employees, a higher-level manager can be invited to sit in on the discussion, thereby discouraging dysfunctional personal attacks and unreasonable stances. To the extent that managers can be trusted to be evenhanded, a third-party approach can facilitate conflict management. Encouraging accommodation usually is preferable to imposing a solution that may only produce resentment of one of the parties.

Progress of the Conflict

It is difficult to manage conflict when the parties are not ready to achieve a reconciliation. Thus it is important to know whether the parties believe that the conflict is escalating. The following example illustrates this point.

During a product strategy meeting, a marketing vice-president carelessly implied that the R&D group tended to overdesign products. The remark was intended to be a humorous stereotyping of the R&D function, but it was interpreted by the R&D vice-president as an attempt to pass on to his group the blame for an uncompetitive product. Later in the meeting, the R&D vice-president took advantage of an opportunity to point out that the marketing vice-president lacked the technical expertise to understand a design limitation. The marketing vice-president perceived this rejoinder as ridicule and therefore as an act of hostility. The R&D vice-president, who believed he had evened the score, was quite surprised to be denounced subsequently by the marketing vice-president, who in turn thought he was evening the score for the uncalled-for barb. These events soon led to a memo war, backbiting, and then to pressure on various employees to take sides.

The important point here is that from the first rejoinder neither party wished to escalate the conflict; each wished merely to even the score. Nonetheless, conflict resolution would have been very difficult to accomplish during this escalation phase because people do not like to disengage when they think they still "owe one" to the other party. Since an even score is subjectively defined, however, the parties need to be convinced that the overall score is approximately equal and that everyone has already suffered enough.

Developing Conflict Management Skills

Strategic decision making usually is portrayed as a unilateral process. Decision makers have some vision of where the organization needs to be headed, and they decide on the nature and timing of specific actions to achieve tangible goals. This portrayal, however, does not take into account the conflict inherent in the decision making process; most strategic decisions are negotiated solutions to conflicts among people whose interests are affected by such decisions. Even in the uncommon case of a unilateral decision, the decision maker has to deal with the conflict that arises when he or she moves to *implement* the decision.

In the presence of conflict at the decision making or decision implementing stage, managers must focus on generating an *agreement* rather than a decision. A decision without agreement makes the strategic direction difficult to implement. By contrast, an agreement on a strategic direction doesn't require an explicit decision. In this context, conflict management is the process of removing cognitive barriers to agreement. Note that agreement does not imply that the conflict has "gone away." The people involved still have interests that are somewhat incompatible. Agreement implies that these people have become committed to a course of action that serves some of their interests.

People make agreements that are less than ideal from the standpoint of serving their interests when they lack the *power* to force others to fully comply with their wishes. On the other hand, if a manager has total power over those whose interests are affected by the outcome of a strategic decision, the manager may not care whether or not others agree, because total power implies total compliance. There are few situations in real life in which managers have influence that even approaches total power, however, and power solutions are at best unstable since most people react negatively to powerlessness per se. Thus it makes more sense to seek agreements than to seek power. Furthermore, because conflict management involves weakening or removing barriers to agreements, managers must be able to diagnose successfully such barriers. The model summarized in Table 6.1 identifies the primary cognitive barriers to agreement.

Competence in understanding barriers to an agreement can be easily honed by making a pastime of conflict diagnosis. The model helps to focus attention on specific aspects of the situation that may pose obstacles to successful conflict management. This pastime transforms accounts of conflicts—from sources ranging from a spouse's response to "how was your day?" to the evening news—into a challenge in which the objective is to try to pinpoint the obstacles to agreement and to predict the success of proposed interventions.

Focusing on the underlying dynamics of the conflict makes it more likely that conflict management will tend toward resolution rather than the more familiar response of suppression. Although the conflict itself—that is, the source—will remain alive, at best, its expression will be postponed until some later occasion; at worst, it will take a less obvious and usually less manageable form.

Knowledge of and practice in using the model is only a starting point for managers and change agents. Their development as professionals requires that conflict management become an integral part of their use of power. Power is a most basic facet of organizational life, yet inevitably it generates conflict because it constricts the autonomy of those who respond to it. Anticipating precisely how the use of power will create a conflict relationship provides an enormous advantage in the ability to achieve the desired levels of control with minimal dysfunctional side effects.

Discussion Questions

1. What indicator suggests that a conflict has been successfully managed?

2. How can an organization member—manager, group member, or lower level employee—learn to empathize with the participants in a conflict?

3. What is the organizing concept of Greenhalgh's diagnostic model?

4. Why does raising a question of principle make conflicts difficult to resolve?

5. How does a divisible issue differ from an issue based on principle?

6. Distinguish "zero-sum" from "positive-sum."

7. What role does leadership play in resolving conflicts?

8. What role can a third party play in the resolution of a conflict?

9. Discuss Greenhalgh's statement "Focusing on the underlying dynamics of the conflict makes it more likely that conflict management will tend toward resolution rather than the more familiar response of suppression."

Negotiating Rationally:
The Power and Impact of the Negotiator's Frame

MARGARET A. NEALE AND MAX H. BAZERMAN

LEARNING OBJECTIVES

After reading "Negotiating Rationally: The Power and Impact of the Negotiator's Frame," by Margaret Neale and Max Bazerman, a student will be able to:

1. Understand when negotiation is required in organizations

2. Know more about how managers can negotiate agreements that maximize their interests

3. Understand how the initial interpretation of a decision—the decision frame—affects the course of negotiations

4. Learn how to avoid being unduly influenced by frames and to improve his or her ability for resolving disputes

Everyone negotiates. In its various forms, negotiation is a common mechanism for resolving differences and allocating resources. While many people perceive negotiation to be a specific interaction between a buyer and a seller, this process occurs with a wide variety of exchange partners, such as superiors, colleagues, spouses, children, neighbors, strangers, or even corporate entities and nations. Negotiation is a decision-making process among interdependent parties who do not share identical preferences. It is through negotiation that the parties decide what each will give and take in their relationship.

The aspect of negotiation that is most directly controllable by the negotiator is how he or she makes decisions. The parties, the issues, and the negotiation environment are often predetermined. Rather than trying to change the environment surrounding the negotiation or the parties or issues in the dispute, we believe that the greatest opportunity to improve negotiator performance lies in the negotiator's ability to make effective use of the information available about the issues in dispute as well as the likely behavior of an opponent to reach more rational agreements and make more rational decisions within the context of negotiation.

The goal of our research has been to help negotiators think rationally. This is important, not because rationality is some end-state we should strive to achieve, but rather because by negotiating rationally, we will improve the likelihood that we will reach better agreements as well as know which opportunities or deals we are better off avoiding.

To this end, we offer advice on how a negotiator should make decisions. However, to follow this advice for analyzing negotiations rationally, a negotiator must understand the psychological forces that limit a negotiator's effectiveness. In addition, rational decisions require that we have an optimal way of evaluating the behavior of the opponent. This requires a psychological perspective for anticipating the likely decisions and subsequent behavior of the other party. Information such as this can not only create a framework that predicts how a negotiator structures problems, processes information, frames the situation, and evaluates alternatives but also identifies the limitations of his or her ability to follow rational advice.

Rationality refers to making the decision that maximizes the negotiator's interests. Since negotiation is a decision-making process that involves other people that do not have the same desires or preferences, the goal of a negotiation is not simply reaching an agreement. The goal of negotiations is to reach a *good* agreement. In some cases, no agreement is better than reaching an agreement that is not in the negotiator's best interests. When negotiated agreements are based on biased decisions, the chances of getting the best possible outcome are significantly reduced and the probabilities of reaching an agreement when an impasse

Source: Margaret A. Neale and Max H. Bazerman, "Negotiating Rationally: The Power and Impact of the Negotiator's Frame," *Academy of Management Executive,* 1992, Vol. 6, No. 3, pp. 42–51. Reprinted by permission.

would have left the negotiator relatively better off are significantly enhanced.

A central theme of our work is that our natural decision and negotiation processes contain biases that prevent us from acting rationally and getting as much as we can out of a negotiation. These biases are pervasive, destroying the opportunities available in competitive contexts, and preventing us from negotiating rationally. During the last ten or so years, the work that we and our colleagues have done suggests that negotiators make the following common cognitive mistakes: (1) Negotiators tend to be overly affected by the frame, or form of presentation, of information in a negotiation; (2) Negotiators tend to nonrationally escalate commitment to a previously selected course of action when it is no longer the most reasonable alternative; (3) Negotiators tend to assume that their gain must come at the expense of the other party and thereby miss opportunities for mutually beneficial trade-offs between the parties; (4) Negotiator judgments tend to be anchored upon irrelevant information—such as, an initial offer; (5) Negotiators tend to rely on readily available information; (6) Negotiators tend to fail to consider information that is available by focusing on the opponent's perspective; and (7) Negotiators tend to be overconfident concerning the likelihood of attaining outcomes that favor the individual(s) involved.

Describing the impact of each of these biases on negotiator behavior is obviously beyond the scope of this article. What we will attempt to do, however, is to focus on one particular and important cognitive bias, *framing,* and consider the impact of this bias on the process and outcome of negotiation. The manner in which negotiators frame the options available in a dispute can have a significant impact on their willingness to reach an agreement as well as the value of that agreement. In this article, we will identify factors that influence the choice of frame in a negotiation.

The Framing of Negotiations

Consider the following situation adapted from Russo and Shoemaker[1]:

You are in a store about to buy a new watch which costs $70. As you wait for the sales clerk, a friend of yours comes by and remarks that she has seen an

identical watch on sale in another store two blocks away for $40. You know that the service and reliability of the other store are just as good as this one. Will you travel two blocks to save $30?

Now consider this similar situation:

You are in a store about to buy a new video camera that costs $800. As you wait for the sales clerk, a friend of yours comes by and remarks that she has seen an identical camera on sale in another store two blocks away for $770. You know that the service and reliability of the other store are just as good as this one. Will you travel two blocks to save the $30?

In the first scenario, Russo and Shoemaker report that about ninety percent of the managers presented this problem reported that they would travel the two blocks. However, in the second scenario, only about fifty percent of the managers would make the trip. What is the difference between the two situations that makes the $30 so attractive in the first scenario and considerably less attractive in the second scenario? One difference is that a $30 discount on a $70 watch represents a very good deal; the $30 discount on an $800 video camera is not such a good deal. In evaluating our willingness to walk two blocks, we frame the options in terms of the percentage discount. However, the correct comparison is not whether a percentage discount is sufficiently motivating, but whether the savings obtained is greater than the expected value of the additional time we would have to invest to realize those savings. So, if a $30 savings were sufficient to justify walking two blocks for the watch, an opportunity to save $30 on the video camera should also be worth an equivalent investment of time.

Richard Thaler illustrated the influence of frames when he presented the following two versions of another problem to participants of an executive development program[2]:

You are lying on the beach on a hot day. All you have to drink is ice water. For the last hour you have been thinking about how much you would enjoy a nice cold bottle of your favorite brand of beer. A companion gets up to make a phone call and offers to bring back a beer from the only nearby place where beer is sold: a fancy resort hotel. She says that the beer might be expensive and asks how much you are willing to pay for the beer. She will buy the beer if it costs as much as or less than the price you state. But if it costs more than the price you state, she will not buy it. You trust your friend and there is no possibility of bargaining with the bartender. What price do you tell your friend you are willing to pay?

Now consider this version of the same story:

You are lying on the beach on a hot day. All you have to drink is ice water. For the last hour you have been thinking about how much you would enjoy a nice cold bottle of your favorite brand of beer. A companion gets up to make a phone call and offers to bring back a beer from the only nearby place where beer is sold: a small, run-down grocery store. She says that the beer might be expensive and asks how much you are willing to pay for the beer. She will buy the beer if it costs as much as or less than the price you state. But if it costs more than the price you state, she will not buy it. You trust your friend and there is no possibility of bargaining with the store owner. What price do you tell your friend you are willing to pay?

In both versions of the story, the results are the same: you get the same beer and there is no negotiating with the seller. Also you will not be enjoying the resort's amenities since you will be drinking the beer on the beach. Recent responses of executives at a Kellogg executive training program indicated that they were willing to pay significantly more if the beer were purchased at a "fancy resort hotel" ($7.83) than if the beer were purchased at the "small, run-down grocery store"($4.10). The difference in price the executives were willing to pay for the same beer was based upon the frame they imposed on this transaction. Paying over $5 for a beer is an expected annoyance at a fancy resort hotel; however, paying over $5 for a beer at a run-down grocery store is an obvious "rip-off!" So, even though the same beer is purchased and we enjoy none of the benefits of the fancy resort hotel, we are willing to pay almost a dollar more because of the way in which we frame the purchase. The converse of this situation is probably familiar to many of us. Have you ever purchased an item because "it was too good of a deal to pass up," even though you had no use for it? We seem to assign a greater value to the quality of the transaction over and above the issue of what we get for what we pay.

Both of these examples emphasize the importance of the particular frames we place on problems we have to solve or decisions we have to make. Managers are constantly being exposed to many different frames, some naturally occurring and others that are purposefully proposed. An important task of managers is to identify the appropriate frame by which employees and the organization, in general, should evaluate its performance and direct its effort.

The Framing of Risky Negotiations

The way in which information is framed (in terms of either potential gains or potential losses) to the negotiator can have a significant impact on his or her preference for risk, particularly when uncertainty about future events or outcomes is involved. For example, when offered the choice between gains of equal expected value—one for certain and the other a lottery, we strongly prefer to take the *certain* gain. However, when we are offered the choice between potential losses of equal expected value, we clearly and consistently eschew the loss for certain and prefer the risk inherent in the *lottery*.

There is substantial evidence to suggest that we are not indifferent toward risky situations and we should not necessarily trust our intuitions about risk. Negotiators routinely deviate from rationality because they do not typically appreciate the transient nature of their preference for risk; nor do they take into consideration the ability of a particular decision frame to influence that preference. Influencing our attitudes toward risk through the positive or negative frames associated with the problem is the result of evaluating an alternative from a particular referent point or base line. A referent point is the basis by which we evaluate whether what we are considering is viewed as a gain or a loss. The referent point that we choose determines the frame we impose on our options and, subsequently, our willingness to accept or reject those options.

Consider the high-performing employee who is expecting a significant increase in salary this year. He frames his expectations on the past behavior of the company. As such, he is expecting a raise of approximately $5000. Because of the recession, he receives a $3500 salary increase. He immediately confronts his manager, complaining that he has been unfairly treated. He is extremely disappointed in what his surprised manager saw as an exceptional raise because the employee's referent point is $1500 higher. Had he known that the average salary increase was only $2000 (and used that as a more realistic referent point), he would have perceived the same raise quite differently and it may have had the motivating force that his manager had hoped to create.

The selection of which relevant frame influences our behavior is a function of our selection of a base line by which we evaluate potential outcomes. The choice of one referent point over another may be the result of a visible anchor, the "status quo," or our expectations. Probably one of the most common referent points is what we perceive to be in our current inventory (our status quo)—what is ours already. We then evaluate offers or options in terms of whether they make us better off (a gain) or worse off (a loss) from what (we perceive to be) our current resource state.

Interestingly, what we include in our current resource state is surprisingly easy to modify. Consider the executive vice-president of a large automobile manufacturing concern that has been hit by a number of economic difficulties because of the recession in the U.S. It appears as if she will have to close down three plants and the employee rolls will be trimmed by 6000 individuals. In exploring ways to avoid this alternative, she has identified two plans that might ameliorate the situation. If she selects the first plan, she will be able to save 2000 jobs and one of the three plants. If she implements the second plan, there is a one-third probability that she can save all three plants and all 6000 jobs but there is a two-thirds probability that this plan will end up saving none of the plants and none of the jobs. If you were this vice president, which plan would you select (#1 or #2)?

Now consider the same options (Plan 1 or Plan 2) framed as losses: If the vice-president implements Plan 1, two of the three plants will be shut down and 4000 jobs will be lost. If she implements Plan 2, then there is a two-thirds probability of losing all three plants and all 6000 jobs but there is a one-third probability of losing no plants and no jobs. If you were presented with these two plans, which would be more attractive? Plan 1 or Plan 2?

It is obvious that from a purely economic perspective, there is no difference between the two choices. Yet, managers offered the plans framed in terms of gains select the first plan about seventy-six percent of the time. However, managers offered the choice between the plans framed in terms of losses only select the first plan about twenty-two percent of the time. When confronted with potential losses, the lottery represented by Plan 2 becomes relatively much more attractive.

An important point for managers to consider is that the way in which the problem is framed, or presented, can dramatically alter the perceived value or acceptability of alternative courses of action. In negotiation, for example, the more risk-averse course of action is to accept an offered settlement; the more risk-seeking course of action is to hold out for future, potential concessions. In translating the influence of the framing bias to negotiation, we must realize that the selection of a particular referent point or

base line determines whether a negotiator will frame his or her decision as positive or negative.

Specifically, consider any recurring contract negotiation. As the representative of Company "A," the offer from Company "B" can be viewed in two ways, depending on the referent point I use. If my referent point were the current contract, Company "B's" offer can be evaluated in terms of the "gains" Company "A" can expect relative to the previous contract. However, if the referent point for Company "A" is an initial offer on the issues under current consideration, then Company "A" is more likely to evaluate Company "B's" offers as losses to be incurred if the contract as proposed is accepted. Viewing options as losses or as gains will have considerable impact on the negotiator's willingness to accept side "B's" position—even though the same options may be offered in both cases.

Likewise, the referent points available to an individual negotiating his salary for a new position in the company include: (1) his current salary; (2) the company's initial offer; (3) the least he is willing to accept; (4) his estimate of the most the company is willing to pay; or (5) his initial salary request. As his referent moves from 1 to 5, he progresses from a positive to a negative frame in the negotiation. What is a modest *gain* compared to his current wage is perceived as a loss when compared to what he would like to receive. Along these same lines, employees currently making $15/hour and demanding an increase of $4/hour can view a proposed increase of $2/hour as a $2/hour gain in comparison to last year's wage (Referent 1) or as a $2/hour loss in comparison to their stated or initial proposal of $19/hour (Referent 5). Consequently, the location of the referent point is critical to whether the decision is positively or negatively framed and affects the resulting risk preference of the decision maker.

In a study of the impact of framing on collective bargaining outcomes, we used a five-issue negotiation with participants playing the roles of management or labor negotiators.[3] Each negotiator's frame was manipulated by adjusting his or her referent point. Half of the negotiators were told that any concessions they made from their initial offers represented losses to their constituencies (i.e., a negative frame). The other half were told that any agreements they were able to reach which were better than the current contract were gains to their constituencies (i.e., the positive frame). In analyzing the results of their negotiations, we found that negatively framed negotiators were less concessionary and reached fewer agreements than positively framed negotiators. In addition, negotiators who had positive frames perceived the negotiated outcomes as more fair than those who had negative frames.

In another study, we posed the following problem to negotiators:

You are a wholesaler of refrigerators. Corporate policy does not allow any flexibility in pricing. However, flexibility does exist in terms of expenses that you can incur (shipping, financing terms, etc.), which have a direct effect on the profitability of the transaction. These expenses can all be viewed in dollar value terms. You are negotiating an $8,000 sale. The buyer wants you to pay $2,000 in expenses. You want to pay less expenses. When you negotiate the exchange, do you try to minimize your expenses (reduce them from $2,000) or maximize net profit, i.e., price less expenses (increase the net profit from $6,000)?

From an objective standpoint, the choice you make to reduce expenses or maximize profit should be irrelevant. Because the choice objectively is between two identical options, selecting one or the other should have no impact on the outcome of the negotiation. What we did find, in contrast, is that the frame that buyers and sellers take into the negotiation can systematically affect their behavior.[4]

In one study, negotiators were led to view transactions in terms of either (1) net profit or (2) total expenses deducted from gross profits. These two situations were objectively identical. Managers can think about maximizing their profits (i.e., gains) or minimizing their expenses (i.e., losses). These choices are linked; if one starts from the same set of revenues, then one way to maximize profits is to minimize expenses and if one is successful at minimizing expenses, the outcome is that profit may be maximized. That is, there is an obvious relationship between profits and expenses. So, objectively, there is no reason to believe that an individual should behave differently if given the instructions to minimize expenses or to maximize profits. However, those negotiators told to maximize profit (i.e., a positive frame) were more concessionary. In addition, positively framed negotiators completed significantly more transactions than their negatively framed (those told to minimize expenses) counterparts. Because they completed more transactions, their overall profitability in the market was higher, although negatively framed negotiators completed transactions of greater mean profit.[5]

The Endowment Effect

The ease with which we can alter our referent points was illustrated in a series of studies conducted by Daniel Kah-

neman, Jack Knetsch, and Richard Thaler.[6] In any exchange between a buyer and a seller, the buyer must be willing to pay at least the minimum amount the seller is willing to accept for a trade to take place. In determining the worth of an object, its value to the seller may, on occasion, be determined by some objective third party such as an economic market. However, in a large number of transactions, the seller places a value on the item—a value that may include not only the market value of the item but also a component for an emotional attachment to or unique appreciation of the item. What impact might such an attachment have on the framing of the transaction?

Let's imagine that you have just received a coffee mug.[7] (In the actual demonstration, coffee mugs were placed before one third of the participants, the "sellers," in the study.) After receiving the mug, you are told that in fact you "own the object (coffee mug) in your possession. You have the option of selling it if a price, to be determined later, is acceptable to you." Next, you are given a list (See Exhibit 6.1) of possible selling prices, ranging from $.50 to $9.50, and are told for each of the possible prices, you should indicate whether you would (a) sell the mug and receive that amount in return, or (b) keep the object and take it home

---

EXHIBIT 6.1

THE COFFEE MUG QUESTIONNAIRE

For each price listed below, indicate whether you would be willing to sell the coffee mug for that price or keep the mug.

If the price is $0.50, I will sell _____; I will keep the mug _____.
If the price is $1.00, I will sell _____; I will keep the mug _____.
If the price is $1.50, I will sell _____; I will keep the mug _____.
If the price is $2.00, I will sell _____; I will keep the mug _____.
If the price is $2.50, I will sell _____; I will keep the mug _____.
If the price is $3.00, I will sell _____; I will keep the mug _____.
If the price is $3.50, I will sell _____; I will keep the mug _____.
If the price is $4.00, I will sell _____; I will keep the mug _____.
If the price is $4.50, I will sell _____; I will keep the mug _____.
If the price is $5.00, I will sell _____; I will keep the mug _____.
If the price is $5.50, I will sell _____; I will keep the mug _____.
If the price is $6.00, I will sell _____; I will keep the mug _____.
If the price is $6.50, I will sell _____; I will keep the mug _____.
If the price is $7.00, I will sell _____; I will keep the mug _____.
If the price is $7.50, I will sell _____; I will keep the mug _____.
If the price is $8.00, I will sell _____; I will keep the mug _____.
If the price is $8.50, I will sell _____; I will keep the mug _____.
If the price is $9.00, I will sell _____; I will keep the mug _____.
If the price is $9.50, I will sell _____; I will keep the mug _____.

amount in return, or (b) keep the object and take it home with you. What is your selling price for the mug?

Another third of the group (the "buyers") were told that they would be receiving a sum of money and they could choose to keep the money or use it to buy a mug. They were also asked to indicate their preferences between a mug and sums of money ranging from $.50 to $9.50. Finally, the last third of the participants (the "choosers") were given a questionnaire indicating that they would later be given an option of receiving either a mug or a sum of money to be determined later. They indicated their preferences between the mug and sums of money between $.50 and $9.50. All of the participants were told that their answers would not influence either the predetermined price of the mug or the amount of money to be received in lieu of the mug.

The sellers reported a median value of $7.12 for the mug; the buyers valued the mug at $2.88; and the choosers valued the mug at $3.12. It is interesting that in this exercise, being a buyer or a chooser resulted in very similar evaluations of worth of the mug. However, owning the mug (the sellers) created a much greater sense of the mug's worth. In this case, it was approximately forty percent greater than the market (or retail) value of the mug.

The explanation for this disparity lies in the fact that different roles (buyer, seller, or chooser) created different referent points. In fact, what seems to happen in such situations is that owning something changes the nature of the owner's relationship to the commodity. Giving up that item is now perceived as a loss and in valuing the item, the owner may include a dollar value to offset his or her perceived loss. If we consider this discrepancy in the value of an item common, then the simple act of "owning" an item, however briefly, can increase one's personal attachment to an item—and typically, its perceived value. After such an attachment is formed, the cost of breaking that attachment is greater and is reflected in the higher price the sellers demand to part with their mugs as compared to the value the buyers or the choosers place on the exact same commodity. In addition, we would expect that the endowment effect intensifies to the extent that the value of the commodity of interest is ambiguous or subjective, the commodity itself is unique, or not easily substitutable in the marketplace.

Framing, Negotiator Bias, and Strategic Behavior

In the previous discussion, we described the negotiator behaviors that may arise from positive and negative frames within the context of the interaction. In this section, we identify some of the techniques for strategically manipulating framing to direct negotiator performance.

Framing has important implications for negotiator tactics. Using the framing effect to induce a negotiating opponent to concede requires that the negotiator create referents that lead the opposition to a positive frame by couching the proposal in terms of their potential gain. In addition, the negotiator should emphasize the inherent risk in the negotiation situation and the opportunity for a sure gain.

As our research suggests, simply posing problems as choices among potential gains rather than choices among potential losses can significantly influence the negotiator's preferences for specific outcomes.

Framing can also have important implications for how managers choose to intervene in dispute among their peers or subordinates. Managers, of course, have a wide range of options to implement when deciding to intervene in disputes in which they are not active principals. If the manager's goal is to get the parties to reach an agreement rather than having the manager decide what the solution to the dispute will be, he or she may wish to facilitate both parties' viewing the negotiation from a positive frame. This is tricky, however, since the same referent that will lead to a positive frame for one negotiator is likely to lead to a negative frame for the other negotiator if presented simultaneously to the parties. Making the use of the effects of framing may be most appropriate when a manager can meet with each side separately. He or she may present different perspectives to each party to create a positive frame (and the subsequent risk-averse behavior associated with such a frame) for parties on both sides of the dispute. Again, if the manager is to effect the frame of the problem in such a way to encourage agreement, he or she may also emphasize the possible losses inherent in continuing the dispute. Combining these two strategies may facilitate both sides' preference for the certainty of a settlement.

Being in the role of buyer or seller can be a naturally occurring frame that can influence negotiator behavior in systematic ways. Consider the curious, consistent, and robust finding in a number of studies that buyers tend to outperform sellers in market settings in which the balance of power is equal.[8] Given the artificial context of the laboratory settings and the symmetry of the design of these field and laboratory markets, there is no logical reason why buyers should do better than sellers. One explanation for this observed difference may be that when the commodity is anonymous (or completely substitutable in a market sense), sellers may think about the transaction in terms of the dollars exchanged. That is, sellers may conceptualize the process of selling as gaining resources (e.g., how many dollars do I gain by selling the commodity); whereas buyers may view transaction in terms of loss of dollars (e.g., how many dollars do I have to give up). If the dollars are the primary focus of the participants' attention, then buyers would tend to be risk seeking and sellers risk averse in the exchange.

When a risk-averse party (i.e., the seller, in this example) negotiates with a risk-seeking party (i.e., the buyer), the buyer is more willing to risk the potential agreement by demanding more or being less concessionary. To reach agreement the seller must make additional concessions to induce the buyer, because of his or her risk-seeking propensity, to accept the agreement. Thus, in situations where the relative achievements of buyers and sellers can be directly compared, buyers would benefit from their negative frame (and subsequent risk averse behavior). The critical issue is that these naturally occurring frames such as the role demands of being a "buyer" or "seller" can easily influence the way in which the disputed issues are framed—even without the conscious intervention of one or more of the parties.

It is easy to see that the frames of negotiators can result in the difference between impasse and reaching an important agreement. Both sides in negotiations typically talk in terms of a certain wage, price, or outcome that they must get—setting a high referent point against which gains and losses are measured. If this occurs, any compromise below (or above) that point represents a loss. This perceived loss may lead negotiators to adopt a negative frame to all proposals, exhibit risk-seeking behaviors, and be less likely to reach settlement. Thus, negotiators, similar to the early example involving the beach and the beer, may end up with no beer (or no agreement) because of the frame (the amount of money I will pay for a beer from a run-down grocery store) that is placed on the choices

rather than an objective assessment of what the beer is worth to the individual.

In addition, framing has important implications for the tactics that negotiators use. The framing effect suggests that to induce concessionary behavior from an opponent, a negotiator should always create anchors or emphasize referents that lead the opposition to a positive frame and couch the negotiation in terms of what the other side has to gain.

In addition, the negotiator should make the inherent risk salient to the opposition while the opponent is in a risky situation. If the sure gain that is being proposed is rejected, there is no certainty about the quality of the next offer. Simultaneously, the negotiator should also not be persuaded by similar arguments from opponents. Maintaining a risk-neutral or risk-seeking perspective in evaluating an opponent's proposals may, in the worst case, reduce the probability of reaching an agreement; however, if agreements are reached, the outcomes are more likely to be of greater value to the negotiator.

An important component in creating good negotiated agreements is to avoid the pitfalls of being framed while, simultaneously, understanding the impact of positively and negatively framing your negotiating opponent. However, framing is just one of a series of cognitive biases that can have a significant negative impact on the performance of negotiators. The purpose of this article was to describe the impact of one of these cognitive biases on negotiator behavior by considering the available research on the topic and to explore ways to reduce the problems associated with framing. By increasing our understanding of the subtle ways in which these cognitive biases can reduce the effectiveness of our negotiations, managers can begin to improve not only the quality of agreements for themselves but also fashion agreements that more efficiently allocate the available resources—leaving both parties and the communities of which they are a part better off.

NOTES

This article is based on the book by Bazerman, M.H., & Neale, M.A. (1992). *Negotiating Rationally*. Free Press: New York.

[1] Adapted from J.E. Russo, & P.J. Schomaker, *Decision traps* (New York: Doubleday, 1989).

[2] R. Thaler, "Using Mental Accounting in a Theory of Purchasing Behavior," *Marketing Science*, 4, 1985, 12–13.

[3] M.A. Neale, & M.H. Bazerman, "The Effects of Framing and

Negotiator Overconfidence," *Academy of Management Journal*, 28, 1985, 34–49.

[4] M.H. Bazerman, T. Magliozzi, & M.A. Neale, "The Acquisition of an Integrative Response in a Competitive Market Simulation," *Organizational Behavior and Human Performance*, 34, 1985, 294–313.

[5] See, for example, Bazerman, Magliozzi, & Neale (1985), op. cit.; Neale and Bazerman, (1985), op. cit.; or M.A. Neale, & G.B.

Northcraft, "Experts, Amateurs and Refrigerators: Comparing Expert and Amateur Decision Making on a Novel Task," *Organizational Behavior and Human Decision Processes,* 38, 1986, 305–317; M.A. Neale, V.L. Huber, & G.B. Northcraft, "The Framing of Negotiations: Context Versus Task Frames," *Organizational Behavior and Human Decision Processes,* 39, 1987, 228–241.

[6] D. Kahneman, J.L. Knetsch, & R. Thaler, "Experimental Tests of the Endowment Effect and Coarse Theorem," *Journal of Political Economy,* 1990.

[7] The coffee mugs were valued at approximately $5.00.

[8] Bazerman et al., (1985), op. cit.; M.A. Neale, V.L. Huber, & G.B. Northcraft, (1987), op. cit.

Discussion Questions

1. Define negotiation.
2. Define rationality.
3. What is the goal of negotiation?
4. List the biases that negotiators typically experience.
5. Why do the authors believe that the frame of a negotiation is of particular importance?
6. How do reference points influence the negotiation process?
7. How can the negotiating processes that Neale and Bazerman discuss be used in Greenhalgh's conflict management framework?

For Further Reading

Brett, J., Goldberg, S., and Ury, W. "Designing Systems for Resolving Disputes in Organizations." *American Psychologist* 45 (1990) 162–170.

Coser, L. *The Functions of Social Conflict.* New York: Free Press, 1956.

Fisher, R., Ury, W., and Patton, B. *Getting to Yes: Negotiating Agreement Without Giving In,* 2nd ed. New York: Penguin, 1991.

Ganster, D. and Schaubroeck, J. "Work, Stress, and Employee Health." *Journal of Management* 17 (1991) 235–261.

Ivancevich, J., Matteson, M., Freedman, S., and Phillips, J. "Worksite Stress Management Interventions." *American Psychologist* 45 (1990) 252-261.

Pondy, L. "Organizational Conflict: Concepts and Models." *Administrative Science Quarterly* 12 (1967).

PART II: CASE 1

FRANK HARRIS, MBA

H. Donald Hopkins

Frank Harris had completed his MBA degree only six years earlier and already his career plans had gone astray. When he graduated, near the top of his class, he had high expectations and was very confident. But he was behind schedule (he wanted to be the general manager of a division or region by age 35) and was now unemployed and looking for another position. His self-confidence was a little shaken, and he wondered out loud about what had gone wrong with his first job after graduation. He recounted the following story to the casewriter.

My first job after graduating from business school with an MBA was with a well-known *Fortune* 100 manufacturer of big-ticket consumer products. Initially I was interviewed for half an hour at a hotel as part of a job conference organized by an employment agency. Following this early hurdle I was called to one of the company's many district sales offices for a full day of interviewing. During this day I spoke with almost a dozen managers as they attempted to both look me over and sell me on their company.

The final interviewer was the district manager, Mr. Robin. By the end of the interview it was clear he wanted to hire me but he didn't actually make an offer at this point. Instead he tried to secure the deal by reviewing the company's strongest selling point, the salaries they gave their managers. He said, "If hired, you will start out as a district trainee at between $18,000 and $31,000; after about two years of training and seasoning you'll make area manager at $25,000 to $45,000 per year; after being area manager in several different territories you'll become a department manager and make between $40,000 and $65,000 per year; and as a general field manager for the whole district you will make somewhere between $50,000 and $80,000."

Upon hearing these amounts I was dumbstruck. My jaw dropped and I was certain I had found paradise. I figured I would be willing to do just about anything for this kind of money. In business school, such salary figures were always being tossed about in cases, but now it was for real. I wasn't about to miss out. They could have me, body and soul, for this kind of money.

I was made an offer later over the phone, and I accepted immediately. My first full day in the district office was spent on clerical duties related to a company sales-incentive program. My official title was "sales analyst," but I did not actually analyze anything. My duties were clerical and included, among other things, opening mail, filing, running errands, making copies, etc. I was amazed that this company was paying me, with my MBA, that much money to do such things. According to the company these clerical duties were important training for my promotion to area manager.

Initially I was very ambitious and I badly wanted to be promoted to area manager. I stayed late almost every night. I took home work over the weekends and tried to fit in. I tried to dress and act like I was a charter member of the company.

Maintaining my ambitious nature was no small feat in light of the unchallenging work, the high pressure, and the highly political climate. To accomplish my objective I applied myself to learning the rules and carrying out my duties in an impeccable manner. I was rewarded with my promotion in less than a year! Along with my promotion came a big jump in salary, a company car, and an expense account. I had made it.

However, despite its trappings this promotion resulted in little job satisfaction. This position involved greater freedom from direct supervision but no real opportunity for individual decision making. My duties were totally spelled out, and a detailed check-list was kept to record results. The workload was the only challenging part of the job.

The first area I was assigned to was in the northeast corner of the state. It took a full day's drive to get to my area from the district office. We were not allowed to live in our area of responsibility but, instead, had to live near the district office. This travel time back and forth left three days each week for me to get my work completed. Once in my area a typical day would often include three or four customer visits, 150 miles of driving within my area, a return to a motel at 6 or 7 P.M., and filling out Customer Contact Reports until very late. Because of bureaucratic and legal requirements, every action an area manager took had to be documented.

Because of the travel and workload, my personal and social life was almost nonexistent. I would go to work on Monday morning and not return home until Friday night. Friday nights were often spent commiserating with other area managers at a bar close to the district office. Sundays were usually spent going through mail and memos, completing a detailed expense report, packing a suitcase and generally preparing for the coming week.

Source: Reprinted by permission of the publisher from "Frank Harris, MBA," by H. Donald Hopkins, *Journal of Management Case Studies*, 3, 277–279. Copyright 1987 by Elsevier Science Publishing Co., Inc.

Probably the worst part of the job was the intense pressure. The company was militaristic and authoritarian. Fear and threats were the prime motivational tools used by the company. We were frequently required to perform duties for the company that made little sense to us because the rationale behind them was not given. Virtually all communication flowed from top to bottom. Area managers were rarely consulted for their expertise on their territory or knowledge of customers or sales trends.

As an area manager, I was placed between the customers and the company, and I was expected to control the behavior of the customers. On the other hand, the customers expected me to get the company to respond to their complaints and special requests. Many of my customers despised the company but had to do business with them because they had no alternative source of supply. In fact, at one point I was physically assaulted by an irate customer.

I had no choice but to be totally committed to the company even though my heart was with my customers. I was making more money than I ever had before, even though I had almost no time to spend it. I was almost never home. I was on the road so much I hardly even needed a place of my own, and I rented the cheapest apartment I could find.

Company politics were played to the hilt. Every aspect of my personal life had to conform to the firm's view. Company politics were at their worst during company social functions. Employees and spouses tried to ingratiate themselves with higher level managers. At these functions the crowd would always gravitate toward the highest level manager in attendance. Few people were interested in talking to the poor guys at the bottom because they couldn't do anybody's career any good.

There was a lot of joking in the office about what one had to do to survive in this company. The competition was so intense that my coworkers changed frequently. There were many early retirements and much job jumping to other companies. Many long-term employees had heart problems, or were pill takers or alcoholics, and there had been many divorces caused by the travel, pressure, and competition.

Career paths in this company were like nothing I had ever seen before. Managers would often move up the ranks for many years and then, incredibly enough, they would start to come back down! My first boss in the company now had a job several levels below me, and the company was trying to force him out.

The company had an unofficial but well-known policy of associating each management position with a specific age. If you fell behind schedule your chances diminished rapidly. Apparently, those who fell behind were blocking the real "comers" who had a genuine chance of reaching the upper levels. Actually, the company would have liked to have fired many of those who were behind schedule but it was too expensive. It was expensive because they had to pay one month's severance pay for each year a manager had been with the company if he was fired. This policy was required because any provisions won by the company's unionized workers were automatically extended to management. If a manager was making $60,000 per year and had been with the company 20 years his severance would amount to $100,000. Because of this, the company would demote people who fell behind and try to humiliate them into leaving on their own.

After a while I became less ambitious. I didn't work as hard as before and tried to enjoy life a little more. I fell seriously behind schedule in the process. And eventually I realized I had to get out. I had saved a bit of money, so I quit without having lined up another job. But the money's starting to run out.

PART II: CASE 2

KEN GARFF: SMALL-BUSINESS ENTREPRENEUR

C. Brooklyn Derr

Although the role of entrepreneurs in American business is acknowledged and respected, the nature and characteristics of entrepreneurs are less well understood. What kind of people are they? Can they be found in fields other than small business? What are their common characteristics? Career theorist Edgar Schein (1982) defined entrepreneurship based on an internal personal orientation:

> *These people discovered early in life that they had an overriding need to create a new business. . . . We are not talking about the inventor or the creative artist here, although some of them may become entrepreneurs. Nor should this group be confused with the creative researcher, market analyst or advertising executive. The entrepreneur's creative urge is specifically toward creating a new organization, product or service that can be identified closely with his or her building efforts, that will survive on its own, and that will permit the making of a fortune by which the success of the enterprise can be measured.*

Sociologists Albert Shapero and Lisa Sokol (1982) contrasted entrepreneur and manager:

> *Many managers take initiative, innovate in the technological sense, and even bring together resources, but if they do not personally share the risk of success or failure, if they do not manage the organization with a considerable degree of autonomy, they have not generated a genuine entrepreneurial event.*

Historian Albro Martin (1982) maintained that entrepreneurs must be owner-innovators, not just owner-managers. They must use their creativity to exploit new ideas and inventions, and to develop marketable new services and products. In contrast to investors who risk only capital, entrepreneurs risk status, reputation, position, and ego.

Psychology, sociology, history, and other disciplines have each contributed much to the study of entrepreneurship but as yet there is no cross-discipline consensus definition of an entrepreneur. Assembled collectively, the research from each field paints an incomplete picture. The case study that follows takes a careers perspective; it is believed that this approach might be useful to further elucidate and delineate the entrepreneurial concept.

A Careers Perspective

A career is typically (1) a long-term work history, (2) which has a sense of direction to it and that over time,(3) includes those private life activities (such as family relationships, self-development, and life-stage events) that act upon and impact the careerist's work.

Entrepreneurship as a career orientation represents a sequence of work-related activities over time, rather than one-time or short-term activities, and hypothesizes that characteristic factors of entrepreneurs will emerge as long-term attitudes and behaviors that sustain entrepreneurial activity.

Entrepreneurial careerists would also display purposeful and projected (or directional) activity with powerful motives, values, and talents, long-range plans, fall-back positions, and working strategies that acknowledge the restrictions imposed on them by their working situation.

The third element of a careers perspective is that the whole person—not just the career—must be considered. A divorce or a midlife crisis will almost certainly impact on work performance. Negative spillover from a boring or stressful job will probably show up in family interactions. Bird's recent qualitative research of Los Angeles entrepreneurs (1984) showed that the boundaries between private and professional life are very elastic and ill defined, a conclusion that most of the psychological research would also support.

"Career Portraiture" is a method currently used by Derr (1984) to study entrepreneurs. In-depth, intensive, and qualitative, this method typically requires ten to fifteen hours of tape-recorded interviews with the subject and four or five cross-checking one-hour interviews with significant others who have an informed perspective about the subject's work history.

It is not possible to generalize about all small-business entrepreneurs from a single case study. Nevertheless, career-portrait methodology has identified entrepreneurs in technical fields, in the arts, and in large organizations. The most important outcome of a careers perspective on entrepreneurs may eventually be identifying a common core of entrepreneurial career orientations and lifestyles that

Source: Reprinted by permission of the publisher from "Ken Garff: Small-Business Entrepreneur," by C. Brooklyn Derr, Professor of Human Resource Management, David Eccles School of Business, University of Utah, *Journal of Management Case Studies*, 2, 188–198. Copyright 1986 by Elsevier Science Publishing Co., Inc.

accommodate different applications as the work setting varies. Technical, small-business, and large-organization entrepreneurs may be differentiated from each other because of the unique demands of their various work environments.

Viewed in this way, the distinction between entrepreneur and small-business person would become moot, allowing for a more intensive and sophisticated study of the similarities and differences of the various types of entrepreneurs. A major contribution to this field of study would then be a clearer understanding of what is required for successful entrepreneurship within diverse settings.

The following case study of Kendall D. Garff, a small-business person, is presented on the theory that the best generalizations emerge from specifics. This abridged career portrait identifies Garff as an entrepreneur (not just a small-business man) and a particular kind of entrepreneur: small business, rather than technical or large business.

The Formative Years (1906–1926)

Kendall Day Garff, the second of Royal B. Garff and Rachel Day Garff's five children, was born in 1906 in Draper, Utah. Both parents were devout Mormons.

The father was affectionate and, according to Garff, "one of the hardest workers I have ever seen." However, he changed occupations often and never abandoned hopes of a fabulous strike from his repeated ventures into mining.

Rachel Garff, a strong-willed woman, handled the family finances and got the family through hard times by personally negotiating a payment schedule with the bankers so the Garff's could keep their properties. Garff recalls, "She taught me not to spend more than I could pay for, and she helped me understand that the only way to build a reputation and get a standing was to have good credit and honor your commitments."

Surrounded by a loving and close-knit extended family who were all committed to self-sufficiency, Garff spent a hardworking but pleasant childhood on his grandfather's 40-acre fruit farm. He typically worked from sunup to sunset every day, but Sunday offered a reprieve for this church-going family. "One of my great motivations in going into business," Ken confesses, "was to not become a row crop farmer. It was just too hard a life."

In about 1921, Royal Garff purchased a small grocery store at E Street and Sixth Avenue in Salt Lake City. Between the ages of 15 and 19 (1921-1925), Ken, with his mother, managed most of the day-to-day running of the operation. Odd products bought in response to an appealing sales pitch, he soon observed, could sit for months on the shelf, whereas staples and recognized brands turned over quickly enough to make a profit. Profits could be increased, as well, if goods were displayed so the ripe produce sold first, and if the perishables were stored to maximize shelf life. "Tutors" at the farmer's market taught him how to buy quality produce at the best prices; Roscoe Eardley, manager of the United Grocery, became an early mentor.

With its good location, the Garff grocery store was well-suited for serving some of Salt Lake's more affluent clientele. Ken delivered printed handbills announcing Saturday sales, telephoned to describe various bargains or let certain customers know when certain fruits and vegetables were available for home canning, took orders by phone, and personally delivered the groceries.

"The customer is king," became the cornerstone of Garff's business philosophy. Years later, associates recount, he could be almost fanatical in his insistence that a merchant should, within reason, do whatever is necessary to satisfy the customer. And he justified this service with a realistic business axiom: "If treated well, the customer will continue to trade with you and will bring you other customers."

During these years, Garff also would accompany his father to the lobby of Salt Lake's Cullen Hotel, where old miners told tales of fabulous strikes. Allured, young Garff spent many Saturday nights taking samples of the ore. Results from the smelter were inevitably discouraging. By the time he reached 20, he was committed to a formula of hard work, good reputation, solid credit, and superb service rather than striking it rich on a gamble.

Ken's school work was easy but uninteresting compared to the store. He graduated from LDS High School in 1926, then earned a business degree from the University of Utah in 1932, partly to please his mother.

Getting Established (1927-1946)

As a volunteer Mormon missionary to Ireland (1927–1928), Garff consolidated some religious and personal values: he liked to work with people; selling suited him; he liked to work for himself, not under bureaucratic controls; and he was an excellent manager as a mission leader. Thus, Garff left this experience confident in his ability to manage his own business and direct a sales force.

Upon returning to Salt Lake City, he worked briefly for United Grocery, but quickly began looking for opportunities in selling. In the summer of 1930, he and a partner were hired by Cache Valley Knitting Works to sell its fine woolen clothes door-to-door in a territory running along the Great Northern Railroad from Havre, Montana, to Williston,

North Dakota, and south to Billings, Montana. The people in this territory were poor; many were out of work. The two salesmen with bulging satchels were not welcome.

After several days of little success and the additional irritant of being tied to a partner (the partner owned the car they used), Garff went alone to a city park. "I took out those samples and looked at them and wondered how I'd make a proper presentation and excite someone to buy. It finally hit me that I had to find out about the family before I made the presentation, and I had to make a startling enough approach that they'd let me in the house. I remember going up to this lady that had turned me down—she was a nice lady—and I said, 'If you could help me, what's the name of the lady next door?' She told me. I said, 'How many children does she have and what does her husband do?' She told me that they had two or three children and about what their ages were, and about the husband and what he did.

"So then, I picked out a sweater about the size of the girl next door, and for the boy a pair of slacks or a little jacket or something, and a nice dress about the mother's size. Then I went up and knocked on the door with the clothes over my arm that might appeal to this home. So when the lady came to the door, these clothes looked very appealing to her and she said, 'Well, this is a pretty dress, but I don't like the color. I'd like something a little different. And that's about right for my boy. How much is it?' And I'd say, 'Well, Mrs. Smith, take these samples and look at them. I'll run out to my car and get my cases and I can show you a dress that I think would more nearly be to your liking. If your boy doesn't need a sweater, I've got a pair of pants he could use,' and so on.

"Then, I'd run and get the samples and get in. And that was the main thing—to get in and show something. Well, I started selling, more and more. The jubilation I found in learning how to sell was overwhelming."

He immediately spent $100 for an old Model T Ford so he'd be free to operate independently, and then began using even more innovative ideas. He would go into the fields and ask farmers to try to pull woolen underwear apart, a test of strength that often clinched the sale of a $26 pair. Garff made large sales to lonely sheepherders by hiking to their camps, or by hanging around cafes during off-hours and displaying clothes to the waitresses.

At the end of a very successful summer, while waiting in Billings, Montana, for his partner, Garff polished up his Model T and sold it for $150 more than he had paid for it, thus discovering that the thrill of making one big sale was even greater than the pleasure of making numerous small ones.

Cache Valley Knitting Works invited Garff and his partner to Logan to honor them and offered Garff a posi-

tion as division manager. *The Ken Garff Biography* (1983), records his response:

> *Ken was intrigued by the offer, but even more interested in a stockpile of returned merchandise in a basement storeroom, still in the original boxes, some of it out of style. People had moved, their circumstances had changed, or for some other reason they had sent the merchandise back—some as long as five years ago.*
>
> *"I just couldn't believe that a company that made such good merchandise would allow it to just sit there," Ken said. He offered the company twenty cents on the dollar for the entire lot, and leased a small store in Idaho Falls. . . .*
>
> *He and Walt Mason had fixed up some pipe racks for dresses and coats. They had overturned big cardboard boxes as display tables for sweaters, socks, and other garments, and in an advertisement offered free stockings and socks to the first ten people in the store.*
>
> *"When I looked out the door at ten o'clock, opening time, I was scared to death," Ken recalls. "There was a line almost all the way around the block. How could we handle that crowd? So I sneaked out a side door and found a policeman to help out."*
>
> *For the first few hours, Walt and Ken allowed only a few people at a time to enter the store. Even so, it was the usual scramble when bargains are offered. At the end of the day, sweaters, socks, dresses, underwear, and coats were all over the store. "It was a real mess," recalls Ken, "but we sold a thousand dollars worth of merchandise with a 50 percent markup."*
>
> *Idaho Falls buyers cleaned out the stock in a week's time, and each partner took $1,500 as his share of the enterprise.*
>
> *"This was another experience that got me enthusiastic about merchandising and dealing with people," says Ken.*

In a class report at the University of Utah, Garff predicted that one day most American families would have two cars, a notion the professor and most of his students found laughable. In 1932, however, Garff leased a Shell Oil service station and planned also to sell a few used cars. When a Shell representative told him he could sell only company products, Ken replied, "Well, I don't want to be in the service station business anyway. I'm going into business for myself—the car business." He leased a 150 × 150-foot lot at

444 South State Street (1932-1937). Good used cars were scarce. Ken would wait outside the door of McBride's, a major used car dealer, and talk to people as they came out. If they were dissatisfied with the price McBride's had offered, he'd offer them a better one.

To free himself up to search for more merchandise, he found, after numerous attempts, one of the best used car salesmen in town. A persistent pattern of Garff's has been to carefully select people, turn parts of the business over to them, and concentrate himself on growth and expansion.

He learned from his brother, then in graduate school at Northwestern University, that there were clean used cars available around Evanston, Illinois. Garff would purchase the cars at wholesale prices and drive them back to Salt Lake at a profit of $150 to $200 per car. Remembering his grocery store, Garff stuck to popular-brand cars, mostly Fords and Chevrolets.

Garff's selection of excellent cars and his "customer is king" services brought him repeat business. Customers also asked him to arrange their new-car purchases. He first purchased a distributorship in a dying company, then, in 1937, he became the inter-mountain distributor for Studebaker trucks and a local dealer for Studebaker cars. With about 70 dealers under his direction as a distributor, he made a 3 percent royalty on each of their sales. He operated from a garage and showroom at 120 East Fifth South, a piece of property he had persuaded another mentor and an established realtor, Graham Doxey, to buy for him less the 6 percent sales commission in return for cars at cost.

One of the key lessons Garff remembered from college was how to analyze companies and purchase undervalued stocks and bonds. He purchased United Bond and Finance Company common stock for ten cents on the dollar. UB&F president Beckstead owned some new apartments on Fifth East and agreed to accept rent in stock. The Garffs acquired a $75 a month apartment for $7.50 a month in stock. By then, Ken and his wife, Marjorie Heiner, had a son, Kendall Gary, born in 1935. (A second son, Robert Heiner, would be born in 1942, and the couple would adopt a daughter, Jane, in 1953.) Beckstead refused stock for a home he had for sale but agreed to accept UB&F bonds, many of which were owned by small investors in Montana towns. Garff drove to these towns and got the towns' bankers to agree that as UB&F bonds had never paid a dividend, one share of Montana Power stock (selling at $40 par) was equivalent to one $200 UB&F bond. With shares of Montana Power stock, Garff then proposed trading the bondholders for their UB&F bonds, giving the bankers' names as a reference. In this way, he acquired $5,250 worth of UB&F bonds at 40 cents on the dollar for $2,100. Beckstead accepted the

bonds, Garff got his home, and he immediately borrowed $3,000 on the home for his business, thus establishing a lifelong pattern of raising capital on real estate.

Just prior to World War II, correctly seeing that few new cars would be sold during the war, Garff leased his Studebaker facility to the Salt Lake City Oldsmobile dealer, reserving some Studebaker buses that he then leased to a nearby air base for a handsome profit. Then, to sell used cars and Studebaker parts, he bought the Shell station he had leased earlier. He also bought a large cattle ranch in central Utah. Although not particularly profitable, the ranch gave him valuable experience for heading, later in life, one of the West's largest ranching enterprises, Deseret Livestock Company.

During the war, the Oldsmobile dealer to whom he had leased his operation died, leaving his widow with the business. Garff declared his intentions to apply for the franchise. Besides his excellent reputation in the Salt Lake car business, he had two points in his favor: GM had a policy against female-owned dealerships, and the Olds operation was already established on Garff's property.

Mrs. Tourssen, the widow, insisted on a $60,000 purchase price and Oldsmobile supported her demand but refused to allow Garff and his associates to check her inventory. Garff scraped up all his available cash, sold the cattle ranch, and persuaded John Wallace, president of Walker Bank, to loan him $30,000 on the strength of his reputation and his business plan. On August 1, 1944, Ken Garff, at age 40, became Salt Lake City's Oldsmobile dealer.

"I took a chance," Ken recalls. "I figure I paid maybe five or ten thousand dollars more than the deal was worth. But I bought it anyway, and then the boom began." Garff sold every car he could get at full list price. "Making the money and having happy customers and getting a reputation in town was a thrill."

The Pinnacle Years: Wheeling and Dealing (1947–1978)

Garff worked for five years to establish his lead and keep his base. By 1952 he was ready to diversify and expand. He formed a partnership with attorney Dave Robinson and financier Dave Freed, their motto was: "Don't take on any deal unless we can still break even in the worse-case scenario."

Garff's role in the partnership was to find deals for his partners to consider. "I guess I just had a flare," he says. As an attorney with extensive experience in accounting, engineering, and business, Robinson, according to Robert Garff, "was everything my Dad wasn't, and the two of them worked well together. Dave was a guy who took things slowly, who analyzed everything, who dotted the i's and crossed the t's. Dad was people oriented and could conceptually visualize the end results."

Garff had first met Freed in 1941 and had received low-interest financing from him at a time when other financiers termed him overextended. As the head of a loan company, Freed had a million-dollar line of credit, an asset that proved as valuable as his penchant for good analysis. Besides being effective partners, Robinson, Freed, and Garff were also, as Robinson says, "closer than brothers; and in all the years we worked together, we've never had a misunderstanding we could not work out."

Another important member of the team was Roberta Harris. She met Garff in 1954 when she worked as a volunteer under his leadership of a United Way fund drive. Impressed with her abilities, he offered her a job, first as his secretary, than as his administrative assistant for over 30 years.

On a typical day, Roberta recalls, Ken would phone her between 6:30 and 7:00 A.M. to get the schedule for the day and discuss what he needed to wear and bring to the office. He would arrive at 9:00 A.M. and work until 7:00 at night. "Energetic and enthusiastic," she says, was how he approached each day. "You'd go to his office," a former employee recalls, "and there were two desks, one for Ken and one for Roberta. Ken would have three or four phones going at once and be doing well on each phone. Roberta would be giving him files and other information from across the room to correspond to each phone call. It was really something to witness."

This was Ken at the height of his career, in the late 1960s and 1970s. But even in 1952 he was on his way. That year the 350,000-acre Deseret Livestock Company became available. Garff and his partners approached Marriner Eccles, chief executive officer of First Security Corporation, with a plan to buy a controlling interest. He agreed to loan them part of the money through the bank and the rest as a personal loan from him and several wealthy Utahans. He required, however, that the undervalued land be liquidated as soon as possible, with the investors receiving a fair share of the profits.

The Deseret Salt Plant, an unsuccessful holding of Deseret Livestock, was promptly sold for $325,000, a considerable loss. However, because of a loophole in the tax laws, the partners reaped a $700,000 government rebate from excess taxes paid two years earlier. As a result, the salt plant sale produced a million dollars of the capital needed to keep the property. The partners then mortgaged the ranch at 4.5 percent interest to generate the necessary capital to buy out Eccles and the other investors, at $35 per share on an original investment of $27 per share. In 1954, the three partners each owned 35 percent of the ranch. Creative

innovations soon made the ranch profitable. One innovation was selling about 2,000 hunting licenses annually at $10 each. Another idea was cross breeding that produced steers weighing 50 pounds more than their predecessors. Breeding two-year-old heifers with small bulls produced one more calf per cow. All profits went back into the operation. In 1974 Garff sold part of the Deseret Livestock Company to a New York investor for about $11 million, a $3 million profit. The partners retained about 26,000 acres in one of the ranch's most productive and beautiful parts. They also owned, as the Skull Valley Partnership, a 45,000-acre winter range in Tooele County and a feedlot in Colorado.

A second profitable venture of the 1950s was mobile homes. Garff had first entered the business in 1938. With Deseret Livestock as collateral, he and his two partners bought Aetna Loan Company, 20 trailer lots, a mobile home insurance agency, an appliance franchise, and then consolidated to become the largest mobile-home business in the world. Thus, they were able to sell mobile homes, space in mobile-home parks, insurance for the units (making about $2 million in premiums over a ten-year period), and Norge appliances for the units. Roberta Harris managed much of the trailer business, which netted the company as much as $500,000 per year before taxes.

About 1972, however, the IRS made an administrative ruling that taxes had to be paid immediately by the owners on the full-time purchase price, including the interest reserve held for the life of the contract. By 1976, the partnership had divested itself of the business.

A third major investment area continued to be the automobile business. Garff added Mercedes-Benz (1958), Honda (1971), and Saab franchises (1977) to his operations. Today, Ken Garff Imports (the Mercedes and Saab components headed by Robert Garff) and the Ken Garff Company (the Oldsmobile and Honda dealership led by Gary Garff) are both substantial and established businesses. Ken Garff Enterprises owns both automobile companies and all the real estate holdings associated with the car businesses.

Although Garff took many of his deals to Robinson and Freed for analysis, he bypassed them many times to wheel and deal with his own money. Freed comments that Garff's imagination could easily outpace his concrete plans, but Harris claims Garff was surprisingly skilled at foreseeing consequences of a deal and could compute propositions in his head with surprising accuracy.

Goliath, Borgward, Renault, Jaquar, MC, and International Harvester were in-the-red franchises. Some speculative real estate deals did not pay dividends and a few of them lost money. During the Korean War, Garff operated an open-pit gold mine in Nevada that, because the war made gasoline and good labor hard to get, turned out to be an unprofitable business although it yielded 1,000 tons per day and has since proven its worth. He has also been involved in a uranium mine, a turkey farm, a cold-storage business, a dry-cleaning business, and a chinchilla farm—none of which can be regarded as successful.

Much of Garff's financial success depended on his personality, which enabled him to generate future funding for his various ventures. His son Robert commented:

> Your relationship with your banker is important. Dad would invite them up to the ranch and show them a great time. It wasn't like, "He's a banker, therefore I'm going to devise this plan to impress him," it was that Dad loved doing it. He loved showing people a good time. It was his nature.
>
> Dad would be up before everybody else, finding ways to show them a great time. He got their breakfasts, he'd locate them in a certain spot and then run around to flush the deer. He would be the first one cleaning the pheasants, making up a bag to give to the guests. It was the kind of service you couldn't hire, but he loved it. It was very genuine.
>
> People would come and be so overwhelmed with his charismatic personality and what he did for them that they went home and just couldn't believe what an experience they had had. That kind of thing made him friends with the corporate giants of America. With those kinds of friends, there were a lot of informal phone calls when they'd hear about a business deal he might be interested in. Many of them were also in a position to put financing together for him, too, and were willing to do it, you see, because they believed in him. They loved him.
>
> Whatever he'd say he'd do, he did. In other words, if he borrowed money from a banker, he always paid it back before the due date. He was a man of his word, and people knew they could count on Ken Garff. His name and his reputation—his integrity—were absolutely impeccable.

In addition to being good business, the ranch gave Ken tremendous personal satisfaction. After acquiring it, Ken began to manifest some of the same enthusiasm for leisure activities as he had previously reserved for work. He had belonged to a duck club since the 1950s but would leave home at 3:30 A.M., hunt ducks, and be back in time for a full day's work. On the ranch, he became both skilled and exuberant as a hunter and as a fisherman.

Gary and Robert became partners in Garff's hunting and fishing excursions and remember having total access to their father during these outings. Their mother became ill during their teen years and died in 1976 but during her illness Garff maintained a stable home for the children. Robert remembers, "Dad would wake me up in the mornings and fix my breakfast and take me to school. I remember him being at that time both father and mother to me. He was my hero."

The boys began working in the car business at an early age and spent much of their after-school time and Saturdays with their father. Though establishing a career had kept Garff away from his boys' school functions and Little League games, both sons describe their father as very committed to his family, keenly motivated to provide for them both financially and emotionally. He was never too busy to be with them, they recall, or talk to them on an "as needed" basis. Robert identifies several important facets of his father's parenting. First, he gave them the opportunity to earn money, not cash. Second, he would not permit waste or ostentatious living. Third, he gave the children as much responsibility as they were willing to assume. To this, Gary adds, Garff never has a "master plan" for his children. They were allowed to experiment, make mistakes, and learn from the consequences.

As Garff became more thoroughly established in his business, he also became more active in community and civic affairs. As early as the 1950s, he gave creative leadership and time to the United Way, the Boy Scouts, the Utah National Guard, the LDS Church, the United Fund, the Republican Party, the Utah Symphony, universities, and the Salt Lake Country Club, among others. He served on the boards of the Detroiter Mobile Homes, the First Security Corporation, the University of Utah, and BYU, among others, and also served as president of the Utah Automobile Association. Adept as a fund-raiser and generous contributor himself, he was a significant patron of the colleges of medicine and business at the University of Utah. The College of Business named its principal office building for him in 1981.

For nine years he served as Republican National Committeeman, becoming one of the best known and most powerful Republicans in Utah. He held several national appointments and was an honorary consul of the Federal Republic of West Germany.

Garff's most important business talents are:

1. The ability to choose good business associates and subordinates. Unlike entrepreneurs whose egos require an entourage of nonthreatening sycophants, Garff "kept looking until I had the person who could do a job as

PART II: CASE 2 Continued

well as I could and then I gave him or her the responsibility."

2. The ability to deal well with people. He knows how to sell creatively, how to satisfy a customer, and how to close a deal. Accepting and nonjudgmental, he makes others feel liked. His personal relationships have fostered his business career—especially as none of his friends have lost money by loaning it to him.

3. Energy and emotional resilience. Freed says, "He's always busy and nothing seems too hard for him. He never gets down for long. He just pushes on."

4. Intuition combined with analysis. A risk-taker, he taught himself early to identify the important information and screen out the rest. As a result, he is able to make decisions quickly and, for the most part, well.

5. Ready capital. By carefully making investments and cultivating trustworthy business relationships, he can move quickly when he sees the right deal.

Like most businessmen with a clearly successful career, Garff is able to articulate the business principles that are most important to him:

1. The more customers you service with good will, the better your long-term sales will be.

2. Don't let business reverses get you down. Cut your losses and move on.

3. Don't try to play the other man's game or be involved in endeavors where you have a competitive disadvantage.

4. Develop good people, give them lots of incentives, and delegate as much responsibility as they can handle.

5. Never go into a deal unless you control it, but once it's going, be willing to turn it over to others.

6. Don't go into any deal unless you enjoy it and are having fun.

The Late Career Years: Winding Down (1977–present)

When asked how he would like to be remembered, Garff replied, "I hope people will say first that I raised good and successful children; that I remained loyal to my religious principles and to my friends; that I'd been successful in busi-

ness but had lived a balanced life and helped the community; and," he paused and grinned, "that I'd had lots of fun in the process."

One of his greatest thrills at age 79 is watching his sons function as successful up-and-comers. His children and grandchildren are "good people," he says, and it gives him boundless satisfaction that they are also his best friends. He feels that successful men his age who have not paid attention to the raising of their children must regret their priorities, especially if their children are not making their own mark.

In 1977 Ken married Betty June Morgan, a widow with children and grandchildren of her own. The two play golf together often and are very active in the Salt Lake social scene. They winter at a condominium in Palm Springs next to the golf course. Partly at Betty's urging, Garff has devoted some of the attention formerly given to business affairs to their relationship, family, friends, and recreation. "I want more balance," he says. He has little tolerance for associates who are unable to retire from their businesses and find other sources of satisfaction. "I enjoyed business—still do—and I'm enjoying other things now," he comments. Ken's friendships have also taken on new meaning. He used to like to see how much money he could raise for worthy causes, but he now moderates the appeals he makes of his friends. The relationships have deepened and become more personal.

Some of his "retirement" pleasures are reading a good novel or visiting an art gallery and collecting art—things he never had time to do before. Garff's creative entrepreneurship is currently channeled into estate planning.

He still checks in with the office regularly by phone and frequently goes in. He is most enthusiastic, associates say, about the ranching business and on days when he doesn't have business meetings he goes to the office in a plaid shirt and cowboy boots. He remains active at the University of Utah, on the First Security Board, in church affairs, and as head of a homeowner's group.

One of his retirement activities is continuing to acquire parts of the city block on which his automobile business and offices are located in downtown Salt Lake City. He now owns all but three small pieces. A story of how he recently got another segment reveals his characteristic ingenuity. An older couple owned a small house on about 2,000 square feet of property. They asked a high price because they didn't see how they could replace the dwelling in today's market for less. Garff found a good deal on a small home, clean and in good condition, in a nicer neighborhood. The sellers wanted to move the house quickly and without encumbrances, so for cash he was able

PART II: CASE 2 Continued

to buy the home and its pleasant furnishings for a very good price.

He then approached the older couple personally, drove them to the new home, completely furnished, comfortable, and tailor-made for an older couple. They liked it very much. Ken swapped the houses straight across, acquiring their property for half of what they had requested, and still had very satisfied customers.

Roberta Harris reports that nowadays on his way to work Garff will also "spot someone driving a four- or five-year old Oldsmobile, Honda, Mercedes, or Saab and get their license plate number. Then he'll find out who they are, call them up, and offer them a very good deal on a new model. About half the time he'll make a sale."

"It's interesting for me to clean up loose ends," Garff says of his retirement. "I still get a big kick out of putting together all these little deals."

References

Bird, Barbara Jean (1984) *Internal Maps of Entrepreneurs.* Unpublished doctoral dissertation, University of Southern California.

Derr, C. Brooklyn (1984) *Career Portraiture.* Unpublished working paper no. 001-84, The Institute for Human Resource Management, Graduate School of Business, University of Utah, Salt Lake City.

Paulson, Jean R. (1983) *The Ken Garff Biography.*

Martin, Albro (1982) Additional aspects of entrepreneurial history. In Calvin A. Kent, et al., *Encyclopedia of Entrepreneurship.* Englewood Cliffs, NJ: Prentice-Hall, pp. 15–20.

Schein, Edgar H. (1982) *Individuals and Careers.* Unpublished technical report no. ONR 19, Office of Naval Research, p. 39.

Shapero, Albert, and Sokol, Lisa (1982) The social dimensions of entrepreneurship. In Calvin A. Kent, et al., *Encyclopedia of Entrepreneurship.* Englewood Cliffs, NJ: Prentice-Hall, pp. 72–90.

THE NATIONAL LEARNING CORPORATION

Barry Allen Gold

Hard Work and No Profits

On November 7, 1987, Dr. Martin Robbins, a child psychologist and owner of two National Learning Center franchises, wrote the following letter to the President of National.

> Dear Mr. Ireland:
>
> We, the undersigned owners of National Learning Centers in Region II, are deeply concerned over our continued struggle to develop, maintain, and build up financially healthy centers.
>
> While in-house operations and educational programs are excellent, our marketing and advertising efforts are failing. Public awareness of and interest in the National name still must be minimal as the monthly number of inquiries is far too low to permit growing enrollments.
>
> Months and years of hard work, long hours, and little progress in our efforts to increase revenues have resulted in widespread frustration and demoralization, which continues to grow. The statistics for our region reveal that almost 50% of the centers are grossing less than $10,000 per month and are losing money. Another 40% are grossing $10,000 to $14,000 and are meeting expenses. Finally, only 10% report revenues above $14,000.
>
> In view of these circumstances, we respectfully request that you seriously investigate mechanisms to provide major marketing and advertising assistance to this stricken segment of the National franchise network. One possibility, for example, would be to channel 3–5 percentage points of our monthly royalties back into a marketing relief fund for Region II.
>
> While we all sincerely recognize our responsibility to help our individual businesses grow, it has become abundantly clear that the prospects for financial growth without substantive corporate assistance are dismal. Indeed, at this point it does not seem unreasonable to ask the question: Does the franchisor not have the responsibility, if not the obligation, to provide the franchisee with the necessary marketing support so that we can do our job and make a reasonable profit?
>
> We look forward to your careful review of this very urgent matter and your prompt reply.

All except eight of the 37 franchisees in Region II signed the letter. The President of National never answered the letter.

A few days after Robbins' complaint was mailed, the franchisees received a letter from Craig Johnson, the President of the Association of National Learning Center Owners (ANLCO) in which he wrote,

> It has been somewhat frustrating at board meetings to be met with responses from Corporate such as "we have never heard this from other owners," or "this is the first time we have heard about this, so it must not be a major issue." The owners association was recently cited by one Corporate officer for "soliciting bad news" when it attempted to deal with an issue it felt was of great concern to the entire membership. This kind of minimizing makes our efforts less effective than they could be.

National's Beginning

Arnold Harrison, a junior high school teacher in an affluent suburb of Miami, always had three or four students in his classes who had difficulty learning. Remedial school programs like Title I seldom helped these students. But when Harrison tutored them after school they always improved significantly.

After ten years as an elementary teacher, Harrison grew tired of classroom routines and started to consider a career change that used his educational skills and entrepreneurial talents. After evaluating several options it occurred to him that the market for tutoring would increase dramatically when the children of the highly educated "baby-boom" generation entered school.

After experimenting, Harrison discovered that high-quality tutoring was possible with one teacher working with three students. This arrangement created a student teacher ratio that was the same as one-to-one instruction; the teacher would instruct one student while the other two worked independently. Even more important, this arrangement could produce high volume and maintain low labor costs. Harrison discovered that a sophisticated version of his moonlighting job had the potential to produce significant profits.

In the summer of 1978 Harrison opened his first tutoring center in the town where he was a teacher. At first business was slow. By April—the third report card of the year—business picked up rapidly and Harrison's Learning

Center was profitable. In the next year he opened two more Centers in nearby towns. One year later he began franchising his educational programs, teaching methods, marketing strategies, and advertising concepts. By June 1981 Harrison had sold 20 franchises.

Acquisition and Expansion

Harrison encountered marketing problems outside Florida and new franchises grew slowly during the next two years. Unexpectedly, in 1983, KidKoKorp, which was diversifying, offered Harrison $4,500,000 for the company. Harrison retired to the U.S. Virgin Islands.

KidKoKorp was one of the largest operators of private day care centers in the United States. It was part of a conglomerate that also owned shoe stores, discount women's apparel stores, portrait studios, a savings and loan association, and a life insurance company. KidKoKorp's stock was traded on NASDAQ.

KidKoKorp appointed John Ireland to be its senior vice president of operations and president and CEO of National. Ireland was regarded as the architect of KidKoKorp's child care division's growth and profitability. Ireland hired Ron Caputo as vice president of operations. Caputo's experience was in the operations of a successful franchised fast-food company. Ireland also hired professional franchise salespeople and began an aggressive campaign to sell franchises.

By 1988 National Learning Centers had grown to over 400 Centers. Most of the Centers were owned by franchisees with KidKoKorp owning and operating 30 Centers in California and suburbs of Boston.

By late 1988 the sale of new franchises dried up because all of the potentially lucrative territories had been sold. The business challenge shifted from selling franchises, which had been extremely successful, to increasing the gross revenues of the franchisees and consequently the royalties to KidKoKorp.

Organization

National's headquarters were in Boulder, Colorado. The president/CEO, vice presidents of operations, education, and finance reported to the president of KidKoKorp. Regional directors and franchise consultants, who served as liaison between the corporation and the franchisees, covered seven regions in the United States. An educational advisory committee, headed by a former Secretary

of Education, monitored the quality and endorsed the educational programs. Advertising and public relations were contracted to prominent firms. Finally, to link Corporate and the franchisees, Ireland established the Association of National Learning Center Owners (ANLCO).

Corporate Strategy

National's goal was to become "The McDonald's of Education." To accomplish this, in addition to rapidly adding franchises, National's executives formulated a strategy to make National the leader in the after school tutoring business. Key elements of the strategy included:

1. Guarantee
National was the only learning center to offer a guarantee. The guarantee stated that,

> *If there is less than one year of growth as measured by standardized tests after 36 hours of instruction, the student will receive 12 lessons free of charge.*

In addition to differentiating National from its competitors, the guarantee was designed to increase enrollment and student length of stay.

2. Advertising
The franchise license required a minimum of $20,000 annually on local advertising for each Center. Each franchisee also contributed one percent of monthly gross revenue to a national advertising fund that was used for ads in women's magazines with national readership.

3. Public Relations
One public relations activity was an educational advisory counsel of prominent educators who wrote testimonial letters and appeared at teacher conferences to endorse National. Another campaign featured a celebrity spokesperson who made occasional guest appearances on syndicated talk shows to emphasize the importance of education.

4. In-Center Marketing Activities
Marketing activities in Centers included seminars for parents of children with learning disabilities, parties for students, and open houses for local teachers.

5. New Programs
The purpose of new programs was to add to the clients served and to increase student re-enrollment. One new program, such as process writing, study skills, and adult literacy, was introduced every two years.

6. Operations Manuals

Center owners were supplied with manuals that specified all procedures for operating a National Learning Center. Topics included were financial planning, marketing, advertising, hiring procedures, educational programs, and daily operations.

7. Quality Control

Quality control was maintained by periodic inspections made by franchise consultants of Center operations. Marketing plans were reviewed, telephone sales scripts were critiqued, parent conference techniques were analyzed, and educational program effectiveness was assessed.

8. Required Meetings

National staged an annual national conference to present new programs, unveil advertising campaigns, and to have franchisees feel that they were part of a growing, dynamic organization. In addition, quarterly regional conferences featured topics such as cost control, improving student length of stay, and employee motivation.

The Franchisees

A typical franchisee was an educator with fifteen years of teaching or administrative experience and little or no business background. In most cases franchisees owned and operated one Center. However, nine percent owned multiple Centers including several investors who owned six. National required each owner and executive director to attend two weeks of training in both the educational and business aspects of a Center.

Investment and Finance

The total investment, including franchise fees and equipment, was $120,000. The projected breakeven of a National Learning Center was calculated on an average monthly enrollment of 30 students. Franchisees set the tuition for their Center according to expenses and the average family income of the communities surrounding their Center. In 1988 the system-wide test fee was $100 and the average tuition was $250 per month.

Major operating expenses were the director's annual compensation of $35,000 plus bonuses, an $11 hourly rate for part-time teachers, rent, advertising, utilities, insurance, telephone, office supplies, taxes, royalty, and insurance. Monthly breakeven costs ranged from $10,500 to $14,000. Variation in rent, the number of full-time employees, and advertising expenses accounted for the range.

The Franchise Agreement

Each franchisee signed an agreement that described the obligations of the franchisor and the franchisee. Key terms were a 10.5 percent royalty based on annual gross revenues payable monthly, specification of the exclusive territory of the franchisee, and a minimum of $20,000 per year to be spent on local advertising by the franchisee.

Other important provisions of the agreement included KidKoKorp's right to audit franchisees financial records and to perform periodic reviews of franchisee operations. The agreement also specified conditions for license sale, restrictions on the use of trademarks, and covenants not to compete. Finally, the agreement enumerated the legal actions the franchisor could take to correct deficiencies in a franchisee but did not specify franchisee remedies against the franchisor.

Operation of a National Learning Center

Location and Design

National Learning Centers were located in professional office buildings. They consisted of a waiting room, an office for the director, a testing room, and a large open-space classroom. The classroom had five tables that accommodated the one teacher for three students instructional arrangement. Study carrels contained computers, language machines, and tape recorders that students used for part of their lessons. Educational materials were displayed on the walls in a colorful array. Also prominent in the classroom was a "store" filled with toys and school supplies that students purchased with tokens they received from instructors. In general, the classroom and offices were cheerful, interesting, well organized, and presented the image of a "professional" service.

Organization

The full-time staff of a Center was an executive director and a director of education. The director had overall responsibility for the educational program, personnel, local advertising, school contacts, and public relations. The director of education conducted student testing and prescribed the educational program. There were as many part-time teachers as enrollment required.

Educational Program

The educational program started with standardized tests to evaluate a student's academic skills. The test results were then presented to the student's parents. If they enrolled, an individualized educational program based on the test results began. A child attended the Center one hour two times each week for a minimum of 36 hours.

Parents met after every ten hours of instruction with the executive director to discuss the student's progress. At the end of the program, the students were retested to measure what was learned.

In-Center Marketing

Because students enrolled for a month and could discontinue at any time, every aspect of center activity involved sales, merchandising, and marketing. For example, student treatment during diagnostic tests was important for encouraging enrollment. Also, the quality of parent conferences influenced the duration of a student's attendance.

National's Competitors

Royden and Remington Learning Centers

Royden Learning Centers and Remington Learning Centers entered the tutoring business at the same time as National. Royden, a subsidiary of the Royden Encyclopedia Corporation, was similar in concept and educational programs to National. However, Royden did not franchise its Centers. In 1988 Royden had 250 Centers throughout the United States. Remington Learning Centers, founded and owned by Joseph Remington, a professor at a state university, were franchised. Remington had 145 Centers in the middle Atlantic states. Both Royden and Remington located their centers in affluent suburban communities, often near a National Learning Center.

Teachers

Other competitors were independent, private tutoring businesses, learning disabilities consultants, and teachers. Teachers were National's most significant competitor because of minimal overhead, scheduling flexibility, and easy access to students.

Critics of Tutoring Businesses

Although National and its competitors often received favorable publicity in newspapers and magazines, there were vocal critics of learning centers. For example, a prominent professor of education claimed in a *New York Times* interview that,

> *The standardized tests that learning centers use do not measure real knowledge or transferable skills, but decoding skills. It's like taking a valuable piece of behavior and becoming good at it. It is not creative thinking.*

Some critics claimed that the high cost of learning centers increased the grades of only students with wealthy parents. In their view this was undesirable because it increased the educational gap between suburban and urban students.

Clients

Families

Because the average monthly tuition for eight lessons at National was $250 (Royden and Remington had similar fees), the majority of students were from middle- and upper-middle-class families. To make its service more accessible, National offered an installment payment plan.

Students who attended National ranged from those who were a year or more below grade level to "enrichment" students who achieved high grades.

Franchisees often had difficulty selling the program to parents. In many cases they were skeptical of the claims that National made, for example, the 36-hour guarantee. In other cases their hesitancy was based on frustration with previously failed attempts to find solutions for their child's inability to learn. One result of parental distrust was that in 20 percent of the cases there was a delay of one year or more between initial contact and student enrollment. Another reason for the delay was that many families viewed attending National as a stigma; they tried other solutions first.

Schools

National encouraged its franchisees to develop relationships with schools. Suggested marketing methods to schools consisted of meetings with teachers, seminars for teachers on new educational methods, and open houses to demonstrate National's programs.

Educational Outcomes

Over 80 percent of students and parents reported that National's educational programs produced the results that they wanted. Only two percent of National's students did not achieve one year of academic growth after 36 hours of instruction; they received the guaranteed 12 free lessons.

Region II: Opportunities and Conflicts

Region II, the subject of Dr. Robbins' letter, had 37 National Learning Centers in a metropolitan tri-state area. Three of the most profitable Centers in the United States were in Region II along with ten that lost $15,000 annually since they opened. A typical Center in this region either fell slightly short of its breakeven or struggled to make a small profit. In 1987 Centers in Region II averaged five years in business.

Advertising Cooperatives

One advantage of purchasing a National franchise was the ability to pool resources to build the business. National's vice presidents of operations and marketing created advertising cooperatives based on patterns of media concentration. All the centers in Region II became members of a co-op.

In Region II, because advertising costs were the highest in the United States—even when costs were distributed among 37 Centers, purchasing the necessary exposures on television and radio was too expensive. The alternative recommended by an advertising agency was a 12-week flight of full-page ads in the regional zone of two major magazines. The cost for this second-best approach was $20,000 for each Center. The franchisees were alarmed because this doubled their annual advertising budgets at a time when many were losing money. In addition, they were concerned about the effectiveness of a burst of advertisements compared with a continuous presence on, for example, cable TV. But cable TV was viewed as ineffective by the advertising agency.

The franchisees were also concerned with nonparticipation by fellow franchisees and with the administrative details of the cooperative. They decided that to protect themselves against legal actions and financial liabilities, and to specify the activities of the cooperative, a set of bylaws was required. They drafted bylaws, had them reviewed by an attorney, and incorporated the cooperative. However, because they were not able to design an advertising plan that they could afford, the cooperative was never operational.

Cooperative advertising did occur on a limited scale among several Centers when a special event—a trade show or teacher convention—affected more than one territory. These efforts were never sustained because benefits were difficult to measure and franchisees who failed to increase their enrollments stopped participating.

College Preparation Program

Another proposal to increase Center revenues was to cooperatively advertise SAT preparation courses. The objective was to develop a larger, more predictable market than the remedial education students. In addition, consumer awareness of SAT preparation was created by Stanley Kaplan and *Princeton Review.*

Although it was debated at length, the proposal was rejected because many franchisees thought that they could not compete successfully. Other Centers had not purchased the SAT program from National and had no intention to. Yet other owners discouraged students from enrolling in SAT programs because past results had been disappointing.

Inter-Center Competition

An important influence on the franchisees in Region II was that several owners competed for the same students in communities that were not within designated territories. Because of this there was resistance to joint advertising and reluctance to share business information. An example of the conflict among owners was that one franchisee advertised in another owner's territory's newspapers using a telephone number without an address. When a potential client called from outside her territory, instead of referring them to the closest Center, they were encouraged to enroll at her Center. When parents discovered the closer Center—which in some cases was ten minutes from their house instead of an hour to the Center that ran the ad—they became irate and withdrew their child from National.

The Franchisees Assess Themselves

After several years of quarterly meetings in which franchisees complained among themselves about the inaction and ineptness of National's officers, continuous losses, and the failure of the cooperative, a consensus emerged among the franchisees that successful owners were lucky, not skillful. In support of this view they pointed to the larger potential student populations of successful Centers or the availability of inexpensive advertising. Many of the owners considered selling their businesses while hoping that things would improve.

Corporate Views the Franchisees

John Ireland's attitude toward franchisees was excitement and optimism during the period of rapid franchise sales. When franchise sales stalled it was replaced with, "Let's wait and see what develops." Eventually his view was that the reason many franchisees were unable to operate profitable businesses was their lack of effort and failure to faithfully implement the National program and strategy. As a result Ireland and his staff emphasized strict compliance with license and program requirements.

Data that supported Ireland's conclusion came from several sources. For example, Ireland and Caputo thought that franchisees did not utilize public relations opportunities provided by their staff. They pointed to the small amounts of money that students donated to an annual Muscular Dystrophy campaign National sponsored. Another example was that Caputo hired a firm to evaluate telephone sales techniques used by franchisees by posing as "secret shoppers." The results indicated that many Centers did not follow the mandated telephone script and, in some cases, failed to return the messages of potential clients. Ireland also thought that student length of stay—a critical factor in profitability— would have been better if Centers implemented marketing activities more aggressively, consistently, and imaginatively. Finally, Phil Martz, vice president of education, reported that a study showed that in many Centers the quality of educational programs suffered from substandard teaching.

Based on this and other evidence, the policy that National's corporate executives developed toward the franchisees was to ignore their complaints and demands. They decided to encourage dissatisfied owners to sell; they would be replaced with owners with the desire to take action to achieve success. Caputo announced at an annual meeting, "Some of you aren't fit to be in this business. In the next few months we'll tell you who you are."

Unwelcome Choices

In September 1988 revenue from royalties increased modestly but many franchisees were paying royalties late, and attendance at regional and national meetings was declining. More franchisees complained among themselves, to the franchise consultants, and to National's headquarters about their inability to make money.

In Region II in 1988 four Centers closed and seven others were for sale. In addition, Royden closed one-third of its Centers and Remington stopped opening new Centers. Similar conditions existed in other regions. At the same time, however, several National Centers established record revenues and profits. KidKoKorp's 1988 Annual Report summarized the situation.

> Although franchise royalties have increased in the current year, total revenues were slightly lower for 1988 due to a gain on the sale of several corporate centers included in the prior year's revenues and a lower number of franchise sales in the current year. Total revenues were $11,222,000 as compared to $12,799,000 in 1987. In addition, management decided to consolidate several corporate centers in the Boston market to maximize future earnings potential in this market. The resulting asset write-offs combined with a loss on the sale of investments resulted in a before taxes loss of $2,652,000 in the prior year.

Under pressure from KidKoKorp's senior management, individual franchisees, and a barrage of complaints from ANLCO, John Ireland and Ron Caputo were forced to consider changing National. Among the possibilities were:

1. Separating KidKoKorp into two corporations—one involved only in child care and tutoring and the other in the retail and financial businesses.
2. Revamping National's national advertising campaign.
3. Developing more effective advertising media.
4. Increasing the effectiveness of regional and local public relations efforts.
5. More careful monitoring of franchise operations with an emphasis on program quality and the placement of local advertising.
6. Developing more types of educational programs to enlarge the client base.
7. Reducing or rebating a percentage of franchise royalties for a year.
8. Purchasing failing franchises in good locations and operating them as corporate Centers.

Two Views of the Future

John Ireland, his staff, and many of the franchisees believed that National's problems were temporary and part of the start-up of a new business. In their view the strategy was correct and the plan for implementing it was sound. In a newsletter Ireland told franchisees to have patience:

We believe that in the next few years our strategy will be very productive. Within a reasonable time National will dominate its market. For the present we need to have dedication, creativity, and most importantly, provide a high-quality value-added service to our students.

Like Dr. Robbins, a growing number of franchisees experienced frustration, disenchantment, and were weary from the conflicts with their fellow franchisees and National. In their view they made a substantial financial investment and faithfully followed corporate policies and procedures. But, in over five years of business, they could not make money. Prospects for improvement in the near future were slender and, as one franchisee put it, "The lights could go out." They demanded immediate action from the franchisor.

PART II: EXPERIENCE 1

THE LEARNING-MODEL INSTRUMENT

Kenneth L. Murrell

Purpose

To determine the type of learners students are.

Time Required

45 minutes.

Group Size

Any number of students.

Preparation

Before the class meeting complete and score the learning-model instrument.

Procedure

After scoring the instrument, the class divides into groups based on learning style: Thinker Planners, Feeling Planners, Task Implementors and Participative Implementors.
Each group discusses the following:

1. What is the ideal learning environment for your learning type?
2. How can learning environments be changed to fit the various types?
3. What are the implications of this experience for understanding other people's learning types?
4. How can the identification of learning types assist a manager in her job?

This is followed by class discussion.

The Learning-Model Instrument

Instructions: For each statement choose the response that is more nearly true for you. Place an X on the blank that corresponds to that response.

1. When meeting people, I prefer
   ___ (a) to think and speculate on what they are like.
   ___ (b) to interact directly and to ask them questions.
2. When presented with a problem, I prefer
   ___ (a) to jump right in and work on a solution.
   ___ (b) to think through and evaluate possible ways to solve the problem.
3. I enjoy sports more when
   ___ (a) I am watching a good game.
   ___ (b) I am actively participating.
4. Before taking a vacation, I prefer
   ___ (a) to rush at the last minute and give little thought beforehand to what I will do while on vacation.
   ___ (b) to plan early and daydream about how I will spend my vacation.
5. When enrolled in courses. I prefer
   ___ (a) to plan how to do my homework before actually attacking the assignment.
   ___ (b) to immediately become involved in doing the assignment.
6. When I receive information that requires action, I prefer
   ___ (a) to take action immediately.
   ___ (b) to organize the information and determine what type of action would be most appropriate.
7. When presented with a number of alternatives for action, I prefer
   ___ (a) to determine how the alternatives relate to one another and analyze the consequences of each.
   ___ (b) to select the one that looks best and implement it.
8. When I awaken every morning. I prefer
   ___ (a) to expect to accomplish some worthwhile work without considering what the individual tasks may entail.
   ___ (b) to plan a schedule for the tasks I expect to do that day.
9. After a full day of work, I prefer
   ___ (a) to reflect back on what I accomplished and think of how to make time the next day for unfinished tasks.

Source: "The Learning-Model Instrument," ©1987, by Dr. Kenneth Murrell, University of West Florida and Empowerment Leadership Systems. Reprinted by permission.

PART II: EXPERIENCE 1 Continued

_____ (b) to relax with some type of recreation and not think about my job.

10. After choosing the above responses, I
_____ (a) prefer to continue and complete this instrument.
_____ (b) am curious about how my responses will be interpreted and prefer some feedback before continuing with the instrument.

11. When I learn something, I am usually
_____ (a) thinking about it.
_____ (b) right in the middle of doing it.

12. I learn best when
_____ (a) I am dealing with real-world issues.
_____ (b) concepts are clear and well organized.

13. In order to retain something I have learned, I must
_____ (a) periodically review it in my mind.
_____ (b) practice it or try to use the information.

14. In teaching others how to do something, I first
_____ (a) demonstrate the task.
_____ (b) explain the task.

15. My favorite way to learn to do something is
_____ (a) reading a book or instructions or enrolling in a class.
_____ (b) trying to do it and learning from my mistakes.

16. When I become emotionally involved with something, I usually
_____ (a) let my feelings take the lead and then decide what to do.
_____ (b) control my feelings and try to analyze the situation.

17. If I were meeting jointly with several experts on a subject, I would prefer
_____ (a) to ask each of them for his or her opinion.
_____ (b) to interact with them and share our ideas and feelings.

18. When I am asked to relate information to a group of people. I prefer
_____ (a) not to have an outline, but to interact with them and become involved in an extemporaneous conversation.
_____ (b) to prepare notes and know exactly what I am going to say.

19. Experience is
_____ (a) a guide for building theories.
_____ (b) the best teacher.

20. People learn easier when they are
_____ (a) doing work on the job.
_____ (b) in a class taught by an expert.

The Learning-Model Instrument Scoring Sheet

Instructions: Transfer your responses by writing either "a" or "b" in the blank that corresponds to each item in the Learning-Model Instrument.

Abstract/Concrete		Cognitive/Affective	
Column 1	Column 2	Column 3	Column 4
1. _b_	2. _b_	11. _a_	12. _a_
3. _a_	4. _b_	13. _b_	14. _a_
5. _a_	6. _b_	15. _a_	16. _b_
7. _b_	8. _b_	17. _b_	18. _a_
9. _b_	10. _a_	19. _b_	20. _a_
Total Circles _2_	_4_	_3_	_3_

Grand Totals _____   _____

Now circle every "a" in Column 1 and Column 4. Then circle every "b" in Column 2 and in Column 3. Next, total the circles in each of the four columns. Then add the totals of Columns 1 and 2; plot this grand total on the vertical axis of the Learning Model for Managers and draw a horizontal line through the point. Now add the totals of Columns 3 and 4; plot that grand total on the horizontal axis of the model and draw a vertical line through the point.

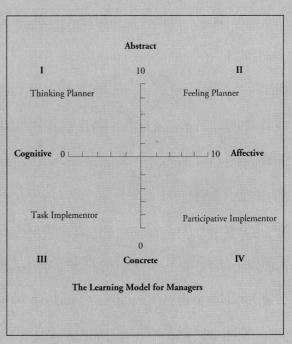

The Learning Model for Managers

The intersection of these two lines indicates the domain of your preferred learning style.

The Learning-Model Instrument Interpretation Sheet

The cognitive-affective axis or continuum represents the range of ways in which people learn. Cognitive learning includes learning that is structured around either rote storing of knowledge or intellectual abilities and skills, or both. Affective learning includes learning from experience, from feelings about the experience, and from one's own emotions.

The concrete-abstract axis or continuum represents the range of ways in which people experience life. When people experience life abstractly, they detach themselves from the immediacy of the situation and theorize about it. If they experience life concretely, they respond to the situation directly with little subsequent contemplation.

The two axes divide the model into four parts or domains. Most people experience life and learn from it in all four domains but have a preference for a particular domain. Liberal arts education has typically concentrated on abstract learning (domains I and II), whereas vocational and on-the-job training usually takes place in the lower quadrants, particularly domain III.

Occupations representative of the four styles include the following: domain I, philosopher or chief executive officer; domain II, poet or journalist; domain III, architect or engineer; domain IV, psychologist or personnel counselor.

Managerial jobs require an ability to learn in all four domains, and a manager's development depends on his or her ability to learn both cognitively and affectively. Thus, management education and development demand the opportunity for the participants to learn how to learn in each domain.

Interpreting the Scores

The next four paragraphs give an interpretation of the four end points of the axes in the Learning Model for Managers. Following these are explanations of the four domains in the model.

Cognitive Learning

A person who scores low on the cognitive-affective axis shows a marked preference for learning through thought or other mental activity. People who grasp intellectually very quickly what they are trying to learn or who simply prefer to use controlled thought and logic will be found on the cognitive end of this axis. Rationality appeals to these individuals, as do logic and other thinking skills that are necessary for this type of learning. Although this statement is not based on hard research, it appears that a high cognitive orientation correlates with a high task orientation rather than with a people orientation. The research about possible left-versus-right brain functioning correlates a cognitive orientation to individuals who are left-brain dominant. Therefore, the left side of the axis was deliberately assigned to the cognitive orientation to serve as an easy reminder.

Affective Learning

A person who scores high on the cognitive-affective axis shows a marked preference for learning in the affective realm. Such an individual is more comfortable with and seeks out learning from his or her emotions and feelings. These individuals desire personal interaction and seek to learn about people by experiencing them in emotional ways. This type of learner would potentially be highly people oriented. A manger with this orientation would probably seek out social interaction rather than to focus exclusively on the task components of the job. In right-brain research, affective learners are said to be more intuitive, more spontaneous, and less linear. They seek out feelings and emotions rather than logic.

Concrete Life Experiencing

People with a preference for the concrete enjoy jumping in and getting their hands dirty. Hands-on experiences are important to them. As managers, these people want to keep busy, become directly involved, and physically approach or touch whatever they are working with. If they work with machines, they will get greasy; if they work with people, they will become involved.

Abstract Life Experiencing

Individuals preferring this style have no special desire to touch, but they want to keep active by thinking about the situation and relating it to similar situations. Their preferred interaction style is internal—inside their own heads.

The Four Learning Domains

A person is unlikely to be on the extreme end of either axis, and no one type of learning is "best." Any mixture of preferences simply represents a person's uniqueness. The model is useful in helping people differentiate themselves, and it offers a method for looking at the way different styles fit together. This section describes the four domains that are represented in the model.

The descriptions of these domains could be of special interest to managers, because they will help the manager understand the relationship between managerial action and learning style. A manager should be capable of learning and functioning well in all four domains, especially if he or she expects to face a variety of situations and challenges. The successful manager is likely to be the one who can operate in both a task and a people environment with the ability to see and become involved with the concrete and also use thought processes to understand what is needed. The normative assumption of the model is that a manager should learn how to learn in each of the four domains. In doing this, the manager may well build on his or her primary strengths, but the versatility and flexibility demanded in a managerial career make clear the importance of all four domains.

Domain I, the Thinking Planner. A combination of cognitive and abstract preferences constitutes domain I, where the "thinking planner" is located. This domain might well be termed the place for the planner whose job is task oriented and whose environment contains primarily things, numbers, or printouts. The bias in formal education is often toward this learning domain, and Mintzberg (1976) was critical of this bias. In this domain things are treated abstractly and often their socio-emotional elements are denied.

The domain-I learner should do well in school, should have a talent for planning, and is likely to be successful as a staff person, or manager in a department that deals with large quantities of untouchable things. This domain represents an important area for management learning. Of the four domains. it seems to receive the heaviest emphasis in traditional university programs and in management-development seminars, particularly those in financial management.

Domain II, the Feeling Planner. A combination of affective and abstract preferences constitutes domain II, where the "feeling planner" is located. The managerial style associated with this domain is that of the thinker who can learn and who enjoys working with people but has limited opportunity to get close to them. This domain is important for the personnel executive or a manager with too much responsibility to interact closely with other employees. Social-analysis skills are represented in this area. Managers in this domain should be able to think through and understand the social and emotional factors affecting a large organization.

Difficulties in this area sometimes arise when good first-line supervisors who have a natural style with people are promoted into positions that prevent them from having direct contact with others and are expected to determine without concrete experience the nature of and solutions to personnel problems.

Domain III, the Task Implementor. A combination of cognitive and concrete preferences constitutes domain III, where the "task implementor" is located. This domain contains decision makers who primarily want to understand the task and who can focus on the details and specifics of the concrete in a thoughtful manner. If these people are allowed to think about a situation, they can see the concrete issues and, after close examination, can make a well-thought-out decision. A person in this domain is often a task-focused doer. If the interpersonal skill demands are low and if the emotional climate is not a problem, this person is likely to do well.

Domain IV, the Participative Implementor. A combination of affective and concrete preferences constitutes domain IV, where the "participative implementor" is located. The manager with people skills who has the opportunity to work closely with people is found in this category. This is the place where implementors and highly skilled organization development consultants reside. This domain is for those who like to become involved and who have the ability and interest in working with the emotional needs and demands of the people in an organization. This is the domain that is emphasized by most of the practical management programs, and it can be used to complement the traditional educational programs of domain I.

REFERENCES

Blake, R. R., and J. S. Mouton. *Managerial Grid.* 3rd ed. Houston, Texas: Gulf, 1984.

Jung, C. C. *Second Impression.* Trans. H. Godwin. New York: Harcourt Brace, 1924.

Kolb, D. A., I. M. Rubin and J. M. McIntyre. *Organizational Psychology: An Experiential Approach.* 2nd ed. Englewood Cliffs, NJ: Prentice-Hall, 1974.

Mintzberg, H. "PIanning on the Left Side and Managing on the Right." *Harvard Business Review,* July-August, 1976, pp. 49–58.

Peters, D. *Directory of Human Resource Development Instrumentation.* San Diego, Ca.: University Associates, 1985.

Pfeiffer, J.W., R. Heslin, and J. E. Jones. *Instrumentation in Human Relations Training.* San Diego, Ca.: University Associates, 1976.

Rogers. C. R. *Freedom to Learn.* Columbus, Ohio: Charles E. Merrill, 1982.

PART II: EXPERIENCE 2

STRESS AND BREATH

Barry Allen Gold

Purpose

The intention of this exercise is to create an awareness of emotional and physical responses to stress and to experiment with methods for controlling stress.

Time Required

Thirty minutes.

Materials

None.

Introduction

Stress in organizations is pervasive. Under certain conditions stress reduces an individual's ability to perform. But in many instances moderate stress—the "flow of adrenaline"—actually increases performance. In either case it is useful to attempt to control levels of stress.

Yoga exercises provide a method of reducing stress through refocusing and controlling consciousness by deliberate efforts to channel breathing patterns.

Procedure

Form groups of four to six students. Read the following descriptions of breathing and suggestions for changing breath patterns.

Breath

In *Yoga and Psychotherapy* (Rama, Ballentine and Ajaya, 1976) the process of breathing is described this way:

> *A normal person will breath through one nostril for two to three hours while the tissues of the other are engorged, closing it off. By the end of this time, the situation will have gradually shifted. He will have begun to breathe though the opposite nostril. Midway through this cycle he passes through a period when both are momentarily open. The*

pattern continues: first one nostril is clear, then the other (1976: 40).

Activities

Close one nostril by placing your thumb against it. Repeat this procedure with the other nostril. Does your breathing pattern conform to the description above? Compare your results with the group members. Does anyone in the group breathe continually through both nostrils? What if you have a cold? What if you breathe through your mouth?

The shifting pattern of breath from nostril to nostril means that:

> *When the right nostril is clear, the right side of the body (and the left hemisphere of the brain) are predominant. During that time one finds he is "in the mood" for more aggressive tasks and assertive interactions. Those yogis who have studied this matter in depth discovered that operating in the world effectively and being assertive is easier during these periods. On the other hand, more passive functions are to be performed when the left nostril is open and the opposite system is predominant. At this time the physiology and mind are inclined toward rest and receptivity (1976: 41).*

This passage implies that certain breath patterns are likely to increase or decrease stress if they fit a particular environment. If there is a mismatch of breath pattern and activity pattern the result will be a less than satisfactory experience.

But according to Rama, Ballentine, and Ajaya, breathing can be consciously controlled.

> *There are maneuvers which are employed for activating one or the other of the nostrils. For example, lying on the right side or keeping a pillow [or your hand] pressed tightly under the right arm will, after several minutes, open the left nostril. However, those who have advanced further in their training, effect control through mental concentration alone (1976: 42).*

Place your hand under the arm *opposite* your open nostril. After five minutes has the nostril you are breathing through changed? If this doesn't work, try to focus your mind on changing your breath.

If you succeeded in changing the nostril through which

PART II: EXPERIENCE 2 Continued

you breathe, has your mood changed? Do you feel more assertive or more relaxed?

If you were unable to change your breathing pattern, try lying on the opposite side of a closed nostril at home tonight.

After-Class Assignment

Use these breathing techniques in your daily life for a day or two. Are you able to reduce stress or increase your energy by controlling your breath? Observe the breathing patterns of others under conditions of stress, moderate tension, and relaxation. How do these people control stress?

Discussion Questions

1. What situations do students typically find stressful? Generate a list of stressful situations.

2. Does stress ever serve a positive function? If yes, how?

3. What techniques are commonly used for dealing with stress? Develop a typology of techniques.

4. In addition to breathing patterns, what other biological processes operate—voluntarily or involuntarily—when a person experiences stress? How do these affect their behavior?

5. What are *organizational devices* that companies use to reduce or cope with employee stress?

6. How can a manager use these insights and techniques to understand workplace stress and reduce it?

REFERENCES

Rama, S., Ballentine, R., and Ajaya, S. 1976. *Yoga and Psychotherapy.* Honesdale, Pa.: The Himalayan International Institute of Yoga Science and Philosophy.

Exploring Individual Behavior: The Dodds-Blackman Case

Barry Allen Gold

Purpose

The purpose of this experience is to create discussion about the roles of perception, personality, motivation, individual decision making, and stress in organizations.

Time Required

One hour.

Materials Needed

The "Dodds-Blackman" case.

Procedure

This short case will be read like a play. The instructor will assign the roles of Dodds, Blackman, and the Narrator to students. Although Dodds and Blackman appear to be men, it is suggested that the case be read several times with these roles assigned to minorities, women, and people of various ages. Altering the characteristics of the actors changes the interpersonal dynamics of the case.

After the case is read, the class should be broken into groups of four to six students. Each group should discuss the case for fifteen minutes using the questions below as guidelines.

The product of the group discussions will be an interpretation that supports either Dodds or Blackman. A consensus should be reached within the group for the position taken.

The group then presents its conclusions with supporting reasons to the entire class.

This is followed by an entire class discussion.

The Dodds-Blackman Case

Dr. Richard Dodds, a physics research worker, entered the office and showed his superior, Dr. Blackman, a letter. This letter was from another research institution, offering Dodds a position. Blackman read the letter.

Dodds: "What do you think of that?"

Blackman: "I knew it was coming. He asked me if it would be all right if he sent it. I told him to go ahead, if he wanted to."

Dodds: "I didn't expect it, particularly after what you said to me last time [pause]. I'm really quite happy here. I don't want you to get the idea that I am thinking of leaving. But I thought I should go and visit him—I think he expects it—and I wanted to let you know that just because I was thinking of going down, that didn't mean I was thinking of leaving here, unless of course, he offers me something extraordinary."

Blackman: "Why are you telling me all this?"

Dodds: "Because I didn't want you hearing from somebody else that I'm thinking of leaving here, you know, unless he offers me something really extraordinary that I can't afford to turn down. I think I'll tell him that, that I am willing to look at his laboratory, but unless there is something unusual for me, I have no intention of leaving here."

Blackman: "It's up to you."

Dodds: "What do you think?"

Blackman: "Well, what? About what? You've got to make up your own mind."

Dodds: "I don't consider too seriously this job. He is not offering anything really extraordinary. But I am interested in what he had to say. I would like to look around his lab."

Blackman: "Sooner or later you are going to have to make up your mind where you want to work."

Dodds replied sharply: "That depends on the offers, doesn't it?"

Blackman: "No, not really; a good man always gets offers. You get a good offer and you move, and as soon as you have moved, you get other good offers. It would throw you into confusion to consider all the good offers you will receive. Isn't there a factor of how stable you want to be?"

Dodds: "But I'm not shopping around. I already told you that. He sent me this letter, I didn't ask

Source: Abraham Zaleznik, *Human Dilemmas* of *Leadership*, New York: Harper and Row, 1966.

him to. All I said was that I should visit him, and to you that's shopping around."

Blackman: "Well, you may choose to set aside your commitment here if he offers you something better. All I am saying is that you will still be left with the question of you've got to stay some place, and where is that going to be?"

The discussion continued on how it would look if Dodds changed jobs at this point, and finally Dodds said:

Dodds: "Look, I came in here, and I want to be honest with you, but you go and make me feel guilty, and I don't like that."

Blackman: "You are being honest as can be."

Dodds: "I didn't come in here to fight. I don't want to disturb you."

Blackman: "I'm not disturbed. If you think it is best for you to go somewhere else, that is O.K. with me."

Again there is a lengthy exchange about what Dodds really wants and how his leaving would look to others. Finally Dodds blurts out:

Dodds: "I don't understand you. I came in here to be honest with you, and you make me feel guilty. All I wanted was to show you this letter, and let you know what I was going to do. What should I have told you?"

Blackman: "That you had read the letter, and felt that under the circumstances it was necessary for you to pay a visit to the professor, but that you were happy here and wanted to stay at least until you had got a job done."

Dodds: "I can't get over it. You think there isn't a place in the world I'd rather be than here in this lab. . . . "

Conclusion: Alternative Perspectives

Abraham Zaleznik, the author of the Dodds-Blackman case, views Dodds as a masochistic, compulsive subordinate. Specifically, according to Zaleznik, Dodds exhibits doubt, attitude reversal, hidden aggression, and denial of responsibility. In Zaleznik's view, given this type of subordinate, Blackman uses the status of his position and expert power to control the situation very well.

Richard Sennett has reinterpreted the Dodds-Blackman case (1981: 97-104). Sennett views Blackman as a paternalistic employer and Dodds as a victimized employee. According to Sennett, Blackman uses the technique of *reversed responses* to control reality and make Dodds defensive, guilty, and dependent. In other words, Blackman abuses his position and power.

These scholars perceive the same data in opposite ways because of their assumptions and how they frame Dodds's and Blackman's decision-making processes.

Discussion Questions

Motivation

1. What is Dodds's motivation?
2. What is Blackman's motivation?

Decision Making

3. How has the question of Dodds's career been framed? By Dodds? By Blackman?
4. Did the frame change at any point in the conversation?

Perception

5. What is Dodds's perceptual style?
6. How does Blackman perceive Dodds?

Communication

7. What is Dodds's communication pattern?
8. What is Blackman's communication style?
9. What, if any, are the problems with the communication between Dodds and Blackman?

Stress and Conflict

10. What are the sources of conflict in this dialogue?
11. How do Dodds and Blackman respond to stress?

REFERENCES

Sennett, R. *Authority.* NY: Vintage, 1982.

Zaleznik, A. *Human Dilemmas of Leadership.* NY: Harper and Row, 1966.

PART
III

BEHAVIOR IN GROUPS

7

GROUP DYNAMICS AND COMMUNICATION

Time and Transition in Work Teams:
Toward a New Model of Group Development

CONNIE J. G. GERSICK

LEARNING OBJECTIVES

After reading Gersick's "Time and Transition in Work Teams: Toward a New Model of Group Development," a student will be able to:

1. Understand traditional models of group development

2. Reconstruct the research methods used to propose a new model of group development

3   Understand the new model of group development

4. Be able to use the implications of this study for improving the behavior of groups in organizations

Groups are essential management tools. Organizations use teams to put novel combinations of people to work on novel problems and use committees to deal with especially critical decisions; indeed, organizations largely consist of permanent and temporary groups (Huse & Cummings, 1985). Given the importance of group management, there is a curious gap in researchers' use of existing knowledge. For years, researchers studying group development—the path a group takes over its life-span toward the accomplishment of its main tasks—have reported that groups change predictably over time. This information suggests that, to understand what makes groups work effectively, both theorists and managers ought to take change over

time into account. However, little group-effectiveness research has done so (McGrath, 1986).

One reason for the gap may lie in what is unknown about group development. Traditional models shed little light on the triggers or mechanisms of change or on the role of a group's environment in its development. Both areas are of key importance to group effectiveness (Gladstein, 1984; Goodstein & Dovico, 1979; McGrath, 1986). This hypothesis-generating study, stimulated by an unexpected set of empirical findings, proposed a new way to conceptualize group development. It is based on a different paradigm of change than that which underlies traditional models, and it addresses the timing and mechanisms of change and groups' dynamic relations with their environments.

Traditional Models of Group Development

There have been two main streams of research and theory about group development. The first stream deals with

Source: Connie J.G. Gersick: "Time and Transition in Work Teams: Toward a New Model of Group Development," *Academy of Management Journal,* 1988, Vol. 31, No. 1, pp. 9–41. Copyright ©1988. Reprinted by permission.

group dynamics, the other with phases in group problem solving. Group dynamics research on development began in the late 1940s, with a focus on the psychosocial and emotional aspects of group life. Working primarily with therapy groups, T-groups, and self-study groups, researchers originally saw a group's task in terms of the achievement of personal and interpersonal goals like insight, learning, or honest communication (Mills, 1979). They explored development as the progress, over a group's life-span, of members' ability to handle issues seen as critical to their ability to work, such as dependency, control, and intimacy (Bennis & Shepard, 1956; Bion, 1961; Mann, Gibbard, & Hartman, 1967; Slater, 1966).

In 1965, Tuckman synthesized this literature in a model of group development as a unitary sequence that is frequently cited today. The sequence, theoretically the same for every group, consists of forming, storming, norming, and performing. Tuckman and Jensen's 1977 update of the literature on groups left this model in place, except for the addition of a final stage, adjourning. Models offered subsequently have also kept the same pattern. Proposed sequences include: define the situation, develop new skills, develop appropriate roles, carry out the work (Hare, 1976); orientation, dissatisfaction, resolution, production, termination (LaCoursiere, 1980); and generate plans, ideas, and goals; choose/agree on alternatives, goals, and policies; resolve conflicts and develop norms; perform action tasks and maintain cohesion (McGrath, 1984).

The second stream of research on group development concerns phases in group problem solving, or decision development. Researchers have typically worked with groups with short life-spans, usually minutes or hours, and studied them in a laboratory as they performed a limited task of solving a specific problem. Studies have focused on discovering the sequences of activities through which groups empirically reach solutions—or should reach solutions—and have used various systems of categories to analyze results. By abstracting the rhetorical form of group members' talk from its content and recording percentages of statements made in categories like "agree" and "gives orientation," researchers have portrayed the structure of group discussion. The classic study in this tradition is Bales and Strodtbeck's (1951) unitary sequence model of three phases in groups' movement toward goals: orientation, evaluation, and control.

Though they differ somewhat in the particulars, models from both streams of research have important similarities. Indeed, Poole asserted that "for thirty years,

researchers on group development have been conducting the same study with minor alterations" (1983b: 341). The resultant models are deeply grounded in the paradigm of group development as an inevitable progression: a group cannot get to stage four without first going through stages one, two, and three. For this reason, researchers construe development as movement in a forward direction and expect every group to follow the same historical path. In this paradigm, an environment may constrain systems' ability to develop, but it cannot alter the developmental stages or their sequence.

Some theorists have criticized the validity of such models. Research by Fisher (1970) and by Scheidel and Crowell (1964) suggested that group discussion proceeds in iterative cycles, not in linear order. Bell (1982) and Seeger (1983) questioned Bales and Strodtbeck's methodology. Poole (1981, 1983a, 1983b) raised the most serious challenge to the problem-solving models by demonstrating that there are many possible sequences through which decisions can develop in groups, not just one.[1] Despite these critiques, however, the classic research continues to be widely cited, and the traditional models continue to be widely presented in management texts as the facts of group development (Hellriegel, Slocum, & Woodman, 1986; Szilagy & Wallace, 1987; Tosi, Rizzo, & Carroll, 1986).

Apart from the question of validity, there are gaps in all the extant models, including those of the critics, that seriously limit their contribution to broader research and theory about groups and group effectiveness. First, as Tuckman pointed out in 1965 and others have noted up to the present (Hare, 1976; McGrath, 1986; Poole, 1983b), they offer snapshots of groups at different points in their life-spans but say little about the mechanisms of change, what triggers it, or how long a group will remain in any one stage. Second, existing models have treated groups as closed systems (Goodstein & Dovico, 1979). Without guidance on the interplay between groups' development and environmental contingencies, the models are particularly limited in their utility for task groups in organizations. Not only do organizational task groups' assignments, resources, and requirements for success usually emanate from outside the groups (Gladstein, 1984; Hackman, 1985), such groups' communications with their environments are often pivotal to their effectiveness (Katz, 1982; Katz & Tushman, 1979).

---

[1] This work was called to my attention by a reviewer.

The Approach of This Study

The ideas presented here originated during a field study of how task forces—naturally-occurring teams brought together specifically to do projects in a limited time period—actually get work done. The question that drove the research was, what does a group in an organization do, from the moment it convenes to the end of its life-span, to create the specific product that exists at the conclusion of its last meeting? I was therefore interested not just in interpersonal issues or problem-solving activities, the foci of past research, but in groups' attention to outside resources and requirements, their temporal pacing, and in short, in whatever groups did to make their products come out specifically the way they did, when they did. Since the traditional models do not attend to these issues, I chose an inductive, qualitative approach to increase the chances of discovering the unanticipated and to permit analysis of change and development in the specific content of each team's work.

This study was designed to generate new theory, not to test existing theory, and the paper is organized to present a new model, not to refute an old one. For clarity, however, differences between the proposed and traditional models of group development are noted after each segment of the Results section.

Methods

Because this study was somewhat unconventional, it may help to start with an overview. I observed four groups (A, B, C, and D in Table 7.1) between winter 1980 and spring 1981, attending every meeting of every group and generating complete transcripts for each. This observation was done as part of a larger study of group effectiveness (Gersick, 1982; Hackman, forthcoming). I also prepared a detailed group-project history for presentation to each team.

After I had completed studies of the four groups it was evident that their lives had not gone the way the traditional models predicted. Not only did no single developmental model fit all the teams, the paradigm of group development as a universal string of stages did not fit the four teams taken together. The sequences of activities that teams went through differed radically across groups. Moreover, activities and issues that most theories described as sequential pro-

gressions were in some cases fully simultaneous or reversed.

Those findings prompted me to reexamine the groups' transcripts. I began formulating a tentative new model of group development through the method of grounded theory (Glaser & Strauss, 1967), identifying similarities and differences across the histories and checking emerging hypotheses against original raw data. The results were rewarding, but since three of the four groups were from the same setting, it seemed important to continue to expand the data base. I sought groups that fit into the research domain but that varied as much as possible in project content and organizational setting. As Harris and Sutton pointed out, "Similarities observed across a diverse sample offer firmer grounding for . . . propositions [about the constant elements of a model] than constant elements observed in a homogeneous sample" (1986: 8). Four additional groups (E, F, C, and H in Table 7.1) were studied in 1982-83. In line with Glaser and Strauss's suggestion, I stopped after observing the second set of groups because all the results were highly consistent.

The Research Domain

Several features distinguish the groups included in the domain of this research. They were real groups—members had interdependent relations with one another and developed differentiated roles over time, and the groups were perceived as such both by members and nonmembers (Alderfer, 1977). Each group was convened specifically to develop a concrete piece of work—the groups' lives began and ended with the initiation and completion of special projects. Members had collective responsibility for the work. They were not merely working side by side or carrying out preset orders; they had to make interdependent decisions about what to create and how to proceed. The groups all worked within ongoing organizations, had external managers or supervisors, and produced their products for outsiders' use or evaluation. Finally, every group had to complete its work by a deadline.

Data Sources

The eight groups in the study (see Table 7.1) came from six different organizations in the Northeast; the three student groups came from the same university. Their life-spans varied in duration from seven days to six months. I did not select groups randomly but did choose them carefully to ensure that they fit within the research domain and that all meetings

TABLE 7.1

THE GROUPS OBSERVED

TEAMS[a]	TASK	TIME-SPAN	NUMBER OF MEETINGS
A. Graduate management students: 3 men	Analyze a live management case.	11 days	8
B. Graduate management students: 2 men, 3 women	Analyze a live management case.	15 days	7
C. Graduate management students: 2 men, 1 woman	Analyze a live management case.	7 days	7
D. Community fundraising agency committee: 4 men, 2 women	Design a procedure to evaluate recipient agencies.	3 months	4
E. Bank task force: 4 men	Design a new bank account.	34 days	4
F. Hospital administrators: 3 men, 2 women	Plan a one-day management retreat.	12 weeks	10
G. Psychiatrists and social workers: 8 men, 4 women[b]	Reorganize two units of a treatment facility.	9 weeks[c]	7
H. University faculty members and administrators: 6 men	Design a new academic institute for computer sciences.	6 months[c]	25

[a] The three student groups were from one large, private university. Team H was from a small university.

[b] Two other members attended only once; one other member attended two meetings.

[c] The actual time-span (shown) differed from the initially expected span (see Table 2).

could be observed from the start to the finish of their projects. The management students were recruited from graduate courses that required group projects. After describing the study to each class, I asked the groups to volunteer. I gained entry to the other five groups through referrals to individual members. Team members were provided with information about the study and with opportunities to ask questions; no team was included without all its members' permission. All teams except team D permitted audio taping.

Data Collection

Every meeting of every team was observed, and handwritten transcripts were made during each meeting to back up the audio tapes. In addition to records of members' verbal communication, the handwritten notes included group-level indicators of the energy members applied to their work (attendance, scheduling, and duration of meetings), the use of physical devices to structure work (writing on blackboards and taking notes), and routines (meeting times, locations, and seating patterns). For the second four groups, I also interviewed members after their projects were over to address aspects of each project's development that I did not directly observe: the project's history, events that happened outside meetings, and members' expectations, perceptions, and evaluations of the project.

Data Analysis

This study follows the tradition of group dynamics research in its qualitative analytical approach. I developed a case history for each of the first four groups after its product was completed, the unit of analysis being the group meeting. I did not reduce teams' activities to a priori categories for three reasons. (1) Existing category systems have measured the frequency of groups' activities without necessarily indicating their meaning; a large percentage of problem-orientation statements, for example, could mean either that a group did a careful job or that it had great difficulty defining its task. (2) A priori categories would have been unable to capture qualitative, substantive revisions in groups' product designs. (3) Category systems may be used for specific hypothesis testing but are inappropriate for inductive discourse analysis in theory development (Labov & Fanshel, 1977: 57).

Instead of using a priori categories, I read transcripts repeatedly and used marginal notes to produce literal descriptions of what was said and done at each meeting that were much like detailed minutes. These descriptions encompassed modes of talk, like production work, arguing, and joking; topics covered; teams' performance strategies, that is, implicit or explicit methods of attacking the work; any immediate or long-term planning they did; patterns of relations among members, such as roles, coalitions, and conflicts; and teams' discussions about or with outside stakeholders and authorities.

The entire course of meetings was searched to pinpoint milestones in the design of the products. This process was similar to that usually followed implicitly when a scholar develops a history of the body of work of an artist, writer, or scientist. I identified ideas and decisions that gave the product its basic shape or that would be the fundamental choices in a decision tree if the finished product were to be diagrammed. I also identified points at which milestone ideas were first proposed, whether or not they were accepted at that time. The expression of agreement to adopt a proposal and evidence that the proposal had been adopted were the characteristics of milestone decisions. When a proposal was adopted, either subsequent discussion was premised on it or concrete action followed from it. The milestones added precision to the qualitative historical portrait of each team's product. I searched the complete string of each team's meetings to identify substantive themes of discussion and patterns of group behavior that persisted across meetings and to see when those themes and patterns ceased or changed.

After the first four histories were complete, I searched them for general patterns by isolating the main points from each team's case, forming hypotheses based on the similarities and differences across groups, and then returning to the data to assess and revise the hypotheses. Analysis of data from the first four groups suggested a new model of group development, which I explored and refined in the second stage of the study.

Analysis of the second set of groups again began with the construction of a detailed project history for each team, but construction of the second set of histories was more systematic. To help preserve the literal completeness of project histories and to forestall premature closure on the developmental model, I condensed each team's transcripts in three successive steps. Every turn members took to speak was numbered and the content condensed to retain the literal meaning in a streamlined form; for example, "628: Rick role-plays president's reaction to the idea of tiering the account." I then condensed these documents by abstracting members' exchanges, a few statements at a time, into a detailed topic-by-topic record of the meeting; for example, "646–656: strategizing how to get soundings from outsiders on whether or not to tier the account." The third condensation produced a concise list of the events—the discussions, decisions, arguments, and questions—of each meeting. The following is a sample item: "Team estimates outsiders' reactions to tiering account. Decides to test the waters before launching full design effort; plans how to probe without losing control over product design." The condensation process reduced transcripts of 50 or more pages to 1-page lists, concise enough to allow an overall view of teams' progress across all meetings, yet documented minutely enough to trace general observations back to the numbered transcripts for concrete substantiation or refutation.

After the second four teams' histories were complete, I used them for another iteration of theory-building work. Transcripts of meetings and interviews were searched to see whether or not features common to the first four groups appeared. Again, similarities and differences among all eight groups were used to extend and refine the model.

Presentation of Results

Qualitative research permits wide exploration but forgoes the great economy and precision with which quantified results can be summarized and tested. This study employed description and excerpts from meetings and interviews to document, in members' words as often as possible, what happened in the teams and how they progressed over time.

Results

An Overview of the Model

The data revealed that teams used widely diverse behaviors to do their work; however, the *timing* of when groups formed, maintained, and changed he way they worked was highly congruent. If the groups had fit the traditional models, not only would they have gone through the same sequence of activities, they would also have begun with an open-ended exploration period. Instead, every group exhibited a distinctive approach to its task as soon as it commenced and stayed with that approach through a period of inertia[2] that lasted for half its allotted time. Every group then underwent a major transition. In a concentrated burst of changes, groups dropped old patterns, reengaged with outside supervisors, adopted new perspectives on their work, and made dramatic progress. The events that occurred during those transitions, especially groups' interactions with their environments, shaped a new approach to its task for each group. Those approaches carried groups through a second major phase of inertial activity, in which they executed plans created at their transitions. An especially interesting discovery was that each group experienced its transition at the same point in its calendar—precisely halfway between its first meeting and its official deadline—despite wide variation in the amounts of time the eight teams were allotted for their projects.

This pattern of findings did not simply suggest a different stage theory, with new names for the stages. The term "stage" connotes hierarchical progress from one step to another (Levinson, 1986), and the search for stages is an effort to "validly distinguish . . . types of behavior" (Poole, 1981: 6–7), each of which is indicative of a different stage. "Stage X" includes the same behavior in every group. This study's findings identified temporal periods, which I termed phases, that emerged as bounded eras within each group, without being composed of identical activities across groups and without necessarily progressing hierarchically. It was like seeing the game of football as progressing through a structure of quarters (phases) with a major half-time break versus seeing the game as progressing in a characteristic sequence of distinguishable styles of play (stages). A different paradigm of development appeared to be needed.

The paradigm through which I came to interpret the findings resembles a relatively new concept from the field of natural history that has not heretofore been applied to groups: *punctuated equilibrium* (Eldredge & Gould, 1972). In this paradigm, systems progress through an alternation of stasis and sudden appearance—long periods of inertia, punctuated by concentrated, revolutionary periods of quantum change. Systems' histories are expected to vary because situational contingencies are expected to influence significantly the path a system takes at its inception and during periods of revolutionary change, when systems' directions are formed and reformed.

In sum, the proposed model described groups' development as a punctuated equilibrium. *Phase 1,* the first half of groups' calendar time, is an initial period of inertial movement whose direction is set by the end of the group's first meeting. At the midpoint of their allotted calendar time, groups undergo a *transition,* which sets a revised direction for *phase 2,* a second period of inertial movement. Within this phase l-transition-phase 2 pattern, two additional points are of special interest: the first meeting, because it displays the patterns of phase l; and the last meeting, or completion, because it is a period when groups markedly accelerate and finish off work generated during phase 2.

Special Aspects of the Model

The importance of the first meeting was its power to display the behaviors (process) and themes (content) that dominated the first half of each group's life. Each group appears to have formed almost immediately a framework of givens about its situation and how it would behave. This framework in effect constituted a stable platform from which the group operated throughout phase 1.

Members occasionally clearly indicated their approach to something, stating their premises and how they planned to behave ("The key issue here is X; let's work on it by doing Y"); however, teams seldom formulated their frameworks through explicit deliberation. Instead, frameworks were established implicitly, by what was said and done repeatedly in the group. That phenomenon was observable on several fronts. The themes, topics, and premises of discussions provided evidence; for example, a group might take as given that its organization's staff is not talented and discuss every project idea in terms of how hard it would be to explain to the sales force. Members' interaction patterns—the roles. alliances, and battles members took on—also revealed implicit frameworks. Performance strategies, or methods of attacking the work, were another indicator. A group's behavior toward its external contexts—for example, acting dependent or acting assertive about outside stakeholders—provided evidence as well. Finally a group's overall standing on its task—whether it was confident of a plan and working on it, deadlocked in disagreement over goals, or explicitly opposed to the assignment and unwilling to begin work[3]—helped to establish its implicit framework.

---

[2] This paper uses the dictionary definition of inertia as the tendency of a body to remain in a condition: if standing still, to remain so; if moving, to keep moving on the same course.

[3] Three dimensions of a group's stance on a task emerged from the data. Members may accept or object to an assignment, may be certain or uncertain what to do about a task, and may converge or *(continued)*

Central approaches and behavior patterns that appeared during first meetings and persisted during phase 1 disappeared at the halfway point as groups explicitly dropped old approaches and searched for new ones. They revised their frameworks. The clearest sign of transition was the major jump in progress that each group made on its project at the temporal midpoint of its calendar. Further comparisons, across meetings within groups and across groups, revealed five empirical earmarks of the transition, a set of events uniquely characteristic of midpoint meetings. The frameworks that groups formed at transition carried them through a second period of momentum, phase 2, to a final burst of completion activities at their last meetings.

Illustration of the Model

Three groups will serve as examples to illustrate each part of the model. Each is representative of the overall model, yet each shows some aspects especially concisely, and the differences between the groups show the diversity within the pattern.

First Meeting and Phase 1

Almost immediately, in every team studied, members displayed the framework through which they approached their projects for the first half of their calendar time. Excerpts show the scope, variety, and nature of those frameworks.

Excerpt 1 (E1). A team of three graduate management students start their first, five-minute encounter to plan work on a group case assignment, defined by the professor as an organizational design problem.[4]

1. Jack: We should try to read the [assigned] material.
2. Rajeev: But this isn't an organizational design problem, it's a strategic planning problem.

---

3. (Jack and Bert agree.)
4. Rajeev: I think what we have to do is prepare a way of growth [for the client].
5. (Nods, "yes" from Jack and Bert.)

Excerpt 1, representing less than one minute from the very start of a team's life, gives a clear view of the opening framework. The team's approach toward its organizational context (the professor and his requirements) is plain. The members are not going to read the material; they disagree with the professor's definition of the task and will define their project to suit themselves.

Their pattern of internal interaction is equally visible. When Rajeev made three consequential proposals—about the definition of the task, the team's lack of obligations to the professor, and the goal they should aim for—everyone concurred. There was no initial "storming" (Tuckman, 1965; Tuckman & Jensen, 1977) in this group. The clip also shows this team's starting approach toward its task: confidence about what the problem is, what the goal ought to be, and how to get to work on it. The team's stated performance strategy was to use strategic planning techniques to "prepare a way of growth."

Excerpt 2 (E2). The following excerpt of the team's next work session, two days later, shows how well the minute of dialogue from the first meeting indicated lasting patterns.

1. Jack: I have not looked at any of the readings—did you look at all?
2. (Bert and Rajeev laugh.)
3. Jack: . . . I was thinking . . . we could do alternatives—different ways to grow . . . like a prospectus for a consulting study.
4. Bert: That's exactly the way I'd go. (Restates Jack's position.)
5. Rajeev: Well . . . we are thinking mostly in the same manner. My idea was . . . (He states the same plan.)
   (After five minutes of discussion about the client and his situation, Rajeev suggests they start work.)
6. Jack: We've got some more time . . . I think it would be premature to describe alternative goals yet. . . .
7. Rajeev: If we can generate some of the assumptions now and talk about the alternatives later—it's a two-step thing.
8. Jack: OK, that's fine. Let's start that.
9. Rajeev: (at blackboard) What are the things on which the business depends?

(continued) diverge with each other about these issues. The dimensions may be arrayed in a 2×2×2 matrix to suggest a number of potential answers to the questions "Where do we stand?" The three dimension are primarily concerned with members' approaches toward context, task, and internal interaction, yet they are closely intertwined.

[4] All names used in this report are pseudonyms.

The dialogue shows that the team is still disregarding the professor (E2, 1 & 2),[5] still working in easy agreement (E2, 4, 5, & 8), and still taking the same approach to the task (E2, 3). It also shows the group *acting* on its expressed intentions, employing a logical, orderly technique to construct its product (E2, 6–9). The team worked within this framework for two full meetings. Rajeev led the group through a structured set of strategic planning questions. At that point, the team had a complete draft outline of a growth plan for its client.

Excerpt 3 (E3).   A group of four bank executives open their first meeting to design a new type of account.

1. Don: What do you think we ought to do to start this, Rick? Just go through each of these? (Referring to a written list of topics.)
2. Rick: Well, I want to explain to Gil and Porter—we had a little rump session the other day just to say "What the hell is this thing? What does it say, and what are the things that we have to decide?" And what we did was run through a group of 'em. . . . These are not necessarily in order of importance—they're in order of the way we thought of 'em, really. . . .

This excerpt of the first 25 seconds in the life of another task force, showing a quite different beginning, also illustrates the team's approach toward its task, and its performance strategy. This team did not choose a product through the whole first half of its life. Given a new set of federal rules, the team's reaction was to ask the questions "What the hell is this thing? What does it say?" The team was uncertain, and as the project began they approached the task as a job of mapping out "the things we have to decide."

The excerpt is also an elegant summary of the group's performance strategies. It shows that the leader prepared for the meeting with one other member, that the preparation consisted of generating a list of topics to be covered, and that this list was arranged only "in order of the way we thought of 'em." This general strategy was followed for every one of the group's meetings. Before each meeting, a pair of members prepared skeletal documents for the group to work from. Items were checked off the documents as they were covered, but discussions were more like pinball games than orderly progressions. Each question ricocheted the conversational ball onto several new ques-

tions, and occasionally bells and lights went off as the team made a decision about a specific point.

The link between the team's pinball-style performance strategies and its approach to its task as "mapping" was strong. As one member, trying to keep track of the discussion, said to another, "It's all intertwined."

For the first two of its four meetings, the dominant activity of this team's members was to generate the questions that needed to be settled in a loosely structured format and to go as far as they could in answering each. Their own definition of where they were, from inception through the end of this period, was that they did not yet know "what we're planning to offer. We're still thinking."

Excerpt 4 (E4).   Five hospital department heads are a few minutes into their first meeting to plan the fourth in a series of management retreats for their peers and division chief. They have just chosen a date and place.

1. Nancy: So, in order of preference, the [dates we want are] the tenth, third, and ninth.
2. Sandra: Sounds great. . . . (to Bernard): I think you probably should talk to the division chief about—did he give you any thoughts about what we should do next?
3. Bernard: I'd say—that's on us. . . .
4. Sandra: Um hum. The only thing I feel strongly about is—it's not time to have an outside [facilitator].
5. Bill: Well, I'm not for or against [that] but—what are we trying to achieve? Trust among—people? . . . the highest value [on the participants' critique of the previous retreat was] developing trust among the managers themselves . . . and not only trust among ourselves. . . . I think there has to be trust—upward.
6. Sandra: And that's the issue we talk about, and walk around the edges of. . . . We say, "Yeah, Tom [division chief], we trust you," but we don't trust you very *well*, 'cause we don't dare say we don't trust you, Tom.
7. Bill: Yep. The sacred cow, like you said earlier.
8. Bernard: There's three levels, aren't there? The people we supervise, peers that we work with, as well as . . . .

The hospital administrators team began at an impasse. After they had swiftly decided where and when to hold the retreat, the pace plummeted with the question of what to

---

[5] The notion "E2, 1" identifies the excerpt (E2) and the line or lines (1) of dialogue.

do with the event. The team's opening framework shows the problem. The members' position toward their organizational context was complicated because the final product had to please the task delegator, the division chief, but he had given no indication of what they "should do next," and the team leader was unwilling to ask (E4, 2–4). The team's approach to its task was closely related to that ambivalence. Members' opening premises were that the retreat ought to deal with trust, especially with regard to the division chief, and that they should run it themselves without bringing in an outside facilitator (E4, 4–6). Those premises put the team in a self-imposed bind as evidenced by the statement " 'cause we don't dare say we can't trust *you*, Tom." The team's key phase 1 question was "What are we trying to achieve?" (E4, 5).

The concern with intradivisional relationships and the feelings of directionlessness in the group continued for the first six weeks of the team's 12-week life-span. In a later interview, a member said, "From [the beginning] to the [end of October] all I can remember is talking. With absolutely no idea of what was going to happen. None." This was so even though members were concerned and *wanted* meetings to be different. Another member said, "It was very frustrating from September 20 until maybe November 1 for me [the first through the sixth weeks]. That's a long time to be frustrated." A third member noted, "It was very difficult to get the work going. We had no direction, only to put together a retreat. . . . Nothing was happening! I was very frustrated." The group made no decisions about what to do at the retreat during its first phase.

Table 7.2 summarizes the findings about first meetings and phase 1. Column 1 presents each team's starting approach toward its task, and column 2 summarizes the central task activity of phase 1, including the first meeting.

Each group immediately established an integrated framework of performance strategies, interaction patterns, and approaches toward its task and outside context. The most concise illustration of this finding comes from the student group, whose (1) easy agreement on (2) a specific plan for its work represented (3) a decision to ignore the outside requirements for its task—all within the same minute of group discussion. Such frameworks embodied the central themes that dominated all through the first half of groups' calendar time, even for teams that were frustrated with the paths they were following. This finding contradicts traditional models, which pose teams' beginnings as a discrete stage of indeterminate duration during which teams orient

themselves to their situation, explicitly debating and choosing what to do.

Though each team began with the formation of a framework, each framework was unique as illustrated by the contrast between the students' instant confidence and the hospital administrators' directionlessness. Some teams began with harmonious internal interaction patterns; others, with internal storms. Teams took very different approaches to authority figures from their outside contexts, as evidenced by the hospital administrator's preoccupation with the division chief versus the students' cheerful disregard for the professor. These findings contradict the typical stage theory paradigm in which it is assumed that all teams essentially begin with the same approach toward their task (e.g., orientation), their team (e.g., forming then storming), and toward authority (e.g., dependency).[6]

The Midpoint Transition

As each group approached the midpoint between the time it started work and its deadline, it underwent great change. The following excerpts from transitional meetings illustrate the nature and depth of this change. Particular points to notice are members' comments about the time and their behavior toward external supervisors.

Excerpt 5 (E5).   The students begin their meeting on the sixth day of an 11-day span.

1. Rajeev: I think what he said today in class—I have, already, lots of criticism on our outline. What we've done now is OK, but we need a lot more emphasis on organization design than what we—I've been doing up to now.
2. Jack: I think you're right. We've already been talking about [X]. We should be talking more about [Y].
3. Rajeev: We've done it—and it's super—but we need to do other things, too.
4. (Bert agrees.)
5. Jack: After hearing today's discussion—we need to say [X] more directly. And we want to say more explicitly that . . . .
6. Rajeev: . . . should we be . . . organized and look at the outline? . . . We should know where we're going.

---

[6] The authority designation comes from Mann, Gibbard, and Hartman (1967).

TABLE 7.2

TEAMS	FIRST MEETING	PHASE 1	TRANSITION	PHASE 2	COMPLETION
A. Student team A	Agreement on a plan.	Details of plan worked out: client's "growth options."	First draft revised; second draft planned.	Details of second plan worked out: organization design.	Homework compiled into paper, finished, and edited.
B. Student team B	Disagreement on task definition.	Argument over how to define task: challenge vs. follow client's problem statement.	Task defined; case analysis rough-outlined.	Details of outline worked out: affirmative action plan, following client's request.	Paper (drafted by one member) finished; edited.
C. Student team C	One member proposes concrete plan: others oppose it.	Argument over details of competing plans ("structured" vs. "minimal") but no discussion of goals.	Goals chosen; case analysis outlined.	Details of outline worked out: "minimalist" U.S. trade policy.	Homework compiled into paper, finished, and edited.
D. Community fundraising agency committee	Agreement on a plan.	Details of plan worked out: "nonthreatening" self-evaluation for member agencies.	First draft revised; second draft planned.	Details of second plan worked out: explicitly allocations-related evaluation plan.	Report (drafted by two members) edited.
E. Bank task force	Uncertainty about new product; federal regulations unclear.	Team "answers questions"; maps possible account features.	Account completely outlined.	Members work through-out bank on systems, supplies for account.	Account finalized for advertising; bank-wide training planned.
F. Hospital administrators	Team fixes on "trust" theme; uncertain what to do with it for program.	Unstructured trial and rejection of program possibilities; disagreement about goals.	Complete program outlined.	Consultant hired to plan program; team arranges housekeeping details.	Responsibility for final preparations delegated.
G. Psychiatrists and social workers	Leader presents "the givens"; team opposes project.	Subgroup reports presented; members object to all plans; leader rebuts objections.	Disagreement persists: leader picks one plan; redelegates task; dissolves team.		
H. University faculty members and administrators	Team divided on whether to accept project; leader proposes diagnosis as first step	Structured exploration: diagnosis of situation.	Team redefines task; commits to project.	Computer institute designed (original task) plus system for university computer facilities planning.	Report (written by leader from members' drafts) edited and approved.

(The group goes quickly through the outline members had prepared for the meeting, noting changes and additions they want to make.)

7. Rajeev: The problem is, we're very short on time.

The students came to this meeting having just finished the outline of the strategic plan they had set out to do at their opening encounter (see E1). At their midpoint, they stopped barreling along on their first task. They marked the completion of that work, evaluated it, and generated a fresh, significantly revised agenda. The team's change in outlook on its task coincided with a change in stance toward the professor. Revisions were made that were based on "what he said today in class" and " hearing today's discussion." Having reaffirmed the value of their first approach to the case, members reversed their original conviction that it was "not an organizational design problem." This was the first time members allowed their work to be influenced by the professor, and at this point, they accepted his influence enthusiastically.

It is significant that Rajeev's remark, "we're very short on time," was only the second comment about the adequacy of the time the group had for the project, and it marked a switch from Jack's early sentiment that "we've got some more time" (E2, 6). A new sense of urgency marked this meeting.

The students knew what they wanted to create at their first meeting; the bank team members started much closer to scratch and they were not nearly as far along as the students at the midpoint. Their transitional meeting was different from the students' in character but similar in scope and magnitude.

Since the bankers scheduled each meeting ad hoc, it is noteworthy that the third one fell on the 17th day of a 34-day span. As he convened the group, Don worried that if they continued their present course, they might not finish on time: "We can explore all the ramifications [of the regulations], but I just hope we don't get *stuck,* toward the end, without . . . " In the first minutes of this meeting, members confirmed their intentions to move to the next step: "Basically, we're gonna lay out the characteristics of the account." The next two hours were spent problem solving with two staff experts who had been invited to the meeting to make sure the account design would fit the bank's computer systems. By the end of that time, the basic design was finished.

The leap forward on the task coincided with a change in the team's relationship with its organizational context. At first, the group decided its meetings would be closed to staff people "[until] . . . we know how we want to handle this . . . ." The third meeting marked that shift. Moreover, one of the members had a key meeting with the bank chairman that afternoon, to argue for the extra resources he now felt were needed to market the team's product successfully.

If the bank team started out less far along in its work than the students, the hospital team was even a step behind the bankers. Though everyone said that intradivision relationships were the key topic to address, the team could not agree on a goal for the retreat and spent the first half of its life describing and rejecting a series of ideas. Statements 1–3 of the following excerpt show how little concrete progress the team had made halfway through its calendar; the remaining lines show how much they then accomplished at the meeting.

Excerpt 6 (E6).   The hospital administrators hold their fifth meeting, in the sixth week of a 12-week span.

1. Bernard (to Bill, just before the meeting): I'm gonna bring Tom [the division chief] to the next meeting, Bill. . . . Last time we were struggling like we are here—Tom [really helped] to sort things out . . . .

2. Bernard (convening meeting): . . . I think we need to . . . brainstorm about [the program]—see what we might come up with, and bounce it off Tom next time. (He recaps an idea he brought to the previous meeting.)

3. Sandra: We'd each be responsible for an hour of the program? As facilitators, or role playing—whatever we decided to do?
    (Later in the meeting, there was a dramatic shift in the discussion when Nancy described a management simulation program on the problems of middle managers, run by a consultant who worked nearby.)

4. Sandra: If awareness is all that comes out of the day . . . I think that's a good—a reasonable goal.

5. Nancy: Understanding, too, some of the forces that operate on us as middle managers—that's where we are, in our relationship with the top manager . . . .

6. Bernard: Yeah . . . that's the thing that we all share together, with the exception of Tom— is that we're in the middle, and it's a difficult spot to be in. And this would show that . . .

7. Sandra: (adds up the time that the simulation and debriefing would take) So—there's

the rest of the day! . . . I think that's reasonable to run by Tom.

(The team endorsed the program and decided to invite the consultant Nancy mentioned to run it. The following are from the close of the meeting.)

8. Bill: We are making progress! I was afraid we weren't moving fast enough!

9. Sandra: I had the same problem! . . . I felt . . . in the beginning there was a lot of talk. . . . That's necessary in some degree—then, I think, you gotta move on it.

10. Bernard: We've made progress, folks. . . . [Next week] Tom'll be here, we'll throw those ideas out to him—Monday, we're going to look at the [conference center]—so we've made progress.

This team's midpoint anxiety about finishing on time showed in the meeting and in interviews: "I was uncomfortable that time was going to run out and we were not going to have it done." "I called Nancy and said 'Look—this needs to start going, or we're going to get to [the program date] wondering what we're going to do!'" Yet in a single session, the team managed to solve all the major problems it had struggled with for six weeks. The theme of the new program design, "being in the middle," was actually not new to the group. It had come up in the very first meeting (see E4, 7) and had been discussed with some enthusiasm at the fourth meeting. But members had been preoccupied trying to make the "trust" idea work. Because "being in the middle" did not fit into the team's original framework, it did not lead to a program design during phase 1.

Two more major changes show in excerpt 6. One was the reversal of the first-meeting approach that members had to run the program themselves (E4, 4) with the decision to get an outside facilitator. Members said in interviews that this change made a tremendous difference. One person captured the whole transition: "The [mood in the team] went down . . . and then all of a sudden, it took kind of a swoop . . . 'Ah! It's going to happen!' We decided what we were going to do. . . . The decision to bring in a facilitator was a great relief! Then we got the division chief—he said 'OK, go ahead,' and the rest was just mechanics."

The second change occurred in the team's approach toward its task delegator, when Bernard reversed his early decision not to ask the division chief for help (E4, 3; E6, 1). Indeed, the anticipation of talking to Tom appeared to spur the team's work at the same time that it marked the end of the talk *about* him.

The structure of the transition period was similar for all the teams, even though the specific details differed widely. Table 7.3 shows the timing of each team's transition meeting, describes the changes that occurred in the work at that point, and documents those changes in members' words. Five major indicators, or earmarks, of the transition are reviewed below.[7]

First, teams entered transition meetings at different stages in their work, but for each, progress began with the completion or abandonment of phase 1 agendas. For example, groups A and D entered transition meetings with complete drafts of plans that had been hatched when they started, and team H finished a system diagnosis just before its midpoint (see Table 1). The hospital administrators dropped key premises that the program would be about trust and run by themselves. Team G's leader unexpectedly pronounced the group's task complete at its midpoint (G, 2),[8] but interviews indicated that members, too, felt it was time to move dramatically: "At that point . . . there was a need to go *up*. But instead of going up, we stopped."

Second, team members expressed urgency about finishing on time. At this time—and no other—members expressed explicit concern about the pace and timeliness of their work: "We ought to be conscious of deadlines" (Team H, transition meeting; see also Table 3: A, 2; B, 1 & 2; D, 4; E, 1; and F, 2). Group G, dissolved with no prior warning (or protest) at its midpoint, was the only team that did not fit this pattern.

Third, teams' transitions all occurred at the midpoints of their official calendars, regardless of the number or length of meetings teams had before or after that.

Fourth, new contact between teams and their organizational contexts played important roles in their transitions. Most often, this contact was between the team and its task delegator. Sometimes it was initiated by the team (E and F), sometimes by both at once (A, D, and H),[9] and sometimes by the task delegators (B and C).

These contacts both fostered decision making and influenced decision outcomes. Five groups showed explicit new interest in the match between their product and out-

[7] Two additional indicators of transition, a pretransition low point and a change in groups' routines, are not covered here because of space limitations. A discussion of all seven indicators is available in Gersick (1984).

[8] In the discussion of indicators, letters identify teams, and numbers identify lines of dialogue in Table 3.

[9] For example, team H decided to schedule a special meeting to confront top administrators about its mission. Just after that, the leader *(continued)*

TABLE 7.3

TRANSITION MEETINGS IN THE EIGHT GROUPS

A. Student team A: Day 6 of 11-day span
Team revises first draft of case analysis; plans final draft.

Opening	(1)	I think, what he said today in class—I have . . . lots of criticism on our outline . . . . We've done it—and it's super—but we need to do other things too.
Closing	(2)	The problem is, we're very short on time.

B. Student team B: Day 7 of 15-day span
Team progresses from argument over how its task should be defined to rough outline of case analysis.

Opening	(1)	This is due next Monday, right?
	(2)	Right. Time to roll.
Later	(3)	Not bad! We spent one hour on one topic, and an hour on another! . . . We're moving along here, too. I feel a lot better at this meeting than I have—
	(4)	Well . . . we're also making decisions to be task-oriented, and take the problem at its face value—

C. Student team C: Day 4 of 7-day span
Team progresses from argument over details of competing plans, with no discussion of overall goals, to goal clarification and complete outline of product.

Opening	(1)	This morning I redesigned the whole presentation! I don't know what the content is, but—
Later	(2)	(Surveying blackboard) OK—we've got goals! Those are the U.S. goals for [X topic]. . . . The [outline for the paper is] the lead-in, the goals, and the strategy.
	(3)	That makes sense! . . .
	(4)	I like it!

D. Community fundraising agency committee: Meeting 3 of 4 preset meetings
Team revises first plan for evaluation procedure; agrees on final plan.

Opening	(1)	Does anyone have any problem with the . . . evaluation draft?
	(2)	Let's be realistic—we don't have the staff time to sit down with each [recipient] agency every year.
	(3)	What are we accomplishing, then? . . . . We need to know [X]. Otherwise I say, "don't bother!"
Later	(4)	(Summing up a revised version of the plan) If you tell [member agencies] they *will* be evaluated . . . and these are questions you'll be asked, so—get your baloney swinging . . . ! [Laughter from team] OK. Let's move on, otherwise we're going to get behind.

E. Bank task force: Day 17 of 34-day span
Team progresses from "answering questions" to designing complete outline of new bank account.

Opening	(1)	I just hope we don't get stuck, toward the end, without—
	(2)	What are we gonna do—just—answer a lot of questions today? —or—
	(3)	. . . basically, we're gonna lay out the characteristics of the account.
Closing	(4)	Oh, I think that's super!
	(5)	I think we got a good product!

F. Hospital administrators: Week 6 of 12-week span
Team progresses from uncertainty and disagreement about goal to a complete program plan.

Opening	(1)	. . . we need to . . . come up with [something to] bounce off Tom next time.
Closing	(2)	We are making progress! I was afraid we weren't moving fast enough!
	(3)	We've made *progress,* folks!

G. Psychiatrists and social workers: Week 9 of 17-week span
Leader chooses one of three reorganization plans to break stalemate; dissolves team.

Opening	(1)	Is [plan A] a reasonable way to go? *That's* the question.
Closing	(2)	We are nearing the completion of our task . . . the next step is turning [the work] over [to Dr. C.] . . . There is disagreement in here, [but] I think . . . we have to come *down* . . . [on one plan]. . . . Then we are—dissolved. . . . Thank you.

H. University faculty member and administrators: Week 7 of 14-week span
Team redefines task; progresses from skepticism to commitment.

Opening	(1)	. . . the task force reached a crossroads last meeting . . . and decided it [must choose] whether it should [continue with its original task] or consider the overall needs. For that reason, we've asked two people at the vice-presidential level to . . . help us deliberate that question.
Closing	(2)	I think we've . . . reached a conclusion today, and that is, we need to include the administrative end [in our task].
	(3)	Hey, I think we're finally giving Connie some good stuff here! Isn't this typical? You go through, you roll along, and then all of a sudden you say, "What are we doing?" Then we go back and *reconstitute* ourselves! Anyway, processes are taking place!

side resources and requirements. Excerpts A and D and the bank's work with computer experts show how groups shaped their products specifically to contextual resources and requirements. The bank group also illustrates the other side of the coin—a team member took his new assessment of the project out to the organization to request more resources. The importance of this contact is highlighted by the exception, team G, whose lack of information about outside requirements exacerbated its inability to choose. A member stated during its pretransition meeting: "*If* we are expected [to do X] then there is no [way to support plan A over plan B, but] . . . that may not be the demand. Obviously, there's a lot of politics outside this room that are going to define what [we] have to do."

Finally, transitions yielded specific new agreements on the ultimate directions teams' work should take. Regardless of how much or how little members argued during phase 1, every team that completed its task agreed at transition on plans that formed the basis for the completion of the work. In teams with easy phase 1 interaction, the agreeableness itself was not a change. But for teams where phase 1 had been conflictual, transition meetings were high points in collaboration. Indeed, in the one team whose members still disagreed at this point, the leader dissolved the group, chose a plan unilaterally, and moved the work forward by shifting it into other hands (G, 2).

Overall, the changes in teams' work tended to be dialectical. Teams that had started fast, with quick decisions and unhesitating construction of their products, paused at their transitions to evaluate finished work and address shortcomings (A and D). For teams that started slowly, unsure or disagreeing about what to do, transitions were exhilarating periods of structuring, making choices, and pulling together (B, C, E, F, and H). In either case, transitional advances depended on the combination of phase 1 learning and fresh ideas. For example, the bankers' transitional raw materials were ideas generated during phase 1, refined and integrated with the help of expertise newly infused into the team. The hospital administrators, newly open to an alternative format, found use for a theme they had discussed but not developed earlier.

Traditional models of group development do not predict a midpoint transition. They present groups as progressing forward if and whenever they accumulate enough work on specific developmental issues—not at a predictable moment, catalyzed by team members' awareness

of time limits. Traditional group development models are silent about team-context relations and the influence of such relations on teams' progress. The findings reported here suggest that there is a predictable time in groups' life cycles when members are particularly influenceable by, and interested in, communication with outsiders. Cases in which task delegators contacted teams at this point suggest this interest might be mutual.

Phase 2

Teams' lives were different after the midpoint transition. In all seven surviving teams, members' approaches toward their tasks clearly changed and advanced (Table 7.2). All seven executed their transitional plans during this period. Posttransitional changes in teams' internal interaction patterns and approaches toward their outside contexts were not so simple. Transitions did not advance every team in these areas, nor did every team use its transition equally well. Internal troubles that went unaddressed during transition sometimes worsened during phase 2, and teams that were lax in matching their work to outside requirements during the transition showed lasting effects.

The student group, which developed strategic "growth options" for its client in phase 1, spent phase 2 building the organizational design, planned at the transitional meeting, to support those options. As the task approach shifted from strategic planning to organizational design, one element of the team's interaction pattern changed. Jack took over from Rajeev as lead questioner. Other than that, the team continued the easy, orderly agreement of its phase 1 interaction style. The team sustained its new perspective on its context, formed at transition, by maintaining attentiveness to the professor's requirements throughout phase 2.

The bankers spent phase 2 executing the details for the account they had designed at transition; they prepared marketing extras, operational machinery, and documents. With this change in focus, the team deepened its transitional move toward working with the organizational context and also dramatically changed its own interaction pattern. The team did not convene as a group during phase Z but met individually and in pairs with staff members throughout the bank.

The hospital team's phase 1 uncertainty about the task and discussion of relationships did not recur. A consultant, engaged shortly after the midpoint, took charge of planning the program the team chose at its transition; the team's work for the next four meetings consisted of supplying the consultant with information and arranging menus, invitations, and materials for the retreat.

Though the hospital administrators were like the other teams in using phase 2 to carry out transitional plans in task work, their phase 2 changes in interaction patterns and approach toward outside context were more extreme and less benign. Internally, the team fell apart just after the transitional meeting. Two members, who had engaged in restrained competition through phase 1 but had supported each other at the transition, had a falling out. The same weekend, the team leader and one other member engendered resentment by making some unilateral decisions outside the group, and the interaction in meetings deteriorated. The team's transitional openness toward its context also regressed after the chief appeared at the post-midpoint meeting.

Excerpt 7 (E7).   The following comes from an interview with the hospital team's leader:

> He says "Do what you want. Spend what you want." Then he came to the damn meeting and was worried about money! Giving me mixed signals! That's when I decided I'm gonna spend what I want and make my own decisions. . . .

By the time the division chief met with the team, the decision to hire the facilitator—the largest expense—had already been made. It was "too late" to be "worried about money," and the team never checked its budget with the chief.

Phase 2 was a second period of inertia in teams' lives, shaped powerfully by the events of their transitions. Teams did not alter their basic approaches toward their tasks within this phase. As one hospital team member stated, "We decided what we were going to do [at the midpoint meeting] . . . and the rest was just mechanics."

Since all teams were doing construction work on their projects during phase 2, similar to "performing" in Tuckman's (1965) synthesis, it was a time when teams were more similar both to each other and to the traditional model than they were in phase 1. However, progress was not so much like traditional models in other respects, since it was not so linear. Some teams started performing earlier than others, without previous conflict; other teams returned to internal conflict after their transition and during phase 2 performance. In every team, transitional work centered explicitly on solving task problems, not on solving internal interaction problems; it is not surprising, then, that some teams' internal processes worsened after the major need for collaborative decision making was past.

Completion

Completion was the phase of teams' lives in which their activities were the most similar to each others'. Three patterns characterized final meetings: (1) groups' task activity changed from generating new materials to editing and preparing existing materials for external use; (2) as part of this preparation, their explicit attention toward outside requirements and expectations rose sharply; and (3) groups expressed more positive or negative feeling about their work and each other. At this point, the major differences among the groups involved not what they were doing but how easily they were doing it. Not surprisingly, groups that had checked outside requirements early on and groups that had paced themselves well all along had easier, shorter final meetings.

The last distinct change in the student team's life occurred the day before the paper was due. This meeting was considerably longer than any other; the team now had to keep working until the case analysis was finished. Members' work activities changed from generating ideas to editing what they had into the form required by the instructor. A sample from that meeting is "I'm not disagreeing with anything you're saying. But I think you got 'em in the wrong section." Though the long hours and the need to edit each others' work made the meeting more difficult than usual, by the time the team was ready to give its presentation, members were expressing their feelings that the project had gone well. The presentation went smoothly and the team received a good grade.

The bank executives' final group meeting marked the "finish [of] all the deliberations" about the design of the account and a shift into activities to educate the public and the branch banks about it: "It's one thing to . . . say we're gonna offer the thing . . . [but now] we've gotta get something out [to the staff] on how to *handle* it." The team went over the account one last time, to get it "written in blood" for the advertising copy, due that day. Then, with two extra staff people, members planned the final approach. After the meeting, everyone rushed off with his own assignment for the new task of getting the whole bank ready for opening day. In interviews later, team members proudly described a memorandum the president had sent congratulating everyone on the success of the account.

By the hospital group's last meeting, its work was mostly done. At this point, the interpersonal tension that had been building during phase 2 erupted in an angry discussion about the handling of the consultant's fee and how to present it to the division chief. But the subject was dropped when a member declared it had been "talked about long enough." The team delegated final responsibilities for the conference and ended the meeting early. On the day of the retreat, half the team members arrived late and left early; otherwise, relations among them appeared smooth. At day's end, the division chief—who had not yet received the bill—toasted the team: "I think this is the best one yet, and I'm looking forward to number five."

In every team, discussion of outsiders' expectations was prominent at the last meeting. As teams anticipated releasing their work into outside hands, they scrutinized it freshly, through outsiders' eyes: "We'll be judged poorly if we . . ."; "You can't promise [X] and then do [Y]." Since phase 2 actions carried out, but did not alter, plans made at transition, teams that entered phase 2 with a poor match between product and requirements had an especially hard time confronting outside expectations at completion. But even teams that discovered in last-day meetings that they had major gaps to fill framed their remaining work as rearranging or fixing what they already had, as these excerpts indicate: "I think our content . . . is good . . . it's just a matter of reorganizing it . . ." (Team B) and "I think we have all the ideas. . . .The main task is how to arrange them" (Team A). Though teams' attention to outside requirements was high at last meetings, completion activities did not undo the basic product revisions established at transition.

Discussion

The traditional paradigm portrays group development as a series of stages or activities through which groups gradually and explicitly get ready to perform, and then perform, their tasks. All groups are expected to follow the same historical path. Proponents of existing models specify neither the mechanisms of change nor the role of a group's environment. In contrast, the paradigm suggested by the current findings indicates that groups develop through the sudden formation, maintenance, and sudden revision of a framework for performance; the developmental process is a punctuated equilibrium. The proposed model highlights the processes through which frameworks are formed and revised and predicts both the timing of progress and when and how in their development groups are likely, or unlikely, to be influenced by their environments. The specific issues and activities that dominate groups' work are left unspeci-

fied in the model, since groups' historical paths are expected to vary.

The proposed model works in the following way: A framework of behavioral patterns and assumptions through which a group approaches its project emerges in its first meeting, and the group stays with that framework through the first half of its life. Teams may show little visible progress during this time because members may be unable to perceive a use for the information they are generating until they revise the initial framework. At their calendar midpoints, groups experience transitions—paradigmatic shifts in their approaches to their work—enabling them to capitalize on the gradual learning they have done and make significant advances. The transition is a powerful opportunity for a group to alter the course of its life midstream. But the transition must be used well, for once it is past a team is unlikely to alter its basic plans again. Phase 2, a second period of inertial movement, takes its direction from plans crystallized during the transition. At completion, when a team makes a final effort to satisfy outside expectations, it experiences the positive and negative consequences of past choices.

The components of this model raise an interesting set of theoretical questions. Why do lasting patterns form so early and persist through long periods of inertia? Why do teams' behavior patterns and product designs undergo dramatic change precisely halfway through their project calendars? What is the role of a team's context in its development? This exploratory study did not test or prove any prior hypotheses; nonetheless, it is appropriate to ask whether established theory provides any basis for understanding the observed results, to help formulate hypotheses and questions for future testing.

Early Patterns

Why do lasting patterns form so early and persist through long periods of inertia? The present findings show that lasting patterns can appear as early as the first few seconds of a group's life. This finding was unexpected, but it is not unheard of. Reports from the psychoanalytic literature show the power of the first minutes of a therapeutic interview to predict the central issues of the session (Ginnette, 1986; Pittenger, Hockett, & Danehy, 1960: 22b). Quite recently, Bettenhausen and Murnighan found that "unique norms formed in each [of several bargaining groups], typically during their very first agreements" (1985: 359).

The sheer speed with which recurring patterns appear suggests they are influenced by material established before a group convenes. Such material includes members' expectations about the task, each other, and the context and their repertoires of behavioral routines and performance strategies. The presence of these factors would circumscribe the influence of the interaction process that occurs in the first meeting but not rule it out. Bettenhausen and Murnighan (1985) discussed norm formation in terms of what happens when team members encounter the scripts (Abelson, 1976) each has brought to a group's first meeting. Pittenger, Hockett, and Danehy (1960: 16–24) described the opening of a therapeutic interview as the interaction of "rehearsed" material brought in by the patient with the therapist's opening gambit. This construction of first meetings suggests that peoples' earliest responses to each other set lasting precedents about how a team is going to handle the issues, ideas, questions, and performance strategies that members have brought in.

In phase 1, groups define most of the parameters of their situation quickly and examine them no further, concentrating their work and attention on only a few factors. The contrast between this model and the traditional idea that groups take time to generate, evaluate, and choose alternative views before getting to work parallels Simon's (1976) contrast between bounded and perfect rationality, and it may be understood through his argument that people must make simplifying assumptions in order to take any action at all.

The Halfway Point

Why do teams' behavior patterns and product designs undergo dramatic change exactly halfway through their project calendars? The transition can be understood through a combination of two concepts: problemistic search (March & Simon, 1958) and pacing. The idea of problemistic search simply extends the theory of bounded rationality. Its proponents posit that innovation is the result of search and that people do not initiate search unless they believe they have a problem. New perspectives appear to enter a group at transition because team members find old perspectives are no longer viable and initiate a fresh search for ideas.

The problem that stimulates search and stimulates it at a consistent moment in groups' calendars may be explained with the construct of pacing. Groups must pace their use of a limited resource, time, in order to finish by their deadlines. The midpoint appears to work like an alarm clock, heightening members' awareness that their time is limited, stimulating them to compare where they are with where they need to be and to adjust their progress accordingly: it is "time to roll." Since the groups in this research are charged with creating novel products, perspectives created quickly at the first meeting are likely to be found wanting in some way. For example, it may be perfectly suitable to begin with the approach "we're mapping out the task," but that approach must change at some time if there is to be a product. Even groups that started with a plan they liked learned by working on it to see flaws that were not visible when the plan was just an idea.

This model has some important qualifications. If the midpoint is primarily a moment of alarm, when groups feel "we need to move forward *now*," then the transition is an opportunity for, not a guarantee of, progress. This allows for the possibility that a group, like an individual, might feel strongly that it is time to move ahead, yet be unable to do so. Similarly, to hypothesize that transitions are catalyzed by groups' comparison of their actual progress with their desired progress leaves room for the chance that a group may—correctly or incorrectly—be largely satisfied and proceed with little visible change. These qualifications are consistent with the observation that groups' historical paths vary, and they provoke further research by posing the question, what factors affect the success of groups' transitions?

Why the consistent midpoint timing? Halfway is a natural milestone, since teams have the same amount of time remaining as they have already used, and they can readily calibrate their progress. Adult development research offers analogous findings. At midlife, people shift their focus from how much time has passed to how much time is left (Jaques, 1955). Levinson found a major transition at midlife, characterized by "a heightened awareness of mortality and a desire to use the remaining time more wisely" (1978: 192). Nonetheless, it would be premature to base the entire weight of these findings on the midpoint timing of the transition. Some groups may work on schedules that make times other than the midpoint highly salient. Ultimately, the midpoint itself is not as important as the finding that groups use temporal milestones to pace their work and that the event of reaching those milestones pushes groups into transitions. This study raises, but cannot answer, the question of what sets the alarm to go off when it does and precisely how it works in groups.

Context

What is the role of a team's context in its development? Traditional group development theory leaves little room for environmental influence on the course of development; all groups are predicted to go through the same steps, and all are predicted to suspend opinions of what they are about until they have thrashed that issue out through their own internal processes. Neither do these theories comment about development-linked changes in interaction between a group and its context. In contrast, the current findings suggest that the outside context may play a particularly important role in a group's developmental path at three points: the design of the group and two well-defined critical periods.

As noted, the speed with which distinctive patterns appear suggests the influence of materials imported into the group. The finding is congruent with, but does not test, a viewpoint from the group-performance research tradition. In that view, the design of a group—the composition of the team, the structure of the task, the contextual supports and circumstances under which the team is formed—precedes and conditions the interaction that transpires among members (Hackman, 1986). In terms of the current model, the pool of materials from which a team fashions its first framework is set by the design and designer of the group.

A critical period is a time in an organism's life within which a particular formative experience will take and after which it will not (Etkin, 1967). Though the analogy is imperfect, there appear to be two critical periods when groups are much more open to fundamental influence than they are at other times. The first is the initial meeting. As a time when the interaction in the group sets lasting precedents, it holds special potential to influence a team's basic approach toward its project.

The transition is the second chance. Not only did teams open up to outside influence at this point—they actively used outside resources and requirements as a basis for recharting the course of their work. The transition appears to be a unique time in groups' lives. It is the only period when the following three conditions are true at once: members are experienced enough with the work to understand the meaning of contextual requirements and resources, have used up enough of their time that they feel they must get on with the task, and still have enough time left that they can make significant changes in the design of their products.

In contrast, teams did not make fundamental changes of course in response to information from their contexts during phase 1 and phase 2, when ideas that did not fit with their approach to the task did not appear to register. That observation does not suggest that teams universally ignore or cut off environmental communication during phases 1 and 2, but it suggests that outsiders are unlikely to turn teams around during those times.

The three example teams showed how groups may insulate themselves from environmental input at some times yet seek it during transition—partly to get help limiting their own choices and moving forward, partly to increase the chances that their product will succeed in their environment. That pattern has interesting implications for the theoretical debate between population ecologists, who argue that environments "select," and advocates of resource dependency, who argue that systems "adapt." Researchers have already observed that organizations change through alternating periods of momentum and revolution (Miller & Friesen, 1984; Tushman & Romanelli, 1985). Further, organizations commonly construct time-related goals for productivity and growth, such as monthly, annual, and five-year plans, as well as possibly much longer-term objectives for their ultimate growth schedules. It appears worth investigating (1) whether pacing or life cycle issues affect the timing or success of organizational revolutions and (2) how organization-environment communication, or lack of it, during revolutionary periods particularly affects outcomes. Interaction with an environment may be very likely to foster and shape adaptation at certain predictable times in a system's life cycle and unlikely to do so at other times. If its environment changes dramatically when an organization is also entering a change phase, that organization may be more likely to adapt. Organizations that are instead in a phase of inertia will be less able to respond and may be selected out. Since this study did not include interviews with external stakeholders or observation of them outside teams' meetings, more research is needed to study the effects of environmental influence attempts during phases 1 and 2, versus during transition.[10]

Limitations of the Study

This study must be interpreted with caution. It was hypothesis-generating, not hypothesis-testing; the model is expressly provisional. One person conducted the analysis. As Donnellon, Gray, and Bougon (1986: 54) pointed out, the use of a single judge is important in discourse analysis, where the goal is to create an in-depth understanding of a whole event, but it increases the need for further research. There are also limits on the type of group to which the findings might apply. The transition involves

---

[10] Gersick (1983) does include and discuss additional evidence of teams dismissing or not understanding outside requirements during phases 1 and 2.

groups' revising their understanding of and approach to their work in response to time limits. Accordingly, results should apply only to groups that have some leeway to modify their work processes and must orient themselves to a time limit. The length of the time span should not matter, though that is a question for empirical research.

Comparison with Past Findings

Why did this study result in findings so different from the findings of previous group development research? An important possibility is that the paradigm of unitary stage theory directed previous researchers' attention away from phenomena of special interest here. The developmental stage paradigm naturally focuses on the stages themselves, not on the process of change, since all systems are assumed to progress through the same stages in a forward direction. Such events as T-groups' characteristic revolt against the leader may be midpoint transitions, but past researchers did not note their timing or think in such terms. The theoretical prominence of the environment is also limited in the traditional models because is does not alter the basic sequence of stages. In contrast, punctuated equilibrium paradigms direct attention to periods of stability and to change processes, provoking questions about what happens within a team and between a team and its context during the short periods of time when systems are especially plastic and labile. Finally, the traditional paradigm raised different questions about group process. Many past studies conceptualized and examined group process at the microanalytic level of members' sentence-by-sentence rhetoric and speech patterns, whereas this study encompassed the more macroanalytic level of group actions, such as revising plans and contacting outside supervisors. Such actions would be undetectable to traditional coding schemes, as would one of the most important clues in the study, the one-shot comments about time that group members made as they began their transitions.

The work of Poole (1983a, 1983b) suggests another possibility. He found that groups developed decisions within single meetings in multiple, not unitary, sequences, and proposed that past research did identify the key components of the development of group decisions, but that outside the controlled conditions and broad category systems of past laboratory research, it is possible to see that groups treat those components as blank spaces on an outline. They may fill in the blank spaces in a variety of sequences, depending on a host of task-related variables. Finally, the nature of its task affects the development of a group (Poole, 1983b). Past research has concentrated on a few types of group and tasks, with little attention to naturally occurring groups responsible for creating concrete products for outside use and evaluation.

Implications for Action

The results reported here have many implications for managers working with groups. Although traditional theory implies that group leaders have plenty of time at a project's beginning before the group will choose its norms and get to work, this model implies that a group's first meeting will set lasting precedents for how the group will use the first half of its time. That finding suggests that group leaders prepare carefully for the first meeting, and it identifies a key point of intersection between group development and group-effectiveness research on team design. According to traditional theory, a group must also expect an inevitable storming stage. In contrast, the proposed model suggests that groups use the first meeting to diagnose the unique issues that will preoccupy them during phase 1.

The proposed model also suggests that a group does not necessarily need to make visible progress with a steady stream of decisions during phase 1 but does need to generate the raw material to make a successful transition. For example, groups that begin with a clear plan may do best to use phase 1 to flesh out a draft of that plan fully enough to see its strong and weak points at the transition. Groups that begin with a deep disagreement may do best to pursue the argument fully enough to understand by transition what is and is not negotiable for compromise. A leader who discovers at the first meeting that the group adamantly opposes the task may do best to decide whether to restart the project or help the group use phase 1 to explore the issues enough to determine, at transition, whether it can reach an acceptable formulation of the task. In such a case, a leader might want to redefine a group's task as a preliminary diagnostic project, with a shorter deadline. Once past the first meeting, phase 1 interventions aimed at fundamentally altering a group, rather than at helping it pursue its first framework more productively, may be unsuccessful because of members' resistance to perceiving truly different approaches as relevant to the concerns that preoccupy them.

The next new implication of the present model is that the midpoint is a particularly important opportunity for groups and external managers to renew communication. Again, note that the teams and supervisors studied did not all automatically do this or do it uniformly well. The special challenge of the transition is to use a group's increased information, together with fresh input from its environment, to revise its framework knowledgeably and to adjust the match between its work and environmental resources and requirements. This is another point of special intersection between group development and group-effectiveness research, since that research should be especially helpful in evaluating and revising a group's situation (Hackman & Walton, 1986). Further research is needed to explore ways to manage the transition process productively.

Once the transition is past, the major outlines of a group's project design are likely to be set; the most helpful interventions are likely to be aimed at helping the group execute its work smoothly. For external managers, this may be an especially important time to insure a group's access to needed resources.

Conclusions

The concepts highlighted here center around the broad theme of change over time in groups' lives. This kind of knowledge about groups is particularly needed now, given the increasing importance of groups in high commitment organizations (Walton & Hackman, 1986) and in young, high technology industries (Mintzberg, 1981).

The pattern of continuity and change, observed directly in eight groups, also matches a punctuated equilibrium pattern that others have postulated at different levels of analysis. These formulations range from Kuhn's (1962) concept of normal science versus scientific revolution, through Abernathy and Utterback's (1982) description of radical versus evolutionary innovation in industries and Miller and Friesen's (1984) model of momentum and revolution in organizations, to Levinson's (1978) theory of adult development as alternating periods of stability and transition. Findings about small groups cannot be generalized directly to individual lives, growing organizations, or developing industries; nevertheless, knowledge about group development should stimulate and enrich our learning about inertia and change in human systems across those levels of analysis.

REFERENCES

Abelson, R. P. 1976. Script processing in attitude formation and decision making. In J. Carroll & J. Payne (Eds.), *Cognition and social behavior:* 33–45. Hillsdale, N.J.: Lawrence Erlbaum Associates.

Abernathy, W., & Utterback, J. 1982. Patterns of industrial innovation. In M. Tushman & W. Moore (Eds.), *Readings in the management of innovation:* 9–108. Boston, Mass.: Pitman Publishing.

Alderfer, C. P. 1977. Group and intergroup relations. In J. R. Hackman & J. L. Suttle (Eds.), *Improving life at work:* 227–296. Santa Monica Calif.: Goodyear Publishing.

Bales, R. F. & Strodtbeck, F. L. 1951. Phases in group problem solving. *Journal of Abnormal and Social Psychology,* 46: 485–495.

Bell, M. A. 1982. Phases in group problem solving. *Small Group Behavior,* 13: 475-495.

Bennis, W. & Shepard, H. 1956. A theory of group development. *Human Relations,* 9: 415–437.

Bettenhausen, K., & Murnighan, J. K. 1985. The emergence of norms in competitive decision-making groups. *Administrative Science Quarterly,* 30: 350–372.

Bion, W. R. 1961. *Experiences in groups.* New York: Basic Books.

Donnellon, A., Gray, B., & Bougon, M. 1986. Communication, meaning, and organized action. *Administrative Science Quarterly,* 31: 43-55.

Eldrege, N. & Gould, S. J. 1972. Punctuated equilibria: An alternative to phyletic gradualism. In T. J. Schopf (Ed.), *Models in paleobiology:* 82–115. San Francisco: Freeman, Cooper and Co.

Etkin, W. 1967. *Social behavior from fish to man.* London: University of Chicago Press.

Fisher, B. A. 1970. Decision emergence: Phases in group decision-making. *Speech Monographs,* 37: 53–66.

Gersick, C. G. 1982. Manual for group observations. In J. R. Hackman (Ed.), *A set of methodologies for research on task performing groups.* Technical report no. 1, Research Program on Group Effectiveness, Yale School of Organization and Management, New Haven, Connecticut.

Gersick C. G. 1983. *Life cycles of ad hoc task groups.* Technical report no. 3, Research Program on Group Effectiveness, Yale School of Organization and Management, New Haven, Connecticut.

Gersick C. G. 1984. *The life cycles of ad hoc task groups: Time, transitions, and learning in teams.* Unpublished doctoral dissertation. Yale University, New Haven, Connecticut.

Ginette, R. 1986. *OK, let's brief real quick.* Paper presented at the 1986 meeting of the Academy of Management, Chicago, Ill.

Gladstein, D. 1984. Groups in context: A model of task group effectiveness. *Administrative Science Quarterly,* 29: 499–517.

Glaser, B., & Strauss, A. 1967. *The discovery of grounded theory: Strategies for qualitative research*. London: Wiedenfeld and Nicholson.

Goodstein, L. D. & Dovico. M. 1979. The decline and fall of the small group. *Journal of Applied Behavioral Science*, 15: 320–328.

Hackman, J. R. 1985. Doing research that makes a difference. In E. Lawler, A. Mohrman, S. Mohrman, G. Ledford. & T. Cummings (Eds.), *Doing research that is useful for theory and practice*: 126–148. San Francisco: Jossey-Bass.

Hackman, J. R. 1986. The design of work teams. In J. Lorsch (Ed.), *Handbook of organizational behavior*: 315–342. Englewood Cliffs, N.J.: Prentice-Hall.

Hackman, J. R. (Ed.). *Groups that work*. San Francisco: Jossey-Bass. Forthcoming.

Hackman, J. R., & Walton, R. E. 1986. Leading groups in organizations. In P. S. Goodman & Associates (Eds.), *Designing effective work groups*: 72–119. San Francisco: Jossey-Bass.

Hare, A. P. 1976. *Handbook of small group research* (2nd ed.). New York: Free Press.

Harris, S., & Sutton, R. 1986. Functions of parting ceremonies in dying organizations. *Academy of Management Journal*, 29: 5–30.

Hellriegel, D., Slocum, J., & Woodman, R. 1986. *Organizational behavior* (4th ed.). St. Paul: West Publishing Co.

Huse, E., & Cummings, T. 1985. *Organization development and change* (3rd ed.). St. Paul: West Publishing Co.

Jaques, E. 1955. Death and the mid-life crisis. *International Journal of Psychoanalysis*, 46: 502–514.

Katz, R. 1982. The effects of group longevity on project communication and performance. *Administrative Science Quarterly*, 27: 81–104.

Katz, R., & Tushman, M. 1979. Communication patterns, project performance, and task characteristics: An empirical evaluation and integration in an R & D setting. *Organizational Behavior and Human Performance*, 23: 139–162.

Kuhn, T. S. 1962. *The structure of scientific revolutions*. Chicago: University of Chicago Press.

Labov, W., & Fanshel, D. 1977. *Therapeutic discourse*. New York: Academic Press.

LaCoursiere, R. B. 1980. *The life cycle of groups: Group developmental stage theory*. New York: Human Sciences Press.

Levinson, D. J. 1978. *The seasons of a man's life*. New York: Alfred A. Knopf.

Levinson, D. J. 1986. A conception of adult development. *American Psychologist*, 41: 3-14.

Mann, R., Gibbard, G., & Hartman, J. 1967. *Interpersonal styles and group development*. New York: John Wiley & Sons.

March, J., & Simon, H. 1978. *Organizations*. New York: John Wiley & Sons.

McCrath, J. E. 1984. *Groups: Interaction and performance*. Englewood Cliffs, N.J.: Prentice Hall.

McGrath, J. E. 1986. Studying groups at work: Ten critical needs for theory and practice. In P. S. Goodman & Associates (Eds.), *Designing effective work groups*: 363–392. San Francisco: Jossey-Bass.

Miller, D., & Friesen, P. 1984. *Organizations: A quantum view*. Englewood Cliffs, N.J.: Prentice Hall.

Mills, T. 1979. Changing paradigms for studying human groups. *Journal of Applied Behavioral Science*, 15: 407-423.

Mintzberg, H. 1981. Organization design, fashion or fit? *Harvard Business Review*, 59(1): 103-116.

Pittenger, R., Hockett. C., & Danehy, J. 1960. *The first five minutes: A sample of microscopic interview analysis*. Ithaca, N.Y.: Paul Martineau.

Poole, M. S. 1981. Decision development in small groups I: A comparison of two models. *Communication Monographs*, 48:1–24.

Poole, M. S. 1983a. Decision development in small groups II: A study of multiple sequences of decision making. *Communication Monographs*, 50: 206–232.

Poole, M. S. 1983b. Decision development in small groups III: A multiple sequence model of group decision development. *Communication Monographs*, 50: 321–341.

Scheidel, T., & Crowell, L. 1964. Idea development in small discussion groups. *Quarterly Journal of Speech*, 50:140–145.

Schutz, W. C. 1958. *FIRO: A three-dimensional theory of interpersonal behavior*. New York: Rinehart & Winston.

Seeger, J. A. 1983. No innate phases in group problem solving. *Academy of Management Review*, 8: 683–689.

Simon, H. A. 1976. *Administrative behavior* (3rd ed.). New York: Free Press.

Slater, P. E. 1966. *Microcosm: Structural, psychological, and religious evolution in groups*. New York: John Wiley & Sons.

Szilagy, A., & Wallace, M. 1987. *Organizational behavior and performance* (4th ed.). Glenview, III.: Scott, Foresman & Co.

Tosi, H., Rizzo, J., & Carroll, S. 1986. *Managing organizational behavior*. Marshfield, Mass.: Pitman Publishing.

Tuckman, B. 1965. Developmental sequence in small groups. *Psychological Bulletin*, 63: 384–399.

Tuckman, B., & Jensen, M. 1977. Stages of small-group development. *Group and Organizational Studies*, 2: 419–427.

Tushman, M. L., & Romanelli, E. 1985. Organizational evolution: A metamorphosis model of convergence and reorientation. In L. Cummings & B. Staw (Eds.), *Research in organizational behavior*, vol. 7: 171–222. Greenwich, Conn.: JAI Press.

Walton, R. E., & Hackman, J. R. 1986. Groups under contrasting management strategies. In P. Goodman & Associates (Eds.), *Designing effective work groups*: 168–201. San Francisco: Jossey-Bass.

DISCUSSION QUESTIONS

1. Outline the group dynamic approach to research and theory with regard to group development.

2. Outline the group problem solving stream of research on group development.

3. What criticisms of traditional research and theory does Gersick present? Evaluate her critique.

4. Discuss the research design of Gersick's study and how it differs from yet improves previous studies.

5. What are the central features of the new model of group development?

6. Discuss the concept of *punctuated equilibrium*.

7. What is the importance of the midpoint transition in the development of a group?

8. What behavior defined the completion phase of the groups observed by Gersick?

9. Discuss the implications for action that the revised perspective on group functioning has for managers and group members.

Genres of Organizational Communication: A Structurational Approach to Studying Communication and Media

Joanne Yates and Wanda J. Orlikowski

LEARNING OBJECTIVES

After reading "Genres of Organizational Communication: A Structurational Approach to Studying Communication and Media" by Joanne Yates and Wanda Orlikowski, a student will be able to:

1. Understand that the development of communication devices is a dynamic process in organizations

2. Utilize elements of both rhetorical theory and the structurational approach for the analysis of communication in organizations

3. Distinguish between communication media and genres of organizational communication

4. Consider ways that a dynamic view of organizational communication may increase organizational effectiveness

Human communication has always been central to organizational action. Today, the introduction of various sophisticated electronic communication technologies and the demand for faster and better forms of interaction are visibly influencing the nature of much organizational communication. These pressures are giving rise to hitherto poorly understood changes in what, how, when, why, and with what effect organizational communication occurs. Yet, such changes are not unprecedented; the nature and role of communication in organizations is always evolving as individual actors interact with social institutions over time (Weick, 1979, 1987).

This ongoing interaction between individuals and institutions can be seen as an instance of what Giddens (1984) termed *structuration*. Structuration theory involves the production, reproduction, and transformation of social institutions, which are enacted through individuals' use of social rules. These rules shape the action taken by individuals in organizations; at the same time, by regularly drawing on the rules, individuals reaffirm or modify the social institutions in an ongoing, recursive interaction. Only a few researchers have drawn on Giddens's (1984) structuration theory in their treatment of organizational communication (Contractor & Eisenberg, 1990; Manning, 1989; McPhee, 1985; Monge & Eisenberg, 1987; Poole & DeSanctis, 1989, 1990; Poole & McPhee, 1983). For example, Poole and DeSanctis (1989) used structurational concepts to examine how groups appropriate the interaction rules of their group decision support systems, thereby structuring their group communication and reinforcing or modifying their systems' influence over time.

This article adapts the concept of *genre* from rhetorical theory and uses it to explain organizational communication as a structuration process. Genre is a literary and rhetorical concept that describes widely recognized types of discourse (e.g., the novel, the sermon). In the context of organizational communication, it may be applied to recognized types of communication (e.g., letters, memoranda, or meetings) characterized by structural, linguistic, and substantive conventions. These genres can be viewed as social institutions that both shape and are shaped by individuals' communicative actions. By situating genres within processes of organizational structuration, the proposed framework captures the continuing interaction between human communicative action and the institutionalized communicative practices of groups, organizations, and societies.

Source: Joanne Yates and Wanda J. Orlikowski: "Genres of Organizational Communication: A Structurational Approach to Studying Comunication and Media," *Academy of Management Review*, 1992, Vol. 17, No. 2, pp. 299–326. Copyright ©1992. Reprinted by permission.

Genres of Organizational Communication

Background and Concept

Rhetoricians and literary critics since Aristotle's time have used genre as the basis for classifying types of rhetorical discourse and literary works. In traditional literary scholarship (e.g., Holman, 1972), the term *genre* was typically and loosely defined to mean a classification based on form and topic, such as a tragedy, a comedy, the novel, and the epic. In rhetoric, discourse was classified into genres such as the elegy or the inaugural address by one or more of a variety of characteristics, including form, subject, audience, or situation. (For extensive reviews of this literature, see Campbell & Jamieson. 1978; Miller, 1984.)

Since the late 1970s, the concept of rhetorical genre has received considerable attention. Rhetoricians have attempted to define the concept more precisely than in the past and have taken a more contextual approach to it. Simons (1978: 42), for example, defined *rhetorical genre* as "a distinctive and recurring pattern of similarly constrained rhetorical practices," in which the constraint is based primarily on purpose and situation. Harrell and Linkugel (1978: 263-264) argued that "rhetorical genres stem from *organizing principles* found in *recurring situations* that generate discourse characterized by a family of *common factors*." Of the most use here, Miller (1984: 159) identified genres "as typified rhetorical actions based in recurrent situations." These attempts at redefinition of rhetorical genre all draw on Bitzer's (1968: 8) concept of a rhetorical situation composed of three critical elements: an exigence (something needing to be done), an audience (who must be affected or influenced), and constraints ("persons, events, objects, and relations which are parts of the situation because they have the power to constrain decision and action needed to modify the exigence").

Miller (1984) modified Bitzer's relatively objective notion of exigence by introducing an element of subjectivity. Drawing on Burke's (1973) notion that motives (i.e., human action as subjectively perceived) rather than objective circumstances constitute the essence of situations, Miller (1984: 157) argued that exigence is neither totally objective nor totally subjective but rather "a form of social knowledge—a mutual construing of objects, events, interests, and purposes that not only links them but also makes them what they are: an objectified social need." In response to this *objectified social need,* humans enact typical rhetori-

cal practices or genres characterized by patterns of form and substance. Thus, genres are typified rhetorical action in the context of socially defined recurrent situations. This concept of rhetorical genre has been used within rhetorical research to study various types of discourse, ranging from the experimental scientific article (Bazerman, 1988) to the documentary film (Gronbeck, 1978). In a study of genre in a professional community, Devitt (1991) used documents from six major accounting firms as a basis for identifying a number of genres common to the tax accounting profession (e.g., opinion letters and memoranda to the file).

Drawing on Miller's concept of rhetorical genres, we propose a similar concept: *genres of organizational communication.* This concept can be applied to a wide range of typical communicative practices occurring in organizations, and it provides a new perspective on organizational communication that is both interactive and socially embedded. Thus, it allows us to examine the production, reproduction, and modification of different types of organization communication over time and under different circumstances.

A genre of organizational communication (e.g., a recommendation letter or a proposal) is a typified communicative action invoked in response to a recurrent situation. The *recurrent situation* or socially defined need includes the history and nature of established practices, social relations, and communication media within organizations (e.g., a request for a recommendation letter assumes the existence of employment procedures that include the evaluation and documentation of prior performance; a request for a proposal is premised on a system for conducting and supporting research). The resulting genre is characterized by similar substance and form. *Substance* refers to the social motives, themes, and topics being expressed in the communication (e.g., the positive or negative recommendation and the supporting characteristics of the recommendee; the proposing of the project including its rationale and design). *Form* refers to the observable physical and linguistic features of the communication (e.g., inside address and salutation of a letter; standard sections of a proposal). There are at least three aspects of form in organizational communication: structural features (e.g., text-formatting devices such as lists and fields and devices for structuring group interactions, such as an agenda and a chairperson for a meeting), communication medium (e.g., pen and paper or face to face), and language or symbol system (which would include linguistic characteristics such as formality and the specialized vocabulary of technical or legal jargon).

To illustrate, consider the meeting genre. Individuals invoke this genre in response to a recurrent organizational situation, defined generally by the set of organized group practices emerging from the socially defined demand for face-to-face interaction underlying contemporary organizational culture. In staging and participating in the meeting, participants draw on the characteristic features that constitute meetings: *substance,* defined generally as the participants' joint execution of assigned tasks and responsibilities, and *form,* including prearrangement of time and place, the face-to-face medium within which the meeting is typically executed, and structuring devices such as an agenda and the chairperson's role. A particular instance of this meeting genre would be, for example, a specific meeting of a personnel committee in a law firm. In this case, the recurrent situation is the institutionalized practice of meeting to evaluate employees, with its existing social relations of authority and legitimacy, and its past interactions. The substance of the meeting concerns evaluating the performance of certain employees. The form is a face-to-face meeting with a formal agenda, chaired by the director of personnel, minutes noted by the firm's secretary, and conducted in informal, everyday language.

Drawing on Giddens' (1984) notion of social rules, we posit that *genres* are enacted through rules, which associate appropriate elements of form and substance with certain recurrent situations. We call these rules *genre rules.* For example, in the case of the business letter, which is invoked in recurrent situations requiring documented communication outside the organization, the genre rules for substance specify that the letter pertain to a business interaction with an external party, and the genre rules for form specify an inside address, salutation, complimentary close, and correct, relatively formal language. The ways in which these genre rules influence the generation of specific communication is central to an understanding of genre as enacted within communities. When individuals draw on the rules of certain genres of organizational communication (genres as the vehicle of communicative action), they also reproduce these genres over time (genres as the outcome of communicative action). For example, when organizational members write business letters or engage in meetings, they implicitly or explicitly draw on the genre rules of the business letter or meeting to generate the substance and form of their documents or interactions. They also, in effect, reinforce and sustain the legitimacy of those rules through their actions.

A particular instance of a genre need not draw on all the rules constituting that genre. For example, a meeting need not include minutes or a formal agenda for it to be recognizable as a meeting. Enough distinctive genre rules,

however, must be invoked for the communicative action to be identified—within the relevant social community—as an instance of a certain genre. A chance encounter of three people at the water cooler, which is not preplanned and lacks formal structuring devices, would not usually be considered a meeting.

Genre rules may operate tacitly, through socialized or habitual use of communicative form and substance, or they may be codified by an individual or body into specific standards designed to regulate the form and substance of communication. Adherence to codified genre rules may be mandated at various social levels, as with laws requiring tax returns to conform to IRS standards, or explicit organizational regulations requiring expense reports that conform to corporate standards. Genre rules also may be standardized by being embedded in a medium, as with preprinted paper forms such as credit or job application blanks, or electronic templates such as the headings provided by electronic mail systems.

Inherent in the notion of genre as presented above is the issue of *level of abstraction.* For example, if the business letter is a genre of organizational communication, what about the recommendation letter? Similarly, if the meeting is a genre, what about the personnel committee meeting? In each case, the variants derived from the more general type differ primarily by being more specific in subject and form. Do they constitute genres? Miller (1984: 162) suggested that genre may be defined at different levels in different cultures and at different times, depending on "our sense of recurrence of rhetorical situations." Applying this notion to organizational genre, the business letter and the meeting might at one point be genres, whereas at another point, these types of communication might be considered too general and the recommendation letter or the personnel committee meeting might better capture the social sense of recurrent situation. Although Miller maintained that genre can only be identified at one of these levels in a specific time and place, Simons (1978: 37) argued that genre need not be identified at a single level: "Rather than haggling over the level at which something becomes a genre as opposed to a family or species, one might better recognize that genres 'exist' at various levels of abstraction, from the very broad to the very specific." Within limits, this flexible approach seems more useful in dealing with the vast range of communication in organizations; that is, the business letter and the recommendation letter, the meeting and the personnel committee meeting may all be designated as genres of organizational communication if there can be identified for each a recurrent situation, a common subject (either very general or more specific), and common formal features. For example, the study of genres in the tax accounting profession (Devitt, 1991) identified six distinct types of letters (e.g., opinion letters and promotional letters) and three types of memoranda (e.g., research memos and administrative memos).

It may be useful to discuss the relationship of genres on different levels of abstraction; if so, we can invoke a notion of *subgenres* within genres. For example, the positive recommendation letter could be viewed as a subgenre of the recommendation letter, which is a subgenre of the business letter. The term subgenre is, of course, relative, because in the posited nesting, the recommendation letter is a subgenre of the business letter, but it is a genre in relation to its subgenre, the positive recommendation letter. Moreover, this nesting, as well as the concept of genre in general, must be understood to be situated in time and context. In the contemporary American climate of plentiful lawsuits and occasional public disclosure of recommendation letters, a situation may be emerging in which almost all recommendation letters are positive and, thus, the three nested genres can be collapsed into two genres.

Related to, but analytically distinct from, level of abstraction is the issue of *normative* scope. That is, how extensively shared must the social norms of a recurrent communicative situation, along with characteristic subject and formal features, be to qualify as a genre?[1] Must a genre be universally meaningful, or may it be shared across certain types of organizations, within a single organization, or within a single group? What if it is widely applied across organizations in one culture, but not in those of another culture? To pose a contrasting case, what if a single individual has developed a consistent pattern of communicative action in response to a personally identified recurrent situation? Because recurrent situations are socially defined, we can disqualify as a genre the pattern invoked only by a single individual, though such patterns may be of interest as stages in the eventual emergence of a socially defined genre.

Because recurrent situations may be socially defined at any level above the personal, we posit that genres of organizational communication may be shared across the following various kinds of social communities: (a) those that are widely accepted in most advanced industrial nations (e.g., the memo and business letter), (b) those that are specific to organizations within certain societies or particular cultures (e.g., the Japanese tea ceremony or a U.S. envi-

ronmental impact statement), (c) those specific to transorganizational groups such as occupations and industries (e.g., audit reports, SEC filings), (d) those that reflect distinct organizational or corporate cultures (e.g., the Procter & Gamble one-page memo), and finally (e) those genres that exist within intraorganizational groups such as departments and teams (e.g., the "complex sheet" used by airline ground crews to coordinate the movement of planes into and out of gates, and the transfer of passengers and baggage into and out of planes, Suchman & Trigg, 1991). It appears that genres with a broad normative scope also are more likely to be at a high level of abstraction, and vice versa. Nevertheless, the two aspects of genre can be distinguished. It is, for example, possible to identify genres and subgenres with the same normative scope (e.g., the business letter and the recommendation letter are both used in organizations throughout the United States).

To allow flexibility in use of the genre concept, we have defined it broadly in terms of both normative scope and level of abstraction. Nevertheless, undue proliferation of genres may also weaken the usefulness of the concept.[2] For example, Devitt's (1991) catalog of genres in tax accounting is useful in understanding various aspects of the tax accounting profession. If, however, such cataloging were extended to every industry, it would result in endless lists of genres comparable to the exhaustive (and exhausting) model letter books common in the 19th century (Weiss, 1945). Thus, there is a tension between too broad and too narrow a definition of genre. In a particular use of the concept, the domain or communicative phenomenon being studied should guide the researcher in determining the useful balance between too narrowly and too broadly construing the genre concept. For example, the Procter & Gamble one-page memo may be considered a genre (or a subgenre of the memo) only for certain limited purposes such as studying the socialization of new Procter & Gamble employees.

Production, Reproduction, and Change over Time

In discussing what constitutes a genre, we have only alluded to the more complex and central dynamic issue of

[1] In his examination of artistic genres, DiMaggio (1987: 448) termed this dimension *universality*.

[2] We are indebted to an anonymous reviewer for elaborating on this possibility.

how genres are produced, reproduced, and changed over time. This aspect of genres will now be elaborated upon.

We have suggested that genres emerge within a particular sociohistorical context and are reinforced over time as a situation recurs. As rhetoricians have also observed, these genres, in turn, shape future responses to similar situations. For example, Bitzer's (1969: 13) discussion of recurrent rhetorical situations notes:

> From day to day, year to year, comparable situations occur, prompting comparable responses; hence rhetorical forms are born and a special vocabulary, grammar, and style are established. . . . The situation recurs and, because we experience situations and the rhetorical responses to them, a form of discourse is not only established but comes to have a power of its own—the tradition itself tends to function as a constraint upon any new response in the form.

This view of communicative practices within sociohistorical contexts is particularly compatible with structuration theory (Giddens, 1984).

In structurational terms, genres are social institutions that are produced, reproduced, or modified when human agents draw on genre rules to engage in organizational communication. As social institutions, genres both shape and are shaped by communicative action. To borrow from Barley and Tolbert (1988: 2) on institutions, genres "are by-products of a history of negotiation among social actors that results in shared typifications which gradually acquire the moral and ontological status of taken-for-granted facts." Figure 7.1 (adapted from Barley, 1986) depicts the processes by which genres are used and reproduced or changed over time in organizational communication.[3] At any given time in a particular firm, genres of organizational communication exist and inform ongoing organizational communication (arrow 1 in Figure 7.1). Organizational members in certain situations draw on the rules of substance and form of established genres in their communicative action (arrow 2 in Figure 7.1). By using (or not using) particular genre rules, individuals enact the established genres (or modified versions) (arrow 3 in Figure 7.1), thus reinforcing and reproducing (or challenging and changing) established genres over time (arrow 4 in Figure 7.1). The

enacted genres then inform future communicative action, and the recursive cycle begins anew.

As this description suggests, although the processes of structuration generally reproduce genres over time, the processes may also change them. That is, even though genres facilitate and constrain communicative choices, genre rules do not create a binding constraint. Instead, human agents continually enact genres, and during such enactment they have the opportunity to challenge and change these genres. Barley and Tolbert (1988:9) recognized three modes of enacting already-established social institutions—maintenance, elaboration, and modification—which can also be used to understand the production and reproduction of genres. When individuals enact the genres by using the rules of substance and form without alteration, they are *maintaining* the existing genres. When they consistently but slightly adapt genre rules to reflect new conditions—such as a new medium or a new locale—without substantially departing from those genre rules, they are *elaborating* the existing genres (e.g., a firm may customize its own memo stationery with an added field for file number). When individuals depart significantly and persistently from the rules of existing genres, they are *modifying* the existing genres (e.g., when prose reports are replaced by tabular, numeric reports in organizations).

Thus, on occasion, individuals modify (deliberately or inadvertently, whether by mandate or spontaneously) some of the established genre rules of substance and form. These modifications may be triggered by material or perceptual changes in the recurrent situation. That is, changes to the social, economic, or technological context (e.g., changed organizational forms, new or less expensive electronic media, revised reporting requirements), or changes in how social groups recognize and respond to situations (e.g., an ad hoc group's redefinition of itself into a regular task force) may occasion a deviation from habitual use of genre rules. Similarly, changes in elements of form, such as available media, structuring devices, and language, may allow or encourage individuals to violate genre rules. Although rules establish continuity with the past, they are not determining forces because communicative action can create variations in the rules of substance and form. As Cohen (1989: 45) noted, "There is no guarantee that agents will reproduce regularities of conduct as they previously have done." Thus, the potential for genre modification is inherent in every act of communication. The extent to which established genres actually are modified will depend on the duration, normative scope, and nature of variation from existing genre rules. Significant and persistent modifications to genre rules that are widely adopted

---

[3] Although this article depicts institutional forces and social actions sequentially in both the discussion and in Figure 7.1, this is for analytical clarity only. Processes of structuration occur simultaneously and are often inseparable in practice.

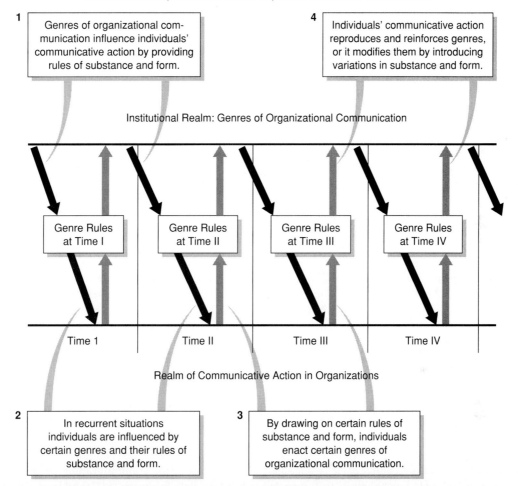

FIGURE 7.1

GENRES OF ORGANIZATIONAL COMMUNICATION:
PRODUCTION, REPRODUCTION, AND CHANGE OVER TIME

1 Genres of organizational communication influence individuals' communicative action by providing rules of substance and form.

4 Individuals' communicative action reproduces and reinforces genres, or it modifies them by introducing variations in substance and form.

Institutional Realm: Genres of Organizational Communication

Genre Rules at Time I

Genre Rules at Time II

Genre Rules at Time III

Genre Rules at Time IV

Time 1   Time II   Time III   Time IV

Realm of Communicative Action in Organizations

2 In recurrent situations individuals are influenced by certain genres and their rules of substance and form.

3 By drawing on certain rules of substance and form, individuals enact certain genres of organizational communication.

result in a modified genre. In some cases, these changes may be so extensive that they lead to the emergence of a new or modified genre (either one that is parallel with an existing genre or one that replaces a genre that has broken down). The result of such ongoing challenges is "that the set of genres is an open class, with new members evolving, old ones decaying" (Miller, 1984: 153).

The structurational account of genre production, reproduction, and change over time helps us to describe and interpret both historical and contemporary changes in communicative practices. It also provides a powerful lens through which to examine the relationships between organizational communication and communication media.

Communication Media and Organizational Genres

Overview of Two Streams of Prior Research

Numerous studies focusing on many different variables have examined the relationship between organizational communication and communication media. Although the approaches adopted by these studies seem disparate, from a structurational point of view, we can identify two dominant streams of research that are characterized by their opposing views of the role played by media in organizational communication. One stream of research focuses on the conditions that influence media choice, thus positing communication media as a dependent variable and examining the technical, economic, psychological, and social factors that influence use of media in organizations. The other stream of research focuses on the communication effects of using media, thus positing communication media as an independent or mediating variable that influences certain communicative behaviors or outcomes in organizations.

Research on Media Choice.   The research on media choice has attempted to determine when and with what consequences individuals choose to use a particular communication medium. Such studies have examined the use and appropriateness of various media for different types of communication under various circumstances. Though there are several theories regarding media choice, such as those of *social presence* (Short, Williams, & Christie, 1976) and *cost minimization* (Reinsch & Beswick, 1990), the most widely studied recent theory, and the one used here to illustrate this stream, is that of *media richness* (Daft & Lengel, 1984, 1986; Daft, Lengel, & Trevino 1987; Trevino, Lengel, & Daft, 1987). This theory posited that media may be ranked on a continuum according to their capacity to provide immediate feedback, to convey multiple cues, to support personalization, and to accommodate linguistic variety. The continuum runs from face-to-face interaction at the "rich" end through telephone communication, electronic mail (included only in later studies), and personally addressed written letters and memos to general bulletins and standardized quantitative reports at the "lean" end. The theory states that effective managers choose richer media to convey equivocal or ambiguous messages and leaner media to convey unequivocal messages.

Empirical studies of media choice have shown some support for the media richness concept and its link with managerial effectiveness (Russ, Daft, & Lengel, 1990; Trevino et al., 1987), as well as the effect of situational and individual factors on media choice (Trevino, Daft, & Lengel, 1990). Other studies, however, have found that executives use certain media more often (Rice & Shook, 1990) or for different types of tasks (Markus, 1988) than the theory would predict. Some conceptual limitations have also been noted. Fulk, Schmitz, and Steinfield (1990), for example, pointed out that this theory is limited by assumptions about the rationality and objectivity of decision makers. Decisions about media do not occur in a vacuum; both decision makers and media are socially

embedded within organizational settings. Fulk and her colleagues (1990) proposed a more comprehensive "social influence" model which explains that media choice is based not simply on objective characteristics of media and tasks, but it is also based on subjective perceptions that are influenced by social and historical factors. The social influence model overcomes many of the difficulties of the media richness assumptions. Despite the incorporation of many social factors, this literature still focuses primarily on the factors determining media use.

Research on Media Consequences.   In contrast, the other main stream of research has concentrated on the consequences of media use for communication structure, process, and outcomes (see reviews by Culnan & Markus, 1987; Kraemer & Pinsonneault, 1990; Williams, 1977). To illustrate, studies have examined the extent to which electronic media filter out many of the cues—nonverbal (Trevino et al., 1990), social context (Sproull & Kiesler, 1986), and social presence (Rice, 1984; Short et al., 1976)—that are associated with face-to-face and other non-computer-mediated forms of communication. For example, one group of researchers (Siegel, Dubrovsky, Kiesler, & McGuire, 1986; Sproull & Kiesler, 1986) found that the language used in electronic communication media was less inhibited than that in face-to-face communication and also included many instances of what they called *flaming* (e.g., emotional outbursts, name-calling, exaggerated emphasis, inappropriate innuendos, sarcasm, and obscene language). More recently, however, the pervasiveness of this phenomenon in social settings has been questioned (Foulger, 1990; Matheson & Zanna, 1989; Rafaeli, 1990). Other researchers have examined the influence of electronic media on communication patterns (Eveland & Bikson, 1988; Feldman, 1987) and language patterns (Ferrara, Brunner, & Whittemore, 1990; Foulger, 1990; Murray, 1985, 1987) within established communities. Despite the focus on social contexts in these studies, this literature still posits media as a relatively fixed influence on social and communicative behaviors.

Limitations of Two Streams of Prior Research

The two streams of research that have been sketched out in the previous section have shed light on numerous aspects of the relationship between media and organizational communication. Several commentators have critiqued this body of work (Contractor & Eisenberg, 1990; Fulk et al., 1990; Krone, Jablin, & Putnam, 1987; Weick,

1983), but the genre perspective on communication in this article highlights two specific areas of concern.

Causal Relationships between Media and Organizational Communication.   As revealed in the previous section, most existing research focuses *either* on how technical, organizational, personal, or social factors influence media choice and use *or* on how media affect organizational communication, but not on both. A structurational view of communication suggests that each of these accounts, by itself, is incomplete for it fails to examine reciprocal and recursive relationships between media and communication in organizations over time. A small number of researchers have used structurational concepts to study communication media in organizations (Contractor & Eisenberg, 1990; Poole & DeSanctis, 1990). These approaches, like the genre perspective presented here, offer a way of resolving the dualism in the two dominant streams of existing research.

Definitions of Media.   The notion of communication media is used variously and inconsistently by different researchers in different studies. In particular, the concept of medium has often been confused with that of genre. Confusion arises when researchers compare genres of communication (e.g., memos or bulletins) with communication media (e.g., electronic mail or fax). Genres, however, may be physically created, transmitted, and stored in various media. Thus, comparing memos with electronic mail, for example, confounds the concept of communication medium with that of communication genre.[4] Though a few researchers have applied the term *genre* to communication in electronic media (Foulger, 1990; Reder & Schwab, 1988), this concept has not been theoretically elaborated. Although our notion of genre is clearly differentiated from that of medium, we recognize their interaction by positing that medium may play a role in both the recurrent situation and the form of a genre. For example, a recurrent situation may include a specific medium (e.g., when an electronic mail message typically evokes an electronic mail response). Alternatively, a medium may be conceived as an aspect of a genre's form (e.g., letters are traditionally conceived of as paper-based).

---

[4] Stohl and Redding (1987: 457) identified this problem using the term *format* rather than *genre*. They wrote: "It must be noted also that the dividing line between 'medium' and 'format' is admittedly fuzzy: for example, between telephone, print, and oral media on the one hand; and conversations, interviews, committee meetings, letters and in-house presentation—all formats—on the other."

The genre perspective on communication presented in this article, which draws on structurational precepts and distinguishes between the physical means of communication (media) and the typified communicative action (genre), affords a powerful alternative approach to studying communication in organizations. To illustrate its usefulness, an exposition of the development over time of a particular organizational genre, the memo, follows.

Genre Evolution: Historical Illustration

In this section the genre approach is used to examine the gradual evolution of the memo genre of internal business correspondence away from the business letter genre of external correspondence in late 19th- and early 20th-century American firms, and the recent elaboration of this genre in electronic mail. This evolution is depicted in structurational terms in Figure 7.2.[5] Beginning in the last quarter of the 19th century, an emerging ideology of management created a newly recognized recurrent situation within firms: the managerially defined need to document internal interactions on paper. This ideology, interacting with other situational factors including communication media, triggered the evolution of new rules of substance and form, resulting in the emergence of a particular genre of internal organizational communication—the memo. In recent years, that genre has influenced communication within new media such as electronic mail. The following historical account is based on Yates (1989a, 1989b) (where detailed historical documentation is provided).

Emergence of the Memo Genre

Business correspondence generated by members of a typical mid-19th century American firm was aimed primarily at external individuals or firms. Such communications followed the genre rules of the business letter, exemplified in many model letter books. Members of the firm having been instructed and socialized in the appropriate form of business correspondence, invoked this genre to conduct and document business with another party (arrow 1 in Figure 7.2).

---

[5] As indicated previously, our sequential discussion and depiction in Figure 7.2 of institutional forces and social action is analytical only. Additionally, the timing of the major stages is only approximate.

FIGURE 7.2

EMERGENCE AND INSTITUTIONALIZATION OF MEMO GENRE
IN ORGANIZATIONAL COMMUNICATION

Institutional Realm: Genres of Organizational Communication

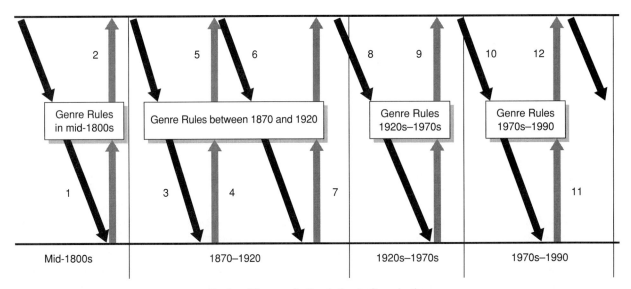

Realm of Communicative Action in Organizations

The substance of this genre was managing the business at hand, often a specific transaction (frequently indicated by an opening reference to a previous letter). The form was characterized by distinctive polite language (e.g., "In response to your esteemed favor of the 2nd inst. . . ." and "Your humble servant . . .") and by several standard structural features, including the placement of date, inside address, complimentary close, and signature. The communication medium associated with business letters was pen and paper. Regular use of the business letter genre in recurrent social situations served to reinforce its status as a social institution within firms (arrow 2 in Figure 7.2). The institutional force of the business letter genre served to shape many communicative transactions among firms of the mid-1800s.

A limited amount of correspondence among members of the same firm existed at this time, primarily to bridge physical distances when one party was not available for face-to-face discussion, as when one partner was away from the firm's headquarters on a buying or selling trip. When all involved parties were at the same physical location, ad hoc oral methods, supplemented by traditional financial accounts, were used to coordinate and control

operations. In writing intrafirm correspondence to bridge distance, firm members invoked the same business letter genre. Internal letters followed the same conventions of form as letters to external parties, though the language often reflected greater shared knowledge and assumptions. The substance in such letters was still primarily managing the business at hand, but such letters tended to be less focused on a specific transaction and more likely to discuss a whole range of topics relevant to the firm.

Between 1870 and 1920, internal correspondence in manufacturing firms mushroomed in volume and changed in social motive, reflecting the broader socioeconomic changes occurring at the time. This period was one of tremendous firm growth. While at midcentury, small, owner-managed firms with only a single level of management (foremen) characterized the manufacturing sector, by the turn of the century many firms had grown, departmentalized, and acquired several layers of management. When these firms were managed by the oral, ad hoc methods of the earlier period, the result was chaos, loss of control by owners and managers, and diseconomies of scale. To improve efficiency and regain control from the workers and foremen, managers developed new approaches and techniques that coalesced into a new managerial philosophy, later labeled *systematic management* (Litterer, 1961). This ideology, which emerged in engineering and management journals of the period, stressed the importance of documenting operational processes and outcomes and of establishing flows of written communication for internal coordination and control. Written documents were preferred to oral exchanges in many cases because documents could be stored for later consultation and analysis. They created a form of organizational memory.

The emphasis on documentation and use of internal information created a new recurrent situation—the managerial defined demand for documentation of internal interactions (vertical or horizontal, within a single site or between company sites) for later reference. Even though the telephone, widely adopted by businesses shortly after its introduction in 1876, facilitated oral communication within and between the growing factories and plants of this period, it did not satisfy management's demand for documentation. To respond to this exigence, managers increasingly turned to internal correspondence, initially invoking the rules of the business letter genre (arrow 3 in Figure 7.2).

The growth and expanded functions of internal correspondence put new demands on media for the creation and storage of written communication, and new media evolved and diffused in response to the demands. The typewriter, introduced in the 1870s, was widely adopted by large firms in the mid-1880s to speed the production of all correspondence.[6] The typewriter influenced emerging genre rules over subsequent decades by making certain structural features (e.g., underlining, all capital letters) easy to distinguish, thus opening the way for increased use of such features as subheads. Tab stops were added to typewriters around the turn of the century, making lists easier to type. Such formatting features were rarely adopted for external letters where the business letter genre continued to hold force. Internally, however, they were more freely adopted to ease the creation and processing of correspondence, hence introducing modifications in the genre rules for internal business letters (arrow 4 in Figure 7.2). Moreover, typists, a new occupational group which quickly emerged to "operate" this new technology, served as agents of standardization of document format within and across

firms. Variation from the business letter genre in internal correspondence thus became common across many organizations, and it was reinforced through ongoing use (arrow 5 in Figure 7.2).

The new systematic methods of management demanded not simply the creation of many internal documents, but also their ready retrieval for subsequent reference. Storage during this period included both bound volumes for copies of outgoing correspondence and individual, book-like letter boxes for storage of incoming documents. Managers' desire for more accessible storage media encouraged the development and adoption of vertical filing systems (introduced in 1893 and widely adopted in the early years of the 20th century) to replace both types of storage and to combine all documents in a single, functional system. This storage medium was intended to make documents more accessible for reference, organizing correspondence by subject rather than chronology.

Vertical files occasioned changes in rules for the substance and form of internal correspondence. The fact that a document could only be filed under a single subject led some firms to institute procedures limiting internal correspondence to a single subject and requiring subject lines to aid file clerks (arrow 6 in Figure 7.2). For example, when Scovill Manufacturing Company adopted vertical files, headquarters explained the new filing system in correspondence with the firm's New York store and issued very specific requirements that each letter cover only one subject, to be designated at the top of the sheet. Such a change to standard practice, however, did not come unopposed. One week after this mandate was issued, headquarters wrote to reprimand some lapses in providing the requested subject lines, ending with this statement: "We are changing our system of filing, and we must INSIST that you pay particular attention to this matter." Through such monitoring and exhortations, headquarters finally achieved general use of these standardized communication rules restricting the substance and introducing a new structural feature into its internal correspondence.

With widespread adoption of vertical files, such rules were widely imposed by other organizations and enacted through individuals' use of these rules (arrow 7 in Figure 7.2). Eventually, new forms of headings (with the familiar To, From, Subject, and Date fields of today's memo headings) evolved to simplify the addressing conventions for internal documents and to put all the pieces of information relevant to identifying, storing, and retrieving the document in clear view of the file clerk and the recipient of the document. Initially, the exact

---

[6] Detailed analysis of the records of specific firms undercuts a technologically deterministic argument, showing that in at least these cases, the typewriter did not *cause* the growth in correspondence, but was adopted after the growth was well under way, as a way of dealing with it (Yates, 1989a).

form of the new headings varied from person to person. Then, either by mandate from management or by hardening custom among typists, the order and placement of heading elements were standardized (though different firms might employ slightly variant elaborations) (arrow 8 in Figure 7.2). The new headings also eliminated some of the language characteristic of the business letter genre: the polite language of salutations and complimentary closes. Some firms also urged the elimination of other standard polite phrases in favor of directness and brevity, though this change was harder to enforce and occurred only gradually.

Thus, over time, changes in communication substance and form were introduced to better accommodate the demands of internal correspondence (Table 7.4 traces the evolution of memo genre rules). Through mandate and habitual use, these changes were gradually accepted, legitimized, and reinforced within organizations (arrow 9 in Figure 7.2), and this pattern of communicative action became recognizable as a new genre of organizational communication. The adoption of the term *memorandum* or *memo* rather than *business letter* to designate internal correspondence was one of the last features to be widely accepted, officially signalling the recognition of a new genre of organizational communication.[7] Although these changes did not eliminate the business letter genre, they did lead to the abandonment of the business letter genre for intraorganizational communication. Over subsequent decades, however, some elements of the business letter genre have decayed and others have been elaborated. Even though the business letter has retained its traditional structural elements and their placement, its language has been simplified and made more direct. In addition, structural devices that emerged in the memo (e.g., subject lines, subheadings, and lists) have been adopted as elaborations to the business letter.

The Memo Genre in Electronic Mail

We now turn to a discussion of both how the established memo genre has influenced communication in electronic

---

[7] During most of the period under discussion, memorandum generally referred to a written note or reminder to oneself. The origin of the term reinforces the central social motive of the emergent genre by emphasizing written documentation for future reference. Although the term was occasionally used in its current sense as early as the late 19th century, its use in that way is not consistent until around 1920.

TABLE 7.4

EMERGENCE AND INSTITUTIONALIZATION OF MEMO GENRE OVER TIME

TIME PERIOD	EXAMPLES OF GENRE RULES	
mid-1800s	**Maintenance of Business Letter Genre**	
	Substance:	Transacting business with external parties.
	Form:	Content and placement of date, inside address, salutation, complimentary close; formal, polite language with extensive use of standard phrases.
1870–1920	**Emergence of Memo Genre for Internal Correspondence**	
	Substance:	Documentation of internal interactions and outcomes; restricted to single subject.
	Form:	Addition of subject lines; compression of inside address and salutation; optional use of subheads or lists; less formal and polite language.
1920–present	**Maintenance of Memo Genre**	
	Substance:	Standard exchange and documentation of internal interactions and outcomes; restricted to a single subject.
	Form:	Standardized memo heading; direct language.
1970s–1990s	**Elaboration of Memo Genre in Electronic Mail**	
	Substance:	Internal and external exchanges and some documentation: not restricted to single subject.
	Form:	Memo heading template embedded in medium; less use of other structural devices; increasingly informal language.

mail and how the widespread adoption and use of electronic mail in organizations has set the stage for the emergence of new computer-mediated genres of organizational communication. The memo genre, as reinforced and elaborated since the 1920s, was created, transmitted, and stored on paper. With the advent of computers and the demand for faster communication and access to information, a new electronic medium of organizational communication—electronic mail—was created. Systems designers embedded the structural features of the memo heading into the new medium. In this case, computers rather than people routed the messages, so the fields of the memo heading were designed to be readable by computers (as well as humans). A typical memo layout for the fields was not required by computers, so its widespread adoption shows that designers (whether implicitly or explicitly) retained elements of an existing and familiar genre in moving to a new medium (arrow 10 in Figure 7.2).

Electronic mail messages often demonstrate other aspects of memo substance and form as described previously, indicating that users are drawing on that familiar genre for some of their communication in this newer medium (as was the case with the early internal correspondence and the business letter genre). For example, some electronic mail messages are used to document internal events or outcomes for future reference, often with subject matter restricted to a single topic. Moreover, the language of such messages often exhibits the direct but noncolloquial usage typical of memos. Further, those electronic mail messages may contain subheadings and lists, in spite of the typically more limited formatting capabilities of most systems. In such cases, then, electronic mail messages may clearly be classified as memos, elaborated within the electronic mail medium (see Table 7.4).

Yet electronic mail differs from paper in its capabilities, creating new options and new constraints affecting the invocation of the memo genre. This medium allows very rapid asynchronous exchanges, both because it is transmitted so rapidly and because intermediaries such as secretaries are usually bypassed. In contrast, editing facilities in electronic mail are often much less sophisticated than those in word processing. The system header format follows that of the memo, except that it uses system identifiers in place of names in the To and From fields. Although these are sometimes clearly recognizable variants on the individuals' names, sometimes they are nonmeaningful sequences of letters and numbers. Also, various local electronic mail systems have been linked by large, multinode networks such as Bitnet and CompuServe, making them useful for interorganizational communication (which would typically call for a letter, informal note, or telephone call rather than a memo).

These differences may help explain some of the variations from memo genre rules that can be observed in many electronic mail messages. For example, messages sometimes contain author-added headers and signoffs, which occasionally resemble those of a letter (e.g., "Dear Chris" and "Regards, Jane") or more often those of an informal note (e.g., "Hi, Chris—" and "Jane"). The language in many electronic mail messages is more informal and colloquial than is generally used in memos, and spelling and grammatical errors considered inappropriate in memos tend to be tolerated in this medium. These deviations may, in part, reflect the typical rapidity of and lack of secretarial mediation in this medium, as well as its weaker editing facilities and the lack of typing skills among many electronic mail users. In terms of substance, electronic mail is often used to convey messages that would not typically be handled through memos and that require no documentation (e.g., a two-line invitation to meet for lunch or a one-word response to a question). The possibility of rapid but nonintrusive exchanges may encourage individuals to use the medium for messages that are ephemeral and too incomplete to stand alone, unlike the memo and the business letter, which are intended for future reference and, hence, are more comprehensive.

Thus, organizational members draw selectively on the memo genre rules in this new medium (arrow 11 in Figure 7.2), sometimes maintaining it and sometimes elaborating it (arrow 12 in Figure 7.2). However, some electronic mail messages resemble genres other than the memo, such as the voicemail message or the informal note, or display unique characteristics. For example, Markus's (1988) study of electronic mail usage found a convention of what she calls *mosaic messages,* which result from the appending of responses to received messages to create continuity and conversational context. Variation in form and substance in response to similar situations reveals, as would be expected within a new medium, some ambiguity among individuals about what genres are appropriately invoked in which situations. Whether unique variations such as the mosaic messages represent the first stage in the emergence of one or more new genres of organizational communication remains to be seen. The emergence of such new genres, however, need not signal the demise of the memo genre, just as the memo genre emerged in parallel with, not in place of, the business letter genre. The memo genre may coexist with any potential new genres that emerge in the new medium, allowing individuals to enact any one genre (or combination of genres) in specific situations.

Explanatory Power of Genre Approach

The explanation of the emergence and institutionalization of the memo genre provided in the previous section shows how the genre approach furnishes a number of advantages vis-à-vis more traditional approaches to organizational communication and media. In particular, it allows us to transcend the two limitations in research on media identified earlier. First, the genre approach allows the integration of the two separate causal perspectives in media research, and second, it addresses the conceptual issues surrounding the nature and role of media in organizational communication.

Integration of Causal Perspectives in Media Research

The concept of genre developed here integrates two approaches to studying media that typically have been treated separately in the literature. It suggests that the conditions influencing media use and the consequences of media use are tightly coupled in a process of structuration over time. Thus, the practice of focusing on one set of relationships at the expense of the other, although useful for certain analytic purposes, may, if overused or used in isolation, encourage a misleading reliance on one-sided explanations—either technological determinism or rational choice (Markus & Robey, 1988; Orlikowski, In press). For example, many individuals do not put opening salutations and closing sign-offs in electronic mail messages. From the perspective of technological determinism, this practice, which could be seen as impersonal in comparison to a letter or a note, may be attributed to the depersonalizing influence of electronic media. From the perspective of rational choice, this practice may be attributed to the rational decision of individuals to avoid redundancy with the system header and, thus, to work efficiently.

The genre perspective, on the other hand, does not attempt to understand the practice as an isolated act or outcome, but as communicative action that is situated in a stream of social practices which shape and are shaped by it. Any time a new communication medium is introduced into an organization, we expect that existing genres of communication will influence the use of this new medium, though the nature of this influence will reflect the interaction between existing genres and human action within specific contexts. In this case, the absence of salutations and sign-offs may be attributed to users drawing on memo genre rules that inhibit the use of openings and closings, an influence encouraged by the memo-like heading of their electronic mail systems. The reciprocal nature of the genre approach also allows us to see the unintended institutional consequences of the users' actions—that such use of genre rules reinforces the legitimacy of the memo genre and extends its reach into electronic media. Conversely, when individuals add greetings and sign-offs, the genre perspective allows us to interpret their actions as invoking other genres, such as the informal note or the letter, or as modifying existing genre rules in ways that may ultimately lead to the emergence of new genres in response to new recurrent situations. Finally, by focusing on process and recursive interaction over time, this approach points researchers toward longer range explanations that put contemporary media such as electronic mail in historical perspective.

Clarification of the Nature and Role of Media

The approach presented here avoids the confusion between medium and genre by allowing us to distinguish between them and to understand how they shape each other. Media are the physical means by which communication is created, transmitted, or stored. Genres are typified communicative actions invoked in recurrent situations and characterized by similar substance and form. Though a genre's form may at one point include the medium, that genre may also expand into other media, as with the memo genre when it is invoked within electronic mail, or as with accounting records that have migrated from clay tablets, to ledger books, to punched cards, and most recently to electronic files.[8]

Further, clarifying the nature of medium and genre may inform previous studies of media. In particular, this distinction raises questions about the media richness continuum, which combines media and genres on a single scale. For example, the memo and bulletin are different genres traditionally associated with the same medium and, thus, should occupy the same point on the continuum. The fact that they occupy separate points suggests that genre mediates the influence of communication media. Recognition of genre's mediating influence on communication may also illuminate phenomena such as flaming, currently attributed primarily to new media. Because the language of flaming is not at all characteristic of the memo and business letter genres, it should not be common in situations in which individuals are enacting these more traditional genres in electronic mail, with their characteristic structural indicators and substance. In cases where flaming occurs, there may be other violations of the rules of these genres, as well as the possible emergence of new genres of which flaming is more characteristic. Thus, the distinction between medium and genre makes possible a richer understanding of communication in new media.

Implications for Future Research

The concept of genres of organizational communication developed and illustrated here, illuminates the complex

---

[8] Note that even though the movement of a genre into a new medium may result in its movement out of the old medium, it is also possible for the genre to continue to be invoked in both media.

ways in which types of organizational communication emerge in interaction with certain sociohistorical conditions, become institutionalized through reinforcing cycles of use, and evolve over time and in relation to changes in situation. This theoretical approach suggests both areas for future research and methodological approaches to such research.

Future Research Topics Using Genres of Organizational Communication

Empirical research is needed to investigate the various social, economic, and technological factors that occasion the production, reproduction, or modification of different genres in different sociohistorical contexts. For example, the case of the memo suggests that under different historical conditions, different factors may influence genre development more strongly. In the late 19th and early 20th centuries, a changing ideology of management significantly shaped the social recognition of a new recurrent situation that led to the emergence of a particular type of communicative action (writing internal correspondence to document organizational interactions and outcomes). At the same time, new communication media (such as the typewriter and vertical files) played a role in shaping the form of the newly emerging memo genre. The recent adoption of new communication media may be triggering the modification of existing genres such as the memo, as well as the emergence of new genres. Electronic mail, for example, may make it convenient to communicate in situations where no communication or a different type of communication would have occurred in the past. To the extent that such situations come to be recognized as recurrent, new genres of organizational communication may emerge, and their form may, in part, reflect the capability of the media. Although some developments in the structural and linguistic features characterizing electronic mail have been noted, without further empirical study it is not clear whether these have become sufficiently widespread or stable within smaller or larger communities to be institutionalized as genres. Further research should also illuminate which factors or conditions influence the possible emergence of such genres in electronic communication media.

Another important factor influencing the development and institutionalization of genres is the national, industrial, organizational, or occupational context. For example, genres with a wide normative scope, such as the memo, cross such boundaries fairly easily, though they may be elaborated to reflect particular local environments. In contrast, genres with a more limited normative scope, sometimes subgenres of the more broadly recognized genres, emerge within particular contexts—for example, opinion letters to clients in the accounting profession (Devitt, 1991) or customer support calls in service organizations (Pentland, 1991). When genre rules are not mandated, they are likely to emerge and be institutionalized in specific contexts and communities first; they will achieve broader acceptance later only if the emerging genre is perceived by a larger community to respond to a common recurrent situation. Comparative research would illuminate the range of influences across different industries, organizations, occupations, and nations. In addition, detailed examinations of genre emergence within organizations may uncover a process by which groups and organizations adopt as genre rules practices originating with individuals.

The concept of genre has much broader implications than those discussed thus far. Because communication is central to organizations, genres of organizational communication can be expected to influence a wide range of organizational phenomena. For example, some areas for study include the influence of genres on information exchange and influence in social networks, the role of genres as carriers of ideologies or cultures at the organizational level, and the use of genres as instruments of impression management at the individual level. Although it is not possible to explore these issues in this article, we briefly describe one such research area—the role of genre in organizational power and prestige.

Within the framework posed in this article, genre rules would function both as instruments and outcomes of organizational power and politics. Scott (1987: 508) observed that institutional rules "are important types of resources, and that those who can shape or influence them possess a valuable form of power." For example, near the end of the 19th century, the president of the Illinois Central Railroad was having trouble getting his middle managers to provide financial analyses of proposed track improvements. Consequently, he tried to impose a new genre rule for such proposals—that they include an assessment of the project's expected return on investment (Yates, 1989a). To the extent that imposed rules become institutionalized through others' continued enactment of them, new genre rules are outcomes of power play. Where they are not adhered to (the president of the Illinois Central Railroad quickly learned that his subordinates simply failed to understand the concept of return on investment and thus provided irrelevant assessments), the exercise of power fails. In fact, such an exercise of power may backfire if superiors accept compliance at face value, not realizing that the information provided is vacuous or distorted.

Power also may be exercised through the manipulation or selective application of existing genre rules. As Eisenberg and Phillips (1991) pointed out, individuals manipulate communication through the strategic use of devices such as ambiguity, politeness, and agenda control. For example, the chair of a meeting may deal with the unexpected raising of a sensitive issue by invoking the formal agenda to suppress the issue, while at other times this same chair may allow discussion of a nonsensitive topic that was not on the formal agenda. In these cases, individuals apply genre rules to their advantage—thereby using the rules as instruments of their power. Both direct imposition and selective application of genre rules may occur at multiple levels, affecting individuals, groups, organizations, occupational communities, and even nations.[9] Genres thus represent another vehicle for the potential implementation of power and influence in and across organizations, with consequences not only for the shaping of organizational communication but also for decision making, information processing, and strategic action.

Methods of Studying Genres of Organizational Communication

The genre phenomenon clearly needs elaboration through further empirical study within particular contexts. Although this phenomenon must be understood both synchronically and diachronically, specific studies may take one or both of these approaches. Synchronic analyses would identify the existing genres influencing communication and media use within certain contexts, either by searching for the presence of well established genres such as the memo or the meeting, or by identifying genres based on detailed analysis of communication form, substance, and the invoking situation. Such analyses also might examine the relationship between genres and other factors such as national culture, communication climates, or work practices. Although synchronic studies focus on a fixed period of time, such studies, nevertheless, must be sensitive to differences in genre dimensions due to diachronic

factors such as emergence, maintenance, modification, and decay.

Diachronic studies would investigate the production, reproduction, and change of genres through communicative action over time. Monge, Farace, Eisenberg, White, and Miller (1984) pointed out the importance of capturing process in the study of communication. Longitudinal studies of genre would explore the process underlying the ongoing evolution of genres of organizational communication. For example, studies could examine communication within an organization or industry before and after the introduction of a new medium, or they could trace the use of a new medium within a particular community over the first several months or years to see how existing genres are maintained or modified and new ones emerge. Such studies could also investigate the interaction between genre production, reproduction, or modification and other variables such as power and corporate culture. In addition to longitudinal studies with time spans restricted to researchers' project durations, the memo example demonstrates the importance of studying developments over much longer time periods. Historical studies (e.g., Bazerman, 1988; Yates, 1989a) can contribute to the understanding of the role of genre in organizational communication through in-depth retrospective analyses. Whether the time period covered is short or long, diachronic analysis is essential to observing the processes of genre emergence, maintenance, elaboration, modification, and decay.

Field studies seem appropriate in both synchronic and diachronic investigations because they allow researchers to investigate the genre phenomenon contextually and without constraining the direction of effects examined. Though laboratory experiments have many advantages (e.g., replicability, greater researcher control, and ability to manipulate variables and minimize confounding effects), they isolate the phenomenon of interest from an organizational context. Thus, such studies would be unable to account for the socially and historically embedded nature of genre, and it would be difficult for researchers to investigate the reciprocal and recursive relationship between organizational communication and genre posited in the theory presented here. In addition, because genres occur within communities ranging from the work group to the organization or professional community, and finally to the national culture, genre studies must be situated within specific contexts and must take into account the normative scope of the genres present in that context.

In conclusion, our genre approach to organizational communication takes into account the inherently situated and dynamic nature of organizational processes. Adapting

---

[9] During the recent Senate confirmation hearings on Supreme Court Justice Clarence Thomas, much political commentary centered on the manipulation and negotiation of the genre rules of such confirmation hearings.

a concept from rhetoric and using the premises of structuration, we have interpreted organizational communication, not as the result of isolated, rational actions, but as part of an embedded social process that over time produces, reproduces, and modifies particular genres of communication. We expect that this concept of genre will provide new and productive ways of understanding communicative action in organizations.

REFERENCES

Barley, S. 1986. Technology as an occasion for structuring: Evidence from observation of CT scanners and the social order of radiology departments. *Administrative Science Quarterly,* 31: 78–108.

Barley, S. R., & Tolbert, P. S. 1988. *Institutionalization as structuration: Methods and analytic strategies for studying links between action and structure.* Paper presented at the Conference on Longitudinal Field Research Methods for Studying Organizational Processes, University of Texas, Austin.

Bazerman, C. 1988. *Shaping written knowledge: The genre and activity of the experimental article in science.* Madison: University of Wisconsin Press.

Bitzer, L. F. 1968. The rhetorical situation. *Philosophy and Rhetoric,* 1: 1–14.

Burke, K., 1973. The rhetorical situation. In *Communication: Ethical and moral issues:* 263–275. New York: Gordon & Breach.

Campbell, K. K., & Jamieson. K. H. 1978. Form and genre in rhetorical criticism: An introduction. In K. K. Campbell & K. H. Jamieson (Eds.), *Form and genre: Shaping rhetorical action:* 9–32. Falls Church, VA: Speech Communication Association.

Cohen, I. J. 1989. *Structuration theory: Anthony Giddens and the constitution of social life.* New York: St. Martin's Press.

Contractor, N. S., & Eisenberg, E. M. 1990. Communication networks and new media in organizations. In J. Fulk & C. W. Sieinfield (Eds.), *Organizations and communication technology:* 143–172. Newbury Park, CA: Sage.

Culnan, M. J., & Markus, M. L. 1937. Information technologies. In F. M. Jablin, L. L. Putnam, K. H. Roberts, & L. W. Porter (Eds)., *Handbook of organizational communication: An interdisciplinary perspective:* 420–443. Newbury Park, CA: Sage.

Daft, R. L., & Lengel, R. H. 1984. Information richness: A new approach to managerial information processing and organization design. In B. Staw & L. L. Cummings (Eds.), *Research in organizational behavior,* 6: 191–233. Greenwich, CT: JAI Press.

Daft, R. L., & Lengel, R. H. 1986. Organizational information requirements, media richness and structural design. *Management Science,* 32: 554–571.

Daft, R. L., Lengel, R. H., & Trevino, L. K. 1987. Message equivocality, media selection, and manager performance: Implications for information systems. *MIS Quarterly,* 11: 355–366.

Devitt, A. J. 1991. Intertextuality in tax accounting: Generic, referential, and functional. In C. Bazerman & J. Paradis (Eds.), *Textual dynamics of the professions: Historical and contemporary studies of writing in professional communities:* 336–357. Madison: University of Wisconsin Press.

DiMaggio, P. 1987. Classification in art. *American Sociological Review,* 52: 440–455.

Eisenberg, E. M. 1984. Ambiguity as strategy in organizational communication. *Communication Monographs,* 51: 227–242.

Eiseniberg, E. M., & Phillips, S. R. 1991. Miscommunication in organizations. In N. Coupland, H. Giles, & J. M. Wiemann (Eds.), *Miscommunication and problematic talk:* 244–258. Newbury Park, CA: Sage.

Eveland, J. D., & Bikson, T. K. 1968. Work group structures and computer support: A field experiment. *ACM Transactions on Office Information Systems,* 6: 354–379.

Fellowman, M. S. 1987. Electronic mail and weak ties in organizations. *Office: Technology and People,* 3: 83–101.

Ferrari, K., Burner, H., & Whitener, G. 1990. Interactive written discourse as an emergent register. *Written Communication,* 8: 8–34.

Fouler, D. A. 1990. *Medium as process: The structure, use, and practice of computer conferencing on IBM PC computer conferencing facility.* Unpublished doctoral thesis, Temple University, Philadelphia, PA.

Fulk, J., Schmitz, J, & Steinfield, C. W. 1990. A social influence model of technology use. In J. Fulk & C. W. Steinfield (Eds.), *Organizations and communication technology:* 117–140. Newbury Park, CA: Sage.

Giddens, A. 1984. *The constitution of society: Outline of the theory of structure.* Berkeley: University of California Press.

Gronbeck B. 1978. Celluloid rhetoric: On genres of documentary. In K. K. Campbell & K. H. Jamiesen (Eds.), *Form and genre: Shaping rhetorical action:* 139–161. Falls Church, VA: Speech Communication Association.

Harrell, J., & Linkugel, W. A. 1978. On rhetorical genre: An organizing perspective. *Philosophy and Rhetoric,* 11: 262–281.

Holman, C. H. 1972. *A handbook to literature* (3rd ed). New York: Odyssey Press.

Kraemer, K. L., & Pinsonneault, A. 1990. Technology and groups: Assessment of the empirical research. In J. Galegher, R. E.

Kraut, & C. Egido (Eds.), *Intellectual teamwork: Social and technological foundations of cooperative work:* 375–405. Hillsdale, NJ: Erlbaum.

Krone, K. J., Jablin, F. M., & Putnam, L. L. 1987. Communication theory and organizational communication: Multiple perspectives. In F. M. Jablin, L. L. Putnam, K. H. Roberts, & L. W. Porter (Eds.), *Handbook of organizational communication: An interdisciplinary perspective:* 18–40. Newbury Park, CA: Sage.

Litterer, J. A. 1961. Systematic management: The search for order and integration. *Business History Review,* 35: 461–476.

Manning, P. K. 1989. *Symbolic communication.* Cambridge, MA: MIT Press.

Markus, M L. 1988. *Electronic mail as the medium of managerial choice.* Working Paper, Anderson School of Management. Los Angles: University of California, Los Angeles.

Markus, M. L., & Robey, D. 1988. Information technology and organizational change: Causal structure in theory and research. *Management Science,* 34: 583–598

Matheson, K., & Zanna, M. 1989. Impact of computer-mediated communication on self-awareness. *Computers in Human Behavior,* 4: 221–233.

McPhee, R. D. 1985. Formal structure and organizational communication. In P. D. McPhee & P. K. Tompkins (Eds.), *Organizational communication: Traditional themes and new directions:* 149–178. Beverley Hills, CA: Sage.

Miller, C. R. 1984. Genre as social action. *Quarterly Journal of Speech,* 70: 151–167.

Monge, P. R., Farace, R. V., Eisenberg, E. M., White, L., & Miller, K. L. 1984. The process of studying process in organizational communication. *Journal of Communication,* 34: 22–43.

Monge, P. R., & Eisenberg, E. M. 1987. Emergent communication networks. In F. M. Jablin, L. L. Putnam, K. H. Roberts, & L. W. Porter (Eds.), *Handbook of organizational communication: An interdisciplinary perspective:* 304–342. Newbury Park, CA: Sage.

Murray, D. 1985. Composition as conversation: The computer terminal as medium of communication. In L. Odell & D. Goswami (Eds.), *Writing in nonacademic settings:* 203–228. New York: Guilford Press.

Murray, D. 1987. Requests at work: Negotiating the conditions for conversation. *Management Communication Quarterly,* 1: 58–83.

Orlikowski, W. J. In press. The duality of technology: Rethinking the concept of technology in organizations. *Organization Science.*

Pentland, B. T. 1991. *Making the right moves: Toward a social grammar of software support hot lines.* Unpublished doctoral thesis, Sloan School of Management, Massachusetts Institute of Technology, Cambridge, MA.

Pole, M. S., & DeSanctis, G. 1989. *Use of group decision support systems as an appropriation process.* Proceedings of the Hawaii International Conference on Information Systems: 149–157.

Poole, M. S., & DeSanctis, G. 1990. Understanding the use of group decision support systems: The theory of adaptive structuration. In J. Fulk & C. W. Steinfield (Eds.), *Organizations and communication technology:* 173–193. Newbury Park, CA: Sage.

Poole, M. S., & McPhee, R. D. 1983. A structurational theory of organizational climate. In L. Putnam & M. Pacanowsky (Eds.), *Organizational communication: An interpretive approach:* 195–219. Newbury Park, CA: Sage.

Rafaeli, S. 1990. *Electronic message to computer-mediated communication hotline.* Comserve Electronic Information Service, April 26.

Reder, S., & Schwab, R. G. 1988. *The communicative economy of the workgroup: Multichannel genres of communication.* Proceedings of the Conference on Computer Supported Cooperative Work, Portland, OR: 354–368.

Reinsch, N. L., & Beswick, R. W. 1990. Voice mail versus conventional channels: A cost minimization analysis of individuals' preferences. *Academy of Management Journal,* 33: 801–816.

Rice, R. E. 1984. Mediated group communication. In R. E. Rice & associates (Eds.), *The new media: Communication, research, and technology:* 33–54. Newbury Park, CA: Sage.

Rice, R. E., & Shook, D. E. 1990. Voice messaging, coordination, and communication. In J. Galegher, R. E. Kraut, & C. Egido (Eds.), *Intellectual teamwork: Social and technological foundations of cooperative work:* 327–350. Hillsdale, NJ: Erlbaum.

Russ, G., Daft, R. L., & Lengel, R. H. 1990. Media selection and managerial characteristics in organizational communications. *Management Communication Quarterly,* 4: 151–175.

Scott, W. R. 1987. The adolescence of institutional theory. *Administrative Science Quarterly,* 32: 493–511.

Short, J., Williams, E., & Christie, B. 1976. *The social psychology of telecommunications.* New York: Wiley.

Siegel, J., Dubrovsky, V., Kiesler, S., & McGuire, T. W. 1986. Group processes in computer-mediated communication. *Organizational Behavior & Human Decision Processes,* 37: 157–186.

Simons, H. W. 1978. "Genre-alizing" about rhetoric: A scientific approach. In K. K. Campbell & K. H. Jamieson (Eds.), *Form and genre: Shaping rhetorical action:* 33–50. Falls Church, VA: Speech Communication Association.

Sproull, L., & Kiesler, S. 1986. Reducing social context cues: Electronic mail in organizational communication. *Management Science,* 32: 1492–1512.

Stohl, C., & Redding, W. C. 1987. Messages and message exchange processes. In F. M. Jablin, L. L. Putnam, K. H. Roberts, & L. W. Porter (Eds.), *Handbook of organizational communication: An interdisciplinary perspective:* 451–502. Newbury Park CA: Sage.

Suchman, L. A., & Trigg, R. H. 1991. Understanding practice:

Video as a medium for reflection and design. In J. Greenbaum & M. Kyng (Eds.), *Design to work:* 65–89. Hillsdale, NJ: Erlbaum.

Trevino, L. K., Daft, R. L., & Lengel, R. K. 1990. Understanding managers' media choices: A symbolic interactionist perspective. In J. Fulk & C. W. Steinfield (Eds.), *Organizations and communication technology:* 71–94. Newbury Park, CA: Sage.

Trevino, L. K., Lengel, R. K., & Daft, R. L. 1987. Media symbolism, media richness, and media choice in organizations. *Communication Research,* 14: 553–574.

Weick, K. 1979. *The social psychology of organizing.* Reading, MA: Addison-Wesley.

Weick, K. 1983. Organizational communication: Towards a research agenda. In L. Putnam & M. Pacanowsky (Eds.), *Organizational communication: An interpretive approach:* 13–29.

Newbury Park, CA: Sage.

Weick, K. 1987. Theorizing about organizational communication. In F. M. Jablin, L. L. Putnam, K. H. Roberts, & L. W. Porter (Eds.), *Handbook of organizational communication: An interdisciplinary perspective:* 97–129. Newbury Park, CA: Sage.

Weiss, H. B. 1945. *American letter-writers: 1698–1943.* New York: New York Public Library.

Williams, E. 1977. Experimental comparisons of face-to-face and mediated communication: A review. *Psychological Bulletin,* 84: 963–976.

Yates, J. 1989a. *Control through communication: The rise of system in American management.* Baltimore, MD: Johns Hopkins University Press.

Yates, J. 1989b. The emergence of the memo as a managerial genre. *Management Communication Quarterly,* 2: 485–510.

DISCUSSION QUESTIONS

1. What does Gidden's term *structuration* mean?

2. In what ways can the structurational approach be used to study other aspects of organizational behavior, for example, organizational socialization?

3. How do the authors use the concept of genre? Describe how genre rules operate.

4. Why is it important to understand the processes of organizational production, reproduction, and change over time?

5. Discuss attempts to do research on media choice and media consequences and the limitations of both efforts.

6. Describe the evolution of the memo and electronic mail as communication genres.

7. What are the implications, if any, for changing organizational behavior through the understanding of the processes of communication as presented by Yates and Orlikowski?

FOR FURTHER READING

Bell, M. "Phases in Group Problem Solving." *Small Group Behavior* 13 (1982) 475–495.

Blau, P. *Exchange and Power in Social Life.* New York: Wiley, 1964.

Giddens, A. *The Constitution of Society: Outline of the Theory of Structure.* Berkeley: University of California Press, 1984.

Fulk, J., and Boyd, B. "Emerging Theories of Communication in Organizations." *Journal of Management* 17 (1991) 407–446.

Luthans, F., and Larsen, J. "How Managers Really Communicate." *Human Relations* 39 (1986)161–178.

Stinchcombe, A. *Information and Organizations.* Berkeley: University of California Press, 1990.

Sundstrom, K., De Meuse, K., and Futrell, D. "Work Teams: Applications and Effectiveness." *American Psychologist* 45 (1990) 120–133.

Thibaut, J., and Kelley, K. *The Social Psychology of Groups.* New York: Wiley, 1959.

Yukl, G., and Falbe, D. "Influence Tactics and Objectives in Upward, Downward, and Lateral Influence Attempts." *Journal of Applied Psychology* 16 (1990) 132–140.

8

POWER AND INFLUENCE

Who Gets Power—And How They Hold on to It: A Strategic Contingency Model of Power

GERALD R. SALANCIK AND JEFFREY PFEFFER

> ## LEARNING OBJECTIVES
>
> After reading "Who Gets Power—And How They Hold on to It: A Strategic Contingency Model of Power" by Salancik and Pfeffer, a student will be able to:
>
> 1. Develop a working definition of power
>
> 2. Understand the sources of power and uses of politics in organizations
>
> 3. Understand the strategic-contingency view of power
>
> 4. Realize how power can help an organization either adapt to its environment or lose touch with it

Power is held by many people to be a dirty word or, as Warren Bennis has said, "It is the organization's last dirty secret."

This article will argue that traditional "political" power, far from being a dirty business, is, in its almost naked form, one of the few mechanisms available for aligning an organization with its own reality. However, institutionalized forms of power—what we prefer to call the cleaner forms of power: authority, legitimization, centralized control, regulations, and the more modern "management information systems" tend to buffer the organization from reality and obscure the demands of its environment. Most great states and institutions declined, not because they played politics , but because they failed to accommodate to the political realities they faced. Political processes, rather than being mechanisms for unfair and unjust allocations and appointments, tend toward the realistic resolution of conflicts among interests. And power, while it eludes definition, is easy enough to recognize by its consequences—the ability of those who possess power to bring about the outcomes they desire.

The model of power we advance is an elaboration of what has been called strategic-contingency theory, a view that sees power as something that accrues to organizational subunits (individuals, departments) that cope with critical organizational problems. Power is used by subunits, indeed, used by all who have it, to enhance their own survival through control of scarce critical resources, through the placement of allies in key positions, and through the definition of organizational problems and policies. Because of the processes by which power develops and is used, organizations become both more aligned and more misaligned with their environments. This contradiction is the most interesting aspect of organizational power, and the one that makes administration one of the most precarious of occupations.

What Is Organizational Power?

You can walk into most organizations and ask without fear of being misunderstood, "Which are the powerful groups

Source: "Who Gets Power—And How They Hold on to It: A Strategic Contingency Model of Power," by Gerald R. Salancik, et al. Reprinted by permission of Publisher, from *Organizational Dynamics,* Winter 1977, ©1977. American Management Association, New York. All rights reserved.

of people in this organization?" Although many organizational informants may be *unwilling* to tell you, it is unlikely they will be *unable* to tell you. Most people do not require explicit definitions to know what power is.

Power is simply the ability to get things done in the way one wants them to be done. For a manager who wants an increased budget to launch a project that he thinks is important, his power is measured by his ability to get that budget. For an executive vice-president who wants to be chairman, his power is evidenced by his advancement toward his goal.

People in organizations not only know what you are talking about when you ask who is influential but they are likely to agree with one another to an amazing extent. Recently, we had a chance to observe this in a regional office of an insurance company. The office has 21 department managers; we asked ten of these managers to rank all 21 according to the influence each one had in the organization. Despite the fact that ranking 21 things is a difficult task, the managers sat down and began arranging the names of their colleagues and themselves in a column. Only one person bothered to ask, "What do you mean by influence?" When told "power" he responded, "Oh," and went on. We compared the rankings of all ten managers and found virtually no disagreement among them in the managers ranked among the top five or the bottom five. Differences in the rankings came from the department heads claiming more influence for themselves than their colleagues had attributed to them.

Such agreement on those who have influence, and those who do not, was not unique to this insurance company. So far we have studied over 20 very different organizations—universities, research firms, factories, banks, retailers, to name a few. In each one we found individuals able to rate themselves and their peers on a scale of influence or power. We have done this both for specific decisions and for general impact on organizational policies. Their agreement was unusually high, which suggests that distributions of influence exist well enough in everyone's mind to be referred to with ease—and we assume with accuracy.

Where Does Organizational Power Come From?

Earlier we stated that power helps organizations become aligned with their realities. This hopeful prospect follows from what we have dubbed the strategic-contingencies

theory of organizational power. Briefly, those subunits most able to cope with the organization's critical problems and uncertainties acquire power. In its simplest form, the strategic-contingencies theory implies that when an organization faces a number of lawsuits that threaten its existence, the legal department will gain power and influence over organizational decisions. Somehow other organizational interest groups will recognize its critical importance and confer upon it a status and power never before enjoyed. This influence may extend beyond handling legal matters and into decisions about product design, advertising production, and so on. Such extensions undoubtedly would be accompanied by appropriate, or acceptable, verbal justifications. In time, the head of the legal department may become the head of the corporation, just as in times past the vice-president for marketing has become the president when market shares were a worrisome problem and, before him, a chief engineer, who had made the production line run as smooth as silk.

Stated in this way, the strategic-contingencies theory of power paints an appealing picture of power. To the extent that power is determined by the critical uncertainties and problems facing the organization and, in turn, influences decisions in the organization, the organization is aligned with the realities it faces. In short, power facilitates the organization's adaptation to its environment—or its problems.

We can cite many illustrations of how influence derives from a subunit's ability to deal with critical contingencies. Michael Crozier described a French cigarette factory in which the maintenance engineers had a considerable say in the plantwide operation. After some probing he discovered that the group possessed the solution to one of the major problems faced by the company, that of troubleshooting the elaborate, expensive, and irrascible automated machines that kept breaking down and dumbfounding everyone else. It was the one problem that the plant manager could in no way control.

The production workers, while troublesome from time to time, created no insurmountable problems; the manager could reasonably predict their absenteeism or replace them when necessary. Production scheduling was something he could deal with since, by watching inventories and sales, the demand for cigarettes was known long in advance. Changes in demand could be accommodated by slowing down or speeding up the line. Supplies of tobacco and paper were also easily dealt with through stockpiles and advance orders.

The one thing that management could neither control nor accommodate to, however, was the seemingly happenstance breakdowns. And the foremen couldn't instruct the workers what to do when emergencies developed since the maintenance department kept its records of problems and solutions locked up in a cabinet or in its members' heads. The breakdowns, were, in truth, a critical source of uncertainty for the organization, and the maintenance engineers were the only ones who could cope with the problem.

The engineers' strategic role in coping with breakdowns afforded them a considerable say on plant decisions. Schedules and production quotas were set in consultation with them. And the plant manager, while formally their boss, accepted their decisions about personnel in their operation. His submission was to his credit, for without their cooperation he would have had an even more difficult time in running the plant.

Ignoring Critical Consequence

In this cigarette factory, sharing influence with the maintenance workers reflected the plant manager's awareness of the critical contingencies. However, when organizational members are not aware of the critical contingencies they face, and do not share influence accordingly, the failure to do so can create havoc. In one case, an insurance company's regional office was having problems with the performance of one of its departments, the coding department. From the outside, the department looked like a disaster area. The clerks who worked in it were somewhat dissatisfied; their supervisor paid little attention to them, and they resented the hard work. Several other departments were critical of this manager, claiming that she was inconsistent in meeting deadlines. The person most critical was the claims manager. He resented having to wait for work that was handled by her department, claiming that it held up his claims adjusters. Having heard the rumors about dissatisfaction among her subordinates, he attributed the situation to poor supervision. He was second in command in the office and therefore took up the issue with her immediate boss, the head of administrative services. They consulted with the personnel manager and the three of them concluded that the manager needed leadership training to improve her relations with her subordinates. The coding manager objected, saying it was a waste of time, but agreed to go along with the training and also agreed to give more priority to the claims department's work. Within a week after the training , the results showed that her workers were happier but that the performance of her department had decreased, save for the people serving the claims department.

About this time, we began, quite independently, a study of influence in this organization. We asked the administrative services director to draw up flow charts of how the work of one department moved onto the next department. In the course of the interview, we noticed that the coding department began or interceded in the work flow of most of the other departments and casually mentioned to him, "The coding manager must be very influential." He said, "No, not really. Why would you think so?" Before we could reply he recounted the story of her leadership training and the fact that things were worse. We then told him that it seemed obvious that the coding department would be influential from the fact that all the other departments depended on it. It was also clear why productivity had fallen. The coding manager took the training seriously and began spending more time raising her workers' spirits than she did worrying about the problems of all the departments that depended on her. Giving priority to the claims area only exaggerated the problem, for their work was getting done at the expense of the other departments. Eventually the company hired a few more clerks to relieve the pressure in the coding department and performance returned to a more satisfactory level.

Originally we got involved with this insurance company to examine how the influence on each manager evolved from his or her department's handling of critical organizational contingencies. We reasoned that one of the most important contingencies faced by all profit-making organizations was that of generating income. Thus we expected managers would be influential to the extent to which they contributed to this function. Such was the case. The underwriting managers, who wrote the policies that committed the premiums, were the most influential; the claims managers, who kept a lid on the funds flowing out, were a close second. Least influential were the managers of functions unrelated to revenue, such as mailroom and payroll managers. And contrary to what the administrative services manager believed, the third most powerful department head (out of 21) was the woman in charge of the coding function, which consisted of rating, recording, and keeping track of the codes of all policy applications and contracts. Her peers attributed more influence to her than could have been inferred from her place on the organization chart. And it was not surprising, since they all depended on her department. The coding department's records, their accuracy and the speed with which they could be retrieved, affected virtually every other operating department in the insurance office. The underwriters depended on them getting the contracts straight; the typing department depended on them in preparing the formal contract document; the claims department depended on them in adjusting claims; and accounting depended on them for billing. Unfortunately, the "bosses" were not aware of these dependencies, for unlike the cigarette factory, there were no massive breakdowns that made them obvious, while the coding manager, who was a hardworking but quiet person, did little to announce her importance.

The cases of this plant and office illustrate nicely a basic point about the source of power in organizations. The basis for power in an organization derives from the ability of a person or subunit to take or not take actions that are desired by others. The coding manager was seen as influential by those who depended on her department, but not by the people on top. The engineers were widely influential because of their role in keeping the plant operating. The two cases differ in these respects: The coding supervisor's source of power was not as widely recognized as that of the maintenance engineers, and she did not use her source of power to influence decisions; the maintenance engineers did. Whether power is used to influence anything is a separate issue. We should not confuse this issue with the fact that power derives from a social situation in which one person has a capacity to do something and another person does not, but wants it done.

Power Sharing in Organizations

Power is shared in organizations; and it is shared out of necessity more than out of a concern for principles of organizational development or participatory democracy. Power is shared because no one person controls all the desired activities in the organization. While the factory owner may hire people to operate his noisy machines, once hired they have some control over the use of the machinery. And thus they have power over him in the same way he has power over them. Who has more power over whom is a mooter point than that of recognizing the inherent nature of organizing as a sharing of power.

Let's expand on the concept that power derives from the activities desired in an organization. A major way of managing influence in organizations is through the designation of activities. In a bank we studied, we saw this principle in action. This bank was planning to install a computer system for routine credit evaluation. The bank,

rather progressive-minded, was concerned that the change would have adverse effects on employees and therefore surveyed their attitudes.

The principle opposition to the new system came, interestingly, not from the employees who performed the routine credit checks, some of whom would be relocated because of the change, but from the manager of the credit department. His reason was quite simple. The manager's primary function was to give official approval to the applications, catch any employee mistakes before giving approval, and arbitrate any difficulties the clerks had in deciding what to do. As a consequence of his role, others in the organization, including his superiors, subordinates, and colleagues, attributed considerable importance to him. He, in turn, for example, could point to the low proportion of credit approvals, compared with other financial institutions, that resulted in bad debts. Now, to his mind, a wretched machine threatened to transfer his role to a computer programmer, a man who knew nothing of finance and who, in addition, had ten years less seniority. The credit manager eventually quit for a position at a smaller firm with lower pay, but one in which he would have more influence than his redefined job would have left him with.

Because power derives from activities rather than individuals, an individual's or subgroup's power is never absolute and derives ultimately from the context of the situation. The amount of power an individual has at any one time depends, not only on the activities that he or she controls, but also on the existence of other persons or means by which the activities can be achieved and those who determine what ends are desired and, hence, on what activities are desired and critical for the organization. One's own power always depends on other people for these two reasons. Other people, or groups or organizations, can determine the definition of what is a critical contingency for the organization and can be also undercut the uniqueness of the individual's personal contribution to the critical contingencies of the organization.

Perhaps one can best appreciate how situationally dependent power is by examining how it is distributed. In most societies, power organizes around scarce and critical resources. Rarely does power organize around abundant resources. In the United States, a person doesn't become powerful because he or she can drive a car. There are simply too many others who can drive with equal facility. In certain villages in Mexico, on the other hand, a person with a car is accredited with enormous social status and plays a key role in the community. In addition to scarcity, power is also limited by the need for one's capacities in a social system. While a racer's ability to drive a car around a 90°

turn at 80 mph may be sparsely distributed in a society, it is not likely to lend the driver much power in society. The ability simply does not play a central role in the activities of the society.

The fact that power revolves around scarce and critical activities, of course, makes the control and organization of those activities a major battleground in struggles for power. Even relatively abundant or trivial resources can become the bases for power if one can organize and control their allocation and the definition of what is critical. Many occupational and professional groups attempt to do just this in modern economies. Lawyers organize themselves into associations, regulate the entrance requirements for novitiates, and then get laws passed specifying situations that require the services of an attorney. Workers had little power in the conduct of industrial affairs until they organized themselves into closed and controlled systems. In recent years, women and blacks have tried to define themselves as important and critical to the social system, using law to reify their status.

In organizations there are obviously opportunities for defining certain activities as more critical than others. Indeed, the growth of managerial thinking to include defining organizational objectives and goals has done much to foster these opportunities. One sure way to liquidate the power of groups in the organization is to define the need for their services out of existence. David Halberstam presents a description of how just such a thing happened to the group of correspondents that evolved around Edward R. Murrow, the brilliant journalist, interviewer, and war correspondent of CBS news. A close friend of CBS chairman and controlling stockholder William S. Paley, Murrow, and the new department he directed, were endowed with freedom to do what they felt was right. He used it to create some of the best documentaries and commentaries ever seen on television. Unfortunately, television became too large, too powerful, and too suspect in the eyes of the federal government that licensed it. It thus became, or at least the top executives believed it had become, too dangerous to have in-depth, probing commentary on the news. Crisp, dry, uneditorializing headlines were considered safer. Murrow was out and Walter Cronkite was in.

The power to define what is critical in an organization is no small power. Moreover, it is the key to understanding why organizations are either aligned with their environments or misaligned. If an organization defines certain activities as critical when in fact they are not critical, given the flow of resources coming into the organization, it is not likely to survive, at least in its present form.

Most organizations manage to evolve a distribution of power and influence that is aligned with the critical realities they face in the environment. The environment, in turn, includes both the internal environment, the shifting situational contexts in which particular decisions get made, and the external environment that it can hope to influence but is unlikely to control.

The Critical Contingencies

The critical contingencies facing most organizations derive from the environmental context within which they operate. This determines the available needed resources and thus determines the problems to be dealt with. That power organizes around handling these problems suggests an important mechanism by which organizations keep in tune with their external environments. The strategic-contingencies model implies that subunits that contribute to the critical resources of the organization will gain influence in the organization. Their influence presumably is then used to bend the organization's activities to the contingencies that determine its resources. This idea may strike one as obvious. But its obviousness in no way diminishes its importance. Indeed, despite its obviousness, it escapes the notice of many organizational analysts and managers, who all too frequently think of the organization in terms of a descending pyramid, in which all the departments in one tier hold equal power and status. This presumption denies the reality that departments differ in the contributions they are believed to make to the overall organization's resources, as well as to the fact that some are more equal than others.

Because of the importance of this idea to organizational effectiveness, we decided to examine it carefully in a large midwestern university. A university offers an excellent site for studying power. It is composed of departments with nominally equal power and is administered by a central executive structure much like other bureaucracies. However, at the same time it is a situation in which the departments have clearly defined identities and face diverse external environments. Each department has its own bodies of knowledge, its own institutions, its own sources of prestige and resources. Because the departments operate in different external environments, they are likely to contribute differently to the resources of the overall organization. Thus a physics department with close ties to NASA may contribute substantially to the funds of the university;

and a history department with a renowned historian in residence may contribute to the intellectual credibility or prestige of the whole university. Such variations permit one to examine how these various contributions lead to obtaining power within the university.

We analyzed the influence of 29 university departments throughout an 18-month period in their history. Our chief interest was to determine whether departments that brought more critical resources to the university would be more powerful than departments that contributed fewer or less critical resources.

To identify the critical resources each department contributed, the heads of all departments were interviewed about the importance of seven different resources to the university's success. The seven included undergraduate students (the factor determining size of the state allocations by the university), national prestige, administrative expertise, and so on. The most critical resource was found to be contract and grant monies received by a department's faculty for research or consulting services. At this university, contracts and grants contributed somewhat less than 50 percent of the overall budget, with the remainder primarily coming from state appropriations. The importance attributed to contract and grant monies, and the rather minor importance of undergraduate students, was not surprising for this particular university. The university was a major center for graduate education: many of its departments ranked in the top ten of their respective fields. Grant and contract monies were the primary source of discretionary funding available for maintaining these programs of graduate education, and hence for maintaining the university's prestige. The prestige of the university itself was critical both in recruiting able students and attracting top-notch faculty.

From university records it was determined what relative contributions each of the 29 departments made to the various needs of the university (national prestige, outside grants, teaching). Thus, for instance, one department may have contributed to the university by teaching 7 percent of the instructional units, bringing in 2 percent of the outside contracts and grants, and having a national ranking of 20. Another department, on the other hand, may have taught one percent of the instructional units, contributed 12 percent to the grants, and be ranked the third best department in its field within the country.

The question was: Do these different contributions determine the relative power of the departments within the university? Power was measured in several ways; but regardless of how measured, the answer was "Yes." Those three resources together accounted for about 70 percent of the variance in subunit power in the university.

But the most important predictor of departmental power was the department's contribution to the contracts and grants of the university. Sixty percent of the variance in power was due to this one factor, suggesting that the power of departments derived primarily from the dollars they provided for graduate education, the activity believed to be the most important for the organization.

The Impact of Organizational Power on Decision Making

The measure of power we used in studying this university was an analysis of the responses of the department heads we interviewed. While such perceptions of power might be of interest in their own right, they contribute little to our understanding of how the distribution of power might serve to align an organization with its critical realities. For this we must look to how power actually influences the decisions and policies of organizations.

While it is perhaps not absolutely valid, we can generally gauge the relative importance of a department of an organization by the size of the budget allocated to it relative to other departments. Clearly it is of importance to the administrators of those departments whether they get squeezed in a budget crunch or are given more funds to strike out after new opportunities. And it should also be clear that when those decisions are made and one department can go ahead and try new approaches while another must cut back on the old, then the deployment of the resources of the organization in meeting its problems is most directly affected.

Thus our study of the university led us to ask the following question: Does power lead to influence in the organization? To answer this question, we found it useful first to ask another one, namely: Why should department heads try to influence organizational decisions to favor their own departments to the exclusion of other departments? While this second question may seem a bit naive to anyone who has witnessed the political realities of organizations, we posed it in a context of research on organizations that sees power as an illegitimate threat to the neater rational authority of modern bureaucracies. In this context, decisions are not believed to be made because of the dirty business of politics but because of the overall goals and purposes of the organization. In a university, one reasonable basis for decision making is the teaching work-load of departments and the demands that follow from that workload. We would expect, therefore, that depart-ments with heavy student demands for courses would be able to obtain funds for teaching. Another reasonable basis for decision making is quality. We would expect, for that reason, that departments with esteemed reputations would be able to obtain funds both because their quality suggests they might use such funds effectively and because such funds would allow them to maintain their quality. A ratio-nal model of bureaucracy intimates, then, that the organi-zational decisions taken would favor those who perform the stated purposes of the organization—teaching under-graduates and training professional scientific talent—well.

The problem with rational models of decision making, however, is that what is rational to one person may strike another as irrational. For most departments, resources are a question of survival. While teaching under-graduates may seem to be a major goal for some members of the university, developing knowledge may seem so to others; and to still others, advising governments and other institutions about policies may seem to be the crucial busi-ness. Everyone has his own idea of the proper priorities in a just world. Thus, goals, rather than being clearly defined and universally agreed upon, are blurred and contested throughout the organization. If such is the case, then the decisions taken on behalf of the organization as a whole are likely to reflect the goals of those who prevail in political contests, namely, those with power in the organization.

Will organizational decisions always reflect the distri-bution of power in the organization? Probably not. Using power for influence requires a certain expenditure of effort, time, and resources. Prudent and judicious persons are not likely to use their power needlessly or wastefully. And it is likely that power will be used to influence organizational decisions primarily under circumstances that both require and favor its use. We have examined three conditions that are likely to affect the use of power in organizations: scarcity, criticality, and uncertainty. The first suggests that subunits will try to exert influence when the resources of the organization are scarce. If there is an abundance of resources, then a particular department or particular indi-vidual has little need to attempt influence. With little effort, he can get all he wants anyway.

The second condition, criticality, suggests that a sub-unit will attempt to influence decisions to obtain resources that are critical to its own survival and activities. Critical-ity implies that one would not waste effort, or risk being labeled obstinate, by fighting over trivial decisions affect-ing one's operations.

An office manager would probably balk less about a threatened cutback in copying machine usage than about a reduction in typing staff. An advertising department head would probably worry less about losing his lettering artists than his illustrator. Criticality is difficult to define because what is critical depends on people's beliefs about what is critical. Such beliefs may or may not be based on experience and knowledge and may or may not be agreed upon by all. Scarcity, for instance, may itself affect conceptions of criticality. When slack resources drop off, cutbacks have to be made—those "hard decisions," as congressmen and resplendent administrators like to call them. Managers then find themselves scrapping projects they once held dear.

The third condition that we believe affects the use of power is uncertainty: When individuals do not agree about what the organization should do or how to do it, power and other social processes will affect decisions. The reason for this is simply that, if there are no clear-cut cri-teria available for resolving conflicts of interest, then the only means for resolution is some form of social process, including power, status, social ties, or some arbitrary process like flipping a coin or drawing straws. Under con-ditions of uncertainty, the powerful manager can argue his case on any grounds and usually win it. Since there is no real consensus, other contestants are not likely to develop counter arguments or amass sufficient opposi-tion. Moreover, because of his power and their need for access to the resources he controls, they are more likely to defer to his arguments.

Although the evidence is slight, we have found that power will influence the allocations of scarce and critical resources. In the analysis of power in the university, for instance, one of the most critical resources needed by departments is the general budget. First granted by the state legislature, the general budget is later allocated to individ-ual departments by the university administration in response to requests from the department heads. Our analysis of the factors that contribute to a department get-ting more or less of this budget indicated that subunit power was the major predictor, overriding such factors as student demand for courses, national reputations of depart-ments, or even the size of department's faculty. Moreover, other research has shown that when the general budget has been cut back or held below previous uninflated levels, leading to monies becoming more scarce, budget alloca-tions mirror departmental powers even more closely.

Student enrollment and faculty size, of course, do themselves relate to budget allocations, as we would expect since they determine a department's need for resources, or at least offer visible testimony of needs. But departments are not always able to get what they need by the mere fact of needing them. In one analysis it was found that high-power departments were able to obtain budget without regard to their teaching loads and, in some cases, actually in inverse relation to their teaching loads. In contrast, low-power departments could get increases in budget only when they could justify the increases by a recent growth in teaching load, and then only when it was far in excess of norms for other departments.

General budget is only one form of resource that is allocated to departments. There are others such as special grants for student fellowships or faculty research. These are critical to departments because they affect the ability to attract other resources, such as outstanding faculty or students. We examined how power influenced the allocations of four resources department heads had described as critical and scarce.

When the four resources were arrayed from the most to the least critical and scarce, we found that departmental power best predicted the allocations of the most critical and scarce resources. In other words, the analysis of how power influences organizational allocations leads to this conclusion: Those subunits most likely to survive in times of strife are those that are more critical to the organization. Their importance to the organization gives them power to influence resource allocations that enhance their own survival.

How External Environment Impacts Executive Selection

Power not only influences the survival of key groups in an organization, it also influences the selection of individuals to key leadership positions, and by such a process further aligns the organization with its environmental context.

We can illustrate this with a recent study of the selection and tenure of chief administrators in 57 hospitals in Illinois. We assumed that since the critical problems facing the organization would enhance the power of certain groups at the expense of others, then the leaders to emerge should be those most relevant to the context of the hospitals. To assess this we asked each chief administrator about his professional background and how long he had been in office. The replies were then related to the hospitals' funding, ownership, and competitive conditions for patients and staff.

One aspect of a hospital's context is the source of its budget. Some hospitals, for instance, are run much like other businesses. They sell bed space, patient care, and treatment services. They charge fees sufficient both to cover their costs and to provide capital for expansion. The main source of both their operating and capital funds is patient billings. Increasingly, patient billings are paid for, not by patients, but by private insurance companies. Insurers like Blue Cross dominate and represent a potent interest group outside a hospital's control but critical to its income. The insurance companies, in order to limit their own costs, attempt to hold down the fees allowable to hospitals, which they do effectively from their positions on state rate boards. The squeeze on hospitals that results from fees increasing slowly while costs climb rapidly more and more demands the talents of cost accountants or people trained in the technical expertise of hospital administration.

By contrast, other hospitals operate more like social service institutions, either as government healthcare units (Bellevue Hospital in New York City and Cook County Hospital in Chicago, for example) or as charitable institutions. These hospitals obtain a large portion of their operating and capital funds, not from privately insured patients, but from government subsidies or private donations. Such institutions rather than requiring the talents of a technically efficient administrator are likely to require the savvy of someone who is well integrated into the social and political power structure of the community.

Not surprisingly, the characteristics of administrators predictably reflect the funding context of the hospitals with which they are associated. Those hospitals with larger proportions of their budget obtain from private insurance companies were most likely to have administrators with backgrounds in accounting and least likely to have administrators whose professions were business or medicine. In contrast, those hospitals with larger proportions of the budget derived from private donations and local governments were most likely to have administrators with business or professional backgrounds and least likely to have accountants. The same held for formal training in hospital administration. Professional hospital administrators could easily be found in hospitals drawing their incomes from private insurance and rarely in hospitals dependent on donations or legislative appropriations.

As with the selection of administrators, the context of organizations has also been found to affect the removal of executives. The environment, as a source of organizational problems, can make it more or less difficult for executives to demonstrate their value to the organization. In the hospitals we studied, long-term administrators came from hospitals with few problems. They enjoyed amicable and stable relations with their local business and social communities and suffered little competition for funding and staff. The small city hospital director who attended civic and Elks meeting while running the only hospital within a 100-mile radius, for example, had little difficulty holding on to his job. Turnover was highest in hospitals with the most problems, a phenomenon similar to that observed in a study of industrial organizations in which turnover was highest among executives in industries with competitive environments and unstable market conditions. The interesting thing is that instability characterized the industries rather than the individual firms in them. The troublesome conditions in the individual firms were attributed, or rather misattributed, to the executives themselves.

It takes more than problems, however, to terminate a manager's leadership. The problems themselves must be relevant and critical. This is clear from the way in which an administrator's tenure is affected by the status of the hospital's operating budget. Naively we might assume that all administrators would need to show a surplus. Not necessarily so. Again, we must distinguish between those hospitals that depend on private donations for funds and those that do not. Whether an endowed budget shows a surplus or deficit is less important than the hospital's relations with the benefactors. On the other hand, with a budget dependent on patient billing, a surplus is almost essential; monies for new equipment or expansion must be drawn from it, and without them quality care becomes more difficult and patients scarcer. An administrator's tenure reflected just these considerations. For those hospitals dependent on private donations, the length of an administrator's term depended not at all on the status of the operating budget but was fairly predictable from the hospital's relations with the business community. On the other hand, in hospitals dependent on the operating budget for capital financing, the greater the deficit the shorter was the tenure of the hospital's principal administrators.

Changing Contingencies and Eroding Power Bases

The critical contingencies facing the organization may change. When they do, it is reasonable to expect that the power of individuals and subgroups will change in turn.

At times the shift can be swift and shattering, as it was recently for powerholders in New York City. A few years ago it was believed that David Rockefeller was one of the ten most powerful people in the city, as tallied by *New York* magazine, which annually sniffs out power for the delectation of its readers. But that was before it was revealed that the city was in financial trouble, before Rockefeller's Chase Manhattan Bank lost some of its own financial luster, and before brother Nelson lost some of his political influence in Washington. Obviously David Rockefeller was no longer as well positioned to help bail the city out. Another loser was an attorney with considerable personal connections to the political and religious leaders of the city. His talents were no longer in much demand. The persons with more influence were the bankers and union pension fund executors who fed money to the city; community leaders who represent blacks and Spanish-Americans, in contrast, witnessed the erosion of their power bases.

One implication of the idea that power shifts with changes in organizational environments is that the dominant coalition will tend to be that group that is most appropriate for the organization's environment, as also will the leaders of an organization. One can observe this historically in the top executives of industrial firms in the United States. Up until the early 1950s, many top corporations were headed by former production line managers or engineers who gained prominence because of their abilities to cope with the problems of production. Their success, however, only spelled their demise. As production became routinized and mechanized, the problem of most firms became one of selling all those goods they so efficiently produced. Marketing executives were more frequently found in corporate boardrooms. Success outdid itself again, for keeping markets and production steady and stable requires the kind of control that comes only from acquiring competitors and suppliers or the invention of more and more appealing products—ventures that typically require enormous amounts of capital. During the 1960s, financial executives assumed the seats of power. And they, too, will give way to others. Edging over the horizon are legal experts, as regulation and antitrust suits are becoming more and more frequent in the 1970s, suits that had their beginning in the success of the expansion generated by prior executives. The more distant future, which is likely to be dominated by multinational corporations, may see former secretaries of state and their minions increasingly serving as corporate figureheads.

The Nonadaptive Consequences of Adaptation

From what we have said thus far about power aligning the organization with its own realities, an intelligent person might react with a resounding ho-hum, for it all seems too obvious: Those with the ability to get the job done are given the job to do.

However, there are two aspects of power that make it more useful for understanding organizations and their effectiveness. First, the "job" to be done has a way of expanding itself until it becomes less and less clear what the job is. Napoleon began by doing a job for France in the war with Austria and ended up Emperor, convincing many that only he could keep the peace. Hitler began by promising an end to Germany's troubling postwar depression and ended up convincing more people than is comfortable to remember that he was destined to be the savior of the world. In short, power is a capacity for influence that extends far beyond the original bases that created it. Second, power tends to take on institutionalized forms that enable it to endure well beyond its usefulness to an organization.

There is an important contradiction in what we have observed about organizational power. On the one hand we have said that power derives from the contingencies facing an organization and that when those contingencies change so do the bases for power. On the other hand we have asserted that subunits will tend to use their power to influence organizational decisions in their own favor, particularly when their own survival is threatened by the scarcity of critical resources. The first statement implies that an organization will tend to be aligned with its environment since power will tend to bring to key positions those with capabilities relevant to the context. The second implies that those in power will not give up their positions so easily; they will pursue policies that guarantee their continued domination. In short, change and stability operate through the same mechanism, and, as a result, the organization will never be completely in phase with its environment or its needs.

The study of hospital administrators illustrates how leadership can be out of phase with reality. We argued that privately funded hospitals needed trained technical administrators, more so than did hospitals funded by donations. The need as we perceived it was matched in most hospitals, but by no means in all. Some organizations did not conform with our predictions. These deviations imply that some administrators were able to maintain their positions independent of their suitability for those positions. By dividing administrators into those with long and short terms of office, one finds that the characteristics of longer-termed administrators were virtually unrelated to the hospital's context. The shorter-termed chiefs on the other hand had characteristics more appropriate for the hospital's problems. For a hospital to have a recently appointed head implies that the previous administrator had been unable to endure by institutionalizing himself.

One obvious feature of hospitals that allowed some administrators to enjoy a long tenure was a hospital's ownership. Administrators were less entrenched when their hospitals were affiliated with and dependent upon larger organizations, such as governments and churches. Private hospitals offered more secure positions for administrators. Like private corporations, they tend to have more diffused ownership, leaving the administrator unopposed as he institutionalizes his reign. Thus he endures, sometimes at the expense of the performance of the organization. Other research has demonstrated that corporations with diffuse ownership have poorer earnings than those in which the control of the manager is checked by a dominant stockholder. Firms that overload their boardrooms with more insiders than are appropriate for their context have also been found to be less profitable.

A word of caution is required about our judgment of "appropriateness." When we argue some capabilities are more appropriate for one context than another, we do so from the perspective of an outsider and on the basis of reasonable assumptions as to the problems the organization will face and the capabilities they will need. The fact that we have been able to predict the distribution of influence and the characteristics of leaders suggest that our reasoning is not incorrect. However, we do not think that all organizations follow the same pattern. The fact that we have not been able to predict outcomes with 100 percent accuracy indicates they do not.

Mistaking Critical Consequences

One thing that allows subunits to retain their power is their ability to name their functions as critical to the organization when they may not be. Consider again our discussion of power in the university. One might wonder why the most critical tasks were defined as graduate education and scholarly research, the effect of which was to lend power to those who brought in grants and contracts. Why not something else? The reason is that the more powerful departments argued for those criteria and won their case, partly because they were more powerful.

In another analysis of this university, we found that all departments advocate self-serving criteria for budget allocation. Thus a department with large undergraduate enrollments argued that enrollments should determine budget allocations, a department with a strong national reputation saw prestige as the most reasonable basis for distributing funds, and so on. We further found that advocating such self-serving criteria actually benefited a department's budget allotments but, also, it paid off more for departments that were already powerful.

Organizational needs are consistent with a current distribution of power also because of a human tendency to categorize problems in familiar ways. An accountant sees problems with organizational performances as cost accountancy problems or inventory flow problems. A sales manager sees them as problems with markets, promotional strategies, or just unaggressive salespeople. But what is the truth? Since it does not automatically announce itself, it is likely that those with proper credibility, or those with power, will be favored as the enlightened. This bias, while not intentionally self-serving, further concentrates power among those who already possess it, independent of changes in the organization's context.

Institutionalizing Power

A third reason for expecting organization contingencies to be defined in familiar ways is that the current holders of power can structure the organization in ways that institutionalize themselves. By institutionalization we mean the establishment of relatively permanent structures and policies that favor the influence of a particular subunit. While in power, a dominant coalition has the ability to institute constitutions, rules, procedures, and information systems that limit the potential power of others while continuing their own.

The key to institutionalizing power always is to create a device that legitimates one's own authority and diminishes the legitimacy of others. When the "Divine Right of Kings" was envisioned centuries ago it was to provide an unquestionable foundation for the supremacy of royal authority. There is generally a need to root the exercise of

authority in some higher power. Modern leaders are no less affected by this need. Richard Nixon, with the aid of John Dean, reified the concept of executive privilege, which meant in effect that what the President wished not to be discussed need not be discussed.

In its simpler form, institutionalization is achieved by designating positions or roles for organizational activities. The creation of a new post legitimizes a function and forces organization members to orient to it. By designating how this new post relates to older, more established posts, moreover, one can structure an organization to enhance the importance of the function in the organization. Equally, one can diminish the importance of traditional functions. This is what happened in the end with the insurance company we mentioned that was having trouble with its coding department. As the situation unfolded, the claims director continued to feel dissatisfied about the dependency of his functions on the coding manager. Thus he instituted a reorganization that resulted in two coding departments. In so doing, of course, he placed activities that affected his department under his direct control, presumably to make the operation more effective. Similarly, consumer-product firms enhance the power of marketing by setting up a coordinating role to interface production and marketing functions and then appoint a marketing manager to fill the role.

The structures created by dominant powers sooner or later become fixed and unquestioned features of the organization. Eventually, this can be devastating. It is said that the battle of Jena in 1806 was lost by Frederick the Great, who died in 1786. Though the great Prussian leader had no direct hand in the disaster, his imprint on the army was so thorough, so imbedded in its skeletal underpinnings, that the organization was inappropriate for others to lead in different times.

Another important source of institutionalized power lies in the ability to structure information systems. Setting up committees to investigate particular organizational issues and having them report only to particular individuals or groups facilitates their awareness of problems by members of those groups while limiting the awareness of problems by the members of other groups. Obviously, those who have information are in a better position to interpret the problems of an organization, regardless of how realistically they may, in fact, do so.

Still another way to institutionalize power is to distribute rewards and resources. The dominant group may quiet competing interest groups with small favors and rewards. Credit for this artful form of co-optation belongs to Louis XIV. To avoid usurpation of his power by the nobles of France and the Fronde that had so troubled his father's reign, he built the palace at Versailles to occupy them with hunting and gossip. Awed, the courtiers basked in the reflected glories of the "Sun King" and the overwhelming setting he had created for his court.

At this point, we have not systematically studied the institutionalization of power. But we suspect it is an important condition that mediates between the environment of the organization and the capabilities of the organization for dealing with that environment. The more institutionalized power is within an organization, the more likely an organization will be out of phase with the realities it faces. President Richard Nixon's restructuring of his White House is one of the better documented illustrations. If we go back to newspaper and magazine descriptions of how he organized his office from the beginning in 1968, most of what occurred subsequently follows almost as an afterthought. Decisions flowed through virtually only the small White House staff; rewards, small presidential favors of recognition, and perquisites were distributed by this staff to the loyal; and information from the outside world—the press, Congress, the people on the streets—was filtered by the staff and passed along only if initialed "bh." Thus it is not surprising that when Nixon met war protesters in the early dawn, the only thing he could think to talk about was the latest football game, so insulated had he become from their grief and anger.

One of the more interesting implications of institutionalized power is that executive turnover among the executives who have structured the organization is likely to be a rare event that occurs only under the most pressing crisis. If a dominant coalition is able to structure the organization and interpret the meaning of ambiguous events like declining sales and profits or lawsuits, then the "real" problems to emerge will easily be incorporated into traditional molds of thinking and acting. If opposition is designed out of the organization, the interpretations will go unquestioned. Conditions will remain stable until a crisis develops, so overwhelming and visible that even the most adroit rhetorician would be silenced.

Implications for the Management of Power in Organizations

While we could derive numerous implications from this discussion of power, our selection would have to depend largely on whether one wanted to increase one's power, decrease the power of others, or merely maintain one's position. More important, the real implications depend on the particulars of an organizational situation. To understand power in an organization one must begin by looking outside it—into the environment—for those groups that mediate the organization's outcomes but are not themselves within its control.

Instead of ending with homilies, we will end with a reversal of where we began. Power, rather than being the dirty business it is often made out to be, is probably one of the few mechanisms for reality testing in organizations. And the cleaner forms of power, the institutional forms, rather than having the virtues they are often credited with, can lead the organization to become out of touch. The real trick to managing power in organizations is to ensure somehow that leaders cannot be unaware of the realities of their environments and cannot avoid changing to deal with those realities. That, however, would be like designing the "self-liquidating organization," an unlikely event since anyone capable of designing such an instrument would obviously be in control of the liquidations.

Management would do well to devote more attention to determining the critical contingencies of their environments. For if you conclude, as we do, that the environment sets most of the structure influencing organizational outcomes and problems, and that power derives from the organization's activities that deal with those contingencies, then it is the environment that needs managing, not power. The first step is to construct an accurate model of the environment, a process that is quite difficult for most organizations. We have recently started a project to aid administrators in systematically understanding their environments. From this experience, we have learned that the most critical blockage to perceiving an organization's reality accurately is a failure to incorporate those with the relevant expertise into the process. Most organizations have the requisite experts on hand but they are positioned so that they can be comfortably ignored.

One conclusion you can, and probably should, derive from our discussion is that power—because of the way it develops and the way it is used—will always result in the organization suboptimizing its performance. However, to this grim absolute, we add a comforting caveat: If any criteria other than power were the basis for determining an organization's decisions, the results would be even worse.

Discussion Questions

1. For what reasons is power used by subunits in organizations?

2. Comment on the contradiction that: Because of the processes by which power develops and is used, organizations become both more aligned and more misaligned with their environments.

3. Define power.

4. What are the sources of power in organizations? What role does uncertainty play in allocating power?

5. Why is power shared in organizations?

6. How can an organization determine what is of critical importance to it?

7. How does power influence organizational decision making?

8. In what ways does the external environment affect internal power? Do changes in the environment create changes in an organization's power structure?

9. Discuss some ways that power can become nonadaptive or dysfunctional for an organization.

10. How can the institutional forms of power result in an organization losing touch with reality?

Organizational Politics against Organizational Culture: A Psychoanalytic Perspective

Howell S. Baum

LEARNING OBJECTIVES

After reading Baum's "Organizational Politics against Organizational Culture: A Psychoanalytical Perspective," students will be able to:

1. Understand the psychoanalytic approach to studying political behavior in organizations

2. Learn why organizational politics creates anxiety that induces workers to withdraw emotionally

3. Know that managers can shape organizational conditions to provide support for the unconscious requirements for intimacy

4. Understand why incentive systems should have the effect of permitting people to balance aggressive work with caring work

Workers' frequent complaints about organizational "politics" indicate that many prevailing organizational cultures do not "feel right." Hoping to attract workers' loyalty, senior managers frequently promote the image of a conflict-free organization, in which all interests are congruent and politics is unnecessary. Nevertheless, while they promulgate mission statements and implement training programs to create integrated organizations, actual company cultures often demand social relations that conflict with workers' wishes for competence and attachment to the organization. For different reasons, managers and workers may be drawn to the organizational ideal, but both suffer from the absence of a sophisticated politics that permits people to promote their interests, even in conflict with others, without being expelled from the organization. Consider the following case.

Michael Anderson has worked for 20 years as a transportation planner with a county planning agency. He began with ambitions of designing an extensive modern transportation system in the county. He received three promotions in his first four years and acquired administrative responsibilities. Nevertheless, there were early signs he was not fitting into the organization.

In explaining his failure to get ahead, he used the following analogy to describe the dangers of acting aggressively or politically at work.

> *Among coyotes, males are born into a pack; you have a whole litter. You have men who will never be leaders because of their biology, their genetics. And you have some more aggressive cubs, and they will do whatever they need to do to become leaders. And they have to eat the pack leader. And he never gives up until he can't resist any longer. I think I was born in that other group. When the puppies are born, they do all sorts of things to give the dominant male his rights, and they will do all sorts of growling, and the puppy will turn over. There are linkages back and forth between humans and coyotes. Somehow I must not ever have given my bosses that yelp and stomach up, and they sensed it. And I never got the membership support I needed.*

Anderson responded to his anxiety about politics in two ways. When he started out in the agency, he went with his director to present his transportation plans to the county council. He argued vehemently for his ideas, but he realized that elected officials considered him out of touch with local politics, and the director eventually stopped taking him along. Anderson reacted by isolating himself from others. He emphasized his autonomy in perfecting proposals without concern about their use.

At the same time, he turned his attention to renovating a houseboat. In part, this was another retreat from the

Source: Howell S. Baum, "Organizational Politics against Organizational Culture: A Psychoanalytic Perspective," (New York: John Wiley & Sons, Inc.) 1989, *Human Resource Management*, 191–206, (1989) Vol. 28; No. 2. Reprinted by permission of John Wiley & Sons, Inc.

dangers of acting aggressively: he could plan and develop the houseboat without fear of opposition. In addition, the move was a physical expression of a growing emotional retreat from the organization. Anxiety about power led him to work in isolation, and the more he focused on his autonomy, the less he felt able to identify with the organization as a whole.

Anderson's jungle analogy for bureaucratic politics expresses in exaggeration some common concerns about the nature of politics and the consequences of acting powerfully to get work done. A boss may seem like a father who insists on dominance and whom a subordinate must harm in order to advance. Often even small initiatives seem like vicious attacks on others, and devastating reprisal seems likely. Anderson's career suggests that anxiety about politics may lead workers to retreat from taking initiatives and to fail to identify with an organization.

This article examines how conventional organizational politics arouses anxiety that induces workers to withdraw emotionally from organizations, thereby defeating managerial hopes that workers will adhere to an integrative culture. The first section looks at aggression, power, and politics in organizations. In the second section, the unconscious, developmental meanings of different power orientations and politics are analyzed. The third examines how conventional politics make it psychologically difficult for workers to feel loyal to an organization. And in the final section, prospects for an integrative organizational culture are considered.

Aggression, Power, and Politics in Work Organizations

Many workers complain that organizational "politics" are something alien and antagonistic to their efforts to work (Baum, 1983, 1986, 1987, 1990, forthcoming). They find themselves in relationships where others treat them calculatingly, and they cannot be open to say what they think and feel.

Yet every organization, at least tacitly, has politics (i.e., procedures for promoting interests to allocate scarce resources). Some who complain about their organization's politics realistically describe practices interfering with their professional autonomy. Others, however, are expressing their discomfort with becoming involved in politics. Some dislike politics because it demands abilities they lack; they have difficulty conceptualizing issues in terms of interests

or are poor strategizers. Others may feel uncomfortable confronting people, especially those who oppose them, and particularly those who seem powerful.

Their unease points to a number of *psychological* problems with politics. The organizational "politics" to which most workers react is a particular type of politics: the win-lose politics of interpersonal conflict. This politics depends on and engenders a specific experience of *power*, and people's largely unconscious reactions to it lead them not simply to complain but to avoid considering conflict productive and to retreat from organizations.

Politics and Aggression

Acting politically means acting *aggressively*—encouraging, persuading, or forcing others to act differently than they otherwise would. Hence people who criticize others for being "political" may be themselves particularly anxious about aggression. They may have legitimate grievances against leaders or managers, but they also hold back from thinking and acting politically in order to isolate themselves from a realm of aggressive activity.

Psychoanalytic theory helps understand people's reactions to politics and power by shedding light on typical patterns of unconscious thoughts and feelings about aggression. People who fear or are ambivalent about aggression often unconsciously associate small aggressive intentions with much larger ones. Then, exaggerating their own aims, they may imagine succeeding in the seeming effort to destroy someone else. In turn, they may feel guilty, fear retribution in kind, or both (Fenichel, 1945). Thus to avoid guilt, anxiety about punishment, or even shame from thinking of themselves as aggressive, they may deny their aggressive wishes and thoughts and attribute them to someone else. By denigrating politics they can even take pleasure in attacking others for what they do not want to accept in themselves (Klein, 1952).

The Fantasy of the Ideal Organization

The flight from aggression may be expressed and reinforced by the fantasy of an aggression-free organization, where politics can be avoided because it is not necessary. In an organization without aggression, so the fantasy goes, all would be close; crucially, all would be one and the same. And all, being one, would be omnipotent and omniscient. Further, all would care for one another; the great organization would care infinitely for everyone. This "organizational ideal," corresponds to an individual's ego ideal: finding in adult life something that represents the power and loving which the self-centeredness of early infancy supplied (Chasseguet-Smirgel, 1985, 1986). Someone who identifies totally with an organizational ideal can feel loved and protected by a powerful entity. He or she can feel powerful without having to act aggressively. Thus some complaints about organizational "politics" register unconscious objections to a world of differences, in which some are larger and others are smaller, in which people are in conflict, and where outcomes are uncertain.

The Need for Aggression

Even though managers may have an easy time with workers who care for the organization and harbor no aggressive wishes against it, they also want subordinates to "work hard" and to "attack problems"—to be aggressive after all. Work requires an individual to act aggressively on materials and people in order to change them and direct them in desired ways. However, it also requires him or her to act with enough care so that materials or people are not physically or psychologically destroyed. Aggression in the task must not be so great that it hinders workers from identifying with one another and the organization.

Thus managers confront a dilemma: to encourage sufficient aggression to get work done, but to elicit enough caring to ensure that workers don't hurt one another and feel loyal to the organization. Unconsciously, workers face the quandary of how aggressively to act to be competent without feeling guilty or anxiously awaiting reprisal.

Yankelovich and Immerwahr's (1983) survey of American workers provides evidence of this dilemma. Eighty-eight percent say they want to work hard and do the best they can on the job, and more than half say they have an inner need to do the best job regardless of pay. Nevertheless, 75% say they could be significantly more effective on the job, and half say they work just hard enough to avoid getting fired. In other words, workers say they want to work aggressively but hold back. Some explain that they don't get paid any more for doing so. Others, pointing to the dilemma about aggression, say that managers provide little incentive to work harder.

Complaints about "politics" and workers' conflicts about working hard both express the problem of aggression in organizations: how to incorporate appropriate aggression in work while permitting realistic attachment to the organization. If a corporate culture is to allow workers to care for a realistically perceived organization, it must be supported by political norms that regulate aggression reassuringly.

Power Orientations and Alternative Politics

Conventional organizational politics is only one possible politics. In general, politics may be defined as the exercise of power to promote interests (for example, Dahl, 1964; and Lasswell, 1958), but there can be as many types of politics as there are types of power. The most common conception of power portrays independent parties asserting themselves to defeat one another. This is the principle of politics in a world of scarcity and conflicting interests. It is a zero-sum politics: when one party wins, another must lose. Normal organizational politics is an example.

Arendt (1958) has conceptualized power differently: as the ability of different parties to achieve something together they could not accomplish individually. This power governs a politics concerned with creating new possibilities in a world where resources may be scarce but some interests may be joined and new resources created. This is a win-win politics: victory is only collective, and one party's loss defeats all. This politics could offer an alternative to current organizational norms.

Significantly, different persons conceive power differently and practice politics differently in the same situation. McClelland's (1975) study of the experience of power finds that everyone acts through one of four "power orientations," which vary according to two dimensions. The *source* of power may be external (another person or a principle) or internal (oneself). The *object* of power, similarly, may be external (influencing or controlling another) or internal (controlling or strengthening oneself). Equally important, drawing on the work of psychoanalyst Erik Erikson, McClelland suggests each power orientation corresponds to a specific stage in individual development. Thus, how people view and take up power is linked to their past developmental accomplishments and their present challenges. See Figure 8.1, adapted from McClelland, and Table 8.1, summarize the power orientations and their links to Erikson's developmental stages.

A Developmental Concept of Stages and Phases

Erikson (1963, 1968) suggests that human development involves progressing through stages defined in terms of internal and interpersonal dilemmas. The infant—and

FIGURE 8.1

CLASSIFICATION OF POWER ORIENTATIONS

Source of Power

Object of Power	Other	Self
Self (to feel stronger)		
Intention:	"It" (God, my mother, my leader, food) will strengthen me.	I will strengthen, control, direct myself.
Action:	Being near a source of strength.	Collecting, accumulating information, things.
	I	II
	IV	III
Other (to influence)		
Intention:	It (religion, laws, my group) will move me to serve, influence other, to do my duty.	I will have an impact (influence) on others.
Action:	Action on higher principle or purpose.	Competing with, affecting others.

Source: Adapted from McClelland (1975), p. 14.

later, the child, the adolescent, and the adult—confronts others in the world and demands that their relationship satisfy certain expectations related to its biological condition and social history. Success at any developmental stage—for example, the older child's need to learn to exercise aggressive initiative without guilt—depends on continuing success at all previous stages and permits advancement to the next challenge. When someone fails a particular developmental test, he or she may remain effective at preceding tasks but have difficulty advancing. This person may have partial success at later tasks, but most of his or her effort is concentrated on the unmet challenge. For example, employees who cannot take initiative without feeling guilty will not only have difficult presenting their position when this means challenging someone, but they will also have problems working competently and securing a work identity. Instead, they will continually practice acting aggressively.

Sometimes a person who has passed a particular developmental stage may encounter a situation that presents a challenge corresponding to that stage, which cannot be readily mastered. When this happens, the individual "regresses" to concerns with the developmental dilemma of that stage, almost as if it were being confronted for the first time. For example, a man who has normally been able to take initiative without guilt may run into a supervisor or situation that makes him feel guilty about how he works or anxious about his or others' aggression. As a result, he will have difficulty continuing to work competently. Losing self-confidence, he may become fixated on the problem of aggression and react to many situations as simply being tests of his ability to take initiative.

The following discussion describes Erikson's developmental stages and shows how they are related to the power orientations McClelland discovered.

TABLE 8.1

Type of Power	Stage of Development	Type of Politics
I ("It will strengthen me.")	Trust vs. Mistrust	Subordinacy
II ("I will strengthen myself.")	Autonomy vs. Shame, Doubt	Isolation
III ("I will have an impact on others.")	Initiative versus Guilt	Interpersonal conflict
IV ("It will move me to serve others.")	Identity vs. Identity Confusion	Collaboration
	Intimacy vs. Isolation	
	Generativity vs. Stagnation	

Types of Power

Type I: Power and the Stage of Trust vs. Mistrust. The infant relating to the mother encounters the first question, in Erikson's terms, of whether it should regard the world with "basic trust" or "basic mistrust," whether it can depend on the mother to provide the fundamental support needed for living. Someone who as an adult still seeks reassurance of the world's basic trustworthiness is likely to take a Type I orientation to power ("It strengthens me"). Not only does this orientation provide security, it also represents the only orientation of which such a person is capable. It expresses a wish to feel powerful by working for someone else who is powerful, and who can therefore be trusted to provide a secure world. It may characterize someone who chooses to advise an elected official or top manager and takes satisfaction in the closeness of loyal service to someone strong.

This does not mean that a staff advisor who enjoys drawing on the strength of a line executive is simply a baby. Everyone to some degree continues to seek reassurance of a nurturing environment in later life; rather, adults differ in their need for this confirmation. People who hold the Type I power orientation may especially need or take pleasure from such reassurance. Similarly, the motives for becoming a staff advisor, for example, are infinitely more complex than those of the infant who wants just to be fed. Moreover, nothing in any unconscious connection between particular advising roles and earlier concerns about a mother's trustworthiness diminishes the validity and value of the activity. Indeed, this power orientation may especially suit someone for advising work. These observations are true for the other three power orientations as well.

Type II: Autonomy vs. Shame and Doubt. Once an infant feels it can trust the world and its agents, it encounters the second dilemma, of "autonomy versus shame and doubt." Can it act independently in the trustworthy world without seeming too small, inept, or inadequate? A child seeks to prove its independence by collecting and controlling objects that represent the substance of the world. An adult who is still worried about autonomy is likely to take a Type II orientation ("I strengthen or control myself"). It expresses a wish to feel powerful by being independent of everyone else, free of contact with others and not bound by their interest or actions. It may characterize someone who is interested in data collection. By accumulating and managing information, a person may gain a sense of control over the objects the data represent.

Type III: Initiative vs. Guilt. As the young child develops a sense of autonomy, it confronts the challenge of "initiative versus guilt." Increasingly mobile, the child asserts him- or herself against others such as parents. Can he or she take initiatives against them without feeling guilty about hurting them? The child must find an answer to this question in the specific terms of the Oedipus complex: at this time, a child normally wishes to defeat the same sex parent in a contest for the affection of the other parent. The outcome of the struggle is decisive for later assumptions the child and adult will make about the meanings and consequences of acting lovingly and aggressively without hurting those one loves.

The Type III power orientation ("I have an impact on others") expresses the perspective of this period. People think of becoming powerful by doing battle with others and defeating them for their possessions or positions. Adults who have not fully resolved the Oedipal dilemma may unconsciously exaggerate the danger of conflict and the likelihood of reprisal or, alternatively, the chances of success and resultant guilt. Professionally, this power orientation may characterize strategists or organizers.

Type IV: Identity and Intimacy vs. Identity Confusion and Isolation. Erikson's last four stages present challenges posed by the search for identity, intimacy, generativity, and integrity. The first of these are especially closely tied to the Type IV power orientation. Adolescents face the challenge of consolidating a cohesive "identity against identity confusion." They decide with which ideas, people and, crucially, occupation or career they want to identify (and be identified) for the rest of their lives. Once adults feel secure about who they are, they face the test of being able to engage in "intimacy," rather than ending up in "isolation." Individuals must face the possibilities of closeness against the risks of vulnerability, exposure, and loss. They practice loving wishes in relations with others equal to themselves. When they succeed, the most important new intimacies are sexual, but friendships and affiliations with work organizations also provide opportunities for attachment. This intimacy is the basis for realistic identification with co-workers and work organizations.

The Type IV power orientation ("It moves me to serve others") expresses a wish to feel powerful by directing others in the name of general principles or collective interests. It involves more or less intimate interaction among people who understand who they are and accept others as their partners. People attempt to resolve differences according to mutually accepted norms, rather than individual wishes. This orientation is the most complex of the four, depending on successful development through adulthood. It entails the ability to take initiative in acting competently and intimately with others who are equal. It may be expressed by managers or leaders who act on collective interests rather than personal loyalties. "Professionals" commonly couch their actions in terms of the "neutrality" of this orientation, directing other people in the name of abstract principles.

Just as the stages of identity formation are developmentally linked, so are McClelland's power orientations. *Success at any power orientation depends on mastering the preceding ones.* For example, someone frightened by a Type III power orientation cannot understand or begin to learn the Type IV orientation. Further, he may retreat to a Type II orientation, where he can be alone, dependent only on his own efforts and resources. At most, he will see power in terms of win-lose conflicts.

In addition, as the earlier discussion suggested, power orientations and stages of identity development are reciprocally related. Political success reinforces accomplishments at a corresponding developmental stage. Failure unsettles achievements at the corresponding stage, as well as subsequent stages. For example, someone who has not found ways of taking initiative without guilt will not be secure or effective in the Type III power orientation. Conversely, someone who has trouble with conflict in the Type III orientation will have difficulty moving beyond autonomy to initiative, as well as meeting later challenges.

Types of Politics

As Table 8.1 indicates, each of the different power orientations and their associated developmental stages encourages a particular type of organizational politics. The Type I orientation leads to a politics of subordinacy, in which people look for others who are strong on whom they can depend. This orientation corresponds to unconscious fantasies about a strong, caring, "politics"-free organization, and may be expressed in wishes for an integrating culture.

The Type II orientation leads to a politics of isolation, in which people try to become self sufficient by accumulating as many resources as possible. People may express this orientation through a cynical retreat from "politics."

The Type IV orientation, which corresponds to Arendt's concept of power, can be the basis for a realistically sophisticated collaborative politics through which workers can promote interests and resolve conflicts while feeling some attachment to co-workers and the organization. If people begin with the assumption that co-workers, including managers, will continue to support one another despite conflicts over real differences, they can assert their interests vigorously but securely. They will be able to solve problems that conventional "politics" masks. Even if specific decisions do not satisfy everyone, people will be more likely to feel the procedures are legitimate.

Finally, the Type III orientation leads to conventional organizational "politics," the politics of win-lose competition for programmatic resources and career opportunities: People characterize this politics as self-interested, rather than collectively oriented. It is concerned with winning rather than collaborating. It is a devious and circuitous rather than direct and straightforward. It is selfishly calculating rather than disinterestedly rational. It favors collusion over competence.

Politics and Regression

Type III politics holds out two dangers. It induces workers with more advanced development to regress in order to participate; and it entails expressions of aggression that make workers anxious and encourage them to regress to defend themselves.

The Regressive Effects of Participation in "Politics"

For those who regard their work in terms of a Type IV power orientation—who see themselves acting on general principle, serving collective interests, or mediating conflicts—Type III politics calls on them to act in ways consistent with a developmentally earlier orientation. Someone acting with a Type III orientation makes it difficult for others to maintain a Type IV orientation: there is no commitment to reasoning together and collaborating. It is tempting—and may be strategically necessary—to step down from the Type IV position.

Sometimes people with Type IV orientations engage in Type III politics while continuing to think of the possibilities for Type IV politics. They do not regress, their previous development is unaffected, and they act relatively effectively. However, "politics" may regressively affect both power orientations and identify development. A Type IV orientation depends on a secure sense of industry, a coherent personal identity, and comfort in intimacy. Because the Type III orientation corresponds to earlier efforts to free initiative from guilt and reprisal, participation in such politics unconsciously recalls childhood anxiety about aggressiveness. Sometimes people with Type IV orientations find Type III situations so difficult they lose some of their sense of competence, identity, or ability to be intimate.

These dangers to personal identity help explain why relatively few workers feel loyal to their organizations. Continuing involvement in Type III politics makes it difficult for a worker to be close to and care for co-workers or to identify with an organization. When workers conceptualize most of their relationships in terms of calculated triumph over rivals, they have trouble thinking of co-workers as persons whose welfare they share. Superficially, people might observe they are so annoyed by "politics" that they don't feel part of the workplace. This statement describes an unconscious connection: "politics" makes intimacy difficult.

Regressive Defenses against the Aggression of Politics

All politics are expressions of aggression, in attempting to influence, move, shape, or harm others or the self. In different ways, Freud (1962 [1930]) and Klein (1975 [1932], 1964 [1937]) argue that social life is possible only if people have opportunities to balance their aggression with expressions of love and caring. Unconsciously, being able to act lovingly toward others compensates for imagined dangers from aggressively harming others, being punished, and feeling guilty.

Type III politics is unconsciously associated with earlier Oedipal conflicts with parents, when the risk of aggression seemed greatest. Success in earlier development depended on learning to act both lovingly and aggressively toward parents and others. At work, managerial exhortations to work hard call for aggression yet fail to provide opportunities for caring for others. Conventional "politics" similarly encourages individuals to set themselves off from others and fight them for scarce rewards. As a result, even when some people benefit from strategic action, engagement in "politics" unconsciously makes many people anxious about aggression that is unbalanced by caring. When workers think in terms of individual achievement, and when they concentrate on attacking co-workers, they become isolated and are unlikely to affiliate deeply with an organization.

Workers may defend themselves against the anxiety of involvement in Type III politics in several ways. For example, some continue to work and act aggressively but try to deny any harm or to express any guilt from their efforts.

Others unconsciously regress to a Type II power orientation and argue cynically that "politics" is immoral and dangerous. They will work well but independently, so they don't have to deal with co-workers, owe them anything, or risk losing to them. Some rationalize their actions in terms of a pseudo-Type IV orientation. They say they are serving "economic efficiency" or "the public interest," and their positions should overrule the selfish actions of "politicians." Claiming moral superiority, they almost magically expect power without coming into contact with co-workers.

A still more regressive defense is fantasizing that the organization is an intimate place where caring pervades and aggression is unnecessary. Regression to this Type I orientation is usually less consistent with getting work done than the Type II defense because it rules out the aggression that most work requires. It depends partly on a magical belief that, if a worker holds back on acting aggressively, identifying with the organization and managers will provide the power to get work done.

These defenses retreat from realistic relationships with co-workers and an organization. By protecting workers from dangers of aggression, they require holding back from aggressive action, not simply in social relations but also in work itself. In addition, these regressions in power orientation have regressive consequences in personal development. They redirect concern to problems of aggression and initiative, autonomy, or basic trust and make it difficult for a worker to maintain a sense of competence. Crucially, workers are developmentally unable to feel secure being close to co-workers or identifying with a real organization.

Regression and Withdrawal

Conventional organizational "politics" often presents workers with a difficult choice: risk regression in order to promote their interests and get work done. Many workers fear not only another person's power to harm or hinder them, but, crucially, *they are afraid of their own regression.* They fear losing the mastery, sense of identity, and possibilities of intimacy that have come with their past development. Workers whose development is insecure find work and "politics" especially threatening and may choose the safety of withdrawal, caring less about work or the organization.

In Sum

Worker's capacity to identify with an organization depends on the fit between their personal development and the norms of organizational politics. Type III politics is appropriate for resolving conflicts among interests where resources are scarce. However, by arousing anxiety about aggression, it encourages people to exaggerate scarcities and conflicts. As a result, people apply Type III norms unthinkingly to many situations where Type IV politics might lead to more constructive solutions (see Argyris, 1982; Argyris and Schön, 1978).

Even effective participation in Type III politics is consciously and unconsciously inconsistent with identification with an organization as a whole. Moreover, when workers feel anxious about Type III and defend themselves by regression, they take power orientations that are still less likely to deal realistically with interests and conflicts. The defenses protecting workers from dangers of aggression require them to hold back on acting aggressively. In addition, such responses as subordinacy, isolation, and unthinking aggression move workers further from experiencing an organization as a place of security and development.

When an organization seems dangerous, both personal development and political sophistication are threatened. Workers retreat from realistic relationships with

co-workers and the organization to power orientations which are unlikely to get work done. Moreover, they are less likely to feel competent and secure in their work. Centrally, conventional "politics" makes it constitutionally difficult for people to identify *as adults* with organizations.

Conventional Politics and the Problem of Organizational Loyalty: Prospects for Organizational Culture

Can managers promote organizational loyalty and identification? They cannot significantly change workers' inner lives, but they can shape the conditions to which workers respond. In particular, managers many succeed in creating an integrative organizational culture to the extent that they support the unconscious requirements for intimacy. This analysis suggests that such a program has four requirements.

First, a culture is not simply a set of rules like work procedures, nor is it merely a compendium of stories managers repeatedly tell. A culture comprises values and norms that affect people because the accompanying actions make sense and feel right. Hence efforts to "create an organizational culture" depend on changes in day-to-day activities (see, for example, Deal and Kennedy, 1982; Schwartz, 1985; and Smircich, 1983).

Second, contemporary work, much of it intellectual and interpersonal service activity, must make new sense in two ways. The traditional work language of "production" and "productivity" does not obviously fit what many people do. They "produce" insights, decisions, or personal relationships, but this is not equivalent to producing an automobile, the prototypical work image. People have difficulty measuring themselves when they spend their days attending meetings, talking on the phone, and exchanging memoranda. Managers need to reconceptualize what workers do in terms that reveal the value of their activities.

At the same time, day-to-day activities must make workers important. They need recognition for specific efforts, such as authorship of reports. They need to see consequences to their actions, by participating in and observing decisions about whether and how their efforts are used (see Yankelovich and Immerwahr, 1983). They need to be associated with things that last, whether tangible products or programs or organizations themselves (see Denhardt, 1981; Schwartz, 1987).

People should be able to produce things they regard as useful, valuable, and lasting. If workers can care for the bit of themselves they see in their products, this loving also repairs imagined damage from working hard or occasionally working against others (see Hirschorn, 1988).

Third, working conditions and incentive systems must have the unconscious effect of allowing people to balance aggressive work with caring work. They should have the opportunity to work collaboratively and be evaluated as team members. If co-workers come to care for one another, this affection will hold them together through conflicts among them, and it will unconsciously compensate for anxiety from working aggressively. In addition, these changes require the creation of Type IV organizational politics.

Fourth, for workers to act with the maturity needed to identify with co-workers and an organization, they must participate in politics that enables them to discover and serve collective interests. They need ways of expressing real differences and resolving conflicts that allow them to remain connected to co-workers and invested in collective work. Type IV politics, as every politics, begins in formal authority relations and spreads to other relationships. If managers and supervisors discuss issues, problems, and conflicts honestly and with concern about subordinates' welfare, subordinates may learn that they can express differences and pursue interests without fear of destructive conflict or anxiety. If managers who must make decisions that displease some can honestly explain their actions in terms of general principles and collective interests, both winners and losers remain loyal to the managers and organization.

Simply, any organizational culture that realistically develops worker loyalty must be accompanied by practices and politics that enable people to work hard, together.

REFERENCES

Arendt, H. *The human condition.* Chicago: University of Chicago Press, 1958.

Argyris, C. *Reasoning, learning, and action.* San Francisco: Jossey-Bass, 1982.

Argyris, C., and Schön, D. A. *Organizational learning.* Reading: Addision-Wesley, 1978.

Baum, H. S. *Planners and public expectations.* Cambridge: Schenkman Publishing Company, 1983.

Baum, H. S. Politics in planners' practice, in *Strategic approaches to planning practice,* edited by B. Checkoway. Lexington: Lexington Books, 1986.

Baum, H. S. *The invisible bureaucracy.* New York: Oxford University Press, 1987.

Baum, H. S. *Organizational Membership: Personal Development in the Workplace.* Albany: SUNY Press, 1990 forthcoming.

Chasseguet-Smirgel, J. *The ego ideal: A psychoanalytic essay on the malady of the ideal.* Translated by Paul Burrows. New York: W. W. Norton and Company, 1985.

Chasseguet-Smirgel, J. *Sexuality and mind: The role of the father and the mother in the psyche.* New York: New York University Press, 1986.

Dahl, R. *Who governs?* New Haven: Yale University Press, 1961.

Deal, T. E., and Kennedy, A. A. *Corporate cultures: The rites and rituals of corporate life.* Reading: Addison-Wesley, 1982.

Denhardt, R. B. *In the shadow of organization.* Lawrence: Regents Press of Kansas, 1981.

Erikson, E. H. *Childhood and society (2nd edition).* New York. W. W. Norton and Company, 1963.

Erikson, E. H. *Identity: Youth and crisis.* New York: W. W. Norton and Company, 1968.

Fenichel, O. *The psychoanalytic theory of neurosis.* New York: W. W. Norton and Company, 1945.

Freud, S. *Civilization and its discontents.* Translated and edited by James Strachey (1962). New York: W. W. Norton and Company, 1930.

Hirschhorn, L. *The workplace within: Psychodynamics of organizational life.* Cambridge: MIT Press, 1988.

Klein, M. Notes on some schizoid mechanism, in *Developments in psycho-analysis.* Edited by Joan Riviere. London: Hogarth, 1952.

Klein, M. Love, guilt, and reparation, in *Love, hate, and reparation,* by Melanie Klein and Joan Riviere. New York: W. W. Norton and Company, 1964.

Klein, M. *The psycho-analysis of children.* Translated by Alix Strachey, revised by Alix Strachey and H. A. Thorner. New York: Dell Publishing Company, 1975.

Lasswell, H. *Politics: Who gets what, when, how.* New York: Meridian Books, 1958.

Martin, J. Stories and scripts in organizational settings, in *Cognitive social psychology*, edited by Albert Hastorf and Alice M. Isen. New York: Elsevier/ North Holland, 1982.

McClelland, D. C. *Power: The inner experience.* New York: Irvington Publishers, 1975.

Schwartz, H. S. The usefulness of myth and the myth of usefulness: a dilemma for the applied organizational scientist, *Journal of Management*, 1985, 11, 31–42.

Schwartz, H. S. Anti-social actions of committed organizational participants: An existential psychoanalytic perspective, *Organization Studies*, 1987, 8, 327–340.

Smircich, L. Concepts of culture and organizational analysis, *Administrative Science Quarterly*, 1983, 28, 339–358.

Yankelovich, D., and Immerwahr, J. *Putting the work ethic to work.* New York: Public Agenda Foundation, 1983.

DISCUSSION QUESTIONS

1. What aspects of politics in organizations lead people to retreat from organizations?

2. How does psychoanalytic theory contribute to understanding people's reactions to politics?

3. Describe the dilemma that Baum thinks managers and workers experience concerning aggression.

4. Discuss the classification of power orientations that Baum develops by combining Erikson's and McClelland's techniques. Are there alternative ways of thinking about power in individuals and organizations?

5. Discuss the problems of Type III politics both for individuals and organizations.

6. In Baum's view why do relatively few workers feel loyalty to the organizations that employ them?

7. How can organizational politics affect an individual's identity development?

8. How does Baum's psychoanalytic approach to politics and power differ from Salancik and Pfeffer's strategic-contingency perspective? Also, consider the differences in Baum's approach and Erikson's analysis of alienation.

FOR FURTHER READING

Crozier, M. *The Bureaucratic Phenomenon.* Chicago: The University of Chicago Press, 1964.

Kanter, R. *Men and Women of the Corporation.* New York: Basic Books, 1977.

Krackhardt, D. "Assessing the Political Landscape: Structure, Cognition, and Power in Organizations." *Administrative Science Quarterly*, 35 (1990) 342–369.

McClelland, D. *Power: The Inner Experience.* New York: Irvington, 1975.

Mechanic, D. "Sources of Power of Lower Level Participants in Complex Organizations." *Administrative Science Quarterly*, 7 (1962) 349–364.

Mintzberg, H. *Power in and around Organizations.* New Jersey: Prentice Hall, 1983.

Pfeffer, J. *Power in Organizations.* Boston: Pitman, 1981.

Wrong, D. *Power: Its Forms, Bases, and Uses.* Chicago: University of Chicago Press, 1988.

9

GROUP DECISION MAKING

Groupthink Reconsidered

GLEN WHYTE

LEARNING OBJECTIVES

After reading "Groupthink Reconsidered" by Glen Whyte, a student will be able to:

1. Understand the concept of groupthink and how it affects group decision making

2. Develop a model of group decision making that includes the concepts of framing, risk seeking, and group polarization

3. Appreciate the widespread nature of decision fiascoes and the difficulty in avoiding them

4. Consider techniques to eliminate or reduce the negative outcomes of groupthink for the management of groups

Several authors (e.g., Bazerman, Giuliano & Appelman, 1984; Janis, 1972, 1982; Jervis, 1976; Staw, 1981; Tuchman, 1984) have written about groups' pursuit of disadvantageous policies after the risks of doing so have become apparent. Janis (1972, 1982) and Tuchman (1984) in particular focused on a variety of historically noteworthy decision fiascoes that moved them to speculate about why people in authority frequently act contrary to enlightened self-interest by making decisions that are likely to be counterproductive. Examples of such decisions include, among others, the American failure in Vietnam, the Kennedy administration's decision to invade Cuba at the Bay of Pigs, and the Watergate cover-up. The critical question from an analytical point of view is whether or not any pattern can be recognized from decisions of this sort, or are these simply difficult decisions that unfortunately went awry?

This paper will advance and integrate some theoretical determinants of excessive risk taking in group decision making, the consequences of which have been described as fiascoes. *Risk,* as it is used here, refers to the probability and the value of the outcomes associated with an act. A risky decision is one that rejects a certain outcome in favor of a gamble of equal or lower expected value. To qualify for inclusion in the analysis, the particular course of action pursued must have been recognized as excessively risky or ill-advised at the time the decision was made, feasible alternative courses of action must have existed, and the policy or decision in question must have been the product of group discussion. More contemporary examples include the decision to launch the space shuttle *Challenger* and the Iran-Contra affair. The examples cited in this article represent instances of defective decision making by a few policy makers in which the option pursued had only a low probability of success. Consequently, the primary focus of this paper is on the process by which a decision is reached rather than on the ultimate consequences of the decision, to which process is not always tightly coupled (Janis, 1982).

Many examples of decision fiascoes are characterized by the group's inability to change a failing policy (Staw, 1981), but other examples such as the Watergate cover-up or the launch of the space shuttle *Challenger* were choices about a specific isolated event rather than about the fate of

Source: Glen Whyte: "Groupthink Reconsidered," *Academy of Management Review,* 1989, Vol. 14, No. 1, pp. 40–56. Copyright ©1989. Reprinted by permission.

an entire course of action. It is suggested that similar theoretical mechanisms underlie risky decision making, regardless of whether the policy was clearly mistaken at the outset or whether its flaws became apparent only as commitment mounted.

Consider, for example, the decision of the Kennedy administration to invade Cuba at the Bay of Pigs in 1963. As a policy decision, the Bay of Pigs fiasco ranks among the worst blunders ever committed by an American administration. The groupthink hypothesis has been invoked as a major causal factor to explain this and other notorious examples of bad decision making (Janis, 1972, 1982). *Groupthink* refers to "a mode of thinking that people engage in when they are deeply involved in a cohesive in-group, when the members' striving for unanimity overrides their motivation to realistically appraise alternative courses of action" (Janis, 1982, p. 9). Janis identified eight main symptoms of groupthink: (a) an illusion of invulnerability, (b) an illusion of morality, (c) rationalization, (d) stereotyping, (e) self-censorship, (f) an illusion of unanimity, (g) direct pressure on dissidents, and (h) reliance upon self-appointed mindguards. By facilitating the development of shared illusions and related norms, these symptoms are used by groups to maintain esprit de corps during difficult times. The price paid to maintain group cohesiveness, however, is a decline in mental efficiency, reality testing, moral judgment, and ultimately it leads to a decline in the quality of decision making.

The groupthink hypothesis is a less-than-comprehensive explanation for why groups may make excessively risky decisions. The main theme of groupthink is concurrence seeking. But concurrence seeking generally occurs in group decision making, and it is not unique to groups that perform poorly such as President Kennedy's team in 1963. The task, after all, of a decision-making group is to produce consensus from the initial preferences of its members. Consensus, moreover, is typically obtained around preferences that are initially dominant within the group, although groupthink sheds no light on what these initial preferences might be.

This is unfortunate because knowledge of the dominant point of view of group members at the onset of discussion, combined with knowledge of the nature of the task and the alternatives being considered, can enable researchers to make accurate predictions about the ultimate choice of the group (Kerr, 1982). Increasingly, evidence suggests that the probability that various alternatives will be chosen arising from even complex decisions can be determined with a high degree of accuracy (e.g., Davis, 1980; Kerr & MacCoun, 1985). This

can be accomplished by relying on social decision schemes (Davis, 1973), which relate the initial distribution of member preferences to the group's decision. In the case of the kind of decisions under discussion, which are judgmental tasks, the best fitting social decision scheme is a majority social combinatory process (Laughlin & Adamopoulous, 1982). That is, groups in these circumstances tend to select the option supported by the majority at the outset of group discussion, and they tend to do so regardless of the presence or absence of groupthink.

An additional gap in the groupthink hypothesis is that it does not take into account some of the current research on group dynamics. One of the most intensively researched phenomena in social psychology during recent years describes the tendency for collective judgment that is the product of group discussion to magnify the dominant initial inclinations of group members. This phenomenon, group polarization, is demonstrated in the field by the excessive risk seeking observed in decision fiascoes such as the Bay of Pigs invasion. Group polarization implies that when individual members of a group are generally disposed toward risk before group discussion, it is reliable that the decision of the group will be even riskier than that of the average group member. Janis (1982) briefly acknowledged group polarization, but the phenomenon was not integrated into the theory of groupthink because such integration is dependent on knowledge of the initial preferences of group members.

This paper develops an alternative explanation of decision fiascoes and explains certain theoretical devices that address the limitations of an approach founded on group dynamics. Such theoretical devices include framing effects (Kahneman & Tversky, 1981), risk seeking in the domain of losses (Kahneman & Tversky, 1979), and group polarization (Myers & Lamm, 1976).

More specifically, it is suggested that decision fiascoes are the product of a choice that is framed to appear as one in the domain of losses. Given such a frame, risk seeking preferences usually are elicited (Kahneman & Tversky, 1979). In group decision making, pressures for uniformity will militate toward a choice that is consistent with the initial risky preferences of a majority of members. Group discussion will also amplify the extent to which the group prefers the risky option via the process of polarization. The net effect of these processes is such that groups whose members frame the choice as one between losses will evidence a normatively inappropriate preference for risk even more frequently and to a greater degree than would their average member.

The Aspiration-Level Concept

The key concept in the model of excessively risky group behavior advanced here is derived from the general notion of an aspiration level. Although this notion is not new, it has been reemphasized in recent models of risky decision-making behavior (e.g., Fishburn, 1977; Kahneman & Tversky, 1979).

The aspiration level concept is important because it helps us to understand attitudes toward risk that contradict the prevailing view about risk attitude in management science research. In the prevailing view, the aspiration level concept is ignored and decision makers are assumed to be uniformly risk averse (Payne, Laughhunn, & Crum 1980). Results from many studies plus field observations (e.g., Janis, 1982; Tuchman, 1984) indicate that such a view is inadequate (Payne et al. 1980). The consensus emerging from a variety of studies is that *risk preference* is more accurately described as a mixture of risk seeking when individuals choose between losses and *risk aversion* when individuals choose between gains.

This characterization of risk preference has been discussed in detail by Kahneman and Tversky (1979) in their explication of prospect theory. More specifically, to be risk seeking is to reject a certain outcome in favor of a gamble with equal or lower expected value. To be risk averse is to prefer a certain outcome to a gamble with an equal or greater expected value. An example of risk seeking in the domain of losses would be the rejection of a certain loss of $60 in favor of a gamble with a 60 percent chance of a $100 loss and a 40 percent chance of no loss at all. An example of risk aversion in the domain of gains would be the acceptance of a $60 gain over a gamble with a 60 percent chance of a $100 gain and a 40 percent chance of no gain whatsoever. Loss aversion is consistent with both risk seeking in the domain of losses and risk aversion in the domain of gains.

Prospect theory differs in two critical ways from the preeminent theory of decision making under risk, the expected utility model. These differences are particularly relevant to the present analysis. First, prospect theory relies on the certainty effect, which implies that a given decrease in the probability of an event will have most effect on judgment when the event is initially considered inevitable, rather than merely possible. The certainty effect promotes risk seeking in choices between losses by exaggerating the distastefulness of losses that are certain, relative to those that are less sure. When choices are made between gains, the certainty effect leads to risk aversion because the attractiveness of positive gambles is diminished relative to sure things.

Second, the manner in which people regard risky options is described in terms of what is referred to as a value function. The value function represents the relation between objectively defined gains and losses and the subjective value a person places on such gains and losses. The value function also implies that people evaluate the outcomes of decisions in terms of gains or losses relative to a subjectively appropriate reference point. Consequently, the selection of that point can have strong and predictable effects on the perceived attractiveness of outcomes because objectively identical options may be evaluated or framed as either gains or losses depending on where the reference point is set.

When a decision maker observes an event and frames a subsequent related decision as a choice between losses, he or she has moved on the value function from Point A to Point B. This is precisely the case when a decision maker is faced with a dilemma in which one option is perceived to be the acceptance of a certain loss and the other would be to possibly avoid those losses at the cost of potentially increasing them. At Point B, further losses do not loom as large in terms of value as do comparable gains. As a result, an individual at Point B is inclined to risk further losses in order to obtain possible gains. Compared to a person at Point A, a person at Point B is more likely to engage in risk-seeking behavior. This situation is graphically described in Figure 9.1 in terms of the value function.

For example, consider an entrepreneur who has lost $1,000 and now is facing a choice between a sure gain of $500 and an even chance to earn $1,000 or nothing. Unless the entrepreneur has adapted to his or her losses, the choice is likely to be considered as one between a sure loss of $500 and a 50 percent chance of a $1,000 loss, rather than as a choice between a sure gain of $500 and a 50 percent chance of a $1,000 gain. As suggested in prospect theory, the former characterization promotes the seeking of risk and a resultant preference for the gamble, whereas the latter characterization does not. A person who has not come to terms with his or her losses and, hence, who has not yet shifted his or her reference point to reflect the status quo is likely to engage in more adventurous behavior than normal (Kahneman & Tversky, 1979).

Framing effects may explain the occurrence of decision fiascoes because many of these decisions share a common structure. Decisions that lead to fiascoes are most naturally framed, whether appropriately or not, as a choice between two or more unattractive options. One option

THE VALUE FUNCTION OF
PROSPECT THEORY

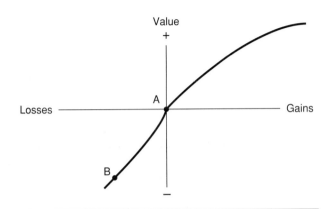

Note: from "Prospect Theory: An Analysis of Decisions under Risk"
by D. Kahneman and A. Tversky, 1979, *Econometrica, 47*, p. 279.
Copyright 1979 by *Econometrica*. Reprinted by permission.

typically involves the immediate recognition of the permanence of an aversive state of affairs. The other option or options entail potentially an even worse situation combined with the possibility that the aversive state of affairs may be avoided. That is, the reference level suggested by the problem leads to the choice being interpreted by those empowered to make it as one between losses, rather than as one between gains or between that status quo versus a potential loss or gain. Typically, the consequence of a person's framing the choice in this manner is the elicitation of risk-seeking preferences, at least at the individual level of analysis. The following will suggest why this may also be true at the group level.

Products of Group Interaction

Uniformity Pressures. The task of a decision-making group is to produce a group position from the initial preferences of its members through the sharing of beliefs, information, and arguments. Although unanimity about the choice is usually unlikely at first, social interaction provides the means by which mutual influence can lead to group convergence and, ultimately, consensus. The socially mediated change that may be necessary if consensus is to be attained can occur through either normative or informational influence (Stasser, Kerr, & Davis, 1980). Normative influence produces conformity in the group through the desire to comply with the expectations or feelings of others. Informational influence occurs when one person relies on another for information about reality. Both modes of influence usually are responsible for socially mediated change because most exchanges communicate information and expectations (Stasser et al., 1980).

The observation that a group's discussion of a problem generates pressures toward uniformity is hardly novel. These pressures result in a tendency for group members to move toward majority positions, even in the absence of external pressure to reach unanimity and independent of the correctness of the majority position (Janis, 1982). The tendency for a member's responses to conform more closely to that of the group after exposure to group discussion has been demonstrated in a variety of contexts, and it has played a significant role in many historic fiascoes. As such, uniformity pressures should form an integral part of any theoretical model that attempts to describe the group process that culminates in a decision fiasco.

The strength of the tendency for group members to conform to the view dominant in the group is contingent on several factors, but it is most powerful under two conditions (Ferrell, 1985). The first condition is uncertainty about the appropriate response, and it is characteristic of decision fiascoes. Rarely in these circumstances is there an obvious correct choice. As a result, group members will be compelled to seek information from others about the selection of the appropriate choice. The second condition that encourages individual conformity to the view of the group is the need to maintain a good relationship with other group members. The organizational context in which most decisions of broad-ranging consequence occur will ensure that this condition is also operative. An organizational setting should induce concerns about social desirability, continued membership in the group, and a desire to maintain the group as a functioning entity.

An important determinant of the direction and extent of normative and informational influence and, hence, of the likelihood that a group will adopt a given alternative is the number of proponents that the alternative has at the outset of group discussion. Assume that a five-person group is required to choose between two options. One option entails a certain loss, and the other entails a potential loss of equal expected value to the certain loss. Assume further that the five group members have been drawn randomly from a population in which 80 percent of individuals are risk seeking in the domain of losses. Such an assumption is tenable in light of previous research (e.g., Toland & O'Neil, 1984) that suggests that approximately this percentage of individuals exhibits an aversion to certain losses in relation to losses of equal or even lower expected value that are less sure.

Based on these assumptions, 94 percent of such five-person groups will contain a majority or more of members who prefer the risky option over the certain loss. Given knowledge of the group decision rule, which is the degree of consensus required for a group decision, and knowledge of the initial preferences of individual group members, it can be determined if the group will attain sufficient consensus in order to make a decision. If majority rule prevails, it is apparent that 94 percent of the groups will have satisfied this criterion at the outset and will prefer the risky option over the certain loss.

Although minority viewpoints can be influential under certain conditions, conformity to the majority view is the dominant form of behavior (Moscovici, 1984). This should particularly be the case with the kind of decision which has been associated with fiascoes in the past. This type of decision is a judgmental task of medium to high uncertainty, for which there is no objectively correct choice. There is strong support for the notion of majority process as characterizing the manner in which groups tend to attain consensus in these circumstances (Davis, 1982; Kerr, 1982). Such evidence supports the notion that reliance on a group, as opposed to an individual, decision process to resolve a judgmental task in the domain of losses will increase the frequency with which the risky option will be preferred.

Group Polarization.   In addition to pressures for uniformity, another well-established product of group interaction is relevant to the occurrence of decision fiascoes. For more than two decades it has been observed that social interaction in small groups can result in group polarization, the tendency for group discussion to enhance the point of view initially dominant within the group. More specifically, the change effect that groups have on individuals in decision-making tasks can be described as a phenomenon in which "the average post-discussion response will tend to be more extreme in the same direction as the average of the pregroup responses. . . . Note that polarization refers to an increase in the extremity of the average response of the subject population responses" (Myers & Lamm, 1976, p. 603).

In the area of risk taking, several studies employing choice dilemmas and other methodologies confirm that a group will be inclined to be more risky than its average member was before participation in group discussion, when that average member had an initial preference for risk (e.g., Burnstein, 1969; Deets & Hoyt, 1970; Doise, 1969; Runyan, 1974; Zaleska, 1974, 1976). Observations in the field also are consistent with the changes implied by the polarization effect (Myers, 1982).

Because group polarization has been well documented, attention has shifted to the processes that are responsible for its occurrence, and two related theories are most commonly advanced (Isenberg, 1986; Myers, 1982). Interpersonal comparison explanations describe polarization in the language of social motivation. Group members alter their views in a manner calculated to maintain an image of social desirability because people need to perceive of and present themselves in a favorable light. Informational influence theories, in contrast, suggest that polarization occurs because the preponderance of arguments and facts adduced during discussion tend to be supportive of the dominant initial position and will therefore reinforce it. Also operative are the biases toward information that are consistent with one's position: the fact that such attention will generate even more arguments in favor of the initially preferred position and the tendency to become committed to a position after espousing support for it (Ferrell, 1985).

It is suggested that group polarization relates to the occurrence of a decision fiasco in the following way. When a required choice is perceived to be between a sure loss and the possibility of a larger loss of equal or even lower expected value, the majority of group members are likely to initially prefer the risky option over the certain loss. Polarization is then hypothesized to occur. That is, the effect of social interaction will be to amplify the dominant initial preference for risk that characterizes individual group members. As a result, a group choice between losses should evidence an even more extreme preference for risk than the average of group members' preferences prior to discussion. The difference in risk preference may not be large, but it should be reliable (Myers & Lamm, 1976).

This increased propensity for risk in choices between a certain loss and a potential loss of equal or lower expected value will manifest itself in at least one of three ways: (a) holding constant the probability of failure if action is taken and the amount of certain loss if no action is taken, groups will be willing to risk even greater potential losses than will individuals to avoid a certain loss; (b) holding constant both the amount and probability of loss if action is taken, groups will be inclined to prefer the action option to a lower value of certain loss than will individuals; (c) holding constant both the certain loss in the event that no action is taken and the potential loss in the event that action occurs but is unsuccessful, groups will find the potential loss option to be preferable at a higher level of probability of loss if action is taken than will individuals.

Relation to Groupthink

Irving Janis (1972, 1982) laid the basis for a theory of the causes and effects of groupthink, "a collective pattern of defensive avoidance" (Janis & Mann, 1977, p. 129). Janis described several shared characteristics of cohesive decision-making groups that have been responsible for some policy debacles. The following quotation from Janis and Mann (1977, p. 130) is a good example.

> Many historic fiascoes can be traced to defective policy making on the part of government leaders who receive social support from their in-group of advisors. A series of historic fiascoes by Janis (1972) suggests that the following four groups of policy advisors, like Kimmel's in-group of naval commanders, were dominated by concurrence seeking or groupthink and displayed characteristic symptoms of defensive avoidance: (1) Neville Chamberlain's inner circle, whose members supported the policy of appeasement of Hitler during 1937 and 1938, despite repeated warnings and events that it would have adverse consequences; (2) President Truman's advisory group, whose members supported the decision to escalate the war in North Korea despite firm warnings by the Chinese Communist government that U.S. entry into North Korea would be met with armed resistance from the Chinese; (3) President Kennedy's inner circle, whose members supported the decision to launch the Bay of Pigs invasion of Cuba despite the availability of information indicating that it would be an unsuccessful venture and would damage U.S. relations with other countries; (4) President Johnson's close advisors, who supported the decision to escalate the war in Vietnam despite intelligence reports and other information indicating that this course of action would not defeat the Vietcong or the North Vietnamese and would entail unfavor-
> able political consequences within the United States. All these groupthink dominated groups were characterized by strong pressures toward uniformity, which inclined their members to avoid raising controversial issues, questioning weak arguments, or calling a halt to soft-headed thinking.

There also is evidence that groupthink was at work in the Nixon entourage, which was responsible for the Watergate cover-up, although there is some question of the cohesiveness of this group (Janis, 1982).

To add a contemporary flavor to the discussion, consider the tragedy of the space shuttle *Challenger*. This situation was the product of a flawed decision as much as it was a failure of technology. The pressures on the National Aeronautics and Space Administration (NASA) to launch the space shuttle at the earliest opportunity were intense, despite evidence that this course of action was inadvisable. A decision to delay the launch was undesirable from NASA's perspective because of the impact it would have on political and public support for the program. In contrast, a successful launch would have appeased the public and the politicians alike, and it would have amounted to another major achievement. NASA engineers claimed that pressure to launch was so intense that authorities routinely dismissed potentially lethal hazards as acceptable risks, reducing such bureaucratic safeguards as the flight readiness review to a meaningless exercise (McConnell, 1987).

Strong pressures for uniformity also characterize the process surrounding the flawed decisions of the Reagan administration to exchange arms for hostages with Iran and to continue commitment to the Nicaraguan Contras in the face of several congressional amendments limiting or banning aid. For example, the Tower Commission report censured Secretary of State Shultz and Defense Secretary Weinberger for not presenting their objections to the arms-for-hostages deal with a sufficient degree of vigor. Also, President Reagan's former national security advisor Robert McFarlane testified before the joint congressional panel investigating the arms-for-hostages deal and the diversion of funds to the Contras that he had reservations about the policies of the Reagan administration. McFarlane, however, said he erred in "not having the guts to stand up and tell the President that. . . . Because if I'd done that, [CIA Director] Bill Casey, [former U.N. ambassador] Jeanne Kirkpatrick, and [Defense Secretary] Cap Weinberger would have said, 'I was some kind of commie, you know'" ("It Was," 1987, p. 19).

The foregoing examples can be described with some degree of accuracy as situations in which groups were faced with a negative deviation from a neutral reference point or, in other words, there would be a sure loss unless action was taken. That is, the groups were at Point B on the value function illustrated in Figure 9.1. In some cases, as in the example of American escalation in the Vietnam War, the U.S. government was responsible for finding itself in this situation. Not all of the deviations from the neutral reference point, however, were attributable to the action of the group that responded to the situation with a decision fiasco. For example, the U.S. government was not directly responsible for the appearance of Castro's regime on America's doorstep. Nor is it easy to characterize the negative deviation from the neutral reference level in terms of resources. For example, the existence of Castro's government did not directly lead to the incurring of costs by the Kennedy administration. Yet the appearance of a communist regime so close to the United States was perceived by anticommunist American policy makers as a decrease in the level of U.S. national security to which they were unwilling or unable to adapt.

Similarly, the situation faced by Nixon's group subsequent to the discovery of the Watergate burglary was such that the likelihood of their escaping detection for various illegal activities had been decreased to an intolerably low level. Their choices were admitting responsibility for the burglary of the Watergate building that was conducted in order to plant eavesdropping equipment in the national headquarters of the Democratic party or fabricating an illegal cover-up. A cover-up entailed the possibility of success, but it also entailed additional grievous consequences in the event of its probable failure.

The decision to launch the *Challenger* also can be described as a choice in the domain of losses. To delay the launch an additional time entailed certain unfortunate consequences for the space shuttle program. Those consequences, however, could possibly have been avoided by the decision to launch, although such a choice entailed additional risks and, hence, additional potential losses.

Understandably, the arms-for-hostages deal also was perceived by those who made it as the product of a choice between losses. The status quo—American nationals held by terrorist groups—was a certain loss to which it would be difficult to adapt. The striking of an arms deal with Iran created the possibility that those losses could be averted, although it was likely that the deal would fail and add to American woes. An important additional element in the trade was also consistent with the view that U.S. decision makers adopted a decision frame for this act consistent with a choice in the domain of losses. The strategic importance of Iran led U.S. policy makers to attempt to reestab-

lish American influence in Iran and "to restore something resembling normal relations with that country" (Tower, Muskie, & Scowcroft, 1987, p. B1).

Finally, consider the decision of the Reagan administration to continue to support the Nicaraguan Contras in the face of a congressional ban on such activity. The administration was attempting to maintain the Contras during a period in which aid was denied by Congress, even though the program of support might eventually have been judged illegal. Apparently, the collapse of the Contra movement was an aversive state of affairs to which White House decision makers were unwilling or unable to adapt. According to President Reagan, without U.S. support for the Contras, the Soviets would gain a dangerous toehold in Central America. Shortly after Congress prohibited aid to the Contras in April, 1985, President Reagan described his congressional opponents as "voting to have a totalitarian Marxist-Leninist government here in the Americas, and there's no way for them to disguise it. So, we're not going to give up" (Hamilton & Inouye, 1987, p. 48). The preferred alternative was the development of a covert program to encourage aid for the Contras which, if successful, would sustain the Contras until additional congressional funding could be obtained. If discovered, however, such activity could lead to indictments for participation in a broad conspiracy to evade the restrictions on military aid, and it could also imperil future congressional support for the Contras. In testimony before the Congressional Committee, former national security adviser Rear Admiral John Poindexter stated: "Very frankly, we were willing to take some risks in order to keep the Contras alive . . . until we could eventually win the legislative battle" (Hamilton & Inouye, 1987, p. 42).

More generally, the initial events that produced the loss or the deviation from the neutral reference point in the preceding examples produced a decision frame for subsequent, related decisions that can be roughly described as follows. One possible subsequent choice becomes the acceptance of losses, whether they are in terms of wasted resources, a decrease in the level of national security, or the admittance of complicity in illegal activity. The other choice, to put it in the boldest relief possible, is to engage in risky behavior. Through such behavior a group may regain what has been lost in the past and return to the neutral reference point. However, such behavior also includes the possibility of exacerbating the situation and of further movement away from the neutral reference point. When decision makers are presented with a decision frame of this description, there is substantial empirical support in laboratory studies employing the method of hypothetical and real choices that the risky option will be preferred, even when it is normatively unacceptable to do so (Kahneman & Tversky, 1979, 1984). In addition, the polarizing effect of group discussion will tend to push the group in the direction of even greater risk and, hence, frequently even greater propensity for error. Figure 8.2 diagrams the relationships among the processes described.

Discussion

Evidence to support the foregoing analysis is far from complete, and it is subject to multiple interpretations. Yet evidence also suggests that for each of the fiascoes discussed by Janis, the frame adopted by decision makers led them to perceive their decision as between a certain loss and potentially greater losses. For example, a major reason for the Bay of Pigs invasion that was offered by informed insiders and the president was the political costs of doing nothing (Schlesinger, 1965). In addition, Truman ran the significant risk of war with Communist China by crossing the 38th parallel into North Korea in part because he favored unification of North and South Korea (Neustadt, 1976). In doing that, the decision to stop at the border amounted to the acceptance of a certain loss. The greater danger of war with China was less than certain and as a result more attractive than accepting the failure of the unification policy.

The failure to fortify the defenses at Pearl Harbor was also most likely seen as the avoidance of certain losses at the expense of potentially greater losses. Kimmel and his group of advisers often discussed at length whether to go on full alert, but they were keenly aware that an alert could only have been put into effect "at the cost of interrupting ongoing training programs and the high priority mission of supplying personnel and equipment to United States outposts close to Japan" (Janis, 1982). The option the group elected to pursue contained "less probable, but more damaging eventualities" (Wohlsetter, 1962).

As in other cases there has been a lack of well-authenticated details about the way the president and his inner circle carried out their decision-making process leading to the escalation of the Vietnam War. However, there has been some support for the view that American policy makers perceived their choice to be in the domain of losses and, hence, were engaged in loss aversion. For example, Ellsberg (1971) argued that President Johnson and his advisers regarded their motions not as "last steps" but

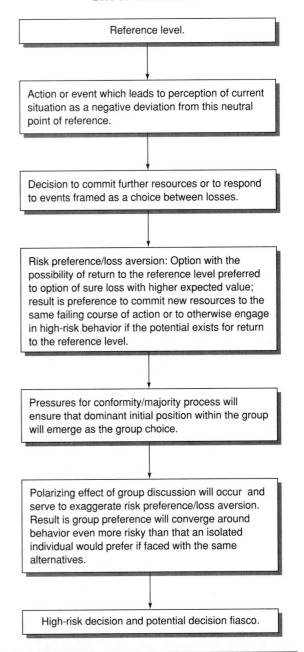

FIGURE 9.2

Proposed Structure of a High-Risk Group Decision

Reference level.

Action or event which leads to perception of current situation as a negative deviation from this neutral point of reference.

Decision to commit further resources or to respond to events framed as a choice between losses.

Risk preference/loss aversion: Option with the possibility of return to the reference level preferred to option of sure loss with higher expected value; result is preference to commit new resources to the same failing course of action or to otherwise engage in high-risk behavior if the potential exists for return to the reference level.

Pressures for conformity/majority process will ensure that dominant initial position within the group will emerge as the group choice.

Polarizing effect of group discussion will occur and serve to exaggerate risk preference/loss aversion. Result is group preference will converge around behavior even more risky than that an isolated individual would prefer if faced with the same alternatives.

High-risk decision and potential decision fiasco.

rather as "holding actions, adequate to avoid defeat in the short run but long shots so far as ultimate success was concerned" (p. 257).

British Prime Minister Neville Chamberlain chose the path of appeasement in response to Hitler's demands, thereby facilitating the outbreak of world war. The decision to agree to Hitler's demands also was the product of a choice in the domain of losses. Chamberlain's private letters and diaries contain several references to his view that the high-risk appeasement policy was chosen in order to save Britain from the perils of otherwise certain war (Janis, 1982).

Finally, it is likely that the Watergate cover-up, undertaken by the White House to prevent knowledge of the link between criminal activities and the Committee to Reelect the President, was the product of a decision framed to appear as a choice in the domain of losses. Nixon was involved in the cover-up once the arrests were made in the Watergate burglary, and he was clear in discussions with his aides that necessary steps should be taken to avoid otherwise certain damage to his reelection campaign (Janis, 1982).

In support of the analysis offered here, note that a variety of researchers have confirmed that the alternative framing of objectively identical decisions can elicit different preferences and can affect attitudes toward risk (e.g., Bazerman, 1983; Levin, Johnson, Russo, & Deldin, 1985; McNeil, Pauker, Sox, & Tversky, 1982; Neale, Huber, & Northcraft, 1987; Schelling, 1981; Slovic, Fischoff, & Lichtenstein, 1982; Tversky & Kahneman, 1981, 1986). Also, risk seeking in choices between losses, which is suggested to underlie the occurrence of decision fiascoes, is a robust form of behavior, and this is consistent with the findings of several social scientists (e.g., Fishburn & Kochenberger, 1979; Hershey & Schoemaker, 1980; Payne et al., 1980; Slovic et al., 1982). This pattern of preference has been observed in choices involving other than financial outcomes, including the duration of pain (Eraker & Sox, 1981) and the loss of human life (Fischoff, 1983; Tversky, 1977). Although it is not possible to say whether it is wrong to seek risk when choosing between losses, it is evident that such a preference, particularly when exacerbated by the polarizing effect of group discussion, often will lead to undesirable outcomes.

Prospect theory was founded on people's reactions to monetary outcomes of varying probabilities, yet this paper advocates the application of prospect theory to situations in which outcomes are not necessarily quantitative and in which the probabilities associated with various outcomes are less than certain. In this regard, Kahneman and Tversky commented (1979, p. 288):

[Prospect] theory is readily applicable to choices involving other attributes [than monetary outcomes], e.g., quality of life or the number of lives that could be lost or saved as a consequence of a policy decision. The main properties of the proposed value function for money should apply to other attributes as well. In particular, we expect outcomes to be coded as gains or losses, relative to a neutral reference point, and losses to loom larger than gains. The theory can also be extended to the typical situation of choice, where the probabilities of outcomes are not explicitly given. In such situations, decision weights must be attached to particular events rather than to stated probabilities, but they are expected to exhibit the essential properties that were ascribed to the weighting function.

An assumption implicit in this analysis is that decision makers often will share a common frame when making a particular decision. Evidence suggests that people tend to rely upon the reference level suggested or implied by the statement of the problem in order to evaluate options (Kahneman & Tversky, 1984; McNeil et al., 1982; Thaler, 1980). Additional factors thought to influence framing include norms, habits, and expectations (Tversky & Kahneman, 1986). Another assumption contained in this analysis for which there is support is that groups will amplify the behavioral tendencies on which prospect theory is founded (McGuire, Kiesler, & Siegel, 1987). These results parallel the findings that group judgments are even more susceptible to the preference reversal phenomenon than those of individuals (Slovic & Lichtenstein, 1983).

Regarding the malady of groupthink, prospect polarization is relevant to, and has predictive utility for, the notion of a concurrence-seeking tendency. Although groupthink posits that such a tendency exists, it is not possible to discern the option toward which such a tendency will be directed, except to say that it will move in the direction of the initial majority. Yet groupthink provides no insight into what that initial majority position will be. Prospect theory implies, however, that when the choice facing a group is framed as one in the domain of losses, a majority of group members will prefer the risky option. It is then reasonable to suggest by reliance on the notions of group polarization and pressures for uniformity that in a choice between losses, concurrence seeking will move most easily toward risk taking. In other words, consensus will be most easily maintainable in the direction of risk and away from the acceptance of a certain loss.

On the one hand, prospect polarization provides leverage with which to discern and predict what the dominant initial preference within the group will be and what will happen to it during the course of group interaction. Groupthink, on the other hand, illuminates the means by which the convergence of the stated views of group members occurs. Using groupthink to explain policy debacles provides only a partial explanation. Although the tendency of group members to conform and the convergence of group members' views around an option can be explained by groupthink, the theory sheds no light on why the group view coalesces around the particular policy option that it does. Prospect polarization can be used to fill this void in the groupthink hypothesis.

Group polarization implies that group pressures toward uniformity will be in the direction of the policy option that is somewhat more extreme than the point of view initially dominant within the group. This point of view can in turn be predicted by knowledge of the decision frame adopted by decision makers. In the context of a choice in the domain of losses and as a result of group interaction, conditions favorable to the occurrence of the distinct processes of group convergence around a high-risk option and group polarization will be established. Unless the tendencies of groups to succumb to these separate and subtle processes are overcome, for example, by systematically approaching the decision-making task, it is likely that consensus around a risky choice will be attained. It is also likely that the option chosen will be even riskier than the choice of an individual acting in isolation and facing the identical situation.

If an option is initially preferred by a majority in a group of decision makers and group discussion serves to heighten that preference, then it is highly likely that this option will be chosen (Stasser et al., 1980). Groupthink symptoms, when they exist, should serve to harden the already existing resolve of individuals in the group to embark upon this initially preferred course of action, regardless of whether or not it makes good sense to do so. Further, groupthink may have an effect by limiting the number of ways available for group members to frame the subject of the decision. But according to this analysis, groupthink is not the proximate cause of any given decision fiasco. That role is accorded to the decision frame initially adopted by decision makers. If we think about the Bay of Pigs invasion, the Watergate cover-up, American involvement in the Vietnam War, or the *Challenger* disaster, it becomes increasingly clear that "the adoption of a decision frame is an ethically significant act" (Kahneman & Tversky, 1981, p. 458).

Implications

Several implications flow from the approach to decision fiascoes adopted here. These implications address the results of the few studies designed to test the groupthink model, and they suggest alternative routes by which to proceed with theory building and future research.

Previous researchers have attempted to examine the effect of those antecedent conditions that were argued by Janis to be necessary for the occurrence of groupthink. Although several antecedent conditions were identified, only group cohesiveness and leader behavior are group-level constraints that identify groupthink as a group, rather than an individual, phenomenon (Leana, 1985). Several studies have found that cohesiveness is not an important antecedent condition of groupthink. Directive leader behavior, however, significantly influences the frequency of groupthink symptoms (Courtwright, 1978; Flowers, 1977; Leana, 1985). These findings are at variance with the groupthink model, but they are consistent with an emphasis on the manner in which the problem is framed at the outset of group discussion, either as a result of directive leadership practices or otherwise.

More generally, this paper links in a theoretically coherent way concepts from cognitive and social psychology and then attempts to demonstrate their relevance for important real-life events. Several testable hypotheses also can be generated from the foregoing analysis of decision fiascoes. Most fundamental, such an approach implies that groups, as well as individuals, will be subject to framing effects. In addition, groups, as well as individuals, should be loss averse, which leads to risk-seeking choices in the domain of losses. Furthermore, groups should be subject to framing effects, and they should manifest a tendency to seek risk in the domain of losses more frequently, and to a greater degree, than individuals. That is, choices made in a social context should be more pronounced, more narrowly distributed, and more consistent with prospect theory than choices made by individuals acting in isolation. A test of prospect theory at the group level of analysis is an important first step in testing the validity of the model advocated here.

Further research is also required on the extent to which the value function is readily applicable to choices that are more than unidimensional. Most policy decisions of consequence do not simply involve choices in which either money or lives may be lost, but involve a variety of potential costs and benefits. What, for example, does the value function look like when decision makers are simultaneously concerned about several issues such as preserving national security, maximizing global influence, and balancing domestic political concerns? Most complex choices are multidimensional. In these circumstances, do decision makers choose as if they possess an aggregate value function, or do they respond to the value function involving that attribute of the situation that is most salient for them? The answer is not yet clear.

Another area that requires attention is derived from the concern in prospect theory with decision making under risk. Prospect theory was based on individual responses to gambles, in which the probabilities and potential losses and gains were precisely specified. Most decisions, however, are made under conditions of uncertainty, in which the amounts at risk and the probabilities of loss or gain are not explicit. Theoretically, there is no reason why prospect theory cannot be extended to the more typical situation of choice under conditions of uncertainty. More compelling would be empirical evidence, currently lacking, which demonstrates this. There is, however, some data suggesting that in the domain of losses, choices under risk and under uncertainty do not differ (Cohen, Jaffray, & Said, 1987).

Further issues requiring investigation are why and how the neutral reference level of prospect theory changes over time to become more consistent with the objective characteristics of the situation. In other words, what determines which reference level will be used to evaluate the outcomes of choice? In some cases, the reference level is a state to which one is accustomed, although it is possible for the reference level to be determined by aspirations (Tversky & Kahneman, 1981). Factors such as the way the problem is presented, personal and cultural values, expectations, and leader behavior also influence the framing of decisions, yet the precise roles of these variables and the ways in which they interact are not well understood. Absent from prospect theory is a formal theory of framing, which makes it difficult to predict the type of frame that decision makers will adopt in a given situation.

Although laboratory studies may be the best way to address some of these issues, the full range of behavioral research methods, including comparative case studies and field experiments in natural settings, could be used to further refine and test the theoretical position advanced here. It is not enough to tailor individual-level explanations for group phenomena to take into account the social context. Ultimately, such explanations must be applicable in the presence of structural attributes of organizations designed to minimize individual limitations in information-processing capability.

In a different vein, there are a number of ways to reduce the occurrence of decision fiascoes. Many of these suggestions, such as those designed to counteract defensive avoidance (Janis & Mann, 1977) and those used to reduce group insularity and directive leadership practices (Janis, 1982), are appropriate regardless of whether or not cognitive or motivational explanations are emphasized. An approach based on prospect theory, however, implies a fundamentally different approach to reduce the incidence of poor decision making. One general hypothesis relates to the effects of training, and it can be stated as follows: Knowledge about the causes and consequences of framing effects will facilitate high quality decision making. More specifically, decision makers should be encouraged to frame a decision problem in a variety of ways in order to investigate the stability of preferences. Perhaps most useful, decision makers should be instructed not to evaluate decision problems in terms of gains or losses from a neutral reference point, as they are inclined to do. Instead, they should be taught to formulate a decision problem in terms of final states or assets, as business students are encouraged to do (Kahneman & Tversky, 1984). Whether any of these strategies will be effective when employed in real decision-making groups faced with important problems has yet to be empirically validated.

The explanation advanced here for the pursuit of policies that have a high risk of failure is not meant to be confined to military or political decisions. It is equally applicable to business decision making, and it is consistent with the previously advanced view (e.g., Singh, 1986) that firms that are performing below target or reference level are more likely to pursue risky options than those that are not (Fiegenbaum & Thomas, 1988). Naturally, the result of the pursuit of such policies is failure in the majority of cases, combined with scattered success.

Conclusion

This article has argued that groupthink, although relevant, is an incomplete explanation for the occurrence of decision fiascoes. Reliance upon prospect polarization to understand excessive risk seeking in group decision making implies that egregious errors in group judgment are not solely the product of group dynamics. Rather, they also are the product of the way group members frame decisions and choose between alternatives. A theory of decision fiascoes, and a theory of choice in general, cannot be descriptively adequate and at the same time ignore the effects of the framing of decisions.

REFERENCES

Abelson, R. P., & Levi, A. (1986) Decision making and decision theory. In G. Lindzey & E. Aronson (Eds.), *The handbook of social psychology* (3rd ed., pp. 231–309). New York: Random House.

Bazerman, M. (1983) Negotiator judgment. *American Behavioral Scientist,* 27, 211–228.

Bazerman, M., Guiliano, T., & Appelman, A. (1984) Escalation of commitment in individual and group decision making. *Organizational Behavior and Human Performance,* 33, 141–152.

Burnstein, E. (1969) An analysis of group decisions involving risk ("The risky shift"). *Human Relations,* 22, 381–395.

Cohen, M., Jaffray, J., & Said, T. (1987) Experimental comparisons of individual behavior under uncertainty for gains and for losses. *Organizational Behavior and Human Decision Processes,* 39, 1–22.

Courtwright, J. (1978) A laboratory investigation of groupthink. *Communications Monographs,* 45, 229–246.

Davis, J. (1973) Group decision and social interaction: A theory of social decision schemes. *Psychological Review,* 80, 97–125.

Davis, J. (1980) Group decisions and procedural justice. In M. Fishbein (Ed.), *Progress in social psychology* (pp. 98–125). Hillsdale, NJ: Erlbaum.

Davis, J. (1982) Social interaction as a combinational process in group decision making. In H. Brandstatter, J. Davis, & G. Stocker-Kreichgauer (Eds.), *Group decision making* (pp. 27–58). New York: Academic Press.

Deets, M., & Hoyt, G. (1970) Variance preferences and variance shifts in group investment decisions. *Organizational Behavior and Human Performance,* 5, 378–386.

Doise, W. (1969) Jugement collectif et prise de risque des petits groups [Risk taking in small group decision making]. *Psychologie Francaise,* 14, 87–95.

Ellsberg, D. (1971) The quagmire myth and the stalemate machine. *Public Policy,* 19, 217–274.

Eraker, S. E., & Sox, H. C. (1981) Assessment of patients' preferences for therapeutic outcomes. *Medical Decision Making,* 1, 29–39.

Ferrell, W. (1985) Combining individual judgments. In G. Wright (Ed.), *Behavioral decision making* (pp. 111–145). New York: Plenum Press.

Fiegenbaum, A., & Thomas, H. (1988) Attitudes toward risk and the risk return paradox: Prospect theory explanations. *Academy of Management Journal,* 31, 86–106.

Fischoff, B. (1983) Predicting frames. *Journal of Experimental Psychology: Learning, Memory, and Cognition,* 9, 103–116.

Fishburn, P. C. (1977) Mean-risk analysis with risk associated with below target returns. *American Economic Review,* 67, 116–126.

Fishburn, P. C., & Kochenberger, G. A. (1979) Two piece Von Newmann–Morgenstern utility functions. *Decision Sciences,* 10, 503–518.

Flowers, M. (1977) A laboratory test of some implications of Janis's groupthink hypothesis. *Journal of Personality and Social Psychology,* 1, 288–299.

Hamilton, L., & Inouye, D. (1987) *Report of the Congressional Committees Investigating the Iran-Contra Affairs* (H. Rept. No. 100–433) Washington, DC: Government Printing Office.

Hershey, J. C., & Schoemaker, P. (1980) Risk taking and problem context in the domain of losses: An expected utility analysis. *Journal of Risk and Insurance,* 47, 111–132.

Isenberg, D. (1986) Group polarization: A critical review and meta-analysis. *Journal of Personality and Social Psychology,* 50, 1141–1151.

It was my idea—Dropping his didn't know defense, Reagan takes credit. (1987, May 25) *Newsweek,* pp. 16–19.

Janis, I. L. (1972) *Victims of groupthink.* Boston: Houghton Mifflin.

Janis, I. L. (1982) *Groupthink.* Boston: Houghton Mifflin.

Janis, I. L., & Mann, L. (1977) *Decision making: A psychological analysis of conflict, choice, and commitment.* New York: Free Press.

Jervis, R. (1976) *Perception and misperception in international politics.* Princeton: Princeton University Press.

Kahneman, D., & Tversky, A. (1979) Prospect theory: An analysis of decisions under risk. *Econometrica,* 47, 263–291.

Kahneman, D., & Tversky, A. (1981) The framing of decisions and the psychology of choice. *Science,* 211, 453–458.

Kahneman, D., & Tversky, A. (1984) Choices, values, and frames. *American Psychologist,* 39, 341–350.

Kerr, N. (1982) Social transition schemes: Model, method and applications. In H. Brandstatter, J. Davis, & G. Stocker-Kreichgauer (Eds.), *Group decision making* (pp. 59–79). London: Academic Press.

Kerr, N., & MacCoun, R. (1985) The effects of jury size and polling method on the process and product of jury deliberation. *Journal of Personality and Social Psychology,* 48, 349–363.

Laughlin, P., & Adamopoulos, J. (1982) Social decision schemes on intellective tasks. In H. Brandstatter, J. Davis, & G. Stocker-Kreichgauer (Eds.), *Group decision making* (pp. 81–94). London: Academic Press.

Leana, C. (1985) A partial test of Janis' groupthink model: Effects of group cohesiveness and leader behavior on defective decision making. *Journal of Management,* 11(1), 5–17.

Levin, I., Johnson, R., Russo, C., & Deldin, P. (1985) Framing effects in judgment tasks with varying amounts of information. *Organizational Behavior and Human Decision Processes,* 36, 362–377.

McConnell, M. (1987) *Challenger: A major malfunction.* New York: Doubleday.

McGuire, T., Kiesler, S., & Siegel, J. (1987) Group and computer mediated discussion effects in risk decision making. *Journal of Personality and Social Psychology,* 52, 917–930.

McNeil, B., Pauker, S., Sox, H., & Tversky, A. (1982) On the elicitation of preferences for alternative therapies. *New England Journal of Medicine,* 306, 1259–1262.

Moscovici, S. (1984) Social influence and conformity. In G. Lindzey & E. Aronson (Eds.), *The handbook of social psychology* (3rd ed., pp. 347–412). New York: Random House.

Myers, D. (1982) Polarizing effects of social interaction. In H. Brandstatter, J. Davis, & G. Stocker-Kreichgauer (Eds.), *Group decision making* (pp. 125–161). London: Academic Press.

Myers, D. G., & Lamm, H. (1976) The group polarization phenomenon. *Psychological Bulletin,* 83, 602–627.

Neale, M., Huber, V., & Northcraft, G. (1987) The framing of negotiations: Contextual versus task frames. *Organizational Behavior and Human Decision Processes,* 39, 228–241.

Neustadt, R. (1976) *Presidential power: The politics of leadership with reflections on Johnson and Nixon.* New York: Wiley.

Payne, J. W., Laughhunn, D. J., & Crum, R. (1980) Translation of gambles and aspiration level effects in risky choice behavior. *Management Science,* 26, 1039–1060.

Runyan, D. (1974) The group risky shift effect as a function of emotional bonds, actual consequences, and extent of responsibility. *Journal of Personality and Social Psychology,* 27, 297–300.

Schelling, T. (1981) Economic reasoning and the ethics of policy. *Public Interest,* 63, 37–61.

Schlesinger, A. (1965) *A thousand days.* Boston: Houghton Mifflin.

Singh, J. V. (1986) Performance, slack, and risk taking in organizational decision making. *Academy of Management Journal,* 29, 562–585.

Slovic, P., Fischoff, B., & Lichtenstein, S. (1982) Response made, framing and information processing effects in risk assessment. In R. Hogarth (Ed.), *New directions for methodology of social and behavioral science: Question framing and response consistency* (pp. 21–36). San Francisco: Jossey Bass.

Slovic, P., & Lichtenstein, S. (1983) Preference reversals: A broader perspective. *American Economic Review,* 73, 596–605.

Stasser, G., Kerr, N. L., & Davis, J. H. (1980) Influence processes in decision making groups: A modeling approach. In P. B. Paulus (Ed.), *Psychology of group influence* (pp. 431–477). Hillsdale, NJ: Erlbaum.

Staw, B. (1981) The escalation of commitment to a course of action. *Academy of Management Review,* 6, 577–587.

Thaler, R. (1980) Toward a positive theory of consumer choice. *Journal of Economic Behavior and Organization,* 1, 39–60.

Toland, A., & O'Neill, P. (1983) A test of prospect theory. *Journal of Economic Behavior and Organization,* 4, 53–56.

Tower, J., Muski, E., & Scowcroft, B. (1987). *Report of the President's Special Review Board.* Washington, DC: Government Printing Office.

Tuchman, B. (1984) *The march of folly.* New York: Knopf.

Tversky, A. (1977) On the elicitation of preferences: Descriptive and prescriptive considerations. In D. Bell, R. Kenney, & H. Raiffa (Eds.), *Conflicting objectives in decisions* (pp. 209–222). New York: Wiley.

Tversky, A., & Kahneman, D. (1981) The framing of decisions and the psychology of choice. *Science,* 211, 453–458.

Tversky, A., & Kahneman, D. (1986) Rational choice and the framing of decisions. *Journal of Business,* 59, S251–S278.

Wohlsetter, R. (1962) *Pearl Harbor: Warning and decision.* Stanford: Stanford University Press.

Zaleska, M. (1974) The effects of discussion on group and individual choices among bets. *European Journal of Social Psychology,* 4, 229–250.

Zaleska, M. (1976) Majority influence on group choices among bets. *Journal of Personality and Social Psychology,* 33, 8–19.

DISCUSSION QUESTIONS

1. Define groupthink.

2. What are some flaws in the groupthink hypothesis?

3. Explain the concept "group polarization" and how it affects risky group decision making.

4. How does prospect theory differ from expected utility models of decision making?

5. According to Whyte, how are most fiasco-related decisions framed?

6. Analyze a recent group decision-making episode and determine if it can be explained by either Janis's model of groupthink or

Whyte's revision. Examples of recent decisions are: the Bush campaign's decision to emphasize family values instead of the economy, the Reagan administration's policy of deregulation, and the decision making that contributed to the decline of IBM and General Motors.

7.   What practical actions can a manager or other group member take to avoid making collective decisions that result in fiascoes?

Participation in Decision Making: When Should It Be Used?

Edwin A. Locke,
David M. Schweiger, and
Gary P. Latham

LEARNING OBJECTIVES

After reading "Participation in Decision Making: When Should It Be Used?" by Locke, Schweiger, and Latham, students will be able to:

1. Critique or support arguments for widespread participation in decision making

2. Understand Locke, Schweiger, and Latham's theory for deciding when participation is appropriate

3. Distinguish between authoritative and participative decision making

4. Develop action principles for knowing under what circumstances participation in decision making will advance organizational goals

For the last few decades, prominent organizational theorists such as Chris Argyris, Warren Bennis, and Rensis Likert have argued that employee participation in decision making is crucial for attaining employee commitment, job satisfaction, and productivity. Discussions of Japanese management techniques such as William Ouchi's *Theory Z* also give participation a prominent role. Indeed, behavioral scientist Marshall Sashkin feels so strongly about the value of participation that he has added another dimension to it. In a recent article in *Organizational Dynamics* (Spring 1984), Sashkin asserts that employee participation is not only effective but that its use by management is an ethical imperative.

But these views of participation fly in the face of extensive research by many different investigators and the experience of top executives, and could lead executives to make serious managerial errors. In this article, we will show that participation is not an ethical imperative but simply a managerial technique that is appropriate only in certain situations. In some circumstances, participation can actually lead to lower employee satisfaction and productivity. In such cases it would be unethical behavior toward both stockholders and employees for managers to use employee participation. In short, we will show that participation is a tool, not a panacea.

Let us be clear about what we mean by *participation*. We mean joint decision making, either by a manager and one employee or a manager and a group of employees. Participation should be clearly distinguished from authoritative decision making, where bosses make decisions on their own, and from delegation, where the employee or employees make the decision alone.

What Does the Research Show?

Let us consider first the studies that Sashkin cites to support the effectiveness of participation. He starts with the now famous research conducted at Western Electric's Hawthorne plant in the late 1930s. At least seven different changes were introduced in these experiments, namely: (1) a simpler, less varied task; (2) a new incentive system (more closely geared to individual effort); (3) more considerate, participative supervision; (4) the use of rest pauses; (5) reduced work hours; (6) improved feedback; and (7) transfer of employees in and out of the experimental group. Given the large number of changes made and the fact that there was no control group to compare with the experimental group, it is impossible for us or Sashkin to know which of the above changes had a direct effect on productivity.

Despite the poor design of the Hawthorne studies, two investigators, Richard Franke and James Kaul, tried

Source: Edwin A. Locke, David M. Schweiger, and Gary P. Latham, "Participation in Decision Making: When Should It Be Used?" *Organizational Dynamics,* 14(3), pp. 65–79, 1986. Reprinted by permission.

251

several years ago to identify cause-effect relationships in
the Hawthorne data by using sophisticated statistical techniques. They concluded that (1) the single biggest boost to
productivity occurred when two less-motivated employees
were removed by management from one work group and
replaced by two more highly motivated employees; (2) the
second biggest source of productivity improvement was
caused by the economic effects of the depression (fear of
job loss); (3) the third most potent factor was the introduction of rest pauses; and (4) the fourth significant factor
was the use of improved incentives. *No productivity increase
could be attributed directly to employee participation.* Contrary to popular belief, there was in fact no *separate* participation intervention divorced from other changes in the
Hawthorne studies.

Similarly, in the well-known Harwood-Weldon studies, nine different changes were introduced. These
included (1) implementing significant technical and production-process improvements; (2) choosing new
employees by using validated tests; (3) improving the
training program; (4) coaching poor performers; (5) firing
low producers and/or those with poor attendance; (6)
changing work standards in several departments; (7)
introducing incentive pay in some departments; (8)
improving feedback systems; and (9) training managers
and supervisors in participation. As with the Hawthorne
studies, no definite conclusions can be drawn about the
effect of any one of these factors.

In a third study cited by Sashkin, Keithley Instruments implemented a participative job-redesign program.
Increases in productivity occurred, but it is not clear
whether they resulted from job enrichment, employee participation, or both.

While the above studies indicated that behavioral science interventions in various combinations can improve
productivity, they did not isolate the effects of employee
participation (or any other factors) per se.

Participation and Performance

The Hawthorne and Harwood studies, however, stimulated many more well-designed experiments that made it
possible to isolate the effectiveness of participation in
achieving higher productivity as such. Fifty of these studies (all that they could find) have been compiled and analyzed by David Schweiger and Carrie Leana. Studies that

looked specifically at participation in setting goals were
separated from studies that looked at the effects of participation in other types of decision making (for example,
work methods, rest periods, or incentive plans). Typically,
effects of job changes or decisions introduced participatively were compared with effects of similar changes introduced authoritatively (without participation). The results
are shown in Exhibit 9.1.

The data show that there is no clear tendency for
participation to result in higher productivity than
authoritative decision making. Although 26% of the
studies of participation in decision making found that
participation led to higher productivity than did authoritative methods, another 26% found that participation
led to lower productivity. And a plurality (49%) found
that the results either were the same in both cases or
depended on certain contingencies (subordinate knowledge, for instance).

Results of studies of participation in goal setting were
similar. Most of these studies were done by Gary Latham
and his colleagues. Typically, employee participation in
goal setting did not lead to better results than when managers simply assigned goals.

Several years ago Edwin Locke and his colleagues
assessed actual productivity gains attributable to such
motivational techniques as employee participation, monetary incentives, goal setting, and job enrichment. Using
only findings from rigorously conducted research in
organizational settings, the data showed participation
contributed least to gains in productivity. In 16 studies,
the median improvement in productivity was only 0.5%
with a range of –24% to +47%. Increases occurred in
only 50% of the studies, and in only 25% of the studies
did these increases amount to 10% or more. In contrast,
monetary incentives, goal setting, and job enrichment
showed median gains of 30%, 16%, and 17%, with
ranges of 3% to 49%, 2% to 57.5% and –1% to 63%,
respectively.

In a recent article Daniel Denison claimed to find support for the value of participation. He found that a decision-making practices measure (relating to participation)
was significantly related to quantitative measures of organizational performance across a sample of 34 companies in
25 different industry groups.

However, for a variety of reasons, no definite conclusions can be drawn from this study: (1) The study was correlational, not experimental (causal). (2) The main
"effect" of participation on performance was observed
three to five years after the participation measurements
were taken, thus suggesting the possibility that other fac-

EXHIBIT 9.1

RESULTS OF 50 STUDIES OF PARTICIPATION

	PARTICIPATIVE SUPERIOR TO AUTHORITATIVE METHODS	AUTHORITATIVE SUPERIOR TO PARTICIPATIVE METHODS	NO DIFFERENCE OR DIFFERENCES ONLY IN CERTAIN GROUPS WITHIN THE STUDY
Participation in Decision Making	9 (26%)	9 (26%)	17 (49%)
Participation in Goal Setting	1 (7%)	1 (7%)	13 (87%)
Total	10 (20%)	10 (20%)	30 (60%)

Note: Percentages across first two columns are calculated from the bases of 35 studies and 15 studies, respectively.

tors intervened during this period. Further, evidence did not show that participation was actually introduced at the time measurements were made. Employee participation may have been introduced years earlier; thus the lag time could be even longer and more questionable. (3) Many different quantitative performance indices were actually tried but only two were reported on. (4) Departments measured in each organization were not randomly selected. (5) The decision-making practices index was actually composed of two items—one relating to involvement in decisions and the other to degree of information sharing throughout the organization. The first item is more motivational in focus while the second is more cognitive. It would have been instructive to look at the two items separately.

We believe that the cognitive benefits of participation are potentially more powerful than motivational benefits. (This issue will be discussed further below.) A more consistently effective measure in this study, incidentally, was an "organization-of-work index" that included an item on clarity of organizational goals.

What conclusions can be drawn about the overall effectiveness of participation based on published studies? Contrary to Sashkin's claims, research shows very clearly that while participation *may* improve productivity, participation does not consistently have this effect and, in some cases, is actually less effective than nonparticipation. If participation works only in certain circumstances, let us consider what they might be.

When Participation Works Best

Using participation intelligently requires an understanding of the mechanisms by which it works and the conditions under which these mechanisms will most likely operate. Motivational and cognitive mechanisms are most important. The motivational mechanism includes such factors as trust, greater control of the work, more ego involvement in the job, increased identification with the organization, more group support (if it is group participation) and, most important, the setting of higher goals and/or increased goal acceptance.

The cognitive mechanism includes more upward communication, better utilization of information (especially when the supervisor does not have sufficient information to make a high-quality decision), and better understanding by employees of the job and the rationale underlying decisions.

As suggested in our previous discussion of Latham's studies, it is apparent that motivation to reach goals can be achieved just as well through assigning goals as through setting them participatively. Sashkin's claim that assigned goals are not accepted as readily as those set participatively is simply false. (See Exhibit 9.1.) Studies repeatedly show that if an employee is assigned a "reasonable" goal (one that is challenging, yet achievable) and is given support and sufficient resources to achieve it, he or she readily accepts it.

Nevertheless, in one study Latham found that participation (through the cognitive mechanism) led to better utilization of skill and knowledge. But participation worked well in this instance because the participants had sufficient task knowledge to make a useful contribution. Including a subordinate in a decision in which he or she lacks knowledge of the particular topic at hand will lead to a low-quality decision at worst and will have a negative motivational impact at best. Employees put in this situation will realize that they should not participate in the decision and will feel embarrassed or inadequate.

During the past decade, Victor Vroom and his colleagues at Yale University have developed and tested a contingency, or situational, model of participative decision making. The model identifies five options for involving subordinates in decisions and seven decision rules that determine the conditions under which each of the five options are effective. The five options are: (1) Make the decision yourself using available information; (2) obtain the necessary information from subordinates, but make the decision yourself; (3) get ideas and suggestions from individuals separately and then make the decision, which may or may not reflect subordinates' input; (4) share the decision with subordinates as a group, and make a decision that may or may not reflect their input; and (5) share the decision with the group and together make the decision.

Using a decision tree, the best option is chosen based on the use of several decision rules. These include: (1) whether the decision has a high-quality requirement; (2) whether the leader has sufficient information to make a high-quality decision; (3) whether the problem is structured; (4) whether acceptance of the decision by subordinates is essential for effective implementation; (5) whether an authoritative decision would be accepted if made; (6) whether conflict among subordinates is likely in the decision; and (7) whether subordinates share the organizational goals to be attained in making the decision. The time available to make the decision can also be considered. These decision rules, together with the five options, suggest that certain options are more effective than others, depending on the situation. Vroom's own research supports the view that decisions made using these rules are of better quality and are more successful than those made when violating the rules.

On the basis of her own research, Rosabeth Moss Kanter suggested that participation should be used to allow knowledgeable individuals to contribute to a decision, to address conflicting approaches or views, or to gain new sources of expertise and experience. Nonparticipative (authoritative) decisions, on the other hand, are preferable when one person clearly has greater expertise on a subject than others; little or no time is available for discussion; and individuals prefer, and are capable of, working alone.

Kanter's principles complement Vroom's. She also noted that a number of implementation factors influence effective use of participation. According to Kanter, managers should give subordinates *reasonable* expectations about their level of involvement in decisions, be explicit about constraints on decisions, provide rewards and feedback, provide a time frame for decisions, specify accountability, reporting relationships, and standards to be met (goals), and provide necessary information and training to help employees make participation work.

The contingency aspect of participation is explicitly recognized by Andrew S. Grove in his book, *High Output Management.* He found that the appropriateness of participation in decision making depends on the employee's or manager's degree of job experience—or, more specifically, what he calls task-relevant maturity. Grove advocates a three-stage decision-making process paralleling the growth in task knowledge. At Stage 1, the employee, who is new to the job, knows very little and therefore should be told what to do by his or her supervisor. As the employee develops some expertise (Stage 2), decisions should be made jointly by superior and employee. When the employee becomes expert at the job (Stage 3), participation evolves into delegation: The employee is allowed to make decisions alone.

Observe that in Grove's model, participation is appropriate at only *one* stage—namely, Stage 2, where the subordinate has partial expertise. If participation is used at the first stage, the subordinate's ideas will most likely be worthless; and if they are accepted and implemented, poor decisions will result. If participation is used at the third stage, the subordinate will be stifled and overmanaged, and his or her expertise will be wasted. Participation would allow too much involvement at Stage 1 but too little at Stage 3.

But even at Stage 3, not all decisions are delegated to the employee or to the manager. Organizations always require leadership, and one thing leaders must do is set the basic direction for the organization. They do this by providing the organization with a sense of mission, a vision, or a strategic goal—to which all activities of individual employees are tied. Participation and delegation are appropriate only in determining subgoals and strategies for attaining larger goals.

In summary, both scientific literature and management experience have shown that, while participation *may* lead to greater involvement and better decisions, it does not necessarily do so. Participation is useful only under some circumstances. A key requirement is that the subordinate has expertise to bring to the decision-making process.

Employee Satisfaction

Let us now consider the contribution of participation to employee morale and satisfaction. People who are unfamiliar with organizational research commonly believe that if employees are happy in their jobs, they will respond with greater organizational commitment and thus higher productivity. Even Sashkin takes this view. It was first proven wrong about 30 years ago and has been shown to be wrong many times since. There's simply no direct connection between job satisfaction and subsequent productivity.

This is not to say that job dissatisfaction has no consequences, but that they vary for different employees and are mediated by many contextual factors. For example, dissatisfaction may lead to absenteeism or to quitting; it may also generate various types of protest—complaints to the boss, unionization, strikes, legal actions, and so forth. For example, unionization, according to Jeanne Brett, is most likely to occur when substantial dissatisfaction with the job is present and when unionization is viewed as an effective means of correcting problems.

Achieving high productivity is a complex task and entails much more than keeping employees satisfied. Key factors that affect productivity are: technology, ability of employees hired, training, management skill in planning and coordination, specificity and difficulty of employee goals, and incentives. Thus managers who take Sashkin at his word would be disillusioned to find that high productivity does not automatically follow when job satisfaction is increased.

Some writers including, to a considerable extent, Sashkin, have declared not only that satisfaction is the key to higher productivity, but also that participation is the key to creating higher satisfaction. Thus the proposed causal sequence is as follows:

Participation → Satisfaction → Productivity

We have just noted that the second part of the sequence is wrong. The first part—the assertion that participation leads to satisfaction—has some degree of plausibility but still is a serious oversimplification of the phenomenon of job satisfaction.

Job satisfaction is the result of attaining one's job values. But employees' values are numerous and their means of fulfillment are considerably more complex than Sashkin suggests. Employee job values fall into at least seven major categories: (1) the work itself, (2) pay, (3) promotion, (4) working conditions, (5) co-workers, (6) supervision, and (7) the organization. An examination of each category will show how employee job values can be satisfied.

Work

Employees want, if possible, work that is personally *interesting* to them. This can be achieved through self-selection on the part of the employee or through job assignment (or job design) by the employer. Employees also like to feel that their job is important or *significant*. Importance of the job in the context of the whole organization can be emphasized, to some extent, by showing the employee how his or her job fits into the "big picture." People also want to feel a sense of achievement, success, or accomplishment (or at least progress) in their work. This is best fostered by giving people specific goals or standards to aim for (for example, projects to complete, deadlines or budgets to meet, or production and quality quotas to attain). Feedback is also valued by employees; they want to know how well they are doing in relation to their goals. Many employees want responsibility and autonomy in their jobs—a chance to use their own judgment, to solve problems, to plan, to make decisions on their own, in short, to make use of their capabilities. Job enrichment or promotion usually provides responsibility and autonomy. Role clarity (the opposite of role ambiguity) gives employees a clear picture of what they are expected to do. Employees also want role congruence (compatible expectations among customers, peers, bosses and so forth), not role conflict. Employees prefer to have some influence in decisions that involve their work, which may be fostered by delegation (as in job enrichment) or by participation. Finally, employees want to be free from physical drudgery, usually by means of mechanization or automation (technology).

Pay

Pay has been perhaps the most overlooked motivator among behavioral scientists (including Sashkin) for the past 50 years. Money undeniably is *the* primary motivator in nonvolunteer organizations. To prove this, perform the mental experiment suggested by former IBM executive

Clair F. Vough: Subtract each work motivator from the job, one by one, and observe the consequences. Clearly, if pay were totally removed, few (if any) people would show up for work. In addition, pay affects decisions to accept a job, to remain, to leave and, under some circumstances, to be absent and to produce.

Pay satisfaction depends on at least five aspects of the pay system: perceived *fairness* of pay relative to market price (what people doing similar work in other firms are getting); perceived *fairness* of pay relative to what others in the same organization are getting (based on type of job and competence); pay in relation to *personal financial needs; benefits* (relative to what other organizations give); and pay *security,* which is really job security. Wage fairness is achieved by doing a market survey and paying at (or above) market price. Internal equity is also achieved in this way, sometimes with the help of a job-evaluation system and a fair and objective performance-appraisal system. Personal needs with regard to pay can be partially satisfied by the use of an incentive or bonus system. Benefits can be pegged to what competitors are giving. Finally, pay security can be granted to some extent, by manpower planning and contingency planning (going to a four-day week in the event of a downturn in business, for example) but, of course, pay security hinges in part on competitive (cost) pressures.

Promotions

Ambitious employees want promotion systems to be fair and clear, and they want promotions to be available soon after they have mastered their current job. Factors that contribute to these desirable conditions include a clear promotion policy, career planning, career ladders, training, and organizational growth.

Working Conditions

Key conditions that employees want to exist with respect to work are: (1) a safe, comfortable, and attractive environment (free of dangerous conditions, poisons, carcinogens, and so forth); (2) hours of work that fit well with one's personal life and off-the-job activities; and (3) resources (for example, space, equipment, time, and money) that help them get the job done. The best way to create a safe work environment is to get top management involved in safety issues and to make them a high priority. Flexitime, where feasible, seems to be the best way to integrate job and off-the-job hours. Obviously, one solution to the resources issue is to provide resources although they are always limited in relation to potential demand.

Co-Workers

Employees want co-workers who cooperate in getting the job done; they want co-workers who are competent and reliable. Proper selection, training, and a good performance-evaluation system can be used toward this end. Employees also prefer co-workers who have values similar to their own.

Supervision

The broadest conclusion that can be drawn from the thousands of studies that have been conducted is employees want *consideration* (a term that emerged out of Ohio State leadership research in the 1950s) from their supervisors. The concept of consideration would seem to subsume such behaviors as being fair, treating each employee as an individual, listening to employees' ideas and concerns, recognizing good performance, giving employees explanations for decisions, being aware of employees' task preferences, asking employees for advice (participation), and so forth.

A neglected element in research on supervision, which has implications for employee satisfaction, is supervisor *competence* (for example, job knowledge, skill at organizing, and ability to get resources for the group). In other words, supervisors need technical and managerial skills in addition to human-relations skills. Organizations can ensure that supervisors have these skills by using proper employee selection, training, and promotion policies.

Organization

Former IBM executive and internationally known consultant David Sirota found that two things employees want most from their organizations are respect and competence. Respect for the individual means respect for his or her values. This principle actually subsumes all the foregoing categories, since the organization's policies determine which employee values are satisfied and how they are satisfied. Ultimately the issue is management philosophy (as practiced, not preached) of the top executive or executive team. Competence means good management and putting out a good product.

The categories discussed above, the associated values, and the means by which these values can be satisfied are summarized in Exhibit 9.2. What is worth noting about this list is that *participation is only one of many values that employees hold for their jobs.*

Sashkin noted correctly that participation is associated with overall job satisfaction. Locke and Schweiger found participation to be more associated with higher morale than was authoritative leadership in about 60% of the studies. In the other 40%, participation led to lower morale or its effects were dependent on contingency factors. However, Sashkin failed to note many of the other attributes that affect satisfaction. Managers and executives would have an extremely narrow and distorted picture of employee values if they believed that participation was the central factor in job satisfaction while everything else was peripheral. Such a view would be especially misleading if one of the consequences were the neglect of such important issues as the nature of the work itself and money. Just as managers would be disillusioned to find out that making employees satisfied would not in itself raise productivity, they would be disappointed to see that introducing participation by itself would not make employees satisfied.

One could argue that since participation as such is simply a method (without specific content), it could be used to help employees satisfy all the values in Exhibit 9.2—in other words, to get everything they want. But such a claim would be extremely naïve. First, no organization

---

EXHIBIT 9.2

BASIC JOB VALUES AND HOW TO PROVIDE THEM

JOB CATEGORIES	VALUE	HOW TO PROVIDE OR ENSURE
Work	Interest	Self-selection, job assignment, and design
	Significance	Provide big picture
	Achievement	Goals, standards
	Feedback	Feedback charts, performance appraisal
	Challenge	Difficult goals, job enrichment
	Responsibility	Job enrichment
	Autonomy	Job enrichment
	Role clarity	Specific goals
	Role congruence	Compatible expectations
	Influence	Delegation, job enrichment, participation
	Freedom from physical drudgery	Mechanization, automation
Pay	Fairness (external)	Market price (wage survey)
	Fairness (internal)	Market price, job evaluation, performance appraisal
	Meet personal needs	Incentive plan
	Benefits	Market
	Security	Manpower planning, contingency plans
Promotions	Fairness	Objectivity
	Clarity	Announced policy
	Availability	Career planning, organizational growth
Working Conditions	Safety	Top management involvement
	Convenient hours	Flexitime
	Resources	Provision of time, equipment, space, help, money
Co-workers	Cooperation	Selection, training, performance appraisal
Supervision	Consideration	Selection, training, promotion
	Managerial competence	Selection, training, promotion
Organization	Respect	Top-management philosophy
	Competence	Top-management competence

could afford to spend the time it would take to allow every employee to participate in every decision about every aspect of the job. Second, even if such participation were encouraged, it would not work because employees differ in what they want, their knowledge, their degree of articulateness in expressing their views, and their degree of assertiveness. Since the organization has limited resources, allowing too much participation would create unrealistic expectations and disappointment or harm to the organization or to employees.

In well-managed organizations, employees get many things they value without participation. They get them as a result of management's respect for employees (for example, pay above the market price, generous benefits, or job security). Input from employees may be solicited in the form of anonymous attitude surveys that help identify problem areas. Problems identified by a majority of employees may be acted on at management's discretion.

While satisfaction does not create productivity, the manager does not have to emphasize one at the expense of the other. He or she can have both under the right conditions. Satisfaction is achieved by providing job attributes (within reason) that employees want. But if the organization is to be productive, at least some things that employees want (for example, high pay) must be provided, not just because they want them, but because they have earned them. Specifically, pay increases, promotions, and other forms of recognition must be based on performance, and incompetence must not be tolerated; in fact, it is usually beneficial to the organization when the least productive employees are dissatisfied because they are not rewarded (or are disciplined).

Some values, such as safe working conditions, convenient hours, and fringe benefits are routinely satisfied, independent of job performance, but this cannot be done for all values without undermining the incentive for goal attainment.

Is Participation an Ethical Issue?

It is Sashkin's assertion that participation is an ethical imperative, more than any other, that prompted us to write this article. Sashkin's argument that participation is an ethical issue is based on the following logic: (1) It is ethically wrong for managers to actively harm subordinates; (2) managers who do not use participation harm people by frustrating

their basic needs; (3) therefore, to be ethical, managers should use participation. The key to this argument is its initial premise. What does Sashkin mean by *harm?* He seems to include in this concept everything from direct physical harm to psychological harm. This harm would include virtually any action or lack of action that would somehow make another person unhappy or frustrated.

We would certainly agree that it is ethically wrong to cause direct physical harm to others—that is, to initiate physical force against them. Initiation of force violates an individual's rights by threatening his or her survival. Force prevents people from acting on their judgment in the furtherance of their life and well-being.

But psychological harm is quite a different matter. Some people may become unhappy because they have unreasonable expectations of another person, or because another person is taking a legitimate action that they do not agree with. If one never were to do anything that might psychologically harm another person, a supervisor would be prohibited, for example, from refusing to hire someone who lacked crucial skills, firing a dishonest employee, redesigning a job in a way that somebody did not like, or requiring an employee to meet quality or service standards that were higher than his or her personal ones.

Sashkin's ethical view is based implicitly on a premise that has become increasingly popular in recent years: Job satisfaction is the employee's "right." Thus the organization is duty-bound to provide it. Some people have even urged that legislation be passed that would penalize organizations that do not provide sufficient job satisfaction for their work force.

We reject this view because of its coercive implications. Job satisfaction is the responsibility of both employer and employee; by this we mean that job satisfaction is worth pursuing in the rational self-interest of both parties. It is important to note that while there is no fundamental conflict of interest between employer and employee, their priorities are not identical. From the standpoint of the employee, his or her own job satisfaction is the primary goal, while the satisfaction of the employer is secondary. For the employer, his or her own satisfaction is primary, while employee satisfaction is secondary.

The goal of employees is to achieve happiness or satisfaction. One way they achieve it is through the job. To get satisfaction from the job, they must derive values from it. But to get these values employees have to do what the employer wants (for example, to get raises and promotions, they have to do competent work). Thus, at least in a well-integrated organization, employees achieve some of their goals by working toward the employer's goals.

Observe that the employer's goals could not be the employee's primary goals; if they were, the employee would be willing to work endless hours on unpleasant tasks for below-market wages—a course of action that would negate the employee's happiness or satisfaction.

The employer also wants to achieve his or her own happiness. One of the ways to accomplish this is by getting the organization to succeed in achieving its goals. In the private sector, the ultimate goal is profitability, whereas in the public sector it is the fulfillment of the organization's function (for example, the function of the police is to protect people from criminals). Employee morale is a means to these ends. Without a reasonable degree of employee satisfaction, an organization would not be able to recruit, retain, or gain the cooperation of a competent work force. In cases of extreme employee dissatisfaction, management might be faced with union militancy, strikes, or worse.

Employee morale could not be an employer's primary goal, however. Imagine the consequences if an organization's major focus was to provide all employees with everything they "wanted," without regard to context (for example, in the areas of pay, promotions, hours of work, benefits, equipment, or co-workers). Conflict and chaos would result—not to mention low productivity, high costs, and ultimate bankruptcy.

Both employee and employer want to achieve their own satisfaction with the help of the other; but each must give the other something in return in order to get it. The employee-employer relationship involves a trade, with each party offering a value (for example, time and effort) in return for a value (such as money). Each attempts to influence terms to protect his or her own interests.

This difference in priorities, while not a fundamental conflict of interest, implies the possibility of disagreement over particulars. A given individual may not always want to help an organization attain its goals, while an organization may not always want, or be able to, concern itself with employee job satisfaction. On the other hand, each has a means of protecting its own ultimate interests in the matter. A dissatisfied employee may quit, while an organization may fire an employee with whom it is not satisfied.

The respective responsibilities of employee and employer are summarized in Exhibit 9.3. Let's consider the individual employee first. To get satisfaction the individual must have rational values, that is, values that do not contradict needs or reality. For example, an employee cannot rationally advocate contradictions, such as a merit system for others and favoritism for himself or herself. Nor can one rationally expect a promotion if one lacks the ability to perform the job in question or a higher salary than

either the market price or what the organization can afford to pay.

Second, the individual must have rational expectations regarding attainment of job values. For example, rewards cannot always be guaranteed or be given immediately after a goal is attained. Every effort does not always pay off. An individual may work very hard on a product for a year only to find that, when marketed, it does not sell. Despite the hard work, a reward is not mandated in such circumstances. And even if the product did sell and a promotion were deserved, a position might not open up in the immediate future.

Third, the individual is responsible for carefully choosing the career and job that is selected. The employee-organizational match is as much the employee's responsibility as it is the organization's. Successful career and job choice requires good decision-making techniques. In addition, the individual must be willing to change careers and/or jobs or to adapt to change if previous choices do not work out as expected. When a person makes a career choice, there is no guarantee that five, or twenty-five years later conditions will not change in ways that no one could have predicted.

Fourth, in whatever career or job a person chooses, he or she must make conscientious efforts to satisfy values through appropriate action, especially through sustained, competent performance and rational persuasion. In lower levels of the blue-collar and white-collar ranks are many individuals who, despite the possession of ability or potential, are not willing to take actions that their professed values require, or who do not have ambition at all. Some people do not want much, and/or are not willing to work for much, and, as a result, do not get much. On the basis of his studies on the mental health of the industrial worker, Arthur Kornhauser concluded:

> . . . the unsatisfactory mental health of working people consists in no small measure of their dwarfed desires and deadened initiative, reduction of their goals and restriction of their efforts to a point where life is relatively empty and only half meaningful.

Of course, material and value impoverishment can result from causes outside the individual's control.

Now let's consider the organization's responsibilities. First, it is in the interest of a company to give realistic pre-employment job previews to prospective employees. Such previews allow employees to better match themselves with jobs and to be aware of what they can realistically expect once hired. In addition, it is important that preemployment (as well as postemployment) promises be kept. If such promises are made contingently, the contingencies

EXHIBIT 9.3

JOINT RESPONSIBILITY FOR JOB SATISFACTION*

The individual's responsibility:
1. A rational code of values, including values that do not contradict needs, reality, or the individual's abilities.
2. Rational expectations (for example, that value attainment cannot be guaranteed; that rewards are not always automatic or immediate).
3. Proper choice of job and willingness to change jobs or careers when previous choices do not work out.
4. Conscientious efforts to obtain values on the job through sustained, competent performance and rational persuasion.

The organization's responsibility:
1. Realistic job previews given to job applicants; preemployment promises kept.
2. Proper selection and placement and willingness to make changes when selection and placement errors occur.
3. Reasonable provision of job values through:
   a. Identifying what employees want.
   b. Providing these values as a condition of employment.
   c. Providing these values in return for competent performance.
4. Giving honest and justifiable reasons for inability to provide certain job values.

*From Edwin Locke's "Job Satisfaction," in *Social Psychology and Organizational Behavior,* edited by M. Gruneberg and T. Wall, Wiley Ltd., 1984. Reprinted by permission of publisher.

should be spelled out (for instance: "We should be able to promote you within two years, if you perform well and we continue our present rate of growth").

Second, the organization will benefit from proper selection of employees. Employers should ensure that the employees they hire have the skills needed to perform effectively (or are given these skills through training); that employees are motivated to use these skills; and that their long-term goals are compatible with organizational opportunities.

Third, the organization will foster satisfaction most effectively if it identifies what its employees want and then attempts, within reason and the limitations of cost to fulfill these wants (a safe work environment or fair pay, for example) or with the opportunity to earn more money.

Fourth, an organization will benefit greatly from being honest and truthful with its employees with respect to the job attributes it can and will offer and with respect to the reasons for its inability to provide attributes it cannot offer.

In practice, no organization could possibly satisfy all job values of all its employees. All employees do not want the same things; thus a condition (for instance, overtime) that satisfies one employee can dissatisfy another. Furthermore, an organization cannot use all of its resources to make employees happy and, at the same time, compete in the marketplace to make a product or provide a service. In

addition, not all employees' values are necessarily rational (one employee, for instance, might want a big pay raise despite the fact that he or she is incompetent and unreliable), so trying to satisfy them would be self-destructive for the organization. Further, employee values can change over time; keeping up with such changes (occurring at different rates in different employees) can be very difficult.

The best an organization can do is choose employees who like what the organization offers and offer what is reasonable in the context of their knowledge, time, and financial position. If a given organization does significantly less well at satisfying employees than most others, eventually the market will force it to conform.

Conclusion

The management of organizations is an extremely complex and demanding task. Executives are not helped in their search for effective managerial techniques by being offered panaceas—techniques that purport to solve all problems and to work without regard to situation or context. There are no panaceas in management. Nor are executives helped by being told to practice arbitrary and irrational "ethical imperatives." Good management is the result of intelligence, experience, and clear thinking and is facilitated by the results of relevant organizational research. With respect to participation, research results are clear. Sometimes par-ticipation is useful and sometimes it is not. We are now beginning to understand some of the conditions under which it will be effective. Until we know more, executives must do what they have always done: integrate what is known from the research with their own good sense.

SELECTED BIBLIOGRAPHY

For a thorough review of the research on participation in decision making up to the late 1970s, see Edwin Locke and David Schweiger's "Participation in Decision Making: One More Look," *Research in Organizational Behavior,* edited by B. Staw (JAI Press, 1979). David Schweiger and Carrie Leana have just completed a more up-to-date review, "Participation in Decision Making," which appears in a book edited by Edwin Locke, *Generalizing from Laboratory to Field Settings* (Lexington Books, 1986). The data in Exhibit 1 are from Schweiger and Leana's article. Gary Latham's work on participation and goal setting is discussed in Edwin Locke and Gary Latham's *Goal Setting: A Motivational Technique That Works* (Prentice-Hall, 1984). Contingency theory of participation is presented in Victor Vroom and Phillip Yetton's *Leadership and Decision Making* (University of Pittsburgh Press, 1973). Rosabeth Moss Kanter's article, "Dilemmas of Managing Participation" appeared in *Organizational Dynamics* (Summer 1982). See also Andrew S. Grove's *High Output Management* (Random House, 1983). Especially interesting is Chapter 12.

William Ouchi's discussion of participation is in *Theory Z* (Addison-Wesley, 1981). Arthur Kornhouser's quotation may be found in his *Mental Health and the Industrial Worker* (Wiley, 1965).

Marshall Sashkin discusses the Hawthorne, Harwood-Weldon, and Keithley studies in his article, "Participative Management Is an Ethical Imperative" (*Organizational Dynamics,* Spring 1984).

We should add that the claim made by Marshall Sashkin that the results of participation studies cannot be interpreted without performing a meta-analysis (a complex, statistical technique) on the data is false. Furthermore, meta-analysis cannot produce significant results when there aren't any.

Daniel Denison asserts that participative companies have better performance records in "Bringing Corporate Culture to the Bottom Line" (*Organizational Dynamics,* Autumn 1984).

Jeanne Brett's article on "Why Employees Want Unions" is in the Spring 1980 issue of *Organizational Dynamics.* For useful references on the topic of employee morale and job satisfaction see Edwin Locke's "The Nature and Causes of Job Satisfaction" in *Handbook of Industrial and Organizational Psychology,* edited by M. Dunnette (Rand McNally & Company, 1976) and Edwin Locke's "Job Satisfaction" in *Social Psychology and Organizational Behavior,* edited by M. Gruneberg and T. Wall (Wiley Ltd., 1984).

The first statistical analysis of the Hawthorne studies is found in Richard Franke and James Kaul's "The Hawthorne Experiments: First Statistical Interpretation" (*American Sociological Review,* 1978, vol. 43, no. 5).

DISCUSSION QUESTIONS

1. Why could it be argued that participation in decision making is an ethical imperative for management? What is the counter-argument?

2. What do the authors mean by participation?

3. What evidence from scientific studies supports the use of widespread participation?

4. Under what conditions does participation work most effectively?

5. What is the relationship between participation and employee morale and satisfaction?

6. Discuss how work, pay, promotion, working conditions, co-workers, supervision, and the organization serve to satisfy employee job values.

7. Discuss the idea that both employers and employees have responsibilities for job satisfaction.

8. What are the key responsibilities of employees?

FOR FURTHER READING

Allison, G. *Essence of Decision.* Boston: Little, Brown, 1971.

Bass, B. *Organizational Decision Making.* Homewood, Illinois: Irwin, 1983.

Cohen, M., March, J., and Olsen, J. "A Garbage Can Model of Organizational Choice." *Administrative Science Quarterly* 45 (1972) 1–25.

Jago, A. "An Assessment of the Deemed Appropriateness of Participative Decision Making for High and Low Hierarchical Levels." *Human Relations* 34 (1981) 379–396.

Janis, I. *Groupthink.* Boston: Houghton Mifflin, 1982.

Staw, B. "Knee-deep in the Big Muddy: A Study of Escalating Commitment to a Chosen Course of Action." *Organizational Behavior and Human Performance* 16 (1976) 27–45.

10

LEADERSHIP

The Ambivalence of Organizational Leaders

ROBERT K. MERTON

LEARNING OBJECTIVES

After reading Merton's "The Ambivalence of Organizational Leaders," a student will be able to:

1. Understand that leaders are subjected to simultaneous incompatible pressures

2. Recognize that ambivalent organizational leader behavior is the result of social structure, not necessarily personality

3. Develop a realistic view of the constraints and opportunities for organizational leaders

4. Consider possible ways to manage the conflicts inherent in the structural conditions of leadership

Consider the popular imagery of the leader in an organization. For some of the many below him in the hierarchy, he is secure, knowing, decisive, powerful, dynamic, threatening, driving, and altogether remote, acting in clear or obscure ways to affect the future of the organization he leads. At eye level, he is more often seen as filled with troubled doubts as he tries to deal with the ambivalences and contradictions of his status. And if his feet are made of a substance more solid than clay, it is because on his climb to the top and with the aid of those who help hold him there, he has learned to still the doubts, to live with the ambivalences, and to cope with the contradictions of his position.

The abundance of people—and if the leader leads, these must inevitably be called the (not necessarily passive) followers—are not altogether unaware of this complex situation. In the political arena, the daily manifestations of the ambivalences and contradictions that afflict the leader have attained the status of a sportive spectacle; periodically, box scores are presented in the press on the current standings of our eminent political figures as their public decisions delight some social strata and alienate others. In other spheres of leadership, too, the contradictions of the position have become public victuals. In a time of recent turmoil, for example, the leaders of our universities have had to set out their dilemmas on the front pages of the newspapers. So, too, with our church leaders, as they seek to bottle the fermenting spirit of their flocks. And, as the world stubbornly refuses to shape itself into accord with our proclaimed national purpose, we see military leaders struggling with the basic conflicts of roles which an objective situation has thrust upon them.

Although many ambivalences of leadership are common to all sorts of organizations—political and economic, religious and academic—this essay will deal primarily with that numerous company of American leaders, the topmost business executives, known, ever since the days of Thorstein Veblen, as captains of industry.

Business—the idea and occasionally the ideal of a more or less private enterprise—has long been a major force in American society. For much of this time, it was ideologized in the American gospel of success and so provided much of the rhetoric and part of the substance of the

Source: Robert K. Merton: "The Ambivalence of Organizational Leaders," in James F. Oates, Jr., *The Contradictions of Leadership* (New York: Appleton-Crofts, 1970), pp. 1–26. Reprinted by permission.

American dream "from rags to riches." And if Americans are no longer as convinced as they were a half-century ago of the self-evident truth of Cal Coolidge's epigram—"The business of America is business"—recent soundings of public opinion show that they are ever more widely convinced of Ted Sorensen's inverted epigram—"The business of business is America."

Routes of Upward Mobility

Whether it is an organization for business or another purpose, there are only two routes to the top: one from within, the other from without. Each has its particular advantages and handicaps; each produces its own syndrome of ambivalence.

The leader coming from within the organization is the more likely to know it well: its signal strengths and weaknesses, its style of management and the quality of its managers, its living history and its aspirations, its markets, products and prospects. But perhaps he will know it too well. Friendships and personality clashes have much the same tendency to induce myopia in a leader. And corporate associations of long standing, except in the case of the most detached and widely experienced of managers, have a way of limiting the leader's horizons, of impairing his vision, of restricting his view of possibilities for the future. What has stood the organization in relatively good stead in the past—in terms of organizational goals and of the methods deployed to move toward them—may continue to be carried on. This may be good enough for the immediate if not the longer-run future. But the very value of his intimate knowledge of the past successes of the organization may induce what Veblen unforgettably described as a "trained incapacity": a state of affairs in which one's abilities come to function as inadequacies. Recurrent actions based upon training, skills, and experiences that have been successfully applied in the past result in inappropriate responses *under changed conditions*. Thus, to adopt a barnyard illustration used in this connection by Kenneth Burke, chickens can be readily conditioned to interpret the sound of a bell as a signal for food. The same bell may now be used to summon the trained chickens to their doom as they are assembled to suffer decapitation. As the leader from within adopts organizational measures in keeping with his past experience and employs them under new conditions that are not recognized as *significantly* different, the

very soundness of training for the past leads to maladaptation in the present. In Burke's almost echolalic phrase: "People may be fit by being fit in an unfit fitness." Their past successes incapacitate them for future ones. To move from the barnyard to the railroad yard, on such sand, for one, has the history of the American railroads been written.

The assumed advantages and handicaps of the internal route to the top are typically reversed with the leader coming from outside the organization. He does not know the company in depth. Practically all of his first months, if not years, will be spent in its study—its past performance gauged against its past potentials, the capabilities of its people, material resources, aggregate aspirations. The organization must endure a period of contemplative inaction. But if his lack of firsthand acquaintance with the organization is a defect, it also has its qualities. He brings few built-in biases toward the particular organization and its parts (although he will, of course, inevitably have his own collection of biases grown outside). But having no emotional involvement with the past of the organization, he is—or the more easily can be—capable of opening himself to all kinds of innovative possibilities. He can more readily perceive ideas that may have been floating around the organization for years. He brings, surely, a fresh—not necessarily a correct—approach to the problems and opportunities of the organization he now leads, and an expertise gained outside the intellectual confinement inherent in every organization. Still, he brings with him from outside no guarantee of success, as is attested by the path of corporate leadership, liberally strewn with the bones of "boy wonders," "financial wizards," and "management geniuses" of all shapes and sizes.

The ambivalences of organizational leadership begin, then, at the beginning. They are found in the route the leader followed to get there, whether from within or from without. They begin with the sum total of his previous organizational experience and with the interaction of his own capability for adaptive growth and all the foibles and creative impulses of the organization he leads.

Varieties of Organizational Ambivalence

Regardless of his origin, the newly made leader of the organization soon confronts another ambivalent situation. As leader, it is his obligation to bring to his position a vision of the future, a sense of direction as to where he wants the organization to go. He must obey the further organizational imperative, on pain of failure, of sharing his private vision with the total organization. For vision that is remote from the values and wants of the many around him becomes transformed into self-defeating fantasy. Within these obligations are planted the seeds of several conflicts and ambivalences.

The more sharply the leader defines his vision, the more confident he is of his own role (and vice versa). But in sharpening his vision he has narrowed his options. And in narrowing his options he has limited the number and kind of his subordinates who will, with enthusiasm, perceive and work toward the goals encompassed in that vision. For people who are to release their energies toward the attainment of goals must have a voice and a hand in shaping those goals. They must have a sense of some mastery over their own destinies. Yet with each slice of power released by the leader—and it is power, i.e., the ability to make something happen, that, in the final analysis and however broadly defined, is the core of leadership—the greater becomes his own condition of uncertainty.

A second kind of conflict is in the offing between the leader who projects his own vision and the organization itself. The more "different" and the more radical that vision happens to be, the greater will be the conflict. For just as the leader comes to his position as the synergistic sum of his experiences, so too he leads an organization which is the synergistic sum of *its* experiences. Indeed, the experiences of the organization will be more deeply ingrained—through its history, traditions, culture, and the sheer inertial structure of all organizational life—than those of any of its individual members. Under such conditions, flexibility in the executive grip may, with only seeming paradox, produce a steadier hand.

Whether his vision is large or small, the leader will want—indeed, will have an emotional need—to shape the organization, to change it, to mold it into a creation that, at least in part, he can claim as his own. Yet, inexorably, he in turn will be shaped, probably without his recognition, by the organization, by its needs, its capabilities, its standards. At some distant time, should he look back, he will be unable to distinguish between the changes he has wrought and the ones that have been wrought in him. "It is a time," wrote Emerson, "when things are in the saddle." Or, to paraphrase a typically Churchillian aphorism: "We shape our organizations and afterwards our organizations shape us." Even the most self-confident of leaders will on occasion find it impossible to disagree.

Another ambivalence confronting the leader is built into the circumstance that although nothing succeeds like success, in organizations increments of success become self-limiting. This means for the leader that the organization will be at one and the same time a continuing source of great pleasure and acute pain. The leader will demand that the organization improve its performance, raise its standards, increase its efficiency. And when, through the objective measurement of the budget or some other device, improvement is discovered and entered into the corporate record, the leader will take great pleasure in it. But to obtain even a tittle of improvement, the leader will find that he must pass through a prolonged period of anguish, during which he feels (and sometimes is) personally responsible for the outcome and, in any case, is held accountable for it. And he will find, too, that unlike an individual who is able to assimilate and use new information for sometimes spectacular improvements in performance, a complex organization functions, for the most part, on precisely the reverse principle: that, after a certain point, as organizational efficiency improves, further improvement becomes increasingly difficult.

Still another ambivalent requirement exacted of the leader calls for him to have pride in his organization, to induce or reinforce the pride of other members of the organization, and still to keep the extent of that collective pride in check. The leader must somehow arrange for that composite of pride that is justified by accomplishment and commitment but, at the same time, he must recognize that pride can become overweening, no longer sustained by continuing accomplishment. This is often expressed in what Theodore Caplow has designated as the "aggrandizement effect": "the upward distortion of an organization's prestige by its own members." Having studied 33 different types of organizations—among them, banks and Skid Row missions, department stores and university departments—he found that members overestimated the prestige of their own organization (as seen by outsiders) eight times as often as they underestimated it. (In judging the prestige of other organizations than their own, people tend to agree.) Now, as Proverbs in the Good Book reminds us in its own brand of organizational sociology: Pride goeth before destruction, and a haughty spirit before a fall. In other words, organizations and their leaders who become happily absorbed in reflecting upon past glories at the expense of providing for new accomplishments are in deep trouble. They come increasingly to live and work in an unreal world of self-induced fantasy. And sooner or later, contact with the world of reality forces the prideful leader and his followers alike to discover that both utilitarian and moral assets waste away if they are not energetically renewed and extended. For the rest of the social system will not stand still. And so organizations which would move with it must continue to engage in both innovative and adaptive change.

While the leader is concerned, perhaps above all else, with pulling the entire organization to higher levels of performance, he will often be put in the contradictory position of being unable to meet the demands for facilities to provide superior performance by the organization's individual parts. He is presented with a classical dilemma of organizational decision. Deeply committed to the goals of the organization, two or more separate departments are each doing their utmost to serve the best interests of the total organization by maximizing their distinctive kinds of contribution to it. But, often, even typically, maximizing the contribution of one part means limiting the contributions of other parts. One thinks of the bright young men and women attracted to the field of electronic data processing who, were the decision in their domain, would systematize the entire universe overnight. There is, in the striving for organizational excellence—although many hesitate to concede it—a balance to be struck that means curbing the single-minded drive for maximum performance by the component parts. The dilemma of decision can be transcended only by having the distinct parts rise to a concern for the whole. Commitment to the goals of the organization then takes precedence over commitment to the goals of the department. All this presents leadership with the geeing-and-hawing that leaves the corporate mule in danger of succumbing to the dead-center obstinacy of noncooperation.

Leadership as Social Exchange

From his relations to his subordinates emerge a variety of other dilemmas, ambivalences, and contradictions for the organizational leader. It is the manager's responsibility, perhaps his very first responsibility, to sustain the people who report to him. He is, in fact as well as in word, "the first assistant of his subordinates." Yet who is to sustain the leader? Granting that topmost leadership is "the loneliest position on earth"—a bit of familiar hyperbole—it is not necessarily so for most organizational leadership; not, that is, under the proper circumstances. Those circumstances have to do, of course, with the kind of support that the

subordinates give to their superior in his position of leadership. Turned half circle and viewed from the position of leadership, this means the degree of confidence that the leader reposes in each of his subordinates.

There is, in every superior–subordinate relationship, a complex of interactions. At the root of them all, when they are effective interactions, is the confidence or trust that each has in the other. For the ultrarationalists among us, it comes hard to recognize that in organizational life, the prime ingredient of reciprocal confidence is not competence alone, although the importance of competent performance of roles should not be underrated. It is the first stone on which confidence is built. After all, no one is better situated than subordinates to distinguish between a superior's authentic competence and its mere appearance.

This reminds us that leadership is not so much an attribute of individuals as it is a social transaction between leader and led, a kind of social exchange. And again, though some leaders sense this intuitively, the rest of us must learn it more laboriously. Leaders assist their associates in achieving personal goals by contributing to organizational goals. In exchange, they receive the basic coin of effective leadership: trust, confidence, and respect. You need not be loved to be an effective leader, but you must be respected.

Identifiable social processes produce the respect required for effective leadership. First, respect expressed *by* the leader breeds respect *for* the leader. As he exhibits a concern for the dignity of others in the organizational system and for their shared values and norms, he finds it reciprocated. Second, as has been said, he demonstrates technical competence in performing his own roles. He does not merely talk about competence, he exhibits it. Third, the effective leader is in continuing touch with the germane particulars of what is going on in the human organization. For this, it helps, of course, to be located at strategic nodes in the network of communication that comprises much of every organization. But structural location is not enough. Once situated there, he provides with calculated awareness for two-way communication. He not only lets the other fellow get an occasional word in edgewise; he lets him get a good number of words in straightaway. And the effective leader listens: both to what is said and to what is not said in so many words but is only implied. He allows for both negative and positive feedback. Negative feedback, as a cue to the possibility that, in his plans and actions, he has moved beyond the zone of acceptability for his colleagues and subordinates; positive feedback, as a cue that he has support for his initiating actions.

Fourth—and on this accounting, finally—although the leader in a position of authority has access to the power that coerces, he makes use of that power only sparingly. He gives up little and gains much in employing self-restraint in the exercise of his power. For once he has gained the respect of associates, it is they, rather than the leader directly, who work to ensure compliance among the rest of their peers. Leaders only deplete their authority by an excess of use, and that excess is not long coming when leaders, having lost the respect of their subordinates, anxiously try to impose their will. Group experiments in sociology have found that the more often group leaders use the coercive power granted them, the more apt are they to be displaced. The experiments confirm what has long been thought; at its most effective, leadership is sustained by *noblesse oblige,* the obligation for generosity of behavior by those enjoying rank and power. Force is an ultimate resource that maintains itself by being sparingly employed.

In a word, what instills confidence between superior and subordinate is joint commitment: commitment to one another and to agreed-upon organizational goals. It is this mutual commitment that encourages even the leader who is temperamentally inclined to retain the reins of power in his own hands to delegate authority as well as responsibility to his subordinates, that allows him to rely more on corporate consensus than on authoritarianism in the making of decisions, and that, in turn, motivates the subordinate to request (or through muted symbolism, to demand) the exercise of responsibility and power commensurate with his position rather than to suffer in silence the close-handed intransigence of the oligarchic leader.

Styles of Organizational Leadership

This train of thought need not be pursued very far in order to identify what has been emerging as one of the major contradictions facing modern organizations, including, as a prime special case, business organizations. This contradiction is found in the tendencies working simultaneously toward democratic rule and the more traditional authoritarian rule. This is something far deeper and more fundamental than a matter of the relationship between two or more individuals or even groups of individuals. It not only affects the style of management, the relationship between organizational units, and the definition and operation of

management, but touches upon the very purposes of the organization itself.

In recent years, behavioral scientists—notably such organizational investigators and theorists as McGregor, Herzberg, Argyris, Likert, Lawrence, and, in his own way, Peter Drucker—have shown to a growing number of corporate executives that efficiency and productivity lie in the direction of a more democratic or participative management. This proposition can be overstated and it often has been. Nevertheless, there is now a growing abundance of evidence testifying that *under certain conditions* democratic leadership is the more efficient in making for productivity of products *and* of valued human by-products.

All the same, styles of leadership continue to vary. The repertoire of styles is extensive; and, it would seem, only few leaders have or acquire the versatility to shift from one to another style as changing circumstances require. There is the authoritarian style in which the leader is insistent, dominating, and apparently self-assured. With or without intent, he creates fear and then meets the regressive needs of his subordinates generated by that fear. He keeps himself firmly at the center of attention and manages to keep communication among the others in the system to a minimum. Ready to use coercion at the slightest intimation of divergence from his definitions of the situation, the authoritarian may be effective for a while in times of crisis when the organizational system is in a state of disarray. But, particularly for organizations in a democratically toned society, extreme and enforced dependence upon the leader means that the organizational system is especially liable to instability.

The democratic style of leadership, in contrast, is more responsive. It provides for extended participation of others, with policies more often emerging out of interaction between leader and led. It provides for the care and feeding of the self-esteem of members of the system, but not in that counterfeit style of spreading lavish flattery on all and sundry egos in the vicinity, after the fashion once advocated by the merchants of interpersonal relations who would have us make pseudo-friends by inauthentic expressions of sentimentality. (Remember G. K. Chesterton's finely wrought distinction: "Sentiment is jam on your bread; sentimentality, jam all over your face.") The democratic style of leadership does not call for indiscriminate and unyielding faith in your fellow man; some people are *not* to be trusted or respected or supported in their incompetence and willful malevolence. What the democratic style does call for is the introduction and maintenance of systems of relations that make for a grounded trust in others and for the human by-product of enabling people in the system to actualize their capacities for effective and responsible action and so to experience both authentic social relations and personal growth, each giving support to the other.

Precisely because one is committed to the ideal of democracy, one must be mindful of countertendencies in organizational systems. To begin with, there is a tendency toward what the German sociologist, Robert Michels, as long ago as 1915, excessively described as "the iron law of oligarchy." He was led to this "law" through which newly organized minorities acquire dominion within organizations by examining the case of democratic organization. He found there the seeming paradox that leaders initially committed to democratic values abandoned those values as their attention turned increasingly to maintaining the organization and especially their own place within it. The danger is plain. Leaders long established are often the last to perceive their own transition toward oligarchy, toward a form of control in which power is increasingly confined to the successively few. And leaders long established are apt to confuse the legitimacy of their rule with the indispensability of themselves. We all remember that royal proclamation by Louis XIV: "L'état, c'est moi!" And we can recall the more recent story of de Gaulle periodically intoning to himself: "Quand je veux savior ce que pense la France, je m'interroge" ("When I want to know what France thinks, I ask myself"). In this specific sense, many a long-established business leader is incorrigibly Gaullist.

The Michels brand of organizational pessimism poses grave problems for the business leader who would be both competitive and compassionate. The temper of the age suggests, however, the necessity of developing a response that utilizes a countervailing force to Michels's iron law. Such a force finds expression in the rule of thumb which says that the solution to the deficiencies of democracy is more democracy.

A particular ailment of organizational leadership was long since diagnosed by Chester Barnard as "the dilemma of the time lag." In this phrase he referred to the problem of discrepancy between organizational requirements for immediate adaptive action and the slow process of obtaining democratic approval of it. This is an authentic dilemma, not easily resolved. Democratically organized groups can cope with it only by having their members come to recognize *in advance* that, remote as they are from the firing line of daily decision, there will be occasions in which decisive action must be taken before it can be fully explored and validated by the membership. This comes hard for democratic organizations whose members often prefer to pay the price of recurrent maladaptations in order

to avoid having their leadership converted into Caesarism or Bonapartism. But to earn the right for leases of independent decision, democratic leaders must provide for continuing accountability. They must be accountable not only in terms of the criteria they themselves propose but in terms of the often more extensive criteria adopted by other members of their organization and by the wider society.

Conflicting Interests

This brings us directly to another kind of ambivalence and dilemma confronting the organizational leader. One of the traditional responsibilities of the corporate leader, no less than the political one, and the cause of many contradictions in which the corporate executive is involved, is the need to balance the interests of groups which have a legitimate (and sometimes not so apparently legitimate) call on the resources of the organization.

The most obvious interest in the business corporation is economic and the most obvious interest groups are composed of employees, owners, and consumers. Striking a balance among these three groups alone—to say nothing here about the needs of increased capitalization, of the local community, and of the society beyond—poses basic contradictions of thought and action. In the one sphere of employee interests, for example, the business leader is often torn by the question of whether he should seek to attract labor at minimum cost or whether he should ensure for the organization a pool of quality labor by paying top salaries; whether he should place more or less emphasis on fringe benefits as opposed to wages and salaries; whether he should ensure security of employment to the possible short-term detriment of the corporation or whether he should seek maximum efficiency (which means, to put it bluntly, staff layoffs during periods of lax activity) to the possible long-term detriment of the corporation. Such questions are not completely resolved in the marketplace. The decisions turn more nearly on the system of values within which the corporation functions. These values, in turn, are imposed not so much by the economic function of the corporation as by its culture, traditions, history of recent experience, and by the personal proclivities of its leaders within the current context of the polity, the economy, and the society.

In this same sphere of employee interests, but now in a wider sense, the corporate leader must balance or arbitrate a secondary and often equally important interest: What is to be the share of the corporate resources allocated to each unit? What percentage of the budget will be allotted to manufacturing, research and development, advertising, computerization, the development of staff, and so on? It is a tempting belief that such questions are resolved in the organizational hierarchy solely by considerations of corporate need based on objective analysis and authoritative projections. But this is seldom the case. The business leader is as much circumscribed as the political leader by "political" constraints internal to the organization. And with all the accounting systems of planning, programming, and budgeting now in force and yet to come, one suspects that this will continue.

All this takes us back to the structural and functional aspects of the position of organizational leader. He is, of course and above all else, a maker of decisions; not, be it noted, *the* decision-maker. He differs from all the other makers of decision in the organization he leads in this: his decisions are ordinarily more consequential for the fate of that organization and for those parts of its environment affected by the ramified results of those decisions. He faces with fearsome regularity the need to assess conflicting interests, conflicting sentiments, and conflicting convictions within the organization. In this regard, there can be no rest for the sometimes weary leader. He is structurally located at the very node of conflicting wants and demands within the organization. His role requires him to acknowledge and work on these conflicts, not to deny them or to cover them over with the rhetoric of feigned consensus. He has the task of alerting the others to the sources of the conflict, to define and redefine the situation for them, to have them acknowledge in turn that decisions gauged in the light of the organization as a whole must often override the particular concerns of its parts.

It is no easy matter to discover what is in the best interest of the total organization, and so there is ample leeway for continuing disagreement. A degree of indeterminacy requires the exercise of reasonably confident judgment rather than the demonstration of certain outcomes. The leader may err in his calculated decisions engaging the conflicting interests and beliefs of his constituency. That is bad enough. But his greatest error comes in trying to evade these conflicts. Nothing catches up with an organizational leader so much as a conscientious policy of evasion that seeks the appearance of peace and quiet by avoiding decisions that might alienate this or that sector of the constituency. And *because* of a degree of indeterminacy about the validity of the decision, it is not merely the substance of his decisions that is consequential for the organization but the mode through which he arrives at them and the mode in which he makes them known. Effective leaders arbitrate and mediate the inevitable conflicts within the organization in such fashion that most of the members involved in his decisions feel most of the time that justice has been done. It is the role of the leader to act for the whole while interpreting for the parts. And so it is that even a substantively mistaken decision—as the limiting case—taken in ways that win the respect of associates and presented in ways that enlist their however reluctant assent will be less damaging than decisions that are substantively sound at the time but have little support in the organization because they are taken as arbitrary and inequitable. The reason for this is plain enough. Organizational decisions become transformed into organizational realities only to the extent that they engage the willing support of those who must translate them into day-by-day practice. Without such support, the initially sound decision has a way of becoming converted into a subsequently unsound one.

Social Environment of the Organization

Just as the corporate leader must balance the interests of interest groups within his organization, so he is caught in the even more difficult dilemma of balancing the interests of interest groups outside his organization. The direct relationship between the portions of economic wealth distributed by the corporation to its various primary "publics" is reasonably well understood. Should dividends greatly increase, there will be less under static conditions for distribution to the workers in the form of wages and to consumers in the form of stable or lower prices. But conditions are not static; indeed, it is one of the functions of the private and public sectors alike to see to it—through innovation, cost control, new efficiencies—that they never become static.

As a business grows in its capacity to create economic wealth, two interrelated phenomena occur, both of which establish new contradictions with which the organizational leader must cope. One is the demands of the traditional interest groups (employees, owners, consumers) for the production of wealth that is not essentially economic, that is, social wealth. The other is the rise of new interest groups that make other demands on the organization's resources for both economic and social wealth. A few topical examples will bring each of these developments to mind.

The rise of consumerism can be ascribed, at least in part, to a growing public which, surfeited with material possessions, now demands that these same possessions be imbued with qualities that are not only economically profitable but socially desirable. Thus, in our autos we demand seat belts rather than chrome strips; in our drugs, efficacy rather than palliatives (or worse); in our health care, adequacy for all rather than for the few. In like fashion, the call for "relevance" and "meaning" in work cannot be ascribed only to the altogether alienated few but must be recognized as also representing the deepest drives for self-actualization and self-esteem among those who, already employed, have found a measure of economic security. Finally, we can discern the faint beginnings of social commitment among at least a few of the twenty-eight million stockholders in this country—the clearest example being the voting of church-owned stock in an effort to achieve, in particular companies, the employment and advancement of minorities.

The second phenomenon is a corollary of business success. That success attracts notice and consequently increased demands, of both an economic and social kind. Thus, eleemosynary associations find their way to the corporate doorstep seeking contributions; quasi-public associations of all kinds place demands on the corporation that are not only financial but managerial (the time of staff) and physical (meeting sites); and on occasion entire communities descend on the successful corporation to seek aid in cleaning up the air and water (which, be it noted, the corporation has often helped to pollute), in employing the unemployed, in creating needed public transportation.

But if success brings enlarged demands, it also brings enlarged obligations for the corporation to engage in public service. The corporation, particularly the large and successful one, cannot stand aloof from the society in which it exists, if for no other reason—and there are other reasons—than its own economic health. In the last analysis, in this democratic republic at least, every corporation exists at the sufferance of society. To continue to exist, the corporation must meet its obligations, and not particularly those that it accepts as its own but those that are placed on it by society.

Thus, the leader of a significant business corporation must be both a "local" and a "cosmopolitan." By a local, I mean one who is largely oriented to his organization or immediate community that dominates his interests, concerns, and values. By a cosmopolitan, I mean one who is oriented toward the larger social world beyond his immediate organization or community, with extended interests, concerns, and values. The effective leader of a major business faces the task of combining both orientations and developing capabilities appropriate for putting both into practice. He must be able to look inward at his organization and outward at its concentric zones of environment. Social change has reduced his realistic options. Now, more than ever before, he must be both local and cosmopolitan. For although organizations have always been part of a larger social system and an ecosystem, the extent and character of those linkages were for a long time not widely noticed. With the spread of education—defective as it often is—all this is changing. Awareness of the interrelations involved in the ecosystem and social system is developing in every sector of our society. For leaders of business the enlarged awareness means that they must abandon the spectacular malapropism of not so long ago: "What's good for business is good for society." They must transform it into the countermaxim: "What's good for society is good for business—even when it's seemingly not."

In short, the leaders of business in the morally more sensitive society of our time are coming to recognize that they must pay the price of a growing commitment to the moral purposes of the larger society. Acting in terms of an authentic moral commitment is not cost-free. It comes at a price, a price paid for what that society has been contributing and continues to contribute to its constituent organizations. For, as the economists tell us in their analyses of market externalities, the price system often fails to account for the benefits received or the costs suffered by those who are not directly parties to a transaction. The beneficiaries of technological change, for example, are at best only a small part of those who suffer from their deleterious secondary consequences (as the report on the assessment of technology by the National Academy of Sciences reminds us) and as we observe for ourselves while suffering our polluted environments of air, water, sound, landscape, and society.

Conceding that the private sector of our economy does have a role in helping to solve public problems, regardless of whether its role is in competition or in cooperation with government, it is evident that the traditional concepts of competition, within and among companies, must be redefined in confronting those problems. One reason is that the problems themselves are so immense that their solution will require all of the organizations' competitive energies; another is that the face of the competitive "enemy" has changed: It is the problem itself, rather than, in the first instance, another company or another industry. These competitions continue, of course, but they are caught up in larger purposes. This notion finds analogy in the American mission-to-the-moon project, which was not a triumph of competition alone (if we put aside the jingoistic impetus to the program: "Beat Russia"). It was a triumph of cooperation (for an imperfectly examined objective). Within that, it was a triumph of managerial ability in getting thousands of organizations and millions of individuals to collaborate in the attainment of one overarching goal. Actually, the contradictions apparent in this example are socially generated rather than inevitably imposed. For as behavioral studies have shown—and as every business leader knows from experience in his own organization—the fruits of cooperation are far more abundant than those of competition. The basic contradictions, then, may lie within our institutions, within our social and cultural patterns, and derivatively in our assumed psychological needs and aspirations.

An Emerging Self-Critical Society

Finally, in raising questions about the very purpose of our business organizations, we find basic ambivalences that must at one time or another plague every corporate executive: Does the successful business try first to profit or to serve? The quick, agile answer—it tries to do both—escapes the dilemma by swift flight from it. Leaders of business have only begun to wrestle with the problem of *how* to do both in appropriate scale. For they are at work in a rapidly changing moral environment which requires them to make new assessments of purpose. This is a tough assignment. I have alluded to the increasing moral sensibility of American society, knowing that I cannot actually demonstrate that increase beyond all reasonable doubt, let alone measure its extent. All the same, it seems to me that evidence for it abounds on every side. Most of all, it is found in our national inventory of self-critical diagnoses. In growing numbers, we Americans direct our critical attention to the shortcomings of our society just as we have long directed our admiring attention to its strengths. The more we demand of our society, the more faults we find in this process of collective self-scrutiny. As we raise our sights and enlarge our moral expectations, we become more sensitive to the inequities of our society, its corruptions, and its unrealized potentials for a humane life. Unlike an apathetic society, or a complacent one, a self-critical society represents a heightened moral sensibility. What was good enough before, in the form of convenient compromises with moral principle, is no longer judged good enough. More and more Americans are stirring themselves out of the complacency induced by affluence to ask the harder questions: affluence for what? and for whom? and what beyond affluence?

Leaders of organizations in this changing moral environment are being pressed to become agents for the enlarging of equity and humane life. The range of their options is becoming delimited. For should they choose to believe that *only* the fiscal record of profit can testify to the success of their organizations, they will find this self-defeating. In due course, they will find that even that restricted index of accomplishment will deteriorate as they remain on the periphery of the great social transformations of our time. With a degree of optimism, one can be persuaded that newly emerging orientations in the private sector of the nation's business, with their attendant contradictions, ambiguities, and doubts, will force a fresh examination of the social role of business and of the business leader, and that this examination will result in an extended, enduring place for the ideal of social commitment in this revolutionary society.

DISCUSSION QUESTIONS

1. What are the strengths and weakness of a leader who comes from within an organization compared with those of a leader who is selected from outside?

2. What is the origin of leadership ambivalence?

3. What types of ambivalence confront a leader when specifying his or her vision for the organization?

4. What are some of the social exchanges that occur between a leader and subordinates?

5. Distinguish between democratic and authoritarian styles of leadership.

6. What is the basic moral ambivalence that leaders must deal with?

7. What are some ways that leaders can cope with the ambivalence of their positions?

Leadership: The Art of Empowering Others

Jay A. Conger

LEARNING OBJECTIVES

After reading "Leadership: The Art of Empowering Others" by Jay Conger, a student will be able to:

1. Understand the concept of empowerment and how it differs from Machiavellian perspectives of leadership

2. Explore the leadership styles of successful executives

3. Identify the organizational contexts of powerlessness

4. Learn about empowerment techniques and strategies

One ought to be both feared and loved, but as it is difficult for the two to go together, it is much safer to be feared than loved . . . for love is held by a chain of obligation which, men being selfish, is broken whenever it serves their purpose; but fear is maintained by a dread of punishment which never fails.

The Prince, Niccolo Machiavelli

In his handbook, *The Prince,* Machiavelli assures his readers—some being aspiring leaders, no doubt—that only by carefully amassing power and building a fearsome respect could one become a great leader. While the shadowy court life of 16th-century Italy demanded such treachery to ensure one's power, it seems hard to imagine Machiavelli's advice today as anything but a historical curiosity. Yet, interestingly, much of the management literature has focused on the strategies and tactics that managers can use to increase their own power and influence.[1] As such, a Machiavellian quality often pervades the literature, encouraging managers to ensure that their power base is strong and growing. At the same time a small but increasing number of management theorists have begun to

explore the idea that organizational effectiveness also depends on the sharing of power—that the distribution of power is more important than the hoarding of power.[2]

While the idea of making others feel more powerful contradicts the stereotype of the all-powerful executive, research suggests that the traditional ways of explaining a leader's influence may not be entirely correct. For example, recent leadership studies argue that the practice of empowering—or instilling a sense of power—is at the root of organizational effectiveness, especially during times of transition and transformation.[3] In addition, studies of power and control within organizations indicate that the more productive forms of organizational power increase with superiors' sharing of power and responsibility with subordinates.[4] And while there is an increasing awareness of this need for more empowering leadership, we have only recently started to see documentation about the actual practices that leaders employ to effectively build a sense of power among organizational members as well as the contexts most suited for empowerment practices.[5]

In this article, I will explore these practices further by drawing upon a recent study of senior executives who proved themselves highly effective leaders. They were selected by a panel of professors at the Harvard Business School and management consultants who were well acquainted with them and their companies. The study included eight chief executive officers and executive vice-presidents of *Fortune 500* companies and successful entrepreneurial firms, representing industries as diverse as telecommunications, office automation, retail banking, beverages, packaged foods, and management consulting. In each case, these individuals were responsible for either the creation of highly successful companies or for performing what were described as remarkable turnarounds. During my study of these executives, I conducted extensive interviews, observed them on the job, read company and other documents, and talked with their colleagues and

Source: Jay Conger: "Leadership: The Art of Empowering Others," *Academy of Management Executive,* 1989; Vol. 3; No. 1, pp. 17–24. Copyright ©1989. Reprinted by permission.

subordinates. While the study focused on the broader issue of leadership styles, intensive interviews with these executives and their subordinates revealed that many were characterized as empowering leaders. Their actions were perceived as building confidence and restoring a sense of personal power and self-efficacy during difficult organizational transitions. From this study, I identified certain organizational contexts of powerlessness and management practices derived to remedy them.

In this article I will also illustrate several of these practices through a series of vignettes. While the reader may recognize some of the basic ideas behind these practices (such as providing greater opportunities for initiative), it is often the creative manner in which the leader deploys the particular practice that distinguishes them. The reader will discover how they have been carefully tailored to fit the context at hand. I might add, however, that these practices represent just a few of the broad repertoire of actions that leaders can take to make an empowering difference in their organizations.

A Word about Empowerment

We can think of empowerment as the act of strengthening an individual's beliefs in his or her sense of effectiveness. In essence, then, empowerment is not simply a set of external actions; it is a process of changing the internal beliefs of people.[6] We know from psychology that individuals believe themselves powerful when they feel they can adequately cope with environmental demands—that is, situations, events, and people they confront. They feel powerless when they are unable to cope with these demands. Any management practice that increases an individual's sense of self-determination will tend to make that individual feel more powerful. The theory behind these ideas can be traced to the work of Alfred Bandura, who conceptualized the notion of self-efficacy beliefs and their role in an individual's sense of personal power in the world.[7]

From his research in psychology, Bandura identified four means of providing empowering information to others: (1) through positive emotional support during experiences associated with stress and anxiety, (2) through words of encouragement and positive persuasion, (3) by observing others' effectiveness—in other words, having models of success with whom people identified—and (4) by actually experiencing the mastering of a task with

success (the most effective source). Each of these sources of empowerment was used by the study executives and will be identified in the practice examples, as will other sources identified by organizational researchers.

Several Empowering Management Practices

Before describing the actual practices, it is important to first draw attention to an underlying attitude of the study participants. These empowering leaders shared a strong and underlying belief in their subordinates' abilities. It is essentially the Theory Y argument;[8] if you believe in people's abilities, they will come to believe in them. All the executives in the study believed that their subordinates were capable of managing their current situations. They did not employ wholesale firings as a means of transforming their organizations. Rather, they retained the majority of their staff and moved those who could not perform up to standard to positions where they could. The essential lesson is that an assessment of staff skills is imperative before embarking on a program of empowerment. This basic belief in employees' abilities underlies the following examples of management practices designed to empower. We will begin with the practice of providing positive emotional support.

1. *The Squirt-gun Shootouts: Providing a Positive Emotional Atmosphere.* An empowering practice that emerged from the study was that of providing positive emotional support, especially through play or drama. For example, every few months, several executives would stage dramatic "up sessions" to sustain the motivation and excitement of their staff. They would host an afternoon-long, or a one- or two-day event devoted solely to confidence building. The event would open with an uplifting speech about the future, followed by a special, inspirational speaker. At these events there would often be films meant to build excitement or confidence—for example, a film depicting a mountain climber ascending a difficult peak. The message being conveyed is that this person is finding satisfaction in the work he or she does at an extraordinary level of competence. There would also be rewards for exceptional achievements. These sessions acted as ceremonies to enhance the personal status and identity of employees and revive the common feelings that binded them together.[9]

An element of play appears to be especially liberating in situations of great stress and demoralization. In the study's examples, play allowed for the venting of frustrations and in turn permitted individuals to regain a sense of control by stepping back from their pressures for a moment. As Bandura suggests, the positive emotional support provided by something like play alleviates, to some extent, concerns about personal efficacy.[10]

For example, one of the subjects of the study, Bill Jackson, was appointed the head of a troubled division. Demand had outstripped the division's ability to maintain adequate inventories, and product quality had slipped. Jackson's predecessors were authoritarian managers, and subordinates were demoralized as well as paranoid about keeping their jobs. As one told me, "You never knew who would be shot next." Jackson felt that he had to break the tension in a way that would allow his staff to regain their sense of control and power. He wanted to remove the stiffness and paranoia and turn what subordinates perceived as an impossible task into something more fun and manageable.

So, I was told, at the end of his first staff meeting, Jackson quietly pulled out a squirt-gun and blasted one of his managers with water. At first, there was a moment of stunned silence, and then suddenly the room was flooded with laughter. He remarked with a smile, "You gotta have fun in this business. It's not worth having your stomach in ulcers." This began a month of squirt-gun fights between Jackson and his managers.

The end result? A senior manager's comment is representative: "He wanted people to feel comfortable, to feel in control. He used waterguns to do that. It was a game. It took the stiffness out of the business, allowed people to play in a safe environment—as the boss says, 'to have fun.'" This play restored rapport and morale. But Jackson also knew when to stop. A senior manager told me, "We haven't used waterguns in nine months. It has served its purpose. The waterfights were like being accepted into a club. Once it achieved its purpose, it would have been overdone."

Interview after interview with subordinates confirmed the effectiveness of the squirt-gun incident. It had been experienced as an empowering ritual. In most contexts, this behavior would have been abusive. Why did it work? Because it is a management practice that fit the needs of subordinates at the appropriate time.

The executive's staff consisted largely of young men, "rough and ready" individuals who could be described as fun-loving and playful. They were accustomed to an informal atmosphere and operated in a very down-to-earth style. Jackson's predecessor, on the other hand, had been stiff and formal.

Jackson preferred to manage more informally. He wanted to convey, quickly and powerfully, his intentions of managing in a style distinct from his predecessor's. He was concerned, however, that his size—he is a very tall, energetic, barrel-chested man—as well as his extensive background in manufacturing would be perceived as intimidating by his young staff and increase their reluctance to assume initiative and control. Through the squirt-gun fights, however, he was able to (1) relieve a high level of tension and restore some sense of control, (2) emphasize the importance of having fun in an otherwise trying work environment, and (3) direct subordinates' concerns away from his skills and other qualities that intimidated them. It was an effective management practice because he understood the context. In another setting, it might have been counter-productive.

2. *The "I Make a Difference" Club: Rewarding and Encouraging in Visible and Personal Ways.* The majority of executives in the study rewarded the achievements of their staffs by expressing personal praise and rewarding in highly visible and confidence-building ways. They believed that people appreciated recognition of their hard work and success. Rewards of high incentive value were particularly important, especially those of personal recognition from the leader. As Rosabeth Kanter notes, a sense of power comes " . . . when one has relatively close contact with sponsors (higher level people who confer approval, prestige, or backing)."[11] Combined with words of praise and positive encouragement, such experiences become important sources of empowerment.

The executives in the study took several approaches to rewards. To reward exceptional performance, one executive established the "I Make a Difference Club." Each year, he selects two or three staff members to be recognized for their excellence on the job. It is a very exclusive club, and only the executive knows the eligibility rules, which are based on outstanding performance. Inductees are invited to dinner in New York City but are not told beforehand that they are about to join the "I Make a Difference Club." They arrive and meet with other staff members whom they believe are there for a staff dinner. During dinner, everyone is asked to speak about what is going on in his or her part of the company. The old-timers speak first, followed by the inductees (who are still unaware of their coming induction). Only after they have given their speeches are they informed that they have just joined the club. As one manager said, "It's one of the most wonderful moments in life."

This executive and others also make extensive use of personal letters to individuals thanking them for their efforts and projects. A typical letter might read,

"Fred, I would personally like to thank you for your contribution to _____ , and I want you to know that I appreciate it." Lunches and dinners are hosted for special task accomplishments.

Public recognition is also employed as a means of rewarding. As one subordinate commented about his boss,

> *He will make sure that people know that so and so did an excellent job on something. He's superb on giving people credit. If the person has done an exceptional job on a task or project, he will be given the opportunity to present his or her findings all the way to the board. Six months later, you'll get a call from a friend and learn that he has dropped your name in a speech that you did well. It makes you want to do it again.*

I found that the investment in rewards and recognition made by many of these executives is unusually high, consuming a significant portion of their otherwise busy day. Yet the payoff appeared high. In interviews, subordinates described these rewards as having an empowering impact on them.

To understand why some of these rewards proved to be so successful, one must understand their organizational contexts. In some cases, the organizations studied were quite large, if not enormous. The size of these organizations did little to develop in employees a sense of an "I"— let alone an "I" that makes a difference. It was easy for organization members to feel lost in the hierarchy and for their achievements to be invisible, for recognition not to be received for personal contributions. The study's executives countered this tendency by institutionalizing a reward system that provided visibility and recognition— for example, the "I Make a Difference Club," presentations to the Board, and names dropped in speeches. Suddenly, you as a member of a large organization stood out—you were special.

Outstanding performance from each of the executives' perspectives was also something of a necessity. All the executives had demanding goals to achieve. As such, they had to tend to subordinates' sense of importance and contribution. They had to structure reward systems that would keep people "pumped up"—that would ensure that their confidence and commitment would not be eroded by the pressures placed on them.

3. *"Praising the Troops": Expressing Confidence.* The empowering leaders in the study spent significant amounts of time expressing their confidence in subordinates' abilities. Moreover, they expressed their confidence throughout

each day—in speeches, in meetings, and casually in office hallways. Bandura comments that "people who are persuaded verbally that they possess the capabilities to master given tasks are likely to mobilize greater sustained effort than if they harbor self-doubts and dwell on personal deficiencies when difficulties arise."[12]

A quote from Irwin Federman, CEO of Monolithic Memories, a highly successful high-tech company, captures the essence and power of a management practice that builds on this process:

> *If you think about it, we love others not for who they are, but for how they make us feel. In order to willingly accept the direction of another individual, it must make you feel good to do so. . . . If you believe what I'm saying, you cannot help but come to the conclusion that those you have followed passionately, gladly, zealously—have made you feel like somebody. . . . This business of making another person feel good in the unspectacular course of his daily comings and goings is, in my view, the very essence of leadership.*[13]

This proactive attitude is exemplified by Bob Jensen. Bob assumed control of his bank's retail operations after a reorganization that transferred away the division's responsibility for large corporate clients. Demoralized by a perceived loss in status and responsibility, branch managers were soon asking, "Where's our recognition?" Bob, however, developed an inspiring strategic vision to transform the operation. He then spent much of his time championing his strategy and expressing his confidence in employees' ability to carry it out. Most impressive was his personal canvass of some 175 retail branches.

As he explained,

> *I saw that the branch system was very down, morale was low. They felt like they'd lost a lot of their power. There were serious problems and a lot of staff were just hiding. What I saw was that we really wanted to create a small community for each branch where customers would feel known. To do that, I needed to create an attitude change. I saw that the attitudes of the branch staff were a reflection of the branch manager. The approach then was a manageable job—now I had to focus on only 250 people, the branch managers, rather than the 3,000 staff employees out there. I knew I had to change their mentality from being lost in a bureaucracy to feeling like the president of their*

own bank. I had to convince them they were special—that they had the power to transform the organization. . . . All I did was talk it up. I was up every night. In one morning, I hit 17 branches. My goal was to sell a new attitude. To encourage people to "pump iron." I'd say, "Hi, how's business?", encourage them. I'd arrange tours of the branches for the chairman on down. I just spent a lot of time talking to these people—explaining that they were the ones who could transform the organization.

It was an important tactic—one that made the branch managers feel special and important. It was also countercultural. As one executive told me, "Bob would go out into the field to visit the operations, which was very unusual for senior people in this industry." His visits heightened the specialness that branch managers felt. In addition, Bob modeled self-confidence and personal success—an important tactic to build a sense of personal effectiveness among subordinates.[14]

I also watched Jack Eaton, president of a regional telephone company, praise his employees in large corporate gatherings, in executive council meetings, and in casual encounters. He explained his philosophy:

I have a fundamental belief and trust in the ability and conscientiousness of others. I have a lot of good people. You can turn them loose, let them feel good about their accomplishments. . . . You ought to recognize accomplishment as well as build confidence. I generally do it in small ways. If someone is doing well, it's important to express your confidence to that person—especially among his peers. I tend to do it personally. I try to be genuine. I don't throw around a lot of b.s.

This practice proved especially important during the transition of the regional phone companies away from the parent organization.

4. *"President of My Own Bank": Fostering Initiative and Responsibility.* Discretion is a critical power component of any job.[15] By simply fostering greater initiative and responsibility in subordinates' tasks, a leader can empower organizational members. Bob Jensen, the bank executive, is an excellent example of how one leader created opportunities for greater initiative despite the confines of his subordinates' positions. He transformed what had been a highly constricted branch manager's job into a branch "president" concept. The idea was simple—every manager was made to feel like the president of his own community

bank, and not just in title. Goals, compensation, and responsibilities were all changed to foster this attitude. Existing measurement systems were completely restructured. The value-of-funds-generated had been the principal yardstick—something over which branch managers had only very limited control because of interest rate fluctuations. Managers were now evaluated on what they could control—that is, deposits. Before, branch managers had rotated every couple of years. Now they stayed put. "If I'm moving around, then I'm not the president of my own bank, so we didn't move them anymore," Jensen explained. He also decentralized responsibilities that had resided higher in the hierarchy—allowing the branch manager to hire, give money to charities, and so on. In addition, a new ad agency was hired to mark the occasion, and TV ads were made showing the branch managers being in charge, rendering personal services themselves. The branch managers even thought up the ad lines.

What Jensen did so skillfully was recognize that his existing managers had the talent and energy to turn their operations around successfully, but that their sense of power was missing. He recognized their pride had been hurt and that he needed to restore a sense of ownership and self-importance. He had to convince his managers through increased authority that they were no longer "pawns" of the system—that they were indeed "presidents" of their own banks.

Another example—this one demonstrating a more informal delegation of initiative—was quite surprising. The setting was a highly successful and rapidly growing computer firm, and the study participant was the vice-president of manufacturing. The vice-president had recently been hired away from another firm and was in the process of revamping manufacturing. During the process, he discovered that his company's costs on its terminal video monitors were quite high. However, he wanted his staff to discover the problem for themselves and to "own" the solution. So one day, he placed behind his desk a black-and-white Sony TV with a placard on top saying $69.95. Next to it he placed a stripped-down version of the company's monitor with a placard of $125.95. Both placards reflected the actual costs of the two products. He never said a word. But during the day as staff and department managers entered their boss's office, they couldn't help but notice the two sets. They quickly got the message that their monitor was costing twice as much as a finished TV set. Within a month, the manufacturing team had lowered the monitor's costs by 40%.

My first impression on hearing this story was that, as a subordinate, I would be hard pressed not to get the point and, more important, I would wonder why the boss was not more direct. Ironically, the boss appears to be hitting subordinates over the head with the problem. Out of context, then, this example hardly seems to make others feel more competent and powerful. Yet staff described themselves as "turned on" and motivated by this behavior. Why, I wondered? A little history will illustrate the effectiveness of this action.

The vice-president's predecessor had been a highly dictatorial individual. He tightly controlled his staff's actions and stifled any sense of discretion. Implicitly, his behavior said to subordinates, "You have no ideas of your own." He fired freely, leaving staff to feel that they had little choice in whether to accept his orders or not. By his actions, he essentially transformed his managers into powerless order-takers.

When the new vice-president arrived, he found a group of demoralized subordinates whom he felt were nonetheless quite talented. To restore initiative, he began to demonstrate the seriousness of his intentions in highly visible and symbolic ways. For example, rather than tell his subordinates what to do, he started by seeding ideas and suggestions in humorous and indirect ways. The TV monitor is only one of many examples. Through these actions, he was able eventually to restore a sense of initiative and personal competence to his staff. While these examples are illustrative of effective changes in job design, managers contemplating job enrichment would be well advised to consult the existing literature and research before undertaking major projects.[16]

5. *Early Victories: Building on Success.* Many of the executives in the study reported that they often introduced organizational change through pilot or otherwise small and manageable projects. They designed these projects to ensure early success for their organizations. For example, instead of introducing a new sales structure nationwide, they would institute the change in one region; a new technology would have a pilot introduction at a single plant rather than systemwide. Subordinates described these early success experiences as strongly reinforcing their sense of power and efficacy. As Mike Beer argues:

> In order for change to spread throughout an organization and become a permanent fixture, it appears that early successes are needed. . . . When individuals, groups, and whole organizations feel more competent than they did before the change, this increased sense of competence reinforces the new behavior and solidifies learning associated with change.[17]

An individual's sense of mastery through actual experience is the most effective means of increasing self efficacy.[18] When subordinates are given more complex and difficult tasks, they are presented with opportunities to test their competence. Initial success experiences will make them feel more capable and, in turn, empowered. Structuring organizational changes to ensure initial successes builds on this principle.

Contexts of Powerlessness

The need to empower organizational members becomes more important in certain contexts. Thus, it is important to identify conditions within organizations that might foster a sense of powerlessness. Certain circumstances, for instance, appear to lower feelings of self-efficacy. In these cases, subordinates typically perceive themselves as lacking control over their immediate situation (e.g., a major reorganization threatens to displace responsibility and involves limited or no subordinate participation),[19] or lacking the required capability, resources, or discretion needed to accomplish a task (e.g., the development of new and difficult-to-learn skills for the introduction of a new technological process).[20] In either case, these experiences maximize feelings of inadequacy and lower self-confidence. They, in turn, appear to lessen motivation and effectiveness.

Exhibit 10.1 identifies the more common organizational factors that affect these self-efficacy or personal power beliefs and contribute to feelings of powerlessness. They include organizational factors, supervisory styles, reward systems, and job design.

For example, during a major organizational change, goals may change—often dramatically—to respond to the organization's new direction. Rules may no longer be clearly defined as the firm seeks new guidelines for action. Responsibilities may be dramatically altered. Power alliances may shift, leaving parts of the organization with a perceived loss of power or increasing political activity. Certain functional areas, divisions, or acquired companies may experience disenfranchisement as their responsibilities are felt to be diminished or made subordinate to others. As a result, employees' sense of competence may be seriously challenged as they face having to accept and acquire new responsibilities, skills, and management practices as well as deal with the uncertainty of their future.

EXHIBIT 10.1

CONTEXT FACTORS LEADING TO POTENTIAL STATE OF POWERLESSNESS

Organizational Factors:

Significant organizational changes/transitions
Start-up ventures
Excessive, competitive pressures
Impersonal bureaucratic climate
Poor communications and limited network-forming systems
Highly centralized organizational resources

Supervisory Style:

Authoritarian (high control)
Negativism (emphasis on failures)
Lack of reason for actions/consequences

Reward Systems:

Noncontingency (arbitrary reward allocations)
Low incentive value of rewards
Lack of competence-based rewards
Lack of innovation-based rewards

Job Design:

Lack of role clarity
Lack of training and technical support
Unrealistic goals
Lack of appropriate authority/discretion
Low task variety
Limited participation in programs, meetings, and decisions that have a direct impact on job performance
Lack of appropriate/necessary resources
Lack of network-forming opportunities
Highly established work routines
Too many rules and guidelines
Low advancement opportunities
Lack of meaningful goals/tasks
Limited contact with senior management

Source: Adapted from J. A. Conger and R. N. Kanungo, "The Empowerment Process: Integrating Theory and Practice," *Academy of Management Review,* July 1988.

In new venture situations, uncertainty often appears around the ultimate success of the company's strategy. A major role for leaders is to build an inspiring picture of the firm's future and convince organizational members of their ability to achieve that future. Yet, market lead times are often long, and tangible results may be slow in coming. Long work hours with few immediate rewards can diminish confidence. Frustration can build, and questions about the organization's future can arise. In addition, the start-up's success and responses to growth can mean constant change in responsibility, pushing managers into responsibilities where they have had little prior experience; thus, failure may be experienced initially as new responsibilities are learned. Entrepreneurial executives may be reluctant to relinquish their control as expansion continues.

Bureaucratic environments are especially conducive to creating conditions of powerlessness. As Peter Block points out, bureaucracy encourages dependency and submission because of its top-down contract between the organization and employees.[21] Rules, routines, and traditions define what can and cannot be done, allowing little room for initiative and discretion to develop. Employees' behavior is often guided by rules over which they have no say and which may no longer be effective, given the present-day context.

From the standpoint of supervision, authoritarian management styles can strip away subordinates' discretion and, in turn, a sense of power. Under an authoritarian manager, subordinates inevitably come to believe that they have little control—that they and their careers are subject to the whims or demands of their boss. The problem becomes acute when capable subordinates begin to attribute their powerlessness to internal factors, such as their own personal competence, rather than to external factors, such as the nature of the boss's temperament.

Rewards are another critical area for empowerment. Organizations that do not provide valued rewards or simply do not reward employees for initiative, competence, and innovation are creating conditions of powerlessness. Finally, jobs with little meaningful challenge, or jobs where the task is unclear, conflicting, or excessively demanding can lower employees' sense of self-efficacy.

Implications for Managers

Managers can think of the empowerment process as involving several stages.[22] Managers might want to

EXHIBIT 10.2

Stages of the Empowerment Process

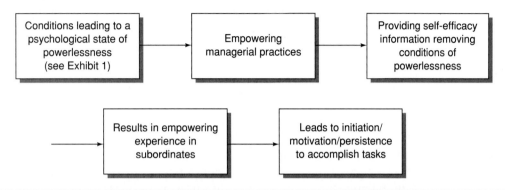

begin by identifying for themselves whether any of the organizational problems and characteristics described in this article are present in their own firms. In addition, managers assuming new responsibilities should conduct an organizational diagnosis that clearly identifies their current situation, and possible problems and their causes. Attention should be aimed at understanding the recent history of the organization. Important questions to ask would be: What was my predecessor's supervisory style? Has there been a recent organizational change that negatively affected my subordinates? How is my operation perceived by the rest of the corporation? Is there a sense of disenfranchisement? Am I planning to change significantly the outlook of this operation that would challenge traditional ways of doing things? How are people rewarded? Are jobs designed to be motivating?

Once conditions contributing to feelings of powerlessness are identified, the managerial practices identified in this article and in the management literature can be used to provide self-efficacy information to subordinates. This information in turn can result in an empowering experience for subordinates and may ultimately lead to greater initiative, motivation, and persistence.

However, in applying these practices, it is imperative that managers tailor their actions to fit the context at hand. For example, in the case of an authoritarian predecessor, you are more likely to need praise and confidence-building measures and greater opportunities for job discretion. With demanding organizational goals and tasks, the practices of confidence building and active rewarding, an element of play, and a supportive environment are per-

haps most appropriate. The specific character of each practice must necessarily vary somewhat to fit your particular situation. For instance, what makes many of the previous examples so important is that the executives responded with practices that organizational members could relate to or that fit their character—for instance, the television and squirt-gun examples. Unfortunately, much of today's popular management literature provides managers with tools to manage their subordinates, yet few highlight the importance of matching the practice to the appropriate context. Empowering is not a pill; it is not simply a technique, as many workshops and articles would lead us to believe. Rather, to be truly effective it requires an understanding of subordinates and one's organizational context.

Finally, although it is not as apparent in the examples themselves, each of the study executives set challenging and appealing goals for their organizations. This is a necessary component of effective and empowering leadership. If goals are not perceived as appealing, it is difficult to empower managers in a larger sense. As Warren Bennis and Burt Nanus argue: "Great leaders often inspire their followers to high levels of achievement by showing them how their work contributes to worthwhile ends. It is an emotional appeal to some of the most fundamental needs—the need to be important, to make a difference, to feel useful, to be part of a successful and worthwhile enterprise."[23] Such goals go hand in hand with empowering management practices. They were and are an integral part of the empowerment process I observed in the companies I studied.

A Word of Caution

In closing, it is important to add a note of caution. First of all, empowerment is not the complete or always the appropriate answer to building the confidence of managers. It can lead to overconfidence. A false sense of confidence in positive outcomes may lead employees and organizations to persist in what may, in actuality, prove to be tactical errors. Thus, a system of checks and balances is needed. Managers must constantly test reality and be alert to signs of "group think."

Some managers may be incapable of empowering others. Their own insecurities may prevent them from instilling a sense of power in subordinates. This is ironic, since often these are the individuals who need to develop such skills. Yet, as Kanter argues, "Only those leaders who feel secure about their own power outward . . . can see empowering subordinates as a gain rather than a loss."[24]

Certain situations may not warrant empowerment. For example, there are contexts where opportunities for greater initiative or responsibility simply do not exist and, in some cases, subordinates may be unwilling or unable to assume greater ownership or responsibility. As Lyman Porter, Edward Lawler, and Richard Hackman point out, research "strongly suggests that only workers with reasonably high strength of desire for higher-order need satisfaction . . . will respond positively and productively to the opportunities present in jobs which are high in meaning, autonomy, complexity, and feedback."[25] Others may not have the requisite experience or knowledge to succeed.

And those given more than they are capable of handling may fail. The end result will be the opposite of what you are seeking—a sense of powerlessness. It is imperative that managers assess as accurately as possible their subordinates' capabilities before undertaking difficult goals and empowering them to achieve.

Second, certain of the empowerment practices described in this article are not appropriate for all situations. For example, managers of subordinates who require structure and direction are likely to find the example of the manager "seeding" ideas with the television set an ineffective practice. In the case of a pressing deadline or crisis, such seeding is inappropriate, given its longer time horizons.

When staging playful or unconventional events, the context must be considered quite carefully. What signals are you sending about yourself and your management philosophy? Like rewards, these events can be used to excess and lose their meaning. It is imperative to determine the appropriateness and receptivity of such practices. You may inadvertently mock or insult subordinates, peers, or superiors.

In terms of expressing confidence and rewarding, both must be done sincerely and not to excess. Praising for nonaccomplishments can make rewards meaningless. Subordinates may suspect that the boss is simply flattering them into working harder.

In general, however, empowerment practices are an important tool for leaders in setting and achieving higher goals and in moving an organization past difficult transitions.[26] But remember that they do demand time, confidence, an element of creativity, and a sensitivity to one's context to be effective.

ENDNOTES

1. See, for example, J. P. Kotter, *Power in Management,* New York: AMACOM, 1979, and J. Pfeffer, *Power in Organizations,* Marshfield, MA: Pitman, 1981.

2. See P. Block, *The Empowered Manager,* San Francisco: Jossey-Bass, 1987; W.W. Burke, "Leadership as Empowering Others," in S. Srivastva (Ed.), *Executive Power,* San Francisco: Jossey-Bass, 1986, pp. 51–77; and R.M. Kanter, *The Change Masters,* New York: Simon & Schuster, 1983.

3. W. Bennis and B. Nanus, *Leaders,* New York: Harper & Row, 1985; R. M. Kanter, "Power Failure in Management Circuits," *Harvard Business Review,* July-August 1979, pp. 65–75.

4. See Kanter, Endnote 3; and A.S. Tannenbaum, *Control in Organizations,* New York: McGraw-Hill, 1968.

5. See J. A. Conger and R. N. Kanungo, "The Empowerment Process: Integrating Theory and Practice," *Academy of Management Review,* July 1988; and R.J. House, "Power and Personality in Complex Organization," in L.L. Cummings and B.M. Staw (Eds.), *Research in Organizational Behavior: An Annual Review of Critical Essays and Reviews,* Vol. 10, Greenwich, CT: JAI Press, 1988. The author is grateful to Rabindra N. Kanungo for his insights and help in conceptualizing the empowerment process.

6. See Conger and Kanungo, Endnote 5.

7. A. Bandura, "Self-Efficiency: Toward a Unifying Theory of Behavioral Change," *Psychological Review,* 1977, 84(2), pp. 191–215.

8. D. McGregor, *The Human Side of Enterprise,* New York: McGraw-Hill, 1960.

9. See J. M. Beyer and H. M. Trice, "How an Organization's Rites Reveal Its Culture," *Organizational Dynamics,* Spring 1987, pp. 4–25.

10. A. Bandura, *Social Foundations of Thought and Action: A Social Cognitive View,* Englewood Cliffs, NJ: Prentice-Hall, 1986.

11. See Kanter, Endnote 3, p. 66.

12. See Bandura, Endnote 10, p. 400.

13. W. Bennis and B. Nanus, *Leaders,* New York: Harper & Row. 1985, pp. 64–65.

14. See Bandura, Endnote 10.

15. See Kanter, Endnote 3.

16. See J. R. Hackman, "The Design of Work in the 1980s," *Organizational Dynamics,* Summer 1978, pp. 3–17.

17. M. Beer, *Organizational Change and Development,* Santa Monica, CA: Goodyear, 1980, p. 64.

18. See Bandura, Endnote 10.

19. F. M. Rothbaum, J. R. Weisz, and S. S. Snyder, "Changing the World and Changing Self: A Two Process Model of Perceived Control," *Journal of Personality and Social Psychology,* 1982, 42, pp. 5–37; and L. Y. Abramson, J. Garber, and M. E. P. Seligman, "Learned Helplessness in Humans: An Attributional Analysis," in J. Garber and M. E. P. Seligman (Eds.), *Human Helplessness: Theory and Applications,* New York: Academic Press, 1980, pp. 3–34.

20. See Kanter, Endnote 2.

21. See Block, Endnote 2.

22. See Conger and Kanungo. Endnote 5.

23. Bennis and Nanus, Endnote 13, p. 93.

24. See Kanter, Endnote 3, p. 73.

25. L.W. Porter, E. E. Lawler, and J. R. Hackman, *Behavior in Organizations,* New York: McGraw-Hill, 1975, p. 306.

26. See N. M. Tichy and M. A. Devanna, *The Transformational Leader,* New York: John Wiley, 1986.

DISCUSSION QUESTIONS

1. What is empowerment?

2. List the empowering management practices that Conger observed.

3. What role does ritual, ceremony, or culture change have in producing empowerment?

4. Describe some of the organizational conditions that cause powerlessness.

6. List the stages that Conger identifies that managers can use to produce empowerment.

7. What are the limitations to the empowerment strategy? Under what conditions can the strategy backfire?

8. How would Merton view Conger's finding that empowered executives "spent significant amounts of time expressing their confidence in subordinates' abilities"? Is there anything in Merton's analysis of leadership and its ambivalences that provides suggestions for the facilitation of empowerment?

FOR FURTHER READING

Bass, B. *Leadership and Performance beyond Expectations.* New York: Free Press, 1985.

Barnes, L., and Kriger, P. "The Hidden Side of Organizational Leadership." *Sloan Manegement Review* (Fall 1986) 15–25.

Bennis, W., and Nanus, B. *Leaders: The Strategies for Taking Charge.* New York: Harper & Row, 1985.

Kirkpatrick, S., and Locke, E. "Leadership: Do Traits Matter?" *Academy of Management Executive* 5 (1991) 48–60.

Kotter, J. *A Force for Change: How Leadership Differs from Management.* New York: Free Press, 1990.

Mintzberg, H. *The Nature of Managerial Work.* New York: Harper & Row, 1973.

Sayles, L. *The Working Leader: The Triumph of High Performance Over Conventional Management Principles.* New York: Free Press, 1993.

Sennett, R. *Authority.* New York: Vintage, 1981.

Thomas, A. "Does Leadership Make a Difference to Organizational Performance." *Administrative Science Quarterly* 33 (1988) 388–400.

PART III: CASE 1

Buying Sneakers

Barry Allen Gold

MOTHER: Ian needs new sneakers. His other pair is too tight. *He's been wearing the same pair for school and play.*

FATHER: OK. We can go to the mall this afternoon.

MOTHER: Good, I think that Herman's is having a sale. We can also try Thom McAnn. Last year they had a "2-for-1" sale. Ian can also use a new pair of penny loafers for Sunday School.

Ian, an eleven-year-old sixth grade student, and his parents, drove fifteen minutes to an enclosed shopping mall to begin their search for high-quality, bargain-priced sneakers.

The first stop was at Thom McAnn. There was no "2-for-1" sale, but the sneakers were cheap—priced from $19.95 to $27.95. The clerk measured Ian's foot, which had increased a full size from his last shoe purchase to size 7. Ian tried on a $24.95 pair that fit well and looked good.

IAN: They're OK, but I already have these. *Can't we look for something new?*

Herman's Sporting Goods was next. There was a sneaker sale but no size 7. The clerk explained that size 7 is not stocked by Herman's.

CLERK: It's too large for boys and too small for men.

Foot Locker was next. There were elaborate displays of the latest models priced from $79.99 to $110. The sale sneakers were priced between $50 to $60. Ian tried on a pair of Air Jordans. They fit fine, looked good, and cost $59.95.

MOTHER: They're a little too expensive. What else do you have?

CLERK: We have pumps on sale for $79. But they're no longer "in." *They're last year's model.*

IAN: Which ones are this year's model?

The salesperson walked to a display and waved his arm elegantly over the sneakers. The prices ranged from $95 to $110.

The family closely inspected each pair. The agreed that they were good sneakers but way beyond their budget.

FATHER: We can get three pairs for that price!

IAN: Do you carry size 7?

CLERK: Yes.

Ian lingered over the Andre Agassi model because of its interesting combination of colors and a large air bubble in its heel. These were the highest fashion and highest tech sneakers in the store. At $110 they were also the most expensive.

MOTHER: Let's look a little more.

Father and Son shoe store was next. It had many sneakers on sale. Air pumps, high tops, and an assortment of old fashioned Converse basketball styles. Ian tried on a $55 high-top air pump in black.

FATHER: The price seems right. It's not $25 but its not $110, either.

MOTHER: He looks clumsy in them. He's walking funny.

After careful deliberation the consensus was that for $55 they should be able to find a better looking sneaker.

FATHER: What about the Converse? When I was a kid I thought they were the greatest. Besides, they're cheap.

IAN: I never heard of Converse. *Nobody wears them.*

It was 4:30 P.M. and there were no other shoe stores in the mall.

MOTHER: Let's give Sears a try. I doubt they'll have anything, but you never know.

Sears had plenty of last year's $25 models that the clerk claimed were the "in thing." To Foot Locker, again.

FATHER: Nice sneakers but too expensive. Who would pay $110 for an eleven-year-old boy's sneakers? In three months he'll outgrow them.

The family left the mall. Drizzle had become soaking rain. It was 4:45 P.M. and they were weary.

On the way home, Ian started a campaign to persuade his parents to stop at Jay's Shoe Box, a neighborhood store.

FATHER: But Jay's doesn't discount. *Why pay top dollar?*

MOTHER: Sometimes they have sales. It's worth a quick look.

Jay's had nothing on sale.

CLERK: We never have sales. But we have the latest models, and expert fit, and, if you have any problems, bring them back and we'll take care of you. You don't get this kind of service at the mall.

Jay's was closing for the evening in ten minutes. Ian and his parents were the only customers in the store. The prices ranged from $69.95 to $110.

CLERK: We have only the latest models. *That's what kids want.*

Ian tried on several pairs in the $70 to $80 range. They looked good and fit fine. It was now 5:10 P.M. and the owner—Jay—was vacuuming, a strong hint that it was time to either purchase something or leave.

[Stop reading. Predict the decision.]

The family deliberated.

FATHER: *There's no rush.* We can look again next week.

IAN: But I want to get them today.
Mother: We've already looked everyplace.

Ian held and admired the Andre Agassi model.

CLERK: Would you like to try them on? I'm pretty sure that I have size 7.

Ian tried on the Andre Agassi Nikes and they looked good and according to Ian they fit the best of any sneakers that he had tried on that day.

After a quick, somewhat pressured debate—the vacuum was coming closer—they decided to buy the $110 Andre Agassi model.

IAN: Thank you. *I really like these!*
FATHER: You're a good boy—straight "A"s on your report card. You deserve nice sneakers.
MOTHER: Yes, Ian is a very good boy.
FATHER: Don't play in the mud in these. OK?

PART III: CASE 2

THE FORGOTTEN GROUP MEMBER

Franklin Ramsoomair

Frank Rasmussen put down the telephone receiver and leaned back in the comfortable swivel chair. He put his hands behind his head, interlocked his fingers, and raised his feet onto the desk. The traffic on University Avenue three floors below him was heavy but he was not really thinking about it. He thought of Janet Simpson, who had just called. She had sounded frustrated and even somewhat defiant. "I cannot fathom why the other group members are against me. I know that you have assigned a group project, but I would like to request permission to do an individual project."

His course outline stated that Business 388 was "heavily group-oriented," and his consent to Janet's request would essentially contradict the conceptual approach he had chosen. He could do it, using the rationale he had proposed so often, that the organization needs to be as flexible as possible in trying to meet the needs of individual members. Either way, there seemed to be a catch. He was not sure at this point how to address the problem.

The Setting and Environment

The University of Ontario School of Business and Economics caters to approximately 1000 students. It has acquired an enviable reputation in the province of Ontario and normally has to turn down numerous applications each year, even though the minimum average percentage required for entry is 83 percent.

Students are exposed to larger classes and a general management program in the first two years of their Bachelor in Business Administration (B.B.A.) program. Classes are smaller in the third year and number 35 on average. Courses are "functional" in orientation and involve areas such as human resources, marketing, production operations, finance, and accounting.

Some of the classes in the third year are run on a group basis. These entail group discussions in class as well as out-of-class group assignments. It is optional for the instructor to have a group-oriented class but in the last five years, departments have been urging instructors to have some measure of group work to increase interaction and interpersonal skills.

Frank Rasmussen teaches Organizational Behavior and he believes in the benefits of group work. He particularly espouses use of the "classroom as organization" model proposed by Cohen,[1] although this is modified to suit the purposes of the class. Thus, members of the class are designated employees of the "Enterprise Corporation." They receive a mission statement and a job description which they have to sign (Exhibits 10.2 and 10.3). Duties include task assignments such as completion of a case analysis by the group as well as maintenance issues such as helping peers in the group. A group facilitator is also selected and the system in this respect varies from semester to semester. There could be a structured set of procedures such as having candidates for the position submit to interviews by Rasmussen. This particular semester saw the facilitator being chosen by the group itself.

Whatever the mode of selection, the facilitator is charged with coordination of the group's activities. Many meetings are held out of class and the facilitator sets the time and place based on input from the members. He/she informs all concerned about meetings and other plans, and then generally initiates activities when members gather together. The participation mark for the course is 20 percent of the total. Rasmussen awards members a number of points out of ten and the facilitator is responsible for the other half. In addition, the instructor scores the facilitator out of twenty and criteria for judging include response of the group in terms of readiness for in-class discussions as well as the quality of the group assignment. As invariably happens, some groups have problems, e.g., the free-rider effect, and the facilitator could then be partially evaluated on how well the situation is handled.

The students who enter the business programme and succeed until third year are high achievers and are marked by the desire to do the best that they possibly can. Group members try to give their optimum and facilitators normally strive for the best group possible. Students aim for A's because they realize the impact that a record such as this could have on their ultimate careers. There is a competitive

Source: Franklin Ramsoomair: "The Forgotten Group Member," *Case Research Journal,* Spring 1992: pp. 63–73. Copyright ©1992. Reprinted by permission.

Exhibit 10.3

THE ENTERPRISE CORPORATION: MISSION STATEMENT

What is an organization? Is the University of Ontario School of Business and Economics an organization? Perhaps it goes without saying, but the buildings, the concrete and mortar do not constitute an organization. These are but facades and the actual organization encompasses people who are working together toward the attainment of a common goal.

Similarly, the Enterprise Corporation consists of you and me, all reaching for the same objective, i.e., to experience the best education possible within the context of this course. Consequently the primary goals of our corporation are:

■ To be adequately prepared for class discussions, by completing the necessary readings
■ To complete the assignments
■ To attend sessions to the best of your ability
■ To strive for the highest grade possible
■ To take part in class discussions

These can be considered the task issues of the corporation. The maintenance issues involve the goals of:

■ Contributing to the efforts of the group
■ Attending group meetings
■ Striving for a cohesive group, while not falling prey to groupthink
■ Assisting the group manager in the managerial functions of planning, leading, and coordinating

You are an integral part of our organization. Your signing of the job description form indicates that you accept the basic tenets of this corporation. Your input is valuable. Given the nature of our venture, it is imperative that you understand the aims of the organization and realize the important part that you, as an individual—with unique perspectives, ideas and criticisms—will play.

In this mission statement, I take the opportunity to welcome you to a different experience. I would ask that, during our time together, you try to carry out the Enterprise Corporation's prime objective, that you try to enjoy our sessions. Once this is achieved, we may then learn something from them.

---

environment and group work, including facilitating, is taken very seriously. In addition, although it may appear to be a minor point, Rasmussen hands out an award at the end of the semester for the best group and peer pressure is such that there is always a notable effort by each group to claim the prize.

The Enterprise Corporation consequently uses an autonomous group conceptual base. Rasmussen attends meetings whenever invited and if his schedule allows. Otherwise the facilitator and the group determine their own schedules and plans in respect of the course. The final product involves completion of the group assignments to the best of the group's ability and also the development of tenets which would allow for a cohesive group. Rasmussen's telephone numbers at his office and home are given to members in case anyone wishes to reach him. He stresses, however, that the outlook of the organization is such that groups should at first attempt to address problems

on their own. He could be *informed* but he generally expects that most problematic issues would be handled at the group level. If this is not possible, the facilitator would discuss the problem with him.

The Semester Begins

Frank Rasmussen left his office and headed to the classroom which was on the same floor. He was in high spirits as was usually the case when he was going into a class for the first time. He looked forward to meeting the new crop of third-year Business Honours students and as the excitement mounted he quickened his pace. What were they going to be like this time around? Would he have an enthusiastic group or would the twelve-week session be lukewarm? Third year marked the students' introduction to group work and sometimes his "classroom-as-organization" model could be a shock to students who had been conditioned to think of

Exhibit 10.4

THE ENTERPRISE CORPORATION: JOB DESCRIPTION

Position Title: Group Member

The group member will be responsible for:

■ Regular attendance on the job.
■ Informing the group manager when attendance is not possible. This should be done, prior to the start of the specific session.
■ Taking part in group discussions.
■ Contributing to the best of his/her ability in making the group case hand-in a success.

■ Contributing to the best of his/her ability in making the oral presentation a success.
■ Contributing to the cohesiveness of his/her group.
■ Putting the best possible effort into the individual project.
■ Supporting the group manager and Enterprise manager wherever possible.

I agree to the above and will endeavor to give of my best to the Enterprise.

Signed:

_____   _____   _____
      Group Member   Group Manager   Enterprise Manager

Date:

_____   _____
                                         Section Designation

---

university life as a series of lectures. He had had positive results with the model, however, and continued to look forward to implementing it. The model provided for an interactive class and even when there were problems in groups, he had learned something about the group dynamics process.

He strode into the classroom and looked around. The class list indicated 34 students. The faces appeared to be stamped with the expression reminiscent of each new class and reflected anticipation. They seemed to be saying to him "O.K. buddy, let's see what you're like."

He gave a brief opening talk outlining the course objectives and method of grading. This was followed by a request to the class to complete a one-page questionnaire. The questions elicited information about work experience, hobbies, as well as attitudes concerning group work. The rest of the class was spent in introductions and discussion. Each participant introduced himself/herself and briefly described the worst job he/she had experienced. The

"pits," as one student described it, was working on a racing track and having to clean up after the horses in full view of the crowd. Needless to say, some very colourful moments were offered.

Rasmussen guided the discussion and selected the factors which made the job the worst. Together they determined that issues such as leadership, job design, culture or power, and politics contributed to the negative effects, and he tied the topics into the course material for the semester.

Later that evening, he fed the information provided by the students into a home-made software programme which focused on a mix of male/female, similar work experience and hobbies. The result was the formation of groups, each consisting of five to seven members. As he completed the process, he thought that he would opt for group selection of facilitators. Members would consequently have to decide whom their facilitators would be.

The second session began with the announcement of the groups. This was punctuated by comments such as, "Oh yeah!" and "Oh no!" The newly formed groups were then asked to select a facilitator by the third session and to communicate this information to the instructor. Rasmussen then initiated a discussion about group dynamics and went through the stages that groups experience such as forming, norming, storming, and performing. There were encouraging responses from participants as the oral analysis of the case for that day began. The case was entitled "Full Speed Ahead."

Third Week of the Semester: Meeting with Rasmussen

"I guess we can begin our meeting." Rasmussen normally met with facilitators at least three times for the semester and this day marked the first meeting with the Business 388 class.

"Can each facilitator begin with a verbal report of how the group is functioning?

The seven members each presented a short report indicating that everything was going fine. This was to be expected as it had been proven with past classes that problems did not develop this early. One facilitator brought up the issue, however, of an unusually shy group member. The assembled group brainstormed and came up with ideas to deal with the point. It was agreed that the facilitator should invite the member to discuss his opinions at the outset of each session and that other members should be privately asked to be as supportive as possible. On the surface, the groups seemed to be going through the forming stage in an inconspicuous manner. Although Rasmussen did not know it, however, the group led by Christine Spencer was already beginning to experience some problems which would ultimately fall onto his plate.

Christine Spencer's Group: The First Group Meeting (End of Week One)

Christine's group consisted of five members. There were two other females, Diane Stuart and Janet Simpson. The male complement consisted of Steve Raison and Mike Thanakos.

The group started out in high spirits and most seemed eager to tackle the group project. The first meeting was called by Christine who coordinated the schedules and selected a suitable time. The meeting was held through mutual agreement at Steve's house since it was close to the university. The group met at four o'clock when no one had classes. The first "order of business," as Christine put it, was to exchange telephone numbers and timetables. Christine also brought up the issue of whether or not they should meet briefly prior to the start of each class to discuss the case for that day. The group consensually agreed that it would not be feasible. Rasmussen had said that he would normally allow for fifteen minutes of class time so that groups could discuss among themselves the major issues of the case. It was decided that the task of each group member was to have the case prepared through "reading and reflecting." They talked among themselves for a while longer.

The session ended with everyone agreeing that Christine would contact each member before the next meeting. She returned to her campus residence and stretched out on her bed for a "pick me up" rest as she called her half-hour catnaps. The meeting went well, she thought, and her mind focused on the group members. She tried to formulate in her mind the impressions she had garnered from their actions, and demeanour in and out of class, as well as from the brief biographies she had requested from each member.

Individual Members

Steve Raison. Steve seems to be a nice guy, thought Christine. He had worked in the Cooperative programme promoted by the School of Business and Economics and had been attached to a managerial accounting firm for the past two work terms. He appeared eager to get the group project going and wanted to have the best product. He seemed to be good at the computer and had already begun talking about the design for the cover of the case analysis, as well as the type font, and the fact that he "could have the analysis sparkle by using a new laser printer."

Diane Stuart. Christine perceived Diane as a quiet, perhaps even shy individual. She hardly said anything, but always had a sensible answer if she was asked a question. Her major was marketing and her placement on the Dean's Honour Roll since the start of university marked her as a good student. Christine got the idea that Diane was capable of solid work and wondered why she appeared so withdrawn. Christine attributed this to the fact that she was slightly overweight.

Mike Thanakos. What a clown, thought Christine. After the first ten minutes of the meeting, Mike had said "Well, I guess we can all go now. . . ." He gave the impression that he was in the group only because it was required. When Christine had posed the question of possibly getting together before each class, he had blurted out "What!" Actually, the remark seemed to be both a question and an exclamation, and she was taken aback by its vociferousness. Mike worked on a "normal programme" basis, meaning that he did not participate in the co-op program. He did not have a major and the response to Christine's questionnaire in this regard was, "I'll choose. There's still lots of time." Sure, she thought.

Janet Simpson. At first, Christine did not think that Janet would attend the meeting. Almost a half-hour had gone by before she appeared. "Sorry" she had said, "'you know how it is when you're working part-time." She seemed quite rushed and a little out of breath. Christine recalled Janet's answers to her questionnaire. "I am presently working at two part-time jobs, two days per week, four hours per day. I hope that I can attend all the meetings." Under the question about extra-curricular activities, Janet had enigmatically stated, "Spending time with my boyfriend." She was a Human Resources major and had stated that she "just managed to get by." At least we have the H.R. in common, thought Christine.

Christine Spencer. Christine thought about herself in relation to the group. She saw herself as a meticulous, organized individual who tried to give her best in anything she did. She was a Human Resources major and really enjoyed the area. She had told the group that she was a people person who saw herself in a senior H.R. position "within the next five to seven years." She also resolved to win the Best Group Prize that Rasmussen was offering.

Fifth Week of the Semester:
The Second Group Meeting

The group case hand-in, due the last week of classes, was the primary topic on the agenda. Rasmussen had continued to mention it in the class, and the group thought that it was time to get started. They were required to analyze a case and decide among themselves what aspect each would

handle. The group case was worth 25 percent of the mark and that figure could be raised or lowered through peer evaluation.

Mike thought that discussion of this item was premature. "We have other assignments. Do we really need to devote time to the case project so early? We should leave it until later. I'm sure we can whip it up in two weeks, man."

"Well, the case has been assigned. I have other projects too and I don't think we should leave major items until the last minute. Believe me, two weeks would be the last minute." It was surprising to hear Diane speak up like this but she clearly had the support of Steve and Christine.

"O.K. already! Just give me the executive summary. I can handle that." Mike laughed loudly as he said this and the group laughed with him.

"You can handle the title page, Mike. What about that?" Christine joined in the good-natured ribbing.

"Gee Chris, that's just about my speed. You've got a deal."

"Did anyone see Janet lately? Is she coming to the meeting?" Steve seemed concerned that all members were not present.

"I spoke with her on campus two days ago and she said she would be here. I guess she's just late," explained Christine.

The meeting went on for approximately three hours. There was much discussion that evening, and not all about the case. Mike insisted on telling the "latest" jokes including his knock-knock specialties.

"Knock, knock."

No one answered. Finally, Diane responded.

"Who's there?" she answered wearily.

"Amos."

"Amos who?"

"A mosquito bit me." Mike laughed the loudest.

"Knock, knock."

"I'm only saying this so you'll be quiet, Mike." "Who's there?" Steve was sounding exasperated.

"Andy. "

"Andy who?"

"And he bit me again."

The group all broke into laughter. They spent the rest of the time assigning various parts of the case. Janet was given the Justification and Implementation sections since these were left over and she had not shown up. The group went to Wolf's university pub after the meeting.

Later that evening, Christine called Janet on the telephone.

"Christine! I'm sorry. I left work and began heading to the meeting. I met Sean, my boyfriend, who had a midterm project to hand in tomorrow and he needed some help with the proofreading and corrections. I'm helping to put him through school and we plan to get married after we graduate, you know. Anyway, before we knew it a few hours had passed and I thought it was too late to come." Janet did not seem to mind when she was told about the sections assigned to her and Christine ended the conversation by telling her about the date for the next meeting.

The Semester Progresses

The members of the group became more familiar with each other during discussion of the cases in class. They usually reviewed the major issues in groups before Rasmussen initiated the class discussion. The instructor would normally spend a few minutes in each group during this time. When he came to Christine's group, he asked how everything was going. Christine smiled warmly and replied that things could not go any better.

She reflected on that remark during her "thinking period" that afternoon, just before her catnap. The group seemed to be coming together and operating cohesively, all things being equal. Mike's performance was still lukewarm, however. Whenever they discussed cases in class, he seemed ill-prepared. Christine would usually admonish him by saying "Oh Mike, you really should read the case." Mike would usually start the discussion by talking about the football game to be played that evening, or the concert the night before. The group would chime in and Christine would bring them back on track with an, "O.K. guys, back to work."

And then there was Janet. Diane had privately remarked that she thought it odd the way Janet would address Mike as "Michael." Whenever the group discussed a case during class, Janet would generally be prepared. When it came to bantering and just talking as friends, she would be very quiet.

Janet Simpson

It was a particularly bad day for Janet. She had two projects due, one for Marketing and the other for Production Operations. She had been pushing herself academically as well as in the job. Earlier, she was working at the restaurant and had delivered an order of stir-fried shrimp to Table 4. The customer in the suit had virtually sputtered with indignation. "You have the wrong order, miss. Besides, I am quite allergic to shrimp and the odour of this dish is upsetting me." Other customers had heard as did the manager and she was reprimanded. She broke into tears at the waitresses' station.

That night she thought about her own situation. She tried her best. Sean seemed to be overly demanding lately and she wondered if the commitment they had made to each other could last—should last. She worked at the two part-time jobs for his sake. In addition, she had to keep up with her courses. Then there was the Organizational Behavior group. What was wrong with them anyway? Did they not like her? They seemed to get along so well together and she got the impression that her presence was merely an intrusion. Could they not see that she was just a human being trying her best at all the many activities in her life?

Seventh Week of the Semester: The Third Group Meeting

Christine had called the meeting for seven o'clock since this time appeared suitable to all. Janet was working that night and could not attend. However, a meeting at any other time would conflict with both Steve's and Mike's schedule. Consequently, she decided this was the best alternative.

They discussed the first drafts of the sections assigned to each individual. Changes were made across-the-board and these included adjustments to the Justification and Implementation sections that Janet had handed in. Mike's section looked like a sea of red when they were finished with it.

Christine tried a number of times that night to reach Janet by telephone. She thought that Janet would be finished by then. There was no answer.

Eighth Week of the Semester: The Classroom Incident

The members of the group had found themselves sitting in the first row next to each other in Rasmussen's class. Mike and Diane were engaged in conversation prior to the beginning of this class. They were early and as Janet took her seat in the last row, she thought it more beneficial to read the case rather than talk with the two members of her group. She couldn't help but overhear their conversation, though.

"Hey, Di, did you see Chris last night? She was dancing up a storm—in the aisles, no less—at the Frozen Ghost gig!" Mike laughed and recalled the event for Diane.

"Well, I prefer a more dignified existence than our beloved leader. I sat quietly and took in the music."

Steve and Christine walked into the classroom, along with some other members of the class.

"Look who I had to pick up from the sidewalk and drag to class, guys. Steve was just about ready to collapse. He had a better time than even little old me last night," Christine teased.

"Yeah? Well I partied after the party."

They laughed. They had not seen Janet until she greeted them from the other side of the room.

Tenth Week of the Semester: The Cafeteria Incident

It was 11:30 a.m. and Janet was just leaving after her accounting class. She had missed breakfast and decided to go to the cafeteria to pick up an order of fries. After emerging from the queue, she looked for a table and much to her surprise she saw her Human Resources group sitting together. She approached the table but they did not notice her. They were busily engrossed in discussion of the group case.

"You guys didn't say you were having a group meeting," blurted Janet.

They looked surprised.

"Well . . . why not join us?" invited Christine. Janet did but hardly said anything.

A similar incident happened the next week. Janet inadvertently came across her group (with the exception of Mike, who was absent). Again they invited her over, saying that they just happened to run into each other.

Eleventh Week of the Semester: An Appeal to Professor Rasmussen

Janet decided that she had to discuss the events with Professor Rasmussen. She explained the situation to the instructor.

"I try my best. I hold down two jobs, but I still devote quality time to my courses. I know I can do well, but the group does not seem to like me. They have formed their own little clique and I seem to be excluded from that circle. The situation is affecting me emotionally and I know it will

affect my grade. I need this course. I can do it. And I don't need the emotional hassle."

Rasmussen thought it would be best for him to speak with Christine. At the next class he asked her about the progress of her group.

"Well, I have no specific complaints. Everything seems to be working out well. Our group members generally contribute to the best of their abilities."

"How is Mike coming along? You had mentioned that he had a heavy course load."

"Okay, I guess. At least he makes an effort."

"What about Janet?"

"I was not really going to bring up Janet's situation, but since you ask, I will fill you in. I know that she is quite busy with her courses and part-time jobs. As a result, she has not really had the opportunity to become part of the group. We meet each other on campus and in fact have been having spontaneous meetings about our case analysis. We are all pretty well a cohesive group in that respect. As facilitator of the group, I realize I have a responsibility to Janet. I've tried to phone her on a number of occasions to fill her in on our meetings. But there never seems to be anyone home. Once I was passing by the discount store where she works and dropped in there to try to catch her, but she was actually working at the restaurant that evening. If you want to know the truth, I was going to keep everything quiet and have Janet share in whatever mark the group obtained."

The next day Rasmussen received a telephone call from Janet.

"I know that your class is group-oriented but I find it difficult to work with a group that excludes me and worse, doesn't like me. The whole situation is disturbing me more than you can imagine. Would you consider letting me do an individual case instead of the group analysis? I promise I will do the best I can and I think I will be more motivated. I would not have to worry about the likes of Christine and her buddies."

Note

1. Allan R. Cohen, "Beyond simulation: Treating the classroom as an organization," Exchange, September 1975, Vol. 1, No. 3.

PRINCIPAL ALONZO'S CHALLENGE: LEADERSHIP, CULTURE, AND THE POLITICS OF ORGANIZATION INNOVATION

Barry Allen Gold

Principal Alonzo Reflects

Two weeks before school opened in September 1991, Sam Alonzo, principal of Lincoln Acres Elementary School, talked about what he had learned during 1990, his first year at the school. Alonzo focused on problems with the faculty's decision-making process.

> There are times, I think, that the committee structure slows things down. It was designed to create shared decision making to keep the innovative vision of the school intact. But more often than not it is a problem for me. There have been countless times when I knew how a decision should be made or what a program would ultimately look like, and it took a committee months to arrive at the same point.
>
> I recognize, however, that committees are useful because they keep things from getting dropped out of the decision-making process. They bring a lot of wisdom from a lot of concerned people to bear on an issue. Also, the committees engage the larger population of the school; they spread ideas around and there are people who speak for this idea and that idea which creates a sense of involvement.
>
> Despite these benefits, shared decision making does slow things down. Sometimes decisions are made by eight people, when one or two decision makers would be appropriate. Often, because of the need for a faculty committee to reach consensus there is reluctance to move forward. I think there is a real fear that if everyone doesn't agree with a decision there will be hurt feelings that will create conflict.

Alonzo concluded,

> I think that I understand the issues that have created this situation—the early failures and conflicts in the school. Now I have to figure out how I'm going to deal with my relationship with the faculty and how I'm going to become a more effective leader.

History of the Lincoln Acres School

The First Year

In 1975, Lincoln Acres School was a new, innovative school. Its major innovations were open space architecture, team teaching, multigraded classrooms, and an organizational mission to involve parents in their children's education. The principal, Ellis Brown, was selected by a committee primarily because of his successful start-up and administration of a similar school. A research report (Gold and Miles, 1981:345–346) characterized the planning and early implementation phases of the school as a

> Collegial Organization. *During the planning period and at early implementation, the faculty defined education as "child-centered," with an emphasis on individualization of instruction and affective growth, along with a program of traditional cognitive skills. Conceptualizing education in this way—as a non-uniform technology—resulted in the intentional creation of a collegial organization, a type of organization congruent both with the value orientations of the faculty and with team teaching. The chief mechanism for guiding instructional tasks was the faculty's internalization of the values and norms of the school. The majority of teachers ignored the external environment; the main device for maintaining organizational boundaries was the delegation of authority to the principal to buffer, negotiate with, and possibly co-opt community groups.*

After two months of operation, the innovations were criticized severely by influential parents and community leaders. They claimed that teachers were unable to implement the educational programs correctly; valuable time was wasted and the students' education suffered. After a series of tense, confrontational meetings involving parents, teachers, central administrators, and the Washingtonville Township school board, one teacher was fired and the school was reorganized into self-contained classrooms. Gold and Miles (1981: 346) characterize the organizing principle of this period as

> Force and Force Threat. *From the time of teacher selection until early implementation of the innovations, community criticism of the educational program intensified. Shortly after implementation, the result of persistent community pressure was a transitional period in the social relations of the school; there was at first disorganization, followed by a coercive compliance structure. During this period, the failure to maintain normal*

functioning of the organization was largely due to the lack of a clear boundary between the organization and its environment; there was no single power center or organizing principle. Community complaints and close scrutiny of school activities by many parents eventually resulted in a forced reorganization of two teaching teams.

Following the resolution of the conflict between the faculty and parents, the teachers behaved in an aggressively defensive way. Gold and Miles (1981: 346) identified teacher behavior as creating a

Conflict Bureaucracy. *In reaction to the firing of a teacher, administrative ineptness, and frequent intervention in school activities by community members, the faculty instituted rules within the school and between the school and community in an attempt to end what the majority of teachers considered the arbitrary use of force. In the process, the original goal of child-centered education was abandoned and replaced with a modified "back-to-basics" educational philosophy. The evolved organizational structure—bureaucracy—was no longer suitable for highly individualized, creative education (to which several teachers were still committed). Nevertheless, the objective of stabilizing the organization was achieved.*

By the end of the first year, the school was no longer innovative, teachers were emotionally exhausted, and Ellis Brown had resigned.

The Second Year

Alberta Bard, a vice principal of a Washingtonville Middle School, was selected by a committee to become the second principal of Lincoln Acres School. Ms. Bard understood her mission as to re-establish harmonious relations between the school and community, revive faculty morale, develop an innovative educational philosophy, and guide the teachers toward innovations. Her first year was characterized by Gold and Miles (1981: 346) as a

Stabilized Quasi-Collegial Organization. *In the second year, following succession to a new leader, the operating model shifted back toward the original collegial model. Hopes for re-implementation appeared, and several teachers actually used aspects of the first year's innovations, including*

team teaching. But bureaucratic procedures were still clearly in evidence, along with a cautious approach toward innovation.

Ms. Bard's Administration

In Alberta Bard's second year as principal, when school-community relationships stabilized, she began to implement her educational vision. According to her,

What I tried to create was a happy and exemplary school. I think an exemplary school is a school where children are learning and happy. This occurs when children are treated with respect by everyone, where they feel valued, where kids and teachers alike have mutual respect. Also, the curriculum has to be an appropriate balance between academic and social instruction.

Alberta described her relationship with the Lincoln Acres teachers as,

My role was to help the teachers do what they wanted to do. Facilitating, coaching, a bit of mentoring, but not much. The Lincoln Acres teachers were extremely dedicated and professional. Unfortunately, as a principal you have to do a lot of other things like deal with bus schedules and bus drivers. A particular problem was the state education bureaucracy, which increased greatly in the past few years.

Early in her eleven-year tenure, Alberta established a school site council composed of teachers, parents, and administrators to be a decision-making body for the school. Because of her administrative style, the relationship between Alberta and the school site council was professional and productive. It re-established trust between the school and community. According to Alberta,

Overall, the school site council worked very well. It was a good way to assure the community that they would be listened to. My relationship with the parents on the council was similar to the way a superintendent works with a Board of Education. We had a cooperative working relationship and pretty much—not always, by any means—they took my advice.

Relations between Alberta and the faculty were harmonious; the teachers appreciated her supportive administrative style and rewarded her with loyalty, hard work, and an absence of the types of conflicts that characterized the school's first year. An illustration of the teachers' attachment to Alberta is that two years after Alberta voluntarily transferred to Green Valley Elementary School to "move to a new set of challenges," she was still missed by the Lincoln Acres faculty. One veteran teacher stated that,

> Alberta created the best educational environment for teachers and students that I have experienced. She treated us like professionals and we behaved like professionals.

Principal Englehard

Sally Englehard, Alberta Bard's successor, was carefully selected from a large pool of applicants by a committee of Lincoln Acres teachers, parents, and central office administrators. The majority of the faculty, including influential and well-respected veteran teachers, viewed Sally as the best choice.

After two months, however, relationships between Ms. Englehard and the faculty were strained. The primary issue was the faculty's negative reaction to Englehard's administrative style; she made all key educational and administrative decisions and ignored teacher suggestions. In addition, Ms. Englehard viewed the principal's role as a disciplinarian. She had no tolerance for the noisy, free-flowing classrooms typical of the school and insisted on strict enforcement of student behavior codes.

In the middle of the year the superintendent of schools, Dr. Fred Barnes, hired an industrial psychologist to discover the reasons for conflict between the faculty and Ms. Englehard. Dr. Barnes suspected that there was also tension between original members of the school and new teachers who had to become socialized into the school's culture. Barnes' rationale for the study was that,

> When the conflict within the faculty is resolved, tensions between Sally and the faculty will disappear.

The industrial psychologist's report, which was based on one day of short interviews with a nonrandom sample of three teachers (there were twenty-eight faculty members), was never shared with the faculty. Because of this, many teachers were suspicious of Barnes, who, despite repeated requests, never made the report public.

As the school year progressed Sally Englehard's leadership style remained the same and faculty dissatisfaction increased. In a series of meetings in March, the teachers organized against Englehard and decided to seek the support of influential parents. In early May they demanded that the central school administration and Board of Education remove Sally Englehard. Their main argument was that Sally Englehard,

> . . . failed to understand the child-centered educational philosophy of the Lincoln Acres Elementary School and administer educational programs to reflect it.

After six weeks of acrimonious meetings the teachers and parents succeeded: Sally Englehard's contract was not renewed. Alberta Bard's view of this was that,

> The thing that absolutely floored me was that the staff wasn't able to be convinced that they didn't really need a principal. I had just been allowing them to do their thing. I was very, very surprised that they could not get their act together and work constructively with Sally—she was brand new. The people there were just saying, "everything is all wrong." They had a principal they couldn't stand. As soon as one individual left—me—the school fell apart. I think that's just a symptom of the problems in education.

The Future of Innovation

Sam Alonzo's First Year

Like his predecessor Sally Englehard, Sam Alonzo was selected to be principal of Lincoln Acres School by a committee of teachers, parents, and administrators. Mr. Alonzo—who requested to be called Sam by the faculty—earned an M.Ed. from a respected state university near the Lincoln Acres School. He had been a middle school teacher in a nearby town for five years and for ten years the principal of a private elementary school in a Chicago suburb.

Early in his first year at Lincoln Acres Alonzo developed a proposal for a Nabisco Next Century School grant. The proposal was to fund programs for "at risk" students and their families. The goal of the proposal was,

To make Lincoln Acres School a place where all youngsters are successful, regardless of any disadvantage they may bring to the schoolhouse door—social, economic, linguistic, behavioral, etc.—and where theory and research about learning are applied and adopted to the specific site.

The proposal included the use of computers to help increase student self-esteem, a mentor project, family intervention programs, and a wide range of teacher training workshops to increase skills for dealing more effectively with special student needs.

Lincoln Acres School was awarded the $265,000 Nabisco grant for 1991–1994.

The Faculty's View of the Nabisco Grant

Initial faculty reaction to the Nabisco proposal was cautious. Because of pressure to meet a deadline, only two teachers participated in writing the proposal. Nevertheless, most teachers supported the goals of the grant. They were concerned, however, that the time required to plan and implement the new programs would divert them from the educational programs that were already working well. They also expressed concern over the possible loss of professional autonomy; the grant could dictate both curriculum and teaching methods, reducing opportunities for professional judgment.

In early autumn 1991, elements of the Nabisco grant were discussed in faculty meetings, and in November implementation began. Although many teachers retained their original concerns, acceptance of the project gradually increased.

The Faculty's View of Sam Alonzo

In faculty meetings Sam acts as an impartial facilitator. For example, he makes certain that everyone has an opportunity to add items to and structure the agenda, raise arguments for or against a topic, or suggest a set of procedures for a discussion. Also, he is patient and encouraging when the teachers attempt to achieve a consensus. When Sam offers his opinion he states that it is his opinion, not school or district policy. On occasion he will remind the faculty of precedents, rules, and policies.

Many of the teachers view these behaviors as symptoms of problems with Sam's leadership. Audry Kohlberg, a fifth grade teacher who has been at the school since it opened in 1974—a respected veteran—reflected the majority faculty view that,

Sam is a very nice person. His problem is that he is too nice. He wants to be liked by everybody.

Alberta Bard, who became principal of Green Valley Elementary School in the Washingtonville district, observed Sam as a colleague and successor. In Alberta's view: "Sam is a really nice guy, but he's not a strong leader."

The Central Administration's View of Lincoln Acres

The superintendent of schools and other central office administrators view the Lincoln Acres faculty as unnecessarily confrontational. A typical conflict with the central administration was provoked by a change in the district-wide date for administering California Achievement Tests. After several meetings, the Lincoln Acres faculty objected to the change because it conflicted with a previously planned school program. There was little agreement, however, on how to demonstrate opposition to the change. After two weeks of lunch-time meetings, the faculty consensus was to enlist the support of the Lincoln Acres school site council and arrange a meeting with Dr. Barnes to demand an alternate date. In these meetings Alonzo suggested less confrontational remedies but eventually reluctantly supported the teachers' action.

Sam's View of the Future

By the end of his first year, Sam Alonzo was becoming increasingly aware that his leadership style was important. Also, Sam was becoming steeped in the history of Lincoln Acres School. He talked with veteran teachers about the early years of the school and read Gold and Miles' research report.

In Sam's view his dilemma was,

I don't want to unintentionally unleash the power that this faculty has used in the past

against people and policies that it doesn't like. On the other hand, I recognize that I have to use my position more effectively to shape decisions and move things along—particularly the Nabisco grant. Otherwise, we'll get bogged down in the process, and that will be all we'll achieve. We run the risk of having consensus over how to do things but without knowing what should be done, or who is going to do it. My problem is:

How can I create meaningful faculty participation without letting the process get in the way of innovation?

REFERENCE

Gold, B., and Miles, M. *Whose School Is It, Anyway?* New York: Praeger, 1981.

PART III: EXPERIENCE 1

The Ambivalence of Social Roles

Barry Allen Gold

Purpose

This experience is designed to introduce students to the complexity of roles in groups and organizations.

Time Required

Fifty-five minutes.

Materials Needed

None.

Introduction

Roles are scripts that guide behavior. But the actor is seldom the sole author of a script and often performs to mixed reviews. One reason is that norms are often contradictory. The sociologist Robert Merton has observed

> that normative structures do not have unified norm-sets. Instead that sociological ambivalence is built into normative structures in the form of incompatible patterned expectations and a "dynamic alternation of norms and counternorms" in social roles (1975:35).

Stated somewhat differently, the norms that govern individual behavior for enacting a role are often at odds with each other. Put differently again, norms seldom add up to a clear set of stage directions for the performance of a role. For example, Mitroff (1974) discovered in a study of scientists that their scientific work was shaped by two opposite sets of norms. On one hand were conventional norms that govern science. On the other hand were counternorms—the rules of how science was *really* done. Here is a partial list of the conventional scientific norms and the counternorms that Mitroff (1974: 79) observed.

Conventional Norms

1. *Faith in rationality.*
2. *Emotional neutrality* as an instrumental condition for the achievement of rationality.
3. *Universalism:* In science all have morally equal claims to the discovery and possession of rational knowledge.
4. *Impartiality:* A scientist concerns himself only with the production of new knowledge and not with the consequences of its use.
5. *Suspension of judgment:* Scientific statements are made only on the basis of conclusive evidence.
6. *Absence of bias:* The validity of a scientific statement depends only on the operations by which evidence for it was obtained and not upon the person who makes it.

Counternorms

1. *Faith in rationality and nonrationality.*
2. *Emotional commitment* as an instrumental condition for the achievement of rationality.
3. *Particularism:* In science some men have special claims to the discovery and possession of rational knowledge.
4. *Partiality:* A scientist must concern himself as much with the consequences of his discoveries as with their production; to do any less is to make the scientist into an immoral agent who has no concern for the moral consequences of his activities.
5. *Exercise of judgment:* Scientific statements are always made in the face of inconclusive evidence; to be a scientist is to exercise expert judgment in the face of incomplete evidence.
6. *Presence of Bias:* In reality the validity of a scientific statement depends on both the operations by which evidence for it was obtained and upon the person who makes it; the presence of bias forces the scientist to acknowledge the operation of bias and to attempt to control it.

Procedure

Form groups of six. Each group should select a leader using any technique—voting, consensus, self-appointment—that the members think is appropriate. The group leader should *appoint* someone to be the group recorder and another person to report the results of the discussion to the class.

The task of the group is to list and discuss the norms and counternorms that compose the roles of student and professor (25 minutes). An example of dual norms for students is "learn for the sake of learning" *but* "only take courses that lead to a high-paying job."

After listing the norms and counternorms, discuss the following questions for the student and professor roles.

PART III: EXPERIENCE 1 Continued

STUDENT ROLE

CONVENTIONAL NORMS	COUNTERNORMS
1.	1.
2.	2.
3.	3.
4.	4.
5.	5.

PROFESSOR ROLE

CONVENTIONAL NORMS	COUNTERNORMS
1.	1.
2.	2.
3.	3.
4.	4.
5.	5.

1. What are the sources of the norms?
2. What are the sources of the counternorms?
3. How does the existence of dual norms affect behavior?
4. Does the perception of conflicting norms result in an inability of an individual to set personal goals and take actions to achieve them? Is it a psychological problem?

3. How does ambivalence affect influence processes and power relations within a group?
4. How does ambivalence affect group decision making?
5. Are there any practical techniques for controlling the pressures created by incompatible norms?

Class Discussion

The group reporter presents a summary of each group's discussion to the entire class (10 minutes).

Class Discussion

The instructor leads an entire class discussion based on the answers for the above questions (10 minutes).

Group Discussion

The groups reform and discuss the following questions (15 minutes).

1. Did the group leaders experience ambivalence? If yes, what were the sources of ambivalence?
2. What sources of ambivalence did the group members experience?

REFERENCES

Merton, R. "Structural Analysis in Sociology." In P. Blau (ed.) *Approaches to the Study of Social Structure.* New York:Free Press, 1975.

Mitroff, I. *The Subjective Side of Science.* New York: Elsevier, 1974.

PART III: EXPERIENCE 2

A Simple—But Powerful—Power Simulation

Lee Bolman and Terrence E. Deal

Purpose

To understand some of the power dynamics in organizations at every level—from the individual to the systemic.

Group Size

24–90 people.

Time Required

60 minutes or more if time permits.

Materials

Each student brings a dollar bill to class.

Room Arrangement Requirements

A room large enough to accommodate two work groups and enough space in a hallway or corridor for a third group.

Procedure

Part A—Simulation
1. *Divide groups* (5 minutes)
   Students turn in a dollar bill to the instructor and are divided into three groups based on criteria given by the instructor, assigned to their work places, and instructed to read the rules and tasks below. The money is divided into thirds, giving two-thirds of it to the top group, one-third to the middle group, and none to the bottom group.
2. *Conduct simulation* (30 minutes)
   Groups go to their assigned work places and complete their tasks.
   Rules:
   a. Members of the top group are free to enter the space of either of the other groups and to communicate whatever they wish, whenever they wish. Members of the middle group may enter the space of the lower group when they wish but must request permission to enter the top group's space (which the top group can refuse). Members of the lower group may not disturb the top group in any

way unless specifically invited by the top. The lower group does have the right to knock on the door of the middle group and request permission to communicate with them (which can also be refused).
   b. The members of the top group have the authority to make any change in the roles that they wish, at any time, with or without notice.
   Tasks:
   a. **Top Group:** To be responsible for the overall effectiveness and learning from the simulation, and to decide how to use its money.
   b. **Middle Group:** To assist the Top Group in providing for the overall welfare of the organization, and to decide how to use its money.
   c. **Bottom Group:** To identify its resources and to decide how best to provide for learning and the overall effectiveness of the organization.

Part B—Debrief
1. *Representatives discuss* (10 minutes)
   Each of the three groups chooses two representatives to go to the front of the class and discuss the following questions with the instructor.
   a. What can we learn about power from this experience? Does it remind us of events we have seen in other organizations?
   b. What did each of us learn individually? How did we think about what power is? Were we satisfied with the amount of power we had? How did we try to exercise or to gain more power?
2. *Class Discussion* (15 minutes)
   The instructor will lead a discussion on the following:
   a. Discuss what occurred within and between the three groups.
   b. What were the in-group, out-group dynamics?
   c. How did trust and mistrust figure into the simulation?
   d. What does this exercise say about structural injustice?
   e. What were some differences of being in the top group versus being in the bottom one?

Source: Lee Bolman and Terrence E. Deal, "A Simple—But Powerful—Power Simulation," *Exchange,* Vol. 4 (3), 1979, pp. 38–42. Copyright ©1979. Reprinted by permission.

PART III: EXPERIENCE 3

THE DESERT SURVIVAL SITUATION

J. Clayton Lafferty, Patrick M. Grady, and Alonzo W. Pond

Introduction

The situation described in this exercise is based on over 2,000 actual cases in which men and women lived or died depending upon the survival decisions they made. Your "life" or "death" will depend upon how well your group can share its present knowledge of a relatively unfamiliar problem so that the team can make decisions that will lead to your survival.

When instructed, read about the situation and do Step 1 without discussing it with the rest of the group.

It is approximately 10:00 a.m. in mid-August, and you have just crash landed in the Sonora Desert in the southwestern United States. The light twin-engine plane, containing the bodies of the pilot and the copilot, has completely burned. Only the air frame remains. None of the rest of you has been injured.

The pilot was unable to notify anyone of your position before the crash. However, he had indicated before impact that you were 70 miles south-southwest from a mining camp that is the nearest known habitation and that you were approximately 65 miles off the course that was filed in your VFR Flight Plan.

The immediate area is quite flat and except for occasional barrel and saguaro cacti appears to be rather barren. The last weather report indicated the temperature would reach 110° that day, which means that the temperature at ground level will be 130°. You are dressed in lightweight clothing: short-sleeved shirts, pants, socks, and street shoes. Everyone has a handkerchief. Collectively, your pockets contain $2.83 in change, $85.00 in bills, a pack of cigarettes, and a ballpoint pen.

Your Task

Before the plane caught fire your group was able to salvage the 15 items listed in the following table. Your task is to rank these items according to their importance to your survival, starting with "1," the most important, to "15," the least important.

You may assume the following:

ITEMS	STEP 1: YOUR INDIVIDUAL RANKING	STEP 2: THE TEAM'S RANKING	STEP 3: SURVIVAL EXPERT'S RANKING	STEP 4: DIFFERENCE BETWEEN STEP 1 AND STEP 3	STEP 5: DIFFERENCE BETWEEN STEP 2 AND STEP 4
Flashlight (4-battery size)					
Jackknife					
Sectional air map of area					
Plastic raincoat (large size)					
Magnetic compass					
Compress kit with guaze					
.45 caliber pistol (loaded)					
Parachute (red and white)					
Bottle of salt tablets (1,000 tablets)					
1 quart of water per person					
A book entitled *Edible Animals of the Desert*					
A pair of sunglasses per person					
2 quarts of 180 proof vodka					
1 top coat per person					
A cosmetic mirror					
Totals (the lower the score, the better)				Your Score, Step 4	Team Score, Step 5

PART III: EXPERIENCE 3 Continued

1. The number of survivors is the same as the number on your team.
2. You are the actual people in the situation.
3. The team has agreed to stick together.
4. All items are in good condition.

Step 1. Each member of the team is to individually rank each item. Do not discuss the situation or problem until each member has finished the individual ranking.

Step 2. After everyone has finished the individual ranking, rank order the 15 items as a team. Once discussion begins do not change your individual ranking. Your instructor will inform you how much time you have to complete this step.

PLEASE COMPLETE THE FOLLOWING STEPS AND INSERT THE SCORES UNDER YOUR TEAM'S NUMBER.	TEAM NUMBER					
	1	2	3	4	5	6
Step 6: Average Individual Score Add up all the individual scores (Step 4) on the team and divide by the number on the team.	___	___	___	___	___	___
Step 7: Team Score	___	___	___	___	___	___
Step 8: Gain Score The difference between the Team Score and the Average Individual Score. If the Team Score is lower than Average Individual Score, then gain "+". If Team Score is higher than Average Individual Score, then gain is "–".	___	___	___	___	___	___
Step 9: Lowest Individual Score on the Team	___	___	___	___	___	___
Step 10: Number of Individual Scores Lower Than the Team Score.	___	___	___	___	___	___

Source: J. Clayton Lafferty, Patrick M. Eady, and Alonzo W. Pond, "The Desert Survival Situation: A Group Decision Making Experience for Examining and Increasing Individual and Team Effectiveness," 8th ed. Copyright © 1974 by Experiential Learning Methods, Inc., 14539 Harbor Island, Detroit, MI 48215, (313) 823-4400. Reprinted by permission.

MANAGING FOR PERFORMANCE

11

ORGANIZATIONAL ENTRY AND SOCIALIZATION

Organizational Culture

EDGAR H. SCHEIN

LEARNING OBJECTIVES

After reading "Organizational Culture" by Edgar Schein, a student will be able to:

1. Define and understand the concept of organizational culture

2. Understand the historical development of organizational culture studies

3. Understand how organizational culture contributes to organizational reproduction

4. Learn how organizational cultures change

To write a review article about the concept of organizational culture poses a dilemma because there is presently little agreement on what the concept does and should mean, how it should be observed and measured, how it relates to more traditional industrial and organizational psychology theories, and how it should be used in our efforts to help organizations. The popular use of the concept has further muddied the waters by hanging the label of "culture" on everything from common behavioral patterns to espoused new corporate values that senior management wishes to inculcate (e.g., Deal & Kennedy, 1982; Peters & Waterman, 1982).

Serious students of organizational culture point out that each culture researcher develops explicit or implicit paradigms that bias not only the definitions of key concepts but the whole approach to the study of the phenomenon (Barley, Meyer, & Gash, 1988; Martin & Meyerson, 1988; Ott, 1989; Smircich & Calas, 1987; Van Maanen, 1988). One probable reason for this diversity of approaches is that culture, like role, lies at the intersection of several social sciences and reflects some of the biases of each—specifically, those of anthropology, sociology, social psychology, and organizational behavior.

A complete review of the various paradigms and their implications is far beyond the scope of this article. Instead I will provide a brief historical overview leading to the major approaches currently in use and then describe in greater detail one paradigm, firmly anchored in social psychology and anthropology, that is somewhat integrative in that it allows one to position other paradigms in a common conceptual space.

This line of thinking will push us conceptually into territory left insufficiently explored by such concepts as "climate," "norm," and "attitude." Many of the research methods of industrial/organizational psychology have weaknesses when applied to the concept of culture. If we are to take culture seriously, we must first adopt a more clinical and ethnographic approach to identify clearly the kinds of dimensions and variables that can usefully lend themselves to more precise empirical measurement and

Source: Edgar H. Schein: "Organizational Culture," *American Psychologist,* February 1990, Vol. 45, No. 2, pp. 109–119. Reprinted by permission.

hypothesis testing. Though there have been many efforts to be empirically precise about cultural phenomena, there is still insufficient linkage of theory with observed data. We are still operating in the context of discovery and are seeking hypotheses rather than testing specific theoretical formulations.

A Historical Note

Organizational culture as a concept has a fairly recent origin. Although the concepts of "group norms" and "climate" have been used by psychologists for a long time (e.g., Lewin, Lippitt, & White, 1939), the concept of "culture" has been explicitly used only in the last few decades. Katz and Kahn (1978), in their second edition of *The Social Psychology of Organizations,* referred to roles, norms, and values but presented neither climate nor culture as explicit concepts.

Organizational "climate," by virtue of being a more salient cultural phenomenon, lent itself to direct observation and measurement and thus has had a longer research tradition (Hellriegel & Slocum, 1974; A. P. Jones & James, 1979; Litwin & Stringer, 1968; Schneider, 1975; Schneider & Reichers, 1983; Tagiuri & Litwin, 1968). But climate is only a surface manifestation of culture, and thus research on climate has not enabled us to delve into the deeper causal aspects of how organizations function. We need explanations for variations in climate and norms, and it is this need that ultimately drives us to "deeper" concepts such as culture.

In the late 1940s social psychologists interested in Lewinian "action research" and leadership training freely used the concept of "cultural island" to indicate that the training setting was in some fundamental way different from the trainees' "back home" setting. We knew from the leadership training studies of the 1940s and 1950s that foremen who changed significantly during training would revert to their former attitudes once they were back at work in a different setting (Bradford, Gibb, & Benne, 1964; Fleishman, 1953, 1973; Lewin, 1952; Schein & Bennis, 1965). But the concept of "group norms," heavily documented in the Hawthorne studies of the 1920s, seemed sufficient to explain this phenomenon (Homans, 1950; Roethlisberger & Dickson, 1939).

In the 1950s and 1960s, the field of organizational psychology began to differentiate itself from industrial psy-

chology by focusing on units larger than individuals (Bass, 1965; Schein, 1965). With a growing emphasis on work groups and whole organizations came a greater need for concepts such as "system" that could describe what could be thought of as a *pattern* of norms and attitudes that cut across a whole social unit. The researchers and clinicians at the Tavistock Institute developed the concept of "socio-technical systems" (Jaques, 1951; Rice, 1963; Trist, Higgin, Murray, & Pollock, 1963), and Likert (1961, 1967) developed his "Systems 1 through 4" to describe integrated sets of organizational norms and attitudes. Katz and Kahn (1966) built their entire analysis of organizations around systems theory and systems dynamics, thus laying the most important theoretical foundation for later culture studies.

The field of organizational psychology grew with the growth of business and management schools. As concerns with understanding organizations and interorganizational relationships grew, concepts from sociology and anthropology began to influence the field. Cross-cultural psychology had, of course, existed for a long time (Werner, 1940), but the application of the concept of culture to organizations *within* a given society came only recently as more investigators interested in organizational phenomena found themselves needing the concept to explain (a) variations in patterns of organizational behavior, and (b) levels of stability in group and organizational behavior that had not previously been highlighted (e.g., Ouchi, 1981).

What has really thrust the concept into the forefront is the recent emphasis on trying to explain why U.S. companies do not perform as well as some of their counterpart companies in other societies, notably Japan. In observing the differences, it has been noted that national culture is not a sufficient explanation (Ouchi, 1981; Pascale & Athos, 1981). One needs concepts that permit one to differentiate between organizations within a society, especially in relation to different levels of effectiveness, and the concept of organizational culture has served this purpose well (e.g., O'Toole, 1979; Pettigrew, 1979; Wilkins & Ouchi, 1983).

As more investigators and theoreticians have begun to examine organizational culture, the normative thrust has been balanced by more descriptive and clinical research (Barley, 1983; Frost, Moore, Louis, Lundberg, & Martin, 1985; Louis, 1981, 1983; Martin, 1982; Martin, Feldman, Hatch, & Sitkin, 1983; Martin & Powers, 1983; Martin & Siehl, 1983; Schein, 1985a; Van Maanen & Barley, 1984). We need to find out what is actually going on in organizations before we rush in to tell managers what to do about their culture.

I will summarize this quick historical overview by identifying several different research streams that today influence how we perceive the concept of organizational culture.

Survey Research

From this perspective, culture has been viewed as a property of groups that can be measured by questionnaires leading to Likert-type profiles (Hofstede, 1980; Hofstede & Bond, 1988; Kilmann, 1984; Likert, 1967). The problem with this approach is that it assumes knowledge of the relevant dimensions to be studied. Even if these are statistically derived from large samples of items, it is not clear whether the initial item set is broad enough or relevant enough to capture what may for any given organization be its critical cultural themes. Furthermore, it is not clear whether something as abstract as culture can be measured with survey instruments at all.

Analytical Descriptive

In this type of research, culture is viewed as a concept for which empirical measures must be developed, even if that means breaking down the concept into smaller units so that it can be analyzed and measured (e.g., Harris & Sutton, 1986; Martin & Siehl, 1983; Schall, 1983; Trice & Beyer, 1984; Wilkins, 1983). Thus organizational stories, rituals and rites, symbolic manifestations, and other cultural elements come to be taken as valid surrogates for the cultural whole. The problem with this approach is that it fractionates a concept whose primary theoretical utility is in drawing attention to the holistic aspect of group and organizational phenomena.

Ethnographic

In this approach, concepts and methods developed in sociology and anthropology are applied to the study of organizations in order to illuminate descriptively, and thus provide a richer understanding of, certain organizational phenomena that had previously not been documented fully enough (Barley, 1983; Van Maanen, 1988; Van Maanen & Barley, 1984). This approach helps to build better theory but is time consuming and

expensive. A great many more cases are needed before generalizations can be made across various types of organizations.

Historical

Though historians have rarely applied the concept of culture in their work, it is clearly viewed as a legitimate aspect of an organization to be analyzed along with other factors (Chandler, 1977; Dyer, 1986; Pettigrew, 1979; Westney, 1987). The weaknesses of the historical method are similar to those pointed out for the ethnographic approach, but these are often offset by the insights that historical and longitudinal analyses can provide.

Clinical Descriptive

With the growth of organizational consulting has come the opportunity to observe in areas from which researchers have traditionally been barred, such as the higher levels of management where policies originate and where reward and control systems are formulated. When consultants observe organizational phenomena as a byproduct of their services for clients, we can think of this as "clinical" research even though the client is defining the domain of observation (Schein, 1987a). Such work is increasingly being done by consultants with groups and organizations, and it allows consultants to observe some of the systemic effects of interventions over time. This approach has been labeled "organization development" (Beckhard, 1969; Beckhard & Harris, 1977, 1987; Bennis, 1966, 1969; French & Bell, 1984; Schein, 1969) and has begun to be widely utilized in many kinds of organizations.

The essential characteristic of this method is that the data are gathered while the consultant is actively helping the client system work on problems defined by the client on the client's initiative. Whereas the researcher has to gain access, the consultant/clinician is provided access because it is in the client's best interest to open up categories of information that might ordinarily be concealed from the researcher (Schein, 1985a, 1987a).

The empirical knowledge gained from such observations provides a much needed balance to the data obtained by other methods because cultural origins and dynamics can sometimes be observed only in the power centers where elements of the culture are created and changed by founders, leaders, and powerful managers (Hirschhorn, 1987; Jaques, 1951; Kets de Vries & Miller, 1984, 1986;

Schein, 1983). The problem with this method is that it does not provide the descriptive breadth of an ethnography nor the methodological rigor of quantitative hypothesis testing. However, at this stage of the evolution of the field, a combination of ethnographic and clinical research seems to be the most appropriate basis for trying to understand the concept of culture.

Definition of Organizational Culture

The problem of defining organizational culture derives from the fact that the concept of organization is itself ambiguous. We cannot start with some "cultural phenomena" and then use their existence as evidence for the existence of a group. We must first specify that a given set of people has had enough stability and common history to have allowed a culture to form. This means that some organizations will have no overarching culture because they have no common history or have frequent turnover of members. Other organizations can be presumed to have "strong" cultures because of a long shared history or because they have shared important intense experiences (as in a combat unit). But the content and strength of a culture have to be empirically determined. They cannot be presumed from observing surface cultural phenomena.

Culture is what a group learns over a period of time as that group solves its problems of survival in an external environment and its problems of internal integration. Such learning is simultaneously a behavioral, cognitive, and an emotional process. Extrapolating further from a functionalist anthropological view, the deepest level of culture will be the cognitive in that the perceptions, language, and thought processes that a group comes to share will be the ultimate causal determinant of feelings, attitudes, espoused values, and overt behavior.

From systems theory, Lewinian field theory, and cognitive theory comes one other theoretical premise—namely, that systems tend toward some kind of equilibrium, attempt to reduce dissonance, and thus bring basic categories or assumptions into alignment with each other (Durkin, 1981; Festinger, 1957; Hebb, 1954; Heider, 1958; Hirschhorn, 1987; Lewin, 1952). There is a conceptual problem, however, because systems contain subsystems, organizations contain groups and units within them, and it is not clear over what range the tendency toward equilibrium will exist in any given complex total system.

For our purposes it is enough to specify that any definable group with a shared history can have a culture and that within an organization there can therefore be many subcultures. If the organization as a whole has had shared experiences, there will also be a total organizational culture. Within any given unit, the tendency for integration and consistency will be assumed to be present, but it is perfectly possible for coexisting units of a larger system to have cultures that are independent and even in conflict with each other.

Culture can now be defined as (a) a pattern of basic assumptions, (b) invented, discovered, or developed by a given group, (c) as it learns to cope with its problems of external adaptation and internal integration, (d) that has worked well enough to be considered valid and, therefore (e) is to be taught to new members as the (f) correct way to perceive, think, and feel in relation to those problems.

The strength and degree of internal consistency of a culture are, therefore, a function of the stability of the group, the length of time the group has existed, the intensity of the group's experiences of learning, the mechanisms by which the learning has taken place (i.e., positive reinforcement or avoidance conditioning), and the strength and clarity of the assumptions held by the founders and leaders of the group.

Once a group has learned to hold common assumptions, the resulting automatic patterns of perceiving, thinking, feeling, and behaving provide meaning, stability, and comfort; the anxiety that results from the inability to understand or predict events happening around the group is reduced by the shared learning. The strength and tenacity of culture derive, in part, from this anxiety-reduction function. One can think of some aspects of culture as being for the group what defense mechanisms are for the individual (Hirschhorn, 1987; Menzies, 1960; Schein, 1985b).

The Levels of Culture

In analyzing the culture of a particular group or organization it is desirable to distinguish three fundamental levels at which culture manifests itself: (a) observable artifacts, (b) values, and (c) basic underlying assumptions.

When one enters an organization one observes and feels its *artifacts*. This category includes everything from the physical layout, the dress code, the manner in which people address each other, the smell and feel of the place, its emotional intensity, and other phenomena, to the more permanent archival manifestations such as company records, products, statements of philosophy, and annual reports.

The problem with artifacts is that they are palpable but hard to decipher accurately. We know how we react to them, but that is not necessarily a reliable indicator of how members of the organization react. We can see and feel that one company is much more formal and bureaucratic than another, but that does not tell us anything about why this is so or what meaning it has to the members.

For example, one of the flaws of studying organizational symbols, stories, myths, and other such artifacts is that we may make incorrect inferences from them if we do not know how they connect to underlying assumptions (Pondy, Boland, & Thomas, 1988; Pondy, Frost, Morgan, & Dandridge, 1983; Wilkins, 1983). Organizational stories are especially problematic in this regard because the "lesson" of the story is not clear if one does not understand the underlying assumptions behind it.

Through interviews, questionnaires, or survey instruments one can study a culture's espoused and documented *values,* norms, ideologies, charters, and philosophies. This is comparable to the ethnographer's asking special "informants" why certain observed phenomena happen the way they do. Open-ended interviews can be very useful in getting at this level of how people feel and think, but questionnaires and survey instruments are generally less useful because they prejudge the dimensions to be studied. There is no way of knowing whether the dimensions one is asking about are relevant or salient in that culture until one has examined the deeper levels of the culture.

Through more intensive observation, through more focused questions, and through involving motivated members of the group in intensive self-analysis, one can seek out and decipher the taken-for-granted, underlying, and usually unconscious *assumptions* that determine perceptions, thought processes, feelings, and behavior. Once one understands some of these assumptions, it becomes much easier to decipher the meanings implicit in the various behavioral and artifactual phenomena one observes. Furthermore, once one understands the underlying taken-for-granted assumptions, one can better understand how cultures can seem to be ambiguous or even self-contradictory (Martin & Meyerson, 1988).

TABLE 11.1

THE EXTERNAL AND INTERNAL TASKS FACING ALL GROUPS

EXTERNAL ADAPTATION TASKS	INTERNAL INTEGRATION TASKS
Developing consensus on: 1. The core mission, functions, and primary tasks of the organization vis-à-vis its environments. 2. The specific goals to be pursued by the organization. 3. The basic means to be used in accomplishing the goals. 4. The criteria to be used for measuring results. 5. The remedial or repair strategies if goals are not achieved.	Developing consensus on: 1. The common language and conceptual system to be used, including basic concepts of time and space. 2. The group boundaries and criteria for inclusion. 3. The criteria for the allocation of status, power, and authority. 4. The criteria for intimacy, friendship, and love in different work and family settings. 5. The criteria for the allocation of rewards and punishments. 6. Concepts for managing the unmanageable—ideology and religion.

Note. Adapted from *Organizational Culture and Leadership* (pp. 52, 56) by E. H. Schein, 1985, San Francisco: Jossey-Bass. Copyright 1985 by Jossey-Bass. Adapted by permission.

As two case examples I present later will show, it is quite possible for a group to hold conflicting values that manifest themselves in inconsistent behavior while having complete consensus on underlying assumptions. It is equally possible for a group to reach consensus on the level of values and behavior and yet develop serious conflict later because there was no consensus on critical underlying assumptions.

This latter phenomenon is frequently observed in mergers or acquisitions where initial synergy is gradually replaced by conflict, leading ultimately to divestitures. When one analyzes these examples historically one often finds that there was insufficient agreement on certain basic assumptions, or, in our terms, that the cultures were basically in conflict with each other.

Deeply held assumptions often start out historically as values but, as they stand the test of time, gradually come to be taken for granted and then take on the character of assumptions. They are no longer questioned and they become less and less open to discussion. Such avoidance behavior occurs particularly if the learning was based on traumatic experiences in the organization's history, which leads to the group counterpart of what would be repression in the individual. If one understands culture in this way, it becomes obvious why it is so difficult to change culture.

Deciphering the "Content" of Culture

Culture is ubiquitous. It covers all areas of group life. A simplifying typology is always dangerous because one may not have the right variables in it, but if one distills from small group theory the dimensions that recur in group studies, one can identify a set of major external and internal tasks that all groups face and with which they must learn to cope (Ancona, 1988; Bales, 1950; Bales & Cohen, 1979; Benne & Sheats, 1948; Bennis & Shepard, 1956; Bion, 1959; Schein, 1988). The group's culture can then be seen as the learned response to each of these tasks (see Table 11.1).

Another approach to understanding the "content" of a culture is to draw on anthropological typologies of universal issues faced by all societies. Again there is a danger of overgeneralizing these dimensions (see Table 11.2), but the comparative studies of Kluckhohn and Strodtbeck (1961) are a reasonable start in this direction.

If one wants to decipher what is really going on in a particular organization, one has to start more inductively

TABLE 11.2

SOME UNDERLYING DIMENSIONS OF ORGANIZATIONAL CULTURE

DIMENSION	QUESTIONS TO BE ANSWERED
1. The organization's relationship to its environment	Does the organization perceive itself to be dominant, submissive, harmonizing, searching out a niche?
2. The nature of human activity	Is the "correct" way for humans to behave to be dominant/proactive, harmonizing, or passive/fatalistic?
3. The nature of reality and truth	How do we define what is true and what is not true; and how is truth ultimately determined both in the physical and social world? By pragmatic test, reliance on wisdom, or social consensus?
4. The nature of time	What is our basic orientation in terms of past, present, and future, and what kinds of time units are most relevant for the conduct of daily affairs?
5. The nature of human nature	Are humans basically good, neutral, or evil, and is human nature perfectible or fixed?
6. The nature of human relationships	What is the "correct" way for people to relate to each other, to distribute power and affection? Is life competitive or cooperative? Is the best way to organize society on the basis of individualism or groupism? Is the best authority system autocratic/paternalistic or collegial/participative?
7. Homogeneity vs. diversity	Is the group best off if it is highly homogeneous, and should individuals in a group be encouraged to innovate or conform?

Note. Adapted from *Organizational Culture and Leadership* (p. 86) by E. H. Schein, 1985, San Francisco: Jossey-Bass. Copyright 1985 by Jossey-Bass. Adapted by permission.

to find out which of these dimensions is the most pertinent on the basis of that organization's history. If one has access to the organization one will note its *artifacts* readily but will not really know what they mean. Of most value in this process will be noting *anomalies* and things that seem different, upsetting, or difficult to understand.

If one has access to members of the organization one can interview them about the issues in Table 11.1 and thereby get a good roadmap of what is going on. Such an interview will begin to reveal *espoused values,* and, as these surface, the investigator will begin to notice inconsistencies between what is claimed and what has been observed. These inconsistencies and the anomalies observed or felt now form the basis for the next layer of investigation.

Pushing past the layer of espoused values into underlying *assumptions* can be done by the ethnographer once trust has been established or by the clinician if the organizational client wishes to be helped. Working with motivated insiders is essential because only they can bring to the surface their own underlying assumptions and articulate how they basically perceive the world around them.

To summarize, if we combine insider knowledge with outsider questions, assumptions can be brought to the surface, but the process of inquiry has to be interactive, with the outsider continuing to probe until assumptions have really been teased out and have led to a feeling of greater understanding on the part of both the outsider and the insiders.

people staying late and expressing excitement about the importance of their work.

If one asks about these various behaviors, one is told that the company is in a rapidly growing high-technology field where hard work, innovation, and rapid solutions to things are important and where it is essential for everyone to contribute at their maximum capacity. New employees are carefully screened, and when an employee fails, he or she is simply assigned to another task, not fired or punished in any personal way.

If one discusses this further and pushes to the level of assumptions, one elicits a pattern or paradigm such as that shown in Figure 11.1. Because of the kind of technology the company manufactures, and because of the strongly held beliefs and values of its founder, the company operates on several critical and coordinated assumptions: (a) Individuals are assumed to be the source of all innovation and productivity. (b) It is assumed that truth can only be determined by pitting fully involved individuals against each other to debate ideas until only one idea survives, and it is further assumed that ideas will not be implemented unless everyone involved in implementation has been convinced through the debate of the validity of the idea. (c) Paradoxically, it is also assumed that every individual must think for himself or herself and "do the right thing" even if that means disobeying one's boss or violating a policy. (d) What makes it possible for people to live in this high-conflict environment is the assumption that the company members are one big family who will take care of each

Two Case Examples

It is not possible to provide complete cultural descriptions in a short article, but some extracts from cases can be summarized to illustrate particularly the distinctions between artifacts, values, and assumptions. The "Action Company" is a rapidly growing high-technology manufacturing concern still managed by its founder roughly 30 years after its founding. Because of its low turnover and intense history, one would expect to find an overall organizational culture as well as functional and geographic subcultures.

A visitor to the company would note the open office landscape architecture; a high degree of informality; frenetic activity all around; a high degree of confrontation, conflict, and fighting in meetings; an obvious lack of status symbols such as parking spaces or executive dining rooms; and a sense of high energy and emotional involvement, of

FIGURE 11.1

The Action Company Paradigm

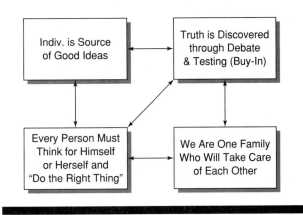

other and protect each other even if some members make mistakes or have bad ideas.

Once one understands this paradigm, one can understand all of the different observed artifacts such as the ability of the organization to tolerate extremely high degrees of conflict without seeming to destroy or even demotivate its employees. The value of the cultural analysis is that it provides insight, understanding, and a roadmap for future action. For example, as this company grows, the decision process may prove to be too slow, the individual autonomy that members are expected to exercise may become destructive and have to be replaced by more disciplined behavior, and the notion of a family may break down because too many people no longer know each other personally. The cultural analysis thus permits one to focus on those areas in which the organization will experience stresses and strains as it continues to grow and in which cultural evolution and change will occur.

By way of contrast, in the "Multi Company," a 100-year-old multidivisional, multinational chemical firm, one finds at the artifact level a high degree of formality; an architecture that puts great emphasis on privacy; a proliferation of status symbols and deference rituals such as addressing people by their titles; a high degree of politeness in group meetings; an emphasis on carefully thinking things out and then implementing them firmly through the hierarchy; a formal code of dress; and an emphasis on working hours, punctuality, and so on. One also finds a total absence of cross-divisional or cross-functional meetings and an almost total lack of lateral communication. Memos left in one department by an outside consultant with instructions to be given to others are almost never delivered.

The paradigm that surfaces, if one works with insiders to try to decipher what is going on, can best be depicted by the assumptions shown in Figure 11.2. The company is science based and has always derived its success from its research and development activities. Whereas "truth" in the Action Company is derived through debate and conflict and employees down the line are expected to think for themselves, in the Multi Company truth is derived from senior, wiser heads and employees are expected to go along like good soldiers once a decision is reached.

The Multi Company also sees itself as a family, but its concept of a family is completely different. Whereas in the Action Company, the family is a kind of safety net and an assurance of membership, in the Multi Company it is an authoritarian/paternalistic system of eliciting loyalty and compliance in exchange for economic security. The paradoxical absence of lateral communication is explained by the deeply held assumption that a job is a person's private turf and that the unsolicited providing of information to

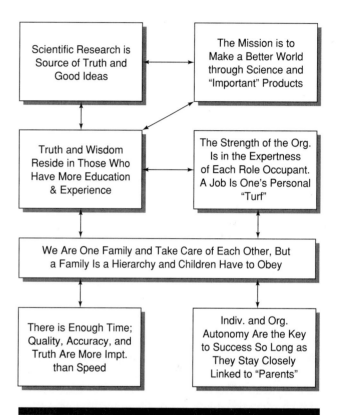

EXHIBIT 11.2

THE MULTI COMPANY PARADIGM

that person is an invasion of privacy and a potential threat to his or her self-esteem. Multi Company managers are very much on top of their jobs and pride themselves on that fact. If they ask for information they get it, but it is rarely volunteered by peers.

This cultural analysis highlights what is for the Multi Company a potential problem. Its future success may depend much more on its ability to become effective in marketing and manufacturing, yet it still treats research and development as a sacred cow and assumes that new products will be the key to its future success. Increasingly the company finds itself in a world that requires rapid decision making, yet its systems and procedures are slow and cumbersome. To be more innovative in marketing it needs to share ideas more, yet it undermines lateral communication.

Both companies reflect the larger cultures within which they exist in that the Action Company is an American firm whereas the Multi Company is European, but each also is different from its competitors within the same country, thus highlighting the importance of understanding *organizational* culture.

Cultural Dynamics: How Is Culture Created?

Culture is learned: hence learning models should help us to understand culture creation. Unfortunately, there are not many good models of how groups learn—how norms, beliefs, and assumptions are created initially. Once these exist, we can see clearly how leaders and powerful members embed them in group activity, but the process of learning something that becomes shared is still only partially understood.

Norm Formation around Critical Incidents

One line of analysis comes from the study of training groups (Bennis & Shepard, 1956; Bion, 1959; Schein, 1985a). One can see in such groups how norms and beliefs arise around the way members respond to critical incidents. Something emotionally charged or anxiety producing may happen, such as an attack by a member on the leader. Because everyone witnesses it and because tension is high when the attack occurs, the immediate next set of behaviors tends to create a norm.

Suppose, for example, that the leader counterattacks, that the group members "concur" with silence or approval, and that the offending member indicates with an apology that he or she accepts his or her "mistake." In those few moments a bit of culture has begun to be created—the norm that "we do not attack the leader in this group; authority is sacred." The norm may eventually become a belief and then an assumption if the same pattern recurs. If the leader and the group consistently respond differently to attacks, a different norm will arise. By reconstructing the history of critical incidents in the group and how members dealt with them, one can get a good indication of the important cultural elements in that group.

Identification with Leaders

A second mechanism of culture creation is the modeling by leader figures that permits group members to identify with

them and internalize their values and assumptions. When groups or organizations first form, there are usually dominant figures or "founders" whose own beliefs, values, and assumptions provide a visible and articulated model for how the group should be structured and how it should function (Schein, 1983). As these beliefs are put into practice, some work out and some do not. The group then learns from its own experience what parts of the "founder's" belief system work for the group as a whole. The joint learning then gradually creates shared assumptions.

Founders and subsequent leaders continue to attempt to embed their own assumptions, but increasingly they find that other parts of the organization have their own experiences to draw on and, thus, cannot be changed. Increasingly the learning process is shared, and the resulting cultural assumptions reflect the total group's experience, not only the leader's initial assumptions. But leaders continue to try to embed their own views of how things should be, and, if they are powerful enough, they will continue to have a dominant effect on the emerging culture.

Primary embedding mechanisms are (a) what leaders pay attention to, measure, and control; (b) how leaders react to critical incidents and organizational crises; (c) deliberate role modeling and coaching; (d) operational criteria for the allocation of rewards and status; and (e) operational criteria for recruitment, selection, promotion, retirement, and excommunication. *Secondary articulation and reinforcement mechanisms* are (a) the organization's design and structure; (b) organizational systems and procedures; (c) the design of physical space, facades, and buildings; (d) stories, legends, myths, and symbols; and (e) formal statements of organizational philosophy, creeds, and charters.

One can hypothesize that as cultures evolve and grow, two processes will occur simultaneously: a process of differentiation into various kinds of subcultures that will create diversity, and a process of integration, or a tendency for the various deeper elements of the culture to become congruent with each other because of the human need for consistency.

Cultural Dynamics: Preservation through Socialization

Culture perpetuates and reproduces itself through the socialization of new members entering the group. The socialization process really begins with recruitment and selection in that the organization is likely to look for new members who already have the "right" set of assumptions, beliefs, and values. If the organization can find such pre-socialized members, it needs to do less formal socialization. More typically, however, new members do not "know the ropes" well enough to be able to take and enact their organizational roles, and thus they need to be trained and "acculturated" (Feldman, 1988; Ritti & Funkhouser, 1987; Schein, 1968, 1978; Van Maanen, 1976, 1977).

The socialization process has been analyzed from a variety of perspectives and can best be conceptualized in terms of a set of dimensions that highlight variations in how different organizations approach the process (Van Maanen, 1978; Van Maanen & Schein, 1979). Van Maanen identified seven dimensions along which socialization processes can vary:

1. *Group versus individual:* the degree to which the organization processes recruits in batches, as in boot camp, or individually, as in professional offices.
2. *Formal versus informal:* the degree to which the process is formalized, as in set training programs, or is handled informally through apprenticeships, individual coaching by the immediate superior, or the like.
3. *Self-destructive and reconstructing versus self-enhancing:* the degree to which the process destroys aspects of the self and replaces them, as in boot camp, or enhances aspects of the self, as in professional development programs.
4. *Serial versus random:* the degree to which role models are provided, as in apprenticeship or mentoring programs, or are deliberately withheld, as in sink-or-swim kinds of initiations in which the recruit is expected to figure out his or her own solutions.
5. *Sequential versus disjunctive:* the degree to which the process consists of guiding the recruit through a series of discrete steps and roles versus being open-ended and never letting the recruit predict what organizational role will come next.
6. *Fixed versus variable:* the degree to which stages of the training process have fixed timetables for each stage, as in military academies, boot camps, or rotational training programs, or are open-ended, as in typical promotional systems where one is not advanced to the next stage until one is "ready."
7. *Tournament versus contest:* the degree to which each stage is an "elimination tournament" where one is out of the organization if one fails or a "contest" in which one builds up a track record and batting average.

Socialization Consequences

Though the goal of socialization is to perpetuate the culture, it is clear that the process does not have uniform effects. Individuals respond differently to the same treatment, and, even more important, different combinations of socialization tactics can be hypothesized to produce somewhat different outcomes for the organization (Van Maanen & Schein, 1979).

For example, from the point of view of the organization, one can specify three kinds of outcomes: (a) a *custodial orientation,* or total conformity to all norms and complete learning of all assumptions; (b) *creative individualism,* which implies that the trainee learns all of the central and pivotal assumptions of the culture but rejects all peripheral ones, thus permitting the individual to be creative both with respect to the organization's tasks and in how the organization performs them (role innovation); and (c) *rebellion,* or the total rejection of all assumptions. If the rebellious individual is constrained by external circumstances from leaving the organization, he or she will subvert, sabotage, and ultimately foment revolution.

We can hypothesize that the combination of socialization techniques most likely to produce a custodial orientation is (1) formal, (2) self-reconstructing, (3) serial, (4) sequential, (5) variable, and (6) tournament-like. Hence if one wants new members to be more creative in the use of their talents, one should use socialization techniques that are informal, self-enhancing, random, disjunctive, fixed in terms of timetables, and contest-like.

The individual versus group dimension can go in either direction in that group socialization methods can produce loyal custodially oriented cohorts or can produce disloyal rebels if countercultural norms are formed during the socialization process. Similarly, in the individual apprenticeship the direction of socialization will depend on the orientation of the mentor or coach.

Efforts to measure these socialization dimensions have been made, and some preliminary support for the above hypotheses has been forthcoming (Feldman, 1976, 1988; G. R. Jones, 1986). Insofar as cultural evolution is a function of innovative and creative efforts on the part of new members, this line of investigation is especially important.

Cultural Dynamics: Natural Evolution

Every group and organization is an open system that exists in multiple environments. Changes in the environment will produce stresses and strains inside the group, forcing new learning and adaptation. At the same time, new members coming into the group will bring in new beliefs and assumptions that will influence currently held assumptions. To some degree, then, there is constant pressure on any given culture to evolve and grow. But just as individuals do not easily give up the elements of their identity or their defense mechanisms, so groups do not easily give up some of their basic underlying assumptions merely because external events or new members disconfirm them.

An illustration of "forced" evolution can be seen in the case of the aerospace company that prided itself on its high level of trust in its employees, which was reflected in flexible working hours, systems of self-monitoring and self-control, and the absence of time clocks. When a number of other companies in the industry were discovered to have overcharged their government clients, the government legislated a system of controls for *all* of its contractors, forcing this company to install time clocks and other control mechanisms that undermined the climate of trust that had been built up over 30 years. It remains to be seen whether the company's basic assumption that people can be trusted will gradually change or whether the company will find a way to discount the effects of an artifact that is in fundamental conflict with one of its basic assumptions.

Differentiation

As organizations grow and evolve they divide the labor and form functional, geographical, and other kinds of units, each of which exists in its own specific environment. Thus organizations begin to build their own subcultures. A natural evolutionary mechanism, therefore, is the differentiation that inevitably occurs with age and size. Once a group has many subcultures, its total culture increasingly becomes a negotiated outcome of the interaction of its subgroups. Organizations then evolve either by special efforts to impose their overall culture or by allowing dominant subcultures that may be better adapted to changing environmental circumstances to become more influential.

Cultural Dynamics: Guided Evolution and Managed Change

One of the major roles of the field of organization development has been to help organizations guide the direction of their evolution, that is, to enhance cultural elements that are viewed as critical to maintaining identity and to promote the "unlearning" of cultural elements that are viewed as increasingly dysfunctional (Argyris, Putnam, & Smith, 1985; Argyris & Schon, 1978; Beckhard & Harris, 1987; Hanna, 1988; Lippitt, 1982; Walton, 1987). This process in organizations is analogous to the process of therapy in individuals, although the actual tactics are more complicated when multiple clients are involved and when some of the clients are groups and subsystems.

Leaders of organizations sometimes are able to overcome their own cultural biases and to perceive that elements of an organization's culture are dysfunctional for survival and growth in a changing environment. They may feel either that they do not have the time to let evolution occur naturally or that evolution is heading the organization in the wrong direction. In such a situation one can observe leaders doing a number of different things, usually in combination, to produce the desired cultural changes:

1. Leaders may unfreeze the present system by highlighting the threats to the organization if no change occurs, and, at the same time, encourage the organization to believe that change is possible and desirable.

2. They may articulate a new direction and a new set of assumptions, thus providing a clear and new role model.

3. Key positions in the organization may be filled with new incumbents who hold the new assumptions because they are either hybrids, mutants, or brought in from the outside.

4. Leaders systematically may reward the adoption of new directions and punish adherence to the old direction.

5. Organization members may be seduced or coerced into adopting new behaviors that are more consistent with new assumptions.

6. Visible scandals may be created to discredit sacred cows, to explode myths that preserve dysfunctional traditions, and destroy symbolically the artifacts associated with them.

7. Leaders may create new emotionally charged rituals and develop new symbols and artifacts around the new assumptions to be embraced, using the embedding mechanisms described earlier.

Such cultural change efforts are generally more characteristic of "midlife" organizations that have become complacent and ill adapted to rapidly changing environmental conditions (Schein, 1985a). The fact that such organizations have strong subcultures aids the change process in that one can draw the new leaders from those subcultures that most represent the direction in which the organization needs to go.

In cases where organizations become extremely maladapted, one sees more severe change efforts. These may take the form of destroying the group that is the primary cultural carrier and reconstructing it around new people, thereby allowing a new learning process to occur and a new culture to form. When organizations go bankrupt or are turned over to "turnaround managers," one often sees such extreme measures. What is important to note about such cases is that they invariably involve the replacement of large numbers of people because the members who have grown up in the organization find it difficult to change their basic assumptions.

Mergers and Acquisitions

One of the most obvious forces toward culture change is the bringing together of two or more cultures. Unfortunately, in many mergers and acquisitions, the culture compatibility issue is not raised until after the deal has been consummated, which leads, in many cases, to cultural "indigestion" and the eventual divestiture of units that cannot become culturally integrated.

To avoid such problems, organizations must either engage in more premerger diagnosis to determine cultural compatibility or conduct training and integration workshops to help the meshing process. Such workshops have to take into account the deeper assumption layers of culture to avoid the trap of reaching consensus at the level of artifacts and values while remaining in conflict at the level of underlying assumptions.

The Role of the Organizational Psychologist

Culture will become an increasingly important concept for organizational psychology. Without such a concept we cannot really understand change or resistance to change. The more we get involved with helping organizations to design their fundamental strategies, particularly in the human resources area, the more important it will be to be able to help organizations decipher their own cultures.

All of the activities that revolve around recruitment, selection, training, socialization, the design of reward systems, the design and description of jobs, and broader issues of organization design require an understanding of how organizational culture influences present functioning. Many organizational change programs that failed probably did so because they ignored cultural forces in the organizations in which they were to be installed.

Inasmuch as culture is a dynamic process within organizations, it is probably studied best by action research methods, that is, methods that get "insiders" involved in the research and that work through attempts to "intervene" (Argyris et al., 1985; French & Bell, 1984; Lewin, 1952; Schein, 1987b). Until we have a better understanding of how culture works, it is probably best to work with qualitative research approaches that combine field work methods from ethnography with interview and observation methods from clinical and consulting work (Schein, 1987a).

I do not see a unique role for the traditional industrial/organizational psychologist, but I see great potential for the psychologist to work as a team member with colleagues who are more ethnographically oriented. The particular skill that will be needed on the part of the psychologist will be knowledge of organizations and of how to work with them, especially in a consulting relationship. Organizational culture is a complex phenomenon, and we should not rush to measure things until we understand better what we are measuring.

REFERENCES

Ancona, D. G. (1988). Groups in organizations: Extending laboratory models. In C. Hendrick (Ed.), *Annual review of personality and social psychology: Group and intergroup processes.* Beverly

Hills, CA: Sage.

Argyris, C., Putnam, R., & Smith, D. M. (1985). *Action science.* San Francisco: Jossey-Bass.

Argyris, C., & Schon, D. A. (1978). *Organizational learning: A theory of action perspective.* Reading, MA: Addison-Wesley.

Bales, R. F. (1950). *Interaction process analysis.* Chicago: University of Chicago Press.

Bales, R. F., & Cohen, S. P. (1979). *SYMLOG: A system for the multiple level observation of groups.* New York: Free Press.

Barley, S. R. (1983). Semiotics and the study of occupational and organizational cultures. *Administrative Science Quarterly, 28,* 393–413.

Barley, S. R., Meyer, C. W., & Gash, D. C. (1988). Culture of cultures: Academics, practitioners and the pragmatics of normative control. *Administrative Science Quarterly, 33,* 24–60.

Bass, B. M. (1965). *Organizational psychology.* Boston: Allyn & Bacon.

Beckhard, R. (1969). *Organization development: Strategies and models.* Reading, MA: Addison-Wesley.

Beckhard, R., & Harris, R. T. (1977). *Organizational transitions: Managing complex change.* Reading, MA: Addison-Wesley.

Beckhard, R., & Harris, R. T. (1987). *Organizational transitions: Managing complex change* (2nd ed.). Reading, MA: Addison-Wesley.

Benne, K., & Sheats, P. (1948). Functional roles of group members. *Journal of Social Issues, 2,* 42–47.

Bennis, W. G. (1966). *Changing organizations.* New York: McGraw-Hill.

Bennis, W. G. (1969). *Organization development: Its nature, origins, and prospects.* Reading, MA: Addison-Wesley.

Bennis, W. G., & Shepard, H. A. (1956) A theory of group development. *Human Relations, 9,* 415–437.

Bion, W. R. (1959). *Experiences in groups.* London: Tavistock.

Bradford, L. P., Gibb, J. R., & Benne, K. D. (Eds.). (1964). *T-Group theory and laboratory method.* New York: Wiley.

Chandler, A. P. (1977). *The visible hand.* Cambridge, MA: Harvard University Press.

Deal, T. W., & Kennedy, A. A. (1982). *Corporate cultures.* Reading, MA: Addison-Wesley.

Durkin, J. E. (Ed.). (1981). *Living groups: Group psychotherapy and general systems theory.* New York: Brunner/Mazel.

Dyer, W. G., Jr. (1986). *Cultural change in family firms.* San Francisco: Jossey-Bass,

Feldman, D. C. (1976). A contingency theory of socialization. *Administrative Science Quarterly, 21,* 433–452.

Feldman, D. C. (1988). *Managing careers in organizations.* Glenview, IL: Scott, Foresman.

Festinger, L. (1957). *A theory of cognitive dissonance.* New York: Harper & Row.

Fleishman, E. A. (1953). Leadership climate, human relations training, and supervisory behavior. *Personnel Psychology, 6,* 205–222.

Fleishman, E. A. (1973). Twenty years of consideration and structure. In E. A. Fleishman & J. G. Hunt (Eds.), *Current developments in the study of leadership* (pp. 1–39). Carbondale: Southern Illinois University Press.

French, W. L., & Bell, C. H. (1984). *Organization development* (3rd ed.). Englewood Cliffs, NJ: Prentice-Hall.

Frost, P. J., Moore, L. F., Louis, M. R., Lundberg, C. C., & Martin, J. (Eds.). (1985). *Organizational culture.* Beverly Hills, CA: Sage.

Hanna, D. P. (1988). *Designing organizations for high performance.* Reading, MA: Addison-Wesley.

Harris, S. G., & Sutton, R. I. (1986). Functions of parting ceremonies in dying organizations. *Academy of Management Journal, 29,* 5–30.

Hebb, D. (1954). The social significance of animal studies. In G. Lindzey (Ed.), *Handbook of social psychology* (Vol. 2, pp. 532–561). Reading, MA: Addison-Wesley.

Heider, F. (1958). *The psychology of interpersonal relations.* New York: Wiley.

Hellriegel, D., & Slocum, J. W., Jr. (1974). Organizational climate: Measures, research, and contingencies. *Academy of Management Journal, 17,* 255–280.

Hirschhorn, L. (1987). *The workplace within.* Cambridge, MA: MIT Press.

Hofstede, G. (1980). *Culture's consequences.* Beverly Hills, CA: Sage.

Hofstede, G., & Bond, M. H. (1988). The Confucius connection: From cultural roots to economic growth. *Organizational Dynamics, 16*(4), 4–21.

Homans, G. (1950). *The human group.* New York: Harcourt, Brace, Jovanovich.

Jaques, E. (1951). *The changing culture of a factory.* London: Tavistock.

Jones, A. P., & James, L. R. (1979). Psychological climate: Dimensions and relationships of individual and aggregated work environment perceptions. *Organizational Behavior and Human Performance, 23,* 201–250.

Jones, G. R. (1986). Socialization tactics, self-efficacy, and newcomers' adjustments to organizations. *Academy of Management Journal, 29,* 262–279.

Katz, D., & Kahn, R. L. (1966). *The social psychology of organizations.* New York: Wiley.

Katz, D., & Kahn, R. L. (1978). *The social psychology of organizations* (2nd ed.). New York: Wiley.

Kets de Vries, M. F. R., & Miller, D. (1984). *The neurotic organization.* San Francisco: Jossey-Bass.

Kets de Vries, M. F. R., & Miller, D. (1986). Personality, culture, and organization. *Academy of Management Review, 11,* 266–279.

Kilmann, R. H. (1984). *Beyond the quick fix.* San Francisco: Jossey-Bass.

Kluckhohn, F. R., & Strodtbeck, F. L. (1961). *Variations in value orientations.* New York: Harper & Row.

Lewin, K. (1952). Group decision and social change. In G. E. Swanson, T. N. Newcomb, & E. L. Hartley (Eds.), *Readings in social psychology* (rev. ed., pp. 459–473). New York: Holt, Rinehart, & Winston.

Lewin, K., Lippitt, R., & White, R. K. (1939). Patterns of aggressive behavior in experimentally created "social climates." *Journal of Social Psychology, 10,* 271–299.

Likert, R. (1961). *New patterns of management.* New York: McGraw-Hill.

Likert, R. (1967). *The human organization.* New York: McGraw-Hill.

Lippitt, G. (1982). *Organizational renewal* (2nd ed.). Englewood Cliffs, NJ: Prentice-Hall.

Litwin, G. H., & Stringer, R. A. (1968). *Motivation and organizational climate.* Boston: Harvard Business School, Division of Research.

Louis, M. R. (1981). A cultural perspective on organizations. *Human Systems Management, 2,* 246–258.

Louis, M. R. (1983). Organizations as culture bearing milieux. In L. R. Pondy, P. J. Frost, G. Morgan, & T. C. Dandridge (Eds.), *Organizational symbolism* (pp. 39–54). Greenwich, CT: JAI Press.

Martin, J. (1982). Stories and scripts in organizational settings. In A. Hastorf & A. Isen (Eds.), *Cognitive social psychology.* New York: Elsevier.

Martin, J., Feldman, M. S., Hatch, M. J., & Sitkin, S. (1983). The uniqueness paradox in organizational stories. *Administrative Science Quarterly, 28,* 438–454.

Martin, J., & Meyerson, D. (1988). Organizational cultures and the denial, channeling, and acknowledgment of ambiguity. In L. R. Pondy, R. J. Boland, & H. Thomas (Eds.), *Managing ambiguity and change.* New York: Wiley.

Martin, J., & Powers, M. E. (1983). Truth or corporate propaganda: The value of a good war story. In L. R. Pondy, P. J. Frost, G. Morgan, & T. C. Dandridge (Eds.), *Organizational symbolism* (pp. 93–108). Greenwich, CT: JAI Press.

Martin, J., & Siehl, C. (1983). Organizational culture and counterculture: An uneasy symbiosis. *Organizational Dynamics, 12,* 52–64.

Menzies, I. E. P. (1960). A case study in the functioning of social systems as a defense against anxiety. *Human Relations, 13,* 95–121.

O'Toole, J. J. (1979). Corporate and managerial cultures. In C. L. Cooper (Ed.), *Behavioral problems in organizations.* Englewood Cliffs, NJ: Prentice-Hall.

Ott, J. S. (1989). *The organizational culture perspective.* Chicago: Dorsey Press.

Ouchi, W. G. (1981). *Theory Z.* Reading, MA: Addison-Wesley.

Pascale, R. T., & Athos, A. G. (1981). *The art of Japanese management.* New York: Simon & Schuster.

Peters, T. J., & Waterman, R. H., Jr. (1982). *In search of excellence.* New York: Harper & Row.

Pettigrew, A. M. (1979). On studying organizational cultures. *Administrative Science Quarterly, 24,* 570–581.

Pondy, L. R., Boland, R. J., & Thomas, H. (1988). *Managing ambiguity and change.* New York: Wiley.

Pondy, L. R., Frost, P. J., Morgan, G., & Dandridge, T. C. (Eds.). (1983). *Organizational symbolism.* Greenwich, CT: JAI Press.

Rice, A. K. (1963). *The enterprise and its environment.* London: Tavistock.

Ritti, R. R., & Funkhouser, G. R. (1987). *The ropes to skip and the ropes to know* (3rd ed.). New York: Wiley.

Roethlisberger, F. J., & Dickson, W. J. (1939). *Management and the worker.* Cambridge, MA: Harvard University Press.

Schall, M. S. (1983). A communication-rules approach to organizational culture. *Administrative Science Quarterly, 28,* 557–581.

Schein, E. H. (1965). *Organizational psychology.* Englewood Cliffs, NJ: Prentice-Hall.

Schein, E. H. (1968). Organizational socialization and the profession of management. *Industrial Management Review (MIT), 9,* 1–15.

Schein, E. H. (1969). *Process consultation.* Reading, MA: Addison-Wesley.

Schein, E. H. (1978). *Career dynamics.* Reading, MA: Addison-Wesley.

Schein, E. H. (1983). The role of the founder in creating organizational culture. *Organizational Dynamics, 12,* 13–28.

Schein, E. H. (1985a). *Organizational culture and leadership.* San Francisco: Jossey-Bass.

Schein, E. H. (1985b). Organizational culture: Skill, defense mechanism or addiction? In F. R. Brush & J. B. Overmier (Eds.), *Affect, conditioning, and cognition* (pp. 315–323). Hillsdale, NJ: Erlbaum.

Schein, E. H. (1987a). *The clinical perspective in fieldwork.* Beverly Hills, CA: Sage.

Schein, E. H. (1987b). *Process consultation* (Vol. 2). Reading, MA: Addison-Wesley.

Schein, E. H. (1988). *Process consultation* (rev. ed.). Reading, MA: Addison-Wesley.

Schein, E. H., & Bennis, W. G. (1965). *Personal and organizational change through group methods.* New York: Wiley.

Schneider, B. (1975). Organizational climate: An essay. *Personnel Psychology, 28,* 447–479.

Schneider, B., & Reichers, A. E. (1983). On the etiology of climates. *Personnel Psychology, 36,* 19–40.

Smircich, L., & Calas, M. B. (1987). Organizational culture: A critical assessment. In F. M. Jablin, L. L. Putnam, K. H. Roberts, & L. W. Porter (Eds.), *Handbook of organizational communication* (pp. 228–263). Beverly Hills, CA: Sage.

Tagiuri, R., & Litwin, G. H. (Eds.). (1968). *Organizational climate: Exploration of a concept.* Boston: Harvard Business School, Division of Research.

Trice, H., & Beyer, J. (1984). Studying organizational cultures through rites and ceremonials. *Academy of Management Review, 9,* 653–669.

Trist, E. L., Higgin, G. W., Murray, H., & Pollock, A. B. (1963). *Organizational choice.* London: Tavistock.

Van Maanen, J. (1976). Breaking in: Socialization to work. In R. Dubin (Ed.), *Handbook of work, organization and society* (pp. 67–130). Chicago: Rand McNally.

Van Maanen, J. (1977). Experiencing organizations. In J. Van Maanen (Ed.), *Organizational careers: Some new perspectives* (pp. 15–45). New York: Wiley.

Van Maanen, J. (1978). People processing: Strategies of organizational socialization. *Organizational Dynamics, 7,* 18–36.

Van Maanen, J. (1988). *Tales of the field.* Chicago: University of Chicago Press.

Van Maanen, J., & Barley, S. R. (1984). Occupational communities: Culture and control in organizations. In B. M. Staw & L. L. Cummings (Eds.), *Research in organizational behavior* (Vol. 6). Greenwich, CT: JAI Press.

Van Maanen, J., & Schein, E. H. (1979). Toward a theory of organizational socialization. In B. M. Staw & L. L. Cummings (Eds.), *Research in organizational behavior* (Vol. 1, pp. 204–264). Greenwich, CT: JAI Press.

Walton, R. (1987). *Innovating to compete.* San Francisco: Jossey-Bass.

Werner, H. (1940). *Comparative psychology of mental development.* New York: Follett.

Westney, D. E. (1987). *Imitation and innovation.* Cambridge, MA: Harvard University Press.

Wilkins, A. L. (1983). Organizational stories as symbols which control the organization. In L. R. Pondy, P. J. Frost, G. Morgan, & T. C. Dandridge (Eds.), *Organizational symbolism* (pp. 81–91). Greenwich, CT: JAI Press.

Wilkins, A. L., & Ouchi, W. G. (1983). Efficient cultures: Exploring the relationship between culture and organizational performance. *Administrative Science Quarterly, 28,* 468–481.

DISCUSSION QUESTIONS

1. What is organizational culture?

2. What recent events in business have created intense interest in studying and understanding how to manage organizational culture?

3. Describe the levels of culture and how they affect behavior.

4. What is the research approach and strategy that Schein thinks is most useful for understanding organizational culture?

5. According to Schein, what are the processes by which culture is created?

6. How does organizational culture contribute to the reproduction of an organization?

7. How do organizational cultures change?

8. What role, if any, can consultants—psychologists, anthropologists, sociologists—perform to help an organization understand or change its culture?

Changing Unethical Organizational Behavior

RICHARD P. NIELSEN

LEARNING OBJECTIVES

After reading Nielsen's "Changing Unethical Organizational Behavior," a student will be able to:

1. Understand how unethical behavior in organizations is affected by socialization, commitment, and an organization's culture

2. See how an individual's action can change unethical behavior

3. Contemplate the limitations and liabilities of the individual and the organization in changing unethical behavior

4. Appreciate the relationship between the individual and the organization—the ethical component of a psychological contract

To be, or not to be: that is the question:
Whether 'tis nobler in the mind to suffer
The slings and arrows of outrageous fortune,
Or to take arms against a sea of troubles,
And by opposing end them?

William Shakespeare, *Hamlet*

What are the implications of Hamlet's question in the context of organizational ethics? What does it mean to be ethical in an organizational context? Should one suffer the slings and arrows of unethical organizational behavior? Should one try to take arms against unethical behaviors and by opposing, end them?

The consequences of addressing organizational ethics issues can be unpleasant. One can be punished or fired; one's career can suffer, or one can be disliked, considered an outsider. It may take courage to oppose unethical and lead ethical organizational behavior.

How can one address organizational ethics issues? Paul Tillich, in his book *The Courage to Be*, recognized, as Hamlet did, that dire consequences can result from standing up to and opposing unethical behavior. Tillich identified two approaches: *being* as an individual and *being* as a part of a group.[1]

In an organizational context, these two approaches can be interpreted as follows: (1) Being as an individual can mean intervening to end unethical organizational behaviors by working against others and the organizations performing the unethical behaviors; and (2) being as a part can mean leading an ethical organizational change by working with others and the organization. These approaches are not mutually exclusive; rather, depending on the individual, the organization, the relationships, and the situation, one or both of these approaches may be appropriate for addressing ethical issues.

Being as an Individual

According to Tillich, the courage to be as an individual is the courage to follow one's conscience and defy unethical and/or unreasonable authority. It can even mean staging a revolutionary attack on that authority. Such an act can entail great risk and require great courage. As Tillich explains, "The anxiety conquered in the courage to be . . . in the productive process is considerable, because the threat of being excluded from such a participation by unemployment or the loss of an economic basis is what, above all, fate means today. . . ."[2]

According to David Ewing, retired executive editor of the *Harvard Business Review,* this type of anxiety is not without foundation.

There is very little protection in industry for employees who object to carrying out immoral,

Source: Richard P. Nielsen: "Changing Unethical Organizational Behavior," *The Academy of Management Executive,* 1989, Vol. 3, No. 2, pp. 123–130. Copyright ©1989. Reprinted by permission.

unethical or illegal orders from their superiors. If the employee doesn't like what he or she is asked to do, the remedy is to pack up and leave. This remedy seems to presuppose an ideal economy, where there is another company down the street with openings for jobs just like the one the employee left.[3]

How can one *be* as an individual, intervening against unethical organizational behavior? Intervention strategies an individual can use to change unethical behavior include: (1) secretly blowing the whistle within the organization; (2) quietly blowing the whistle, informing a responsible higher-level manager; (3) secretly threatening the offender with blowing the whistle; (4) secretly threatening a responsible manager with blowing the whistle outside the organization; (5) publicly threatening a responsible manager with blowing the whistle; (6) sabotaging the implementation of the unethical behavior; (7) quietly refraining from implementing an unethical order or policy; (8) publicly blowing the whistle within the organization; (9) conscientiously objecting to an unethical policy or refusing to implement the policy; (10) indicating uncertainty about or refusing to support a cover-up in the event that the individual and/or organization gets caught; (11) secretly blowing the whistle outside the organization; or (12) publicly blowing the whistle outside the organization. Cases of each are considered below.

Cases

1. Secretly blowing the whistle within the organization. A purchasing manager for General Electric secretly wrote a letter to an upper-level manager about his boss, who was soliciting and accepting bribes from subcontractors. The boss was investigated and eventually fired. He was also sentenced to six months' imprisonment for taking $100,000 in bribes, in exchange for which he granted favorable treatment on defense contracts.[4]

2. Quietly blowing the whistle to a responsible higher-level manager. When Evelyn Grant was first hired by the company with which she is now a personnel manager, her job included administering a battery of tests that, in part, determined which employees were promoted to supervisory positions. Grant explained:

There have been cases where people will do something wrong because they think they have no choice. Their boss tells them to do it, and so they do it, knowing it's wrong.

They don't realize there are ways around the boss. . . . When I went over his [the chief psychologist's] data and analysis, I found errors in assumptions as well as actual errors of computation. . . . I had two choices: I could do nothing or I could report my findings to my supervisor. If I did nothing, the only persons probably hurt were the ones who "failed" the test. To report my findings, on the other hand, could hurt several people, possibly myself.

She spoke to her boss, who quietly arranged for a meeting to discuss the discrepancies with the chief psychologist. The chief psychologist did not show up for the meeting; however, the test battery was dropped.[5]

3. Secretly threatening the offender with blowing the whistle. A salesman for a Boston-area insurance company attended a weekly sales meeting during which the sales manager instructed the salespeople, both verbally and in writing, to use a sales technique that the salesman considered unethical. The salesman anonymously wrote the sales manager a letter threatening to send a copy of the unethical sales instructions to the Massachusetts insurance commissioner and the *Boston Globe* newspaper unless the sales manager retracted his instructions at the next sales meeting. The sales manager did retract the instructions. The salesman still works for the insurance company.[6]

4. Secretly threatening a responsible manager with blowing the whistle outside the organization. A recently hired manager with a San Francisco Real Estate Development Company found that the construction company his firm had contracted with was systematically not giving minorities opportunities to learn construction management. This new manager wrote an anonymous letter to a higher-level real estate manager threatening to blow the whistle to the press and local government about the contractor unless the company corrected the situation. The real estate manager intervened, and the contractor began to hire minorities for foremen-training positions.[7]

5. Publicly threatening a responsible manager with blowing the whistle. A woman in the business office of a large Boston-area university observed that one middle-level male manager was sexually harassing several women in the office. She tried to reason with the office manager to do something about the offensive behavior, but the manager would not do anything. She then told the manager and several other people in the office that if the manager did not do something about the behavior, she would blow the whistle to the personnel office. The manager then told the offender that if he did not stop the harassment, the personnel office would be brought in. He did stop the behavior, but he and several other employees refused to talk to the woman who initiated the actions. She eventually left the university.[8]

6. *Sabotaging the implementation of the unethical behavior.* A program manager for a Boston-area local social welfare organization was told by her superior to replace a significant percentage of her clients who received disability benefits with refugee Soviet Jews. She wanted to help both the refugees and her current clients; however, she thought it was unethical to drop current clients, in part because she believed such an action could result in unnecessary deaths. Previously, a person who had lost benefits because of what the program manager considered unethical "bumping" had committed suicide: He had not wanted to force his family to sell their home in order to pay for the medical care he needed and qualify for poverty programs. After her attempts to reason with her boss failed, she instituted a paperwork chain with a partially funded federal agency that prevented her own agency from dropping clients for nine months, after which time they would be eligible for a different funding program. Her old clients received benefits and the new refugees also received benefits. In discussions with her boss, she blamed the federal agency for making it impossible to drop people quickly. Her boss, a political appointee who did not understand the system, also blamed the federal agency office.[9]

7. *Publicly blowing the whistle within the organization.* John W. Young, the chief of NASA's astronaut office, wrote a 12-page internal memorandum to 97 people after the Challenger explosion that killed seven crew members. The memo listed a large number of safety-related problems that Young said had endangered crews since October 1984. According to Young, "If the management system is not big enough to stop the space shuttle program whenever necessary to make flight safety corrections, it will not survive and neither will our three space shuttles or their flight crews." The memo was instrumental in the decision to broaden safety investigations throughout the total NASA system.[10]

8. *Quietly refraining from implementing an unethical order/policy.* Frank Ladwig was a top salesman and branch manager with a large computer company for more than 40 years. At times, he had trouble balancing his responsibilities. For instance, he was trained to sell solutions to customer problems, yet he had order and revenue quotas that sometimes made it difficult for him to concentrate on solving problems. He was responsible for signing and keeping important customers with annual revenues of between $250,000 and $500,000 and for aggressively and conscientiously representing new products that had required large R&D investments. He was required to sell the full line of products and services, and sometimes he had sales quotas for products that he believed were not a good match for the customer or appeared to perform marginally. Ladwig would quietly not sell those products, concentrating on selling the products he believed in. He would quietly explain the characteristics of the questionable products to his knowledgeable customers and get their reactions, rather than making an all-out sales effort. When he was asked by his sales manager why a certain product was not moving, he explained what the customers objected to and why. However, Ladwig thought that a salesman or manager with an average or poor performance record would have a difficult time getting away with this type of solution to an ethical dilemma.[11]

9. *Conscientiously objecting to an unethical policy or refusing to implement it.* Francis O'Brien was a research director for the pharmaceutical company Searle & Co. O'Brien conscientiously objected to what he believed were exaggerated claims for the Searle Copper 7 intrauterine contraceptive. When reasoning with upper-level management failed, O'Brien wrote them the following:

> *Their continued use, in my opinion, is both misleading and a thinly disguised attempt to make claims which are not FDA approved. . . . Because of personal reasons I do not consent to have my name used in any press release or in connection with any press release. In addition, I will not participate in any press conferences.*

O'Brien left the company ten years later. Currently, several lawsuits are pending against Searle, charging that its IUD caused infection and sterility.[12]

10. *Indicating uncertainty about or refusing to support a cover-up in the event that the individual and/or organization gets caught.* In the Boston office of Bear Stearns, four brokers informally worked together as a group. One of the brokers had been successfully trading on insider information, and he invited the other three to do the same. One of the three told the others that such trading was not worth the risk of getting caught, and if an investigation ever occurred, he was not sure he would be able to participate in a cover-up. The other two brokers decided not to trade on the insider information, and the first broker stopped at least that type of insider trading.[13]

11. *Secretly blowing the whistle outside the corporation.* William Schwartzkopf of the Commonwealth Electric Company secretly and anonymously wrote a letter to the Justice Department alleging large-scale, long-time bid rigging among many of the largest U.S. electrical contractors. The secret letter accused the contractors of raising

bids and conspiring to divide billions of dollars of contracts. Companies in the industry have already paid more than $20 million in fines to the government in part as a result of this letter, and they face millions of dollars more in losses when the victims sue.[14]

12. Publicly blowing the whistle outside the organization. A. Earnest Fitzgerald, a former high-level manager in the U.S. Air Force and Lockheed CEO, revealed to Congress and the press that the Air Force and Lockheed systematically practiced a strategy of underbidding in order to gain Air Force contracts for Lockheed, which then billed the Air Force and received payments for cost overruns on the contracts. Fitzgerald was fired for his trouble, but eventually received his job back. The underbidding/cost overruns, on at least the C-5/A cargo plane, were stopped.[15]

Limitations of Intervention

The intervention strategies described above can be very effective, but they also have some important limitations.

1. The individual can be wrong about the organization's actions. Lower-level employees commonly do not have as much or as good information about ethical situations and issues as higher-level managers. Similarly, they may not be as experienced as higher-level managers in dealing with specific ethical issues. The quality of experience and information an individual has can influence the quality of his or her ethical judgments. To the extent that this is true in any given situation, the use of intervention may or may not be warranted. In Case 8, for example, if Frank Ladwig had had limited computer experience, he could have been wrong about some of the products he thought would not produce the promised results.

2. Relationships can be damaged. Suppose that instead of identifying with the individuals who want an organization to change its ethical behavior, we look at these situations from another perspective. How do we feel when we are forced to change our behavior? Further, how would we feel if we were forced by a subordinate to change, even though we thought that we had the position, quality of information, and/or quality of experience to make the correct decisions? Relationships would probably be, at the least, strained, particularly if we made an ethical decision and were nevertheless forced to change. If we are wrong, it may be that we do not recognize it at the time. If we know we are wrong, we still may not like being forced to change. However, it is possible that the individual forcing us to change may justify his or her behavior to us, and our relationship may actually be strengthened.

3. The organization can be hurt unnecessarily. If an individual is wrong in believing that the organization is unethical, the organization can be hurt unnecessarily by his or her actions. Even if the individual is right, the organization can still be unnecessarily hurt by intervention strategies.

4. Intervention strategies can encourage "might makes right" climates. If we want "wrong" people, who might be more powerful now or in the future than we are, to exercise self-restraint, then we may need to exercise self-restraint even when we are "right." A problem with using force is that the other side may use more powerful or effective force now or later. Many people have been punished for trying to act ethically both when they were right and when they were wrong. By using force, one may also contribute to the belief that the only way to get things done in a particular organization is through force. People who are wrong can and do use force, and win. Do we want to build an organization culture in which force plays an important role? Gandhi's response to "an eye for an eye" was that if we all followed that principle, eventually everyone would be blind.

Being as a Part

While the intervention strategies discussed above can be very effective, they can also be destructive. Therefore, it may be appropriate to consider the advantages of leading an ethical change effort (being as a part) as well as intervening against unethical behaviors (being as an individual).

Tillich maintains that the courage to be as a part is the courage to affirm one's own being through participation with others. He writes,

> *The self affirms itself as participant in the power of a group, of a movement. . . . Self-affirmation within a group includes the courage to accept guilt and its consequences as public guilt, whether one is oneself responsible or whether somebody else is. It is a problem of the group which has to be expiated for the sake of the group, and the methods of punishment and satisfaction . . . are accepted by the individual. . . . In every human community, there are outstanding members, the bearers of the traditions and leaders of the future. They must*

distance in order to judge and to change. They must take responsibility and ask questions. This unavoidably produces individual doubt and personal guilt. Nevertheless, the predominant pattern is the courage to be a part in all members of the . . . group. . . . The difference between the genuine Stoic and the neocollectivist is that the latter is bound in the first place to the collective and in the second place to the universe, while the Stoic was first of all related to the universal Logos and secondly to possible human groups. . . . The democratic-conformist type of the courage to be as a part was in an outspoken way tied up with the idea of progress. The courage to be as a part in the progress of the group to which one belongs. . . .[16]

Leading Ethical Change

A good cross-cultural conceptualization of leadership is offered by Yoshino and Lifson: "The essence of leadership is the influential increment over and above mechanical compliance with routine directives of the organization."[17] This definition permits comparisons between and facilitates an understanding of different leadership styles through its use of a single variable: created incremental performance. Of course, different types of leadership may be more or less effective in different types of situations; yet, it is helpful to understand the "essence" of leadership in its many different cultural forms as the creation of incremental change beyond the routine.

For example, Yoshino and Lifson compare generalizations (actually overgeneralizations) about Japanese and American leadership styles:

In the United States, a leader is often thought of as one who blazes new trails, a virtuoso whose example inspires awe, respect, and emulation. If any individual characterizes this pattern, it is surely John Wayne, whose image reached epic proportions in his own lifetime as an embodiment of something uniquely American. A Japanese leader, rather than being an authority, is more of a communications channel, a mediator, a facilitator, and most of all, a symbol and embodiment of group unity. Consensus building is necessary in decision making, and this requires patience and an ability to use carefully cultivated relationships to get all to agree for the good of the unit. A John Wayne in this situation might succeed temporarily

by virtue of charisma, but eventually the inability to build strong emotion-laden relationships and use these as a tool of motivation and consensus building would prove fatal.[18]

A charismatic, "John Wayne type" leader can inspire and/or frighten people into diverting from the routine. A consensus-building, Japanese-style leader can get people to agree to divert from the routine. In both cases, the leader creates incremental behavior change beyond the routine. How does leadership (being as a part) in its various cultural forms differ from the various intervention (being as an individual) strategies and cases discussed above? Some case data may be revealing.

Cases

1. Roger Boisjoly and the Challenger launch.[19] In January 1985, after the postflight hardware inspection of Flight 52C, Roger Boisjoly strongly suspected that unusually low temperatures had compromised the performance effectiveness of the O-ring seals on two field joints. Such a performance compromise could cause an explosion. In March 1985, laboratory tests confirmed that low temperatures did negatively affect the ability of the O-rings to perform this sealing function. In June 1985, the postflight inspection of Flight 51B revealed serious erosion of both primary and backup seals that, had it continued, could have caused an explosion.

These events convinced Boisjoly that a serious and very dangerous problem existed with the O-rings. Instead of acting as an individual against his supervisors and the organization, for example, by blowing the whistle to the press, he tried to lead a change to stop the launching of flights with unsafe O-rings. He worked with his immediate supervisor, the director of engineering, and the organization in leading this change. He wrote a draft of a memo to Bob Lund, vice-president of engineering, which he first showed and discussed with his immediate supervisor to "maintain good relationships." Boisjoly and others developed potential win-win solutions, such as investigating remedies to fix the O-rings and refraining from launching flights at too-low temperatures. He effectively established a team to study the matter, and participated in a teleconference with 130 technical experts.

On the day before the Challenger launch, Boisjoly and other team members were successful in leading company executives to reverse their tentative recommendation to launch because the overnight temperatures were predicted to be too low. The company recommendation was to launch only when temperatures were above 53 degrees. To this point, Boisjoly was very effective in leading a change toward what he and other engineering and management people believed was a safe and ethical decision.

However, according to testimony from Boisjoly and others to Congress, the top managers of Morton Thiokol, under pressure from NASA, reversed their earlier recommendation not to launch. The next day, Challenger was launched and exploded, causing the deaths of all the crew members. While Boisjoly was very effective in leading a change within his own organization, he was not able to counteract subsequent pressure from the customer, NASA.

2. Dan Phillips and Genco, Inc.[20] Dan Phillips was a paper products group division manager for Genco, whose upper-level management adopted a strategy whereby several mills, including the Elkhorn Mill, would either have to reduce costs or close down. Phillips was concerned that cost cutting at Elkhorn would prevent the mill from meeting government pollution-control requirements, and that closing the mill could seriously hurt the local community. If he reduced costs, he would not meet pollution-control requirements; if he did not reduce costs, the mill would close and the community would suffer.

Phillips did not secretly or publicly blow the whistle, nor did he sabotage, conscientiously object, quietly refrain from implementing the plan, or quit; however, he did lead a change in the organization's ethical behavior. He asked research and development people in his division to investigate how the plant could both become more cost efficient and create less pollution. He then asked operations people in his division to estimate how long it would take to put such a new plant design on line, and how much it would cost. He asked cost accounting and financial people within his division to estimate when such a new operation would achieve a breakeven payback. Once he found a plan that would work, he negotiated a win-win solution with upper-level management: in exchange for not closing the plant and increasing its investment in his division, the organization would over time benefit from lower costs and higher profitability. Phillips thus worked with others and the organization to lead an inquiry and adopt an alternative ethical and cost-effective plan.

3. Lotus and Brazilian Software Importing.[21] Lotus, a software manufacturer, found that in spite of restrictions on the importing of much of its software to Brazil, many people there were buying and using Lotus software. On further investigation, the company discovered that Brazilian businessmen, in alliance with a Brazilian general, were violating the law by buying Lotus software in Cambridge, Massachusetts and bringing it into Brazil.

Instead of blowing the whistle on the illegal behavior, sabotaging it, or leaving Brazil, Lotus negotiated a solution: In exchange for the Brazilians' agreement to stop illegal importing, Lotus helped set them up as legitimate licensed manufacturers and distributors of Lotus products in Brazil. Instead of working against them and the Lotus salespeople supplying them, the Lotus managers worked with these people to develop an ethical, legal, and economically sound solution to the importing problem.

And in at least a limited sense, the importers may have been transformed into ethical managers and business people. This case may remind you of the legendary "Old West," where government officials sometimes negotiated win-win solutions with "outlaw gunfighters," who agreed to become somewhat more ethical as appointed sheriffs. The gunfighters needed to make a living, and many were not interested in or qualified for such other professions as farming or shop-keeping. In some cases, ethical behavior may take place before ethical beliefs are assumed.

4. Insurance company office/sales manager and discrimination.[22] The sales-office manager of a very large Boston-area insurance company tried to hire female salespeople several times, but his boss refused to permit the hires. The manager could have acted against his boss and the organization by secretly threatening to blow the whistle or actually blowing the whistle, publicly or secretly. Instead, he decided to try to lead a change in the implicit hiring policy of the organization.

The manager asked his boss why he was not permitted to hire a woman. He learned that his boss did not believe women made good salespeople and had never worked with a female salesperson. He found that reasoning with his boss about the capabilities of women and the ethics and legality of refusing to hire women was ineffective.

He inquired within the company about whether being a woman could be an advantage in any insurance sales areas. He negotiated with his boss a six-month experiment whereby he hired on a trial basis one woman to sell life insurance to married women who contributed large portions of their salaries to their home mortgages. The woman he hired was not only very successful in selling this type of life insurance, but became one of the office's top salespeople. After this experience, the boss reversed his policy of not hiring female salespeople.

Limitations to Leading Ethical Organizational Change

In the four cases described above, the individuals did not attack the organization or people within the organization, nor did they intervene against individuals and/or the organization to stop an unethical practice. Instead, they worked with people in the organization to build a more ethical organization. As a result of their leadership, the organizations used more ethical behaviors. The strategy of leading an organization toward more ethical behavior, however, does have some limitations. These are described below.

1. In some organizational situations, ethical win-win solutions or compromises may not be possible. For example, in 1975 a pharmaceutical company in Raritan, New Jersey decided to enter a new market with a new product.[23] Grace Pierce, who was then in charge of medical testing of new products, refused to test a new diarrhea drug product on infants and elderly consumers because it contained high levels of saccharin, which was feared by many at the time to be a carcinogen. When Pierce was transferred, she resigned. The drug was tested on infant and elderly consumers. In this case, Pierce may have been faced with an either-or situation that left her little room to lead a change in organizational behavior.

Similarly, Errol Marshall, with Hydraulic Parts and Components, Inc.,[24] helped negotiate the sale of a subcontract to sell heavy equipment to the U.S. Navy while giving $70,000 in kickbacks to two materials managers of Brown & Root, Inc., the project's prime contractor. According to Marshall, the prime contractor "demanded the kickbacks. . . . It was cut and dried. We would not get the business otherwise." While Marshall was not charged with any crime, one of the upper-level Brown & Root managers, William Callan, was convicted in 1985 of extorting kickbacks, and another manager, Frank DiDomenico, pleaded guilty to extorting kickbacks from Hydraulic Parts & Components, Inc. Marshall has left the company. In this case, it seems that Marshall had no win-win alternative to paying the bribe. In some situations it may not be possible to lead a win-win ethical change.

2. Some people do not understand how leadership can be applied to situations that involve organizational-ethics issues. Also, some people—particularly those in analytical or technical professions, which may not offer much opportunity for gaining leadership experience—may not know how to lead very well in any situation. Some people may be good leaders in the course of their normal work lives, but do not try to lead or do not lead very well when ethical issues are involved. Some people avoid discussing ethical, religious, and political issues at work.

For example, John Geary was a salesman for U.S. Steel when the company decided to enter a new market with what he and others considered an unsafe new product.[25] As a leading salesman for U.S. Steel, Geary normally was very good at leading the way toward changes that satisfied customer and organizational needs. A good salesman frequently needs to coordinate and spearhead modifications in operations, engineering, logistics, product design, financing, and billing/payment that are necessary for a company to maintain good customer relationships and sales. Apparently, however, he did not try to lead the organization in developing a win-win solution, such as soliciting current orders for a later delivery of a corrected product. He tried only reasoning against selling the unsafe product and protested its sale to several groups of upper-level engineers and managers. He noted that he believed the product had a failure rate of 3.6% and was therefore both unsafe and potentially damaging to U.S. Steel's longer-term strategy of entering higher technology/profit margin businesses. According to Geary, even though many upper-level managers, engineers, and salesmen understood and believed him, "the only desire of everyone associated with the project was to satisfy the instructions of Henry Wallace [the sales vice-president]. No one was about to buck this man for fear of his job."[26] The sales vice-president fired Geary, apparently because he continued to protest against sale of the product.

Similarly, William Schwartzkopf of Commonwealth Electric Co.[27] did not think he could either ethically reason against or lead an end to the large-scale, long-time bid rigging between his own company and many of the largest U.S. electrical contractors. Even though he was an attorney and had extensive experience in leading organizational changes, he did not try to lead his company toward an ethical solution. He waited until he retired from the company, then wrote a secret letter to the Justice Department accusing the contractors of raising bids and conspiring to divide billions of dollars of contracts among themselves.

Many people—both experienced and inexperienced in leadership—do not try to lead their companies toward developing solutions to ethical problems. Often, they do not understand that it is possible to lead such a change; therefore, they do not try to do so—even though as the cases here show, many succeed when they do try.

3. Some organizational environments—in both consensus-building and authoritarian types of cultures—discourage leadership that is nonconforming. For example as Robert E. Wood, former CEO of the giant international retailer Sears, Roebuck, has observed, "We stress the advantages of the free enterprise system, we complain about the totalitarian state, but in our individual organizations we have created more or less a totalitarian system in industry, particularly in large industry."[28] Similarly, Charles W. Summers, in a *Harvard Business Review* article, observes, "Corporate executives may argue that . . . they recognize and protect . . . against arbitrary termination through their own internal procedures. The simple fact is that most companies have not recognized and protected that right."[29]

David Ewing concludes that "It [the pressure to obey unethical and illegal orders] is probably most dangerous however, as a low-level infection. When it slowly bleeds the individual conscience dry and metastasizes insidiously, it is most difficult to defend against. There are no spectacular firings or purges in the ranks. There are no epic blunders. Under constant and insistent pressure, employees simply give in and conform. They become good 'organization people.'"[30]

Similar pressures can exist in participative, consensus-building types of cultures. For example, as mentioned above, Yoshino and Lifson write, "A Japanese leader, rather than being an authority, is more of a communications channel, a mediator, a facilitator, and most of all, a symbol and embodiment of group unity. Consensus building is necessary to decision making, and this requires patience and an ability to use carefully cultivated relationships to get all to agree for the good of the unit."[31]

The importance of the group and the position of the group leaders as a symbol of the group are revealed in the very popular true story, "Tale of the Forty-Seven Ronin." The tale is about 47 warriors whose lord is unjustly killed. The Ronin spend years sacrificing everything, including their families, in order to kill the person responsible for their leader's death. Then all those who survive the assault killed themselves.

Just as authoritarian top-down organizational cultures can produce unethical behaviors, so can participative, consensus-building cultures. The Japanese novelist Shusaku

Endo, in his *The Sea and Poison,* describes the true story of such a problem.[32] It concerns an experiment cooperatively performed by the Japanese Army, a medical hospital, and a consensus-building team of doctors on American prisoners of war. The purpose of the experiment was to determine scientifically how much blood people can lose before they die.

Endo describes the reasoning and feelings of one of the doctors as he looked back at this behavior:

> "At the time nothing could be done. . . . If I were caught in the same way, I might, I might just do the same thing again. . . . We feel that getting on good terms ourselves with the Western Command medical people, with whom Second [section] is so cosy, wouldn't be a bad idea at all. Therefore we feel there's no need to ill-temperedly refuse their friendly proposal and hurt their feelings. . . . Five doctors from Kando's section most likely will be glad to get the chance. . . . For me the pangs of conscience . . . were from childhood equivalent to the fear of disapproval in the eyes of others—fear of the punishment which society would bring to bear. . . . To put it quite bluntly, I am able to remain quite undisturbed in the face of someone else's terrible suffering and death. . . . I am not writing about these experiences as one driven to do so by his conscience . . . all these memories are distasteful to me. But looking upon them as distasteful and suffering because of them are two different matters. Then why do I bother writing? Because I'm strangely ill at ease. I, who fear only the eyes of others and the punishment of society, and whose fears disappear when I am secure from these, am now disturbed. . . . I have no conscience, I suppose. Not just me, though. None of them feel anything at all about what they did here." The only emotion in his heart was a sense of having fallen as low as one can fall.[33]

What to Do and How to Be

In light of the discussion of the two approaches to addressing organizational ethics issues and their limitations, what should we do as individuals and members of organizations? To some extent that depends on the circumstances and our own abilities. If we know how to lead, if there's time for it, if the key people in authority are reasonable, and if a win-win solution is possible, one should probably try leading an organizational change.

If, on the other hand, one does not know how to lead, time is limited, the authority figures are unreasonable, a culture of strong conformity exists, and the situation is not likely to produce a win-win outcome, then the chances of success with a leadership approach are much lower. This may leave one with only the choice of using one of the intervention strategies discussed above. If an individual wishes to remain an effective member of the organization, then one of the more secretive strategies may be safer.

But what about the more common, middle range of problems? Here there is no easy prescription. The more win-win potential the situation has, the more time there is, the more leadership skills one has, and the more reasonable the authority figures and organizational cultures are, the more likely a leadership approach is to succeed. If the opposite conditions exist, then forcing change in the organization is the likely alternative.

To a large extent, the choice depends on an individual's courage. In my opinion, in all but the most extreme and unusual circumstances, one should first try to lead a change toward ethical behavior. If that does not succeed, then mustering the courage to act against others and the organization may be necessary. For example, the course of action that might have saved the Challenger crew was for Boisjoly or someone else to act against Morton Thiokol, its top managers, and NASA by blowing the whistle to the press.

If there is an implicitly characteristic American ontology, perhaps it is some version of William James' 1907 *Pragmatism,* which, for better or worse, sees through a lens of interactions the ontologies of being as an individual and being as a part. James explains our situation as follows:

What we were discussing was the idea of a world growing not integrally but piecemeal by the contributions of its several parts. Take the hypothesis seriously and as a live one. Suppose that the world's author put the case to you before creation, saying: "If I am going to make a world not certain to be saved, a world the perfection of which shall be conditional merely, the condition being that each several agent does its own 'level best.' I offer you the chance of taking part in such a world. Its safety, you see, is unwarranted. It is a real adventure, with real danger, yet it may win through. It is a social scheme of co-operative work genuinely to be done. Will you join the procession? Will you trust yourself and trust the other agents enough to face the risk?" . . . Then it is perfectly possible to accept sincerely a drastic kind of universe from which the element of "seriousness" is not to be expelled. Who so does so, it seems to me, a genuine pragmatist. He is willing to live on a scheme of uncertified possibilities which he trusts; willing to pay with his own person, if need be, for the realization of the ideals which he frames. What now actually are the other forces which he trusts to co-operate with him, in a universe of such a type? They are at least his fellow men, in the stage of being which our actual universe has reached.[34]

In conclusion, there are realistic ethics leadership and intervention action strategies. We can act effectively concerning organizational ethics issues. Depending upon the circumstances including our own courage, we can choose to act and be ethical both as individuals and as leaders. Being as a part and leading ethical change is the more constructive approach generally. However, being as an individual intervening against others and organizations can sometimes be the only short or medium term effective approach.

Acknowledgments

I would like to acknowledge and thank the following people for their help with ideas presented in this article: the members of the Works in Progress Seminar of Boston College particularly Dalmar Fisher, James Gips, John Neuhauser, William Torbert, and the late James Waters; Kenneth Boulding of the University of Colorado; Robert Greenleaf; and, Douglas Steere of Haverford College.

NOTES

1. Paul Tillich, *The Courage to Be.* New Haven, CT: Yale University Press, 1950.

2. See Endnote 1, page 159.

3. David Ewing, *Freedom Inside the Organization.* New York: McGraw-Hill, 1977.

4. The person blowing the whistle in this case wishes to remain

anonymous. See also Elizabeth Neuffer, "GE Managers Sentenced for Bribery," *The Boston Globe,* July 26, 1988, p. 67.

5. Barbara Ley Toffler, *Tough Choices: Managers Talk Ethics.* New York: John Wiley, 1986, pp. 153–169.

6. Richard P. Nielsen, "What Can Managers Do about Unethical Management?" *Journal of Business Ethics,* 6, 1987, 153–161. See also Nielsen's "Limitations of Ethical Reasoning as an Action Strategy," *Journal of Business Ethics,* 7, 1988, pp. 725–733, and "Arendt's Action Philosophy and the Manager as Eichmann, Richard III, Faust or Institution Citizen," *California Management Review,* 26, 3, Spring 1984, pp. 191–201.

7. The person involved wishes to remain anonymous.

8. The person involved wishes to remain anonymous.

9. See Endnote 6.

10. R. Reinhold, "Astronauts Chief Says NASA Risked Life for Schedule," *The New York Times,* 36, 1986, p. 1.

11. Personal conversation and letter with Frank Ladwig, 1986. See also Frank Ladwig and Associates' *Advanced Consultative Selling for Professionals.* Stonington, CT.

12. W. G. Glaberson, "Did Searle Lose Its Eyes to a Health Hazard?" *Business Week,* October 14, 1985, p. 120–122.

13. The person involved wishes to remain anonymous.

14. Andy Pasztor, "Electrical Contractors Reel under Charges That They Rigged Bids," *The Wall Street Journal,* November 29, 1985, pp. 1, 14.

15. A. Ernest Fitzgerald, *The High Priests of Waste.* New York: McGraw-Hill, 1977.

16. See Endnote 1, pp. 89, 93.

17. M. Y. Yoshino and T. B. Lifson, *The Invisible Link: Japan's Saga Shosha and the Organization of Trade.* Cambridge, MA: MIT Press, 1986.

18. See Endnote 17, p. 178.

19. Roger Boisjoly, address given at Massachusetts Institute of Technology on January 7, 1987. Reprinted in *Books and Religion,* March/April 1987, 3–4, 12–13. See also Caroline Whitbeck, "Moral Responsibility and the Working Engineer," *Books and Religion,* March/April 1987, 3, 22–23.

20. Personal conversation with Ray Bauer, Harvard Business School, 1975. See also R. Ackerman and Ray Bauer, *Corporate Social Responsiveness.* Reston, VA: Reston Publishing, 1976.

21. The person involved wishes to remain anonymous.

22. The person involved wishes to remain anonymous.

23. David Ewing, *Do It My Way or You're Fired.* New York: John Wiley, 1983.

24. E. T. Pound, "Investigators Detect Pattern of Kickbacks for Defense Business," *The Wall Street Journal,* November 14, 1985, pp. 1, 25.

25. See Endnote 23. See also Geary vs. U.S. Steel Corporation, 319 A. 2nd 174, Supreme Court of Pa.

26. See Endnote 23, p. 86.

27. See Endnote 14.

28. See Endnote 3, p. 21.

29. C. W. Summers, "Protecting All Employees against Unjust Dismissal," *Harvard Business Review,* 58, 1980, pp. 132–139.

30. See Endnote 3, pp. 216–217.

31. See Endnote 17, p. 187.

32. Shusaku Endo, *The Sea and Poison.* New York: Taplinger Publishing Company, 1972. See also Y. Yasuda, *Old Tales of Japan.* Tokyo: Charles Tuttle Company, 1947.

33. See Endnote 32.

34. William James, *Pragmatism: A New Name for Some Old Ways of Thinking.* New York: Longmans, Green and Co., 1907, p. 290, 297–298.

DISCUSSION QUESTIONS

1. What does Tillich's idea of "being as an individual" mean within the context of modern organizations?

2. What is unethical behavior? How does it differ from illegal behavior?

3. What common elements, if any, do the twelve interventions for changing unethical organizational behavior have?

4. Supply examples of whistle blowing from your personal experience or news accounts.

5. What are the consequences for the individual and the organization if an intervention to change unethical behavior is based on incorrect information?

6. According to Nielsen, under what conditions is it more appropriate to lead a change effort as part of a group rather than as an individual?

7. What happens when an individual or group effort to change organizational ethics fails?

8. What aspects of organizational socialization and culture can be changed to reduce the opportunities for unethical behavior?

For Further Reading

Gellerman, S. "Managing Ethics from the Top Down." *Sloan Management Review,* Winter (1989) 73–79.

Hofstede, G., Neuijen, B., Ohayv, D., and Sanders, G. "Measuring Organizational Cultures: A Qualitative and Quantitative Study across Twenty Cases." *Administrative Science Quarterly* 35 (1990) 286–316.

Jackall, R. *Moral Mazes: The World of Corporate Managers.* NY: Oxford University Press, 1988.

Martin, J. *Cultures in Organizations: Three Perspectives.* New York: Oxford University Press, 1992.

Pascale, R., and Athos, A. *The Art of Japanese Management.* New York: Simon & Schuster, 1981.

Schein, E. *Organizational Culture and Leadership.* San Francisco: Jossey-Bass, 1985.

Trice, H., and Beyer, J. *The Cultures of Work Organizations.* New Jersey: Prentice-Hall, 1993.

12

JOB DESIGN

A New Strategy for Job Enrichment

J. RICHARD HACKMAN, GREG OLDHAM,
ROBERT JANSON, AND KENNETH PURDY

LEARNING OBJECTIVES

Hackman, Oldham, Janson, and Purdy's article "A New Strategy for Job Enrichment" will enable students to understand:

1. A theory for redesigning work

2. Ways to diagnose existing jobs

3. A method for translating diagnostic results into specific action

4. How psychological theory can be translated into management practice to improve organizational behavior

personally "turned on" to their work. The theory shows what kinds of jobs are most likely to generate excitement and commitment about work, and what kinds of employees it works best for.

2. A set of action steps for job enrichment based on the theory, which prescribe in concrete terms what to do to make jobs more motivating for the people who do them.

3. Evidence that the theory holds water and that it can be used to bring about measurable—and sometimes dramatic—improvements in employee work behavior, in job satisfaction, and in the financial performance of the organizational unit involved.

We present here a new strategy for going about the redesign of work. The strategy is based on three years of collaborative work and cross-fertilization among the authors—two of whom are academic researchers and two of whom are active practitioners in job enrichment. Our approach is new, but it has been tested in many organizations. It draws on the contributions of both management practice and psychological theory, but it is firmly in the middle ground between them. It builds on and complements previous work by Herzberg and others, but provides for the first time a set of tools for *diagnosing* existing jobs—and a map for translating the diagnostic results into specific action steps for change. What we have, then, is the following:

1. A theory that specifies when people will get

The Theory Behind the Strategy

What Makes People Get Turned on to Their Work?

For workers who are really prospering in their jobs, work is likely to be a lot like play. Consider, for example, a golfer at a driving range, practicing to get rid of a hook. His

Source: Copyright © 1990 by The Regents of the University of California. Reprinted from the *California Management Review,* Vol. 32, No. 4, pp. 57–71. By permission of The Regents.

activity is *meaningful* to him; he has chosen to do it because he gets a "kick" from testing his skills by playing the game. He knows that he alone is *responsible* for what happens when he hits the ball. And he has *knowledge of the results* within a few seconds.

Behavioral scientists have found that the three "psychological states" experienced by the golfer in the above example also are critical in determining a person's motivation and satisfaction on the job.

Experienced meaningfulness. The individual must perceive his work as worthwhile or important by some system of values he accepts.

Experienced responsibility. He must believe that he personally is accountable for the outcomes of his efforts.

Knowledge of results. He must be able to determine, on some fairly regular basis, whether or not the outcomes of his work are satisfactory.

When these three conditions are present, a person tends to feel very good about himself when he performs well. And those good feelings will prompt him to try to continue to do well—so he can continue to earn the positive feelings in the future. That is what is meant by "internal motivation"—being turned on to one's work because of the positive internal feelings that are generated by doing well, rather than being dependent on external factors (such as incentive pay or compliments from the boss) for the motivation to work effectively.

What if one of the three psychological states is missing? Motivation drops markedly. Suppose, for example, that our golfer has settled in at the driving range to practice for a couple of hours. Suddenly a fog drifts in over the range. He can no longer see if the ball starts to tail off to the left a hundred yards out. The satisfaction he got from hitting straight down the middle—and the motivation to try to correct something whenever he didn't—are both gone. If the fog stays, it's likely that he soon will be packing up his clubs.

The relationship between the three psychological states and on-the-job outcomes is illustrated in Figure 12.1. When all three are high, then internal work motivation, job satisfaction, and work quality are high, and absenteeism and turnover are low.

What Job Characteristics Make It Happen?

Recent research has identified the "core" characteristics of jobs that elicit the psychological states described above.[1–3] These five core job dimensions provide the key to objectively measuring jobs and to changing them so that they have high potential for motivating people who do them.

Toward Meaningful Work   Three of the five core dimensions contribute to a job's meaningfulness for the worker:

1. *Skill variety.* The degree to which a job requires the worker to perform activities that challenge his skills and abilities. When even a single skill is involved, there is at least a seed of potential meaningfulness. When several are involved, the job has the potential of appealing to more of the whole person, and also of avoiding the monotony of performing the same task repeatedly, no matter how much skill it may require.

2. *Task identity.* The degree to which the job requires completion of a "whole" and identifiable piece of work—doing a job from beginning to end with a visible outcome. For example, it is clearly more meaningful to an employee to build complete toasters than to attach electrical cord after electrical cord, especially if he never sees a completed toaster. (Note that the whole job, in this example, probably would involve greater skill variety as well as task identity.)

3. *Task significance.* The degree to which the job has a substantial and perceivable impact on the lives of other people, whether in the immediate organization or the world at large. The worker who tightens nuts on aircraft brake assemblies is more likely to perceive his work as significant than the worker who fills small boxes with paper clips—even though the skill levels involved may be comparable.

Each of these three job dimensions represents an important route to experienced meaningfulness. If the job is high in all three, the worker is quite likely to experience his job as very meaningful. It is not necessary, however, for a job to be very high in all three dimensions. If the job is low in any one of them, there will be a drop in overall experienced meaningfulness. But even when two dimensions are low the worker may find the job meaningful if the third is high enough.

Toward Personal Responsibility   A fourth core dimension leads a worker to experience increased responsibility in his job. This is *autonomy,* the degree to which the

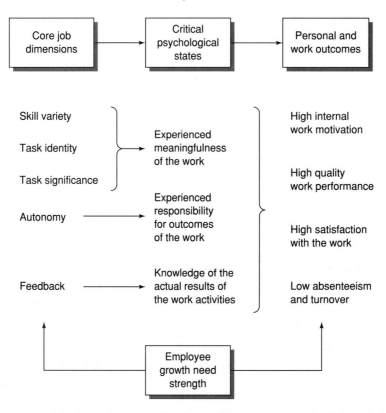

FIGURE 12.1

RELATIONSHIPS AMONG CORE JOB DIMENSIONS, CRITICAL PSYCHOLOGICAL STATES, AND ON-THE-JOB OUTCOMES

job gives the worker freedom, independence, and discretion in scheduling work and determining how he will carry it out. People in highly autonomous jobs know that they are personally responsible for successes and failures. To the extent that their autonomy is high, then, how the work goes will be felt to depend more on the individual's own efforts and initiatives—rather than on detailed instructions from the boss or from a manual of job procedures.

Toward Knowledge of Results The fifth and last core dimension is *feedback.* This is the degree to which a worker, in carrying out the work activities required by the job, gets information about the effectiveness of his efforts. Feedback is most powerful when it comes directly from the work itself—for example, when a worker has the responsibility for gauging and otherwise checking a com-

ponent he has just finished, and learns in the process that he has lowered his reject rate by meeting specifications more consistently.

The Overall "Motivating Potential" of a Job Figure 12.1 shows how the five core dimensions combine to affect the psychological states that are critical in determining whether or not an employee will be internally motivated to work effectively. Indeed, when using an instrument to be described later, it is possible to compute a "motivating potential score" (MPS) for any job. The MPS provides a single summary index of the degree to which the objective characteristics of the job will prompt high internal work motivation. Following the theory outlined above, a job high in motivating potential must be high in at least one (and hopefully more) of the three dimensions that lead to experienced meaningfulness and high in both autonomy and feedback as well. The MPS provides a quantitative index of the degree to which this is in fact the case (see Appendix for detailed formula). As will be seen later, the MPS can be very useful in diagnosing jobs and in assessing the effectiveness of job-enrichment activities.

Does the Theory Work for Everybody?

Unfortunately not. Not everyone is able to become internally motivated in his work, even when the motivating potential of a job is very high indeed.

Research has shown that the *psychological needs* of people are very important in determining who can (and who cannot) become internally motivated at work. Some people have strong needs for personal accomplishment, for learning and developing themselves beyond where they are now, for being stimulated and challenged, and so on. These people are high in "growth-need strength."

Figure 12.2 shows diagrammatically the proposition that individual growth needs have the power to moderate the relationship between the characteristics of jobs and work outcomes. Many workers with high growth needs will turn on eagerly when they have jobs that are high in the core dimensions. Workers whose growth needs are not so strong may respond less eagerly—or, at first, even balk at being "pushed" or "stretched" too far.

Psychologists who emphasize human potential argue that everyone has within him at least a spark of the need to grow and develop personally. Steadily accumulating evidence shows, however, that unless that spark is pretty strong, chances are it will get snuffed out by one's experiences in typical organizations. So, a person who has worked for 20 years in stultifying jobs may find it difficult or impossible to become internally motivated overnight when given the opportunity.

We should be cautious, however, about creating rigid categories of people based on their measured growth-need strength at any particular time. It is true that we can predict from these measures who is likely to become internally motivated on a job and who will be less willing or able to do so. But what we do not know yet is whether or not the growth-need "spark" can be rekindled for those individuals who have had their growth needs dampened, by years of growth-depressing experience in their organizations.

Since it is often the organization that is responsible for currently low levels of growth desires, we believe that the organization also should provide the individual with the chance to reverse that trend whenever possible, even if that means putting a person in a job where he may be "stretched" more than he wants to be. He can always move back later to the old job—and in the meantime the embers of his growth needs just might burst back into flame, to his surprise and pleasure, and for the good of the organization.

FIGURE 12.2

THE MODERATING EFFECT OF EMPLOYEE GROWTH-NEED STRENGTH

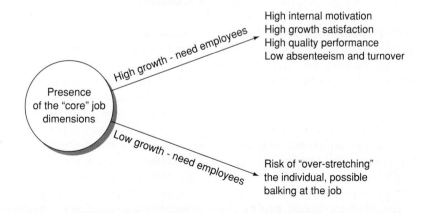

From Theory to Practice: A Technology for Job Enrichment

When job enrichment fails, it often fails because of inadequate *diagnosis* of the target job and employees' reactions to it. Often, for example, job enrichment is assumed by management to be a solution to "people problems" on the job and is implemented even though there has been no diagnostic activity to indicate that the root of the problem is in fact how the work is designed. At other times, some diagnosis is made—but it provides no concrete guidance about what specific aspects of the job require change. In either case, the success of job enrichment may wind up depending more on the quality of the intuition of the change agent—or his luck—than on a solid base of data about the people and the work.

In the paragraphs to follow, we outline a new technology for use in job enrichment which explicitly addresses the diagnostic as well as the action components of the change process. The technology has two parts: (1) a set of diagnostic tools that are useful in evaluating jobs and people's reactions to them prior to change—and in pinpointing exactly what aspects of specific jobs are most critical to a successful change attempt; and (2) a set of "implementing concepts" that provide concrete guidance for action steps in job enrichment. The implementing concepts are tied directly to the diagnostic tools; the output of the diagnostic activity specifies which action steps are likely to have the most impact in a particular situation.

The Diagnostic Tools

Central to the diagnostic procedure we propose is a package of instruments to be used by employees, supervisors, and outside observers in assessing the target job and employees' reactions to it.[4] These instruments gauge the following:

1. *The objective characteristics of the jobs themselves,* including both an overall indication of the "motivating potential" of the job as it exists (that is, the MPS score) and the score of the job on each of the five core dimensions described previously. Because knowing the strengths and weaknesses of

the job is critical to any work-redesign effort, assessments of the job are made by supervisors and outside observers as well as the employees themselves—and the final assessment of a job uses data from all three sources.

2. *The current levels of motivation, satisfaction, and work performance of employees* on the job. In addition to satisfaction with the work itself, measures are taken of how people feel about other aspects of the work setting, such as pay, supervision, and relationships with co-workers.

3. *The level of growth-need strength of the employees.* As indicated earlier, employees who have strong growth needs are more likely to be more responsive to job enrichment than employees with weak growth needs. Therefore, it is important to know at the outset just what kinds of satisfactions the people who do the job are (and are not) motivated to obtain from their work. This will make it possible to identify which persons are best to start changes with, and which may need help in adapting to the newly enriched job.

What, then, might be the actual steps one would take in carrying out a job diagnosis using these tools? Although the approach to any particular diagnosis depends upon the specifics of the particular work situation involved, the sequence of questions listed below is fairly typical.

Step 1. Are Motivation and Satisfaction Central to the Problem?

Sometimes organizations undertake job enrichment to improve the work motivation and satisfaction of employees when in fact the real problem with work performance lies elsewhere—for example, in a poorly designed production system, in an error-prone computer, and so on. The first step is to examine the scores of employees on the motivation and satisfaction portions of the diagnostic instrument. (The questionnaire taken by employees is called the Job Diagnostic Survey and will be referred to hereafter as the JDS.) If motivation and satisfaction are problematic, the change agent would continue to Step 2; if not, he would look to other aspects of the work situation to identify the real problem.

Step 2. Is the Job Low in Motivating Potential?

To answer this question, one would examine the motivating potential score of the target job and compare it to the MPS of other jobs to determine whether or not *the job itself* is a probable cause of the motivational problems documented in Step 1. If the job turns out to be low on the MPS, one would continue to Step 3; if it scores high, attention should be given to other possible reasons for the motivational difficulties (such as the pay system, the nature of supervision, and so on).

Step 3. What Specific Aspects of the Job Are Causing the Difficulty?

This step involves examining the job on each of the five core dimensions to pinpoint the specific strengths and weaknesses of the job as it is currently structured. It is useful at this stage to construct a "profile" of the target job, to make visually apparent where improvements need to be made. An illustrative profile for two jobs (one "good" job and one job needing improvement) is shown in Figure 12.3.

Job A is an engineering maintenance job and is high on all of the core dimensions; the MPS of this job is a very high 260. (MPS scores can range from 1 to about 350; and "average" score would be about 125.) Job enrichment would not be recommended for this job; if employees working on the job were unproductive and unhappy, the reasons are likely to have little to do with the nature or design of the work itself.

Job B, on the other hand, has many problems. This job involves the routine and repetitive processing of checks in the "back room" of a bank. The MPS is 30, which is quite low—and indeed, would be even lower if it were not for the moderately high task significance of the job. (Task significance is moderately high because the people are handling large amounts of other people's money, and therefore the quality of their efforts potentially has important consequences for their unseen clients.) The job provides the individuals with very little direct feedback about how effectively they are doing it; the employees have little autonomy in how they go about doing the job; and the job is moderately low in both skill variety and task identity.

For Job B, then, there is plenty of room for improvement—and many avenues to examine in planning job changes. For still other jobs, the avenues for change often turn out to be considerably more specific; for example, feedback and autonomy may be reasonably high, but one

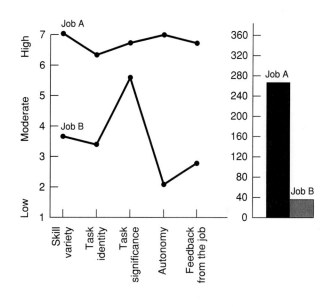

FIGURE 12.3

THE JDS DIAGNOSTIC PROFILE FOR A "GOOD" AND A "BAD" JOB

or more of the core dimensions that contribute to the experienced meaningfulness of the job (skill variety, task identity, and task significance) may be low. In such a case, attention would turn to ways to increase the standing of the job on these latter three dimensions.

Step 4. How "Ready" Are the Employees for Change?

Once it has been documented that there is need for improvement in the job—and the particularly troublesome aspects of the job have been identified—then it is time to begin to think about the specific action steps which will be taken to enrich the job. An important factor in such planning is the level of growth needs of the employees, since employees high on growth needs usually respond more readily to job enrichment than do employees with little need for growth. The JDS provides a direct measure of the growth-need strength of the employee. This measure can be very helpful in planning how to introduce the changes to the people (for instance, cautiously versus dramatically), and in deciding who should be among the first group of employees to have their jobs changed.

FIGURE 12.4

The Full Model: How Use of the Implementing Concepts Can Lead to Positive Outcomes

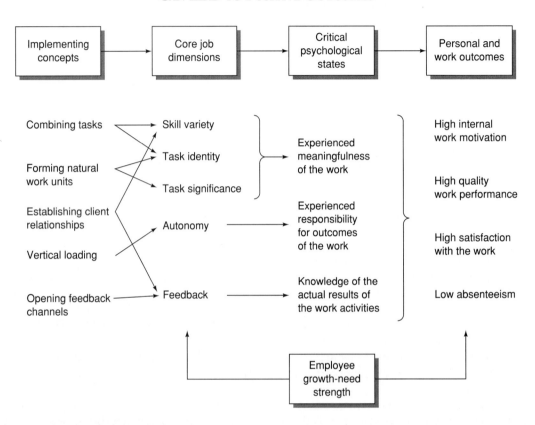

In actual use of the diagnostic package, additional information is generated which supplements and expands the basic diagnostic questions outlined above. The point of the above discussion is merely to indicate the kinds of questions which we believe to be most important in diagnosing a job prior to changing it. We now turn to how the diagnostic conclusions are translated into specific job changes.

The Implementing Concepts

Five "implementing concepts" for job enrichment are identified and discussed below.[5] Each one is a specific action step aimed at improving both the quality of the working experience for the individual and his work productivity. They are: (1) forming natural work units; (2) combining tasks; (3) establishing client relationships; (4) vertical loading; (5) opening feedback channels.

The links between the implementing concepts and the core dimensions are shown in Figure 12.4—which illustrates our theory of job enrichment, ranging from concrete action steps through the core dimensions and the psychological states to the actual personal and work outcomes.

After completing the diagnosis of a job, a change agent would know which of the core dimensions were most in need of remedial attention. He could then turn to Figure 12.4 and select those implementing concepts that specifically deal with the most troublesome parts of the existing job. How this would take place in practice will be seen below.

Forming Natural Work Units The notion of distributing work in some logical way may seem to be an obvious part of the design of any job. In many cases, however, the logic is one imposed by just about any consideration, except job-holder satisfaction and motivation. Such considerations include technological dictates, level of worker training or experience, "efficiency" as defined by industrial engineering, and current workload. In many cases the cluster of tasks a worker faces during a typical day or week is natural to anyone *but* the worker.

For example, suppose that a typing pool (consisting of one supervisor and ten typists) handles all work for one division of a company. Jobs are delivered in rough draft or dictated form to the supervisor, who distributes them as evenly as possible among the typists. In such circumstances the individual letters, reports, and other tasks performed by a given typist in one day or week are randomly assigned. There is no basis for identifying with the work or the person or department for whom it is performed, or for placing any personal value upon it.

The principle underlying natural units of work, by contrast, is "ownership"—a worker's sense of continuing responsibility for an identifiable body of work. Two steps are involved in creating natural work units. The first is to identify the basic work items. In the typing pool, for example, the items might be "pages to be typed." The second step is to group the items in natural categories. For example, each typist might be assigned continuing responsibility for all jobs requested by one or several specific departments. The assignments should be made, of course, in such a way that workloads are about equal in the long run. (For example, one typist might end up with all the work from one busy department, while another handles jobs from several smaller units.)

At this point we can begin to see specifically how the job-design principles relate to the core dimensions (cf., Figure 12.4). The ownership fostered by natural units of work can make the difference between a feeling that work is meaningful and rewarding and the feeling that it is irrelevant and boring. As the diagram shows, natural units of work are directly related to two of the core dimensions: task identity and task significance.

A typist whose work is assigned naturally rather than randomly—say, by departments—has a much greater chance of performing a whole job to completion. Instead of typing one section of a large report, the individual is likely to type the whole thing, with knowledge of exactly what the product of the work is (task identity). Furthermore, over time the typist will develop a growing sense of how the work affects co-workers in the department serviced (task significance).

Combining Tasks   The very existence of a pool made up entirely of persons whose sole function is typing reflects a fractionalization of jobs that has been a basic precept of "scientific management." Most obvious in assembly-line work, fractionalization has been applied to nonmanufacturing jobs as well. It is typically justified by efficiency, which is usually defined in terms of either low costs or some time-and-motion type of criteria.

It is hard to find fault with measuring efficiency ultimately in terms of cost-effectiveness. In doing so, however, a manager should be sure to consider *all* the costs involved. It is possible, for example, for highly fractionalized jobs to meet all the time-and-motion criteria of efficiency, but if the resulting job is so unrewarding that performing it day after day leads to high turnover, absenteeism, drugs and alcohol, and strikes, then productivity is really lower (and costs higher) than data on efficiency might indicate.

The principle of combining tasks, then, suggests that whenever possible, existing and fractionalized tasks should be put together to form new and larger modules of work. At the Medfield, Massachusetts plant of Corning Glass Works the assembly of a laboratory hot plate has been redesigned along the lines suggested here. Each hot plate now is assembled from start to finish by one operator, instead of going through several separate operations that are performed by different people.

Some tasks, if combined into a meaningfully large module of work, would be more than an individual could do by himself. In such cases, it is often useful to consider assigning the new larger task to a small *team* of workers—who are given great autonomy for its completion. At the Racine, Wisconsin plant of Emerson Electric, the assembly process for trash disposal appliances was restructured this way. Instead of a sequence of moving the appliance from station to station, the assembly now is done from start to finish by one team. Such teams include both men and women to permit switching off the heavier and more delicate aspects of the work. The team responsible is identified on the appliance. In case of customer complaints, the team often drafts the reply.

As a job-design principle, task combination, like natural units of work, expands the task identity of the job. For example, the hot-plate assembler can see and identify with a finished product ready for shipment, rather than a nearly invisible junction of solder. Moreover, the more tasks that are combined into a single worker's job, the greater the variety of skills he must call on in performing the job. So task combination also leads directly to greater skill variety—the third core dimension that contributes to the overall experienced meaningfulness of the work.

Establishing Client Relationships   One consequence of fractionalization is that the typical worker has little or no contact with (or even awareness of) the ultimate user of his product or service. By encouraging and enabling employees to establish direct relationships with the clients of their work, improvements often can be realized simultaneously on three of the core dimensions. Feedback increases, because of additional opportunities for the individual to receive praise or criticism of his work outputs directly. Skill variety often increases, because of the necessity to develop and exercise one's interpersonal skills in maintaining the client relationship. And autonomy can increase because the individual often is given personal responsibility for deciding how to manage his relationships with the clients of his work.

Creating client relationships is a three-step process. First, the client must be identified. Second, the most direct contact possible between the worker and the client must be established. Third, criteria must be set up by which the client can judge the quality of the product or service he receives. And whenever possible, the client should have a means of relaying his judgments directly back to the worker.

The contact between worker and client should be as great as possible and as frequent as necessary. Face-to-face contact is highly desirable, at least occasionally. Where that is impossible or impractical, telephone and mail can suffice. In any case, it is important that the performance criteria by which the worker will be rated by the client must be mutually understood and agreed upon.

Vertical Loading   Typically the split between the "doing" of a job and the "planning" and "controlling" of the work has evolved along with horizontal fractionalization. Its rationale, once again, has been "efficiency through specialization." And once again, the excess of specialization that has emerged has resulted in unexpected but significant costs in motivation, morale, and work quality. In vertical loading, the intent is to partially close the gap between the doing and the controlling parts of the job—and thereby reap some important motivational advantages.

Of all the job-design principles, vertical loading may be the single most crucial one. In some cases, where it has been impossible to implement any other changes, vertical loading alone has had significant motivational effects.

When a job is vertically loaded, responsibilities and controls that formerly were reserved for high levels of management are added to the job. There are many ways to accomplish this:

Return to the job holder greater discretion in setting schedules, deciding on work methods, checking on quality, and advising or helping to train less experienced workers.

Grant additional authority. The objective should be to advance workers from positions of no authority or highly restricted authority to positions of reviewed, and eventually, near-total authority for their own work.

Time management. The job holder should have the greatest possible freedom to decide when to start and stop work, when to break, and how to assign priorities.

Troubleshooting and crisis decisions. Workers should be encouraged to seek problem solutions on their own, rather than calling immediately for the supervisor.

Financial controls. Some degree of knowledge and control over budgets and other financial aspects of a job can often be highly motivating. However, access to this information frequently tends to be restricted. Workers can benefit from knowing something about the costs of their jobs, the potential effect upon profit, and various financial and budgetary alternatives.

When a job is vertically loaded it will inevitably increase in *autonomy.* And as shown in Figure 12.4, this increase in objective personal control over the work will also lead to an increased feeling of personal responsibility for the work, and ultimately to higher internal work motivation.

Opening feedback channels. In virtually all jobs there are ways to open channels of feedback to individuals or teams to help them learn whether their performance is improving, deteriorating, or remaining at a constant level. While there are numerous channels through which information about performance can be provided, it generally is better for a worker to learn about his performance *directly as he does his job*—rather than from management on an occasional basis.

Job-provided feedback usually is more immediate and private than supervisor-supplied feedback, and it increases the worker's feelings of personal control over his work in the bargain. Moreover, it avoids many of the potentially disruptive interpersonal problems that can develop when the only way a worker has to find out how he is doing is through direct messages or subtle cues from the boss.

Exactly what should be done to open channels for job-provided feedback will vary from job to job and organization to organization. Yet in many cases the changes involve simply removing existing blocks that isolate the worker from naturally occurring data about performance—rather than generating entirely new feedback mechanisms. For example,

■   Establishing direct client relationships often removes blocks between the worker and natural external sources of data about his work.

- Quality-control efforts in many organizations often eliminate a natural source of feedback. The quality check on a product or service is done by persons other than those responsible for the work. Feedback to the workers—if there is any—is belated and diluted. It often fosters a tendency to think of quality as "someone else's concern." By placing quality control close to the worker (perhaps even in his own hands), the quantity and quality of data about performance available to him can dramatically increase.

- Tradition and established procedure in many organizations dictate that records about performance be kept by a supervisor and transmitted up (not down) in the organizational hierarchy. Sometimes supervisors even check the work and correct any errors themselves. The worker who made the error never knows it occurred—and is denied the very information that could enhance both his internal work motivation and the technical adequacy of his performance. In many cases it is possible to provide standard summaries of performance records directly to the worker (as well as to his superior), thereby giving him personally and regularly the data he needs to improve his performance.

- Computers and other automated operations sometimes can be used to provide the individual with data now blocked from him. Many clerical operations, for example, are now performed on computer consoles. These consoles often can be programmed to provide the clerk with immediate feedback in the form of a CRT display or a printout indicating that an error has been made. Some systems even have been programmed to provide the operator with a positive feedback message when a period of error-free performance has been sustained.

Many organizations simply have not recognized the importance of feedback as a motivator. Data on quality and other aspects of performance are viewed as being of interest only to management. Worse still, the *standards* for acceptable performance often are kept from workers as well. As a result, workers who would be interested in following the daily or weekly ups and downs of their performance, and in trying accordingly to improve, are deprived of the very guidelines they need to do so. They are like the golfer we mentioned earlier, whose efforts to correct his hook are stopped dead by fog over the driving range.

The Strategy in Action: How Well Does It Work

So far we have examined a basic theory of how people get turned on to their work; a set of core dimensions of jobs that create the conditions for such internal work motivation to develop on the job; and a set of five implementing concepts that are the action steps recommended to boost a job on the core dimensions and thereby increase employee motivation, satisfaction, and productivity.

The remaining question is straightforward and important: *Does it work?* In reality, that question is twofold. First, does the theory itself hold water, or are we barking up the wrong conceptual tree? And second, does the change strategy really lead to measurable differences when it is applied in an actual organizational setting?

This section summarizes the findings we have generated to date on these questions.

Is the Job-Enrichment Theory Correct?

In general, the answer seems to be yes. The JDS instrument has been taken by more than 1,000 employees working on about 100 diverse jobs in more than a dozen organizations over the last two years. These data have been analyzed to test the basic motivational theory—and especially the impact of the core job dimensions on worker motivation, satisfaction, and behavior on the job. An illustrative overview of some of the findings is given below.[6]

1. People who work on jobs high on the core dimensions are more motivated and satisfied than are people who work on jobs that score low on the dimensions. Employees with jobs high on the core dimensions (MPS scores greater than 240) were compared to those who held unmotivating jobs (MPS scores less than 40). As shown in Figure 12.5, employees with high MPS jobs were higher on

FIGURE 12.5

EMPLOYEE REACTIONS TO JOBS HIGH AND LOW IN MOTIVATING POTENTIAL FOR TWO BANKS AND A STEEL FIRM

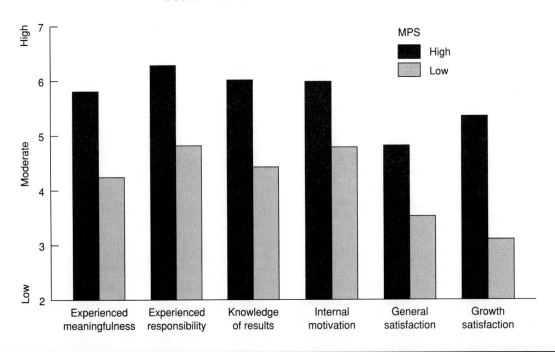

(a) the three psychological states, (b) internal work motivation, (c) general satisfaction, and (d) "growth" satisfaction.

2. Figure 12.6 shows that the same is true for measures of actual behavior at work—absenteeism and performance effectiveness—although less strongly so for the performance measure.

3. Responses to jobs high in motivating potential are more positive for people who have strong growth needs than for people with weak needs for growth. In Figure 12.7 the linear relationship between the motivating potential of a job and employees' level of internal work motivation is shown, separately for people with high versus low growth needs as measured by the JDS. While both groups of employees show increases in internal motivation as MPS increases, the *rate* of increase is significantly greater for the group of employees who have strong needs for growth.

How Does the Change Strategy Work in Practice?

The results summarized above suggest that both the theory and the diagnostic instrument work when used with real people in real organizations. In this section, we summarize a job-enrichment project conducted at The Travelers Insurance Companies, which illustrates how the change procedures themselves work in practice.

The Travelers project was designed with two purposes in mind. One was to achieve improvements in morale, productivity, and other indicators of employee well-being. The other was to test the general effectiveness of the strategy for job enrichment we have summarized in this article.

The work group chosen was a keypunching operation. The group's function was to transfer information from printed or written documents onto punched cards for computer input. The work group consisted of 98 keypunch operators and verifiers (both in the same job classification), plus seven assignment clerks. All reported to a

FIGURE 12.6

ABSENTEEISM AND JOB PERFORMANCE FOR EMPLOYEES WITH JOBS HIGH AND LOW IN MOTIVATING POTENTIAL

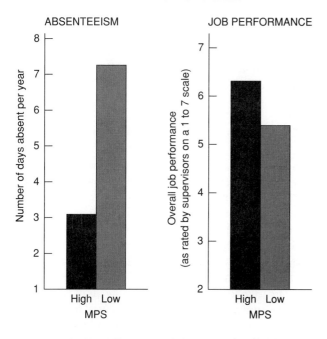

jobs for due dates before sending them to the computer. Errors detected in verification were assigned to various operators at random to be corrected.

The computer output from the cards was sent to the originating department, accompanied by a printout of errors. Eventually the printout went back to the supervisor for final correction.

A great many phenomena indicated that the problems being experienced in the work group might be the result of poor motivation. As the only person performing supervisory functions of any kind, the supervisor spent most of his time responding to crisis situations, which recurred continually. He also had to deal almost daily with employees' salary grievances or other complaints. Employees frequently showed apathy or outright hostility toward their jobs.

Rates of work output, by accepted work-measurement standards, were inadequate. Error rates were high. Due dates and schedules frequently were missed. Absenteeism was higher than average, especially before and after weekends and holidays.

supervisor who, in turn, reported to the assistant manager and manager of the data-input division.

The size of individual punching orders varied considerably, from a few cards to as many as 2,500. Some work came to the work group with a specified delivery date, while other orders were to be given routine service on a predetermined schedule.

Assignment clerks received the jobs from the user departments. After reviewing the work for obvious errors, omissions, and legibility problems, the assignment clerk parceled out the work in batches expected to take about one hour. If the clerk found the work not suitable for punching it went to the supervisor, who either returned the work to the user department or cleared up problems by phone. When work went to operators for punching, it was with the instruction, "Punch only what you see. Don't correct errors, no matter how obvious they look."

Because of the high cost of computer time, key-punched work was 100 percent verified—a task that consumed nearly as many man-hours as the punching itself. Then the cards went to the supervisor, who screened the

FIGURE 12.7

RELATIONSHIP BETWEEN THE MOTIVATING POTENTIAL OF A JOB AND THE INTERNAL WORK MOTIVATION OF EMPLOYEES (SHOWN SEPARATELY FOR EMPLOYEES WITH STRONG VERSUS WEAK GROWTH-NEED STRENGTH)

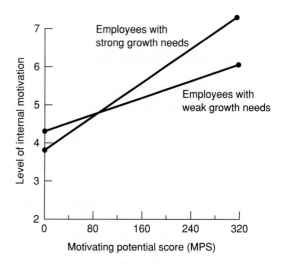

The single, rather unusual exception was turnover. It was lower than the company-wide average for similar jobs. The company has attributed this fact to a poor job market in the base period just before the project began, and to an older, relatively more settled work force—made up, incidentally, entirely of women.

The Diagnosis

Using some of the tools and techniques we have outlined, a consulting team from the Management Services Department and from Roy W. Waters & Associates concluded that the keypunch-operator's job exhibited the following serious weaknesses in terms of the core dimensions.

Skill variety. There was none. Only a single skill was involved—the ability to punch adequately the data on the batch of documents.

Task identity. Virtually nonexistent. Batches were assembled to provide an even workload, but not whole identifiable jobs.

Task significance. Not apparent. The keypunching operator was isolated by an assignment clerk and a supervisor from any knowledge of what the operation meant to the using department, let alone its meaning to the ultimate customer.

Autonomy. None. The operators had no freedom to arrange their daily tasks to meet schedules, to resolve problems with the using department, or even to correct, in punching, information that was obviously wrong.

Feedback. None. Once a batch was out of the operator's hands, she had no assured chance of seeing evidence of its quality or inadequacy.

Design of the Experimental Trial

Since the diagnosis indicated that the motivating potential of the job was extremely low, it was decided to attempt to improve the motivation and productivity of the work group through job enrichment. Moreover, it was possible to design an experimental test of the effects of the changes to be introduced: the results of changes made in the target work group were to be compared with trends in a control work group of similar size and demographic make-up. Since the control group was located more than a mile away, there appeared to be little risk of communication between members of the two groups.

A base period was defined before the start of the experimental trial period, and appropriate data were gathered on the productivity, absenteeism, and work attitudes of members of both groups. Data also were available on turnover; but since turnover was already below average in the target group, prospective changes in this measure were deemed insignificant.

An educational session was conducted with supervisors, at which they were given the theory and implementing concepts and actually helped to design the job changes themselves. Out of this session came an active plan consisting of about 25 change items that would significantly affect the design of the target jobs.

The Implementing Concepts and the Changes

Because the job as it existed was rather uniformly low on the core job dimensions, all five of the implementing concepts were used in enriching it.

Natural units of work. The random batch assignment of work was replaced by assigning to each operator continuing responsibility for certain accounts—either particular departments or particular recurring jobs. Any work for those accounts now always goes to the same operator.

Task combination. Some planning and controlling functions were combined with the central task of keypunching. In this case, however, these additions can be more suitably discussed under the remaining three implementing concepts.

Client relationships. Each operator was given several channels of direct contact with clients. The operators, not their assignment clerks, now inspect their documents for correctness and legibility. When problems arise, the operator, not the supervisor, takes them up with the client.

Feedback. In addition to feedback from client contact, the operators were provided with a number of additional sources of data about their performance. The computer department now returns incorrect cards to the operators who punched them, and operators correct their own errors. Each operator also keeps her own file of copies of her errors. Each operator receives weekly a computer printout of her errors and productivity, which is sent to her directly, rather than given to her by the supervisor.

Vertical loading. Besides consulting directly with clients about work questions, operators now have the authority to correct obvious coding errors on their own. Operators may set their own schedules and plan their daily work, as long as they meet schedules. Some competent operators have been given the option of not verifying their work and making their own program changes.

Results of the Trial

The results were dramatic. The number of operators declined from 90 to 60. This occurred partly through attrition and partly through transfer to other departments. Some of the operators were promoted to higher-paying jobs in departments whose cards they had been handling—something that had never occurred before. Some details of the results are given below.

Quantity of work. The control group, with no job changes made, showed an increase in productivity of 8.1 percent during the trial period. The experimental group showed an increase of 39.6 percent.

Error rates. To assess work quality, error rates were recorded for about 40 operators in the experimental group. All were experienced, and all had been in their jobs before the job-enrichment program began. For two months before the study, these operators had a collective error rate of 1.53 percent. For two months toward the end of the study, the collective error rate was 0.99 percent. By the end of the study the number of operators with poor performance had dropped from 11.1 percent to 5.5 percent.

Absenteeism. The experimental group registered a 24.1 percent decline in absences. The control group, by contrast, showed a 29 percent *increase.*

Attitudes toward the job. An attitude survey given at the start of the project showed that the two groups scored about average, and nearly identically, in nine different areas of work satisfaction. At the end of the project the survey was repeated. The control group showed an insignificant 0.5 percent improvement, while the experimental group's overall satisfaction score rose 16.5 percent.

Selective elimination of controls. Demonstrated improvements in operator proficiency permitted them to work with fewer controls. Travelers estimates that the reduction of controls had the same effect as adding seven operators—a saving even beyond the effects of improved productivity and lowered absenteeism.

Role of the supervisor. One of the most significant findings in the Travelers experiment was the effect of the changes on the supervisor's job, and thus on the rest of the organization. The operators took on many responsibilities that had been reserved at least to the unit leaders and sometimes to the supervisor. The unit leaders, in turn, assumed some of the day-to-day supervisory functions that had plagued the supervisor. Instead of spending his days supervising the behavior of subordinates and dealing with crises, he was able to devote time to developing feedback systems, setting up work modules and spearheading the enrichment effort—in other words, managing. It should be noted, however, that helping supervisors change their own work activities when their subordinates' jobs have been enriched is itself a challenging task. And if appropriate attention and help are not given to supervisors in such cases, they rapidly can become disaffected—and a job-enrichment "backlash" can result.[7]

Summary

By applying work-measurement standards to the changes wrought by job enrichment—attitude and quality, absenteeism, and selective administration of controls—Travelers was able to estimate the total dollar impact of the project. Actual savings in salaries and machine rental charges during the first year totaled $64,305. Potential savings by further application of the changes were put at $91,937 annually. Thus, by almost any measure used—from the work attitudes of individual employees to dollar savings for the company as a whole—The Travelers test of the job-enrichment strategy proved a success.

Conclusions

In this article we have presented a new strategy for the redesign of work in general and for job enrichment in particular. The approach has four main characteristics;

1. It is grounded in a basic psychological theory of what motivates people in their work.
2. It emphasized that planning for job changes should be done on the basis of *data* about the jobs and the people who do them—and a set of diagnostic instruments is provided to collect such data.
3. It provides a set of specific implementing concepts to guide actual job changes, as well as a set of theory-based rules for selecting *which* action steps are likely to be most beneficial in a given situation.
4. The strategy is buttressed by a set of findings showing that the theory holds water, that the diagnostic procedures are practical and informative, and that the implementing concepts can lead to changes that are beneficial both to organizations and to the people who work in them.

We believe that job enrichment is moving beyond the stage where it can be considered "yet another management fad." Instead, it represents a potentially powerful strategy for change that can help organizations achieve their goals for higher quality work—and at the same time further the equally legitimate needs of contemporary employees for a more meaningful work experience. Yet there are pressing questions about job enrichment and its use that remain to be answered.

Prominent among these is the question of employee participation in planning and implementing work redesign. The diagnostic tools and implementing concepts we have presented are neither designed nor intended for use only by management. Rather, our belief is that the effectiveness of job enrichment is likely to be enhanced when the tasks of diagnosing and changing jobs are undertaken *collaboratively* by management and by the employees whose work will be affected.

Moreover, the effects of work redesign on the broader organization remain generally uncharted. Evidence now is accumulating that when jobs are changed, turbulence can appear in the surrounding organization—for example, in supervisory-subordinate relationships, in pay and benefit plans, and so on. Such turbulence can be viewed by management either as a problem with job enrichment, or as an opportunity for further and broader organizational development by teams of managers and employees. To the degree that management takes the latter view, we believe, the oft-espoused goal of achieving basic organizational change through the redesign of work may come increasingly within reach.

The diagnostic tools and implementing concepts we have presented are useful in deciding on and designing basic changes in the jobs themselves. They do not address the broader issues of who plans the changes, how they are carried out, and how they are followed up. The way these broader questions are dealt with, we believe, may determine whether job enrichment will grow up—or whether it will die an early and unfortunate death, like so many other fledgling behavior-science approaches to organizational change.

Appendix

For the algebraically inclined, the Motivating Potential Score is computed as follows:

$$MPS = \left\{ \frac{\begin{array}{c} Skill\ variety + Task\ indentity \\ + Task\ significance \end{array}}{3} \times Autonomy \times Feedback \right\}$$

It should be noted that in some cases the MPS score can be *too* high for positive job satisfaction and effective performance—in effect overstimulating the person who holds the job. This paper focuses on jobs which are toward the low end of the scale—and which potentially can be improved through job enrichment.

Acknowledgments   The authors acknowledge with great appreciation the editorial assistance of John Hickey in the preparation of this paper, and the help of Kenneth Brousseau, Daniel Feldman, and Linda Frank in collecting the data that are summarized here. The research activities reported were supported in part by the Organizational Effectiveness Research Program of the Office of Naval Research, and the Manpower Administration of the U.S. Department of Labor, both through contracts to Yale University.

NOTES

1 A. N. Turner and P. R. Lawrence. *Industrial Jobs and the Worker* (Cambridge, Mass.: Harvard Graduate School of Business Administration, 1965).

2 J. R. Hackman and E. E. Lawler. "Employee Reactions to Job Characteristics," *Journal of Applied Psychology Monograph,* 1971, pp. 259–286.

3 J. R. Hackman and G. R. Oldham. *Motivation Through the Design of Work: Test of a Theory,* Technical Report No. 6 (New Haven, Conn.: Department of Administrative Sciences, Yale University, 1974).

4 J. R. Hackman and G. R. Oldham. "Development of the Job Diagnostic Survey," *Journal of Applied Psychology,* 1975, pp. 159–170.

5 R. W. Walters and Associates. *Job Enrichment for Results* (Cambridge, Mass.: Addison-Wesley Publishing Co., Inc., 1975).

6 Hackman and Oldham. *Motivation.*

7 E. E. Lawler III, J. R. Hackman, and S. Kaufman. "Effects of Job Redesign: A Field Experiment," *Journal of Applied Social Psychology,* (1973), pp. 49–62.

DISCUSSION QUESTIONS

1. What are the three psychological states that are experienced by a person who enjoys their work? How do they contribute to internal motivation?

2. What are the consequences if one of the psychological states is missing?

3. How does *autonomy*, a core dimension of jobs, affect worker attitudes?

4. Under what conditions and for what types of people is the theory ineffective?

5. Discuss the procedures for diagnosing a job. Are they usable in most organizational settings?

6. What makes the concept *vertical loading* the most crucial for job redesign?

7. According to the authors, how well does job redesign work? What are its limitations?

8. Following the principles presented in this article, how could you redesign either your job or that of someone you know?

The New Plant Approach: A Second Generation Approach

EDWARD E. LAWLER III

LEARNING OBJECTIVES

After reading Lawler's "The New Plant Approach: A Second Generation Approach" students will understand:

1. How the design of organizations affects job design

2. The Second Generation organization and job design approach

3. Implications of participative management on job design, particularly in creating employee involvement in an organization

4. That job design is part of a total management philosophy

The creation of a new manufacturing location represents an excellent opportunity to apply a new management approach. In a new setting, all the systems in an organization can be designed from the beginning to be consistent with a particular management strategy. Whole new methods of organizing and managing work can be put into place virtually overnight. In 1978 I wrote an article "The New Plant Revolution" (*Organizational Dynamics,* Vol. 6 No. 3, 1978, pp. 2–12), which described a new approach to management that was being used by a number of companies when they created new plants. This New Plant Approach is much more participative in its management practices than is traditional management; its structure allows it to incorporate a number of innovations.

More recently, in 1990, I wrote an article that reviewed the New Plant Approach. "The New Plant Revolution Revisited" (*Organizational Dynamics,* Winter, 1990) noted that companies such as Procter & Gamble and Mead used this management style for all their new plants, and that some companies have successfully converted their old plants to it as well. In addition, many of the specific practices that are part of the New Plant

Approach have spread to existing plants and have become standard operating procedure in a large number of manufacturing settings.

Even though the New Plant Approach has proven to be quite successful, there are opportunities to improve upon it. After all, a great deal has changed in American business since its initial introduction more than 20 years ago. Significant new management technologies have developed, particularly in areas concerned with the management of quality and the use of information technology. In addition, the business environment has changed in many respects. Many markets have become global, and as a result performance standards with respect to quality, speed, and costs have grown.

The focus of this article is on the need to develop a new or next-generation management model for settings that are managed with a participative management approach. Although I am building on work that was originally done in manufacturing settings, much of what I have to say applies to any organizational setting in which a product or service is being produced or delivered.

The major feature that differentiates the Second Generation Approach from the New Plant Approach is the degree to which the former places information, power, knowledge, and rewards in the hands of individuals who are actually creating the products and services. The intention is to develop a high level of business involvement among all employees. The expectation is that doing so will lead to performance improvements in speed, quality, and costs because lower level employees will be able to act more quickly and in a more informed, more motivated manner.

The original New Plant Approach, for a variety of reasons, focused heavily on being sure that individuals had control over, and information about, their piece of the production process. It might best be called a productivity involvement or plant operations involvement approach to

Source: Edward E. Lawler III, "The New Plant Approach: A Second Generation Approach." From *Organizational Dynamics,* Summer 1992, pp. 5–14. Copyright ©1992. Reprinted by permission.

management. Getting individuals involved in the business of the organization represents a significant step beyond this type of involvement.

It requires the adoption of the same practices—for example, work teams, an all salary workforce, and skill-based pay—that are part of the New Plant Approach, but it requires going beyond these in a number of areas as well. It requires that individuals receive new information, have additional skills, be rewarded differently, and ultimately have the power to influence many parts of the business process.

With this in mind, let us turn to a consideration of the features that need to be built into an organization if it is to involve individuals in the business.

Organization Design

The New Plant Approach includes a flat organization design and the extensive use of self-managing teams. This basic design approach is appropriate for a business involvement plant design as well. It is particularly important for business involvement that teams have the responsibility for producing a whole product or completely serving an identifiable customer base. Without this, it is impossible for individuals to feel that they have a business that they control in a bottom-line sense. In a manufacturing setting, a team needs to be given responsibility for producing an entire product and for dealing as directly as possible with both customers and suppliers. The teams, in essence, need to be responsible for all the value-added activities that occur with respect to a particular product.

In the case of service teams, the same principle holds. Employee teams need to be given responsibility for performing all activities with respect to a particular customer. This principle means, for example, that work teams charged with processing and managing mortgages, or handling credit card business, need to be given responsibility for the entire service process with respect to a particular customer.

In creating teams, a clear bias needs to exist toward establishing a customer-supplier relationship for each work team. These can be internal customer-supplier relationships; where possible, however, there is a definite advantage to creating external customer-supplier relationships. This provides the most "real" business experience for individuals and keeps them in contact with the competi-

tive business environment that they are in and the kinds of demands that the organization faces from its external markets and suppliers.

To facilitate team management of a business, it often is important to include staff support members in the production teams. For example, engineers and accountants may need to be placed on the teams so that the teams can handle a full scope of business issues and, in effect, operate as mini-business enterprises.

The physical layout of the facility should be designed to facilitate teams owning an entire product or customer. Equipment needs to be positioned so that employees who are on the same teams are located together. Staff support individuals need to be located in the production areas they support. Blocks to communication, including walls, need to be minimized or eliminated, as do all symbols that indicate differences in power and status. Hierarchical symbols work against all individuals feeling responsible for organizational success, and they encourage decision making on the basis of hierarchy rather than expertise.

The sociotech approach to work design and the total quality management approach both argue for building teams around key workflow interdependencies. Total quality programs also stress the importance of establishing a clear customer relationship. Thus, both the total quality and sociotech approaches are compatible with creating business involvement plants. The sociotech approach has in fact frequently been used in the design of new plants. Neither the sociotech approach nor the quality approach, however, will necessarily create teams that are responsible for whole products or services—nor do they always create teams that have external customers. Both of these are critical elements in establishing the kinds of teams that encourage business involvement.

There are some interesting examples of organizations giving teams responsibility for taking a product from suppliers to completion. For example, the Digital Equipment plant at Enfield, Connecticut allows work team members to deal directly with suppliers and gives them direct contact with the customers for the electronic boards that the teams make. This contact is facilitated by giving the team members business cards and including an 800 phone number with the product so that customers can call them directly with questions or problems. The teams are also encouraged to visit customers and to invite their suppliers into the plant to work with them in assuring high quality supplies.

Volvo's new Swedish car manufacturing facility carries the team model further than any other manufacturing facility of which I am aware. The customers, through information technology, place an order directly with the manufacturing team. The team informs the customer of the "build schedule" for the car and invites the customer to be on hand when the car is built. Once the car is completed, the team delivers the car to the customer—but the process does not end there. The team makes arrangements with the customer to maintain an ongoing performance record for the car. Team members can also communicate with the customer through information technology that ties them to the dealership and therefore to the customer. This approach has the potential to tie the entire manufacturing team to an individual customer over a sustained period of time. It allows the team to receive continuous feedback about the quality of each car produced, and to respond directly to customer questions and issues.

Total Team Environment

The New Plant Approach stresses the use of teams at the production level, but it does not stress the use of teams in other areas of the plant. The jobs of managers, office personnel, and staff support individuals end up being different from what they are in a traditional plant because they have to deal with teams—yet they are not in a team structure. This inconsistency in some respects has limited the effectiveness of the New Plant Approach because staff support groups do not have the same kind of flexibility and performance gains that are characteristic of the production area.

The obvious solution to the problem of differences existing between the production area and the rest of the plant is to make the plant a total team environment. Several organizations have done this by placing as many support people as possible in production teams and by creating management and staff support teams. These teams meet regularly to allocate their time and effort and, like production teams, do a considerable amount of self-managing. They usually are not as flexible as the production teams, since it is harder for individuals to learn other jobs in staff and managerial roles. Nevertheless, with cross-training they are still in a good position to take advantage of some of the flexibility inherent in the team concept—and, consequently, to engage in a fair amount of self-management.

The use of team structures throughout the organization should contribute to an even flatter approach than is typical of the New Plant Approach. In plants using a team approach, the organization is usually quite flat with wide spans of control but there is a limit to just how flat it can be because of the need to have a supervisor for at least every three or four work teams. This can be partially overcome by having a team supervision approach so that individuals in managerial jobs can help each other out and cover the work load imbalances that are inherent in supervising a number of teams.

Business Integration

The typical New Plant Approach has been used primarily in locations that do only manufacturing. Consequently, employees in the manufacturing area have had little input or contact with individuals who are doing product development and little contact with individuals doing sales, customer service, or customer relations. This is an obvious limitation with respect to business involvement. Individuals who could provide valuable feedback are not involved in the total value creation process of the organization and do not have external customer contacts. This can be corrected, however, by co-locating and better integrating other functions with the manufacturing process. The use of concurrent engineering by an increasing number of organizations represents just such a positive step.

Product development and design can be co-located at manufacturing sites, so that individuals in the manufacturing areas can be involved in these issues and vice-versa. Production employees may not have great amounts of customer knowledge, but they do have a great deal of knowledge about manufacturability; it is important to capture this expertise in the product development process. Similarly, if the marketing and sales organizations are co-located with manufacturing, it can provide individuals in the manufacturing area with an opportunity to deal with customers more directly and to have inputs to the marketing and sales process.

The co-location of product development, manufacturing, and marketing/sales is not necessary in order to get individuals involved in all phases of the business process. Task forces represent one way to create involvement up and down the value-added chain without co-location. Information technology can also be used to allow individuals in the manufacturing area to have input to product design as well as sales and marketing activities. With networked computers, a task force can be given the opportunity to comment on new product designs and, in some cases, to answer marketing and sales questions about the products and services that they produce.

Reward System

Two important and visible features of the New Plant Approach are the extensive use of skill-based pay and the commitment to job security. In the Second Generation Approach, there is no reason to change either of these; both are consistent with a business involvement approach that pushes information, power, knowledge, and rewards downward. Indeed, what is needed is an extension of the commitment to skill-based pay.

In the New Plant Approach, skill-based or competency pay is applied only to individuals who are in self-managing work teams, which in effect means it applies only to production area employees. With the use of teams throughout the organization, it is appropriate to extend skill-based pay to all employees in the organization. This means that staff, managerial, and clerical teams would all have skill-based pay just as do production teams. Few organizations have done this so far, although Polaroid stands out as a notable exception. The advantages of applying skill-based pay to all employees are essentially the same as those that are derived when it is applied to manufacturing divisions. It has the potential to create a more flexible and knowledgeable workforce, and it is highly congruent with a team-based management approach that stresses learning and continuous improvement.

Completely missing in the New Plant Approach are reward systems based on organization and business performance. This is an enormous void, and one that must be filled in a Second Generation Approach based on business involvement.

Individuals need to be accountable for the results of the business, and the best way to do this is to make their pay at least partially dependent on the success of the business for which they are responsible. This can be done through gainsharing plans, profit sharing plans, and employee ownership. The approach that works best is determined by specific organizational conditions. Critical factors are just how much of the business process an individual plant or location can be held accountable for and how those responsibilities relate to the rest of the organization. In many cases, more than one pay-for-performance method are likely to be needed. The key is to make

compensation variable based on controll mance. In the case of the new start-up, it appropriate to put a gainsharing or other plant level plan in at the beginning. It is often difficult to implement a good gainsharing plan then because it is hard to know what to measure and even harder to know what the standard is above which a bonus should be paid. What can be done at start-up is to make a commitment to the development of a gainsharing or profit sharing plan, and to begin the development process within several years after the start-up of the new location.

An important feature of the reward system in the New Plant Approach is skill-based pay. It helps assure the development of the right competencies in the work force. There is no reason to change this. In fact, with the greater use of teams in the Second Generation Approach, it is important to extend skill-based pay to white-collar and managerial teams. In some respects it can be harder to do skill-based pay in nonproduction areas because the quantification of performance and skill acquisition is more difficult. Nevertheless, this important feature needs to be built into these work teams as well. Without it, teams cannot control a very important feature of their environment that influences performance.

Information Technology

When the New Plant Approach was developed, there was very little use of computers and no use of computer networking by organizations. This limited the kinds of decisions that work team members could be involved in because it made it difficult to deliver information to them in a timely fashion. With the advent of relatively inexpensive computing and sophisticated information system networks, the situation has changed dramatically. It is now possible for all employees to have access to PCs or terminals that are linked to company-wide information systems. Employees can get a great deal of information about the business, their local operations, and, indeed, operations in other plants. This in turn means that they can be involved in a wide range of decisions and get feedback in areas where it was not practical before.

The Second Generation Approach needs to take advantage of information technology so that individuals have the ability to access the latest data about what is occurring in other areas of the company, how their product or service is performing, how customers are reacting to it, and how much it is costing to produce. This tremendous increase in the amount of feedback employees get can also change decision-making processes so that more than just quality and production numbers are being considered. It can allow everyone to understand the economic tradeoffs that are involved in his or her performance and thus enable business involvement.

If adapted correctly, information technology can also help with problem solving and education. For example, it can allow employees to communicate with each other when they have a technical problem and avoid the entire process of going up and down the hierarchy to find out who has a particular expertise and what the correct solution is for a problem. In some Procter & Gamble plants, for example, individuals or teams with production problems can access an electronic bulletin board and ask for help from anyone within the organization. It is also possible for employees to compare production rates and numbers from plant to plant so that they are aware of how much can be done with the equipment for which they are responsible.

Networked computers can also be used to expand the input opportunities of employees. With the New Plant Approach, attitude surveys and focus groups are often used to sense how the employees are feeling about their job situation, but this is inherently a slow and limited approach to gathering data. IBM and other organizations are now converting this to an information technology-based system in which survey questions are simply put on the network and individuals are allowed to respond to them online. In addition, key strategy or policy decisions can be put on the information system for comment and debate. This can mean that even employees in overseas locations have a chance to give input on new policies and practices that previously would have been decided by a corporate staff group and senior management.

Finally, television screens can be used to help link employees who are involved in different aspects of the production or service process. This can take the form of video tapes that show employees in the manufacturing environment what employees outside that area are doing, or have been doing in some plants. Individuals earlier in the production process can be linked to those later in the production process by closed-circuit video. This has the obvious advantage of improving communication and understanding throughout the production process. It can also help individuals conceptualize what is going on elsewhere in the production process so that they can identify with the total product and suggest improvements.

Television and electronic mail can also be used to support business involvement by reporting on financial results and key company events. In some companies this is already being done on a regular basis. In one company, in fact, a quarterly state-of-the-business video tape is sent to every employee's home. Other companies do television broadcasts on a weekly basis in order to keep employees up-to-date on what is happening.

Quality Technology

When the New Plant Approach was first implemented in the 1960s, very little was known in the United States about the quality programs being used in Japan. The situation has changed dramatically since then; virtually every major corporation has a total quality management system based on the work of Juran, Deming, and Crosby. These so-called quality gurus have strongly transformed the way quality management is perceived in the United States. They stress the importance of employee involvement in producing high-quality products and offer a number of specific management tools to improve quality.

In many respects, the total quality concept of involvement is much more limited than that of the New Plant Approach. However, this does not mean that the quality tools they offer are inappropriate. Indeed, many of the tools need to be adopted because they can help work teams and plants do a better job of managing themselves and understanding their production processes.

Statistical process control, cost of quality measurement, and some of the problem-solving approaches inherent in the quality technology fit well with the Second Generation Approach. When these are installed in a business involvement-oriented plant, they can substantially improve the ability of teams to understand their production process and become more self-managing. Also potentially useful are quality improvement teams and task forces that are targeted at improving particular features of the production or service process. In contrast with traditionally managed locations, however, fewer of these teams should be needed in those organizations that adopt the Second Generation Approach. The reason for this is simple. The work teams should handle much of the improvement process activities themselves without the need for special groups and the extra cost that is involved in creating them and supporting them. Some organization-wide issues or some in-depth sticky problems may crop up that affect several teams; such problems may require individuals dedicated to solving them over a substantial period of time. In these cases the use of problem-solving teams makes sense.

Overall, the correct stance with respect to quality technology is to adopt those elements that improve the problem-solving process, bring more information and knowledge into the work teams, and allow them to be more self-managing. Several plants that started in the 1970s with the New Plant Approach have done a good job of this. They have trained their employees in statistical process control, problem analysis, and process management. This has helped them improve their organizational performance and advance further in the areas of business involvement and self-management.

Human Resource Management

A heavy commitment to selection and training is a critical element of the New Plant Approach. This typically includes realistic job previews as well as team-based selection processes. But the Second Generation Approach, if anything, requires a greater commitment to selection and development. In the area of development, for example, it requires a commitment to individuals learning a great deal about quality technology. It also requires individuals to learn more about the business impact of their roles in the organization. This means they need to get extensive economic education, as well as being educated in the technical details of the manufacturing or service process.

In essence, individuals in the production area need to be treated more like managers as far as the training, information, and pay rates they receive. In terms of skill-based pay, they need to be able to progress higher in total compensation in return for learning vertical or upward skills. This has implications for the kind of individuals that are selected, since much more is expected of them than just the ability to work in a team and control a production process. They need to develop an understanding of the business.

The Second Generation Approach demands a great deal of managers. They must be coaches, leaders, and expert resources. Getting the right kind of manager cannot be left to chance. The selection process needs to be able to identify them—and of course, training and support should be available to them. In the area of selection, assessment centers and simulations can help to identify the right individuals. The training and development process needs to include peer and staff assessment data and behavioral learning experiences.

Renewal/Improvement Process

The New Plant Approach does not have any built-in renewal or improvement structures. Total quality programs appropriately stress the importance of taking a continuous improvement approach to management. Such an approach can, and should, be combined with a focus on competitive benchmarking. This can help reinforce the necessity for continuous improvement because the simple fact of the matter is that performance standards, with respect to most products and services, are constantly rising.

Continuous improvement can be done within work teams if they are given the appropriate information and support, but it also may require separate structures to get the appropriate amount of attention and an organization-wide perspective. This suggests that organizations regularly need to create task forces or design teams that can assess the organization and look at its competitive position. They need to use such tools as attitude surveys and competitive benchmarking to see how well the organization is operating—and then to involve people within the organization in the improvement process.

It is difficult to predict exactly how often an extensive organizational renewal or assessment process should be undertaken, but a rough guess is that it should be done at least every two years, with benchmarking being done at least annually. One suggested approach that can help facilitate an assessment is to invite customers and suppliers to be involved in the assessment process. Similarly, outside experts in critical areas can be brought in to help describe the newest management technologies. The key is to help the organization update itself and assure that it stays on the cutting edge.

The Second Generation New Plant in Practice

When I wrote my first article about the New Plant Approach, I was able to report that a number of plants already followed this model. The same is not true with respect to the Second Generation Model. I know of no example that fits it perfectly, although a number of organizations are clearly moving toward creating plants that will adhere to the new model. Organizations such as Mead, TRW and Digital already have plants that possess many of the necessary features. Thus, my prediction is that before too long there will be a number of good examples.

Because the Second Generation Approach clearly represents a significant step beyond the New Plant Approach,

adopting it involves some risk. But with the growing emphasis and acceptance of employee involvement as a management strategy, it is likely that more plants will explore Second Generation strategies. If, as seems likely, the new approach can offer efficiencies in the areas of reduced overhead, greater commitment to the business, and overall, greater flexibility and responsiveness, its use may very well grow rapidly and in fact become widespread.

SELECTED BIBLIOGRAPHY

My original article on this subject was "The New Plant Revolution" (*Organizational Dynamics,* Vol. 6 No. 3, 1978, pp. 2–12) and in 1990 I wrote an article reviewing the New Plant Approach entitled "The New Plant Revolution Revisited" (*Organizational Dynamics,* Winter 1990).

Data on the adoption of participative management practices are provided in Carla O'Dell's *People, Performance and Pay* (American Productivity Center, 1987) and in Edward E. Lawler, Gerald E. Ledford and Susan A. Mohrman's *Employee Involvement in America* (American Productivity and Quality Center, 1989).

See the following for a description of the different approaches to participative management: Edward E. Lawler's *High Involvement Management* (Jossey-Bass, 1986); a chapter on "Beyond Self Managing Work Teams," by Charles Manz, published in a work edited by Robert W. Woodman and William A. Posmore, *Research in Organizational Change and Development,* Volume 4, JAL, 1990, pp. 273–299.

For a discussion of quality circles, see Edward E. Lawler and Susan A. Mohrman's "Quality Circles after the Fad" (*Harvard Business Review,* Volume 85 No. 1, pp. 64–71) and by the same authors "Quality Circles: After the Honeymoon" (*Organizational Dynamics,* Volume 15 No. 4, 1987, pp. 42–54).

For a discussion of team effectiveness, see *Groups That Work* edited by J. Richard Hackman (Jossey-Bass, 1990) and an article by J. P. MacDuffie, "The Japanese Auto Transplants: Challenges to Conventional Wisdom" (*ILR Report,* Volume 26 No. 1, 1988, pp. 12–18), which discusses the practices of Japanese companies.

Two works by Edward E. Lawler discuss gainsharing and skill-based pay, *Pay and Organizational Development* (Addison-Wesley, 1981) and *Strategic Pay* (Jossey-Bass, 1990). There is also an article by Richard E. Walton and Leonard A. Schlesinger, "Do Supervisors Thrive in Participative Work Systems?" (*Organizational Dynamics,* Volume 8 No. 3, 1979, pp. 25–38) that looks at the role of managers in a participative management system.

DISCUSSION QUESTIONS

1. What are the advantages of the New Plant Approach?

2. What are the major differences between the New Plant Approach and the Second Generation Approach?

3. In what ways does the Second Generation Approach get individuals involved in the business of the organization?

4. What does Lawler mean when he says that teams should "own" an entire product or customer?

5. How does the Second Generation Approach deal with total quality management?

6. In your view, would the approach that Volvo uses to create a relationship between the workers and customers be transferable to the U.S. automobile industry?

7. What are the advantages of locating marketing, sales, and customer service functions with manufacturing?

8. How does skill-based pay work? What are its implications for work teams and job design?

9. In what ways does the Second Generation Approach change the job design of managers?

FOR FURTHER READING

Aldag, J., and Brief, A. *Task Design and Employee Motivation.* Glenview, Illinois: Scott, Foresman, 1979.

Hackman, J., and Oldham, G. *Work Redesign.* Reading, Mass.: Addison-Wesley, 1980.

Roberts, K., and Glick, W. "The Job Characteristics Approach to Job Design: A Critical Review." *Journal of Applied Psychology,* April (1981) 193–217.

Walton, R. "How to Counter Alienation in the Plant." *Harvard Business Review,* Nov.-Dec. (1972) 70–81.

13

MAINTAINING PERFORMANCE

Goal Setting—A Motivational Technique That Works

GARY P. LATHAM AND EDWIN A. LOCKE

LEARNING OBJECTIVES

After reading "Goal Setting—A Motivational Technique That Works" by Latham and Locke students will understand that:

1. Members of organizations require motivation

2. There is an empirical, scientific foundation for motivating people based on laboratory and field experimentation

3. There are practical methods managers can use to improve work performance, such as motivating organization members by having them set goals

4. There are limitations to goal setting as a motivation technique; goal setting does not remedy inadequate management or unsatisfactory working conditions

The problem of how to motivate employees has puzzled and frustrated managers for generations. One reason the problem has seemed difficult, if not mysterious, is that motivation ultimately comes from within the individual and therefore cannot be observed directly. Moreover, most managers are not in a position to change an employee's basic personality structure. The best they can do is try to use incentives to direct the energies of their employees toward organizational objectives.

Money is obviously the primary incentive, since without it few if any employees would come to work. But money alone is not always enough to motivate high performance. Other incentives, such as participation in decision making, job enrichment, behavior modification, and organizational development, have been tried with varying degrees of success. A large number of research studies have shown, however, that one very straightforward technique—goal setting—is probably not only more effective than alternative methods, but may be the major mechanism by which these other incentives affect motivation. For example, a recent experiment on job enrichment demonstrated that unless employees in enriched jobs set higher, more specific goals than do those with unenriched jobs, job enrichment has absolutely no effect on productivity. Even money has been found most effective as a motivator when the bonuses offered are made contingent on attaining specific objectives.

The Goal-Setting Concept

The idea of assigning employees a specific amount of work to be accomplished—a specific task, a quota, a performance standard, an objective, or a deadline—is not new. The task concept, along with time and motion study and

Source: "Goal Setting—A Motivational Techique That Works," by Gary Latham and Edwin A. Locke. Reprinted by permission of Publisher, from *Organizational Dynamics,* Autumn 1979, © 1979. American Management Association, New York. All rights reserved.

incentive pay, was the cornerstone of scientific management, founded by Frederick W. Taylor more than 70 years ago. He used his system to increase the productivity of blue collar workers. About 20 years ago the idea of goal setting reappeared under a new name, management by objectives, but this technique was designed for managers.

In a 14-year program of research, we have found that goal setting does not necessarily have to be part of a wider management system to motivate performance effectively. It can be used as a technique in its own right.

Laboratory and Field Research

Our research program began in the laboratory. In a series of experiments, individuals were assigned different types of goals on a variety of simple tasks—addition, brainstorming, assembling toys. Repeatedly it was found that those assigned hard goals performed better than did people assigned moderately difficult or easy goals. Furthermore, individuals who had specific, challenging goals outperformed those who were given such vague goals as to "do your best." Finally, we observed that pay and performance feedback led to improved performance only when these incentives led the individual to set higher goals.

While results were quite consistent in the laboratory, there was no proof that they could be applied to actual work settings. Fortunately, just as Locke published a summary of the laboratory studies in 1968, Latham began a separate series of experiments in the wood products industry that demonstrated the practical significance of these findings. The field studies did not start out as a validity test of laboratory theory, but rather as a response to a practical problem.

In 1968, six sponsors of the American Pulpwood Association became concerned about increasing the productivity of independent loggers in the South. These loggers were entrepreneurs on whom the multimillion-dollar companies are largely dependent for their raw material. The problem was twofold. First, these entrepreneurs did not work for a single company; they worked for themselves. Thus they were free to (and often did) work two days one week, four days a second week, five half-days a third week, or whatever schedule they preferred. In short, these workers could be classified as marginal from the standpoint of their productivity and attendance, which were considered highly unsatisfactory by conventional company standards. Second, the major approach taken to alleviate this problem had been to develop equipment that would make the industry less dependent on this type of worker. A limitation of this approach was that many of the

logging supervisors were unable to obtain the financing necessary to purchase a small tractor, let alone a rubber-tired skidder.

Consequently, we designed a survey that would help managers determine "what makes these people tick." The survey was conducted orally in the field with 292 logging supervisors. Complex statistical analyses of the data identified three basic types of supervisor. One type stayed on the job with their men, gave them instructions and explanations, provided them with training, read the trade magazines, and had little difficulty financing the equipment they needed. Still, the productivity of their units was at best mediocre. second-rate

The operation of the second group of supervisors was slightly less mechanized. These supervisors provided little training for their workforce. They simply drove their employees to the woods, gave them a specific production goal to attain for the day or week, left them alone in the woods unsupervised, and returned at night to take them home. Labor turnover was high and productivity was again average.

The operation of the third group of supervisors was relatively unmechanized. These leaders stayed on the job with their men, provided training, gave instructions and explanations, and in addition, set a specific production goal for the day or week. Not only was the crew's productivity high, but their injury rate was well below average.

Two conclusions were discussed with the managers of the companies sponsoring this study. First, mechanization alone will not increase the productivity of logging crews. Just as the average tax payer would probably commit more mathematical errors if he were to try to use a computer to complete his income tax return, the average logger misuses, and frequently abuses, the equipment he purchases (for example, drives a skidder with two flat tires, doesn't change the oil filter). This increases not only the logger's downtime, but also his costs which, in turn, can force him out of business. The second conclusion of the survey was that setting a specific production goal combined with supervisory presence to ensure goal commitment will bring about a significant increase in productivity.

These conclusions were greeted with the standard, but valid, cliché, "Statistics don't prove causation." And our comments regarding the value of machinery were especially irritating to these managers, many of whom had received degrees in engineering. So one of the companies decided to replicate the survey in order to check our findings.

The company's study placed each of 892 independent logging supervisors who sold wood to the company into one of three categories of supervisory styles our survey had identified—namely, (1) stays on the job but does not set specific production goals; (2) sets specific production goals but does not stay on the job; and (3) stays on the job and sets specific production goals. Once again, goal setting, in combination with the on-site presence of a supervisor, was shown to be the key to improved productivity.

Testing for the Hawthorne Effect

Management may have been unfamiliar with different theories of motivation, but it was fully aware of one label—the Hawthorne effect. Managers in these wood products companies remained unconvinced that anything so simple as staying on the job with the men and setting a specific production goal could have an appreciable effect on productivity. They point out that the results simply reflected the positive effects any supervisor would have on the work unit after giving his crew attention. And they were unimpressed by the laboratory experiments we cited—experiments showing that individuals who have a specific goal solve more arithmetic problems or assemble more tinker toys than do people who are told to "do your best." Skepticism prevailed.

But the country's economic picture made it critical to continue the study of inexpensive techniques to improve employee motivation and productivity. We were granted permission to run one more project to test the effectiveness of goal setting.

Twenty independent logging crews who were all but identical in size, mechanization level, terrain on which they worked, productivity, and attendance were located. The logging supervisors of these crews were in the habit of staying on the job with their men, but they did not set production goals. Half the crews were randomly selected to receive training in goal setting; the remaining crews served as a control group.

The logging supervisors who were to set goals were told that we had found a way to increase productivity at no financial expense to anyone. We gave the ten supervisors in the training group production tables developed through time-and-motion studies by the company's engineers. These tables made it possible to determine how much wood should be harvested in a given number of manhours. They were asked to use these tables as a guide in determining a specific production goal to assign their employees. In addition, each sawhand was given a tallymeter

(counter) that he could wear on his belt. The sawhand was asked to punch the counter each time he felled a tree. Finally, permission was requested to measure the crew's performance on a weekly basis.

The ten supervisors in the control group—those who were not asked to set production goals—were told that the researchers were interested in learning the extent to which productivity is affected by absenteeism and injuries. They were urged to "do your best" to maximize the crew's productivity and attendance and to minimize injuries. It was explained that the data might be useful in finding ways to increase productivity at little or no cost to the wood harvester.

To control for the Hawthorne effect, we made an equal number of visits to the control group and the training group. Performance was measured for 12 weeks. During this time, the productivity of the goal-setting group was significantly higher than that of the control group. Moreover, absenteeism was significantly lower in the groups that set goals than in the groups who were simply urged to do their best. Injury and turnover rates were low in both groups.

Why should anything so simple and inexpensive as goal setting influence the work of these employees so significantly? Anecdotal evidence from conversations with both the loggers and the company foresters who visited them suggested several reasons.

Harvesting timber can be a monotonous, tiring job with little or no meaning for most workers. Introducing a goal that is difficult, but attainable, increases the challenge of the job. In addition, a specific goal makes it clear to the worker what it is he is expected to do. Goal feedback via the tallymeter and weekly recordkeeping provide the worker with a sense of achievement, recognition, and accomplishment. He can see how well he is doing now as against his past performance and, in some cases, how well he is doing in comparison with others. Thus the worker not only may expend greater effort, but may also devise better or more creative tactics for attaining the goal than those he previously used.

New Applications

Management was finally convinced that goal setting was an effective motivational technique for increasing the productivity of the independent woods worker in the South.

The issue now raised by the management of another wood products company was whether the procedure could be used in the West with the company logging operations in which the employees were unionized and paid by the hour. The previous study had involved employees on a piece-rate system, which was the practice in the South.

The immediate problem confronting this company involved the loading of logging trucks. If the trucks were underloaded, the company lost money. If the trucks were overloaded, however, the driver could be fined by the Highway Department and could ultimately lose his job. The drivers opted for underloading the trucks.

For three months management tried to solve this problem by urging the drivers to try harder to fill the truck to its legal net weight, and by developing weighing scales that could be attached to the truck. But this approach did not prove cost effective, because the scales continually broke down when subjected to the rough terrain on which the trucks traveled. Consequently, the drivers reverted to their former practice of underloading. For the three months in which the problem was under study the trucks were seldom loaded in excess of 58 to 63 percent of capacity.

At the end of the three-month period, the results of the previous goal setting experiments were explained to the union. They were told three things—that the company would like to set a specific net weight goal for the drivers, that no monetary reward or fringe benefits other than verbal praise could be expected for improved performance, and that no one would be criticized for failing to attain the goal. Once again, the idea that simply setting a specific goal would solve a production problem seemed too incredible to be taken seriously by the union. However, they reached an agreement that a difficult, but attainable, goal of 94 percent of the truck's legal net weight would be assigned to the drivers, provided that no one could be reprimanded for failing to attain the goal. This latter point was emphasized to the company foremen in particular.

Within the first month, performance increased to 80 percent of the truck's net weight. After the second month, however, performance decreased to 70 percent. Interviews with the drivers indicated that they were testing management's statement that no punitive steps would be taken against them if their performance suddenly dropped. Fortunately for all concerned, no such steps were taken by the foremen, and performance exceeded 90 percent of the truck's capacity after the third month. Their performance has remained at this level to this day, seven years later.

The results over the nine-month period during which this study was conducted saved the company $250,000.

This figure, determined by the company's accountants, is based on the cost of additional trucks that would have been required to deliver the same quantity of logs to the mill if goal setting had not been implemented. The dollars-saved figure is even higher when you factor in the cost of the additional diesel fuel that would have been consumed and the expenses incurred in recruiting and hiring the additional truck drivers.

Why could this procedure work without the union's demanding an increase in hourly wages? First, the drivers did not feel that they were really doing anything differently. This, of course, was not true. As a result of goal setting, the men began to record their truck weight in a pocket notebook, and they found themselves bragging about their accomplishments to their peers. Second, they viewed goal setting as a challenging game: "It was great to beat the other guy."

Competition was a crucial factor in bringing about goal acceptance and commitment in this study. However, we can reject the hypothesis that improved performance resulted solely from competition, because no special prizes or formal recognition programs were provided for those who came closest to, or exceeded, the goal. No effort was made by the company to single out one "winner." More important, the opportunity for competition among drivers had existed before goal setting was instituted; after all, each driver knew his own truck's weight, and the truck weight of each of the 36 other drivers every time he hauled wood into the yard. In short, competition affected productivity only in the sense that it led to the acceptance of, and commitment to, the goal. It was the setting of the goal itself and the working toward it that brought about increased performance and decreased costs.

Participative Goal Setting

The inevitable question always raised by management was raised here: "We know goal setting works. How can we make it work better?" Was there one best method for setting goals? Evidence for a "one best way" approach was cited by several managers, but it was finally concluded that different approaches would work best under different circumstances.

It was hypothesized that the woods workers in the South, who had little or no education, would work better with assigned goals, while the educated workers in the

West would achieve higher productivity if they were allowed to help set the goals themselves. Why the focus on education? Many of the uneducated workers in the South could be classified as culturally disadvantaged. Such persons often lack self-confidence, have a poor sense of time, and are not very competitive. The cycle of skill mastery, which in turn guarantees skill levels high enough to prevent discouragement, doesn't apply to these employees. If, for example, these people were allowed to participate in goal setting, the goals might be too difficult or they might be too easy. On the other hand, participation for the educated worker was considered critical in effecting maximum goal acceptance. Since these conclusions appeared logical, management initially decided that no research was necessary. This decision led to hours of further discussion.

The sample questions were raised again and again by the researchers. What if the logic were wrong? Can we afford to implement these decisions without evaluating them systematically? Would we implement decisions regarding a new approach to tree planting without first testing it? Do we care more about trees than we do about people? Finally, permission was granted to conduct an experiment.

Logging crews were randomly appointed to either participative goal setting, assigned (nonparticipative) goal setting, or a do-your-best condition. The results were startling. The uneducated crews, consisting primarily of black employees who participated in goal setting, set significantly higher goals and attained them more often than did those whose goals were assigned by the supervisor. Not surprisingly, their performance was higher. Crews with assigned goals performed no better than did those who were urged to do their best to improve their productivity. The performance of white, educationally advantaged workers was higher with assigned rather than participatively set goals, although the difference was not statistically significant. These results were precisely the opposite of what had been predicted.

Another study comparing participative and assigned goals was conducted with typists. The results supported findings obtained by researchers at General Electric years before. It did not matter so much *how* the goal was set. What mattered was *that* a goal was set. The study demonstrated that both assigned and participatively set goals led to substantial improvements in typing speed. The process by which these gains occurred, however, differed in the two groups.

In the participative group, employees insisted on setting very high goals regardless of whether they had attained their goal the previous week. Nevertheless, their productivity improved—an outcome consistent with the theory that high goals lead to high performance.

In the assigned-goal group, supervisors were highly supportive of employees. No criticism was given for failure to attain the goals. Instead, the supervisor lowered the goal after failure so that the employee would be certain to attain it. The goal was then raised gradually each week until the supervisor felt the employee was achieving his or her potential. The result? Feelings of accomplishment and achievement on the part of the worker and improved productivity for the company.

These basic findings were replicated in a subsequent study of engineers and scientists. Participative goal setting was superior to assigned goal setting only to the degree that it led to the setting of higher goals. Both participative and assigned-goal groups outperformed groups that were simply told to "do your best."

An additional experiment was conducted to validate the conclusion that participation in goal setting may be important only to the extent that it leads to the setting of difficult goals. It was performed in a laboratory setting in which the task was to brainstorm uses for wood. One group was asked to "do your best" to think of as many ideas as possible. A second group took part in deciding with the experimenter, the specific number of ideas each person would generate. These goals were, in turn, assigned to individuals in a third group. In this way, goal difficulty was held constant between the assigned-goal and participative groups. Again, it was found that specific, difficult goals—whether assigned or set through participation—led to higher performance than did an abstract or generalized goal such as "do your best." And, when goal difficulty was held constant, there was no significant difference in the performance of those with assigned as compared with participatively set goals.

These results demonstrate that goal setting in industry works just as it does in the laboratory. Specific, challenging goals lead to better performance than do easy or vague goals, and feedback motivates higher performance only when it leads to the setting of higher goals.

It is important to note that participation is not only a motivational tool. When a manager has competent subordinates, participation is also a useful device for increasing the manager's knowledge and thereby improving decision quality. It can lead to better decisions through input from subordinates.

A representative sample of the results of field studies of goal setting conducted by Latham and others is shown in Figure 13.1. Each of these ten studies compared the performance of employees given specific challenging goals with those given "do best" or no goals. Note that goal setting has been successful across a wide variety of jobs and industries. The effects of goal setting have been recorded

FIGURE 13.1

REPRESENTATIVE FIELD STUDIES OF GOAL SETTING

RESEARCHER(S)	TASK	DURATION OF STUDY OR OF SIGNIFICANT EFFECTS	PERCENT OF CHANGE IN PERFORMANCE[a]
Blumenfield & Leidy	Servicing soft drink coolers	Unspecified	+27
Dockstader	Keypunching	3 mos.	+27
Ivancevich	Skilled technical jobs	9 mos.	+15
Ivancevich	Sales	9 mos.	+24
Kim and Hamner	5 telephone service jobs	3 mos.	+13
Latham and Baldes	Loading trucks	9 mos.[b]	+26
Latham and Yukl	Logging	2 mos.	+18
Latham and Yukl	Typing	5 weeks	+11
Migliore	Mass production	2 years	+16
Umstot, Bell, and Mitchell	Coding land parcels	1–2 days[c]	+16

[a] Percentage changes were obtained by subtracting pre-goal-setting performance from post-goal-setting performance and dividing by pre-goal-setting performance. Different experimental groups were combined where appropriate. If a control group was available, the percentage figure represents the difference of the percentage changes between the experimental and control groups. If multiple performance measures were used, the median improvement on all measures was used. The authors would like to thank Dena Feren and Vicki McCaleb for performing these calculations.

[b] Performance remained higher for seven years.

[c] Simulated organization.

for as long as seven years after the onset of the program, although the results of most studies have been followed up for only a few weeks or months. The median improvement in performance in the ten studies shown in Figure 13.1 was 17 percent.

A Critical Incidents Survey

To explore further the importance of goal setting in the work setting, Dr. Frank White conducted another study in two plants of a high-technology, multinational corporation on the East Coast. Seventy-one engineers, 50 managers, and 31 clerks were asked to describe a specific instance when they were especially productive and a specific instance when they were especially unproductive on their present jobs. Responses were classified according to a

reliable coding scheme. Of primary interest here are the external events perceived by employees as being responsible for the high-productivity and low-productivity incidents. The results are shown in Figure 13.2.

The first set of events—pursuing a specific goal, having a large amount of work, working under a deadline, or having an uninterrupted routine—accounted for more than half the high-productivity events. Similarly, the converse of these—goal blockage, having a small amount of work, lacking a deadline, and suffering work interruptions—accounted for nearly 60 percent of the low-productivity events. Note that the first set of four categories are all relevant to goal setting and the second set to a lack of goals or goal blockage. The goal category itself—that of pursuing an attainable goal or goal blockage—was the one most frequently used to describe high- and low-productivity incidents.

The next four categories, which are more pertinent to Frederick Herzberg's motivator-hygiene theory—task interest, responsibility, promotion, and recognition—are

FIGURE 13.2

EVENTS PERCEIVED AS CAUSING HIGH AND LOW PRODUCTIVITY*

EVENT	PERCENT OF TIMES EVENT CAUSED	
	HIGH PRODUCTIVITY	LOW PRODUCTIVITY
Goal pursuit/Goal blockage	17.1	23.0
Large amount of work/Small amount of work	12.5	19.0
Deadline or schedule/No deadline	15.1	3.3
Smooth work routine/Interrupted routine	5.9	14.5
Intrinsic/Extrinsic factors	50.6	59.8
Interesting task/Uninteresting task	17.1	11.2
Increased responsibility/Decreased responsibility	13.8	4.6
Anticipated promotion/Promotion denied	1.3	0.7
Verbal recognition/Criticism	4.6	2.6
People/Company conditions	36.8	19.1
Pleasant personal relationships/Unpleasant personal relationships	10.5	9.9
Anticipated pay increase/Pay increase denied	1.3	1.3
Pleasant working conditions/Unpleasant working conditions	0.7	0.7
Other (miscellaneous)	—	9.3

*N = 152 in this study by Frank White.

less important, accounting for 36.8 percent of the high-productivity incidents (the opposite of these four categories accounted for 19.1 percent of the lows). The remaining categories were even less important.

Employees were also asked to identify the responsible agent behind the events that had led to high and low productivity. In both cases, the employees themselves, their immediate supervisors, and the organization were the agents most frequently mentioned.

The concept of goal setting is a very simple one. Interestingly, however, we have gotten two contradictory types of reaction when the idea was introduced to managers. Some claimed it was so simple and self-evident that everyone, including themselves, already used it. This, we have found, is not true. Time after time we have gotten the following response from subordinates after goal setting was introduced: "This is the first time I knew what my supervisor expected of me on this job." Conversely, other managers have argued that the idea would not work, precisely *because* it is so simple (implying that something more radical and complex was needed). Again, results proved them wrong.

But these successes should not mislead managers into thinking that goal setting can be used without careful planning and forethought. Research and experience suggest that the best results are obtained when the following steps are followed:

Setting the Goal   The goal set should have two main characteristics. First; it should be specific rather than vague: "Increase sales by 10 percent" rather than "Try to improve sales." Whenever possible, there should be a time limit for goal accomplishment: "Cut cost by 3 percent in the next six months."

Second, the goal should be challenging yet reachable. If accepted, difficult goals lead to better performance than do easy goals. In contrast, if the goals are perceived as unreachable, employees will not accept them. Nor will employees get a sense of achievement from pursuing goals that are never attained. Employees with low self-confidence or ability should be given more easily attainable goals than those with high self-confidence and ability.

There are at least five possible sources of input, aside from the individual's self-confidence and ability, that can be used to determine the particular goal to set for a given individual.

The scientific management approach pioneered by Frederick W. Taylor uses time and motion study to determine a fair day's work. This is probably the most objective technique available, but it can be used only where the task is reasonably repetitive and standardized. Another drawback is that this method often leads to employee resistance, especially in cases where the new standard is substantially higher than previous performance and where rate changes are made frequently.

More readily accepted, although less scientific than time and motion study, are standards based on the average past performance of employees. This method was used successfully in some of our field studies. Most employees consider this approach fair but, naturally, in cases where past performance is far below capacity, beating that standard will be extremely easy.

Since goal setting is sometimes simply a matter of judgment, another technique we have used is to allow the goal to be set jointly by supervisor and subordinate. The participative approach may be less scientific than time and motion study, but it does lead to ready acceptance by both employee and immediate superior in addition to promoting role clarity.

External constraints often affect goal setting, especially among managers. For example, the goal to produce an item at a certain price may be dictated by the actions of competitors, and deadlines may be imposed externally in line with contract agreements. Legal regulations, such as attaining a certain reduction in pollution levels by a certain date, may affect goal setting as well. In these cases, setting the goal is not so much the problem as is figuring out a method of reaching it.

Finally, organizational goals set by the board of directors or upper management will influence the goals set by employees at lower levels. This is the essence of the MBO process.

Another issue that needs to be considered when setting goals is whether they should be designed for individuals or for groups. Rensis Likert and a number of other human relations experts argue for group goal setting on grounds that it promotes cooperation and team spirit. But one could argue that individual goals better promote individual responsibility and make it easier to appraise individual performance. The degree of task interdependence involved would also be a factor to consider.

Obtaining Goal Commitment If goal setting is to work, then the manager must ensure that subordinates will accept and remain committed to the goals. Simple instruction backed by positive support and an absence of threats or intimidation were enough to ensure goal acceptance in most of our studies. Subordinates must perceive the goals as fair and reasonable and they must trust management, for if they perceive the goals as no

more than a means of exploitation, they will be likely to reject the goals.

It may seem surprising that goal acceptance was achieved so readily in the field studies. Remember, however, that in all cases the employees were receiving wages or a salary (although these were not necessarily directly contingent on goal attainment). Pay in combination with the supervisor's benevolent authority and supportiveness were sufficient to bring about goal acceptance. Recent research indicates that whether goals are assigned or set participatively, supportiveness on the part of the immediate superior is critical. A supportive manager or supervisor does not use goals to threaten subordinates, but rather to clarify what is expected of them. His or her role is that of a helper and goal facilitator.

As noted earlier, the employee gets a feeling of pride and satisfaction from the experience of reaching a challenging but fair performance goal. Success in reaching a goal also tends to reinforce acceptance of future goals. Once goal setting is introduced, informal competition frequently arises among the employees. This further reinforces commitment and may lead employees to raise the goals spontaneously. A word of caution here, however: We do not recommend setting up formal competition, as this may lead employees to place individual goals ahead of company goals. The emphasis should be on accomplishing the task, getting the job done, not "beating" the other person.

When employees resist assigned goals, they generally do so for one of two reasons. First, they may think they are incapable of reaching the goal because they lack confidence, ability, knowledge, and the like. Second, they may not see any personal benefit—either in terms of personal pride or in terms of external rewards like money, promotion, recognition—in reaching assigned goals.

There are various methods of overcoming employee resistance to goals. One possibility is more training designed to raise the employee's level of skill and self-confidence. Allowing the subordinate to participate in setting the goal—deciding on the goal level—is another method. This was found most effective among uneducated and minority group employees, perhaps because it gave them a feeling of control over their fate. Offering monetary bonuses or other rewards (recognition, time off) for reaching goals may also help.

The last two methods may be especially useful where there is a history of labor-management conflict and where employees have become accustomed to a lower level of effort than currently considered acceptable. Group incentives may also encourage goal acceptance, especially where there is a group goal, or when considerable cooperation is required.

Providing Support Elements   A third step to take when introducing goal setting is to ensure the availability of necessary support elements. That is, the employee must be given adequate resources—money, equipment, time, help—as well as the freedom to utilize them in attaining goals, and company policies must not work to block goal attainment.

Before turning an employee loose with these resources, however, it's wise to do a quick check on whether conditions are optimum for reaching the goal set. First, the supervisor must make sure that the employee has sufficient ability and knowledge to be able to reach the goal. Motivation without knowledge is useless. This, of course, puts a premium on proper selection and training and requires that the supervisor know the capabilities of subordinates

when goals are assigned. Asking an employee to formulate an action plan for reaching the goal, as in MBO, is very useful, as it will indicate any knowledge deficiencies.

Second, the supervisor must ensure that the employee is provided with precise feedback so that he will know to what degree he's reaching or falling short of his goal and can thereupon adjust his level of effort or strategy accordingly. Recent research indicates that, while feedback is not a sufficient condition for improved performance, it is a necessary condition. A useful way to present periodic feedback is through the use of charts or graphs that plot performance over time.

Elements involved in taking the three steps described are shown in Figure 13.3, which illustrates in outline form our model of goal setting.

FIGURE 13.3

GOAL-SETTING MODEL

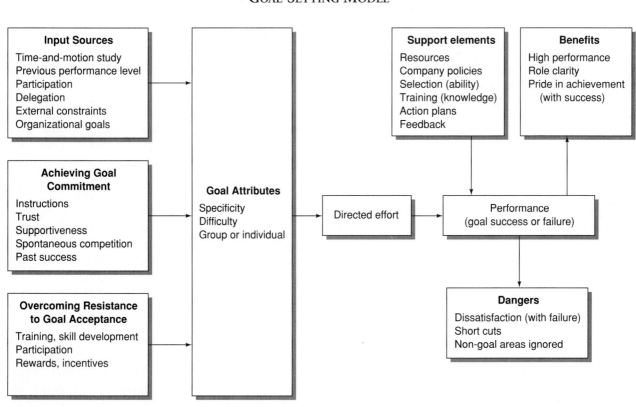

Conclusion

We believe that goal setting is a simple straightforward and highly effective technique for motivating employee performance. It is a basic technique, a method on which most other methods depend for their motivational effectiveness. The currently popular technique of behavior modification, for example, is mainly goal setting plus feedback, dressed up in academic terminology.

However, goal setting is no panacea. It will not compensate for underpayment of employees or for poor management. Used incorrectly, goal setting may cause rather than solve problems. If, for example, the goals set are unfair, arbitrary, or unreachable, dissatisfaction and poor performance may result. If difficult goals are set without proper quality controls, quantity may be achieved at the expense of quality. If pressure for immediate results is exerted without regard to how they are attained, short-term improvement may occur at the expense of long-run profits. That is, such pressure often triggers the use of expedient and ultimately costly methods—such as dishonesty, high-pressure tactics, postponing of maintenance expenses, and so on—to attain immediate results. Furthermore, performance goals are more easily set in some areas than in others. It's all too easy, for example, to concentrate on setting readily measured production goals and ignore employee development goals. Like any other management tool, goal setting works only when combined with good managerial judgment.

SELECTED BIBLIOGRAPHY

A summary of the early (mainly laboratory) research on goal setting may be found in E. A. Locke's "Toward a Theory of Task Motivation and Incentives" (*Organization Behavior and Human Performance*, May 1968). More recent reviews that include some of the early field studies are reported by G. P. Latham and G. A. Yukl's "Review of Research on the Application of Goal Setting in Organizations" (*Academy of Management Journal*, December 1975) and in R. M. Steers and L. W. Porter's "The Role of Task-Goal Attributes in Employee Performance" (*Psychological Bulletin*, July 1974).

An excellent historical discussion of management by objectives, including its relationship to goal-setting research, can be found in G.S. Odiorne's "MBO: A Backward Glance" *(Business Horizons,* October 1978).

A thorough review of the literature on participation, including the relationship of participation and goal setting, can be found in a chapter by E. A. Locke and D. M. Schweiger, "Participation in Decision-Making: One More Look," in B. M. Staw's edited work, *Research in Organizational Behavior* (Vol. 1, Greenwich, JAI Press, 1979). General Electric's famous research on the effect of participation in the appraisal interview is summarized in H. H. Meyer, E. Kay, and J. R. P. French, Jr.'s "Split Roles in Performance Appraisal" (*Harvard Business Review*, January–February 1965).

The relationship of goal setting to knowledge of results is discussed in E. A. Locke, N. Cartledge, and J. Koeppel's "Motivational Effects of Knowledge of Results: A Goal Setting Phenomenon?" (*Psychological Bulletin*, December 1968) and L. J. Becker's "Joint Effect of Feedback and Goal Setting on Performance: A Field Study of Residential Energy Conservation" (*Journal of Applied Psychology*, August 1978). Finally, the role of goal setting in virtually all theories of work motivation is documented in E. A. Locke's "The Ubiquity of the Technique of Goal Setting in Theories of and Approaches to Employee Motivation" (*Academy of Management Review*, July 1978).

DISCUSSION QUESTIONS

1. What are the intellectual and practical origins of goal-setting theory?

2. How does goal setting differ from other motivation theories, for example, Maslow's hierarchy of needs?

3. Are Latham and Locke justified in claiming that the results they obtained in laboratory experiments are generalizable to actual work settings?

4. What is the "Hawthorne effect" and how did it affect outcomes of field experiments on motivation?

5. What was the key variable in determining the degree of participation appropriate for a worker to participate in goal setting? Why was the outcome of the experiment that included this variable unexpected?

6. What is the advantage in worker participation in setting goals?

7. What are the specific steps that a manager can follow to set goals for organizational participants?

U.S. Quality Improvement in the Auto Industry: Close but No Cigar

ROBERT COLE

LEARNING OBJECTIVES

Robert Cole's article "U.S. Quality Improvement in the Auto Industry: Close but No Cigar" will provide students with:

1. An overview of recent attempts by the U.S. auto industry to improve quality

2. A comparison of U.S. and Japanese quality improvement efforts

3. An understanding of the problems that U.S. automobile companies have created for themselves in their approach to improved quality

4. Reasons for the inability of U.S. automakers to maintain and improve product quality

The public statements made by managers tell us a great deal about how they handle challenges. In the late 1970s, U.S. automakers developed a "new" conventional wisdom for explaining the differences in quality between domestic and Japanese cars. In a November 1978 interview with the *Detroit Free Press,* Ford Chairman and CEO Philip Caldwell announced that Ford owners are happier with the quality of their cars than with that of any other domestic producer.[1] He made no mention of the foreign automobile competition. In a 1980 Associated Press story, John Manoogian, Ford's newly appointed Executive Director for Product Assurance, conceded that "the Japanese have a slight edge in quality delivered to the dealer." Later in that same year, Ford Vice President Bidwell told the *Detroit Free Press* that "the high quality of Japanese cars is to some extent real and to some extent perceived."[2] In a November 1980 issue of GM's *Tech Center News* (an internal organ), GM's President-elect James McDonald first extolled GM quality, but then resorted to the familiar fit-and-finish argument: "We think we have not always given enough attention to some appearance items. And to our potential customers, quality is often determined by the first impression of these fit and finish items."[3] Much of the debate during this period focused on the issue of to what extent quality problems were caused by poorly motivated and poorly disciplined workers. Management responsibility was notably absent from the public discussions.

Privately, the Big Three's commissioned surveys were telling them that there were massive gaps in quality performance. However, as the McDonald quote demonstrates, they had trouble stating that publicly even to their own employees. Nevertheless, by the early 1980s most auto executives were admitting publicly that they had a serious quality problem and were making commitments to do something about it. By denying the problem as long as they did, however, they made the mobilization of their employees on behalf of quality improvement far more difficult.

Management has come to recognize that management behavior is the root cause of quality problems. If one looks at the statements made by chief executives at those companies that have been successful in revitalizing their product quality, the responsibility of managers to manage quality emerges as a recurrent and dominant theme.[4] Concepts like "changing our corporate culture is key to quality improvement" are now becoming commonplace. There is widespread recognition, if not always the practice, that designing quality in (a management function) during the product development cycle is central to producing quality products. There has been a powerful demonstration effect provided by the production of high quality products at the Japanese "transplant" facilities operating with American workers and Japanese management systems. The New United Motor Manufacturing Inc. (NUMMI), General Motors' joint venture with Toyota, symbolizes this success; NUMMI has consistently scored close to or at the top of GM's internal quality ratings.

TABLE 13.1

QUALITY PERFORMANCE BY LOCATION OF PARENT FIRM AND PLANT

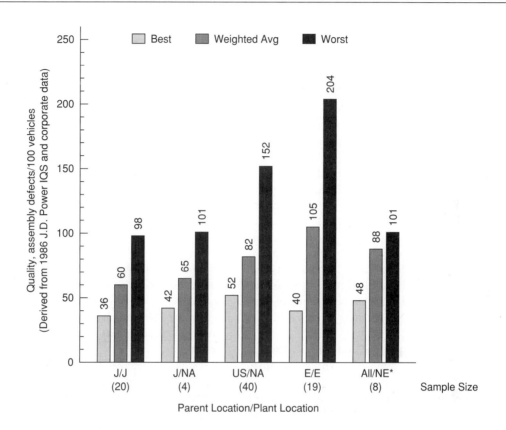

J/J	=	Japanese company with Japanese plants
J/NA	=	Japanese company with North American plants
US/NA	=	U.S. company with North American plants
E/E	=	European companies with European plants
All/NE	=	All new entrant companies with local plants

Source: John Paul MacDuffie and John Krafcik, "Flexible Production Systems and Manufacturing Performance: The Role of Human Resources and Technology," paper presented at the Academy of Management, August 1989.

To the extent that workers constitute a roadblock to quality improvement, it is not because of a lack of interest in quality. Workers and the UAW have greeted the quality movement with some enthusiasm.[5] U.S. management has consistently underestimated the appeal of quality among workers. Setting high quality standards gives workers dignity by telling them that what they are doing is important.

In this area, the problem is not workers per se but the failure of public education, limited and poorly conceived in-plant training, the failure of management to fully utilize the talents of employees, and—above all—poor management systems.

An important lesson of the 1980s is that technology in itself provides no easy fix to the quality problem.

Unless you remove the underlying system problems and solve the human relations problems, automation may simply allow you to produce poor quality products more rapidly. The Japanese did not achieve their initial quality advantage in the 1970s through high-technology solutions, and there were many documented examples of older Japanese plants producing better quality than newer, seemingly more technologically advanced American plants. In the 1980s, GM's Hamtramck plant became a symbol of misguided high-technology investment. Conceived as part of GM's strategy to leapfrog the competition and designed to achieve major cost reduction through the use of state-of-the-art technology, it had a dismal quality and productivity performance after opening in 1985.

A somewhat comparable situation existed at GM's Buick City assembly plant. In the late 1980s, GM was able to turn both plants around, but only through a drastic *reduction* in the level of plant automation. These changes, along with dramatic improvements in plant-level teamwork, led to rapid improvement in the quality rankings of the Buick LeSabre (produced at Buick City) and the Buick Riviera (produced at Hamtramck). Despite the improvements in productivity, however, the Hamtramck plant to this date still has the lowest productivity of any GM North American plant.[6]

In contrast, studies of Japanese capital investment patterns show that Japanese automakers often automate specifically to achieve quality and flexibility objectives rather than having cost reduction as the primary concern.[7] In short, both the conditions under which automation occurs and the objectives driving that decision have powerful effects on quality.

Got the Problem Just about Licked?

American auto managers have undergone rapid attitudinal and behavioral change. Most major U.S. auto manufacturers and supplier companies have made substantial progress in product quality over the last decade. Indeed, the progress has been impressive in many cases. Much of that progress has come from manufacturing people taking direct responsibility for quality. This represented a sharp break with past practices where quality was strictly a responsibility of the Quality Control Department. Increasingly, managers have come to understand that the objective is prevention not inspection. It is now openly recognized that customer perception is reality and that quality and cost are not tradeoffs.

How bad was it in the late 1970s and early 1980s and how far have the U.S. auto firms come? Data submitted by Ford Motor Company in the mid-1980s to the Federal Trade Commission show that, adjusted for volume, in 1981 the U.S. Big Three had customer-reported defects that were approximately 250% more than the average for Japanese producers. However, by 1981 the Big Three had already begun their rapid improvement; if one looked at data for the late 1970s, the U.S. makers were reporting defects on the order of 300% more than the Japanese. Current data reveal that this gap has been cut to approximately 50%. That is a tremendous improvement over a ten-year period.

More general support for this closing of the gap comes from the work of John Paul MacDuffie and John Krafcik.[8] Data based on 1988 performance (shown in Table 13.1) show the American final assembly plants in America were producing only 37% more defects than the Japanese plants in Japan.[9] However, this data set is designed to uncover only those defects that assembly plants can affect, ignoring such areas as engine and transmission performance and reliability. The emphasis is on fit and finish of body panels and trim pieces, paint quality, and integrity of electrical connections.

Consumer Reports magazine's frequency of repair ratings for 1989 model cars and trucks, by contrast, suggest a continuing large gap. Converted to a 4.0 grading scale, the three top Japanese auto companies selling vehicles in the U.S. (Honda, Toyota, and Nissan) receive an average score of 3.32 while the American Big Three receive an average score of 1.07.[10]

To be sure, there are reports that paint a brighter picture for the American producers in this general area of reliability. A new study by J.D. Power and Associates examines owner satisfaction with their overall ownership experience of four- to five-year-old vehicles. The study relies on a "vehicle dependability index" and the initial survey of 1985 model cars at the end of 1989 resulted in an average score of 104 for Asian producers (primarily Japanese at this time) and 99 for American producers.

Underlying the use of all this data is a narrow view of quality; quality is measured primarily by a car's reliability. A broader view identifies a variety of dimensions. David Garvin lists seven such dimensions beyond reliability: performance, features, conformance, durability, serviceability, aesthetics and perceived quality.[11] Of particular relevance, especially for performance and features, is the ability of producers to put advanced technology into their cars. There is every reason to believe that the Japanese have a substantial lead and may be extending it in this area. In short, while the progress of American producers has been tremendous, the remaining gap is hardly an insignificant one—close, but no cigar.

The significant reduction in the Japanese lead in reliability has led a lot of American experts, however, to proclaim a new conventional wisdom. In the September 1987 issue of *Automotive News,* GM Chairman and CEO Roger Smith declared that "by 1990, quality differences won't be important at all in the market." Industry analysts and other company officials echo this line as they talk about "quality becoming the price of entry—table stakes." They stress the shift to the costs of capital and marketing and design as the new competitive factors that will replace quality.

A recent Gallup study sponsored by the American Society of Quality Control surveyed 601 senior executives across a representative sample of American manufacturing and service industries. The findings show that only 9% saw Japan as providing the greatest competitive challenge in quality for them, down from 22% the year before. There seems to be a developing consensus within U.S. management circles, not just auto industry officials, that the gap with the Japanese is being rapidly closed.

The Danger of Declaring Victory

What can we say about these perspectives? First, even in those industries in which the Japanese are competing essentially against each other such as consumer electronics, there continues to be fierce competition over quality. A major reason for this continued fierce competition is that Japanese managers accept as fact, not rhetoric, that continued quality improvement is essential to continued cost reduction, employee mobilization, and interdepartmental cooperation. These are seen as keys to marketplace success, which involves winning the trust of the customer.

To focus only on defects that end up in the hands of the customer is a basic error. As the Japanese have reminded us, we need to focus on the process that produces a given outcome. Firms could be getting a reduction of defects in the hands of the customer but not getting the cost reduction that should go with it. In fact, firms could

be adding costs. This is an outcome of trying to inspect in quality. There is little doubt that some of the American producers' quality improvement has come about in this wrong fashion.

Consider the following explanation that I was given in an October 1989 interview with a medium-size automotive supplier to one of our OEMs. The respondent said that after seven years of aiming for quality improvement, "we are still having trouble with rework. We don't ship bad product so our perceived quality as seen by the customer is high but we do an awful lot of inspection, rework, and hassling in the plant to get it that way." In other words, it is 1989 and they are still adding cost to get that higher quality rather than getting their processes under control. Conversely, one sees many cases in day-to-day work processes in the industry where quality problems are not addressed because they are seen as too costly to do so (typically these are problems that are defined as not likely to lead to safety-related problems nor large costs to the consumer). They can, however, well be the source of considerable customer irritation. These practices are becoming fewer as the new quality systems take hold.

Nevertheless, the pull of past practices is so strong that even when companies have moved to new modern approaches to quality, they have sometimes regressed. Some automotive assembly plants, for example, eliminated end-of-line inspections a few years back as part of their effort to put responsibility for quality improvement in the hands of the workers. They found, however, that too many problems were getting through the system and recently have returned to using inspectors. Without getting their processes more fully under control, the only viable option under today's competitive market conditions is "containment" of error. This, however, is a short-term solution that does not bode well for cost reduction efforts.

The problem with claiming victory in advance of winning is that the troops tend to lose their motivation. The Japanese understand that all too well. Even when they haven't got much of a battle on their hands, they magnify—not diminish—the challenge in order to rally the troops to still greater efforts. Quality improvement is not one of those issues where we can tell everyone not to worry because "our three experts" in that area will take care of things. The modern approach to quality requires the involvement of all employees; therefore, companies need to keep all employees motivated for quality improvement. Quality also seems to have the distinctive character whereby drift and regression set in if you are not making improvements. Moreover, from a relative point of view, maintaining the status quo is equivalent to moving backwards because of the rapid improvement of the competition.

For employees to stay motivated, they need to feel that they are buying into some kind of challenge. Announcing victory in advance just doesn't fit that model. This applies to managers as well as workers. For manufacturing managers to push for deep change, they have to become convinced that the company has serious problems. Unless they are convinced they are in trouble, they won't search for a solution. And unless they continue to believe that, they will not continue to make improvements.

A Slowdown in the Rate of Improvement

When I talk to auto executives, and for that matter executives in manufacturing firms in general, I get a sense that many companies believe that the rate of their quality improvement efforts is either slowing down or even plateauing. Ford Motor Co., generally recognized as the domestic leader in quality improvement, acknowledges that it is having trouble continuing its high rate of quality improvement. Ray Rogal, Ford's Director of Corporate Quality, states that the dramatic improvements in quality made by Ford slowed after the early to mid-1980s.[12]

In the September/October 1989 issue of *Harvard Business Review*, the President of Velcro USA discusses his own company's recent slowdown in quality improvement and notes that the easiest gains have already been made—the cream has been skimmed. New gains in product quality are coming more slowly and appear to be getting more expensive. As one auto executive described it, "the slop has been taken out of the old systems but to make major further advances, new management systems have to be put in place." This is the real challenge and it is one that faces all American companies competing in the global marketplace.

What makes this of special concern is that while a number of our companies are worried about slowing down or plateauing, there are indications that the Japanese quality improvement effort continues unabated. Consider what the data from the J.D. Power's survey tell us if we compare not 1980 data to 1990 data, but 1988 data to 1990 data. In the 1990 survey of problems per 100 cars reported by owners after 90 days of ownership, the domes-

tic firms improved 24 points to 153 over 1988. But the Japanese, starting from a lower base of reported problems, improved 25 points over the same two-year period to 119. In percentage terms, the Japanese firms improved 17% while the American firms improved 14%. This runs counter to our notion that it should get harder to make big gains as you come down the curve.

This slowdown in the rate of quality improvement among U.S. firms relative to their Japanese competitors could be, of course, just a temporary development. I spent the first half of 1989 in Japan interviewing the top person responsible for quality (typically the general manager or secretary general of the Total Quality Control Office at Corporate headquarters) at 20 major Japanese corporations known for their quality achievements. Based on those interviews, I rather doubt that this is a chance outcome. In firm after firm, I received documented examples of major quality improvements over the last few years and plans for further advances. At Matsushita Electrical Industrial Company, the company has set a 1991 goal of cutting the percentage of its rejects to one tenth of its 1987 performance. Of the 30–40 products it puts out a year, its current objective is to score the best in consumer quality evaluations vis-à-vis its competitors in over half of these products. Clearly, Japanese firms continue to drive hard for quality improvement under the assumption that it will yield powerful results in the marketplace. Matsushita officials asserted that its automative products, destined primarily for Toyota, have the highest quality of its products because of how incredibly demanding Toyota is. In short, it would be dangerous to assume that the Power's data for 1988–1990 are just blips on the screen. For American firms to act on that assumption, given how much they have to lose were they to be wrong, could be fatal.

The Nature of the Competition

Some observers might make the following argument: the differences reported in the J.D. Power's data come down to the fact that customers report that U.S. cars have 1.6 defects per car and the Japanese 1.2. That's a difference of only 0.4. As one *Wall Street Journal* writer said to me, "So, what's the big deal? Customers aren't going to notice such small differences." Moreover, both figures are in fact pretty low now given the complexity of the product and how many things could be wrong with it. This is a position that some industry officials have taken as well. Is too much being made of some very small differences?

I decided to put the question to the 20 companies I was interviewing. I asked my respondents the following hypothetical question. Suppose we have an industry producing a fairly complicated product with a lot of parts in which two large firms are competing. A consumer survey reports the number of defects per product to average 1.6 for one company and 1.2 for the other. Moreover, let's say that viewed from the perspective of product performance, these defects are not so significant with the defects being more in the way of scratches and the like. In other words, I tried to make it hard for the respondents to argue that these were important differences.

I described for my respondents two ways of thinking about this situation and asked them to tell me which one their company would follow. The first scenario would be for the company to take the position that these differences were so small that they were not likely to be noticed or of concern to the customer. Consequently, competition between the two companies would probably turn to other matters like marketing and design. The second possible response was for the company to seek to eliminate these differences taking the position that these differences in quality might conceal other deficits in capability and that in any case it was important to be Number One in quality.

The overwhelming response (16 out of 20) was that these are serious differences. They saw a small gap in quality as reflecting gaps in capability in all sorts of other areas relating to cost and quality. Consequently, the company with the higher score should struggle to improve its quality. One respondent argued that even if the problems are not so serious, employees will hone their problem-solving skills in dealing with them and this will feature in the Japanese approach to quality: problems are seen as an opportunity and as sources of information for improvement, and they believe that this will ultimately be reflected in bottom-line improvements.[13]

The most powerful response I received came from Honda Motor Co. Since they are regarded as one of the major quality leaders among Japanese auto companies, I have reproduced part of Mr. Takagi's response. Mr. Takagi is the head of the quality department at Honda.

I would answer that there is a world of difference between 1.6 and 1.2. Quality is based on customer satisfaction. In order for a customer of a certain country to feel satisfaction, he or she has to be buying the Number One product in that country. So a necessary quality standard for a corporation is to have its customer ride in its cars with this kind of pride. This is our basic philosophy. Therefore, if ours was the company with 1.6, I would feel that it was a huge problem. I would immediately notify our top officers so that we could begin an analysis of the causes and aim for recovery. We would have a project on this up and running within a week. This type of thing is done all the time in our company.

Coming in first, being on top, only thinking of being Number One, not Number Two—this kind of racing spirit is what drives us in our business. These figures are extremely critical, and it is impossible for us to think that there is not much of a difference here. If J.D. Power announced these figures, we would start action as soon as they were announced if ours was the 1.6 company.

For us it is not so much a matter of whether the consumer is aware of the difference between 1.6 and 1.2, but as a company, as long as this fact exists, we feel the need to rectify the situation toward customers who would buy Honda products. It is not a question here of what the customer thinks, but we work with the mind set that we will offer the best product in the world. So, in this context, we do not put very much weight on market research about the customer. If we took action with the thought that our customers probably wouldn't care about this difference, we would never beat the competition. I would think that if we behaved differently, there would be something wrong with our management philosophy. And our top management thinks exactly the same as I do.

One may see many different meanings in this response but the theme that impresses me is the way Honda uses quality as the driver and focus of corporate competitive behavior. In that context, to accept Number Two status is a kind of corporate suicide. You would lose face with your employees, salespeople, and customers as to what the company and its products were supposed to be all about. It is a view which assumes that salespeople sell better and employees work better when they are selling the Number One product in the business. It would be a mistake to write off Mr. Takagi's response as one of those mission statements that lack any connection with reality; his comments strongly suggest this is the way Honda management not only thinks but acts.

Quality Ratings, Years in Production, and Learning

The J.D. Power's survey makes no attempt to adjust the quality ranking for the number of years a car has been in production. Yet, we might expect that when a car has been in production several years, management should have invested in identifying and solving most of the product's quality problems. In other words, there ought to be a learning curve. As one of my Japanese respondents said, a manager is not worth his salt if he still has significant quality problems in a product that has been on the market for several years. If the product's quality problems are caused by poor design to begin with, it should be quickly redesigned.

In light of this, one has to wonder about the managers responsible for the Chevy Caprice in its 12th year of production (see Figure 13.1). In *Consumer Reports'* annual auto

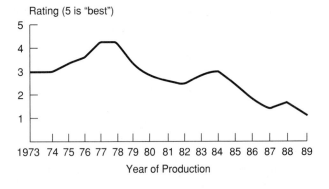

FIGURE 13.1

CHEVROLET CAPRICE V8 AVERAGE "TROUBLE INDEX" RATING

Rating (5 is "best")

Year of Production

Note: "Best" is 35% above mean.
Source: *Consumer Reports*

issue ratings, the Caprice has at best received average ratings; and relative to other cars, it has actually declined in quality. It should be kept in mind that the average quality score for all models was rising for the period between roughly 1980 and 1988; *Consumer Reports* evaluates each model relative to the average quality performance of all models.[14]

It is my experience with U.S. manufacturing managers generally that they tend to applaud *Consumer Reports* when it shows their products on top. However, when the quality reports for their products are poor they tend to dismiss it. For its annual auto issue, the magazine polls only the magazine's readers and these respondents do not constitute a representative sample. This is a clear limitation. Yet, pointing out—as some industry officials do—that readers of a consumers' magazine are likely to be more critical than the average customer, while plausible, does not explain the higher rankings received by Japanese cars.

Not only does the Caprice not go down the learning curve during much of its life, but as shown in Figure 13.1, it actually goes "up the learning curve" relative to the competition! Its quality ratings rose gradually from 1973 to 1977, but after the major redesign involved in the downsizing for the 1977 model year, we see a flat and then declining trajectory until 1982 (it received a modest "face lift" in 1980), followed by a slight rise and then sharp decline after 1984. Why the sharp decline after 1984? It has been a common practice in the U.S. car industry, once a company made a decision to discontinue a model in the near future, not to put much new investment in that product (e.g., tooling) and simply reap the benefits of past investments. As a consequence, quality tends to decline. We do not know whether this happened to the Chevy Caprice in an absolute sense, but at a minimum it occurred in a relative sense in that GM let the Caprice's quality decline compared to the rapidly improving competition of the 1980s. These practices are disappearing, but in market segments in which competition is limited to domestic competitors (the Caprice's only real competitors in recent years are Ford's full-sized Crown Victoria and Grand Marquis), they survive.

It would be extremely rare for a Japanese auto company to make this kind of decision at the tail end of a model run. Their view of quality is to deliver superior products to satisfied customers "whose trust they must win"—a phrase I often heard in my interviews. To leave a less than acceptable product out on the market grossly violates that concept. Even if the particular model in question had very few serious competitors, it would damage their *corporate reputation* among customers were they to let quality decline. From their point of view, their corporate reputation is a very fragile commodity and one not to be tampered with.

Lest this convey the impression of the Japanese as somehow given to divine wisdom, it is clear that even they can overestimate their capabilities. Any system, even a very good one, has its limits. In the context of the hyper competition currently occurring in the Japanese market, the auto companies have been shortening the time between introductions of new and reengineered models. The spate of recalls in the Japanese market in late 1989 of new and recently reengineered models combined with booming sales suggests that quality has been sacrificed under pressure of production and bringing new product to market. These recent events should not divert us from the track record of the Japanese auto producers in this regard relative to the Americans. We can get a sense of this track record by comparing the Chevy Caprice experience with that of the Honda Accord shown in Figure 13.2. There is a strong learning curve for the Accord relative to the competition! This upward curve is apparent despite three major reengineerings of the Accord in the 1982, 1986, and 1990 models. With American-produced vehicles, we typically expect downturns to show up in years immediately following major reengineering. As shown in Figure 13.2, no downturn is evident in the case of the reengineered Accords for which we have data. Contrary to some economic models, the learning curve can operate over successive car models if there is a concerted effort to incorporate the results of past problem solving and general learning into new designs.

There are some U.S. cars that have been on the road for a long time that do have high quality scores. One might think that my Japanese respondent would praise this outcome. He took the position, however, that such an achievement is no great accomplishment from a quality point of view. He argued instead that quality achievement requires that one also puts the most technologically advanced and proven products on the market as well. Viewed from this mindset, failure to redesign the product at frequent intervals incorporating the latest technology is a sign of quality failure.

The Japanese producers generally display a remarkable ability to produce high quality even in the first year of production. The top quality rankings achieved by Acura and the 1989 reengineered Nissan Maxima in their first year of production testify to this success. Compare that to the highly successful Ford Taurus, which had significant quality problems in its first year. U.S. producers still have a long way to go to match the Japanese in designing in quality from the start of a production cycle.

If we assume that the Japanese have traditionally shorter model cycles and are reengineering existing models more often and more thoroughly, then the seemingly modest gaps in the quality ratings reported by J.D. Power and Associates take on added significance. Support for this view comes from Takeshi Tanuma, President of Nissan Research and Development. His data show that Japanese automakers (represented by Honda, Nissan, and Toyota) redesign 82% of their models in a five-year period compared to the Americans (Chrysler, GM, and Ford), who redesign only 40% of their models during this same time period.[15]

FIGURE 13.2

HONDA ACCORD AVERAGE "TROUBLE INDEX" RATING

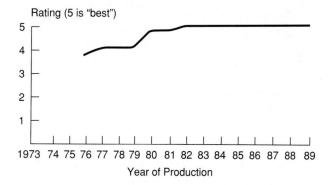

Note: "Best" is 35% above mean.
Source: *Consumer Reports*

On average, the Japanese producers conducted model changes every 4.8 years in the period between 1965 and 1988 while the American producers carried them out on average every 6.3 years. In addition, the ratio of new parts to new model vehicles is higher in the Japanese market. Tanuma estimates the ratio to be about 30% in the U.S. compared to 55–70% in Japan. These data are consistent with the observation that with a few exceptions, chiefly small-volume specialty vehicles, the Japanese sell models not much older than three or four years.[16]

Based on these observations, we can only conclude that because of the longer learning curve available to the Americans, the seeming modesty of the reported quality gap is misleading. The Japanese are not only achieving higher quality and are incorporating more-advanced technology in each new model, but they are doing it with shorter time available for learning once the car is on the market. This is only possible because they are able to solve many of the quality problems in the design stage.

Conclusion

U.S. car companies are in a protracted competitive struggle. Those American managers who are saying that they just about got the quality problem licked are doing American workers and American industry an enormous disservice. The U.S. car companies have come a long way, but they have a lot of work yet to do.

Beyond the concept of defect prevention, which has been the primary focus here, there is the "state of the art definition" of total quality control. This involves meeting and, where possible, exceeding customer expectations. A high quality product or service is one with a quality process; that is, for firms to achieve high quality products and services, they need to focus on improving the quality of every work process in the firm (as measured by the needs of internal and external customers). While American auto managers are beginning to grasp the importance of perfecting the quality of every business process, they lag greatly on its implementation. Clearly, a moving target, such as the Japanese automakers present, allows for no complacency or self-congratulation.

The pursuit of quality has an incredible potential for organizing employees around common corporate objectives and for building alliances with the unions. This is not because quality is more important than traditional objectives such as cost reduction, cash flow management, and market share, rather it is because quality improvement can operate as a centerpiece that provides the opportunity to reach these other objectives as well. For companies not to grasp that and instead proclaim that the campaign on quality will soon be over is both unwise and dangerous.

References

[1] "Stung by Recalls, Ford Creating New Cars More Slowly," *Detroit Free Press,* November 24, 1978, p. 12c.

[2] "Challenges Facing the Automotive Industry," *Detroit Free Press,* September 28, 1980, p. 1c.

[3] "McDonald Assures Quality is Priority," *Tech Center News,* November 17, 1980, p. 1.

[4] See, for example, the statements by Douglas Danforth, Chairman of Westinghouse Electric Corp. in "At the Helm," *Quality Progress* (April 1986), pp. 14–17. See also Brad Stratton, "The Refined Focus of Automative Quality," *Quality Progress* (October 1989), pp. 47–50.

[5] Helen Fogel and David Sedgwick, "UAW May Bid for GM 'Quality' Strikes," *The Detroit News,* March 21, 1990, p. 1e.

[6] John Lippert, "GM is Close to Shifting Productivity into High Gear," *Detroit Free Press,* January 2, 1990, p. 3e.

[7] Watanabe Susumu, *Microelectronics, Automation and Employment in the Automobile Industry* (New York, NY: John Wiley & Sons, 1987).

[8] John Paul MacDuffie and John Krafcik, "Flexible Production Systems and Manufacturing Performance: The Role of Human Resources and Technology," paper presented at the Academy of Management, August 1989.

[9] Defects for this data set are calculated using consumer perceptions as reported in J.D. Power's data from the 1985 and 1987 new car initial quality survey.

[10] Bradley Stertz, "Big Three Boost Car Quality but Still Lag," *Wall Street Journal,* March 27, 1990.

[11] David Garvin, *Managing for Quality* (New York: NY: The Free Press, 1988), pp. 549–550.

[12] "Still 'Running Scared,' Poling Faces New Problems at Ford," *Automotive News,* February 26, 1990, p. 51.

[13] John Paul MacDuffie is currently conducting a field study of problem-solving approaches and finds strong supporting evidence for these propositions. He also identifies a number of characteristic behaviors and structures associated with the Japanese approach to problem solving. Personal Conversation, Ann Arbor, MI, February 22, 1990.

[14] Owners of cars produced in a given year are surveyed annually. The score shown in Figure 1 for a given model year is the average of its scores in the first and subsequent years up to a maximum of six years. Thus, to calculate a 1980 model rating, we add up that model's scores for each year through 1986 and divide by 6.

$$\text{1980 model score} = \frac{(\text{1981 score} + \text{1982 score} + \text{1983 score} + \text{1984 score} + \text{1985 score} + \text{1986 score})}{6}$$

[15] Takeshi Tanuma, "The Key to the Challenge: Black Box Engineering," paper presented to the University of Michigan, Management Briefing Seminar, August 7–11, 1989, Traverse City, MI.

[16] "Newest Models Make the Gains as Ford and Japan Climb," *Automotive News,* February 5, 1990, p. 1.

DISCUSSION QUESTIONS

1. How have U.S. automobile executives responded to the Japanese challenge, especially concerning quality?

2. In what ways did the denial of a quality problem by the auto industry make employee mobilization more difficult?

3. Whose responsibility is it to improve, maintain, and increase product quality?

4. What is the role of technology in solving problems of product quality?

5. What factors have contributed to the quality improvement of U.S. automobiles?

6. According to Cole, what are the dangers for American industry—especially automobile companies—in declaring that the quality gap with Japan has been closed?

7. How do the Japanese maintain and even improve quality? Can the U.S. borrow and implement these techniques?

8. Could Latham and Locke's goal-setting theory be applied to the automobile industry to improve quality?

FOR FURTHER READING

Heneman, R. *Merit Pay: Linking Pay Increases to Performance Ratings.* Reading, Mass.: Addison-Wesley, 1992.

Lawler, E., and Mohrman, S. "Quality Circles: After the Honeymoon." *Organizational Dynamics* 15 (1987) 42–54.

Locke, E., and Latham, G. *A Theory of Goal Setting & Task Performance.* New Jersey: Prentice Hall, 1990.

Seligman, M. *Learned Optimism.* New York: Knopf, 1991.

PART IV: CASE 1

THE AMERICAN FOOD CORPORATION

Barry Allen Gold

"The cooperative type of organization is our greatest strength and our greatest weakness," observed the Chairman of the American Food Corporation. Few members of American, the largest retailer-owned food-merchandising cooperative in the United States, would disagree with his assessment. Since its founding 30 years ago, there has been persistent conflict among members and tension between member needs and the requirements of the corporation. Nevertheless, because of adroit management and the economies of large scale, the cooperative has been successful. Recently, however, novel organizational problems have developed, and the cooperative is confronting the most turbulent competitive environment in its history.

History

Early Years

Founded in 1955 by men whose business experience was family owned butcher shops, wholesale produce companies, and diverse small businesses, American began as a grocery-buying cooperative. Members of the cooperative benefited from volume discounts from grocery manufacturers, which enabled them to be more competitive in their small neighborhood stores. Along with low grocery prices, the featured department in this easy-entry, labor-intensive business was the service meat department, which was operated by the butcher–buyer–manager–owner.

In 1958 a Buy-Mart logo was formulated to identify the retailers to customers as members of a cooperative. At this time joint advertising programs were also initiated and a private-label grocery product line was introduced.

In the early years growth was rapid. New members were admitted into the cooperative, and the original members either opened new stores or relocated to larger ones. In 1958 the annual sales volume of the American warehouse was $450,000. By 1962 sales volume was over $1 billion, and in 1969 it approached $2 billion annually and served 29 member firms.

During this period the variety of products available from the American warehouse increased and expanded to include meat, dairy, produce, frozen foods, health and beauty aids, general merchandise, tobacco products, prescription drugs, alcoholic beverages, and a full line of private-label products.

The Formation of NewKirk Operators

The year 1969 was pivotal for the American Food Corporation. The largest member firm, whose president was credited with being the creative force in American, withdrew from the cooperative. The reason for the departure was chronic conflict with other members over retail store locations. In retail food merchandising location is critical for success; approval of sites by the American Board of Directors became a political, time-consuming process. By leaving the cooperative NewKirk could open stores in any location including those in direct competition with Buy-Marts.

NewKirk merged with several other Buy-Mart members, and today NewKirk operates 120 supermarkets in the same trading area as Buy-Mart (Buy-Mart operates 179 stores) and has surpassed Buy-Mart in average weekly store sales. NewKirk also owns 30 home-improvement centers and 15 department stores. It is recognized nationally as a well-managed, growth-oriented industry leader.

The departure of NewKirk, which reduced the American warehouse volume by 32 percent, caused many remaining members to fear that the cooperative could not survive. Although the initial impact was severe, after three years of retrenchment that included modernization of warehouse management and the addition of stores, American regained a significant share of lost volume. Aiding this recovery was the strategic withdrawal from the market of two nationwide chains—Safeway and Acme—on the rationale that competition was too severe. At the same time A&P began its long decline as a major competitor. Nevertheless, despite the rapid recovery, the departure of NewKirk affected American over the long term as it has continued to be its most aggressive competitor. In addition, NewKirk's withdrawal set the stage for a ten-year conflict between factions of American's membership.

The Intensification of the Conflict Culture

Upon leaving American, NewKirk relinquished its stock, thereby creating an opportunity for the redistribution of this stock among remaining members. American's officers redistributed the stock, with the result of increasing the power of smaller member firms as stock ownership determines election of members to the board of directors.

After the redistribution, the largest member firm initiated a lawsuit claiming that the redistribution violated American's bylaws, was illegal under state corporate law,

Source: Reprinted by permission of the publisher from "The American Food Corporation," by Barry Allen Gold, *Journal of Management Case Studies*, 2, pp. 312–326. Copyright 1986 by Elsevier Science Publishing Co., Inc.

and was "a blatant attempt to usurp control of the corporation." After ten years of legal maneuvering and personal and corporate conflict a United States Appellate Court found for the defendants.

As the lawsuit dragged on growth was sharply curtailed because of uncertainty over the outcome and the possibility that the cooperative might again lose its largest member. Also, the conflict diverted energy from the operating business; its resolution became an obsession for many members.

A lasting product of the protracted legal battle was intensification of the already conflict-prone organizational culture. Although there was rapprochement between the former litigants, a pervasive atmosphere of distrust and factionalism was embedded in the culture; today it is not uncommon for members to threaten litigation against each other.

A positive element of the corporate culture from American's founding until the present is the entrepreneurial character of its members. The founders and members are pragmatic, aggressive, tough, and essentially optimistic. Thus, despite their diverse personal styles, interpersonal intrigues, and corporate conflicts the entrepreneurial Weltanschauung, combined with the benefits of economies of large size, held the cooperative together.

To reaffirm the cooperative philosophy and the goals of the corporation, in 1980, shortly after the resolution of the lawsuit, American restated its purpose in a "Credo." The Credo is:

American/Buy-Mart is a retailer-owned cooperative. Its members consist of entrepreneurial families who have banded together to secure merchandise and services that they could not obtain economically or retail competitively if they acted individually.

They have accepted the creed of the cooperative movement because they recognize the value of people working together for their mutual benefit.

They assume the sacrifice of time and effort in order to achieve common goals.

They accept these burdens because they believe in the far-reaching benefits through cooperative methods.

The social purpose of American Food Corporation and the Buy-Mart stores, shall be to raise the standard of living of the consumers served by our stores by providing better merchandise at lower prices.

The next two sections describe the organizational structure, operations and social processes that were designed

to manage the company, and, in several instances, have evolved to regulate the tension between the entrepreneurial goals of the members and the system requirements of the cooperative.

The Member Firms

Twenty-six companies are currently members of the cooperative (see Figure 13.1). Member firms vary in size from one to 38 stores. Eleven members operate one store each, and nine members operate between two and eight stores each. These companies are closely held, with management primarily the responsibility of family members. The four largest member firms each have between 20 and 38 stores. Stock in these companies is traded on the American Stock Exchange, but ownership and control are retained by the founding families, who remain active in management.

Retail store sales volume ranges from $200,000 to $900,000 weekly with the average store at $365,000. Average gross profit is currently 22 percent and net profit less than one percent. In its primary trading area Buy-Mart currently has 14 percent of the market.[1]

Member Philosophy and Retail Strategy

Since its founding, in addition to the ideology of the cooperative movement, two principles have guided American's business philosophy: competitive pricing and extensive variety of merchandise.

In its price structure Buy-Mart has consistently attempted either to match or beat the prices of competitors. It usually succeeds; it is the low-price leader in its market. One result of this strategy has been reduced profit margins; to compensate for low margins continuous increase of sales volume is required.

Extensive product variety has been implemented successfully, surpassed in the last five years only by NewKirk.[2] Extensive merchandise variety requires large sales areas, raising operating expenses and, once again, increasing the necessity of high sales volume.

---

[1]Detailed financial data are not included in this case for several reasons. First, of the 26 member firms only the four with stock on the American Stock Exchange provide public financial information. Second, the nature of the business is that profitability can vary greatly from one quarter to another and from one year to the next. Third, American does not publish public financial data.
[2]NewKirk's merchandising philosophy is similar to Buy-Mart's, with the critical difference that NewKirk stores have high-profit, expanded general-merchandise departments. This fact permits price reduction of food items yet creates a high overall profit structure.

FIGURE 13.1

ORGANIZATION OF THE AMERICAN FOOD CORPORATION

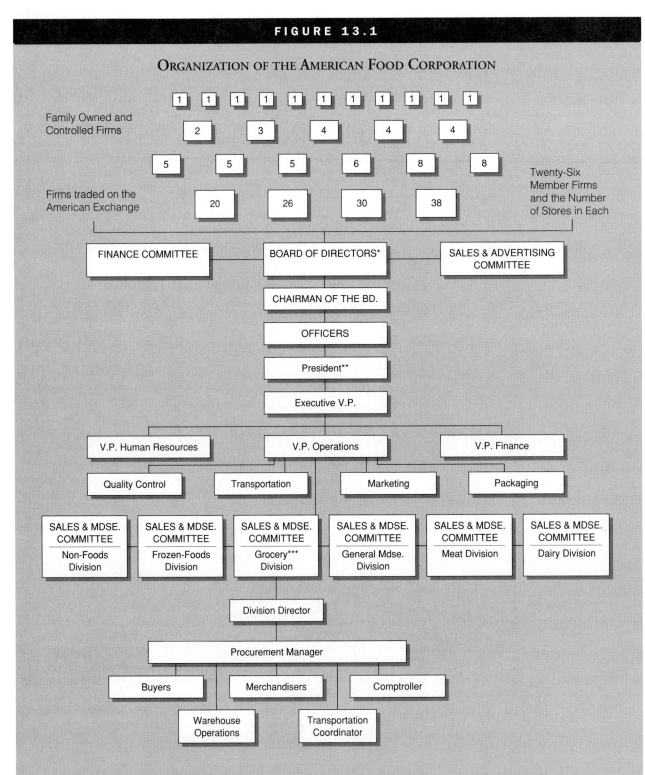

Family Owned and Controlled Firms

Firms traded on the American Exchange

Twenty-Six Member Firms and the Number of Stores in Each

*   Upper case indicates member positions.
** Lower case indicates managerial positions.
*** Each division is organized the same way as the Grocery Division.

Although the merchandising strategy is adhered to by members—joint advertising programs limit opportunities for deviation—there is no prototype Buy-Mart store. Each owner is permitted to set his own prices on nonsale merchandise and to arrange departments and store decor as he desires; the only uniformity among the stores is some display material and logos. At present, a merchandising strategy that is accelerating the historical trend in food retailing, inclusion of specialty departments within each store, is being introduced.

Management Styles of Member Companies

The leadership styles of members vary considerably and are reflected in the management of their companies. Representative of the sophisticated management style is a continuously profitable 30-store company that is organized in what the owner-president calls a "matrix" structure. There are distinct authority structures for both operations and merchandising, decision making is decentralized to the level of the retail store, and staff positions are designed to facilitate the store manager, who is the focal point of the organization. In this company there is substantial investment of time and personnel in employee training and motivation. A management-by-objectives program integrates and guides the organization. Finally, there is a strategic plan for the growth of the company and a plan for the evolution of management techniques. Several other companies have developed similar approaches to management.

The most prevalent management style is found in firms that range in size from three to 38 stores. Despite recurrent attempts to improve, these companies alternate between autocratic and laissez-faire approaches to management. Which style is used depends on the issue involved, the nature and immediacy of the competition, and the short-term profitability of the business. The result of this ambivalent management style is uneven operations and erratic long-term profitability.

Finally, about one-third of the firms improvise operations and tactics to meet the daily demands confronting their businesses. These members, primarily single store owners but also several medium-size firms, frequently operate in a "crisis" atmosphere. To some extent this is caused by the nature of the business ("NewKirk lowered the price of milk. How should we respond?") and the personalities of the owner–managers. Although several of these members are unable to systematize their businesses and are only marginally profitable, others appear to benefit from anarchistic organization; it permits instantaneous adaptation to local competition.[3]

There is minimal diffusion of management philosophy and style from the sophisticated, consistently profitable companies to the less successful, crisis-oriented companies even though the characteristics of the retail stores are similar.

Retail Store Structure

The management of a supermarket typically consists of one general manager, three assistant managers, and department managers.[4] Also part of the management structure are supervisors and merchandising specialists.

Each store has two unions: retail clerks and meatcutters. A store employs between 15 and 20 members of the meatcutter's union (including delicatessen workers) and between 50 and 70 retail clerks, two-thirds of whom are cashiers. Hourly wages average $12.50 for meatcutters and $10.50 for retail clerks. Extensive employee benefits increase payrolls by 25 percent of wages.

Store Operations: Labor and Technology

Despite the gradual introduction of technological innovations, the retail food store is a labor-intensive workplace. In addition to scheduling workers, interacting with customers, and handling merchandising and security, store management must deal with replenishment of the 15,000 different products carried in the store.[5] Daily store volumes range from $30,00 to $200,000, creating a continuous need for restocking, which is done at night. Each worker unpacks several hundred containers; technological advances have had no impact on this critical function.

An area where technology has had significant effect on retail operations is "box" beef. Box beef is cattle that is fabricated on assembly lines in Midwestern factories instead of being cut in the retail store from hanging quarters of cattle.

Technological innovation has had the greatest impact on point-of-purchase procedures. "Scanning," the use of lasers to decode Universal Product Codes, has increased the accuracy and speed of customer transactions. Continuous inventory and reorder functions available with scanning have not been implemented by American.

---

[3]Of course, despite periodic operating losses—even losses for several consecutive quarters—annual member compensation averages

$150,000. One source of income for many members in addition to the retail business is rent from ownership of the real estate occupied by the operating business.

[4]Department managers are union members. They differ from other union members because they are responsible for ordering products from the warehouse.

[5]Store-level management does not set prices or select items to be advertised; American management in consultation with members performs these tasks.

Along with reduction of operating costs, a result of technological changes has been union attempts to reduce the impact on workers of new technologies by negotiating manpower clauses in contracts.[6] Technological innovations have also decreased worker morale and strained relations between management and labor. For example, two consequences of technology are deskilling and the nondifferentiation of skills; opportunities for either more satisfying jobs or meaningful advancement are reduced; under these conditions there are limited organizational methods for motivating employees.

With few exceptions, the introduction of technologies into the stores is dependent on either manufacturers, as with box beef, or, more often, the committee process of American, which is described in the next section.

The American Warehouse

Corporate Philosophy

The cornerstone of American's management philosophy is to decentralize warehouse operations. Another goal is to promote professionalism through employee participation in decision making; a management-by-objectives program was established to achieve this along with an attempt to create a "Theory Y" corporate culture. Finally, in the past five years there has been a shift in management philosophy from a narrow focus on the operation of the distribution center to active concern with the problems of the retail stores.

Organization Structure

At the top of American's management hierarchy is the Board of Directors (see Chart 13.1). The chairman of the board of directors, with the officers, formulates policy and strategy for the corporation. Board members also serve as chairmen of corporate committees. Board members spend considerable time acting as brokers and buffers for member factions.

Below the directors is the executive committee, composed of the president, executive vice president, vice president for operations, vice president for finance and vice president for human resources. Along with performing their technical roles, this group formulates policy and strategy in consultation with the board of directors and is a liaison between members and the product divisions of the warehouse.

---

[6]An example of union action to delay the impact of technology and protect jobs is a local meatcutter union's contractual redefinition of meat products to include frozen dinners and pet food. The union claim is that its members should handle all meat products, not only fresh meat.

At the next organizational level decentralization was implemented by organizing each product division—meat, dairy, frozen food, etc.—into its own company with the division director serving as "president." The tasks of each division are to procure merchandise, select sale items, formulate advertisements, and operate the warehouse effectively.

The Role of Members

Relationships between members and professional managers are complex. Generally, directors, who are elected from the membership, support the president and executive committee. However, the director's and other members' entrepreneurial frame of mind is frequently uncomfortable with the "bureaucratic" style of the executive committee. The members are pragmatic, impatient, action oriented, and more informed and concerned with the retail aspect of the business than with warehouse operations. In addition, they are occasionally embroiled in disputes—for example, the lawsuit discussed above—and are continuously maneuvering for individual short- and long-term advantages.

Another influence on the behavior of the members and board of directors is variation in their perceptions of the type of management appropriate for American, its competitive position, and their vision of the corporate future. These multiple conflicting perspectives reflect the diverse management styles of their own firms. Because of this, board consensus—either on an internal problem or in response to competition—is infrequent and, when achieved, is often the product of reluctant compromise.

The role of the board of directors and members is diffuse—the boundaries for the use of influence are unclear—and this creates tension within the organization. After interviewing key personnel a consultant observed that:

> The executive committee is seen as a unit of management which is at the beck and call of the ownership. Alarming in this instance is the lack of understanding on the part of the division directors and managers with regard to the necessary liaison activities between the ownership and the rest of American which are fulfilled at the executive level. Therefore, the executive director's role vis à vis the ownership remains unclarified.

In many ways the diffuse member roles and conflict affect the professional managers' interpretation of events and actions. The managers spend considerable effort avoiding conflicts and positioning within the separate power structures of the members and the corporate hierarchy. Another result is that many managers complain that their expertise is underutilized and their decision-making authority diminished because of member intervention.

Warehouse Operations and Technology

Before describing the objectives, structure, and decision-making process of the division committees an account of warehouse operations and technology is required.

In 1985 American's annual sales to its member firms was $3 billion. It operates three warehouses that ship daily to 179 retail stores supplying 90 percent of the products required to merchandise a supermarket (the remaining products are supplied through direct delivery by local and national vendors).

The work process at the distribution centers involves two sets of routine, repetitive tasks. The first task is receiving weekly deliveries of several hundred railcars and tractor trailers from manufacturers throughout the country. Once received, these shipments are allocated space in the warehouse. The second task is selection of orders placed by the retail stores. Forklifts are used to pick merchandise from the warehouse shelves and load it onto trucks (American operates a fleet of 1,500 tractor trailers).

This flow of products is created by a stream of orders between the stores and the warehouse and the warehouse and manufacturers. A bureaucratic structure coordinates and controls warehouse operations (see Chart 13.1). However, major merchandising and policy decisions are made by committees chaired by members.

Committee Purpose and Structure

Product divisions conduct weekly sales and merchandising meetings. The objectives of these meetings are to review the previous weeks' sales, pricing, write advertisements for the following weeks, and give advice and direction to the division director. These meetings are chaired by a member appointed by the chairman of the board and are attended by members, the division director, buyers, and merchandising, marketing, quality assurance, and advertising personnel.

Committee Processes

The decision-making processes used in sales and merchandising committees vary. Several chairmen encourage debate and try to achieve consensus, or, in some situations, resort to a formal vote. In other committees the chairman autocratically decides all major issues. Independent of each chairman's style, there is a pervasive tension that affects corporate decision making. Three competing sets of concerns shape the tension; the magnitude of tension varies with the importance of the topic.

The first tension is created by the dual role of members. Members are, of course, concerned about their own corporate problems and goals. The other concern a member has is to advance American's goals, which, on occasion, may not be in his firm's interest (for example, technological innovations that would improve operations but require capital investment that would burden an individual firm's finances). A second concern is the division director's sales objectives and profit projections (warehouse profit is distributed as an annual rebate to members). Finally, the participants in meetings—managers and members—often champion particular merchandising philosophies.

To illustrate this tension, a complex debate can arise over a mundane product like hot dogs. The dairy division director's goal is to increase the tonnage of hot dogs shipped from the warehouse; the member's concern is that refrigerated shelf space is limited and hot dogs are low-profit items; the merchandiser's desire, adhering to the philosophy of extensive variety, is to have many types of hot dogs available to customers. To resolve these tensions the decision is to stock 60 varieties of hot dogs in the warehouse and put ten brands on sale in each advertisement.

Similar dynamics can be activated over any issue; these committees often become mired in trivia, ritualism, the idiosyncratic needs or views of a member, and, on occasion, the expression of power by groups within the cooperative. Although detailed records of product movement and advertisement effectiveness are referred to during meetings, the use of information and expertise is often subordinated to other considerations.

However, when a major decision approaches, or a member or director has a strong view on an issue, an attempt is made to structure the debate and control the committee assigned to the issue. The control method is extensive telephone conversations among members prior to the meeting. Support is sought on the basis of friendship, previous political alignments, common competitive situations, or a shared understanding of corporate goals, opportunities, and constraints. Implicit or explicit exchanges for support on future issues are part of the negotiations, creating a pattern that reinforces member allegiances. When this tactic succeeds, rather than acting as decision-making structures, the committees function as forums for members to "sell" their decisions, refine concepts, and formulate implementation plans.

When a telephone campaign is either impractical or unsuccessful, it is common for members to circumvent the committee process by directly approaching a division director, the president, or the chairman.

In sum, the diversity of interests represented by members and managers are axes on which temporary disagreements can develop, and enduring conflicts thrive. This structural feature of the cooperative coexists with and contributes to the conflict corporate culture. How these structurally generated tensions are managed determines the quality of corporate decisions. Presented below are examples of decision making in the areas of marketing strategy, technological innovation, and store location.

Decision Making I—Marketing Strategy

A competitive tool introduced and featured in advertisements by American's major competitors is generic, no-frill products. These products are staple consumer items—peanut butter, peas, facial tissue—that are nongraded, but nutritionally standard, products packaged with plain labels and priced below national and private-label products.

Shortly after competitors introduced generic merchandise debate among American members focused on the possible negative effects on Buy-Mart of stocking no-frills products, including lower gross profit and erosion of private-label sales. But market research indicated that competitors were successful with generic items. In addition, manufacturers offered attractive costs on generic products and needed little advance notice to start production.

Because of key member resistance, generic products were available to Buy-Mart stores two years after they were introduced by competitors. Implementation of the generic program within Buy-Mart varied; some companies installed full-scale displays of the merchandise to emulate competitors, some located it next to national brands, and others minimized its sale by stocking limited quantities of advertised items.

Members of the executive committee viewed the member decision-making process as too lengthy, cumbersome, and as a missed opportunity for a rapid response to competition on a major issue.

Decision Making II—Technological Innovation

Another example of decision making is the change from electronic cash registers to computerized, scanning, point-of-purchase equipment. Aside from the cost for each member ($250,000 for each store) the major barrier to introducing scanning was the ongoing cost of a staff of computer experts to support it. Nevertheless, the advantages of scanning included inventory control and reduction of operator error, resulting in higher gross profit.

The earliest user of scanning was the chairman of the board. After initial technical problems, his experience with IBM equipment and service was successful. Eventually, other members selected machines manufactured by National Cash Register, Monroe-Sweda, and Digital Equipment. Because each manufacturer required different support systems, American had to select one. Guidelines for the decision were ease of operation, service, and innovativeness of the manufacturer.

Judgments on the available equipment from the committees with responsibility for store operations varied substantially. The board of directors was required to intervene. The board authorized American to supply computer support for equipment manufactured by four companies.

Decision Making III—Site Location

The location of a retail store is a critical decision; location determines sales volume, and, independent of management skill, volume can determine the success or failure of a store. Throughout American's history approval of member applications for retail locations was an area of conflict. Site approval was the domain of a subcommittee of the board of directors with an appeal process to the entire board. Politics, power, and friendship permeated the site-location process.

In 1980 a quasiautonomous site-location committee was established to evaluate member applications. To depoliticize the process the committee was composed of a professor of retailing, a retired supermarket executive from another chain, and a bank president. This committee's recommendations are seldom reversed.

Decision Making and Leadership in the Future

Many of the original members of the cooperative are either semiretired or retired. In several instances sons and daughters have assumed leadership roles successfully; in other firms the transition is taking place slowly with uneven results.

The second generation is composed of people with diverse educational backgrounds and interests. They view the future of American with cautious optimism and plan to manage it by emphasizing technical expertise rather than the entrepreneurial instincts of their fathers. At present, many members feel constrained by their fathers and are impatient to assume roles with greater responsibility. They are also experienced in and concerned about the tradition of political intrigue and conflict that form American's culture; evidence suggests that the younger members view the conflict culture as detrimental and desire a change toward a more rational corporation.

Compounding the complex dynamics of succession in a family business—in this case a multifamily business—key members of the executive committee are considering retirement. Selecting successors satisfactory to members could be a treacherous and possibly divisive process.

These leadership changes are occurring at a time when many American members and managers view the food-distribution industry and American as entering a transitional phase. One member of the executive committee expressed a sense of ennui and pessimism about the future. In his opinion, compared with other forms of business organization, cooperatives have truncated life cycles; American has plateaued and is entering a period of organizational decline. Other managers and members are more optimistic but acknowledge that to prevent deterioration changes in American may be needed. The ambitions of the emerging leadership, together with influential senior members' views, will influence not only American's decision-making process but also its strategy for the future.

The Competitive Environment

Strategic Competitive Changes

The competitive environment of the supermarket industry since World War II has been turbulent. In the American trading area, the most dynamic in the nation, strategic changes in the marketing practices of retail food chains occur every few years.

One recent strategic change made by an American competitor was A&P's introduction of limited variety stores under the "Plus" logo. These stores offer a limited variety of grocery items—no meat or produce—and limited customer services in exchange for reduced prices.

Currently, in another strategic change, A&P is closing conventional stores, expanding the variety and quality of products, and modernizing and reopening under the name "Superfresh." The competitive advantage, aside from emulating the Buy-Mart merchandising format, is that these stores have a union contract requiring considerably lower wages than competitors.

Grand Union, until recently a minor Buy-Mart competitor because of a higher price structure, has also developed limited-variety or "warehouse" stores. More important, however, Grand Union has remodeled its conventional stores and installed a price structure equal to Buy-Mart and NewKirk. To emphasize this, Grand Union television commercials end with the phrase: "We are going to meet or beat your prices, Buy-Mart and NewKirk—FOREVER."

NewKirk has remained the chief Buy-Mart competitor in its primary trading area. NewKirk, with 120 supermarkets, has sustained a program of new store development and remodeling and expansion of existing units. An increasing number of NewKirk stores are 50,000 square feet, full-line stores, with highly competitive prices and often superior locations compared with competing Buy-Marts.

An important redirection of NewKirk's strategy was signaled by its recent acquisition of a 40-store chain in a trading area contiguous to its concentration of stores. Fifteen of these new stores are 60,000 square foot warehouse stores that could serve as pilots for development of a prototype of future NewKirks that would be developed in the Buy-Mart trading area.

Finally other chains have made progress with new formats, particularly large warehouse stores. The impact of these chains has been minimal because they have been prevented from penetrating Buy-Mart's primary trading area because of lack of locations.

A significant difference in the current competitive environment, compared with previous changes such as A&P's Warehouse Economy Outlets (WEO), which lasted two years, is that it appears that A&P's Superfresh and Grand Union's low-price strategy will be sustained. These companies are now owned by foreign-headquartered multinational corporations; long periods of losses in the retail food industry can be offset by profits in other industries until a market niche is established.[7]

Buy-Mart's Competitive Strategies

The aggressiveness, cohesiveness, and scope of Buy-Mart's competitive strategy varies with the perceived threat of competition. In the case of the A&P Plus stores key members felt that the new format had to be stopped; if it was not, chains outside the region would be encouraged to enter the market as limited-variety stores require little investment because of the small sales area and the absence of expensive refrigerated equipment. The cooperative acted as a unit with the advertising slogan "Price-PLUS." "Price" indicated that Buy-Mart's prices were competitive with A&P and the "PLUS" reinforced its commitment to full customer service. The result of the concerted effort was that within one year all Plus stores in the Buy-Mart trading area were closed.

In the case of Grand Union and its low-price, full-service strategy, the threat is perceived as not affecting the majority of stores, and the Buy-Mart response is localized. As in other instances of regionally concentrated competitors, member preference is to subsidize sale merchandise for stores directly in competition. How readily and for how long a member is supported in his attempt to thwart competition depends on the potential competitive threat other members feel as well as the political connections of the member.

Generally, Buy-Mart's response to competition, including NewKirk, is that chances for success are increased by being all things to all customers; competition would be warded off because Buy-Mart would absorb or buffer their

---

[7]The trend toward multinationalism and diversification is exemplified by Sir James Goldsmith, who controls Grand Union and recently acquired Crown Zellerback, a forest products company.

challenges by incorporating all of the innovations and promotions in the marketplace. This strategy has accelerated recently with the inclusion in stores of specialty departments such as custom meat shops, service gourmet cheese shops, fresh pizza departments, video departments, travel agencies, 24-hour photo development, banks, salad bars, and other attractions. These departments and services, which often require capital investment and additional labor expenses, offer customers convenience and low prices.

Within the strategy outlined above, to facilitate responsiveness to everyday, nonextraordinary competition American provides each member with a price structure geared to his primary competitor. In addition, each member has available stronger competitive devices ranging from special promotions to "double coupons."

Along with the strategy of comprehensiveness, targeted price zones, and devices such as double coupons, there is a stream of print and television advertisements emphasizing the low-price image. There are also several major promotions each year with a particular theme such as merchandise freshness, double-money-back guarantees on fresh meat, and "super" coupons.

Occasionally, a radical reinforcement of the low-price theme is launched. An example of this was the promotion of turkeys for Thanksgiving 1984. Store volumes suffered dramatically as the result of a five-week meatcutter strike that ended in mid-September. When the strike was over, despite the liberal use of coupons in addition to regular advertising, customer counts and store volumes remained lower than during the same quarter the previous year. Members were alarmed by the situation; money had been lost because of the strike, volume was not returning, the new contract increased labor costs, and profitable fall and winter quarters are essential.

After exhaustive discussion the directors decided that a potentially costly solution, but one that would have the greatest impact, would be to give a free turkey to customers who collected $350 of Buy-Mart register tapes during the four weeks preceeding Thanksgiving. The program was implemented and competition was unprepared for the unprecedented offer of free turkeys. Eventually, several chains developed a similar giveaway and others reduced turkey prices from 89 cents to 29 cents a pound.

The immediate result of the turkey promotion for Buy-Mart was significant increases in store volumes, reestablishment of its low-price image, and an average loss for each store of $60,000. The long-term effect on volume depended on the particular store and follow-up promotions used by the owner. Overall, however, volume gains were not as enduring as anticipated; customer-survey data indicate that shoppers are no longer loyal to a particular store but frequently switch to the store with the lowest advertised prices.

Because of the relative success of these competitive strategies Buy-Mart has decided not to experiment with new formats such as warehouse or limited-variety stores. They have also decided not to diversify. Other factors influencing these decisions are the sunk costs of existing facilities and lack of the financial and organizational resources necessary to initiate and sustain changes similar to those undertaken by A&P, NewKirk, and Grand Union. Nevertheless, for the past five years American/Buy-Mart sales volumes have been stagnant.

Barriers to Growth

Several factors besides the turbulent environment have contributed to American's stagnation. First, there are few locations available for stores in its traditional trading area. Several members have opened stores in nearby states but, despite sales volumes at projected levels, the high cost of advertising in a new market has resulted in financial losses and discouraged further expansion. Second, the cost of expansion has increased because of high interest rates and real estate, building, and equipment expenses. Start-up expenses for a 50,000 square foot supermarket are approximately $5 million, with a break-even sales volume of $500,000 weekly. Third, because competition is severe, resulting in depressed sales volumes and low profit margins, alternative investments are attractive.

Compounding the inability to expand, in recent years several member firms have experienced financial difficulty. A six-store company, facing extensive losses and internal conflict after an unsuccessful attempt to expand, liquidated its assets. Another multiunit company has been operating nonprofitably for several years and survives only because of American's reluctant extension of credit. A third company (which operates the highest-volume supermarkets in the nation) currently perches on the brink of bankruptcy after it opened two new stores near NewKirks, which started a price war. The largest publicly traded company has become the possible target of a takeover and liquidation by a real estate company. Finally, even though profitable, to avoid becoming embroiled in the protracted politics of American, one member surreptitiously sold his four stores to NewKirk.

An unintended result of member business failures is American's absorption of members of another food retail cooperative. This process began when a member of the competing cooperative purchased the assets of a near-bankrupt American member. Because of his positive experience with American he encouraged members of his former cooperative to switch. However, many of these stores are substandard in either size or location; they are not permitted to display the Buy- Mart logo but do purchase inventory from American.

Corporate Culture and the Future

Member financial problems have exacerbated the corporate culture of distrust and conflict. The primary cause of the renewed conflict is unequal treatment of members. For example, a member who opened his second store requested financial relief from the chairman of the board after six weeks of operation. Without consulting other members, the chairman authorized American to purchase the store; today American operates it with substantial losses. Another firm is permitted to purchase inventory from American even though its payments are continuously delinquent. However, in other cases, modest requests, for example, extension of credit to alleviate cash-flow problems, are denied. At present one member is demanding that American purchase a new but unprofitable store that is threatening the solvency of his company. There is strong member opposition to the request.

A related factor contributing to member conflict is competition over the acquisition of stores that are for sale. Because suitable sites are scarce, several different members often want to purchase the same store; political and philosophical factions clash until a single candidate emerges.

Resolving the complex issue of member equity—which is at the core of member conflict—has major implications for American's future as a cooperative.

PART IV: CASE 2

BILL KADOTA'S PROBLEM

J. Malcolm Walker

The years of single-minded dedication to his education and then to his work were beginning to pay off for Bill Kadota. He had become a first-line supervisor and believed that if he performed well, a career in management would be open to him. Arriving in this country in the 1970s with very little money, Bill had worked his way to a masters degree in engineering (with several business courses as part of his program). He was promoted to a supervisory position after three years of work in the electronics industry, the last 18 months at Dandy Electronics, a medium-sized firm in the Southwest. Bill was proud of his achievements both at the university and in his work life.

Bill Kadota was anxious to show that he could be a good supervisor. He saw his promotion as a challenging opportunity to find out how well he could handle supervising responsibilities. Yet he wondered whether the people whom he would be supervising would work well for him, and he felt he would have to prove himself quickly, because be believed that opportunities for promotion in management were limited and the company didn't give people long to show how well they could perform. Bill was anxious to please his new boss, John Davidson, and he wondered how much cooperation he would get from him. In talking with Bill about his new position, Davidson had emphasized the importance of meeting production deadlines. Bill formed the impression that Davidson might be personally supportive, but he was not sure.

Bill was taking over the Production Control (PC) section, which had responsibility for some aspects of product testing, evaluation, and shipping. The section included nine non-exempt technicians, in addition to the supervisor. The previous supervisor, Tom Brown, had left the company before Bill was notified of his promotion. For the six weeks before Bill took over the section, John Davidson (the department manager) had directly supervised the PC section.

Before moving into his new position, Bill talked with two people who had previously worked in the PC section in order to get information about the quality of the employees now in the section. According to the former members of the section, most of the current employees were at least reasonably conscientious and regular in their work. They told Bill that one of the workers, Joe Calonico, had been a "buddy" of the previous supervisor, had exercised a lot of freedom to come and go pretty much as he pleased, and hardly put in more than four or five hours a day of real working time. Bill felt than Calonico might be a problem.

On hearing of Tom Brown's resignation, Joe Calonico had approached John Davidson to ask for promotion to section supervisor. Davidson denied his request and gave the following reasons: (1) Calonico was not qualified for the position, because he had neither a university degree nor the six years of experience required as a substitute for the degree; (2) he lacked experience in one of the section's work areas and in coordinating work with other departments; and (3) he had no supervisory experience that would demonstrate his ability to work under pressure in performing high-priority tasks.

Calonico was unhappy with this decision. He told Davidson that he was a top performer as a technician. He also reminded Davidson that he had been promoted to "engineer" (an exempt but nonsupervisory position) two years earlier, and had held that position for ten months until he and many other employees were demoted to their previous positions during one of the quite frequent periods of company cutbacks (a characteristic of many firms in the electronics industry). Calonico retained his engineer's salary despite his demotion to special technician. He had also been put through several technical and a few "human relations" courses in house training programs.

When Bill took over as supervisor of the PC section he discussed work tasks, work flow relationships, and task priorities with each employee in the section individually. By doing this he hoped to learn much about each employee's abilities and to establish good relations with all employees from the start. He left task assignments and work flow much as they had been, although he changed some output priorities in line with some new directives from the department manager.

Bill was satisfied with the performance of most of the section employees but he immediately sensed an attitude of personal hostility on the part of Joe Calonico, who also seemed apathetic toward his own work. Calonico would accept a task assignment, then either fail to perform it or take what Bill felt to be an unduly long time to complete it. He would give no reason to Bill, or he stated that he simply hadn't had enough time, or gave what Bill felt were vague excuses.

Bill thought that perhaps Calonico felt he could get away with this behavior because he expected to get a job in

Source: Reprinted by permission of the publisher from "Bill Kadota's Problem," developed by J. Malcolm Walker, Professor Emeritus, San Jose State University, *Journal of Management Case Studies*, 2, pp. 70–75. Copyright 1986 by Elsevier Science Publishing Co., Inc.

another department for which he was bidding. Calonico was unsuccessful in securing this other job. Bill never found out why; he thought that perhaps the manager who had advertised the opening didn't really have such an opening immediately available but was simply scouting for good candidates for the time when such an opening should become available. Calonico was upset about his lack of success in getting that job. Bill noted that Calonico became even more careless about completing his tasks. He sometimes reported late for work. Bill observed him sitting idly or talking with employees from other sections for long periods. On a few days, Calonico stayed away from work without notifying Bill, who felt that he must be looking for a job outside the company. Although other employees in the section sometimes depended on Calonico to help accomplish their tasks, they exerted no informal pressure on him. Bill felt this was because Calonico had been around longer than most of the other employees and had a forceful personality. Calonico sometimes argued with Bill about job assignments and work methods in the presence of other employees.

Trying to find out more about Calonico, Bill discovered that his predecessor had given Calonico favorable performance appraisals, although Bill noticed that most of the supervisor's comments were of a very general nature. These appraisals indicated that Calonico had done the job well, had done good work, and had put in the effort required to solve some special problems. Bill didn't know what to make of these appraisals. He thought that perhaps they had been influenced by personal friendship between Tom Brown and Calonico, or that Brown had simply wanted to be sure he kept Calonico in light of the company cost control practice of not replacing people who were transferred or fired.

Calonico's behavior puzzled and disturbed Bill because he felt Calonico lacked the qualifications to perform the supervisory job. Yet it was not unusual, in Bill's experience, to find technicians who felt they could do jobs that require real engineering know-how. It seemed to Bill that there were many people like that in the electronics industry. Bill felt that Calonico should recognize that he lacked such qualifications and get on with doing good work in his present position (which he felt Calonico had the ability to do). Bill never felt that he understood why Calonico behaved as he did. The section's workload was heavy, output was in continuous danger of falling behind schedule, and Bill had to meet a succession of output objectives to meet company deadlines and pressure from Davidson. He frequently told Calonico that he was too indifferent to his work, was working inefficiently, and was weak on punctuality. Bill also indicated that Calonico should improve in each of these areas. Bill's actions had little effect but, having wanted to establish good

relations right from the start he kept hoping Calonico would improve.

Bill had talked with John Davidson about Calonico' behavior. Davidson made no proposals about how to solve the problem but indicated that Bill must solve it. "You're the manager of the PC section," Davidson said. He would quickly shift discussion to technical and output issues. Bill felt he had inherited the problem of Calonico, and whereas it should have been solved earlier, it was now his own responsibility. He worried about it a great deal at work and during his leisure time.

After two months on the job, Bill felt that pointing out Calonico's performance inadequacies was not having much effect, and that Calonico had had enough time to show improvement. He then decided to try to motivate Calonico to perform more effectively. He did not want to take a hard line and desired to maintain good relations in the section. Especially because he was still quite new, he did not wish to appear to be domineering or to put on too much pressure in the section. He wished "to be employee-oriented" and to avoid "close supervision." These approaches seemed consistent with ideas emphasized by his instructors in his college business courses and in a human relations course taken at Dandy Electronics. He also felt that Calonico might be personally hostile because Bill had obtained the job that Calonico had badly wanted. While continuing to point out Calonico's performance problems and the necessity to improve, Bill tried to establish favorable relations with him by socializing during coffee and lunch breaks. Bill felt that this would help make Calonico "feel part of the group" and show him that Bill would treat him objectively and fairly. As Bill saw it, he was trying to "turn him on by way of motivation . . . to win him over."

Calonico's job performance did not improve and Bill felt his efforts had been in vain; nothing would work, Calonico just didn't care and would never accept Bill as his supervisor. After two weeks of trying to be friendly with Calonico, Bill felt he had to take a firm stand. At this point another department requested early resolution of a quality control problem that had been sitting on Calonico's desk for two weeks. Bill told him to solve the problem and provide recommendations within two days. Calonico agreed. On the afternoon of the second day, the following discussion took place:

KADOTA: Do you have the results and recommendations on the Production department problem?

CALONICO: No. I haven't gotten around to it yet.

KADOTA: Joe, what have you been doing in the past week?

CALONICO: Some of those customer requirement projects.

KADOTA: Which customer projects?

CALONICO: Oh . . . you know, some of those we have had around.

KADOTA: You aren't working at half speed, even though you're the highest-paid special technician in the division.

CALONICO: I get as much done in four hours as anyone else does in eight.

Bill broke off the discussion. He decided to take a very firm stand to settle the Calonico problem once and for all. Because he wasn't sure just how to accomplish this, he called the Organization Development specialist for advice. He had heard about MBO, Managerial Grid, and related programs run by the OD specialist, and felt that the OD man—whom everyone in the company was authorized to contact directly and informally—should be able to help in a problem of this type. The OD specialist's secretary told Bill to call back after two weeks because the OD man was attending an important OD conference in New York.

Bill wanted to act right away. It occurred to him that maybe it was just as well that the OD specialist was out of town; now that he thought more about it, he remembered that the OD man concentrated on helping to solve problems related to output and productivity failures of work groups. Bill decided to go to the Personnel Department, even though he wasn't sure how much help he could get from that department in solving problems in his section. He did know that the Personnel Department had a formal responsibility to help resolve differences between employees and to act as a sort of "mediator," whatever that meant.

Bill described the Calonico issue to a personnel specialist who suggested that Bill give Calonico a formal written warning, putting him on probation and indicating that failure to improve in all areas would lead to dismissal. To Bill, this sounded like the kind of tough action that was needed. It would represent a formal recognition of the problem and lead to formal involvement of John Davidson, whose endorsement of the formal warning would be required. Davidson approved of this approach when Bill told him what he intended to do.

In his formal letter to Calonico, Bill criticized (1) his failures to complete assignments on time; (2) the adverse impact of his attitude on achievement of section output objectives; and (3) his irresponsibility. Bill cited examples of failures to perform specific tasks and of tardiness. He told Calonico that he would be dismissed after one month if he did not improve his productivity, show a greater sense of responsibility and a more positive attitude, and get to work on time. Bill also told Calonico to provide a daily report on tasks completed, progress in ongoing tasks, and problems being met in completing tasks.

After Calonico read the letter he threw it at Bill and made abusive comments to the effect that the letter was "ridiculous," "stupid," and "a lot of nonsense." Calonico accused Bill of incompetence. Calonico also refused to sign the letter (which would be a formal acknowledgment that he had received it). Calonico then went off to complain to the personnel manager. The next day Bill took Calonico into the department manager's office, where Calonico repeated his criticisms, accused Bill of being incompetent and of having failed to provide enough direction in the section, and attempted to refute each item in the letter. Davidson replied that he believed everything in the letter. When Calonico continued to refuse to sign it, Davidson signed the letter himself, to formally witness that refusal. Davidson also told Calonico that he had the right to file a reply to the probationary letter.

Bill now felt that Calonico "would have to toe the line" or get out. Bill's experience was that employees at Dandy Electronics couldn't challenge their bosses and get away with it. As with many companies in the electronics industry, Dandy Electronics experienced periodic sales downturns—sometimes due to poor product or market decisions—that resulted in periodic layoffs. Bill felt the company kept an eye out for "troublemakers" and that layoff times were used as occasions to get rid of them. He felt that Calonico would now be scared of losing his job. Bill felt rather sorry for Calonico.

Later that week the personnel manager called in Bill to talk about Calonico's probation, and reviewed in detail the probationary letter. The personnel manager then asked Bill to withdraw the probationary letter. Bill was upset and told the personnel manager that he was responsible to the company for the efficient and profitable operation of his section, and could not tolerate an ineffective and disrespectful employee. Bill refused to withdraw the letter, and the meeting ended. Bill felt that his stand was "adamant, but rational," and that he had to treat his subordinates "within the boundaries set by my own boss." Bill also felt he had persuaded the personnel manager of the correctness of his position. Since the Personnel Department did not have the formal authority to reverse Bill's position, he felt his decision would stand.

The following week Calonico again met with John Davidson to find out exactly how he was to remove his probationary status. When Davidson reviewed the situation with Bill, Bill told him that Calonico's work behavior had not improved and that the sooner he was fired, the sooner a replacement might be hired to deal with the backlog of work. Davidson told Bill that he agreed with this perspective. Later that day Davidson called Bill and Calonico together. Davidson said, "I believe that a personality conflict exists between you two and that it might well be impossible to resolve this conflict. Maybe you fellows can never work together." Davidson then presented the following options and told Calonico to select one of them:

1. stay in his present job, improve his performance, and show the proper respect toward Bill Kadota.
2. write a formal rebuttal letter to Bill's formal charges, which Davidson would then evaluate.
3. find a job in another department.
4. resign.
5. accept a transfer into another section within Davidson's department and, in order to remove his probationary status, show that he could perform effectively in that section.

Calonico chose the fifth alternative.

A few days later—three months into his supervisory job—Bill Kadota expressed some feelings while he shared a few beers at a local bar. "I'm pleased that Calonico is gone from the section. The problem seems finally over. But I'm uneasy about the way things have gone. So much seemed to go wrong along the way. Things have been pretty unpleasant. There's a lot of pressure, and I don't seem to get much cooperation. You know, Dandy seems a cruel place sometimes. It's tough to manage. Why won't people just get on with their work, do what they're paid to do?"

PART IV: CASE 3

A Student Dilemma: Unethical Practices or Competitive Advantage?

Howard D. Feldman and Morton Cotlar

Professor Simon looked out his office window and watched a group of students coming into the business school. He thought about what had happened during the last few weeks and wondered what had gone wrong. What made his students do what they had done? What should he do? Should he fail the students, have them suspended, slap them on the wrist and ask them not to do it again, or choose another course of action?

The First Class Meeting

Professor Simon had welcomed 37 students into his senior business policy class. The course was a mixture of cases, lectures, and a business simulation game—*Corporate Planning*—that he had not played before. Much of the first class meeting was spent discussing the simulation game and how Simon would evaluate student performance (see Appendix A). To get their attention, Simon told the students of a classroom incident that took place several years past. At the end of the semester, one group revealed that they had taken a competing team member out for drinks, hoping to obtain information regarding her company's strategies and decisions. As Simon had expected, the story caught the students' interest but it didn't stimulate the discussion for which he hoped. They had laughed, but that was all.

One of Simon's last comments that day was, "students could use anything to help their decision making process in order to play the game." Now he wondered whether he should have explicitly cautioned, "anything legal and ethical." It certainly had not crossed his mind that his statements *could* be interpreted any other way. Had be been negligent? Had his comments encouraged the very student actions that he was now being asked to judge?

The Incident

The game had been running smoothly until the Friday of week eight. That morning, three students from ExecuCorp had come in to see him. Joe Cannon started: "I was working at the Engineering School last night and overheard two students talking about a business game. One was describing how he and his roommate had 'broken into' a disk. I approached him and asked a few questions about what they had done. I realized that he was talking about our game, but the only thing I could think of was that some of my classmates were cheating! At that point, I just 'lost it' and pinned him against the wall. Suffice to say, he didn't get out of that room until I got a lot more information. It turned out that

his roommate, who he identified, is in our class. The two of them had searched through the game disk and extracted passwords for two of the teams in the game, including ours. What ticked me off most was that this guy was bragging that it had been easy to get into the disk, that they could manipulate the game, and they could change the decisions made by other teams without their knowledge. Can they do that? Has our performance been affected by what they did?"

Obtaining another team's password was a serious matter, if true. The disk was copyrighted and each team had a secret password that allowed them to access only their files. Although each disk contained the data for every team in the game, passwords were supposed to provide security against unauthorized access by other individuals. In addition, the game had a feature which allowed the administrator to detect any tampered files. If a team had broken the code and obtained information that could help them, this was a serious problem. Each team's grade was affected by their relative performance to the first place team, and Joe's team was in last place. Were they there because another team was manipulating the game?

Joe continued, "after I left the Engineering School, I got together with the rest of my group to talk about what I had heard and to decide what to do. We thought we should first come talk to you. And by coincidence, on our way over here we ran into two members of the other group. We told them we were coming to see you and why. They denied it at first, but finally admitted they had seen our spreadsheets. I guess they started to panic, because they offered to share their information with us. Can you believe it? They also asked if their CEO could talk to us before we came up here, but we said no."

It was obvious that the group was upset, but they refused to provide any names, preferring to see if the other group would first "confess" to their "crime." After the students left his office, Professor Simon went downstairs to talk to the Undergraduate Dean and alert him to the situation. What were his options if the story proved to be true? The Dean suggested he wait a week for the students to come in of their own volition. If they didn't, they would deal with the situation then.

Source: Howard D. Feldman and Morton Cotlar, "A Student Dilemma: Unethical Practices or Competitive Advantage?" From *Case Research Journal*, Spring 1990, pp. 17–34. Copyright ©1990. Reprinted by permission.

Meeting the Accused

The following Monday, Sally Mason and Debby Hofberg, members of the first place team, came in to Professor Simon's office. It was their team that had been involved in the alleged cheating scandal. Craig Miner, their team CEO, would see him that afternoon and Laura Thompson, the fourth team member, had not been involved, so Sally and Debby decided to come without her. The women confirmed all of Joe's allegations; Craig and his roommate had obtained the passwords of two teams and printed their financial spreadsheets. Sally and Debby had tried to use the information but it was virtually useless; it was historical data only. The women hadn't questioned how and from where Craig had gotten this information and they wanted Simon to know their only involvement was using what they were given. No data was tampered with, no decisions were changed, and they had no idea why Craig's roommate had said such things. In their minds, this wasn't cheating. Maybe they had made a mistake, but they hadn't cheated.

Professor Simon's attempts to calm them were only partially successful. Nothing definite could be said because the dean had the final say, or so Simon believed. Was this incident serious enough to expel or flunk students, particularly students scheduled to graduate in a few short weeks? Simon didn't think so, but since an engineering student was involved, that complicated matters. An engineering student helped break into the disk, and his school was known to take a hard-line stance in dealing with "cheaters." What message would be sent to students if the consequences chosen by the Business School were less severe (or more severe) than those of the Engineering School? No matter how hard one tried to keep this type of affair private, it was bound to come out sooner or later. And what would be communicated to students, faculty, and administrators about the school's tolerance of cheating? Or were the students right—was this merely an act of competitive intelligence gathering similar to what they read about all-too-frequently in the business press?

Later that afternoon, Craig talked with Professor Simon. Craig didn't believe he had done something wrong. The focus was on winning the game, and this was just one way to help ensure reaching his team's goal. In fact, Sally and Debbie had said the same thing earlier that morning. They felt remorse that their actions might have affected other students' grades, but the ethics, not to mention the legality of "breaking into" the password file was ignored as an issue.

Professor Simon asked the group to meet with the instructor of the Business and Society classes. Perhaps their situation could be put to use as a learning experience in ethics. Furthermore, he asked that each member of the group describe their involvement in the incident, along with the thoughts, emotions, motivations, etc. they had experienced to this point. (See Appendices B, C, D, and E for student papers). Professor Simon wanted time—to think, and to talk with those people whose counsel he respected.

The Recommendations of the Deans

During the next few days, Professor Simon spoke to several faculty members and administrators whose opinion he respected. The dean and associate dean thought that expulsion was too harsh, but a failing grade could easily be justified for Craig. After all, he had broken into the password file. They weren't quite so sure about the others. They thought Debby and Sally should at least fail some portion of the game (see Appendix A for the grade allocations). They suggested giving Laura a strongly worded warning since it appeared she was only marginally involved, if at all.

The deans also suggested the possibility that the matter be taken out of Professor Simon's hands by convening the Academic Ethics Committee. This required Simon ask the committee to hear a case of "alleged" academic dishonesty. The committee consisted of three faculty members and three students and their mission was to ensure students accused of academic misconduct received a fair hearing. They could recommend anything from a polite hand slap to a failing grade plus suspension or expulsion.

Other Recommendations

A variety of alternatives were recommended, including: failing all four students; having them apologize publicly to their class and explain their actions; having them lead a discussion on ethics in the Business and Society classes; letting the incident die a slow death without any further action; and finally, rewarding them for their resourcefulness. One faculty member from another school suggested that any consequences chosen should be based on "what was learned" (see Appendix F). Another colleague gave Simon the state statute defining computer crime, along with a segment from a textbook discussing data theft (see Appendix G) and suggested "the punishment should fit the crime."

Several faculty played the devil's advocate—how does this differ from students who use test files; wouldn't most students do the same if given the chance? Didn't you encourage this behavior by your statements at the beginning of the semester? Misconstrued or not, didn't you have some responsibility at the beginning of the semester to immediately and publicly condemn any type of unethical or illegal behavior that might take place? A few students even suggested, "didn't you give them carte blanche to do this by not stating specifically on your syllabus—NO CHEATING ALLOWED?"

Complications

On Wednesday morning, Joe Cannon talked to Professor Simon. He was terribly upset, worried about what might happen to the members of Craig's team. He was a good friend of several of them and was feeling guilty. Had he overreacted? Should he and his team have gone to Craig's group first and tried to work it out among themselves rather than going to Professor Simon? Joe offered to be a "character witness," attesting to his friends' good qualities. The idea of being a "whistleblower" was not sitting well with him, but it was too late to change.

After Joe left, Professor Simon leaned back in his office chair and loosened his necktie. The students had done everything he had asked of them—they had met with him as well as the faculty member teaching the business ethics course, and they had submitted their write-ups (Appendices B–E). Now he had to make some decisions.

Appendix A

*Corporate Planning Simulation Game**

Each student will be given an opportunity to run their own company during the course of this game. Some of the companies will be in very high growth industries, and some may be in declining industries. Even though each of you will have your own company, you will also be part of a team. In other words, each team will operate a portfolio of companies.

Each quarter you will receive a newsletter which will tell you about the conditions and events in each of 12 different industries in which you can compete. In addition, you will be able to examine the profit and sales performance of all companies in each industry.

Every team will start with the same portfolio of businesses and the same amount of cash. The winner will be the team that increases its portfolio worth the most over the length of the simulation. You'll know exactly where you stand each quarter, and your mark in this simulation will be directly reflected as part of your grade in this course.

The portfolio rank is only one measure of team performance. Other measures such as total profits, total asset value and performance consistency will be used to create a more

---

*Partial syllabus plus excerpted text of an electronic mail message given to students at the beginning of the semester to inform them of the game and the evaluation criteria to be used. Adapted from the actual simulation game manual.

complete measure of each team's performance. A team's performance will also be measured in more qualitative ways. For example, each team must submit a strategic plan at the beginning of the game and a summary report at the end. Periodic reports summarizing performance and describing future plans can be included to enhance the final report as can anything else that you have done during this semester to help you better manage your firm.

Simulation Grading (35% of the final grade)

Students will be evaluated on 3 components:

1. Team performance (15%)—Based on a team's final ranking and average portfolio standing.
2. Individual Performance (10%)—Based on peer evaluations by team members and as measured by certain individual performance tracking charts.
3. Team's final written report and presentation (10%). The final report includes your written analyses of the industries in which you operated, an evaluation of your team's performance, any charts, graphs, etc., that illustrate your points, an analysis of your industry environments, market shares, recommendations on how your businesses should have been managed, etc. In addition, a preliminary report is due in the second week of the game highlighting your team's proposed strategy for competing, your mission, goals and objectives and the operating policies which your firm adopts. Explain how things changed (if they did) from your initial strategy. What did you learn that made you change? The presentation should be a short (20–30 minute) summary of the final paper.

Appendix B

Craig Miner, CEO

How It Started

My motivation to obtain extra information started at the beginning of the semester. In the very first class, Professor Simon discussed the computer strategy game, trying to get the class excited for the upcoming challenge. I thought this game would be a great learning experience, so I chose to be a CEO and was looking forward to getting started. At the end of Simon's discussion, he gave an example of the kind of behavior seen in the past—how some students get "into" the game. He described how one team got a competitor drunk and convinced her to talk about her team's decisions and strategies. I began to think that perhaps it was okay to date each other to get inside information. The game sounded like it would be full of real-life situations, testing the skills gained during four years in the business school. I thought this would be a great way to apply what I had learned about running a company as well as using my imagination to make good creative decisions.

Obtaining the Passwords

After a couple of weeks, I was approached by students from several other teams who came up to me and jokingly asked for my team's password. Playing along, I gave them an "idea" of what it might be. I thought to myself, "I wonder what you could do if you had another team's password" and remembered that Professor Simon had once asked me to loan my disk to another team. That team was having disk problems and needed our disk to copy their company results. Obviously, our disk contained files belonging to other teams. With that realization, I decided to test my theory. After some trial and error, my roommate and I opened a file containing all of the passwords used in the game. Although encoded, we eventually were able to figure out the passwords for two other teams. Once we had those it was easy to print out each company's data, but it wasn't worth the effort. All I was able to obtain was historical information, and we already had plenty of that.

The Balloon Is Burst

One week later, at our next group meeting, trouble started when Sally and Debby came to the meeting in a frenzy. They had been confronted by several members of another team, ExecuCorp, and accused of cheating. Larry Bell, their CEO and Joe Cannon, another team member, wanted to talk to me as soon as possible. I thought I could straighten them out and stop the accusations. Then I could talk to Professor Simon about what I had done, instead of what I was accused of doing.

On Sunday night, Debby called me after a study session with Joe Cannon. She told me that ExecuCorp's group members had already gone to Professor Simon and that he had been very upset about what had happened. Supposedly, Simon had already gone to the dean. After I heard this, I was really upset. The situation was getting blown out of proportion and no one even knew the facts. This was the start of a two-and-a-half day headache that consumed my every waking moment.

Meeting with Simon

I talked with Professor Simon the next day. The meeting went well but he wanted to talk to the dean before making

any hasty decisions. Monday night was miserable, no sleep and virtually nothing accomplished for Tuesday, which included an exam in Professor Simon's class. The next morning was a little better, but I still felt lousy. The test went poorly. When it was over, Professor Simon talked with our group and asked us to meet Professor Gary Hunter, who taught the Business and Society classes. After our talk with Simon, life seemed to slow down and I was finally able to get a good night's sleep. Our talk with Dr. Hunter also went well, because we were able to talk openly about ethics. He knew how difficult it is to distinguish the fine line that separates an ethical from an unethical act.

Craig's Final Thoughts

I had planned on telling the class what I had done during our final presentation, but we obviously didn't make it to that point. Instead, my plans blew up in my face. It was especially frustrating to get into trouble for doing something that was of no benefit to us in the first place, but I have learned something from this experience. I learned that although difficult, even in a game one must look at the consequences before one acts. I didn't think that what I was doing was cheating. Perhaps I should have consulted Professor Simon right after I got the other teams' passwords— maybe all of this trouble could have been avoided.

Appendix C

Sally Mason

Sally's Involvement

I was glad the week was almost over, tired of getting up early but being late to school, and excited about making decisions for the next quarter of our business simulation game. Our team had been in first place since the beginning of the game so our decisions were requiring more analysis, and taking longer to make.

Knowing how important my decisions were, I came to our weekly meeting well-prepared with my analyses and initial decisions. As I sat down to enter my decisions on Craig's disk, he handed me another team's spreadsheet. Being somewhat naive, I looked at it and saw how it differed from mine. Craig and I discussed the differences but my analyses of the industry reports, historical performances, and the game's newsletter had already accounted for these. I wondered how Craig had gotten another team's spreadsheet, but since my decisions had already been made, I didn't give it too much thought. When our meeting was over, we all went our merry way, not realizing that weeks of hard work may have been tossed out the window by our momentary lack of foresight.

One week later, Debby met me after one of my classes. She was on the verge of tears. She had been confronted by a furious Joe Cannon who told her that we had cheated. He had written "Die Craig" all over his notebook! I suspect that I would have been just as upset if I were told that the team in first place had manipulated the game to favor one group over another.

Reality Sets In

Debby was shocked and so was I. Both of us had wondered how Craig had gotten the spreadsheets. Perhaps it had been through some illicit or unethical action. But, for whatever reason, neither of us had done anything about it during the past week. Now we were in a predicament. We decided to talk to Craig to get the facts straight, but just as we were leaving, we were confronted by several members of the ExecuCorp team. We were accused of cheating and being part of a conspiracy to destroy everybody else's grade in the game. It was definitely time to speak to Craig.

Craig's Response

Talking to Craig helped a little. His motivation, or so I gathered, was to see if another team's information could help our poorly performing businesses. As far as making the game favor one team over another, Craig said he wouldn't do that because all the challenge of winning would be gone, plus, it might not allow other teams the opportunity of learning how to formulate a winning strategy. I was somewhat relieved to find out the game had not been tampered with, but I knew we had a major problem on our hands.

The Pressure Builds

I wasn't able to go to class or sit still for the rest of the day. I went home and discussed the situation with my mother and my father. Once they realized I understood the consequences of my actions, they assured me they would support me and fight any battle that arose to keep me enrolled in school. That helped but the weekend was miserable. I was stressed-out, trying to prepare for two tests, a major case project and paper, two job interviews, and thinking about this mess.

Monday finally arrived and Debby and I decided we had to see Professor Simon. I think both Debby and I were stunned at the seriousness with which he was treating this problem. As I sat there listening to him identify the range of possible consequences, all I could think about was: here were four bright, trusted, and respected students whose promising futures were about to be thrown down the drain because of a very unfortunate mistake. He asked us to come back as a group in two days. More waiting. More anxiety.

What Went Wrong?

During this time I thought about what happened. Obviously I had not approached this game with the seriousness which it required. I wanted to learn how the game worked and how various factors affected the success of different industries. I didn't care if my team won or lost, just so long as I learned how to run a couple of businesses, in addition to obtaining some insights into the operation of a multi-business corporation. I also didn't keep my facts straight. The syllabus stated that 15% of everybody's final grade depended on their team's performance in the game. However, I thought this meant that final grades wouldn't be based on a team's performance, but rather on the presentation of their strategy. And I didn't think about the consequences of my actions until it was too late. Regardless of the others, I made a very stupid, unthinkable mistake. I never realized that what I had done could be construed by others as using "insider information" and could hurt another classmate's grade. Finally, I can't say I'm completely sorry this happened because the next time I'm faced with a situation like this one, I will think twice about my actions.

Appendix D

Laura Thompson

The "Scandal" Breaks

I have so many mixed feelings about the "scandal" in the *Corporate Planning* game that I hardly know where to begin. My perspective is somewhat different from that of my colleagues since I didn't know what was going on. Of course, not knowing kept me out of trouble, but the "guilt by association," made it just as difficult.

The first I heard of our "dishonor," I was at our weekly team meeting. Craig and I were the only ones there when Sally and Debby arrived screaming, "We're dead!" They were extremely upset . . . I was confused! I'm sure you've heard the story already, but one thing you may not have known was that Craig and his roommate Bill, a "computer whiz" from the Engineering School, had spent 48 hours to get the two passwords. They could have obtained the other ones as well, but apparently it would have taken so much time they decided to quit after the first two. I wasn't there when Craig handed out the spreadsheets—I came late—and when I asked about them, I didn't get an answer. I guess, technically, I knew that something was up, but I thought that perhaps Craig had glanced over someone's shoulder in the computing lab.

Craig's Response

At our next group meeting, I began to realize what a conflict differing ethics and morals can create. Craig felt he hadn't done anything wrong. His actions were simply a "strategy"—doing what it takes to win the game. "After all," he said, "in the business world, financial data is available to the public. The essence of doing business is figuring out how to interpret such figures and to predict competitors' future behavior." Unlike Craig, I thought if the information on the disk was supposed to be "publicly available," it would have been either supplied to us or there would be no need for secret passwords.

Laura's Final Thoughts

My lack of involvement kept me out of trouble. But what amazed me was my reaction to not knowing! I felt that I had been left out of my group! This is not to say I would have approved had I been included; on the contrary, I would have been greatly upset. But still, I had been left out and not given the choice to participate. Perhaps I might have said something at the outset that could have prevented us from getting into this mess.

I didn't need the other teams' spreadsheets; my company had captured the largest market share, the largest amount of sales, the highest profit, and had the highest investment base in the industry. I couldn't believe that our dominant position was jeopardized by doing something so stupid. Now, of course, our integrity is nonexistent. I know this has been a learning experience, but we are all frustrated and confused. I guess the best thing to do now is just move on and realize that this will not be the last time we will encounter a conflict of morals. I hope others can learn from our mistakes.

Appendix E

Debby Hofberg

I knew I was in trouble the minute a classmate told me our secret was out. He knew our group had inside information on some of the other teams in our class, including his. Yet I honestly had no idea what we had gotten ourselves into.

I Didn't Cheat

Many people—students, professors, and businesspeople—have asked about my motives. In all honesty, I really don't know. We had been in first place in the game's overall standings since the first quarter, so there was really no need to do what we did. I know that when the spreadsheets from the other two teams were handed to me, cheating didn't even cross my mind. If I had known that using the spreadsheets would be considered cheating, I would never have gotten involved.

Should You Be Punished for Doing Something That You Didn't Know Was Wrong When You Did It?

I have spoken to many people about this situation and some feel that we should be commended for our resourcefulness while others feel we should be severely punished. Although I agree what was accomplished was resourceful, how can I be punished for an act that I didn't understand was wrong when I was committing it? This is the hardest part to accept. When I used the spreadsheets I honestly didn't understand the full implications of my actions. If nothing else, I have learned from this experience, and will never allow it to happen again. Most students never learn what I have in the past five weeks. And they should because they could easily have a problem like mine. For example, test files are used by lots of students, but how many actually check to see if the file has been approved by a professor? And what about students who do a group project and obtain information and/or help from someone who's taken the course before and did the same project? I'm not implying that these actions are cheating, I'm simply trying to show that no student questions situations such as these. I did the same thing, I never questioned what I was doing nor why.

Can't We Be Taught to Think?

Children are taught not to question or think, just to read and acknowledge. My senior year of college is the first time I've been taught to think critically, to read between the lines, and to realize that books can't always provide an answer to the questions we face. In the business world, adults are faced with ethical and value-based questions daily. Where do they go for answers? They can refer to the legal system. Most students refer to their childhood and adolescent experiences for help. However, many of the earliest decisions with which children are confronted are made for them by family members or other adults. There is little opportunity to learn about borderline ethical questions. In order to do that, I feel we must look to the academic system. Instead of teaching facts, professors should teach the art of learning through questioning. It's as simple as that.

Please don't misunderstand, I am not blaming my situation on the academic system, I am simply trying to turn what I have experienced into a positive learning situation for other students facing similar circumstances. Hopefully, whether or not students feel they have done something wrong, they can at least refer back to my dilemma and maybe it will allow them to avoid some of the things that I am currently going through.

Appendix F*

Dear Professor Simon,

I've thought about the decision you face and I must admit I don't envy you. While I don't have any answers, perhaps the following suggestions might help a bit.

I hesitate to call it "cheating" for a variety of reasons. According to your message to me, you had told students at the outset that they could use "anything" to help their decision making in order to win the game. "Industrial espionage" is a concept that may be more appropriate to a simulation, while "cheating" is a term more appropriate to a "game." Also, cultural differences are often so subtle that what is obviously wrong to some people may be entirely acceptable to others.

It seems to me that getting the issue into the proper perspective is very important. You are confronting a situation within an institution of higher education. The emphasis should be placed on learning, rather than on rewards and punishment. The issues of responsibilities, clearly stated policies, and means-end relationships, should be in focus. The management concepts of participation, consensus and mutual support are also involved. The importance of grade and grade point average ought not to transcend the importance of relationships with others and learning from structured experiences. Competitive spirit is critical, but acceptable behavior is far more important.

I teach "situational ethics," and I think you have a great opportunity to focus on what has happened as a concrete way of exposing some hard ethical issues. I plan to use your incident as a discussion topic when our spring break is over, because it is one to which everyone will relate, enough to make the points relevant. That is ordinarily hard to achieve.

One key issue is the fact that you told students "anything goes" in the simulation of the real world. Even if you didn't mean what you said, the communication process with all of its real problems is another issue worth discussion. The responsibility for communication should rest primarily with the communicator, but responsibility for questioning vague elements lies with the students.

Still another important issue deals with the benefits and detriments to the various people involved. There might have been no expectation of direct harm to competitors (other than their compromised privacy). Also, there is the potential for you saving competitors from harm, by provid-

*A computer-mail message sent by a tenured faculty member at another university in response to Professor Simon's request was initiated by Professor Simon because the game was being played via telecommunications in conjunction with students in Professor Dean's business classes, and any action taken would also affect his class.

ing a bonus grade to those who operated within accepted standards of behavior.

Perhaps peripheral to the central issue is the responsibility for avoiding attractive temptations. The simulation is structured so that everyone has competitors' data literally in their hands, protected from view by only a few keystrokes. I think this is a major flaw in the physical and logical structure of this game. It deserves a special caution to all users at the outset of the simulation, and in the absence of that caveat, one may be perceived as Adam in the presence of a luscious apple.

I think you might now convince everyone that accessing other organizations' books is not acceptable behavior in our current society. I think you could penalize the "offenders" for not asking specifically what "anything goes" meant, but if you do penalize them for that, I think you might also reward them for their resourcefulness (which often "pays" in the real world), as well as others (who may have been harmed) with a bonus for conforming to generally accepted behavior. I think (based on my limited awareness of the particulars) that expulsion or course failure would be disproportionate and harsh treatment. The ultimate question might be, "was anything important learned" and by how many, as a result of the entire situation (including all of the subsequent discussion). The parallel issue of what benefit might come from any penalty is also well worth consideration. Thanks for the opportunity to ponder your "problem." I'll put it to good use.

Sincerely,

Paul Dean
Professor of Management

Appendix G

Computer Crime and Data Theft

Computer Crime (1) Any person who knowingly uses any computer, computer system, computer network, or any part thereof for the purpose of devising or executing any scheme or artifice to defraud; obtaining money, property, or services by means of false or fraudulent pretenses, representations, or promises; using the property or services of another without authorization; or committing theft commits computer crime. (2) Any person who knowingly and without authorization uses, alters, damages, or destroys any computer, computer system, or computer network . . . or any computer software, program, documentation, or data contained in such computer, computer system, or computer network commits computer crime.[1]

[1] State Revised Statute, 1987. in Professor Dean's business classes, and any action taken would also affect his class.

PART IV: CASE 3 Continued

Data Theft. Theft of important data is a serious problem in business today. In many highly competitive industries, both quantitative and qualitative information about one's competitors are constantly being sought. . . . The courts have long upheld that data stored in a company's computer is private and cannot be used without the company's permission. In California, data theft can lead to conviction of violating a trade secret, punishable by a ten year prison sentence. Trade secret laws are not unique to California. In one very important case, the Encyclopedia Britannica Company accused the computer operators on its night shift of copying nearly three million names from the computer file containing the company's most valued customer list. Employees were accused of selling the list to a direct mail advertiser. Encyclopedia Britannica claimed that the list was worth three million dollars. In another case, a California man was accused of dialing his competitor's number, bypassing the computer security system and copying information as needed. There are many other cases on record of an individual dialing into a company's computer and accessing privileged information.[2]

---

[2] From *Accounting Information Systems* 3rd ed. by George Bodnar and William Hopwood, Allyn and Bacon, Inc.: Boston, MA, 1987, p. 680.

ETHICS QUESTIONAIRE

Gene E. Burton

Purpose

To help students gain a better appreciation for the complexity of differentiating between ethical and unethical behavior.

Time Required

45 minutes
  Step 1: Individual activity (15 minutes)
  Step 2: Small-group activity (20 minutes)
  Step 3: Class discussion (10 minutes)

Materials Needed

None.

Procedure

Step 1: Each student should complete and score The Ethics Questionnaire.

Step 2: Each group of six should compute its average scores and develop group responses to the discussion questions.

Step 3: A representative from each group will present the group's findings for class discussion.

_____

Source: Gene E. Burton, *Exercises in Management,* Third Edition, pp. 285–288. Copyright ©1990 by Houghton Mifflin Company. Used with permission.

THE ETHICS QUESTIONNAIRE

STATEMENT	STRONGLY AGREE	SLIGHTLY AGREE	NOT SURE	SLIGHTLY DISAGREE	STRONGLY DISAGREE
1. It's OK for management to pay for lavish entertainment to land a big contract.	1	2	3	4	5
2. It's OK for a worker to falsify his/her time card when late to work.	1	2	3	4	5
3. A manager should not use a company car for personal use.	5	4	3	2	1
4. A worker should not call in sick to get an extra day off.	5	4	3	2	1
5. For management, the goal-achievement end usually justifies the means used.	1	2	3	4	5
6. A worker may use the office copier to copy personal documents.	1	2	3	4	5
7. It is wrong for management to give gifts/favors in exchange for favors that help the firm.	5	4	3	2	1
8. A worker should not conduct personal business on company time.	5	4	3	2	1
9. A manager may exaggerate a bit on quality or delivery date, if it means getting a big order.	1	2	3	4	5
10. It's acceptable to pad an expense report up to about 10%.	1	2	3	4	5
11. Management should be allowed to conceal minor product deficiencies from the public.	1	2	3	4	5

12. Employees should not take pencils, tools, etc. home for personal use.	5	4	3	2	1
13. Managers should not set unreasonable goals to push for better worker performance.	5	4	3	2	1
14. It's acceptable for a worker to work slower than he/she is capable of working.	1	2	3	4	5
15. A manager may tell a worker to violate rules to help the firm meet a shipping date.	1	2	3	4	5
16. There's no problem if an employee takes extra time for lunch or break time.	1	2	3	4	5
17. A manager should not violate a safety rule even if it means losing a big order.	5	4	3	2	1
18. WATS lines should never be used by employees for personal long-distance telephone calls.	5	4	3	2	1
19. Management should not divulge confidential information about an employee.	5	4	3	2	1
20. An employee should not accept gifts from salespersons in exchange for preferential treatment.	5	4	3	2	1

THE ETHICS QUESTIONNAIRE SCORING SHEET

Transfer your numeric responses from the questionnaire onto this scoring sheet and sum the items to find your scores. Place an X on each of the continuums to indicate your scores.

MANAGERIAL ETHIC		EMPLOYEE ETHICS	
QUESTION NO.	SCORE	QUESTION NO.	SCORE
1	_____	2	_____
3	_____	4	_____
5	_____	6	_____
7	_____	8	_____
9	_____	10	_____
11	_____	12	_____
13	_____	14	_____
15	_____	16	_____
17	_____	18	_____
19	_____	20	_____
Total:	_____	Total:	_____

Grand Total: _____

(*continued*)

PART IV: EXPERIENCE 1 Continued

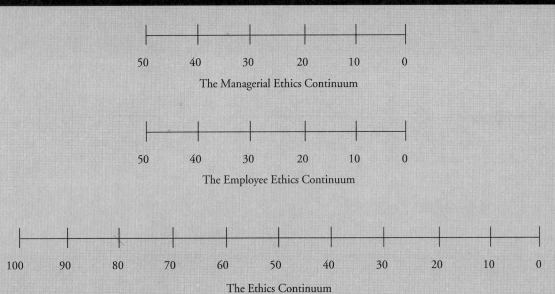

The Managerial Ethics Continuum

The Employee Ethics Continuum

The Ethics Continuum

Questions for Discussion

1. Was there greater agreement on Managerial Ethics Scores or on Employee Ethics Scores? Why?

2. What might account for differences of opinions on the definition of ethical behavior?

3. How can the results of this questionnaire be put to constructive use?

1. 4
3. 5
5. 3
7. 4
9. 5
11. 3
13. 4
15. 4
17. 4
19. 5

45

2. 5
4. 5
6. 5
8. 5
10. 2
12. 5
14. 4
16. 5
18. 5
20. 5

46

PART IV: EXPERIENCE 2

AFFIRMATIONS: POSITIVE SELF-TALK

Marian K. Prokop

Purpose

To understand the nature and purpose of affirmation.
To offer members of a group the opportunity to practice developing and using affirmations.

Time Required

Approximately one hour.

Group Size

The class should be divided into groups of six.

Materials

1. One copy of the Affirmations Action Plan for each participant.
2. A newsprint sheet or chalkboard prepared in advance with the following affirmation guidelines:
   Effective affirmations:
   ■ Begin with "I, (name);"
   ■ Use the present tense;
   ■ Use positive verbs;
   ■ Are phrased as if the desired results were already present.
3. Several sheets of newsprint or adequate chalkboard space.

Procedure

1. The instructor and students read and discuss the following:
   "An affirmation is a positive thought that you deliberately choose to put into your consciousness. You might know affirmations as positive thinking or positive self-talk. An affirmation works in the following way; what you believe influences your emotions, which influence your actions, which then affect your life. Negative thoughts and beliefs lead to negative results; positive thoughts and beliefs lead to positive results.
   Affirmations are reminders to yourselves that although we may not have control over the people, situations, and events in our lives, we do have control over our relations to such things. We can choose our attitudes, our actions, and how we choose to think about stressors in our lives."

2. The instructor posts the newsprint sheet (or writes on the chalkboard) affirmations guidelines and reviews the guidelines with the participants.
3. The participants choose partners for the next part of the activity. Each participant should have a copy of the Affirmations Action Plan, several sheets of blank paper, a pencil, and a clipboard or other portable writing surface. The facilitator reviews the instructions with the participants and answers questions as needed. The participants are asked to work with their partners to complete an individual action plan and to reproduce the action plan on a sheet of newsprint or on the chalkboard. (Twenty minutes).
4. The facilitator calls time, reconvenes the total group, and asks participants to take turns presenting their action plans to the class. Each action plan is posted or written on the chalkboard so that it is visible to all participants. (Fifteen minutes).
5. The facilitator leads a discussion of the action plans based on the following questions:
   a. What are you thinking or feeling about affirmations now?
   b. What themes do the action plans have in common? How do they differ?
   c. What have you learned about affirmations? What generalizations can you make about affirmations?
   d. How can you use affirmations to improve or maintain your academic or work performance?
   e. In what ways can you use affirmations in situations outside of school or work? (Fifteen minutes).

Affirmations Action Plan

1. Discuss the following sentence stem with your partner and complete the sentence with a phrase acceptable to both you and your partner:
   I feel stressed when _____.

Source: Marian K. Prokop, "Affirmations: Positive Self-Talk," *1991 Annual: Developing Human Resources,* San Diego, CA: Pfeiffer & Company. Copyright 1991. Reprinted by permission.

PART IV: EXPERIENCE 2 Continued

2. Rephrase that sentence as an affirmative goal statement. For example, if your sentence reads "I feel stressed when I do not have the resources I need to complete my job tasks effectively," you might rephrase that as a goal as follows: "I ask for the resources I need in order to complete my job tasks effectively." Remember to phrase your goal in the first person as if it were already accomplished.
Goal Statement:_____.

3. Write at least ten positive results that will come from achieving this goal:
   a. _____
   b. _____
   c. _____
   d. _____
   e. _____
   f. _____
   g. _____
   h. _____
   i. _____
   j. _____

4. Use your affirmation to write action steps that you personally can take. For example, for the sample goal listed previously, an action step would be, "I make a list of the resources I need to do my job effectively." Write as many action steps as you need to achieve your goal.
   a. _____
   b. _____
   c. _____
   d. _____
   e. _____

5. Write the following statement at the end of your action steps:
   "I am willing to take the action steps needed to accomplish my goals and I release myself from responsibility for circumstances that I cannot control."

6. Copy your action plan onto a newsprint sheet or chalkboard. When the facilitator calls time, present your action plan to the rest of the class.

For Further Reading

Ellis, A., and Harper, R. *A New Guide to Rational Living.* CA: Wilshire Book Company, 1961.

Seligman, M. *Learned Optimism.* NY: Knopf, 1991.

HOLD THE HAMBURGER: A FIELD EXPLORATION OF JOB DESIGN AND ORGANIZATIONAL CULTURE

Barry Allen Gold

Purpose

The purpose of this exercise is to analyze the design of service jobs and explore how organizational culture works. It is a field experiment using as the experimental subjects employees of a fast-food restaurant. For casual research projects fast-food outlets are excellent research sites because their architecture usually has minimal separation between the frontstage and backstage areas of the organization. This permits customers—for our purposes, the researcher—to observe employees who have direct contact with the public as well as production workers and managers.

Time Required

This field experiment requires approximately one hour outside class for each student. Class discussion time is 30 minutes.

Materials Needed

A fast food restaurant.
Enough money to purchase a hamburger.

Introduction

Organizations differ in the degree to which they permit workers to exercise discretion in their work. For example, some organizations design jobs with detailed rules that are to be followed without deviation. Other organizations provide workers with policy statements and allow them to design their own work procedures as long as organizational goals are met. Organizational culture often influences job design and the extent to which the organization attempts to control its employees and customers.

Procedure

Step 1: Locate a fast-food restaurant (for example, McDonald's, Roy Rogers, or Hardee's).
Step 2: Order a hamburger with cheese and ask the order taker to "hold" everything except the bun and the cheese (be certain to insist that the hamburger be "held").
Step 3: Observe the behavior of the order taker and other personnel as they respond to your request.
Step 4: If you encounter questions from the order taker insist that you *do not* want the hamburger in your order (if necessary negotiate with the order taker).
Step 5: Purchase the product that results from your order.
Step 6: Using the Fieldwork Observation Form below record as accurately as possible the behavior of the order taker and any other employees involved with your order.

Class Meeting

Each student should report the findings of their experiment to the class. The objective of these reports is to locate the range of behaviors observed in the restaurants. The class should then attempt to explain the observed variation according to job design, organizational culture, and other variables. The following questions should guide the discussion.

1. Overall, what does this field experiment suggest about the interaction of job design and organizational culture?
2. What are alternate ways of organizing and managing service sector jobs?
3. What are other ways of collecting data concerning job design and organizational culture?

Note: The results of this experiment vary depending on the location of the restaurant (urban, suburban, rural, shopping mall, highway, downtown, etc.), the time of day (lunch is different from 10 a.m.), and to some extent, if there is a supply of already prepared food in the warming bins. The instructor may want to have students conduct the experiment under varying conditions.

Fieldwork Observation Form

A. Researcher-Worker Interaction

1. What was the order taker's reaction to your request to hold everything but the bun and cheese?
   a. Did the order taker process it routinely? If not, what issues were raised?
   b. Did the order taker consult with a supervisor or colleague? What did they discuss?
   c. If the order taker refused your request or suggested that you order something on the menu, what reasons were offered?
2. Assuming your order was processed:
   a. How long did it take to receive the order compared with an order from the menu?
   b. Was there any observable change in the production process when the order was prepared?
   c. Was there an adjustment in the price to reflect the absence of major ingredients?

B. Job Design

1. Describe the key aspects of the jobs that you can observe (order taker, hamburger cook).
2. What elements do these jobs have in common?
3. What is the role of machines in the design of these jobs?

C. Organizational Culture

1. Describe the displayed aspects of the culture of the fast-food restaurant.
2. Are there any artifacts that shape the culture for employees (employee of the month plaques, uniforms, etc.)?

3. How does the culture shape the worker's job and performance?
4. Overall, what energy level and enthusiasm did the workers display?

D. Performance

1. How did the job design characteristics and organizational culture affect your request to "hold" the hamburger?
2. How could the jobs you observed be redesigned?
3. Could the culture be changed to improve worker performance and customer satisfaction?

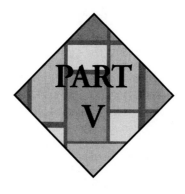

PART V

THE LARGER CONTEXT OF ORGANIZATIONAL BEHAVIOR

14

THE ENVIRONMENT

Transplanted Organizations:
The Transfer of Japanese Industrial
Organization to the U.S.

RICHARD FLORIDA AND MARTIN KENNEY

LEARNING OBJECTIVES

After reading "Transplanted Organizations: The Transfer of Japanese Industrial Organization to the U.S." by Florida and Kenney, a student will understand:

1. The theory that organizations are shaped by their environment

2. The perspective that organizations shape their environment

3. The impact of Japanese transplant organizations on internal organizational behavior and the U.S. environment

4. The implications of environmental and organizational forces for the shaping of individual and group work behaviors

Organization theory and industrial sociology suggest that organizations are closely tied to their environments. Both imply that it is difficult to transfer organizations from one environment to another and suggest that organizations that are transferred will gradually take on characteristics of the new environment. Japanese organizations are closely tied to their environment and thus may be particularly difficult to transfer.

We explore the cross-national transfer of organizational forms and practices and hypothesize that such forms and practices can be taken from their original environ-ments and implanted into new ones. We contend that certain types of organizations (e.g., large, resource-rich, powerful organizations) have sufficient resources to alter the new environment in light of their functional requirements. Therefore, we suggest that the organization/environment relation is reciprocal. We address these issues in light of the recent debate over new forms of production and work organization, production subcontracting, and interfirm production networks (Piore and Sabel 1984; Sabel 1989; Perrow 1990; Kenney and Florida 1988; Florida and Kenney 1990a, 1990b; Lazonick 1990; Womack, Jones, and Roos 1990).

Japanese automobile manufacturing plants in the United States, which we refer to as the "transplants," provide an ideal test of these hypotheses because they have been transferred from a supportive to a nonsupportive environment. The U.S. environment is typically characterized in terms of "diversity," "individualism," and unrestrained market forces, while Japan is characterized in terms of "homogeneity," "familism," "paternalism," and/or "welfare corporatism" (Dore 1973). The ideal-typical large U.S. industrial organization is distinguished by high levels of functional specialization, large numbers of job classifications, extensive internal labor markets (Edwards 1979), adversarial labor-management relations (Kochan, Katz, and McKersie 1986; Katz 1985) and "arm's length" rela-

Source: Richard Florida and Martin Kenny: "Transplanted Organizations: The Transfer of Japanese Industrial Organization to the U.S.," *American Sociological Review,* 1991, Vol. 56 (June: 381–398). Copyright ©1991. Reprinted by permission.

tions between corporations and their suppliers (Altshuler, Anderson, Jones, Roos, and Womack 1984; Womack et al. 1990), whereas the ideal-typical large Japanese manufacturing firm is characterized by small numbers of job classifications (Aoki 1988), team-based work organization (Koike 1988), consensual relations between labor and management (Shirai 1983), and long-term supplier relations (Dore 1983, 1986, 1987).[1]

We examine the transfer of Japanese intraorganizational practices, such as work and production organization, and interorganizational characteristics, such as just-in-time supplier relations, to the United States in light of three related research questions: (1) Are organizations derivative of the environments in which they are embedded, or can they be removed from an original environment and successfully implanted in a new one? (2) What strategies do organizations devise to adapt, respond, and/or cope with a new environment? (3) Do they take on charcteristics of the environment, or do they act on the new environment to bring it into line with their needs?

Theoretical Context

Organization theory suggests that organizations that are transferred from one environment to another will take on characteristics of the new environment. A few researchers would argue for a tight, deterministic connection between environment and organizations; most suggest that organizations gradually take on characteristics of the new environment and/or of organizations with which they interact (DiMaggio and Powell 1983; Meyer and Rowan 1977; Zucker 1977; Granovetter 1985; Hannan and Freeman 1977; McKelvey and Aldrich 1983).

A few theorists focus explicitly on organizational influences on the environment. In his classic studies of innovation in capitalism, Schumpeter (1947) differentiated between "creative" responses that alter social and economic situations and the more typical "adaptive" responses of firms and economic organizations. Pfeffer and Salancik (1978) suggested that while organizations tend to adapt to their environments, they will sometimes alter the environ-

ment in line with their needs. Weick (1979) argued that the ability of an organization to influence, construct or "enact" its environment is a function of size. Young (1988) suggested that organizations can change their environments by strategic use of resources.

The literature on Japanese development is generally pessimistic regarding the transfer of Japanese organization. It suggests that Japanese organizations derive from cultural factors such as homogeneity, familism, and group loyalty (Nakane 1970; Benedict 1946). For Abegglen (1958), Japanese organizational characteristics like team-based work organization and long-term tenure reflect a general close alignment between persons and groups. Dore (1973) contrasted the Japanese model of "welfare corporatism" and the Anglo-American model of "market individualism." Cole (1971) suggested that Japan's cultural legacy informs unique organizational solutions to general development problems. Recent research continues to be pessimistic about the transfer of Japanese organization (Cool and Legnick-Hall 1985).

Recent work (Shimada 1986; Shimada and MacDuffie 1986; Aoki 1988; Koike 1988) has concluded that Japanese work organization is a set of organizational forms that are relatively autonomous from culture and the environment. Several historical studies support this view. Taira (1961, 1964, 1970) documented the emergence of permanent employment from Japanese industrialists' need to cope with high rates of labor mobility and a desire to exert more efficient control over the labor force. Gordon (1985) indicated that team-based work organization is the product of postwar industrial unrest over worker control of production (also see Kenney and Florida 1988). Empirical research (Lincoln and Kalleberg 1985, 1990) supports the view that Japanese organization rather than culture is the source of work-force motivation, control, and commitment.

Currently, there is a general debate over the rise of alternative forms of industrial organization, including new forms of work and production organization (Kenney and Florida 1988; Florida and Kenney 1990a; Lazonick 1990; Best 1990; Morris-Suzuki 1988; Zuboff 1988), new mechanisms for generating work-force control and commitment (Lincoln and Kalleberg 1990), new supplier relations (Dore 1983; Sako 1989), interfirm networks and production subcontracting (Piore and Sabel 1984; Lazerson 1988; Perrow 1990; Florida and Kenney 1990b), and ways of organizing the division of labor inside and outside the firm (Richardson 1972; Williamson 19875, 1981, 1983; Robins 1987; Perrow 1981, 1986). A growing body of work argues that the key to the current transition lies in the emergence of new forms of organization at the point of production, such as work teams, task rotation,

---

[1] These are ideal-typical characterizations of large manufacturing firms, particularly automobile firms, in these countries, designed to focus attention on salient differences highlighted in the literature. In reality, there are significant differences among firms in each country and there may even be "mixed" forms.

the application of workers' intelligence in production, and the integration of innovation and production (Florida and Kenney 1990a; Womack et al. 1990; Lazonick 1990; Best 1990). Taking a different perspective, Piore and Sabel (1984) contend that "flexibly specialized" communities of small firms are supplanting the older model of "fordist" industrial mass production (Aglietta 1979); others suggest that flexible specialization may be a transitory phenomenon (Powell 1987) or even a misreading of current trends (Gertler 1988).

A number of studies explore the role of Japanese organizational forms in this more general process. The flexible specialization school views the Japanese model as part of the global convergence toward small-firm networks (Piore and Sabel 1984; Sabel 1989; Friedman 1988). However, detailed empirical studies of Japanese interorganizational relations suggest that it is a distinctive system centered around large companies (Sayer 1986; Sako 1989; Florida and Kenney 1990b). Others see the Japanese system as an advanced and efficient form of fordist mass production (Dohse, Jurgens, and Malsch 1986; Parker and Slaughter 1988). Still others see Japanese production organization as a unique model. According to Womack et al. (1990), Japanese organizational practices constitute a new form of "lean production" toward which firms all over the world are converging. Kenney and Florida (1988; forthcoming) see the Japanese model as a successor to fordism that uses new organizational forms to harness the intellectual as well as the physical capabilities of workers. Our research explores the "generalizability" of these new organizational forms.

The empirical evidence regarding the transfer of Japanese organization is mixed. Yoshino (1976) suggested that the absence of Japanese sociocultural conditions in other countries is a serious obstacle to transfer. Cole (1979) was guardedly optimistic: "There are those who would argue that they [quality control circles] have their basis in Japanese cultural and institutional conditions, with their unique group orientation, practice of permanent employment, and strong employee commitment to organizational goals. Consequently they are held not to be applicable to the United States. My own judgment is they may well be applicable if appropriate adaptations are made to accommodate the circles to U.S. conditions" (Cole 1979, p.255). White and Trevor (1983) concluded that Japanese organizational traits were not transferred to Japanese firms operating in the U.K. However, Oliver and Wilkinson (1989), Kumazawa and Yamada (1989), and Morris (1988) concluded that the Japanese management system has been successfully transferred to Japanese firms in the U.K. A study of Nissan in the U.K. (Crowther and Garrahan 1988) documented the emergence of a Japanese-style automobile production complex comprising a main assembly plant and supplier firms.

Research on the transfer of Japanese organization to the U.S. is less extensive and the findings are inconclusive. Case studies of the GM-Toyota joint venture automobile assembly plant, NUMMI, in Fremont, California (Krafcik 1986; Brown and Reich 1989) provide evidence of successful transfer of Japanese organization. Mair, Florida, and Kenney (1988) documented the emergence of a complex of Japanese automotive assemblers and suppliers in the midwestern United States. A University of Tokyo study (Institute of Social Science 1990) concluded that automotive plants have been the most successful in transferring Japanese practices, while consumer electronics firms have tended to adapt or conform to the U.S. environment and semiconductor firms occupy a middle position. Fucini and Fucini (1990) reported interviews with Mazda workers as evidence of adaptation problems, including high rates of injury, worker discontent, and labor-management conflict. Most of these studies suffer from very small sample sizes, reliance on case-specific data, and a narrow conceptual focus on managerial practices. Our research remedies such problems by providing a theoretically-informed empirical study of the transfer of intra- and interorganizational forms and practices to Japanese automotive transplants in the United States.

Research Design

"Transplants" are defined as firms that are either wholly Japanese-owned or have a significant level of Japanese participation in cross-national joint ventures located in the U.S. We developed a database of Japanese transplant assemblers and suppliers from data provided by the Japan Economic Institute, U.S. government sources, industry trade journals, and newspaper reports. Eight assembly centers were identified in the United States, of which one operated two plants at one site and the rest operated single plants. In addition, 229 transplant suppliers were identified; this number has since grown to approximately 270.

The study population is heavily concentrated in a "transplant corridor" of the lower Midwest and upper South—an area with a legacy of traditional U.S. (fordist) organizational practices. Four of the assembly transplants, Mazda, NUMMI, Diamond-Star, and the Ford-Nissan joint venture are unionized; four others, Honda, Nissan, Toyota, and Subaru-Isuzu (SIA), are not. Three assembly transplants are joint ventures with U.S. producers: NUMMI, a GM-Toyota joint venture managed by Toyota, Diamond-Star, a joint venture between Chrysler and Mitsubishi, and Ford-Nissan.

Site visits were conducted at six of the seven operating transplant assembly plants in the U.S. (Honda, Nissan, Toyota, Mazda, NUMMI, and Subaru-Isuzu) and at various supplier firms including Nippondenso, which has the largest investment in the U.S. of any transplant supplier.[2] More than 100 personal interviews were conducted. Interviews with Japanese and American executives focused on investment strategies, location, production and organization, supplier relations, and interorganizational linkages. To reduce the potential for bias and increase reliability, the interviewees in assembly plants and suppliers were asked similar questions. Interviews with present and former shopfloor workers and engineers, trade union officials, and state and local government officials provided an additional check against respondent bias. A member of the research team visited Honda's main assembly facility in Japan as well as several automotive parts suppliers to provide a comparative context for the analysis.

A mail survey was administered to the universe of Japanese-owned or Japanese-U.S. joint venture suppliers in the United States. Establishments were the unit of analysis (rather than firms) to capture differences among plants owned by the same firm because establishments may make different components and use different management and organizational practices. Moreover, the research required responses from plant management familiar with the actual operations of the plant. The suppliers responding to the survey were relatively evenly distributed by the assemblers they supply, thereby reducing the possibility for idiosyncratic practices of one or two end-users to significantly affect the survey results.

The survey instrument obtained background information such as start-up date, employment, sales, industry, end-users, information on intraorganizational characteristics such as work organization, number of job classifications, use of teams, rotation, quality control circles, wages and wage determination, employment security and workforce characteristics, and information on interorganizational relationships such as delivery times, frequency of communication, shared personnel, and cooperation in R&D and product design. Addresses were located for 196

of the 229 suppliers in the original database. (Some of the firms for whom addresses were unavailable likely had not yet begun operations). Each establishment was then contacted by telephone to identify the appropriate person to complete the survey.

The survey was mailed in 1988. A series of follow-up post cards and letters resulted in 73 completed surveys for a response rate of 37.2 percent, which is comparable to the rates in other research of this type. Lincoln and Kalleberg (1985), for example, obtained a response rate of 35 percent from U.S. manufacturing firms and 40 percent from Japanese manufacturing firms. Further, Japanese-owned firms in the U.S. may have been reticent to respond because of the highly charged political climate surrounding their activities. We have no reason to believe there was any bias between respondents and nonrespondents.

Transfer of Intraorganizational Forms and Practices

Work and Production Organization

Table 14.1 summarizes the main characteristics of work and production organization for transplant assemblers and for a representative Big Three automobile company. Table 14.2 presents similar information for transplant suppliers.[3]

Work teams. In Japan, work is organized on the basis of teams that are responsible for planning and carrying out production tasks (Aoki 1988; Koike 1988). Teams socialize production tasks and assign immediate managerial tasks to shopfloor workers. Table 14.1 indicates that work teams are used by all of the transplant assemblers. At Honda, Toyota, and NUMMI teams meet daily to discuss production improvements and redesign of tasks; meetings at the other transplants take place at least once a week. More than three-fourths of transplant suppliers organize production on the basis of work teams (Table 14.2).

Task rotation. Rotation of workers among tasks within a team is a key feature of Japanese production organization. Rotation functions to train workers in multiple tasks and to reduce the incidence of repetitive motion injuries. While rotation is used by all transplant assemblers, its frequency varies, as it does in Japan. Toyota, Honda, and

---

[2] We were unable to arrange a visit to Diamond-Star and the Ford-Nissan venture was not yet operational.

[3] Here we note that not all Japanese automobile firms are organized the same way; each has its own "personality."

| | TABLE 14.1 |

PRESENCE OF JAPANESE INTRAORGANIZATIONAL PRACTICES
IN TRANSPLANT ASSEMBLERS: U.S., 1990

| ASSEMBLER | WORK ORGANIZATION | | NUMBER OF JOB CLASSIFICATIONS | WORKER QUALITY CONTROL | AVERAGE ANNUAL WAGES | HOURLY WAGES FOR PRODUCTION WORKERS | PRESENCE OF UNION |
	WORK TEAMS	ROTATION					
Honda	+	+	3	○	$33,685	$14.55	No
Nissan	+	+	4	○	$32,579	$13.95	No
NUMMI	+	+	4	○	$36,013	$16.81	Yes
Toyota	+	+	3	○	$29,598	$14.23	No
Mazda	+	+	2	○	$32,970	$15.13	Yes
Subaru-Isuzu (SIA)	+	+	3	○	$28,995	$13.94	No
Big Three U.S.	−	−	90	−	$36,089	$16.41	Yes

Source: Wage data for each transplant and average for Big Three producers are from Jackson (1990); data on intraorganizational practices of transplant assemblers are from site visits and personal interviews; data on intraorganizational practices of a representative Big Three automaker are from U.S. General Accounting Office (1988).

Note: + = similar to Japan; ○ = modified; − = different from Japan.

NUMMI rotate workers in the same team quite frequently. Toyota workers in high stress jobs, e.g., jobs that require the use of a high impact "torque gun" or involve constant bending or lifting, rotate as frequently as once an hour, others rotate at break times, at lunch, or every other day. According to a NUMMI worker: "We would be rotating every time we had a break or change. If we had a break in the morning, we rotated. And then lunchtime, we rotated. And we had a break in the afternoon, we rotated. Every time the line stopped, a break or whatever, we rotated." Rotation is less frequent at Mazda, Nissan, and SIA. While these companies consider rotation a long-term goal, each has slowed or even stopped the use of rotation during production ramp-ups. Our interviews with Mazda workers confirm that infrequent rotation has been a major cause of repetitive motion injury at the Mazda plant. Rotation from team to team is less common both in Japan and in the transplants. In Japan, this type of rotation is typically mandated by management; in the U.S., it is more common for workers to apply for job transfers.

According to the supplier survey, roughly 87 percent of suppliers rotate workers within teams, while approximately 66 percent rotate among teams. Nippondenso rotates workers in high stress jobs every hour or two and encourages workers to apply for rotation from team to team. Both U.S. and Japanese managers at all the transplants we visited, as well as many workers, felt that it was too early for implementation of a full Japanese-style rotation system and that it may be a few years before workers have enough basic skills and knowledge to be moved regularly from team to team.

Inventory control. In Japan, production takes place according to the "just-in-time" system of inventory control in which materials are forwarded as needed and inventory is kept to a minimum (Monden 1982; Cusumano 1985). All the assemblers and over two-thirds of suppliers (68.5 percent) use a just-in-time system of production control.

The supplier survey asked: "How similar is your manufacturing process to one that might be found in Japan?" Eighty-six percent of the respondents said that their U.S. manufacturing practice was either "exactly the same" or "very similar" to one that might be found in Japan; only one supplier said that it was not at all similar.

The Division of Labor

Job classifications. Few job classifications are a key characteristic of the Japanese model. This contrasts sharply with traditional U.S. production organization in which virtually

TABLE 14.2

PERCENTAGE OF TRANSPLANT PARTS
SUPPLIERS WITH SELECTED JAPANESE
INTRAORGANIZATIONAL PRACTICES:
U.S., 1988

CHARACTERISTIC	PERCENT	NUMBER OF CASES
Work Organization		
Work teams	76.7	73
Rotation within teams	87.0	69
Rotation between teams	66.2	68
Just-in-time inventory control	68.5	73
Worker Involvement		
Production workers maintain their own machines	79.5	73
Production workers do routine quality control	98.6	73
Production workers help design their own jobs	60.9	69
Division of Labor		
Number of job classifications:		
1	34.3	67
2	14.9	67
3	16.4	67
4	14.9	67
5	6.0	67

every job has its own classification and job classifications are seen by workers and unions as a "job ladder" that provides the basis for wage increases and employment security. Kochan et al. (1986) report that the unionized plants in a multidivisional U.S. manufacturing firm had an average of 96 job classifications. Table 14.1 indicates that transplant assemblers use no more than four job classifications, whereas a representative traditional U.S. Big Three auto maker had 90. The implementation of few job classifications might seem especially difficult at transplants which employ a large number of managers and workers that were originally socialized to traditional Big Three practices, e.g., NUMMI, which has a large percentage of former GM workers. However, our interviews with NUMMI officials and workers indicated few adaptation problems.

More than 85 percent of transplant suppliers use five or fewer job classifications for production workers; and one-third use only one job classification. Several indicate that they have instituted more job classifications than would be ideal (as many as ten) to keep American workers happy by providing the appearance of an internal career ladder.

Team leaders. Japanese production organization includes a class of workers, referred to as "team leaders," who are members of shopfloor work groups but also have managerial responsibility for immediate production activities. There are no foremen or low-level managers whose job is to supervise shopfloor workers. Team leaders are used at all the transplant assemblers we visited, and 84 percent of suppliers use them as well. At Honda, Toyota, NUMMI, Nissan, and SIA team leaders are the first line of supervision and play a crucial role in the organization, design, and allocation of work on a daily basis. At some transplants, team leaders are selected by management, while at others, especially the unionized transplants, team leaders are selected by joint labor-management committees. All the transplants consider the input of workers to be an important criterion for the selection of team leaders.

Status distinctions. Overt status distinctions between management and blue-collar workers are less evident in Japan than in the U.S. For example, in Japan workers and managers eat in the same cafeteria; middle level managers wear the same uniforms as shopfloor workers. Managers typically do not have enclosed offices but sit at desks on a large open floor adjacent to the production facility. All transplants we visited had single cafeterias. At Nippondenso, all executives including the President work at desks on the floor. Nissan is the only transplant in which status distinctions are more visible, e.g., a separate parking lot for top managers' cars and plush "American-style" offices. This may be because Nissan has a much higher percentage of former American automobile executives than other transplants. All the transplants provide uniforms, although some give workers the option of wearing street clothes. Transplant officials we interviewed suggested that uniforms create an identification between workers and the company. Most top executives wear company uniforms, although Nissan is again the exception. In fact, the transplants tend to have greater visible status equality than obtains in Japan where top executives have chauffeured company automobiles and wear suits and ties rather than work uniforms.

Hierarchy. Lincoln, Hamada, and McBride (1986) indicated that management hierarchies are taller in Japan than in the U.S. Our findings suggest that management hierarchies in the automotive transplants are relatively flat. At Honda, there are nine levels in the internal hierarchy:

associate, team leader, coordinator, department manager, plant manager, assistant vice president, senior vice president, executive vice president, and president. This structure is typical of the other transplants as well. At Honda, the various vice presidents do not form separate levels in the reporting structure, but are part of Honda's senior management team, which includes the plant manager and the president of Honda of America Manufacturing. This senior management team makes decisions as a group and thus functions to some extent as a single reporting level. The president of Honda America is a member of and reports to the Board of Directors for Honda Japan. A number of shopfloor workers have risen to management ranks at Honda and the company actively encourages such mobility. Toyota officials indicate that shopfloor workers are recruited for middle-level management positions in the factory and the front office.

Worker Participation and Quality Control

It is important to distinguish between the form of Japanese organization and its substance, i.e., its effects on worker behavior. A main objective of the Japanese system of work and production organization is to harness the collective intelligence of workers for continuous product and process improvement (Kenney and Florida 1988, 1989). This stands in sharp contrast to traditional American automobile industry practices in which there are formal and informal organizational barriers and norms that inhibit the use of worker intelligence (Braverman 1974). In Japan, workers actively participate in company suggestion programs and quality control circles as well as informal, everyday "*kaizen*," or continuous improvement activities. In Japan, different automobile corporations emphasize different aspects of *kaizen* activity. Toyota places greater emphasis on team activities, like quality circles, whereas Honda emphasizes individual initiative and innovation. Japanese scholars use the concept of "voluntarism" to explain the extraordinary initiative of workers in Japan. However, Japanese automobile companies vary significantly in their ability to generate "voluntaristic" behavior—with Toyota being the most effective.

Worker initiative. Transplants encourage worker initiative through the delegation of managerial authority and responsibility to shopfloor workers. Workers at the transplants, especially Honda and Toyota, have significant input into the design of their jobs. More than 60 percent of respondents to the supplier survey indicate that workers are involved in the design of their tasks. At Toyota and Nippon-

denso, work teams actually design standardized task descriptions for their work units and post them in the form of drawings and photographs with captions at their work stations. Roughly 80 percent of suppliers indicate that workers are responsible for routine maintenance on their own machines.

Japanese corporations use suggestion systems to harness workers' knowledge and ideas. Honda and Toyota have fairly well-developed suggestion systems. Although Mazda has a suggestion system, Mazda workers have occasionally boycotted it to express their dissatisfaction with management policy. SIA does not yet have a suggestion system, although management indicates that the company will institute one in the future. Thirty percent of transplant suppliers provide cash awards for worker suggestions, and two-thirds report that "willingness to suggest new ideas" is a key criterion for evaluating production workers for wage increases.

Quality circles. Quality circles are an important element of the Japanese system (Cole 1989a; Lillrank and Kano 1989). In Japan, quality circles are groups of workers who devote effort outside regular working hours to improving an element of the production process. According to Lincoln et al. (1986, p. 354), 76 percent of employees in a sample of Japanese plants participated in quality circles compared to 27 percent of workers in U.S. plants. The transplants vary in the extent and intensiveness with which they employ quality circles. Toyota and Honda use quality circles extensively, Mazda and NUMMI "moderately," and SIA not at all. Slightly less than half of suppliers use quality circles, and 68 percent of those who do not use quality control circles plan to do so in the future.

Transplant assemblers pay workers for quality circle activity. Of suppliers that use quality circles, 83 percent pay workers for hours spent working on quality circles. In both transplant assemblers and suppliers, participation in quality circles usually occurs immediately before or after shift work. Several transplants conduct competitions between quality control circles and use prizes, plaques, and cash awards as additional incentives for quality circle participation. Some transplants have sent American quality circles to Japan to participate in annual company competitions. All the transplant assemblers and suppliers that we visited indicated that they will devote significant effort to establishing quality control circles on a par with Japan. We thus agree with Cole's assessment (1989, pp. 111–12) that it is still too early in the transfer process to expect full use of quality control circles. Such activity will likely increase as the transplants complete the process of implanting organizational forms and move on to more subtle techniques of shaping and motivating worker initiative.

We also asked Japanese managers to tell us how much, in percentage terms, Japanese *kaizen* or continuous improvement activity they have been able to replicate in their American work force. Honda executives feel they have completely replicated Japanese practice in their Marysville, Ohio plant. A Toyota manager who has worked in numerous Toyota plants in Japan as well as at NUMMI and Georgetown, Kentucky, indicated the Georgetown plant is at 60 percent of Japanese practice and NUMMI at 40 to 50 percent. Management is actively trying to implement greater *kaizen* activities. Nippondenso, a Toyota group member, has also closely replicated Japanese practice. Mazda and Nissan have had more difficulty implementing *kaizen* activity, and stand at roughly 50 percent of Japanese practice. Executives of SIA, which is the most recent transplant, estimate that the plant is currently at about 30 percent of Japanese practice. Still, the progress of the transplants on this dimension is remarkable, given the limited time they have had to socialize American workers to the requirements of Japanese production.

The central role played by worker initiative and the use of workers' knowledge contradicts the view that the Japanese model is simply an extension of fordist mass production. It lends support to the alternative conceptualization that it is a new and potential successor model based upon harnessing workers' intellectual and physical capabilities.

Transplants recognize this deficit and are working hard to replicate the worker initiative and voluntaristic behavior of Japanese firms. Numerous Japanese executives see the lack of independent initiative of American workers as a product of previous attitudes and socialization, and suggest that it can be changed by education and socialization to Japanese practices. According to the Japanese president of a transplant supplier, education and effort is required to "remove American barriers to worker initiative." Managers at the transplants indicate that they will concentrate on this issue in the next few years. Going even further, Toyota is working with the local school system to redesign curriculum and other socialization mechanisms to impart group-oriented behavior, problem solving, and initiative to students. SIA has also sent local school officials to Japan so that they can learn more about Japanese group-oriented educational practice.

Work Force Selection and Socialization

Japanese corporations do not simply impose Japanese production organization and manufacturing practice on their American work forces. Instead, they use a number of selection and socialization mechanisms to ensure effective transfer.

Selection. Recruitment and selection processes identify workers who possess initiative, are dedicated to the corporation, work well in teams, and do not miss work. The process differs from the recruitment policies of Japanese corporations in Japan (Rosenbaum and Kariya 1989) but serves a similar function. Moreover, the process differs markedly from the typical U.S. practice of hiring "off the street." The transplants subject potential workers to cognitive and psychological tests and other screening procedures to identify workers who "fit" the Japanese model. Previous job records or high school records are scrutinized for absenteeism. Potential employees go through extensive interviews with personnel officials, managers, and even members of their potential work teams to rate their initiative and group-oriented characteristics. While theorists have generally treated the so-called "loyalty" of the Japanese work force as a product of Japanese culture, the screening and selection process constitutes an organizational mechanism that selects potential "loyal" workers from a large, diverse population. Simply put, this long held "cultural" effect is also a product of organizational practice.

Socialization. Prior to start-up, all the assembly transplants sent key employees (e.g., managers and team leaders) to Japanese sister plants for three to six months. There they received both formal training and informal socialization to Japanese practice (e.g., team work and *kaizen*). They worked closely with veteran Japanese "trainers," who transfer formal and tacit knowledge of production and who function as role models to some extent. Workers and trainers also spent time together outside work to continue the socialization process. These trainers then came to the U.S. for periods from three months to two years to work alongside the same U.S. employees and their teams. The supplier survey indicates that 33 percent of American managers were sent to Japan for training. According to workers at different transplants, "trainers" provided the most substantial and significant exposure to Japanese practices.

The transplants use ongoing training and socialization programs to acclimate workers to Japanese production. Most employees begin with a six- to eight-week introductory session that includes an overview of automotive assembly and fairly rigorous socialization in the Japanese model. After this, workers are assigned to teams where they continue to learn from senior employees. According to the survey, suppliers provide an average of eight days of training for factory workers before they assume shopfloor activities (range = 0–180 days); assemblers have longer training periods. This is supplemented by an average of 61 days additional training on the shopfloor (range = 1–302 days).

Adaptation. Shopfloor workers in the U.S. have experienced few problems adapting to the Japanese system. NUMMI workers who previously worked for GM indicate that they prefer the Japanese model to U.S. fordist practice. According to one: "I was at GM and the part I didn't like—which I like now—is that we had a lot of drug and alcohol problems. It was getting to the point, even with me, when it got around lunchtime I had to go out . . . and take down two or three beers." Mazda has had the most adaptation problems including significant worker discontent and the recent election of a new union local that is less conciliatory toward management. However, Mazda workers indicate that such adaptation problems are largely due to management's failure to fully implement Japanese production organization, e.g., by not rotating workers to prevent repetitive motion injury.

Management has been the source of recurring adaptation problems at the transplants. During site visits and interviews, we were told repeatedly that American middle managers, especially those recruited from U.S. automobile corporations, have experienced great difficulty adapting to Japanese production organization and management. Honda officials indicate that the previously formed attitudes and prejudices of U.S. middle managers toward factory workers are a serious problem. White and Trevor (1983) documented a similar problem in U.K. transplants. NUMMI workers complain that American managers still operating in the GM style are a major obstacle to implementation of a full-blown Japanese system that they see as more favorable to workers than the old fordist system. According to a NUMMI worker: "A lot of things have changed. But see, you hear people talk. You hear them saying once in a while: 'Oh, we're going back to the GM ways,' I hope not. That was rough. . . . I think to completely bring back the Japanese way, Japan would have to take over the plant completely and have nothing to do with General Motors at all." Japanese transplant managers indicate that problems with American middle managers have encouraged them to promote shopfloor workers to supervisory positions.

Wages and Labor-Management Relations

In any industrial system, the immediate organization of production is reflected in rules, regulations, and norms that form the context in which production takes place. This broader production environment includes wage rates, wage determination, the organization and function of the internal labor market, degree of tenure security, type of unionization, and pattern of labor relations. These factors create incentives for work effort, establish the context for labor-management relations, and form the framework for mobilizing employee demands and mediating disputes. In Burawoy's (1979) terminology, they provide the social context for the "manufacture of consent."

Wages and bonuses. The Japanese "*nenko*" system of wage determination is based on a combination of seniority, job-related performance, and the ability to work in a group context (Suzuki 1976; Gordon 1985; Kagono, Nonaka, Sakikabara, and Okumura 1985). Semiannual bonuses constituting roughly 30 percent of total remuneration are used to supplement regular pay (Aoki 1988).

As in Japan, transplant assemblers and suppliers pay relatively high wages. Transplant assembler pay average annual wages between $28,598 and $36,013 dollars, compared to an average of $36,089 for Big Three auto makers (Table 14.1). Workers in transplant assembly plants can earn over $50,000 when overtime is included. Hourly wages for regular production workers in transplant assembly plants range between $13.94 and $16.81 per hour, compared to an average of $16.41 at Big Three firms (Table 14.1). Transplant suppliers also pay relatively high wages, $7.21 per hour to start and $8.00 after a year on the job for "low skill" workers—a rate which is slightly below the wage levels at U.S. parts suppliers (U.S. International Trade Commission 1987). Total annual compensation at the transplant suppliers averages $21,200 per year. This wage differential between assemblers and suppliers is roughly similar to that in Japan.

The wage levels and wage determination policies of the transplants are more standardized and uniform than in Japan. This is somewhat striking because academic studies and conventional wisdom contrast American "individualism" to Japanese "familism." Transplant assemblers pay uniform wages for each class of workers, with raises at regular intervals. Transplant suppliers report that work effort, absenteeism, "willingness to work in teams," and "willingness to suggest new ideas" are the major criteria used to evaluate workers for wage increases and promotions.

Bonuses are not as common in the transplants as they are in Japan, and they are not an important component of employee wages. Bonuses at the transplants tend to be across-the-board, equal-percentage wage supplements to all workers. Honda provides a monthly bonus of $100 for perfect attendance. Bonuses represent only 1 percent of total compensation for transplant suppliers. However, 49 percent of transplant suppliers provide small cash awards for suggestions, and 18 percent provide small cash awards for participation in quality circles.

Job security. "Permanent employment," or more appropriately, long-term employment tenure, is a much discussed feature of the Japanese system (Abegglen 1958; Taira 1970; Dore 1973; Cole 1979; Lincoln and Kalleberg 1985). The pattern of employment security differs between unionized and nonunionized assembly transplants, and between assemblers and suppliers. Our review of the labor-management agreements for the unionized assembly transplants indicates that all of them have formal contractual agreements that stipulate tenure security, "guaranteeing" jobs except under conditions that jeopardize the financial viability of the company. Both NUMMI and Mazda have fulfilled their commitment to no layoffs. NUMMI has kept full employment during periods of up to 30 percent reduction in output by eliminating overtime, slowing the work pace, offering workers voluntary vacation time, placing workers in special training programs, or transferring them to other jobs. Mazda workers have been loaned to local governments during slowdowns. The nonunionized transplants provide informal assurance of tenure security, although this is not reflected in contractual agreements with workers. Nissan and Toyota have redeployed workers to other jobs to avoid layoffs. However, it is impossible to know at this stage whether the nonunionized transplants will remain committed to tenure security in the event of a severe economic downturn.

Transplant suppliers do not offer formal guarantees of tenure security. However, more than two-thirds of the supplier respondents indicate that the Japanese long-term employment system should be transferred to the U.S. Nevertheless, they offered a wide range of opinions on this issue—some saw long-term employment as a source of long-run productivity increases, others saw the threat of termination as a way to motivate American workers.

Unionization. The Japanese system of unionization is one of enterprise or "company" unions (Taira 1961; Shirai 1983), which differs markedly from the prevailing U.S. practice of industrial unionism. However, Levine (1958), Taira (1961), and Koike (1988) observed that the U.S. has always had a system of decentralized plant-specific "locals" that operate in a way that is similar to enterprise unions by aggregating worker demands and establishing the context of labor-management relations at the plant level.[4]

---

[4] The U.S. industrial relations system is experiencing a general decentralization of such functions to the local level. For example, the new GM Saturn plant in Tennessee has instituted an agreement with unique provisions.

The transplants have developed two basic strategies to cope with U.S. labor relations and to recreate some elements of Japanese industrial relations. Most automobile transplants have simply chosen to avoid unionization. Only 4 our of the 71 supplier respondents were unionized. The four nonunionized assemblers—Honda, Toyota, Nissan and SIA—have chosen rural "greenfield locations" at least in part to avoid unionization. Nissan went to great lengths to defeat a unionization drive. SIA has implemented an in-plant video system to communicate messages to workers in anticipation of a unionization campaign. Nonunionized transplants, notably Nissan and Toyota, use employee "handbooks" that provide plant rules and regulations and have formed "employee associations" that collect employee input and create a stable structure through which work-related grievances can be addressed. The unionized transplants, Mazda, NUMMI, and Diamond-Star, have established independent agreements with their respective union locals that enlist the union in the implementation of Japanese work organization. These agreements allow fewer job classifications and more flexible work rules and utilize pay systems that differ markedly from the typical U.S. assembly plant.

Work force segmentation. The transplants are recreating aspects of Japan's highly segmented or "dual" labor markets (see Koike 1988; Kalleberg and Lincoln 1988). In Japan, for example, a large manufacturing facility will typically have nonunionized temporary workers or lower-paid workers from subcontractors working side-by-side with regular employees. The transplants use part-time or temporary employees to provide flexibility. At both Mazda and Diamond-Star, temporary employees were laid off during a downturn in the automobile market in early 1990 (Guiles and Miller 1990). The use of temporary workers has been a source of ongoing labor-management conflict at Mazda where (in contrast to Japan) union leaders see temporary workers as a threat to labor solidarity.

Gender is the most common basis of work force segmentation in Japan. Japanese women are prohibited from working in assembly plants by Japanese laws that make it illegal for women to work the night shift. The transplants do not show the extreme pattern of gender-based segmentation that is common in Japan. The supplier survey indicates that women comprise 34 percent of production workers. However, women are only 10 percent of the management work force.

Race is a typical line of work force segmentation in the U.S. Earlier research (Cole and Deskins 1988) inferred racial bias from the site selection and work force composition of Japanese transplants. We did not see large or even representative numbers of minorities in site visits. According to the supplier survey, minorities fill 11 percent of production positions and 9 percent of management slots. Recent data indicate that the transplant assemblers are hiring relatively more minority workers in production jobs. For example, Honda has increased minority employment from 2.8 percent in 1989 to 10.6 percent in 1990. Similarly, Toyota in Kentucky reports that 15 percent of its employees are nonwhite (also see Cole 1989b). In all likelihood, this is a response to the political pressure that resulted from publicizing earlier hiring practices.

Effects and implications. The Japanese transplants have been successful in economic terms. In 1990, the transplants produced nearly 20 percent of all U.S. cars and are projected to increase this to between 40 and 50 percent of the U.S. market over the next five to ten years (Wharton Econometric Forecasting Associates 1990). Productivity comparisons done by the International Motor Vehicle Program at the Massachusetts Institute of Technology indicate that the transplants have productivity ratings that are as good as or better than U.S.-owned automobile assembly plants and comparable to their Japanese sister plants (Krafcik 1989; Womack et al. 1990).

The combined economic and organizational success of the transplants is exerting a powerful demonstration effect on U.S. automobile corporations, resulting in the imitation and diffusion of Japanese practices. The diffusion process has been accelerated by joint ventures with Big Three auto makers, some of which (e.g., NUMMI) were organized explicitly to educate U.S. managers. Furthermore, union leadership is pressing to apply transplant job security provisions to U.S. firms. Each of the Big Three auto makers currently operates plants (e.g., GM's Saturn) that use the "team concept," few job classifications, pay-for-performance, and other organizational practices that have been influenced by the Japanese. However, a recent study (Kochan and Cutcher-Gershenfeld 1988) suggests that U.S. reforms are essentially "hybrid forms" in which workers are grouped in teams but not given decentralized decision-making authority. Whereas the literature predicts convergence of Japanese transplants toward the U.S. model, the reverse is occurring as U.S. producers adopt elements of the Japanese model. This further reinforces the contention that the Japanese model is a potentially generalizable successor to fordist mass production.

Summary. Our findings indicate that both transplant assemblers and suppliers have been remarkably successful in implanting the Japanese system of work organization in the U.S. environment. The basic form of Japanese work organization has been transferred with little if any modification. There are differences in the extent to which the transplants have been able to replicate Japanese behavior in *kaizen*, quality circles and other such activity, but they are working hard to increase the participation of U.S. workers in these activities. Japanese wage determination and labor relations practices have been somewhat modified to fit the U.S. context. However, these practices still resemble Japanese more than U.S. traditions. In sum, our findings are in line with the hypothesis that the Japanese model is a set of organizational practices that can be removed from the Japanese environment and successfully implanted elsewhere. However, we do not imply that the transfer process has occurred automatically. Japanese firms have taken great care to select and even to alter the environment to make it conducive to new organizational forms.

Transfer of Interorganizational Relations

The Japanese system of interorganizational relations differs markedly from that of the U.S. The Japanese "just-in-time" system of supplier relations is characterized by close geographic proximity of producers, long-term relationships, and tight interfirm linkages characterized by personnel sharing, joint participation in product development, and regular communication and interaction (Asanuma 1985; Odaka, Ono and Adachi 1988). In Japan, suppliers provide as much as 70 percent of a car's components, while U.S. automobile assemblers rely on suppliers for 30 to 50 percent of inputs (Mitsubishi Research Institute 1987; U.S. International Trade Commission 1987). The Japanese supplier system is organized in a pyramidal structure with 500 first-tier suppliers, a few thousand second-tier suppliers and more than 20,000 tertiary automotive parts suppliers (Sayer 1986; Nishiguchi 1987; Sheard 1983). The parent or "hub" company plays a key role by structuring linkages and coordinating flows within the network (Florida and Kenney 1990b). The Japanese supplier system is embedded in a set of organizational relationships that structure economic behavior. Dore (1983) advanced the concept of "relational contracting" to capture elements of the Japanese system and to contrast it with the "arm's length" system of the U.S. (Altshuler et al. 1984).

Japanese assembly transplants initially located facilities in the lower Midwestern region of the United States to take advantage of the indigenous infrastructure of domestic automobile parts suppliers. However, indigenous supplier firms were unable to adapt to the delivery and quality requirements of Japanese just-in-time system. Dismayed by the performance of U.S. suppliers, assembly transplants encouraged their first-tier Japanese suppliers to locate in the U.S. The Japanese suppliers, in turn, found it in their interest to expand overseas. In effect, the creation of a Japanese system of interorganizational relations in the U.S. was a "creative response" (Schumpeter 1947) to the deficiencies of the U.S. environment.

Transplant assemblers have played an active role in the creation of this new production environment by financing and helping to set up U.S. branches for key suppliers. For example, Honda encouraged two of its Japanese suppliers to form Bellemar Parts to supply it with seat subassemblies. In another instance, Honda provided technical and financial assistance to a group of Japanese suppliers to form KTH Parts Industries, a company that took over U.S. production of chassis parts that were once produced in-house by Honda at Marysville. Nearly half of Honda's main suppliers in Japan now operate U.S. plants. The supplier survey indicates that 12 of 73 suppliers are partially owned by the assemblers they supply.

Furthermore, assemblers played a key role in influencing both the original decision of transplant suppliers to relocate production in the U.S. and their choice of locations in the U.S. According to the supplier survey, more than 75 percent set up U.S. operations to maintain close ties to a major Japanese customer, and 90 percent chose their specific locations to be close to a major customer. Traditional environmental factors like the local labor market or local labor costs have had relatively little impact on locational choices. Recently, other Japanese parts suppliers have opened U.S. plants on their own initiative to access the growing market for their products. Most of the supplier plants are located in states with transplant assembly plants. The strong role played by large assemblers in orienting and structuring the transplant supplier complexes contradicts the claim (Sabel 1989; Friedman 1988) that the Japanese model is converging toward small-firm flexible specialization.

Supplier Relations

Table 14.3 summarizes data from the supplier survey on the main characteristics of relations among transplant assemblers and suppliers. This table reports the responses of 73 transplant suppliers on their supply relationships with transplant assemblers and with their own "second-

TABLE 14.3

PERCENTAGE OF TRANSPLANT FIRST-TIER SUPPLIERS WITH SELECTED JAPANESE INTERORGANIZATIONAL LINKAGES: U.S., 1988

CHARACTERISTIC	LINKAGES TO ASSEMBLERS		LINKAGESS TO SECOND-TIER SUPPLIERS	
	%	N	%	N
Transit time				
1/2 hour	6.9	72	—	—
1/2 hour-2 hours	33.3	72	—	—
2-8 hours	38.9	72	—	—
8-24 hours	9.7	72	—	—
Deliver according to just-in-time schedule	80.0	70	43.1	72
Immediate feedback on defective parts	97.2	72	97.2	72
Customers' engineers visit plant site				
For quality control problems	96.8	62	96.9	65
For production problems	74.2	62	83.1	65
Interaction in design				
Close interaction between supplier and customer	50.0	72	33.8	71
Supplier bids on customer design	31.9	72	62.0	71
Supplier can alter customer design	22.2	72	11.3	71
Supplier designs subject to customer approval	15.3	72	11.3	71
Supplier designs but customer can alter	6.9	72	8.5	71

tier" suppliers. Geographic proximity is a basic characteristic of the Japanese supplier relations (Sayer 1986). Among transplant suppliers, 40 percent are located within a two-hour shipping radius of end-users, and almost 90 percent are located within an eight-hour radius. Eighty percent make just-in-time deliveries. Still, the distances separating end-users from suppliers are somewhat greater in the United States than in Japan. Transplant complexes are essentially "stretched out" versions of Japan's geographically concentrated just-in-time system of interorganizational linkages. This is likely due to the greater availability of land, well-developed highway systems, larger trucks, and greater storage capacity in the U.S.

Interaction and information exchange. Table 14.3 reveals a continuous exchange of information between transplant assemblers and suppliers. Approximately 97 percent of transplant suppliers are contacted immediately by phone when they deliver a defective product. Eight-two percent indicate that engineers from their major customer came on-site while they were setting up U.S. operations, three-quarters report that engineers from their major customer make ongoing site visits to deal with production problems, and 97 percent indicate that engineers from their major customer make ongoing site visits to deal with quality control problems.

Joint product development. Joint participation in design and development is another key characteristic of Japanese supplier relations. Fifty percent of suppliers said they participate closely with assemblers in the development of new products. This includes interaction with U.S.-owned firms as well. Honda engineers, for example, developed new production techniques for a small Ohio plastics firms that became a Honda supplier. Honda, Toyota, and SIA send teams of engineers and shopfloor workers to consult with suppliers on new product designs and production machinery. Honda intends to use its Marysville R&D center to integrate both transplant and U.S. suppliers into the future design of cars. We thus conclude that Japanese interorganizational practices like high levels of interaction, joint development, and long-term contracts, which typically have been viewed as a function of Japan's sociocultural environment, are actually a product of the organizational relation itself.

Supplier tiers. In Japan, first-tier suppliers play a critical role in organizing and coordinating supply flows between lower-level suppliers and main assembly plants. They are located close to assemblers, interact frequently with them, and often are at least partially owned by them (Asanuma 1985). First-tier suppliers are probably more important in transplant complexes. For example, the windshields for Honda's American-made vehicles originate at PPG, an American producer. PPG supplies windshields to a Japanese supplier, AP Technoglass, twice a week. AP Technoglass screens them for defects, cuts and grinds them, and delivers them to a Honda subsidiary, Bellemar Parts, twice a day. Bellemar, which is located one mile from the Honda plant, applies rubber seals to the windshields and makes just-in-time deliveries to Honda every two hours. Bellemar also screens for defects, so that Honda receives much higher quality windshields than it would without its suppliers. In this way, suppliers serve as a "buffer" between assemblers and the environment.

Table 14.3 reveals the pyramidal nature of transplant supplier relations. Second-tier suppliers, who supply to the first-tier suppliers, have less interaction in design or development of new products. One-third of first-tier suppliers integrate second-tier suppliers in a new product development. Just 43 percent of the first-tier suppliers receive just-in-time deliveries from their second-tier suppliers, whereas in Japan, tight interorganizational relations extend to second- and third-tier suppliers. However, this may be due to the fact that the transplant complex is still in the process of formation so linkages are at an early stage of development. Other evidence indicates that linkages are being extended down through the hierarchy to producers of basic inputs like steel, rubber and tires, and automotive plastics (Kenney and Florida 1991).

Integration of and diffusion to U.S. suppliers. Transplant assemblers are forging interorganizational linkages to U.S. producers, leading to the rapid diffusion of Japanese practices among U.S. producers. Over half of Mazda's U.S. suppliers are U.S.-owned firms: 43 of Mazda's 96 suppliers are independent U.S.-owned firms, 10 are owned by Ford, and 43 are Japanese-owned or Japanese-U.S. joint ventures (*Automotive News* 1989). Helper (1990) indicated that 41 percent of 437 U.S. automotive suppliers surveyed supplied at least one component to the transplants.

Transplant assemblers work with U.S. suppliers to accelerate the diffusion of Japanese practices. As in Japan, Toyota has set up an organization of its Kentucky suppliers, the Bluegrass Automotive Manufacturers Association (BAMA), and has held meetings with U.S. suppliers in Las Vegas and Japan to encourage diffusion of Japanese practices. NUMMI has organized a supplier council of 70 mostly U.S.-owned suppliers to share information and facilitate product improvement (Krafcik 1986). SIA has organized teams of engineers, purchasing representatives, and manufacturing people who work with suppliers to improve quality. Johnson Controls, an American-owned automotive supplier in Georgetown, Kentucky, is now the sole source supplier of seats for the Toyota Camry. Toyota has worked with the company to implement a full-blown Japanese production system. Johnson Controls delivers completed subassemblies to Toyota according to just-in-time requirements every four hours. We visited a ten-person small machine shop in rural Ohio that formerly rebuilt tractor engines, but now rebuilds robot heads for Honda and Honda suppliers.

The emergence of a new system of Japanese supplier relations in the U.S. is exerting a sizable demonstration effect on U.S. practice. Helper (1989) provided empirical evidence of U.S. convergence toward the Japanese model. Rather than taking on characteristics of U.S. suppliers or the broader environment of U.S. supplier relations, the Japanese transplants are transforming existing patterns of interorganizational relations in the U.S.

Summary. Our research indicates that the Japanese system of interorganizational relationships has been successfully transferred to the U.S. The Japanese transplants show little sign of conforming to the prevailing U.S. model of organization. Instead, the transplants have acted on the environment to create the resources and conditions they need to function. Furthermore, our findings reveal considerable symmetry or congruence between intra- and interorganizational relations. The Japanese transplants replicate in their external relations with suppliers the long-term relations, high levels of interactions, and joint problem-solving typical of their internal relations. Features such as mutual dependence, shared problem solving, and continuous interaction, which are thought to be a function of Japan's sociocultural environment, can be better explained as part of the interorganizational relationship itself.

Conclusion

Our findings may come as a surprise, given the legacy, conceptual orientation, and predictions of industrial sociology and organization theory. These theories imply that the environment has a strong effect on organizations, that it is difficult to transfer organizations between dissimilar environments, and that once transferred, organizations tend to take on characteristics of the new environment. At the intraorganizational level, however, the transplants have effectively recreated the basic Japanese system of production organization and are working hard to implant it fully. At the interorganizational level, the transplants have recreated Japan's "relational contracting" system, establishing a new production environment for automobile manufacture. Thus, our findings suggest that too much explanatory power has been given to cultural factors in organizational development. Outside the plant as well as inside, the Japanese model forms a set of organizational practices that has been effectively transferred to the U.S.

On a more general level, our research suggests a general symmetry between intra- and interorganizational characteristics. The Japanese transplants have replicated long-term, interactive, participative, and/or mutually dependent relations at both the intra- and interorganizational levels. These findings are not specific to the trans-

plants but are reflected in comparative institutional research—the U.S. pattern of short-term adversarial labor-management relations is reflected in the short-term "arm's length" pattern of U.S. supplier relations. We believe that there may be an underlying rationale for such symmetry. Organizational pressures and incentives may lead to increasing continuity in the governance structures inside and outside the firm. Firms that effectively organize intraorganizational activity are likely to replicate it in dealings with external firms as well. More research and theory-building are needed on this crucial issue, using other sectors, industries, and types of organizations.

Our research indicates that organizations can and do shape their environments. Thus, the concept of environmental "embeddedness" should be revised to incorporate measures of the power, intentions, and purposeful activities of organizations. Transferring organizational practices and forms from one society to another means that they must be uncoupled from the environment in which they are embedded and recreated in the new environment. The transplants provide clear evidence that organizational forms can be effectively lifted from an originally supportive context and transferred to a foreign environment. Furthermore, they show that organizations can mold the new environment to their needs and to some degree create the conditions of their own embeddedness. In general terms then, organizations have the resources to alter the environment. Large powerful firms, for example, can control the machines, the organization of production, the hiring of employees, and the establishment of interorganizational connections. These organizational resources can be used to offset and transform the "social matrix" of the environment.

We do not wish to imply that any type of organization can be made to fit any environment. The German automobile manufacturer, Volkswagen, failed to implement its production organization in the U.S. context—its U.S. plant experienced high levels of worker discontent, serious strikes, and was closed after less then ten years of operation. Successful organizational transfer is neither natural nor automatic; it hinges on the strategic actions organizations take to shape the environment to meet their requirements. Based on our findings, we conclude that the organizational-environmental tie works in both directions.

Finally, our research provides useful insights for the debate over new forms of production and industrial organization. The findings resonate with the general notion of a movement toward new models of production organization; the transplants reflect the more general restructuring of production organization, supplier relations, and industrial networks. However, we find little evidence to support the claim made by Sabel (1989) that the Japanese model, as manifested by the transplants, is converging toward flexible specialization. In fact, the evidence clearly suggests that U.S. firms are converging toward the Japanese model. By focusing on what is or can be transferred, our research reveals three defining features of the Japanese model: (1) high levels of task integration, (2) integration of workers' intelligence as well as physical capabilities, and (3) tightly networked production complexes. In organizational terms, the transplants, and the Japanese model in general, display a high degree of *functional integration* that differs markedly from previous forms of functional (and/or flexible) specialization. Based on our findings here and related research on U.S. high-technology industrial organization (Florida and Kenney 1990a, 1990b), we believe that these features may be the underlying and defining elements that will determine the success, survival, and diffusion of the competing models of production organization that are emerging around the world. It remains for future research to further assess the broad generality of these trends.

References

Abegglen, James. 1958. *The Japanese Factory.* Cambridge, MA: MIT Press.

Aglietta, Michel. 1979. *A Theory of Capitalist Regulation: The U.S. Experience.* London: New Left Books.

Altshuler, Alan, Martin Anderson, Daniel Jones, Daniel Roos, and James Womack. 1984. *The Future of the Automobile.* Cambridge: MIT Press.

Aoki, Masahiko. 1988. *Information, Incentives and Bargaining in the Japanese Economy.* Cambridge: Cambridge University Press.

Asanuma, Banri. 1985. "The Organization of Parts Purchases in the Japanese Automotive Industry." *Japanese Economic Studies* 13:32–53.

Automotive News. 1989. "Mazda: $1 Billion to Suppliers." 23 Oct., p. E29.

Benedict, Ruth. 1946. *The Chrysanthemum and the Sword.* Boston: Houghton-Mifflin.

Best, Michael. 1990. *The New Competition: Institutions of Industrial Restructuring.* Cambridge: Harvard University Press.

Braverman, Harry. 1974. *Labor and Monopoly Capital.* New York: Monthly Review Press.

Brown, Clair and Michael Reich. 1989. "When Does Union-Management Cooperation Work: A Look at NUMMI and GM-Van Nuys." *California Management Review* 31:26–44.

Burawoy, Michael. 1979. *Manufacturing Consent.* Chicago: University of Chicago.

Cole, Robert. 1971. *Japanese Blue Collar.* Berkeley: University of California Press.

_____. 1979. *Work, Mobility and Participation.* Berkeley: University of California Press.

_____. 1989a. *Strategies for Learning.* Berkeley: University of California Press.

_____. 1989b. "Reflections on Japanese Corporate Citizenship: Company Reactions to a Study of Hiring Practices in the United States." *Chuo Koron* 10:122–135.

Cole, Robert and Donald Deskins. 1988. "Racial Factors in Site Location and Employment Patterns of Japanese Automobile Firms in America." *California Business Review* 31:9–22.

Cool, Karel and Cynthia Legnick-Hall. 1985. "Second Thoughts on the Transferability of the Japanese Management Style." *Organization Studies* 6:1–22.

Crowther, Stuart and Philip Garrahan. 1988. "Invitation to Sunderland: Corporate Power and the Local Economy." *Industrial Relations Journal* 19:51–59.

Cusumano, Michael. 1985. *The Japanese Automobile Industry.* Cambridge: Harvard University Press.

DiMaggio, Paul and Walter Powell. 1983. "The Iron Cage Revisited: Institutional Isomorphism and Collective Rationality in Organizational Fields." *American Sociological Review* 48:147–60.

Dohse, Knuth, Ulrich Jurgens and Thomas Malsch. 1986. "From Fordism to Toyotism? The Social Organization of the Labor Process in the Japanese Automobile Industry." *Politics and Society* 14:45–66.

Dore, Ronald. 1973. *Japanese Factory, British Factory.* Berkeley: University of California Press.

_____. 1983. "Goodwill and the Spirit of Market Capitalism." *British Journal of Sociology* 34:459–82.

_____. 1986. *Flexible Rigidities.* Stanford: Stanford University Press.

_____. 1987. *Taking Japan Seriously.* Stanford: Stanford University Press.

Edwards, Richard. 1979. *Contested Terrain.* New York: Basic Books.

Florida, Richard and Martin Kenney. 1990a. *The Breakthrough Illusion: Corporate America's Failure to Move from Innovation to Mass Production.* New York: Basic Books.

Florida, Richard and Martin Kenney. 1990b. "High-Technology Restructuring in the USA and Japan." *Environment and Planning A* 22:233–52.

Freidman, David. 1988. *The Misunderstood Miracle: Industrial Development and Political Change in Japan.* Ithaca: Cornell University Press.

Fucini, Joseph and Suzy Fucini. 1990. *Working for the Japanese: Inside Mazda's American Auto Plant.* New York: Free Press.

Gertler, Meric. 1988. "The Limits to Flexibility: Comments on the Post-fordist Vision of Production and Its Geography." *Transactions of the Institute of British Geographers* 13:419–32.

Gordon, Andrew. 1985. *The Evolution of Labor Relations in Japan: Heavy Industry, 1985–1955.* Cambridge: Harvard University Press.

Granovetter, Mark. 1985. "Economic Action and Social Structure: The Problem of Embeddedness." *American Journal of Sociology* 91:481–510.

Guiles, Melinda and Krystal Miller. 1990. "Mazda and Mitsubishi-Chrysler Venture Cut Output, Following Big Three's Lead." *Wall Street Journal,* 12 Jan., pp. A2, A12.

Hannan, Michael and John Freeman. 1977. "The Population Ecology of Organizations." *American Journal of Sociology* 82:929–64.

Helper, Susan. 1989. "Changing Supplier Relationships in The U.S.: Results of Survey Research." Department of Economics, Case Western Reserve University, Cleveland. Unpublished manuscript.

_____. 1990. "Selling to Japanese Automobile Assembly Plants: Results of a Survey." Department of Economics, Case Western Reserve University, Cleveland. Unpublished manuscript.

Institute of Social Science. 1990. "Local Production of Japanese Automobile and Electronic Firms in The United States: The 'Application' and 'Adaptation' of Japanese Style Management." University of Tokyo, Tokyo, Japan.

Jackson, Kathy. 1990. "Transplant Wages Will Rise to Match Any Gains at Big 3," *Automotive News,* 2 July, p. 60.

Kagono, Tadao, Ikujiro Nonaka, Kiyonori Sakakibara, and Akihiro Okumura. 1985. *Strategic vs. Evolutionary Management.* Amsterdam: North Holland.

Kalleberg, Arne and James Lincoln. 1988. "The Structure of Earnings Inequality in the United States and Japan." *American Journal of Sociology* 94:S121–53.

Katz, Harry. 1985. *Shifting Gears.* Cambridge: MIT Press.

Kenney, Martin and Richard Florida. 1988. "Beyond Mass Production: Production and the Labor Process in Japan." *Politics and Society* 16:121–58.

Kenney, Martin and Richard Florida. 1989. "Response to the Debate Over 'Beyond Mass Production'" (in Japanese). *Mado* no. 2:210–13.

_____. 1991. "How Japanese Industry Is Rebuilding the Rustbelt." *Technology Review* 94:24–33.

_____. Forthcoming. *Mass Production Transformed: The Japanese Industrial Transplants in the United States.* New York: Oxford University Press.

Kochan, Thomas and Joel Cutcher-Gershenfeld. 1988. "Institutionalizing and Diffusing Innovation in Industrial Relations." U.S. Department of Labor, Bureau of Labor-Management Relations and Cooperative Programs, Washington, DC.

Kochan, Thomas, Harry Katz and Robert McKersie. 1986. *The Transformation of American Industrial Relations.* New York: Basic Books.

Koike, Kazuo. 1988. *Understanding Industrial Relations in Modern Japan.* New York: St. Martin's.

Krafcik, John. 1986. "Learning From NUMMI." Massachusetts Institute of Technology, International Motor Vehicle Program. Unpublished manuscript.

_____. 1989. "A New Diet for U.S. Manufacturers." *Technology Review* 92:28–38.

Kumazawa, Makoto and Jun Yamada. 1989. "Jobs and Skills Under the Lifelong Nenko Employment Practice." Pp. 102–26 in *The Transformation of Work,* edited by Stephen Wood. London: Unwin Hyman.

Lazerson, Mark. 1988. "Organizational Growth of Small Firms: An Outcome of Markets and Hierarchies?" *American Sociological Review* 53:330–42.

Lazonick, William. 1990. *Competitive Advantage on the Shopfloor.* Cambridge: Harvard University Press.

Levine, Solomon. 1958. *Industrial Relations in Postwar Japan.* Urbana: University of Illinois Press.

Lillrank, Paul and Noriaki Kano. 1989. "Continuous Improvement: Quality Control Circles in Japanese Industry." Center for Japanese Studies, The University of Michigan, Ann Arbor.

Lincoln, James and Arne Kalleberg. 1985. "Work Organization and Workforce Commitment: A Study of Plants and Employees in the U.S. and Japan." *American Sociological Review* 50:738–760.

_____. 1990. *Culture, Control and Commitment: A Study of Work Organization and Work Attitudes in the United States and Japan.* New York: Cambridge University Press.

Lincoln, James, Mitsuyo Hanada, and Kerry McBride. 1986. "Organizational Structures in Japanese and U.S. Manufacturing." *Administrative Science Quarterly* 31:338–64.

Mair, Andrew, Richard Florida and Martin Kenney. 1988. "The New Geography of Automobile Production: Japanese Transplants in North America." *Economic Geography* 64:352–73.

McKelvey, Bill and Howard Aldrich. 1983. "Populations, Natural Selection and Applied Organizational Science." *Administrative Science Quarterly* 28:101–28.

Meyer, John and Brian Rowan. 1977. "Institutionalized Organizations: Formal Structure as Myth and Ceremony." *American Journal of Sociology* 83:340–63.

Mitsubishi Research Institute. 1987. *The Relationship Between Japanese Auto and Auto Parts Makers.* Tokyo: Japanese Automobile Manufacturers Association, Inc.

Monden, Yasuhiro. 1982. *Toyota Production System.* Norcross, GA: Industrial Engineering and Management Press.

Morris, Jonathan. 1988. "The Who, Why and Where of Japanese Manufacturing Investment in the U.K." *Industrial Relations Journal* 19:31–40.

Morris-Suzuki, Tessa. 1988. *Beyond Computopia: Information, Automation and Democracy in Japan.* London: Kegan Paul International.

Nakane, Chie. 1970. *Japanese Society.* Berkeley: University of California Press.

Nishiguchi, Toshihiro. 1987. "Competing Systems of Automotive Components Supply: An Examination of the Japanese 'Clustered Control' Model and the 'Alps' Structure." International Motor Vehicle Program, Massachusetts Institute of Technology, Cambridge, MA. Unpublished manuscript.

Odaka, Konosuke, Keinosuke Ono, and Fumihiko Adachi. 1988. *The Automobile Industry in Japan: A Study of Ancillary Firm Development.* Tokyo: Kinokuniya. Distributed by Oxford University Press.

Oliver, Nick and Barry Wilkinson. 1989. "Japanese Manufacturing Techniques and Personnel and Industrial Relations Practice in Britain: Evidence and Implications." *British Journal of Industrial Relations* 27:73–91.

Parker, Mike and Jane Slaughter. 1988. "Management by Stress." *Technology Review* 91:36–44.

Perrow, Charles. 1981. "Markets, Hierarchies and Hegemony: A Critique of Chandler and Williamson." Pp. 371–386 in *Perspectives on Organization Design and Behavior,* edited by Andrew Van de Ven and William Joyce. New York: Wiley Interscience.

———. 1986. "Economic Theories of Organization." *Theory and Society* 15:11–45.

———. 1990. "Small Firm Networks." Paper presented at the Harvard University Conference on Networks, August, Cambridge, MA.

Pfeffer, Jeffery and Gerald Salancik. 1978. *The External Control of Organizations: A Resource Dependence Perspective.* New York: Harper and Row.

Piore, Michael and Charles Sabel. 1984. *The Second Industrial Divide.* New York: Basic Books.

Powell, Walter. 1987. "Hybrid Organizational Arrangements: New Form or Transitional Development." *California Management Review* 30:47–87.

Richardson, G.B., 1972. "The Organization of Industry." *Economic Journal* 82:883–96.

Robins, James. 1987. "Organizational Networks: Notes on the Use of Transaction Cost Theory in the Study of Organizations." *Administrative Science Quarterly* 32:68–86.

Rosenbaum, James and Takehiko Kariya. 1989. "From High School to Work: Market and Institutional Mechanisms in Japan." *American Journal of Sociology* 94:1334–65.

Sabel, Charles. 1989. "Flexible Specialization and the Re-emergence of Regional Economies." Pp. 17–70 in *Reversing Industrial Decline? Industrial Structure and Policies in Britain and Her Competitors,* edited by Paul Hirst and Jonathan Zeitlin. New York: St. Martin's.

Sako, Mari. 1989. "Neither Markets nor Hierarchies: A Comparative Study of the Printed Circuit Board Industry in Britain and Japan." London School of Economics. Unpublished manuscript.

Sayer, Andrew. 1986. "New Developments in Manufacturing: The Just-in-Time System." *Capital and Class* 30:43–72.

Schumpeter, Joseph. 1947. "The Creative Response in Economic History." *Journal of Economic History* 7:149–59.

Sheard, Paul. 1983. "Auto Production Systems in Japan: Organizational and Locational Features." *Australian Geographical Studies* 21:49–68.

Shimada, Haruo. 1986. "Japanese Industrial Relations in Transition." (Working Paper No. 1854–88). Sloan School of Management, Massachusetts Institute of Technology, Cambridge, MA.

Shimada, Haruo and John MacDuffie. 1986. "Industrial Relations and 'Humanware'" (Working Paper No. 1855–88). Sloan School of Management, Massachusetts Institute of Technology, Cambridge, MA.

Shirai, Taishiro, ed. 1983. *Contemporary Industrial Relations in Japan.* Madison: University of Wisconsin Press.

Suzuki, H. 1976. "Age, Seniority and Wages." *International Labour Review* 113:67–83.

Taira, Koji. 1961. "Japanese Enterprise Unionism and Inter-Firm Wage Structure." *Industrial and Labor Relations Review* 15:33–51.

———. 1964. "The Labour Market in Japanese Development." *British Journal of Industrial Relations* 2:209–27.

———. 1970. *Economic Development and the Labor Market in Japan.* New York: Columbia University Press.

U.S. General Accounting Office. 1988. *Foreign Investment: Growing Japanese Presence in the U.S. Auto Industry.* Washington, DC: U.S. General Accounting Office.

U.S. International Trade Commission. 1987. *U.S. Global Competitiveness: The U.S. Automotive Parts Industry.* Washington, DC: U.S. Government Printing Office.

Wharton Economic Forecasting Associates. 1990. *North American Light Vehicle Outlook.* Philadelphia, PA.

Weick, Karl, 1979. *The Social Psychology of Organizing.* New York: Random House.

White, Michael and Malcolm Trevor. 1983. *Under Japanese Management.* London: Heinemann Educational Books.

Williamson, Oliver. 1975. *Markets and Hierarchies.* New York: Free Press.

———. 1981. *The Economic Institutions of Capitalism.* New York: Free Press.

———. 1983. "Organizational Innovation: The Transaction Cost

Approach." Pp. 101–33 in *Entrepreneurship,* edited by Joshua Ronen. Lexington, MA: Lexington Books.

Womack, James, Daniel Jones, and Daniel Roos. 1990. *The Machine That Changed the World.* New York: Rawson Associates.

Yoshino, M. 1976. *Japan's Multinational Enterprises.* Cambridge: Harvard University Press.

Young, Ruth. 1988. "Is Population Ecology a Useful Paradigm for the Study of Organizations." *American Journal of Sociology* 94:1–24.

Zuboff, Shoshana. 1988. *In the Age of the Smart Machine.* New York: Basic Books.

Zucker, Lynne. 1977. "The Role of Institutionalization in Cultural Persistence." *American Sociological Review* 42:726–43.

DISCUSSION QUESTIONS

1. What theory of organization–environment relations do Florida and Kenney test?

2. How does the U.S. environment differ from the Japanese environment?

3. What are the typical differences between U.S. and Japanese industrial organizations?

4. Are organizations a derivative of their environment, or can they be removed from the original environment and become implanted in a new one?

5. What strategies do organizations develop to adapt and respond to a new environment?

6. Do transplanted organizations take on characteristics of the new environment, or do they act on the new environment to bring it into line with their needs?

7. In what ways do transplanted organizations change the behavior of American workers?

8. Is the Japanese model of organization one toward which firms throughout the world are converging?

Managing Globally Competent People

NANCY J. ADLER AND SUSAN BARTHOLOMEW

LEARNING OBJECTIVES

After reading "Managing Globally Competent People" by Adler and Bartholomew, students will be able to:

1. Understand the expansion of the environment of organizational and managerial behavior from the domestic to the global environment

2. Learn a set of skills required by managers to become globally competent

3. Understand the differences between a corporation's human resource strategies and their business strategies

4. Discover that much of current thinking about global management is based on a set of illusions about global human resource management

"Top-level managers in many of today's leading corporations are losing control of their companies. The problem is not that they have misjudged the demands created by an increasingly complex environment and an accelerating rate of environmental change, nor even that they have failed to develop strategies appropriate to the new challenges. The problem is that their companies are incapable of carrying out the sophisticated strategies they have developed. Over the past 20 years, strategic thinking has far outdistanced organizational capabilities."[1]

Today, people create national competitiveness, not, as suggested by classical economic theory, mere access to advantageous factors of production.[2] Yet, human systems are also one of the major constraints in implementing global strategies. Not surprisingly therefore, human resource management has become "an important focus of top management attention, particularly in multinational enterprises."[3]

The clear issue is that strategy (the *what*) is internationalizing faster than implementation (the *how*) and much faster than individual managers and executives themselves (the *who*). "The challenges [therefore] are not the 'whats' of what-to-do, which are typically well-known. They are the

'hows' of managing human resources in a global firm."[4]

How prepared are executives to manage transnational companies? How capable are firms' human resource systems of recruiting, developing, retaining, and using globally competent managers and executives? A recent survey of major U.S. corporations found only six percent reporting foreign assignments to be essential for senior executive careers, with forty-nine percent believing foreign assignments to be completely immaterial.[5]

Which firms are leading in developing globally competent managers and executives, and which remain in the majority and lag behind? That majority, according to a recent survey of 1500 CEOs, will result in a lack of sufficient senior American managers prepared to run transnational businesses, forcing U.S. firms to confront the highest executive turn-over in history.[6]

This article recommends changes in global human resource management at two levels: individual and systemic. First, from an individual perspective, it recommends skills required by individual managers to be globally competent, highlighting those which transcend the historic competencies required of international and expatriate managers. Second, from a systems perspective, it recommends a framework for assessing globally competent human resource systems. It then shows that the majority of North American firms have much room for improvement in developing both globally competent managers and globally effective human resource systems.

By contrast, it describes the approaches of some of the world's leading firms that distinguish them from the majority. There is no question that world business is going global; the question raised in this article is how to create human systems capable of implementing transnational business strategies. Based on their research, the authors support the conclusion of the recent *21st Century Report* that "executives who perceive their international opera-

Source: Nancy J. Adler and Susan Bartholomew: "Managing Globally Competent People," *Academy of Management Executive*, 1992, Vol. 6, No. 3, pp. 52–65. Reprinted by permission.

tions as shelves for second-rate managers are unsuited for the CEO job in the year 2000, or indeed any managerial job today."[7]

Transnationally Competent Managers

Not all business strategies are equally global, nor need they be. As will be described, a firm's business strategy can be primarily domestic, international, multinational, or transnational. However, to be effective, the firm's human resource strategy should be integrated with its business strategy. Transnational firms need a transnational business strategy. While superficially appearing to be a truism, transnational firms also need a transnational human resource system and transnationally competent managers.

As summarized in Table 14.4, transnationally competent managers require a broader range of skills than traditional international managers. First, transnational managers must understand the worldwide business environment from a global perspective. Unlike expatriates of the past, transnational managers are not focused on a single country nor

limited to managing relationships between headquarters and a single foreign subsidiary. Second, transnational managers must learn about many foreign cultures' perspectives, tastes, trends, technologies, and approaches to conducting business. Unlike their predecessors, they do not focus on becoming an expert on one particular culture. Third, transnational managers must be skillful at working with people from many cultures simultaneously. They no longer have the luxury of dealing with each country's issues on a separate, and therefore sequential, basis. Fourth, similar to prior expatriates, transnational managers must be able to adapt to living in other cultures. Yet, unlike their predecessors, transnational managers need cross-cultural skills on a daily basis, throughout their career, not just during foreign assignments, but also on regular multi-country business trips and in daily interaction with foreign colleagues and clients worldwide. Fifth, transnational managers interact with foreign colleagues as equals, rather than from within clearly defined hierarchies of structural or cultural dominance and subordination. Thus, not only do the variety and frequency of cross-cultural interaction increase with globalization, but also the very nature of cross-cultural interaction changes.

The development of transnationally competent managers depends on firms' organizational capability to design and manage transnational human resource systems. Such

TABLE 14.4

TRANSNATIONALLY COMPETENT MANAGERS

TRANSNATIONAL SKILLS	TRANSNATIONALLY COMPETENT MANAGERS	TRADITIONAL INTERNATIONAL MANAGERS
Global Perspective	Understand worldwide business environment from a global perspective	Focus on a single foreign country and on managing relationships between headquarters and that country
Local Responsiveness	Learn about many cultures	Become an expert on one culture
Synergistic Learning	Work with and learn from people from many cultures simultaneously	Work with and coach people in each foreign culture separately or sequentially
	Create a culturally synergistic organizational environment	Integrate foreigners into the headquarters' national organizational culture
Transition and Adaptation	Adapt to living in many foreign cultures	Adapt to living in a foreign culture
Cross-cultural Interaction	Use cross-cultural interaction skills on a daily basis throughout one's career	Use cross-cultural interaction skills primarily on foreign assignments
Collaboration	Interact with foreign colleagues as equals	Interact within clearly defined hierarchies of structural and cultural dominance
Foreign Experience	Transpatriation for career and organization development	Expatriation or inpatriation primarily to get the job done

systems, in turn, allow firms to implement transnational business strategies. Before investigating firms' capability to implement transnational business strategies, let us briefly review a range of global business strategies along with each strategy's requisite managerial skills.

The Globalization of Business: Strategy, Structure, and Managerial Skills

Since World War II, industry after industry has progressed from dominantly domestic operations toward more global strategies. Historically, many firms progressed through four distinct phases: domestic, international, multinational, and transnational.[8] As firms progress towards global strategies, the portfolio of skills required of managers undergoes a parallel shift.

Domestic. Historically, most corporations began as domestic firms. They developed new products or services at home for the domestic market. During this initial domestic phase, foreign markets, and hence international managerial skills, were largely irrelevant.

International. As new firms entered, competition increased and each company was forced to search for new markets or resign itself to losing market share. A common response was to expand internationally, initially by exporting to foreign markets and later by developing foreign assembly and production facilities designed to serve the largest of those markets. To manage those foreign operations, firms often restructured to form a separate international division. Within the new international division, each country was managed separately, thus creating a multidomestic nature. Because the foreign operations were frequently seen as an extension—and therefore a replication—of domestic operations, they generally were not viewed as state of the art.

During this international phase, a hierarchical structure exists between the firm's headquarters and its various foreign subsidiaries. Power and influence are concentrated at corporate headquarters, which is primarily staffed by members of the headquarters' national culture. It is during this phase that firms often send their first home country managers abroad as expatriates. Cross-cultural interaction between expatriate managers and local subsidiary staff thus takes place within a clearly defined hierarchy in which headquarters has both structural and cultural dominance.

During this phase, international management is synonymous with expatriation. To be effective, expatriate managers must be competent at transferring technology to the local culture, managing local staff, and adapting business practices to suit local conditions. Specifically, international expatriate managers require cultural adaptation skills—as does their spouse and family—to adjust to living in a new environment and working with the local people. They must also acquire specific knowledge about the particular culture's perspectives, tastes, trends, technologies, and ways of doing business. Learning is thus single country focused—and culturally specific—during the international phase.

Multinational. As competition continues to heighten, firms increasingly emphasize producing least-cost products and services. To benefit from potential economies of scale and geographic scope, firms produce more standardized products and services. Because the prior phase's multidomestic structure can no longer support success, firms restructure to integrate domestic and foreign operations into worldwide lines of business, with sourcing, producing, assembling, and marketing distributed across many countries, and major decisions—which continue to be made at headquarters—strongly influenced by least-cost outcomes.

During the multinational phase, the hierarchical relationship remains between headquarters and foreign subsidiaries. In addition, with the increased importance of foreign operations to the core business, headquarters more tightly controls major decisions worldwide. However, headquarters' decisions are now made by people from a wider range of cultures than previously, many of whom are local managers from foreign subsidiaries posted on temporary "inpatriate" assignments at corporate headquarters. These "inpatriates" are not encouraged to express the diversity of national perspectives and cultural experience they represent. Rather, they are asked to adapt as the firm implicitly and explicitly integrates them into the organizational culture which is still dominated by the values of the headquarters' national culture. While multinational representation increases at headquarters, cultural dominance of the headquarters' national culture continues, remaining loosely coupled with structure.

For the first time, senior managers, those leading the worldwide lines of business, need to understand the world business environment. Similarly for the first time, senior managers must work daily with clients and employees from around the world to be effective. International and cross-cultural skills become needed for managers throughout the firm, not just for those few imminently leaving for foreign postings. Expatriates and "inpatriates" still require cultural adaptation skills and specific local knowledge, but these are not the dominant international skills required by most managers in a multinational firm. For the majority, learning needs grow beyond local context to encompass a need to understand the world business environment. In addition, multinational managers need to be skilled at working with clients and employees from many nations (rather than merely from a single foreign country), as well as at standardizing operations and integrating people from around the world into a common organizational culture.

Transnational. As competition continues to increase and product lifecycles shorten dramatically, firms find it necessary to compete globally, based simultaneously on state-of-the-art, top quality products and services and least-cost production. Unlike the prior phase's emphasis on identical products that can be distributed worldwide, transnational products are increasingly mass-customized—tailored to each individual client's needs. Research and development demands increase as does the firm's need for worldwide marketing scope.

These dynamics lead to transnational networks of firms and divisions within firms including an increasingly complex web of strategic alliances. Internationally, these firms distribute their multiple headquarters across a number of nations. As a result, transnational firms become less hierarchically structured than firms operating in the previous phases. As such, power is no longer centered in a single headquarters that is coincident with or dominated by any one national culture. As a consequence, both structural and cultural dominance are minimized, with cross-cultural interaction no longer following any pre-defined "passport hierarchy." It is for these firms that transnational human resource strategies are now being developed that emphasize organizational learning along with individual managerial skills.

To be effective, transnational managers need both the culturally specific knowledge and adaptation skills required in international firms, and the ability to acquire a worldwide perspective and to integrate worldwide diversity required in multinational firms. As a consequence, one of the transnational manager's primary skills is to exercise discretion in choosing when to be locally responsive and when to emphasize global integration.

Moreover, the integration required in transnational firms is based on cultural synergy—on combining the many cultures into a unique organizational culture—rather than on simply integrating foreigners into the dominant culture of the headquarters' nationality (as was the

norm in prior phases). Transnational managers require additional new skills to be effective in their less hierarchical, networked firms: first, the ability to work with people of other cultures as equals; second, the ability to learn in order to continually enhance organizational capability. Transnational managers must learn how to collaborate with partners worldwide, gaining as much knowledge as possible from each interaction, and, transmitting that knowledge quickly and effectively throughout the worldwide network of operations. This requires managers who both want to learn and have the skills to quickly and continuously learn from people of other cultures.[9]

Transnational Human Resource Systems

The development of such "transnationally competent managers," as discussed previously, depends upon firms' capability to design and manage transnational human resource systems. The function of human resource systems, in general, is to recruit, develop, and retain competent managers and executives. Beyond these core functions, we add utilization: human resource systems facilitate the effective "utilization" of those managers who have been recruited, developed, and retained. Therefore, a transnational human resource system is one that recruits, develops, retains and utilizes managers and executives who are competent transnationally.[10]

Three Dimensions of a Transnational Human Resource System

For a transnational human resource system to be effective, it must exhibit three characteristics: transnational scope, transnational representation, and transnational process. We will describe each briefly, and then discuss their implications for recruiting, developing, retaining, and using human resources.

Transnational Scope. Transnational scope is the geographical context within which all major decisions are made. As Bartlett and Ghoshal have stated, global management is a "frame of mind," not a particular organizational structure.[11] Thus, to achieve global scope, executives and managers must frame major decisions and evaluate options relative to worldwide business dynamics. Moreover, they must benchmark their own and their firm's performance against worldclass standards. They can neither discuss nor resolve major issues within a narrower national or regional context. An example is Unilever's "Best Proven Practices." This British-Dutch consumer products firm identifies superior practices and innovations in its subsidiaries worldwide and then diffuses the outstanding approaches throughout the worldwide organization.[12]

Transnational Representation.   Transnational representation refers to the multinational composition of the firm's managers and executives. To achieve transnational representation, the firm's portfolio of key executives and managers should be as multinational as its worldwide distribution of production, finance, sales, and profits. Symbolically, firms achieve transnational representation through the well balanced portfolio of passports held by senior management. Philips, for example, maintains transnational representation by having "the corporate pool." This pool consists of mobile individuals representing more than fifty nationalities, each having at least five years of experience and ranked in the top twenty percent on performance, and all financed on a corporate budget.[13]

Transnational Process.   Transnational process reflects the firm's ability to effectively include representatives and ideas from many cultures in its planning and decision-making processes. Firms create transnational process when they consistently recognize, value, and effectively use cultural diversity within the organization; that is, when there is "no unintended leakage of culture specific systems and approaches."[14] Transnational process, however, is not the mere inclusion of people and ideas of many cultures; rather, it goes beyond inclusion to encompass cultural synergy— the combination of culturally diverse perspectives and approaches into a new transnational organizational culture. Cultural synergy requires "a genuine belief . . . that more creative and effective ways of managing people could be developed as a result of cross-cultural learning."[15] To create transnational process, executives and managers must be as skilled at working with and learning from people from outside their own culture as with same culture nationals.

Today's Firms: How Transnational?

A survey was conducted of fifty firms headquartered in the United States and Canada from a wide variety of industries

to determine the extent to which their overall business strategy matched their current human resource system, as well as identifying the extent of globalization of their human resource strategies. The results paint a picture of extensive global business involvement. Unfortunately, however, similar involvement in recruiting, developing, retaining, and using globally competent managers is lacking.

Global Strategic Integration

The fifty firms made almost half of their sales abroad, and earned nearly forty percent of their revenues and profits outside of their headquarters' country (the United States or Canada). Similarly, almost two fifths of the fifty firms' employees worked outside the headquarters' country. Yet, when these firms reviewed their human resource systems as a whole, and their senior leadership in particular, they could not reveal nearly as global a portrait.

For example, in comparing themselves with their competitors, the fifty firms found themselves to be more global on overall business strategy, financial systems, production operations, and marketing. However, they found their human resource systems to be the least global functional area within their own organization. Moreover, unlike their assessment in other functional areas, they did not evaluate their human resource systems as being more global than those of their competitors.

Similarly, the senior leadership of the surveyed firms was less global on all three global indicators—scope, representation, and process—than each firm's overall business performance. For example, an average of only eight countries were represented among the most senior one hundred executives in each firm. Half of the companies reported fewer than four nationalities among the top one hundred executives. Firms therefore have less than a quarter of the international representation in their senior leadership (eight percent) as they have in their global business performance (i.e., sales, revenues, and profits: forty percent). Similarly, of the same top one hundred executives in each firm, only fifteen percent were from outside of North America. This represents less than half the internationalization of the senior executive cadre (fifteen percent) as of business performance (forty percent). Moreover, using experience, rather than representation, yields similar results. Of the same one hundred leaders, almost three quarters lacked expatriate experience, with only a third reporting any international experience at all. Not surprisingly, less than one in five spoke a foreign language. On no measure of international experience is the senior leadership of these North American firms as international as the business itself.

Transnational Human Resource Integration

Firms' organizational capability to implement transnational business strategies is supported by transnational human resource management systems. As discussed, such systems should exhibit all three dimensions—transnational scope, transnational representation, and transnational process. These three global dimensions are clearly important for each of the four primary components of human resource systems—recruiting, developing, retaining, and utilizing globally competent people. Each will therefore be discussed separately. Unfortunately, the results of this study indicate that firms' human resource management systems have not become global either as rapidly or as extensively as have their business strategies and structures.

Recruiting.   For recruiting decisions, transnational scope requires that firms consider their business needs and the availability of candidates worldwide. Similar to the firm's strategic business decisions, some recruiting decisions must enhance worldwide integration and coordination, others local responsiveness, and others the firm's ability to learn.[16] Local responsiveness requires that firms recruit people with a sophisticated understanding of each of the countries in which they operate; this includes recruiting host nationals. Worldwide integration requires that recruiting be guided by worldclass standards in selecting the most competent people from anywhere in the world for senior management positions. Individual and organizational learning requires that people be selected who are capable of simultaneously working with and learning from colleagues from many nations: people who are capable of creating cultural synergy.

Transnational representation in recruiting requires that firms select managers from throughout the world for potential positions anywhere in the world. In a literal sense, it requires that talent flows to opportunity worldwide, without regard to national passport.

Transnational process in recruiting requires that firms use search and selection procedures that are equally attractive to candidates from each target nationality. Selection criteria, including the methods used to judge competence, must not be biased to favour any one culture.

Similarly, incentives to join the firm must appeal to a broad range of cultures. The antithesis of transnational process was exhibited by one U.S. firm when it offered new college recruits from the Netherlands one of the same incentives it offers its American recruits: free graduate education. The Dutch candidates found this "benefit" amusing given that graduate education in the Netherlands—unlike in the United States—is already paid for by the government and thus free to all students.

Rather than encouraging high potential candidates, this particular incentive made Dutch students hesitate to join a firm that demonstrated such parochialism in its initial contact with them.

The fifty surveyed firms reported that their recruitment and selection activities were less than global in terms of scope, representation, and process. For a summary, see Exhibit 14.1: Transnational Recruiting.

Development.   In managerial development, transnational scope means that managers' experiences both on-the-job and in formal training situations prepare them to work anywhere in the world with people from all parts of the world; that is, it prepares them to conduct the firm's business in a global environment. Transnational firms search worldwide for the best training and development options and select specific approaches and programs based on worldclass standards.

EXHIBIT 14.1

TRANSNATIONAL RECRUITING

The 50 surveyed firms reported that their recruitment and selection activities were less than transnational in terms of scope, representation, and process. In selecting future senior managers, the 50 firms ranked an outstanding overall track record as the most important criterion, with foreign business experience, demonstrated cultural sensitivity and adaptability, and a track record for outstanding performance outside the home country ranked as somewhat, but not highly, important. Moreover, foreign language skills were not considered at all important. Similarly, while considering three out of four transnational scope and process skills to be somewhat important for promotion to senior management (understanding world issues and trends; working effectively with clients and colleagues from other countries; and, demonstrating cultural sensitivity), none was considered highly important. Once again, foreign language skills were not considered important for promotion. Similarly, on transnational representation, only a third of the 50 firms stated that they "recruit managers from all parts of the world in which . . . [they] conduct business."

To achieve transnational representation, training and development programs must be planned and delivered by multinational teams as well as offered to multinational participants. To be transnational, programs cannot be planned by one culture (generally representatives of the headquarters' nationality) and simply exported for local delivery abroad. By contrast, using a transnational approach, American Express created a multinational design team at headquarters to develop training approaches and programs which were subsequently localized for delivery around the world. At no time did American cultural values dominate either the process or the programs.

Transnational process in development requires that the approaches taken effectively include all participating cultures. Thus, the process cannot encourage greater participation by one nationality to the exclusion of other nationalities. Ericsson and Olivetti provide examples of a transnational development approach. Each company created a management development center in which both the staff and executive participants come from all regions of the world. To minimize the possibility of headquarters' cultural dominance, neither company located its management development center in the headquarters' country—Sweden or Italy—but rather both chose another more culturally neutral country.[17]

For transnational firms, foreign assignments become a core component of the organizational and career development process. "Transpatriates" from all parts of the world are sent to all other parts of the world to develop their worldwide perspective and cross-cultural skills, as well as developing the organization's cadre of globally sophisticated managers. Foreign assignments in transnational firms are no longer used primarily to get a job done in a foreign country (expatriation) or to socialize foreign country nationals into the home country headquarters' culture ("inpatriation"), but rather to enhance individual and organizational learning in all parts of the system ("transpatriation"). Using a "transpatriation" approach, Royal Dutch Shell, for example, uses multifunctional and multinational experience to provide corporate wide, transnational skills. Shell's "aim is that every member of an operating company management team should have had international experience and that each such team should include one expatriate . . . [Similarly, at IBM], international experience is [considered] indispensable to senior positions."[18]

In the survey, the fifty firms reported that their training and development opportunities were less than global on all three dimensions of human resource strategy:

transnational scope, transnational representation, and transnational process (for a summary of the research, see Exhibit 14.2: Transnational Development). Similar to recruitment, training and development approaches currently are not nearly as global as are overall business strategies. To reduce the gap between the relative globalization of firms' strategies and their less-than-global human resource systems, firms must learn how to recognize, value, and use globally competent managers. As one surveyed executive summarized, closing the gaps begins by having "the key organizational development activity . . . focused on allowing people of different nationalities to meet and to get to know each other, and, through these linkages, to meet the needs of the company."

Retaining. Transnational scope in retaining managers means that decisions about career paths must consider the firm's needs and operations worldwide. Performance

---

EXHIBIT 14.2

TRANSNATIONAL DEVELOPMENT

In the survey, the 50 firms reported that their training and development opportunities were less than transnational on all three dimensions of human resource strategy: scope, representation, and process. Fewer than one in four of the firms reported that the content of their training programs was global in focus, that they had representatives of many nations attending each program, or that their programs were designed or delivered by multinational training teams. Only four percent reported that cross-cultural training was offered to all managers. However, the firms did report offering a greater number of general development opportunities worldwide than specific international training programs. A third of the firms provide equivalent development opportunities for managers worldwide and 42 percent provide such opportunities for managers of all nationalities.

In reviewing foreign assignments, the 50 firms report using expatriates primarily to "get the job done abroad," not to develop the organization, nor to develop the individual manager's career. Given their emphasis on getting the immediate job done, it is not surprising that they did not report consistently selecting the "stars" (either high potential junior managers or very senior, top-performing executives) for expatriate positions. To increase globalization in their development programs, the surveyed executives strongly recommended "transferring different nationalities to different countries several times in their career" and "making it clear to these employees that international assignments are important to career development." However, to date, the majority of the surveyed firms do not have such recommended programs in place.

incentives, rewards, and career opportunities must meet worldclass standards such that the firm does not lose its most competent people. Firms must benchmark excellence in their human resource systems against their most significant global competitors in the same ways that they assess the relative competitiveness of their research and development, production, marketing, and financial systems.

Transnational representation requires that organizational incentives and career path opportunities be equally accessible and appealing to managers from all nationalities. Firms with transnational human resource systems do not create a glass ceiling beyond which only members of the headquarters' nationality can be promoted.

Transnational process requires that the performance review and promotion systems include approaches which are equally appropriate to a broad range of nationalities. The process by which promotion and career path decisions are made should not be innately biased towards any one culture, nor should it exclude particular cultures. The underlying dynamic in transnational process is not to institute identical systems worldwide, but rather to use approaches which are culturally equivalent. Shell for example, ensures this transnational orientation by having managers' "career home" be in "a business function rather than a geographical place."[19] As one surveyed senior executive summarized, firms considered to be outstanding in transnational human resource management are "flexible enough in systems and practices to attract and retain the best people regardless of nationality."

Utilizing.   Transnational scope in utilization means that managers' problem solving skills are focused on the firm's worldwide operations and competitive environment, not just on the regional, national, or local situation. To assess the competitive environment in transnational human resource management, the fifty surveyed firms identified leading North American, European, and Asian companies. The top North American firm was perceived to be IBM, followed by General Electric, and Citicorp. The surveyed firms identified Royal Dutch Shell as the leading European firm, followed by Nestle and Philips, along with British Petroleum and Unilever. Sony was selected as the leading Asian firm, followed by Honda, Toyota, and Mitsubishi. Yet, in reviewing the pattern of responses, a significant proportion of the surveyed firms do not appear to be benchmarking excellence in global human resource management at all, and an even greater number appear to be geographically limiting their perspective to a fairly narrow, parochial scope. For instance, almost a fifth of the surveyed firms (all of which are North American) could not name a single

leading North American firm. Even more disconcerting, more than a third could not identify a single excellent European firm, and half could not name a single excellent Asian firm.[20]

Beyond scope, transnational representation in utilization means that managers and executives of many nationalities are included in the firm's critical operating and strategic planning teams. Managers from outside of headquarters are not "out of sight and out of mind;" rather they are integrated into the worldwide network of knowledge exchange, continual learning, and action. For example, as Unilever's director of management development explains:

> *In recent years, I have had several product group directors . . . [want] an expatriate on the board of the local company. Not just because they haven't got a national, not just because it would be good for the expatriate, but because it would be good for the company to have a bit of challenge to the one-best-way of doing things.*[21]

Transnational process in human resource utilization means that the organization culture does not inherently bias contributions from or towards any particular cultural group. The human resource system recognizes the firm's cultural diversity and uses it either to build culturally synergistic processes that include all cultures involved or to select the particular process that is the most appropriate for the given situation.

Illusions and Recommendations

From the prior discussion, it is clear that transnational human resource systems are both fundamentally important for future business success and qualitatively different from prior approaches to human resource management. Equally evident is the fact that North American firms' human resource systems are not nearly as global as their business operations on any of the three fundamental human resource dimensions: transnational scope, transnational representation, and transnational process. Competitive demands appear to have "outrun the slow pace of organizational change and adjustment . . . [with] top management beginning to feel that the organization itself is the biggest barrier to competitive and strategic development."[22] It is telling that in most cases the respondents found the survey itself to be important and yet very difficult to complete, primarily because their firms did not systematically collect or keep data on any aspect of global human resource management.

The remaining question is why. There appears to be a series of illusions—of mind traps—that are preventing firms from acting in a global manner, including recognizing the mental gap between their current human resource approaches and those necessary to succeed in a highly competitive transnational business environment. Many of the surveyed executives recognized that their firms simply "lack global thinking" and "lack global business strategies," largely due to the "massive U.S. imprint on human resource practices." According to many of the American executives, firms must "stop thinking that the world begins and ends at U.S. borders," "stop having a U.S. expatriate mentality," and begin to "realize that the world does not revolve around us." This pattern of responses suggests the following seven illusions.

Illusion One: If business has gone well, it will continue to go well. No, today is not like yesterday, nor will tomorrow be a projection of today. Business has fundamentally changed, and human resource systems must undergo similar transformational changes to stay relevant, let alone effective. As Kenichi Ohmae has pointed out, "Today and in the twenty-first century, management's ability to transform the organization and its people into a global company is a prerequisite for survival because both its customers and competitors have become cosmopolitan."[23]

Illusion Two: We have always played on a level playing field and won. No. The North American economies (and therefore North American firms) have had an advantage: they were the only developed economies left intact following World War II and were thus "the only game in town." Today, Asia, Europe, and the Americas each have highly competitive firms and economies, none of which will continue to prosper without being excellent at including people and business worldwide. As Ohmae has observed, "The key to a nation's future is its human resources. It used to be its natural resources, but not any more. The quality and number of its educated people now determines a country's likely prosperity or decline"; so too with global firms.[24]

Illusion Three: If we manage expatriates better, we will have an effective global human resource system. No. Doing better at what was necessary in the past (expatriate management) is not equivalent to creating systems capable of sustaining global competitiveness today. Whereas the temptation is to attempt to do better at that which is known (in this case, the simple expatriation of managers), the real challenge is to excel at that which is new. Transnational firms need transnational human resource systems to

succeed. Better managed expatriate transfers will only improve one small aspect of existing human resource management, not create an overall transnational system.

Illusion Four: If we're doing something, we must be doing enough. No. Focusing on only one of the three transnational dimensions—scope, representation, or process—is not enough to transform domestic, international, or multinational human resource approaches into truly transnational systems. Bringing a "foreigner" onto the board of directors, for example, gives the illusion of globalization, but is insufficient to underpin its substance.

Illusion Five: If "foreigners" are fitting in at headquarters, we must be managing our cultural diversity well. No. This is a multinational paradigm trap. In multinationals, foreigners must adapt to the headquarters' culture, including learning its native language. Multinationals typically see cultural differences "as a nuisance, a constraint, an obstacle to be surmounted."[25] In transnational firms, all managers make transitions, all managers adapt, and all managers help to create a synergistic organizational culture which transcends any one national culture.

Illusion Six: As national wealth increases, everyone will become more like us. No. To the extent that the world is converging in its values, attitudes, and styles of doing business, it is not converging on a single country's national pattern, even that of the world's wealthiest nation. "The appealing 'one-best-way' assumption about management, the belief that different cultures are converging at different paces on the same concept of organization, is dying a slow death."[26] Moreover, transnational firms need to create transnational cultures that are inclusive of all their members, not wait for the world to converge on a reality that looks like any particular firm's national culture, even one that looks "just like us."

Illusion Seven: If we provide managers with cross-cultural training, we will increase organizational capability. No. Increased cognitive understanding does not guarantee increased behavioral effectiveness, nor is enhanced individual learning sufficient for improved organizational effectiveness. Simply increasing the number of cross-cultural training programs offered to individual managers does not ensure that they will actually use the skills on a regular basis, nor that the firm as a whole will benefit from the potentially improved cross-cultural interaction. To benefit, the individual must want to learn that which is not-invented-here and the organization must want to learn from the individual. To enhance organizational capability, managers must continually work with and learn from people worldwide and disperse that knowledge throughout the firm's worldwide operations.

Despite the seemingly insurmountable challenges, firms are beginning to address and solve the dilemmas posed by going global. To date, no firm believes it has "the answer," the solution to creating a truly transnational human resource system. However, a number of firms are currently inventing pieces of the solution which may cohere into just such a system. For example, as John Reed, CEO of Citicorp, describes:

> *There are few companies in the world that are truly global. . . . Our most important advantage is our globality. Our global human capital may be as important a resource, if not more important, than our financial capital. Look at the Policy Committee, the top thirty or so officers in the bank. Almost seventy-five percent have worked outside the United States; more than twenty-five percent have worked in three or more countries. Half speak two or more languages other than English. Seven were born outside the United States.[27]*

Perhaps, then, a primary role of transnational human resource executives today is to remain open to fundamental change and to continue to encourage the openness and experimentation needed to create truly global systems.

NOTES

The authors would like to thank the Ontario Centre for International Business for generously funding this research. See "Globalization and Human Resource Management," (Nancy J. Adler and Susan Bartholomew) in *Research in Global Strategic Management: Corporate Responses to Global Change,* Alan M. Rugman and Alain Verbeke (eds.), Vol. 3, (Greenwich, Conn.: JAI Press, 1992) for further details of the research design and results of the study.

[1] Christopher A. Bartlett and Sumantra Ghoshal, "Matrix Management: Not a Structure, a Frame of Mind" *Harvard Business Review,* July-August 1990, 138.

[2] See Michael E. Porter, *The Competitive Advantage of Nations* (New York: The Free Press, 1990).

[3] Paul A. Evans, Yves Doz, and Andre Laurent, *Human Resource Management in International Firms* (London: Macmillan Press, 1989), xi–1.

[4] Ibid.; also see Gunnar Hedlund "Who Manages the Global Corporation? Changes in the Nationality of Presidents of Foreign Subsidiaries of Swedish MNCs During the 1980s," Working Paper, (Institute of International Business and the Stockholm School of Economics, May 1990).

[5] See Donald C. Hambrick, Lester B. Korn, James W. Frederickson, and Richard M. Ferry, *21st Century Report: Reinventing the CEO* (New York: Korn/Ferry and Columbia University's Graduate School of Business, 1989), 1–94.

[6] Ibid.

[7] Ibid., 57.

[8] See Nancy J. Adler and Fariborz Ghadar "International Strategy from the Perspective of People and Culture: The North American Context," in Alan M. Rugman (ed.), *Research in Global Strategic Management: International Business Research for the Twenty-First Century; Canada's New Research Agenda,* Vol. 1, (Greenwich, Conn.: JAI Press, 1990) 179–205; and "Strategic Human Resource Management: A Global Perspective," in Rudiger Pieper (ed.), *Human Resource Management in International Comparison* (Berlin, de Gruyter, 1990), 235–260.

[9] See Gary Hamel, Yves Doz, and C.K. Prahalad "Collaborate With Your Competitors and Win," *Harvard Business Review,* 89(1), 1989, 133–139.

[10] For a review of international human resource management, see Nancy J. Adler, *International Dimensions of Organizational Behaviour,* 2nd ed. (Boston: PWS Kent, 1991); Peter J. Dowling "Hot Issues Overseas," *Personnel Administrator,* 34(1), 1989, 66–72; Peter J. Dowling & R. Schuler, *International Dimensions of Human Resource Management* (Boston: PWS Kent, 1990); Peter J. Dowling & Denise E. Welch, "International Human Resource Management: An Australian Perspective," *Asia Pacific Journal of Management,* 6(1) 1988, 39–65; Yves Doz & C.K. Prahalad "Controlled Variety: A Challenge for Human Resource Management in the MNC," *Human Resource Management,* 25(1), 1986, 55–71; A. Edstrom & J.R. Galbraith "Transfer of Managers as a Coordination and Control Strategy in Multinational Firms," *Administrative Science Quarterly,* 22, 1977, 248–263; Evans, Doz, & Laurent, (1989) op. cit.; Andre Laurent "The Cross-Cultural Puzzle of International Human Resource Management," *Human Resource Management,* 25(1), 1986, 91–101; E.L. Miller, S. Beechler, B. Bhatt, & R. Nath, "The Relationship Between the Global Strategic Planning Process and the Human Resource Management Function," *Human Resource Planning,* 9(1), 1986, 9–23; John Milliman, Mary Ann Von Glinow, & Maria Nathan, "Organizational Life Cycles and Strategic International Human Resource Management in Multinational Companies: Implications for Congruence Theory," *Academy of Management Review,* 16(2), 1991, 318–339; Dan A. Ondrack, "International Human Resources Management in European and North American Firms," *Human Resource Management,* 25(1), 1985, 121–132; Dan A. Ondrack, "International Transfers of Managers in North American and European MNEs," *Journal of International Business Studies,* 16(3), 1985, 1–19; Vladimir Pucik, "The International Management of Human Resources," in C.J. Fombrun, N.M. Tichy, & M.A.

Devanna (eds.), *Strategic Human Resource Management* (New York: Wiley, 1984); Vladimir Pucik & Jan Hack Katz, "Information, Control and Human Resource Management in Multinational Firms," *Human Resource Management*, 25(1), 1986, 121–132; and Rosalie Tung, *The New Expatriates: Managing Human Resources Abroad* (New York: Harper & Row 1988), and "Strategic Management of Human Resources in Multinational Enterprises," *Human Resource Management*, 23(2), 1984, 129–143; among others.

[11] Op. cit., 1990.

[12] Unilever's "Best Proven Practice" technique was cited by Philip M. Rosenzweig and Jitendra Singh, "Organizational Environments and the Multinational Enterprise," *Academy of Management Review*, 16(2), 1991, 354, based on an interview that Rosenzweig conducted with Unilever.

[13] See Paul Evans, Elizabeth Lank, and Alison Farquhar, "Managing Human Resources in the International Firm: Lessons from Practice," in Paul Evans, Yves Doz, and Andre Laurent, 1989, op. cit., 138.

[14] Kenichi Ohmae, *The Borderless World: Power and Strategy in the Interlinked Economy* (New York: Harper Business, 1990), 112.

[15] Andre Laurent, op. cit., 1986, 100.

[16] See C.K. Prahalad and Yves Doz, *The Multinational Mission: Balancing Local Demands and Global Vision* (New York: Free Press, 1987); also, for a discussion of global integration versus local responsiveness from a business strategy perspective, see Michael E. Porter, "Changing Patterns of International Competition," *California Management Review*, 28(2), 1986, 9–40; and Christopher A. Bartlett, "Building and Managing the Transnational: The New Organizational Challenge," in M.E. Porter (ed.) *Competition in Global Industries* (Boston: Harvard Business School Press, 1986), 367–401, who explicitly developed the concepts, along with initial work and elaboration by: Christopher A. Bartlett & Sumantra Ghoshal, *Managing*

Across Borders: The Transnational Solution (Boston: Harvard Business School Press, 1989); Yves Doz, "Strategic Management in Multinational Companies," *Sloan Management Review*, 21(2), 1980, 27–46; Yves Doz, Christopher A. Bartlett, & C.K. Prahalad, "Global Competitive Pressures and Host Country Demands: Managing Tensions in MNCs," *California Management Review*, 23(3), 1981, 63–73; and Yves Doz & C.K. Prahalad, "Patterns of Strategic Control Within Multinational Corporations," *Journal of International Business Studies*, 15(2), 1984, 55–72.

[17] See Evans, Lank and Farquhar, op. cit., 1989, 119.

[18] Ibid., 130–131; 139.

[19] Ibid., 141.

[20] An even more disconcerting display of ignorance was that four surveyed firms listed 3M, Citicorp, Ford, and General Motors as European firms, and in another four responses, Dupont, Eastman Kodak, Coca-Cola, and Wang were identified as leading Asian firms.

[21] Evans, Lank, and Farquhar, op. cit., 122.

[22] Paul Evans and Yves Doz, "The Dualistic Organization," in Evans, Doz, & Laurent, op. cit., 1989, 223: based on the earlier work of Doz, "Managing Manufacturing Rationalization Within Multinational Companies," *Columbia Journal of World Business*, 13(3), 1978, 82–94; and Prahalad and Doz, op. cit., 1987.

[23] *Beyond National Borders* (Homewood, Illinois: Dow Jones-Irwin, 1987), 93.

[24] Ibid., 1.

[25] Evans, Lank & Farquhar, op. cit., 115.

[26] Ibid., 115.

[27] Noel Tichy and Ram Charan, "Citicorp Faces the World: An Interview with John Reed," *Harvard Business Review*, November-December, 1990, 137.

DISCUSSION QUESTIONS

1. Why are global business strategies more advanced than global management and human resource strategies?

2. What are the skills required of transnational managers compared with traditional international managers?

3. What is a transnational human resource system?

4. To what extent are corporations transnational in the 1990s?

5. What does it mean to develop a global benchmark for human resource systems?

6. What are the implications of the illusions held by North American firms concerning their ability to develop transnational management systems?

7. How does Adler and Bartholomew's view of the development of global human resource systems fit with the findings of Florida and Kenney? Specifically, what is the relationship between the organization and its environment?

For Further Reading

Adler, N. *International Dimensions of Organizational Behavior,* 2nd ed. Boston, Mass.: PSW-Kent, 1991.

Aldrich, H. *Organization and Environments.* New Jersey: Prentice-Hall, 1979.

Lawrence, P. and Lorsch, J. *Organization and Environment.* Boston: Harvard University Graduate School of Business Administration, Division of Research, 1967.

Hannan, M. and Freeman, J. *Organizational Ecology.* Cambridge: Harvard University Press, 1989.

15

TECHNOLOGY

Automate/Informate:
The Two Faces of Intelligent Technology

SHOSHANA ZUBOFF

LEARNING OBJECTIVES

After reading Zuboff's "Automate/Informate: The Two Faces of Intelligent Technology" a student will be able to:

1. Understand how technology can be used

2. Know the limitations of technology when automation is used to reduce skill and labor requirements

3. Understand the potential of technology in becoming an informational tool used to increase innovation in organizations

4. Learn how to manage technology to increase long-term organizational success

Put your eye to the kaleidoscope and hold it toward the light. You see a burst of color, tiny fragments in an intricate composition. Imagine a hand slowly turning the kaleidoscope's rim until hundreds of angles collapse, merge, and separate to form a new design. A fundamental change in an organization's technological infrastructure wields the power of the slow-moving hand at the turning rim. Technology defines the horizon of our material world as it shapes the limits of what is possible and what is barely imaginable; it erodes assumptions about the nature of our reality, the "design" in which we dwell; and it creates new choices. An innovation like the steam engine, the telephone, the electric light, or the computer is not only an ele-

ment within the pattern; it is a force that turns the rim, a concrete presence that silently evokes a new vision of the potential for relatedness and, in the end, provides the occasion for a new design.

It is in this sense that technology cannot be considered neutral. It is brimming with valence and specificity in the opportunities that it creates and forecloses. Air travel has allowed us to conquer time and distance in a new way by knitting the planet together and giving us access to other peoples, places, and cultures. The electric light rescued the night from darkness. Telephones permit us to pursue intimate contact without bodies that touch or eyes that meet. The litany of dramatic new organizations of reality engendered by new technologies is a long one.

But between the turning rim and the emergence of a new pattern, another force infuses the final configuration of elements with meaning. This is the human activity of choice. As the limits of the possible are newly defined, so too is the opportunity for choice multiplied. Shall I fly or drive or take a train? What is my destination? Shall I use the telephone to maintain intimate contact with friends I rarely see? If so, whom shall I call, how often, and for how long shall we speak? The metaphor of kaleidoscopic change is finally a limited one. Those pretty fragments align themselves without meaning, but change in human societies is not quite as blind. Though intentions do not necessarily predict consequences, human beings do proceed by constructing meaning, assessing interests and, with varying degrees of awareness, making choices. It is in the realm of choice that technology reveals a certain indeterminacy. Though it redefines the horizon of possibility, it cannot determine what choices will be made and for what purposes.

In these final decades of the twentieth century, many long-standing assumptions about how work is organized are being challenged by a new technological presence. Advanced computer-based information technology is providing a new infrastructure that mediates many of the productive and communicative activities most central to organizational life. This article will examine the role that information technology can play in restructuring the work place. Having interviewed approximately 500 workers and managers at ten research sites representing six companies, in industries as diverse as banking, telecommunications, and paper and pulp production, I shall discuss some themes that cut across organizational boundaries and seem to have relevance to a wide range of settings. Specifically, this article will sketch two divergent conceptions of information technology and their respective implications for the organization of work.

Automate/Informate: The Duality of Intelligent Technology

As the logic of Frederick Taylor's scientific management began to take hold earlier in this century, the substitution of machine power for human labor became the obvious solution for increasing the speed and volume of production. Beginning with Ford's Highland Park auto-assembly plant in 1915, technology would be relied on to complement or supplant human direction. In *Mechanization Takes Command,* Siegfried Giedion describes this process:

> The instruction cards on which Taylor set so much value Ford was able to discard. The conveyer belt, the traveling platform, the overhead rails and material conveyers take their place. . . . Motion analysis has become largely unnecessary, for the task of the assembly-line worker is reduced to a few manipulations. Taylor's stopwatch nevertheless remains, measuring the time of operations to the fraction of a second.

H. L. Arnold, an industrial journalist, wrote enthusiastically about the Ford innovations that maximized the continuity of assembly. He summarized the key elements of the productivity strategy: First, all needless motions were eliminated from the workman's actions and second, the task was organized to require the least expenditure of will power, and . . . . brain fatigue." This formula is of enduring significance as it has dominated the design of mass-production technologies throughout the twentieth century. It calls for simplification (and sometimes intensification) of effort, while skill is increasingly subsumed by technology.

In the 1980s, the rapid development and diffusion of advanced information technology have focused new attention on the underlying logic of technology deployment. To what extent will applications of this powerful new technology reproduce the formula of labor substitution, which was perfected through decades of economic success in the mass-production industries?

Managers typically invest in new information technology because they believe it will allow them to accomplish their operations more quickly and at less cost. Increasingly managers are beginning to appreciate the more complex ways in which information technology can provide new sources of competitive advantage. In either case, when managers harness information technology to their strategic goals, they usually plan to accomplish one or more of three interdependent operational objectives— to increase the *continuity* (functional integration, enhanced automaticity, rapid response), *control* (precision, accuracy, predictability, consistency, certainty), and *comprehensibility* (visibility, analysis, synthesis) of productive functions.

In a manufacturing environment, for example, microprocessor-based devices such as programmable logic controllers (PLCs) or sensors can be integrated into production equipment and linked to a hierarchy of computer systems, thus increasing both the continuity and the control of production operations. In an office environment, the standardization, real-time updating, and orderly storage of transaction histories made possible by computer systems enhance both the control and the continuity of office functions.

Information technology also increases the comprehensibility of the very processes that have been automated. Indeed, greater comprehension is both a condition and a consequence of such applications. Any activity, from a clerical transaction to spraying paint on an automobile, if it is to be computerized, must first be broken down into its smallest components and analyzed so that it can be translated into the binary language of a computer system. For most organizations, this step prepares the way for automation and simultaneously creates a deeper understanding of the activity itself. Once they are automated, the intelligence of the very devices that increase control or continuity generates new streams of data that provide an opportunity to develop an even more penetrating understanding of the operation. For example, PLCs or microprocessor-based sensors not only apply programmed instructions to equipment; they also convert the current state of product or process into data, thus creating the possibility of increased comprehension. Similarly, the same systems that make it possible to automate office transactions create an overview of real-time organizational functioning and coordinate many levels of data, which are then available for tracking, reporting, and analysis.

By its very nature, then, information technology is characterized by a fundamental duality that has not been fully appreciated. First, the technology can be applied to *automate* operations. The reasoning behind such applications is essentially the same as that applied to Ford's early assembly plant. The aim is to replace human effort and skill with a technology that enables the same processes to be performed at less cost and with more control and continuity.

Second, technology can be used to create information. Even when a given application is designed to automate, it simultaneously generates information about the underlying processes through which an organization accomplishes its work. The word that I have coined to describe this process is *informate*. It is meant to capture that aspect of this technology that may include but also go beyond automation. We see the informating power of intelligent technology at work in the manufacturing environment where microprocessor-based devices such as robots, PLCs, or sensors translate the three-dimensional production process into two-dimensional digital data. Such data are then typically made available on a video display terminal or computer printout, in the form of electronic symbols—numbers, letters, and graphics. This is information that did not exist before. In the office environment the combination of on-line transaction systems and communications systems create a vast information presence that includes many data formerly lodged in people's heads, in face-to-face conversations, in discrete file drawers, and on various pieces of paper widely dispersed in time and space. In its capacity to automate, information technology has a prodigious ability to displace human effort and to substitute for much that has been familiar as human skill. As an *informating* technology, its implications are equally significant, although not yet well understood.

Information technology can make a powerful contribution to the objectives of increasing control and continuity, but its uniqueness lies in its informating capacity, which can enhance comprehension of the operations through which an organization does its work. Thus far I have pointed to this informating process as if it were autonomous and unintended. However, an organization can choose to emphasize and exploit the informating potential of intelligent technology. The extent to which either of information technology's two capacities is emphasized will play a central role in determining the organizational consequences of technological change. The choice of emphasis is above all a question of strategy and derives from management's conception of the contribution that this technology can make to the business. Informating may proceed as an unintended and undermanaged consequence of computer-based automation, but it can also be part of a conscious management policy designed to exploit the new information presence to create a different and potentially more penetrating, comprehensive, and insightful grasp of the business. This, in turn, can serve as the catalyst for significant improvement and innovation in the production and delivery of goods and services, thus strengthening the competitive position of the firm.

Yet even as managers begin to recognize and appreciate the informating power of new technology, a strategic approach to technology deployment will in many cases fall short of achieving the desired outcomes. One conclusion from my research is that organizational innovations are necessary to support technological innovations if a firm is to fully benefit from the informating process. It is a process that has implications for the kinds of skills that organization members must develop, the articulation of roles and functions, and the design of systems and structures that support and reward participation in an informated organization.

The Database as Organization Surrogate

As organizations apply information technology, they tend to develop mechanisms that allow information to be automatically generated and captured. As automation proceeds, they search for ways to integrate information and make it valid, immediate, and accessible. Some organizations have already reached a level where they have been able to recreate their own images in the form of detailed, real-time, integrated databases, which give access to internal operations and external business data and can be reflexive enough to organize, summarize, and analyze aspects of their own content. In a highly informed organization, the database takes on a life of its own. It becomes an autonomous domain, a public symbol of organizational experience, much of which previously had been fragmented, private, and implicit. For example, in one highly automated pulp plant built around a microprocessor base of instrumentation, a computerized database included all vital business and personnel data as well as real-time record of operations—created by continual measurements of the 2,500 key pieces of plant equipment, which were updated several times per minute. A powerful information system like this one becomes an on-line, symbolic surrogate for much of the dynamic detail of an organization's daily life. The fact that the database assumes the status of organization surrogate is even more compelling in the context of the traditionally information-intensive organizations: banks, insurance companies, airlines, and so forth. Indeed, a recent speech found the chairman of MCI Communications referring to changes in financial services with the statement, "Banks are becoming more like databases."

But what does it mean for an organization to "become a database?" In organizations where informating proceeds as an undermanaged and autonomous phenomenon, the growth of the database is experienced as overwhelming and incomprehensible—hence the term *information overload*. An approach to technology deployment that assumes minimal skills at the information interface along with a hierarchical and fragmented division of labor tends to create organizations with a minimal capacity to plumb newly available information in ways that would add value to business activities.

When the informating process is pursued as part of a conscious strategy, the new information presence can be felt at every level of organizational activity. The information presence invites organization members to pose questions and generate hypotheses. As aspects of organization functioning are brought to light or seen in different ways, new insights are engendered. The organization can become a learning environment in that work itself becomes a process of inquiry, and the contributions that members can make are increasingly a function of their ability to notice, reflect, explore, hypothesize, test, and communicate.

Mastery at the Information Interface

The quality of skills that people bring to the new information is usually an important determinant of whether the emerging database is experienced as overload or as an opportunity to reach for a new level of comprehension and innovation. My understanding of these emerging skill demands derives from detailed interviews with people who have grappled with the need to make sense of their work when information about their tasks comes to them primarily through the medium of a computer-based system.

Mastery at the information interface depends upon what I define as *intellective skill*. The central problem that confronts the person who must accomplish a significant portion of his or her work through the information interface is that of reference. People find themselves asking, "To what do these data refer? What is their meaning?" Intellective skills become necessary for creating meaning and so grappling with the problem of reference.

The intellective skill base has three crucial dimensions. The first is the ability to think abstractly. For many people—like the mill operator who interacted directly with machinery, the clerical worker whose tasks involved specific pieces of paper and interpersonal routines, or the manager who culled information from meeting and talking with people—work tasks have tended to be embedded in concrete activities. But as work becomes more computer-mediated, it also becomes more abstract and remote from physical cues. Learning what information might mean when it is separated from its action context requires a new emphasis on abstract thinking and relies on the ability to make explicit the inferences that link data to a concrete world. An operator in an automated mill described his experience in a computerized control room:

> Anytime you mash a button you should have in mind exactly what is going to happen. You need to have in your mind where it is at, what it is doing and why it is doing it. Out there in the plant you can know things just by habit. You can know them without knowing that you know them. In here you have to watch the numbers whereas out there you have to watch the actual process.

The second component of intellective skill is inductive reasoning. Because information in a computer system tends to be reduced to quantitative terms, people must be able to approach data analytically, grasp the potential relationships among variables, and use data to build and test hypotheses. A systems engineer who had worked closely with operators in another highly automated plant described how successful operators managed the production process through the computerized control interface:

> When you want to know what is going on in a part of the plant, you roll through several screens of data. You must keep important data in your mind as you continue to scan. People learn how to organize data in their minds. They build models in their heads about what is really happening, and they build on the model with data until they have a complete picture.

The ability to perform such inductive reasoning ultimately depends on having a theoretical conception of the processes to which the data refer. This is a third dimension of intellective skill; it is this theoretical grasp that provides a guide through the data, a basis from which to generate hypotheses, and clues as to where to search for evidence of the consequences of any given course of action. Consider the words of one account officer for whom a powerful information system provided a real-time overview of his loan portfolio:

> Certain things can be less apparent because there is so much information. We have to spend time pinpointing the major factors we are looking for. You have to know what is significant in order to know how to discern it.

Or, in the words of another plant operator:

> The more I learn theoretically, the more I can see in the information. Raw data turn into information with my knowledge. I find that you have to be able to know more in order to do more. It is your understanding of the process that guides you.

Of course, people learn from and about their work in many ways. When tasks become computer-mediated, people will often look for ways to check back with the pre-computer action context to assure themselves that they are doing things correctly. For example, a clerical operation might be performed in both manual and automated modes until people trust the new system. Plant workers sometimes leave the control room to check on equipment, just to see if the computer system accurately reflects "what is really going on." But often these older contexts are organized out of the new environment—there's no going back to check because there's nothing to go back to. Older equipment and instrumentation is dismantled; paper forms and the office routines built around them disappear.

When this happens, intellective skill becomes a prerequisite for operating competently in the new computer-mediated environment. Those without it can feel lost.

Two Roads Diverge

In one manufacturing organization, the plant manager had a heated debate with his leadership group over the strategic conception that would guide technology deployment. "Are we all going to be working for a smart machine," he asked, "or will we have smart people around the machine?" The response to this question becomes the keystone of any strategy for mutually developing technology applications and the organizational innovations that support them. In this context, "smart people" are organization members who can contribute to and learn from the systems through which they perform their work. A strategy that emphasizes automation focuses on the smart machine. An informating strategy recognizes the value and function of the smart machine, but only in the context of its interdependence with smart people. It is the knowledge and understanding in people's heads—their "intellective skill"—that turns smart machines into an opportunity for fundamental business improvement. Mastery of inference through inductive reasoning and theoretical understanding provides the basis from which those at the information interface can construct, integrate, and synthesize the meaning of information.

Perhaps the most compelling reason that managers are driven to a narrow emphasis on automation is the web of economic logic in which they must operate. Conventional accounting formulas treat technology as a capital substitution for labor. As many managers have learned, "to justify a computer we have to show job eliminations." These lines of economic force cut a deep path and carry certain inevitable implications. For example, organizational resources are channeled in ways that support the fundamental technology strategy. Investment dollars and staff know-how are dedicated to enhancing automation through technology design, application, maintenance, and upgrading. It is a simple and obvious fact that such choices have long-term consequences in terms of which organizational potentialities become robust, atrophy, or are stillborn.

The emphasis on automation is further bolstered by the middle manager's role, which has been largely defined as one of collecting, manipulating, disseminating, or withholding information. As organizations grew in size, middle managers became the information conduits through which planning and execution could be coordinated and controlled. But there is deeper significance to the manager's information function. Managers have traditionally been considered the representatives of ownership. Only they could be counted on for the loyalty and dedication that this symbolic investment of property rights implied. It followed that significant information could be entrusted only to those who could be relied on to serve the interests of ownership. But the informating process unleashed by new technology can provide the nonexempt worker at the information interface with access to data that convey a broad scope of the organization's functioning. One corporate vice-president put the problem this way:

> An issue that the technology is forcing us to face involves the loss of managerial control . . . . There is a legal definition that management is the steward for the owners of the enterprise. They are expected to be loyal and unswervingly dedicated to achieving the objectives of the owners. They are expected to not let the situation ever get out of control . . . . New information technology introduces some very new problems. Suddenly the folks who work with these systems are interfacing with a tremendous technology power—power to see all the functions of the operation. That is pretty scary to some managers.

For middle managers who measure their worth in terms of their ability to exert control and maximize the certainty of outcomes, the choice to create "smart people" can be a threat. Even those willing to consider the obsolescence of their traditional function can find the ambiguity of their emerging role painful enough to elicit resistance. As one manager explained, "As we face change, the big issue is, 'What's in it for me?' If I can keep the box narrowly defined, then I know my worth as a manager. I don't know what my new skills will need to be, so that is uncomfortable."

To the extent that managers confront these dilemmas by emphasizing automation, the structure of Taylorism is likely to be replicated, along with all of its inherent antagonisms. Consider the voice of a worker in a plant that had invested heavily in automatic control systems:

> They need the workers to help them figure out what the computer should do. But why should you

tell a man all your knowledge about how this place runs so he can put it into a machine and then it's going to take your job away? It robs me of my dignity, it robs me of what I know how to do . . . . If they don't like me they can hard time me, as I am more expendable now, because my knowledge is in the system.

Or as a clerical worker in the back office of another company put it:

> Because you are dealing with the tube everyday, you can't beat it. You can't get ahead with it. It's just an inanimate object that stands on your desk and you have to fight it every day. And the tube is going to tally what you have worked . . . . It's like a fight that you cannot win. With the tube you do not have a chance.

Under these conditions certain organizational consequences become more likely than others. Productivity will increase, at least in the short run, as routine jobs are eliminated. Authority will tend to become more centralized as managers set objectives for the machine system. Design efforts will tend to maximize the self-regulatory capacity of computer systems and minimize the need for human interaction, understanding, and contribution. Members of the technical and managerial elite are likely to become more powerful, as they will have the intellective skill needed to monitor, improve, or override the automatic systems. In such a scenario the remaining work force tends to become an adjunct to the machine system, with little or no critical understanding of its functions. Such dependence on automation means that the problems of reliability will be critical. Automatic controls that can provide fail-safe measures to guard against systems errors will be needed, since the ripple effects of such failures can escalate with alarming speed in a highly automatic and interdependent machine system.

Despite the compelling economic, organizational, and psychological exigencies that press managers to exclusively emphasize the automating opportunities offered by information technology, many of the managers with whom I spoke had come to feel that this emphasis tended to prevent their organizations from using the newly generated information as an opportunity for business improvement and innovation.

In one plant converting to a microprocessor-based control system that would allow workers to interact remotely with the production process through a centralized information interface, one of the managers complained:

*We have cut out so many people, there is no one
to do the neat things we could use the information for. We need to look at added value and
we don't know how. We need to let hourly
people make a contribution, but we will go
mean and lean as pure profit drives us in the
end. Unfortunately, no one is considering the
trade-offs.*

The ill-considered trade-offs involve the special characteristics of an informating technology. As long as the technology vision is limited to staff reductions and
characterized by the assumption that more technology
means diminished skill requirements, then the informating capacity of new technology cannot possibly be
exploited. It may be true that the quickest route to
increased profits is through this kind of labor substitution.
It may also be true that for many businesses long-term
profitability, innovation, and growth will depend on a different approach to technology deployment—one that is
able to use "smart people" to exploit the opportunities for
competitive advantage that are offered by more, different,
and better information.

In one organization, corporate senior managers were
trying to assess the experience of their manufacturing
sites caught up in the problems of computerization.
They began to realize that any attempt to profit from the
upward spiral of information availability would require
more profound organizational change than anyone had,
as yet, seriously considered. One corporate vice president reflected:

*With the new technology it seems there is an
almost inevitable kind of development, if you have
as a goal maximizing all business variables and
harnessing the entire organization to contribute to
that effort. I now think you must choose to
distribute information and authority in a new
way if you want to achieve that. If you do not, you
will give up an important component of competitive advantage.*

If it is assumed that the availability of new applications will rapidly equalize any competitive advantage
gained from being an early technology leader, then it follows that a sustained advantage is likely to come from an
organization's ability to exploit the learning opportunities
offered by new information. In many businesses,
improvement and innovation in products and services
made possible by increased levels of comprehension and
insight can make an important contribution to competi-

tive position. These organizations will distinguish themselves by exploiting the informating potential of the new
technology. For example, one bank, in the process of creating an on-line integrated database to provide valid,
internally consistent numbers on front- and back-end
banking operations, understood the emerging "database
environment" as the source of new product development.
Banking "products" were being redefined in terms of their
informational content and the procedures used to analyze
that information. The hope for such a database was that
it would provide the flexibility needed to manipulate data
in new ways—and thus create new products. As one bank
officer explained:

*Eighty percent of the bank's products can be
produced with 150 procedures. The other 20%
of the products require at least as many
procedures. We want a database that will give
us all the pieces—an integrated view of our
entire business. It will be like a pictorial view
of the bank. Then, any idea that we come up
with can immediately be converted into a
product. If you use the same procedure in a
different order you would get a different
product, or you could eliminate one procedure
and you'd get a different product. This will
give us a truly flexible bank. The challenge will
be to train our people to think of products as a
conceptual thing, not as a material thing. Our
business will depend on data and procedures
and the conceptual thinking to come up with
new ideas.*

If such a vision is to bear fruit, each level of the
organization must be empowered to respond effectively
to the information that is most relevant to its functional
concerns. Such empowerment depends on two elements.
First, those closest to information relevant to their functions must have the authority to respond. Such authority will only emerge from a strategy that stresses the
importance of smart people. This both implies and
reflects a second requirement—that the organization
make a commitment to the development of intellective
skill at the information interface. Without a depth of
these skills, people will not be able to engage in the quality of "sense making" that can add value. As one worker
in a newly computerized plant reflects: "Before, we did
not have any way to know what we were learning or to
understand the effects of our actions. Now we have so
much information and feedback—not to be able to conceptualize it is the real crime."

A New Division of Labor

Informating implies a division of labor different from the logic of work organization inherited from scientific management, perfected in the mass-production industries, and widely applied in white-collar bureaucracies. With scientific management, the worker's implicit know-how was analyzed to generate data that could serve as the basis for developing a series of management functions. These functions allowed management to take responsibility for coordination and control of the production process, including the fragmentation and standardization of tasks.

When intelligent technology creates (or provides new access to) information and when that information is made available to those at the point of production, the essential logic of Taylorism is shattered. For the first time, technology returns to the worker what it once took away, but with a great deal more as well. The worker's knowledge had been implicit in his or her actions. Informating makes that knowledge explicit; it is a mirror reflecting what was tacitly known but now is in a form that is public and precise. It also expands the range of what can be known, since the newly available information often extends beyond the narrow boundaries of a conventional job definition. Intellective skill becomes the means by which one can reappropriate and expand upon one's own knowledge and engage in the kind of learning process that makes information valuable. As one factory worker put it:

> All the information that you can get through this system gives you an opportunity to see how things could have been done better or how they could done differently . . . . That is the real potential of this equipment. That would never have occurred if we had just stayed with the old technology.

Informating invites a new vision of the organization: a group of people gathered around a central core—that is the automated database. Individuals relate to the electronic information interface according to their responsibilities, which vary in range and comprehensiveness. Intellective skill becomes one of the organization's most precious resources, and the company invests in maintaining and upgrading that skill base in measures comparable to the investment in technology itself. In this vision, the organization becomes a learning institution of which a fundamental objective is the expansion of knowledge about the business and the opportunities it faces. Such an approach implies a departure from most current practice. Today, it is not unusual for an organization to spend millions on technology purchases and installation, while even the most rudimentary training fails to show up as a line item in the annual budget.

Managers who want to pursue this vision will need to appreciate the intricacies of life at the information interface. Too often it is assumed that human beings will respond to data displays like obedient servomechanisms, immediately recognizing the data's significance and responding appropriately. But the image of the human subject as another factor in the feedback loop is not realistic. The meaning with which people invest their work, their levels of motivation and commitment, and the quality of their skills will each mediate the relationship between the information interface and the human observer.

Indeed, as the work that people do and the effort they must make become more abstract, the need for their motivation becomes all the more crucial. For the first-line manager, the contingencies of supervision are altered. In a conventional environment it is relatively easy for a manager to determine that a worker has not properly repaired a boiler (it continues to malfunction) or failed to type a document properly (it is full of errors). But how does a manager determine that an employee failed to respond to some element in the data? How does a manager evaluate the possibility of missed opportunities to learn more about the business or improve operations in some way? In the final analysis it is only the employee's skill and commitment that can ensure that intellective effort will be exerted and that opportunities made available by an informating technology will be exploited.

A New Language and a New Vision

Anyone applying an informating strategy will come up against a variety of organizational barriers, some of which have been identified in this discussion. These barriers are only part of the problem; a deeper issue to confront, one that is both philosophical and ideological in character, involves the limitations of language. We remain, in these final years of the twentieth century, prisoners of a language that has its roots in a day of life and a way of work that are fast becoming obsolete. Consider the workplace vocabulary available to us: Managers require workers; superiors have subordinates; jobs have definitions that are specific, detailed, narrow, and task-related; and organizations have levels that, in turn, create chains of command and spans of control that are either centralized or decentralized. The guiding metaphors are military; the relationships are contractual and often adversarial; the foundational image is one of a manufacturing enterprise in which raw materials are transformed through physical labor and machine power into finished goods. Because production is complex, expensive, and sometimes dangerous, the prevailing notion is that it requires a kind of precise planning and direction that only the management edifice can provide.

For some organizations, because of the nature of their products, processes, or markets, this approach will continue to be most appropriate. But for many others, organizational success will depend less on competent execution of the status quo than it will on increased understanding of functions, innovations in products and processes, opportunities to expand or develop new markets with customized services, and so forth. In these organizations, informating will be a core process. But for informating to become a conscious strategy, it will be necessary to create a vision that transcends the limitations of our current language. The images associated with physical labor can no longer guide our conception of work. The work place, which may no longer be a "place" at all, might come to be thought of as an arena through which information circulates, information to which intellective effort is applied. The quality, not the quantity, of effort is the source from which added value will be derived. Economists can continue to measure labor productivity as if the entire world of work could be adequately symbolized by the assembly line, but their measures are likely to be systematically indifferent to what is most valuable in the informated organization.

Such a world as this calls for a new vocabulary, one that introduces the possibilities of colleagues and co-learners, of exploration, experimentation, and innovation; one reflecting jobs that are comprehensive, tasks that are abstractions depending on insight and synthesis, and power that is a roving force that comes to rest according to function and need. A new vocabulary cannot be assigned; it will have to be developed by those engaged in breaking ties with an industrial logic that has ruled the imaginative life of our century.

Industrial technology has been liberating; it has created vast wealth and decreased the demands on the human body: It has also been seductive—promising to fulfill the dream of perfect automaticity while healing egos wounded by their need for certainty and control. Part of the dream is an image of "people serving a smart machine." In the shadow of the dream, human beings have lost the experience of critical judgment. But only such judgment can initiate the kind of human action that moves over and against the vortex of stimuli, not merely to respond, but to "know better than," to ask questions, to invent, to say *no*. The dream of automation brings us dangerously close to Hannah Arendt's dark vision of a behaviorist world come true:

> *The last stage of the laboring society, the society of jobholders, demands of its members a sheer automatic functioning, as though individual life had actually been submerged in the overall life process of the species and the only active decision still required of the individual were to let go, so to speak, to abandon his individuality, the still individually sensed pain and trouble of living, and acquiesce in a dazed, "tranquilized," functional type of behavior. The trouble with modern theories of behaviorism is not that they are wrong, but that they could become true, that they actually are the best possible conceptualization of certain obvious trends in modern society. It is quite conceivable that the modern age—which began with such an unprecedented outburst of human activity—may end in the deadliest, most sterile passivity history has ever known.*

That managers may give themselves over to this dream out of inertia or convenience rather than cogent analysis is all the more disturbing. Organizations that take steps toward a purely automating strategy can set a course that is not easily reversed. The message communicated to the work force and the depletion of skills that would be needed in value-adding activities represent losses that are not easily retrieved.

An informating strategy requires a comprehensive vision that appreciates the unique capacities of intelligent technology and recognizes the need to use the organization to liberate those capacities. It means forging a new logic of technology deployment based on that vision. A coherent rationale will be necessary, particularly as the tide of conventional thinking and familiar assumptions begins to submerge many important value-laden choices regarding basic technology design. As one plant manager pointed out:

> *The technology is going in the direction that says one person operates the master controls. Is the technology right? We don't believe it is, and we are working hard to convince vendors to leave the design flexible enough so that it does not preclude the uses we want to make of it.*

The informated organization does move in another direction. It relies on the human capacities for teaching and learning, criticism, and insight. It has an approach to business improvement that rests on the innovation made possible by an enhanced comprehension of core processes. And it reflects the interdependence between the human mind and some of its most sophisticated productions. As one worker mused:

If you don't let people grow and develop and make more decisions, it is a waste of human life—a waste of human potential. If you don't use your knowledge and skill it's a waste of life. Using the new technology to its full potential means using the person to his or her full potential.

SELECTED BIBLIOGRAPHY

Hannah Arendt develops an historical and philosophical perspective on labor and its status in the modern world in *The Human Condition* (University of Chicago Press, 1958). Siegfried Giedion surveys the mechanization of every aspect of human endeavor, from agriculture to the domestic environment, in *Mechanization Takes Command* (Norton, 1969).

The Five Dollar Day: Labor Management and Social Control in the Ford Motor Company, 1908–1921 (State University of New York Press, 1981), by Stephen Meyer, explores the evaluation of mass-production technology in the Ford Motor Company and its role in shaping the relations between workers and managers.

Michael E. Porter and Victor E. Millar's "How Information Gives You Competitive Advantage," an article which appears in the *Harvard Business Review* (July–August 1985), provides a useful framework for analyzing the strategic significance of information technology.

Richard Walton's "Challenges in the Management of Technology and Labor Relations" (which appears in *Human Resource Management: Trends and Challenges,* edited by Richard Walton and Paul Lawrence, Harvard Business School Press, 1985) describes the ways in which computer technologies can be deployed that either exacerbate adversarial relationships or contribute to greater mutuality and cooperation between labor and management.

DISCUSSION QUESTIONS

1. What are the uses of information technologies in relation to automation?

2. How does "informate" differ from automate?

3. What are the products of information technology?

4. In what way can informating be an unintended consequence of information technology?

5. What organizational innovations are necessary to support technological changes to take advantage of informating?

6. How does a database assume the status of organization surrogate?

7. What are the components of the "intellective" skill base?

8. Why do managers resist fully implementing technologies throughout an organization?

Technology as an Occasion for Structuring: Evidence from Observations of CT Scanners and the Social Order of Radiology Departments

STEPHEN R. BARLEY

LEARNING OBJECTIVES

After reading Steven Barley's "Technology as an Occasion for Structuring: Evidence from Observations of CT Scanners and the Social Order of Radiology Departments" a student will be able to:

1. Understand the complexities and interrelationships among technology, organizational behavior, and structure

2. Understand how new technologies can alter the role relationships of workers and, consequently, organizational structure

3. Learn how technology is a social, rather than a physical, object and structure is a process rather than an entity

4. Consider the implications of technological change for the management of human relations in organizations

From the standpoint of social science, organizational theorists could hardly pose a more plausible thesis than that technology shapes organizational structure. Anthropologists, sociologists, historians, and economists have repeatedly shown that technologies transform societies by altering customary modes and relations of production. Since most production in industrial society occurs within formal organizations, when modern technologies alter relations of production they should also, by implication, shift organizational forms (Blau et al., 1976). However, as most investigators admit, after two and a half decades of research our evidence for technology's influence on organizational structure is, at best, confusing and contradictory (Hickson, Pugh, and Pheysey, 1969; Mohr, 1971; Blau et al., 1976; Gerwin, 1981; Fry, 1982).

To salvage the thesis that technology shapes the organization of work, theorists have therefore proposed numerous strategies for untangling the empirical confusion. For example, the Aston group admonished researchers to control for the effects of size (Hickson, Pugh, and Pheysey, 1969). Child (1972) suggested that managers' decisions be taken as intervening variables. Comstock and Scott (1977) argued against the "creative use of indicators," the presumption of "modal technologies," and the tendency to confuse levels of analysis. After observing that different researchers have attributed similar characteristics to both technology and structure, Stanfield (1976) even urged researchers to pay closer attention to categorization. Yet, despite the long history of clarification, results remain inconclusive (Gerwin, 1981; Fry, 1982).

Rather than continue to scrutinize research for additional methodological and conceptual flaws, a more fruitful ploy may be simply to embrace the contradictory evidence as a replicated finding. One could then seek alternate theoretical frameworks that would explain technology's link to structure while treating inconsistent outcomes as a matter of course. This paper draws on recent sociological thought on the relation between institution and action to sketch such a perspective.

Source: Stephen R. Barley, "Technology as an Occasion for Structuring: Evidence from Observations of CT Scanners and the Social Order of Radiology Departments," *Administration Science Quarterly,* Volume 31, No. 1, (March 1986) pp. 78–108. Copyright © 1986. Reprinted by permission.

Earlier versions of this paper were presented at the Second Conference on the Interpretive Study of Organizations held in Alta, UT, August 1983, and at the 44th Annual Academy of Management Meetings in Boston, MA, August 1984. Over time, my thinking has profited by careful, insightful comments supplied by patient colleagues: Tove Hammer, Dave Krackhardt, Gideon Kunda, Barbara Lawrence, Peter Manning, Ed Schein, Sim Sitkin, Bob Stern, Pam Tolbert, and John Van Maanen. The research was sponsored in part by a Doctoral Dissertation Grant (HS 05004) from the National Center of Health Services Research.

Technology and the Structuring of Structure

Most students of technology and organization have used the term structure to denote abstract, formal relations that constrain day-to-day action in social settings. When structure has been treated as an autonomous, formal constraint, three other presumptions have typically followed: that technology is a material cause, that relations between technology and structure are orderly, and that these relations hold regardless of context. Moreover, since relations are usually held to transcend contexts, researchers have tended to study technology's influence on structure at organizational levels of analysis. That such a notion of structure and its corollaries undergird organizational research on technology is substantiated not only by the prevalence of cross-sectional research designs but by the determinism that haunts the literature in such phrases as the "technological imperative" (e.g., Khandwalla, 1974; Fry, 1982).

In contrast to this dominant notion of structure, organizational theorists such as Silverman (1971), Weick (1979), Van Maanen (1977, 1979), and Manning (1977) have advocated an alternate formulation that views structure as patterned action, interaction, behavior, and cognition. Unlike in the first usage, in which structure stands outside of and prior to human endeavor, in the second, structure is understood as an emergent property of ongoing action. The contrast reflects the essential difference between those sociological traditions that portray structure as a template for action and those that treat structure as a contour of human behavior (see Burrell and Morgan, 1979; Salaman and Thompson, 1980). Although this alternate conception of structure legitimates the probability of multiple outcomes, it has yet to seriously penetrate the study of technology.

Taken alone, however, neither conception may adequately represent the way technology influences the structure of a workplace. As Goffman (1983) was fond of observing, in everyday life actors are simultaneously the marks as well as the shills of social order. While it is difficult to see how social structure can arise except out of the actions of people, people's actions are also surely shaped by forces beyond their control and outside their immediate present. A full account of structural change therefore appears to require a synthetic view of structure as both a product of and a constraint on human endeavor.

Negotiated-order theory and structuration theory represent two recent attempts to forge such a synthesis. As articulated by Strauss (1978, 1982), negotiated-order theory derives from symbolic interactionism and takes as its point of departure the events of everyday life. In contrast, structuration theory attempts to broach functionalist and phenomenological notions of social order at the level of social theory (Giddens, 1976, 1979). But while the two approaches differ substantially in scope and detail, both share the premise that adequate theories must treat structure as both process and form.

Noting that action is "constituted by" and "constitutive of" social organization, Giddens suggested that structure be understood as a duality: ". . . by the duality of structure I mean that the structural properties of social systems are both the medium and the outcome of practices that constitute those systems" (Giddens, 1979: 69). Similarly, Strauss (1978) argued that even though social order is a product of negotiations that take place as interacting individuals attempt to define situations, all negotiations are nevertheless constrained by prior interaction that has become institutionalized. Both perspectives liken social order to language. Structures consist of sets of rules that specify parameters of acceptable conduct, but structures are also modified by the actions they inform, just as languages are altered over time by everyday speech.

Both theories therefore attempt to bridge the gap between a deterministic, objective, and static notion of structure, on one hand, and its voluntaristic, subjective, and dynamic alternative, on the other, by positing two realms of social order (analogous to grammar and speech) and by shifting attention to the processes that bind the two together. Structure can be viewed simultaneously as a flow of ongoing action and as a set of institutionalized traditions or forms that reflect and constrain that action. More important than either realm, however, is the interplay that takes place between the two over time. Through this interplay, called the process of structuring, institutional practices shape human actions which, in turn, reaffirm or modify the institutional structure. Thus, the study of structuring involves investigating how the institutional realm and the realm of action configure each other.

Negotiated-order and structuration theories concur that structuring is driven by actors' interpretations of events, by differential access to resources, and by moral frameworks that legitimate a setting's social order. To these engines of stability and change should be added the intended and unintended consequences of decisions and the press of forces, such as technological innovation and economic change, that are initially exogenous to the setting but that impinge and occasion response (Ranson, Hinings, and Greenwood, 1980; Archer, 1982). The structuring of a social setting may be understood to unfold as actors draw on institutional patterns of signification, domination, and legitimation to construct roles and to interpret persons, objects, and events in their environment (Giddens, 1979: 82).

To the degree that actors' behaviors and interpretations give life to these abstractions, the institutional structure is recreated. But since acts of communication, power, and moral sanction necessarily entail the vagaries of interaction, some slippage will occur between the institutional template and the exigencies of daily life. The likelihood of slippage increases when a social system encounters exogenous shocks, such as the acquisition of new members or the arrival of a new technology. Slippages are inconsequential for the institutional structure when they are momentary and random or when they can by subsumed under a framework of prior action, interaction, and interpretation (Meyer, 1982). However, when slippages persist, they become replicated patterns whose contours depart, perhaps ever so slightly, from former practice. Eventually, changed patterns of action reconfigure the setting's institutional structure by entering the stock of everyday knowledge about "the way things are" (Berger and Luckmann, 1967: 56–61).

Approaching the question of technology's relationship to structure from the foregoing vantage point frees researchers from three practices that may have sustained the inconsistencies that have plagued research on technology. First, since structuring implies a process, its temporal nature enjoins researchers to adopt longitudinal as well as cross-sectional perspectives on technical change. Second, since the social context of actions and interpretations is important, it becomes unsound practice to lump together organizations with radically different institutional histories and ecological milieux. Finally, since technologies exist as objects in the realm of action, one cannot hope to understand a technology's implications for structuring without investigating how the technology is incorporated into the everyday life of an organization's members.

Taken together, these epistemological and methodological axioms challenge the presumption that technologies cause organizational structure. Rather, from the point of view of a theory of structuring, technologies are better viewed as occasions that trigger social dynamics which, in turn, modify or maintain an organization's contours. Since these dynamics are likely to be multifaceted, to vary with time, and to reflect the situational context, it is quite likely that identical technologies used in similar contexts can occasion different structures in an orderly fashion. To grasp order in disorder requires a research strategy sensitive to the contextual dynamics by which structuring unfolds.

Mapping the Evolution of Structure

Several organizational theorists have recently noted the value of a theory of structuring for the study of organizational phenomena (Ranson, Hinings, and Greenwood, 1980; Willmott, 1981; Sitkin and Boehm, 1984). But, with the exception of Manning's (1982) careful analysis of how police officers enact the occupational structure of policing and Riley's (1983) study of two subsidiaries of a large corporation, few have actually investigated the structuring of organizational worlds. Manning explicated the logic of a mundane encounter between police and citizen to demonstrate how institutional structures shape and are shaped by the minutia of interaction. In contrast to Manning's emphasis on unfolding behavior, Riley coded interview data, using Giddens' categories of signification, domination, and legitimation, to show that one can account for organizational differences in terms of the dynamics that undergird an organization' s traditions. Thus, Riley's work suggests that organizational differences can in fact be understood in terms of structuring processes, while Manning's analysis indicates how structures are produced and reproduced by situated action.

Although both Manning and Riley explicated Giddens' premise that structure's duality is evident in all instances of action, neither specified how articulations between institution and action evolve. But as Ranson and his colleagues emphasized, to account for change as well as stability requires a temporal model of the structuring process. Evolutionary visions are particularly important for studying technical change, since technologies occasion adaptations whose implications may congeal but slowly as actors redefine their situation (Ranson, Hinings, and Greenwood, 1980: 13). The present research therefore extends and specifies previous work by modelling the dynamics of structuring sequentially rather than concurrently.

The sequential model of structuring that guides the analysis is shown in Figure 15.1. The two realms of social organization, action and institution, are depicted as parallel, horizontal arrows signifying contiguous flows through time. The institutional realm represents the setting's social logic: an abstract framework of relations derived from prior action and interaction on which actors draw to enact their daily lives. In contrast, the realm of action refers to actual arrangements of people, objects, and events in the minute-by-minute flow of the setting's history. Since the institutional realm encodes idealized patterns derived from past practice, it may be considered equivalent to what

FIGURE 15.1

SEQUENTIAL MODEL OF THE STRUCTURING PROCESS

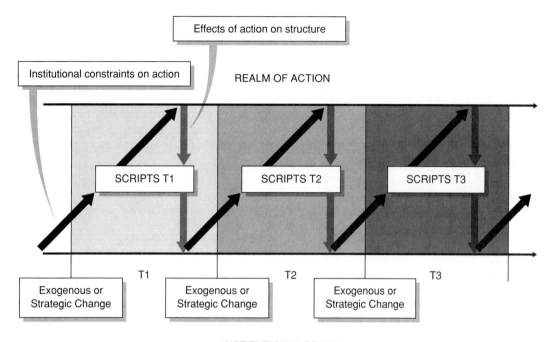

Note: The progressively denser backgrounds signify structuring's cumulative effects.

Ranson, Hinings, and Greenwood (1980) call "realized structure." [1] The realm of action parallels Goffman's (1983) "interaction order."

As shown in Figure 15.1, the present analysis parses structuring's ceaseless flow into temporal phases (Tl, T2, T3, etc.) to better specify the interaction between structure's realms and to highlight changes that accumulate gradually. To avoid arbitrary partitionings, changes in circumstance recognized as significant by an organization's members and brought about by exogenous events or shifts in organizational strategy signal the start of each phase. The diagonal and vertical arrows linking the two realms

indicate the duality of the structuring process: the diagonal arrows signify institutional constraints on action while the vertical arrows represent action's shaping of the institution. The sequential nature of the process is captured by the relation of the diagonal and vertical arrows to the phases' temporal boundaries. Institutional patterns provide programs of action and interpretation at the beginning of each phase, while actions modify institutions within phases. Social practices therefore constitute institutions synchronically while institutions constrain action diachronically. The progressively denser backgrounds in Figure 15.1 signify structuring's cumulative effects.

The sequential model of structuring points to a broad empirical strategy for investigating social dynamics occasioned by technology. Since most technologies enter established contexts whose institutions will influence subsequent events, researchers must document traditional patterns of behavior, interaction, and interpretation before the technology arrives. Such assessment is critical not only because

[1] While I concur with Ranson, Hinings, and Greenwood (1980) that it is often useful to distinguish analytically between "prescribed structure" (the organization's formal dicates) and "realized structure" (patterns of actual practice), I submit that only those aspects of prescribed structure that become embedded in realized structure influence the round of life in social settings.

institutional patterns influence the action that surrounds the technology's adoption, but because such patterns set contextually specific baselines for judging structural stability and change. Once the technology arrives, attention shifts from the institutional context to the social practices that envelop the technology's use, in order to document behaviors and cognitions, which are the raw material from which interaction orders emerge. To map emergent patterns of action and interpretation accurately requires at least partial reliance on participant observation to record who interacts with whom in what ways at what times and to elicit actors' immediate interpretations of events. Retrospective accounts and archival data are insufficient for these purposes, since individuals seldom remember, and organizations rarely record, how behaviors and interpretations stabilize over the course of the structuring process. As an interaction order solidifies, one's analytic focus shifts back to the institutional realm, where the contours of practices that form the interaction order are specified and compared to prior patterns to assess the extent to which the technology has occasioned replication or modification of the previous structure.

While the presumption of sequentiality enjoins researchers to oscillate from one realm to the other, it provides no analytic or empirical fulcrum for pivoting between the two realms. However, such a mechanism can be found in the notion that scripts link the institutional realm to the realm of action (see Goffman, 1959, 1967). Scripts are outlines of recurrent patterns of interaction that define, in observable and behavioral terms, the essence of actors' roles (Schank and Abelson, 1977). As manifested in the flow of behavior, scripts appear as standard plots of types of encounters whose repetition constitutes the setting's interaction order. Scripts can be specified by sampling interactional episodes that occur in the social context under investigation. From details of actual behavior and speech, the analyst abstracts each episode's logic in terms of turns, roles, and categories of acts that outline the episode's unfolding. More specifically, actors' identities are replaced by the positions they play, their behaviors and speech are reduced to generic form and content, and the action's unfolding is charted as a sequence of turns composed of typical acts. Once each episode has been reduced to its essential plot, the frequency of plots can be counted. Recurring plots signify forms of interaction common to the setting and constitute scripts germane to the interaction order. This method of identifying scripts parallels the technique by which structural anthropologists uncover the syntax of myth and narrative (see Propp, 1958; Lévi-Strauss, 1963). By analogy, scripts can therefore be viewed as behavioral grammars that inform a setting's everyday action.

Just as scripts can be conceived of as behavioral grammars that shape instances of action and interaction, what we traditionally call formal organization can be viewed as the grammar of a set of scripts. From this vantage point, global principles of organization such as centralization, formalization, and specialization represent core attributes of scripts that characterize a setting's activity. The link between action and formal structure can be visualized as a chain of successive encodings that abstract, first, from instances of action and interaction to properties of scripts and, then, from scripts to properties of formal organization. The role that scripts play in the structuring process is also shown in Figure 15.1. Although action modifies institutional patterns along vertical arrows and institutional patterns constrain action along diagonal arrows, scripts mediate both flows.

Thus to occasion the structuring of organizations, technologies must first disturb or confirm ingrained patterns of action to reformulate or ratify scripts, which, in turn, delimit the organization's institutional structure. However, since technology is but one among many elements of social context that influence patterns of action, even identical technologies may occasion processes that lead to different scripts and, hence, to different organizational structures in different settings. Such a situation occurred in the radiology departments of two community hospitals where I was a participant observer during the year that each began to operate its first whole-body, computed tomography (CT) scanner.

Sites and Methods

Urban and Suburban were two of four community hospitals in Massachusetts whose radiology departments received CT scanners in 1982. Both departments employed six radiologists and approximately fifty other individuals, both performed a standard range of radiological procedures, and both purchased identical machines, Technicare 2060's. Although Urban had operated a first-generation EMI head scanner since 1977, the body scanner represented Suburban's first experience with CT. However, since the Technicare scanner and Urban's EMI scanner were technically quite different, and since an ability to read head scans is no qualification for interpreting body scans, Urban's experience with head scanning proved relatively unimportant to the evolution of its body-scanning operation.

The research initially focused on documenting traditional radiological practice to establish a comparative base for determining the extent to which the scanners would affirm or modify institutional patterns in the two departments. Historical data on the technical and social organization of the specialty were gathered from published sources and from interviews with senior radiologists at two large medical centers. However, since actual practice in a specific hospital may depart from the occupation's norms and institutions, it was also critical to study traditional operations at each research site. Consequently, I began observation at both Urban and Suburban in June 1982, four months before the scanners began to operate.

Since radiography and fluoroscopy form the traditional technical core of radiology, from June to September observation centered on the actions and interactions of radiologists and technologists performing x-ray and fluoroscopic procedures in Urban's and Suburban's x-ray areas. As throughout the study, I gathered data by attending individual examinations in their entirety. The occurrence and timing of events were recorded chronologically during the course of each exam in small spiral notebooks to create behavioral records for every procedure observed. Conversations between participants were either taped or written in a shorthand devised for the purpose of documenting setting-specific argots. In addition to behavioral records, I also sought and recorded participants' interpretations of events at the time they occurred or shortly thereafter.

Once the scanners went on-line in late September, observation shifted from the x-ray areas to the two newly created CT areas. However, the method of observing and recording detailed behavioral information remained constant. Over the course of the study approximately 400 complete radiological examinations, including 96 CT scans, were observed. With the exception of a six-week hiatus during the Christmas holidays, data were collected at the two sites on alternate working days for a period of a year. The text of field notes and tape recordings collected during observation of the two CT scanners provided raw data for the analysis.

Analysis began by identifying breakpoints to define phases of structuring at each site. Mapping phases before scripts avoided temporal distinctions based on knowledge of the scripts themselves. To have used distributions of scripts to locate breakpoints would have risked theoretically propitious, but historically spurious, partitionings by maximizing the homogeneity and heterogeneity of scripts within and between phases. As indicated in the discussion of the sequential model of structuring, phases should start with significant exogenous events or shifts in organizational strategy, as judged by insiders. Aside from the arrival of the scanners themselves, alterations in the scanner's staffing pattern were uniformly viewed by members of both departments as crucial disjunctures. Consequently, such shifts were taken to mark the temporal boundaries of structuring's phases at each site. Field notes revealed that, by this criterion, Suburban experienced two and Urban four phases of structuring.

The second step in the analysis entailed recursive scrutiny of the interactions that took place between radiologists and technologists, to isolate scripts characteristic of each area's interaction order. All recorded interactions between radiologists and CT technologists were culled from the field notes and were arranged by site in chronological order. Each episode was then reduced to an initial plot, using the approach described in the previous section. Generic plot statements were refined by comparing episodes, and each plot's frequency was tabulated across the phases of structuring at each site. By examining the relative frequency of the plots in each hospital over time, I identified scripts characteristic of interaction in each CT area during each phase of its structuring. The scripts' content and form provided a basis for comparing role relations in the two CT areas with their analogues in the x-ray areas, while the scripts' temporal distributions traced the scanners' evolving interaction orders.

The third and final stage of analysis linked the scripted parameters of the two interaction orders to properties of each CT area's formal structure. Centralization was deemed particularly relevant, for both substantive and empirical reasons. As is explained more fully below, prescribed distributions of discretion and authority lie at the core of radiology's traditional division of labor. Moreover, data were available for constructing measures of centralization that were independent of the scripts and the interactions from which they were derived. Consequently, by focusing on centralization it was possible to examine the link between the two interaction orders and one of radiology's fundamental institutions by using data independent of the scripts.

Measures of centralization were constructed by coding instances of routine decision making found in the field notes. Regardless of hospital, all CT scans were punctuated by nine operational decisions: (1) when to start a new patient, (2) where to start scanning, (3) how far to scan, (4) what techniques to use, (5) whether to reposition the patient, (6) whether to inject contrast, (7) what windows and centers to use, (8) whether the radiologist should view the scans, and (9) when to end the exam. Since each decision was made as a scan unfolded and since each resulted in overt action, as part of my observational regimen I routinely recorded the identity of the decision maker. My field notes documented 91 scans in sufficient detail to determine whether the radiologist who was nominally in charge or a technologist had made each decision. Thus, the percentage of decisions made by a radiologist during the course of a scan constituted the index of centralization. Plots of the indices over time were interpreted as a department's centralization profile.

If institution and action in the CT areas were in fact linked via the structuring process, then the shape of each department's centralization profile should parallel trends revealed by a chronological analysis of scripts. This hypothesis was tested by regressing each department's centralization scores on the day of operation on which the scans took place, as well as the square of that value, to test for linear and curvilinear trends suggested by the analysis of the scripts. Day of operation was measured as an interval variable from the start of each department's scanning operations. The centralization scores were also used to validate the adequacy of the phases defined for each department's structuring. If phases were identified correctly, then a scatterplot of each department's centralization indices should evidence similar periodicity. To examine the adequacy of the phasing, each department's centralization scores were regressed on a series of dummy vectors that defined a two-stage and a four-stage model for Suburban and Urban, respectively. Each scan was assigned to a stage by the date on which it was performed. If phasing was accurate, one would expect a model constructed from the combined phases to predict Suburban's and Urban's data no better than the two phase and the four-phase model, respectively.

The data analysis thus traced the analytic logic suggested by the sequential model of the structuring process. In keeping with this analytic flow, the following discussion of Urban's and Suburban's experience begins with a brief description of patterns of traditional radiological work in the two hospitals' x-ray areas: the background against which structuring occurred.

Radiology's Institutional Context and Traditions

Radiology's ascent from a scientific association, formed soon after the discovery of x-rays in 1895, to its current status as a medical specialty traces the rise of a "professional monopoly" (Larson, 1977) and the institutionalization of a system of "professional dominance" (Friedson, 1970). As Larkin (1978) and Brown (1973) have documented, by the 1950s radiologists had secured an exclusive license to interpret medical images by excluding physicists and engineers from medical radiography, by barring other physicians from interpreting films, and by controlling the education and registry of radiology technologists. The profession's dominance therefore was built on and maintained by a distribution of expertise that separates radiology's productive and interpretive work.

In Suburban's and Urban's x-ray areas, radiological technologists, individuals with associate's degrees, managed patients during examinations and produced films for the radiologists. In turn, the radiologists extracted diagnostic information from films and provided referring physicians with readings. Although the "techs" were trained to run equipment and to recognize anatomy, they were not taught to interpret. Thus, even after years of experience, most x-ray techs recognized few pathologies revealed by a set of x-rays (Barley, 1984). In contrast, the radiologists were taught to operate x-ray equipment as well as interpret, and although they rarely developed the technologist's finesse, they routinely took control of the equipment, particularly during fluoroscopy. This pattern of expertise created a hierarchy of authority in which radiologists knew what technologists knew, but not the reverse.

The radiologists' dominance was routinely enacted as x-ray techs and radiologists at Urban and Suburban went about their daily work. Perhaps because radiography and fluoroscopy are well understood and because the occupational traditions surrounding this work are well encoded, traditional practice was similar in the two departments. Most interactions between members of the two groups involved a radiologist giving a technologist orders, which the technologist then carried out. During fluoroscopy, for example, interactions between radiologists and technologists consisted almost entirely of imperative sentences spoken by the radiologist and directed toward the technologist. Radiologists rarely provided technologists with justification for their commands and preferences (Barley, 1984). Radiologists also rarely sought an x-ray tech's opinion, even on matters regarding the use of a technology. Technologists, however, routinely awaited directions from radiologists, even when they knew the appropriate action was obvious. Similarly, radiologists never sought from x-ray techs, and only occasionally volunteered, information on a patient's pathology. And while technologists were free to ask radiologists about pathological signs, few actually did. These interactional patterns instantiated the radiologists' institutional dominance and the x-ray techs' corresponding dependence. Not only were x-ray techs prohibited from making numerous routine decisions, but in most interactions information flowed from the radiologist to the technologist. Thus, even in mundane matters, authority was centralized.

Although the radiologist's interpretive monopoly and the x-ray technologist's subordination arose from institutionalized and socially enacted power, it is important to recognize that radiology's traditional structure is linked to its technical history. Until the late 1960s, most technical change in radiology came as incremental improvements to existing machines (Dewing, 1962). Augmentation of the profession's diagnostic knowledge was similarly gradual. Thus, as recently as twenty years ago, the work of a radiology department consisted entirely of procedures performed with technologies that had existed for decades. In this era of incremental technical change it was relatively easy for radiologists to remain proficient in the use of machines as well as in the interpretation of films.

Over the past fifteen years, however, computer-driven technologies such as ultrasound, the CT scanner, and nuclear magnetic resonance have revolutionized medicine's ability to peer inside the human body. Each innovation not only operates by principles dramatically different from traditional machines, but each has created a completely new system of diagnostic signs that radiologists have had to master. If, as at Urban and Suburban, few radiologists follow the professional literature on a new technology until faced with the necessity of using the machine themselves, then when departments acquire new technologies most members will know little about the machine or its images.[2] At both research sites, Technicare's standard four-day orientation program was the only formal training that radiologists or technologists received before the scanners went on-line. The training focused exclusively on the scanner's routine operation and had nothing to do with interpreting anatomical or pathological signs. There was also little discussion of how the scanner worked or how one might troubleshoot problems.

---

[2] Interviews with senior radiologists at medical centers indicated that the practice of waiting to learn a new technology until the time of adoption is widespread. However, one might expect radiologists to seek interpretive training as soon as they know they will acquire a new imaging technology. At Urban and Suburban, at least, the radiologists did not embark on such a course of action. Instead, both departments hired young radiologists trained in CT to serve as shadow consultants for the others, who learned by doing.

Since radiology's professional dominance arises from traditional distributions of expertise, the implications of a situation in which a department's members are relatively ignorant of the technology and its system of signs are that prior structures are likely to be more difficult to maintain and opportunities for structuring are likely to be occasioned. Such was the case when the scanners arrived at Suburban and Urban.

The Structuring of Suburban's CT Operation

Phase 1: Negotiation of Discretion

Since none of Suburban's personnel had experience with CT scanning or could interpret a scanner's images, the department faced the untenable prospect of scanning patients without the necessary expertise. To alleviate the problem, Suburban hired a sixth radiologist who had recently completed a fellowship in computed tomography and charged him with coordinating the start of CT operations. In addition, the department recruited two technologists previously employed by one of the region's first body-scanning installations and transferred two of its x-ray techs to the CT area. The two experienced technologists, the two inexperienced technologists, and the new radiologist brought the scanner on-line.

These personnel decisions and the scanner's arrival signaled the start of the first phase of structuring at Suburban. Since the CT area had no standard procedures, none of the personnel had operated a Technicare machine, and the radiologist and the technologists had never worked together, interactions during the first weeks of the scanner's operation centered on clarifying roles, particularly with regard to who had what competencies and would assume what duties. Field notes from this period document several forms of interaction that differed substantially from those characteristic of the scanner's later operation.

Unsought Validation.   As the CT techs worked to complete early scans, they frequently acted without inquiring whether the experienced radiologist thought their action desirable. Usually the radiologist either failed to note what the technologists had done or chose not to comment on the act. However, on some occasions, the radiologist did question a technologist's decision. Generally, the radiologist framed his interrogation in terms of a request for information or a rationale. In response, the techs recounted facts to justify their action. The radiologist then usually commented on the action's suitability and, more often than not, agreed with the decision, offering compliments on a choice well made. The script of such interactions, which may be called "unsought validation," evidenced the following structure: (1) a technologist took action, (2) a radiologist questioned the action, (3) the technologist provided a justification, and (4) the radiologist confirmed the action as appropriate.

An actual example of unsought validation will clarify the script's role-making relevance and demonstrate how scripts summarize instances of interaction. Several days after Suburban began to operate its scanner, the experienced radiologist was called to the control room to view a patient's scans on the scanner's video monitor. Unknown to him, the technologists had decided among themselves to construct the images using a 512-pixel matrix rather than the 256-pixel matrix that had been used up to that time.[3] Consequently, the images were sharper than usual. As the scans appeared on the monitor, the following exchange occurred between the radiologist and an inexperienced technologist:

Rad:	*(Incredulously)* These are 256's?
Tech:	*(Matter of factly)* No, these are 512's.
Rad:	*(Surprised)* They're 512's?
Tech:	Yes. We reconstructed them at 512.
Rad:	Oh! That's good! I was wondering on the way over here if you could reconstruct at 512 and do quicklooks too. Well, that's great! It's real important.[4]

As can be readily seen, the interaction unfolded in the sequence specified by the script's plot. Except for the fact that the subject matter pertained to CT scanning, the specifics of conversation were irrelevant to the script's unfolding. The example also suggests how unsought validations created unsolicited opportunities for technologists

---

[3] A pixel, loosely speaking, is a small, square unit of a video image that can take on a unique data value. CT images are constructed by assigning values to each pixel in a matrix of pixels and by then correlating these values to shades of grey ranging from white to black. Since a 512-pixel matrix has four times as many pixels as a 256-pixel matrix, more precise images can be constructed.

[4] "Quicklooks" are images constructed with half the pixels of a 256 matrix. They are displayed after each scan is taken and are used to locate one's current position in the patient's body and to initially identify pathological structures.

and radiologists to negotiate knowledge. By confirming the advisability of a technologist's action, the radiologist publicly recognized the tech's competence to make a type of decision about the course of a scan. At the same time, the radiologist's questioning and subsequent acceptance revealed his own understanding of CT work, since he raised questions about acts that might bypass a novice. Although the script subtly maintained the radiologist's dominant role by instancing the radiologist's right to question a technologist, as a whole it affirmed both parties' expertise at neither's expense.

Anticipatory Questioning. In contrast to unsought validation, the anticipatory-question script, a script common to the early days of Suburban's CT operation, unfolded when technologists conferred with the radiologist before taking action. Like all scripts, anticipatory questions followed a plot that subsumed numerous interactional episodes: (1) a technologist asked the radiologist a direct question, (2) the radiologist provided the technologist with a direct answer, (3) the technologist made a statement about his or her next course of action, and (4) the radiologist confirmed the technologist's stated plan as appropriate. Although the initial question often resembled a genuine request for information, the situational context and the tech's subsequent statement framed the question as rhetorical. Since anticipatory questions presumed their answers, they were typically posed by the experienced technologists, who were better positioned to demonstrate knowledge of scanning protocols. For example, during an early scan, an experienced technologist inquired about an injection she perceived to be imminent:

Tech:	Are you going to inject the patient, doctor?
Rad:	Yeah.
Tech:	I'll go draw up the dye. A hundred cc's?
Rad:	Yeah.

Although the encounter appears as a simple request for information, in fact, much more was communicated. To ask the question, the technologist had to surmise, either from the images or the patient's requisition, that an injection was probable, since the radiologist had not stated his intention to inject. By waiting until the radiologist had almost completed his viewing, she demonstrated that she knew how to time an injection. Her question therefore carried the message: "From the looks of things an injection is likely, and if it's going to happen it should happen soon." Moreover, by stating that she would draw up 100 cc's of dye, the technologist acknowledged her role at this point in a procedure and demonstrated that she was willing to execute her duty without being told. Thus did the anticipatory question venture, and the radiologist's affirmation confirm, the experienced technologist's expertise. By initiating encounters with anticipatory questions the techs also maintained the veneer of deference that typified interaction in the x-ray area. In the present case, use of the term, "doctor," underscored the technologist's deference. Since anticipatory questions validated the tech's expertise while preserving the radiologist's status, it is not surprising that the form of interaction was common during the scanner's early operation.

Preference Stating. Regardless of their experience with the technology, the CT techs expected radiologists' knowledge of disease, anatomy, and diagnostic signs to surpass their own. Moreover, they stood willing to accept radiologists' technical preferences, so long as they seemed reasonable. Since radiologists customarily state opinions on technical matters in the x-ray area, it was hardly surprising that Suburban's experienced radiologist freely informed the CT techs of his preferences in conducting scans. However, interchanges scripted as preference stating went beyond the mere giving of directions common in the x-ray department: (1) the experienced radiologist not only made his preferences known, (2) he also provided a rationale for his preferences.

The radiologist usually justified a preference by explaining how his suggestion would either make the scanner's operation less burdensome or provide more conclusive diagnostic evidence. The latter type of explanation often led the radiologist to discuss the signs of pathology in a scan. These interchanges often involved lengthy conversations about disease and interpretation that were uncharacteristic of the x-ray area.[5] Moreover, by outlining the grounds for his preference, the radiologist established his credibility and competence while treating technologists as if they deserved reasoned explanations. Since the radiologist offered justifications, the technologists rapidly came to expect them.

Interactions scripted as unsought validations, anticipatory questions, and preference stating shaped the early definition of role relations in Suburban's CT area. Although the fledgling interaction order reaffirmed the radiologist's traditionally greater authority and expertise, it

[5] In only 14 percent of the 74 procedures I observed performed in Suburban's x-ray area did radiologists inform technologists about the pathological signs in a sign in a set of films. In contrast, such discussions occurred in 40 percent of CT scans I observed at Suburban (Barley, 1984).

also ratified the technologists' claim to occupational knowledge. As the techs demonstrated responsibility and competence, the radiologist began to grant them greater discretion. By the end of the third week a tentative climate of joint problem solving arose to create an atmosphere that more closely resembled the ideal of complementary professions working in concert. The radiologist became less involved in routine decisions and the experienced techs began to administer injections, a highly symbolic event, since no other technologists at Suburban were allowed to inject. However, the technologists' gains in discretion were trivial when compared to the windfall of autonomy that accrued during the next phase of structuring.

Phase 2: Usurping Autonomy

Although the CT-inexperienced radiologists sporadically attended scans during the first three weeks of the operation, the newly hired radiologist was always present and clearly in charge. In fact, field notes reveal that aside from social conversation, the inexperienced radiologists rarely interacted with the technologists. Instead they addressed their questions regarding the scanner to their experienced colleague. During the fourth week, however, the radiologists decided to rotate CT duty on a weekly basis. The experienced radiologist subsequently resumed primary assignments in other areas of the radiology department and rotated through CT on the same schedule as his colleagues. The decision to share CT duty marked the beginning of the second phase of structuring at Suburban. At first, the technologists tried to enact scripts that had evolved during the first phase of the scanner's operation. But former interaction patterns were quickly transformed as role relations between radiologists and technologists shifted.

Clandestine Teaching. Accustomed to exercising authority in other areas of the department, the inexperienced radiologists were also inclined to initiate encounters with CT techs by stating preferences or by raising questions reminiscent of those that had cued unsought validations. However, since these earlier interactions presumed knowledge of the scanning context, and since such knowledge was precisely what the inexperienced radiologists lacked, their preferences and questions could not sustain the former interaction patterns. Instead, their questions and preferences often led to exchanges in which technologists responded to a radiologist's inquiry or suggestion by attempting to teach without appearing to do so.

Instances of clandestine teaching typically began when a radiologist posed questions or made statements that would not have been made by someone familiar with the technical context of CT work. For the technologists to have openly corrected a radiologist's faulty question or preference would have been to risk affront and boldly invert the institutionalized status system. Therefore, the technologists typically responded to the radiologist with a question or statement that tangentially supplied information necessary for the radiologist to reformulate his presentation of self as a knowledgeable partner to the interchange. Picking up the cue, the radiologist then adjusted his claim or action to be more in line with standard protocol. Interactions scripted as clandestine teaching unfolded when (1) a radiologist asked an irrelevant question or made a faulty suggestion, (2) the technologist offered corrective information, and (3) the radiologist adjusted his claim.

Clandestine teaching threatened the institutionalized roles of radiologists and technologists. Under radiology's traditional system, radiologists taught technologists, but the reverse was uncommon and nearly taboo. Only the radiologist's front of self-assurance and the technologist's deference, both of which were encoded in the semantics and pragmatics of the exchange, kept clandestine teaching from becoming open instances of role reversal. Yet, open role reversals did occur with some frequency after the fourth week of the scanner's operation.

Role Reversals. In the most important type of role reversal a radiologist asked a technologist directly whether a scan evidenced pathology. Discussions of pathology between radiologists and technologists in the x-ray area occurred only when radiologists volunteered interpretations. Thus, diagnostic knowledge always flowed from radiologist to technologist, in keeping with the radiology's institutional division of labor. But the traditional distribution of diagnostic expertise was difficult to sustain in the CT area, since the inexperienced radiologists initially knew less about the images than did the experienced technologists. Although the radiologists tried to avoid conferring with CT techs on interpretive matters, daily exigencies occasionally necessitated consultations, especially when radiologists were pressed to give referring physicians immediate readings. These occasions inverted the script of typical interpretive discussions in that (1) the radiologist now questioned the technologist about pathology and (2) the technologist provided the radiologist with an interpretation. In the following exchange, the radiologist explicitly inquired whether spinal scan revealed pathology:

Rad:	*(Sitting down at the console)* You just photographing them?
Tech:	Yes, I'm rematrixing.
Rad:	*(Pointing)* Is that a fracture?
Tech:	No, that's probably a foramen [one part of a vertebra].
Rad:	Did you see a disk here? [Was the disk ruptured or bulging?]
Tech:	I just saw a little bit. It's so small you can't see it.

Although instances of clandestine teaching revealed the radiologist's ignorance, the script maintained the patina of their traditional professional dominance. If need be, the actors could claim that nothing unusual was going on, since techs were supposed to know how to operate the scanner and recognize certain anatomical signs. However, role reversals blatantly violated institutional mores by mandating that technologists assume the interpretive role. Since radiologists and technologists both perceived this inversion of the institutional order, role reversals generated anxiety. After the incident recounted above, the radiologist rushed awkwardly out of the room and the technologist nervously confided to the author, "I don't like it when doctors ask me what a film means. It's not my job to tell them how to do their job."

Blaming the Technologist. Of all the interaction patterns that arose in the second period of structuring, none was more indicative of how the interaction order had changed than the tendency for radiologists to mistake machine problems for a technologist's incompetence. On such occasions, the radiologist (1) stated or questioned a perceived problem, (2) insinuated or directly claimed that the problem was the technologist's fault, and (3) rejected the technologist's claim that the nature of the problem lay with the technology. The following typifies the script:

Rad:	*(Brusquely)* This is pretty bad. The films on the last patient are pretty dark. Can you do anything about it?
Tech:	I don't know.
Rad:	What do you mean you don't know?
Tech:	The problem is either in the processor or the camera there. I don't know how to set them. Dr. X knows how to set the camera. Maybe we should get him to come over and set the camera and I'll rematrix them.
Rad:	*(Pointing to diagonal lines through the basal portion of the brain, in a head scan)* Is this all artifact here?
Tech:	Yes. There's nothing you can do about it.

Rad: Why not? You mean there's nothing *you* can do about it?

Tech: I believe it's all bone artifact. [Bone artifact in the basal brain was a chronic problem with all Technicare 2060's.]

As role reversals, clandestine teaching, and incidents of blaming the technologist gradually defined a new interaction order, the radiologists' moral authority tarnished and the technologists began to regard the inexperienced radiologists with disdain. To account for the new interaction patterns, the technologists formulated the view that the radiologists knew less than they rightfully should and that their ignorance created unnecessary work and kept the CT operation from running smoothly. The radiologists were also uncomfortable with the situation. Unaccustomed to having their knowledge perceived as inadequate, anxious that they might make a serious mistake, and baffled by the computer technology, they began to express hostility toward the technologists.

As anxiety, hostility, and disdain increased, both technologists and radiologists acted to reduce their occurrence. The technologists began to take responsibility for routine decisions where in the past they would have consulted a radiologist before acting. At first the techs took such steps hesitantly. But when autonomous action elicited no repercussions, as was usually the case, the technologists assumed similar responsibility in subsequent exams. At the same time, the radiologists began to withdraw from the scanner's minute-by-minute operation to save face. When assigned to CT duty, most radiologists remained in the radiologists' office and several even went so far as to close the door to the office and shut the window between their desk and the secretary's desk. Another radiologist stayed in the x-ray department whenever he was assigned to CT and visited the CT area only to pick up films. Thus, as an upshot of the interaction patterns that arose during the second phase of structuring, Suburban's CT technologists gained a large measure of autonomy over their day to-day work.

The Structuring of Urban's CT Operation

Phase 1: Negotiating Dependence

Although Urban also faced the prospect of operating a body scanner without experienced personnel, it mobilized to meet the problem by relying solely on knowledgeable radiologists. Two months before the scanner arrived, Urban hired a young radiologist who had specialized in CT scanning during his residency. The second radiologist charged with organizing the scanner's operation was a long-time member of the department who had dominated Urban's head scanner and who had followed the body-scanning literature even though he lacked practical experience with the technology. To complete the scanner's staff Urban assembled a group of eight technologists: four drawn from the head scanner and four from other areas of the department. As at Suburban, these personnel decisions combined with the scanner's arrival to signal the first phase of structuring, but the interaction order that evolved substantially differed from Suburban's.

Direction Giving. Since all of Urban's technologists were novices at body scanning, their initial problem was not to demonstrate technical competence but to discover what it entailed. Moreover, since the four days of training offered by the scanner's vendor were little more than an orientation, responsibility for training fell mainly to the radiologists. But, because they had never developed training programs, since they were themselves unfamiliar with the Technicare scanner, and because the work of scanning patients posed countless exigencies that undermined structured pedagogy, the radiologists resorted to giving directions as a primary means of teaching the technologists. The script underlying such interaction was simple and direct: (1) a radiologist told a technologist what to do and (2) the technologist carried out the radiologist's orders, often without asking for clarification or reason. In most cases, the radiologist's utterance was imperative and pertained to minute details of the scanning process.

Direction giving's order-act unit rapidly became the fundamental building block of interaction between radiologists and technologists during the scanner's early period. Direction giving was frequently the only form of verbal communication that passed between radiologist and technologist over the course of a scan. The following example, which begins as a radiologist discovers that a tech has not entered the patient into the scanner's computer, illustrates how incidents of direction giving could be chained together to support lengthy interactions:

Rad: *(Perturbed)* You don't have her in yet?

Tech: Not yet.

Rad: *(Noting the prompts on the terminal, the radiologist tells the technologist what to enter.)* Default . . . Default . . . Default . . . Oral

IV contrast.

Tech: *(Hits the return key three times and begins to enter the label as the radiologist spells.)*

Rad: O . . R . . A . . L . . I . . V . . C . . O . . N . . T . . R . . A . . S . . T. Now, what technique are we going to use?

Tech: Let's see. This is an abdomen so we use "A." Manual select and then A? *(referring to two buttons on the scanner's console).*

Rad: Yeah. Ok. Set 40. *(The tech pushes the button.)* Push "pause scan." *(The tech pushes the button.)* And then, "start scan." *(The tech pushes the button.)* Now, you're not going to do quicklooks, just 512's.

Direction giving differed from preference stating in that the experienced radiologists offered no justification for their suggestions. The script's success as a training strategy therefore hinged on the technologist's ability to form habits and abstract rules of action. That the excerpt above occurred over a month after the scanner came on-line, and that a more routine aspect of CT scanning could scarcely be found, casts doubt on the script's effectiveness. Direction giving failed as a training strategy because it was predicated on one-way communication in which the radiologist assumed the role of conceiver-of-action and the technologist the role of executor-of-action. Consequently, the interaction pattern not only failed to train, it reaffirmed the radiologists' professional dominance by extending their authority to such mundane matters as when to push what button. Even in the x-ray area a radiologist's directions were rarely so detailed.

Countermands. That technologists were unable to infer rules from radiologists' directions was partially explained by a second common interaction pattern whose script also consisted of an order-act sequence but whose context differed from direction giving. Simple direction giving presumed that radiologists would communicate preferences before technologists acted. But the radiologists did not always formulate orders prospectively. On numerous occasions radiologists recognized only in retrospect that an alternate course of action would have been more desirable. When such realizations struck, they typically redirected the exam, regardless of whether they thereby contradicted earlier directions. Order-act sequences that invalidated previous directions composed the script of a countermand.

Occasions for countermands were multiple. Radiologists countermanded directions for diagnostic reasons when they noticed unexpected signs of pathology while viewing a patient's images. More frequently, countermands arose from the radiologists' personal proclivities and rivalries. Unlike their counterparts at Suburban, Urban's experienced radiologists were intrigued by the scanner's technical capabilities and enjoyed testing its limits by posing on-the-spot hypotheses about what the scanner could do. Moreover, the two experts often disagreed as to how the scanner should be operated. Consequently, the radiologists requested numerous alterations as a result of side debates and routinely countermanded each other's orders. Since the radiologists rarely justified changes and since the technologists were not usually privy to the radiologists' side debates, from the technologists' perspective countermands appeared capricious. As unpredictable order-act sequences that could occur anywhere in the context of a scan, countermands underscored the radiologists' authority, undercut opportunities for the technologists to infer rules of informed action, and reinforced the technologists' subservience, since countermands provided no basis for action other than blind obedience to a radiologist's orders.

Usurping the Controls. Urban's experienced radiologists did not limit their interventions to commands and countermands. As early as the first scan, the radiologists also literally took the scanner's controls away from technologists at the console. This practice became so well established that for the first two months of observation no day passed without an instance of a radiologist usurping the scanner. In sharp contrast, Suburban's radiologists rarely took control of the scanner until asked to review images, and even then they limited their manipulations to altering the video display. Unlike previous interaction patterns, usurping the controls was purely behavioral and required no verbal exchange. Its script consisted of a radiologist (1) approaching the console and (2) interrupting the technologist's work by pushing buttons or typing commands at the keyboard.

Urban's technologists treated usurpation as an emotionally charged event that signified disregard for their role and disdain for their abilities. At first the technologists challenged the radiologists' right to usurp control of the scanner, but as it became clear that the technologists could not quell the behavior, they gradually accepted the encounters as routine. However vociferously they might complain to each other, when a radiologist made a play for the console, the technologists acquiesced passively.

Direction Seeking. Aside from direction giving, encounters between Urban's radiologists and technologists in the first phase of structuring were most frequently scripted as incidents of direction seeking. Direction giving and direction seeking were interactional complements. A radiologist's orders initiated the first type of encounter and a technologist's request for guidance cued the second, but both forms of interaction specified the task the technologist should perform next. Direction seeking's script was as simple as direction giving's: (1) a technologist inquired about an appropriate course of action, (2) the radiologist answered, and (3) the technologist acted. Like direction giving, direction seeking initially grew out of the technologists' need to learn, but direction seeking persisted even after the technologists gained experience. The key to the pattern's stability lay in a subtle shift in its social purpose.

All three scripts therefore affirmed the radiologist's dominance and created a work environment that the technologists perceived as arbitrary. To make sense of the seeming caprice, the technologists formulated an interpretive framework, a constitution of work, whose preamble was to uncover and cater to the radiologists' idiosyncratic preferences. If the world of CT was ruled by personal preference, then the fact that acts could not be codified made sense. Tellingly, by the third week of operation techs ceased to inquire what should be done and instead began to ask each other, "What did he say he wanted?" The technologists therefore continued to seek directions from radiologists not only because they did not know what to do, but because they were convinced that radiologists could potentially say what they wished. Over time, direction seeking became both a reaction to the radiologists' authority and a guarantee of the technologists' dependency. Perversely, however, by continually seeking directions the technologists fostered a perception among the radiologists that the technologists were not attempting to learn, a perception that encouraged the radiologists to exert even greater control. Thus the evolving interaction order drew heavily on institutional patterns of action common in the x-ray area to recreate the technologists' traditionally dependent and the radiologists' traditionally dominant role. All that was left was for the interaction order to be sealed.

Phases 2 and 3: Constructing and Ensuring Ineptitude

Since the technologists were not learning as rapidly as the radiologists had hoped, at the end of the fourth week of operation the department instituted a new duty system. Rather than rotate duty on a daily basis, each technologist would run the scanner on a staggered two-week shift At the same time, the radiologists resolved to spend more time in their office to break the technologists' dependency. Ironically, the radiologists' retreat signaled a second phase of structuring that actually amplified the technologists' dependence.

Unexpected Criticisms.   In the radiologists' absence, the technologists experienced no sudden infusion of confidence and no remission in their conviction that scanning protocols were capricious. However, since they were physically separated from the radiologists, they could no longer seek directions spontaneously. The technologists now confronted their formerly tacit dilemma explicitly: to act independently and risk making a poor choice or seek advice and risk seeming ignorant. That the dilemma had become salient could be seen in the technologists' open debates over whether a radiologist should be consulted before they acted. Given the perceived trade-off, the technologists usually chose to consult.

However, since the radiologists were no longer in the control room, direction seeking required the technologists to walk to the radiologist's office. When the technologist arrived, the radiologist was invariably involved in another activity. Consequently, the technologists' questions breached the flow of the radiologist's experience, thereby amplifying direction seeking's salience. Since the radiologists were now more than ever conscious of the technologists' dependency in routine matters, they became increasingly irritated and began to respond to the technologists' questions in a derisive manner.

Direction seeking was thus transformed into a new form of interaction, unexpected criticism, whose script had the following twist: (1) a technologist asked a radiologist how to proceed and (2) the radiologist responded with a sarcasm. Since technologists' questions now elicited ire as well as information, after being approached several times in the course of a scan, the radiologists became exasperated and often left their office to see what was going on. Once in the control room, the radiologist usually remained for the rest of the scan, and subsequent interaction reverted to patterns typical of earlier weeks.

Accusatory Questions.   As the radiologists became increasingly perturbed at the techs' continuing dependency, they began to claim that the technologists were incompetent, an account that fueled their proclivity to intervene when technologists sought directions or made mistakes. Moreover, since the radiologists expected ineptitude, they often found it, even when it did not exist. The self-fulfilling aspect of the radiologists' perceptions underwrote accusatory questioning, a second interactional pattern that congealed during the second phase of structuring. The accusatory question's script was marked by (1) a radiologist's accosting a technologist with insinuations of incompetence after (2) a technologist took action without seeking direction.

A telling example of accusatory questioning involved a technologist who had spent fifteen minutes successfully puzzling through a computer problem. The problem arose when the radiologist on duty requested that the technologist use parameters the scanner was not programmed to accept. As the technologist finished solving the problem, the radiologist entered the control room and demanded: "What have you been doing all this time?" As was usually the case in such encounters, the tech responded meekly. She told the radiologist that she had encountered a technical problem, but she did not mention that she knew the problem arose from his earlier request. Such encounters rapidly extinguished tentative steps toward initiative and reinforced the tendency to seek direction. At the same time, the technologists' failure to rebut the accusations strengthened the radiologists' suspicion of incompetence, since they read the technologists' deference as guilt.

Unaware of how their own actions contributed to the situation, by the end of the sixth week the radiologists concluded that the technologists were indeed inept and that scans were taking too long to complete. From their vantage point, the experiment of granting the technologists autonomy had failed. To resolve these difficulties, on the fortieth day of operation the radiologists dropped all pretense of aloofness and resumed their former habit of remaining in the control room while patients were being scanned. This decision marked the beginning of a third phase of structuring during which scripts developed in the first phase became firmly ensconced in an interaction order that closely replicated the traditional roles of radiologists and technologists in an x-ray area.

Phase 4: Toward Independence

Urban's interaction order remained stable until the sixteenth week, when four technologists whom the radiologists labeled as least competent at body scanning were permanently transferred to the head scanner. At the same time, the experienced radiologists resumed duties in other areas of the radiology department so that the inexperienced radiologists could rotate through CT. By redistributing the relative balance of practical experience in favor of the remaining technologists, these changes triggered a fourth phase of structuring during which new patterns of interaction emerged reminiscent of those that developed at Suburban.

Technical Consultation. Whereas the technical education of Suburban's inexperienced radiologists took place clandestinely beneath a veneer of self-assurance, Urban's inexperienced radiologists made no pretense that they were not ignorant in technical matters and openly turned to the technologists for aid. These consultations inverted the interaction order established during Urban's earlier structuring. In stark contrast to what had gone before, radiologists now became seekers and technologists givers of directions. The script of a technical consultation resembled direction seeking's script except that the actors' parts were switched: (1) the radiologist inquired about an appropriate course of action and (2) the technologist provided the radiologist with an answer.

Rad: *(Referring to the computer's repetitive display of alternate images)* How do I stop this?

Tech: *(Leaning over the radiologist's shoulder to type at the keyboard)* You type L . . . R . . . O . . . to turn "Load Review Off."

Rad: That's good, LRO. Now, how do I get the 512? *(He types a command into the computer.)*

Tech: Wait!!! That's not what you want. *(She pushes the correct button.)*

Rad: Oh! I see! Wonderful! Thank you.

Mutual Execution. Although technical consultations inverted scripts institutionalized in previous months, the inversion did not threaten the radiologists' authority. Unlike role reversals at Suburban, where radiologists sought interpretations, in mutual consultations radiologists merely sought technical information from technologists. Though uncommon, such reliance on technologists was not taboo, since radiology's occupational rhetoric had always touted technologists to be technical experts. Perhaps for this reason, Urban's novice radiologists did not withdraw from the scanner's daily operation as did their counterparts at Suburban. But since the inexperienced radiologists could not issue minute-by-minute directions and since they willingly acknowledged the technologists' skill in technical matters, interactions between members of the two groups acquired a novel form.

The new interaction pattern, mutual execution, was more complex than any discussed so far. Mutual execution involved a balanced display of direction seeking and direction giving on the part of both technologist and radiologist. Moreover, the technologists began to offer suggestions about how to proceed, and the radiologists began to compliment technologists on their acumen:

Rad: (*Looking at the scan on the monitor*) How far are you going?

Tech: I was going to go to the top of the pancreas.

Rad: Only do ten more millimeters.

Tech: After you do the bolus you want to try a dynamic scan?[6]

Rad: Oh! Can you?

Tech: Well, I did one yesterday on a phantom.[7]

Rad: So you're prepared to do it! Great! What are you doing now?

Tech: Waiting on two more scans to process.

Rad: Oh good! Bring the table back ten millimeters and we'll start her. Now, how does it work with the lights? How does she time her breathing?

Tech: The lights [inside the gantry] will blink red three times and stay solid.

In such interchanges the identity of the lead actor shifted as both parties pooled their knowledge. Because instances of direction seeking and direction giving were interspersed with their inverses, the interaction pattern maintained the radiologists' authority. But the shifting lead also allowed technologists to demonstrate expertise, which was confirmed by the radiologists' acceptance of their suggestions. The turn taking of mutual execution therefore constituted an interaction pattern with greater equanimity than existed in earlier phases of structuring. As technical consultations and mutual execution became frequent, technologists began to exercise more discretion and radiologists loosened their control over day-to-day operations. Thus, role relations became less rigid, and Urban's interaction order moved toward a role structure in which radiologists and technologists behaved as if each possessed valuable, complementary skills.

The Sedimentation of Alternate Organizational Forms

Figure 15.2 displays the number of times the scripts discussed in this paper appeared in field notes taken during

---

[6] "Bolus" is a term for a rapid injection of iodine dye. The "dynamic scan" was a software routine that allowed a series of scans to be taken in extremely rapid succession. At this point, Urban had rarely used the software.

[7] A "phantom" is an object used to tune and practice with the scanner.

each period of structuring in both hospitals. The solid vertical line separates Suburban's and Urban's scripts, while the solid horizontal line separates each department's phases of structuring. Dotted vertical lines cluster the scripts from each site into sets corresponding to the phase in which they gained ascendancy. By reading across the rows of the table one can ascertain the number of times a given script occurred during a particular phase of structuring in one of the two hospitals. Columns record the frequency of a specific script during all phases at both hospitals. The quadrants on the main diagonal formed by the solid lines show the occurrence of scripts in the hospital where they were central to the evolving interaction order. Off-diagonal quadrants represent the frequency of each hospital's scripts in the field notes collected at the other.

The pattern of frequencies in the upper right quadrant of Figure 15.2 substantiates the claim that Suburban experienced two phases of structuring and that each sired a qualitatively different interaction order. No instances of clandestine teaching, role reversal, or blaming the technologist were observed during the first phase of structuring. However, once the inexperienced radiologists assumed CT duty, these scripts became frequent, and instances of scripts common during the first phase of structuring declined. In fact, the few cases of unsought validation, anticipatory questioning, and preference stating observed in the second phase occurred in the first few days after the transition when the experienced radiologist was called to the CT area to assist inexperienced radiologists.

The shift in Urban's interaction order in Phase 4 is substantiated by the lower right quadrant of Figure 15.2 which displays the frequency of Urban's scripts during the four phases of the department's structuring. In field notes from the first three phases of Urban's structuring, no instances of technical consultation or mutual execution were recorded. Instead, most encounters between radiologists and technologists were patterned as direction giving and seeking, as countermands, as cases of usurping the controls, or as unexpected criticism and accusatory questioning. However, with the inexperienced radiologists' arrival, instances of these earlier scripts decreased dramatically, while technical consultations and mutual executions became as common as the other forms of interaction.

Both scanners upset the distribution of expertise that undergirds radiology's traditional division of labor. Both also occasioned dynamics that transformed role relations to yield CT techs more discretion than was typical of technologists in an x-ray area. Yet, the interaction orders differed. As the off-diagonal quadrants of Figure 15.2 attest, scripts prevalent at Suburban were uncommon at Urban, and those

FIGURE 15.2

FREQUENCY IN FIELD NOTES OF SCRIPTS THAT GAINED ASCENDANCY DURING PHASES OF STRUCTURING AT URBAN AND SUBURBAN HOSPITALS

Hospital Phase		Suburban						Urban							
		PHASE 1			PHASE 2			PHASE 1				PHASE 2		PHASE 4	
		UV	AQ	PS	CT	RR	BT	DG	CM	UC	DS	UCRIT	AcQ	TC	ME
Suburban	1	6	9	0	0	0	0	10	0	0	5	0	0	0	0
	2	2	3	2	13	14	7	11	0	0	5	0	1	9	7
Urban	1	0	0	10	0	0	1	47	12	12	21	0	2	0	0
	2	0	0	1	0	0	2	14	1	7	13	11	6	0	0
	3	0	0	1	1	0	0	50	4	9	33	4	7	0	0
	4	0	0	0	0	1	0	13	0	3	11	1	0	11	10

Legend:
UV = unsought validation
AQ = anticipatory question
PS = preference stating
CT = clandestine teaching
RR = role reversal
BT = blaming the technologist
DG = direction giving

CM = countermand
UC = usurping the controls
DS = direction seeking
UCrit = unexpected critisism
AcQ = accusatory question
TC = technical consultation
ME = mutual execution

common at Urban were rare at Suburban. Preference stating was the only script from Suburban that occurred with frequency at Urban. In fact, preference stating actually appeared more often in field notes from Urban's first phase of structuring than it did in notes from Suburban's initial phase. To understand why preference stating was nevertheless more figural at Suburban, one must consider the interactional distinction between the two scripts as well as their relative frequency at each site. While both scripts enabled radiologists to make demands, only when stating preferences did the radiologists justify their demands. Preference stating therefore implied that technologists deserved reasons for action while direction giving merely presumed that technologists should do what they were told. As can be calculated from the data in Figure 15.2, the ratio of preference stating to direction giving was 1 to 1.7 during Suburban's first phase. The same ratio was 1 to 4.7 for Urban's initial phase. Thus, by mere frequency, direction giving overshad-owed preference stating at Urban and thereby strongly reinforced the technologists' perception of radiologists' professional dominance. Because the two scripts were more evenly balanced at Suburban, direction giving's bold enactment of the radiologists' dominance was moderated by preference stating's emphasis on collegiality.

Technical consultation and mutual execution also appear as exceptions to the larger pattern in Figure 15.2. Both scripts occurred almost as frequently at Suburban after the inexperienced radiologists began CT duty as during Urban's corresponding phase of structuring. However, at Suburban the two scripts were interspersed with instances of clandestine teaching, role reversal, and blaming the technologists. These latter scripts were not only more salient for Suburban's personnel, they almost never occurred at Urban. Consequently, the two sites appear to have evolved different interaction orders, even though the two CT areas' scripts did not form mutually exclusive sets.

However, from the perspective of the sequential model of structuring, identical technologies lead to different organizational structures only when they occasion interaction orders that vary in a consistent and coherent manner. For alternate organizational structures to arise it is insufficient for two interaction orders to be composed of different scripts. The scripts in each interaction order must also consistently embody overarching properties that differentiate the two systems. Thus, if structure is viewed as a grammar of scripts, the two scanners can be said to have occasioned different structures if and only if each department's scripts inscribe alternate, coherent blueprints for action.

Institutional patterns of interaction between radiologists and technologists were predicated on the radiologists' dominance, which was legitimated by the authority of expertise. As a formal property of interaction, dominance by expertise is encoded by the direction in which information flows. As Blau (1964) and Emerson (1972) have argued, to possess and send information is to enact power over its recipient, at least for the duration of an encounter. Defined in terms of communicative exchange, dominance finds expression as a structural property of organizations in the concept of centralization. In centralized organizations, decisions are not only made by actors with superior hierarchical status, but information and decisions also flow, by definition, down the status hierarchy

In terms of the direction of information flow, the scripts that compose the two interaction orders coherently and consistently display quite different formal patterns. Suburban's scripts indicate that structuring progressed from an interaction order characterized by mutual exchange to an interaction order in which technologists became the senders and radiologists the recipients of most information. In contrast, Urban's structuring moved from an interaction order in which radiologists possessed and sent all information to an interaction order marked by a more balanced sharing of information. Consequently, on the basis of scripts, it would appear that the scanners not only occasioned a more decentralized structure at Suburban but that Suburban's interaction order thereby departed more significantly from tradition than did Urban's.

Independent verification that Suburban was more decentralized can be obtained by examining the proportion of a scan's routine decisions made by a radiologist. Figure 15.3 plots these indices for Suburban and Urban as a function of the day of operation on which the scan was conducted. The postulated phases of structuring at each site are indicated by vertical bars. The figure shows that the proportion of decisions made by radiologists was generally

much lower at Suburban than at Urban. In 78 percent of Suburban's 49 scans radiologists made less than half the decisions, while the corresponding percentage for Urban's 42 scans was 26 percent.

Moreover, the plots suggest that each department moved toward a more decentralized structure at rates intimated by the analysis of structuring at the two sites. Although radiologists initially made most of the routine decisions in each CT area, their involvement at Suburban fell, at what appears to be a geometrically declining rate. On the other hand, the radiologists' involvement at Urban appears to have declined gradually in a linear fashion. By regressing the proportion of routine decisions made by a radiologist first on a linear model specified by the day of operation on which the scan was conducted and then on a quadratic model constructed by adding the square of that value, one may test whether the visual differences are significant. If structuring progressed as suggested, then a quadratic model should predict Suburban's data better than a linear model, while in Urban's case no improvement should be found. The regression analysis displayed in Table 15.1 shows precisely such a result: addition of the quadratic term to the linear model significantly increases the proportion of explained variance only for Suburban's data.

The plots also show the adequacy of the phases of structuring identified for each department. Suburban's plot suggests that an inflection point occurs shortly after Suburban's second phase was alleged to have begun. The plot therefore appears to verify a rapid increase in the CT techs' discretion shortly after Suburban's inexperienced radiologists assumed CT duty. Urban's data also trace the alleged sequence of phases. Note that Urban's radiologists' involvement in routine decisions fell briefly in the second phase of structuring when the experienced radiologists momentarily withdrew from the control room. However, involvement rose during the third phase when the radiologists abandoned their strategy of restraint. Finally with the arrival of Urban's inexperienced radiologists during the fourth phase, Urban's scores once again fell.

To determine if the centralization scores support each site's alleged phasing, the proportion of decisions radiologists made at each site was first regressed on a series of dummy variables that coded each scan's date in terms of the phase during which it allegedly occurred. Since Suburban was said to have experienced two phases and Urban four, Suburban's data were regressed on one dummy variable representing the first phase of structuring while Urban's data were regressed on three variables representing Urban's first three phases. Each site's data were then regressed on all four dummy variables in a combined

PROPORTION OF OPERATIONAL DECISIONS MADE BY RADIOLOGISTS AT SUBURBAN AND URBAN HOSPITALS

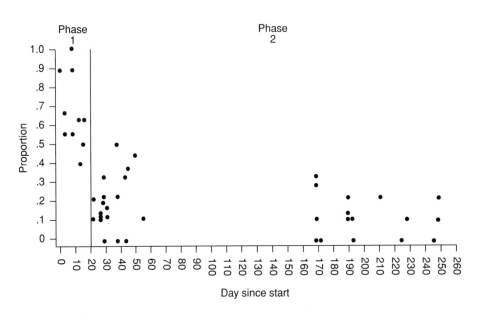

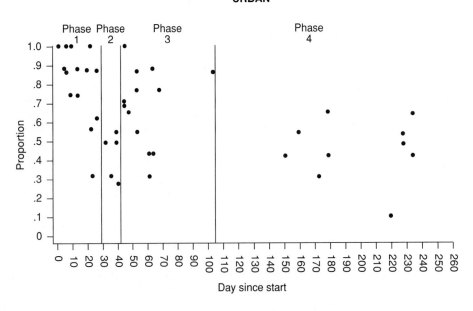

* The missing data between days 80 and 145 represent weeks during which no fieldwork was conducted.

TABLE 15.1

LINEAR AND QUADRATIC TRENDS IN THE PROPORTION OF
OPERATIONAL DECISIONS INVOLVING RADIOLOGISTS*

HOSPITAL	MODEL	INTERCEPT	DAY	DAY²	R^2	Df	F
Suburban	Linear	.40	−.001				
		(9.14)••	(−4.20)••		.27••		
	Quadratic	.53	-.006	2.15 (10⁻⁵)			
		(8.94)••	(−3.67)••	(2.88)••	.38••	(1,46)	8.36••
Urban	Linear	.77	−.002				
		(17.29)••	(−3.60)••		.24••		
	Quadratic	.86	−.005	1.41(10⁻⁵)			
		(13.38)••	(−2.63)••	(1.83)	.30••	(1,39)	3.33

* Numbers in parentheses are t-tests for corresponding parameters.

•p < .05, ••p < .01

analysis. If each site's phasing was adequately defined then the combined model should predict radiologists' involvement no better than the model constructed to depict the site's own phases of structuring. Table 15.2, which presents the regression analysis, shows such a pattern of results: in neither case did the combined model substantially increase the proportion of variance explained by the hospital's own model. Consequently, the data are consistent with the claim that Suburban evolved through two phases of structuring while Urban experienced four.

Conclusions

If nothing else, the foregoing analysis demonstrates that by treating technology as an occasion for structuring, researchers will confront contradictory results head-on because of structuring's central paradox: identical technologies can occasion similar dynamics and yet lead to different structural outcomes. Despite the fact that both structuring processes conformed to the sequential model of reciprocal articulation and despite the fact that roles in each department changed in similar directions, one department became far more decentralized, because formal properties governing the scripts of the two inter-

action orders diverged. One suspects that traditional cross-sectional studies that seek large sample size and ignore contextually embedded dynamics would risk concluding that scanners have no implications for the social organization of radiology because differences in formal structures would tend to cancel each other in correlational analysis. However, to view technology as an occasion for structuring is not to deny the worth of previous work on technology's relation to structure, but rather to modify and specify that work.

A materialist, for example, might argue that the CT scanners' physical properties occasioned structural change by impinging on the organization of radiological work. In the literature on technology and structure, technical complexity is often considered relevant in this regard. Materialists would likely point to the scanner's technical complexity and to the complexity of its diagnostic signs to argue that role structures loosened because the scanners introduced uncertainty into a world hitherto well understood. The present approach would concur. At both hospitals the scanners' technical complexity and the radiologists' lack of familiarity with CT's diagnostic signs threatened the inexperienced radiologists' authority and forced them to rely more heavily on the technologists. However, from the perspective of structuring theory, complexity and uncertainty are functions of how the machine merged with the social system; they are not attributes of the machine itself. That is, the scanners occasioned change

TABLE 15.2

ADEQUACY OF EACH DEPARTMENT'S OWN MODEL OF STRUCTURING FOR PREDICTING THE PROPORTION OF OPERATIONAL DECISIONS INVOLVING RADIOLOGISTS*

HOSPITAL	MODEL	INTERCEPT	SUBURBAN PHASE 1	URBAN PHASE 2	URBAN PHASE 2	URBAN PHASE 3	R^2	Df	F
Suburban	Suburban	.17	.50						
		(7.46)••	(9.96)••				.67••		
	Combined	.13	.53	.01	.07	.14			
		(3.99)••	(6.91)••	(0.21)	(1.31)	(2.12)•	.71••	(3,44)	1.43
Urban	Suburban	.47		.36	−.04	.22			
		(8.20)••		(4.77)••	(0.39)	(2.90)••	.45••		
	Combined	.47	.22	.21	−.04	.22			
		(8.66)••	(2.34)•	(2.19)•	(0.41)	(3.06)••	.52••	(3,37)	1.54

*Numbers in parentheses are t-tests for corresponding parameters.

•p < .05, ••p < .01

because they became social objects whose meanings were defined by the context of their use. Suburban's scanner generated more uncertainty and mounted a greater challenge to professional dominance because Suburban hired experienced technologists and because the inexperienced radiologists assumed CT duty at an early date. At Urban, the scanner's threat was mitigated because the department staffed the scanner with novice techs and relied longer on knowledgeable radiologists.

These differences surely influenced the relative distribution of expertise that constrained the structuring process. But the constraints only partially account for Urban's greater centralization. If the actors at each site had negotiated their roles differently, if, for example, Suburban's radiologists had assumed a stance similar to Urban's novices, then structuring would have evolved differently in spite of the distribution of expertise. Alternately, had Urban's radiologists realized the self-sealing aspect of their behavior, the interaction order they helped create might have been transformed. Furthermore, if all radiologists had studied CT scanning prior to adoption, then the scanners would have surely occasioned other interaction orders and, by implication, other formal structures. In short, structuring theory holds that technical uncertainty and complexity are social constructions that vary from setting to setting even when identical technologies are deployed. Although this phenomenological point was stressed by Perrow's (1967) classic paper on technology

and structure, its implication for a diversity of outcomes has never been fully appreciated.

A voluntaristic theory of technology's ramifications, such as the one found in Child's (1972) work, might claim that the data show how decision makers actually determine technology's implications, since structuring unfolded as radiologists made staffing decisions. Staffing decisions did signal the beginning of each phase of structuring and were indeed influential in shaping structuring's dynamics at each site. But that the radiologists intended the consequences of their decisions is questionable. While the radiologists hired and assigned personnel in certain sequences, the data do not suggest that they intended to affect the degree of centralization. Suburban's radiologists hired experienced technologists to reduce the odds of exposing patients to incompetence and themselves to malpractice suits. Urban used inexperienced technologists because of the hospital's policy of promoting insiders. There is even evidence that some staffing decisions shaped the structuring process in directions opposite of what was intended. For example, Urban's radiologists withdrew in the second period of structuring to discourage rather than encourage the technologists' dependence. Thus from the perspective of structuring theory, decision makers may in fact influence the evolution of interaction orders, but the structural consequences of their decisions are likely to be unanticipated.

Structuring theory thus departs from previous approaches to the study of technology by postulating that technologies are social objects capable of triggering dynamics whose unintended and unanticipated consequences may nevertheless follow a contextual logic. Technologies do influence organizational structures in orderly ways, but their influence depends on the specific historical process in which they are embedded. To predict a technology's ramifications for an organization's structure therefore requires a methodology and a conception of technical change open to the construction of grounded, population-specific theories. For example, to devise a theory of how technology alters radiological work, one would need not only to account for relative distributions of expertise but to develop a taxonomy of scripts to explain how distributions of expertise can be accommodated differently in daily interaction. Structuring theory is a form of soft determinism that searches for regularity by looking down time lines to see how diversity is occasioned by specifiable social processes. Such an idiographic approach is warranted, because structure is viewed as the abstract of a social history written by ongoing interaction. No one is surprised that families are constrained by histories and ritualistic patterns that relatives unwittingly author and sustain in systematic ways. Why should the structures of larger collectives be different in kind?

REFERENCES

Archer, Margaret S.
1982 "Morphogenesis versus structuration: On combining structure and action." *British Journal of Sociology,* 33: 455–483.

Barley, Stephen R.
1984 "The professional, the semi–professional, and the machine: The social implications of computer based imaging in radiology." Unpublished Ph.D. dissertation, Massachusetts Institute of Technology.

Berger, Peter L., and Thomas Luckmann
1967 *The Social Construction of Reality.* New York: Doubleday.

Blau, Peter
1964 *Exchange and Power in Social Life.* New York: Wiley.

Blau, Peter M., Cecilia McHugh Falbe, William McKinley, and Phelps K. Tracey
1976 "Technology and organization in manufacturing." *Administrative Science Quarterly,* 21: 20–40.

Brown, Carol A.
1973 "The division of laborers: Allied health professions." *International Journal of Health Services,* 3: 434–444.

Burrell, Gibson, and Gareth Morgan
1979 *Sociological Paradigms and Organizational Analysis.* London: Heinemann.

Child, John
1972 "Organizational structure, environment, and performance: The role of strategic choice." *Sociology,* 6: 1–22.

Comstock, Donald E., and W. Richard Scott
1977 "Technology and the structure of subunits: Distinguishing individual and workgroup effects." *Administrative Science Quarterly,* 22: 177–202.

Dewing, S. B.
1962 *Modern Radiology in Historical Perspective.* Springfield, IL: Charles C. Thomas.

Emerson, Richard M.
1972 "Exchange theory part 1: A social psychological basis for social change." In J. Berg et al. (eds.), Sociological Theories in *Progress,* 2: 38–93. Boston: Houghton Mifflin.

Friedson, Eliot
1970 *Professional Dominance: The Social Structure of Medical Care.* New York: Atherton Press.

Fry, Louis W.
1982 "Technology-structure research: Three critical issues." *Academy of Management Journal,* 25: 532–552.

Gerwin, Donald
1981 "Relationships between structure and technology." In Paul Nystrom and William Starbuck (eds.), *Handbook of Organization Design,* 2: 3–38. Cambridge: Cambridge University Press.

Giddens, Anthony
1976 *New Rules of Sociological Method.* London: Hutchinson.
1979 *Central Problems in Social Theory.* Berkeley, CA: University of California Press.

Goffman, Erving
1959 *Presentation of Self in Everyday Life.* New York: Anchor.
1967 *Interaction Ritual.* New York: Anchor Books.
1983 "The interaction order." *American Sociological Review,* 48: 1–17.

Hickson, David J., D. S. Pugh, and Diana C. Pheysey
1969 "Operations technology and organization structure: An empirical reappraisal." *Administrative Science Quarterly,* 14: 378–397.

Khandwalla, Pradip N.
1974 "Mass output orientation of operations technology and organizational structure." *Administrative Science Quarterly.* 19: 74–97.

Larkin, Gerald
1978 "Medical dominance and control: Radiographers in the division of labor." *Sociological Review,* 26: 843–858.

Larson, Margali S.
1977   *The Rise of Professionalism.* Berkeley, CA: University of California Press.

Lévi-Strauss, Claude
1963   *Structural Anthropology,* vol. 1. New York: Basic Books.

Manning, Peter K.
1977   *Police Work.* Cambridge, MA: MIT Press.
1982   "Organizational work: Structuration of environments." *British Journal of Sociology,* 16: 444–459.

Meyer, Alan
1982   "Adapting to environmental jolts." *Administrative Science Quarterly,* 27: 515–537.

Mohr, Lawrence B.
1971   "Organizational technology and organizational structure." *Administrative Science Quarterly,* 16: 444–459.

Perrow, Charles
1967   "A framework for the comparative analysis of organizations." *American Sociological Review,* 32: 194–208.

Propp, Vladimir
1958   *The Morphology of the Folktale.* Austin, TX: University of Texas Press.

Ranson, Stewart, Bob Hinings, and Royston Greenwood
1980   "The structuring of organizational structures." *Administrative Science Quarterly,* 25: 1–17.

Riley, Patricia
1983   "A structurationist account of political cultures." *Administrative Science Quarterly,* 28: 414–437

Salaman, Graham, and Kenneth Thompson
1980   *Control and Ideology in Organizations.* Cambridge, MA: MIT Press.

Schank, R. C., and R. P. Abelson
1977   *Scripts, Plans, Goals and Understanding.* Hillsdale, NJ: Erlbaum.

Silverman, David
1971   *The Theory of Organizations.* New York: Basic Books.

Sitkin, Sim, and Michael Boehm
1984   "Structural relations in organizations: On the relationship between behavior, beliefs, and formal structure." Paper presented at the 44th Annual Academy of Management Meeting, Boston.

Stanfield, Gary G.
1976   "Technology and organization structure as theoretical categories." *Administrative Science Quarterly,* 21: 489–493.

Strauss, Anselm
1978   *Negotiations.* San Francisco: Jossey-Bass.
1982   "Interorganizational negotiations." *Urban Life,* 11: 350–367.

Van Maanen, John
1977   "Experiencing organizations: Notes on the meaning of careers and socialization." In J. Van Maanen (ed.), *Organizational Careers: Some New Perspectives:* 15–45. New York: Wiley.
1979   "The self, the situation and rules of interpersonal relations." In W. Bennis et al. (eds.), *Essays in Interpersonal Dynamics:* 43–101. Homewood, IL: Dorsey.

Weick, Karl
1979   *The Social Psychology of Organizing,* 2d ed. Reading, MA: Addison-Wesley.

Willmott, Hugh
1981   "The structuring of organizational structure: A note." *Administrative Science Quarterly,* 26: 470–474.

DISCUSSION QUESTIONS

1. What is the current understanding of the relationship between technology and organizational form?

2. Discuss the various ways that organizational structure is conceptualized. Which formulation does Barley prefer? How does this differ from conceptions of structure that focus on arrangements found in organization charts?

3. How does the organization's context and history affect understanding of the relationship between technology and structure?

4. Describe how scripts function in organizations.

5. What is the traditional hierarchy of authority in a radiology department?

6. In Suburban what were the social processes by which role reversals occurred? How did role reversals affect the departmental social structure?

7. Describe the differences in social structure in Suburban and Urban as a result of the new technology.

8. What are the implications of Barley's analysis for the management of new technology?

FOR FURTHER READING

Blau, P., Falbe, C., McKinley, W., and Tracy, P. "Technology and Organization in Manufacturing." *Administrative Science Quarterly* 21 (1976) 20–40.

Barley, S. "The Alignment of Technology and Structure through Roles and Networks." *Administrative Science Quarterly,* 35 (1990) 61–103.

Miller, C., Glick, W., Wang, Y., and Huber, G. "Understanding Technology–Structure Relationships: Theory Development and Meta-Analytic Theory Testing." *Academy of Management Journal* 34 (1991) 370–399.

Turnage, J. "The Challenge of New Workplace Technology for Psychology." *American Psychologist* 45 (1990) 171–178.

16

ORGANIZATIONAL STRUCTURE AND DESIGN

In Praise of Hierarchy

ELLIOTT JAQUES

LEARNING OBJECTIVES

"In Praise of Hierarchy" by Elliott Jaques will help students understand:

1. What a hierarchy is

2. Why hierarchy has been viewed as ineffective

3. How hierarchy works in organizations

4. How to manage hierarchy to the advantage of both management and workers

At first glance, hierarchy may seem difficult to praise. Bureaucracy is a dirty word even among bureaucrats, and in business there is a widespread view that managerial hierarchy kills initiative, crushes creativity, and has therefore seen its day. Yet 35 years of research have convinced me that managerial hierarchy is the most efficient, the hardiest, and in fact the most natural structure ever devised for large organizations. Properly structured, hierarchy can release energy and creativity, rationalize productivity, and actually improve morale. Moreover, I think most managers know this intuitively and have only lacked a workable structure and a decent intellectual justification for what they have always known could work and work well.

As presently practiced, hierarchy undeniably has its drawbacks. One of business's great contemporary problems is how to release and sustain among the people who work in corporate hierarchies the thrust, initiative, and adaptability of the entrepreneur. This problem is so great that it has become fashionable to call for a new kind of organization to put in place of managerial hierarchy, an organization that will better meet the requirements of what is variously called the Information Age, the Services Age, or the Post-Industrial Age.

As vague as the description of the age is the definition of the kind of new organization required to suit it. Theorists tell us it ought to look more like a symphony orchestra or a hospital or perhaps the British raj. It ought to function by means of primus groups or semiautonomous work teams or matrix overlap groups. It should be organic or entrepreneurial or tight-loose. It should hinge on skunk works or on management by walking around or perhaps on our old friend, management by objective.

All these approaches are efforts to overcome the perceived faults of hierarchy and find better ways to improve morale and harness human creativity. But the theorists' belief that our changing world requires an alternative to hierarchical organization is simply wrong, and all their proposals are based on an inadequate understanding of not only hierarchy but also human nature.

Hierarchy is not to blame for our problems. Encouraged by gimmicks and fads masquerading as insights, we have burdened our managerial systems with a makeshift scaffolding of inept structures and attitudes. What we need is not simply a new, flatter organization but an understanding of how management hierarchy functions—how it relates to the complexity of work and how we can use it to achieve a more effective deployment of talent and energy.

The reason we have hierarchical organization of work is not only that tasks occur in lower and higher degrees of complexity—which is obvious—but also that there are sharp discontinuities in complexity that separate tasks into a series of steps or categories—which is not so obvious. The same discontinuities occur with respect to mental work and to the breadth and duration of accountability. The hierarchical kind of organization we call bureaucracy did not emerge accidentally. It is the only form of organization that can enable a company to employ large numbers of people and yet preserve unambiguous accountability for the work they do. And that is why, despite its problems, it has so doggedly persisted.

Hierarchy has not had its day. Hierarchy never did have its day. As an organizational system, managerial hierarchy has never been adequately described and has just as certainly never been adequately used. The problem is not to find an alternative to a system that once worked well but no longer does; the problem is to make it work efficiently for the first time in its 3,000-year history.

What Went Wrong . . .

There is no denying that hierarchical structure has been the source of a great deal of trouble and inefficiency. Its misuse has hampered effective management and stifled leadership, while its track record as a support for entrepreneurial energy has not been exemplary. We might almost say that successful businesses have had to succeed despite hierarchical organization rather than because of it.

One common complaint is excessive layering—too many rungs on the ladder. Information passes through too many people, decisions through too many levels, and managers and subordinates are too close together in experience and ability, which smothers effective leadership, cramps accountability, and promotes buck passing. Relationships grow stressful when managers and subordinates bump elbows, so to speak, within the same frame of reference.

Another frequent complaint is that few managers seem to add real value to the work of their subordinates. The fact that the breakup value of many large corporations is greater than their share value shows pretty clearly how much value corporate managers can *subtract* from

their subsidiary businesses, but in fact few of us know exactly what managerial added value would look like as it was occurring.

Many people also complain that our present hierarchies bring out the nastier aspects of human behavior, like greed, insensitivity, careerism, and self-importance. These are the qualities that have sent many behavioral scientists in search of cooperative, group-oriented, nonhierarchical organizational forms. But are they the inevitable companions of hierarchy, or perhaps a product of the misuse of hierarchy that would disappear if hierarchy were properly understood and structured?

. . . And What Continues to Go Wrong

The fact that so many of hierarchy's problems show up in the form of individual misbehavior has led to one of the most widespread illusions in business, namely, that a company's managerial leadership can be significantly improved solely by doing psychotherapeutic work on the personalities and attitudes of its managers. Such methods can help individuals gain greater personal insight, but I doubt that individual insight, personality matching, or even exercises in group dynamics can produce much in the way of organizational change or an overall improvement in leadership effectiveness. The problem is that our managerial hierarchies are so badly designed as to defeat the best efforts even of psychologically insightful individuals.

Solutions that concentrate on groups, on the other hand, fail to take into account the real nature of employment systems. People are not employed in groups. They are employed individually, and their employment contracts—real or implied—are individual. Group members may insist in moments of great esprit de corps that the group as such is the author of some particular accomplishment, but once the work is completed, the members of the group look for individual recognition and individual progression in their careers. And it is not groups but individuals whom the company will hold accountable. The only true group is the board of directors, with its corporate liability.

None of the group-oriented panaceas face this issue of accountability. All the theorists refer to group authority, group decisions, and group consensus, none of them to group accountability. Indeed, they avoid the issue of accountability altogether, for to hold a group accountable, the employment contract would have to be with the group, not with the individuals, and companies simply do not employ groups as such.

To understand hierarchy, you must first understand employment. To be employed is to have an ongoing contract that holds you accountable for doing work of a given type for a specified number of hours per week in exchange for payment. Your specific tasks within that given work are assigned to you by a person called your manager (or boss or supervisor), who *ought to be held accountable* for the work you do.

If we are to make our hierarchies function properly, it is essential to place the emphasis on *accountability for getting work done.* This is what hierarchical systems ought to be about. Authority is a secondary issue and flows from accountability in the sense that there should be just that amount of authority needed to discharge the accountability. So if a group is to be given authority, its members must be held accountable as a group, and unless this is done, it is very hard to take so-called group decisions seriously. If the CEO or the manager of the group is held accountable for outcomes, then in the final analysis, he or she will have to agree with group decisions or have the authority to block them, which means that the group never really had decision-making power to begin with. Alternatively, if groups are allowed to make decisions without their manager's seal of approval, then accountability as such will suffer, for if a group does badly, the group is never fired. (And it would be shocking if it were.)

In the long run, therefore, group authority *without* group accountability is dysfunctional, and group authority *with* group accountability is unacceptable. So images of organizations that are more like symphony orchestras or hospitals or the British raj are surely nothing more than metaphors to express a desired feeling of togetherness—the togetherness produced by a conductor's baton, the shared concern of doctors and nurses for their patients, or the apparent unity of the British civil service in India.

In employment systems, after all, people are not mustered to play together as their manager beats time. As for hospitals, they are the essence of everything bad about bureaucratic organization. They function in spite of the system, only because of the enormous professional devotion of their staffs. The Indian civil service was in many ways like a hospital, its people bound together by the struggle to survive in a hostile environment. Managers do need authority, but authority based appropriately on the accountabilities they must discharge.

Why Hierarchy?

The bodies that govern companies, unions, clubs, and nations all employ people to do work, and they all organize these employees in managerial hierarchies, systems that allow organizations to hold people accountable for getting assigned work done. Unfortunately, we often lose sight of this goal and set up the organizational layers in our managerial hierarchies to accommodate pay brackets and facilitate career development instead. If work happens to get done as well, we consider that a useful bonus.

But if our managerial hierarchical organizations tend to choke so readily on debilitating bureaucratic practices, how do we explain the persistence and continued spread of this form of organization for more than 3,000 years? And why has the determined search for alternatives proved so fruitless?

The answer is that managerial hierarchy is and will remain the *only* way to structure unified working systems with hundreds, thousands, or tens of thousands of employees, for the very good reason that managerial hierarchy is the expression of two fundamental characteristics of real work. First, the tasks we carry out are not only more or less complex but they also become more complex as they separate out into discrete categories or types of complexity. Second, the same is true of the mental work that people do on the job, for as this work grows more complex, it too separates out into distinct categories or types of mental activity. In turn, these two characteristics permit hierarchy to meet four of any organization's fundamental needs: to add real value to work as it moves through the organization, to identify and nail down accountability at each stage of the value-adding process, to place people with the necessary competence at each organizational layer, and to build a general consensus and acceptance of the managerial structure that achieves these ends.

Hierarchical Layers

The complexity of the problems encountered in a particular task, project, or strategy is a function of the variables involved—their number, their clarity or ambiguity, the rate at which they change, and, overall, the extent to which they are distinct or tangled. Obviously, as you move higher in a managerial hierarchy, the most difficult problems you have to contend with become increasingly complex. The biggest problems faced by the CEO of a large corporation are vastly more complex that those encountered on the shop floor. The CEO must cope not only with a huge array of often amorphous and constantly changing data but also with variables so tightly interwoven that they must be disentangled before they will yield useful information. Such variables might include the cost of capital, the interplay of corporate cash flow, the structure of the international competitive market, the uncertainties of Europe after 1992, the future of Pacific Rim development, social developments with respect to labor, political developments in Eastern Europe, the Middle East, and the Third World, and technological research and change.

That the CEO's and the lathe operator's problems are different in quality as well as quantity will come as no surprise to anyone. The question is—and always has been—where does the change in quality occur? On a continuum of complexity from the bottom of the structure to the top, where are the discontinuities that will allow us to identify layers of hierarchy that are distinct and separable, as different as ice is from water and water from steam? I spent years looking for the answer, and what I found was somewhat unexpected.

My first step was to recognize the obvious, that the layers have to do with manager-subordinate relationships. The manager's position is in one layer and the subordinate's is in the next layer below. What then sets the necessary distance between? This question cannot be answered without knowing just what it is that a manager does.

The managerial role has three critical features. First, and *most* critical, every manager must be held accountable not only for the work of subordinates but also for adding value to their work. Second, every manager must be held accountable for sustaining a team of subordinates capable of doing this work. Third, every manager must be held accountable for setting direction and getting subordinates to follow willingly, indeed enthusiastically. In brief, every manager is accountable for work and leadership.

In order to make accountability possible, managers must have enough authority to ensure that their subordinates can do the work assigned to them. This authority must include at least these four elements: (1) the right to veto any applicant who, in the manager's opinion, falls below the minimum standards of ability; (2) the power to make work assignments; (3) the power to carry out performance appraisals and, within the limits of company policy, to make decisions—not recommendations—about raises and merit rewards; and (4) the authority to initiate

removal—at least from the manager's own team—of anyone who seems incapable of doing the work.

But defining the basic nature of the managerial role reveals only part of what a managerial layer means. It cannot tell us how wide a managerial layer should be, what the difference in responsibility should be between a manager and a subordinate, or, most important, where the break should come between one managerial layer and another. Fortunately, the next step in the research process supplied the missing piece of the puzzle.

Responsibility and Time

This second step was the unexpected and startling discovery that the level of responsibility in any organizational role—whether a manager's or an individual contributor's—can be objectively measured in terms of the target completion time of the *longest* task, project, or program assigned to that role. The more distant the target completion date of the longest task or program, the heavier the weight of responsibility is felt to be. I call this measure the responsibility time span of the role. For example, a supervisor whose principal job is to plan tomorrow's production assignments and next week's work schedule but who also has ongoing responsibility for uninterrupted production supplies for the month ahead has a responsibility time span of one month. A foreman who spends most of his time riding herd on this week's production quotas but who must also develop a program to deal with the labor requirements of next year's retooling has a responsibility time span of a year or a little more. The advertising vice president who stays late every night working on next week's layouts but who also has to begin making contingency plans for the expected launch of two new local advertising media campaigns three years hence has a responsibility time span of three years.

To my great surprise, I found that in all types of managerial organizations in many different countries over 35 years, people in roles at the same time span experience the same weight of responsibility and declare the same level of pay to be fair, regardless of their occupation or actual pay. The time-span range runs from a day at the bottom of a large corporation to more than 20 years at the top, while the felt-fair pay ranges from $15,000 to $1 million and more.

Armed with my definition of a manager and my time-span measuring instrument, I them bumped into the second surprising finding—repeatedly confirmed—about layering in managerial hierarchies: the boundaries between successive managerial layers occur at certain specific time-span increments, just as ice changes to water and water to steam at certain specific temperatures. And the fact that everyone in the hierarchy, regardless of status, seems to see these boundaries in the same places suggests that the boundaries reflect some universal truth about human nature.

Figure 16.1 shows the hierarchical structure of part of a department at one company I studied, along with the approximate responsibility time span for each position. The longest task for manager A was more than five years, while for B, C, and D, the longest tasks fell between two and five years. Note also that according to the organization chart, A is the designated manager of B, B of C, and C of D.

In reality, the situation was quite different. Despite the managerial roles specified by the company, B, C, and D all described A as their "real" boss. C complained that B was "far too close" and "breathing down my neck." D had the same complaint about C. B and C also admitted to finding it very difficult to manage their immediate subordinates, C and D respectively, who seemed to do better if treated as colleagues and left alone.

In short, there appeared to be a cutoff at five years, such that those with responsibility time spans of less than five years felt they needed a manager with a responsibility time span of more than five years. Manager D, with a time span of two to three years, did not feel that C, with a time span of three to four, was distant enough hierarchically to take orders from. D felt the same way about B. Only A filled the bill for *any* of the other three.

As the responsibility time span increased in the example from two years to three to four and approached five, no one seemed to perceive a qualitative difference in the nature of the responsibility that a manager discharged. Then, suddenly, when a manager had responsibility for tasks and projects that exceeded five years in scope, everyone seemed to perceive a difference not only in the scope of responsibility but also in its quality and in the kind of work and worker required to discharge it.

I found several such discontinuities that appeared consistently in more than 100 studies. Real managerial and hierarchical boundaries occur at time spans of three months, one year, two years, five years, ten years, and twenty years.

These natural discontinuities in our perception of the responsibility time span create hierarchical strata that people in different companies, countries, and circumstances all seem to regard as genuine and acceptable. The

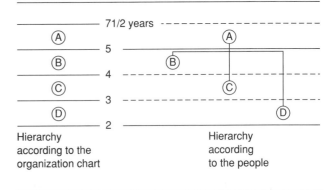

FIGURE 16.1

MANAGERIAL HIERARCHY IN
FICTION AND IN FACT

existence of such boundaries has important implications in nearly every sphere of organizational management. One of these is performance appraisal. Another is the capacity of managers to add value to the work of their subordinates.

The only person with the perspective and authority to judge and communicate personal effectiveness is an employee's accountable manager, who, in most cases, is also the only person from whom an employee will accept evaluation and coaching. This accountable manager must be the supervisor one real layer higher in the hierarchy, not merely the next higher employee on the pay scale.

As I suggested earlier, part of the secret to making hierarchy work is to distinguish carefully between hierarchical layers and pay grades. The trouble is that companies need two to three times as many pay grades as they do working layers, and once they've established the pay grades, which are easy to describe and set up, they fail to take the next step and set up a different managerial hierarchy based on responsibility rather than salary. The result is too many layers.

My experience with organizations of all kinds in many different countries has convinced me that effective value-adding managerial leadership of subordinates can come only from an individual one category higher in cognitive capacity, working one category higher in problem complexity. By contrast, wherever managers and subordinates are in the same layer—separated only by pay grade—subordinates see the boss as too close, breathing down their necks, and they identify their "real" boss as the next manager at a genuinely higher level of cognitive and task complexity. This kind of overlayering is what produces the typical symptoms of bureaucracy in its worst form—too much passing problems up and down the system, bypassing, poor task setting, frustrated subordinates, anxious managers, wholly inadequate performance appraisals, "personality problems" everywhere, and so forth.

Layering at Company X

Companies need more than seven pay grades—as a rule, many more. But seven hierarchical layers is enough or more than enough for all but the largest corporations.

Let me illustrate this pattern of hierarchical layering with the case of two divisions of Company X, a corporation with 32,000 employees and annual sales of $7 billion. As shown in Figure 16.2, the CEO sets strategic goals that look ahead as far as 25 years and manages executive vice presidents with responsibility for 12- to 15-year development programs. One vice president is accountable for several strategic business units, each with a president who works with critical tasks of up to 7 years duration.

One of these units (Y Products) employs 2,800 people, has annual sales of $250 million, and is engaged in the manufacture and sale of engineering products, with traditional semiskilled shop-floor production at Layer I. The other unit (Z Press) publishes books and employs only 88 people. Its funding and negotiations with authors are in the hands of a general editor at Layer IV, assisted by a small

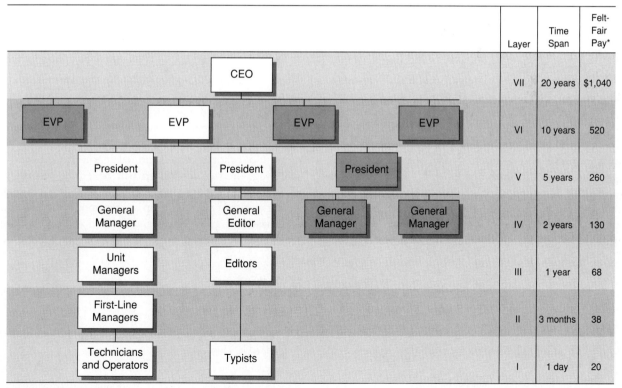

FIGURE 16.2

TWO DIVISIONS OF CORPORATION X

	Layer	Time Span	Felt-Fair Pay*
CEO	VII	20 years	$1,040
EVP EVP EVP EVP	VI	10 years	520
President President President	V	5 years	260
General Manager General Editor General Manager General Manager	IV	2 years	130
Unit Managers Editors	III	1 year	68
First-Line Managers	II	3 months	38
Technicians and Operators Typists	I	1 day	20

*(In thousands of dollars)

group of editors at Layer III, each working on projects that may take up to 18 months to complete.

So the president of Y Products manages more people, governs a greater share of corporate resources, and earns a lot more money for the parent company than does the president of Z Press. Yet the two presidents occupy the same hierarchical layer, have similar authority, and take home comparable salaries. This is neither coincidental nor unfair. It is natural, correct, and efficient.

It is the level of responsibility, *measured in terms of time span*, that tells you how many layers you need in an enterprise—not the number of subordinates or the magnitude of sales or profits. These factors may have a marginal influence on salary; they have no bearing at all on hierarchical layers.

Changes in the Quality of Work

The widespread and striking consistency of this underlying pattern of true managerial layers leads naturally to the question of why it occurs. Why do people perceive a sudden leap in status from, say, four-and-a-half years to five and from nine to ten?

The answer goes back to the earlier discussion of complexity. As we go higher in a managerial hierarchy, the most difficult problems that arise grow increasingly complex, and, as the complexity of a task increases, so does the complexity of the mental work required to handle it. What I found when I looked at this problem over the course of ten years was that this complexity, like responsibility time span, also occurs in leaps or jumps. In other words, the most difficult tasks found within any given layer are all characterized by the same type or category of complexity, just as water remains in the same liquid state from 0° to 100° Celsius, even though it ranges from very cold to very hot. (A few degrees cooler or hotter and water changes in state, to ice or steam.)

It is this suddenly increased level of necessary mental capacity, experience, knowledge, and mental stamina that allows managers to add value to the work of their subordinates. What they add is a new perspective, one that is broader, more experienced, and, most important, one that extends further in time. If, at Z Press, the editors at Layer III find and develop manuscripts into books with market potential, it is their general editor at Layer IV who fits those books into the press's overall list, who thinks ahead to their position on next year's list and later allocates resources to their production and marketing, and who makes projections about the publishing and book-buying trends of the next two to five years.

It is also this sudden change in the quality, not just the quantity, of managerial work that subordinates accept as a natural and appropriate break in the continuum of hierarchy. It is why they accept the boss's authority and not just the boss's power.

So the whole picture comes together. Managerial hierarchy or layering is the only effective organizational form for deploying people and tasks at complementary levels, where people can do the tasks assigned to them, where the people in any given layer can add value to the work of those in the layer below them, and, finally, where this stratification of management strikes everyone as necessary and welcome.

What we need is not some new kind of organization. What we need is managerial hierarchy that understands its own nature and purpose. Hierarchy is the best structure for getting work done in big organizations. Trying to raise efficiency and morale without first setting this structure to rights is like trying to lay bricks without mortar. No amount of exhortation, attitudinal engineering, incentive planning, or even leadership will have any permanent effect unless we understand what hierarchy is and why and how it works. We need to stop casting about fruitlessly for organizational Holy Grails and settle down to the hard work of putting our managerial hierarchies in order.

DISCUSSION QUESTIONS

1. Why has hierarchy been viewed as a negative aspect of organizations?

2. Why does Jaques believe that the search for a replacement for hierarchy is wrong?

3. What are some of the benefits of hierarchy?

4. Why is the idea of accountability important for understanding management?

5. What explains the creation of hierarchical layers?

6. What role does time play in determining the responsibility of a level in a hierarchy?

7. According to Jaques what is the key to making hierarchy work?

8. In your opinion, are Jaques' observations correct? Is the solution to current business problems more hierarchy and not flatter organizations? What other alternatives are there?

The New Web of Enterprise

ROBERT REICH

LEARNING OBJECTIVES

After reading Robert Reich's "The New Web of Enterprise" a student will be able to:

1. Understand the nature of "high-value" enterprise

2. Critically evaluate the idea that hierarchy is no longer a useful way to structure organizations and control organization behavior

3. Understand the role of problem-solvers, problem-identifiers, and strategic brokers in emerging forms of organization

4. Learn about new types of managerial and organizational skills and behaviors that are required for successfully operating high-value organizations

There was . . . a mysterious rite of initiation through which, in one way or another, almost every member of the team passed. The term that the old hands used for this rite . . . was "signing up." By signing up for the project you agreed to do whatever was necessary for success. You agreed to forsake, if necessary, family, hobbies, and friends—if you had any of these left (and you might not if you had signed up too many times before). . . . Labor was no longer coerced. Labor volunteered.

Tracy Kidder,
The Soul of a New Machine (1981)

The high-value enterprise has no need to control vast resources, discipline armies of production workers, or impose predictable routines. Thus it need not be organized like the old pyramids that characterized standardized production, with strong chief executives presiding over ever-widening layers of managers, atop an even larger group of hourly workers, all following standard operating procedures.

In fact, the high-value enterprise *cannot* be organized this way. The three groups that give the new enterprise most of its value—problem-solvers, problem-identifiers, and strategic brokers—need to be in direct contact with one another to continuously discover new opportunities. Messages must flow quickly and clearly if the right solutions are to be applied to the right problems in a timely way. This is no place for bureaucracy.

Anyone who has ever played the children's game Telephone—in which one person whispers a phrase to the next person in line, who then whispers the phrase to the next, and so on, until the last person announces aloud a phrase that invariably bears no resemblance to the original—knows what can happen when even the simplest messages are passed through intermediaries: "Have a nice day" turns into "Get out of my way." If problem-identifiers had to convey everything they were learning about the needs of their customers upward to top management through layers and layers of middle managers, while problem-solvers had to convey everything *they* were learning about new technologies upward through as many layers, and then both groups had to await top management's decisions about what to do—decisions which then had to travel back down through the same bureaucratic channels—the results would be, to say the least, late and irrelevant, and probably distorted.

Thus one of the strategic broker's tasks is to create settings in which problem-solvers and problem-identifiers can work together without undue interference. The strategic broker is a facilitator and a coach—finding the people in both camps who can learn most from one another, giving them whatever resources they need, letting them go at it long enough to discover new complements between technologies and customer needs, but also providing them with enough guidance so that they don't lose sight of mundane goals like earning a profit.

Creative teams solve and identify problems in much the same way whether they are developing new software,

Source: "The New Web of Enterprise," from *The Work of Nations: Preparing Ourselves for 21st-Century Capitalism* by Robert B. Reich, Copyright ©1991 by Robert B. Reich. Reprinted by permission of Alfred A. Knopf, Inc.

473

dreaming up a new marketing strategy, seeking a scientific discovery, or contriving a financial ploy. Most coordination is horizontal rather than vertical. Because problems and solutions cannot be defined in advance, formal meetings and agendas won't reveal them. They emerge instead out of frequent and informal communications among team members. Mutual learning occurs within the team, as insights, experiences, puzzles, and solutions are shared—often randomly. One solution is found applicable to a completely different problem; someone else's failure turns into a winning strategy for accomplishing something entirely unrelated. It is as if team members were doing several jigsaw puzzles simultaneously with pieces from the same pile—pieces which could be arranged to form many different pictures. (Such intellectual synergies can be found, on rare occasions, even in university departments.)

Instead of a pyramid, then, the high-value enterprise looks more like a spider's web. Strategic brokers are at the center, but there are all sorts of connections that do not involve them directly, and new connections are being spun all the time. At each point of connection are a relatively small number of people—depending on the task, from a dozen to several hundred. If a group was any larger it could not engage in rapid and informal learning.[1] Here individual skills are combined so that the group's ability to innovate is something more than the simple sum of its parts. Over time, as group members work through various problems and approaches together, they learn about one another's abilities. They learn how they can help one another perform better, who can contribute what to a particular project, how they can best gain more experience together. Each participant is on the lookout for ideas that will propel the group forward. Such cumulative experience and understanding cannot be translated into standard operating procedures easily transferable to other workers and other organizations. Each point on the "enterprise web" represents a unique combination of skills.

II

Speed and agility are so important to the high-value enterprise that it cannot be weighed down with large overhead costs like office buildings, plant, equipment, and payroll. It must be able to switch direction quickly, pursue options when they arise, discover new linkages between problems and solutions wherever they may lie.

In the old high-volume enterprise, fixed costs such as factories, equipment, warehouses, and large payrolls were necessary in order to achieve control and predictability. In the high-value enterprise, they are an unnecessary burden. Here, all that really counts is rapid problem-identifying and problem-solving—the marriage of technical insight with marketing know-how; blessed by strategic and financial acumen. Everything else—all of the more standardized pieces—can be obtained as needed. Office space, factories, and warehouses can be rented; standard equipment can be leased; standard components can be bought wholesale from cheap producers (many of them overseas); secretaries, routine data processors, bookkeepers, and routine production workers can be hired temporarily.

In fact, relatively few people actually work for the high-value enterprise in the traditional sense of having steady jobs with fixed salaries. The inhabitants of corporate headquarters, who spend much of their time searching for the right combinations of solutions, problems, strategies, and money, are apt to share in the risks and returns of their hunt. When a promising combination is found, participants in the resulting project (some at the center of the web; some at connecting points on the periphery) also may share in any profits rather than take fixed salaries.

With risks and returns broadly shared, and overhead kept to a minimum, the enterprise web can experiment. Experimentation was dangerous in the old high-volume enterprise because failures (like Ford's notorious Edsel) meant that the entire organization had to change direction—retool, retrain, redirect sales and marketing—at a huge cost. But experimentation is the lifeblood of the high-value enterprise, because customization requires continuous trial and error.

Sharing risks and returns has an added advantage. It is a powerful creative stimulus. If they are to spot new opportunities in technologies and markets, problem-solvers, -identifiers, and brokers must be highly motivated. Few incentives are more powerful than membership in a small group engaged in a common task, sharing the risks of defeat and the potential rewards of victory. Rewards are not only pecuniary. The group often shares a vision as well; they want to make their mark on the world.

At the web's outer edges, suppliers of standard inputs (factories, equipment, office space, routine components, bookkeeping, janitorial services, data processing, and so

---

[1] Information technologies have dramatically reduced the costs of coordinating even relatively large numbers of people without relying on standard operating procedures and other bureaucratic structures. See, for example, T. Malone, J. Yates, and R. Benjamin, "Electronic Markets and Electronic Hierarchies," *Communications of the AGM*, Vol. 30, No. 6 (June 1987).

forth) contract to provide or do specific things for a certain time and for a specified price. Such arrangements are often more efficient than directly controlling employees.[2] Suppliers who profit in direct proportion to how hard and carefully they do their jobs have every incentive to find increasingly efficient ways of accomplishing their tasks. Consider the owner of a McDonald's franchise who works fifteen-hour days and keeps the outlet sparkling clean; or the machine operator who, owning the equipment and contracting to do jobs with it (and keep the profits), maintains the machine in perfect condition.[3]

III

Enterprise webs come in several shapes, and the shapes continue to evolve. Among the most common are:

Independent profit centers. This web eliminates middle-level managers and pushes authority for product development and sales down to groups of engineers and marketers (problem-solvers and -identifiers) whose compensation is linked to the unit's profits. Strategic brokers in headquarters provide financial and logistical help, but give the unit discretion over how to spend money up to a certain amount. By 1990, Johnson & Johnson comprised 166 autonomous companies; Hewlett-Packard, some 50 separate business units. General Electric, IBM, AT&T, and Eastman Kodak, among others, were also adopting this

approach. For much the same reason, large publishing houses were busily creating "imprints"—small, semiautonomous publishing houses within the structure of the parent firm, each comprising a dozen or so people with considerable responsibility for acquiring and publishing books on their own.

Spin-off partnerships. In this web, strategic brokers in headquarters act as venture capitalists and midwives, nurturing good ideas that bubble up from groups of problem-solvers and -identifiers and then (if the ideas catch on in the market) spinning the groups off as independent businesses in which the strategic brokers at headquarters retain a partial stake. Xerox and 3M have pioneered this form in the United States, but it is nothing new to the Japanese. Hitachi, for example, is actually more than 60 companies, 27 of which are publicly traded. Some venture-capital firms and leveraged-buyout partnerships are coming to resemble the same sort of web, in which risks and returns are shared between headquarters and the managers of the separate businesses.

Spin-in partnerships. In this web, good ideas bubble up outside the firm from independent groups of problem-solvers and -identifiers. Strategic brokers in headquarters purchase the best of them, or form partnerships with the independents, and then produce, distribute, and market the ideas under the firm's own well-known trademark. This sort of arrangement is common to computer software houses. In 1990, for example, over 400 tiny software-developing firms were purchased by big software companies such as Microsoft, Lotus, and Ashton-Tate. The software developers thus received a nice profit on their efforts, while the larger firms maintained a steady supply of new ideas.

Licensing. In this web, headquarters contracts with independent businesses to use its brand name, sell its special formulas, or otherwise market (that is, find applicable problems for) its technologies. Strategic brokers at the center of the web ensure that no licensee harms the reputation of the brand by offering inconsistent or poor quality, and also provide licensees with special bulk services like computerized inventory management or advertising. Most of the ownership and control, however, is left in the hands of licensees. One example is franchises, which are among the fastest-growing businesses in every advanced economy, now selling everything from tax preparation and accounting services to hotel accommodations, cookies, groceries, printing and copying, health care, and bodybuilding. In 1988, American franchisees comprised 509,000 outlets and accounted for $640 billion in sales, amounting to more than 10 percent of the entire national product.[4]

Pure brokering. In the most decentralized kind of web, strategic brokers contract with independent businesses for

---

[2] A number of studies have revealed a marked increase in outsourcing and the use of part-time workers during the 1980s. Part of the motive in the United States surely is to avoid paying employee benefits mandated by union contracts or legislation. But interestingly, the same pattern is observable in many other advanced economies where union contracts or legislated benefits are not affected. See I. W. Sengenberger and G. Loveman, *Smaller Units of Employment: A Synthesis of Research on Industrial Organization in Industrial Countries* (Geneva: International Institute for Labor Studies, 1988). Good surveys of the trend toward outsourcing and temporary work can be found in E. Appelbaum, "Restructuring Work: Temporary, Part-time, and At-home Employment," in H. Hartmann (ed.), *Computer Chips and Paper Clips: Technology and Women's Employment* (Washington, D.C.: National Academy Press, 1987); S. Christopherson, "Flexibility in the U.S. Service Economy and the Emerging Spatial Division of Labour," *Transactions of the British Institute of Geographies,* Vol. 14 (1989).

[3] This example is not hypothetical. A Finnish paper company, burdened by tree-harvesting machinery always in need of repair, sold the machines to its operators, and gave them contracts to do their old jobs. Productivity soared, as the operators now kept the machines in better condition and used them with far greater care than before. See *The Economist,* December 24, 1988, p. 16.

problem solving and identifying as well as for production. This web is ideal for enterprises that need to shift direction quickly. By 1990, for example, Compaq Computers of Houston (which did not exist in 1982 but eight years later had revenues of $3 billion) was buying many of its most valuable components on the outside (microprocessors from Intel, operating systems from software houses like Microsoft, liquid-crystal screens from Citizen), and then selling the resulting machines through independent dealers to whom Compaq granted exclusive sales territories. The Apple II computer cost less than $500 to build, of which $350 was for components purchased on the outside.[5] Meanwhile, the Lewis Galoob Toy Company sold more than $50 million worth of tiny gadgets conceived by independent inventors and novelty companies, designed by independent engineers, manufactured and packaged by suppliers in Hong Kong (who contracted out the most labor-intensive work to China and Thailand), and then distributed in America by independent toy companies. Movie studios that once relied on their own facilities, crews, and exclusive stables of actors, directors, and screenwriters were contracting on a project-by-project basis with independent producers, directors, actors, writers, crews, and cinematographers, using rented space and equipment, and relying on independent distributors to get the films into appropriate theaters. Book publishers were contracting not only for authors but also for printing, graphics, artwork, marketing, and all other facets of production. Even automakers were outsourcing more and more of what they produced. (By 1990, Chrysler Corporation directly produced only about 30 percent of the value of its cars; Ford, about 50 percent. General Motors bought half its engineering and design services from 800 different companies.)

IV

Americans love to debate old categories. Does manufacturing have a future or are we becoming a service economy? Are big businesses destined to expire like prehistoric beasts, to be superseded by small businesses, or are big businesses critical to our economic future? Such questions provide endless opportunities for debate, not unlike the arguments of thirteenth-century Scholastics over how

many angels could comfortably fit on a pinhead. Such debates are socially useful in that they create excuses for business seminars, conferences, and magazine articles and thus ensure gainful employment for many. But such debates are less than edifying. Debaters usually can find evidence to support whatever side they choose, depending on how they define their terms. Whether manufacturing is being replaced by a service economy depends on how "manufacturing" and "service" are defined; whether small businesses are replacing large depends equally on what these adjectives are taken to mean. In fact, all manufacturing businesses are coming to entail services, and all large businesses are spinning into webs of smaller businesses.

The federal government's Standard Industrial Classification system is as unhelpful and anachronistic here as before. It defines "establishment" as any business, including one that may be part of a larger company.[6] Thus, not surprisingly, official statistics show that the number of small "establishments" nearly doubled between 1975 and 1990, creating millions of new jobs—just as the high-volume, hierarchical corporation was transforming into a high-value, decentralized enterprise web. But even discounting this statistical sleight of hand, the shift from high-volume hierarchies to high-value webs would create the appearance of a dwindling core simply because core corporations no longer employ many people directly and their webs of indirect employment defy easy measurement.

As stated earlier, by most official measures, America's 500 largest industrial companies failed to create a single net new job between 1975 and 1990, their share of the civilian labor force dropping from 17 percent to less than 10 percent. Meanwhile, after decades of decline, the number of people describing themselves as "self-employed" began to rise.[7] And there has been an explosion in the number of new businesses (in 1950, 93,000 corporations were created in the United States; by the late 1980s, America was adding about 1.3 million new enterprises to the economy each year).[8] Most of the new jobs in the economy appear to come from small businesses,[9] as does most

---

[4] Figures from *Business Week,* November 13, 1989, p. 83.

[5] Apple initially got its microprocessors from Synertek, other chips from Texas Instruments and Motorola, video monitors from Hitachi, power supplies from Astec, and printers from Qume. See James Brian Quinn et al., "Beyond Products: Service-Based Strategy," *Harvard Business Review,* March–April 1990, pp. 58–60.

[6] U.S. Office of Management and Budget, SIC Manual (1987), p. 12.

[7] In 1975, only 6.9 percent of the U.S. nonfarm work force was "self-employed"; by 1986, it was 7.4 percent. Data from *The State of Small Business: Report of the President* (Washington, D.C.: U.S. Government Printing Office, various issues).

[8] David L. Birch, "The Hidden Economy," *The Wall Street Journal,* June 10, 1988, p. 23R.

[9] Data from Douglas P. Handler, *Business Demographics* (New York: Dun & Bradstreet, Economic Analysis Department, 1988).

of the growth in research spending.[10] A similar transformation has been occurring in other nations.[11]

But to draw the natural conclusion from these data—that large businesses are being *replaced* by millions of tiny businesses—is to fall into the same vestigial trap as in the debate over "manufacturing" versus "services": both ignore the weblike relationships that are shaping the new economy. Here, the core corporation is no longer a "big" business, but neither is it merely a collection of smaller ones. Rather, it is an enterprise web. Its center provides strategic insight and binds the threads together. Yet points on the web often have sufficient autonomy to create profitable connections to other webs. There is no "inside" or "outside" the corporation, but only different distances from its strategic center.

The resulting interconnections can be quite complex, stretching over many profit centers, business units, spin-offs, licensees, franchisees, suppliers, and dealers, and then on to other strategic centers, which in turn are linked to still other groups. Throughout the 1980s, for example, IBM (which, as you recall, had jealously guarded its independence even to the point of departing India rather than sharing profits with Indian partners) joined with dozens of companies—Intel, Merrill Lynch, Aetna Life and Casualty, MCI, Comsat, and more than eighty foreign-owned firms—to share problem-solving, problem-identifying, and strategic brokering. Similarly, AT&T (which for seventy years had prided itself on having total control over its products and operating systems) found itself in a newly deregulated, unpredictable world of telecommunications, which required hundreds of alliances and joint ventures, and thousands of subcontracts.[12] Core corporations in other mature economies are undergoing a similar transformation. Indeed, as we shall see, their increasingly decen-

tralized enterprise webs are becoming undifferentiated extensions of our own.[13]

The trend should not be overstated. Even by the 1990s there remain large corporations of bureaucratic form and function, which directly employ many thousands of workers and which own substantial physical assets. But these corporations are coming to be the exceptions. That they survive and prosper is despite, rather than because of, their organization. The most profitable firms are transforming into enterprise webs. They may look like the old form of organization from the outside, but inside all is different. Their famous brands adhere to products and services that are cobbled together from many different sources outside the formal boundaries of the firm. Their dignified headquarters, expansive factories, warehouses, laboratories, and fleets of trucks and corporate jets are leased. Their production workers, janitors, and bookkeepers are under temporary contract; their key researchers, design engineers, and marketers are sharing in the profits. And their distinguished executives, rather than possessing great power and authority over this domain, have little direct control over much of anything. Instead of imposing their will over a corporate empire, they guide ideas through the new webs of enterprise.

Forms of the Corporation," in J. Meyer and J. Gustafson (eds.), *The U.S. Business Corporation* (Cambridge, Mass.: Ballinger, 1988). See also Jordan D. Lewis, *Partnerships for Profit: Structuring and Managing Strategic Alliances* (New York: Free Press, 1990).

[13] For a description of the pattern in Europe, see D. J. Storey and S. Johnson, *Job Generation and Labour Market Changes* (London: Macmillan, 1987).

---

[10] According to the National Science Foundation, small firms with fewer than 500 employees doubled their share of America's corporate research and development spending during the 1980s, from 6 percent to 12 percent. National Science Foundation, Research Report (Washington, D.C.: National Science Foundation, November 1990), pp. 12–14.

[11] See, for example, "München Management," *The Economist,* October 14, 1989, p. 25.

[12] My interviews (see "A Note on Additional Sources") confirm the findings of other surveys. See, for example, R. Johnston and Paul Lawrence, "Beyond Vertical Integration: The Rise of the Value-Added Partnership," *Harvard Business Review,* July–August 1988; R. Miles, "Adapting to Technology and Competition: A New Industrial Relations System for the 21st Century," *California Management Review,* Winter 1988; and J. Badaracco, Jr., "Changing

DISCUSSION QUESTIONS

1. How does high-value enterprise differ from traditional forms of organization?

2. Why is bureaucracy inappropriate for emerging forms of organization?

3. What are the tasks of problem-solvers, problem-identifiers, and strategic brokers? How do these roles differ from traditional managerial roles specifically in terms of behavioral requirements?

4. What role does overhead play in the high-value organization? What role does overhead play in the high-volume organization?

5. What are the forms that enterprise webs take and what are their various functions?

6. What are the implications for average workers of the newly proposed type of structure? For example, will more people work at computer terminals located in their homes?

7. Speculate on the nature of managerial functions such as planning, motivating, leading, and controlling as they will be performed in enterprise webs.

8. Evaluate Jaques' arguments for hierarchy in light of Reich's claims that pyramidal forms of organization are obsolete.

FOR FURTHER READING

Evan, W. *Organization Theory: Research and Design.* New York: Macmillan, 1993.

Galbraith, J. *Organizational Design.* Reading, Mass.: Addison-Wesley, 1977.

Perrow, C. *Complex Organizations: A Critical Essay,* 3rd ed. New York: Random House, 1986.

17

MANAGING CHANGE

Central Problems in the Management of Innovation

ANDREW H. VAN DE VEN

LEARNING OBJECTIVES

After reading Van de Ven's "Central Problems in the Management of Innovation," a student will be able to:

1. Develop a definition of organizational innovation

2. Understand the basic factors that affect innovation

3. Appreciate the problems that managers have to confront during innovative periods

4. Understand Van de Ven's framework for the management of innovation

Introduction

Few issues are characterized by as much agreement as the role of innovation and entrepreneurship for social and economic development. Schumpeter's (1942) emphasis on the importance of innovation for the business firm and society as a whole is seldom disputed. In the wake of a decline in American productivity and obsolescence of its infrastructure has come the fundamental claim that America is losing its innovativeness. The need for understanding and managing innovation appears to be widespread. Witness, for example, the common call for stimulating innovation in popular books by Ouchi (1981), Pascale and Athos (1981), Peters and Waterman (1982), Kanter (1983), and Lawrence and Dyer (1983).

Of all the issues surfacing in meetings with over 30 chief executive officers of public and private firms during the past few years, the management of innovation was reported as their most central concern in managing their enterprises in the 1980's (Van de Ven 1982). This concern is reflected in a variety of questions the CEOs often raised.

1. How can a large organization develop and maintain a culture of innovation and entrepreneurship?
2. What are the critical factors in successfully launching new organizations, joint ventures with other firms, or innovative projects within large organizations over time?
3. How can a manager achieve balance between inexorable pressures for specialization and proliferation of tasks, and escalating costs of achieving coordination, cooperation, and resolving conflicts?

Given the scope of these questions raised by CEOs, it is surprising to find that research and scholarship on organizational innovation has been narrowly defined on the one hand, and technically oriented on the other. Most of it has focused on only one kind of organizational mode for

Source: Andrew H. Van de Ven: "Central Problems in the Management of Innovation," *Management Science,* May 1986, Vol. 32, No. 5, pp. 590–607. Copyright © 1986. Reprinted by permission.

innovation—such as internal organizational innovation (Normann 1979), or new business startups (e.g., Cooper 1979)—or one stage of the innovation process—such as the diffusion stage (Rogers, 1981)—or one type of innovation—such as technological innovation (Utterback 1974). While such research has provided many insights into specific aspects of innovation, the encompassing problems confronting general managers in managing innovation have been largely overlooked.

As their questions suggest, general managers deal with a set of problems that are different from and less well understood than functional managers. We concur with Lewin and Minton's (1985) call for a general management perspective on innovation—one that begins with key problems confronting general managers, and then examines the effects of how these problems are addressed on innovation effectiveness. The purpose of this paper is to present such a perspective on the management of innovation. Appreciating these problems and their consequences provides a first step in developing a research program on the management of innovation.

The process of innovation is defined as the development and implementation of new ideas by people who over time engage in transactions with others within an institutional context. This definition is sufficiently general to apply to a wide variety of technical, product, process, and administrative kinds of innovations. From a managerial viewpoint, to understand the process of innovation is to understand the factors that facilitate and inhibit the development of innovations. These factors include ideas, people, transactions, and context over time. Associated with each of these four factors are four central problems in the management of innovation which will be discussed in this paper.

First, there is *the human problem of managing attention* because people and their organizations are largely designed to focus on, harvest, and protect existing practices rather than pay attention to developing new ideas. The more successful an organization is the more difficult it is to trigger peoples' action thresholds to pay attention to new ideas, needs, and opportunities.

Second, *the process problem is managing ideas into good currency* so that innovative ideas are implemented and institutionalized. While the invention or conception of innovative ideas may be an individual activity, innovation (inventing and implementing new ideas) is a collective achievement of pushing and riding those ideas into good currency. The social and political dynamics of innovation become paramount as one addresses the energy and commitment that are needed among coalitions of interest groups to develop an innovation.

Third, there is *the structural problem of managing part-whole relationships,* which emerges from the proliferation of ideas, people and transactions as an innovation develops over time. A common characteristic of the innovation process is that multiple functions, resources, and disciplines are needed to transform an innovative idea into concrete reality—so much so that individuals involved in individual transactions lose sight of the whole innovation effort. How does one put the whole into the parts?

Finally, the context of an innovation points to *the strategic problem of institutional leadership.* Innovations not only adapt to existing organizational and industrial arrangements, but they also transform the structure and practices of these environments. The strategic problem is one of creating an infrastructure that is conducive to innovation.

After clarifying our definition of innovation, this paper will elaborate on these four central problems in the management of innovation. We will conclude by suggesting how these four problems emerge over time and provide an overall framework to guide longitudinal study of innovation processes.

Innovative Ideas

An Innovation is a new *idea,* which may be a recombination of old ideas, a scheme that challenges the present order, a formula, or a unique approach which is perceived as new by the individuals involved (Zaltman, Duncan, and Holbek 1973; Rogers 1982). As long as the idea is perceived as new to the people involved, it is an "innovation," even though it may appear to others to be an "imitation" of something that exists elsewhere.

Included in this definition are both technical innovations (new technologies, products, and services) and administrative innovations (new procedures, policies, and organizational forms). Daft and Becker (1979) and others have emphasized keeping technical and administrative innovations distinct. We believe that making such a distinction often results in a fragmented classification of the innovation process. Most innovations involve new technical and administrative components (Leavitt 1965). For example Ruttan and Hayami (1984) have shown that many technological innovations in agriculture and elsewhere could not have occurred without innovations in institutional and organizational arrangements. So also, the likely success of developments in decision support systems by management scientists largely hinges on an appreciation of the interdependence between technological hardware and software innovations on the one hand, and new theories of administrative choice behavior on the other. Learning to understand the close connection between technical and administrative dimensions of innovations is a key part of understanding the management of innovation.

Kimberly (1981) rightly points out that a positive bias pervades the study of innovation. Innovation is often viewed as a good thing because the new idea must be useful—profitable, constructive, or solve a problem. New ideas that are not perceived as useful are not normally called innovations; they are usually called mistakes. Objectively, of course, the usefulness of an idea can only be determined after the innovation process is completed and implemented. Moreover, while many new ideas are proposed in organizations, only a very few receive serious consideration and developmental effort (Wilson 1966; Maitland 1982). Since it is not possible to determine at the outset which new ideas are "innovations" or "mistakes," and since we assume that people prefer to invest their energies and careers on the former and not the latter, there is a need to explain (1) how and why certain innovative ideas gain good currency (i.e., are implemented), and (2) how and why people pay attention to only certain new ideas and ignore the rest. These two questions direct our focus to problems of managing ideas into good currency and the management of attention.

The Management of Ideas

It is often said that an innovative idea without a champion gets nowhere. *People* develop, carry, react to, and modify ideas. People apply different skills, energy levels and frames of reference (interpretive schemas) to ideas as a result of their backgrounds, experiences, and activities that occupy their attention. *People become attached to ideas over time through a social-political process of pushing and riding their ideas into good currency,* much like Donald Schon (1971) describes for the emergence of public policies. Figure 17.1 illustrates the process.

Schon states that what characteristically precipitates change in public policy is a disruptive event which threatens the social system. Invention is an act of appreciation, which is a complex perceptual process that melds together judgments of reality and judgments of value. A new

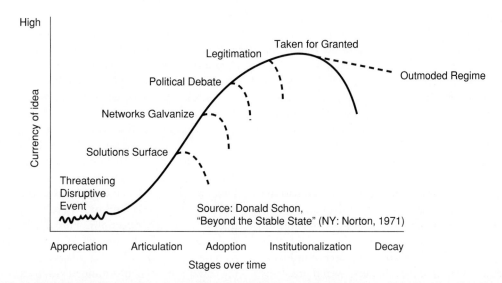

FIGURE 17.1

MANAGING LIFE CYCLE OF IDEAS IN GOOD CURRENCY

appreciation is made as a problem, or opportunity is recognized. Once appreciated, ideas gestating in peripheral areas begin to surface to the mainstream as a result of the efforts of people who supply the energy necessary to raise the ideas over the threshold of public consciousness. As these ideas surface networks of individuals and interest groups gravitate to and galvanize around the new ideas. They, in turn, exert their own influence on the ideas by further developing them and providing them with a catchy slogan that provides emotional meaning and energy to the idea.

However, Schon indicates that ideas are not potent to change policy unless they become an issue for political debate and unless they are used to gain influence and resources. The debate turns not only on the merits of the ideas, but also on who is using the ideas as vehicles to gain power. As the ideas are taken up by people who are or have become powerful, the ideas gain legitimacy and power to change institutions. After this, the ideas that win out are implemented and become institutionalized—they become part of the conceptual structure of the social system and appear obvious, in retrospect. However, the idea remains institutionalized for only as long as it continues to address critical problems and as long as the regime remains in power.

Schon's description of the stages by which ideas come into good currency is instructive in its focus on the social-political dynamics of the innovation process. The description emphasizes the *centrality of ideas as the rallying point around which collective action mobilizes*—organizational structures emerge and are modified by these ideas. Moreover, it is the central focus on *ideas* that provides the vehicle for otherwise isolated, disconnected, or competitive individuals and stakeholders to come together and contribute their unique frames of reference to the innovation process. Schon (1971, p. 141) states that these stages characteristically describe the process features in the emergence of public policies "regardless of their content or conditions from which they spring." Analogous descriptions of this social-political process have been provided by Quinn (1980, especially p. 104) for the development of corporate strategies, and by March and Olsen (1976) for decision making in educational institutions.

However, there are also some basic limitations to the process that lead to inertia and premature abandonment of some ideas. First, there tends to be a short-term problem orientation in individuals and organizations, and a facade of demonstrating progress. This has the effect of inducing premature abandonment of ideas because even if problems are not being solved, the appearance of progress requires

moving on to the next batch of problems. Thus, "old questions are not answered—they only go out of fashion" (Schon 1971, p. 142). Furthermore, given the inability to escape the interdependence of problems, old problems are relabeled as new problems. As a result, and as observed by Cohen, March and Olsen (1972), decision makers have the feeling they are always working on the same problems in somewhat different contexts, but mostly without results.

Except for its use in legislative bodies, the idea of formally managing the sociopolitical process of pushing and riding ideas into good currency is novel. However, as Huber (1984, p. 938) points out, the decision process is similar to project management and program planning situations. Thus, Huber proposes the adoption of proven project management and program planning technologies (e.g., PERT, CPM and PPM) for managing the production of ideas into good currency. For example, based upon a test of the Program Planning Model, Van de Ven (1980a, b) concluded that the PPM avoids problems of decision flight and falling into a rut that are present in March and Olsen's (1976) garbage can model of anarchical decision making. This is accomplished by the PPM's three-way matching of phased tasks with different decision processes and with different participants over time in a program planning effort.

A second limitation of the process is that the inventory of ideas is seldom adequate for the situation. This may be because environmental scanning relevant to an issue does not uncover the values and partisan views held by all the relevant stakeholders. Gilbert and Freeman (1984) point out that with the general concept of environmental scanning, current models of strategic decision making gloss over the need to identify specific stakeholders to an issue and to examine their underlying values which provide reasons for their actions. Viewing the process from a game theoretic framework, they state that "effective strategy will be formulated and implemented if and only if each player successfully puts himself or herself in the place of other players and engages in trying to see the situation from the others' viewpoints" (Gilbert and Freeman 1984, p. 4).

A third, and even more basic problem is the management of attention—how do individuals become attached to and invest effort in the development of innovative ideas? Human beings and their organizations are mostly designed to focus on, harvest, and protect existing practices rather than to pave new directions. This is because people have basic physiological limitations of not being able to handle complexity, of unconsciously adapting to gradually changing conditions, of conforming to group and organizational norms, and of focusing on repetitive activities (Van de Ven and Hudson 1985). One of the key questions in the management of innovation then becomes how to trigger the action thresholds of individuals to appreciate and pay attention to new ideas, needs and opportunities.

The Management of Attention

Much of the folklore and applied literature on the management of innovation has ignored the research by cognitive psychologists and social-psychologists about the limited capacity of human beings to handle complexity and maintain attention. As a consequence, one often gets the impression that inventors or innovators have superhuman creative heuristics or abilities to "walk on water" (Van de Ven and Hudson 1985). *A more realistic view of innovation should begin with an appreciation of the physiological limitations of human beings to pay attention to nonroutine issues, and their corresponding inertial forces in organizational life.*

Physiological Limitations of Human Beings

It is well established empirically that most individuals lack the capability and inclination to deal with complexity (Tversky and Kahneman 1974; Johnson 1983). Although there are great individual differences, most people have very short spans of attention—the average person can retain raw data in short-term memory for only a few seconds. Memory, it turns out, requires relying on "old friends," which Simon (1947) describes as a process of linking raw data with pre-existing schemas and world views that an individual has stored in long-term memory. Most individuals are also very efficient processors of routine tasks. They do not concentrate on repetitive tasks, once they are mastered. Skills for performing repetitive tasks are repressed in subconscious memory, permitting individuals to pay attention to things other than performance of repetitive tasks (Johnson 1983). Ironically as a result, what most individuals think about the most is what they will do, but what they do the most is what they think about the least.

In complex decision situations, individuals create stereotypes as a defense mechanism to deal with complexity. For the average person, stereotyping is likely to begin when seven (plus or minus two) objects or digits are involved in a decision—this number being the information processing capacity of the average individual (Miller 1956). As decision complexity increases beyond this point, people become more conservative and apply more subjective criteria which are further and further removed from reality (Filley, House, and Kerr 1976). Furthermore, since the correctness of outcomes from innovative ideas can rarely be judged, the perceived legitimacy of the decision *process* becomes the dominant evaluation criterion. Thus, as March (1981) and Janis (1982) point out, as decision complexity increases, solutions become increasingly error prone, means become more important than ends, and rationalization replaces rationality.

It is generally believed that crises, dissatisfaction, tension, or significant external stress are the major preconditions for stimulating people to act. March and Simon (1958) set forth the most widely accepted model by arguing that dissatisfaction with existing conditions stimulates people to search for improved conditions, and they will cease searching when a satisfactory result is found. A satisfactory result is a function of a person's aspiration level, which Lewin et al. (1944) indicated is a product of all past successes and failures that people have experienced. If this model is correct (and most believe it is), then scholars and practitioners must wrestle with another basic problem.

This model assumes that when people reach a threshold of dissatisfaction with existing conditions, they will initiate action to resolve their dissatisfaction. However, because individuals unconsciously adapt to slowly changing environments, their thresholds for action are often not triggered while they adapt over time. In this sense, individuals are much like frogs. Although we know of no empirical support for the frog story developed by Gregory Bateson, it goes as follows.

> *When frogs are placed into a boiling pail of water, they jump out—they don't want to boil to death.*
> *However, when frogs are placed into a cold pail of water, and the pail is placed on a stove with the heat turned very low, over time the frogs will boil to death.*

Cognitive psychologists have found individuals have widely varying and manipulable adaptation levels (Helson 1948, 1964). When exposed over time to a set of stimuli that deteriorate very gradually, people do not perceive the gradual changes—they unconsciously adapt to the worsening conditions. Their threshold to tolerate pain, discomfort, or dissatisfaction is not reached. As a consequence, they do not move into action to correct their situation, which over time may become deplorable.

Opportunities for innovative ideas are not recognized, problems swell into metaproblems, and at the extreme, catastrophes are sometimes necessary to reach the action threshold (Van de Ven 1980b).

These worsening conditions are sometimes monitored by various corporate planning and management information units and distributed to personnel in quantitative MIS reports of financial and performance trends. However, these impersonal statistical reports only increase the numbness of organizational participants and raise the false expectation that if someone is measuring the trends then someone must be doing something about them.

When situations have deteriorated to the point of actually triggering peoples' action thresholds, innovative ideas turn out to be crisis management ideas. As Janis (1982) describes, such decision processes are dominated by defense mechanisms of isolation, projection, stereotyping, displacement, and retrospective rationalizations to avoid negative evaluations. As a result, the solutions that emerge from such "innovative" ideas are likely to be "mistakes."

Group and Organizational Limitations

At the group and organizational levels, the problems of inertia, conformity, and incompatible preferences are added to the above physiological limitations of human beings in managing attention. As Janis (1982) has clearly shown, groups place strong conformity pressures on members, who collectively conform to one another without them knowing it. Indeed, the classic study by Pelz and Andrews (1966) found that a heterogeneous group of interdisciplinary scientists when working together daily became homogeneous in perspective and approach to problems in as little as three years. Groups minimize internal conflict and focus on issues that maximize consensus. "Group Think" is not only partly a product of these internal conformity pressures, but also of external conflict— "out-group" conflict stimulates "in-group" cohesion (Coser 1959). Consequently, it is exceedingly difficult for groups to entertain threatening information, which is inherent in most innovative ideas.

Organizational structures and systems serve to sort attention. They focus efforts in prescribed areas and blind people to other issues by influencing perceptions, values, and beliefs. Many organizational systems consist of programs, which create slack through efficient repetitive use of procedures believed to lead to success (Cyert and March 1963). But as Starbuck (1983) argues, the programs do not necessarily address causal factors. Instead, the programs

tend to be more like superstitious learning, recreating actions which may have little to do with previous success and nothing to do with future success. As a result, the older, larger, and more successful organizations become, the more likely they are to have a large repertoire of structures and systems which discourage innovation while encouraging tinkering. For example, strategic planning *systems* often drive out strategic thinking as participants "go through the numbers" of completing yearly planning forms and review cycles.

The implication is that without the intervention of leadership (discussed below), structures and systems focus the attention of organizational members to routine, not innovative activities. For all the rational virtues that structures and systems provide to maintain existing organizational practices, these "action generators" make organizational participants inattentive to shifts in organizational environments and the need for innovation (Starbuck 1983). It is surprising that we know so little about the management of attention. However, several useful prescriptions have been made.

Ways to Manage Attention

At a recent conference on strategic decision making (Pennings 1985), Paul Lawrence reported that in his consulting practice he usually focuses on what management is *not* paying attention to. Similarly based on his observations in consulting with large organizations, Richard Normann observed that well-managed companies are not only close to their customers, they search out and focus on their *most demanding customers*. Empirically, von Hippel (1977) has shown that ideas for most new product innovations come from customers. Being exposed face-to-face with demanding customers or consultants increases the likelihood that the action threshold of organizational participants will be triggered and will stimulate them to pay attention to changing environmental conditions or customer needs. In general, we would expect that *direct personal confrontations with problem sources* are needed to reach the threshold of concern and appreciation required to motivate people to act (Van de Van 1980b).

However, while fact-to-face confrontations with problems may trigger action thresholds, they also create stress. One must therefore examine the effects of stress on the innovative process. Janis (1985) outlines five basic patterns of coping with stress, and states that only the vigilance pattern generally leads to decisions that meet the main criteria for sound decision making. Vigilance involves an extended search and assimilation of information, and a careful appraisal of alternatives before a choice is made. Janis proposes that vigilance tends to occur under conditions of moderate stress, and when there may be sufficient time and slack resources to made decisions. Under conditions of no slack capacity or short-time horizons (which produce stress) the decision process will resemble crisis decision-making—resulting in significant implementation errors (Hrebiniak and Joyce 1984).

Argyris and Schon (1982) focus on single loop and double loop learning models for managing attention that may improve the innovation process. In single loop learning, no change in criteria of effective performance takes place. Single loop learning represents conventional monitoring activity, with actions taken based on the findings of the monitoring system. Because it does not question the criteria of evaluation, single loop learning leads to the organizational inertia which Starbuck (1983) indicates must be unlearned before change can occur. Double loop learning involves a change in the criteria of evaluation. Past practices are called into question, new assumptions about the organization are raised, and significant changes in strategy are believed to be possible.

While double loop learning can lead to change, it can also lead to low trust, defensive behavior, undiscussibles, and to bypass tactics. Thus, the management of attention must be concerned not only with triggering the action thresholds of organizational participants, but also of channeling that action toward constructive ends. Constructive attention management is a function of how two other central problems are addressed: part-whole relations and institutional leadership—which we will now discuss.

The Management of Part-Whole Relationships

Proliferation of ideas, people, and transactions over time is a pervasive but little understood characteristic of the innovation process, and with it come complexity and interdependence—and the basic structural problem of managing part-whole relations.

The proliferation of ideas is frequently observed in a single individual who works to develop an innovation from concept to reality. Over time the individual develops a mosaic of perspectives, revisions, extensions, and applications of the initial innovative idea—and they accumu-

late into a complex set of interdependent options. However, as the discussion of managing ideas into good currency implies, innovation is not an individual activity—it is a collective achievement. Therefore, over time there is also a proliferation of people (with diverse skills, resources, and interests) who become involved in the innovation process. When a single innovative idea is expressed to others, it proliferates into multiple ideas because people have diverse frames of reference, or interpretive schemas, that filter their perceptions. These differing perceptions and frames of reference are amplified by the proliferation of transactions or relationships among people and organizational units that occur as the innovation unfolds. Indeed, management of the innovation process can be viewed as managing increasing bundles of transactions over time.

Transactions are "deals" or exchanges which tie people together within an institutional framework (which is context). John R. Commons (1951), the originator of the concept, argued that transactions are dynamic and go through three temporal stages: negotiations, agreements, and administration. Most transactions do not follow a simple linear progression through these stages. The more novel and complex the innovative idea, the more often trial-and-error cycles of renegotiation, recommitment, and readministration of transactions will occur. Moreover, the selection of certain kinds of transactions is always conditioned by the range of past experiences and current situations to which individuals have been exposed. Therefore, people have a conservative bias to enter into transactions with parties they know, trust, and with whom they have had successful experiences. As a consequence, what may start as an interim solution to an immediate problem often proliferates over time into a web of complex and interdependent transactions among the parties involved.

There is an important connection between transactions and organizations. Transactions are the micro elements of macro organizational arrangements. Just as the development of an innovation might be viewed as a bundle of proliferating transactions over time, so also, is there proliferation of functions and roles to manage this complex and interdependent bundle of transactions in the institution that houses the innovation.

The prevailing approach for handling this complexity and interdependence is to divide the labor among specialists who are best qualified to perform unique tasks and then to integrate the specialized parts to recreate the whole. The objective, of course, is to develop synergy in managing complexity and interdependence with an organizational design where the whole is greater than the sum of its parts. However, the whole often turns out to be less than or a meaningless sum of the parts because the parts do not add to, but subtract from one another (Hackman 1984). This result has been obtained not only when summing the products of differentiated units within organizations, but also the benefits member firms derive from associating with special interest groups (Maitland 1983, 1985). Kanter (1983), Tushman and Romanelli (1983), and Peters and Waterman (1982) have shown that this "segmentalist" design logic is severely flawed for managing highly complex and interdependent activities. *Perhaps the most significant structural problem in managing complex organizations today, and innovation in particular, is the management of part-whole relations.*

For example, the comptroller's office detects an irregularity of spending by a subunit and thereby eliminates an innovative "skunkworks" group; a new product may have been designed and tested, but runs into problems when placed into production because R&D and engineering overlooked a design flaw; the development of a major system may be ready for production, but subcontractors of components may not be able to deliver on schedule or there may be material defects in vendors' parts. Typical attributions for these problems include: lack of communication or misunderstandings between scientific, engineering, manufacturing, marketing, vendors and customers on the nature or status of the innovation; unexpected delays and errors in certain developmental stages that complicate further errors and rework in subsequent stages; incompatible organizational funding, control, and reward policies; and ultimately significant cost over-runs and delayed introductions into the market.

Peters and Waterman (1982) dramatized this problem of part-whole relationships with an example of a product innovation which required 223 reviews and approvals among 17 standing committees in order to develop it from concept to market reality. Moreover, they state that

> *The irony, and the tragedy, is that each of the 223 linkages taken by itself makes perfectly good sense. Well-meaning, rational people designed each link for a reason that made sense at the time. . . . The trouble is that the total picture as it inexorably emerged . . . captures action like a fly in a spider's web and drains the life out of it. (Peters and Waterman 1982 pp. 18–19).*

This example clearly illustrates a basic principle of contradictory part-whole relationships—*impeccable micro-logic often creates macro nonsense,* and vice versa.

Is there a way to avoid having the whole be less than or a meaningless sum of its parts? Perhaps a way is needed to

design the whole into the parts, as Gareth Morgan (1983a, b, 1984) has been pursuing with the concept of a *hologram.* He concluded that the brain, with its incredible complexity, manages that complexity by placing the essential elements of the whole into each of its parts—it is a hologram.

Most organizations, however, are not designed with this logic, but if possible ought to be. The hologram metaphor emphasizes that organization design for innovation is not a discrete event but a process for integrating all the essential functions, organizational units, and resources needed to manage an innovation from beginning to end. It requires a significant departure from traditional approaches to organizing innovation.

Traditionally the innovation process has been viewed as a sequence of separable stages (e.g., design, production, and marketing) linked by relatively minor transitions to make adjustments between stages. There are two basic variations of this design for product innovation. First, there is the technology-driven model where new ideas are developed in the R&D department, sent to engineering and manufacturing to produce the innovation, and then on to marketing for sales and distribution to customers. The second, and currently more popular, design is the customer or need-driven model, where marketing comes up with new ideas as a result of close interactions with customers, which in turn are sent to R&D for prototype development and then to engineering and manufacturing for production. Galbraith (1982) points out that the question of whether innovations are stimulated by technology or customer need is debatable.

> *"But this argument misses the point." As reproduced in Figure 17.2, "the debate is over whether [technology] or [need] drives the downstream efforts. This thinking is linear and sequential. Instead, the model suggested here is shown in Figure [2b]. That is, for innovation to occur, knowledge of all key components is simultaneously coupled. And the best way to maximize communication among the components is to have the communication occur intrapersonally—that is, within one person's mind. If this is impossible, then as few people as possible should have to communicate or interact." Galbraith 1982, pp. 16–17).*

As Galbraith implies, with the hologram metaphor the innovation process is viewed as consisting of iterations of inseparable and simultaneously-coupled stages (or functions) linked by a major ongoing transition process. Whereas the mechanical metaphor of an assembly line of stages characterizes the most current views of the innova-

FIGURE 17.2

Linear Sequential Coupling Compared with Simulaneous Coupling of Knowledge

(a) Linear Sequential Coupling

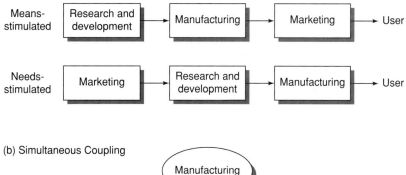

(b) Simultaneous Coupling

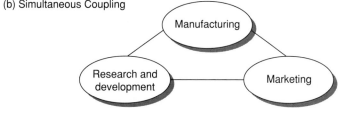

Source: Jay R. Galbraith (1982).

tion process, the biological metaphor of a hologram challenges scholars and practitioners to find ways to place essential characteristics of the whole into each of the parts.

Although very little is known about how to design holographic organizations, four inter-related design principles have been suggested by Morgan (1985) and others: self-organizing units, redundant functions, requisite variety, and temporal linkage.

First, the hologram metaphor directs attention to identifying and grouping together all the key resources and interdependent functions needed to develop an innovation into one organizational unit, so that it can operate as if it were an *autonomous unit.* (Of course, no organizational unit is ever completely autonomous.) The principle of autonomous work groups has been developed largely by Trist (1981), and is consistent with Thompson's (1967) logical design principle of placing reciprocally-interdependent activities closely together into a common unit in order to minimize coordination costs. By definition, autonomous groups are self-organizing, which implies that management follows the "princi-

ple of minimum intervention" (Hrebiniak and Joyce 1984, p. 8). This allows the group to self-organize and choose courses of action to solve its problems within an overall mission and set of constraints prescribed for the unit by the larger organization.

Second, flexibility and a capacity for self-organizing is needed by creating *redundant functions,* which means that people develop an understanding of the essential considerations and constraints of all aspects of the innovation in addition to those immediately needed to perform their individual assignments. Redundant functions does not mean duplication or spare parts as may be implied by the mechanistic metaphor, nor does it eliminate the need for people to have uniquely-specialized technical competencies. It means that all members of an innovation unit develop the capacity to "think globally while acting locally." The principle of redundant functions is achieved through training, socialization, and inclusion into the innovation unit so that each member not only comes to know how his or her function relates to each other functional specialty, but also understands the essential master blueprint of the overall innovation. The former is needed for interdependent action; the latter is essential for survival and reproduction of the innovative effort.

Third, following Ashby's (1956) principle of *requisite variety,* learning is enhanced when a similar degree of complexity in the environment is built into the organizational unit. This principle is a reflection of the fact that any autonomous organizational unit at one level is a dependent part of a larger social system at a more macro level of analysis. Requisite variety means placing critical dimensions of the whole environment into the unit, which permits the unit to develop and store rich patterns of information and uncertainty that are needed in order to detect and correct errors existing in the environment. The principle of requisite variety is not achieved by assigning the task of environmental scanning to one or a few boundary spanners, for that makes the unit dependent upon the "enactments" (Weick 1979) of only one or a few individuals whose frames of reference invariably filter only selective aspects of the environment. Requisite variety is more nearly achieved by making environmental scanning a responsibility of all unit members, and by recruiting personnel within the innovation unit who understand and have access to each of the key environmental stakeholder groups or issues that affect the innovation's development.

Whereas the principles of redundant functions and requisite variety create the slack needed to integrate members of the unit and between the unit and its environment (respectively), the principle of *temporal linkage* integrates parts of time (past, present, and future events) into an overall chronology of the innovation process. While innovations are typically viewed as making additions to existing arrangements, Albert (1984c) proposes another arithmetic for linking the past, present and future. Given a world of scarcity, Albert (1984a, b) notes that the implementation of innovations often results in eliminations, replacements, or transformations of existing arrangements. As a consequence, the management of innovation must also be the management of termination, and of transitioning people, programs, and investments from commitments in the past toward the future. In common social life, funerals and wakes are used to commemorate and bereave the passing of loved ones and to make graceful transitions into the future. As Albert suggests, there is a need to create funerals, celebrations, and transitional rituals that commemorate the ideas, programs, and commitments falling out of

currency in order to create opportunities for ushering in those that must gain good currency for an innovation to succeed.

Institutional Leadership and Innovation Context

Innovation is not the enterprise of a single entrepreneur. Instead, it is a network-building effort that centers on the creation, adoption, and sustained implementation of a set of ideas among people who, through transactions, become sufficiently committed to these ideas to transform them into "good currency." Following holographic principles, this network-building activity must occur both within the organization and in the larger community of which it is a part. *Creating these intra- and extra-organizational infrastructures in which innovation can flourish takes us directly to the strategic problem of innovation, which is institutional leadership.*

The extra-organizational context includes the broad cultural and resource endowments that society provides, including laws, government regulations, distributions of knowledge and resources, and the structure of the industry in which the innovation is located. Research by Ruttan and Hayami (1983) and Trist (1981) suggests that innovation does not exist in a vacuum and that institutional innovation is in great measure a reflection of the amount of support an organization can draw from its larger community. Collective action among institutional leaders within a community becomes critical in the long run to create the social, economic, and political infrastructure a community needs in order to sustain its members (Astley and Van de Ven 1983). In addition, as Aldrich (1979) and Erickson and Maitland (1982) indicate, a broad population or industry purview is needed to understand the societal demographic characteristics that facilitate and inhibit innovation.

Within the organization, institutional leadership is critical in creating a cultural context that fosters innovation, and in establishing organizational strategy, structure, and systems that facilitate innovation. As Hackman (1984, p. 40) points out, "an unsupportive organizational context can easily undermine the positive features of even a well-designed team." There is a growing recognition that innovation requires a special kind of supportive leadership.

This type of leadership offers a vision of what could be and gives a sense of purpose and meaning to those who would share that vision. It builds commitment, enthusiasm, and excitement. It creates a hope in the future and a belief that the world is knowable, understandable, and manageable. The collective energy that transforming leadership generates, empowers those who participate in the process. There is hope, there is optimism, there is energy (Roberts 1984, p. 3).

Institutional leadership goes to the essence of the process of institutionalization. It is often thought that an organization loses something (becomes rigid, inflexible, and loses its ability to be innovative) when institutionalization sets in. This may be true if an organization is viewed as a mechanistic, efficiency-driven tool. But, as Selznick (1957) argued, an organization does not become an "institution" until it becomes infused with value; i.e., prized not as a tool alone, but as a source of direct personal gratification, and as a vehicle for group integrity. By plan or default, this infusion of norms and values into an organization takes place over time, and produces a distinct identity, outlook, habits, and commitments for its participants—coloring as it does all aspects of organizational life, and giving it a social integration that goes far beyond the formal command structure and instrumental functions of the organization.

Institutional leadership is particularly needed for organizational innovation, which represents key periods of development and transition when the organization is open to or forced to consider alternative ways of doing things. During these periods, Selznick emphasized that the central and distinctive responsibility of institutional leadership is the creation of the organization's character or culture. This responsibility is carried out through four key functions: defining the institution's mission, embodying purpose into the organization's structure and systems, defending the institution's integrity, and ordering internal conflict. Selznick (1957, p. 62) reports that when institutional leaders default in performing these functions, the organization may drift. "A set of beliefs, values and guiding principles may emerge in the organization that are counterproductive to the organization's mission or distinctive competence. As institutionalization progresses the enterprise takes on a special character, and this means that it becomes peculiarly competent (or incompetent) to do a particular kind of work" (Selznick 1957, p. 139). Organization drift is accompanied by loss of the institution's integrity, opportunism, and ultimately, loss of distinctive competence.

Lodahl and Mitchell (1980, pp. 203–204) insightfully apply Selznick's perspective by distinguishing how institutional and technical processes come into play to transform innovative ideas into a set of guiding ideals—see Figure 17.3. First there are the founding ideals for an innovation or an enterprise, followed by the recruitment and socialization of members to serve those ideas. Leadership and formalization guide and stabilize the enterprise.

When viewed as a set of technical or instrumental tasks, the process is operationalized into setting clear goals or ends to be achieved; establishing impersonal and universal criteria for recruitment, developing clear rules and

---

FIGURE 17.3

INSTITUTIONAL AND TECHNICAL PROCESSES

INSTITUTIONAL PROCESSES	IDEA	TECHNICAL PROCESSES
Creation, Elaboration of Ideology	Founding Ideals	Statement of Organizational Goals
Use of Personal Networks; Selection Based on Values and Ideals	Recruitment	Broad Search: Use of Universalistic Criteria
Face-to-Face Contact with Founders: Sharing Rituals, Symbols	Socialization	Rules and Procedures Learned through Colleagues
Charismatic, Mythic Images (Transforming)	Leadership	Problem Solving and Consensus Making (Transactional)
Ideals Paramount: Structure Tentative	Formalization	Early Routinization; Uncertainty Reduction

Source: T. Lodahl and S. Mitchell (1980).

procedures for learning and socialization; analytical problem solving and decision making; and routinizing activities in order to reduce uncertainty. Institutional processes are very different from this well-known technical approach.

As Figure 17.3 illustrates, institutional processes focus on the creation of an ideology to support the founding ideals; the use of personal networks and value-based criteria for recruitment; socialization and learning by sharing rituals and symbols; charismatic leadership; and the infusion of values as paramount to structure and formalize activities.

Lodahl and Mitchell (1980, p. 204) point out that an innovation is an institutional success to the degree that it exhibits authenticity, functionality, and flexibility over time. Authenticity requires that the innovation embodies the organization's ideas; functionality requires that the innovation work; and flexibility requires that the innovation can incorporate the inputs and suggestions of its members. If these tests are met, organizational members will make a commitment to the innovation. In contrast, if institutional skills are not used while technical skills are in operation, the innovation may be an organizational success but an institutional failure. In that case, there will be evidence of drift and disillusionment. Such a result will be characterized by individual self-interest, differentiation, and technical efficiency.

These distinctions between institutional and technical processes have three significant implications for addressing the problems of managing attention, ideas, and part-whole relations discussed in previous sections. These implications draw upon cybernetic principles and the hologram metaphor, as Morgan (1983b, 1984) proposes.

First, organizational members can develop a capacity to control and regulate their own behavior through a process of *negative feedback,* which means that goals are achieved by avoiding not achieving the goal. In other words, deviations in one direction initiate action in the opposite direction at every step in performing an activity so that in the end no error remains. In order for learning through negative feedback to occur, an organization must have values and standards which define the critical limits within which attention to innovative ideas is to focus. Whereas technical processes focus attention on clear-cut goals and targets to be achieved, institutional processes define the constraints to avoid in terms of values and limits. Institutional leadership thus involves a choice of limits (issues to avoid) rather than a choice of ends. As Burgelman (1984, p. 1349) points out, "top management's critical contribution consists in strategic recognition rather than planning." As a result, a space of possible actions is

defined which leaves room for innovative ideas to develop and to be tested against these constraints.

Second, whereas single loop learning involves an ability to detect and correct deviations from a set of values and norms, double loop learning occurs when the organization also learns how to detect and correct errors in the operating norms themselves. This permits an institution to adjust and change the ideas considered legitimate or to have good currency.

From an institutional view legitimate error stems from the uncertainty inherent in the nature of a situation. The major problem in dealing with uncertainty is maintaining a balance on organizational diversity and order over time (Burgelman 1984). Diversity results primarily from autonomous initiatives of technical units. Order results from imposing standards and a concept of strategy on the organization. Managing this diversity requires framing ideas and problems so that they can be approached through experimentation and selection. The process of double-loop learning is facilitated by probing into various dimensions of a situation, and of promoting constructive conflict and debate between advocates of competing perspectives. Competing action strategies lead to reconsideration of the organization's mission, and perhaps a reformulation of that mission.

Finally, although technical processes of formalization press to reduce uncertainty, institutional processes attempt to preserve it. Just as necessity is the mother of invention, preserving the same degrees of uncertainty, diversity, or turbulence within an organization that is present in the environment are major sources of creativity and long-run viability for an organization. Embracing uncertainty is achieved by maintaining balance among innovative subunits, each designed according to the holographic principles of autonomous groups, requisite variety, and redundant functions discussed above. Application of these principles results in mirroring the turbulence present in the whole environment into the decision processes and other activities of each of the organization's parts. As a consequence, innovation is enhanced because organizational units are presented with the whole "law of the situation."

Concluding Discussion

Innovation has been defined as the development and implementation of new ideas by people who over time engage in transactions with others within an institutional context. This definition is particularly relevant to the general manager for it applies to a wide variety of technical, product, process, and administrative kinds of innovations that typically engage the general manager. From a managerial viewpoint, to understand the process of innovation is to be able to answer three questions: How do innovations develop over time? What kinds of problems will most likely be encountered as the innovation process unfolds? What responses are appropriate for managing these problems? Partial answers to these questions can be obtained by undertaking longitudinal research which systematically examines the innovation process, problems, and outcomes over time. Undertaking this research requires a conceptual framework to guide the investigation. The main purpose of this paper has been to develop such a framework by suggesting what key concepts, problems, and managerial responses should be the guiding focus to conduct longitudinal research on the management of innovation.

As our definition of innovation suggests, four basic concepts are central to studying the innovational process over time: ideas, people, transactions, and context. Associated with these four concepts are four central problems in the management of innovation: developing ideas into good currency, managing attention, part-whole relationships, and institutional leadership. Although these concepts and problems have diverse origins in the literature, previously they have not been combined into an interdependent set of critical concepts and problems for studying innovation management.

An invention or creative idea does not become an innovation until it is implemented or institutionalized. Indeed by most standards, the success of an innovation is largely defined in terms of the degree to which it gains good currency, i.e., becomes an implemented reality and is incorporated into the taken-for-granted assumptions and thought structure of organizational practice. Thus, a key measure of innovation success or outcome is the currency of the idea, and a basic research question is how and why do some new ideas gain good currency while the majority do not? Based on work by Schon (1971), Quinn (1980), and others, we think the answer requires longitudinal study of the social and political processes by which people become invested in or attached to new ideas and push them into good currency.

But what leads people to pay attention to new ideas? This is the second major problem to be addressed in a research program on innovation. We argued that an understanding of this issue should begin with an appreciation of the physiological limitations of human beings to pay atten-

tion to nonroutine issues, and their corresponding inertial forces in organizational life. The more specialized, insulated, and stable an individual's job, the less likely the individual will recognize a need for change or pay attention to innovative ideas. It was proposed that people will pay attention to new ideas the more they experience personal confrontations with sources of problems, opportunities, and threats which trigger peoples' action thresholds to pay attention and recognize the need for innovation.

Once people begin to pay attention to new ideas and become involved in a social-political process with others to push their ideas into good currency, a third problem of part-whole relationships emerges. A common characteristic in the development of innovations is that multiple functions, resources, and disciplines are necessary to transform innovative ideas into reality—so much so that individuals involved in specific transactions or parts of the innovation lose sight of the whole innovative effort. If left to themselves, they will design impeccable micro-structures for the innovation process that often result in macro nonsense. The hologram metaphor was proposed for designing the innovation process in such a way that more of the whole is structured into each of the proliferating parts. In particular, application of four holographic principles was proposed for managing part-whole relationships: self-organizing groups, redundant functions, requisite variety, and temporal linkage.

However, these holographic principles for designing innovation units simultaneously require the creation of an institutional context that fosters innovation and that links these self-organizing innovative units into a larger and more encompassing organizational mission and strategy. The creation of this macro context for innovation points to the need to understand and study a fourth central problem, which is institutional leadership. Innovations must not only adapt to existing organizational and industrial arrangements, but they also transform the structure and practices of these environments. The strategic problem for institutional leaders is one of creating an infrastructure that is conducive to innovation and organizational learning.

Three cybernetic principles were proposed to develop this infrastructure. First, the principle of negative feedback suggests that a clear set of values and standards are needed which define the critical limits within which organizational innovations and operations are to be maintained. Second, an experimentation-and-selection approach is needed so that the organization develops a capacity for double-loop learning, i.e., learning how to detect and correct errors in the guiding standards themselves. Third, innovation requires preserving (not reducing) the uncertainty and diversity in the environment within the organization because necessity is the mother of invention. Embracing uncertainty can be achieved at the macro level through the principles of requisite variety and redundancy of functions.

It should be recognized that this has been a speculative essay on key problems in the management of innovation. Little empirical evidence is presently available to substantiate these problems, their implications, and proposed solutions. However, the essay has been productive in suggesting a core set of concepts, problems, and propositions to study the process of innovation over time, which is presently being undertaken by a large group of investigators at the University of Minnesota. A description of the operational framework being used in this longitudinal research is available (Van de Ven and Associates 1984). As

this research progresses we hope to provide systematic evidence to improve our understanding of the central problems in the management of innovation discussed here.[1]

[1] The author wishes to gratefully recognize the stimulation of ideas for this paper from faculty and student colleagues involved in the Minnesota Innovation Research Program. Helpful comments on earlier drafts of this paper were provided by George Huber, William Joyce, Arie Lewin, Kenneth Mackenzie, and Donald Schon. This research program is supported in part by a major grant from the Organizational Effectiveness Research Programs, Office of Naval Research (Code 4420E), under Contract No. N00014-84-K-0016. Additional research support is being provided by 3M, Honeywell, Control Data, Dayton-Hudson, First Bank Systems, Cenex, Dyco Petroleum, and ADC Corporations.

REFERENCES

Albert, S., "A Delite Design Model for Successful Transitions," in J. Kimberly and R. Quinn (Eds.), *Managing Organizational Transitions,* Irwin, Homewood, Il., 1984a, Chapter 8, 169–191.

_____, "The Sense of Closure," in K. Gergen and M. Gergen (Eds.), *Historical Social Psychology,* Lawrence Erlbaum Associates, 1984b, Chapter 8, 159–172.

_____, "The Arithmetic of Change," University of Minnesota, Minneapolis, unpublished paper, 1984c.

Aldrich, H., *Organizations and Environments,* Prentice Hall, Englewood Cliffs, N.J., 1979.

Argyris, C. and D. Schon, *Reasoning, Learning, and Action,* Jossey-Bass, San Francisco, 1983.

Ashby, W. R., *An Introduction to Cybernetics,* Chapman and Hall, Ltd., London, 1956.

Astley, G. and A. Van de Ven, "Central Perspectives and Debates in Organization Theory," *Admin. Sci. Quart.,* 28 (1983), 245–273.

Burgelman, R. A., "Corporate Entrepreneurship and Strategic Management: Insights from a Process Study," *Management Sci.,* 29, 12 (1983), 1349–1364.

Cohen, M. D., J. G. March and J. P. Olsen, "A Garbage Can Model of Organizational Choice," *Admin. Sci. Quart.,* 17 (1972), 1–25.

Commons, J., *The Economics of Collection Action,* MacMillan, New York, 1951.

Cooper, A., "Strategic Management: New Ventures and Small Business," in D. Schendel and C. Hofer (Eds.), *Strategic Management,* Little, Brown and Company, Boston, 1979.

Coser, L., *The Functions of Social Conflict,* Routledge and Kegan Paul, New York, 1959.

Cyert, R. M. and J. G. March, *A Behavioral Theory of the Firm,* Prentice-Hall, Englewood Cliffs, N.J., 1963.

Daft, R. and S. Becker, *Innovation in Organization,* Elsevier, New York, 1978.

Erickson, B. and I. Maitland, "Healthy Industries and Public Policy," in Margaret E. Dewar (Ed.), *Industry Vitalization: Toward a National Industrial Policy,* Elmsford, N.Y., 1982.

Filley, A., R. House and S. Kerr, *Managerial Process and Organizational Behavior,* Scott Foresman, Glenview, Il., 1976.

Galbraith, J. R., "Designing the Innovating Organization," *Organizational Dynamics,* (Winter 1982), 3–24.

Gilbert, D. and E. Freeman, "Strategic Management and Environmental Scanning: A Game Theoretic Approach," presented to the Strategic Management Society, Philadelphia, October 1984.

Hackman, J. R., "A Normative Model of Work Team Effectiveness," Yale School of Organization and Management, New Haven, Conn., Research Program on Group Effectiveness, Technical Report #2, 1984.

Helson, H., "Adaptation-Level as a Basis for a Quantitative Theory of Frames of Reference," *Psychological Rev.,* 55 (1948), 294–313.

_____, "Current Trends and Issues in Adaptation-Level Theory," *American Psychologist,* 19 (1964), 23–68.

Huber, G., "The Nature and Design of Post-Industrial Organizations," *Management Sci.,* 30, 9 (1984), 928–951.

Janis, I., *Groupthink,* 2nd edition, Houghton Mifflin, Boston, 1982.

_____, "Sources of Error in Strategic Decision Making," in J. Pennings (Ed.), *Strategic Decision Making in Complex Organizations,* Jossey-Bass, San Francisco, 1985.

Johnson, Paul E., "The Expert Mind: A New Challenge for the Information Scientist," In M. A. Bemmelmans (Ed.), *Beyond Productivity: Information Systems Development for Organizational Effectiveness,* North Holland Publishing, Netherlands, 1983.

Kanter, R., *The Change Masters,* Simon and Schuster, New York, 1983.

Kimberly, J., "Managerial Innovation," in Nystrom, P. and W. Starbuck (Eds.), *Handbook of Organizational Design,* Volume 1, Oxford University Press, Oxford, 1981, 84–104.

Lawrence, P. and P. Dyer, *Renewing American Industry,* Free Press, New York, 1983.

Leavitt, H. J., "Applied Organizational Change in Industry: Structural, Technological, and Humanistic Approaches," Chapter 27 in J. March (Ed.), *Handbook of Organizations,* Rand McNally, Chicago, 1965, 1144–1170.

_____, "Applied Organizational Change in Industry: Structural, Technological, and Humanistic Approaches," Chapter 25, in J. March (Ed.), *Handbook of Organizations,* Rand McNally, Chicago, 1965, 1144–1170.

Lewin, Arie Y., and John W. Minton, "Organizational Effectiveness: Another Look, and an Agenda for Research," *Management Sci.,* 32, 5 (May 1986).

Lewin, K., T. Dembo, L. Festinger, and P. Sears, "Level of Aspiration," Chapter 10 in J. McV. Hunt (Ed.), *Personality and the Behavior Disorders,* Vol. 1, Ronald Press, New York, 1944.

Lodahl, T. and S. Mitchell, "Drift in the Development of Innovative Organizations," in J. Kimberly and R. Miles (Eds.), *The Organizational Life Cycle,* Jossey-Bass, San Francisco, 1980.

Maitland, I., "Organizational Structure and Innovation: The Japanese Case," in S. Lee and G. Schwendiman, *Management by Japanese Systems,* Prager, New York, 1982.

_____, "House Divided: Business Lobbying and the 1981 Budget," *Research in Corporate Social Performance and Policy,* 5 (1983), 1–25.

_____, "Interest Groups and Economic Growth Rates," *J. Politics,* (1985).

March, James G., "Decisions in Organizations and Theories of Choice," in A. Van de Ven and W. F. Joyce (Eds.), *Perspectives on Organizational Design and Behavior,* Wiley, New York, 1981.

_____ and J. P. Olsen, *Ambiguity and Choice in Organizations,* Universitetsforlaget, Bergen, 1976.

_____ and H. Simon, *Organizations,* Wiley, New York, 1958.

Miller, G. A., "The Magical Number Seven, Plus or Minus Two: Some Limits on our Capacity for Processing Information," *Psychological Rev.,* 63 (1956), 81–97.

Morgan, G., "Action Learning: A Holographic Metaphor for Guiding Social Change," *Human Relations,* 37, 1 (1983a), 1–28.

_____, "Rethinking Corporate Strategy: A Cybernetic Perspective," *Human Relations,* 36, 4 (1983b), 345–360.

_____, "Images of Organizations," York University, Downsview, Ontario, Prepublication manuscript, 1986.

Normann, R., *Management for Growth,* Wiley, New York, 1977.

_____, "Towards an Action Theory of Strategic Management," in J. Pennings (Ed.), *Strategic Decision Making in Complex Organizations,* Jossey-Bass, San Francisco, 1985.

Ouchi, W., *Theory Z,* Addison-Wesley, Reading, Mass., 1981.

Pascale, R. and A. Athos, *The Art of Japanese Management,* Warner Books, New York, 1981.

Pelz, D. and F. Andrews, *Scientists in Organizations,* Wiley, New York, 1966.

Pennings, J., *Strategic Decision Making in Complex Organizations,* Jossey-Bass, San Francisco, 1985.

Peters, R. and R. Waterman, *In Search of Excellence: Lessons from America's Best-Run Companies,* Harper and Row, New York, 1982.

Quinn, James Brian, *Strategies for Change: Logical Incrementalism,* Irwin, Homewood, Ill., 1980.

Roberts, N., "Transforming Leadership: Sources, Process, Consequences," presented at Academy of Management Conference, Boston, August 1984.

Rogers, E., *Diffusion of Innovations,* 3rd Ed., The Free Press, New York, 1982.

Ruttan, V. and Hayami, "Toward a Theory of Induced Institutional Innovation," *J. Development Studies,* 20, 4 (1984), 203–223.

Schon, D., *Beyond the Stable State,* Norton, New York, 1971.

Schumpeter, J., *Capitalism, Socialism, and Democracy,* Harper and Row, New York, 1942.

Selznick, P., *Leadership in Administration,* Harper and Row, New York, 1957.

Simon, H. A., *Administrative Behavior,* Macmillan, New York, 1947.

Starbuck, W., "Organizations as Action Generators," *Amer. J. Sociology,* 48, 1 (1983), 91–115.

Terryberry, S., "The Evolution of Organizational Environments," *Admin. Sci. Quart.,* 12 (1968), 590–613.

Trist, E., "The Evolution of Sociotechnical Systems as a Conceptual Framework and as an Action Research Program," in A. Van de Ven and W. Joyce (Eds.), *Perspectives on Organization Design and Behavior,* Wiley, New York, 1981, 19–75.

Tushman, M. and E. Romanelli, "Organizational Evolution: A Metamorphosis Model of Convergence and Reorientation," in B. Staw and L. Cummings (Eds.), *Research in Organizational Behavior,* Vol. 7, JAI Press, Greenwich, Conn., 1985.

Tversky, A. and D. Kahneman, "Judgment under Uncertainty: Heuristics and Biases," *Science,* 185 (1974), 1124–1131.

Utterback, J., "The Process of Technological Innovation within the Firm," *Acad. Management J.,* 14 (1971), 75–88.

Van de Ven, A., "Problem Solving, Planning, and Innovation. Part 1. Test of the Program Planning Model," *Human Relations,* 33 (1980a), 711–740.

_____, "Problem Solving, Planning, and Innovation. Part 2. Speculations for Theory and Practice," *Human Relations,* 33 (1980b), 757–779.

_____, "Strategic Management Concerns among CEOs: A Preliminary Research Agenda," Presented at Strategic Management Colloquium, University of Minnesota, Minneapolis, October 1982.

_____ and Associates, "The Minnesota Innovation Research Program," Strategic Management Research Center, Minneapolis, Discussion Paper #10, 1984.

_____ and R. Hudson, "Managing Attention to Strategic Choices," in J. Pennings (Ed.), *Strategic Decision Making in Complex Organizations,* Jossey-Bass, San Francisco, 1984.

von Hippel, E., "Successful Industrial Products from Customer Ideas," *J. Marketing,* (January 1978), 39–40.

Weick, Karl, *The Social-Psychology of Organizing,* Addison-Wesley, Reading, Mass., 1979.

Wilson, J., "Innovation in Organizations: Notes toward a Theory," in J. Thompson (Ed.), *Approaches to Organizational Design,* University of Pittsburgh Press, Pittsburgh, 1966.

Zaltman, G., R. Duncan and J. Holbek, *Innovations and Organizations,* Wiley, New York, 1973.

Discussion Questions

1. What is an innovation?

2. Discuss the statement: The more successful an organization is the more difficult it is to trigger people's action thresholds to pay attention to new ideas, needs, and opportunities.

3. Through what processes do ideas influence innovation?

4. How do the physiological limitations of human beings affect innovation in organizations?

5. Why is it difficult for groups to deal effectively with threatening ideas that are created by innovations?

6. What does Van de Ven mean by the management of part-whole relationships?

7. What role does institutional leadership play in the process of innovation?

Why Change Programs Don't Produce Change

Michael Beer, Russell A. Eisenstat,
and Bert Spector

LEARNING OBJECTIVES

After reading Beer, Eisenstat, and Spector's "Why Change Programs Don't Produce Change," students will:

1. See why change programs don't produce change

2. Understand "the fallacy of programmatic change"

3. Learn where and why successful change programs begin in large, complex organizations

4. Understand the author's six steps for implementing successful organizational change

In the mid-1980s, the new CEO of a major international bank—call it U.S. Financial—announced a companywide change effort. Deregulation was posing serious competitive challenges—challenges to which the bank's traditional hierarchical organization was ill-suited to respond. The only solution was to change fundamentally how the company operated. And the place to begin was at the top.

The CEO held a retreat with his top 15 executives where they painstakingly reviewed the bank's purpose and culture. He published a mission statement and hired a new vice president for human resources from a company well-known for its excellence in managing people. And in a quick succession of moves, he established companywide programs to push change down through the organization: a new organizational structure, a performance appraisal system, a pay-for-performance compensation plan, training programs to turn managers into "change agents," and quarterly attitude surveys to chart the progress of the change effort.

As much as these steps sound like a textbook case in organizational transformation, there was one big problem: two years after the CEO launched the change program, virtually nothing in the way of actual changes in organizational behavior had occurred. What had gone wrong?

The answer is "everything." Every one of the assumptions the CEO made—about who should lead the change effort, what needed changing, and how to go about doing it—was wrong.

U.S. Financial's story reflects a common problem. Faced with changing markets and increased competition, more and more companies are struggling to reestablish their dominance, regain market share, and in some cases, ensure their survival. Many have come to understand that the key to competitive success is to transform the way they function. They are reducing reliance on managerial authority, formal rules and procedures, and narrow divisions of work. And they are creating teams, sharing information, and delegating responsibility and accountability far down the hierarchy. In effect, companies are moving from the hierarchical and bureaucratic model of organization that has characterized corporations since World War II to what we call the task-driven organization where what has to be done governs who works with whom and who leads.

But while senior managers understand the necessity of change to cope with new competitive realities, they often misunderstand what it takes to bring it about. They tend to share two assumptions with the CEO of U.S. Financial: that promulgating companywide programs—mission statements, "corporate culture" programs, training courses, quality circles, and new pay-for-performance systems—will transform organizations, and that employee behavior is changed by altering a company's formal structure and systems.

In a four-year study of organizational change at six large corporations (see the insert, "Tracking Corporate Change" on page 503; the names are fictitious), we found that exactly the opposite is true: the greatest obstacle to revitalization is the idea that it comes about through companywide change programs, particularly when a corporate staff group such as human resources sponsors them. We call this "the fallacy of programmatic change." Just as important, formal organization structure and systems cannot lead a corporate renewal process.

While in some companies, wave after wave of programs rolled across the landscape with little positive impact, in others, more successful transformations did take place. They usually started at the periphery of the corporation in a few plants and divisions far from corporate headquarters. And they were led by the general managers of those units, not by the CEO or corporate staff people.

The general managers did not focus on formal structures and systems; they created ad hoc organizational arrangements to solve concrete business problems. By aligning employee roles, responsibilities, and relationships to address the organization's most important competitive task—a process we call "task alignment"—they focused energy for change on the work itself, not on abstractions such as "participation" or "culture." Unlike the CEO at U.S. Financial, they didn't employ massive training programs or rely on speeches and mission statements. Instead, we saw that general managers carefully developed the change process through a sequence of six basic managerial interventions.

Once general managers understand the logic of this sequence, they don't have to wait for senior management to start a process of organizational revitalization. There is a lot they can do even without support from the top. Of course, having a CEO or other senior managers who are committed to change does make a difference—and when it comes to changing an entire organization, such support is essential. But top management's role in the change process is very different from that which the CEO played at U.S. Financial.

Grass-roots change presents senior managers with a paradox: directing a "nondirective" change process. The most effective senior managers in our study recognized their limited power to mandate corporate renewal from the top. Instead, they defined their roles as creating a climate for change, then spreading the lessons of both successes and failures. Put another way, they specified the general direction in which the company should move without insisting on specific solutions.

In the early phases of a companywide change process, any senior manager can play this role. Once grass-roots change reaches a critical mass, however, the CEO has to be ready to transform his or her own work unit as well—the top team composed of key business heads and corporate staff heads. At this point, the company's structure and sys-

tems must be put into alignment with the new management practices that have developed at the periphery. Otherwise, the tension between dynamic units and static top management will cause the change process to break down.

We believe that an approach to change based on task alignment, starting at the periphery and moving steadily toward the corporate core, is the most effective way to achieve enduring organizational change. This is not to say that change can *never* start at the top, but it is uncommon and too risky as a deliberate strategy. Change is about learning. It is a rare CEO who knows in advance the fine-grained details of organizational change that the many diverse units of a large corporation demand. Moreover, most of today's senior executives developed in an era in which topdown hierarchy was the primary means for organizing and managing. They must learn from innovative approaches coming from younger unit managers closer to the action.

The Fallacy of Programmatic Change

Most change programs don't work because they are guided by a theory of change that is fundamentally flawed. The common belief is that the place to begin is with the knowledge and attitudes of individuals. Changes in attitudes, the theory goes, lead to changes in individual behavior. And changes in individual behavior, repeated by many people, will result in organizational change. According to this model, change is like a conversion experience. Once people "get religion," changes in their behavior will surely follow.

This theory gets the change process exactly backward. In fact, individual behavior is powerfully shaped by the organizational roles that people play. The most effective way to change behavior, therefore, is to put people into a new organizational context, which imposes new roles, responsibilities, and relationships on them. This creates a situation that, in a sense, "forces" new attitudes and behaviors on people. (See Table 17.1, "Contrasting Assumptions about Change.")

One way to think about this challenge is in terms of three interrelated factors required for corporate revitalization. *Coordination* or teamwork is especially important if an organization is to discover and act on cost, quality, and product development opportunities. The production and sale of innovative, high-quality, low-cost products (or ser-

TABLE 17.1

CONTRASTING ASSUMPTIONS ABOUT CHANGE

PROGRAMMATIC CHANGE	TASK ALIGNMENT
Problems in behavior are a function of individual knowledge, attitudes, and beliefs.	Individual knowledge, attitudes, and beliefs are shaped by recurring patterns of behavioral interactions.
The primary target of renewal should be the content of attitudes and ideas; actual behavior should be secondary.	The primary target of renewal should be behavior; attitudes and ideas should be secondary.
Behavior can be isolated and changed individually.	Problems in behavior come from a circular pattern, but the effects of the organizational system on the individual are greater than those of the individual on the system.
The target for renewal should be at the individual level.	The target for renewal should be at the level of roles, responsibilities, and relationships.

vices) depend on close coordination among marketing, product design, and manufacturing departments, as well as between labor and management. High levels of *commitment* are essential for the effort, initiative, and cooperation that coordinated action demands. New *competencies* such as knowledge of the business as a whole, analytical skills, and interpersonal skills are necessary if people are to identify and solve problems as a team. If any of these elements are missing, the change process will break down.

The problem with most companywide change programs is that they address only one or, at best, two of these factors. Just because a company issues a philosophy statement about teamwork doesn't mean its employees necessarily know what teams to form or how to function within them to improve coordination. A corporate reorganization may change the boxes on a formal organization chart but not provide the necessary attitudes and skills to make the new structure work. A pay-for-performance system may force managers to differentiate better performers from poorer ones, but it doesn't help them internalize new standards by which to judge subordinates' performances. Nor does it teach them how to deal effectively with performance problems. Such programs cannot provide the cultural context (role models from whom to learn) that people need to develop new competencies, so ultimately they fail to create organizational change.

Similarly, training programs may target competence, but rarely do they change a company's patterns of coordination. Indeed, the excitement engendered in a good corporate training program frequently leads to increased frustration when employees get back on the job only to see their new skills go unused in an organization in which nothing else has changed. People end up seeing training as a waste of time, which undermines whatever commitment to change a program may have roused in the first place.

When one program doesn't work, senior managers, like the CEO at U.S. Financial, often try another, instituting a rapid progression of programs. But this only exacerbates the problem. Because they are designed to cover everyone and everything, programs end up covering nobody and nothing particularly well. The are so general and standardized that they don't speak to the day-to-day realities of particular units. Buzzwords like "quality," "participation," "excellence," "empowerment," and "leadership" become a substitute for a detailed understanding of the business.

And all these change programs also undermine the credibility of the change effort. Even when managers accept the potential value of a particular program for others—quality circles, for example, to solve a manufacturing problem—they may be confronted with another, more pressing business problem such as new product development. One-size-fits-all change programs take energy *away* from efforts to solve key business problems—which explains why so many general managers don't support programs, even when they acknowledge that their underlying principles may be useful.

This is not to state that training, changes in pay systems or organizational structure, or a new corporate philosophy are always inappropriate. All can play valuable roles in supporting an integrated change effort. The problems come when such programs are used in isolation as a kind of "magic bullet" to spread organizational change rapidly through the entire corporation. At their best, change programs of this sort are irrelevant. At their worst, they actually inhibit change. By promoting skepticism and cynicism, programmatic change can inoculate companies against the real thing.

Six Steps to Effective Change

Companies avoid the shortcomings of programmatic change by concentrating on "task alignment"—reorganizing employee roles, responsibilities, and relationships to solve specific business problems. Task alignment is easiest in small units—a plant, department, or business unit—where goals and tasks are clearly defined. Thus the chief problem for corporate change is how to promote task-aligned change across many diverse units.

We saw that general managers at the business unit or plant level can achieve task alignment through a sequence of six overlapping but distinctive steps, which we call the *critical path.* This path develops a self-reinforcing cycle of commitment, coordination, and competence. The sequence of steps is important because activities appropriate at one time are often counterproductive if started too early. Timing is everything in the management of change.

1. *Mobilize commitment to change through joint diagnosis of business problems.* As the term task alignment suggests, the starting point of any effective change effort is a clearly defined business problem. By helping people develop a shared diagnosis of what is wrong in an organization and what can and must be improved, a general manager mobilizes the initial commitment that is necessary to begin the change process.

Consider the case of a division we call Navigation Devices, a business unit of about 600 people set up by a large corporation to commercialize a product originally designed for the military market. When the new general manager took over, the division had been in operation for several years without ever making a profit. It had never been able to design and produce a high-quality, cost-competitive product. This was due largely to an organization in which decisions were made at the top, without proper involvement of or coordination with other functions.

The first step the new general manager took was to initiate a broad review of the business. Where the previous general manager had set strategy with the unit's marketing director alone, the new general manager included his entire management team. He also brought in outside consultants to help him and his managers function more effectively as a group.

Next, he formed a 20-person task force representing all the stakeholders in the organization—managers, engineers, production workers, and union officials. The group visited a number of successful manufacturing organizations in an attempt to identify what Navigation Devices might do to organize more effectively. One high-performance manufacturing plant in the task force's own company made a particularly strong impression. Not only did it highlight the problems at Navigation Devices but it also offered an alternative organizational model, based on teams, that captured the group's imagination. Seeing a different way of working helped strengthen the group's commitment to change.

The Navigation Devices task force didn't learn new facts from this process of joint diagnosis; everyone already knew the unit was losing money. But the group came to see clearly the organizational roots of the unit's inability to compete and, even more important, came to share a common understanding of the problem. The group also identified a potential organizational solution: to redesign the way it worked, using ad hoc teams to integrate the organization around the competitive task.

2. *Develop a shared vision of how to organize and manage for competitiveness.* Once a core group of people is committed to a particular analysis of the problem, the general manager can lead employees toward a task-aligned vision of the organization that defines new roles and responsibilities. These new arrangements will coordinate the flow of information and work across interdependent functions at all levels of the organization. But since they do not change formal structures and systems like titles or compensation, they encounter less resistance.

At Navigation Devices, the 20-person task force became the vehicle for this second stage. The group came up with a model of the organization in which cross-functional teams would accomplish all work, particularly new product development. A business-management team composed of the general manager and his staff would set the unit's strategic direction and review the work of lower level teams. Business-area teams would develop plans for specific markets. Product-development teams would manage new products from initial design to production. Production-process teams composed of engineers and production workers would identify and solve quality and cost problems in the plant. Finally, engineering-process teams would examine engineering methods and equipment. The teams got to the root of the unit's problems—functional and hierarchical barriers to sharing information and solving problems.

To create a consensus around the new vision, the general manager commissioned a still larger task force of about 90 employees from different levels and functions, including union and management, to refine the vision and obtain everyone's commitment to it. On a retreat away from the workplace, the group further refined the new organizational model and drafted a values statement, which it presented later to the entire Navigation Devices work force. The vision and the values statement made sense to Navigation Devices employees in a way many corporate mission statements never do—because it grew out of the organization's own analysis of real business problems. And it was built on a model for solving those problems that key stakeholders believed would work.

3. *Foster consensus for the new vision, competence to enact it, and cohesion to move it along.* Simply letting employees help develop a new vision is not enough to overcome resistance to change—or to foster the skills needed to make the new organization work. Not everyone can help in the design, and even those who do participate often do not fully appreciate what renewal will require until the new organization is actually in place. This is when strong leadership from the general manager is crucial. Commitment to change is always uneven. Some managers are enthusiastic; others are neutral or even antagonistic. At Navigation Devices, the general manager used what his subordinates termed the "velvet glove." He made it clear that the division was going to encourage employee involvement and the team approach. To managers who wanted to help him, he offered support. To those who did not, he offered outplacement and counseling.

Once an organization has defined new roles and responsibilities, people need to develop the competencies to make the new setup work. Actually, the very existence of the teams with their new goals and accountabilities will force learning. The changes in roles, responsibilities, and relationships foster new skills and attitudes. Changed patterns of coordination will also increase employee participation, collaboration, and information sharing.

But management also has to provide the right supports. At Navigation Devices, six resource people—three from the unit's human resource department and three from corporate headquarters—worked on the change project. Each team was assigned one internal consultant, who attended every meeting, to help people be effective team members. Once employees could see exactly what kinds of new skills they needed, they asked for formal training programs to develop those skills further. Since these courses grew directly out of the employees' own experiences, they were far more focused and useful than traditional training programs.

Some people, of course, just cannot or will not change, despite all the direction and support in the world. Step three is the appropriate time to replace those managers who cannot function in the new organization—after they have had a chance to prove themselves. Such decisions

are rarely easy, and sometimes those people who have difficulty working in a participatory organization have extremely valuable specialized skills. Replacing them early in the change process, before they have worked in the new organization, is not only unfair to individuals; it can be demoralizing to the entire organization and can disrupt the change process. People's understanding of what kind of manager and worker the new organization demands grows slowly and only from the experience of seeing some individuals succeed and others fail.

Once employees have bought into a vision of what's necessary and have some understanding of what the new organization requires, they can accept the necessity of replacing or moving people who don't make the transition to the new way of working. Sometimes people are transferred to other parts of the company where technical expertise rather than the new competencies is the main requirement. When no alternatives exist, sometimes they leave the company through early retirement programs, for example. The act of replacing people can actually reinforce the organization's commitment to change by visibly demonstrating the general manager's commitment to the new way.

Some of the managers replaced at Navigation Devices were high up in the organization—for example, the vice president of operations, who oversaw the engineering and manufacturing departments. The new head of manufacturing was far more committed to change and skilled in leading a critical path change process. The result was speedier change throughout the manufacturing function.

4. *Spread revitalization to all departments without pushing it from the top.* With the new ad hoc organization for the unit in place, it is time to turn to the functional and staff departments that must interact with it. Members of teams cannot be effective unless the department from which they come is organized and managed in a way that supports their roles as full-fledged participants in team decisions. What this often means is that these departments will have to rethink their roles and authority in the organization.

At Navigation Devices, this process was seen most clearly in the engineering department. Production department managers were the most enthusiastic about the change effort; engineering managers were more hesitant. Engineering had always been king at Navigation Devices; engineers designed products to the military's specifications without much concern about whether manufacturing could easily build them or not. Once the new team structure was in place, however, engineers had to participate on product-development teams with production workers.

This required them to reexamine their roles and rethink their approaches to organizing and managing their own department.

The impulse of many general managers faced with such a situation would be to force the issue—to announce, for example, that now all parts of the organization must manage by teams. The temptation to force newfound insights on the rest of the organization can be great, particularly when rapid change is needed, but it would be the same mistake that senior managers make when they try to push programmatic change throughout a company. It short-circuits the change process.

It's better to let each department "reinvent the wheel"—that is, to find its own way to the new organization. At Navigation Devices, each department was allowed to take the general concepts of coordination and teamwork and apply them to its particular situation. Engineering spent nearly a year agonizing over how to implement the team concept. The department conducted two surveys, held off-site meetings, and proposed, rejected, then accepted a matrix management structure before it finally got on board. Engineering's decision to move to matrix management was not surprising, but because it was its own choice, people committed themselves to learning the necessary new skills and attitudes.

5. *Institutionalize revitalization through formal policies, systems, and structures.* There comes a point where general managers have to consider how to institutionalize change so that the process continues even after they've moved on to other responsibilities. Step five is the time: the new approach has become entrenched, the right people are in place, and the team organization is up and running. Enacting changes in structures and systems any earlier tends to backfire. Take information systems. Creating a team structure means new information requirements. Why not have the MIS department create new systems that cut across traditional functional and departmental lines early in the change process? The problem is that without a well-developed understanding of information requirements, which can best be obtained by placing people on task-aligned teams, managers are likely to resist new systems as an imposition by the MIS department. Newly formed teams can often pull together enough information to get their work done without fancy new systems. It's better to hold off until everyone understands what the team's information needs are.

What's true for information systems is even more true for other formal structures and systems. Any formal system is going to have some disadvantages; none is perfect. These imperfections can be minimized, however, once people

have worked in an ad hoc team structure and learned what interdependencies are necessary. Then employees will commit to them too.

Again, Navigation Devices is a good example. The revitalization of the unit was highly successful. Employees changed how they saw their roles and responsibilities and became convinced that change could actually make a difference. As a result, there were dramatic improvements in value added per employee, scrap reduction, quality, customer service, gross inventory per employee, and profits. And all this happened with almost no formal changes in reporting relationships, information systems, evaluation procedures, compensation, or control systems.

When the opportunity arose, the general manager eventually did make some changes in the formal organization. For example, when he moved the vice president of operations out of the organization, he eliminated the position altogether. Engineering and manufacturing reported directly to him from that point on. For the most part, however, the changes in performance at Navigation Devices were sustained by the general manager's expectations and the new norms for behavior.

6. *Monitor and adjust strategies in response to problems in the revitalization process.* The purpose of change is to create an asset that did not exist before—a learning organization capable of adapting to a changing competitive environment. The organization has to know how to continually monitor its behavior—in effect, to learn how to learn.

Some might say that this is the general manager's responsibility. But monitoring the change process needs to be shared, just as analyzing the organization's key business problem does.

At Navigation Devices, the general manager introduced several mechanisms to allow key constituents to help monitor the revitalization. An oversight team—composed of some crucial managers, a union leader, a secretary, an engineer, and an analyst from finance—kept continual watch over the process. Regular employee attitude surveys monitored behavior patterns. Planning teams were formed and reformed in response to new challenges. All these mechanisms created a long-term capacity for continual adaptation and learning.

The six-step process provides a way to elicit renewal without imposing it. When stakeholders become committed to a vision, they are willing to accept a new pattern of management—here the ad hoc team structure—that demands changes in their behavior. And as the employees discover that the new approach is more effective (which will happen only if the vision aligns with the core task), they have to grapple with personal and organizational changes they might otherwise resist. Finally, as improved coordination helps solve relevant problems, it will reinforce team behavior and produce a desire to learn new skills. This learning enhances effectiveness even further and results in an even stronger commitment to change. This mutually reinforcing cycle of improvements in commitment, coordination, and competence creates a growing sense of efficacy. It can continue as long as the ad hoc team structure is allowed to expand its role in running the business.

The Role of Top Management

To change an entire corporation, the change process we have described must be applied over and over again in many plants, branches, departments, and divisions. Orchestrating this companywide change process is the first responsibility of senior management. Doing so successfully requires a delicate balance. Without explicit efforts by top management to promote conditions for change in individual units, only a few plants or divisions will attempt change, and those that do will remain isolated. The best senior manager leaders we studied held their subordinates responsible for starting a change process without specifying a particular approach.

Create a market for change. The most effective approach is to set demanding standards for all operations and then hold managers accountable to them. At our best-practice company, which we call General Products, senior managers developed ambitious product and operating standards. General managers unable to meet these product standards by a certain date had to scrap their products and take a sharp hit to their bottom lines. As long as managers understand that high standards are not arbitrary but are dictated by competitive forces, standards can generate enormous pressure for better performance, a key ingredient in mobilizing energy for change.

But merely increasing demands is not enough. Under pressure, most managers will seek to improve business performance by doing more of what they have always done—overmanage—rather than alter the fundamental way they organize. So, while senior managers increase demands, they should also hold managers accountable for fundamental changes in the way they use human resources.

For example, when plant managers at General Products complained about the impossibility of meeting new business standards, senior managers pointed them to the corporate organization-development department within human resources and emphasized that the plant managers would be held accountable for moving revitalization along. Thus top management had created a demand system for help with the new way of managing, and the human resource staff could support change without appearing to push a program.

Use successfully revitalized units as organizational models for the entire company. Another important strategy is to focus the company's attention on plants and divisions that have already begun experimenting with management innovations. These units become developmental laboratories for further innovation.

There are two ground rules for identifying such models. First, innovative units need support. They need the best managers to lead them, and they need adequate resources—for instance, skilled human resource people and external consultants. In the most successful companies that we studied, senior managers saw it as their responsibility to make resources available to leading-edge units. They did not leave it to the human resource function.

Second, because resources are always limited and the costs of failure high, it is crucial to identify those units with the likeliest chance of success. Successful management innovations can appear to be failures when the bottom line is devastated by environmental factors beyond the unit's control. The best models are in healthy markets.

Obviously, organizational models can serve as catalysts for change only if others are aware of their existence and are encouraged to learn from them. Many of our worst-practice companies had plants and divisions that were making substantial changes. The problem was, nobody knew about them. Corporate management had never bothered to highlight them as examples to follow. In the leading companies, visits, conferences, and educational programs facilitated learning from model units.

Develop career paths that encourage leadership development. Without strong leaders, units cannot make the necessary organizational changes, yet the scarcest resource available for revitalizing corporations is leadership. Corporate renewal depends as much on developing effective change leaders as it does on developing effective organizations. The personal learning associated with leadership development—or the realization by higher management that a manager does not have this capacity—cannot occur in the classroom. It only happens in an organization where the teamwork, high commitment, and new competencies we have discussed are already the norm.

The only way to develop the kind of leaders a changing organization needs is to make leadership an important criterion for promotion, and then manage people's careers to develop it. At our best-practice companies, managers were moved from job to job and from organization to organization based on their learning needs, not on their position in the hierarchy. Successful leaders were assigned to units that had been targeted for change. People who needed to sharpen their leadership skills were moved into the company's model units where those skills would be demanded and therefore learned. In effect, top management used leading-edge units as hothouses to develop revitalization leaders.

But what about the top management team itself? How important is it for the CEO and his or her direct reports to practice what they preach? It is not surprising—indeed, it's predictable—that in the early years of a corporate change effort, top managers' actions are often not consistent with their words. Such inconsistencies don't pose a major barrier to corporate change in the beginning, though consistency is obviously desirable. Senior managers can create a climate for grass-roots change without paying much attention to how they themselves operate and manage. And unit managers will tolerate this inconsistency so long as they can freely make changes in their own units in order to compete more effectively.

There comes a point, however, when addressing the inconsistencies becomes crucial. As the change process spreads, general managers in the ever-growing circle of revitalized units eventually demand changes from corporate staff groups and top management. As they discover how to manage differently in their own units, they bump up against constraints of policies and practices that corporate staff and top management have created. They also begin to see opportunities for better coordination between themselves and other parts of the company over which they have little control. At this point, corporate organization must be aligned with corporate strategy, and coordination between related but hitherto independent businesses improved for the benefit of the whole corporation.

None of the companies we studied had reached this "moment of truth." Even when corporate leaders intellectually understood the direction of change, they were just beginning to struggle with how they would change themselves and the company as a whole for a total corporate revitalization.

This last step in the process of corporate renewal is probably the most important. If the CEO and his or her management team do not ultimately apply to themselves what they have been encouraging their general managers to do, then the whole process can break down. The time to tackle the tough challenge of transforming company-wide systems and structures comes finally at the end of the corporate change process.

At this point, senior managers must make an effort to adopt the team behavior, attitudes, and skills that they have demanded of others in earlier phases of change. Their struggle with behavior change will help sustain corporate renewal in three ways. It will promote the attitudes and behavior needed to coordinate diverse activities in the company; it will lend credibility to top management's continued espousal of change; and it will help the CEO identify and develop a successor who is capable of learning the new behaviors. Only such a manager can lead a corporation that can renew itself continually as competitive forces change.

Companies need a particular mind-set for managing change: one that emphasizes process over specific content, recognizes organization change as a unit-by-unit learning process rather than a series of programs, and acknowledges the payoffs that result from persistence over a long period of time as opposed to quick fixes. This mind-set is difficult to maintain in an environment that presses for quarterly earnings, but we believe it is the only approach that will bring about successful renewal.

Discussion Questions

1. How do organizational change efforts usually begin? Who manages them?

2. What is "the fallacy of programmatic change"?

3. Why do successful changes start at the periphery or lower level of organizations?

4. What can the top management of an organization do to create change?

5. Comment on the author's statement, "We believe that an approach to change based on task alignment, starting at the periphery and moving steadily toward the corporate core, is the most effective way to achieve enduring organizational change."

6. What is the role of individual employees' attitudes and values in the process of change?

7. Discuss the idea that coordination, commitment, and competencies are central to organizational change.

8. Why are the six steps to effective change sequential?

9. Since change efforts usually encounter resistance, how can the author's change strategy deal with resistance in its various forms?

Tracking Corporate Change

Which strategies for corporate change work, and which do not? We sought the answers in a comprehensive study of 12 large companies where top management was attempting to revitalize the corporation. Based on preliminary research, we identified 6 for in-depth analysis: 5 manufacturing companies and 1 large international bank. All had revenues between $4 billion and $10 billion. We studied 26 plants and divisions in these 6 companies and conducted hundreds of interviews with human resource managers; line managers engaged in change efforts at plants, branches, or business units; workers and union leaders; and, finally, top management.

Based on this material, we ranked the 6 companies according to the success with which they had managed the revitalization effort. Were there significant improvements in interfunctional coordination, decision making, work organization, and concern for people? Research has shown that in the long term, the quality of these 4 factors will influence performance. We did not define success in terms of improved financial performance because, in the short run, corporate financial performance is influenced by many situational factors unrelated to the change process.

To corroborate our rankings of the companies, we also administered a standardized questionnaire in each company to understand how employees viewed the unfolding change process. Respondents rated their companies on a scale of 1 to 5. A score of 3 meant that no

RESEARCHERS AND EMPLOYEES— SIMILAR CONCLUSIONS

EXTENT OF REVITALIZATION

COMPANY	RANKED BY RESEARCHERS	RATED BY EMPLOYEES	
		Average	Standard Deviation
General Products	1	4.04	.35
Fairweather	2	3.58	.45
Livingston Electronics	3	3.61	.76
Scranton Steel	4	3.30	.65
Continental Glass	5	2.96	.83
U.S. Financial	6	2.78	1.07

change had taken place; a score below 3 meant that, in the employee's judgment, the organization had actually gotten worse. As the table suggests, with one exception—the company we call Livingston Electronics—employees' perceptions of how much their companies had changed were identical to ours. And Livingston's relatively high standard of deviation (which measures the degree of consensus among employees about the outcome of the change effort) indicates that within the company there was considerable disagreement as to just how successful revitalization had been.

FOR FURTHER READING

Beer, M. and Walton, E. "Developing the Competitive Organization: Interventions and Strategies." *American Psychologist* 45 (1990) 154–161.

Kanter, R. *The Change Masters.* New York: Simon & Schuster, 1983.

Tichy, N. *Managing Strategic Change: Technical, Political and Cultural Dynamics.* New York: Wiley, 1983.

Burke, W. *Organizational Development: A Normative View.* Reading, Mass.: Addison-Wesley, 1987.

18

DIVERSITY IN THE WORKPLACE—MANAGING IN THE TWENTY-FIRST CENTURY

The Multicultural Organization

TAYLOR COX, JR.

LEARNING OBJECTIVES

After reading "The Multicultural Organization" by Taylor Cox, Jr., a student will be able to:

1. See how U.S. organizations are becoming increasingly diverse in terms of gender, race, ethnicity, and nationality

2. Understand the potential benefits of cultural diversity, such as improved decision making, innovation, and success in marketing to different types of customers

3. Understand the potential limitations of multiculturalism, particularly the possibility of increased turnover, interpersonal conflict, and communication breakdown

4. Recognize the characteristics of a multicultural organization and how to work productively within it

As we begin the 1990s, a combination of workforce demographic trends and increasing globalization of business has placed the management of cultural differences on the agenda of most corporate leaders. Organizations' workforces will be increasingly heterogeneous on dimensions such as gender, race, ethnicity and nationality. Potential benefits of this diversity include better decision making, higher creativity and innovation, greater success in marketing to foreign and ethnic minority communities, and a better distribution of economic opportunity. Conversely, cultural differences can also increase costs through higher turnover rates, interpersonal conflict, and communication breakdowns.

To capitalize on the benefits and minimize the costs of worker diversity, organizations of the '90s must be quite different from the typical organization of the past. Specifically, consultants have advised organizations to become "multicultural."[1] The term refers to the degree to which an organization values cultural diversity and is willing to utilize and encourage it.[2]

Leaders are being charged to create the multicultural organization, but what does such an organization look like, and what are the specific ways in which it differs from the traditional organization? Further, what tools and techniques are available to assist organizations in making the transition from the old to the new?

This article addresses these questions. I have used an adaptation of the societal-integration model developed by Milton Gordon, as well as available information on the early experience of American organizations with managing diversity initiatives, to construct a model of the multicultural organization.

Conceptual Framework

In his classic work on assimilation in the United States, Milton Gordon argued that there are seven dimensions

---

along which the integration of persons from different ethnic backgrounds into a host society should be analyzed.[3] I use "integration" to mean the coming together and mixing of people from different cultural identity groups in one organization. A cultural identity group is a group of people who (on average) share certain values and norms distinct from those of other groups. Although the boundaries of these groups may be defined along many dimensions, I am primarily concerned with gender, race, ethnicity, and national origin. Gordon's seven dimensions are:

1. Form of acculturation
2. Degree of structural assimilation
3. Degree of intergroup marriage
4. Degree of prejudice
5. Degree of discrimination
6. Degree of identification with the dominant group of the host society
7. Degree of intergroup conflict (especially over the balance of power)

Although Gordon's interest was in societal-level integration, I believe his model can be easily and usefully adapted for analysis of cultural integration for organizations. Therefore, an adaptation of his seven-point framework is used here as a basis for describing organizational models for integrating culturally divergent groups. Exhibit 18.1 shows my proposed six-dimensional adaptation of the Gordon framework along with definitions of each term.

Acculturation is the method by which cultural differences between the dominant (host) culture and any minority culture groups are resolved or treated. There are several alternatives, the most prominent being: 1. a unilateral process by which minority culture members adopt the norms and values of the dominant group in the organization *(assimilation)*; 2. a process by which both minority and majority culture members adopt some norms of the other group *(pluralism)*; and 3. a situation where there is little adaptation on either side *(cultural separatism)*.[4] Pluralism also means that minority culture members are encouraged to enact behaviors from their alternative culture as well as from the majority culture. They are therefore able to retain a sense of identity with their minority-culture group. Acculturation is concerned with the cultural (norms of behavior) aspect of integration of diverse groups, as opposed to simply their physical presence in the same location.

Structural integration refers to the presence of persons from different cultural groups in a single organization. Workforce profile data has typically been monitored under traditional equal opportunity and affirmative action guidelines. However, to get a proper understanding

EXHIBIT 18.1

CONCEPTUAL FRAMEWORK FOR ANALYSIS OF ORGANIZATIONAL CAPABILITY FOR EFFECTIVE INTEGRATION OF CULTURALLY DIVERSE PERSONNEL

DIMENSION	DEFINITION
1. Acculturation	Modes by which two groups adapt to each other and resolve cultural differences
2. Structural Integration	Cultural profiles of organization members including hiring, job-placement, and job status profiles
3. Informal Integration	Inclusion of minority-culture members in informal networks and activities outside of normal working hours
4. Cultural Bias	Prejudice and discrimination
5. Organizational Identification	Feelings of belonging, loyalty and commitment to the organization
6. Inter-group Conflict	Friction, tension and power struggles between cultural groups

of structural integration it is important to look beyond organization-wide profile data, and examine cultural mix by function, level, and individual work group. This is because, it is commonplace in American companies for gaps of fifteen to thirty percentage points to exist between the proportion of minority members in the overall labor force of a firm, and their proportion at middle and higher levels of management.[5]

Even within levels of an organization, individual work groups may still be highly segregated. For example, a senior human resource manager for a Fortune 500 firm who is often cited as a leader in managing diversity efforts, recently told me that there are still many "white-male bastions" in his company. As an assistant vice-president with responsibility for equal opportunity, he indicated that breaking down this kind of segregation was a focal point of his current job.

The *informal integration* dimension recognizes that important work-related contacts are often made outside of normal working hours and in various social activities and organizations. This item looks at levels of inclusion of minority-culture members in lunch and dinner meetings, golf and other athletic outings, and social clubs frequented by organization leaders. It also addresses mentoring and other informal developmental relationships in organizations.

Cultural bias has two components. Prejudice refers to negative attitudes toward an organization member based on his/her culture group identity, and discrimination refers to observable adverse behavior for the same reason. Discrimination, in turn, may be either personal or institutional. The latter refers to ways that organizational culture and management practices may inadvertently disadvantage members of minority groups. An example is the adverse effect that emphasizing aggressiveness and self promotion has on many Asians. Many managers that I have talked to are sensitive to the fact that prejudice is a cognitive phenomenon and therefore much more difficult than discrimination for organization managers to change. Nevertheless, most acknowledge the importance of reducing prejudice for long range, sustained change.

Prejudice may occur among minority-culture members as well as among dominant-culture members. Putting the debate over whether rates of prejudice differ for different groups aside, it must be emphasized that the practical impact of prejudice by majority-culture members is far greater than that of minority-culture members because of their far greater decision-making power (except under extraordinary conditions, such as those of South Africa).

Organizational identification refers to the extent to which a person personally identifies with, and tends to define himself or herself as a member in the employing organization. Levels of organizational identification have historically been lower in the United States than in other countries (notably Japan). Indications are that recent changes in organizational design (downsizing and de-layering) have reduced organizational identification even further. Although levels of organizational identification may be low in general in the U.S. workforce, we are concerned here with comparative levels of identification for members of different cultural identity groups.

Finally, *inter-group conflict* refers to levels of culture-group-based tension and interpersonal friction. Research on demographic heterogeneity among group members suggests that communication and cohesiveness may decline as members of groups become dissimilar.[6] Also, in the specific context of integrating minority-group members into organizations, concerns have been raised about backlash from white males who may feel threatened by these developments. It is therefore important to examine levels of inter-group conflict in diverse workgroups.

Types of Organizations

This six-factor framework will now be employed to characterize organizations in terms of stages of development on cultural diversity.[7] Three organization types will be discussed: the monolithic organization, the plural organization and the multicultural organization. The application of the six-factor conceptual framework to describe the three organization types appears in Exhibit 18.2.

Monolithic Organization

The most important single fact about the monolithic organization is that the amount of structural integration is minimal. The organization is highly homogeneous. In the United States, this commonly represents an organization characterized by substantial white male majorities in the overall employee population with few women and minority men in management jobs. In addition, these organizations feature extremely high levels of occupational segregation with women and racioethnic minority men (racially and/or culturally different from the majority)

EXHIBIT 18.2

ORGANIZATIONAL TYPES

DIMENSION OF INTEGRATION	MONOLITHIC	PLURAL	MULTICULTURAL
Form of Acculturation	Assimilation	Assimilation	Pluralism
Degree of Structural Integration	Minimal	Partial	Full
Integration into Informal Org.	Virtually none	Limited	Full
Degree of Cultural Bias	Both prejudice and discrimination against minority-culture groups is prevalent	Progress on both prejudice & discrimination but both continue to exist especially institutional discrimination	Both prejudice and discrimination are eliminated
Levels of Organizational Identification*	Large majority-minority gap	Medium to large majority-minority gap	No majority-minority gap
Degree of Intergroup Conflict	Low	High	Low

*Defined as difference between organizational identification levels between minorities and majorities.

concentrated in low-status jobs such as secretary and maintenance. Thus, the distribution of persons from minority-cultural backgrounds is highly skewed on all three components of function, level, and workgroup.

To a large extent, the specifications on the framework's other five dimensions follow from the structural exclusion of people from different cultural backgrounds. Women, racioethnic minority men, and foreign nationals who do enter the organization must adopt the existing organizational norms, framed by the white male majority, as a matter of organizational survival.

Ethnocentrism and other prejudices cause little, if any, adoption of minority-culture norms by majority group members. Thus, a unilateral acculturation process prevails. The exclusionary practices of the dominant culture also apply to informal activities. The severe limitations on career opportunities for minority-culture members creates alienation. and thus the extent to which they identify with the organization can be expected to be low compared to the more fully enfranchised majority group.

One positive note is that intergroup conflict based on culture-group identity is minimized by the relative homogeneity of the workforce. Finally, because this organization type places little importance on the integration of cultural minority group members, discrimination, as well as prejudice, are prevalent.

While the white-male dominated organization is clearly the prototypical one for the monolithic organization, at least some of its characteristics are likely to occur in organizations where another identity group is dominant. Examples include minority-owned businesses, predominantly Black and predominantly Hispanic colleges, and foreign companies operating in the United States.

Aside from the rather obvious downside implications of the monolithic model in terms of under-utilization of human resources and social equality, the monolithic organization is not a realistic option for most large employers in the 1990s. To a significant degree, large U.S. organizations made a transition away from this model during the '60s and '70s. This transition was spurred by a number of societal forces, most notably the civil-rights and feminists movements, and the beginnings of changes in workforce demographics, especially in the incidence of career-oriented women. Many organizations responded to these forces by creating the plural organization.

Plural Organization

The plural organization differs from the monolithic organization in several important respects. In general, it has a more heterogeneous membership than the monolithic organization and takes steps to be more inclusive of persons from cultural backgrounds that differ from the dominant group. These steps include hiring and promotion policies that sometimes give preference to persons from minority-culture groups, manager training on equal opportunity issues (such as civil rights law, sexual harassment, and reducing prejudice), and audits of compensation systems to ensure against discrimination against minority group members. As a result, the plural organization achieves a much higher level of structural integration than the monolithic organization.

The problem of skewed integration across functions, levels, and work groups, typical in the monolithic organization, is also present in the plural organization. For example, in many large U.S. organizations racioethnic minorities now make up twenty percent or more of the total workforce. Examples include General Motors, Chrysler, Stroh Brewery, Phillip Morris, Coca-Cola, and Anheuser-Busch. However, the representations of non-whites in management in these same companies averages less than twelve percent.[8] A similar picture exists in workgroups. For example, while more than twenty percent of the clerical and office staffs at General Motors are minorities, they represent only about twelve percent of technicians and thirteen percent of sales workers. Thus, the plural organization features partial structural integration.

Because of the greater structural integration and the efforts (cited previously) which brought it about, the plural organization is also characterized by some integration of minority-group members into the informal network, substantial reductions in discrimination, and some moderation of prejudicial attitudes. The improvement in employment opportunities should also create greater identification with the organization among minority-group members.

The plural organization represents a marked improvement over the monolithic organization in effective management of employees of different racioethnic, gender, and nationality backgrounds. The plural organization form has been prevalent in the U.S. since the late 1960s, and in my judgment, represents the typical large firm as we enter the 1990s. These organizations emphasize an affirmative action approach to managing diversity. During the 1980s increased evidence of resentment toward this approach among white males began to surface. They argue that such policies, in effect, discriminate against white males and therefore perpetuate the practice of using racioethnicity, nationality, or gender as a basis for making personnel decisions. In addition, they believe that it is not fair that contemporary whites be disadvantaged to compensate for management errors made in the past. This backlash effect, coupled with the increased number of minorities in the organization, often creates greater inter-group conflict in the plural organization than was present in the monolithic organization.

While the plural organization achieves a measure of structural integration, it continues the assimilation approach to acculturation which is characteristic of the monolithic organization. The failure to address cultural aspects of integration is a major shortcoming of the plural organization form, and is a major point distinguishing it from the multicultural organization.

The Multicultural Organization

In discussing cultural integration aspects of mergers and acquisitions, Sales and Mirvis argued that an organization which simply contains many different cultural groups is a plural organization, but considered to be multicultural only if the organization *values* this diversity.[9] The same labels and definitional distinction is applied here. The meaning of the distinction between *containing* diversity and *valuing* it follows from an understanding of the shortcomings of the plural organization as outlined previously. The multicultural organization has overcome these shortcomings. Referring again to Exhibit 18.2, we see that the multicultural organization is characterized by:

1. Pluralism
2. Full structural integration
3. Full integration of the informal networks
4. An absence of prejudice and discrimination
5. No gap in organizational identification based on cultural identity group
6. Low levels of intergroup conflict

I submit that while few, if any, organizations have achieved these features, it should be the model for organizations in the 1990s and beyond.

Creating the Multicultural Organization

As I have discussed issues of managing diversity with senior managers from various industries during he past year, I have observed that their philosophical viewpoints cover all three of the organizational models of Exhibit 18.2. The few who are holding on to the monolithic model often cite geographic or size factors as isolating their organizations from the pressures of change.

Some even maintain that because American white males will continue to be the single largest gender/race identity group in the U.S. workforce for many years, the monolithic organization is still viable today. I think this view is misguided. By understanding the generic implications of managing diversity (that is, skill at managing work groups which include members who are culturally distinct from the organization's dominant group), it becomes clear that virtually all organizations need to improve capabilities to manage diverse workforces. Further, focusing too much attention on external pressures as impetus for change, misses the fact that gross under-utilization of human resources and failure to capitalize on the opportunities of workforce diversity, represent unaffordable economic costs.

Fortunately, the monolithic defenders, at least among middle and senior managers seem to represent a minority view. Based on my observations, the majority of managers today are in plural organizations, and many are already convinced that the multicultural model is the way of the future. What these managers want to know is how to transform the plural organization into the multicultural organization. Although progress on such transformations is at an early stage, information on the tools that have been successfully used by pioneering American organizations to make this transformation is beginning to accumulate.

Exhibit 18.3 provides a list of tools that organizations have used to promote organization change toward a multicultural organization. The exhibit is organized to illustrate my analysis of which tools are most helpful for each of the six dimensions specified in Exhibit 18.1.

Creating Pluralism

Exhibit 18.3 identifies seven specific tools for changing organizational acculturation from a unilateral process to a reciprocal one in which both minority-culture and major-ity-culture members are influential in creating the behavioral norms, values, and policies of the organization. Examples of each tool are given below.

Training and Orientation Programs.   The most widely used tool among leading organizations is managing or valuing cultural diversity training. Two types of training are most popular: awareness and skill-building. The former introduces the topic of managing diversity and generally includes information on workforce demographics, the meaning of diversity, and exercises to get participants thinking about relevant issues and raising their own self-awareness. The skill-building training provides more specific information on cultural norms of different groups and how they may affect work behavior. Often, these two types of training are combined. Such training promotes reciprocal learning and acceptance between groups by improving understanding of the cultural mix in the organization.

Among the many companies who have made extensive use of such training are McDonnell Douglas, Hewlett Packard, and Ortho Pharmaceuticals. McDonnell Douglas has a program ("Woman-Wise and Business Savvy") focusing on gender differences in work-related behaviors. It uses same-gender group meetings and mixed-gender role-plays. At its manufacturing plant in San Diego, Hewlett Packard conducted training on cultural differences between American-Anglos and Mexican, Indochinese, and Filipinos. Much of the content focused on cultural differences in communication styles. In one of the most thorough training efforts to date, Ortho Pharmaceuticals started its three-day training with small groups (ten to twelve) of senior managers and eventually trained managers at every level of the company.

Specific data on the effectiveness of these training efforts is hard to collect, but a study of seventy-five Canadian consultants found that people exposed to even the most rudimentary form of training on cultural diversity are significantly more likely to recognize the impact of cultural diversity on work behavior and to identify the potential advantages of cultural heterogeneity in organizations.[10]

In addition, anecdotal evidence from managers of many companies indicates that valuing and managing diversity training represents a crucial first step for organization change efforts.

New member orientation programs are basic in the hiring processes of many organizations. Some companies are developing special orientations as part of their managing diversity initiatives. Proctor and Gamble's "On Boarding" program, which features special components for women and minority hires and their managers is one example.

EXHIBIT 18.3

CREATING THE MULTICULTURAL ORGANIZATION: TOOLS FOR ORGANIZATION CHANGE

MODEL DIMENSION	TOOLS
I. Pluralism *Objective/s*: —create a two-way socialization process —ensure influence of minority-culture perspectives on core organization norms and values	1. Managing/valuing diversity (MVD) training 2. New member orientation programs 3. Language training 4. Diversity in key committees 5. Explicit treatment of diversity in mission statements 6. Advisory groups to senior management 7. Create flexibility in norm systems
II. Full Structural Integration *Objective/s* —no correlation between culture-group identity and job status	1. Education programs 2. Affirmative action programs 3. Targeted career development programs 4. Changes in manager performance appraisal and reward systems 5. HR policy and benefit changes
III. Integration in Informal Networks *Objective/s* —eliminate barriers to entry and participation	1. Mentoring programs 2. Company sponsored social events
IV. Cultural Bias *Objective/s* —eliminate discrimination —eliminate prejudice	1. Equal opportunity seminars 2. Focus groups 3. Bias reduction training 4. Research 5. Task forces
V. Organizational Identification —no correlation between identity group and levels of organization identification	1. All items from the other five dimensions apply here
VI. Intergroup Conflict *Objective/s* —minimize interpersonal conflict based on group-identity —minimize backlash by dominant-group members	1. Survey feedback 2. Conflict management training 3. MVD training 4. Focus groups

Language training is important for companies hiring American Asians, Hispanics, and foreign nationals. To promote pluralism, it is helpful to offer second language training to Anglos as well as the minority-culture employees, and take other steps to communicate that languages other than English are valued. Leaders in this area include Esprit De Corp, Economy Color Card, and Pace Foods. For many years, the women's clothier Esprit De Corp has offered courses in Italian and Japanese. At Economy Color Card, work rules are printed in both Spanish and English. Pace Foods, where thirty-five percent of employees are Hispanic, goes a step farther by printing company policies and

also conducting staff meetings in Spanish and English. Motorola is a leader in the more traditional training for English as a second language where classes are conducted at company expense and on company time.

Insuring Minority Group Input and Acceptance. The most direct and effective way to promote influence of minority-culture norms on organizational decision making is to achieve cultural diversity at all organization levels. However, an important supplemental method is through ensuring diversity on key committees. An example is the insistence of *USA Today* President Nancy

Woodhull on having gender, racioethnic, educational, and geographic diversity represented in all daily news meetings. She attributes much of the company's success to this action.

Another technique is explicitly mentioning the importance of diversity to the organization in statements of mission and strategy. By doing this, organizations foster the mindset that increased diversity is an opportunity and not a problem. Examples of organizations that have done this are The University of Michigan and the Careers Division of the National Academy of Management. The latter group has fostered research addressing the impact of diversity on organizations by explicitly citing this as part of its interest.

Another way to increase the influence of minority-group members on organizational culture and policy is by providing specially composed minority advisory groups direct access to the most senior executives of the company. Organizations which have done this include Avon, Equitable Life Assurance, Intel, and U.S. West. At Equitable, committees of women, Blacks and Hispanics (called "Business Resource Groups") meet with the CEO to discuss important group issues and make recommendations on how the organizational environment might be improved. CEO John Carver often assigns a senior manager to be accountable for following up on the recommendations. U.S. West has a thirty-three member "Pluralism Council" which advises senior management on plans for improving the company's response to increased workforce diversity.

Finally, a more complex, but I believe potentially powerful, tool for promoting change toward pluralism is the development of flexible, highly tolerant climates that encourage diverse approaches to problems among all employees. Such an environment is useful to workers regardless of group identity, but is especially beneficial to people from nontraditional cultural backgrounds because their approaches to problems are more likely to be different from past norms. A company often cited for such a work environment is Hewlett Packard. Among the operating norms of the company which should promote pluralism are: 1. Encouragement of informality and unstructured work; 2. Flexible work schedules and loose supervision; 3. Setting objectives in broad terms with lots of individual employee discretion over how they are achieved; 4. A policy that researchers should spend at least ten percent of company time exploring personal ideas. I would suggest that item 4 be extended to all management and professional employees.

Creating Full Structural Integration

Education Efforts.   The objective of creating an organization where there is no correlation between one's culture-identity group and one's job status implies that minority-group members are well represented at all levels, in all functions, and in all work groups. Achievement of this goal requires that skill and education levels be evenly distributed. Education statistics indicate that the most serious problems occur with Blacks and Hispanics.[11]

A number of organizations have become more actively involved in various kinds of education programs. The Aetna Life Insurance Company is a leader. It has initiated a number of programs including jobs in exchange for customized education taught by community agencies and private schools, and its own in-house basic education programs. The company has created an Institute for Corporate Education with a full-time director. Other companies participating in various new education initiatives include PrimAmerica, Quaker Oats, Chase Manhattan Bank, Eastman Kodak, and Digital Equipment. In Minnesota, a project headed by Cray Research and General Mills allows businesses to create schools of their own design. I believe that business community involvement in joint efforts with educational institutions and community leaders to promote equal achievement in education is critical to the future competitiveness of U.S. business. Business leaders should insist that economic support be tied to substantive programs which are jointly planned and evaluated by corporate representatives and educators.

Affirmative Action.   In my opinion, the mainstay of efforts to create full structural integration in the foreseeable future, will continue to be affirmative action programs. While most large organizations have some kind of program already, the efforts of Xerox and Pepsico are among the standouts.

The Xerox effort, called "The Balanced Workforce Strategy," is noteworthy for several reasons including: an especially fast timetable for moving minorities up; tracking representation by function and operating unit as well as by level; and national networks for minority-group members (supported by the company) to provide various types of career support. Recently published data indicating that Xerox is well ahead of both national and industry averages in moving minorities into management and professional jobs, suggests that these efforts have paid off (*Wall Street Journal,* November 5, 1989).

Two features of Pepsico's efforts which are somewhat unusual are the use of a "Black Managers Association" as a supplemental source of nominees for promotion to management jobs, and the practice of hiring qualified minorities directly into managerial and professional jobs.

Career Development.   A number of companies including Mobil Oil, IBM, and McDonalds have also initiated special career development efforts for minority personnel. IBM's long standing "Executive Resource System" is designed to identify and develop minority talent for senior management positions. McDonald's "Black Career Development Program" provides career enhancement advice, and fast-track career paths for minorities. Company officials have stated that the program potentially cuts a fifteen year career path to regional manager by fifty percent.

Revamping Reward Systems.   An absolutely essential tool for creating structural integration is to ensure that the organization's performance appraisal and reward systems reinforce the importance of effective diversity management. Companies that have taken steps in this direction include The Federal National Mortgage Association (Fannie Mae), Baxter Health Care, Amtrak, Exxon, Coca-Cola, and Merck. Fannie Mae, Baxter, Coca-Cola, and Merck all tie compensation to manager performance on diversity management efforts. At Amtrak, manager promotion and compensation are tied to performance on affirmative action objectives, and at Exxon, evaluations of division managers must include a review of career development plans for at least ten women and minority men employees.

For this tool to be effective, it needs to go beyond simply including effective management of diversity among the evaluation and reward criteria. Attention must also be given to the amount of weight given to this criterion compared to other dimensions of job performance. How performance is measured is also important. For example, in addition to work-group profile statistics, subordinate evaluations of managers might be useful. When coded by cultural group, differences in perceptions based on group identity can be noted and used in forming performance ratings on this dimension.

Benefits and Work Schedules.   Structural integration of women, Hispanics, and Blacks is facilitated by changes in human resource policies and benefit plans that make it easier for employees to balance work and family role demands. Many companies have made such changes in areas like child care, work schedules, and parental leave. North Carolina National Bank, Arthur Anderson, Levi Strauss, and IBM are examples of companies that have

gone farther than most. NCNB's "select time" project allows even officers and professionals in the company to work part-time for several years and still be considered for advancement. Arthur Anderson has taken a similar step by allowing part-time accountants to stay "on-track" for partnership promotions. Levi Strauss has one of the most comprehensive work-family programs in the country covering everything from paternity leave to part-time work with preservation of benefits. These companies are leaders in this area because attention is paid to the impact on advancement opportunities and fringe-benefits when employees take advantage of scheduling flexibility and longer leaves of absence. This kind of accommodation will make it easier to hire and retain both men and women in the '90s as parents struggle to balance work and home time demands. It is especially important for women, Hispanics, and Blacks because cultural traditions put great emphasis on family responsibilities. Organization change in this area will promote full structural integration by keeping more racioethnic minorities and white women in the pipeline.

Creating Integration in Informal Networks

Mentoring and Social Events.   One tool for including minorities in the informal networks of organizations is company-initiated mentoring programs that target minorities. A recent research project in which a colleague and I surveyed 800 MBAs indicated that racioethnic minorities report significantly less access to mentors than whites. If company-specific research shows a similar pattern, this data can be used to justify and bolster support among majority-group employees for targeted mentoring programs. Examples of companies which have established such targeted mentoring programs are Chemical Bank and General Foods.

A second technique for facilitating informal network integration is company-sponsored social events. In planning such events, multiculturalism is fostered by selecting both activities and locations with a sensitivity to the diversity of the workforce.

Support Groups.   In many companies, minority groups have formed their own professional associations and organizations to promote information exchange and social support. There is little question that these groups have provided emotional and career support for members who traditionally have not been welcomed in the majority's informal groups. A somewhat controversial issue is whether these groups hinder the objective of informal-network integration. Many believe that they harm integration by fostering a "we-versus-they" mentality and reducing incentives for minorities to seek inclusion in informal activities of majority-group members. Others deny these effects. I am not aware of any hard evidence on this point. There is a dilemma here in that integration in the informal networks is at best a long-term process and there is widespread skepticism among minorities as to its eventual achievement. Even if abolishing the minority-group associations would eventually promote full integration, the absence of a support network of any kind in the interim could be a devastating loss to minority-group members. Therefore, my conclusion is that these groups are more helpful than harmful to the overall multiculturalism effort.

Creating a Bias-Free Organization

Equal opportunity seminars, focus groups, bias-reduction training, research, and task forces are methods that organizations have found useful in reducing culture-group bias and discrimination. Unlike prejudice, discrimination is a behavior and therefore more amenable to direct control or influence by the organization. At the same time, the underlying cause of discrimination is prejudice. Ideally, efforts should have at least indirect effects on the thought processes and attitudes of organization members. All of the tools listed, with the possible exception of task forces, should reduce prejudice as well as discrimination.

Most plural organizations have used equal opportunity seminars for many years. These include sexual harassment workshops, training on civil rights legislation, and workshops on sexism and racism.

Focus Groups. More recently, organizations like Digital Equipment have used "focus groups" as an in-house, on-going mechanism to explicitly examine attitudes, beliefs, and feelings about culture-group differences and their effects on behavior at work. At Digital, the center piece of its "valuing differences" effort is the use of small groups (called Core Groups) to discuss four major objectives: 1. stripping away stereotypes; 2. examining underlying assumptions about outgroups; 3. building significant relationships with people one regards as different; 4. raising levels of personal empowerment. Digital's experience suggests that a breakthrough for many organizations will be achieved by the simple mechanism of bringing discussion about group differences out in the open. Progress is made as people become more comfortable directly dealing with the issues.

Bias-Reduction Training. Another technique for reducing bias is through training specifically designed to create attitude change. An example is Northern Telecom's 16-hour program designed to help employees identify and begin to modify negative attitudes toward people from different cultural backgrounds. Eastman Kodak's training conference for its recruiters is designed to eliminate racism and sexism from the hiring process. This type of training often features exercises that expose stereotypes of various groups which are prevalent but rarely made explicit and may be subconscious. Many academics and consultants have also developed bias-reduction training. An example is the "Race Relations Competence Workshop," a program developed by Clay Alderfer and Robert Tucker of Yale University. They have found that participants completing the workshop have more positive attitudes toward Blacks and inter-race relations.

Leveraging Internal Research. A very powerful tool for reducing discrimination and (to a smaller extent) prejudice, is to conduct and act on internal research on employment experience by cultural group. Time Inc. conducts an annual evaluation of men and women in the same jobs to ensure comparable pay and equal treatment. A second example comes from a large utility company which discovered that minority managers were consistently under-represented in lists submitted by line managers for bonus recommendations. As a result of the research, the company put pressure on the managers to increase the inclusion of minority managers. When that failed, the vice president of human resources announced that he would no longer approve the recommendations unless minorities were adequately represented. The keys to the organization change were, first obtaining the data identifying the problem and then acting on it. My experience suggests that this type of research-based approach is underutilized by organizations.

Task Forces. A final tool for creating bias-free organizations is to form task forces that monitor organizational policy and practices for evidence of unfairness. An example of what I consider to be a well-designed committee is the affirmative action committee used by Phillip Morris which is composed of senior managers and minority employees. This composition combines the power of senior executives with the insight into needed changes that the minority representatives can provide. Of course, minority culture-group members who are also senior managers are ideal but, unfortunately, such individuals are rare in most organizations.

Minimizing Intergroup Conflict

Experts on conflict management have noted that a certain amount of interpersonal conflict is inevitable and perhaps even healthy in organizations.[12] However, conflict becomes destructive when it is excessive, not well managed, or rooted in struggles for power rather than the differentiation of ideas. We are concerned here with these more destructive forms of conflict which may be present with diverse workforces due to language barriers, cultural clash, or resentment by majority-group members of what they may perceive as preferential, and unwarranted treatment of minority-group members.

Survey Feedback.   Probably the most effective tool for avoiding intergroup conflict (especially the backlash form that often accompanies new initiatives targeting minority-groups of the organization) is the use of survey feedback. I will give three examples. As one of the most aggressive affirmative action companies of the past decade, Xerox has found that being very open with all employees about the specific features of the initiative as well the reasons for it, was helpful in diffusing backlash by whites. This strategy is exemplified by the high profile which Chairman David Kearns has taken on the company's diversity efforts.

A second example is Proctor and Gamble's use of data on the average time needed for new hires of various culture groups to become fully integrated into the organization. They found that "join-up" time varied by race and gender with white males becoming acclimated most quickly, and black females taking the longest of any group. This research led to the development of their "on-boarding program" referred to earlier.

A final example is Corning Glass Works' strategy of fighting white-male resistance to change with data showing that promotion rates of their group was indeed much higher than that of other groups. This strategy has also been used by U.S. West which recently reported on a 1987 study showing that promotion rates for white men were seven times higher than white women and sixteen times higher than non-white women.

The beauty of this tool is that it provides the double benefit of a knowledge base for planning change, and leverage to win employee commitment to implement the needed changes.

Conflict-Resolution Training.   A second tool for minimizing intergroup conflict is management training in conflict resolution techniques. Conflict management experts can assist managers in learning and developing skill in applying alternative conflict management techniques such as mediation and superordinate goals. This is a general management skill which is made more crucial by the greater diversity of workforces in the '90s.

Finally, the managing and valuing diversity training and focus group tools discussed previously are also applicable here. AT&T is among the organizations which have explicitly identified stress and conflict reduction as central objectives of its training and focus group efforts.

Conclusion

Increased diversity presents challenges to business leaders who must maximize the opportunities that it presents while minimizing its costs. To accomplish this, organizations must be transformed from monolithic or plural organizations to a multicultural model. The multicultural organization is characterized by pluralism, full integration of minority-culture members both formally and informally, an absence of prejudice and discrimination, and low levels of inter-group conflict; all of which should reduce alienation and build organizational identity among minority group members. The organization that achieves these conditions will create an environment in which all members can contribute to their maximum potential, and in which the "value in diversity" can be fully realized.

ENDNOTES

[1] See, for example, Lennie Copeland, "Valuing Workplace Diversity," *Personnel Administrator,* November 1988; Badi Foster et al. "Workforce Diversity and Business," *Training and Development Journal,* April 1988, 38–42: and R. Roosevelt Thomas, "From Affirmative Action to Affirming Diversity," *Harvard Business*

Review, Vol. 2, 1990, 107–117.

[2] This definition has been suggested by Afsavch Nahavandi and Ali Malekzadeh, "Acculturation in Mergers and Acquisitions," *Academy of Management Review,* Vol. 13, 83.

[3] In his book, *Assimilation in American Life* (New York; Oxford Press, 1964) Gordon uses the term assimilation rather than integration. However, because the term assimilation has been defined in so many different ways, and has come to have very unfavorable connotations in recent years for many minorities, I will employ the term integration here.

[4] These definitions are loosely based on J.W. Berry, 1983. "Acculturation: A Comparative Analysis of Alternative Forms," in R.J. Samuda and S.L. Woods: *Perspectives in Immigrant and Minority Education,* 1983, 66–77.

[5] This conclusion is based on data from nearly 100 large organizations as cited in "Best Places for Blacks to Work," *Black Enterprise,* February 1986 and February 1989 and in Zeitz and Dusky, *Best Companies for Women,* 1988.

[6] Examples of this research include, Harry Triandis, "Some Determinants of Interpersonal Communication," *Human Relations,* Vol. 13, 1960, 279–287 and J.R. Lincoln and J. Miller, "Work and Friendship Ties in Organizations," *Administrative Science Quarterly,* Vol. 24. 1979, 181–199.

[7] The concept of stages of development toward the multicultural organization has been suggested in an unpublished paper titled "Toward the Multicultural Organization" written by Dan Reigle

and Jarrow Merenivitch of the Proctor and Gamble Company. I credit them with helping me to recognize the evolutionary nature of organizational responses to workforce diversity.

[8] See note 5.

[9] A.L. Sales and P.H. Mirvis, "When Cultures Collide: Issues of Acquisitions," in J.R. Kimberly and R.E. Quinn, *Managing Organizational Transition,* 1984, 107–133.

[10] For details on this study see, Nancy J. Adler, *International Dimensions of Organizational Behavior,* (Kent Publishing Co., 1986), 77–83.

[11] For example, see the book by William Julius Wilson which reviews data on educational achievement by Blacks and Hispanics in Chicago, *The Truly Disadvantaged: Inner City, the Underclass and Public Policy* (The University of Chicago Press, 1987). Among the facts cited is that less than half of all Blacks and Hispanics in inner city schools graduate within four years of high school enrollment and only four in ten of those who do graduate read at the eleventh grade level or above.

[12] For example, see *Organization Behavior: Conflict in Organizations,* by Gregory Northcraft and Margaret Neale, (The Dryden Press, 1990), 221.

Discussion Questions

1. What is multiculturalism? Why should managers be concerned with multiculturalism?

2. Explain how Milton Gordon's work on assimilation in the United States can be used to understand multicultural organizations.

3. Discuss the meaning of cultural bias and how it operates in organizations.

4. How does the plural organization differ from the multicultural organization?

5. What is the defining characteristic of multicultural organizations?

6. What is the argument against creating multicultural organizations and maintaining monolithic ones? Is Cox's argument for multiculturalism defensible? If not, why?

7. What are some methods currently in use by major companies to promote culturally diverse organizations?

8. In your view, what are the prospects for the widespread development of multicultural organizations in the United States during the next decade?

On the Idea of Emancipation in Management and Organization Studies

MATS AVESSON AND HUGH WILLMOTT

LEARNING OBJECTIVES

"On the Idea of Emancipation in Management and Organization Studies" by Mats Alvesson and Hugh Willmott will provide students with:

1. A framework for the critical evaluation of management and organizational behavior theory and practice

2. Knowledge of the Frankfurt School of Critical Theory and its focus on human emancipation

3. An understanding of possible new directions that organizational science will take in the 1990s

4. An opportunity to reflect on their philosophy of management and how they would implement it in modern organizations

The objective of this article is to reevaluate the concept of emancipation, developed by the Frankfurt School and other proponents of Critical Theory (CT)[1] in the light of recent critiques from poststructuralism, especially Foucault. Emancipation describes the process through which individuals and groups become freed from repressive social and ideological conditions, in particular those that place socially unnecessary restrictions upon the development and articulation of human consciousness. The intent of CT is to facilitate clarification of the meaning of human need and expansion of autonomy in personal and social life. Ultimately, its purpose is to enable "members of a society to alter their lives by fostering in them the sort of self-knowledge and understanding of their social conditions which can serve as the basis for such an alteration" (Fay,

1987: 23). Examples of authors in management and organization theory whose work is explicitly guided by this concern include Alvesson and Willmott (1992, In press), Burrell and Morgan (1979), Deetz (1992a), Deetz and Kersten (1983), Frost (1980), Jermier (1985), Mumby (1988), Stablein and Nord (1985), and Steffy and Grimes (1986). The more specific aim of this article is to apply and relate the idea of emancipation to the context of management and organization studies (i.e., a field of study that is ostensibly oriented to practical considerations).

Within mainstream management and organization studies (MOS), two dominant attitudes to the notion of emancipation can be found. One immediate, "hard-nosed" response to talk of emancipation is to reject any suggestion that management is in any way associated with such a fancy idea as emancipation. The role of management, it is argued, is to ensure the survival/growth/profitability of the organization or to satisfy shareholders/customers/(and to some extent) workers, or more cynically, to keep the shareholders/customers/workers off the backs of managers. The business of management, managerialists and Marxists might agree, is about safeguarding the interests of shareholders by controlling the productive capacity of workers (Storey, 1985). It has nothing to do with emancipation.

An alternative, "softer" response, closer but still at considerable distance from the position of CT (and of this article), is that much modern management theory is concerned with freeing employees from unnecessarily alienating forms of work organization. From human relations through quality of work life (QWL) programs to corporate culture, a priority of humanistic management theory has been to redesign material and symbolic conditions of work to facilitate the realization of higher order human needs (e.g., self-actualization), to improve job satisfaction, and to raise productivity. When management provides opportunities deemed to satisfy such needs, the

---

[1] We acknowledge the danger of lumping together members of the Frankfurt School who developed distinctive positions. See Connerton (1980), Held (1980), and Jay (1973) for comparatively accessible introductions to the complex and evolving positions of major figures within the School.

Source: Mats Alvesson and Hugh Willmott: "On the Idea of Emancipation in Management and Organization Studies," *Academy of Management Review,* July 1992, pp. 432–464. Copyright © 1992. Reprinted by permission.

"emancipation" of employees from alienating conditions of work is said to be complete.

From a perspective informed by CT, which is advanced in this article, this "softer" approach to "emancipation" can be given a reserved welcome. Critical theorists recognize employees as subjects who have higher order needs and appreciate the value of managing people in a caring, responsible manner. The welcome is qualified, however, because this "softer" approach is based upon a narrow and mystifying understanding of key prerequisites of emancipation. Such an approach mobilizes a discourse—a way of communicating about and, thereby, constituting the social world—of (bourgeois) humanism in which the emancipation of individuals is identified with the provision of opportunities for the fulfillment of their needs (as long as this fulfillment coexists with and, especially, improves organizational performance).

From a CT perspective, which is examined in depth in the following section, emancipation necessarily involves an active process (or struggle) for individual and collective self-determination. According to this perspective, researchers are skeptical about—though not necessarily implacably opposed to—the effects of top-down change, which are salient in most versions of humanistic management theory. For CT, emancipation is not a gift bestowed upon employees; rather it necessitates the (often painful) resistance to, and overcoming of, socially unnecessary restrictions, such as the fear of failure and sexual and racial discrimination. In the absence of this struggle, increased discretion bestowed by "soft" varieties of management theory is understood to have the (paradoxical) effect of weakening employees' capacity to reflect critically on their work situation, for example, where delegation of responsibility is accompanied by the (centralized) strengthening of corporate culture.[2]

Regarding CT, any substantial and lasting form of emancipatory change must involve a process of critical self-reflection and associated self-transformation. From this perspective, emancipation is not to be equated with, or reduced to, piecemeal social engineering directed by a somewhat benevolent management. Rather, its conception of the emancipatory project encompasses a much broader set of issues that includes the transformation of gender relations, environmental husbandry, the development of workplace democracy, and so forth.

Our concern, then, is to explore how the emancipatory impulse of Critical Theory may be retained, albeit in

revised form, in the face of theoretical and practical critiques from poststructuralist and practitioner positions. Without disregarding the contribution of CT's panoramic, utopian vision to the project of emancipation, we are concerned with making it more relevant and accessible to the more mundane world of management and organization. In particular, we seek to correct and go beyond CT's tendency to put down conventional wisdom. By engaging in a kind of conversation between these three orientations—of Critical Theorists, poststructuralists, and practitioners—we explore what space there may be for advancing the emancipatory project. First, a brief account of CT is provided and then three kinds of critique that believers of CT, particularly in the context of MOS, must take seriously are reviewed and formulated. Next, a framework for a modified understanding of emancipation as a response to this critique is described, a reconceptualization that is facilitated by distinguishing key dimensions of an emancipatory project. Finally, specific suggestions for emancipatory research are offered concerning ways of listening, writing, and reading where space is given to critical reflection/enhancement of emancipation as well as to other, more traditional aims.

The discussion circles around various topics—power, knowledge, improvement, autonomy, ends, and so on. Arguments, comments, critiques, and countercritiques arise from, and are directed against, each of the three orientations. Exploratory and perhaps provocative in nature, this article does not presume to have definitive answers to the questions it raises, nor does it claim to provide an integration or a reconciliation of the positions it examines. It does offer a set of brief exchanges, comments, and ideas as a contribution to a debate about the idea of emancipation in management studies, with CT taking center stage. Because the various themes explored in the article have more or less salience for the various voices that appear in the article, these can be heard at different times and to different effect. This discussion is highly tentative; it is meant to encourage greater dialogue between the mainstream and critical areas of management, but without harboring any illusions about differences in their respective positions. Therefore, our discussion is as open-ended as possible.

The Critical Theory Project of Emancipation

Critical theorists work within the Enlightenment tradition—a tradition originally dedicated to changing institu-

---

[2] Moreover, if a more participative management philosophy is combined with a corporate culture that successfully instills a restricted number of values into its employees, its emancipatory effects are severely dampened.

tions such as the divine right of Kings, the church, feudal bondage, and prejudiced and superstitious ideas. Researchers in this area have combined a philosophical understanding of the human basis of seemingly divine or superhuman (e.g., scientific) authority with an empirical investigation of contemporary ideas, dogmas, and prejudices. A fundamental claim of the proponents of CT is that social science can and should contribute to the liberation of people from unnecessarily restrictive traditions, ideologies, assumptions, power relations, identity formations, and so forth, that inhibit or distort opportunities for autonomy, clarification of genuine needs and wants, and thus greater and lasting satisfaction (e.g., Fay, 1987; Fromm, 1976; Habermas, 1971, 1984; Horkheimer & Adorno, 1947; Marcuse, 1964). The combination of philosophy with empirical investigation is of fundamental importance. Without philosophy, empirical study is understood to solidify and legitimize existing dogmas and prejudices. It appears to *mirror* reality. But it achieves this affect by disregarding how the behavior and belief (e.g., of employees) are historically and culturally conditioned and by paying no attention to the way research methodology and instrumentation are involved in producing and sustaining a *construction* of reality. Central to CT is the emancipatory potential of reason to *reflect* critically on how the reality of the social world, including the construction of the self, is socially produced and, therefore, is open to transformation. The task of Critical Theory is to combine philosophy with social science to facilitate the development of change in an emancipatory direction.

In Horkheimer's (1937/1976: 220) original formulation of CT, *critical thinking* is understood to be

> *motivated by the effort really to transcend the tension and to abolish the opposition between the individual's purposefulness, spontaneity, and rationality, and those work-process relationships on which society is built. Critical thought has a concept of man [sic] as in conflict with himself until this opposition is removed.*

This alienated state of consciousness is regarded as irrational when it is remembered that human beings are the producers, and not simply the receivers or products, of this knowledge. CT challenges the dominant, common-sense view of individuals as insular seats of consciousness that exist independently of the historical processes through which a (bourgeois) sense of being an autonomous individual is generated. In the absence of democratic control of the institutional media, including industry and science through which the consciousness of individuals is formed,

the representation and self-understanding of the subject as free and autonomous are viewed as an expression of "false-consciousness." Accordingly, a key objective of CT is to challenge those forms of knowledge and practice that serve to sustain the illusion of autonomy and to replace the illusion with a structure of social relations in which "autonomy" in the guise of individualism is transformed from a pillar of bourgeois ideology into a practical reality.

Through CT, researchers share the understanding that the value of science, including social science, resides in its potential to develop conditions (material and symbolic) that are beneficial to human beings. The tradition of the Enlightenment, out of which modern science emerged, offers the promise of applying the critical powers of reason to expose and remove contemporary forms of unreason, superstition, and dogmatism. In the field of management, one powerful dogma, challenged by "softer" philosophies of management, has been the belief that man is economically rational and that Taylorism provides the one best way of designing and managing work. The challenge illustrates another central thesis of CT: that science (recall Taylor's description of his principles as "scientific") can be used to legitimize new dogmas. With reference to the "softer," behavioral approaches to management, CT enables researchers to reflect critically upon their scientific credentials and practical limits (for overviews, see Alvesson & Willmott, 1992, In press). Uncritical acceptance of behavioral scientists' understanding of human needs, critical theorists suggest, amounts to the development of a new dogma that preserves conditions of work that deny or place socially unnecessary restrictions on processes of self-determination.

The dominant tendency of CT has been to dismiss modern management theory as an expression of technocratic thinking that seeks to manipulate human potential and desire in order to bolster a falsely naturalized status quo (Alvesson, 1987; Tinker & Lowe, 1984). Management theorists are criticized for failing to appreciate the historical, socially constructed nature of existing work processes and for interpreting individual employees' needs (e.g., for money, security, and self-actualization) as essential to human nature, rather than as a manifestation of the structure of social relations in which these needs are constructed and interpreted. When the existing order is viewed as a given, the fulfillment of individuals' needs can be satisfied only in terms of capitalism, an understanding that severely confines the space for integration between individuals and organizations. In the contemporary context, the authority of science and technology (for example, technocratic methods of decision making) as well as ideologies of managerialism (in which managerial expertise is viewed as the high priest/chief interpreter of rationality) are regarded as sources of mystification and restriction, equivalent to witchcraft and feudal bondage. In the workplace, the favoring of technocratic rather than democratic forms of organization and philosophies of management, and the equation of freedom with the perfection of market relations, are regarded as major (ideological as well as practical) obstacles to greater autonomy.

From a CT perspective, scope for realizing purposefulness, spontaneity, and rationality through the piecemeal reform of existing structures is understood to be limited, though nonetheless worth undertaking so long as these limits are recognized and appreciated. If the ideals of CT are to be fully realized, social structures must be radically changed so that they actively support and facilitate, rather than selectively and instrumentally exploit, expansion of purposiveness, creativity, and rationality. More specifically, the emphasis in decision making about how to manage and organize human and material resources must shift from a narrow focus on seemingly technically rational choices about the efficiency of alternative means (e.g., Fordism versus post-Fordism) to self-consciously rational choices about alternative ends (e.g., autonomy versus efficiency).

Given its attack upon established conceptions of science, policy, and practice, it is not surprising that CT has itself been marginalized by mainstream theorists and practitioners. Arguably, its marginality is associated with its apparent lack of realism and practical application. Clearly, CT is not something that can simply be plugged into existing systems to improve their emancipatory performance. And, for this reason, it may seem remote, aloof, and idealistic. There has been a reluctance to engage more directly with the microdynamics of everyday life, including the mundane world of management and organization. In common with other esoteric forms of analysis, CT has assumed a highly abstract, inaccessible form of communication that is easily perceived to express an elitist, pontificating attitude toward understanding people and change. Not only is the work of key figures in this tradition (e.g., Habermas, Adomo, and even Marcuse) dense, convoluted, and difficult to understand, it is also not assisted by what can easily seem to be a cavalier and dismissive attitude toward the mundane detail of key institutions and features of modern society, such as contemporary developments in management theory and practice. A large chasm exists between the experiences of employees (including managers) in today's corporations and Habermas's philosophical reflections on the ideal speech situation—communication free from the distortions of asymmetrical power relations and ideology—even though the application of the latter undoubtedly has potential to yield penetrating insights into processes of communication within modern organizations (Forester, 1989, 1992).

However, despite justifiable antagonism toward the holier-than-thou attitude of CT, we believe that it is right (a) to stress the connection between science and emancipation and (b) to highlight how this connection is weakened and distorted, if not entirely lost, in the sciences of management, including their "softer" variations. A central argument of this article, then, is that CT researchers' understanding of the emancipatory potential of (social and management) science must be preserved, but that criticism of their aloofness and idealism must also be taken seriously. This criticism has been most incisively developed by poststructuralists, such as Foucault (1980, 1982), who have questioned the assumption that "truth" can be separated from "power" and, relatedly, that the autonomous subject is an attainable ideal. This challenge strikes at the heart of CT because it confronts the basis of CT's "totalizing" critique of ideology and false consciousness.[3] Critiques found in poststructuralism (PS) are guided by a more skeptical understanding of the possibilities of emancipation. They emphasize how all forms of knowledge express relations of power that have the potential to become a new source of domination, and that any structure of social relations inevitably enables and constrains the autonomy of subjects. Accordingly, poststructuralists suggest a more cautious, less idealistic vision of emancipatory transformation. Nonetheless, they retain a commitment to questioning or "deconstructing" seemingly incontrovertible "truths" that exercise a constitutive, spellbinding power over modern subjectivity. In this key respect, poststructuralist critique, which stresses the ambiguous, open quality of seemingly fixed, taken-for-granted structures, is in sympathy with the emancipatory project of Critical Theory.

Critiques of Critical Theory

In this section we explore further some reservations about CT by elaborating three types of problems with critical the-

---

[3] In taking this focus, we recognize that there are significant differences and tensions within Critical Theory (e.g., between Adomo and Habermas), and we also are aware that the poststructuralism label has been actively resisted by many of the theorists to which it has been applied, including Foucault. For us, the contribution of these authors is more important than the labels that are attached to their work. Although the entire body of Foucault's work cannot be identified with poststructuralism, his work on the relation between power, truth, and subjectivity does have close affinities with the central concerns of poststructuralism (Weedon, 1988).

orists' ideal of social science as a facilitator of emancipation. Criticisms concerned with its *intellectualism* and *essentialism* are discussed first before relating its *negativism* to the marginalization of CT within management and organization studies. The types of critique differ substantially, but we believe that they are equally important. Finally, we argue that these three criticisms can be answered in a way that is responsive to the respective objections.

Intellectualism

At the heart of Critical Theory is an assumption that human reason is an emancipatory force that is constrained and distorted by historical conditions. These conditions, it is asserted, inhibit and deflect the ability of human beings to determine their own needs and shape their own destinies. Individuals *either* experience unnecessary frustration and suffering, or they are victims of alienation in which independence and reflection are weakened, for example, through the impact of science, technology, and mass media,which reduce the individual to a passive object of ego administration. As Fay (1987: 83), stressing the suffering aspect, observed:

> *Critical social science arises out of, and speaks to, situations of social unhappiness, as situations which it interprets as the result both of the ignorance of those experiencing these feelings and of their domination by others. It is this experience of unhappiness which is the wedge a critical theory uses to justify its entrance into the lives of those it seeks to enlighten and emancipate.*

In reflecting further upon the claims of CT, Fay questioned whether the sequence suffering → critical reflection → emancipation is as unproblematical as Habermas, for example, has suggested. In particular, he doubts the emancipatory powers attributed to human reason, a doubt that can be applied with no less force to the capacity of reason to reflect critically upon the passivity and alienation associated with social conditions which, far from inducing feelings of suffering, support almost uninterrupted consumption in which desires, and associated identities, are constituted and secured through the acquisition and disposal of a stream of commodities. Critical theorists acknowledge the appeal and power of consumption in producing feelings of pleasure and belonging, but they insist that feelings of emptiness and unfulfillment lie beneath the surface (Fromm, 1976; Scitovsky, 1976; Wachtel, 1983).

Without denying that reason is a potent source of emancipatory force, Fay (1987) argued that powers of reason are *inherently limited* by somatic learning, in which the logic of the contemporary social order becomes deeply anchored in the body. Crucially, change is not simply a matter of changing ideas because the influence of tradition and socialization affects the whole person. According to Fay, the person's cultural identity inhibits his or her capacity to exercise critical reason. Because human beings are "historical, embodied, traditional, and embedded creatures" (Fay, 1987), the responsiveness of subjectivity to rational, critical argument is quite limited. As a consequence, the highly abstract, cognitive emphasis of CT may prove less than effective in communicating its message and promoting critical self-reflection, let alone emancipatory practice. Indeed, the emphasis on reflection, evaluation, and freedom in social life may simply lead to recurrent self-questioning and suspicion of all social arrangements. Tendencies that lead a person to speculate on what he or she is doing and the optimality of the social order are, perhaps, as likely to create despair as to inspire a process of personal and social reconstruction. As Sartre reminded us, the burden of autonomy is not light.

In response to this criticism of CT, it is first worth noting that major proponents of CT, such as Horkheimer and Adomo (1947) and Marcuse (1964), were very conscious of the limitations of human reason but had no way of dealing with this problem. Their broad-brush critiques of the "totally administrated" or "one-dimensional" society were as much statements of despair as they were serious efforts to stimulate emancipation, even though Marcuse's book, *One-Dimensional Man,* had the paradoxical effect of contributing directly to a widespread questioning of dominant values (e.g., consumerism) and social arrangements which, he claimed, had been disabled by modern, technocratic consciousness.

Our response to these doubts about CT is to retain and foster a belief in the power of reason to question conventional wisdom and current practice but, at the same time, to acknowledge its limitations. Moreover, instead of understanding this power as either something universal or endemic to modern society, we are inclined, in the aftershock of the Holocaust, McCarthyism, and the Gulags, to regard the critical deployment of reason as a historical phenomenon that is salient during different eras. In our view, the means of sustaining, and perhaps reviving, the (limited and depleted) potency of critical reason is to develop CT in a direction that is less preoccupied with grand theorizing and is more prepared to learn from, and contribute to, localized theoretical and practical concerns—a criticism of the intellectualist bias of CT authors that is paralleled in poststructuralist arguments against metanarratives and totalizing critiques, to which we now turn.

Essentialism

The criticism of CT for being essentialist is directed at its inclination to reduce or totalize phenomena so that they fit into the interpretive powers of a single, integrated framework. Poststructuralists have complained about the totalism inherent in the proposal of an integrated framework that speaks with *one voice* (excluding others) (Calás & Smircich, 1987; Cooper & Burrell, 1988; Lyotard, 1979). A second issue, central to the challenge of PS, has been the assault on the idea of an autonomous subject. Against the essentialist idea of an integrated, coherent, homogeneous individual, PS theorists highlight the irrationality of values and seek to preserve fragmentation, inconsistency, undecidability, variation, and heterogeneity.

According to humanist theory, including humanist MOS and the radical humanism of CT (Burrell & Morgan, 1979), it is assumed that beneath the alienated, fragmented surface of human consciousness there is an autonomous individual striving to come out.[4] Or as Weedon (1988: 21, emphasis added) puts the argument, humanism "presupposes an *essence* at the heart of the individual which is unique, fixed and coherent." It is precisely this assumption that is challenged by PS. According to PS, subjectivity is the product of diverse and contradictory discourses and practices through which individuals are routinely identified, and identify themselves, as more or less autonomous subjects. For proponents of PS, "The individual is both the site for a possible range of subjectivity and, at any particular moment of thought and speech, a subject, subjected to the regime of meaning of a particular discourse and enabled to act accordingly" (Weedon, 1988: 34).

As noted previously, humanistic MOS (Argyris, 1964; McGregor, 1960) researchers are inclined to assume the existence of a fixed set of needs which, when fulfilled by the employer, maximizes the individual's productivity as well as his or her job satisfaction. Critical theorists, in contrast, reject the (bourgeois humanist) idea that the full expansion of human autonomy can be accommodated

within the constraints of capitalist work organizations. According to CT, the death of God is the beginning, not the end, of the humanist project. Although modem individuals have been freed from feudal illusions (e.g., the divine rights of Kings), they/we are ensnared by contemporary illusions—such as the idea that freedom is fully realized by the opportunity to sell labor, participate in representative democracy, and apply science to rationalize existing means of organization without regard for the rationality of ends (which, according to positivist science, lie beyond the scope of rational evaluation, Habermas, 1971, 1972).

To justify their critique of contemporary illusions and social unhappiness, CT researchers have appealed to the idea that, at the core of individuals, is a (potentially) unified, rational autonomous subject—a subject that is currently alienated and degraded by the socially unnecessary demands of capitalist work organizations. (In MOS, this thesis is paralleled by McGregor's [1960] opinion that the autonomous core of individuals can be freed by shifting from a Theory X to a Theory Y philosophy of management.) Marcuse (1955), for example, identified human instincts as a possible drive against the totalizing control of advanced society. At present, however, the cognitivist version of CT proposed by Habermas is dominant. In his recent work, Habermas (1984) argued that the idea of autonomy and solidarity is a condition of every communicative act, however deceptive or distorted specific acts may be. Central here is the anticipation in every speech act of a free dialogue in a nonauthoritarian society in which the potentials in language for questioning, checking, and arguing are utilized.

Habermas assumed that, in principle, knowledge can be cleansed of power, and subjectivity emancipated, by achieving symmetry in its relations. The poststructuralist, in contrast, contends that the true/false, alienation/emancipation dichotomies are unsupportable. More specifically, Foucault (1980) has challenged the idea, central to CT, that the relationship between "knowledge" and "power" is purely negative and, relatedly, that the ideological aspects of the former can be eliminated by removing the latter. He argued that most, if not all, power relations incorporate elements that are positive for, and valued by, those populations whose subjectivity they constitute; moreover, any form of knowledge, however enlightened, exerts truth effects that are potentially contradictory in their consequences. So, for example, the idea that human reason has emancipatory potential can produce a form of critical theory (namely, Critical Theory), which privileges abstract theorizing and critiques over the

---

[4] The intellectual origins of humanism can be traced to the Enlightenment, when Man [sic], through the agency of reason, "postulated the human, as opposed to a divine, construction of the ideal" (Dawe, 1979: 375).

fostering of critical insights into mundane philosophies and practices.

Turning away from grand critiques based upon the idea of society as a totality, Foucault focused attention on what he termed the *microphysics* of power, that is, power as exercised in the context of a complicated network of power relations and struggles rather than as a purely repressive mechanism originating from a single unified source (such as capitalism, top management, the state, the union, or even mass culture or consumptionist ideology). The principle value of this approach, we believe, resides in the theorists' capacity to appreciate the complex and precarious dynamics of social organization without reducing its messy and often paradoxical qualities to a product of an essential, predetermined cause. In turn, this orientation opens up the possibility of appreciating the frailty and vulnerability of processes which, from a totalizing perspective, appear inevitable and unshakable. What, from a more distant or abstracted position, is too readily categorized and dismissed as an expression of "bourgeois ideology" or as a generator of "false consciousness" is appreciated as a more ambiguous phenomenon that, on closer examination, is contradictory in its formation and effects.

Negativism

The third complaint against CT concerns its negativism. Without denying the importance of questioning conventional beliefs and assumptions—a major task of academic knowledge, which is seriously underrepresented in MOS—there is a tendency to one-sidedness in many critical projects (including some of our own works), a one-sidedness which, in some respects, parallels the one-dimensional technicism that dominates conventional management theory (Alvesson & Willmott, In press). The negativity of CT creates problems both (a) in terms of how the objects and subjects of critique are represented and (b) in terms of demonstrating the relevance of the researchers' concerns.

This negative aspect, in combination with the intellectualism and essentialism in CT, may account for its very marginal presence within and impact on MOS. Although this position is largely attributable to the dominance of values that are antithetic to those of CT, antagonism is fueled by blanket dismissals of the preoccupations of practitioners and of MOS researchers as well as the inaccessibility of the language employed within CT. Difficulty in publishing critical research, especially in the United States, means that the critical approach has been marginalized and

silenced (Calás & Smircich, 1987). CT in management then hardly reaches a position from which "resistance" (and even less so, opposition) to mainstream management and organization theory can be exercised. Though mainstream researchers and gatekeepers bear considerable responsibility for limited interest in reflections on the role of interests and ideology in knowledge production, proponents of CT (including the authors of this text) are also culpable when their arguments are unnecessarily one-sided, negative, and unconstructive.

CT is marginalized not only because it is critical of the assumptions on which orthodox MOS is based but also because its researchers tend to adopt a holier-than-thou attitude, which is fundamentally uncompassionate and, as a consequence, uncommunicative. It is uncommunicative because it is perceived to simply "put down" conventional wisdom. Of course, conventional wisdom should not be spared critical examination, but there also must be a willingness for critical researchers to communicate in ways that are understandable and, it is hoped, amenable to others. What often makes critical theorists' critiques unacceptable, we suspect, is that (a) they fail to acknowledge the benefits of conventional wisdom as perceived by those who are committed to it and (b) they are arrogant in the sense of taking for granted the authority of their criticism. CT is not cared about because it appears to be uncaring. Paradoxically, a reluctance of CT researchers to engage in a dialog with mainstream, technicist, objectivist, and promanagerial researchers has contributed to its marginalization. Counter to its intentions, CT leaves the domination of the technocratic consciousness undisturbed, thereby confirming and refueling its contempt for conventional MOS.

To translate this criticism into the terminology of CT, outright dismissals of managerial ideology are *undialectical* insofar as they disregard or marginalize the contradictions and countertendencies within management philosophies. Because of the concentration on the *differences* between the contents of mainstream MOS theories and the emancipatory ideals of CT, the points they *share* are overlooked. There is a reluctance to recognize the most progressive potentialities in certain theories—for example, the contemporary role of at least some of the neohuman relations and corporate culture philosophies in problematizing some theory and practice concerning the widespread preference for an excessively narrow conception of rationality based on quantitative techniques of decision making. Excluded from the design of work processes, they observe, is the productive contribution of irrational, intuitive, and idiosyncratic actions. Shared here is a concern for how a purely technical conception of rationality inhibits creativity and exerts a deadening effect upon human organization. Shared, too, are the beliefs that people will respond positively to opportunities that enable them to expand their discretion or autonomy, and when they do so, they are more likely to act responsibly toward others.

In our view, these potentially emancipatory elements within parts of the conventional literature should be more adequately acknowledged. Without disregarding their manipulatory and negative features, their more progressive aspects should be recognized and welcomed *as a basis for exposing their ideological effects.* Instead of simply dismissing such theories as so much managerial hocus-pocus, it is important to appreciate how their power depends upon an ability to offer and provide a degree of emancipation, albeit circumscribed and contradictory, from the irrationalities of existing work processes. Insofar as opportunities for self-determination are promoted and facilitated, a central thesis of CT is to some extent confirmed: that an expansion of (behavioral) autonomy is possible without degeneration into anarchy.

At the same time, acknowledgment of these elements should not distract attention from the very limited potential of, for example, corporate culture theory to expand human autonomy. Its impact in the reverse direction—reduction of the opportunities for critical thought, rational self-clarification, and autonomy—is often more profound (Willmott, 1991b), and CT critique is here entirely relevant. The optimistic tone of neohuman relations and corporate culture, its portrayal of (potentially) contradiction-free social relations and human conditions within the given (unquestioned) order, and its (equally taken-for-granted) ends merit sustained critical examination from CT and PS.

A Rejoinder to the Critiques of CT

Having reviewed a number of criticisms of CT, primarily from PS but also from the position of conventional management theory and practice, we must add that these criticisms, in some cases, are a bit double-edged: Other forms of critical analysis, including PS, are not necessarily more innocent in terms of intellectualism, essentialism, and negativism.

A potential shortcoming of poststructuralists is their fascination with the ambiguous and comparatively open character of social processes, which becomes an end in itself, a focus that can deflect attention from the embeddedness of such processes within a wider, historical context. As Dews (1986: 33) argued in defense of Critical Theory (and Habermas, in particular) against poststructuralist critique:

> It is true that Habermas' work does not hold up a mirror to contemporary experiences of fragmentation, loss of identity, and libidinal release, in the manner which has enabled poststructuralist writing to provide the "natural" descriptive vocabulary. . . . But neither does it pay for its expressive adequacy and immediacy with a lack of theoretical and historical prospective.

Although this rebuttal of poststructuralism is more relevant for the arguments of Lyotard (1984) and many authors more interested in deconstruction than the analyses of Foucault, it nevertheless is important to direct attention to the esoteric and unconstructive features of poststructuralists' criticism of Critical Theory. Work that emphasizes the open, ambiguous character of language and devotes attention to the precarious nature of writings and texts easily lends itself to an exclusive, intellectual, intrascientific enterprise. In terms of accessibility and constructive critique, it is not necessarily an improvement upon CT. In fact, the negativity of CT (more so in the earlier versions than in Habermas) to contemporary society and its institutions is paralleled in poststructuralists' negativity to what is referred to as *grand narratives* (i.e., all forms of large-scale frameworks and projects, including the idea of a progressive development, which are said to be totalitarian) (Lyotard, 1979). (On this particular point PS harbors its own essentialism, in which all sorts of grand narratives, except its own, are viewed as essentially totalitarian, in an indiscriminate way [cf. Kellner, 1988].) It is arguable that the progressive ideals associated with the emancipatory project make the *mixture* of positive/constructive and negative/critical (and deconstructive) elements in CT less alien to practitioners and MOS than the more consistently "uncommitted" position of PS.

Foucault cannot be accused of being esoteric and intellectualistic. But neither does he leave his readers in an optimistic state concerning the chances for liberation. As Hoy (1986) pointed out, some interpreters view Foucault as writing a story of "the Rise of Unfreedom." For Foucault, disciplinary power lurks everywhere, also behind seemingly humanistic intentions and arrangements. Rorty (1985: 172) remarked that Foucault "forbids himself the tone of the liberal sort of thinker who says to his fellow-citizens: 'We know that there must be a better way to do things than this; let us look for it together.'" To counter this objection, it is relevant to insert a quotation from Foucault, which was generated by a (rarely expressed) impatience with critiques that rely upon essentialist assumptions of utopian schemes rather than engaging more directly in analysis of the microphysics of modem institutions:

> It seems to me that the real political task in a society such as ours is to critique the working of institutions which appear to be both neutral and independent, to criticise them in such a manner that the political violence which has always exercised itself obscurely through them will be unmasked, so that one can fight them. (Foucault in Elders, 1974: 171, cited in Rabinow, 1986: 6)

Even though we want to mobilize Foucault's writing in a project basically positive to emancipation, we realize that his ideas are not without ambiguity in this enterprise. This ambiguity is both a strength and a weakness. It is a strength because it injects a healthy dose of skepticism into the heady, intellectualistic realms of CT (as well as into the naive optimism of MOS). In particular, Foucault's contribution to PS has been to demonstrate the possibility of undertaking genealogical analyses of mundane processes and institutions (e.g., prisons and prison-like organizations) in a way that casts new light on their oppressive consequences and, thereby, contributes to a critique of these practices. But it is also a weakness because Foucault's position lacks any consistent normative orientations. Of course, for some, this weakness is a strength because, in principle, it inhibits the elevation of Foucault into an authority (although the current fascination for his work would seem to belie such an effect).

Summary and a Brief "Confirmative" Response to the Critique

To sum up, critical theorists are not alone in being guilty of intellectualism, essentialism, and negativism. What these slightly pejorative labels point to can also be described in more celebratory terms, which acknowledge the well-meaning intent that underpins the CT project. Nonetheless, these features of CT must be corrected if it is to have greater relevance for actors in ordinary organizational settings. In our opinion, this does not necessitate the jettisoning of the idea of emancipation as a guiding value of analysis. On the contrary, the idea of emancipation must be retained and reconstructed if social science is not to become a nihilistic enterprise in which the generation of knowledge is completely divorced from the values that

inspire and guide its production. Even if the idea of emancipation cannot be justified by appealing to rationality as a universal, it can be defended pragmatically by appealing to values that resonate with its concerns (Rorty, 1989).

A slackening of interest in grand critique facilitates an expansion of interest in the critical analysis of ordinary, everyday power relations and struggles. To paraphrase Geertz (1973), who argued that the (anthropological) concept of culture should be cut down in size so that it covers less and reveals more, the concept of intellectual emancipation should in a similar fashion be cut down in size in a way that allows it to tell a story that avoids too grandiose claims and, thereby, provides more space for other considerations and ideals (ranging from technical problem solving to the securing of tradition and identity) in a way that acknowledges the limited, but still vital, place of the idea of emancipation in human affairs.

Reconceptualizing Emancipation

Microemancipation

Our engagement with poststructuralist critiques of the "strong" program of Critical Theory leads us to emphasize *microemancipation*, in which attention is focused on concrete activities, forms, and techniques that offer themselves not only as means of control, but also as objects and facilitators of resistance and, thus, as vehicles for liberation. In this formulation, processes of emancipation are understood to be uncertain, contradictory, ambiguous, and precarious. Where power techniques are in operation, "loopholes" can be found. The idea of microemancipation is to search for such loopholes in managerial and organizational control that arise from the contradictory character of power techniques and their ideological reproduction. As Deetz (1992a: 336) expressed it, "With every 'positive' move in disciplinary practices, there is an oppositional one." Control is conceptualized not only as discipline and restriction of the space for action, but also as a potential source of critical thought and emancipation. All sorts of control efforts are understood to bring along signs or messages that can trigger suspicion, resistance, and critical reflections (i.e., emancipatory impulses).

Of course, the dialectic of control and resistance has been treated by several authors (e. g., Edwards, 1979), but mainly as a succession of conflicts between major, integrated managerial control strategies and large-scale or aggregates of similar small-scale reactions to these control forms. What we emphasize is the relevance and significance of another level and another type of emancipatory action, which is less visible and less grandiose. For example, it might be the redefinition of a verbal symbol launched by management for a particular purpose: Instead of being a vehicle for managerial control and integration, the symbol becomes a manifestation of irony and distance (e.g., Smircich, 1983). Similarly, status symbols such as office space, luxury equipment, controlled access to privileged areas, and so forth, often reinforce formal hierarchy and feelings of superiority/inferiority and support careerism; these also may draw attention to the arbitrariness and political nature of corporate arrangements, thus leading to skepticism rather than tighter discipline (Kunda, 1991).

Inherent in the concept of microemancipation is an emphasis on partial, temporary movements that break away from diverse forms of oppression, rather than successive moves toward a predetermined state of liberation. This micro view of emancipation differs markedly from the traditional conception of a one-way transformation of consciousness from "false" to "true" as the crucial element in the change from an oppressive social order to one that is in harmony with clarified wants and ethical principles. In our view, this view is consistent with critical theorists who have been consistently skeptical about the more grandiose claims of orthodox Marxism. The critical project is thus formulated as a precarious, endless enterprise; its believers fight continuously in order to create more space for critical reflection and to counteract the effects of traditions, prejudices, the ego administration of mass media, and so forth, which reduce the ways in which the social world can be understood and enacted (cf. Deetz, 1992a,b). It portrays the emancipatory idea not as one large, tightly integrated project, but rather as a group of projects, each limited in terms of space, time, and success.

The Costs and Paradoxes of Emancipation

Emancipation is seen as an element in struggles between the exercise of power and reactions to power techniques. It is important to recognize that power involves, apart from a possible starting point for emancipation, subordination as well as the expansion of productive capacities. Emancipation might involve a loss of gross productive capacities. For example, women emancipating themselves from dominant socialization patterns and gender roles may reduce

their interest in, and capacity for, caring. Employees freeing themselves from a Protestant work ideology may be less committed to and less capable of acting as socially responsible citizens. More generally, a critical questioning of beliefs and values might not only facilitate more rational thinking, recognition and clarification of neglected needs, ideas about fairness, and so on, but, in doing so, may estrange the individual from the tradition that has formed his or her very subjectivity. Anxiety, identity loss, and other severe problems might follow (Fay, 1987).

The costs of emancipation must be acknowledged, especially in critical studies of management and organization where present knowledge about effective and productive organizing can come into conflict with unrestricted emancipatory thinking. The price that has to be paid for many forms of liberation from dominant ideologies and external constraints may be high. For example, enhanced ecological consciousness and greater freedom and creativity at work—likely priorities emerging from emancipatory change—may result in bankruptcy and unemployment. The assumption that only irrationality, apart from the repressive power of an egoistic social elite, stands in the way of liberation, is far too simplistic. Emancipation will involve a trade-off between certain gains and certain losses. People might have persuasive reasons for refusing emancipatory invitations, including both fear of failure and fear of the effects of successful emancipation.

Simply paying attention to certain aspects of management and organization inevitably means that complex phenomena are selectively represented and illuminated, which easily creates a closed and fixed appearance of an open and ambiguous phenomenon. An antiemancipatory potential runs through all projects, even those with the best intentions and preceded by careful reflection. The dynamics and dialectics of emancipation mean that an idea, or an intended practice, can be subverted in its practical application. Even if it begins by opening up understanding or facilitating reflection, it can end up locking people into a certain, fixed, unreflective thinking (Willmott, 1991a). Critique and liberation from old dogmas is then followed by new dogmas. Somewhere in the process a theory guided by critical, emancipatory intent turns into an antiemancipatory force (cf. Horkheimer & Adorno's [1947] critique of the dialectics of enlightenment). The dark side of CT's emancipatory project must be acknowledged. Having said that, we must also resist defeatism. It may be acknowledged that Habermas's (1984) ideas on communicative action and reflective dialogue, for example, contain potentially antiemancipatory elements (i.e., an intellectualist ideology that stresses cognitive capacity and communicative skills as core values and offers a "total" framework [and thereby possibly excluding other voices] and arguably a pro-male bias [Meisenhelder, 1989]). But, on the whole, it would be fair to say that few, if any, socially and politically relevant theories or frameworks run so small a risk of turning into a totalitarian, antiemancipatory force.

The general point about the equivocality of theory has particular relevance for humanistic management and organization theory and practice. Awareness of the antiemancipatory elements in all good suggestions and prescriptions encourages deeper reflection of how seemingly humanistic ideas lend themselves to ideological usage. By considering antiemancipatory as well as emancipatory dimensions and potentials of humanistic management theory, some authors might be taken less seriously and less widely (and superficially) read, and it would improve the likelihood of the net result of the work being more in accordance with its stated intent.

A Note on Emancipation Myopia

Having argued for the virtues of emancipatory microprojects as well as the ambiguities of emancipation (irrespective of scope and intention), we must warn against an overreliance on local projects of emancipation. To reduce the emancipatory project to struggles around local practices might leave virtually undisturbed the vital sources of oppression associated with the laws and principles of capitalism, historically and culturally anchored gender stereotypes, and the domination of professional and managerial ideologies. Efforts to make space for increased discretion and autonomy on the purely local level may lead to a narrow kind of liberation in which local difficulties are (temporarily) ameliorated, but the deeper, structural problems mainly escape attention and correction.

Instead of understanding organizations as sites for emancipation only as a tightly integrated chain of institutions operating according to the logic of the iron cage, as Critical Theorists do, or as a setting in which fragmentary, uncoupled forms of micropower and local struggles are at play, as poststructuralists do, researchers could view organizations as loosely coupled orders harboring elements of oppression, that is, opportunities for emancipation that are to varying degrees connected to or are the products of a macrocontext. Within the context of MOS, the localized analysis is perhaps most relevant, but an emphasis on this should be accompanied with an understanding of the larger setting of local struggles. Acknowledging the signif-

icance of micropower and the problems of totalizing frameworks should not lead to a neglect or denial of the historical and macrosocial conditions of management and organizational practice. We are not prepared to trade totalizing thinking for myopia.

Emancipation: Types and Focuses

To elaborate our reconceptualization of emancipation further, it is necessary to develop a more refined understanding of the nature and object of emancipatory efforts. To this end, a distinction can be drawn between the *type* of emancipatory project and the *focus* of its interest. As with many such distinctions, its value is heuristic: In practice the different types and foci of emancipation merge into one another. Nonetheless, this heuristic provides a point of departure and offers a stimulus for developing a more adequate conceptualization of some key dimensions of emancipatory projects.

On the first dimension we distinguish a questioning from a utopian type of emancipatory project. The first involves the challenging and critiquing of dominant forms of thinking. Existing thinking and social arrangements are met by suspicion and are scrutinized. The aim is to combat the self-evident and the taken-for-granted. This kind of project is primarily concerned with investigating and problematizing. It strives to challenge and resist authority (and its disciplining effects) without proposing an alternative agenda or set of prescriptions. In contrast, another type anticipates a utopian state or an overall "vision," which avoids or minimizes the current problems. Perhaps, it should be stressed that the utopian element is not a matter of providing a recipe for the good life or fixing the mind in a narrowly specified direction. CT is antiauthoritarian and aims only to counteract ideologies and social arrangements that obstruct human freedom, not filling the latter with particular contents. The utopian element emerges when the current conditions are confronted with a new form of ideal, which aims at opening up consciousness for engagement with a broader repertoire of alternatives. Utopianism then represents alternative thinking rather than the suggestion of a ready-made, better alternative or the providing of courses for action. Between these types, we identify projects that favor and articulate an incremental or reformistic type of emancipation, in which liberation from certain forms of oppression is indicated.

These types often concentrate on participatory processes. Of course, questioning and incremental approaches often involve a utopian element. A critique implicitly assumes a possible superior state or emancipatory change of direction. Some proponents of PS might object to this idea. But in many cases ideas about deconstruction are influenced by an alternative set of ideas, which "drives" their efforts in a certain direction. Authors who draw on ideas about deconstruction as well as feminism are an example (e.g., Martin, 1990).

At this point we consider the focus or the primary object of emancipatory efforts. Here we make an analytical distinction among means, social relations, and ends. Again, it is necessary to acknowledge the purely heuristic quality of this distinction. Means refer to discourses and practices that are valued for their supposed ability to make ends achievable. Emancipatory projects that address means challenge the necessity and value of established methods of organization, such as the hierarchical and fragmented division of labor, certain leadership styles, or technocratic modes of control that have been questioned by humanistic as well as radical analyses. Ends refer to the purpose of organizational or managerial activity. The emancipation of ends is concerned with unfreezing institutionalized priorities and, thereby, opening up debate about the practical value of economic growth, consumption, the quality of life and so on. Finally, the inclusion of social relations as a focus draws attention to distributions of equalities/inequalities in terms of privileges and power. Of course, social relations cannot be divorced from either means or ends. But the focus on social relations moves beyond the overall ends that dominate the organizations and the particular means utilized for achieving these ends. Means such as participatory styles of coordinating work for the attainment of goals (e.g., ecologically sound production) do not necessarily touch upon issues like segmented labor markets, pay differences, or other forms of class, gender, or race inequalities. Emancipation directed against oppressive means and taken-for-granted ends does not empty the prospects for emancipation. Similarly, it is possible to imagine relatively successful emancipation that is directed at social relations (e.g., reduced power asymmetries) but that does not affect ends and means. Workplace democracy, for example, does not necessarily exclude high productivity as a taken-for-granted goal or an extensive division of labor as the appropriate means. A focus on social relations serves to highlight the ways in which the selection of particular means may be consistent with the ends to which they are directed—the use of bureaucratic means to achieve democratic ends is an obvious example.

In the workplace, "progressive," humanistic methods of organizing work are not necessarily or unproblematically emancipatory, even in an incremental way, despite their provision of better working conditions, reduced use of rules, and expansion of discretion. Not only may such reforms make little contribution to self-determination within a division of labor governed and preserved by inequalities of class, gender, and race, but, as noted previously, it is questionable whether this kind of reform will facilitate a change in practical consciousness in the direction of increased self-determination.

Figures such as the matrix in the preceding section do not mirror the intentions of people who are engaged in emancipatory projects. Rather, the figure presents a framework for guiding critical reflection on the character and scope of the discourses and practices that comprise MOS. Limitations of space prevent us from discussing the diverse ways in which the dimensions of emancipation are articulated within particular discourses and practices. We will illustrate only how the matrix can illuminate the content of theories. We start from the three foci and briefly explore types of emancipatory projects in relationship to these.

The primary object of study in MOS is *means*. Mainstream MOS is preoccupied with means in a purely technical, nonemancipatory fashion. Sociotechnical and QWL movements and some versions of corporate culture often express aspirations to be emancipatory. However, an instrumental rationality tends to dominate their actions. Such approaches are problematic in relationship to less compromised ideas about emancipation (Alvesson, 1987). The emancipatory potential is, however, worth noting. In terms of type, their position is incremental, whereas the questioning and utopian elements are weak.

When it comes to emancipatory projects aiming at changing *social relations* there is greater variety in terms of the type emphasized. Some contributions to participation are, like most means-focusing research, also incrementally oriented, but they incorporate a more ambitious interest in modifying social relations (e.g., Gustavsen, 1985). Typically, the interest lies in facilitating workplace democracy, often through action research and sometimes in collaboration with unions (Sandberg, 1981). Most Marxist-inspired approaches (e.g., Braverman, 1974; Clegg & Dunkerley, 1980) conceptualize emancipation as a matter of radically changing social relations. Their emphasis is typically utopian (and often questioning). They push for a classless society in which work is coordinated based on consensual social relations.

We can contrast this focus with authors who are suspicious of the wisdom of assuming the unequivocal value of pursuing dominating *ends*. CT-inspired authors and other radical humanists normally challenge these ideas and are more interested in the realization of somewhat abstract goals, such as human freedom, creativity, and rational dialogue. They are generally concerned with ideology critique (e.g., the critique of scientism), with a rather pure questioning orientation (Alvesson, 1987; Mumby, 1988). Sometimes there is an interest in more incremental projects, such as Habermas's (1984) ideas on undistorted communication and, based on that, include suggestions for improved professional practices such as in planning (Forester, 1989) and utopian ones, like Schumacher's (1974) ideas on small scale, ethical production or Burrell and Morgan's (1979) antiorganization theory.

As we argued previously, it is virtually impossible to maintain a hard and fast distinction between truly emancipatory discourse and practice in which the objective is strong yet flexible, and falsely emancipatory discourse and practice, which is more dubious and deceptive. However, although we are skeptical about the possibility and value of "purist" formulations of CT and, therefore, open for the possibility that emancipatory and deceptive elements might go together, we believe that it is important to foster an approach that facilitates efforts to define (theoretically and practically) a space between orthodox CT and humanistic MOS. It is especially important to resist the equation of micro-emancipation with (pseudo)humanistic versions of MOS, which promise full integration of human needs and dominating bureaucratic ideals, thereby devaluing if not denying the emancipatory impulse as it contributes to manipulative forms of practice and obscures contradictions.

When reflecting upon the emancipatory potential of discourse and practice, researchers' efforts should not be restricted to the narrow space covered by only one of the boxes in Figure 18.1. Emancipation, even in a macroversion, should encourage thinking and acting that transcend a singular type or focus, whether it is means, social relations or ends, or questioning, incrementalism, or utopianism. A narrow targeting of a specific space within the matrix of Figure 18.1 fragments and subverts the idea of emancipation, which is to open up, challenge and transcend constraints. In this case, it might be understood that we are arguing for a holistic version of emancipation. As we argued previously, we do not see this as the primary task within the context of management and organization theory. Combatting a narrow targeting of emancipation, which means that this label becomes inappropriate, does not necessarily lead to grand critique. Again, it is the space in between that we are seeking to open up.

The argument against restricting the project of emancipation to only one focus or type does not strike solely against grand versions of improvement and liberation. Even though it is insufficient in emancipatory projects to exclude the more mundane levels of incremental change and of means—and thereby, the concerns of organizational participants—it is also unsatisfactory to improve means without critically considering the wider context of social relations or alternative ends. Without the latter, we can hardly talk about emancipation. Many (most?) forms of organizational development and neohuman relations are disqualified (Alvesson, 1987). So are ideas about women in management and other issues of gender equality when they are reduced to social relations associated with equal access to career possibilities without any consideration of the

FIGURE 18.1

A MATRIX SUMMARIZING THE TYPES AND FOCI OF EMANCIPATION

TYPE OF EMANCIPATORY PROJECT	QUESTIONING	INCREMENTAL	UTOPIAN
Foci of emancipatory intent			
Means			
Social relations			
Ends			

more profound relationship between gender relations and organizational arrangements and goals (Alvesson & Billing, 1992; Ferguson, 1984). Such a constrained and constraining view of gender relations falls well short of the ideal of emancipation: Emancipation is incompatible with any effort at improvement that directs attention to a very narrow target and away from the social context in which it is produced. Certainly, the idea of emancipation as myriad small scale projects concentrates efforts on local problems and possibilities. But, in so doing, attention is paid to the social context and a view of the social macro-order as given and unproblematical is challenged.

Finally, we stress that recognition of the historical context of particular organizational and managerial manifestations is relevant. Emancipatory discourses and practice simply cannot be adequately developed without consideration of macrolevel ideas, ideologies, class, race and gender structures, economic principles and laws, and so forth, that organize the world of organization and management. Taking the idea of emancipation seriously (even when it is revised along the lines suggested here) does not leave the social totality unexamined, taken for granted, or undisturbed.

Reorienting Emancipatory Studies

So far, we have argued that the problems exposed by the critiques of Critical Theory invite a reformulation of the idea of emancipation in social science in general, and in management and organization studies in particular. An important element in such a project is the development of a new research strategy in which a "strong version" of Critical Theory (including its promises of fulfilling an emancipatory project of freeing people from frozen social relations) is suspended in favor of an eclectic framework, which includes perspectives/voices other than CT. The abstract, totalizing attack on the prevalent social order (late capitalism, class society, etc.) or another larger entity (management ideology, distorted communication, etc.) is set aside as space is made for analysis that draws attention to aspects of research objects that are unexplored within a purist formulation of CT.

Given the critique and suggestions made in the preceding sections, what research strategy might be fruitful? In response to this question, the purpose of this section is to point out some ways in which a new version of CT can

be materialized. Again, limitations of space place restrictions on the scope of our discussion. Here we concentrate on the contribution of academic emancipatory discourse and practice by considering (a) the value of ethnography for emancipatory studies, (b) a new approach to writing and the transmission of ideas, and (c) new modes of reading in the interpretation of ideas. We examine the conduct of researchers, the act of writing research and scholarship, and the assessment and reinterpretation of other (e.g., conventional) texts. We recognize that these proposals are neither comprehensive nor are they without precedent. Our purpose is not to recommend novelty as an end in itself but to highlight possibilities for reclaiming and reaccenting the idea of emancipation in the theory and practice of management and organization.

Listening to People

Letting people in organizations speak for themselves by conducting ethnographic studies is a vital means of moderating "totalizing" accounts of management and organization. Ethnography is a research process in which the researcher "closely observes, records, and engages in the daily life of another culture . . . and then writes accounts of this culture, emphasizing descriptive detail" (Marcus & Fischer, 1986: 18). In ethnography, the researcher is not just interested in behavior and structures, but also, and quite often more so, he or she is interested in symbols and meanings (Rosen, 1991). Researchers of critical ethnography accommodate and take more seriously the complexity, ambiguity, and inconsistency of people's discourse and practice, without falling into the empiricist trap of naturalizing the ideology, power, and communicative distortions (including the ambiguity of language) that are an integral part of management and organization. In opposition to those using interpretive ethnography, researchers using the critical version are sensitive to how meanings may carry privileged interests (Deetz, 1992a). A challenge for the critical ethnographer is to simultaneously concentrate on local actors' meanings, symbols, and values; to place these within a wider political, economic, and historic framework; and to prevent such a framework from pressing the material into a particular theory and language (a dominating voice), thus obscuring the ambiguities and variations of the empirical situation and the multiple ways in which it can be accounted for. The trick for the researcher is to be sensitive to all three elements and to avoid ignorance as well as hypersensitivity. Multiple voices is one slogan, but not all voices can speak at the same time, nor are all equally important to raise.

Creating space for pro- as well as antimanagement voices in the same text can be suggested as a part of a less heady emancipatory project. In-depth interviews are more likely to provide insights into how organizational members can hold both affirmative and critical opinions about a particular organization and how it is managed. The ethnographer's role is then one of "uncovering, reading, and making visible to others the critical perspectives and possibilities for alternatives that exist in the lives of his subjects" (Marcus & Fischer, 1986: 133).

Such a proposal is not entirely novel. There are now a number of examples of ethnographic-type studies of organizational work that have been informed by a broadly critical standpoint (e.g., Filby & Willmott, 1988; Knights & Collinson, 1987; Rosen, 1985). These studies have demonstrated the potential for applying CT in order to illuminate and challenge the oppressive and self-defeating features of modem organizations. Critique is made concrete through the presentation and analysis of empirical data. Instead of using or reducing an extract from an interview transcript to illustrate or confirm a grand theory, critique is performed often in an eclectic fashion, in order for the theorist to interpret the data in ways that are believed to carry emancipatory resonances for the reader.

However, these studies depart somewhat from the approach we advocate insofar as the negative, self-defeating aspects of organizational work are stressed without the authors fully acknowledging or exploring the more positive, productive features. Such an objective has been necessary and valuable as a corrective to mainstream, functionalist accounts of management and organization in which the negative aspects are either undisclosed, naturalized, or explained away by authors' interpreting them as symptomatic of individual managerial incompetence. But, there is also a danger of critical ethnographies alienating readers who, potentially, are open to their insights. Too often, the effect is not to unsettle existing preconceptions and dogmas but to convey a sense of self-righteousness and superiority which seems, paradoxically, to be dismissive of, or to poke fun at, the dilemmas and struggles of the people whose practices are the targets of critique. Of course, critical analysis demands a deflation of pretensions, including the (self)deceptions of those who occupy positions of relative power and advantage. But users of CT must also be sensitive to the accomplishments of those in power, and in particular relate such pretensions to the historical and existential conditions within which their subjectivity is constituted (Knights & Willmott, 1989). Otherwise, the critique is too readily interpreted and dismissed as one-sided and negative and, thus,

becomes self-defeating in its mission to communicate the value of emancipatory change.

One possibility is to undertake ethnographic studies that proceed from, and include, not only different critical perspectives, but a combination of "critical" and "noncritical" (e.g., managerial) perspectives, paying attention to the needs for liberation as well as the value of the efficient management of concrete organizational problems under contemporary conditions and restrictions. By addressing conflicts and contradictions as well as consensual matters, such an approach would be more novel and comprise a possibility for reducing the gap between CT and conventional MOS.

New Styles of Writing

The development of an empirically grounded, more accessible form of CT-inspired research can also be facilitated by new styles of writing. Current ideas about writing and experimenting might provide valuable sources of inspiration for CT researchers, but for reason of space we do not describe these (e.g., Calás & Smircich, 1991; Clifford & Marcus, 1986; Jeffcutt, 1991; Marcus & Fischer, 1986). To some extent this article, which encompasses three positions, illustrates the possibility of developing texts that are committed to a less abstract, intellectualistic, and negative view of emancipation.

A more general idea is to alternate between practitioner-friendly and critical-emancipatory textual elements. Such alternation can be more or less frequent, and the critical voice can be more or less salient. Given the traditional understanding of MOS as not being primarily in the business of emancipation, one could imagine a supplementary (or opposite) role of CT in writings typically concerned with traditional topics. Emancipation can reside in the wings, taking center stage in a text only when there is something of direct importance to say. Instead of focusing strongly on emancipation and critique in the overall approach, more muted and limited expressions of these impulses would be presented. Perhaps, critical reflection is more likely when, instead of providing a definitive, seemingly devastating critique of conventional wisdom, more explorations of (and scope for) competing interpretations are allowed and encouraged. Through *critical signaling* (using sentences or portions of texts that point to problems through the use of particular words, such as capitalism, male domination, manipulation, distorted communication, repression, etc.), suspicion and critical reflection are stimulated. Emancipation would be encouraged by drawing the reader's attention to particular issues in portions of a text, rather than by presenting the full critical story or complete writing within a critical discourse. The ideal of emancipation then enters in the form of interruptions or asides in the text.

Another important issue in terms of writing concerns self-reflection. Wherever possible, the text should stimulate reflection not only on the object of critique but also on the authority of the critique. Of course, this point is relevant not only for CT, but also for all writings (and not least those of mainstream MOS). The dangers associated with an exchange of the authority of one account for the authority of another must be recognized and reduced, if not eliminated. If the selection and interpretation of the material illuminates problems and tensions that are widely encountered and struggled with, then perhaps it is less likely that the account will be stored as another nugget of knowledge rather than applied, through a process of critical self-reflection, in order to illuminate and, to some degree, transform practice.[5]

Sometimes a text that is written with another kind of intention can be reinterpreted to assume a more emancipation-oriented character.[6] An example is Pondy's discussion of myths and metaphors. He believes that these are important because "they place explanation beyond doubt and argumentation. . . . In myth, the ordinary rules of logic are suspended, anomaly and contradiction can be resolved within the mythical explanation" (1983: 63). Therefore, myths and metaphors fulfill important functions.

Here Pondy makes a point that parallels the deconstructionist arguments of poststructuralists who seek to reveal how a sense of closure is accomplished by a text. In this case, closure is achieved through the use of metaphors and myths that effectively neutralize alternative, and potentially disruptive, accounts of the organizational reality. From the standpoint of CT, the presence of myths is oppressive when they frustrate reflection and thereby inhibit emancipatory change. However, from Pondy's managerialist standpoint, myths are uncritically embraced on the grounds that "attention to symbolic aspects is necessary for the effective management of organizations" (1983: 163).

Although emancipation presupposes doubt, and is encouraged by anomaly and contradiction, Pondy's observations have an antiemancipatory interest. The article would have encouraged the reverse kind of thinking if, instead, it had incorporated the understanding that critical attention to symbolic aspects is necessary for discovery of anomaly and contradiction, and—through that—the development of critical reflection among organizational participants.

This conclusion is fully consistent with Pondy's argument that myths and symbols obscure contradictions, but it triggers ideas and thoughts in an other, emancipatory, direction. Another possibility would, of course, be to present both types of conclusion or to make alternative and parallel readings and interpretations of a particular phenomenon. In such a case, a distinct critical-emancipatory interpretation could then follow, or be followed by, other kinds of readings without any compulsion to integrate the different readings. Creating a series of tensions and (precarious) resolutions within a text can make it more stimulating and enjoyable.

Looking for Emancipatory Elements in Texts

A third illustration of how a reconstructed concept of emancipation can be applied is in the reading of texts. As noted previously, users of orthodox Critical Theory are inclined to be dismissive of ideas that are intended to enhance the capacity of managers to raise the productivity of labor (such as Taylor's scientific management, human relations, and corporate culture). On the rare occasions when these ideas are considered by critical theorists, the focus is placed on their manipulative features without giving much attention to their (limited) progressive qualities or the contradictory consequences of their application (Alvesson, 1987; Fischer, 1984; Marcuse, 1964).

---

[5] The banking concept of knowledge is drawn from Freire (1972). It is a notion that directly echoes Horkheimer's (1937: 222) critique of the Cartesian understanding of knowledge, in which the "essential unchangeableness between subject, theory, and object" is assumed. The idea that all forms of knowledge can be subjected to a "banking" mentality also serves to expose the limitations of Habermas's notion of critique, which (as he has been obliged to concede) allows, if it does not actively encourage, the "banking" of its own insights rather than stimulating their application through a process of critical self-reflection on practical experience (Habermas, 1982: 233). The intent of Habermas's writing has been in the direction of totalizing critiques of modern society and transcendental defenses of the basis of such critiques rather than the development of methodologies for illuminating mundane practices in ways that are found to be rich in their emancipatory consequences for their participants. Some authors have, however, drawn upon Habermas's ideas in this direction (e.g., Forester, 1983, 1989; Gustavsen, 1985).

[6] Of course, we recognize that intentions are always ascribed (by authors or their readers) by mobilizing those interpretive schemes that are deemed to be more plausible or persuasive within particular (interpreted) contexts (Shotter & Gergen. 1989).

Yet, similar to humanistic management theory (e.g., McGregor, 1960; Weisbord, 1987), the corporate culture literature (Kanter, 1983; Peters & Waterman, 1982) and Critical Theory challenge the adequacy of theories that reduce human nature to a more or less sophisticated form of economic rationality. In each case, the application of a predominantly technical, universal conception of rationality is recognized to inhibit creativity and to exert a generally depressing effect on morale. By acknowledging employees' creative capacities, and by expanding opportunities for them to respond to situations in an innovative and "responsible" way, progressive management theory prescribes the replacement of rigid rules and procedures with an approach that allows flexibility and innovation within the parameters set by a few core values.

The basic argument of corporate culture writers is that improved corporate performance can be achieved by encouraging employees to identify with, and internalize, a limited number of superordinate corporate values:

> Let us suppose that we were asked for one all-purpose bit of advice for management, one truth that we were able to distill. . . . We might be tempted to reply, "Figure out your value system. Decide what your company stands for. What does your enterprise do that gives everyone the most pride?" (Peters & Waterman, 1982: 279)

It is not difficult to appreciate how such prescriptions can be interpreted as manipulative and ideological (Willmott, 1991b). Managers are being advised (a) to commit resources to defining and promoting a definition of the nature and purpose of their company and (b) to exploit their employees' desire for social recognition and meaning by producing an image that compensates for a lack of self-esteem and meaningful work. Deal and Kennedy (1982: 16) provided a more concrete illustration of this ideal:

> A strong culture enables people to feel better about what they do. . . . When a sales representative can say "I'm with IBM," rather than "I peddle typewriters for a living," he will probably hear in response: "Oh, IBM is a great company isn't it?" He quickly figures out he belongs to an outstanding company with a strong identity. For most people, that means a great deal. The next time they have the choice of working an extra half hour or sloughing off, they'll probably work.

Again, it is not difficult to see how the insecurity of individuals is being exploited by marketing a corporate image to employees (as well as customers) in a way that encourages them to reduce their insecurity by identifying more closely with the superordinate values of the company for which they work. However. in the process, employees are invited to question the necessity and value of many established forms of organizational control. It is stressed that people are more complex and have greater potential than is generally attributed to them (Deal & Kennedy, 1982, Chapter 3). According to the gurus of corporate culture, the goal is not simply to train or control people to work accurately and productively on the job which they are currently doing, but to regard their work as an opportunity for applying and developing their ability to innovate and to exercise their discretion. Within the boundaries defined by the culture (and here is the rub for Critical Theory), "people are encouraged to stick out, to innovate" (Peters & Waterman, 1982: 106).

It is rather easy to expose the limitations and antiemancipatory impulses of such a philosophy. The chief objection is that, in implementing this philosophy, corporations become more illiberal, if not totalitarian, institutions in which there is no tolerance of employees who question their sacred values (Soeters, 1986; Willmott, 1991b): "You either buy into their values or get out" (Peters & Waterman, 1982: 77). Certainly, corporations remain shackled to the task of achieving profitable growth to which the strengthening of corporate culture is currently perceived to be a relevant means. Yet, their attentiveness to the innovative and creative potential of employees also opens up opportunities for human growth, albeit distorted by corporate demands, which other philosophies of management control deny. In principle, the corporate culture enables employees to expand, albeit within well-defined limits, their sphere of "objective" autonomy and responsibility and, in doing so, constitutes subjects whose sights about the quality of their working lives are continuously raised by the expectations that the corporation instills into them.

Gains, however small in terms of increased discretion and improved job satisfaction should be appreciated as such, and they should not be measured exclusively against utopian visions of autonomy, creativity, and democracy—visions that have little meaning for the everyday life experiences and struggles of most organizational participants. This aspect should not be disregarded or dismissed when drawing attention to the more sinister and oppressive features of the corporate culture philosophy. Instead of simply rejecting the thesis that "autonomy is the product of discipline" as authoritarian and/or managerial, it is possible to acknowledge that the development of autonomy is impeded by insecurity and uncertainty without accepting that the discipline provided, or imposed, by corporate culture is consistent with autonomy in the sense of collective self-determination.

To be clear, we are not saying that the corporate culture approach qualifies as (micro)emancipation. The antiemancipatory elements are too salient, and it concentrates solely on means, taking corporate goals and management prerogatives as given, thus cementing these particular constraints (Stablein & Nord, 1985). But we are saying that corporate culture should not be a target of blanket rejection, for it can be mobilized in a version of CT committed to "small wins" and an interest in organizational practitioners. Observations of the importance of people's functioning regarding creativity, freedom, and meaning can be drawn upon as a basis for more sustained questioning of the priorities and ends of companies and working life.

Summary and Conclusion

In this article, we have sought to initiate and develop a discussion about humanistic management theory, Critical Theory (CT), and poststructuralism (PS). We have developed some ideas for management and organization studies guided by an idea of emancipation that takes account of PS critiques and tries to avoid the problem of being perceived as irrelevant.

Proponents of orthodox CT challenge the assumptions of consensus of values and the legitimacy of managerial prerogative that are taken for granted and celebrated within conventional management philosophies. However, CT's utopian, abstract orientation serves to expose antiemancipatory elements in humanistic management philosophy, to the exclusion of a sustained consideration of their contributions, albeit limited and compromised, to a questioning and/or incremental type of emancipatory project. We have suggested that an appreciation of key insights of PS facilitates a reconceptualization of the idea of emancipation that supports less grandiose and less remote forms of critical research and scholarship. In turn, this appreciation enhances the prospects of communicating with those who are open to questioning and reforming the truths of established management theory. To this end, we have constructed a framework for guiding a less ambitious and more compromise-oriented critical approach to management theory. Following this idea, we demonstrated how

our reconceptualization of emancipation can be applied so that the user can appreciate and assess the contribution of a variety of discourses and practices to the project of microemancipation. Finally, we illustrated how this project might be continued by encouraging new, experimental approaches to research, writing, and reading.

Scaling down CT is consistent with the recognition that, in common with all forms of knowledge, it is power-laden and can become a source of oppression. In the absence of critical reflection on their own claims, Critical Theorists can overlook how their identification of ideology and autonomy is historically (situationally) accomplished, an oversight that engenders the abstraction of knowledge from the social relations of its production. The challenge is to minimize the antiemancipatory elements and to foster the emancipatory impulse by encouraging questioning, reflection, and openmindedness. At the same time, if the emancipatory project is to be sustained, it is necessary to avoid the nihilistic tendencies within PS, where a concern to avoid contributing to "totalizing thinking" can become a stronger motive than taking the risk of trying to contribute to something positive and constructive. For us, the reconceptualization of CT (e.g., through critical ethnography) can make more concrete and relevant CT's established critique of technocratic consciousness in a way that promotes an appreciation and deflation of the grandiose, rationalistic pretensions of so much management and organization literature.

Encouraging a dialogue between CT and PS, especially the work of Foucault, we have suggested, is supportive of less abstract, ethnographically based studies of management and organization that render more accessible the rather remote, philosophical arguments of CT. This dialogue encourages an approach to writing and reading that is more open to the ambivalence both within management theory which, arguably, is not wholly "antiemancipatory," and in the arguments of CT which, with the benefit of a PS perspective, are not unambiguously emancipatory.

In a space between Critical Theorists' commitment to critical reason and radical change, the skepticism of poststructuralists about metanarratives and efforts to separate power and knowledge, and humanistic ideas for reducing the gap between human needs and corporate objectives, we locate an agenda for microemancipation. This agenda favors incremental change but, because it has open boundaries to more utopian ideas, it does not take as given the contemporary social relations, corporate ends, and the constraints associated with a particular macro-order. The preservation of the concept of emancipation (including microemancipation) from dilution or submersion by approaches that aim at other ideals and are often antie-mancipatory in their effect is of vital importance. A healthy interest in avoiding grandiosity in terms of the scope of the critique must not lead to a phobia about con-ceptualizing the significance and influence of the wider historical context of organizational thought and action. Otherwise, the microemancipation project becomes con-flated with the task of social engineering.

REFERENCES

Alvesson, M. 1987. *Organization theory and technocratic conscious-ness: Rationality, ideology and quality of work.* Berlin/New York: de Gruyter.

Alvesson, M., & Billing, Y. D. 1992. Organization and gender. Towards a differentiated understanding. *Organization Studies,* 13: 75-105.

Alvesson, M., & Willmott, H. In press. *Making sense of management: A critical analysis.* London: Sage.

Alvesson, M., & Willmott, H. (Eds.). 1992. *Critical management studies.* London: Sage.

Argyris, C. 1964. *Integrating the individual and the organization.* New York: Wiley.

Braverman, H. 1974. *Labor and monopoly capital.* New York: Monthly Review Press.

Burrell, G., & Morgan, G. 1979. *Sociological paradigms and organi-zational analysis.* London: Heinemann.

Calás, M., & Smircich, L. 1987. *Is the organizational culture litera-ture dominant but dead?* Paper presented at the 3rd Interna-tional Conference on Organizational Symbolism and Corporate Culture, Milan.

Calás, M., & Smircich, L. 1991. Voicing seduction to silence lead-ership. *Organization Studies,* 12: 567-601.

Clegg, S., & Dunkerly, D. 1980. *Organization, class and control.* London: Routledge & Kegan Paul.

Clifford, J., & Marcus, G. E. (Eds.). 1986. *Writing culture.* Berke-ley: University of California Press.

Connerton, P. 1980. *The tragedy of enlightenment.* Cambridge: Cambridge University Press.

Cooper, R., & Burrell, G. 1988. Modernism, postmodernism and organizational analysis: An introduction. *Organization Studies.* 9: 91-112.

Dawe, A. 1979. Theories of social action. In T. Bottomore & R. Nisbet (Eds.). *A history of sociological analysis:* 362-417. London: Heinemann.

Deal, T. E., & Kennedy, A. A. 1982. *Corporate cultures: The rites and rituals of corporate life.* Reading, MA: Addison-Wesley.

Deetz, S. 1992a. *Democracy in an age of corporate colonization: Devel-opments in communication and the politics of everyday life.* Albany: State University of New York Press.

Deetz, S. 1992b. Disciplinary power in the modem corporation: Discursive practice and conflict suppression. In M. Alvesson &

H. Willmott (Eds.), *Critical management studies.* London: Sage.

Deetz, S., & Kersten, S. 1983. Critical models of interpretive research. In L. Putnam & M. Pacanowsky (Eds.), *Communica-tion and organization:* 147-171. Beverly Hills. CA: Sage.

Dews, P. (Ed.). 1986. *Habermas: Autonomy and solidarity.* London: Verso.

Edwards, R. 1979. *Contested terrain.* London: Heineman.

Elders, F. (Ed.). 1974. *Reflexive water: The basic concerns of mankind.* London: Souvenir.

Fay, B. 1987. *Critical social science.* Cambridge, England: Polity Press.

Ferguson, K. 1984. *The feminist case against bureaucracy.* Philadel-phia: Temple University Press.

Filby, I., & Willmott, H. 1988. Ideologies and contradictions in a public relations department: The seduction and impotence of living myth. *Organization Studies,* 9: 335-349.

Fischer, F. 1984. Ideology and organization theory. In F. Fischer & C. Sarianni (Eds.), *Critical studies in organization and bureau-cracy:* 179-190. Philadelphia: Temple University Press.

Forester, J. 1983. Critical theory and organizational analysis. In G. Morgan (Ed.), *Beyond method:* 234-246. Beverly Hills. CA: Sage.

Forester, J. 1989. *Planning in the face of power.* Berkeley: University of California Press.

Forester, J. 1992. Fieldwork in a Habermasian way: The extraordi-nary character of ordinary professional work. In M. Alvesson & H. Willmott (Eds.), *Critical management studies.* London: Sage.

Foster, H. (Ed.). 1985. *Postmodern culture.* London: Pluto Press.

Foucault, M. 1980. *Power/knowledge.* New York: Pantheon.

Foucault, M. 1982. The subject and power. *Critical Inquiry,* 8: 777-795.

Freire, P. 1972. *Pedagogy of the oppressed.* Hammondsworth, Eng-land: Penguin.

Fromm, E. 1976. *To have or to be?* New York: Harper & Brothers.

Frost, P. 1980. Toward a radical framework for practicing organiza-tional science. *Academy of Management Review,* 5: 501-507.

Geertz, C. 1973. *The interpretation of cultures.* New York: Basic Books.

Gustavsen, B. 1985. Workplace reform and democratic dialogue. *Economic and Industrial Democracy*, 6: 4.

Habermas, J. 1971. *Toward a rational society*. London: Heinemann.

Habermas, J. 1972. *Knowledge and human interest*. London: Heinemann.

Habermas, J. 1982. A reply to my critics. In J. Thompson & D. Held (Eds.), *Habermas: Critical debates*. London: Macmillan.

Habermas, J. 1984. *The theory of communicative action* (vol. 1). Boston: Beacon Press.

Held, D. 1980. *Introduction to critical theory*. London: Hutchinson.

Horkheimer, M. 1976. Traditional and critical theory. In P. Connerton (Ed.), *Critical sociology:* Harmondsworth, England: Penguin (Original work published in 1937).

Horkheimer, M., & Adomo, T. 1947. *The dialectics of enlightenment*. London: Verso.

Hoy, D. C. (Ed.). 1986. *Foucault: A critical reader*. Oxford: Blackwell.

Jay, M. 1973. *The dialectical imagination*. Boston: Little, Brown.

Jeffcutt, P. 1991. *From interpretation to representation in organisational analysis: Postmodernism, ethnography and organisational culture*. Paper presented at the Towards a New Theory of Organization Conference, Keele University.

Jermier, J. 1985. When the sleeper wakes: A short story extending themes in radical organization theory. *Journal of Management*, 11(2): 67-80.

Kanter, R. M. 1983. *The change masters. Innovations for productivity in the American corporation*. New York: Simon & Schuster.

Kellner, D. 1988. Postmodernism as social theory: Some challenges and problems. *Theory, Culture & Society*, 5: 239-269.

Knights. D., & Collinson, D. 1987. Disciplining the shopfloor: A comparison of the disciplinary effects of managerial psychology and financial accounting. *Accounting, Organizations and Society*, 12: 457-477.

Knights, D., & Willmott, H. C. 1989. Power and subjectivity at work: From degradation to subjugation in social relations. *Sociology*, 23: 535-558.

Kunda, G. 1991. *Ritual and the management of corporate culture: A critical perspective*. Paper presented at the 8th International Conference on Organizational Symbolism, Copenhagen.

Lyotard, J.-F. 1984. *The postmodern condition: A report on knowledge*. Manchester: Manchester University Press.

Marcus, G., & Fischer, M. 1986. *Anthropology as cultural critique*. Chicago: University of Chicago Press.

Marcuse, H. 1955. *Eros and civilization*. Boston: Beacon Press.

Marcuse, H. 1964. *One-dimensional man*. Boston: Beacon Press.

Martin, J. 1990. Deconstructing organizational taboos: The suppression of gender conflict in organizations. *Organization Science*, 1: 339-359.

McGregor, D. 1960. *The human side of enterprise*. New York: McGraw-Hill.

Meisenhelder, T. 1989. Habemmas and feminism. The future of critical theory. In R. A. Wallace (Ed.), *Feminism and sociological theory:* 119-132. Newbury Park, CA: Sage.

Mumby, D. 1988. *Communication and power in organizations: Discourse, ideology and domination*. Norwood, NJ: Ablex.

Peters, T. J., & Waterman, R. H. 1982. *In Search of excellence*. New York: Harper & Row.

Pondy, L. R. 1983. The role of metaphors and myths in organization and in the facilitation of change. In L. R. Pondy, P. J. Frost, G. Morgan. & T. C. Dandridge (Eds.), *Organizational symbolism*. Greenwich. CT: JAI Press.

Rabinow, P. (Ed.). 1986. *The Foucault reader*. Harmondsworth, England: Penguin.

Rorty, R. 1985. Habermas and Lyotard on postmodernity. In R. J. Bernstein (Ed.), *Habermas and Modernity:* 161-175. Cambridge. MA: MIT Press.

Rorty, R. 1989. *Contingency, irony and solidarity*. Cambridge: Cambridge University Press.

Rosen, M. 1985. Breakfast at Spiro's: Dramaturgy and dominance. *Journal of Management*, 11(2): 31-48.

Rosen, M. 1991. Coming to terms with the field: Understanding and doing organizational ethnography. *Journal of Management Studies*, 28: 1-24.

Sandberg, Å. (Ed.). 1981. *Forskning för förändring* [Research for change]. Stockholm: Centre for Working Life.

Schumacher, F. 1974. *Small is beautiful*. London: Abacus.

Scitovsky, T. 1976. *The joyless economy*. Oxford: Oxford University Press.

Shotter, T., & Gergen, K. (Ed.). 1989. *Texts of identity*. London: Sage.

Smircich, L. 1983. Organizations as shared meanings. In L. R. Pondy, P.J. Frost, G. Morgan, & T.C. Dandridge (Eds.), *Organizational symbolism*. Greenwich, CT: JAI Press.

Soeters, J. 1986. Excellent companies as social movements. *Journal of Management Studies*, 23: 299-312.

Stablein, R., & Nord, W. 1985. Practical and emancipatory interests in organizational symbolism. *Journal of Management*, 11(2): 13-28.

Steffy, B., & Grimes. A. 1986. A critical theory of organization science. *Academy of Management Review*, 11: 322-336.

Storey, J. 1985. Management control as a bridging concept. *Journal of Management Studies*, 22: 269–291.

Tinker, T., & Lowe, E. 1984. One-dimensional management science: The making of technocratic consciousness. *Interfaces*, 14: 40-56.

Wachtel, P. 1983. *The poverty of affluence. A psychological portrait of the American way of life*. New York: Free Press.

Weedon, C. 1988. *Feminist practice and poststructuralist theory.* Oxford, England: Blackwell.

Weisbord, M. 1987. *Productive workplaces.* San Francisco: Jossey-Bass.

Willmott, H. 1991a. *Breaking the paradigm mentality.* Working paper, Manchester School of Management, University of Manchester Institute of Science and Technology.

Willmott, H. 1991b. *Strength is ignorance: Slavery is freedom: Managing culture in modern organizations.* Paper presented at the 8th International Conference on Organizational Symbolism, Copenhagen.

DISCUSSION QUESTIONS

1. What are the objectives and tasks of Critical Theory?

2. Describe the two mainstream views in management studies regarding the idea of emancipation.

3. Are the criticisms of Critical Theory—intellectualism, essentialism, and negativism—correct or essentially ill-founded as Alvesson and Willmott suggest?

4. What is microemancipation? Why do Alvesson and Willmott think that microemancipation is a useful avenue for research and practice?

5. In your view is the concept of emancipation as developed in this article an appropriate concern for managers? What about for workers, stockholders, and organizational researchers?

6. Speculate on changes in the nature of organizations (for example, management–worker relations, the role of women, ethnicity, handicapped persons) if emancipation were to become a central value and practice in industrial societies.

7. What forces are there at the current time that will either contribute to or suppress emancipation in the structuring and operation of organizations?

8. How do the main ideas of this article—the development of Critical Theory and emancipation—relate to the preceding articles? For example, which articles in this book are concerned with emancipation or a related concept, and which are concerned with control processes?

FOR FURTHER READING

Aktouf, O. "Management and Theories of Organizations in the 1990's: Toward a Critical Radical Humanism?" *Academy of Management Review* 17 (1992) 407–431.

Goldstein, I. and Gilliam, P. "Training System Issues in the Year 2000." *American Psychologist* 45 (1990) 134–143.

Kiernan, M. "The New Strategic Architecture: Learning to Compete in the Twenty-first Century." *Academy of Management Executive* 7 (1993) 7–21.

Morrison, A. and Von Glinow, M. "Women and Minorities in Management." *American Psychologist* 45 (1990) 200–208.

Nkomo, S. "The Emperor Has No Clothes: Rewriting "Race in Organizations." *Academy of Management Review* 17, (1992) 487–513.

Offermann, L. and Gowing, M. "Organizations of the future: Changes and Challenges." *American Psychologist* 45 (1990) 95–108.

JOHNSON CONTROLS AND PROTECTIVE EXCLUSION
FROM THE WORKPLACE (A)

Anne T. Lawrence

In 1990, Cheryl Cook was employed in a nontraditional job: she ran the ball mill, a two-story tall machine that made lead oxide at the Johnson Controls automotive battery plant in Bennington, Vermont. To get the job, the 34-year-old mother of two had had to undergo surgical sterilization. Under a "fetal protection" policy, adopted in 1982, Johnson Controls had decided to hire only infertile women for production jobs, because of the possible effects of maternal exposure to lead on unborn children. The United Auto Workers, the union representing most of the company's production workers, believed that the company's policy was illegal. In 1984, the union filed suit on behalf of all adversely affected employees, charging sex discrimination under Title VII of the Civil Rights Act. Like many women who worked for Johnson Controls, Cheryl Cook expressed resentment at the company's assumption that she was unable to make responsible reproductive decisions on her own. "[Y]ou should choose for yourself," she told a reporter. "Myself, I wouldn't go in there if I could get pregnant. But they [company managers] don't trust you." [1]

Johnson Controls, for its part, vigorously defended its policy of protective exclusion, despite the apparently discriminatory impact of the policy and the tough decisions it forced many female job applicants and employees to make. Medical evidence clearly showed, the company believed, that maternal exposure to lead could interfere with fetal development, causing neurological damage and other birth defects. "To knowingly poison unborn children," the company reasoned, was "morally reprehensible."

Moreover, the company argued that it had a legitimate right to protect itself from the expensive liability lawsuits that could result if a child were born with impairments traceable to its mother's occupational exposure. The company, which was in compliance with Occupational Safety and Health Administration (OSHA) lead standards for adult exposure, maintained that there was no technologically or economically feasible way to reduce lead levels in the battery-making process sufficiently to eliminate risk to the fetus.

After a long journey through the judicial system, the dispute between Johnson Controls and employees who believed themselves victimized by its policy came before the U.S. Supreme Court. In March 1991 after a series of contradictory decisions by lower courts, the high court would decide the legality of the Johnson Controls policy of protective exclusion in a landmark case that appeals court Judge Frank Easterbrook called "likely the most important sex discrimination case in any court since 1964, when Congress enacted Title VII [of the Civil Rights Act]." In the balance hung not only the fate of female employees and job applicants at Johnson Controls, but also that of perhaps as many as 20 million other women whose jobs exposed them to substances potentially hazardous to the fetus.

Johnson Controls, Inc.

At the time of the Supreme Court decision, Johnson Controls, Inc., was one of the nation's leading manufacturers of automotive lead batteries, particularly for the replacement parts market. Between its founding at the turn of the century and the late 1970s, Johnson Controls was engaged chiefly in the production of environmental controls, automotive seating, and miscellaneous plastic products. In 1978, the company purchased Globe Union, Inc., an independent battery manufacturer that had been in business for over 50 years. In 1990, the Globe Battery Division of Johnson Controls operated fourteen plants, extending from Bennington, Vermont, to Fullerton, California, and accounted for 16 percent of Johnson's sales and 20 percent of its income. That year, the company as a whole posted sales of $4.5 billion and employed 43,500 workers—approximately 5400 of them in the battery division.

Prior to the 1960s, few if any women worked in production jobs at Globe Union, reflecting long-standing historical patterns of gender segregation in which men worked in production jobs and women in office and support roles. In the 1970s, at Globe Union—as in many other businesses in those years—women began moving in increasing numbers into traditionally male occupations. Even by the mid-1980s, however, only a small percentage of women had production jobs. In the Bennington, Vermont, plant, for

Source: Anne T. Lawrence. "Johnson Controls and Protective Exclusion from the Workplace (A) and (B)." *Case Research Journal* Winter 1993: pp. 1–14. Copyright © 1993. Reprinted by permission.

example, only 5 percent of the production work force was female. Women never penetrated the top echelons of the company: in 1990, the company's fifteen top executives and twelve directors were all men.

The production process used in Johnson Controls' Globe Battery Division plants necessarily entailed exposure to lead, which is the element that enables an automotive battery to store and deliver electricity. As Denise Zutz, director of corporate communications at Johnson, bluntly put it, "[Without lead] no one would be driving a car."[2] To make a battery, Johnson Controls workers mixed lead oxide to form a paste, which was then compressed to form lead plates in the core of the battery. Lead dust and vapors were produced at multiple points in the production process. Johnson Controls, like other battery manufacturers, had made numerous efforts to develop a nonlead-based battery. Although several alternatives were currently in the experimental stage—including a zinc-bromide battery that Johnson had been researching for several years—none had yet been successfully developed for commercial use.

Lead Toxicity

Lead, a heavy metal, is one of the oldest known toxins. When lead particles are inhaled or ingested, they damage the central nervous, immune, reproductive, cardiovascular, and excretory systems of the body. At low levels, lead causes fatigue and irritability, at high levels, loss of consciousness, seizures, and eventually death. Lead-exposed individuals run a heightened risk of heart attack and stroke. According to the Centers for Disease Control (CDC), lead becomes dangerous to adults at blood levels of 50 micrograms per deciliter (mg/dl). Children suffer toxic effects from lead at even lower levels. Lead poisoning in children is caused mainly by inhaling leaded gasoline fumes and by swallowing peeling, leaded paint in older, poorly maintained buildings. At blood levels of around 25 mg/dl, children begin to show characteristic signs of lead poisoning: irritability, hyperactivity, lowered attention span, and learning difficulties. Higher doses, as in adults, can have even more serious consequences.

Lead also adversely affects the unborn. Lead in a pregnant woman's bloodstream crosses the placenta and enters the fetus's blood, at concentration levels similar to the mother's. Because its central nervous system develops rapidly, the fetus is particularly sensitive to lead. Exposure in the womb may lead to irreversible brain damage, resulting in intellectual and motor retardation, behavioral abnor-

malities, and learning deficiencies. It can also cause spontaneous abortion, low birth weight, premature delivery, and stillbirth. Adverse effects to the fetus have been detected at blood levels as low as 10 μg/dl, well below the CDC standard for adults.

One of the special difficulties with protecting the fetus is that lead is an accumulative toxicant, building up over time in the blood, soft tissues, and bones. Lead's half-life in the body is 5 to 7 years, and it often remains long after an individual has been removed from a high-lead environment. By a cruel twist of medical fate, pregnancy may actually increase levels of lead in the blood, since bones often decalcify during pregnancy to provide calcium to the developing fetus, mobilizing lead stored in the bones. Studies have shown that maternal lead blood levels may as much as double during pregnancy, even without additional exposure. Thus removing a woman from a high-lead workplace when a pregnancy is discovered—or even when one is planned—does not eliminate the risk of lead-caused damage to the fetus.

The effects of lead on male reproductive health are less well understood and more controversial. Lead affects male reproductive capacity: lead-exposed men may experience reduced sexual drive and, at high levels, impotence. Lead may also cause genetic damage to sperm, leading to birth defects. Most of the evidence for male-mediated effects comes from animal studies. A 1990 University of Maryland study, for example, found that lead-exposed male rats mated with unexposed females produced offspring whose brains developed abnormally. The researchers were unable to explain the biological mechanisms by which such male-mediated effects occurred, however, and the results of this study were not confirmed for humans.

Government Regulation of Lead Exposure

In view of the medical evidence on the hazards of lead, the Occupational Safety and Health Administration (OSHA) in 1978 adopted a standard requiring that employees be removed from worksites when their blood levels reached 50 μg/dl, based on an average of three consecutive blood tests. These employees were permitted to return when their blood levels fell to 40 μg/dl or below.

In setting its lead standard, OSHA also considered the impact of lead exposure on the fetus and the possible need to exclude pregnant or fertile women from high-lead workplaces. The agency concluded:

[T] here is no basis whatsoever for the claim that women of child-bearing age should be excluded from the workplace in order to protect the fetus or the course of pregnancy.[3]

OSHA did not set a separate standard for fetal exposure. However, the agency did recommend that individuals of both sexes who planned to conceive a child maintain blood levels below 30 μg/dl "because of the demonstrated adverse effects of lead on reproductive function in both males and females as well as the risk of genetic damage of lead on both the ovum and sperm."[4]

The Johnson Controls Lead Hygiene Program

Well before the OSHA lead standard was established, Globe Union and its successor, Johnson Controls, moved to protect their employees from the adverse effects of lead. In 1969 Dr. Charles Fishburn, then working for Globe Union and later the chief architect of Johnson's fetal protection policy, introduced a comprehensive lead hygiene program at the company. Globe (and later Johnson) instituted "housekeeping" measures and engineering controls to reduce lead dust and vapors in the air. For example, the company installed pumps to supply clean air to workstations and central vacuum systems and powered floor scrubbers and sweepers to keep its plants as free as possible of lead dust.

To prevent workers from carrying home lead particles, work clothing and footwear were provided by the company, and employees were given paid time at the day's end to shower and change into their personal attire. The company provided respirators and taught employees how to use them. Johnson maintained an active program of blood testing, and employees with blood levels above 50 μg/dl were transferred without loss of pay or benefits to jobs where the average level of workers was below 30. After purchasing Globe in 1978, Johnson invested $15 million in additional environmental engineering controls at its battery division plants.

Many observers, including those from the union, agreed that Globe Union, and later Johnson Controls, made significant progress in their industrial hygiene programs during the 1970s and 1980s. During this period, the company remained in substantial compliance with OSHA lead standards.[5]

Instituting a Voluntary Policy

In 1977, partly in response to the growing number of women in production jobs in its plants, Globe Union established its first policy on women in lead-exposed jobs. In promulgating this policy, the company noted:

[Protection] of the unborn child is the immediate and direct responsibility of the parents. While the medical profession and the company can support them in the exercise of this responsibility, it cannot assume it for them without simultaneously infringing their rights as persons. . . .

Since not all women who can become pregnant wish to become mothers, . . . it would appear to be illegal discrimination to treat all who are capable of pregnancy as though they will become pregnant.[6]

Observing that scientific evidence at that time had not conclusively established the risk of lead exposure to the fetus, the company did not officially exclude women capable of bearing children from jobs that exposed them to lead. However, the company issued the following warning:

[We] do feel strongly that those women who are working in lead exposure . . . and those women who wish to be considered for employment be advised that there is risk, [and] . . . we recommend not working in lead if they are considering a family.[7]

The company also required each woman to sign a statement saying that she understood the company's recommendation.

Globe Union did not guarantee transfers for women requesting removal from high-lead-exposure jobs, nor did it guarantee equal wage rates for those who did transfer.

The 1982 Fetal Protection Policy

In 1982, the company—now under the management of Johnson Controls—instituted a new "fetal protection" program in all its battery plants. Citing its ethical obligation not to engage in any activity threatening the well-being of any person, Johnson reversed its voluntary policy and announced its intention to exclude all fertile women from high-lead-exposure jobs in its battery manufacturing plants. It stated its policy as follows:

> [I]t is the [Globe Battery] Division's policy that women who arc pregnant or who are capable of bearing children will not be placed into jobs involving lead exposure or which could expose them to lead through the exercise of job bidding, bumping, transfer or promotion rights. This policy is intended to reduce or eliminate the possible unhealthy effects of lead on the unborn children of pregnant employees or applicants [8]

Johnson defined as "capable of bearing children" any woman under the age of 70 who could not provide medical documentation of sterility, regardless of her age, marital status, sexual orientation, fertility of her partner, use of contraception, or intention to bear children. The company explicitly stated that it was not its intention to encourage surgical sterilization:

> [The policy] is in no way intended to support or encourage women of childbearing capability to seek to change this status. Employees are strongly advised against any such action. [9]

For women already employed in lead-exposed positions, Johnson Controls applied a "grandfather" clause: they could continue to work at their present positions as long as they were able to maintain blood levels below 30 μg/dl in regular tests. If blood levels rose, they were permitted to transfer to other jobs without loss of pay, seniority, or benefits.

The fetal protection policy applied to all jobs in which any employee had recorded a blood level over 30 μg/dl, or where any air sample had exceeded 30 μg per cubic meter, during the previous year. Such high-lead-exposure jobs typically made up less than half of all production jobs. In practice, however, Johnson Controls' new policy excluded fertile women from virtually all production jobs, since most positions—even if not lead-exposed—were connected by chains of job bidding, transfer, or promotion to jobs that were exposed.

Justifying the New Policy

In justifying its move from a voluntary policy to one of protective exclusion, the main argument of Johnson Controls

was that the old policy had not worked. Between 1977 and 1982, at least six women in high-lead positions had become pregnant while maintaining blood levels above 30 μg/dl. One of the children born to these mothers, according to the company's occupational physician, showed some signs of hyperactivity, although this condition was never definitively traced to the mother's occupational exposure to lead. In addition, the company claimed that increased scientific understanding of the risk of lead exposure to the fetus since 1977 had heightened its concern for fetal health.

The company informed its employees that it had considered and rejected several less discriminatory policies, including voluntary exclusion, limiting exclusion to women actually pregnant or planning to become so, and transferring women whose blood lead levels rose above certain levels. Many pregnancies are unplanned, the company argued. Moreover, women often are unaware of pregnancy during the initial weeks, and—in any case—removal from the job after pregnancy has begun may be insufficient to eliminate fetal risk. To protect the unborn, therefore, Johnson officials argued they had no choice but to bar fertile women from high-lead jobs altogether.

Although the main stated reason of Johnson Controls for adopting an exclusionary policy was its concern for the unborn, the company was also influenced by fears of liability lawsuits from children adversely affected by their mother's occupational exposure to lead. The company believed it had a legal obligation to avoid injuries to "third parties," such as fetuses, resulting from the hazards of its manufacturing operations. In a brief filed later before the Supreme Court, the company's attorneys maintained:

> In this day and age, it cannot seriously be disputed that a company's desire to avoid direct harm to its employees and their families, its customers, and its neighbors from its own toxic hazards goes to the heart of its "normal operation."

The brief went on to quote with approval an opinion in an earlier court decision:

> [The] normal operation of a business encompasses ethical, legal and business concerns about the effect of an employer's activities on third parties. An employer might be validly concerned on a variety of

grounds both practical and ethical with the hazards of his workplace on the children of his employees.[10]

Although it delicately avoided addressing the issue directly, the company's point was clear: it was concerned about potential liability risk.

In assessing the extent of the company's exposure to possible liability lawsuits, Johnson Controls managers faced considerable uncertainty. Although employee suits against employers for injury at work are preempted by workers' compensation laws, most states permit the live-born child of an employee to sue its mother's employer for injuries caused in utero by the employer's negligence. Such suits, however, have historically been difficult to win. The causes of most birth defects are elusive. Moreover, in a situation in which an employer had followed all OSHA regulations and warned the mother of known hazards, a child would be hard-pressed to prove employer negligence. Prior to the time the Supreme Court considered the Johnson Controls case, in only one instance had a child sued an employer for its mother's occupational exposure to lead; this case had resulted in a jury verdict in favor of the employer, even though the employer had violated OSHA's maximum exposure rules.[11]

Women's Workplace Rights

Johnson Controls' new policy of protective exclusion—at the time probably the most comprehensive of any in place in U.S. industry—represented a bold challenge to the Civil Rights Act of 1964 and its subsequent amendments. The company's position raised serious questions about the nature of women's rights in the workplace, and how these were to be balanced against possible rights of the fetus and the employer.

Title VII of the Civil Rights Act of 1964 prohibits discrimination in employment on the basis of sex, as well as on the basis of race, color, religion, and national origin. In 1978, Congress passed the Pregnancy Discrimination Act (PDA), which amended Title VII by providing that the term "on the basis of sex" include "because of or on the basis of pregnancy, childbirth, or related medical conditions." That is, pregnant workers (and others distinguished by "related" conditions, such as potential for pregnancy) must, for all employment purposes, be afforded the same treatment as other workers with similar abilities.

In interpreting Title VII, as amended, the courts subsequently developed two frameworks for analyzing discrimination claims. If an employment policy is discriminatory on its face—for example, if it overtly excludes women from a particular job—it is permitted only if the employer can demonstrate that gender is a bona fide occupational qualification (BFOQ). In practice, the courts have interpreted BFOQs narrowly. For example, a department store may legitimately hire only men to model male fashions, but a fire department may not hire only men as fire fighters simply because the position is physically demanding.

On the other hand, if an employment policy is neutral on its face but in fact has an adverse impact on members of a protected class, the courts apply a weaker standard. In such so-called "disparate impact" cases, the employer need only demonstrate that its policy is dictated by a "business necessity." According to the United States Court of Appeals for the Fourth Circuit, "[The] test is whether there exists an overriding legitimate business purpose such that the practice is necessary to the safe and efficient operation of the business."[12]

In practice, the courts have held that employment practices that have a disparate impact are defensible only if they are clearly job-related. For example, a police department may be permitted to use written employment tests, even if minorities perform less well on them than do whites, if it can demonstrate that the tests accurately predict successful job performance.

The entry of increasing numbers of women into hazardous jobs in the 1970s and 1980s—and the subsequent efforts of employers to exclude them in the name of fetal protection—called the legal question: Were gender-based policies of exclusion to protect the unborn legal or illegal? And should specific policies be judged under the more restrictive BFOQ or the less restrictive "business necessity" standard? In 1982, when Johnson Controls managers adopted their fetal protection policy, these difficult matters of law remained unresolved.

The United Auto Workers Lawsuit

The union representing Johnson Controls employees, the United Auto Workers (UAW), believed that protective exclusion was unfair—and illegal. In 1984 the union filed suit, charging that Johnson Controls' fetal protection policy constituted illegal sex discrimination under Title VII and the Pregnancy Discrimination Act. Individual plaintiffs in the case included Mary Craig, a young woman who underwent sterilization in 1983 to keep her job; Elsie Nason, a 50-year-old divorcee whose pay was cut when she was forced to transfer out of a high-lead-exposure job; and Donald Penney, who was denied a transfer out of a high-lead area that he requested because he intended to start a family.

The union's key argument was that the policy of Johnson Controls violated Title VII of the Civil Rights Act because sterility was not a bona fide occupational qualification. The UAW brief argued that the company's policy was discriminatory on its face:

> Because Johnson Controls policy excludes women—
> and only women—from certain jobs precisely
> because of their capacity to bear children—that
> policy is facially discriminatory under the statute
> [Title VII] as amended by the PDA.[13]

Therefore, Johnson Controls would have to demonstrate a BFOQ. But sterility, the union insisted, had nothing to do with batterymaking: "Fertile women . . . produce batteries as efficiently and proficiently as anyone else."[14]

Since fertile women were just as capable of effectively performing the work as were men and infertile women, the employer had not demonstrated a BFOQ. In response to the contention of Johnson Controls that reproductive risks were mediated exclusively through the mother, the union presented medical evidence showing that lead posed a reproductive hazard for men as well as for women. Thus, the appropriate response was not to exclude women, but to reduce workplace exposures to lead for all workers, male and female. The union did not dismiss the employer's concern for fetal health as trivial or insincere. Indeed, the UAW acknowledged in its brief that "certain ethical and moral goals, including promoting child and fetal health, are widely accepted in this society."[15] However, it maintained that the determinants of fetal health were complex and influenced by many factors in addition to workplace hazards. In fact, the union argued, exclusionary policies themselves may be hazardous to fetal health, by pushing women out of jobs with good pay and medical benefits:

> [T]he relationship between fetal health and female
> employment is a complex one. There are . . . fetal
> risks both in the processes and materials used in

> many workplace situations and in depriving fertile
> and pregnant women of income through denial of
> employment opportunities.[16]

The plaintiffs also attacked the policy for assuming that women were unable to make independent, intelligent decisions about the conditions under which to bear children. The plaintiffs' attorney, Marsha Berzon, stated in her oral argument before the Supreme Court:

> The policy . . . is based on a negative behavioral
> stereotype about how women who are faced with
> possible fetal harm will behave. . . . In today's day
> and age, women in general can control whether or
> not they are going to have children.[17]

The mother, not the employer, she maintained, was best situated to assess possible risks and what was best for the child.

The union also argued that the fetal protection policy violated women's privacy. The UAW brief stated:

> Requiring proof of sterility as a precondition to
> obtaining or retaining a job is, in itself, a serious
> intrusion into very sensitive matters, even for those
> whose personal reproductive situation conforms to
> the employer's requirement.

The policy had the effect, furthermore, of pressuring some women to undergo sterilization, although the company explicitly denied that this was their intent.

Some women workers, the union noted, "are as a practical matter forced to choose between their job opportunities and their childbearing capacity. Since many women are economically dependent on their jobs, putting women to that choice conditions employment for women, but not for men, upon the ability to exercise 'the right to have offspring . . . one of the basic civil rights of man.'"[18]

Finally, the union argued that the policy of Johnson Controls, if upheld, would open the door to the exclusion of women from a very wide range of jobs entailing possible hazards to the fetus, thus effectively resegregating the work force. According to studies by the Bureau of National Affairs cited by the union, as many as 20 million jobs held by women involved exposure to possible fetotoxins; many millions more involved exposure to other risks, such as

PART V: CASE 1 Continued

infectious agents, stress, noise, radiation, or even ordinary physical accidents such as falls or automobile accidents.

The union also noted that in practice fetal protection policies had generally been limited to male-dominated occupations. For example, policies like Johnson Controls' were most common in production facilities in the chemical, automotive, and paint industries—all areas in which women constituted a minority. By contrast, women had rarely, if ever, been excluded on the basis of fetal protection from surgical nursing, childcare, or secretarial jobs, where they dominate the work force—even though anesthetic gases, rubella viruses, and radiation emitted by video display terminals were all documented fetal hazards. The union maintained that employers had not excluded women from these work settings, despite the possibility of fetal risk, for the simple reason that women were indispensable.[19]

If upheld by the courts, the union argued, fetal protection policies would therefore have the practical effect of reversing many of the gains women made in the 1970s and 1980s in moving into formerly male-dominated occupations and industries. Union attorney Berzon told the court:

> The net effect of upholding a policy of this type . . . would be to sanction the resegregation of the work force, particularly because the economics of the situation are that employers are going to install fetal protection policies in instances in which they are not dependent on women workers for the work force and not instigate them where they are highly dependent on women workers, because they would have nobody to do the job.[20]

By upholding the position of Johnson Controls, the union concluded, the court would "cut the heart out of Title VII and out of the Pregnancy Discrimination Act."

REFERENCES

1. Peter T. Kilborn. "Who Decides Who Works at Jobs Imperiling Fetuses." *The New York Times,* 2 September 1990: A1, A12.

2. Cathy Trost. "Business and Women Anxiously Watch Suit on 'Fetal Protection.'" *The Wall Street Journal,* 8 October 1990: A3.

3. Brief for the Petitioners at 2-3. International Union, United Automobile, Aerospace, and Agricultural Implements Workers of America. *UAW v. Johnson Controls, Inc.,* 111 S. Ct. 1196 (1991) (No. 89-1215).

4. *International Union UAW v. Johnson Controls,* 886 F.2d 871, 918 (7th Cir. 1989), rev'd, 111 S. Ct. 1196 (1991).

5. Kilborn, A1.

6. Brief for the Petitioners, at 2.

7. *International Union UAW v. Johnson Controls,* 886 F.2d at 876.

8. *International Union UAW v. Johnson Controls,* 886 F.2d, at 877.

9. *International Union UAW v. Johnson Controls,* 886 F.2d., at 878.

10. Brief for the Petitioners, at 18–19.

11. The case was *Security National Bank v. Chloride, Inc.,* 1985; it is discussed in the circuit court opinion in *International Union UAW v. Johnson Controls,* 886 F.2d at 886.

12. Margaret Post Duncan. "Fetal Protection Policies: Furthering Sex Discrimination in the Marketplace." *Journal of Family Law,* 28 (1989–1990): 733.

13. Brief for the Petitioners, at 20.

14. Brief for the Petitioners, at 31.

15. Brief for the Petitioners, at 37.

16. Brief for the Petitioners, at 39.

17. Official Transcript of Proceedings Before the U.S. Supreme Court at 8. *International Union UAW v. Johnson Controls,* No. 89-1215, October 10, 1990.

18. Brief for the Petitioners, at 16.

19. For further discussion of this point, see Mary E. Becker, "From *Muller v. Oregon* to Fetal Vulnerability Policies," *University of Chicago Law Review,* 53 (1986); M. Paul, C. Daniels, and R. Rosofsky, "Corporate Responses to Reproductive Hazards in the Workplace: Results of the Family, Work, and Health Survey," *American Journal of Industrial Medicine,* 16 (1989); and Deborah A. Stone, "Fetal Risks, Women's Rights: Showdown at Johnson Controls," *American Prospect,* Fall 1990.

20. Official Transcript of Proceedings Before the U.S. Supreme Court at 11-12. *International Union UAW v. Johnson Controls,* No. 89-1215, October 10, 1990.

Johnson Controls and Protective Exclusion from the Workplace (B)

On March 20, 1991, the Supreme Court, in a 6 to 3 decision, overturned the fetal protection policy of Johnson Controls, Inc., ruling that employers may not exclude women from jobs in which exposure to toxic substances could harm a fetus.

On the key point of the legality of Johnson Controls' exclusionary policy, the justices were unanimous. Since the company's policy was discriminatory on its face, the justices reasoned, the employer carried the burden of proving that incapacity to bear children was a bona fide occupational qualification, or BFOQ. All the justices agreed that because infertility was not a skill or aptitude related to the job, Johnson Controls' policy of fetal protection violated Title VII of the Civil Rights Act, as amended, and was therefore illegal.

In summarizing the opinion of the majority, Justice Harry A. Blackmun wrote:

> [W]omen as capable of doing their jobs as their male counterparts may not be forced to choose between having a child and having a job. . . . Employment late in pregnancy often imposes risks on the unborn child, . . . but Congress indicated that the employer may take into account only the woman's ability to get the job done. . . . Decisions about the welfare of future children must be left to the parents who conceive, bear, support and raise them rather than to the employers who hire those parents. Congress has mandated this choice through Title VII, as amended by the Pregnancy Discrimination Act. Johnson Controls has attempted to exclude women because of their reproductive capacity. Title VII and the P.D.A. simply do not allow a woman's dismissal because of her failure to submit to sterilization.[1]

Although all agreed that Johnson Controls' policy was illegal, the justices were divided on whether protective exclusion was ever justified. The court majority, led by Justice Blackmun, argued that Title VII prohibited all fetal protection policies. A minority of three, however, led by Justice Byron R White, maintained that the company's concern with fetal health was legitimate and that employers should be permitted to defend specific fetal protection poli-

cies in trial. Justice White was also more sympathetic to the argument that companies had a right to protect themselves against potential liability. In his minority opinion, he stated:

> Common sense tells us that it is part of the normal operation of business concerns to avoid causing injury to third parties, as well as to employees, if for no other reason than to avoid tort liability and its substantial costs.[2]

For their part, the union and many women's groups expressed great satisfaction at the outcome. The UAW's attorney, Marsha Berzon, expressed hope that the decision would lead to a reduction of workplace hazards for all workers and indicated that the union would press for back pay and other remedies. Joan E. Bertin, an attorney with the American Civil Liberties Union who had filed an amicus brief, reacted to the Supreme Court's decision by saying, "This is the end of fetal protection policies, and it reaffirms my faith in the judicial system."[3]

Some representatives of the business community, however, reacted differently. Quentin Riegel, deputy general counsel for the National Association of Manufacturers, said that the decision "will make it harder for companies to produce products safely and efficiently [and raises] a tough policy issue that Congress will have to address soon."[4] Jerry J. Jasinowski, president of the National Association of Manufacturers, was even more forceful in a newspaper guest editorial a few days later:

> There is no doubt in my mind that we'll see contingency-fee lawyers trying to dip into the "deep pockets" of responsible companies on behalf of damaged children as a result of this court decision. U.S. manufacturers are as innovative and productive as our foreign competitors. But our backward liability laws force companies to spend millions of dollars on legal fees instead of on new product research and development . . . Until Congress wakes up and allows reasonable exceptions to the Pregnancy Discrimination Act, future children will continue to be at risk and employers will face an impossible situation.[5]

PART V: CASE 1 Continued

References

1. "Excerpts from Court Ruling on 'Fetal Protection' Policy in Job Screening." *The New York Times,* 21 March 1991: A14. The full text of the decision appears in *UAW v. Johnson Controls,* 111 S. Ct. 1196 (1991) (No. 89-1215).

2. Linda Greenhouse. "Court Backs Right of Women to Jobs with Health Risks." *The New York Times,* 21 March 1991: A14.

3. Greenhouse, A14.

4. Joann S. Lublin. "Decision Poses Dilemma for Employers." *The Wall Street Journal,* 21 March 1991: Bl.

5. Jerry J. Jasinowski. "Protect Employers from Irrational Laws. " *USA Today,* 25 March 1991: 6A.

MANAGING ORGANIZATIONAL CHANGE: THE CASE OF A HOSTILE TAKEOVER

Barry Allen Gold

Alliance Energy's Problems and Prospects

In September 1987, John D. Molloy, CEO and President of Alliance Energy, Inc., was in the final stages of arranging financing to take the company private through a management-led leveraged buyout. By late October 1987, because of the stock market crash, credit markets collapsed; the inability to place debt instruments postponed Molloy's buyout plan.

By December 1987, Alliance, an independent producer of electric, steam, and alternative energy sources, struggled to survive. The unexpected simultaneous departure of three major customers caused a plunge in revenue.

These rapid business reversals forced Malloy to reconsider his plans for Alliance.

The Officers Meet

After exhaustive evaluation of the options—including a proposal to reorganize under Chapter 11 of the Federal Bankruptcy Code—Molloy and the other corporate officers decided to continue with plans to take the company private. The consensus of the officers according to Molloy was that,

> What created our problem was an unfortunate combination of a temporary business downturn and an historical aberration. In a relatively short time we'll find new customers or regain our old ones and the stock market will rebound. We have a successful track record, dedicated employees, and a good management team.

The officers changed the plan. They decided to sell selected assets immediately to reduce operating losses and improve the prospects of obtaining financing. Also, they decided to sell major parts—possibly put the entire company in play—three years after the buyout.

Alliance's History

Alliance was incorporated in 1982 by three former executives of a well-respected investment banking firm. Their experience was in financing energy and energy-related businesses. They also had sophisticated knowledge of the oper-

ational aspects of the energy business, government energy regulations, and federal tax law.

Alliance's business strategy was to produce energy using technologies that public utilities either neglected or had marginal interest in developing. A financial incentive was that private energy generation facilities were not regulated by rate of return restrictions that applied to public utilities.

Alliance's business developed in four closely related areas. Through a subsidiary it leased two coal-fired electric generating facilities that supplied power to public and private power users at wholesale rates. Alliance Thermal Energy Corporation owned and operated the steam systems in four major U.S. cities. Alliance also developed resource recovery facilities to convert solid waste to electric and thermal energy. Finally, the company acquired and operated alternative fuel technologies including one hydroelectric and two cogeneration plants.

Alliance, Inc. in 1987

Corporate Goal

From its inception Alliance's overarching goal was to increase revenues and profits at extraordinary rates. To achieve this goal management wanted rapid expansion through acquisitions financed with capital raised on public markets. This objective was pursued more aggressively in 1987 with the decision to take the company private.

Organizational Stucture

In December 1987 with John Molloy, who had spent seventeen years in investment banking, as its CEO and President, Alliance had 175 employees headquartered in Cleveland, Ohio. Sales in 1987 were $492,000,000 compared to 1982 sales of $10,000,000. During this period Alliance's profits steadily increased and were slightly above industry standards.

Alliance's organizational structure was designed to be minimal. There was no organization chart and key functions such as finance, sales, and operations were shared among the top and middle managers. Accountants and administrative assistants acted as a support staff. To maintain staffing flexibility most lower level positions in the company were performed by either outside contractors, such as maintenance or construction firms, or by independent contractors that often included operations personnel at generating facilities.

The guiding principle for this arrangement was senior management's philosophy of "constructive improvisation." This phrase encapsulated their belief that too much administration would limit opportunities for creative, quick decision making. A minimal administrative apparatus would permit employees to focus on essential business issues.

Consistent with their business philosophy, the senior managers spent little time in the corporate office. They preferred to meet with clients and bankers to create deals. As a result, administrative responsibilities were delegated to middle level managers and administrative assistants, many of whom had little experience in the energy industry. Another example of the management style was the deliberate absence of policies for employee sick days, vacations, or travel and entertainment expenses. Employees were expected to use their own judgment in these matters. The results were a few blatant abuses, some conflict over the control of resources, and an overall assessment by most employees that Alliance was a good place to work.

Alliance's Corporate Culture

Alliance's corporate culture resembled that of an investment banking firm. Instead of a clear, comprehensive business strategy, employees were exhorted to "go prospecting." Consistent with this approach executives were rewarded with large bonuses upon completing a deal. The result was to motivate employees to aggressively close deals to generate increased corporate revenue. But according to one middle level executive:

> Several of us sometimes worried that this produced excessively opportunistic and potentially fragile deal making. But we were making a lot of money and put our concerns aside.

In addition to the absence of centralized authority to structure and coordinate deal making, there was no systematic monitoring of contracts and customer satisfaction once deals were made. One consequence of the lack of integration was that employees at all levels were frequently "putting out fires" for dissatisfied customers. Some employees thought there were better ways to run a business, but most accepted frequent customer complaints as an inherent aspect of any business.

An example of a major deal that went awry was a 1985 steam generating contract for a midwestern city. Alliance's senior management negotiated a lucrative contract to supply steam for municipal buildings—including public hospitals—by a negotiated delivery date. Construction delays caused by strikes resulted in cost overruns and the inability to meet the deadline. The contract was invalidated and the city signed an agreement with another firm. A senior manager observed later that this episode was typical of Alliance's aggressiveness, which led to overly optimistic expectations of project completion. In his view,

> The basic contract was excellent. But it promised too much too fast. Unpredictable events—work stoppages, material shortages— were almost never taken into account when we made a deal.

This organizational structure, management style, and culture reflected the philosophy of Alliance's founders and managers. One of the initial partners recalled that:

> We saw certain problems and opportunities out there and found solutions to them or took immediate advantage of them. We tended not to focus on long-range plans but on survivability. That's how we understood our business. If the short term went well, the long term would fall into place. We liked to make quick deals. We didn't want to manage an organization.

Transition I

Molloy Announces the Buyout to Employees

On December 15, 1987, John Molloy presented details of the proposed management buyout and formation of Beta Energy, Ltd. to all Alliance employees. He did this for several reasons. First, he wanted to correct potentially destructive rumors concerning a corporate restructuring that were circulating throughout the company. Second, as a result of the rumors, many employees were extremely concerned about their jobs; anxiety created low morale and reduced productivity. Finally, the proposed leveraged buyout required the cooperation of the employees.

In the meeting Molloy explained the restructuring and the intention to sell assets. He also announced that the reorganization would take approximately one year and that financing was proceeding according to plans. In response to questions he acknowledged that the organization would be, "downsized in the near future but that most jobs were secure." In conclusion Molloy emphasized that Alliance intended to conduct "business-as-usual."

Employee Reaction

Despite Molloy's assurances that their jobs were not in immediate jeopardy, four percent of the employees left the company within two weeks. Another six percent were planning to leave. A typical employee comment was:

> Why should I stay here? Alliance was a good place to work but now everything has changed—the uncertainty is tremendous. There are plenty of jobs available and I'll find another good one.

During this period two employee factions formed. One group was a small number of employees familiar with the details of the buyout either because they worked on the SEC filings or were selected to be members of the new company. The second, larger group continued to learn details of the organizational changes through rumors; their increasing uncertainty over their futures with the company distracted them from work. A typical panic producing rumor was, "By next Wednesday everyone not already part of Beta will be fired."

Managing Internal Uncertainty

After several months of declining morale that further reduced employee productivity, Molloy reluctantly decided that it was necessary to offer a stop-gap motivation package. The objective of the plan was to reduce employee departures and restore efficient operations. The incentive plan was aimed at employees who were not involved in planning the buyout or promised employment in the new company.

To implement the plan Molloy sent an individualized letter to each employee. The letter restated the rationale for taking the company private, the need to sell selected assets, and the proposed reductions in staff. Each letter also contained an employment termination date for each employee, a monetary incentive—a large bonus—for staying until ter-

mination, and a list of tasks to be successfully completed before termination.

Because the monetary incentives were substantial, most employees—even those with fewer than six months before termination—decided to remain. Generally, compared to their performance before the monetary incentive they now worked harder.

Transition II

Enter Alfred T. Cronen, Jr.

But in April 1988, four months before Molloy's plan to reorganize as Beta Energy, Ltd. could be completed, Alliance became the target of a hostile takeover by an investor group led by Alfred T. Cronen, Jr.

Cronen was attracted to the independent energy business because of improved industry conditions created by the Public Utility Regulatory Policies Act of 1987. The Act required public utilites to buy power from privately operated facilities that complied with statutory standards. This created potentially larger and more stable customers for Alliance. But what really interested Cronen in Alliance was its precarious financial position.

After intense, complex negotiations, on July 11, 1988, Molloy's investment group unwillingly lost control of the company to Cronen. Despite difficulty in arranging financing Cronen pieced together enough capital to outbid Molloy's group. His bid was facilitated because the stock was thinly traded over-the-counter and the proposed price satisfied the Board of Directors. Also, because the company was small and virtually unknown outside the energy industry, no organized employee or community opposition interfered with the deal. Upon gaining control he started to restructure Alliance into the ATC Energy Group, Inc.

Cronen's Reputation

Alfred T. Cronen's reputation as a ruthless corporate raider preceded him to Alliance's employees. Cronen and his father had attempted, and in several instances succeeded, in highly publicized hostile takeovers of energy companies during the ten years prior to his bid for Alliance. Following the successful takeovers, the Cronens rapidly dismantled the companies to profit from the value of their assets. In the unsuccessful takeovers, the Cronens would end their hostile takeover actions when management bought their stock for a premium. The press labeled this tactic "greenmail."

Critics charged that these tactics distracted and ultimately weakened the management of otherwise well-run companies. The Cronens were also admonished because in their successful takeovers one result was massive employee layoffs. They countered that inept management created the opportunity for a takeover. Employee layoffs, they argued, were simply the result of prudent trimming of bloated payrolls.

Cronen's Strategy

Initial Actions

The "business-as-usual" atmosphere that Malloy's personal letter to each employee had created lasted only until rumors of Cronen's bid for Alliance reached the water coolers. Dismay, confusion, distrust, and diffuse anxiety affected all employees.

To quell the situation, the day after the tender offer was completed, Cronen held a company-wide meeting to present his vision for the ATC Energy Group, Inc.

In his forty-five minute presentation he painstakingly characterized his current management style and business philosophy as "totally different" than the "negative, error-filled media hype you have probably seen." To demonstrate the difference he announced that no ATC employees would be terminated (Molloy and two other senior managers had already resigned). He then explained that his strategic plan for ATC was different than both Molloy's, which was to sell the company, and his father's past practice of spinning off parts for asset values. Cronen told the employees:

> I have no intention to liquidate the company. We will sell only unproductive assets to help build and expand the remaining businesses. In my view the independent energy business has an extremely promising future. I'm here for the long haul.

Despite his straightforward approach and apparent sincerity, this meeting unsettled employees. Morale problems intensified and employee performance decreased; after his talk, another ten percent resigned.

Managing Internal Uncertainty Again

When Cronen became aware of the dispiriting effect of his ownership of ATC on employees, he had his chief operating

officer—whom he brought from outside—meet privately with every employee to explain ATC's business plan. The COO also outlined the employees' future with the company and answered questions. In these meetings no monetary incentives were offered other then regular salary for continuing work for ATC.

Within six weeks of Cronen's takeover only two Alliance executives remained at ATC. Increasing exits affected all levels in the organization; by the end of 1988, thirty-eight percent of the employees had resigned.

For many employees the departure of senior management and other personnel contributed to uncertainty. But Cronen viewed it as an opportunity to significantly change the company. He immediately implemented a new organizational structure and corporate culture designed to reflect his goals for ATC.

The Organization of ATC

Corporate Goals

Cronen's goals were corporate survival: to revitalize revenue and profits; to develop the business gradually—within a reasonable time frame; and to diversify through acquisitions. To accomplish this he thought it was necessary to set realistic short- and long-term objectives. Most importantly, according to Cronen, "The goals should be *corporate* goals, not *individual* goals."

Management Style

On taking control of ATC Cronen assumed an active, aggressive, and visible leadership style. To draw attention to the differences of his management from his predecessors', Cronen often referred to the Alliance's management style as, "shooting-from-the-lips."

The key members of Cronen's management team were a chief operating officer and a chief financial officer. The responsibilities of the COO were to direct and control the daily operations of the energy production facilities. The CFO's mandate was to develop a comprehensive financial plan and develop sources of funds for corporate acquisitions.

During the nine months after the takeover key decisions were made solely by Cronen, the COO, and the CFO. Eventually, when Cronen began to trust the remaining

Alliance personnel, he instituted weekly management meetings with other senior members from the finance, accounting, and operations groups. Cronen was the dominant actor in these meetings.

Organizational Structure

In addition to centralizing decision making, Cronen reorganized each functional division into hierarchical positions. He emphasized clear reporting relationships and specific managerial spans of control. He also had all middle level managers set short- and long-range goals, and produce written plans for achieving them. For example, each manager was required to specify goals and actions to improve customer service. These were reviewed by senior management—Cronen, the COO, and CFO—to determine if they fit corporate goals.

To prevent the new organizational structure from dissolving into Alliance's investment bank deal-making orientation, Cronen decided that only achievement of prespecified objectives would earn bonuses. In addition, he implemented policies intended to provide work satisfaction and career development within ATC, for example, a job posting system.

After one year senior management began to encourage and facilitate group decision making throughout the organization. At this time "trans-functional" groups that cut across departments were formed to coordinate corporate actions. Finally, by the end of the first year, comprehensive personnel policies were implemented concerning areas such as vacations, employee benefits, and expense accounts.

ATC's Corporate Culture

The culture that Cronen attempted to introduce into ATC was shaped by and intended to reflect his leadership style. For example, he insisted that all employees call him "Mr. Cronen." He also insisted that the chain of command be followed. He practiced and demanded punctuality. In addition, he and the senior officers formulated policies, established procedures, and enforced rules. Finally, Cronen and the senior managers frequently restated their intention to conduct business with a long-term orientation.

Cronen created ceremonial occasions such as corporate dinners to acknowledge the completion of a major business deal such as the acquisition of a generating plant or signing of a major customer. Other new rituals included corporate-sponsored family picnics, softball games, and celebration of employee birthdays.

Cronen's rationale for attempting to gain control of the corporate culture was based on his analysis of Alliance's culture and its consequences. He observed,

> We recognized that an "entrepreneurial" spirit existed at Alliance. At first it was useful—it got the company up and running. But it quickly got out of control and developed into an "every-man-for-himself" situation. There was an obsession with deals regardless of how they were put together. Many otherwise good deals fell apart because of this.
>
> We have tried to shift the emphasis to the "making" side of the equation but, at the same time, not forgetting about the other side of the equation—the deal. Alliance only saw the "deal" side of the equation. Just how much the culture can affect this remains to be seen—but I think that it can.

Assessing the Takeover

Corporate Performance

By December 1990, with gross revenues of $560,000,000, improved return on investment, and record profits, ATC Energy Group, Inc. had substantially outperformed its predecessor, Alliance Energy, Inc. Alfred T. Cronen, Jr., senior managers, and outside observers attributed the improved performance primarily to the reorganization of ATC. Another positive action was the sale of under-performing assets. Finally, part of ATC's success was attributed to improvements in the business environment of the independent energy industry.

Cronen's Views

When Cronen reflected on his accomplishments he was pleased. He was surprised that his plans were implemented more rapidly and with fewer problems than he had expected. A possible negative issue for Cronen, however, was the possibility that the new organization structure would become too rigid. He was also concerned about the evolution of the corporate culture. Cronen wanted it to develop into a creative set of values, not foster "unthinking loyalty to a stagnant company."

As Cronen viewed it, a paradox was that his successful strategy for achieving efficient operations could displace other corporate goals. If not intelligently managed, he was convinced that the organization structure, administrative procedures, and possibly even the culture could "stifle" ATC.

ATC's Future: Visions and Decisions

Thinking about the Future

When he was thinking about his annual report to the Board of Directors, Cronen decided that he would present a preliminary picture of a new phase in the management of ATC. The objective would be: "To manage the company into the 1990s to establish a foundation for new business opportunities in the twenty-first century."

The key issue for ATC's future according to Cronen was to find ways to inject aspects of Alliance's creative, entrepreneurial spirit into ATC's stable, bureaucratic structure. The problem, however, was to avoid reverting to the practices and disastrous consequences of the "investment banking" approach to the energy industry.

Acting on the Future

On a flip chart in his office Cronen began to organize his thoughts by writing in bold letters:

Future

Leadership

Culture

He then started to draw a diagram to represent the next phase in the organization of the ATC Energy Group, Inc.

The diagram located the functional departments and corporate positions in a hierarchical order. He had second thoughts and ripped the last page from the easel. Cronen then added to the original list:

Growth

Profits

Participation

Committment

Vision

He then decided to meet with his CFO and COO, and selected middle managers to explore ATC's future organizational structure and culture. But before writing a memo announcing the meeting he telephoned Dr. Marc Miller, a consultant whom his father frequently used to review the management of his companies.

PART V: CASE 3

THE CSEPEL MACHINE TOOL COMPANY

Joseph Wolfe and Jozsef Poor

Gabor Hajnoczy, the managing general director of Csepel Machine Tool Company, knew the time had come to put together a strategy for this Hungarian firm, but a number of issues stood in the way. Should Csepel replace the plant's kerosene lanterns with electric lights? How could its creditors be persuaded to wait a few more months for payment? Could Csepel make do with the existing pool of bicycles for interplant transportation? (Although still usable, they weren't very stylish.) Hajnoczy hoped to confer with American manufacturing experts during his upcoming trip to the United States. Perhaps he could bring home some innovative management ideas from the business school he expected to visit.

The year 1989 seemed to be good for the Csepel Machine Tool Company. Since 1985 sales had increased an average of 7.5 percent a year despite Hungary's financial crisis through most of the 1980s. Management had been able to lessen the firm's dependence on domestic sales (particularly important because of Hungary's stagnant economy), and it had increased its vital hard-currency sales 23 percent in just 1 year.

Something, however, was seriously wrong. After allowing for Hungary's double-digit inflation, sales revenues were actually falling, and high costs were causing profits to decline. Accordingly, various managers questioned Csepel's customizing strategy, with its high attendant manufacturing costs, and called for the institution of strict cost controls and a modernization of the company's aging product line, a legacy of the past government's central-planning investment in outdated technology. Csepel faced the upcoming decade with a number of thorny issues and problems and no clear course of direction.

Machine Tools and the Machine-Tool Industry

The demand for machine tools (tools using rotary motion to smooth, sharpen, or otherwise "machine" surfaces) in 1990 was highly dependent on the amount of metalworking activity conducted in both heavy and light industry. Automobile manufacturers and their suppliers had been the largest customers. Therefore, the demand for machine tools during the 1980s had been high in Western Europe and Japan and relatively low in the United States and Canada,

as the Big Three car manufacturers deferred their purchases in the face of losses.

Machine-tool manufacturers in the United States had been faced with a sales growth that was less than growth in gross national product and profit margins of only 2.03 percent of sales. Thus, they had been forced to restructure or diversify out of the industry. In the near term, demand for machine tools by American automobile manufacturers was not expected to rebound. At the same time, as new materials replaced iron and steel, developing new technology to machine these new materials became important.

On the other hand, Japanese machine-tool manufacturers had been relatively bullish on the long-term prospects for the industry. They had been developing machines with improved efficiency and higher end-product quality and had been broadening the product lines they exported to the United States and other world markets.

The Hungarian Environment

Hungary was a relatively industrialized country in 1990; the industrial sector, generating about 40 percent of the gross domestic product (GDP), provided employment for over 40 percent of the labor force and accounted for about 75 percent of the country's merchandise exports. The economy was highly trade dependent, with over 40 percent of the GDP traded internationally. Hungary traded with two markets—the socialists, primarily CMEA countries, and the Free World. The CMEA (Council for Mutual Economic Assistance or COMECON) was a political and economic union of most East European countries that governed trade and investment between member states.

Hungary's central-planning method had led to many market inefficiencies. It encouraged firm managers to hide the genuine capabilities of their firms and to obtain easy plans that could be achieved even if supplies did not arrive on time. Furthermore, under this system, the administered prices

---

reflected neither resource abundance or scarcity nor world market prices. Enterprises were unable to perform economic evaluations of investment projects or determine the proper mix of imports and exports, which reinforced the need for central control of production, investment, and foreign trade.

In 1980 a new wave of reform was begun to increase the competitiveness of the economy in the international market, which would, the reformers hoped, generate hard-currency exports to service the country's foreign debt. The economy also faced a labor shortage because of very slow growth in population and labor productivity. The only way to increase economic growth and generate hard currency was considered to be increasing labor productivity. The newest reforms were intended to create more market functions in the allocation of credit and to improve individual firms' access to export markets.

As with other formerly centrally planned economies, Hungary's industries in 1990 faced difficult problems as they attempted to join the world's markets. One of the thorniest problems within the Hungarian reform process concerned trade between Hungary and various Eastern European countries, particularly the Soviet Union. The trade relations with these countries were not based on the principle of free markets and had little to do with the world economy. Rather, each country in the East Bloc was assigned in quota, which was determined years in advance at rather inflexible prices. Settlement of accounts took place with transfer rubles. Rubles had very restrictive liquidation policies attached to them; they were only accepted as payment by the country that initially paid them. In other words, if Hungary sold machine tools to Poland, and Poland paid in transfer rubles, Hungary could not use those rubles to buy metal in Czechoslovakia. Hungary's own currency, the forint, had been overvalued by about 20 percent since the late 1970s. Although the forint was not convertible in 1990, the government did attempt to maintain its value at a rate close to true conversion through periodic devaluations.

The Csepel Complex

The Csepel Machine Tool Company had its origins in the Manfred Weiss manufacturing complex, which manufactured primarily iron, steel, and military equipment in the late 19th century. By 1929 the company was also producing bicycles and airplanes as well as machine tools for its own use. In 1930 the company began to sell machine tools to other firms both inside and outside Hungary.

In the early 1940s, having formally declared war on the USSR, Great Britain, and the United States, the company supplied the Axis war effort under the guise of the Hermann Goering Werke. The Weiss family had been forced out.

After a series of military defeats, Hungary made peaceful overtures toward the Allies. In 1944, however, German forces occupied the country, a right-wing puppet regime was installed, and more than 450,000 Hungarians were deported to German extermination camps in Poland. Soviet troops invaded in the fall of 1944, and Hungary was forced to sign an armistice with the Allies in Moscow. Under Soviet military occupation, Hungary restored full diplomatic relations with Moscow and signed a long-term agreement with the USSR allowing close Soviet control of Hungary's domestic economy. In effect, Hungary became a Soviet puppet. Under a Three Year Plan introduced in 1947, the government nationalized nearly 600 industrial firms, including Manfred Wiess, which became the Csepel Iron and Metalworking Trust.

From its nationalization in 1946 until 1983, the company operated within various Soviet industrial concepts. Hungary had a centralized form of economy characterized by a rigid top-down approach to macro- and microeconomic planning. A Hungarian Council of Ministers set output targets drawn up by a Central Planning Office. Targets were intended to ensure economic growth at a predetermined rate. Each state-owned company received hundreds, even thousands, of performance targets every year.

Performance targets fell into four broad categories: physical output goals; input goals regarding material and parts specifications, as well as supplier references, labor quotas, and wage allowances; financial guidelines for profits, maximum allowable debt capacity, and production costs; and strategic instructions covering new product and technology introductions and various capital investments to be made over the course of the year. While all plan elements were mandatory, some carried greater weight than others.

The state government assumed control of Csepel's import/export effort through the Ministry of Commerce, and the company's R&D function was transferred to the Institution for Mechanical Industry Research in Budapest. During this time, the company expanded its physical facilities and diversified its product line from drilling and milling machines to include lathes, grinding machines, and other precision equipment.

Hungary began moving from a planned economy to a market economy through various reform movements initiated in 1968. In late 1983, the company reorganized into an independent state-owned company. One of Hungary's largest industrial conglomerates, it was divided into 13 autonomous companies ranging from a bicycle venture to an education-and-development company. The new entity faced a difficult period, because it was burdened with nearly 700 million forints of debt and delinquent accounts receivable of 500 million. This situation forced the company to find new sources of cash to stabilize its operations.

In 1986 the company obtained equity financing by transforming itself into a publicly held shareholder corporation in an effort to allow the market to determine investment and capital formation. With this step, Csepel became a pioneer within the Hungarian economy. (Although the government had encouraged the creation of several secondary financial markets, including the first bond market in a communist country in 1984, a stock market was not established until 1989, at which time shares were issued in state-owned companies.)

In October 1988, the company split into two stock corporations: the Csepel Machine Tool Company and the Csepel Fixture and Tool Corporation. The Csepel Machine Tool Company (see organization structure in Exhibit 18.4), capitalized at 860 million forints, manufactured drilling and milling machines, lathes, and machining centers. The Csepel Fixture and Tool Corporation, capitalized at 160 million forints, manufactured small fixtures, tools, and parts.

While Csepel's sales continued to climb, to about 2.6 billion forints in 1989, the firm's profits declined after the peak in 1987 (see Exhibit 18.5). Company financial statements are in Exhibits 18.6 and 18.7; Exhibit 18.8 displays the source of Csepel's sales by general market areas for 1985-1989. Over the next 3 to 4 years, Csepel expected to boost its sales to over 3.5 billion forints. Forecasts for 1990 revenues ranged from 2.05 to 2.19 billion forints and for profits from –55.6 to 66.6 million forints. Included in this amount was an estimated 700 million forints in new contracts for parts under joint ventures with Western companies to take advantage of recent government programs freeing import and export restrictions. Csepel's joint-venture activities were part of a planned revival of the flourishing business the firm had with the West in the 1970s.

The Foreign Investments Act of 1988 gave Hungary one of the most liberal foreign-investment environments in Eastern Europe. Foreign investors were assured freedom from adverse discrimination, compensation in original currency in the event of nationalization, the right to own up to 100 percent of firms, and the ability to transfer abroad dividends and up to 50 percent of wages. A big stumbling block for foreign investors in Hungary was eliminated in 1989 when investors' profits were allowed to be repatriated in convertible currency. To encourage international trade further, the government established reciprocal trade agreements with 25 countries, including France, Ireland, India, and China.

Within the Hungarian economy itself, Csepel was one 1 of only 3 machine-tool manufacturers. Of them, SZIM Machine Tool Company, with 10 billion forints in revenue, was the largest. The other domestic competitor, DIGEP Mechanical Factory, had only 0.3 billion forints in revenue.

Products and New Product Development

The Csepel Machine Tool Company produced five types of machine tools: radial drilling machines, computer numerically controlled (CNC) machining centers, CNC lathes, high-precision systems, and special-purpose systems. Exhibit 18.9 provides details of Csepel's product line. As can be seen, Csepel received different prices for its products in different geographical markets. In addition to standard products, Csepel made a significant amount of orders to customer specification; the proportion of custom work ranged from 2 percent of radial drilling machines to 100 percent of special-purpose systems. Csepel's products had gained a reputation for quality and low prices, and the company had no difficulty obtaining custom orders.

The slow rate of new-product development at Csepel was a major source of concern within the company. A shortage of skilled labor existed, and despite 58 state-supported colleges and universities, only 7.9 percent of the adult population possessed a university degree. In the words of Levente Godri, the Central Plant's chief designer,

> We don't have enough engineers in the first place, and those we do have get too involved in daily operations—so much so, they don't have any time to do new-product development. We could hire some good people from the Technical University in Budapest, and they could staff a new R&D

EXHIBIT 18.4

The Csepel Machine Tool Company

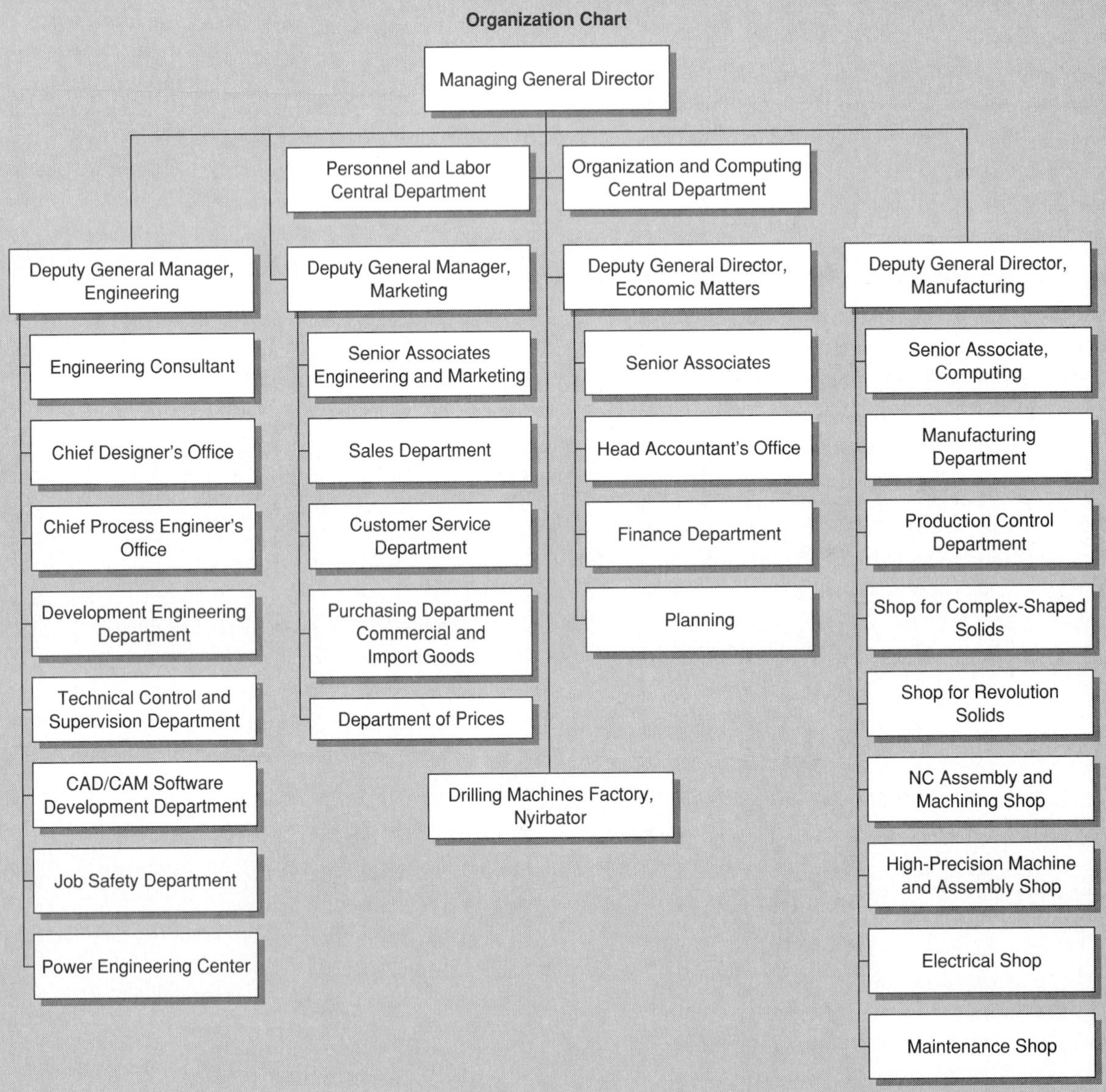

Organization Chart

Managing General Director

- Personnel and Labor Central Department
- Organization and Computing Central Department

Deputy General Manager, Engineering
- Engineering Consultant
- Chief Designer's Office
- Chief Process Engineer's Office
- Development Engineering Department
- Technical Control and Supervision Department
- CAD/CAM Software Development Department
- Job Safety Department
- Power Engineering Center

Deputy General Manager, Marketing
- Senior Associates Engineering and Marketing
- Sales Department
- Customer Service Department
- Purchasing Department Commercial and Import Goods
- Department of Prices

Drilling Machines Factory, Nyirbator

Deputy General Director, Economic Matters
- Senior Associates
- Head Accountant's Office
- Finance Department
- Planning

Deputy General Director, Manufacturing
- Senior Associate, Computing
- Manufacturing Department
- Production Control Department
- Shop for Complex-Shaped Solids
- Shop for Revolution Solids
- NC Assembly and Machining Shop
- High-Precision Machine and Assembly Shop
- Electrical Shop
- Maintenance Shop

EXHIBIT 18.5

THE CSEPEL MACHINE TOOL COMPANY

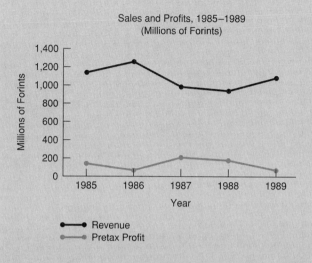

Sales and Profits, 1985–1989
(Millions of Forints)

81.2 million in 1987, then declined to 55.7 million in 1988 and 18.7 million in 1989. Budgeted R&D for 1990 totaled 15.0 million forints.

Factories and Manufacturing Operations

The company manufactured its machine tools and parts in two locations. The Central Plant and executive offices were in Budapest, and the second plant was located in Nyirbator, a city of about 30,000 people in northeastern Hungary. The specialization of the plants prevented either plant from building a complete machine tool. The Nyirbator Plant focused mainly on parts fabrication and subassembly, while the Central Plant produced some parts and completed final assemblies of the machine tools.

Outside experts considered the manufacturing equipment and techniques at both plants to be outdated and inefficient, although the newer Nyirbator Plant was slightly better. Overall, about 15 percent of the production equipment was less than 10 years old, 37 percent was 11 to 20 years old, and 48 percent was over 20 years old. The firm owned only 24 numerically controlled machines (standard production equipment for the most modern machine manufacturers), and 59 percent of its equipment had been fully depreciated to scrap value.

Although maintenance and repair of the older manufacturing equipment consumed significant resources, replacement of old equipment would require large investments. Experts estimated that $4.7 to $6.0 million would be required to modernize Csepel's production equipment. In addition, $12.0 million would be needed to introduce advanced production control and information systems and to provide the necessary production resources to extend the current product lines.

In the past, engineers and a highly skilled work force had bridged the technological gap at Csepel. By 1989, however, the workers had become dissatisfied with the working conditions and forced overtime. Consequently, the Central Plant had begun losing its cross-trained senior factory technicians and their trainees to local private-sector machine shops and small factories in the area. The Nyirbator Plant had not experienced as much of a loss because of limited alternative employment opportunities in that area.

The employment dilemma was exacerbated by Hungary's problems in human resources. Its population of

Department, but I don't know if that would really solve our problem.

Whatever we're doing, we have to do a better job than we're doing now. Unfortunately, our bonus system is based on the on-time delivery of machines, so our R&D people spend time in the shop helping to get orders delivered instead of spending time developing new products.

In the middle of this explanation, as if to underscore Godri's observations, the leader of the CNC-Assembly Machining Shop telephoned to demand that an engineer be sent immediately to the production unit to make a substitute part in the Maintenance Department. Godri sent the engineer, even though each shop had an on-duty technical assistant to handle these minor crises. He explained that this type of problem persisted because Csepel's part-numbering system did not disclose or cross-reference part substitutions.

In addition to the problems listed by Godri, the company's R&D expenditures had fluctuated widely in the past four years. They rose from 27.1 million forints in 1986 to

EXHIBIT 18.6

THE CSEPEL MACHINE TOOL COMPANY

INCOME STATEMENTS
(UNAUDITED; IN THOUSANDS OF FORINTS)

	1985	1986	1987	1988	1989
Revenues					
Domestic	484.7	605.8	814.2	567.0	542.5
Exports					
CMEA* ruble market	352.8	466.4	694.7	981.4	1,058.9
Hard currency	1,151.0	1,263.6	982.2	898.1	1,016.9
Total 1,988.6	2,335.8	2,491.1	2,446.5	2,618.3	
Direct manufacturing cost	1,044.4	1,173.7	1,277.8	1,294.7	1,385.8
Operating profit	944.2	1,162.2	1,213.3	1,151.8	1,232.5
Overhead cost					
Factory overhead	351.2	478.0	478.4	282.0	352.6
Admin. overhead	325.5	293.8	299.2	505.8	689.8
R&D expense 37.3	27.1	81.2	55.7	18.7	
Customer service	11.3	16.2	12.5	22.1	17.0
Land rent	4.0	3.7	0.0	0.0	0.0
Miscellaneous 53.4	64.9	70.4	97.1	8.1	
Total 782.7	883.7	941.7	962.7	1,086.2	
Additional expenses	156.3	129.8	107.4	62.9	137.2
Other income					
Export support 123.0	16.0	60.7	0.0	0.0	
Ministry support	2.1	35.7	79.1	129.2	35.1
R&D subsidy 5.0	0.0	51.2	35.7	5.9	
Vendor penalties	6.1	2.4	2.4	0.0	3.4
Other	2.5	5.7	3.0	0.0	8.3
Total 138.7	59.8	196.4	164.9	52.7	
Profit before taxes	143.9	208.4	360.6	291.1	61.8
Taxes	109.6	133.1	151.4	49.3	.3
Profit after taxes	34.1	75.3	209.2	241.8	61.5

*Council for Mutual Economic Assistance.

10.6 million had been declining since 1985, and the size of the work force fell 3.4 percent in the 1980s. The population was expected to continue to decline at an annual rate of about 0.15 percent, despite the government's attempts to reverse the trend. Many Hungarian workers were excessively tired from working multiple jobs or, alternatively, lacked dedication to their principal employer. Some observers believed that the labor force had begun to work itself to the point of psychological and physical exhaustion.

EXHIBIT 18.7

THE CSEPEL MACHINE TOOL COMPANY

	BALANCE SHEET (UNAUDITED; IN MILLIONS OF FORINTS)	
	1988	1989
ASSETS		
Current assets		
Cash	1,139	3,230
Bank account	32,646	16,276
Additional accounts	13,896	–32,949
Bonds	-0-	-0-
Domestic buyer	203,731	192,807
Foreign buyer	666,332	978,162
Total	917,744	1,157,526
Employee fund	657	-0-
State budget fund	-0-	2,882
Total		870,720 1,173,851
Inventories		
Goods in process	192,216	216,533
Finished goods	36,315	23,362
Total	229,687	239,895
Raw material	428,644	678,293
Purchased stocks	123,201	99,229
Total	551,845	777,522
Total		781,532 1,017,417
Contingency fund	-0-	-0-
Other active accounts	257,231	45,158
Temporary account	-0-	-0-
Total	257,231	45,158
Shares held	6,000	228,000
Assets held	-0-	-0-
Foreign investments	6,000	228,000
Fixed plant and equip.	928,097	1,091,681
Less depreciation	735,634	786,716
Plant additions	22,559	82,249
Net book value	215,022	387,214
Total assets	2,177,030	2,838,030

EXHIBIT 18.7 (CONTINUED)

	BALANCE SHEET (UNAUDITED; IN MILLIONS OF FORINTS)	
	1988	1989
LIABILITIES		
Accounts payable	-0-	840,399
Domestic deliverer	812,413	188,014
Foreign deliverer	89,070	221,510
Investment deliverer	24,962	12,935
Factoring	30,000	113,810
Creditors	308	36,144
Salaries payable	10,511	17,933
Soc. sec. payable	21,747	34,077
Prepaid taxes	−125,762	−33,389
Other accounts	200,270	262,972
Total	1,063,519	1,694,405
Paid-in capital	835,000	835,000
Retained earnings	−99	323,344
Total	834,901	1,158,344
Income tax liability	−35,910	−53,613
Profit account	−3,716	−22,428
Profit	318,236	61,489
Total liabilities	2,177,030	2,838,197

Central Plant Operations

About 5 percent of the company's 24,000 parts and sub-assemblies were manufactured in the Central Plant. (The other 95 percent were manufactured by the Nyirbator Plant or were purchased.) The Central Plant handled parts requiring extreme accuracy and/or state-of-the-art technology. The nature of the products and the availability of production equipment in the Central Plant had led to a complex manufacturing process and material flow (see Exhibit 18.10). The plant layout was not rational, although efforts were underway to improve it.

Manufacturing Operations at the Central Plant produced a monthly manufacturing schedule for both Central and Nyirbator. Based on the sales forecast, the department also produced a portfolio of shop cards (raw-material requisitions) and time and labor charges by order number. The complete portfolio went to the Production Department,

which launched a new shop order to the shop manager. The shop manager assigned the order to a shop foreman, who scheduled the workers and the tools and gathered the raw materials as required by the shop order. Each worker inspected his/her own work and signed off on the order as the assignment was completed.

A conversation with Arpad Koknya, deputy general director in charge of the Central Plant's manufacturing operations, revealed certain problems in the planning and manufacturing process:

We have a stupid quality-control system that works well for simple, small things, but for complicated subassemblies like ours, it doesn't work so well. It can really cause big problems if the assembly is produced in a number of steps.

The system is a mixture of worker self-inspection and staff quality-control inspection. The worker says

EXHIBIT 18.8

THE CSEPEL MACHINE TOOL COMPANY

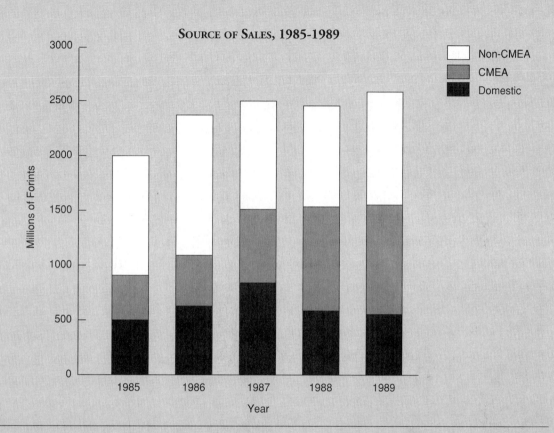

SOURCE OF SALES, 1985-1989

whether his own part is good or not, while the Quality Control Department looks at the entire subassembly when it's complete. Many of our workers sign off that their work is up to standard, but it isn't, and we don't find out about it until it shows up in the final assembly or, even worse, after it's been delivered. We should really punish these guys, but the present employment situation (shortage of labor) doesn't allow us to do this. The quantitative bonus system we use in parts production adds to this problem.

Parts scheduling also causes problems. Each month our department sets up a parts shortage list (PSL). The PSL contains a list of final products and all the missing parts, along with the part identification number required to complete that product. This list is a key input into the parts-manufacturing operation. Items on the PSL get

higher priority on the production schedule. Unfortunately, the computer can't handle the six-plus-one-digit code number very well, so a lot of part searches kick out "Out of Stock" messages even though they're really in stock. Too often we're making parts we don't need on a high-priority basis, which slows up our regular production.

Creating a production plan for assembly operations isn't complicated, but coordinating the production is difficult. Because of how sales orders come in, we only have to deliver about 20 units per month in the first part of the year, but about 60 to 100 units a month in the last part. Workers get very overworked by the end of the year; sometimes our best workers get sick from stress. But life isn't so easy for management either. These swings in production cause headaches for everybody. If the

EXHIBIT 18.9

The Csepel Machine Tool Company

1989 Product Mix and Product Prices by Geographical Market

Machine Type	Model Number	Product Price (in thousands of forints)			Annual Production	Life-Cycle Position	Competitive Strength
		Hungarian Market	U.S. Dollar Market	CMEA Countries			
Radial drilling machines	RF-50	747.7	577.5	577.9	200 for entire group	All very late	All weak
	RFh-75	1,449.4	1,116.4	909.6			
	RFh-100	2,015.7	2,056.1	1,558.2			
CNC machining centers	Yasda	n.a.*	23,951.4	n.a.	30 to 40	Early	Average
	MK-500	11,683.4	9,460.0	12,072.9	35 to 55	Early	Average
	MV16	10,903.6	n.a.	n.a.	10 to 15	Relative late	Weak
	MVI10	11,989.6	13,294.9	n.a.	6 to 8	Relatively early	Average
CNC lathes	SDNC 610 1000	8,951.5	10,581.9	6,566.2	35 to 50	Relative early	Strong
	SDNC 610 1500	n.a.	4,742.4	8,464.1		Relative early	Strong
	RS-100	5,516.3	9,258.8	n.a.	15 to 25	Very early	Average
	TCFM-100	1,616.2	n.a.	2,047.2	25 to 30	Very early	Strong
High-precision systems	FKP-326-10	7,315.5	10,851.5	7,259.4	35 to 40	Mature	Weak
	UP-I	15,726.0	n.a.	n.a.	5 to 10	Very early	Strong
Special-purpose systems	PTC-71-180	n.a.	n.a.	4,431.7	10 to 15	Mature	Weak
	SMC-71-180	n.a.	n.a.	5,539.8		Mature	Weak

*Product not available in this market.

Source: Company internal records and consultant's estimates.

EXHIBIT 18.10

THE CSEPEL MACHINE TOOL COMPANY

Central Plant Manufacturing Sequence

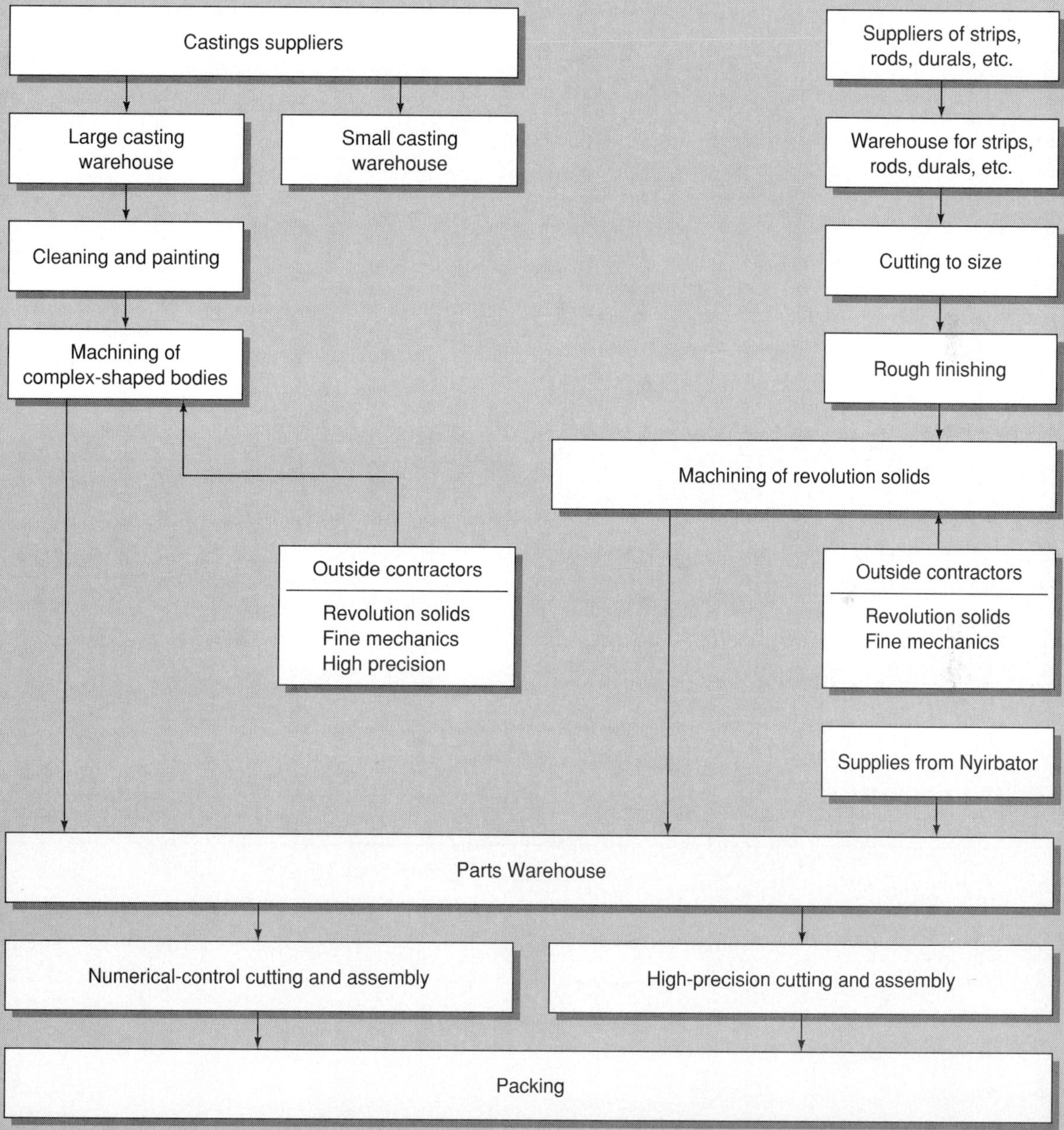

```
Castings suppliers                          Suppliers of strips,
                                            rods, durals, etc.
        │                                           │
        ▼                    ▼                       ▼
Large casting          Small casting        Warehouse for strips,
warehouse              warehouse            rods, durals, etc.
        │                                           │
        ▼                                           ▼
Cleaning and painting                       Cutting to size
        │                                           │
        ▼                                           ▼
Machining of                                Rough finishing
complex-shaped bodies                               │
        ▲                                           ▼
        │                              Machining of revolution solids
        │                                           ▲
   Outside contractors                      Outside contractors
                                           
   Revolution solids                        Revolution solids
   Fine mechanics                           Fine mechanics
   High precision
                                            Supplies from Nyirbator
        │                         │                 │
        ▼                         ▼                 ▼
              Parts Warehouse
        │                                           │
        ▼                                           ▼
Numerical-control cutting and assembly    High-precision cutting and assembly
        │                                           │
        ▼                                           ▼
                    Packing
```

Note: About 5.0 percent of the company's 24,000 parts and subassemblies were manufactured in the Central Plant. The plant handled parts requiring extreme accuracy and/or state-of-the-art technology.

Sales Department could just forecast sales better, we'd have fewer problems down the line.

Exhibit 18.11 provides information on inventory levels for Csepel.

Nyirbator Plant

The Nyirbator Plant was originally created to manufacture parts for all Csepel products, under the government's plan to bring industrial economic development to the country's rural areas. Currently, the plant produced the company's basic drilling machines and parts for all other machine types. The original labor supply was drawn from unskilled agricultural workers, who had to be intensively trained in company-run technical training programs. Over the years, Csepel had been a strong supporter of the city's technical school, which was now the firm's major source of skilled labor. In 1989 the plant employed about 740 people, and it generated sales of 649.1 million forints. The plant's manufacturing flow is shown in Exhibit 18.12, and its organization in Exhibit 18.13.

Managers at the Nyirbator Plant believed they were unnecessarily constrained by Csepel management. The drilling-machine plant's director of Economic Matters, Janos Fazekas, described several issues of contention:

First of all, our plant has to manufacture Csepel's low-profit items. As bad as that is, many times we get urgent orders by FAX from the Central Plant, which forces us to shut down our machines to supply them. We argue about these things all the time.

We want to be more independent and to have more power in these discussions with Production Control and Planning. These departments consider us to be their slaves and don't consider our specific bottleneck problems, and they continue to bother us with their special orders, which overuse our special machines.

Also, headquarters' sales operations are very slow in processing domestic orders. We could do a faster job on these sales if we could set up our own sales department.

Nyirbator's Engineering director, Istvan Szatmari, thought his department should be free to pursue new-product designs for the facility:

In recent years, we've brought in new engineers for new-product development, but all their time is spent in operations. They want to design new tools but can't. We're also in conflict with the Central

---

EXHIBIT 18.11

THE CSEPEL MACHINE TOOL COMPANY

INVENTORY TYPE	INVENTORY LEVELS (IN THOUSANDS OF FORINTS)				
	1985	1986	1987	1988	1989
Purchased stocks and raw materials	450.6	678.6	610.9	551.8	777.5
Goods in process	185.5	139.8	171.6	192.3	216.5
Finished goods	15.5	17.4	31.8	36.3	10.0
Total	651.7	635.2	814.3	780.4	1,017.4

Source: Internal company records.

Plant's R&D operations, because they won't give us the freedom to operate on our own.

The Nyirbator Plant was approximately 250 kilometers from headquarters. The telephone service at the plant was spotty, and the internal auditing controls lax. The Nyirbator managers occasionally took advantage of these conditions to evade Csepel's control. In one instance, they were able to buy a nonauthorized Xerox machine by listing it as a production part.

Headquarters Operations

Except for Istvan Rakoczy, the head of the company's computer services, Csepel's headquarters staff had been promoted after long service in production. Hajnoczy, the managing general director, exemplified their pace and management style. Two or three mornings a week, beginning just after the shift opened, he toured the plants' shops with Koknya. These rounds, which were conducted at both plants, could last up to three hours and occurred more often if problems were plaguing a particular production run. Hajnoczy was very familiar with the plant operations and knew many employees on a first-name basis. Should he see something that appeared to be wrong, he would immediately order a change in either the production method or the order's schedule.

Hajnoczy was closely involved with many plant activities. During a two-hour afternoon conversation, he was interrupted many times by short telephone calls from plant personnel and brief conferences with his secretary. He also had to sign a number of technical orders and a

EXHIBIT 18.12

THE CSEPEL MACHINE TOOL COMPANY

Nyirbator Manufacturing Sequence

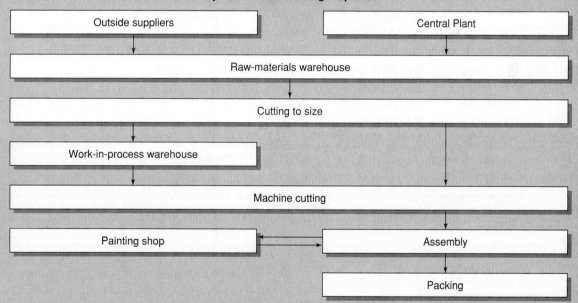

Note: Almost 90 percent of Csepel's parts and subassemblies were manufactured in this factory. The process technology was simpler than that used in the Central Plant. Nyirbator's products were easier to assemble than those produced in the Central Plant, but their unit value was significantly lower. Except for high-precision parts, the plant was self-sufficient.

EXHIBIT 18.13

THE CSEPEL MACHINE TOOL COMPANY

Organization Chart for Nyirbator Plant

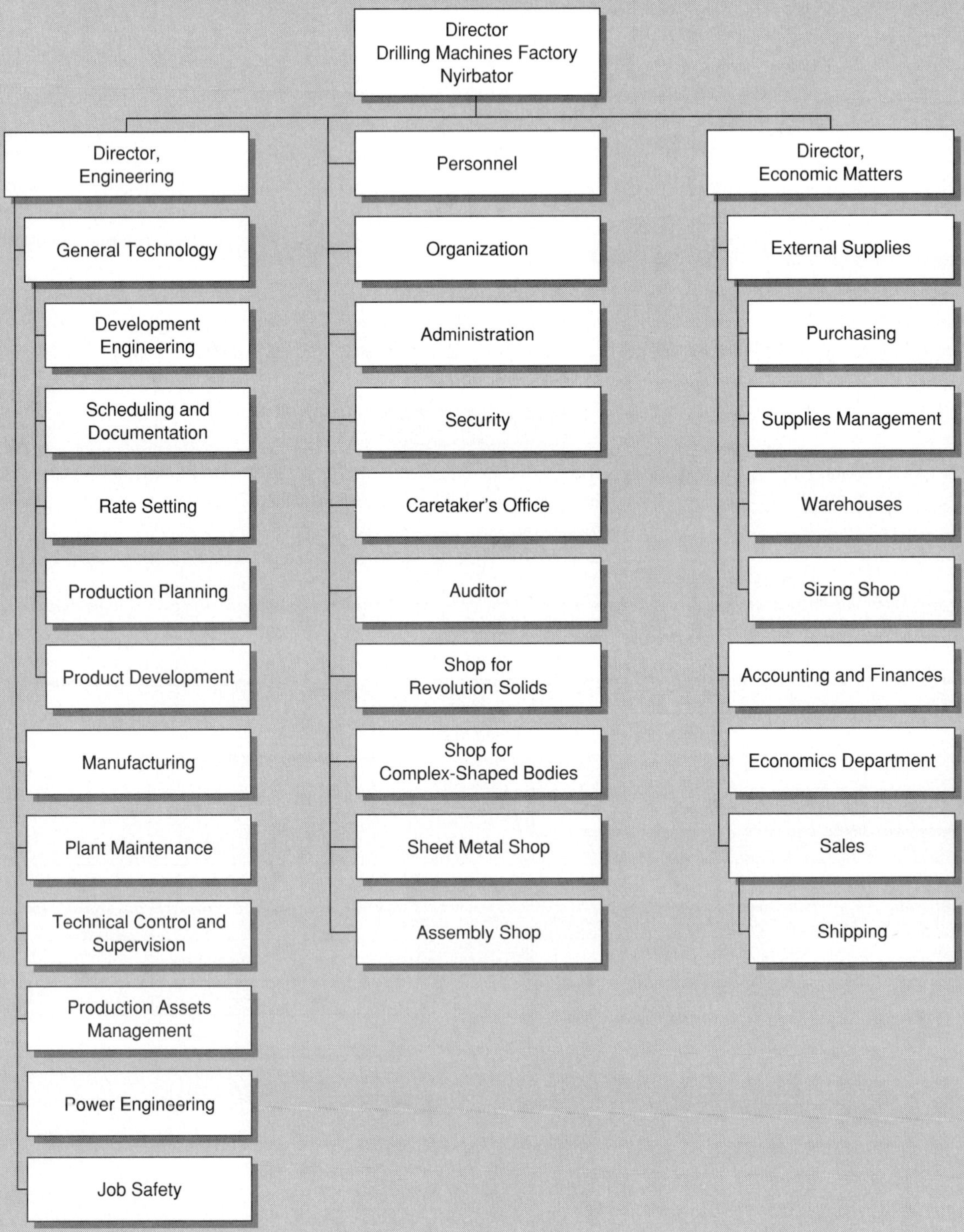

Director
Drilling Machines Factory
Nyirbator

Director, Engineering

- General Technology
  - Development Engineering
  - Scheduling and Documentation
  - Rate Setting
  - Production Planning
  - Product Development
- Manufacturing
- Plant Maintenance
- Technical Control and Supervision
- Production Assets Management
- Power Engineering
- Job Safety

Personnel

- Organization
- Administration
- Security
- Caretaker's Office
- Auditor
- Shop for Revolution Solids
- Shop for Complex-Shaped Bodies
- Sheet Metal Shop
- Assembly Shop

Director, Economic Matters

- External Supplies
  - Purchasing
  - Supplies Management
  - Warehouses
  - Sizing Shop
- Accounting and Finances
- Economics Department
- Sales
  - Shipping

request for computer supplies. Several lengthy telephone calls dealt with decisions about where pieces of shop equipment should be placed for a shopfloor layout change that was under way.

Although some employees appreciated the accessibility of top management and their intimate working knowledge of plant operations, others thought they showed too much concern for production and the bonuses attached to on-time production deliveries at the expense of other company functions. The head of the Central Plant's Sales Department, Gabor Nagy, commented:

> Sometimes our general manager gets orders on his own when he's out in the field . . . and when he comes back, he simply gives these orders directly to the Production Department. This is bad for us in Sales, because we can't tell how effective we've been. We don't know if we got the order because of him or because we had been developing the same customer over the past few months. By doing things this way, we can't tell why the sale was ever made. . . . Top management's manufacturing bias is the company's major problem; it keeps us from being flexible.

Nagy was also concerned about Technoimpex, Csepel's foreign-trading firm. Lately, Technoimpex had broadened its product line and de-emphasized machine tools. As a result, Csepel now employed service representatives in

EXHIBIT 18.14

THE CSEPEL MACHINE TOOL COMPANY

	1990 PRO FORMA INCOME STATEMENTS UNDER THREE SCENARIOS (IN MILLIONS OF FORINTS)		
	A	B	C
Revenues			
Domestic	407.0	430.0	450.0
Exports			
CMEA ruble market	648.0	231.4	130.0
Hard currency	993.2	1,428.0	1,610.0
Total	2,048.2	2,089.4	2,190.0
Manufacturing costs			
Direct	1,124.1	1,145.2	1,182.6
Overhead	900.0	900.0	900.0
Total	2,024.1	2,045.2	2,082.6
Other income			
U.S. dollar support	0.0	0.0	32.2
Ruble export	−86.3	−30.0	−13.0
Profit before taxes	−55.6	34.2	66.6
Less taxes	0.0	17.1	33.3
Profit after taxes	−55.6	17.1	33.3

Source: Company internal forecast.

Romania, West Germany, and the United States to boost sales and service quality. In countries where Csepel had no representatives, it used Austria's Intertrade, a steel and machine-tool specialist.

Looking to the Future

For Istvan Rakoczy, head of Organization and Computing, exciting years were ahead:

> I've recently convinced top management they should buy the MAS-MCS [Management Accounting System-Management Control System] integrated software package from the British software firm Hoykens. It's being introduced at the Hungarian firms VIDETON, BHG, and SZIM, and it's a system that can manage the MIS [management information system] problems for a company our size—production planning, all the paperwork controls, operations scheduling, and operations finance.
>
> We bought a used IBM 4361 from a German firm late last year. We are installing 70 work stations at the Central Plant, as well as some in Nyirbator. It's the first time we've tried to implement a real integrated management system. It'll cost the company nearly 100 million forints, but it should be completed in 1991. If this implementation is successful, I'd like to make the department

> into a separate money-making operation. This would allow us to serve Csepel, keep our own people busy, and help them earn more money.

For Peter Toth, general manager of Economic Matters, the future was a bit more cloudy. The order book was low (particularly for domestic clients), prices were rising overall, the government was cutting support for CMEA exports, and optimal production lot sizes had not been established. Exhibit 18.14 contains three scenarios developed by Toth after consulting top management. The scenarios, ranging from "pessimistic" (A) to "optimistic" (C), made assumptions regarding the growth of the economy and Csepel's market penetration. Toth's suggestions for improving 1990's company performance entailed the following:

- dismiss 15 percent of all personnel (about 200 employees);
- raise the salaries of all remaining personnel by 20 percent;
- reduce costs in general, including the stock level of various finished goods;
- investigate opportunities for new ruble exports;
- maintain the company's traditionally good relationships with its creditors;
- accelerate the rate at which products are delivered to customers;
- find a joint-venture partner.

PART V: EXPERIENCE 1

THE PROBLEM WITH MEN/WOMEN IS . . . SEX-ROLE ASSUMPTIONS

J. Rose Farber

Purposes

1. To help students identify their own and others' assumptions about role expectations for men and women.
2. To explore attitudes and feelings that surface when students begin comparing their assumptions and role expectations.
3. To allow students to experience arguing in favor of a point of view with which they personally disagree.

Time Required

Approximately two hours [it can be split into hour sessions].

Group Size

Four subgroups of four participants each. For this structured experience to have impact, the students should represent heterogeneous viewpoints regarding sex-role assumptions. (For example, an all-feminist group is not recommended).

Materials

1. One complete set of expectation statements, with each statement cut apart along the dashed lines. These statements, which appear at the end of this structured experience, are printed in consecutive groups of four. (Note the number and letter code in the upper-right corner of each statement. The first group consists of 1-A, 1-B, 1-C, and 1-D; the second group consists of 2-A, 2-B, 2-C, and 2-D; and so on.) The statements are to be distributed so that each participant receives four separate pieces that form a single group. For example, one participant receives statements 1-A, 1-B, 1-C, and 1-D; the next participant receives statements 2-A, 2-B, 2-C, and 2-D; another receives 3-A, 3-B, 3-C, and 3-D; and so on.
2. A section of chalkboard or newsprint for each subgroup.

Procedure

1. Each student is given four separate expectation statements (see the Materials section) and selects two of the four that he or she agrees with more than the remaining two.
2. Students assemble into subgroups of four, preferably choosing to work with others that they do not know well. The subgroups should review all of the statements

that the members selected as well as all of the ones that were rejected. Then, if one member has selected any statements with which another member agrees more strongly, the members may trade statements; however, the member who holds the preferred statements must agree to the exchange and should relinquish only those statements that he or she does not wish to include in the final two. At the end of this step each student should still have two statements. After fifteen minutes the instructor collects all rejected statements.

3. Students spend the next ten minutes milling around and reviewing each participant's selected statements. At the end of this period each student joins three others whose selected statements are very similar to his or her own.
4. The members of the new subgroups are instructed to spend five minutes sharing their combined eight statements and selecting six that they all agree are the most important. After five minutes the instructor collects all rejected statements.
5. Each subgroup will spend approximately three minutes meeting with each other subgroup, in turn, to review the other subgroup's selected statements. At the end of this process each subgroup will be asked to join another subgroup whose statements are *dissimilar* to or *different from* its own, thereby forming groups of eight participants each. These groups meet for three minutes.
6. Each subgroup joins with another as explained in the previous step to exchange statements. Each subgroup of four then separates from the other subgroup of four to choose the one statement from the new batch with which the subgroup members *disagree* the most.
7. Each subgroup spends twenty minutes determining the best possible arguments for convincing others to *agree* with the statement chosen in Step 6. At the end of the twenty-minute period each subgroup will present its arguments to the total group.
8. After twenty minutes each subgroup presents its arguments.
9. The instructor leads a concluding discussion by asking the following questions:

Source: J. Rose Farber, "The Problem With Men/Women Is . . . Sex-Role Assumptions." Reprinted from J.W. Pfeiffer (Ed.), *The 1988 Annual: Developing Human Resources*, San Diego, CA: Pfeiffer & Company. Copyright © 1988. Reprinted by permission.

a.   What was it like to have to choose statements? What did you think and feel as you chose them?

b.   If you were to summarize the statements you selected, what would the summary suggest about your attitude toward men? Your attitude toward women?

c.   What did you think and feel when others selected statements that you disagreed with? How did you feel when you realized that you were selecting statements that others disagreed with?

d.   When you exchanged final statements with another subgroup, how did you react to the other subgroup's statements? What might your reactions suggest about your typical reactions when confronted with opposing viewpoints?

e.   What was it like to argue in favor of a point of view that you personally disagreed with? Was there a difference in your feelings about that issue before and after you argued it? If so, what was that difference?

f.   What does this experience suggest about the assumptions and expectations you have about the roles of men and women? How are those assumptions and expectations helpful or hindering in your daily life?

g.   What would you like to do about what you have discovered as a result of this experience?

The Problem with Men/Women Is . . . Expectation Statements

1-A

There are basic differences between men and women, and it is important to account for these differences in day-to-day life.

1-B

Men are stronger than women, both physically and mentally.

1-C

Women work harder than men.

1-D

The roles of men and women should be clearly divided for efficiency, but it does not matter who has what role; each can do any job equally as well.

2-A

Men do not seem to have the ability to take care of children properly.

2-B

Women typically earn less money than men, but they deserve less because they do not work as hard.

2-C

Women are more reliable than men.

2-D

Birth control is the responsibility of both partners.

3-A

If a woman makes more money than her mate, this will certainly cause problems in their relationship.

3-B

Men are at a disadvantage—often forced to work at jobs they do not like in order to support their families. Women, for the most part, do not have to work if they do not want to.

3-C

Women are basically smarter than men.

3-D

There are no major differences between what a man can do and what a woman can do.

4-A

Women are not as capable of handling their emotions as men are.

4-B

A family is much better off if the firstborn child is a male.

4-C

Men have a real advantage in this world.

4-D

Men and women should share equally in financial, domestic, and child-rearing tasks.

5-A

It is O.K. for a woman to pursue a career; but when there are children in a family, the woman is still the better caretaker.

5-B

Men are more reliable than women.

5-C

In today's world it is more important for women to be assertive and competitive than it is for men.

5-D

The differences between men and women are both innate and cultural, but mostly cultural.

6-A

It is important in a relationship for the man to make more money than the woman.

6-B

A man can still be attractive in his later years, even if he has gray hair and a pot belly.

6-C
Women consistently earn less money than men. The reality is that women deserve more money because they work harder than men do.

6-D
Women have as many opportunities in this world as men do.

7-A
It is a sign of weakness for a man to cry.

7-B
Women have a real advantage in this world.

7-C
Men do not think of women as people; they think of women as bodies.

7-D
As much as possible, little girls and little boys should be treated the same.

8-A
Men who want to stay home as "house husbands" are basically lazy.

8-B
Women nag more than men.

8-C
Women are more responsible than men.

8-D
How much money someone earns is not affected by his or her sex.

9-A
Birth control is basically a woman's responsibility.

9-B
Men are basically smarter than women.

9-C
Men have a much harder time handling their emotions than do women.

9-D
Women have a right to choose to do anything in this world that they want.

10-A
Assertiveness and competitiveness are more appropriate traits for a man than for a woman.

10-B
Men are more responsible than women.

10-C
Men have more opportunities in this world than women do.

10-D
A person's intelligence is not determined by his or her sex.

11-A
The differences between men and women are both innate and cultural, but mostly innate.

11-B
Women are indecisive.

11-C
In the long run, a woman is a better supervisor than a man.

11-D
It is a valid option for the woman to work and the man to take care of the children.

12-A
It is the man's responsibility to support his family.

12-B
In the long run, a man is a better supervisor than a woman.

12-C
Men would be lost without women.

12-D
It is unfair to expect a woman to work at a job all day and then come home and prepare meals, clean the house, and take care of the children.

13-A
The man should earn a living, and the woman should take care of the house; this arrangement is the most efficient.

13-B
Women have a real advantage in the business world; they can get ahead by "sleeping with the boss."

13-C
Men want to be taken care of.

13-D
Regardless of how hard a man works, it is still his responsibility to assume an equal role in taking care of his children.

14-A
Men should never be seen crying.

14-B
Women do not know what they really want.

14-C
Women can take care of themselves better than men can.

14-D
A woman can still be attractive in her later years, even if she has gray hair and a pot belly.

15-A
Women do not belong in the corporate world.

15-B
Men can take care of themselves better than women can.

15-C
If it were up to women, there would be no war.

PART V: EXPERIENCE 1 Continued

15-D
If a mother wishes to pursue a career, the father can be just as effective in caring for the children.

16-A
It is more natural for a man to be the aggressor in a sexual relationship.

16-B
Women would be lost without men.

16-C
Men have more needs for power and control than women do.

16-D
Regardless of how hard each parent works, both parents have an obligation to assume major roles in caring for their children.

PART V: EXPERIENCE 2

CAREERS IN INTERNATIONAL MANAGEMENT

Nancy J. Adler

Purpose

Given the substantial increases in international trade and global operations over the last decade, it has become increasingly important for managers and corporations to understand the career aspirations of business students. This questionnaire is designed to increase your understanding of your own career aspirations.

Time Required

Approximately 45 minutes.

Materials

The International Management Career Questionnaire.

Procedure

After each student answers the questionnaire class discussion should focus on the employment opportunities that currently exist for international management careers. Another area for discussion is the availability of appropriate training including the design of courses and the sequencing of corporate jobs that will lead to an international position.

Questionnaire

Background: How Prepared Are You?

1. Counting your maternal language, which languages do you speak (relatively well)?

	Adequate			Fluent	
_____	1	2	3	4	5
_____	1	2	3	4	5
_____	1	2	3	4	5
_____	1	2	3	4	5
_____	1	2	3	4	5

2. How many years have you studied outside of your country of citizenship (from grade 1 on)?

   _____ total number of years in _____.
   country/countries

3. How many months outside your country of citizenship have you traveled, lived, or worked? _____

4. Did either of your parents travel internationally for their work? _____

5. How many of your friends are neither from your country of citizenship nor from the country in which you are currently living?

   a. _____ none   b. _____ a few   c. _____ about half

   d. _____ most   e. _____ all

What Are Your Career Plans?

The following section asks you a number of questions about your career plans. In the questions

   Home Country is your country of citizenship.

   An *International Assignment* is one in which the company sends an employee for a single assignment of a year or more to a foreign country.

   An *International Career* is a series of foreign assignments in different foreign countries.

   International Travel is a business trip to a foreign country without the employee moving there.

   An *Expatriate* is an employee who is sent by the company to live and work in a foreign country.

How true is each of the following statements for you?

1. I am seriously considering pursuing an international career. _____

2. I would like my first job after my degree to be in a foreign country. _____

3. If offered an equivalent position in my home country or in the foreign country of my choice, I would rather work at home. _____

_____

Source: Nancy J. Adler, *International Dimensions of Organizational Behavior* (second edition). MA: PWS Kent, © 1991: pp. 285–290. Reprinted by permission of Wadsworth Publishing Company.

4. While continuing to live in my home country, I would like to travel internationally more than 40% (approximately 20 weeks/year) of my time. _____

5. I would like to have an *International Assignment* at some time in my career. _____

6. I would like to follow an *International Career* in which I had a series of foreign assignments. _____

7. I had never thought about taking an international assignment until I read this questionnaire. _____

There are many reasons why people choose not to pursue an international career. Which of the following would discourage *you* from pursuing an international career or taking an international assignment? *(Circle one number for each statement or write NA if not applicable.)*

8. I like living in my home country. _____

9. I do not want to learn another language. _____

10. I do not want to adjust to another culture. _____

11. My spouse would not want to move to a foreign country. _____

12. It is not good to move children. _____

13. I want my children to be educated in my home country. _____

14. I do not want to live in:

    a. Any foreign location _____

    b. North America _____

    c. Europe _____

    d. Latin or South America _____

    e. Asia _____

    f. Africa _____

    g. the Middle East _____

    h. my home country _____

    i. other (specify) _____

15. International jobs involve too much travel. _____

16. If I live in a foreign country, my children will not gain a sense of national identity. _____

17. My spouse would not want to interrupt his or her career. _____

18. I will lose my sense of identity, my roots. _____

19. Foreign assignments put too much strain on a marriage. _____

20. When you are on a foreign assignment you become "invisible" to the company and tend to be forgotten for promotions. _____

21. It would be difficult to come back home after having lived and worked for a long time in a foreign country. _____

22. I do not want to be exposed to the political instability in some parts of the world. _____

23. I would be more socially isolated and lonely in a foreign country. _____

24. I would be exposed to more personal danger in a foreign country. _____

In comparing potential domestic and international careers, which do you think could give you the greatest professional opportunities?

	DOMESTIC CAREER	ABOUT SAME	INTERNATIONAL CAREER
25. I could succeed faster in	_____	_____	_____
26. I could earn a higher salary in	_____	_____	_____
27. I could have greater status in	_____	_____	_____
28. I could be more recognized for my work in	_____	_____	_____
29. I could have a more interesting professional life in	_____	_____	_____

30. I could have a more
satisfying personal life _____ _____ _____

In comparing male and female business students, who do
you think will have the greater chance of being

| | EQUAL | |
| MALES | CHANCES | FEMALES |

31. Selected for an
international
assignment? _____ _____ _____

32. Effective on an
international
assignment? _____ _____ _____

33. Successful in
advancing in an
international
career? _____ _____ _____

34. Effective on
domestic
assignments? _____ _____ _____

35. Successful in
advancing in a
domestic career? _____ _____ _____

36. Socially isolated and
lonely in a foreign
country? _____ _____ _____

37. Exposed to personal
danger in a foreign
country? _____ _____ _____

In Your Opinion

1. What are the main reasons that would lead *you* to
accept an international assignment?

    a. _____

    b. _____

    c. _____

2. What are the main reasons why *you* would turn down
an international assignment?

    a. _____

    b. _____

    c. _____

3. What, if any, are the blocks for women successfully
pursuing international careers that include foreign
assignments (which do *not* exist for men)?

    a. _____

    b. _____

    c. _____

PART V: EXPERIENCE 3

Managing Organizational Change

Barry Allen Gold

Purpose

The purpose of this experience is to demonstrate processes involved in changing organizational behavior through planned managerial action.

Time Required

Two hours (if two class sessions are required the first class should end after Step IV).

Materials

Directions for "How to Make a Panda." One hundred 6" pieces of paper (the number should be adjusted for class size).

Introduction

Planned change in organizations is a complex sequence of activities. One theory of organizational change is Kurt Lewin's (1951) model of unfreezing, movement, and refreezing. An additional phase, diagnosis, is often added to the model.

A Model of Organizational Change

Phase 1
Diagnosis:

A. Finding the problem
B. Selecting a solution

Phase 2
Unfreezing

C. Preparing for change
D. Generating ownership

Phase 3
Movement

E. Making the changes

Phase 4
Refreezing

F. Institutionalizing the changes

Procedure

The class should be divided into two equal groups. One group will be Optimal Organizational Consultants, Inc. (OOCI) and the other will be Paper Panda Ltd. (PPL).

Step I: Company Formation (10 Minutes)
A. Both companies should select a President, Vice Presi-dent, and Treasurer. If they desire they can also have supervisors, quality control experts and other posi-tions.
B. Both companies should develop brief corporate mis-sion statements.
C. The company officers should introduce themselves to the entire class and read their company mission statement.

Step II: Making Pandas (20 minutes)
A. *Training:* Using the Directions for Paper Pandas the officers of PPL should train their employees in making Pandas (20 minutes).
B. *Organization:* The group should decide how to pro-duce Pandas. Assembly line, craft or another type of production method can be used.
C. *Quality:* PPL should decide what quality control the Pandas will have (for example, are the folds straight and crisp, do the heads fit on the bodies correctly?).
D. *Quantity:* PPL should decide how many Pandas it can produce in ten minutes and purchase the exact amount of raw material from the instructor.

Step III: Production 1 (10 minutes)
A. PPL produces Pandas for ten minutes.

**Instructions for Optimal
Organizational Consultants, Inc.**

While Paper Panda, Ltd. organizes and produces pandas OOCI observes. The purpose of the observation is to diag-nose PPL's operations and plan ways to improve PPL's per-formance by at least 20% in the second ten minute production run.

OOCI should decide:
A. The number of Pandas to be produced in Production 2 (at least 20% more than Production 1).
B. What quality improvements are required, if any?
C. Is retraining necessary?
D. Should PPL be reorganized?

Note: OOCI is not permitted to interact with PPL during Steps II and III. In Phase IV OOCI cannot fire or otherwise dismiss PPL employees. In addition, OOCI cannot add staff to PPL as a way to increase production.

Step IV: Changing Paper Panda, Ltd. (20 minutes)
A. OCCI should reorganize PPL to increase production by a minimum of 20% while maintaining or improv-ing product quality.

1.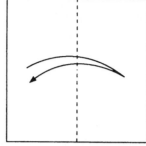

2.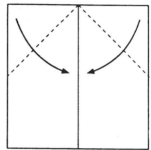

3.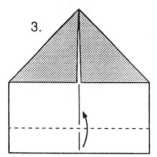

7.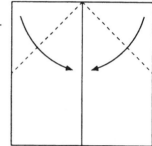

8.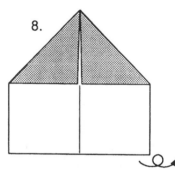

9.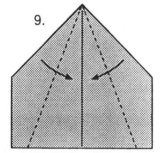

11.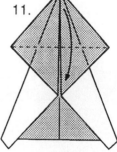

12.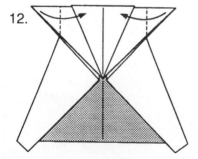

13.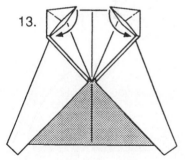

15.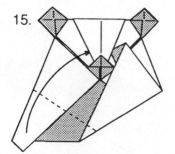

16.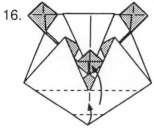

4.

5.

6.

10.

14.

Step V: Production 2 (10 minutes)

A. PPL produces Pandas for 10 minutes under the reorganization by OOCI.

Step VI: OOCI Reviews PPL Production (10 minutes)

A. OOCI counts and inspects the Pandas produced by PPL in the second production run.

B. The instructor determines if the 20% production increase and quality specifications were met.

Step VII: Discussion (30 Minutes)

A. Company discussion: Members of OOCI and PPL should meet separately to discuss the following questions (10 minutes).

1. Was there resistance to change? What were the sources of resistance? What behaviors demonstrated resistance?

2. What factors facilitated change? How were these expressed behaviorally and verbally?

3. What was the experience of company officers?

4. What did the PPL and OOCI employees experience?

5. How could this change process be improved?

B. Class discussion: Following the separate company discussions the entire class should discuss the same questions and any additional issues that were raised during the experience (20 minutes).

Directions For Paper Pandas

Material

Use two paper squares, 6″ (15cm) or larger, black on one side and white on the other (plain white paper will do).

Legs

1. With white side of paper up, fold paper in half. Unfold.
2. Fold upper corners to the middle crease.
3. Fold lower edge up, leaving white space showing.
4. Reverse fold both bottom corners in between the two layers of paper.
5. Fold the sides back, leaving the two bottom corners on the front untouched. Tuck the two loose corners in the middle under.
6. To make the legs stand up, crease the paper in the middle and let the legs rest at right angles to each other.

Head

7. With white side of paper up, fold paper in half. Unfold. Fold upper corners to the middle crease.
8. Turn paper over.
9. Bring folded edges to the middle.
10. Find the hidden corners underneath and bring them to the outside.
11. Fold the top corner down, creasing through the middle of the black square.
12. Fold the outer corners toward the middle. Note where bottom of the crease starts.
13. Poke your finger into the pocket of the triangle on the upper left corner to open it. Then squash it on the top to form square. Repeat on the right side.
14. Form the mouth by folding up the corner in the center. Fold the upper edge back through the middle of the small squares at the sides. Swing the corners of the squares up to reveal the ears. Fold the right lower corner up, tucking the black tip just slightly under the pocket above the mouth.
15. Fold the left lower corner up in the same way.
16. Fold bottom tip up. Then fold bottom edge up again to cover just a little of the black. Crease sharply.

Rest the folded-over edge of the head on top of the legs.

REFERENCE

Lewin, K. *Field Theory in Social Science.* New York: Harper & Row, 1951.

APPENDIX: THE SCIENTIFIC METHOD

Examining "Untangling the Relationship between Displayed Emotions and Organizational Sales"

Barry Allen Gold

Purpose

The purpose of this exercise is to examine the research design and data collection method used in Robert Sutton and Anat Rafaeli's "Untangling the Relationship between Displayed Emotions and Organizational Sales" (page 68) to determine if a different design and method would produce different research findings and interpretations.

Preparation

Reread Sutton and Rafaeli's "Untangling the Relationship between Displayed Emotions and Organizational Sales."

Time Required

Approximately one hour. Forty-five minutes for group discussion and fifteen minutes for class discussion.

Introduction

Displayed emotions play a role in organizations. But as Sutton and Rafaeli discovered in their study of convenience stores the role emotions play is not self evident. To the researcher's surprise the positive display of emotions did not account for higher sales volume in retail stores. In fact, stores with clerks who displayed lower levels of positive emotion—those with indifferent or rude clerks—had higher sales.

Because this finding is counterintuitive it is useful to ask: Was the study designed and conducted correctly? Before continuing, however, it should be noted that we have two advantages that Sutton and Rafaeli did not have. First, the quantitative deductive study was designed by the research director of the company, not Sutton and Rafaeli. Second, Sutton and Rafaeli provide an excellent description of the research design and the findings which makes locating improvements comparatively easy.

Procedure

Form groups of six. One person should be the group leader and another should act as group recorder/reporter. The leader should guide the discussion and the recorder/reporter preserve the key points and at the end of the discussion report them to the entire class.

A.   Missing Variables

The predictor variable is display of positive emotion which is hypothesized by both management and the researchers to positively affect total store sales, the cri-

terion variable. In addition, there are eight control variables which through statistical manipulation attempt to hold constant a variety of influences on store sales. They are the clerks' gender, customer's gender, clerk's image, a store's stock level, length of line, store ownership, supervision costs, and geographical region.

What other variables affect the sales volume of a convenience store? List additional variables.

1. _____
2. _____
3. _____
4. _____
5. _____

Why do people shop in a convenience store? Do customers expect courteous service from convenience store clerks? List customer expectations.

1. _____
2. _____
3. _____
4. _____
5. _____

B.   Generalization of Findings
What other types of businesses could be included in a sample to increase the generalizability of the findings? What additional variables would be introduced to the study? List other types of organizations and how they differ from convenience stores.

Type of Business	Differences	Additional variable
1._____	1._____	1._____
2._____	2._____	2._____
3._____	3._____	3._____
4._____	4._____	4._____
5._____	5._____	5._____

C.   Hypothesis
Based upon the new variables what additional hypotheses should a revised study examine?

1. _____
2. _____
3. _____
4. _____
5. _____

APPENDIX: THE SCIENTIFIC METHOD

D. Study Design
   With additional variables and a comparative perspective how might this study be redesigned?
   1. Variation according to type of service?
   2. Variation based on commodity price?
   3. Variation according to complexity of service and goods?

E. Research Methods
   What research methods would be appropriate for the redesigned study?
   1. How would a quantitative study be designed?
   2. How would a qualitative study be designed?
   3. How would quantitative and qualitative elements be integrated into one design?

F. Data Collection
   How should the data be collected?
   1. How could the variables be measured and operationalized?
   2. What techniques would be appropriate for collecting data?

G. Data Analysis
   How should the data be analyzed?
   1. What methods could be used to analyze quantitative data?
   2. What methods could be used to analyze qualitative data?

H. Findings
   What would be some of the possible findings of the redesigned study?

1. _____

2. _____

3. _____

5. _____

4. _____

I. Data Presentation
   How should the research findings be presented?
   1. What is the most appropriate way to write a report for an audience interested in improving sales volume in retail stores?
   2. How should a report be written for students and researchers interested in further research into the role of emotions in organizations?

J. Implications
   How could these findings influence training programs designed to improve interaction between retail employees and customers?
   1. _____
   2. _____
   3. _____
   4. _____
   5. _____

K. Reports
   After forty-five minutes the groups should report the results of their findings to the entire class.

Credits

2   Karl E. Weick, "Perspectives on Action in Organizations," Jay W. Lorsch, ed., *Handbook of Organizational Behavior*, © 1987, pp. 10–28. Reprinted by permission of Prentice-Hall, Inc., Englewood Cliffs, New Jersey.

23   "A Model for Diagnosing Organizational Behavior," by David A. Nadler and Michael T. Tushman. Reprinted by permission of Publisher, from *Organizational Dynamics*, Autumn 1980, © 1980. American Management Association, New York. All rights reserved. Reprinted by permission.

36   William Foote Whyte, "From Human Relations to Organizational Behavior: Reflections on the Changing Scene," *Industrial and Labor Relations Review*, Vol 40, No. 4 (1987), pp. 487–500. © Cornell University, 1987. Reprinted by permission.

48   David Vogel, "Business Ethics Past and Present." Reprinted with permission of the publisher and the author from: *The Public Interest*, No. 102 (Winter 1991), pp. 49–64. © 1991 by National Affairs, Inc.

58   Kai Erickson, "On Work and Alienation," from *The Nature of Work: Sociological Perspectives*, ed. Kai Erikson and Steven Peter Vallas, pp. 19–35 (Yale University Press, 1990). Reprinted by permission.

68   Robert Sutton and Anat Rafaeli, "Untangling the Relationship between Displayed Emotions and Organizational Sales: The Case of Convenience Stores, *Academy of Management Journal*, 1988; Vol. 31; No. 3. Copy-right © 1988. Reprinted by permission.

87   Barbara Levitt and James G. March, Organizational Learning. Reprinted from the *Annual Review of Sociology*, 14 (1988) pp. 319–340, with the permission of the authors and the publishers. All rights for subsequent reproduction are retained by the authors and the original publishers.

102 Reprinted by permission of *Harvard Business Review*, "Power is the Great Motivator," David C. McClelland and David H. Burnham, March–April 1976. Copyright © 1976 by the President and Fellows of Harvard College; all rights reserved.

113 Allen I. Kraut, Patricia R. Pedigo, D. Douglas McKenna, and Marvin D. Dunnette, "The Role of the Manager: What's Really Important in Different Management Jobs," *Academy of Management Executive* 1989; Vol 3; No 4. Copyright © 1989. Reprinted by permission.

123 Herbert A. Simon, "Making Management Decisions: The Role of Intuition and Emotion," *Academy of Management Executive*, February 1987, pp. 57–64. Copyright © 1987. Reprinted by permission.

133 Leonard Greenhalgh, "SMR Forum: Managing Conflict," *Sloan Management Review*, Summer 1986. Copyright © 1986. Reprinted by permission.

139 Margaret A. Neale and Max H. Bazerman, "Negotiating Rationally: The Power and Impact of the Negotiator's Frame," *Academy of Management Executive* 1992; Vol 6; No. 3. Copyright © 1992. Reprinted by permission.

147 Reprinted by permission of the publisher from "Frank Harris, MBA," by H. Donald Hopkins, *Journal of Management Case Studies*, 3, pp. 277–279. Copyright 1987 by Elsevier Science Publishing Co., Inc.

149 Reprinted by permission of the publisher from "Ken Garff: Small-Business Entrepreneur," by C. Brooklyn Derr, Professor of Human Resource Management, David Eccles School of Business, University of Utah, *Journal of Management Case Studies*, 2, pp. 188–198. Copyright 1986 by Elsevier Science Publishing Co., Inc.

164 "The Learning-Model Instrument," © 1987, by Dr. Kenneth Murrell, University of West Florida and Empowerment Leadership Systems. Reprinted by permission.

174 Connie J. G. Gersick, "Time and Transition in Work Teams: Toward a New Model of Group Development," *Academy of Management Journal* 1988; Vol 31; No. 1. Copyright © 1988. Reprinted by permission.

196 Joanne Yates and Wanda J. Orlikowski, "Genres of Organizational Communication: A Structurational Approach to Studying Communication and Media," *Academy of Management Review*, 1992; Vol 17; No. 2. Copyright © 1992. Reprinted by permission.

214 "Who Gets Power—And How They Hold on to It: A Strategic Contingency Model of Power" by Gerald Salancik

and Jeffrey Pfeffer. Reprinted by permission of Publisher, from *Organizational Dynamics,* Winter 1977, © 1977. American Management Association, New York. All rights reserved.

227 Howell S. Baum, "Organizational Politics against Organizational Culture: A Psychoanalytic Perspective," (New York: John Wiley & Sons, Inc.) 1989, *Human Resource Management,* 191–206, (1989) Vol. 28; No. 2. Reprinted by permission of John Wiley & Sons, Inc.

237 Glen Whyte, "Groupthink Reconsidered," *Academy of Management Review,* 1989; Vol. 14; No. 1, pp. 40–56. Copyright © 1989. Reprinted by permission.

251 Edwin A. Locke, David M. Schweiger, and Gary P. Latham, "Participation in Decision Making: When Should It Be Used?" *Organizational Dynamics,* 14(3), pp. 65–79, 1986. Reprinted by permission.

263 Robert K. Merton: "The Ambivalence of Organizational Leaders," in James F. Oates, Jr., *The Contradictions of Leadership* (New York: Appleton-Crofts, 1970), pp. 1–26. Reprinted by permission.

272 Jay Conger, "Leadership: The Art of Empowering Others," *Academy of Management Executive,* 1989; Vol 3; No. 1, pp. 17–24. Copyright © 1989. Reprinted by permission.

284 Franklin Ramsoomair, "The Forgotten Group Member," *Case Research Journal,* Spring 1992: pp. 63–73. Copyright © 1992. Reprinted by permission.

298 Lee Bolman and Terrence E. Deal, "A Simple—But Powerful—Power Simulation," *Exchange,* Vol. 4(3), 1979, pp. 38–42. Copyright © 1979.

299 J. Clayton Lafferty, Patrick M. Eady, and Alonzo W. Pond, "The Desert Survival Situation: A Group Decision Making Experience for Examining and Increasing Individual and Team Effectiveness," 8th ed. Copyright © 1974 by Experiential Learning Methods, Inc., 14539 Harbor Island, Detroit, MI 48215, (313) 823–4400. Reprinted by permission.

302 Edgar H. Schein, "Organizational Culture," *American Psychologist,* February 1990, Vol. 45, No. 2, pp. 109–119. Copyright 1990 by the American Psychological Association. Reprinted by permission.

306, 307 **For tables included with *American Psychologist* article:** Tables 11.1 and 11.2 from the February 1990 issue of *American Psychologist.* Adapted from Edgar H. Schein's *Organizational Culture and Leadership: A Dynamic View,* pp. 52, 56, 86. Copyright 1985 by Jossey-Bass Inc., Publishers. Reprinted by permission.

317 Richard Nielsen, "Changing Unethical Organizational Behavior," *Academy of Management Executive,* 1989; Vol 3; No. 2, pp. 123–130. Copyright © 1989. Reprinted by permission.

328 J. Richard Hackman; Greg Oldham; Robert Janson; and Kenneth Purdy, "A New Strategy for Job Enrichment," *California Management Review,* 1975; Vol 32, No 4; pp. 57–71

344 Edward E. Lawler III, "The New Plant Approach: A Second Generation Approach," From *Organizational Dynamics,* Summer 1992, pp. 5–14. Copyright © 1992. Reprinted by permission.

352 "Goal Setting—A Motivational Technique That Works," by Gary Latham and Edwin A. Locke. Reprinted by permission of Publisher, from *Organizational Dynamics,* Autumn 1979, © 1979. American Management Association, New York. All rights reserved.

362 Robert Cole, "U.S. Quality Improvement in the Auto Industry: Close but No Cigar," *California Management Review,* Summer 1990; Vol 32, No. 4.

372 Reprinted by permission of the publisher from "The American Food Corporation," by Barry Allen Gold, *Journal of Management Case Studies,* 2, pp. 312–326. Copyright 1986 by Elsevier Science Publishing Co., Inc.

382 Reprinted by permission of the publisher from "Bill Kadota's Problem," developed by J. Malcolm Walker, Professor Emeritus, San Jose State University, *Journal of Management Case*

Studies, 2, pp. 70–75. Copyright 1986 by Elsevier Science Publishing Co., Inc.

386 Howard D. Feldman and Morton Cotlar, "A Student Dilemma: Unethical Practices or Competitive Advantage?" *Case Research Journal,* Spring 1990, pp. 17–34. Copyright © 1990. Reprinted by permission.

394 Burton, Gene E., *Exercises in Management,* Third Edition. Copyright © 1990 by Houghton Mifflin Company. Used with permission.

397 Marian K. Prokop, "Affirmations: Positive Self-Talk." Reprinted from J.W. Pfeiffer (Ed.), *The 1991 Annual: Developing Human Resources,* San Diego, CA: Pfeiffer & Company, 1991. Used with permission.

402 Richard Florida and Martin Kenney, "Transplanted Organizations: The Transfer of Japanese Industrial Organizations to the U.S.," *American Sociological Review* 56 (1991): pp. 381–398. Copyright 1991. Reprinted by permission.

420 Nancy J. Adler and Susan Bartholomew, "Managing Globally Competent People," *Academy of Management Executive* 1992; Vol 6; No. 3. Copyright © 1992. Reprinted by permission.

432 "Automate / Informate: The Two Faces of Intelligent Technology," by Shoshana Zuboff. Reprinted by permission of Publisher, from *Organizational Dynamics,* Autumn 1985, © 1985. American Management Association, New York. All rights reserved.

442 Stephen R. Barley, "Technology as an Occasion for Structuring: Evidence from Observations of CT Scanners and the Social Order of Radiology Departments," *Administrative Science Quarterly,* Volume 31, No. 1, (March 1986) pp. 78–108. Copyright © 1986. Reprinted by permission.

466 Reprinted by permission of *Harvard Business Review,* "In Praise of Hierarchy," by Elliot Jacques, January–February 1990. Copyright © 1990 by the President and Fellows of Harvard College; all rights reserved.

473 "The New Web of Enterprise," from *The Work of Nations: Preparing Our-*

Index

Supervision and alienation, 63
Sutton, R., 176

T

Taira, Koji, 403
Task forces, 176–193
Taylor, Frederick W., 353
Team structure, 346
Technology
  and organizational structure, 443–463
Technology, information, 432–441
  automate v. "informate," 433–436
  organizational barriers to "informat-
    ing," 439–441
  role in restructuring workplace,
    432–441
Thaler, Richard, 140, 143
Theory Z, 251
Thorngate, W., 8
Thorsrud, Einar, 43
Tillich, Paul, 317–318, 320
Training, management, 120

Transplant organizations, 402–416
  and interorganizational relations,
    412–415
  organization of, 405–412
  research design of, 404–405
Trist, Eric, 43, 487
Tuchman, B., 237
Tuckman, B., 175, 180
Turner, Arthur, 41
Tversky, A., 239, 245

U

Unions
  role of in human relations, 38
  in transplant organizations, 411
Unitary stage theory, 192
Utterback, J., 193

V

Veblen, Thorstein, 263
Vroom, Victor, 254

W

Walker, Charles, 38, 41
Walzer, Michael, 48
Warner, W. Lloyd, 37
Waterman, R. H., Jr., 70, 479
Wealth and Poverty, 54
Wealth of Nations, The, 52, 53
Weber, Max, 36, 38, 48
Weick, Karl, 403, 443
Woodward, Joan, 42–43
White, Frank, 357
Whitehead, Alfred N., 8
Whistle-blowing, 318–320
Willis, R. J., 13

Y

Yankelovich, D., 229
Yoshino, M., 321, 404

Z

Zaleznik, Abraham, 110
Zimbardo, P. G., 4